Contents

Maps and plans

Introduction

On 29 August 2000 the New York Times ran a story on the sinking of Venice—a topical matter for all those who hold dear the destiny of this most unique of cities. An American archaeologist, it seems, had discovered that the water level has risen as much in recent years as it has since the beginning of recorded history; and that if the present trend in global warming continues, Venice will 'sink' beneath the rising sea more, and faster, every year. Technical impediments, such as the movable floodgates recently proposed to thwart the phenomenon, will prove as useless as they are expensive (the system is considered the most costly public-works project ever conceived), and what is now a vibrant, living city will become an archaeological curiosity, a sort of Pompeii to be visited by boat.

Though the sinking of Venice is certainly the most dramatic environmental issue that Italy has faced in recent years, it is not the only one. As the country gradually takes stock of its California-like disposition towards earthquakes, landslides, drought and flooding, and of the aggravating factors brought by prosperity and development, Italians are beginning to realise that the proper attitude towards the land is one of watchful care, not heedless exploitation. In a word, they are rediscovering Nature. Especially in the northern regions, the proliferation of small, profitable industries that, in the not-so-distant past, had turned demographic patterns topsy-turvy (causing the country folk to move to the cities) and created an urgent demand for infrastructures (more roads!) has slowed, thanks largely to the information revolution. The service sector, rather than industry, is the fastest growing employer, and telecommuting is increasingly common. The result: the populations of Milan and other major cities are decreasing as the affluent middle class (often with dotcoms and smart, craft-based businesses in tow) rediscovers the simple pleasures of small-town life.

This is good news for travellers like us. It translates as more good restaurants, charming hotels, tastefully renovated bed-and-breakfasts, music festivals, theatre festivals, film series, galleries, museums and exhibitions even in out-of-the-way places. And more hiking trails, cycling trails, back-country ski trails, parks and nature reserves. Today a new and more adventurous northern Italy awaits you.

The area covered in this book ranges from the Alps down through the wide Po Valley to Emilia Romagna at the foot of the Apennines. It stretches west through Liguria to the French border, and east along the Adriatic coast to Trieste, now on the Slovenian frontier. It includes some of the more important historic cities of Italy—such as Milan, Turin, Genoa, Venice, Padua, Verona and Bologna—and numerous beautiful small towns, such as Ferrara, Vicenza, Mantua, and Bergamo. It also takes in the famous lakes of Garda, Maggiore and Como as well as the vast Alpine parklands. The Veneto region is well known for its many country villas, and the splendid Byzantine mosaics of Ravenna, in Romagna, make that region, too, one you will not want to miss.

The eleventh edition of Blue Guide Northern Italy offers a detailed description of the most interesting cities, towns, and natural areas of this fascinating territory. Places are arranged in geographic 'bundles', leaving you the freedom to choose the route best suited to your personal tastes. Each bundle forms a chapter, at the beginning of which you'll find suggestions on how to get there and back, what to do and when, where to stay and where to eat. A lot of care has gone into the selection of these creature comforts, in the conviction that pleasant accommodation, delicious food and good wine can go a long way to determining the success or failure of a holiday.

You might find yourself leafing through the guide rather more than you expect: for although its general organisation is loose and open, the specific places are dealt with intensely, offering walking tours that take you round the major sights (or through the finest countryside) step by step. In most cases these walks are designed to last about two hours, after which you'll be more than ready for some form of refreshment, or—in the case of larger towns like Milan (where you'll be ambling about for a full day or more)—even for a cat-nap.

Finally, a word of warning: Italy possesses some two-thirds of the world's artistic heritage, and it's an old heritage, in constant need of conservation and restoration. If during your visit some of the works of art and architecture described in the guide are covered (in the case of buildings or public sculpture) or away for cleaning (paintings), don't let it spoil your day: just move on. The more memorable moments of a foreign journey are often those one least expects—and Italy is indeed a land of the unexpected.

Acknowledgements

The author is indebted to all those people who contributed in various ways to the making of the book. Acknowledgement is also due to the *Ente Nazionale Italiano di Turismo* (Italian State Tourist Office) for their generous assistance, and to the regional, provincial and local tourist boards whose co-operation was indispensable to the accurate preparation of the guide. Special thanks are owed to the many friends who assisted in the gathering of information, particularly Alexandra Massini and Christopher Wellington, who travelled extensively through northern Italy; to Alta Macadam, author of previous editions of the guide, whose friendship and advice has been invaluable; and to Isabella Toraldo di Francia, who provided encouragement and support throughout the preparation of the guide. As with other volumes in the *Blue Guide* series, suggestions for the correction or improvement of the guide are gratefully welcomed.

Highlights of the region

Here are just a few of the magnificent sights that await you in northern Italy.

Valle d'Aosta
Aosta has some important Roman remains, and many of the castles that line the valley can be visited. The Parco Nazionale del Gran Paradiso has fine mountain scenery.

Piedmont
Turin has a 17C–18C aspect and some very fine museums (including an important Egyptian collection), and grand Savoy residences on the outskirts. On the picturesque Lago d'Orta is the charming, well-preserved village of Orta San Giulio. The Langhe and Roero districts, famous for their vineyards, have pretty landscapes and excellent restaurants.

Lombardy
Milan is one of the more interesting cities in Italy, with a splendid Gothic cathedral, the Brera Gallery containing a superb collection of paintings, Leonardo da Vinci's famous fresco of the *Last Supper*, La Scala, renowned for opera, and numerous museums (including the delightful Poldi Pezzoli), and churches (notably Sant'Ambrogio, San Satiro, Sant'Eustorgio, and San Lorenzo Maggiore).

The Italian lakes have been visited for centuries for their beautiful scenery: on Lago Maggiore, the charming Isole Borromei have lovely gardens; on Lago di Como, the most attractive towns are Como itself, Bellagio and Varenna, and there are fine gardens on its shores. Perhaps the most beautiful lake of all is Lago di Garda, with the spectacular Roman villa at Sirmione.

Mantua is a lovely old town, famous for its huge Palazzo Ducale with its frescoes by Mantegna, and for the handsome Palazzo Te. The upper town of Bergamo is particularly well-preserved with some important art treasures, and Cremona is a pleasant city. Brescia has interesting Roman and Lombard remains. The small towns of Castiglione Olona, with its Renaissance works, and Sabbioneta, laid out in the 16C, are of the greatest interest. There are important prehistoric rock carvings in the Valle Camonica.

Trentino-Alto Adige
Trento, Bolzano and Bressanone all merit a day's visit. The Alpine valleys offer boundless opportunities for summer and winter sports, and the area's many large nature reserves are perfect for hiking, swimming, cross-country and alpine skiing, birdwatching, etc.

Veneto
Apart from the world-famous city of Venice (also the subject of a separate *Blue Guide*), the Veneto includes Verona, a particularly beautiful city with fine churches and piazze, and a celebrated Roman amphitheatre. The lively university town of Padua has interesting monuments including important frescoes by Giotto, and the town of Vicenza, laid out by the great 16C architect Palladio, is unusually well-preserved. All over the Veneto are splendid country villas, some

built in the early 16C by Palladio, others by 17C and 18C architects. Attractive small towns include Treviso, Asolo and Bassano del Grappa. Montagnana and Cittadella have very well-kept walls. The area around the Delta of the Po has a remarkable landscape, and there is fine mountain scenery in the Venetian Dolomites.

Friuli-Venezia Giulia

The 18C city of Trieste has a distinctive atmosphere, and Pordenone and Gorizia are agreeable towns. Udine possesses some fine frescoes by Giovanni Battista Tiepolo, and the little town of Cividale has beautiful Lombard works. Aquileia is an important Roman site, and it also has superb early-Christian mosaics. The medieval village of Venzone, carefully reconstructed after earthquake damage, is one of the more remarkable sights in northeastern Italy.

Liguria

Genoa is a historic city with fine palaces and magnificent art collections. The peninsula of Portofino is particularly beautiful, and in the gulf of La Spezia is the picturesque village of Portovenere. The most unspoiled part of the coast is the Cinque Terre, with a series of delightful little remote villages in spectacular scenery.

Emilia Romagna

Bologna, an important, large university town with a pleasant atmosphere, is well worth a visit: it has numerous interesting churches and museums. Ravenna has the most important Byzantine mosaics in western Europe, and in Rimini there are Roman monuments and the famous Renaissance Tempio Malatestiano. Parma has a splendid Baptistery and many masterpieces by Correggio. Faenza is famous for its ceramics. Ferrara, home of the Renaissance Este dukes, is a particularly pleasing and well-preserved town.

PRACTICAL INFORMATION

 Planning your trip

When to go

The best time to visit northern Italy is late spring (May–June) or early autumn (September–October). The earlier spring and later autumn months are often wet and unexpectedly chilly, with strong northerly winds. The height of the summer is unpleasantly hot, especially in the Po Valley and the larger towns; and winter days are sometimes as cold and wet as in Britain. The upper Alpine valleys of Piedmont, Lombardy and the Dolomites are cool in summer, and the winter sports season in the Alpine resorts is extended even to midsummer in the high Alps. Seaside resorts are crowded from mid-June to early September; before and after this season many hotels are closed and the beaches are practically deserted.

What to bring

Due to the difference in temperature between morning/evening and midday, and to the overall unpredictability of weather in the Mediterranean, you will be most comfortable if you dress in layers that can be donned or removed as the need arises. Evening dress is generally casual, except for special events such as theatre and opera, at which a jacket and tie or an evening dress are suggested. Light trainers or water-resistant walking shoes are best for exploring cities; on country and mountain trails, the nature of the terrain almost always requires you to wear lightweight hiking boots with ankle support. Wherever you are, a backpack or shoulder bag will come in handy to carry snacks, water, camera, sunscreen, etc., and effective rain gear (a lightweight parka or Gore-Tex jacket) will keep you dry when the odd storm breaks.

Try to travel lightly—especially if you are using public transport. Most Italian train stations require you to drag your bags up and down stairs to reach the platforms. For this important reason, and because baggage capacity in buses and trains is limited, you would do well to restrict luggage to two small bags per person. If you are starting and ending your trip in the same city, additional luggage may be left at the first hotel and picked up at the end of the trip.

Passports and formalities

Passports or ID cards are necessary for EU travellers entering Italy; North American travellers must carry passports. No visa is required for visits of less than 90 days for EU, US or Canadian citizens holding a valid passport. Citizens of other countries should check current visa requirements with the nearest Italian consulate before departure.

Italian law requires travellers to carry some form of identification at all times. A stolen or lost passport can be replaced with little trouble by your embassy in

Rome. All foreign visitors to Italy must register with the police within three days of arrival. If you are staying at a hotel, this formality is attended to by the management. If staying with friends or in a private home, you must register in person at the nearest *questura* (police station).

National tourist boards

Information may be obtained abroad from ENIT (Ente Nazionale Italiano per il Turismo), whose local name changes from place to place.

UK Italian State Tourist Office, 1 Princes Street, London W1R 8AY, ☎ 020 7408 1254, fax 020 7493 6695, e-mail: enitland@globalnet.co.uk

USA Italian Government Tourist Board, c/o Italian Trade Commission, 499 Park Avenue Avenue, New York, NY 10022, ☎ 212 843 6885, fax 212 843 6886

Italian Government Travel Office, 401 North Michigan Avenue, Suite 3030, Chicago 1, IL 60611, 312 644 0996, fax 312 644 30197

Italian Government Travel Office, 12400 Wilshire Blvd, Suite 550, Los Angeles, CA 90025, ☎ 310 820 0098, fax 310 820 6357, email: enitla@earthlink.net

Canada Italian Government Travel Office, 1 Place Ville Marie, Suite 1914, Montreal, Québec H3B 3M9, ☎ 514 866 7667, fax 514 866 0975, email: initaly @ucab.net

Australia Italian Government Travel Ofice, c/o Italian Chamber of Commerce and Industry, Level 26, 44 Market St, Sydney, NSW 2000, ☎ 02 9262 1666; fax 02 9262 5745

Netherlands Stadhoudeskade 2, 1054 ES Amsterdam, ☎ (003) 120 616 8244; fax 120 618 8515

Websites on Italy

Let's roam Italy: tqd.advanced.org/2838

Italytour.com: www.italytour.com/

Italy online: www.italy.initaly.com/

Tour operators

Tour operators in **Britain** who sell tickets and book accommodation, and also organise inclusive tours to some parts of northern Italy, include:

Abercrombie and Kent, Sloane Square House, Holbein Place, London SW1W 8NS, ☎ 020 7730 9600, fax 020 7730 9376, e-mail: info@ abercrombiekent.co.uk.

Citalia, Marco Polo House, 3–5 Lansdowne Road, Croydon CR9 1LL, ☎ 020 8686 5533, fax 020 8686 0328, e-mail: ciao@citalia.co.uk; www.citalia.co.uk

Ilios Travel Ltd, 18 Market Square, Horsham, West Sussex RH12 1EU, ☎ 01403 259788, fax 01403 211699.

Italian Escapades, 227 Shepherds Bush Road, London W6 7AS, ☎ 020 8748 2661, fax 020 8748 6381.

Italiatour, 205 Holland Park Avenue, London W11 4XB, ☎ 020 7371 1114, fax 0207 602 6172.

Magic of Italy, 227 Shepherds Bush Road, London W6 7AS, ☎ 020 8748 7575, fax 020 8748 3731.

Martin Randall Travel, 10 Barley Mow Passage, Chiswick, London W4 4PH, ☎ 020 8742 3355, fax 020 8742 1066, e-mail: info@martinrandall.co.uk.

Page and Moy Ltd, 136–140 London Road, Leicester LE2 1EN, ☎ 0116 254

9949; e-mail: holiday@page-moy.co.uk.
Prospect Music and Art Tours Ltd, 36 Manchester Street, London W1M 5PE, ☎ 020 7486 5704, fax 020 7486 5868; e-mail: enquiries@prospecttours.com.
Specialtours, 81a Elizabeth Street, London SW1W 9PG, ☎ 020 7730 2297, fax 020 7823 5035.
Vacanze in Italia, Bignor, Pulborough, West Sussex RH20 1QD, ☎ 01798 869485, fax 09700 780190; e-mail: holidays@indiv_travellers.com, specialise in self-catering accommodation in Italy.

The many **North American** agents offering individual and group tours to Italy include:
Central Holidays, 206 Central Avenue, Jersey City, NJ 07307, ☎ 201 475 4559 (toll-free 1 800 935 5000), fax 201 963 0966; Los Angeles Office 577 W. Century Blvd, Los Angeles, CA 90045, ☎ 1 800 CHT WEST.
Donna Franca Tours, 470 Commonwealth Avenue, Boston, MA 02215, ☎ 617 375 9400 (toll-free 1 800 225 6290).
The Travel Bug, 220 Montgomery Street, Suite 1034, San Francisco, CA 94104, ☎ 415 981 1331 (toll-free 1 800 221 2264), fax 415 296 0714.

Disabled travellers

All new public buildings are now obliged by law to provide easy access and specially designed facilities for the disabled. Unfortunately the conversion of historical buildings, including many museums and monuments, is made problematic by structural impediments such as narrow sidewalks (which make mobility difficult for everyone). Barriers therefore continue to exist in many cases. Hotels that are able to give hospitality to the disabled are indicated in the annual list of hotels published by the local tourist boards. Airports and railway stations provide assistance, and certain trains are equipped to transport wheelchairs. Access is allowed to the centre of towns (normally closed to traffic) for cars with disabled drivers or passengers, and special parking places are reserved for them. For further information, contact the tourist board in the city of interest.

Maps

The *TCI* (*Touring Club Italiano*) publishes several sets of excellent maps, including *Carta Stradale d'Europa: Italia* on a scale of 1:1,000,000; *Atlante Stradale Touring* (1:800,000); and *Carta Stradale d'Italia* (1:200,000). The latter is divided into 15 sheets covering the regions of Italy. These are also published as an atlas (with a comprehensive index) called the *Atlante Stradale d'Italia*, in three volumes. The ones entitled *Centro* and *Nord* cover Northern Italy. These maps are available in Italy from the *TCI* offices and at many booksellers. In London they can be purchased at **Stanfords**, 12–14 Long Acre, London WC2 9LP, ☎ 0207 836 1321.

The **Istituto Geografico Militare**, Via Cesare Battisti 10, Florence, publishes a map of Italy on a scale of 1:100,000 in 277 sheets, and a field survey, partly 1:50,000, partly 1:25,000, both of which are invaluable for the detailed exploration of the country, especially its more mountainous regions; the coverage is, however, still far from complete at the larger scales and some of the maps are out of date. For the computer-literate, ***Route 66 Geographic Information Systems BV*** of Veenendaal, The Netherlands, distributes software that calculates and displays routes from any origin to any destination in Italy.

Health and insurance

British citizens, as members of the EU, have the right to claim health services in Italy if they have an E111 form (issued by the Department of Health and Social Security). You are also recommended to take out private holiday health insurance policies. Italy has no medical programme covering US or Canadian citizens, who are advised to take out an insurance policy before travelling. First-aid services (*Pronto Soccorso*) are available at all hospitals, railway stations and airports. For emergencies, ☎ 113 (*Polizia di Stato*) or 112 (*Carabinieri*).

Currency

The Italian national currency is the *lira* (pl. *lire*). Italy is one of the European Community countries that accept the single European currency, the euro (1 euro = 1936 lire). The euro will replace the lira as the official curency in 2002. Meanwhile, both euros and lire are accepted.

Travellers' cheques and Eurocheques are the safest way of carrying money while travelling, and most credit cards are now generally accepted in hotels, shops, restaurants and, increasingly, petrol stations.

Getting there

By air

Direct air services operate throughout the year between the UK and Bologna, Milan, Turin, Venice and Verona, and from several North American cities to Milan, Rome and Venice, where connections may be made with internal lines to other northern Italian airports.

From Britain

Alitalia, ☎ 0870 544 8259, www.alitalia.co.uk.
British Airways, ☎ 0990 444000 (flight information), ☎ 0345 222111 (reservations); www.british-airways.com.
British Midland, ☎ 0870 6070 555, www.iflybritishmidland.com.
Buzz, ☎ 0870 240 7070, www.buzzaway.com.
Go, ☎ 0845 605 4321, www.go-fly.com.
Meridiana, ☎ 020 7839 2222, www.meridiana.it.
Ryanair, ☎ 0870 156 9569, www.ryanair.com.

Air France (☎ 0845 0845 111), *Lufthansa* (☎ 0345 737747) and *Sabena* (☎ 020 8780 1444) offer flights connecting through Paris, Frankfurt, and Brussels, respectively. These may cost less than the direct flights.

From the USA and Canada

Alitalia (☎ 1 800 223 5730, www.alitaliausa.com) flies non-stop from New York (JFK or Newark) to Rome or Milan, from Boston and Chicago to Rome, from San Francisco to Milan and from Los Angeles to Rome or Milan.
American (☎ 212 489 7004, www.aa.com) from Chicago to Milan.
Canadian (☎ 613 247 5000, www.cdnair.com) from Toronto and Montreal to Rome.
Continental (☎ 1 800 2310856, www.continental.com) from New York to

Rome, www.continental. com.

Delta (☎ 1 800 241 4141, www.delta-air.com) from New York to Milan and Rome.
TWA (☎ 1 800 8924141, www.twa.com) from New York to Rome and Milan and from Los Angeles to Rome.
United (☎ 1 800 5382929, www.ual.com) from Washington DC to Rome.

Air France, *British Airways*, *KLM*, *Lufthansa* and *Sabena* offer flights connecting through Paris, London, Amsterdam, Frankfurt or Munich and Brussels. These are often more economical than the direct flights.

Agencies in the USA and Canada

Many agencies specialise in discount tickets from North America. These include:
Access International, 101 West 3 St, Suite 104, New York, NY 10001 (☎ 1 800 TAKE OFF).
Nouvelles Frontières, 800 Boulevard de Maisonneuve Est, Montreal, PQ H2L 4L8 (☎ 1 514 288 9942).
Stand Buys, 311 West Superior St, Chicago, IL 60610 (☎ 1 800 331 0257).
Travel Brokers, 50 Broad St, New York, NY 10004 (☎ 1 800 999 8748).

Students may find special bargains through youth-travel agencies such as:
Council Travel, 205 East 42 St, New York, NY 10017 (☎ 212 661 1450).
STA, 48 East 11 St, New York, NY 10003 (☎ 212 477 7166).
Travel Cuts, 187 College St, Toronto, ON M5T 1P7 (☎ 1 416 979 2406).

For tickets on the Internet, try *Expedia UK* (www: expedia.co.uk) and, in North America, *Travelocity* (www: travelocity.com).

By rail

From Britain

To travel from London to northern Italy by train is an adventure, but it is not significantly cheaper than flying. It makes sense only if you're thinking of stopping at other destinations along the way.

The principal Italian cities are linked with Britain by a variety of rail routes, the most direct being from London via Paris and Turin, or via Paris and Milan. These services have sleeping cars (first class: single or double compartment; second class: three-berth compartments) and couchettes (seats converted into couches at night: first class: four; second class: six). Couchettes and sleeping compartments should be booked well in advance, although those that are not occupied at the time of departure can be hired directly from the conductor without paying a supplement. Reciprocal booking arrangements exist with Austria, Belgium, Denmark, France, Great Britain, Hungary, Luxembourg, the Netherlands, Portugal, Spain and Switzerland.

Information on and tickets for Italian State Railways (*Ferrovie dello Stato* or *FS*) can be obtained from *European Rail Ltd*, ☎ 020 7387 0444, fax 020 7387 0888; also from *Rail Choice Ltd*, ☎ 020 7939 9915, www.railchoice.co.uk. See also websites: www.fs-on-line.com, www.itwg.com/home.asp, www.raileurope.co.uk.

From the USA and Canada

In North America contact the following *Citalia* offices:
CIT New York: 15 West 44th Street, 10th Floor, New York, NY 10036. (800) CIT-

TOUR for tour information, email tour@cittours.com.
CIT Chicago (CIT RAIl): 9501 West Devon Avenue, Suite 1, E Rosemont, IL 60018. (800) CIT-RAIL for rail information, email: rail@cit-rail.com.
CIT Montreal: 1450 City Counselers ST Quebec, Montreal H3A2E6. (800) 361 7799 for the Montreal area, local area dial (514) 845 9101.
CIT Toronto: 80 Tiverton Crt, Suite 401, Markham, ON L3R0G4. (800) 387 0711 for the Toronto area, local area dial (905) 415 1060.
For general information contact your local travel agent or call 1 (800) 248 8687.
The Italian State Railways' web site is www.fs-on-line.com.

By coach

From Britain

A coach service operates in two days between London (Victoria Coach Station) and Rome (Piazza della Repubblica) via Dover, Paris, Mont Blanc, Aosta, Turin, Genoa, Milan, Bologna and Florence, daily from June to September, and once or twice a week for the rest of the year. Reductions are available for students. Information in London from the *National Express* office at Victoria Coach Station (☎ 0990 808080), from local National Express agents, and from *SITA* offices in Italy.

By car

The easiest approaches to Italy by road are the motorways through the San Bernard, Frejus or Mont Cenis tunnels, or over the Brenner Pass. The Mont Blanc tunnel is closed and will probably remain so for several years. British drivers taking their own cars by any of the routes across France, Belgium, Luxembourg, Switzerland, Germany and Austria need the vehicle registration book, a valid national driving licence, an international insurance certificate (check with your insurance broker) and a nationality plate (fixed to the rear of the vehicle so as to be illuminated by the rear lights). A Swiss motorway pass is needed for Switzerland and can be obtained from the *Royal Automobile Club* (☎ 01345 333 1133), the *Automobile Association* (☎ 0990 500 600), or at the Swiss border. Motorists who are not owners of the vehicle must possess the owner's permit for its use abroad. Foreign drivers hiring a car in Italy need only a valid national driver's licence. Additional route information is available from www.autostop.it/.

By sea

Adriatic Italy is connected by car-ferry and hydrofoil to Greece (Patras, Igoumenitsa, Corfu), Albania (Durres, Vlore), and Croatia (Split). Information and reservations from:
A.K. Ventouris, L. Posidonos 73, Piraeus (☎ 01 938 9280-7, fax 01 938 9289; branch offices in Patras, Igoumenitsa, and Brindisi).
Agoumidos Lines, Kapodistriou 2, Piraeus (☎ 01 412 6680, fax 01 422 0595; branch offices in Brindisi, Corfu, and Igoumenitsa).
Fragline, 5a Rethymnou St, Athens (☎ 01 821 4171, fax 01 821 3095; branch offices in Brindisi, Rome, Milan, Corfu, Igoumenitsa and Patras).
Illyria Lines, 5 Ifestou St, Athens (☎ 01 964 3124, fax 01 962 7042; branch offices in Brindisi, Durres and Vlore).
Misano Alta Velocità, Via Tunisi 10, Brindisi (☎ 0831 562043, fax 0831

562005; branch offices in Milan, Genoa, and Rome).
Società Adriatica di Navigazione, Zattere 1141, Venice (☎ 041 781611, fax 041 781894; branch offices in Ancona, Bari, Brindisi, Corfu, Durres, Igoumenitsa, Patras, Split, Trieste).

Where to stay

Hotels
In this guide a selection of hotels has been given at the beginning of each chapter. They have been classified in a very relative manner, as expensive, moderate or inexpensive. Generally speaking, you should expect a double room at an expensive hotel to cost L 400,000 (200 euros) per night or more; at a moderate hotel, L 200,000–400,000 (100–200 euros), and at an inexpensive hotel, under L 200,000 (100 euros). The hotels listed, regardless of their cost, have been chosen on the basis of their personality or character: all have something special about them (beautiful surroundings, distinctive atmosphere), and even the humblest are quite comfortable. The local tourist offices will help you find accommodation on the spot; nevertheless, you should try to book well in advance, especially if you're planning to travel between May and October. Hotels equipped to offer hospitality to the disabled are indicated in the tourist boards' hotel lists.

In all hotels the service charges are included in the rates. The total charge is exhibited on the back of the door of the hotel room. Breakfast is by law an optional extra charge, although many hotels try to include it in the price of the room. When booking a room, always specify whether you want breakfast or not. If you are staying in a hotel in a town, it is usually well worthwhile going round the corner to the nearest café for breakfast. Hotels are now obliged by law (for tax purposes) to issue an official receipt to customers: you should not leave the premises without this document.

Bed and breakfast
Bed-and-breakfast accommodation is now offered in most areas. Rooms are usually in private homes, villas, etc., and may be booked through a central agency. Contact *Caffelletto*, Via di Marciola 23, 50020 San Vincenzo a Torri (Firenze) Italy; ☎ 055 730 9145, fax 055 768121; e-mail: info@caffelletto.it. You can visit their website at www.caffelletto.it.

Residences
A new type of hotel, called a *residenza*, has been introduced into Italy. Residences are normally in a building or group of houses of historic interest, often a castle or monastery. They may have only a few rooms, and sometimes offer self-catering accommodation. They are listed separately in the tourist information offices' hotel lists, with their prices.

Farm stays
Recently developed throughout Italy, the short-term rental of space in villas and farmhouses (*agriturismo*) provides an interesting form of accommodation in the

countryside. Terms very greatly, from bed-and-breakfast to self-contained flats. These are highly recommended for travellers with their own transport, and for families, as an excellent (and usually cheap) way of visiting the Italian country-side. Some farms require a stay of a minimum number of days. Cultural or recre-ational activities, such as horse-riding, are sometimes also provided. Details are supplied by the local tourist information offices. The main organisations in Italy concerned with agriturismo are:

Agriturist, Via Isonzo 27, Milan, ☎ 02 58302122, www.agriturist.it.
Terranostra, Via Marocco 8, Milan, ☎ 02 2613083, www.terratnostra.it. Terranostra publish an annual list of agriturismo accommodation under the title *Vacanze Natura.*
Turismo Verde, 19 Via Cornalia, Milan, ☎ 02 5591316.

Camping
Camping is well organised throughout Italy. Camping sites are listed in the local information offices' publications. Full details of the sites in Italy are published annually by the *Touring Club Italiano*, Corso Italia 10, 20122 Milan (☎ 02 85261, fax 02 852 6362) in *Campeggi e Villaggi Turistici in Italia*. The national headquarters of the *Federazione Italiana del Campeggio*, at 11 Via Vittorio Emanuele, 50041 Calenzano (Firenze) (☎ 055 882 391, fax 055 882 5918, www.camping.it), also publishes an annual guide (*Guida Camping d'Italia*) and maintains an information office and booking service.

Hostels
The *Associazione Italiani Alberghi per la Gioventù* (Italian Youth Hostels Association), Via Cavour 44, 00184 Rome (☎ 06 487 1152) runs many hostels, which are listed in its free annual guide. A membership card of the AIAG or the International Youth Hostel Federation is required for access to Italian youth hos-tels. Details from the *Youth Hostels Association*, Trevelyan House, 8 St Stephen's Hill, St Albans, Herts AL1 2DY (☎ 01727 845047) and from the National Offices of *American Youth Hostels Inc.*, Washington DC 20013-7613.

Religious institutions
Religious institutions sometimes offer simple but comfortable accommodation at very reasonable prices. For listings of convents, monasteries and other religious institutions offering accommodation, contact the Arcivescovado of the city of your choice (for Milan, for instance, the address is: *Arcivescovado di Milano, Milano, Italia*), or the local tourist information office.

 # Getting around

By rail
The Italian State Railways (*FS*—Ferrovie dello Stato) now run nine categories of trains:
• *ES* (*Eurostar*), high-speed trains running between major Italian cities.
• *EC* (*Eurocity*), international express trains running between the main Italian

and European cities.
- *EN* (*Euronotte*), overnight international express trains with sleeping-car or couchette service.
- *IC* (*Intercity*), express trains running between major Italian cities.
- *E* (*Espressi*), long-distance trains not as fast as the Intercity trains.
- *D* (*Diretti*), intermediate-distance trains making more stops than the Espressi.
- *IR* (*Interregionali*), the new name for Diretti.
- *R* (*Regionali*), local trains stopping at all stations.
- *M* (*Metropolitani*), surface or underground commuter trains.

Booking seats

Seats can be booked in advance, as early as two months and as late as 30mins before departure, from the main cities at the station booking office (usually open daily 07.00–22.00), or at travel agencies representing the Italian State Railways. The timetable of the train services changes in late September and late May every year. Excellent timetables are published twice a year by the Italian State Railways (*In Treno*; one volume covers the whole of Italy; trains with facilities for the disabled are marked) and by several independent publishers. These can be purchased at news-stands and train stations.

Tickets

Tickets must be bought at the station (or from travel agents representing the Italian State Railways) before starting a journey, otherwise a fairly large supplement has to be paid to the ticket-collector on the train. Most tickets are valid for 60 days after the date of issue. Time should be allowed for buying a ticket, as there are often long queues at the station ticket counters. Some trains charge a special supplement, and on others seats must be booked in advance. It is therefore always necessary to specify which train you are intending to take as well as the destination when buying tickets. And don't forget: you must stamp the date of your journey on the ticket in the meters located on or near the station platforms *before you get on the train*. If you buy a return ticket, you must stamp your ticket before beginning the outward-bound *and* return journeys. In the main stations the better-known credit cards are now generally accepted (although a special ticket window must sometimes be used when buying a ticket with a credit card). There are limitations on travelling short distances on some trains.

Fares and reductions

Fares in Italy are still much lower than in Britain or North America. Children under four travel free, and between four and twelve pay half price. There are also reductions for families and for groups of as few as two persons.
- For travellers over the age of 60 (with Senior Citizen Railcards), the *Rail Europ Senior* card offers a 30 per cent reduction on Italian rail fares.
- The *Inter-rail* card (valid one month), which can be purchased in Britain or North America by young people up to the age of 26, and the *Inter-rail 26+* card for those over 26 years of age, are valid in Italy.
- In Italy the *Carta d'Argento* and the *Carta Verde* (both valid one year) allow a 20 per cent reduction on rail fares respectively for those over 60 and between the ages of 12 and 26.
- A *Biglietto Chilometrico* (Cumulative Ticket) is valid for 3000 kilometres over a two-month period and can be used by up to five people at the same time.

- The *Euro Domino* and *Euro Domino Junior* cards, available to those resident out side Italy, gives freedom of the Italian railways for three, five, or ten days. These cards can be purchased in Britain or at main stations in Italy.
- The *Carta Blu* is available for the disabled.

Other forms of discounted travel are *Rail Inclusive Tours*, which offer transport, accommodation, excursions, etc., in a single package; the *Tessera di Autorizzazione* (Special Concession Card), which provides a 20 per cent discount and exemption from special supplements for frequent travel in first class, second class or both. The *Carta Primaclasse* enables one person or two people travelling together to buy up to eight first-class tickets at a 50 per cent discount; it is valid for 60 days from the time of purchase.

Website For timetables and other information on rail services in Italy only, visit the Italian State railways' website: www.fs-on-line.it.

Restaurant cars
Restaurant cars are attached to most international and internal long-distance trains. Some trains also have self-service restaurants. Snacks, hot coffee and drinks can often be purchased from a trolley wheeled down the train during the journey. At every large station snacks are on sale from trolleys on the platform, and you can buy them from the train window. These include carrier-bags with sandwiches, drink and fruit (*cestini da viaggio*) or individual sandwiches (*panini*).

Additional services and information
Additional services available at main stations include assistance for the disabled; special car-hire offers; automatic ticketing; porterage; and left luggage offices (open 24hrs at the main stations; often closed at night at smaller stations). Porters are entitled to a fixed amount, shown on notice boards at all stations, for each piece of baggage.

By bus
Local and long-distance coaches between the main towns in northern Italy are not as frequent as they once were, for service is diminishing as increasing num-bers of residents become independently mobile. Except in areas of particular interest to non-residents (such as the summer and winter resorts), most coaches now carry schoolchildren from the villages to the towns in the early morning, and from the towns to the villages in the afternoon. Coaches still serve most towns not reached by rail at least once a day, leaving major cities from a depot usually at or near the train station. Excellent timetables are published twice a year by the Italian State Railways. Accurate timetables for other areas can be obtained from the local tourist boards.

City buses are an excellent means of getting about in most towns. In Milan the underground (*Metro*, marked 'M') is the swiftest and easiest means of moving across town. Almost everywhere, tickets must be purchased before boarding (at tobacconists, bars, news-stands, information offices, etc.) and stamped on board.

By car
Regardless of whether you are driving your own car or a hired vehicle, Italian law requires you to carry a valid driving licence when travelling. You must also keep a red triangle in the car in case of accident or breakdown. This serves as a warning

to other traffic when placed on the road at a distance of 50m from the stationary car. It can be hired from ACI for a minimal charge and returned at the frontier.

It is now compulsory to wear seat-belts in cars in Italy, and crash helmets are compulsory when driving or riding a motorcycle. Traffic is generally faster (and often more aggressive) than in Britain or America. As 80 per cent of the goods transported travel by road, lorries pose a constant hazard on the open road, and the degree of congestion in even the smallest towns defies the imagination. Road signs are now more or less standardised to the international codes, and state-of-the-art technology is used to enforce speed limits: 130km/h (80mph) on motorways, 90km/h (56mph) on major highways, 50km/h (31mph) in urban areas.

Certain customs differ radically from those of Britain or America. Pedestrians have the right of way at zebra crossings, although you're taking your life in your hands if you step into the street without looking. Unless otherwise indicated, cars entering a road or roundabout from the right are given precedence. Trollies and trains always have the right of way from either left or right. If an oncoming driver flashes his headlights, it means he is proceeding and not giving you precedence. In towns, Italian drivers frequently change lanes without warning. They also tend to ignore pedestrian crossings. In the south they view red lights with a certain contempt. Everywhere the drivers of motorbikes, mopeds, and Vespas weave in and out of traffic, snapping up the right of way. The concept of the safe braking distance is unknown, and if you leave a gap between your car and the vehicle in front of you it will be filled immediately.

Roads in Italy

Italy probably has the finest motorways in Europe, called *autostrade* (for information: www.autostrade.it). They are indicated by green signs or, near the entrance ramps, by large boards of overhead lights. Tolls are charged according to the rating of the vehicle and the distance covered. All autostrade have service areas open 24hrs, and most have SOS points every 2km. At the entrance to motorways, the two directions are indicated by the name of the most important town (and not by the nearest town), which can be momentarily confusing. Similar to autostrade, but not provided with service stations, SOS points, or emergency lanes, are the dual-carriageway fast roads called *superstrade* (also indicated by green signs).

Northern Italy has an excellent network of secondary highways (*strade statali* or *provinciali*, indicated by blue signs marked, respectively, SS or SP; on maps simply by a number), usually good roads which provide fine views of the countryside. Local traffic can be extremely heavy in densely populated areas and on many arteries.

Throughout Italy, buildings of historic interest are often indicated by yellow signs (although there are long-term plans to change the colour to brown); towns (*comuni*) and their component villages (*frazioni*), by white signs. The territory of a comune is often much larger than the town of the same name that is its administrative centre—another source of confusion.

Petrol stations

Petrol stations are open 24hrs a day on motorways, elsewhere 07.00–12.00, 15.00–20.00; winter 07.30–12.30, 14.30–19.30. 24hr self-service stations can also be found in or near the larger towns. Pumps are operated by L 10,000 or L 50,000 banknotes, or by credit cards. All varieties of petrol (including diesel and unleaded) are now readily available in Italy, although they cost more than in

Britain, and considerably more than in North America. Most stations offer basic maintenance service (motor oil, brake fluid, and so on), but mechanical assistance must be sought from a *meccanico* (mechanic), *elettrauto* (auto electrician), *gommaio* (tyre shop), *carrozziere* (body shop), and so on. Temporary membership of the **ACI** (*Automobile Club d'Italia*) can be taken out on the frontier or in Italy (the headquarters of **ACI** are at Via Marsala 8, Rome, with branch offices in all the main towns). They provide a breakdown service (*Soccorso ACI*, ☎ 116) and other advantages.

Parking

Many cities in northern Italy have taken the wise step of closing their historic centres to traffic (except for residents), which makes them much more pleasant to visit on foot. Access is allowed to hotels and for the disabled. It is always advisable to leave your car in a supervised car park, though with a bit of effort it is frequently possible to find a place to park free of charge away from the town centre. However, to do so overnight is not advisable. Always lock your car when parked, and never leave anything of value inside it.

Car hire

Car hire is available in most Italian cities. Arrangements can be made before departure through the airlines (at specially advantageous rates in conjunction with their flights) or in Italy through any of the principal car-hire firms (the best known include **Maggiore/Budget**, **Avis** and **Hertz**), which offer daily, 5-day, weekly, and weekend rates. Special leasing rates are available for periods of 30 days and over. Italian State Railways also offers special rail-car combinations (see above).

Car and driver service is a convenient, though somewhat expensive way to visit northern Italy, especially metropolitan areas such as Milan and its environs, where traffic is harrowing and a knowledge of alternative routes saves time and fatigue. Details from the local tourist boards.

By air

Frequent internal flights are operated between most main towns. Reductions are available for early booking and weekend travel.

Cycling and walking

Cycling and walking have become more popular in Italy in recent years, and more information is now available locally. The local offices of the **CAI** (***Club Alpino Italiano***) and the **WWF** (***Worldwide Fund for Nature***) provide all the information necessary. Maps are published by the *Istituto Geografico Militare* , *CAI* and several private publishers at scales of 1:50,000 and 1:25,000.

Taxis

These are hired from ranks or by telephone; there are no cruising cabs. Before engaging a taxi, it is advisable to make sure it has a meter in working order. Fares vary from city to city but are generally cheaper than London taxis, though considerably more expensive than New York taxis. No tip is expected, but L 1000 or so can be given. Supplements are charged for late-night journeys and for luggage. There is a heavy surcharge when the destination is outside the town limits (ask roughly how much the fare is likely to be).

Language

Even a few words of Italian are a great advantage in Italy, where any attempt to speak the language is met with approval and encouragement. Local dialects vary greatly and are usually unintelligible to the foreigner, but even where dialect is universally used, nearly everybody can speak and understand Italian. A simple series of instructions for pronouncing Italian words follows.

Words should be pronounced well forward in the mouth, and no nasal intonation exists in Italian. Double consonants call for special care as each must be sounded. Consonants are pronounced roughly as in English with the following exceptions:

c and *cc* before e and i have the sound of *ch* in chess.

sc before e and i is pronounced like *sh* in ship.

ch before e and i has the sound of *k*.

g and *gg* before e and i are always soft, like *j* in jelly.

gh is always hard, like *g* in get.

gl is nearly always like *lli* in million (there are a few exceptions, for example, *negligere*, where it is pronounced as in English).

gn is like *ny* in lanyard.

gu and *qu* are always like *gw* and *kw*.

s is hard like *s* in six, except when it occurs between two vowels, when it is soft, like the English *z* or the *s* in rose.

ss is always hard.

z and *zz* are usually pronounced like *ts*, but occasionally have the sound of *dz* before a long vowel.

Vowels are pronounced much more openly than in southern English and are given their full value. There are no true diphthongs in Italian, and every vowel should be articulated separately. The stress normally falls on the last syllable but one; in modern practice an accent-sign is written regularly only when the stress is on the last syllable, for example, *città*, or to differentiate between two words similarly spelt but with a different meaning: for example *e* (and); *è* (is).

Customs and etiquette

Attention should be paid to the more formal manners of the Italians. It is customary to open conversation in shops and such places with the courtesy of *buon giorno* (good day) or *buona sera* (good evening). The deprecatory expression *prego* (don't mention it) is everywhere the obligatory and automatic response to *grazie* (thank you). The phrases *per piacere* or *per favore* (please), *permesso* (excuse me), used when pushing past someone (essential on public vehicles), *scusi* (sorry; also, I beg your pardon, when something is not heard), should not be forgotten. A visitor will be wished *Buon appetito!* before beginning a meal, to which he should reply *Grazie, altrettanto*. This pleasant custom may be extended to fellow passengers taking a picnic meal on a train. Shaking hands is an essential part of greeting and leave-taking. In shops and offices a certain amount of self-assertion is taken for granted, since queues are not the general rule and it is incumbent on the inquirer or customer to get him or herself a hearing.

Galleries, museums and churches

The opening times of museums, sites, and monuments are given in the text, but they often change without warning. The provincial tourist authority in major cities keeps updated timetables of most museums. National museums and monuments are usually open Tues–Sun 09.00–14.00 or 19.00, plus evening hours in summer. Archaeological sites generally open at 09.00 and close at dusk. Naturally, as opening times are constantly being altered, care should be taken to allow enough time for variations in the hours shown in the text when planning a visit to a museum or monument.

Some museums are closed on the main public holidays: 1 January, Easter, 1 May, 15 August and 25 December. Several smaller museums have suspended regular hours altogether and are now open by appointment only. Their telephone numbers are included in the text, and visits may be reserved by calling ahead. Entrance fees to Italian museums vary (from free to L 12,000) according to your age and nationality; British citizens under 18 and over 60 are entitled to free admission to national museums and monuments because of reciprocal arrangements in Britain. During the *Settimana per i Beni Culturali e Ambientali* (Cultural and Environmental Heritage Week), usually held early in December, entrance to national museums is free for all.

Churches in northern Italy open quite early in the morning (often for 06.00 Mass), but are normally closed for a considerable period during the middle of the day (12.00–15.00, 16.00, or 17.00), although cathedrals and some of the large churches may be open without a break during daylight hours. Smaller churches and oratories are often open only in the early morning, but the key can usually be found by inquiring locally. The sacristan will also show closed chapels and crypts, and a small tip should be given. Some churches now ask that sightseers do not enter during a service, but normally visitors may do so, provided they are silent and do not approach the altar in use. At all times they are expected to cover their legs and arms, and generally dress with decorum. An entrance fee is becoming customary for admission to treasuries, bell-towers, and so on. Lights (operated by L 500 coins) have been installed in many churches to illuminate frescoes and altarpieces. In Holy Week most of the pictures are covered and are on no account shown.

Entertainment

Annual **music**, **drama** and **film festivals** take place in many towns, famous ones including the opera festival in the Verona Arena, and the international song festival in San Remo. The **opera** season in Italy usually begins in December and continues until June: the principal opera house in Northern Italy is the Teatro alla Scala in Milan.

Traditional festivals are celebrated in most towns and villages in commemoration of a local historical or religious event and are often very spectacular—with fireworks, processions, music and dancing, food and drink, etc. The major festivals have been indicated in the text; see the local tourist information office or your hotel staff for further details.

At present there are no agencies in the UK or North America authorised to sell opera and concert tickets. You may write directly to the theatre or ask your travel agent if he/she can obtain tickets though his/her representatives in Italy. The desk staff at hotels will also assist guests in obtaining tickets for performances.

Sport

Cycling This is Italy's leading participant sport. Every man, woman and child, from eight to eighty, has or knows someone who has a racing bicycle, and many can be seen out riding the back roads on weekends. Amateur bicycle races are numerous and fun to watch or even participate in. The hills of Piedmont, the Veneto and Venezia-Giulia are excellent for cycling, and the Alpine passes of the Dolomites are as beautiful as they are challenging.

Fishing Italy's many lakes, rivers, mountain streams and miles of coastline afford abundant fishing. Mountain waters are rich in trout, grayling, char, etc., and other waters contain bleak, chub, carp, tench, pike, perch, etc. Sea fishing is free, but a special licence is required for inland waters. The licence is very inexpensive and is valid for one year. In addition, membership must be taken out in the *Federazione Italiana della Pesca Sportiva*, which administers 90 per cent of Italian waters. Membership can be obtained without formality at all provincial offices of the federation or at the central headquarters in Rome, Viale Tiziano 70, ☎ 06 394754.

No licence is required for spear fishing, which is allowed everywhere except in harbours. However, regulations forbid the use of oxygen tanks and nets for underwater fishing. Not more than 5kg of fish, crustacea and shellfish may be caught.

Golf Golf has only recently come into vogue in Italy, and although the game does not enjoy the same popularity as in Britain and North America, there are quite a few beautiful and challenging courses. Details are given in the text.

Horse-riding Arrangements for riding can be made through most hotels. For more information, contact the *Federazione Italiana Sport Equestri*, Viale Tiziano 70, Roma, ☎ 06 36851.

Hunting Restrictions are strictly enforced on the importation and use of firearms, and the disproportionate number of hunters, with respect to prey, makes hunting in Italy frankly boring. Information from the *Federazione Italiana Caccia*, Viale Tiziano 70, 00196 Roma, ☎ 06 3685 8344.

Skiing Downhill skiing is extremely popular throughout northern Italy, and there are many miles of excellent slopes. Exact locations are given in the text.

Cross-country, back-country and alpine skiing, as well as snow-shoeing, are acquiring a growing public in the Alpine resorts. Many trails are now marked with phosphorescent flashes.

Spectator sports Soccer is by far the most popular spectator sport in Italy. Every Sunday, from September to June, enthusiastic fans pack into Italian soccer stadiums. The most important teams in the north are *Milan* and *Inter* (Milano), *Torino* (Turin), *Sampdoria* (Genoa) and the homeless *Juventus* (who play in Turin). Basketball, cycling, ice-hockey and volleyball are other major spectator sports. Life grinds to a halt for the *Giro d'Italia* bicycle race (June) and the European Cup and World Cup soccer championships.

Swimming and water sports The clear Mediterranean waters of Italy's coasts make for marvellous swimming, water-skiing, kajaking, diving, etc. Motor boats (including jet-skis) must stay at least 300m from public beaches. Many hotels have pools, and most towns have at least one Olympic-size public pool. Details from your hotel staff.

Tennis There are numerous tennis courts in all larger cities, and most holiday centres and many hotels have at least one or two courts. Ask your hotel staff for the nearest ones.

Walking, hiking and climbing These are probably the fastest-growing sports in Italy. Trails and back-country lodges, from the Alps to the Apennines, are maintained by individuals, towns, provinces and regions, and by the *CAI* (*Club Alpino Italiano*) headquarters at Via Ugo Foscolo 3, 20122 Milan, ☎ 02 7202 3085), with local branches in major cities and resorts.

Yachting The Italian coastline has numerous natural harbours, which make it ideal for yachting. Permission to anchor must be obtained from the *Capitaneria di Porto* (harbour master) in each harbour. Information from the *Federazione Italiana Vela* (Viale Brigata Bisagno 2/17, 16129 Genova, ☎ 010 565723, fax 010 592864) or *Federazione Italiana Motonautica* (Via Piranesi 44/b, 20137 Milano, ☎ 02 761 0502). The latter also furnish lists of yacht-chartering companies.

Additional information

Banking services

Money can be changed at banks, post offices, travel agencies and some hotels, restaurants and shops, though the rate of exchange can vary considerably from place to place. The best way to obtain lire while in Italy is to use your cashpoint card or credit card: in most cities ATM machines are open 24hrs a day, require no waiting and offer the best exchange rates.

Banks are open Mon–Fri, 08.30–13.30, 14.30–15.30 and are closed on Saturday, Sunday and holidays. The afternoon one-hour opening may vary from bank to bank, and many banks close early (about 11.00) on days preceding national holidays. Exchange offices are usually open seven days a week at airports and most main railway stations. A limited amount of lire can be obtained from conductors on international trains and at certain stations. For small amounts of money, the difference between hotel and bank rates may be negligible, as banks tend to take a fixed commission on transactions.

Crime and personal security

Pickpocketing is a widespread problem in towns all over Italy: it is always advisable not to carry valuables in handbags, and be particularly careful on public transport. Never wear conspicuous jewellery, including necklaces and expensive watches; women, when walking, should keep their handbags on the side of their bodies nearer the wall (never on the street side). Crime should be reported at once to the police or the local *carabinieri* office (found in every town and small village). A detailed statement has to be given in order to get an official document confirming loss or damage (essential for insurance claims). Interpreters are provided.

For emergencies, ☎ 113 (*Polizia di Stato*) or 112 (*Carabinieri*).

Electric current

The electrical current in Italy is AC 220 volts/50 cycles. If you are carrying electrical appliances having a different current (for instance, 100volts/60 cycles), you should buy a lightweight transformer either before leaving home or at an electrical appliance shop in Italy. Check the voltage with your hotel before using electrical appliances. Plugs have prongs that are round, not flat, therefore an adaptor plug is needed for appliances manufactured in the UK or North America. Many electrical appliances, such as travel irons, hair dryers and laptop computers are available in the UK or North America for use abroad without the need of separate transformers or adaptors.

Embassies and consulates

Help is given to British, US, and Canadian travellers who are in difficulty by the British, Canadian and United States embassies in Rome, and by the Canadian and United States consulates in Milan. **Canadian Consulate**: Via Vittor Pisani 19, Milan (☎ 02 669 7451; night line 02 669 4970). **United States Consulate**: Via Principe Amedeo 2/10, Milan (☎ 02 290 351).

Emergency numbers

For emergencies, ☎ 113 (*Polizia di Stato*) or 112 (*Carabinieri*).
Medical assistance ☎ 118

Newspapers

The most widely read newspapers are *Corriere della Sera* of Milan, *La Stampa* of Turin, and *Repubblica* and *Messaggero* of Rome. Genoa's *Secolo XIX* and Bologna's *Il Resto del Carlino* are locally important. *Il Sole 24 Ore*, Milan's answer to the *Financial Times* and the *Wall Street Journal*, has an excellent cultural page on Sunday. Foreign newspapers are sold at central street kiosks and railway stations.

Opening hours

Government offices usually work Mon–Sat 08.00/09.00–13.00/14.00; businesses Mon–Fri 08.30/09.00–12.30/13.00 and 14.30/15.00–18.00. Shops generally open Mon–Sat 08.30/9.00–13.00 and 15.30/16.00–19.30/20.00.

Shops selling clothes and other goods are usually closed on Monday morning, food shops on Wednesday afternoon, except from mid-June–mid-September, when all shops are closed instead on Saturday afternoon. In resorts, during July and August many shops remain open from early morning until late at night.

Pharmacies

Pharmacies (*farmacie*) are usually open Mon–Fri 09.00–13.00, 16.00–19.30 or 20.00. A few are open also on Saturdays, Sundays and holidays (listed on the door of every pharmacy). In all towns there is also at least one pharmacy open at night (also shown on the door of every pharmacy).

Photography

There are few restrictions on photography in Italy, but permission is necessary to photograph the interiors of churches and museums and may sometimes be withheld. Care should also be taken before photographing individuals, notably members of the armed forces and the police. Photography is forbidden on railway stations and civil airfields, as well as in frontier zones and near military installations.

Public holidays

The Italian national holidays when offices, shops, and schools are closed are as follows:

1 January	25 April (Liberation Day)
Easter Sunday and Easter Monday	1 May (Labour Day)
15 August (Assumption)	1 November (All Saints' Day)
8 December (Immaculate Conception)	25 December (Christmas Day)
26 December (St Stephen)	

Each town keeps its patron saint's day as a holiday.

Public toilets

There is a notable shortage of public toilets in Italy. All cafés should have toilets available to the public (generally speaking, the larger the café, the better the facilities). It is customary to make a small purchase if using the toilet. Nearly all museums now have toilets.

Religion

There is an **Anglican church** in Milan (All Saints, Via Solferino 12, ☎ 02 6552258). **Synagogues** can be found in Alessandria (Via Milano 7, ☎ 0131 62224), Bologna (Via Combruti 9, ☎ 051 232066), Casale Monferrato (Vicolo Salomone Olper 44), Ferrara (Via Mazzini 95, ☎ 0532 34240), Genoa (Via Bertora 6, ☎ 010 891513), Mantua (Via Govi 11, ☎ 0376 321490), Merano (Via Schiller 14, ☎ 0463 36127), Milan (Via Eupili 6, ☎ 02 345 2096), Modena (Piazza Mazzini 26, ☎ 059 223978, Padua (Via Santi Martino e Solferino 5, ☎ 049 23524), Parma (Via Cervi 4), Turin (Via San Pio V 12, ☎ 011 669 2387), Trieste (Via San Francesco 19, ☎ 040 768171), Vercelli (Via Foà 70) and Verona (Via Portici 3, ☎ 045 21112).

Sales tax rebates

If you're a non-European Union resident, you can claim tax back on purchases made in Italy, provided the total expenditure is more than L 300,000. Ask the vendor for a receipt describing the goods acquired and send it back to him when you get home (but no later than 90 days after the date of the receipt). The receipt must be checked and stamped by Italian Customs upon leaving Italy. On receipt of the bill, the vendor will forward the sales tax rebate (the present tax rate is 20 per cent on most goods) to your home address.

Telephone and postal services

Stamps are sold at tobacco shops (*tabacchi*, marked with a large white 'T') and post offices. *Posta ordinaria* is regular post; *posta prioritaria* receives priority handling, including transport by air mail, and is only slightly more expensive. Correspondence can be addressed to you in Italy c/o the post office by adding 'Fermo Posta' to the name of the locality.

There are numerous **public telephones** all over Italy, and card-operated phones are becoming increasingly common in major cities and resort areas. Local calls cost L 200. Cards offering L 5000, L 10,000 or L 20,000 in prepaid calls are available at post offices, tobacconists and some news-stands. They are particularly convenient for phoning abroad. All **calls in Italy**, local and long-distance, are made by dialling the city code (for instance, 02 for Milan), then the telephone number; international and intercontinental calls, by dialling 00 plus the country code, then the city code (for numbers in Britain, without the initial zero), and the telephone number (for instance, the central London number 020 7855 2000 would be 0041 20 7855 2000). You can reach an *AT&T* operator at ☎ 172 1011, *MCI* at 172 1022, or *Sprint* at 172 1877.

For **directory assistance** ☎ 12 (numbers in Italy) or 176 (international numbers). You can receive a wake-up call on your phone by dialling 114 and following the prompts (in Italian).

Most car rental agencies can arrange the rental of mobile (cellular) phones.

Time

Italy is one hour ahead of Greenwich Mean Time and six hours ahead of Eastern Standard Time in North America. Daylight savings time in Italy usually runs from April to October inclusive.

Tipping

A service charge of 15–18 per cent is added to **hotel** bills. The service charge is already included when all-inclusive prices are quoted, but it is customary to leave an additional tip in any case. As a guideline and depending on the category of your hotel, the following tips are suggested: chambermaid, L 1000/day; concierge, L 3000/day (additional tip for extra services); bellhop or porter, L 1500/bag; doorman (for calling a cab), L 1000; room-service waiter, L 1000 and up (depending on amount of bill); valet service, at least L 1000; hotel bar, 15 per cent.

A service charge of approximately 15 per cent is added to all **restaurant** bills. It is customary, however, to leave a small tip (5–10 per cent) for good service. In cafés and bars, leave 15 per cent if you were served at a table and if a bill does not already include service; and L 100–500 while standing at a counter or bar drinking coffee, cocktails, etc.

At **opera**, **concerts** and the **theatre**, tip ushers L 1000 and up, depending on the price of your seat.

Tourist information

ENIT has information offices at the border crossings with Austria (*Valico Autostradale Lupo di Brennero*) and France (*Casello Roverino di Ventimiglia*) as well as at Milano Linate, Roma Leonardo da Vinci and Napoli Capodichino airports. Within Italy each 'region' has information services organised on the regional, provincial, and local levels; where possible, these have been indicated in the text. A general reorganisation of the Italian tourist authorities will, when completed, lead to the concentration of resources traditionally divided between the *EPT* (*Enti Provinciali del Turismo*) and the *AA* (*Aziende Autonome di Cura, Soggiorno e Turismo*) under a single authority, the *APT* (*Aziende di Promozione Turistica*). In some areas this transition has already taken place.

Weights and measures

Italians use the metric system of weights and measures. The *metro* is the unit of length, the *grammo* of weight, the *ara* of land measurement, the *litro* of capacity. Greek-derived prefixes (*deca-, etto-, chilo-*) are used with those names to express multiples; Latin prefixes (*deci-, centi-, milli-*) to express fractions (1 *chilometro* = 1000 *metri*, 1 *millimetro* = 1000th part of a *metro*).

For approximate calculations:
the *metro* (or metre) may be taken as 39 inches
the *chilometro* (kilometre) as 0.6 mile
the *litro* (litre) as 1.75 pint, an *etto* as 3.5 oz
the *chilo* (kilogram) as 2.2 lb.

Food and drink

Italian food is usually good and inexpensive. Generally speaking, the least pretentious *ristorante* (restaurant), *trattoria* (simple restaurant) or *osteria* (inn or tavern) provides the best value. A selection of restaurants has been given at the beginning of each chapter. The restaurants listed have been chosen for the quality and distinction of their cuisine and the extent of their wine lists; even the simplest are quite good. Like hotels, they have been graduated by price (expensive, moderate, inexpensive). Consider an expensive meal as one costing L 100,000 (50 euros) or more; a moderate meal, L 40,000–100,000 (20–50 euros), an inexpensive meal, under L 40,000 (20 euros). As a rule, the more exclusive eating places are slightly cheaper at midday. You should telephone for details *and* to reserve, as all the establishments listed provide good value for price and are likely to be crowded. Where no restaurants have been indicated at the beginning of a chapter, I have felt that none merit special mention; naturally, many establishments in the area will nonetheless be capable of providing a satisfactory meal.

Restaurants are now obliged by law (for tax purposes) to issue a receipt to customers: you can be fined if you leave the premises without this document. Prices on the menu do not include a cover charge (marked *coperto*, usually at the bottom of the page), which is added to the bill. The service charge (marked *servizio*) is now almost always automatically added at the end of the bill; tipping is therefore not strictly necessary, but a few thousand lire are appreciated. Many simpler establishments do not offer a written menu, and here, although the choice is limited, the standard of cuisine is usually quite acceptable.

> ### A gourmet primer
> Here, for quick reference, is a translation of some common menu listings.
>
> **antipasti** (hors d'œuvre): *prosciutto e melone*, ham (raw) and melon; *carciofi o finocchio in pinzimonio*, raw artichokes or fennel with an olive-oil dip; *antipasto misto*, mixed cold hors d'œuvre; *antipasto di mare*, seafood hors dœuvre; *crostini*, toast with fresh liver or vegetable paté.
>
> **primi piatti** (first course): *brodo*, clear soup; *gnocchi*, a nugget-like pasta made from potato, flour and eggs; *ravioli*, egg pasta, filled with spinach and ricotta cheese or minced veal; *spaghetti al pomodoro*, spaghetti with tomato sauce; *spaghetti al sugo* or *al ragù*, spaghetti with meat sauce; *spaghetti alle vongole*, spaghetti with clams; *tortellini*, small coils of pasta filled with a rich meat stuffing; *zuppa*, thick soup.
>
> **secondi piatti** (entrées): *agnello*, lamb; *coniglio*, rabbit; *fagiano*, pheasant; *lepre*, hare; *maiale*, pork; *manzo*, beef; *piccione*, pigeon; *pollo*, chicken; *vitello*, veal; *acciughe*, anchovies; *calamari*, squid; *cozze*, mussels; *dentice*, dentex; *gamberi*, prawns; *orata*, bream; *sarde*, sardines; *tonno*, tuna; *trota*, trout; *arrosto*, roast; *bollito*, boiled; *fritto*, fried; *alla griglia*, grilled.
>
> **contorni** (vegetables): *asparagi*, asparagus; *fagioli*, beans; *funghi*, mushrooms; *insalata*, salad; *melanzane*, aubergines; *patate*, potatoes; *peperoni*, red peppers; *pomodori*, tomatoes; *spinaci*, spinach; *zucchine*, courgettes.
>
> **dolci** (sweets): *crostata*, fruit flan; *pasta*, pastry; *torta*, tart; *zabaione*, whipped eggs with Marsala wine.
>
> **frutta** (fruit): *albicocche*, apricots; *anguria* or *cocomero*, water melon; *arance*, oranges; *ciliege*, cherries; *fichi*, figs; *fragole*, strawberries; *fragoline di bosco*, wild strawberries; *mele*, apples; *melone*, melon; *pere*, pears; *pesche*, peaches; *uva*, grapes; *macedonia di frutta*, fruit salad; *con panna*, with cream; *con limone*, with lemon.

A full **Italian meal** usually consists of an appetiser (*antipasto*), a first course (*primo piatto*) of soup or pasta, a main course (*secondo piatto*) of meat (*carne*) or fish (*pesce*) accompanied by a vegetable (*contorno*), then salad, fruit and/or dessert. Odd as it may seem, this combination is not fattening, as the various food groups are all present in carefully established proportions and, generally speaking, are consumed slowly. If you want to be on the safe side, though, try having pasta and a salad at lunch (you'll burn off the calories in the afternoon), and your meat and vegetables in the evening. Or just go with a **pizza**, which is made to order in a *pizzeria* but can be bought on the run in cafés, bakeries, and any number of other places. Excellent refreshments, including sandwiches and salads, can also be found in cafés, many of which have outside tables. As a rule, if you eat at the bar you must pay the cashier first, then present your receipt to the barman in order to get served. If you sit at a table the charge is usually higher, and you will be given waiter service (so, you should not pay first).

A *vinaio* or *enoteca* often sells wine by the glass and simple food for very reasonable prices. Sandwiches are made up on request at *alimentari* (grocery shops), and *fornai* (bakeries) often sell delicious individual pizze, focaccie or schiacciate (bread with oil and salt), cakes and so on.

Pizza

Pizza is today at least as well-known as spaghetti, and perhaps even more so. Suffice it to recall here that there is an infinite variety of pizza recipes, all based on bread dough. The secret of a successful pizza is a blazing hot oven. Only violent heat, in fact, is capable of cooking the pizza in such a way that it is soft, yet crunchy at the same time; if the oven is not hot enough, the dough becomes tough as shoe leather. A wood-fired oven is best, although it is possible to produce an acceptable pizza in an electric or gas oven.

Remember always that **pasta** is *the* essential ingredient of Italian cuisine—and the one where the Italian culinary fantasy is at its best. An ordinary Italian supermarket usually stocks about 50 different shapes, but some experts estimate that there are more that 600 shapes in all. *Pasta corta* (i.e. *rigatoni*) is much more varied than *pasta lunga* (i.e. *spaghetti*). The latter may be tubular (like *macaroni*), or threadlike (*spaghetti, vermicelli, capellini*); smooth (*fettucce, tagliatelle, linguine*), ruffled (*lasagne ricce*), or twisted (*fusilli*). Pasta corta comes in the shape of shells (*conchiglie*), stars (*stelle*), butterflies (*farfalle*), etc., and may be smooth (*penne*) or fluted (*rigatoni*). The differences of shape translate into differences of flavour, even when the pasta is made from the same dough, or by the same manufacturer. The reason for this is that the relation between the surface area and the weight of the pasta varies from one shape to another, causing the sauce to adhere in different ways and to different degrees. But even when pasta is served without a sauce, experts claim to perceive considerable differences in flavour due to the fact that different shapes cook in different ways. In northern Italy most regional dishes call for *pasta all'ovo*, which is made with egg batter, rather than *pastasciutta*, a simple flour-and-water paste.

A short history of pasta

Whereas the invention of egg pasta is generally credited to the Chinese, the origin of *pastasciutta* may well be Italian. The Etruscan Tomb of the Reliefs at Cerveteri, near Rome, has stucco decorations representing pasta-making tools: a board and a rolling pin for rolling out the dough, knives, even a toothed cutting-wheel for making decorative borders. References to lasagne may be found in Cicero and other Roman writers; the name itself is probably derived from the Latin *lagana* or *lasana*, a cooking pot.

By the end of the Middle Ages pasta was known throughout Italy. The 14C *Codice del l'Anonimo Toscano*, preserved in the library of Bologna University, contains several serving suggestions; and the poet Boccaccio, in his masterpiece, the *Decameron*, describes an imaginary land of grated parmesan cheese inhabited by people whose only pastime is the making of '*maccheroni e raviuoli*'. Of course, tomato sauce was unheard of until the discovery of America: Boccaccio's contemporaries cooked their macaroni and ravioli in chicken broth and dressed them with fresh butter.

Coffee and ice cream

Bear in mind also that Italy is considered to have the best **coffee** in Europe. *Caffè* (or *espresso*, black coffee) can be ordered *alto* or *lungo* (diluted), *corretto* (with a liquor), or *macchiato* (with hot milk). A *cappuccino* is an *espresso* with more hot milk than a *caffè macchiato* and is generally considered a breakfast drink. It is less substantial than a *caffè latte*, half coffee and half milk. A glass of hot milk with a dash of coffee in it, called *latte macchiato*, is another early-morning favourite. In summer, many customers take *caffè freddo* (iced coffee). **Ice cream** (*gelato*) is another widely famed Italian speciality. It is always best in a *gelatria*, where it is made on the spot.

Regional cuisine

The cuisine of northern Italy reveals all the treasures of its marvellous landscape—a landscape of blue seas and and fertile plains, hills festooned with sun-drenched vineyards, and highland plains abounding with aromatic herbs and juicy berries. From village to village, province to province, these diverse topographical conditions, coupled with different historical and cultural traditions, have given rise to an almost countless number of local specialities. What follows is therefore a brief summary of the kind of local fare you can expect to find as you move across northern Italy.

Valle d'Aosta

The inhabitants of the rugged Valle d'Aosta have always made the best of this mountainous region. Game, wild herbs, vegetables, nuts and berries, grains and potatoes are the basic ingredients of a simple but suprisingly tasty and nutritious culinary tradition. In the Valle d'Aosta proper a Provençal French tradition prevails, but in the Gressoney side valley, where the local population is of Germanic descent, the cuisine is more similar to that of the Alto Adige.

Characteristic dishes, which you will find throughout the region, are the appetiser *mocetta* (cured chamoix or goat ham); the first courses *polenta concia* (cornmeal polenta and fontina cheese, sometimes made *au gratin*) and *soupe cogneintze* (a soup of rye bread, fontina cheese, rice and meat broth, cooked in a clay pot and baked in the oven before serving); the main courses *camoscio o capriolo alla valdostana* (usually a leg or fillet of chamoix or mountain goat marinated in spiced red wine, browned in its own marinade, sprinkled with grappa and served with fresh or grilled polenta) and *carbonade* (salted and spiced beef sliced thin and cooked in a wine and onion sauce); and the desserts *blanc manger* (a pudding of milk, sugar and vanilla) and *brochat* (a dense cream of milk, wine and sugar eaten with rye bread). *Caffè valdostano* is strong, hot coffee served in a wooden cup with four, six or eight spouts (you'll want to drink it with friends), flavoured with lemon and lots of grappa, and served *flambé*.

Piedmont

Although other Italians consider the Piedmontese to be quiet, unexpressive, even gruff or crusty, they do not hesitate to acknowledge that Piedmontese cuisine is full of imagination, creativity and flair. And no wonder: Piedmont's plains, hills, mountains, lakes, rivers, forests and high pastures yield an unimaginable variety of products that Piedmontese chefs prepare with unsurpassed skill.

Outstanding regional dishes include the appetisers *vitello tonnato* (*vitel tonné* in dialect, made with boiled spiced veal sliced thin and smothered in a sauce of tuna, anchovies and capers) and *cipolle ripiene* (baked onions stuffed with parmesan cheese, egg, butter, spices and, sometimes, braised beef or sausage).

Good first courses are *agnolotti* (ravioli of Provençal origin; *agnolotti grassi* are made with veal and other meats mixed with egg and cheese; *agnolotti magri* with spinach, cream, egg and cheese) and *fonduta* (a hot dip with fontina cheese, milk, and egg yolks sprinkled with truffles and white pepper).

Delicious main courses include *bagna cauda* (a hot spicy sauce with garlic and anchovies used as a dip for raw vegetables), *brasato al barolo* (beef marinated in a Barolo wine sauce with lard, carrots and spices, then slowly braised in the marinade together with meat broth and tomatoes) and *volliti misti con salsa verde* (various types of meat stewed together with a green sauce made with herbs).

A very special Piedmontese dessert is *zabaione* (named after San Giovanni Baylon, the patron saint of pastry chefs: egg yolks, Marsala wine and sugar whipped together in a double boiler and served, usually, with dry bisquits).

Turin was the first city in Europe to process cocoa. The most famous expression of this tradition is the *giandujotto*, the famous candy made from cocoa and hazel nuts, named after the Torinese Carnival character Giandjua. In the Langhe, where the preparation of food is considered a fine art on a par with painting, sculpture and architecture, the white truffle of Alba vies with *tajarin*, the only authentically Piedmontese pasta (thin ribbon-like egg noodles, handmade and served with meat drippings, butter and sage), as the most typical item.

Lombardy

Although Lombardy is the most prosperous region of Italy, its many industries represent only half of its wealth: the other half comes from farming. The biggest 'crop' here is livestock—mainly beef and dairy cattle, but also pigs, sheep and goats. Lombard cuisine therefore is characterised by abundant meat and cheese, and by the use of butter rather than olive oil in the preparation of traditional dishes.

The tastiest appetisers come from the Valtellina. They are: *bresaola* (salted, air-dried beef sliced thin and served with olive oil, lemon and pepper), *cicc* (a thin focaccia made with buckwheat polenta and cheese, fried in lard) and *sciatt* (soft, round buckwheat pancakes dressed with cheese and grappa: the word, in dialect, means 'toad').

Good first courses are the ravioli, typical of Bergamo and Brescia, known as *casonei* (made with salame, spinach, egg, raisins, *amaretti*, cheese and breadcrumbs, served in a butter and sage sauce); *risotto alla milanese* (rice toasted with butter, onion and beef marrow, then cooked in meat broth with saffron); *pizzoccheri* from the Valtellina (ribbons of buckwheat pasta boiled together with potatoes and vegetables and dressed with a sauce of sautéed garlic, butter and bitto cheese); and the Mantuan *tortelli di zucca* (large tortellini filled with amaretti, pumpkin, egg, spiced apples and parmesan cheese, usually served in a butter and cheese sauce).

As a main course, try *costoletta alla milanese* (a breaded veal cutlet fried in butter); *osso buco*, another Milanese dish (sliced veal shin cooked slowly in tomato sauce and *gremolada*, a mixture of lemon zest, rosemary, sage and parsley, usually served with rice); *lavarelli al vino bianco* (lake fish sautéed in butter, parsley and white wine), especially popular around the Lombard lakes; and the signature dish of Pavia, *rane in umido*, frogs cooked in a sauce of tomatoes and leeks.

An interesting local *contorno* (usually served with boiled meats) is *mostarda di Cremona* (a fruit compote made with honey and white wine and seasoned with mustard and other spices).

Good Lombard desserts include the Milanese Christmas cake *panettone* (made with flour, natural leavening, butter, sugar, egg, candied fruit and raisins); Bergamasque *polenta dolce* (cornflour cooked with milk, egg yolks, amaretti, butter and cinnamon); and Mantuan *torta sbrisolona* (wheat and cornflour, sugar, egg yolks, chopped almonds, baked until dry then crumbled rather than sliced).

Trentino-Alto Adige

The regional specialities of the Trentino-Alto Adige combine the rustic character of Alpine cuisine with the naturalness and digestibility of Italian cooking—taking the best from both traditions.

The cuisine of the Trentino is a medley of Venetian, Lombard, and Tyrolean influences. The basic ingredients here are polenta and cheese. The most typical Trentine polenta is made from potatoes; dressed with cream, it is found in traditional dishes such as smacafam (baked with lard and sausage). Many dishes are hand-me-downs from the Austro-Hungarian tradition; examples include *canederli*, the Trentine version of *Knödel* (large stuffed bread balls), *gulasch*, smoked meat with sauerkraut, and *zelten alla trentina* (bread dough baked with eggs and dried fruit). Other distinctive dishes are the first course, *strangolapreti* (vegetable gnocchi), and the main courses *anguilla alla trentina* (eel seasoned with cinnamon) and *pollo ripieno alla trentina* (chicken boiled and filled with walnuts, pine nuts, raisins and marrow). Sweets include *fiadoni alla trentina* (pastries stuffed with a mixture of almonds, honey and rum).

In Bolzano, Bressanone, and the Dolomites a marked Germanic bias prevails. Distinctive dishes that can be eaten as a first or as a main course include *Knödel* (canederli), *Gertensuppe* (barley soup with chopped speck), *Frittatensuppe* (soup with strips of omelette), *Milzschittensuppe* (served with toast with spleen spread), *Rindgulasch* (beef gulash), *Schmorbraten* (stew), *Gröstl* (boiled diced beef and boiled potatoes, sautéed), various sausages (*Würstel*) and speck. The incomparable sweets of the region include strudel, *Zelten* (Christmas cake of rye bread dough with figs, dates, raisins, pine nuts and walnuts) and *Kastanientorte* (chestnut cake served with cream).

Veneto

In the area around Venice rice is served in a variety of ways, especially with seafood and vegetables. Classic specialities are *risi e bisi* (risotto with peas) and **risotto nero** (coloured and flavoured with the ink of cuttlefish). Thick soups are also popular. The best of these is *pasta e fasioi* (pasta and beans), which is eaten lukewarm, having been left to 'set up' for an hour or so before being served—generally in deep plates or, better yet, clay bowls. The classical *pasta e fasioi* once called for *bigoli*, a local variant of spaghetti. Bigoli are homemade in a special press, and their composition, with just water and buckwheat or wholewheat flour, is such that the pasta is dark. But bigoli are rare today and have been replaced with other types of pasta that range from *subiotino* to *ditalini* to *lingue di passero* to lasagna to tagliatelle—always with flour and water, but without eggs.

Fish and seafood form the basis of Venice's best main courses. Local specialities include *granseola* (lagoon crabs), *sarde in saor* (marinated sardines) and *seppioline nere* (cuttlefish cooked in their own ink). An outstanding seafood dish is the *brodetto di pesce or boreto di Grado*—rigorously *in bianco* (without tomatoes), which testifies to its origins in an age before the discovery of America. Cornmeal polenta is another staple, often served with the famous *fegato alla venziana* (calves' liver and onions). *Tiramisù* is the favourite dessert, though you'll also find rich cakes and pastries of Austrian inspiration.

Paduan cuisine is basically Venetian with local variations, as in the case of risi e bisi, to which the Paduans add *oca in onto* (pieces of goose preserved in their own fat). Distinctive first courses are rice and tagliatelli in *brodo d'anatra* (duck broth), and *risotto con rovinasassi* (chicken giblets). Sweets include *pinza* (a cake made with cornmeal and white flour), *fugassa*, *smegiazza* (both with crumbled polenta, toasted bread, milk and molasses) and *sugoli* (grape-juice preserve).

Rice is a basic ingredient of the cuisine of Vicenza, too. It was once grown extensively on the low, wet plains at the foot of the Alps. Here, along with the usual risi e bisi you'll find a wide range of risotti—with squash, asparagus, hops and quail, flanked by bigoli in duck sauce. Nevertheless, the best-known of local specialties is *baccalà alla vicentina* (salt cod stewed with milk and onions and grilled polenta), followed closely by *bovoloni*, *bovoletti* or *bogoni* (snails in butter, garlic, and parsley), *piccioni torresani allo spiedo* (pigeon on the spit) and *cappone alla canavera* (capon cooked inside an ox bladder). These are all served as main courses. Among the better local sweets are *focaccia vicentina* and amaretti.

Many Veronese specialities are common also in other cities of the Veneto. Distinctive dishes are *zuppa scaligera*, a rich version of the more popular *sopa coada* (see Treviso), made with chicken and white wine as well as pigeon. Another Veronese speciality is *gnocchi* in butter or tomato sauce, or topped with the famous *pastizzada de caval* (horsemeat stewed with aromatic herbs). Distinctive main courses include fish from Lago di Garda, including a rare variety of carp, and *boliti misti* with *pearà* (a sauce of breadcrumbs, butter, ox marrow, parmesan cheese, salt and pepper). Among Veronese sweets, the most delectable are certainly the great fluffy cake *pandoro* and the less well-known *natalini* and Easter *brasadella*.

The leading role in Trevisan cuisine is played by *radicchio trevigiano* (the long, narrow heads of Treviso's red lettuce), which is eaten in salads, grilled, fried or in risotto. Other specialities are *risotto al tajo* (made with shrimp and eel), *risotto alla sbiraglia* (with chicken and chicken stock), *zuppa di trippe* (tripe soup), *oca arrosto col sedano* (roast goose with celery), *anguille e gamberi di San Polo* (a stew of shrimp and eel), *sopa coada* (boned pigeon baked with bread) and *salsiccia trevisana* or *luganega*, cooked whole with rice in consumé (*risi e luganega*) or grilled. Trevisans claim to have invented the rich dessert *tiramisù*, a combination of creamy mascarpone cheese, finger biscuits, coffee and cocoa.

In the hills and woodlands to the north, around Belluno, Feltre and Asolo, local dishes present a singular combination of alpine and Venetian influences. Characteristic first courses include *gnocchi alla cadorina*, *casunzei* (ravioli with pumpkin or spinach, ham and cinnamon), *lasagne da formel* (dressed with a sauce of nuts, raisins, dried figs and poppy seeds), and *riso alla lamonese* (with lamon beans); favourite main courses feature game stewed in a rich sauce (*salmì*).

Friuli-Venezia Giulia

Situated in the extreme northeast of Italy, Friuli-Venezia Giulia extends from the Alps to the Adriatic between the Veneto, Carinthia and Slovenia. Subjected to wave after wave of foreign invasion, it has known centuries of war, poverty and devastation during which nutrition was reduced to the bare essentials: little meat (generally pork), and porridges made of millet, buckwheat and corn with milk, cheese, vegetables and wine were the traditional fare here. The dishes for which the region is best known today developed during the 19C and sink their roots in Bohemian, Austrian, Hungarian, Jewish, Slavic, Greek and Turkish traditions.

Triestine cuisine features a variety of bittersweet specialities, such as *pistum* (bread balls with aromatic herbs and raisins, served in broth), *lasagne al papavero* (lasagne dressed with sugar, butter and poppy seeds), *gnocchi di prugne* (potato gnocchi stuffed with a dried prune), and *lepre alla boema* (stuffed hare in a sauce of white vinegar and sugar). Old favourites include *iota* (bean soup, common throughout the region), *brovada* (white turnips fermented in the dregs of pressed grapes and served with polenta meal; or else beans, potatoes, sauerkraut and rind of lard), and the traditional *gulasch*. There is an excellent choice of fish, including *sardoni in savor* (marinated sardines) and *granseola alla triestina* (the spiky scarlet spider-crabs of the Adriatic, dressed with oil and lemon and served in their own shell). Other distinctive dishes are *zuf* (corn porridge) and *cevapcici* (grilled meatballs). Among the regional sweets are *gubana* and *presnitz* (almond puff pastry).

Rice is a major ingredient of the cuisine of Udine and its environs, *ris e lujanis* (rice and beans) and *risotto e asparagi* (with asparagus) being two of the more common specialities. In daily use bean soup with barley and vegetables—*la jota*—is popular. Square-shaped homemade pasta (*blecs*) is served with various meat or game sauces. Also typical are *bisna* (cornmeal polenta with sauerkraut), *cialzons* (ravioli filled with cheese, meat, eggs and aromatic herbs, or else calf's brain, chicken and herbs), *brovada* (white turnips fermented in grape dregs, cut in strips) with *cotechino* (stuffed pig's trotter), and *salame alla friulana* (cut in slices, sautéed and served with polenta).

The most typical main courses are *boliti* (boiled meats) served with marinated vegetables; stews with rich sauces accompanied by abundant polenta; and last but not least, goulash and tripe. In the right season you any number of game dishes, particularly birds on the spit or in a sauce with polenta. Omelettes are made with wild herbs (*primaverile*), wild or cultivated vegetables such as hops (*urtizon*), poppies (*confernon*), butcher's broom (*riscli*), valerian (*ardielut*) and chickory (*radicchio*). Winter lettuces are sautéed with lard or bacon and vinegar. The lightly salted *prosciuto di San Daniele* is considered the best in Italy. The typical sweet is *gubana*; other sweets are made with ricotta cheese, aromatic herbs and fruit.

Liguria

Liguria huddles by its sea (the *Mar Ligure* to Italians) like a lone individual cut off from the 'family 'of Italian regions by steep, rugged mountains. In some areas the mountains plunge directly into the sea and have had to be terraced to permit the cultivation of the olive and vine; in other areas the small alluvial basins of mountain torrents are intensely planted with fruit orchards and vegetable gardens. In both cases the farmer's life in Liguria is a hard one (not by chance, young people are rapidly abandoning the countryside for the city). Even the fishing, in the shallow waters of the Mar Ligure, is meagre.

The end result is that Ligurian cooking is *povera*, 'poor' in terms of ingredients, but rich in fantasy. And to the immense good fortune of Ligurians and outsiders alike, the best regional dishes are prepared with delicious local olive oil and seasoned with fresh spices, many of which grow wild in the rocky, sun-baked hills.

Partly because of the region's material poverty, and partly because imagination rarely respects traditional boundaries, little distinction is made in Liguria between appetisers, first courses and main courses. In fact the region's two great contributions to Italian cuisine are *focaccia*, the low, soft, salty bread that can be used as a support for just about anything, and *torta salata*, the 'savoury pie' that can be filled with anything and everything. Also distinctive is *pesto*, the famous sauce made from fresh basil, garlic, pine nuts and ewe's cheese and served with *trofie*, *trenette* or other pastas.

Good things to try in Liguria are *torta pasqualina* (the most famous of Ligurian *torte salate*, traditionally made for Easter but now available throughout the spring: a flaky pastry stuffed with beet greens, milk curd, parmesan and eggs), *cappon magro* (a Genoese treat made with a large fish and several oysters or shellfish, various vegetables, and a rich sauce of anchovies, garlic, pine nuts, capers, hard-boiled egg yolk, olives, parsley, oil and vinegar), *corzetti* (a small butterfly pasta usually dressed with butter, sweet marjoram and pine nuts, but also with the rich, spicy meat sauce *tòcco*), *buridda di seppie* (sliced cuttlefish cooked with olive oil, tomatoes, spices and fresh peas), *coniglio in umido* (rabbit browned in olive oil and butter, then stewed with garlic, rosemary, onion, white wine, black olives and pine nuts), *vitello all'uccelleto* (diced veal browned in olive oil and butter, with bay, white wine and sliced artichokes, when in season), *pandolce* (Ligurian panettone, less fluffy than the Milanese cake, with plenty of candied fruit and raisins) and *latte alla crema* (a rich vanilla and cinnamon custard, served in a deep bowl).

Emilia Romagna

Emilia Romagna stands on the border between the 'land of butter' and the 'land of olive oil'—between the European tradition of northern Italy and the Mediterranean culture of Tuscany, Umbria and Italy south of the Apennines. The region has a prevalently agrarian economy, thanks to the fertile Po River Basin, which is perfect for grains, fruit, vegetables and livestock.

Ostensibly one region, in reality Emilia Romagna is two entities with very different characters, histories and traditions. There is an 'inland' part—Emilia strictly speaking—comprising the five provinces of Bologna, Modena, Reggio Emilia, Parma and Piacenza, and an Adriatic seaboard, with the provinces of Ferrara, Ravenna, Forli and Rimini, which make up Romagna.

Although both are fond of the good life—including good cooking—*emiliani* and *romagnoli* are different by temperament. Where the former are easygoing and fun-loving, the latter are hot-tempered and resolute. These character differences reappear at the table. Emilian cuisine, which glides along softly and persuasively on flavours tempered in the amalgam of delicious butter and of delicate sauces, becomes increasingly sharp and aggressive as one crosses the invisible border of Romagna.

A cross-cultural sampling of appetisers might include *belecott* (boiled ground pork spiced with cinnamon, cloves and nutmeg, from the area around Ravenna but similar to the Modenese *cotechino*), *erbazzone* or *scarpazzone* (a simple country dish popular throughout the region, made with boiled spinach sautéed with spiced lard, mixed with parmesan cheese and egg, then baked in a crust) and the famous *piada* or *piadina* of Romagna (which bears a tell-tale resemblance to the unleavened breads of Greece and the Middle East: made with flour, water and lard, it is often stuffed to make a fold-round sandwich).

First courses not to be missed include *anolini di parma* (fresh egg pasta stuffed with braised beef sauce, breadcrumbs, parmesan cheese, egg and other ingredients, usually served in broth), *bomba di riso* (one of the few Emilian rice dishes, made in a mould with boneless stewed pigeon and mushrooms), *brodetto alla romagnola* (a rich fish-and-tomato soup), *lasagne alla bolognese* (the classic dish of oven-baked pasta squares, meat sauce, white sauce and parmesan cheese) and *pasticcio alla ferrarese* (a sumptuous legacy of the Este court: maccheroni or other short pasta in a pie crust with meat sauce, white sauce and mushrooms).

Delicious main courses are *agnello alla romagnola* (lamb browned in lard and butter then stewed with tomatoes and fresh peas), *bocconcini alla modenese* (little sandwiches made with ham, cheese and possibly truffle, dipped in milk and egg and fried in lard), *capretto alla piacentina* (goat browned in oil and butter, stewed in white wine and broth, and seasoned with garlic and parsley before serving), *costoletta alla bolognese* (breaded and fried veal cutlet, layered with prosciutto, fresh parmesan and tomato sauce, then baked) and the Modenese *zampone* (stuffed pig's trotter served with lentils, beans or mashed potatoes and spinach).

Characteristic sweets are *buricchi* (an invention of the Emilian Jewish community: little square pastries filled with almonds and sugar), *erbazzone dolce* (an interesting twist on the classic erbazzone described above: the beet greens are mixed with ricotta cheese, sugar, almonds and other ingredients) and *torta nera* (a rich Modenese cake made with almonds, sugar, butter, chunks of chocolate, cocoa, eggs, coffee and sometimes rum)

Wine

Most Italian wines take their names from the geographical area in which they are produced, the blend of grapes of which they are made, and the estate on which the grapes were grown. The best come in numbered bottles and are marked **DOC** (*di origine controllata*) or **DOCG** (*di origine controllata e garantita*), which, freely translated into English, means 'no fooling around'. The vinification of DOC and DOCG wines is carefully monitored from beginning to end by an independent authority, and only the best barrels of vintners located in a particular geographic area are admitted to this exclusive club (the others are packaged and sold under the generic name *vino da tavola*, 'table wine').

Wine-making is still very much an art in Italy, and each region has its own characteristic varieties, of which inhabitants are duly proud. To make the most of your stay you might want to take a brief look at the breakdown of regional wines offered below.

Valle d'Aosta

Vineyards in the Valle d'Aosta are necessarily small, stolen from the mountainside. But winemaking is heavily subsidised, which has enabled young people to maintain and modernise methods and facilities, and to devote new energies to the making of high-quality wines in small quantities.

A single DOC (*Valle d'Aosta/Vallée d'Aoste*) covers the whole region, embracing *Müller Thurgau, Pinot Nero, Pinot Grigio, Chardonnay, Petite Arvine, Premetta, Fumin* and *Petit Rouge* single varietal wines, plus *coupages* (blends) called simply Bianco, Rosso, Rosato and Novello. A particularly good geographical sub-appellation is *Chambave*, which is vinified as Moscato, Moscato Passito, and Rosso (a *coupage* of Petit Rouge, Dolcetto, Gamby and Pinot Nero grapes), while the autoctonous Blanc de Morgex grape is used in the delicious *Valle d'Aosta Blanc de Morgex* and *La Salle*.

> ## Ordering wines
> Red wines are *vini rossi* on the wine list; white wines, *vini bianchi*; rosés, *chiaretti* or *rosati*. Dry wines are *secchi*; sweet wines, *amabili* or *dolci*. *Vino novello* is new wine. *Moscato* and *passito* is wine made from grapes that have been left on the vine or dried before pressing.
>
> When ordering, remember also that many DOC wines come in versions labelled *spumante, liquoroso, recioto* and *amarone*. *Spumante* is the Italian equivalent of champagne and uses some of the same methods to obtain its foamy (*spumante*) effervescence. It is much bubblier than sparkling whites such as *Prosecco*, which is popular both before meals and as a light dinner wine. *Liquoroso* means 'liqueur-like' and usually refers to dessert wines. The term *recioto* is applied to wines made from grapes that have been dried like raisins; *amarone* is the dry, mellow version of *recioto*.
>
> Many wine critics predict that the 1997 vintage will be the best of the 20C for Italian wines. Other excellent years are '90 and '88.

Piedmont

Piedmont is one of the better wine-growing areas in Italy. The region counts 49 DOC and DOCG wines, and one district—Asti—is second only to the Chianti in terms of quantity of wine produced. There is a plan to make the region one huge DOC vineyard, and the more prestigious areas, such as Barolo, are defining *crus* or sub-areas.

Dolcetto Among Piedmontese reds, *Dolcetto* is a dry single varietal red wine that takes its name from the intense sweet flavour of the dolcetto grape. Grown throughout Piedmont, it has a robust structure, intense spicy nose, rich colour and is high in tannins and alcohol. The most famous is *Dolcetto d'Alba*, from the Langa Albese, mainly in the province of Cuneo.

Freisa is a single varietal red available in secco and amabile versions. Garnet red to light cherry red in colour, it takes on orange nuances with ageing. It has delicate raspberry and rose scents and a fresh flavour. The best comes from Asti and from Chieri; *Freisa di Chieri* is also vinified *frizzante* and *spumante*.

Grignolino is the signature wine of Asti and the Monferrato. Difficult to make, it has a light, ruby-red colour that develops orange shades with aging; the flavour is grassy and tart, dry and tannic, with a pleasantly bitter aftertaste.

Nebbiolo As many as 12 Piedmontese DOC wines, including Barbaresco, Roero and the world-famous Barolo, are made from the *Nebbiolo* grape (the oldest in the region, documented since the 13C). Served with robust first courses or with red meat, these wines are intense ruby red, tending toward granate red when aged. They have a light, delicate nose recalling raspberries and violets, which grows and improves with age. Pleasantly tannic when young, they age well to become full-bodied, smooth and harmonic. *Barolo, possibly Italy's best red wine, is grown in a small area south of Alba. It is rich, tannic, strong (minimum 13 per cent alcohol), dry but wonderfully deep and fragrant; it can age up to 15 years and is *riserva* after five.

Barbera is a single varietal wine made from grapes grown on the hills around Alba, Asti and in the Monferrato. Ruby red when young, it tends toward granate red after ageing. It has an intense, delicate nose and a dry, full-bodied and pleasantly bitter flavour that mellows with ageing to become rounder and more harmonious. Barbera's popularity in the past as a low-priced table wine has tarnished its reputation, which is now improved thanks to new growing and vinification techniques. *Barbera del Monferrato*, made with a small percentage of Freisa, Grignolino and/or Dolcetto grapes, can be lightly sparkling.

Cortese is a single varietal white wine grown in three areas: Alto Monferrato, Gavi and Colli Tortonesi. Sometimes made with small percentages of other non-aromatic whites, it is perfect with appetisers, delicate pasta and rice dishes, and soups. Light straw-yellow in colour, sometimes with a touch of green, it has a delicate but persistent nose and a dry, pleasantly bitter flavour. It is Piedmont's oldest and most familiar dry white wine. *Gavi, probably the most famous white wine of Piedmont, is grown in a small area between Gavi and Novi Ligure. Made with the Cortese grape, it has a straw-yellow colour and distinctive dry, fresh, harmonic flavour. Good with fish and seafood, it is also vinified *spumante naturale* or *frizzante naturale*.

Lombardy

Lombardy has one DOCG and 15 DOC wines. The DOCG, *Franciacorta, is the most famous and important (as well as the most expensive). It is vinified red, white, chiaretto and spumante. Franciacorta red is made from Cabernet Franc and Cabernet Sauvignon grapes blended with Barbera, Nebbiolo and Merlot. Franciacorta white is Chardonnay and Pinot Bianco.

Valtellina Probably the most interesting Lombard wines are the Valtellina reds, made from Nebbiolo grapes (described in the 'Piedmont' section, above), here called *Chiavennasca*, by small 'boutique' growers. The DOCs *Valtellina* and *Valtellina Superiore* are divided into four sub-appellations: *Grumello, Inferno, Sassella* and *Valgella*, all delicious with red and white meat. Late-pressed (forced) grapes make the rich, strong (16 per cent alcohol) and very special *Sfurzat*. The spectacular *vineyards of the Valtellina cling like moss to the rocks of this steep Alpine valley, in terraces at altitudes as high as 800m.

Also interesting in Lombardy are the Lake Garda wines, which offer outstanding quality at a relatively low price, and the table wines of the Oltrepò Pavese (the area south of the Po, bordering ion Emilia-Romagna), fragrant whites and full-bodied reds, some of which are surprisingly smooth and complex.

Alto Aldige

Because the Alto Adige is bilingual, its wine labels are in Italian and German. The DOC wines, whose area of production embraces the entire province of Bolzano-Alto Adige, carry the designation *Alto Adige* after the name (in German, the term *Südtiroler* precedes the name); these wines are the reds, *Cabernet, *Lagrein Scuro* (*Lagrein Dunkel*), *Lagrein Rosato* (*Kretzer*), *Malvasia* (*Malvasier*), *Merlot, Pinot Nero* (*Blauburgunder*, also spumante made as a white), *Schiava* (*Vernatsch*); and the whites *Chardonnay, Pinot Bianco* (*Weissburgunder*, also spumante), *Pinot Grigio* (*Rulander*, also spumante), *Riesling Italico* (*Welschriesling*), *Riesling Renaro* (*Rheinriesling*), *Riesling Sylvaner* (*Müller-Thurgau*), *Sauvignon, Sylvaner* and *Traminer Aromatico* (*Gewürztraminer*). To these must be added *Moscato Giallo* (*Goldenmuskateller*), *Moscato Rosa* (*Rosenmuskateller*) and *Spumante dell'Alto Adige* (*Südtiroler Sekt*). The Müller-Thurgau, Pinot Grigio, Sylvaner, Traminer Aromatico and Veltliner whites produced in the Valle dell'Isarco bear the denomination *Valle Isarco* (or *Bressanone*, in German *Eisacktaler*).

From hills around Bolzano come the two reds *Colli di Bolzano* (*Bozner Leiten*) and *Santa Maddalena*. The light red *Lago di Caldaro* (*Kalterersee*) comes from the vineyards on the lake of the same name. *Terlano* (*Terlaner*) is a white wine produced east of Bolzano. The denomination *Valdadige* or *Etschtaler* regards that territory which extends also into the provinces of Trent and Verona.

Veneto

The shores of Lake Garda, the Soave district, the Valpolicella and the Valdadige produce Veronese DOC wines. From Garda come the red *Bardolino*, *Bardolino Chiaretto* and *Bardolino Classico*, and the *Bianco di Custoza* and *Lugana* whites. Soave makes an excellent dry white wine, while the Valpolicella region makes *Valpolicella* and *Valpantena* reds. Bardolino, Soave and Valpolicella *classico* are made from grapes grown in the oldest vineyards. The denomination *Valdadige* applies to just a small part of Verona province; for details see Trentino-Alto Adige.

The DOC wines of Vicenza come from *Gambellara*, from the *Colli Bèrici* and from the *Breganzese*. Gambellara is always white, whereas the Colli Bèrici wines include *Cabernet*, *Merlot*, and *Tocai Rosso* reds as well as *Garganega*, *Pinot Bianco*, *Sauvignon* and *Tocai Bianco* whites. The Breganzese area produces *Breganze Bianco* and *Breganze Rosso*, *Cabernet* and *Pinot Nero* reds as well as *Pinot Bianco*, *Pinot Grigio* and *Vespaiolo* whites.

Three different regional denominations precede the names of Trevisan DOC wines: *Conegliano Valdobbiadene*, *Montello e Colli Asolani* and *Piave*. The first is limited to *Prosecco* white, which can also be called *Prosecco di Valdobbiadene* and *Prosecco di Conegliano*; the long name *Conegliano Valdobbiadene Prosecco Superiore di Cartizze* is reserved for the product of a very small area in the commune of Valdobbiadene. *Montello e Colli Asolani* makes *Cabernet* and *Merlot* reds as well as Prosecco white. The Piave growing area, shared with the province of Venice, produces *Cabernet*, *Merlot*, *Pinot Nero* and *Raboso* reds, in addition to *Pinot Bianco*, *Pinot Grigio*, *Tocai* and *Verduzzo* whites.

The Euganean Hills are where Paduan wines are made. The best are the *Colli Euganei Bianco* and *Rosso*, the *Cabernet* and *Merlot* reds and the *Moscato*, *Pinot Bianco* and *Tocai Italico* whites.

The indication *Trentino* precedes the name in almost all the DOC wines from the vineyards in this province; in addition to *Trentino Bianco* and *Trentino Rosso* there are the reds *Cabernet*, *Cabernet Franc*, *Cabernet Sauvignon*, *Lagrein Rubino* (there is also a *Lagrein Rosato*), *Marzemino*, *Merlot*, *Pinot Nero*; the whites *Chardonnay* (also spumante), *Müller-Thurgau*, *Nosiola*, *Pinot Bianco* (also spumante), *Pinot Grigio* (also spumante), *Riesling Italico*, *Riesling Renano* and *Traminer Aromatico*; and finally, three desert wines, *Moscato Giallo* (also liquoroso), *Moscato Rosa* (also liquoroso) and *Vin Santo*. The other wines of the province are *Casteller* red, *Sorni* white and red and *Teroldego Rotaliano* (rosé and red). The denomination *Valdadige* (white, red, rosé, Pinot Grigio and Schiava) refers to a territory that also includes parts of the provinces of Bolzano and Verona.

Friuli-Venezia Giulia

The best wines of the Trieste area include the three DOC wines that carry the name of the Carso, the plateau behind the city: they are the white *Malvasia del Carso* and the reds *Rosso del Carso* and *Terrano del Carso*.

The DOC wines of Udine come from three distinct growing districts, indicated on the labels respectively as *Grave del Friuli*, *Aquileia e Latisana* and *Colli Orientali del Friuli*. Common to these denominations are Cabernet and Merlot reds, a pleasant rosé (*rosato*), and the *Pinot Bianco*, *Pinot Grigio*, *Chardonnay*, *Verduzzo Friulano*, *Sauvignon*, *Traminer Aromatico* and *Tocai Friulano* whites.

Produced exclusively in the Colli Orientali del Friuli are the red *Pinot Nero* and the white *Sauvignon* and *Tocai Friulano*. The Grave del Friuli area also produces the *Cabernet Franc*, *Cabernet Sauvignon*, *Pinot Nero*, *Refosco dal Peduncolo Rosso* reds and the white *Riesling Renano*; the Aquileia e Latisana area makes the *Cabernet Franc*, *Cabernet Sauvignon*, *Refosco di Acquileia* and *Refosco dal Peduncolo Rosso di Latisana* reds; the Colli Orientali del Friuli the *Riesling Renano*, *Ribolla Gialla*, *Picolit*, *Ramandolo* and *Malvasia Istriana* whites and the *Refosco*, *Schioppettino* and *Pinot Nero* reds.

Liguria

The lay of the land in Liguria—a strip of steep hills hinged between sea and mountains—makes all farming, and especially grape-growing, difficult. So, one understands why winemaking is a dying art here, and why Ligurian wines are made in such small quantities that they rarely make it out of the region.

The growing districts are located at the two ends of the region: the Riviera di Levante produces the legendary *Cinque Terre* and *Sciacchetrà* whites, the *Colli di Luni* white and red, and the *Colline di Levanto* and *Golfo del Tigullio* red, white and rosé. The Riviera di Ponente makes *Vermentino*, *Pigato*, *Ormeasco* and **Rossese di Dolceacqua*. This is undoubtedly the finest Ligurian wine. It takes its name from a small village in the Valle Nervina but is made throughout Imperia Province and around Ventimiglia. It is a light, sincere red, with a colour somewhere between ruby and granate and a soft, aromatic, warm flavour. It is made in very small quantities.

Emilia Romagna

Emilia Romagna is traditionally considered the homeland of sparkling wines, where quantity triumphs over quality. This judgement is not altogether fair, for the vast and varied market offers, if not great wines, excellent quality/price relationships. The only DOCG is *Albana di Romagna*, a white made in the provinces of Ravenna, Forlì and Bologna. It is vinified *secco*, *amabile*, *dolce* and *passito*. *Albana secco* is dry and somewhat tannic, warm and harmonic, good with fish, soups and egg dishes. *Albana amabile* has a characteristic fragrant nose and is good with cakes and fruit.

The DOC *Colli Bolognesi*, which also appears on labels as *Monte San Pietro* or *Castelli Medioevali*, covers seven or eight kinds of grape: Barbera, Cabernet Sauvignon, Merlot, Pignoletto, Pinot Bianco, Riesling Italico, Savignon and Chardonnay, and is often subdivided by territory.

The best-known wine of Emilia, *Lambrusco*, is a fresh, fruity, dry or sparkling red good with heavy meat sauces and pork dishes.

BACKGROUND INFORMATION

Historical introduction

By John Law

To the visitor, northern Italy can appear as part of a united nation. Italian is the predominant language. Roman Catholicism appears as the established religion. Certain social mores are common throughout: a seemingly well-ordered existence; a resigned deference to bureaucracy; the conspicuousness of family life; café society; the *passeggiata* (the fashion-conscious parade—on wheels or heels—around noon or in the early evening); the flourishing state of small—often family—businesses in shops, restaurants and bars; the interest in sport (above all in football) and in the byzantine complexities of the political situation. Good and bad taste vie for predominance: carefully preserved town centres and appalling urban sprawl; exquisite craftsmanship and sordid neglect.

The legacy of Rome

Behind such initial impressions more fundamental signs of unity present themselves. Throughout, the legacy of Rome is apparent in place names and the layout of cities, in civic monuments and the direction of roads. The region of Friuli is called after the Roman colonies established in the first century BC, like *Forum Iulii* (now Cividale). The street plan of central Verona is predominantly Roman, while buildings, like its Arena or Roman amphitheatre, are still in use. The modern Via Emilia follows the line of the Roman Via Aemilia from the Adriatic through Bologna to Piacenza.

Moreover, the legacy of Rome should be understood in terms of an ongoing influence. This influence was probably at its most intense and fruitful during the Renaissance, from the mid-14C to the mid-16C. This was the period when artists, architects and scholars—and their patrons—sought a rebirth, or 'renaissance' of ancient Rome. Hence the delight of the poet Francesco Petrarch (1304–74) when he discovered a neglected collection of letters of Cicero in the cathedral library in Verona. Hence the almost archaeological interest in Antiquity displayed by the painter Andrea Mantegna (1431–1506).

But the impact of Rome can be detected both earlier and later. Virgil, from Mantua, was revered in the Middle Ages as a prophet and a magician before his poetry was subjected to a more scholarly appreciation in the Renaissance. Roman Law shaped the statutes of the medieval communes and provided the law curriculum at the University of Bologna, one of the earliest of medieval Europe, founded in the 12C. Roman architectural designs and ornament influenced all periods of architecture down to the 20C, only seriously challenged by the Gothic from the 13C to the 15C. The expansion of Rome, its military and political strength, influenced the political aspirations of many regimes, from the Holy Roman Empire to Fascism.

Diversity in language, religion and art

The Fascist period (1922–45) was noted for the effort made to foster a sense of Italian unity, but this was a process begun with the *Risorgimento*, the unification—literally the renewal or revival—of Italy in the 19C. It is a process which has continued to the present day, and it can heighten the impression of unity: the monuments to the heroes of the Risorgimento; the street names and memorials to the First World War, which defended and extended Italian unity; the presence in major cities of a large military establishment and grandiose public buildings; the standardised lay-out of railway stations and the far-reaching railway network; the superbly engineered *autostrade*.

But on closer scrutiny, the homogeneity of northern Italy can appear more superficial. The survival of regional and even local dialects shows little sign of weakening; in some areas Italian can reveal the influence of foreign languages, as is the case with French in Piedmont. German is the majority language in the province of Bolzano in the region of the Alto Adige, acquired by Italy from Austria only in 1919. In the same region, a distinct romance language, Ladino, also survives. And linguistic survivals from German immigration in the Middle Ages can still be detected in the Dolomites as well as in Friuli, where pockets of Slavonic can also be found.

Again, while Catholicism is certainly the predominant religion, Piedmont is the centre for the earliest surviving 'protestant' church, that of the Waldensians (*Chiesa Evangelica Valdese*). This owed its origins to a 12C reformer, Peter Waldo, his followers finding sanctuary from persecution in the valleys of the Alps; one particularly savage wave of persecution inspired Milton's sonnet *Avenge, O Lord, thy slaughtered saints* (1655). At a time of tension between the papacy and the House of Savoy, the Waldensians finally received royal recognition (1848), and the 19C also saw increased support from other Protestant churches; J.C. Beckwith, a veteran of the battle of Waterloo, established Waldensian schools and encouraged the use of Italian rather than French in services. The church has established small congregations elsewhere, for example in Milan and Venice.

Diversity can also be detected in architecture and the arts. In the Alpine valleys, stone and wood are used to a much greater extent than in Lombardy, where brick, terracotta and marble are more prevalent. In artistic terms, regional schools can be detected in the medieval and Renaissance periods. Because of long political and commercial connections with the eastern Mediterranean, Venetian art and architecture register a strong Byzantine influence, seen strikingly in the church of San Marco; the embellishment and maintenance of that building encouraged the art of mosaic to survive more vigorously and for longer than in the rest of northern Italy. Again, in Piedmont and Friuli, the Middle Ages and Renaissance saw the creation of elaborately carved wooden altarpieces, familiar enough in northern Europe, but largely unknown in the rest of Italy.

Finally, the monumental presence of the state in public buildings and works exists in a creative tension with strong regional, provincial and communal autonomy. For example, the Valle d'Aosta, whose strategic importance at the foot of the St Bernard Passes had secured it privileges in the Middle Ages, enjoys regional status in modern Italy. In 1972, the state gave special powers to the region of the Trentino and Alto Adige and to its provinces of Trento and Bolzano to assuage separatist opinion. However, from the 1980s the issue of greater regional autonomy has been rather overtaken by movements demanding the separation—though how completely?—of the north—though within which frontiers?—from the rest of Italy.

Unification in the 19th century

That the nature of the Italian state is still a matter of debate is hardly surprising: the unification of the country is relatively recent. The House of Savoy, ruling the kingdom of Sardinia, comprised of that island and the mainland regions of Liguria and Piedmont, acquired Lombardy from the Austro-Hungarian empire in 1859 and most of the rest of the peninsula in 1860. The first national parliament was held in Turin in 1861 and the Kingdom of Italy was proclaimed on 14 March. The Veneto was added in 1866, while the First World War brought the acquisition of the Trentino, the Alto Adige, Venezia Giulia and Istria.

This is the period of the Risorgimento, and while it still retains a prominent place in national history and mythology, it was not a story of unalloyed victory and patriotic fervour. The first attempt by the House of Savoy to expand its frontiers (1848–49) met with heavy defeat from Austro-Hungary, despite the valiant resistance of Venice. The successes of 1859–60, 1866 and 1919 were in part due to developments on the European stage; for example, French intervention assisted in the acquisition of Lombardy. But there were losses as well as gains. French support was paid for, in 1861, with the cession of Savoy—the ancestral lands of Italy's ruling house—and Nice—the birthplace of Giuseppe Garibaldi, the patriotic military genius who won Sicily and southern Italy for the new kingdom.

The ill-judged participation of Italy on Germany's side in the Second World War led to the loss of territory to the former Yugoslavia. In northern Italy itself, the record of plebiscites—still commemorated in central *piazze*—can suggest overwhelming support for the national cause. However, as some foreign observers noted, Austro-Hungarian rule was not as oppressive or unpopular as Italian patriots claimed; indeed some believed that conditions in Venice had improved since the overthrow of the noble oligarchy that had ruled the city down to 1797. In fact, the Risorgimento was driven by a minority of committed enthusiasts and skilful opportunists, and their vision of a united Italy ranged widely, from support for the House of Savoy, to solutions of a republican or federalist nature. Camillo Cavour, prime minister of the Kingdom of Sardinia from 1852 and a principal architect of the successes of 1859–60, preferred to speak French rather than Italian, while his actions reveal him to have been a shrewd pragmatist rather than a visionary patriot.

The issue of unity in Italian history

The northern boundaries reached by Italy at the end of the First World War are close to those established by the reign of the first Roman emperor, Augustus (27 BC–AD 14); this has more to do with natural frontiers imposed by the Alpine chain than historical precedent. Roman expansion began in the late 3C BC and continued after Hannibal's invasion in the early 2C BC, encompassing (from west to east) the Ligurians, the Celts and the Veneti. Romanisation was both signalled and encouraged by the planting of colonies (e.g. Aquileia and Aosta), the construction of roads, the elevation of urban centres to the privileged status of *municipium*, the spread of Roman Law and the Latin language.

This was the longest period of stable political unity the north was to experience; it was brought to an end by waves of barbarian invaders and settlers from north of the Alps. For example, the Ostrogothic kingdom of Italy lasted from 493 to 553, and was at its height under Theodoric the Great (493–526). After his death, his successors were overwhelmed between 535 and 553 by the armies of the eastern Roman, or Byzantine, empire with its capital at Constantinople. This 'Roman' recovery was virtually destroyed by the invasions of the Lombards, whose kingdom encompassed much of the north between 568 and 774. In turn, it succumbed to another northern conqueror, the Franks under Charlemagne (768–814). His imperial coronation by the pope in Rome (800) incorporated the kingdom of Italy within a western empire, known from the 13C as the Holy Roman Empire. Ruled by the Habsburg dynasty from the 15C, this empire lasted —at least in name—down to 1806 when Francis II surrendered the title under pressure from Napoleon.

At the height of Napoleon's power as king of Italy (1805–14), all of northern Italy was either directly under his rule or dependent on the French empire; after the battle of Waterloo, there appeared to be an emphatic return to the status quo, with the reinstatement of the principal powers in the region. The House of Savoy was restored and added Genoa to its dominions. The Habsburgs added the Trentino and the Veneto to Lombardy, and client states were set up in Parma and Modena. In addition, papal authority was restored in Emilia Romagna.

However, the Revolutionary and Napoleonic periods had far-reaching consequences. They encouraged radical political and social ideas. They had seen constitutional experiments, for example the setting up of a more democratic Ligurian Republic in Genoa (1798–1800). They had brought about the abolition of customs barriers and the remnants of the feudal system, as well as a massive reduction in the property of the Church. There had also been a reaction against the demands made upon Italy by foreign, French, rulers, but in general old orders had been seriously questioned and a new mood was prevalent, if only among elements of the political class. These changes contributed to the movement for independence which saw the whole of northern Italy come under the House of Savoy.

Why did the periods of unity in Italy between the Roman empire and the 19C prove—on the whole—to be either fragile or superficial? In part, the answer lies with the incorporating states themselves: they could not maintain the resources necessary to impose their authority in the area or defend themselves from external enemies. Hence the efforts of the Hohenstaufen emperors Frederick I (Barbarossa) (1123–90) and his grandson Frederick II (1194–1250) to make good imperial authority were thwarted by a combination of internal resistance and the hostility of the papacy. The popes were anxious to maintain the position of Rome and the States of the Church, and the northern states lay across some of the principal routes to Rome, a secular and religious capital that for centuries attracted aspiring conquerors. For the north itself, the Alps presented a formidable barrier, but they were pierced by passes, while the rivers and lakes of northern Italy—and the great Lombard plain itself—facilitated the movement of armies; an attempt to counteract such movement can be seen in the system of heavy defences built by the Habsburgs on the borders of the Veneto and Lombardy in the early 19C—the 'Quadrilateral' based on Mantua, Peschiera, Verona and Legnago. And lastly, northern Italy was a prize in itself in terms of its communications, its natural resources and its large number of taxable cities.

Many of these points can be illustrated from the early history of Venice. The lagoons had had only peripheral importance in the Roman Empire, but they became a haven for refugees trying to escape the barbarian invasions. These settlements were protected not only by the lagoons, but also by Byzantine naval power, the head of the Adriatic remaining under that empire long after its authority had been driven from the rest of northern Italy. However, as the Venetians grew in prosperity—as fishermen, salt manufacturers and traders— the Byzantine Empire declined. The balance of power between capital and frontier province changed. From the early 9C the Venetians began to supply ships to defend the empire, in return securing commercial privileges. And the Venetian duke—or *doge*—began to lose the character of a Byzantine representative and to assume that of a Venetian official.

The rise of the communes

The emergence of Venice can also be seen in its rejection of the authority of the western empire, and this introduces a further reason for the failure of powers seeking to unify northern Italy—the resistance of the northern Italians themselves, with the rise of the communes. As in the case of Venice, these were urban-based associations which owed their political and social prominence to the recovery of the Italian economy in the 10C and 11C. The aims of the communes included the protection and advancement of the interests of their members— their citizens—and resistance to the feudal nobility, the bishop or the emperor and his representatives.

In Italian historiography, the rise of the communes in the 11C and 12C has been seen in heroic terms and coupled with such grand issues as the defeat of feudal and foreign power and the rise of capitalism and the bourgeoisie. In the 19C and early 20C, the communes were seen as prototypes for modern Italy, democratic and free from foreign rule; the great—and patriotic—composer Giuseppe Verdi captured this spirit in his opera *La Battaglia di Legnano* (1849), which celebrated the victory of the Lombard communes over Frederick Barbarossa in 1176.

Inevitably historians have sought to tone down this view. The communes were not early experiments in democracy; real power was always held by a narrow, if changing, élite of wealthy landowners, entrepreneurs and professional men—and noble families were never totally excluded. Their political tolerance was low: critics faced heavy taxation, loss of office, exile, execution. From the 13C to the end of the Middle Ages, the communes were dominated by a relentless conflict between two parties, the Guelfs and the Ghibellines operating— albeit opportunistically—under the banners of pope and emperor respectively. Shakespeare's *Romeo and Juliet*—in any case drawn from Italian literary sources—was a not too distant reflection of a world of vendetta.

Finally, a preoccupation with the history of the communes can disguise the fact that most of northern Italy in the late medieval and Renaissance periods was ruled by different types of regime. Most cities came under the rule of signorial, or lordly, dynasties, generally from powerful local families who seized or acquired power to dominate or manipulate the republican constitutions of the communes they ruled. The leading examples here are the Este of Ferrara (1209–1598), the Della Scala of Verona (1260–1387), the Gonzaga of Mantua (1329–1708), the Carrara of Padua (1337–1405), the Visconti of Milan (1277–1447) and the Sforza of Milan (1450–1499). To some contemporaries, and to later historians, the *signori* are seen to conflict, in political and ideological terms, with the communes they came to rule, but the majority of the *signori* did not rule from behind fortifications as aloof and capricious dictators. Rather they needed and sought the cooperation of at least an élite of the citizenry and generally sought to project their governments as legitimate and mindful of the welfare of their subjects. Moreover, in other areas of the north, where urban life was less advanced, princely governments of various types had even earlier and longer histories. For example, the prince-bishopric of Trento was established by the western emperors as early as the 11C and lasted until 1801.

Foreign intervention and rule

The number and diversity of northern Italian states had profound consequences. For historians of the nation state these can appear in a negative light: the economic resources and political will of the northern cities may have defeated the Hohenstaufen in the 12C and 13C, but the on-going divisions of the region encouraged intervention from France, the Habsburg Empire and Spain in the late 15C and early 16C, the period of the 'Italian Wars': Italy became—and remained—caught up in the rivalries of the major powers. At the time, this was seen as a disaster, and in the main the Italian historical tradition has continued to see it in this light, seeking to pin blame on individual rulers, the state system, methods of government and military organisation.

However, the impact of foreign intervention and rule should not be exaggerated. It did not involve the settlement of foreign peoples as had occurred with the collapse of the Roman Empire. On the whole, foreign rule was not savagely enforced; repression of that kind was not experienced until the Second World War (1943–45) as the Third Reich delayed the advance of the Allies northwards; the situation was compounded by a vicious civil war between those who remained loyal to Mussolini and anti-Fascist partisans. Earlier, foreign rule could prove temporary: the lands of the House of Savoy were largely under French rule from 1536 to 1559, but the dynasty recovered its duchy and skilfully exploited its position on the frontier between French and imperial spheres of influence, attaining royal status with the acquisition of Sardinia in 1720.

And the hegemony of foreign powers could be exploited in other ways. The merchants and bankers of Genoa were able to profit from Spanish conquests in the New World. The Genoese statesman and admiral Andrea Doria (1466–1560) used an alliance with the Habsburgs to rule the city, virtually as prince after 1528. Alessandro Farnese, duke of Parma and Piacenza (1545–92), brought fame and fortune to both himself and his dynasty by serving Philip II of Spain in the Mediterranean and the Low Countries.

Finally, of the northern states only Milan and central Lombardy remained constantly under direct foreign rule; its last Italian duke, Francesco II Sforza, died in 1535 and the duchy was annexed to the Habsburg Empire. Otherwise, the northern Italian states long retained at least nominal independence, even if their freedom of action on the international stage was restricted. Thus the Gonzaga ruled Mantua to 1708. The Venetian Republic lasted until 1797 in a state of watchful neutrality protected by diplomacy and massive fortifications.

Cultural heritage

The fall of the republic was symbolised by the transport of the famous bronze horses from the façade of San Marco to Paris by Napoleon. They were returned, but war and invasion have contributed to the destruction, damage and dispersal of the 'cultural heritage' of northern Italy. An earlier French invasion, in 1498, led to the removal of the fine library built up by the Visconti and Sforza dukes of Milan; Allied bombing in the Second World War severely damaged Mantegna's fresco cycle, the *Martyrdom of St James*, in the Ovetari Chapel, Padua. But much has survived intact and in place, and undoubtedly the political divisions of northern Italy contributed to enriching its 'cultural heritage'.

Major cities—Venice, Milan, Genoa—did of course act as magnets, but the north had no traditional, effective, central capital with a first call on men of talent and their patrons: the sense of the 'provincial' is largely absent from the cities of northern Italy. So, for example, in Verona—subject to Venice from 1405 to 1797—an intense interest was maintained from the Renaissance in the geology, flora and fauna, antiquities, history and musical and literary traditions of the area, finding expression in the founding of such learned socities as the Accademia Filarmonica—a musical academy—in the 16C and the Accademia di Scienze, Lettere ed Arti in the 18C. A similar phenomenon can be detected in smaller centres: an academy was established in Rovereto in the Trentino in 1750. The conscious maintenance of such traditions helps to account for the present rich and varied cultural activity of the towns and cities of northern Italy, from folklore to festivals of music and film, from pageantry to art exhibitions and the celebration of local saints.

Architecture provides another—older and more continuous—expression of political diversity. City walls and fortresses were built to protect republican and princely governments. Churches such as Sant' Antonio in Padua were embellished to celebrate local cults. Ruling dynasties like the Visconti of Milan and the Gonzaga of Mantua built palaces to proclaim their authority and magnificence. As that suggests, political and cultural competition within states could be mirrored by rivalries within them; from the end of the Middle Ages, the Grand Canal in Venice, some islands in the lagoons—like Murano—and some areas of the mainland—as on the banks of the Brenta—became prized sites for families to demonstrate their wealth and nobility, notably in the construction of palaces, villas and gardens.

But explanations for the rich heritage of the north lie in more than political diversity. Historically, the region has been of great economic importance, even if its wealth has not been evenly spread in geographical or social terms. Christianity, however, has been, and religious observance has contributed vitally to the cultural life of the region. This can be seen in the patronage of parish, monastic and friary churches—and the chapels and altars within them—as well as in the support of hospitals, for the spiritual good of an individual, a family or a collective, like a guild or confraternity.

Motives could also be utilitarian, as seen in the construction of bridges, fountains, markets and halls—*palazzi*—for the conduct of government. And cultural patronage could also seek to delight or instruct a more restricted circle of courtiers or cognoscenti, for example in the tapestry-like frescoes depicting the labours and pleasures of the months painted for the prince-bishop of Trento around 1400, or the collection of antiquities established by the Veronese scholar Scipione Maffei in 1714.

However, it would be misleading to insist on single or predominant motives behind cultural patronage. Three members of the Della Scala, the rulers of Verona, had free-standing tomb monuments built in the centre of the city in the 14C to commemorate and celebrate the dynasty, to express its piety, to proclaim its authority, aims enhanced by their employment of innovative and gifted Gothic sculptors. In 1456, Francesco Sforza, Duke of Milan, appointed the highly regarded architect and sculptor Antonio Filarete to design a major hospital for the city; the project was intended to improve the welfare of his subjects while enhancing the duke's reputation for good government. The stone bridge at the Rialto in Venice was designed by Antonio da Ponte (1588–91) to impress; it also served a very practical function at the commercial heart of the city. When in 1729 Vittorio Amedeo II of Savoy commissioned Filippo Juvara to build a palace, the Stupinigi, near Turin it was intended as a hunting lodge and a rural retreat; he was also seeking to emulate the magnificence of the French crown.

Travellers to Italy

Palaces and villas, often enhanced by gardens and collections of antiquities and works of art, drew generations of admiring and envious foreign visitors. But northern Italy had long attracted foreigners: from mercenary soldiers to pilgrims heading for Rome or the Holy Land (via Venice); from merchants and diplomats to musicians seeking to benefit from the taste for northern singers and composers in the courts of Renaissance Italy; from students frequenting the great universities of Padua and Bologna to refugees from political and religious persecution—particularly marked in the 15C and the 16C with the spread of Islam and Protestantism. Cultural tourism probably has its origins in the curiosity of pilgrims and the enthusiasm of scholars and collectors; from the 15C pilgrim guides and accounts are increasingly descriptive while from the 16C impressions left by the traveller seeking to broaden his education—like Sir Philip Sidney (1554–86)—become steadily more numerous.

Drawn to court societies and concentrations of Roman antiquities, participants in the Grand Tour tended to head further south, but Venice's remarkable site, its reputation as a more open society, the achievements of such widely regarded artists as Titian (1490–1576) and architects as Andrea Palladio (1508–80) ensured that it remained a magnet for travellers, as the demand for painters like Canaletto (1697–1768) and Guardi (1712–93) demonstrates. From the late 18C, an appreciation of the scenery of the Alps and the northern lakes—an appreciation which had existed since Roman times, as is suggested by the villa, associated with the poet Catullus, at Sirmione on Lake Garda—was heightened with Romanticism. The Alpine passes and the northern lakes became major subjects for artists like J.M.W. Turner (1773–1857) and followers and assistants like James Hakewill (1778–1843). The following century was to see a growing interest in the art and architecture of medieval Italy, which heightened the interest of travellers and scholars, like the Scottish historian and collector James Dennistoun (1803–55), in the northern cities.

The succession of European wars, from the French Revolution to the Risorgimento, did little to deter foreign travellers; indeed, sympathy with Italian Unification—together with the development of the railway network—increased the number of foreign visitors. Both a cause and an effect of this was the growth in guide books and accounts. The first Murray guide (by Sir Francis Palgrave) appeared in 1842, the first Baedeker (in English) in 1870. As early as 1840 the *Edinburgh Review* was complaining about the anodyne character of many accounts of the country, if the *Quarterly Review*—in a more charitable mood in 1847—welcomed further descriptions of Italy. Not all travellers were consistently impressed. Wordsworth complained that 'improvements' to the Simplon Pass made on the orders of Napoleon had ruined its natural beauty. Most of northern Italy, with the exceptions of Venice, Verona and—eventually—Genoa, seems to have depressed Charles Dickens on his tour of 1844–45. Ruskin's fascination for Venice was tinged with reservations and disappointments; he was certainly critical of the railway bridge linking it to the mainland and of the insensitive restoration of its principal monuments.

Hans Christian Andersen (1835) and Thomas Mann (1912) were among those who detected a sinister quality to Venice, but that did not prevent a sizeable foreign community from establishing itself in the course of the 19C, drawn by the advocacy of Ruskin and others, as well as by its art market, low rents and cosmopolitan—and apparently tolerant—society. Even earlier, a much larger foreign community settled on the Riviera whose climate was highly regarded. Its history and legacy are remarkable. For example, an English entrepreneur, Sir Thomas Hanbury, established a botanical garden near Ventimiglia in 1867, while in 1888 another Englishman, Clarence Bicknell, founded an archaeological museum at Bordighera. Edward Lear and his cat Foss set up home in San Remo in 1871.

An insight into these foreign communities is provided by the career of the Scottish Presbyterian minister Alexander Robertson, who lived in Italy from 1882 to 1933. He first settled at San Remo, where he ministered to a Presbyterian congregation; that this was only one of a number of flourishing Protestant churches on the Riviera is suggestive—together with the presence of libraries, clubs and consulates—of the large and varied foreign community. From 1888 Robertson was in Venice, where he established a church—again, one of several Protestant churches in the city—and where he wrote prolifically on Venetian and Italian affairs. Though now largely forgotten as a writer, the *pastore scozzese* made himself known and useful to a large number of visitors to Venice, one of whom—the poet Ezra Pound—affectionately mimicked the sound and fury of his sermons in his *Cantos*. Pound is now buried near to Robertson in the cosmopolitan Protestant section of the cemetery island of San Michele in the Venetian lagoons.

This historical introduction is dedicated to the memory of Harry Hearder, 1924–96.

Italian place names

Many of the place names in Italian towns and cities have ancient origins. The names assigned to public buildings, market places, towers, bridges, gates and fountains frequently date back to the Middle Ages; this is strikingly so with the *rii* (canals), *calli* (alleys) and *fondamente* (quays) of Venice. But the practice of formally naming all streets and squares began in the 19C. Frequently local—even parochial—patriotism determines the choice as the community celebrates its own history and its own political, literary, religious, artistic and scientific figures, as well as famous foreign visitors.

On the other hand, some individuals transcend the local and are widely commemorated. For example, **Dante Alighieri** (1265–1321), **Francesco Petrarch** (1304–74) and **Giovanni Boccaccio** (1303–75), pioneering masters of the Italian language, emerge as national heroes. And events and issues of national history are also prominently represented. Thus a united republican Italy can be celebrated in terms of concepts (for instance **Via della Repubblica**, **della Libertà**, **della Vittoria**), events (**Via del Plebiscito**, recalling the vote that preceded a region uniting with the Kingdom of Italy), or by drawing on the gazetteer of Italian rivers, mountains, seas and cities.

Broadly speaking the national figures and events chosen tend to be representative of four phases in recent Italian history. Probably the most emotive and frequently commemorated is the **Risorgimento** (the Resurgence), the movement that led to the unification and independence of Italy in the 19C; among the battles commemorated are **Custoza**, **Lissa**, **Solferino**, **Magenta**, **Montebello** and **Mentana**. For some historians, Italy's entry to the First World War represents the final phase in the pursuit of national unity; the battles and campaigns between Italy and her allies and the Central Powers are also frequently recorded in place names: **Isonzo**, **Monte Pasubio**, **Caporetto**, **Monte Grappa**, **the Piave**, **Vittorio Veneto**. Opposition to Fascism and the ending of the Second World War are also commemorated, as are the statesmen and events associated with the country's reconstruction, economic development and membership of the EC. Casualties in Italy's successful struggle against political terrorism (**Aldo Moro**, murdered by the Red Brigades in 1978) and the less successful war against organised crime (**Alberto della Chiesa**, killed by the Mafia in 1982) are also entering the pantheon.

Of course, the political climate changes. So the **Arco della Pace** in Milan was originally intended as part of a Neo-classical complex celebrating Napoleon's victories, but appropriated by the Austro-Hungarian Empire, it came to celebrate his defeat. Largely censored and deleted from the more recent record are the events and personalities closely linked to **Fascism**, Italy's empire and the reigns of the last two members of the House of Savoy, Vittorio Emanuele III (1900–46) and Umberto II (1946). However, the keen-eyed observer might be able to identify traces of Fascist insignia and the Fascist system of dating (1922, when Mussolini was invited to lead the government, is year 1) on public buildings and monuments, and some street names still recall territories once ruled from Rome (e.g. **Dalmazia, Albania, Libia**).

Below is listed a selection of the more prominent figures and events from recent Italian history the traveller is likely to encounter time and again.

People

Vittorio Alfieri (1749–1803), poet and dramatist

Cesare Balbo (1789–1853), political thinker and historian

Cesare Battisti, Italian patriot, executed by the Habsburg regime in Trento, 12 July 1916

Cesare Beccaria (1738–94), legal theorist and political economist

Don Bosco (the Blessed Giovanni, 1815–88), educationalist and founder of the Salesian Order

Giosuè Carducci (1835–1907), patriotic poet and literary critic

Camillo Cavour (1810–61), statesman and cautious architect of Italian unification

Francesco Crispi (1818–1901), statesman

Gabriele d'Annunzio (1863–1938), poet, novelist, dramatist, nationalist

Massimo d'Azeglio (1798–1866), painter, man of letters, patriot

Armando Diaz (1861–1928), leading Italian general of the First World War

Ugo Foscolo (1778–1827), poet and patriot

Giuseppe Garibaldi (1807–82), inspirational political and military leader in the Risorgimento

Vincenzo Gioberti (1801–52), political thinker, philosopher

Antonio Grasmsci (1891–1937), political thinker, Marxist, opponent of Fascism

Daniele Manin (1804–57), Venetian patriot and statesman, defender of that city against the Habsburgs, 1848–49

Alessandro Manzoni (1785–1873), poet and novelist

Guglielmo Marconi (1874–1937), electrical engineer and radio pioneer

Margherita of Savoy (1851–1926), wife of Umberto I, noted for her piety, good works and cultural patronage

Martiri della Resistenza (or **della Libertà**), opponents of Fascism and German occupation 1943–45

Giacomo Matteotti (1885–1924), socialist politician, assassinated by Fascists

Giuseppe Mazzini (1805–82), leading republican figure of the Risorgimento

Guglielmo Oberdan (1858–82), patriot executed by the Habsburg regime in Trieste

Bettino Ricasoli (1809–80), Florentine statesman, instrumental in securing Tuscany's adherence to the Kingdom of Italy in 1860

Aurelio Saffi (1819–1890), man of letters and hero of the Risorgimento

Umberto I of Savoy, King of Italy 1878–1900

Giuseppe Verdi (1813–1901), prolific opera composer whose output was often associated with the cause of a united Italy. His surname could be read as the initials of 'Vittorio Emanuele Re d'Italia'

Vittorio Emanuele II of Savoy, King of Sardinia-Piedmont from 1849, King of Italy 1861–78

Events

XI Febbraio: 11 February 1929, formal reconciliation between the papacy and the Kingdom of Italy

XXIX Marzo: 29 March 1943, armistice between Italy and the Allies

XXVII Aprile: 27 April 1945, Benito Mussolini captured in northern Italy. The Fascist leader was quickly tried and executed on 28 April

XXIV Maggio: 24 May 1915, Italy enters the First World War

II Giugno: 2 June 1946, referendum designed to favour a republican constitution

XX Settembre: 20 September 1870, Italian forces enter Rome, overthrowing papal rule

IV Novembre: 4 November 1918, proclamation of the armistice between Italy and Austria

Further reading

E. Baudo, *The Charm of the Western Riviera* (Genoa, 1995)

A. Cole, *Art of the Italian Renaissance Courts* (London, 1995)

C. Duggan, *A Concise History of Italy* (Cambridge, 1994)

D. Hay (ed.), *The Longman History of Italy* (London, 1980)

H. Hearder, *Italy: a Short History* (Cambridge, 1990)

M. Hollingsworth, *Patronage in Renaissance Italy* (London, 1994)

D. Mack Smith, *Italy and its Monarchy* (London, 1992.

J. Morris, *Venice* (London, 1983)

T. Parks, *Italian Neighbours* (London, 1993)

T. Parks, *An Italian Education* (London, 1994)

J. Pemble, *The Mediterranean Passion* (Oxford, 1988)

J. Pemble, *Venice Rediscovered* (Oxford, 1995)

D.P. Waley, *The Italian City-Republics* (London, 1978)

VALLE D'AOSTA

The Valle d'Aosta extends from Piedmont to the border with France and Switzerland at the Italian end of the Mont Blanc and Great St Bernard tunnels, two of the more important entrances to Italy across the Alps. The Dora Baltea River runs the length of the valley, the head of which is surrounded by high Alpine peaks (Mont Blanc, the Matterhorn and Monte Rosa all exceed 4000m). The region has numerous ski resorts, and just south of Aosta the Gran Paradiso Massif (4061m) rises in the centre of the Parco Nazionale del Gran Paradiso, the first national park to be created in Italy (in 1922). A stretch of the Roman road from Milan to Gaul (which went over the St Bernard Pass) can still be seen, including three Roman bridges; and the ancient town of Aosta has more impressive Roman remains. Medieval monuments include the imposing castles that once defended the valley, on the steep slopes above the Dora Baltea. The most important of these were built by the powerful Challant family in the 14C and 15C and are now owned by the region: five of them can be visited. The resorts of the side valleys are popular both in summer and for winter sports.

The Valle d'Aosta has always been a place of transit for travellers and armies entering Italy. One of the earlier visitors was Sir Roger Newdigate (1774), but the valley was 'discovered' in the early 19C by British alpinists and excursionists who came to explore and admire the mountain scenery. Murray's guide of 1838 was the first guide to the region in any language, and many well-known alpinists who made ascents in the mountains (the Rev. Henry Budden, John Ball and Douglas William Freschfield, for example) published descriptions of their travels illustrated with engravings. The guides of Valtournenche and Courmayeur are world-famous, and many have accomplished first ascents in Switzerland, America, Africa and among the Himalayas.

The valley is now visited also for downhill and cross-country skiing, and besides the famous resorts of Courmayeur and Cervinia, numerous other resorts (including Pila, La Thuile, Cogne, Champoluc and Gressoney-la-Trinité) have hotels and winter sports facilities. These places are also visited by mountaineers, rock climbers and walkers.

Under the Italian Constitution of 1948 the valley was granted a statute of administrative and cultural autonomy, with a Regional Council of 35 members, sitting in Aosta. The region also sends one deputy and one senator to the Italian parliament. Although never for long under French dominion, the valley had a long tradition of bilingualism under the Savoy kings: most of the 118,000 inhabitants can speak both French and Italian, even though the French language was severely prohibited during the Fascist regime. Italian and French are now both official languages of the region. Signage carries both languages and French is obligatory in schools, even though Italian is the common language heard all over the valley. *Patois*, a French-Italian dialect, is spoken in the villages. An interesting relic of the colonisation of the valley from the Swiss Valais remains in the German dialect that survives at Gressoney.

The most important industry in the valley from the Second World War up to the 1960s was the Cogne steel mill outside Aosta, now in decline (the magnetite mines in the mountains above Cogne were closed down in 1974). Agriculture is subsidised by the regional government, and the brown-and-white cows (with loud bells) are taken up to pasture in the high alps from May to the end of September. The valley is noted for its *fontina* cheese, some of which is still made in the old farm buildings raised on stone bases and wooden stilts, with slate roofs. The slopes of the valley are covered with trellised vineyards. These yield some excellent wines, including *Aymavilles* (*Torrette*) and *Donnas* red, and *Chambave*, *Nus* and *Morgex* white.

Unfortunately there is a lot of undistinguished new building throughout the valley, and the motorway (still being completed) detracts from the otherwise impressive natural beauty. The Valle d'Aosta is also now visited for its casino at St-Vincent, the second most important in Europe after Monte Carlo.

Aosta

Once the chief town of the Gallic Salassi, Aosta was captured by Terentius Varro in 24 BC and renamed Augusta Praetoria. You can still see the Roman influence in its regular, gridlike street plan—a characteristic evolved from the Roman battle camp. The character of the later city, however, is southern French rather than Italian. The architecture is essentially Burgundian, and the people speak a French dialect. Throughout the later Middle Ages, town and valley owed allegiance to the great house of Challant, viscounts of Aosta. Later the dukedom was a prized apanage of the house of Savoy. The most famous native of Aosta is St Anselm (1033–1109), Archbishop of Canterbury from 1093.

Today Aosta is a pleasant small town (583m; population 35,000) surrounded by snow-capped mountains. The old centre, less than 2km square, is still enclosed by well-preserved Roman walls and contains many Roman monuments including the main gate, a *cryptoporticus* of the forum, and a theatre. A suburban villa and Roman baths are in the process of excavation. Sant'Orso and the cathedral are both interesting medieval buildings with remarkable 11C paintings, and the cathedral museum has numerous works of art. The outskirts now have unattractive buildings, and the huge steelworks, once important to the economy of the whole valley, are sadly abandoned.

Practical information

Getting there and getting around
By air

If you're flying to the Valle d'Aosta intercontinentally, you can choose between the international airports at Geneva or Milan and proceed by car via Chamonix or Turin, respectively. From London and other European capitals the choice is between Milan Malpensa and Turin Caselle, respectively 160km and 107km away. Both have domestic and international flights.

By road

The quickest route to Aosta from Turin is the A5; on Fri and Sun evenings, traffic is thick with escaping/returning *Torinesi*. From Milan take the A4 west to the junction at Santhia, then the A5 north, bypassing Turin. The main road from Pont-St-Martin to Aosta and Courmayeur is 26. There are bus services from Turin and Milan to Aosta (see below) with some international services through the tunnels. **Car parking** (free) in Aosta in Piazza Plouves.

By rail

Slow *Diretti* and *Regionali* only from Turin and Milan to Aosta via Chivasso, where a change is sometimes necessary. The 100km run from Turin, on a single track after Chivasso, is made in 2hrs–2hrs 15mins.

Information offices

Piazza Chanoux 3, ☎ 0165 236627. For hiking and alpine or cross-country ski trails: *Club Alpino Italiano*, Piazza Chanoux 8, ☎ 0165 40194.

Where to stay

Ambassador, Via Duca degli Abruzzi 2, ☎ 0165 42230, fax 0165 236851; a warm, rustic family-run establishment; inexpensive.
Europe, Via Emilia 65, ☎ 0165 236363, fax 0165 40566; elegant and friendly, in the city centre; moderate.
Roma, Via Torino 7, ☎ 0165 43645, fax 0165 361377; calm and comfortable, near the Roman theatre; closed Jan; inexpensive.

Eating out
Restaurants

Le Foyer, Corso Ivrea 146, ☎ 0165 32136, is one of the better restaurants in town, with traditional local dishes; closed Mon evening, Tues, Jan and Jul; moderate.
Taverna da Nando, Via de Tillier 41, ☎ 0165 44455, is a family-run restaurant serving excellent regional specialities; closed Mon and Jun–Jul; inexpensive. Other good restaurants are located in the environs of Aosta (see p 65).

Cafés

Aosta's best café is the *Nazionale*, Piazza Chanoux 9, but if you're looking for fresh pastries, you'll be better off at *Pasticceria Boch*, Via De Tillier 2. *Enoteca la Cave*, Via Festaz 53, carries fine wine from the valley; you can get cheese to go with it at *Latteria Gerard Lale*, Via De Sales 14. There are picnic places in the small gardens outside the southern stretch of walls, in the gardens in front of the station, and in the small garden off Via Hotel des Monnais (behind Sant'Orso).

Night life

Teatro Giocoso, with a theatre and music season, Nov–Mar.

Shopping

Market day in Aosta is Tuesday, in Piazza Cavalieri di Vittorio Veneto.

Special events

Fair of Sant'Orso, 30 and 31 Jan, with local artisans' products exhibited in the streets.

Sports

Walking and **skiing** throughout the valley, see p 66.

The city centre

Piazza Emile Chanoux is the centre of the town, site of the **hôtel de ville**, the grand town hall of 1837, with a war monument (1924) by Pietro Canonica outside. There is an attractive old-fashioned café here. Via Porta Pretoria exits the piazza on the east side. Under an archway on the left, an alley leads to a terrace overlooking the Roman theatre (described below), near recently excavated houses with pebble pavements on a Roman road once lined with a portico. At no. 41 is the house of Philippe-Maurice de Challant (1724–1804), the last descendant of the important family who built numerous castles in the valley. Opposite, no. 46 is one of the few old houses to survive in the town.

The *Porta Praetoria, a massive, well-preserved double Roman gateway of three arches, stands at the end of the street. This was the main gate of the city. The two fortified gates, built in puddingstone, are separated by a small square defended by two towers. The side facing away from the city was originally faced in marble. The side arches were used by pedestrians and the central one by carriages. The level of the Roman road was 2.6m below the present pavement. The gate was incorporated in a medieval fortress until the 18C, and the main arches and those on the right were blocked up. This explains

The Porta Praetoria

why the axis of Via Porta Pretoria is not aligned with the gate.

Beside the gate is the entrance to the *Roman theatre (open 09.30–12.00, 14.00–16.30 or 18.30), comparable with that of Orange in Provence. The most conspicuous part of the monument is the tall façade, 22m high, decorated with arched windows. Behind it are remains of the seats in the *cavea* and the foundations of the *scena*.

A long stretch of the **Roman walls** can be seen on the east side of the theatre. A road leads north outside the walls past several medieval buildings, including the **Tour Fromage** (now used for exhibitions) and the **Torre del Baillage**, a 12C addition at the northeast angle of the walls. Eight arches of the Roman amphitheatre, a building once capable of holding about 20,000 spectators, are visible in the nearby convent of Santa Caterina (ring to get in). Some of the arches have been built into the wall of the convent; the others run through the orchard.

Via Sant'Anselmo continues east from the Porta Praetoria to Via Sant'Orso, which you follow left. Here are the priory and collegiate church of **Sant'Orso**, or St-Ours, founded by St Anselm. The church has a campanile finished in 1131 and a late-Gothic façade, 16C stalls and an 11C crypt with 12 plain Roman columns. In the roof vaulting are remarkable Ottonian *frescoes, dating from 1030 or 1040. A custodian shows them at close range from a system of platforms and walkways (open Tues–Sun 10.00–16.45; in summer 09.30–12.00,

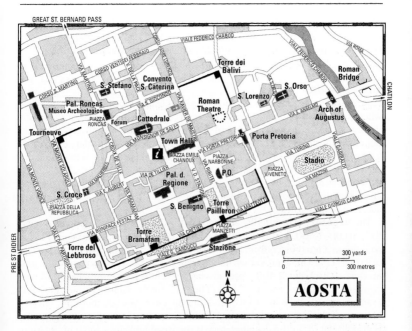

14.00–17.30). Two of the scenes represent the *Miracles on Lake Gennesaret* and at the *Marriage at Cana*; they were damaged in the 15C by the construction of the nave vault. These frescoes, together with those found beneath the cathedral roof (described below), are among the very few mural paintings of this date to have survived in Italy.

To the right of the church façade is the ***cloister** (open as the frescoes in the church), with fascinating Romanesque capitals, carved in white marble but covered at a later date with a dark patina. Placed at the top of unusually low columns, they date from c 1132. They illustrate biblical scenes (*Story of Jacob*, *Childhood of Christ*, *Raising of Lazarus*, *Noli Me Tangere*, *Stoning of St Stephen*), two episodes relating to the priory, fantastic and stylised animals, a fable of Aesop (*The Wolf and the Stork*) and prophets. This and the cloister of Monreale in Sicily are the only surviving examples in Italy of large Romanesque cloisters with representations of historical and legendary scenes. The carvings are suffering from pollution. The priory (1494–1506), with an octagonal tower, has fine terracotta decoration.

A passage opposite Sant'Orso leads round the deconsecrated church of San Lorenzo to a **5C chapel** excavated beneath the church's east end (open Tues–Sun 10.00–16.45; in summer 09.30–12.00, 14.00–17.30). The Latin-cross chapel, with apses at the end of each arm, was the burial place of the first bishops of Aosta (the sarcophagus of Bishop Agnello, who died in 528, is preserved here). It was destroyed in the Carolingian era.

Via Sant'Anselmo continues to the ***Arch of Augustus**, a triumphal arch erected in 24 BC to commemorate the defeat of the Salassi. Decorated with ten Corinthian columns, the arch was drawn and engraved many times in the 19C, and before that by Sir Roger Newdigate, who gave his drawing to Piranesi when he reached Rome. The roof was added in 1716. Further on, beyond the modern bridge over the Buthier, is a remarkable single-arched **Roman bridge**, still in use, over a dried-up channel.

The Cathedral

From Piazza Emile Chanoux, Via Hotel des Etats leads to Via Monsignor De Sales, where remains of Roman baths dating from the 1C AD have been excavated. To the left is the Cathedral, founded in the early Christian age but rebuilt in the Romanesque and Gothic styles and given a sculptured west portal in 1526, now framed by a Neo-classical façade of 1848. Inside you can see remains of the early-Christian baptistery and traces of the original 3C–4C church. The stained glass dates from the late 14C and early 15C. 16C frescoes, a 16C painted lunette illustrating the legend of St Grato and a 13C stone effigy of the Blessed Bonifacio adorn the south aisle.

The ***treasury** is beautifully arranged in the deambulatory (open in summer, daily 10.00–12.00, 15.00–17.00; in winter, Sun and holidays 15.00–17.45). It contains precious objects from the cathedral and from churches in the valley. The oldest pieces are an agate cameo dating from the 1C (in a 13C gold setting), and an ivory diptych dated 406. Cases display 13C church silver and beautiful processional crosses of the 13C–15C. The 15C tombs include those of Count François de Challant (c 1430) and Bishop Oger Moriset, both by Etienne Mossettaz. The bishop's missal, illuminated around 1420 by Giacomo Jaquerio, is also displayed. In the deambulatory is the wood-and-silver tomb of St Grato, exquisitely decorated between 1415 and 1458. Nearby is a crucifix of 1499, removed from below the Arch of Augustus. A beautiful illuminated codex and cope both belonged to Bishop François de Prez. Above you can see the tomb of Thomas II of Savoy (c 1425–35), attributed to Mossettaz. The chapel of the reliquaries contains the reliquary of San Giocondo (1615).

In the **choir** are interesting mosaic pavements dating from the 12C and 14C, one with the *Labours of the Months*, the other depicting lively animals and the Tigris and Euphrates; 15C stalls and a crucifix dating from 1397. The crypt has a miscellany of Roman and medieval columns. The Ottonian *frescoes in the roof, discovered in 1979, have been meticulously restored. They are the upper band of a fresco cycle illustrating the story of St Eustachio and biblical scenes (with a frieze of animals, some of them symbolic) that once decorated the nave and was covered when the 15C vault of the church was constructed. Thought to be by the same hand as those in Sant'Orso and dating from 1030 or 1040, they, like the latter, are rare survivals in Italy of mural paintings of this date.

The cloister, on the north side of the church, dates from 1460. It is reached by way of Via Conte Tomaso and Via San Bernardo, and can be seen through a locked gate. Some of the pillars have inscriptions instead of carvings.

Relics of Rome and Gaul

In a sunken garden beside the cathedral façade are some remains of the **Roman forum**, with the base of a temple now part of the foundations of a house. From here you can enter a splendid underground ***Roman *cryptoporticus*** (open 09.00–12.00, 14.00–17.00; if closed enquire at the Museo Archeologico). The double north walk is over 92m long.

Via Forum and Via San Bernardo lead northwest to Piazza Roncas, where a 17C palace houses the **Museo Archeologico Regionale** (open 09.00–12.00, 14.00–18.30). The first two rooms illustrate the history of the city from the 4C BC onwards by means of diagrams, models, and objects found in excavations in the city, including an exquisite bronze of the 2C AD, once part of a horse's bridle, showing a battle scene between Romans and barbarians. Stairs lead down to the excavations of one of the four Roman gates of the city and part of the walls.

Across the courtyard is a room (unlocked on request) with the remarkable *numismatic collection of Andrea Pautasso (1911–85), particularly notable for its Celtic coins found in northern Italy (many of them, in gold, silver and bronze, in imitation of Greek coins). There are also examples from the Roman, Byzantine and medieval periods, as well as the 19C.

On the left side of the palace is a little public fountain, on a canal where the water is regulated by a sluice gate.

Via Martinet leads to the church of **St Etienne** (or Santo Stefano), which has an elaborate high altar and a little museum of 15C–18C liturgical objects. The striking wood statue of *St Christopher* was carved in the 15C.

Via Croix de Ville, on the line of the *cardo maximus* of the Roman town, leads south to the medieval market place and a cross set up in 1541 to commemorate the expulsion of the Calvinists from the town. Via Tillier leads back to Piazza Chanoux past the 15C chapel of San Grato, with frescoes.

The *Roman walls, forming a rectangle 724m long and 572m wide, are best preserved on the southern and western sides of the town. Standing across the west wall is the medieval **Torre del Lebbroso**. Recently restored, it is now used for exhibitions. Near the **Torre Bramafan**, an 11C relic of the lords of Challant, remains of the Roman *Porta Principalis Dextera* have been unearthed; and the **Torre del Pailleron**, with Roman masonry, stands in a garden near the station.

On the northern outskirts of the town lies the **Villa della Consolata**, a Roman villa that has been excavated and may be opened to the public.

A cable car from behind the railway station up to the modern ski resort of Pila (1800m) operates frequently, taking 20mins.

The Valle d'Aosta

This chapter follows the Valle d'Aosta upstream from its entrance, on the Piedmont Plateau, to its end, at the foot of the 4000m peak of Mont Blanc. It also explores the four main side valleys—the Val di Gressoney, Valtournenche, Great St Bernard Valley and Val di Cogne—renowned for their immaculate farms, stony little villages and majestic alpine vistas.

Practical information

Getting there and getting around
By air

See p 58.
By road

The main road from Pont-St-Martin, at the foot of the valley, to Courmayeur, at its head, is 26.
By bus

Buses run all year from Aosta (opposite the train station) to centres of the Valle d'Aosta to Turin and Milan; via the Great St Bernard Tunnel to Martigny, and via Courmayeur and the Mont Blanc Tunnel to Chamonix. For the side valleys a change is usually necessary at the town at the beginning of the valley.
By rail

A pretty line built between the two World Wars continues from Aosta to Pré-St-Didier, a few kilometres south of Courmayeur, in c 50mins.

Information offices
BREUIL-CERVINIA, Via Carrel 29, ☎ 0166 949136.
CHAMPOLUC, Via Varasch, ☎ 0125 307113.
COGNE, Piazza Chanoux 36, ☎ 0165 74040.
COURMAYEUR, Piazzale Monte Bianco 3, ☎ 0165 842060.
GRESSONEY-LA TRINITÉ, Town hall, ☎ 0125 366143
GRESSONEY-ST-JEAN, Villa Margherita, ☎ 0125 355185.
ST-VINCENT, Via Roma 48, ☎ 0166 512239.
VILLENEUVE (Gran Paradiso National Park), Comunità Montana Gran Paradiso, ☎ 0165 95055.

Where to stay
BREUIL-CERVINIA *Bucaneve*, Piazza Jumeaux 10, ☎ 0166 949119, fax 0166 948308; calm, restful and centrally located, with good views of the Matterhorn and Grandes Murailles; open Nov–Apr and Jul–Sep; moderate.
Hermitage, Strada Cristallo, ☎ 0166 948998, fax 0166 949032; a warm, atmospheric place steeped in tradition, with stunning views over the Matterhorn and Grandes Murailles; open Dec–Apr and Jul–Sep; expensive.
Hostellerie des Guides, Via Carrel 32, ☎ 0166 949473, fax 0166 948824; simple but rich in atmosphere, with antique furniture and ample documentation of alpinists in the Valtournenche; open Nov–Apr and Jul–Aug; moderate.
CHAMPOLUC *Villa Anna Maria*, Via Croues 5, ☎ 0125 307128, fax 0125 307984; set amid pines and wildflowers, with warm, woody interiors and friendly staff; inexpensive.
COGNE *Bellevue*, Via Gran Paradiso 22, ☎ 0165 74825, fax 0165 749192; lovely building, locally crafted antiques, staff in traditional dress and a small collection of arts and crafts from the valley; open Jan–Sep; expensive.
Miramonti, Viale Caagnet 31, ☎ 0165 74030, fax 0165 749378; a restful family-managed place rich in atmosphere, with views of the Gran Paradiso; moderate. *Sant'Orso*, Via Bourgeois 2, ☎ 0165 74821, fax 0165 74822; a tranquil place, with pleasant garden and good views of the Gran Paradiso; closed May and Nov; moderate.
COURMAYEUR *Dolonne*, at Dolonne (across the Dora from Courmayeur), ☎ 0165 846674, fax 0165 846671; in a 17C farmhouse with good views over the valley and mountains; inexpensive.
Palace Bron, at Plan Gorret, ☎ 0165 846742, fax 0165 844015; beautifully located in the woods above Courmayeur, with stunning views; open Dec–Apr and Jul–Sep; moderate.

GRESSONEY-SAINT-JEAN *Gran Baita*,
Strada Castello Savoia 26, at
Gresmatten,
☎ 0125 356441, fax 0125 356441;
just 12 rooms in an 18C lodge with stupendous views of Monte Rosa; open
Dec–Apr and Jul–Sep; moderate.

SAINT-VINCENT *Elena*, Piazza Monte
Zerbion, ☎ 0166 512140, fax 0166
537459; calm and efficient; closed
Nov–Dec; inexpensive.

Grand Hotel Billia, Viale Piemonte 72,
☎ 0166 5231, fax 0166 523799;
large, traditional hotel in a lovely park,
with direct underground access to the
casino; expensive.

Accommodation can also be found in
numerous **back-country lodges** and
mountain huts.

Eating out

ARNAD (MACHABY) *Lo
Dzerby*, Frazione Machaby, ☎
0125 966067; farmhouse serving hot
meals by reservation; open Sat and Sun,
May–Oct; inexpensive.

ALLEIN (27km north of Aosta on 27).
Lo Ratelé, Frazione Ville 2, ☎ 0165
78265; good farm lunches in a former
stable; open by reservation only; inexpensive.

In the village, *Enoteca La Croix
Blanche* has a wide selection of wines
from the region.

8km down the road at Etroubles, *Luca
Tamone*, Rue des Verges 13, grows all
sorts of berries.

ARVIER *Café du Bourg*, Via Lostan 14,
☎ 0165 99094; wine bar serving *fonduta* and other traditional dishes; closed
Thur and midday, Jun and Oct; inexpensive.

CHATILLON *Privé Parisien*, regione
Panorama 1, ☎ 0166 537053; traditional restaurant, with rooms; closed
midday (except Sat, Sun and holidays),
Thur and Jul; expensive.

COGNE *Pasticceria Elda Perret*, Via
Bourgeois 57, makes delicious pastries,

notably the local Christmas cake called
meculin.

Les Pertzes, Via Grappein 93, ☎ 0165
749227; wine bar and brasserie offering
good, simple fare; closed Tues and midday Wed, Nov and May–Jun; inexpensive.

Lou Ressignon, Rue Mines de Cogne
23, ☎ 0165 4034; rustic osteria, with
game and other mountain dishes; closed
Tues (and Mon evening in low season),
Jun, Sep and Nov; moderate.

Lou Tchappè, Frazione Lillaz, ☎ 0165
74379; traditional restaurant in a
mountain cabin; closed Mon (except
Jul–Aug), Jun and Nov; moderate.

COURMAYEUR *Gallia Gran Baita*,
Strada Larzey, ☎ 0165 844040; hotel
restaurant offering innovative interpretations of traditional recipes; closed May
and Nov; moderate.

Grill Royal e Golf, Via Roma 87, ☎
0165 846787; refined regional cuisine,
in the Royal e Golf hotel; open Dec–Mar
and Jul–Aug, closed midday and Mon
(except Aug and 25 Dec); moderate.

GIGNOD (LA CLUSAZ) *Locanda La
Clusaz*, ☎ 0165 56075; trattoria (with
rooms) offering delicious local fare;
closed Tues, May–Jun and Oct–Nov;
inexpensive.

GRESSAN (AOSTA). *Hostellerie de la
Pomme Couronée*, Frazione Resselin 3,
☎ 0165 251010; an old farmhouse
with good regional dishes, especially
recipes with apples; closed Tues; moderate.

MORGEX *Café Quinson Vieux Bistrot*,
Piazza Principe Tommaso 9, ☎ 0165
809499; wine bar and café; closed Tues,
Jun and Oct; moderate.

NUS *Maison Rosset*, Via Risorgimento
39, ☎ 0165 767176; farmhouse in the
village, offering rustic dinners by a roaring fire; open evenings only (midday on
Sun and holidays), closed Mon; inexpensive.

SAINT-CHRISTOPHE (AOSTA) *Sanson*,
regione Chabloz, ☎ 0165 541410; tra-

ditional restaurant in a panoramic position above the city; closed Wed and Jul; moderate.

SAINT-PIERRE (HOMENÉ-SAINT-MARGUERITE) *Les Ecureuils*, Località Homené Dessus, ☎ 0165 903831; farmhouse (with rooms) in a village at 1500m, famous for its seasonal cuisine; open evenings, by reservation, Nov–Jun (summer for guests only); closed Jan–Feb; inexpensive.

SAINT-RHEMY EN BOSSES *Suisse*, Via Roma 21, ☎ 0165 780906; restaurant with rooms, open Dec–Apr and Jun–Sep; moderate.

SAINT-VINCENT *Batezar*, Via Marconi 1, ☎ 0166 513164; traditional restaurant serving delicious regional delicacies; closed midday (except, Sat, Sun and holidays), Wed, Nov and Jun; expensive.

Le Grenier, Piazza Monte Zerbion 1, ☎ 0166 512224; good traditional fare, in an old granary; closed Tues, midday Wed, Jan and Jul; moderate.

SARRE *Mille Miglia*, on the main road at San Maurizio 15, ☎ 0165 257227; a family-run place serving good local dishes; closed Mon and Nov, inexpensive.

VALGRISENCHE (BONNE) *Perret*, Località Bonne 2, ☎ 0165 97107; trattoria (with rooms) offering strictly local fare; closed Jun and Nov, inexpensive.

VERRES *Chez Pierre*, Via Martorey 73, ☎ 0125 929376; restaurant (with rooms), offering excellent regional delicacies and summer seating outside; closed Tues; moderate.

Shopping
Local artisans' products are sold in *IVAT* shops in Aosta, Cogne, Courmayeur, Valtournenche, and Gressoney-St-Jean. Market day in Aosta is Tues, in Piazza Cavalieri di Vittorio Veneto.

Special events
COGNE The *Veillà*, a local artisans' fair, is held on a Sat in mid-Jul and in mid-August.

The *Battaglia delle Regine*, a contest between horned cattle, is held in various heats throughout the valley (the finals in late Oct usually take place in a field outside the castle of Fénis).

PONT ST-MARTIN *Carnival* is celebrated with a traditional festa on Shrove Tuesday at Pont-St-Martin, when the devil is 'hung' from the Roman bridge, followed by a party in the castle of Verrès.

FONTAINEMORE A *procession* every 3 or 4 years in summer across the mountains to the sanctuary of Oropa in Piedmont.

PERLOZ In Oct there is a *contest between mountain goats*.

GRESSONEY-ST-JEAN A *procession in local costume* is held on 24 Jun and 15 Aug. **AYMAVILLES** On the last Sunday of May there is a *music festival* in the park of the castle of Aymavilles.

Sports
Skiing. There are good cross-country and Alpine back-country trails throughout the Valle d'Aosta, especially around Cogne and in the Gran Paradiso National Park. Courmayeur and Cervinia are the most famous of the downhill ski resorts. There are numerous marked trails all over the region for **walkers** and **hikers**. The most spectacular mountaineering routes for experienced hikers are the two 'Alte Vie' which cover 282km at altitudes ranging from 1200m to 3296m (best undertaken Jun–Sep). They lead from Gressoney-St-Jean via Valtournenche and St Rhémy to Courmayeur (no. 1) and from Courmayeur via La Thuile, Valgrisenche and the Gran Paradiso National Park to Champorcher (no. 2); information from the information bureaus and CAI offices.

From Pont-St-Martin to Mont Blanc

Pont-St-Martin lies on the southernmost border of the region of Valle d'Aosta. It has a well-preserved Roman *bridge (1C BC), with a single arch over the Lys, which can be crossed on foot (the bridge downstream was built in 1876). Above are the ruins of a 12C castle. Just beyond **Donnas** you can see the best surviving stretch in the valley of the **Roman road to Gaul** above the modern road on the right. It was built just above the level of the river, to avoid flooding, and ran mostly along the left bank, where the warmth of the sun (stronger here than on the other side) helped to melt the snow in winter. A conspicuous arch cut into the rock by the Romans survives here—a demonstration of the skill required by the stoneworkers, who in places had to construct the road out of the sheer rock face. A round column serves as a milestone (35 miles from Aosta). The road was in use up to the 19C, and if you look closely you can see the ruts made by cartwheels.

The interesting castle of **Bard**, an 11C foundation, was largely reconstructed in the 19C. At present only the courtyard can be visited, but there are plans to open the whole castle. In 1800 Napoleon's progress was halted here for a week by the defenders of the castle, but in the end he managed to pass unnoticed with his army during the night; they went through the narrow gorge in silence, having protected the wheels of the gun carriages with straw. As an over-liberal young officer, Camillo Cavour was despatched to this remote garrison by Carlo Felice of Savoy, King of Sardinia and Piedmont, in 1830–31.

The church of **Arnad**, founded in the 11C and restored in the early 15C, is one of the older churches in the valley. The exterior frescoes in late-Gothic style are part of the 15C restoration.

The castle of **Verrès** (open 09.00–19.00; winter 10.00–17.00) commands the mouth of the Val d'Ayas. A road leads up to the car park (or a path ascends in 15 minutes from Piazza Chanoux in Verrès village), from where a steep path continues up the hill, taking you to the entrance in 5–10 minutes. This four-square castle, with sheer walls 30m high, was founded by the Challant family in 1390 and strengthened by them in 1536 (it was acquired by the state in 1894). Never a residence, it was used purely for defensive purposes, and its bare interior has huge fireplaces, an old kitchen built into the rock, and an imposing staircase. Just below the castle is the abbey of St Gilles, founded c 1050 (now a school).

On the other side of the river is the castle of *Issogne, rebuilt by Georges de Challant in 1497–98. This is a splendid example of a late medieval residence (open as the Castle of Verrès). It retains some of its original furnishings and lovely Gothic double doors carved in wood. It was donated to the state in 1907. Notice the 16C frescoed lunettes with scenes of everyday life, including a guard-house with a game of backgammon in progress and various shops, beneath the arches in the courtyard. The unusual wrought-iron fountain, in the form of a pomegranate tree, was made in the 16C. The little walled garden has box hedges. Next to the dining room is the kitchen, with three fireplaces. The chapel has a lovely late 16C altarpiece and an unusual lunette fresco of the *Death of the Virgin*. Stairs continue up to the loggia on the top floor. Off the main staircase is the bedroom of Georges de Challant, which has a pretty wood ceiling and a little oratory with a *Crucifixion* and the kneeling figure of Challant. Another room has views of the two castles of Verrès and Arnad. A small room used as a school-room has sums scratched on the walls. The Sala baroniale has delightful painted walls depicting the *Judgement of Paris*, and lovely landscapes with birds behind painted crystal columns.

Near Champdepraz is the **Parco Naturale di Mont Avic**, a protected area surrounding the pointed mountain of Avic (3006m). Marked trails lead up through the park's pine and larch woods to crystalline alpine lakes.

> ### On Italy's highest mountains
> *The great ones, the giants of Alps, stood about us here and there in a cloudless sky, a burning serenity. Their immobility never seems to me static; it has a vitality that seems to us repose, like that of a humming top at rest on its axis, spinning along its orbit in space.* Freya Stark, *Traveller's Prelude*, 1950

St-Vincent is the second most important town in the valley, after Aosta. It is famous for its casino and has numerous hotels. The approach road passes the remains of a Roman bridge that collapsed in the 19C. Beside the Art Nouveau Hotel Billia (1910), and a congress hall built in 1983, is the **Casinò**, which was opened in the 1950s and renovated in the 1970s. The Region of Valle d'Aosta has a majority holding in the Casino, which is closed to residents of the valley. It is the most important gambling house in Italy (and considered the second in Europe after Monte Carlo). It is frequented mostly by Italians, and there are direct train and bus services from Turin to St-Vincent in the afternoon. The casino is open 15.00–02.00, although *chemin-de-fer* is usually played throughout the night.

The **old church**, built on a prehistoric and Roman site, has a 14C fresco in a niche outside the apse. The interior, with Romanesque columns, has 15C and 16C frescoes and a little museum. The frescoes in the window jambs are attributed to the school of Jaquerio.

St-Vincent has been known since 1770 as a health resort, and the spa (open May–Oct) is reached by a funicular railway from the centre of the town in 3 minutes. The **Palazzo delle Fonti** was built in 1960 above the source of the mineral spring (*fons salutis*).

Châtillon is built on the Marmore torrent, with 19C foundries, mills and forges on its banks. On high ground across the valley stands the castle of Ussel (1351). Chambave, beneath the ruined castle of Cly, is noted for its *Moscato* wine.

The castle of **Fénis** (open Mon–Sat 10.00–17.00, Sun and holidays 10.00–18.00; closed Tues; visitors admitted every 30mins; recorded guide available) is the most famous medieval fortress in the Valle d'Aosta and former seat of the Challant family. With numerous towers, it is enclosed by double walls (the outer circuit was reconstructed in 1936). It was rebuilt c 1340 by Aimone de Challant and heavily restored at the end of the 19C. The charming courtyard, with wooden balconies and a lovely semicircular staircase, has remarkable *frescoes in a refined International Gothic style by Giacomo Jaquerio and his school (15C), including *St George and the Dragon* and a frieze of philosophers and prophets holding scrolls with proverbs in Old French. The first floor, with a chapel also frescoed by Jaquerio, has been closed since 1981. The rooms of the castle have interesting local furniture, although not all of it is authentic. The furnished guardroom contains a model of the castle.

The valley expands into the fertile basin of Aosta, with a small airfield. A large steel mill south of the town is very prominent.

Beyond Aosta stands the 13C castle of **Sarre**, rebuilt in 1710 (open Jul–Aug 09.00–20.00). It is notable for its hall decorated with thousands of hunting trophies, including numerous ibex shot by Vittorio Emanuele II in the Gran Paradiso park. The castle of **St-Pierre** was first built in the 12C but transformed in the 19C, when the four cylindrical towers and castellations were added. In a splendid position on an isolated rock, above the church and bell tower of St-Pierre, it has a good view of the snow-capped mountain of La Grivola. It is owned by the city of St-Pierre and houses the Museo Regionale di Scienze Naturali (open Apr–Oct, 09.00–19.00; Nov–Mar 09.00–12.00 and 14.00–18.00), founded in 1850 and opened here in 1985. A display of minerals, mostly from Mont Blanc, occupies the stable block; other rooms have exhibits illustrating the geology, flora and fauna of the area, including 290 ibex antlers. The little summer resort of **St-Nicolas** (1126m) lies in a good position above St-Pierre.

Low down on the river is the castle of **Sarriod de la Tour**, dating in part from the 14C, which may one day be used as an exhibition centre. **Morgex** is the principal village in the Valdigne, the upper valley of the Dora. The church, founded in the 6C, has an unusual onion-shaped steeple and contains early 16C frescoes.

Courmayeur (1228m) is a famous ski resort in a deep vale at the southern foot of Mont Blanc. It has a much milder climate than Chamonix, on the other side of the mountain in Savoy. A museum illustrates the history of alpinism in the area. La Palud is the starting point of the *cable railway to Chamonix, which crosses over Mont Blanc in c 1hr 30 mins. It runs every hour (weather permitting) and provides a magnificent panorama of the Graian Alps and the south side of the Pennine Alps. It crosses the French frontier at an altitude of 3462m.

Mont Blanc (4807m) is the highest mountain in western Europe (the summit, in France, is fully described in *Blue Guide France*). It was first climbed from Chamonix in 1786. The Col de la Seigne (2512m), on the French frontier, is the watershed between the basins of the Po and the Rhône. The Mont Blanc Tunnel, built through the mountains in 1958–65, is 11.6km long (temporarily closed). The road descends over 100m from the Italian to the French side.

The side valleys

The tributaries of the Dora Baltea rush and tumble through steep, wooded alpine valleys that are every bit as interesting as the main Valle d'Aosta and often more dramatic in their natural beauty.

The **Val di Gressoney**, which leads towards Monte Rosa, is ascended by road from Pont-St-Martin. It contains the largest and oldest of the German-speaking colonies formed by settlers who crossed over from Valais in the Middle Ages. The people of this valley, known as the Walsers, are mentioned as early as 1218. They were subjects of the Bishop of Sion and have kept their language and customs even more distinct from their Italian neighbours than have the people of Alagna or Macugnaga. The attractive chalets (*rascards*) in the lower valley, the farmhouses (*stadel*) in the upper valley, and the costume of the women (which is brightly coloured in red and black, with a remarkable headdress adorned with hand-made gold lace) all suggest a northern origin.

Fontainemore has a lovely medieval single-arched bridge across the Lys. **Issime** (939m) has an interesting German Walser dialect, known as *titsch*, and the signs here are written in all three languages. The church, rebuilt after 1567, has a fresco of the *Last Judgement* on the façade, opposite which is a pretty porch with niches, painted in 1752. Inside is a little museum. The elaborate high altar, in gold and turquoise, is decorated with numerous statues (1690–1710). At the west end is an interesting judge's chair, with a chain collar for those found guilty: it was used up to 1770 in the piazza.

Gaby, where the poet Giosuè Carducci used to stay at the end of the 19C, is a French-speaking village (1032m), but the German dialect is used again at **Gressoney-St-Jean** (1385m), the principal village in the valley and a summer and winter resort. You can still see some old houses (*stadel*) here, and there is a fine view of snow-covered Monte Rosa (4637m) at the head of the valley. The town hall occupies Villa Margherita, a remarkable Art Nouveau building built for Queen Margherita at the end of the 19C.

Across the river in fir and larch woods is the turreted Gothic-revival **castle of Gressoney** (or Castel Savoia; open Fri–Wed 09.00–12.00, 15.00–18.00; guided visits every 30mins), built in 1899–1904 by Emilio Stramucci for Queen Margherita, who spent every summer here up to 1925. This period piece—the decoration of the wooden stairs is particularly successful—contains a bronze bust of a woman wearing the local headdress by Pietro Canonica. The veranda enjoys a splendid view of Monte Rosa (the mountain was frequently visited by the queen). The kitchen was in a separate building, connected to the castle by a miniature railway.

The pretty little village is German in atmosphere. The church has a bust of Queen Margherita on the façade and a Baroque interior with charming wooden altars and a small museum. A statue of Umberto I graces the adjoining piazza.

The sister village of Gressoney-la-Trinité (1628m), is a ski resort for Monte Rosa, with a view of the grand line of snow peaks from Monte Rosa to the Gran Paradiso.

The **Val d'Ayas** leaves the main valley at Verrès and follows the River Evançon. The ruined 13C castle of Graines stands on a prehistoric site in an attractive landscape with cherry trees. The valley has pine forests and massive wooden chalets. Antagnod (1710m) has a fine church. Champoluc (1570m), surrounded by splendid forests, is an important ski resort for Monte Rosa.

The **Valtournenche**, extending from Châtillon to the base of the Matterhorn along the Marmore valley, has numerous resorts, including Valtournenche (1528m). **Breuil-Cervinia** (2004m) has become one of the more popular ski resorts in Italy, with numerous cableways ascending the main ridge of the Alps, dominated by the Matterhorn and Breithorn (4171m) on either side of the Theodule pass on the Swiss frontier. Most of the early attempts to scale the **Matterhorn** (4478m: *Monte Cervino* in Italian) were started from Breuil, but the summit was not reached from this side by a direct route until 1867.

The passes

The Valle del Gran San Bernardo extends north from Aosta to the Swiss frontier on the Passo del Gran San Bernardo. The busy tunnel (approached by a stretch of motorway) was built in 1958–64 (toll). It is 5.8km long and rises slightly from the Italian side (1875m) to the Swiss (1918m).

The road over the **Passo del Gran San Bernardo** is usually closed Nov–Jun. It was known and used by Celts and Romans. The latter called it Mons Jovis (Mont Joux) after a temple of Jupiter Paeninus that once stood on the Plan de Jupiter, near the saddle. It acquired its present name in the 12C. The pass was much used by pilgrims and clerics bound to or from Rome, and between 774 and 1414 it was crossed 20 times by medieval emperors, including Frederick Barbarossa in 1162. Coaches that entered Italy here in the 18C had to be dismantled and carried piece by piece over the pass on the backs of local mountaineers. Both French and Austrian soldiers crossed the pass in the campaigns of 1798–1800. The most famous passage was made by Napoleon, who on 14–20 May 1800 led 40,000 troops by this route into Italy and a month later defeated the Austrians at the Battle of Marengo. Numerous engravings were made of the pass after this event and throughout the 19C. A proper road was constructed only in 1905.

Just beyond the Swiss frontier is the **Hospice du Grand-St-Bernard** (2469m), a massive stone building on the summit of the pass, exposed to storms from the northeast and southwest. On the northwest it is sheltered by the peak of Chenalette (2889m), on the southeast by Mont Mort (2867m). The hospice was supposedly founded in the 11C by St Bernard of Menthon, archdeacon of Aosta, a native of Savoy; by 1215 it was kept by Austin canons from Martigny. Since 1925 the hospice has been managed by 10 or 12 canons and a number of lay brothers called *aumoniers*. In their rescue of snow-bound travellers the canons are assisted by the famous St Bernard dogs, a breed said to be a cross between the Pyrenean sheepdog and the Newfoundland.

The **Passo del Piccolo San Bernardo** (2188m) is just over the French frontier, on the watershed between the Dora Baltea and the Isère. Nearby is the Colonne de Joux, probably a Roman monument of *cipollino* marble, with a statue of St Bernard added in 1886. A little below it is an Iron Age stone circle just over 73m in diameter, in which Gaulish and Roman coins have been discovered. The trail across the pass was transformed into a road for carriages in 1871. The ruined Hospice du Petit-St-Bernard (2152m), founded c 1000, used to offer free hospitality to poor travellers. The botanical garden established here in 1897 by Abbot Pierre Chanoux is being reconstructed and is open to the public.

The Parco Nazionale del Gran Paradiso

The whole of the Gran Paradiso Massif (4061m) to the south of Aosta, above the valleys of Cogne, Valnontey, Valsavarenche and Val di Rhêmes, lies within the **Parco Nazionale del Gran Paradiso**, an area of some 70,000 hectares and the oldest national park in Italy (established in 1922). The natural beauty of the park has been threatened by attempts to open up part of the Valsavarenche as a resort for skiers. The park was created as a hunting reserve for Vittorio Emanuele II in 1856 and presented to the state by Vittorio Emanuele III in 1919. Many of the bridlepaths made by Vittorio Emanuele II are still in use. This is the only part of the Alps in which the ibex (*stambecco*) has survived in its natural state (some 5000 live here). The chamois and Alpine marmot are also common. The flowers are at their best May and June. To find out about **climbs and walks**, contact the *Comunità Montana Gran Paradiso*, località Champagne 18, Villeneuve (☎ 0165

95055), and the information office in Cogne. There are three entrances from the Valle d'Aosta: at Valnontey, Valsavarenche and Val di Rhêmes (the rest of the park lies within Piedmont).

The most direct road from Aosta follows the delightful **Val di Cogne**, the upper reaches of which border the national park. The road passes the unusual castle of Aymavilles, altered in the 18C when the turrets were added and it was surrounded by a park. Just off the road, a by-road (signposted) descends right to the tiny isolated hamlet of **Pondel**, with a remarkable *****Roman bridge** that once also served as an aqueduct. As the inscription states, it was built privately by two Paduans in the 3C BC; 50m long and 50m high, it crosses the ravine made by the Grand'Eyvia Torrent. A splendid covered passageway, still practicable, runs beneath the aqueduct channel. It is extremely well preserved and is one of the more interesting sites in the Valle d'Aosta. The valley on the other side of the bridge is well known for its butterflies (you can take lovely walks in the area along marked trails). There is a good view from here of the peak of the Grivola mountain (3969m) at the top of the valley. The pretty little resort of Ozein (1300m), with a few hotels and a fine view of the peak of the Grivola, stands above the main road.

The valley opens out into a wide basin at **Cogne** (1533m), just outside the limits of the national park. It has a large common (where you can often see ibex in May), across which rises the snow-capped Gran Paradiso. Cogne was developed as a resort after the magnetite mines were closed down in 1974. You can see remains of the mines, at an altitude of some 2000m on the hillside (the miners were transported by lift), and there is a museum (open May–Sep) in the mining village of Boutillère. Next to the church are a small museum illustrating the craft of lace-making, for which Cogne is famous, and the modest hunting lodge of Vittorio Emanuele III.

A by-road ends at **Lillaz** (also reached by a path along the river from Cogne), where most of the houses preserve their typical slate roofs. A path leads past a number of waterfalls. The other road from Cogne enters the park along the **Valnontey**, which runs due south to the Gran Paradiso and ends at Valnontey, an attractive group of houses with a few simple hotels, the starting point of numerous nice walks in the park. The Paradisia alpine garden (1700m), founded here in 1955, is open July–September.

PIEDMONT

The ancient principality of Piedmont, the cradle of the Italian nation, is divided into the provinces of Turin, Cuneo, Alessandria, Asti, Vercelli, Biella, Novara and Verbania. The region occupies the upper basin of the Po—mainly *al pie' dei monti*, 'at the foot of the mountains' which encircle it: the Pennine, Graian, Cottian, and Maritime Alps. The cultural relations of Piedmont with France have always been very close, and the French language was long used at the court and parliament of Turin. Its influence survives in the Piedmontese dialects.

Historically Piedmont combines the territories of the old marquisates of Ivrea and Monferrato and the county of Turin; the name Piemonte does not appear until the 13C. In 1045 the territory of Turin came into the hands of the House of Savoy by the marriage of Adelaide of Susa with Otho (Oddone), son of Humbert, Count of Savoy. In the 14C, under the guidance of Amedeo VI and VII, the princely house gained so much power that Amedeo VIII was made Duke of Savoy by the Holy Roman Emperor in 1391.

Saluzzo and Monferrato were added to Piedmont in the 16C and 18C. Further territory was gained when Vittorio Amedeo II, appointed king of Sicily in 1713, was awarded the kingdom of Sardinia in 1720 in exchange for the more distant island. The Piedmontese kingdom, like all other Italian states, was obliterated by the Napoleonic conquests; but the Treaty of Vienna reinstated the Savoy kings at Turin and gave them suzerainty over Liguria in addition.

The decades following the Napoleonic interlude witnessed the emergence of Piedmont as the principal agent of Italian nationhood. Vittorio Emanuele II, thanks to the astuteness of his minister Cavour, won the goodwill of France and England by taking part in the Crimean War, then turned this privilege to his advantage by calling Napoleon III to his aid when the second War of Italian Independence broke out in 1859. The war was fought against Austria, which occupied northern Italy from Milan to Trieste. The Austrian army was crushed in a succession of defeats, and Lombardy was annexed to Piedmont after the final victory of Solferino. The Piedmontese dominions west of the Alps (Savoy and Nice) were handed over to France, and the remaining Italian provinces (except the areas north and east of Venice, acquired after the First and Second World Wars, respectively) were added one by one to Vittorio Emanuele's kingdom. In 1865 he transferred his capital from Turin to Florence, and the history of Piedmont became merged in the history of Italy.

Turin

Turin, in Italian *Torino*, is the most important city of Piedmont (population 919,000) and one of the more important industrial centres of Italy. Long a centre of metalworking, it has been famous since 1899 as the home of the Fiat motor company. The regular Roman street plan of its ancient core, consciously developed when the city was enlarged in the 17C–18C, gives it the air of a French rather than an Italian town. The centre of the city, with some splendid palaces and churches built in a late Baroque style by Guarino Guarini and Filippo Juvarra, is remarkably homogeneous. Trams still traverse the long straight streets, and there are quite a few elegant old-fashioned cafés.

In its heyday—the 18C—Turin must have been a very striking place indeed. The English writer Horace Walpole, who passed through on his 1739 tour of Italy, wrote of it as 'by far one of the prettiest cities [in Italy], clean and compact, very new and very regular'. His travelling companion Thomas Gray called it 'a place of many beauties', expressing particular regard for the 'streets all laid out by the line, regular uniform buildings, fine walks that surround the whole, and in general a good lively, clean appearance'. Post-industrial Turin is a bit scruffy with respect to the 18C city that Walpole and Gray saw, but it still retains the orderly, rational aspect that they found so appealing. And there is an ongoing effort to restore it to its past splendour (which you can see particularly well in the brilliant recovery of Piazza San Carlo), the master-plan for which encompasses everything from commercial signage to the most minute details of colour and materials in building façades.

Ideally, you should allow at least a couple of days to tour the city and its fine artistic and archaeological collections, and and another day or two to explore the several large parks and grand Savoy residences in the immediate environs.

Practical information

Getting there
By air

Turin's Sandro Pertini International Airport, at Caselle Torinese 16km north of the city, is connected by daily flights to most European capitals. There is an air terminal (Map 1) in Corso Inghilterra (corner of Via Sacchi). Buses to Caselle (30–40mins) run c every hour; to Milan Malpensa (c 2hrs) three times daily. For flight information, ☎ 011 567 6361/62.

By road

The quickest way to Turin from Milan is by the A4; from Bologna, by A1/A21; from Genoa, A10/A26 and A21; from Savona, A6. From Geneva, use the San Bernardo tunnel while work is underway on the Mont Blanc tunnel; from Lyon or Grenoble, the Mont Cenis (Fréjus) tunnel and E70/A5. Direct buses connect Turin with Geneva, London, Madrid, Paris and other European capitals; as well as with centres in Piedmont and Italy. The bus terminal is located at Corso Inghilterra 3; details from the Tourist Information Office.

By rail

The main train station in Turin is Porta Nuova (**Map 9**), though Milan-bound trains often stop also at Porta Susa (**Map**

1), and Genoa-bound trains at Lingotto. *Eurocity* trains originating in Paris or Lyon make the run from Chambery (the last important stop in France) to Turin in c 2hrs 20mins. *Intercity* trains (some originating in Venice or Trieste) from Milan to Turin in 1hr 50mins. *Eurostar* and *Intercity* trains (originating in Naples, Rome or Florence) from Genoa to Turin in 90mins. There are also slow, local connections to places throughout Piedmont and western Liguria.

Getting around

The centre of Turin is closed to motor traffic, although you can enter adjacent zones with your car by paying a toll.

Car parking

As a rule, car parking is difficult, though not impossible. There is an underground car park in Via Roma. Limited car parking is available also in Corso Galileo Ferraris, Via Ventimiglia, Corso Re Umberto, Piazza Bodoni, Piazzale Valdo Fusi, Longotto Fiere, Piazza Emanuele Filiberto, at the Cittadella and near Porta Nuova railway station (Piazza Carlo Felice; Map 9, 10).

Public transport

Public transport (run by *Azienda Torinese Mobilita*, ☎ 011 800 019152) is the quickest way to get around, though you can walk across central Turin in about 40 minutes.

Tram

4. Via XX Settembre (near the main railway station) to the Duomo.
1. Stazione Porta Nuova—Corso Vittorio Emanuele II—Stazione Porta Susa.
15. Station (Corso Vittorio Emanuele)—Via XX Settembre—Piazza Castello—Via Po—Piazza Vittorio Veneto—Via Napione—Corso Regina Margherita—Corso Belgio—Corso Casale—Sassi (for the Superga cog railway).
13. Stazione Porta Susa—Via

Cernaia—Via Micca—Piazza Castello—Via Po—Piazza Vittorio Veneto—Piazza Gran Madre di Dio (at the foot of Monte dei Cappuccini).
16. Piazza Repubblica—Corso Regina Margherita—Via Rossini—Corso San Maurizio—Via Bava—Piazza Vittorio Veneto—Corso Cairoli—Corso Vittorio Emanuele II—Corso Massimo d'Azeglio (Parco del Valentino).

Bus

67. Largo Marconi—Corso Marconi—Corso Massimo d'Azeglio—Piazza Zara—Corso Moncalieri—Moncalieri.
35. Stazione Porta Nuova—Lingotto.
Suburban buses 41. Corso Vittorio—Stupinigi. **36**. Corso Francia—Rivoli.

Country buses depart from the bus station, 3 Corso Inghilterra (**Map 1**), to Sestriere, Milan, Valle d'Aosta, etc, and from Corso Marconi (corner of Via Nizza; **Map 9**) to Cuneo, Saluzzo, Alba, etc.

Taxi

☎ 011 5737, 011 5730, 011 3399.

Sightseeing tours

Tours of the city centre and the royal residences (Palazzina di Caccia di Stupinigi, Castello di Rivoli, Reggia di Venaria Reale) depart daily at 14.30 from Piazza Castello; for reservations ☎ 011 576 4590. The historic cog railway from Torino Sassi to the Basilica of Superga (660m) will return to operation in 2000 (for information and reservations, ☎ 011 576 4590). Boat trips on the Po River, lasting c 1hr 30mins, depart from the Murazzi (quays) and Borgo Medioevale; for information and reservations, ☎ 011 576 4590.

Information offices

Piazza Castello 161, ☎ 011 535181, with a branch office at Porta Nuova Station, ☎ 011 531327. *Informagiovani*, Via Assarotti 2, ☎ 011 442 4976.

Where to stay

There seems to be an opportunity here, if you like buying and developing property. Most hotels in Turin are geared to business people in town for the auto show, the book fair (increasingly important) or some other commercial event. Naturally, they all have beds and showers—but little else.

Possible exceptions to this rule are *Relais Villa Sassi*, Strada al Traforo di Pino 47 (at the base of the hill of Superga), ☎ 011 898 0556, fax 011 898 0095; an 18C villa in a lovely park, with an excellent restaurant, closed Aug, expensive; and *Victoria*, Via Nino Costa 4, ☎ 011 561 1909, fax 011 561 1806, an elegant, friendly place in the heart of town; moderate.

Also acceptable are: *Grand Hotel Sitea*, Via Carlo Alberto 35, ☎ 011 517 0171, fax 011 548090; central and classy, with another famous restaurant; expensive. *Piemontese*, Via Berthollet 21, ☎ 011 669 8101, fax 011 669 0571; small and comfortable, in a quiet street of the city centre; moderate. *Turin Palace*, Via Sacchi 8, ☎ 011 562 5511, fax 011 561 2187; an older, more traditional establishment, next to Porta Nuova Station; expensive.

Youth hostel, 1 Via Alby 1, ☎ 011 660 2939.

Eating out

Turin is a fabulous place for gourmets. Delicious candies and pastries line the windows of cafés and confectioners everywhere in the city centre, and there are quite a few good restaurants around town—some with their original 18C or 19C décor.

Restaurants

Al Gatto Nero, Corso Turati 14, ☎ 011 590414; restaurant famous for its grill; closed Sun and Aug; moderate.

Antiche Sere, Via Cenischia 9, ☎ 011 385 4347; an excellent traditional osteria in the working-class quarter of Borgo San Paolo; open evenings only, closed Sun, Aug and Dec–Jan; moderate.

Balbo, Via Andrea Doria 11, ☎ 011 812 5566; restaurant renowned for its delicious regional dishes; closed Mon and Jul–Aug; expensive.

Caval'd Brôns, Piazza San Carlo 157, ☎ 011 5627483; another well-known traditional restaurant; closed midday Sat and Sun; moderate.

C'era una Volta, Corso Vittorio Emanuele 41, ☎ 011 650 4589; restaurant famous for its large portions of traditional regional fare, open evenings only, closed Sun and Aug; moderate.

Da Benito, Corso Siracusa 142, ☎ 011 309 0353; restaurant famous for its seafood; closed Mon and Aug; moderate.

Dai Saletta, Via Belfiore 37, ☎ 011 668 7867; good trattoria near the Parco del Valentino and Torino Esposizioni; closed Sun and Aug; moderate.

Del Cambio, Piazza Carignano 2, ☎ 011 543760; restaurant famous for its 19C décor; expensive.

Ij Brandé, Via Massena 5, ☎ 011 537279; restaurant serving *Barolo*-braised beef and other regional specialities; closed Sun, midday Mon and Aug; moderate.

L'Agrifoglio, Via Accademia Albertina 38d, ☎ 011 837064; small, friendly and declicious restaurant in the heart of town; closed Sun, midday Mon and Jul–Aug; inexpensive.

La Prima Smarrita, Corso Unione Sovietica 244, ☎ 011 317 9657; delicious, innovative Mediterranean cuisine, with lots of fish; closed Mon and Aug; moderate.

L'Osto dël Borgh Vej, Via Torquato Tasso 7, ☎ 011 436 4843; another tiny place offering good regional cuisine, near the duomo and Palazzo di Città; closed Sun and Aug; moderate.

Locanda Mongreno, Strada Mongreno 50, ☎ 011 898 0417; osteria serving creative variations of traditional recipes, in the hills outside the city centre; open evenings only, closed Mon, Aug and Jan; inexpensive.

Ostu, Via Cristoforo Colombo 63, ☎ 011 596789; popular osteria and wine bar; closed Sun and Jul–Aug; inexpensive.

Porta di Savona, Piazza Vittorio Veneto 2, ☎ 011 817 3500; the traditional place to go for honest, wholesome regional cuisine, in a warm friendly setting (crowded in the evening); closed Mon, midday Tues and Aug; inexpensive.

Torricelli, Via Torricelli 51, ☎ 011 599814; restaurant serving traditional dishes with an innovative twist; closed Sun, Aug and Jan; moderate.

Tre Galline, Via Bellezia 37, ☎ 011 436 6553; traditional restaurant, in the same spot for three centuries; closed Sun, midday Mon and Aug; moderate.

Cafés, confectioners and pastry shops

San Carlo, *Torino* and *Stratta*, all in Piazza San Carlo, are the city's top venues for pastries and candies.

Mulassano and *Baratti*, both in Piazza Castello, are well-known cafés.

Al bicerin, Piazza della Consolata, takes its name from a drink combining coffee, chocolate, cream—even if you're not hungry or thirsty, go there to see the ˚décor. *Fiorio*, 8 Via Po, and *Platti*, Corso Vittorio Emanuele II 72, also have good coffee, cakes and candies.

Caffetteria Viennese, Corso Re Umberto 19g, delicious hot chocolate.

Avvignano and *T.R.*, in Piazza Carlo Felice, *giandujotti* and other local candies. *Gertosio*, Via Lagrange 34, and *Giordano*, Via San Domenico 21, chocolates and pastries.

Other special food shops

Il Vinaio, Via Cibrario 38, sells collector wines, especially *Barolo*.
Other good places for wines are *Il Bottigliere*, Via San Francesco da Paola 43 (with snacks; open until midnight);

and *La Petite Cave*, Via De Gasperi 2. *Delicatesses*, Via Madama Cristina 62, is an excellent choice for picnic supplies. For *agnolotti* and other fresh pastas, try *Giulio Gallo*, Corso Sebastopoli 161. **CHIERI** *San Domenico*, Via San Domenico 2b, ☎ 011 941 1864; restaurant specialising in fish; closed Mon and Aug; moderate.

Entertainment
Theatre

Teatro Alfa, Via Casalborgone 16/l.

Adua, Corso Giulio Cesare 67.
Agnelli, Via Sarpi 111.
Alfieri, Piazza Solferino 4.
Carignano, Piazza Carignano 6.
Colosseo, Via Madama Cristina 71/A.
Erba, Corso Moncalieri 241.
Gianduja, Via Santa Teresa 5.
Juvarra, Via Juvarra 15.
Nuovo, Corso Massimo D'Azeglio 17.
Torino, Piazza Massaua 9.

Opera, ballet and concerts

Teatro Regio, Piazza Castello 215.
Teatro Stabile, Piazza San Carlo 161.
Auditorium Giovanni Agnelli–Lingotto, Via Nizza 262/43.
Auditorium Rai, Piazza Rossaro, corner of Via Rossini.
Conservatorio Giuseppe Verdi, Via Mazzini 11.
Palastampa, Corso Ferrara 30.

Shopping

The main shopping streets in central Turin are Via Roma, Via Lagrange, Via Carlo Alberto, Via Mazzini, Via Cavour, Via Maria Vittoria, Via Santa Teresa, Via Pietro Micca, Via Monte di Pietà, Via Garibaldi, Via Barbaroux, Via dei Mercanti, Via Sant' Agostino, Via San Tommaso and Via Po. Here you'll find mainly **designer clothing, furniture and housewares**.

The things for which Turin is most famous, however, are chocolate, wine and breads (especially breadsticks, *grissini*).

The best **chocolate** is at *Baratti & Milano*, Piazza Castello 29; *Confetteria Giordano*, Piazza Carlo Felice 69; *Peyrano Pfatisch*, Corso Vittorio Emanuele II 76; *Laboratorio Artigianale del Gianduiotto*, Via Cagliari 19B; *Peyrano*, Corso Moncalieri 47; *Pfatisch*, Via Sacchi 42; and *Stratta*, Piazza San Carlo 191. The most characteristic form of chocolate is the *giandujotto*, the famous long, tringular ingot that comes in a gold or silver wrapper; the chocolate is mixed with toasted, chopped hazel nuts. While shopping for your *giandujotti*, be sure to pause for a *bicerin*, a delightful blend of chocolate, coffee and cream (especially good at *Bicerin*, Piazza della Consolata 5).

The outstanding **wines** are *Barolo* (produced in the hills between Alba and Cuneo), *Barbaresco* (made from the same *nebbiolo* grape), *Dolcetto* (from vineyards around Dogliani, Alba, Asti, Acqui and Ovada) and *Barbera* (the object of a historic rivalry between Alba and Asti).

For **grissini**, try *Marta Bera*, Via San Tommaso 12; *Guala*, Piazza Statuto 13; *Panaté*, Via Palazzo di Città 6; and *Panificio Serra*, Via Palazzo di Città, Chieri.

A daily food and garment **market** and a periodic **antiques market** (second Sunday of the month) are held at Porta Palazzo (Piazza della Repubblica).

Special events

Festa di San Giovanni Battista (patron saint, 24 Jun), celebrated with music, food, fireworks on the Po River and a famous bonfire in Piazza San Carlo which, depending on which way it falls, bodes ill or well for the coming year. *Ad Ovest di Paperino*, cabaret festival, Jun–Jul. *Biennale Internazionale di Fotografia*, internation biennial photography exhibition in odd years, Sep–Oct. *Colonna Sonora*, music festival, Jul. *Festival delle Colline Torinesi*, theatre festival in castles, villas, churches and villages in the hills around Turin, summer. *Settembre Musica*, chamber music series, with an accent on contemporary composers, September. *Torino Danza*, biennial contemporary dance festival, even years. *Torino Film Festival*, Nov. *Torino International Jazz Festival*, Jul.

CHIERI *Nel Borgo di Landolfo*. Pageant in 14C costume, late May.

MONCALIERI *Il Beato Bernardo* (patron saint). Pageant in medieval costume, second Saturday in Jul.

RIVOLI *C'era una Volta un Re*. Historic re-enactment of the abdication of vittorio Amedeo II in favour of his son Carlo Emanuele II, second week in Sep.

Sports

The official Torinese **soccer** team is *Toro*, but the homeless *Juventus*, for those without a team to cheer for, is hosted in Turin. Both teams play at the Stadio delle Alpi, Strada Altessano 131; tickets available at the stadium 2hrs before games.

Canoeing and sailing: *Amici del Fiume*, Corso Moncalieri 18, ☎ 011 660 4121; *Riverside*, Piazza Emanuele Filiberto 8, ☎ & fax 011 436 3159.

Golf is available at the follwoing clubs: *Golf Club Stupinigi*, Corso Unione Sovietica 506/a, Torino, ☎ 011 347 2640.

Le Fronde, Via Sant'Agostino 68, Avigliana, ☎ 011 932 8053.

I Roveri, Rotta Cerbiatta 24, Fiano Torinese, ☎ 011 923 5719.

Torino, Via Grange 136, Fiano Torinese, ☎ 011 923 5450.

Vinovo, Via Stupinigi 18, Vinovo, ☎ 011 965 3880.

I Ciliegi, Strada Valle Sauglio 130, Pecetto, ☎ 011 860 9802.

I Ginepri, Località Pian del Colle,

Frazione Melezet, Bardonecchia, ☎ 0122 901406. *Claviere*, Strada Nazionale 45, Claviere, ☎ 0122 878917.
Sestriere, Piazzale G. Agnelli 4 , Sestriere, ☎ 0122 799411.
Limone, Località San Bernardo 9, Limone Piemonte, 0171 929166.

For details of **walking and skiing** contact *ATL Montagne Doc*, Via Giolitti 7, 10064 Pinerlo, ☎ 0121 595589 or 011 744003, fax 0121 794932; Piazza Garambois 2, 0056 Oulx ; ☎ 0122 831596 or 011 831789, fax 0122 831880.

History

No one knows who established Turin, but it is fairly clear that the city began as a Celtic or Ligurian settlement. It was Romanised as Julia Augusta Taurinorum in the 1C BC, and the Goths, Lombards and Franks held sway in the Middle Ages. The marriage of Countess Adelaide, heiress of a line of French counts of Savoy, to Oddone (Otho), son of Humbert 'the White-Handed', united the Cisalpine and Transalpine possessions of the House of Savoy in 1046, with Turin as their capital. After a period of semi-independence in the 12C–13C, the city consistently followed the fortunes of the princely house of Savoy. It was occupied by the French in 1506–62, but was awarded to Duke Emanuele Filiberto 'the Iron-Headed' by the Treaty of Cateau-Cambrésis (1559). It was besieged in 1639–40, and again in 1706, when it was saved from the French by the heroic action of Pietro Micca (see p 89).

From 1720 Turin was capital of the kingdom of Sardinia, and after the Napoleonic occupation (1798–1814) it became a centre of Italian nationalism and the headquarters of Camillo Cavour (1810–61), a native of the town and the prime mover of Italian liberty. Carlo Alberto, who succeeded to the Savoy throne in 1831, had a profound influence on the appearance of the city, and most of its important art collections date from his time. The writer Silvio Pellico lived here from 1838 until his death in 1854. In 1861–65 Turin was the capital of Vittorio Emanuele II (1820–78) as king of Italy. Allied air raids caused heavy damage during the Second World War. After the war anonymous new suburbs grew up around the city to accommodate the huge number of immigrants from the south of Italy who came here to find work. The novelist Primo Levi (1919–87), and Carlo Levi (1902–75), writer and painter, are among famous modern natives of Turin.

Exploring Turin

The centre of Turin is the large quadrangular area lying between Corso Vittorio Emanuele, Corso Galileo Ferraris, Corso Regina Margherita, Corso San Maurizio, and the Po. Roughly bisecting this area is the fashionable Via Roma (**Map 6**), lined with wide arcades, which connects the main railway station with Piazza Castello; on either side of it and parallel with it are streets laid out at right angles. Porta Nuova Station (**Map 9**) was built in 1868 and has a monumental façade in the form of an arch which was designed to close the vista from Via Roma. It faces Piazza Carlo Felice (1823–55), with a garden.

Impressions of Turin

The historic centre of Turin is blessed with beautiful buildings, many of which, alas, could use some fresh paint. Their nobility is nevertheless quite evident, and the impression they left on past visitors—initially brilliant, but later somewhat damped—can be gleaned from the following lines:

My arrival at Turin was the first and only moment of intoxication I have found in Italy. It is a city of palaces.
William Hazlitt, *Notes of a Journey through France and Italy*, 1826

This is a remarkably agreeable place. A beautiful town, prosperous, thriving, growing prodigiously... crowded with busy inhabitants; full of noble streets and squares.
Charles Dickens, letter, 1853, in Forster, *Life of Dickens*, 1872–3

In the matter of roominess it transcends anything that was ever dreamed of before, I fancy. It sits in the middle of a vast dead-level, and one is obliged to imagine that land may be had for the asking, and no taxes to pay, so lavishly do they use it.
Mark Twain, *A Tramp Abroad*, 1880

Turin is not a city to make, in vulgar parlance, a fuss about, and I pay an extravagant tribute to subjective emotion in speaking of it as ancient.... Relatively speaking, Turin is diverting; but there is, after all, no reason in a large collection of shabbily stuccoed houses, disposed in a rigidly rectangular manner, for passing a day of deep, still gaiety. The only reason, I am afraid, is the old superstition of Italy—that property in the very look of the written word, the evocation of a myriad images, that makes any lover of the arts take Italian satisfactions upon easier terms than any other. Italy is an idea to conjure with, and we play tricks upon our credulity even with such inferior apparatus as is offered to our hand at Turin.
Henry James, 'Italy Revisited', 1877, in *Portraits of Places*, 1883

Turin is a very large city, rectangular in form and spirit.
Arnold Bennett, *Journal 1929*, 1930.

Piazza San Carlo

Halfway along Via Roma is the arcaded ***Piazza San Carlo** (Map 6), a handsome monumental square begun in 1640. Here are the twin churches of San Carlo and Santa Cristina, the latter with a façade by Filippo Juvarra (1715–18) and 18C stucco decoration in the interior. The monument to *Duke Emanuele Filiberto* (1838), whose equestrian figure ('El caval d'brôns' in dialect) is shown sheathing his sword after the victory of St Quentin (1557), is considered the masterpiece of the sculptor Carlo Marochetti. The two long yellow-and-grey palazzi have wide porticoes, beneath which are several cafés, including, on the corner of Via San Teresa, the well-known *Caffè San Carlo*. On the opposite side of the piazza, Palazzo Solaro del Borgo (No. 183), partly reconstructed by Benedetto Alfieri in 1753, is the seat of the Accademia Filarmonica and the Circolo del Whist, an exclusive club with delightful 18C premises.

The Museo Egizio and the Galleria Sabauda

At the end of the piazza (right; entrance on Via Accademia delle Scienze) is the **Palazzo dell'Accademia delle Scienze** (Map 6), with a fine exterior, built for the Jesuits by Guarino Guarini (1678). The Academy of Science, founded in 1757, has had its seat here since 1783. The building also houses the Museo Egizio and the Galleria Sabauda.

Museo Egizio

The famous *Museo Egizio (open summer, Tues–Fri 09.00–21.00, Sat 09.00–24.00, Sun and holidays 09.00–20.00; winter Tues–Sat 09.00–19.00, Sun and holidays 09.00–14.00) has the third most important collection of Egyptian antiquities in existence, after Cairo and London. The real founder of this remarkable museum was Carlo Felice, who in 1824 bought the collections of Bernardo Drovetti, the trusted counsellor of Mohammed Ali. Later important acquisitions came from the expeditions of Schiaparelli (1903–20) and Farina (1930–37), notably in the Theban region, at Ghebelein (Aphroditopolis), Qau el-Kebir (Antaepolis, near Assiut) and Heliopolis. The museum played a leading part in the rescue digs in Nubia before the completion of the Aswan high dam and was rewarded with the rock temple of Ellessya, which was transported by sea in sections via Genoa in 1967 and then reconstructed.

On the **ground floor** are large sculptures. Room **I**. Black diorite statue of *Rameses II* (1299–33 BC), statues of *Amenhotep II* and *Thothmes I*; *Horemheb* and his wife; figures of *Sekhmet* and *Ptah*. Room **II**. Seated figure of *Thothmes III* (1496–1422 BC) and statue of *Tutankhamen*, with the god Amen-ra. Another room contains the reconstructed rock temple of Ellessya (15C BC), with its bas-relief frieze showing Thothmes III. In an underground room (where you can see parts of the Roman wall of Turin) are finds from the excavations of Schiaparelli, including a fragment of painted linen from c 3500 BC.

Steps or a lift bring you to the **first floor**. In room I (right) are the most important discoveries from Heliopolis, Qau el-Kebir (limestone heads), Ghebelein, and Deir el Medina (tomb-gateway and wooden statuettes). Room **II** contains mummies and mummy-cases, scarabs, amulets, Canopic vases, ushabti figures, etc. In room **III** is archaeological material arranged chronologically, from the Predynastic to the Coptic periods, giving an excellent idea of the evolution of Egypt over the centuries. The reconstructed tomb of Khaiè, director of the works at the Necropolis of Thebes, and his wife Meriè (XVIII Dynasty) preserves intact its furniture, food, cooking utensils, etc. The small room **IV** contains textiles. Room **V** contains administrative and literary papyri with architectural plans and plans of gold mines; a love poem; the *Royal Papyrus*, with a list of the kings of Egypt from the Sun to the XVII Dynasty; the *Papyrus of the Palace Conspiracy* (XX Dyn.); writing materials, rolls of papyrus, etc. Room **VI**. Objects showing the daily life of the Egyptians: clothes, furniture, toilet articles and some interesting jewels. Room **VII** has statuettes of animal deities. Room **VIII** contains mural paintings from the tomb of Iti at Ghebelein (c 2100 BC).

Galleria Sabauda

The *Galleria Sabauda (open Tues, Wed, Fri, Sat 09.00–14.00, Thur 10.00–19.00, Sun and holidays 09.00–20.00), on the second floor, had as a nucleus the collections of paintings made by the princes of the House of Savoy, from the 16C onwards, and was first opened to the public in 1832 by Carlo Alberto. Remarkably rich in Flemish and Dutch works acquired in 1741 through Eugenio of Savoy, it is interesting also for its paintings by Venetian and Piedmontese masters, some of them hardly represented elsewhere. Recent acquisitions include

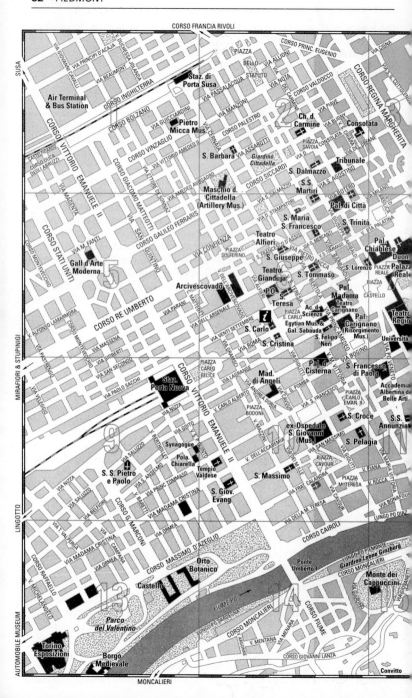

CORSO FRANCIA RIVOLI

SUSA

Air Terminal & Bus Station

Staz. di Porta Susa

PIAZZA BELLO

STATUTO

CORSO PRINC. EUGENIO

VIA CIGNA

CORSO REGINA MARGHERITA

VIA BEAUMONT

VIA GIOVANNI CAVALLI

VIA PRINCIPI D'ACAJA

VIA DUCHESSA JOLANDA

CORSO INGHILTERRA

CORSO BOLZANO

Pietro Micca Mus.

VIA GUICCIARDINI

VIA CERNAIA

VIA MANZONI

CORSO PALESTRO

VIA ASSAROTTI

CORSO VALDOCCO

VIA DEL CARMINE

VIA PIAVE

Ch. d. Carmine

VIA BLIGNY

Consolata

CASTELFIDARDO

CORSO DUCA DEGLI ABRUZZI

CORSO VITTORIO EMANUELE II

CORSO VINZAGLIO

VIA VITTORIO AMEDEO II

CORSO GIACOMO MATTEOTTI

VIA ETTORE DE SONNAZ

VIA AMEDEO AVOGADRO

S. Barbara

Giardino Cittadella

CORSO SICCARDI

VIA DI D.

PIAZZA SAVOIA CONSOLATA

VIA D. CHIARA

VIA DEL DRONE

S. Dalmazzo

Tribunale

VIA S. AGOSTINO

VIA BOTERO

VIA MILANO

BASILICA

Maschio d. Cittadella (Artillery Mus.)

VIA D. DALMAZZO

S.S. Martiri

VIA STAMPATORI

VIA DELLA BASILICA

Pal. di Città

VIA MAGENTA

CORSO STATI UNITI

VIA M. FANTI

VIA SAN QUINTINO

CORSO GALILEO FERRARIS

VIA CONFIENZA

PIAZZA SOLFERINO

S. Maria
S. Francesco

Teatro Alfieri

VIA D. MERCANTI

VIA PIETRO MICCA

S. Giuseppe

S. Trinita

PTA. PALATINA

Pal. Chiablese

Duomo

CORSO MONTEVECCHIO

Gall d'Arte Moderna

CORSO RE UMBERTO

Teatro Gianduja

VIA ALFIERI

VIA S. TERESA

P.O.

Arcivescovado

VIA DELL'ARCIVESCOVADO

VIA DELL'ARSENALE

Teresa

S. Tommaso

S. Lorenzo

PIAZZA REALE

Palazzo Reale

PIAZZA CASTELLO

Pal. Madama

Teatro Carignano

Teatro Regio

VIA ALFONSO LAMARMORA

CORSO MONTEVECCHIO

VIA MASSENA

VIA GIOBERTI

VIA VENTI SETTEMBRE

VIA ROMA

S. Carlo

S. Cristina

Ac. d. Scienze

Egytian Mus. & Gal. Sabauda

S. Felipo Neri

Pal. Carignano (Risorgimento Mus.)

Universita

VIA PASTRENGO

VIA SAN SECONDO

VIA PAOLO SACCHI

Staz. Porta Nuova

CORSO VITTORIO EMANUELE II

VIA NIZZA

Mad. di Angeli

VIA LAGRANGE

VIA ANDREA DORIA

VIA G. POMBA

VIA S. FRANCESCO

Pal. d. Cisterna

S. Francesco di Paola

Accademia Albertina di Belle Arti

LINGOTTO

MIRAFIORI & STUPINIGI

VIA SALUZZO

VIA BERTHOLLET

Synagogue

Pola Chiarella

Tempio Valdese

S. Giov. Evang.

VIA GOITO

VIA S. PIO V

VIA CARLO ALBERTO

PIAZZA BODONI

VIA MAZZINI

VIA DELL'ACCADEMIA

ex-Ospedale S. Giovanni (Mus.)

PIAZZA CARLO EMAN. II

S. Croce

S. Pelagia

S.S. Annunziata

S. S. Pietro e Paolo

VIA S. ANSELMO

VIA PRINC TOMMASO

VIA MADAMA CRISTINA

S. Massimo

PIAZZA CAVOUR

VIA GIOLITTI

VIA MARIA VITTORIA

VIA BELFIORE

CORSO G. MARCONI

VIA BARETTI

VIA ORMEA

VIA CAMPANA

VIA FRAT CALANDRA

VIA DELLA ROCCA

PIAZZA M. TERESA

VIA S. MASSIMO

VIA ROCCA

VIA BONAFOUS

AUTOMOBILE MUSEUM

VIA RAFFAELLO

VIA MICHELANGELO

VIA T. VALPERGA

CORSO MASSIMO D'AZEGLIO

VIA ORMEA

Orto Botanico

Castello

Parco del Valentino

CORSO CAIROLI

Ponte Umberto I

FIUME PO

LUNGO PO DIAZ

LUNGO PO CADORNA

CORSO MONCALIERI

Giardino Leone Ginzburg

Monte dei Cappuccini

Torino Esposizioni

Borgo Medievale

LUNGO PO SARDEGNA

CORSO MONCALIERI

V. MENTANA

CORSO FIUME

CORSO GIOVANNI LANZA

Convitto

MONCALIERI

TURIN

works by Rubens, Defendente Ferrari and David Teniers. The works are arranged in two distinct groupings: the Savoy family collections, and the acquisitions made after 1832. Rearrangement has been in progress since 1987.

The **first section** illustrates the birth of the collection with works acquired c 1550–1630. Works by Roger van der Weyden, Gaudenzio Ferrari, Mantegna (*Madonna*), Veronese, court painters (including Moncalvo), Orazio Gentileschi (*Annunciation*, painted in 1623 for Carlo Emanuele I), Guercino, Morazzone, Giulio Cesare Procaccini, Cerano and Rubens.

The **second section** traces the history of the collection from the time of Vittorio Amedeo I to Vittorio Amedeo II (1630–1730), through works by Francesco Duquesnoy, Francesco Albani, Francesco Cairo (1598–1674), and Guercino. The *Children of Charles I* (1635) by van Dyck was presented by Henrietta Maria, Charles' queen, to her sister Cristina of Savoy.

The **third section** has works reflecting the artistic taste of the Savoy court from 1730 to 1830. These include two *Views of Turin* commissioned by Carlo Emanuele III in 1745 from Bernardo Bellotto, and works by Carlo Andrea van Loo, Sebastiano Conca, Pompeo Batoni, Anton Raphael Mengs and Elisabeth Vigée-Lebrun. The copies on porcelain of famous works owned by the Tuscan grand-dukes and acquired by Carlo Alberto in 1826 are by Abraham Constantin.

The **fourth section** is dedicated to the works collected by Prince Eugenio in 1737–41, including some by Nicolas Poussin, Carlo Cignani, Francesco Albani and Guido Reni (*St John the Baptist*). The superb Flemish and Dutch collection includes works by Cornelis Engelbrechtsz, Jan van Eyck, Petrus Christus, Rembrandt (*Old Man Asleep*, perhaps the artist's father), Willem van de Velde the Younger, Jacob van Ruisdael, Hans Memling (*Passion of Christ*), Bernart van Orley, Paulus Potter, David Teniers the Younger, Jan van Huysum, Jan Breughel, Phillipe Wouwerman, Paul Mignard, Jan de Heem, Gerard Dou, Holbein the Younger and van Dyck (*Madonna and Child*). The portrait of a *Young Boy* was formerly attributed to van Dyck.

The **fifth section** contains the works acquired by the gallery from 1832 onwards. The Piedmontese school is represented by Macrino d'Alba, Gaudenzio Ferrari, Bernardino Lanino, Girolamo Giovenone, Defendente Ferrari and Giovanni Martino Spanzotti. Among the Tuscan works are a *Madonna* (c 1433) by Fra Angelico, *Tobias and the Archangel Raphael* by Piero and Antonio Pollaiolo, *Tobias and the Three Archangels* by Filippino Lippi, and a *Madonna and Saints* by Sodoma. The schools of Lombardy (Bergognone, Moretto, Savoldo, Giampietrino and Cesare da Sesto and Venice (Giovanni Bellini, Veronese, Tintoretto and Francesco Bassano) are also represented.

The Gualino collection, donated to the museum in 1928, contains Italian paintings (including a *Madonna* attributed to Duccio di Buoninsegna, and works by Taddeo di Bartolo, Veronese, and Jacopo Sansovino), German paintings, ancient sculpture, Roman and medieval ivories, goldsmiths' work, Chinese works, medieval furniture and lace. The modern collection, with works by Italian painters between the two World Wars, was not on view at the time of writing.

Opposite the palace, on the corner of Via Accademia delle Scienze, is the large church of **San Filippo Neri** (Map 6), rebuilt by Filippo Juvarra (c 1714), with a Corinthian pronaos by Giuseppe Talucchi (1823). The fine Baroque interior (with, unexpectedly, a parquet floor) has a high altar by Antonio Bertola (1697) with an altarpiece by Carlo Maratta, and a painting by Francesco Trevisani.

Just beyond, in Piazza Carignano, is **Palazzo Carignano** (Map 6), the residence of the princes of Savoy until 1831. It has an interesting Baroque front, faced with brick, by Guarino Guarini (1679), and an oval vestibule with a pretty double staircase. The east façade, facing Piazza Carlo Alberto, dates from 1864–71. The palace was the birthplace (1798) of Carlo Alberto and (1820) of Vittorio Emanuele II. It was used for the meetings of the lower house of the Subalpine Parliament (1848–59) and of the first Italian Parliament (1861–64). On the *piano nobile* (first floor) is the Museo Nazionale del Risorgimento (open Tues–Sat 09.00–18.00; Sun and holidays 09.00–12.00), founded in 1878 and one of the more important museums of this crucial period in Italian history. The fine hall of the Subalpine Parliament is also shown.

Piazza Carlo Alberto has a bronze equestrian statue of Carlo Alberto by Marochetti (1861). The Biblioteca Nazionale here has over 850,000 volumes and some 5000 manuscripts, mainly from religious institutions in Piedmont. The 17C Palazzo Graneri della Roccia, at Via Bogino 9, is the seat of the Circolo degli Artisti, founded in 1855 and closed to women until 1987.

In Piazza Carignano, with a monument by Giovanni Albertoni (1859) to the philosopher Vincenzo Gioberti (1801–52), is the Teatro Carignano, reconstructed in 1787 by Giovanni Battista Feroggio. Vittorio Alfieri's tragedy *Cleopatra* was was first performed in the theatre, in 1775. The Ristorante del Cambio, famous as a meeting place during the Risorgimento, overlooks the square.

Piazza Castello

Via Roma ends in the huge, rectangular Piazza Castello (Map 6; 7), the centre of the city. The square was laid out by Ascanio Vittozzi in 1584 around the castle, now called Palazzo Madama, and is surrounded by uniform monumental buildings with porticoes.

Near Via Roma is a skyscraper of 1934. Beneath the porticoes, on the corner nearest Via Accademia delle Scienze, are two elegant cafés (*Mulassano* and *Baratti*, with elaborate decorations by Edoardo Rubino) on either side of the Galleria dell'Industria Subalpina (Map 6), a delightful shopping arcade built in 1873–74 by Pietro Carrera. A monument to the Duke of Aosta (d. 1931) by Eugenio Baroni (1937), and war memorials by Vincenzo Vela (1859) and Pietro Canonica (1923), stand in the centre of the square.

Palazzo Madama (Map 6; 7), the most imposing of the old buildings of Turin, is a four-square castle of the 15C, one side of which has been replaced by a wing and façade of 1718–21 by Filippo Juvarra. A castle was begun here after 1276 by William VII of Monferrato on the site of the Roman Porta Praetoria, the east gate of the ancient city. The palace takes its present name from the two regents, Maria Cristina, widow of Vittorio Amedeo I, and Giovanna Battista, widow of Carlo Emanuele II; both were entitled Madama Reale, and both resided here and remodelled the old castle. The palazzo was the seat in 1848–60 of the Subalpine Senate and in 1861–65 of the Italian Senate.

Since 1935 the palace has housed the *Museo Civico di Arte Antica (closed at time of writing), displaying the municipal collections of old master paintings, sculpture and applied arts. Here you can see Romanesque, Gothic and Renaissance sculpture, including works by Tino da Camaino and Bambaia. The precious collection of codexes includes the illuminated 14C statutes of the city of Turin and the celebrated *Book of Hours* of the Duc de Berry (*Les Très Riches Heures de Milan*, c 1450), illustrated by Jan van Eyck. The paintings include a *Portrait of a Man* by Antonello da Messina, signed and dated 1476, one of his best and last works.

On the first floor, beyond the central hall, seat of the senate, are the **Royal Apartments**. Some of the furniture here dates from the time of Carlo Emanuele II (d. 1675), but the fittings are mainly in early-18C style, with paintings by Vittorio Amedeo Cignaroli and sculptures by Simon Troger. One room was frescoed by Domenico Guidobono (1714), with 18C tapestries of local weave, after Cignaroli.

The Teatro Reggio occupies the northeast corner of the square, beneath the arcades. Rebuilt in 1973, it has a disappointing interior. Remnants of the old theatre, burnt down in 1936, survive behind the modern buildings. Further on, beneath the portico, is the Prefettura (no. 201).

At no. 191 is the entrance to the *Armeria Reale* (Map 7; visitors are admitted every 45mins, Tues and Thur 14.30–19.30; Wed, Fri and Sat 09.00–14.00), housed in a wing of the Palazzo Reale (the palace as a whole is described below). The royal armoury, one of the more important in Europe, includes some remarkable pieces by the great Bavarian and Austrian armourers and gunsmiths. It was transferred here by Carlo Alberto and opened to the public in 1837. The monumental staircase, designed by Filippo Juvarra and built by Benedetto Alfieri, leads up to the three 18C–19C galleries. These provide a magnificent setting for the collection. The *rotonda* was decorated in 1841–45 by Pelagio Pelagi. The collections of the last princes of the House of Savoy and arms and ensigns of the *Risorgimento* period are displayed here. The splendid Galleria Beaumont, designed by Filippo Juvarra in 1733, is named after Claudio Francesco Beaumont who painted the vault in 1738–64, and contains a superb display of about 30 complete suits of armour (12 equestrian), some of which were made for the Martinengo family of Brescia. Oriental arms are displayed in the Medagliere.

The Biblioteca Reale has 150,000 volumes, 5000 manuscripts, and many miniatures and drawings collected by Carlo Alberto, including a self-portrait of Leonardo da Vinci and works by Dürer, Rembrandt and Raphael.

Palazzo Reale and the Cathedral

The Piazzetta Reale, with railings by Pelagio Pelagi of 1842 surmounted by statues of the *Dioscuri* by Abbondio Sangiorgio, precedes **Palazzo Reale** (Map 7; open Tues–Sun 09.00–19.00). The former royal residence, built for Madama Reale Maria Cristina of France, has a façade on the piazzetta by Amedeo di Castellamonte (1646–60). The Cappella della Sacra Sindone was built in 1694 to contain the Holy Shroud in the west wing of the palace, adjoining the apse of the cathedral (described below). You have a good view of its delightful spiral dome by Guarino Guarini from here.

The state apartments, on the first floor (shown on conducted tours), were lavishly decorated from the mid-17C to the mid-19C, with some good ceilings and floors; they contain furniture (some by Pietro Piffetti), porcelain and tapestries. The *Gabinetto Cinese* is a delightful work by Filippo Juvarra. The Galleria del Daniele was begun in 1684 by Daniel Seyter. The charming Neo-classical dancing figures in the Sala da Ballo were painted by Carlo Bellosio and Francesco Gonino (1842). The *Scala degli Forbici is an ingenious staircase by Filippo Juvarra (1720).

The **Giardino Reale**, approached through the palace, is normally open May–Oct, daily 09.00–dusk. The garden was enlarged by André Le Nôtre in 1697 for Carlo Emanuele II but has since been altered. A fountain by Simone Martinez (c 1750) stands at the centre.

In Piazza Castello is the church of **San Lorenzo** (**Map 7**), formerly the royal chapel, a superb Baroque work by Guarino Guarini, with a delightful cupola and lantern. It has a complex, beautifully lit *interior of 1667.

The **Cathedral** (**Map 7**) was built in 1491–98 for Archbishop Domenico della Rovere by Meo del CaprinoArt;Meo del Caprino and other Tuscans, after three churches had been demolished to make way for it. It has a Renaissance façade and a campanile (1468–70) completed by Juvarra in 1720.

Inside are 15C tombs and a *polyptych, in a fine Gothic frame, attributed to Giovanni Martino Spanzotti, with delightful little pictures of the life of Sts Crispin and Crispinian, including scenes of mercantile life. Behind the apse is the **Cappella della Sacra Sindone** (open daily 09.00–12.00, 15.00–19.00), the chapel of the Holy Shroud built by Guarino Guarini in 1668–94 and restored after a fire of 1997. It has dark marble walls and family monuments erected in 1842 by Carlo Alberto. The urn that traditionally held the Holy Shroud, in which the body of Christ is believed to have been wrapped after his descent from the Cross, is on the altar. The Shroud itself is periodically displayed in a special case.

The Story of the Holy Shroud

This greatly revered sacred relic was said to have been taken from Jerusalem to Cyprus, and from there to France in the 15C, and to have been brought to Turin by Emanuele Filiberto in 1578. On the linen shroud (4.36 x 1.10m) is the negative image of a crucified man. In 1988 the Archbishop of Turin announced that scientific research using carbon 14 dating had proved that this icon must have been made between 1260 and 1390, but discussion still continues about its origins. It is kept in a silver casket inside an iron box enclosed in a marble case. When the shroud is shown is not easily discovered in advance; it was shown during part of 2000, with an acccompanying website—www.giubileo.piemonte.it—but future plans are unknown. Check at local information offices.

Beside the campanile are pretty railings in front of a wing of Palazzo Reale, built in 1900. Here are the ruins of a Roman theatre of the 1CAD. On the left, in an unattractive setting, is a stretch of Roman and medieval wall beside the impressive *Porta Palatina** (**Map 7**), an exceptionally well-preserved two-arched Roman gate flanked by two 16-sided towers. This was the *Porta Principalis Sinistra* in the wall of the Roman colony of Augusta Taurinorum.

A garden house of Palazzo Reale (entrance at Corso Regina Margherita 105) holds the **Museo di Antichità** (open Tues–Sat 09.00–19.00, Sun and holidays 14.00–19.00), with archaeological material discovered mainly in Piedmont and Liguria and dating from the Stone Age to the Barbarian invasions. Roman finds include the Marengo treasure, discovered in 1928, with a silver bust of Emperor Lucius Verus (r. 161–69).

Via Garibaldi

The handsome Via Garibaldi (**Map 6, 2**), a street about 1km long, closed to motor vehicles and lined with characteristic 18C balconied palaces, leads west from Piazza Castello. One block along, on the north side of the street, is the church of the **Trinità** (1590–1606), by Ascanio Vittozzi, with a marble interior by Filippo Juvarra (1718). It contains fine carved confessionals.

In Via Porta Palatina to the right is the church of **Corpus Domini** (1607–71), also by Vittozzi, with a lavishly decorated interior by Benedetto Alfieri. Jean-Jacques Rousseau abjured the Protestant faith in this church in 1728. A few paces further on is Piazza di Palazzo di Città, laid out in 1756 by Benedetto Alfieri, with a bronze monument to the 'Green Count' Amadeus VI (d. 1383), the conqueror of the Turks, by Pelagio Pelagi (1853). Here is **Palazzo di Città** (**Map 6**), the town hall, begun in 1659 by Francesco Lanfranchi and modified a century later by Benedetto Alfieri. The nearby church of **San Domenico** (**Map 2**) dates from 1354; its belfry, from 1451. It has a painting by Guercino and a chapel with 14C frescoes.

Via Milano, a less elegant street, leads from San Domenico past the huge elliptical domed church of Santi Maurizio e Lazzaro, begun in 1679 by Carlo Emanuele Lanfranchi, with a Neo-classical façade by Carlo Bernardo Mosca. Beyond lies the large Piazza della Repubblica (**Map 3**), known locally as Porta Palazzo, the scene of a popular general market (and, on Saturday and the second Sunday of the month, of the Balôn antiques market). Two noted charitable institutions of Piedmontese origin lie in Via Cottolengo to the north: the Cottolengo, founded for the aged infirm in 1828 by St Joseph Benedict Cottolengo (1786–1842), and the Istituto Salesiano, established in 1846 by St John Bosco (1815–88) for the education of poor boys, with the basilica of Maria Santissima Ausiliatrice by Antonio Spezia (1865–68).

Return to Via Garibaldi by Via Milano and turn right. The church of the **Santi Martiri**, on the south side of the street (**Map 6**), was begun in 1577, probably by Pellegrino Tibaldi. It has an 18C cupola by Bernardino Quadri and a Baroque interior. The frescoed ceiling is by Luigi Vacca (1836), and the high altar by Filippo Juvarra.

Next door is the **Cappella dei Banchieri e Mercanti** (No. 25; **Map 2, 6**; open Sat afternoon or by appointment, ☎ 011 5627226), a delightful Baroque chapel dating from the late 17C, with paintings by Andrea Pozzo, Stefano Maria Legnano, Carlo Innocenzo Carlone and others, in huge black frames decorated in gold. The painted wood statues are by Carlo Giuseppe Plura, and the vault is frescoed by Legnano. The high altar is by Filippo Juvarra. The benches and lanterns survive intact, and the organ dates from 1748–50. In the sacristy is an ingenious mechanical calendar constructed by Antonio Plana in 1831.

Further west along Via Garibaldi, Via della Consolata leads right, through Piazza Savoia, with an obelisk, to the church of the **Consolata** (**Map 2**). This popular place of worship was made by joining two churches by Guarino Guarini (1679), one oval, the other hexagonal. In Via Piave, which also diverges right from Via Garibaldi, is the 18C church of the **Sudario**, next to a museum dedicated to the Holy Shroud.

Via Garibaldi ends in Piazza dello Statuto, laid out in 1864, with a monument of 1879 to the engineers of the Mont Cenis railway tunnel.

West of the centre

Via Santa Teresa leads west from Piazza San Carlo to **Santa Teresa** (Map 6), a Baroque church probably by Andrea Costaguta (1642–74), hemmed in between two modern buildings. It contains an altarpiece by Sebastiano Conca. Next to the church is the **Teatro Gianduja**, the puppet theatre of the Lupi family (performances on Sun and holidays at 16.00), with a delightful museum (open 09.00–13.00, Sun 15.00–18.00; closed Sat), displaying puppets, backcloths, etc. collected by the family since the 18C.

Via Santa Teresa continues to the large Piazza Solferino. Here Via Pietro Micca (**Map 6**), an elegant street with a portico on one side, leads towards Piazza Castello. Laid out in 1894 on a diagonal line, it has a conspicuous Gothic-revival building by Carlo Ceppi.

Via Cernaia continues the line of Via Santa Teresa west to the **Maschio** (**Map 2**), or keep, of the old citadel (1564–68), the rest of which was demolished in 1857. It contains the **Museo Nazionale di Artiglieria** (open for special exhibitions only), founded by Carlo Emanuele III in 1731 and on this site since 1899. Further on, the RAI (Radiotelevisione Italiana) skyscraper rises on the corner of Via Guicciardini. Turn left here to visit the Museo Pietro Micca (entrance at Via Guicciardini 7, **Map 1**; open Tues–Sun 09.00–19.00), dedicated to the French siege of 1706. The museum is named after the Piedmontese sapper who exploded a mine on this site and saved the city from the French at the cost of his own life. From the museum you can visit part of the remarkable underground defence works, which extend for several kilometres beneath the city.

Corso Galileo Ferraris leads south from the Maschio for nearly 1km across Corso Vittorio Emanuele II to Via Magenta. Here, on the west, is the **Galleria Civica d'Arte Moderna e Contemporanea** (**Map 5**; open Tues–Sun 09.00–19.00). Founded in 1863 and reopened in 1993, the gallery houses one of the more important collections of 19C and 20C painting in Italy. Highlights include 19C Italian works by Francesco Hayez, Antonio Canova, Massimo d'Azeglio, Vincenzo Vela, Giuseppe Pellizza da Volpedo, Vincenzo Gemito, the Macchiaioli group of post-Impressionist realist painters (Telemaco Signorini, Silvestro Lega, Giovanni Fattori), and works by French artists (Renoir, Courbet), on the second floor; and paintings by Umberto Boccioni, Giacomo Balla, Giorgio De Chirico, Gino Severini, Felice Casorati, Giorgio Morandi, Carlo Carrà, Alberto Savinio, Filippo De Pisis and the artists known as the *Gruppo dei Sei* (influential in Turin from about 1928 until 1935), on the first floor. Another wing has an extensive collection of works from the 1950s and 1960s. Contemporary works are displayed on the ground floor.

Nearby, at Via Bricherasio 8, is the **Museo Civico di Numismatica, Etnografia e Arte Orientale** (open Tues–Sun 09.00–19.00). It contains Greek, Roman and Byzantine coins; ethnographical material collected from 1864 onwards; and a section on Oriental art.

East of the centre

The arcaded Via Po (**Map 7, 11**), the main street of the eastern district of Turin, leads from Piazza Castello towards the river. The University (**Map 7**) stands on the left, with a brick façade facing Via Verdi. The college, which has a chequered history dating back to the early 15C, has occupied its present site since 1720. Erasmus took a degree here in theology in 1506. The church of San Francesco di Paola, containing 17C sculptures by Tommaso Carlone, rises on the right.

In Via dell'Accademia Albertina (right) is the Accademia Albertina di Belle Arti (**Map 11**), an academy of fine arts founded in 1678.The **Pinacoteca dell'Accademia Albertina** (open Tues–Sun 09.00–13.00, 15.00–19.00), in the same building, is interesting mainly for its 60 drawings by Gaudenzio Ferrari, the eminent Piedmontese painter, and his workshop. There are also paintings by Filippo Lippi, Bernardino Lanino, and Piedmontese masters.

Via Accademia leads through Piazza Carlo Emanuele II, with a monument to Cavour by Giovanni Dupré (1873), to the former hospital of San Giovanni (**Map 10**), where the university museums of zoology, anatomy, mineralogy and geology are being arranged; ☎ 011 670 2951 for further information on their opening.

Off the other side of Via Po, in Via Montebello, rises the ***Mole Antonelliana** (**Map 11**), the symbol of Turin. Begun in 1863 as a synagogue, it is the most famous work of the Piedmontese architect Alessandro Antonelli. Its extraordinary shape and enormous height make it an amazing feat of engineering skill. It was finished by the municipality in 1897 as monument of Italian Unity (the *Risorgimento* museum, now in Palazzo Carignano, was first opened here). It was much admired by Nietzsche. The terrace (86m; view) is reached by a lift (open Tues–Fri, 10.00–16.00; Sat–Sun and holidays 09.00–19.00; closed Mon); the granite spire, 167m high, was rebuilt in aluminium after it lost its upper 47m in a gale in 1953.

The interior has been restored to house the **Cinema Museum** (due to open in 2000), which has an absorbing collection founded in the 1950s. The collection illustrates the history of photography and cinema in Italy and abroad, and incorporates an important film library.

At Via Po 55 is the **Museo Pietro Occorsi**, with 26 rooms housing a collection of antiques and objets d'art assembled by the eminent 20C antiquarian. Open for guided visits Tues–Sun 09.00–19.00.

Via Po ends in the spacious Piazza Vittorio Veneto (**Map 11**), laid out in 1825–30, beyond which the Ponte Vittorio Emanuele I leads across the river.

Across the Po

The chill white façade of the **Gran Madre di Dio** (**Map 15**) dominates the east end of the Ponte Vittorio Emanuele I. The Neo-classical church was built by Ferdinando Bonsignore in 1818–31, in imitation of the Pantheon at Rome, to celebrate the return from exile of Vittorio Emanuele I (1814). The king's monument, by Giuseppe Gaggini, stands in front of the porch. On the banks of the river here are pleasant public gardens.

From Piazza di Gran Madre di Dio, Via Villa della Regina leads straight to the Baroque **Villa della Regina** (**Map 15**; closed at the time of writing), built for Cardinal Maurizio of Savoy on a design probably by Ascanio Vittozzi, executed by Amedeo di Castellamonte in 1620. It was altered in the 18C by Filippo Juvarra. The villa is named after Marie-Anne d'Orléans, queen of Vittorio Amedeo II, who resided here. It has a beautiful park and garden laid out in terraces on the hillside in the style of a Roman villa.

Via Giardino ascends from Corso Moncalieri (right) to the wooded Monte dei Cappuccini (283m; **Map 15**), on whose summit are a Capuchin church by Ascanio Vittozzi (1596), with its convent, and the **Museo Nazionale della Montagna Duca degli Abruzzi** (open Sat–Mon 09.00–12.30, 14.45–19.15; Tues–Fri 08.30–19.15). Founded by the Club Alpino Italiano in 1863, the museum illustrates the history of mountaineering, with mementoes of famous ascents in Italy. A section with relief maps and models is dedicated to the geology of the mountains and their vegetation. There is also an observatory with a panorama of the western Alps, including Monte Rosa.

The southern districts

The beautiful **Parco del Valentino (Map 14, 13)**, laid out on the left bank of the Po and opened in 1856, borders the city centre on the south. It contains a fine botanic garden (open Apr–Sept, Sat–Sun and holidays 09.00–13.00, 15.00–19.00, Mon–Fri for guided tours, by appointment only, ☎ 011 6707447), founded in 1729, with a museum and library. The latter contains the remarkable *Iconographia Taurinensis*, a collection of 7500 botanical drawings dated 1752–1868. The Castello del Valentino, now used by the university, was built in 1630–60 by Maria Cristina in the style of a French château.

The **Borgo e Rocca Medievali**, reproductions of a medieval Piedmontese village (open daily 09.00–19.00) and of a castle in the Valle d'Aosta (open Tues–Sun 09.00–19.00) were erected for the Turin exhibition of 1884. Nearby is the fine equestrian monument of Prince Amedeo, the masterpiece of Davide Calandra (1902). At the southwest end of the park is an exhibition ground with various buildings erected between 1938 and 1950, notably Palazzo Torino-Esposizioni, whose spectacular vaulted ceiling was designed by architect and engineer Pier Luigi Nervi. It was built in 1948 for the first Turin Motor Show.

Corso Massimo d'Azeglio borders the Valentino on the west, changing its name to Corso Unità d'Italia at the park's southern end. It's a good half-hour walk along this busy thoroughfare to the splendid *Museo dell'Automobile Carlo Biscaretti di Ruffia* (Corso Unità d'Italia 40; open Tues–Sun 10.00–18.30), founded in 1933. The building, designed by Amedeo Albertini, contains an international collection of vehicles, admirably displayed and technically documented. Further on still, overlooking the river, is the huge Palazzo del Lavoro, designed by Pier Luigi Nervi for the 1961 exhibition.

In Via Nizza (**Map 9**), parallel to Corso Unità d'Italia to the west, beside the railway, is the huge Lingotto Fiat factory, which started production in 1923 and closed down in 1983. The interesting building, which has played an important part in the history of the industrialisation of the city, has a test circuit on the roof. In 1991 part of the factory was demolished and part-converted by Renzo PianoArt;Piano, Renzo into an exhibition and congress centre (also used for concerts). The Turin Motor Show is now appropriately held here (biennially in April–May). The Mirafiori Fiat factory, built in 1935–38 and extended 1958–70, where the Fiat motorworks now operate, is to the west, across Corso Unione Sovietica and Corso Giovanni Agnelli.

Environs of Turin

The most interesting momument in the immediate environs of Turin is the basilica of **Superga** (open daily 08.00–12.30; 14.30–18.30), splendidly situated on a wooded hilltop on the right bank of the Po (beyond **Map 16**). The church was built in 1717–31 by Vittorio Amedeo II in fulfilment of a thanksgiving vow for the deliverance of Turin from the French in 1706. It is considered Filippo Juvarra's finest work. It has an impressive exterior, with a columned portico, a dome, and two campanili; and a fine interior with the tombs of the kings of Sardinia, from Vittorio Amedeo II (d. 1732) to Carlo Alberto (d. 1849), in the crypt.

Superga is reached by a cog railway which, after years of inactivity, is being returned to operation as this book goes to press.

Moncalieri, also on the right bank of the Po (beyond **Map 13**), lies 8km from the centre of Turin and can be reached by train and bus. It is an industrial town with a castle (open Thur, Sat–Sun 09.00–13.00, 15.00–18.00) reconstructed in the 15C and enlarged in the 17C–18C. It was the favourite residence of Vittorio Emanuele II; Vittorio Amedeo II (1732) and Vittorio Emanuele I (1824) died here. The apartment of the Savoy princess Letizia Bonaparte, and the 19C royal apartments can be visited.

At **Stupinigi**, 10km southwest of the centre (beyond **Map 9**; bus **41**), is the magnificent **Palazzina di Caccia**, a royal hunting lodge built for Vittorio Amedeo II in 1729–30 by Filippo Juvarra on an ingenious and complex plan. Surrounded by a fine park, it is now the property of the Mauritian Order. The palace has been undergoing restoration since 1988, but it is open (summer Tues–Sun 09.00–18.00, winter 10.00–17.00) and contains a museum of furniture, arranged in some 40 rooms. The queen's apartment has ceiling paintings by Carle van Loo and Giovanni Battista Crosato, and the splendid central hall is frescoed by Giuseppe and Domenico Valeriani (1732). The apartments of Carlo Felice and Carlo Alberto are also shown. The original 18C bronze stag by Francesco Ladatte, which used to crown the roof of the elliptical central hall, is now displayed inside the palace. A stable block is used for exhibitions.

Rivoli, 13km west of the city centre (bus **36**), was once a favourite residence of the Counts of Savoy. The so-called Casa del Conte Verde is a typical early 15C patrician house. The huge, square castle was left unfinished by Filippo Juvarra in 1715. It was restored and modernised in 1984 to house the splendid ***Museo d'Arte Contemporanea** (open Tues–Fri 10.00–17.00; Sat–Sun and holidays 10.00–19.00). Here you can see an outstanding selection of international contemporary art displayed in rooms that merit a trip in themselves. Highlights include works by Anselmo, Baumgarten, Byars, Castellani, Charlton, Cucchi, Dibbets, Fabro, Förg, Kirkeby, Kounellis, Long, Mainolfi, Calzolari, Fontana, Melotti, Merz, Oldenburg-VanBruggen, Paolini, Penck, Penone, Pistoletto, Salvadori, Toroni, Vedova , Vercrysse, Zorio and others. Near Piazza Rivoli is Villa La Tesoriera, built in 1714 by Jacopo Maggi; the garden is open to the public.

To visit the other places of interest around Turin you really need a car, as public transport is too infrequent and complicated to be useful.

The **Castello della Venaria Reale**, 9km north of central Turin, is a royal hunting lodge built for Carlo Emanuele II in 1660 by Amedeo di Castellamonte and destroyed by French troops in 1693. It was reconstructed by Juvarra in 1714–28 and is now open (Tues, Thur, Sat–Sun and holidays 09.00–13.00; Mon, Wed, Fri 14.30–17.00) as a museum. A long avenue of plane trees leads to the **Castello della Mandria**, built for Vittorio Amedeo II in 1713 by Filippo Juvarra, in a large park (open daily) that was once a hunting reserve.

South of Turin near the Po, is **Carignano**, an ancient lordship long associated with the royal house of Savoy. The cathedral (1757–67) is the masterpiece of Benedetto Alfieri. The banks of the Po in this area are protected and of interest for their vegetation and birdlife.

To the east of Turin is the pleasant little industrial town of **Chieri**. The ***Cathedral**, built in 1405–36, has a 13C baptistery with a 15C fresco cycle and a small 9C–10C crypt incorporating Roman work. The 14C church of San Domenico and remains of the Commandery of the Templars are also worth seeing.

The northwest

The northwest of Piedmont is not just a land of great natural beauty. It is also a place of historical significance, the theatre of religious struggles whose violence and duration made 'Piedmont' sound in the 17C as 'Ulster' sounded in the 20C.

Practical information

 Getting there and getting around
By road

If you take Turin as the hub of your explorations, you can most easily reach Pinerolo by 589; Susa by the A5/E70 or 25; Ivrea by A5 or 11 and 26. From these places local roads wind their way over hill and dale to the Alpine parks and resorts.

By rail

The main line between Turin and Chambery (France) traverses the Val di Susa. Slow *Regionali* and *Diretti* reach Bussoleno (where there are connections for Susa, just 5mins away) in 45mins and Oulx-Claviere-Sestriere in 1hr 15mins. Fast *Eurocity* trains rush non-stop to Oulx-Claviere-Sestriere in 50mins, leaving Italy 10min later at Bardonecchia and entering France at Modane.

Ivrea is c 1hr from Turin on the Aosta line; a change is sometimes necessary at Chivasso. Minor lines run from Turin Porta Nuova Station to Pinerolo (40min), where there are connections to Torre Pellice (25mins more); and from Turin Porta Susa or Dora Station to Lanzo Torinese (65mins), with some trains continuing to Ceres (20mins more).

 Information offices
IVREA Corso Vercelli 1, ☎ 0125 618131.
LANZO TORINESE Via Umberto I 9, ☎ 0123 28080.
PINEROLO Viale Giolitti, 7/9, ☎ 0121 795589.

VAL DI SUSA Piazza Garambois 5, Oulx, ☎ 0122 831596.

Where to stay

CHIAVERANO *Castello San Giuseppe*, Località San Giuseppe, ☎ 0125 424370, fax 0125 641278; a pleasant old convent with garden and views; moderate.

IVREA *La Serra*, Corso Carlo Botta 30, ☎ 0125 44341, fax 0125 49313; central and comfortable, with its own little collection of antiquities; moderate.

Sirio, Via lago di Sirio 85, ☎ 0125 424247, fax 0125 48980; a family-managed place with a popular restaurant, on Lake Sirio; moderate.

QUINCINETTO *Mini Hotel Praile*, Via Umberto I 5, ☎ 0125 757188, fax 0125 757349; small, friendly and inexpensive.

SAUZE D'OULX *Il Capricorno*, Via Case Sparse 21, Le Clotes, ☎ 0122 850273, fax 0122 850273; a cordial, family-run place with 7 rooms, in the forest at 1800m; open Jun–Sep and Nov–May; moderate.

SESTRIERE *Grand Hotel Principi di Piemonte*, Via Sauze, ☎ 0122 7941, fax 0122 755411; *the* place to stay in *the* resort in Piedmont; open Dec–Apr and Jul–Aug, expensive.

Eating out

BARDONECCHIA *La Ciaburna*, Località Melezet 48, ☎ 0122 999849; rustic restaurant with good food and excellent wines; inexpensive.

CAVOUR *La Posta*, Via dei Fossi 4, ☎ 0121 69989; restaurant (with rooms) in a historic building, renowned for its delicious regional cuisine; closed Fri and Jul–Aug; inexpensive.

CERESOLE REALE *Chalet del Lago*, Località Pian della Balma, ☎ 0124 953128; trattoria (with rooms), in a mountain chalet on the south side of the Gran Paradiso National Park; open daily Jun–Sep; inexpensive.

IVREA *La Trattoria*, Via Aosta 47, ☎ 0125 48998; trattoria strong on local tradition; closed Sun and Jul; inexpensive. Pasticceria Balla, Via Gozzano 2, has good pastries.

LESSOLO *La Miniera*, Via delle Miniere 9, Località Valcava, ☎ 0125 58618; good country cooking in an old mine; closed Mon–Wed and Jan; inexpensive.

LORANZÉ *Panoramica*, Via San Rocco 7, ☎ 0125 669966; restaurant (with rooms and views) offering local dishes with an innovative twist; closed Sun evening, Dec–Jan and Jul–Aug; moderate.

MEZZENILE *Antica Società*, Via Sabbione 3, ☎ 0123 581210; small, quiet restaurant in the Valli di Lanzo; closed Mon, Oct and Feb; inexpensive.

PINEROLO *Locanda della Capreria Occitana*, Via Nazionale 370r, Abbadia Alpina; famous cheese-makers, also seerving country meals; open Fri–Sat evenings, all day Sun; moderate.

QUINCINETTO *Da Giovanni*, Via Fontana Riola 3, Montellina, ☎ 0125 757447; good views, great food; closed Tues evening and Wed; moderate.

ROLETTO *Il Ciabòt*, Via Costa 7, ☎ 0121 542132; warm, friendly restaurant offering wholesome local dishes; closed Mon and Jul–Aug; moderate.

SAN GIORGIO CANAVESE *Trattoria della Luna*, Piazza Ippolito San Giorgio 12, ☎ 0124 32184; good, simple lunches; closed evenings, Mon and Jul–Aug; inexpensive.

SANT'ANTONIO DI SUSA *Il Sentiero dei Franchi*, Borgata Cresto 16, ☎ 011 9631747; traditional *trattoria* in a clifftop hamlet above Sant'Antonio; closed Tues and Jun; moderate.

SCARMAGNO *La Pergola*, Via Montalenghe 59, Masero; good traditional restaurant, 5km south of Ivrea; closed Mon and Jan; moderate.

TORRE PELLICE *Flipot*, Corso Gramsci 17, ☎ 0121 91236; excellent regional cooking in an old farmhouse;

closed Mon and Tues (except Jun–Sep); moderate.

 Special events
In Chivasso, *Assedio di Chivasso* is the re-enactment of a siege of 1705, last weekend in September. *Carnival* celebrations have been held at Ivrea for some 200 years.

The most important events take place from the Thursday before Ash Wednesday (with a famous battle of oranges).

Sports
Walking and **skiing** throughout the area.

The Valli Valdesi

The Valle del Chisone and the Valle del Pellice, also known as the **Valli Valdesi**, have been inhabited for centuries by the Protestant Waldensians or Vaudois. This religious community originated in the south of France about 1170, under the inspiration of Peter Waldo, a Lyons merchant who sold his goods and started preaching the gospel. His adherents were formally condemned by the Lateran Council in 1184, and persecution drove them to take refuge in these remote valleys. About 1532 the Vaudois became absorbed in the Swiss Reformation. When renewed persecution broke out in 1655 under Carlo Emanuele II, assisted by the troops of Louis XIV, a strong protest was raised by Cromwell in England, and Milton wrote his famous sonnet (box). Still further persecution followed the revocation of the Edict of Nantes (1685), but the remnant of the Vaudois, about 2600 in number, were allowed to retreat to Geneva. In 1698 Henri Arnaud led a band of 800 to the reconquest of their valleys, and a rupture between Louis XIV and Vittorio Amedeo of Savoy was followed by their recognition as subjects of Savoy, in a spirit of religious tolerance. At the beginning of the 19C much interest was taken in Protestant countries on their behalf, and an Englishman, General Charles Beckwith, helped them personally and built their church in Turin (1849). Since 1848 they have been allowed complete religious liberty. Towards the end of the 19C large colonies emigrated to Sicily, Uruguay and the Argentine Republic.

> ### On the Valdesi
> *Avenge, O Lord, they slaughter'd saints, whose bones*
> *Lie scatter'd on the Alpine mountains cold;*
> *Ev'n them who kept thy truth so pure of old*
> *When all our Fatheres worship Stocks and Stones,*
> *Forget not: in thy book record their groanes*
> *Who were thy Sheep, and in their antient Fold*
> *Slayn by the bloody Piemontese that roll'd*
> *Mother with Infant down the Rocks...*
> John Milton, 'Sonnet—On the Late Massacher in Piedmont', May 1655, *Poems*, 1673.

Pinerolo, the historic capital of the Princes of Acaia, ancestors of the Savoy kings, is in a beautiful position at the foot of the hills where the Chisone and Lemina valleys merge into the Piedmontese plain. The fortress of Pignerol was under French control from 1630 to 1706 and, because of its remoteness from Paris, was used as a state prison.

The hub of life in Pinerolo is the large Piazza Vittorio Veneto, with the adjacent Piazza Cavour, beyond which are the public gardens and the Waldensian church (1860). In the military school, founded in 1849 and closed down in 1943, is a museum dedicated to the history of Italian cavalry regiments. The restored Gothic cathedral stands at the centre of the old town. Via Trento and Via Principi d'Acaia (right), with ancient houses, ascend to the early 14C palace of the Princes of Acaia and the contemporaneous church of San Maurizio, reconstructed in 1470, where eight princes are buried. South of Pinerolo is **Cavour**, ancestral home of the great statesman's family. Giovanni Giolitti, five times prime minister of Italy, died here in 1928.

The Valle del Chisone is remarkable for the *fortifications built in 1727 by Vittorio Amedeo II and his son Carlo Emanuele III to defend **Fenestrelle** (1154m), now a summer resort surrounded by forests between the peaks of the Orsiera (2878m) and the Albergian (3043m). The fortifications climb up the hillside from the Chisone to Pra Catinat, with numerous forts, barracks, bridges, a five-storeyed palace used also as a prison, and a church, connected by a splendid covered ramp with 4000 steps, about 1km long. The buildings are now abandoned, but have been partly restored and can be visited by appointment (☎ 0121 83600). Pragelato is noted for its alpine flowers and for the honey they produce. The famous ski resort of Sestriere is described below.

In the Valle del Pellice is **Torre Pellice**, the main centre of the Waldensians and a pleasant little town with some good 19C buildings, including a Waldensian church and college, and a museum illustrating their history.

The Valle di Susa

The Valle di Susa in the western corner of Piedmont, some 50km west of Turin, has been traversed by travellers and armies on their way across the Alps for many centuries. It belonged to the Dauphiny until it was transferred to Turin in 1713 (the carved symbol of the dolphin can still be seen in some places in the valley). Three roads across the Alps from France now converge here, the busiest of which is via the Mont Cenis Tunnel. The main ski resorts in the valley are Sestriere, Sauze d'Oulx, and Bardonecchia.

In the lower Valle di Susa is the abbey church of *Sant'Antonio di Ranverso**, one of the more interesting medieval buildings in Piedmont. Founded in 1188, it was extended in the 13C–14C, and the apse and the unusual façade were added in the 15C. The interior (ring for the custodian except Fri and Mon) has 15C frescoes and a polyptych of the Nativity by Defendente Ferrari (1531) on the high altar. The presbytery and sacristy contain frescoes by Giacomo Jaquerio. The tower and the little cloister are Romanesque.

Avigliana, an ancient little town with many fine 15C mansions, is dominated by a ruined castle of the Counts of Savoy. The church of San Giovanni contains two paintings by Defendente Ferrari. Above the valley, with a fine view of the Alps, is the Sacra di San Michele (open 09.00–12.30, 15.00–17.00 or 18.00), an important abbey founded c 1000, enlarged in the 12C, and suppressed in 1622.

Susa, on the Dora Riparia, is on the main roads from France through the Mont

Cenis tunnel and over the passes of Mont Cenis and Montgenèvre. It preserves some interesting buildings of Roman Segusium, the seat of the Gaulish chief Cottius, who received the dignity of prefect from Augustus and gave his name to the surrounding Cottian Alps (Alpi Cozie). The town was burned in 1173 by Barbarossa in revenge for its rebellion against him in 1168.

San Giusto, a cathedral since 1772, is an interesting 11C church with a massive tower. It has 14C stalls; an incomplete polyptych attributed to Bergognone, and the *triptych of Rocciamelone; a Flemish brass of 1358 (shown on 5 August).

Via Archi ascends from the 4C **Porta Savoia** past the Parco d'Augusto to the *Arco di Augusto**, an arch erected in 8 BC by Cottius in honour of Augustus, decorated with processional reliefs. Higher up is a double Roman arch, with remains of an aqueduct and Roman baths. Piazza della Torre, with the best of the town's medieval mansions (13C), lies below a tower of the **Castle of Countess Adelaide** (11C; small archaeological museum). Southwest of the town is the 13C church of San Francesco, with ruined 15C frescoes, near a small Roman amphitheatre (2C AD).

North of Susa is the **Mont Cenis Pass** (Colle del Moncenisio; 2083m), one of the historic passes over the Alps, crossed by Pepin the Short (755), Charlemagne (774) and Charles the Bald (877), and many other sovereigns with their armies. **Novalesa** has remains of a Benedictine abbey founded in 726, a famous centre of learning in the Middle Ages (Charlemagne stayed here in 773). It was suppressed under Napoleon, but the Benedictines returned here in 1973, and now run a restoration centre for books. The main church was rebuilt in 1712, but several 11C chapels survive, one of them dedicated to St Heldrad (died 842), abbot here for 30 years. In the parish church of Novalesa are some paintings donated by Napoleon in 1805 to the abbot of the hospice of Mont Cenis, including a good copy of the *Crucifixion of St Peter* by Caravaggio.

That's progress

Before the carriage road was constructed by Napoleon in 1803–13 the old road to Italy terminated here, and travellers continued on mule-back or were carried over the pass in a wicker chair. Edward Gibbon, on his way from Lausanne to Rome in 1764, chose the latter means of transport and praised the 'dexterous and intrepid Chairmen of the Alps'.

Beyond the French frontier is the huge lake of Moncenisio (1974m), used to generate electricity, which submerged the hospice of Mont Cenis built by Louis I of France c 815 at the request of St Heldrad. The road winds down to Lanslebourg (see *Blue Guide France*).

In the upper Valle di Susa is the fort of Exilles (strengthened by Vauban in 1799), on the site of many previous impregnable fortifications that defended the frontier here with the Dauphiny. **Salbertrand** was the site of a famous defeat of the French by the Waldensians in 1689. It has a fine parish church (1506–36). The lovely woods on the left bank of the Dora Riparia are now in a protected area. **Sauze d'Oulx** (1510m) is a well-known ski resort.

Bardonecchia is another ski resort (1312m) in a wide basin at the junction of several valleys. It is at the end of the Mont Cenis road tunnel (Traforo del

Fréjus), the second longest road tunnel in Europe. It was begun by France and Italy in 1974–75 and opened to traffic in 1980. The motorway through the tunnel (toll) descends from 1296m to 1228m at the French exit at Modane (see *Blue Guide France*). The railway tunnel across the frontier was begun in 1857 and finished in 1871 on the plans of the engineers Sommeiller, Grandis, and Grattoni. The first great Transalpine tunnel, it reaches a summit level of 1295m. It had an immediate effect on world communications, speeding the transmission of mail from the East to northern Europe by several days, with Brindisi replacing Marseilles as the transit port. Originally 12.2km long, the tunnel was realigned in 1881 and again after the Second World War, and is now 12.8km long. Cars were carried by train through the tunnel from 1935 until the opening of the road tunnel.

Southwest of Oulx is Cesana Torinese, where the painter Paul Cézanne spent much time in his family home. Claviere is another ski resort (1765m) on the French frontier. The **Col du Montgenèvre** (1860m), the frontier before 1947, is one of the older, as well as one of the lower passes over the main chain of the Alps. It was crossed by the armies of Marius, Augustus, Theodosius and Charlemagne, and again in 1494 by Charles VIII of France and his army, dragging with them 600 cannon. The present road was constructed by Napoleon in 1802–07. French armies entered Italy by it in 1818 and 1859; and in 1917–18 French reinforcements were sent to the Italian armies over this pass. The road descends to Briançon (see *Blue Guide France*).

A little to the south, and almost from a common source, rise the Dora, which flows through the Po into the Adriatic, and the Durance, flowing through the Rhône into the Mediterranean.

Sestriere (2030m), the most fashionable ski resort in Piedmont, has become one of the better-known resorts in Europe since it was first developed in 1928–32. Unfortunately, this has led to a lot of new building.

The Valli di Lanzo

The Valli Di Lanzo are three scenic Alpine valleys (the Valle di Viù, Valle di Ala and Val Grande) northwest of Turin, extending to the French frontier. They are the heart of the Graian Alps, which lie between the valleys of the Dora Riparia and Dora Baltea, and are visited by climbers and skiers. The main centre is Lanzo Torinese, with a 14C tower and bridge.

Ivrea and the Canavese

The pleasant old town of Ivrea was the Roman *Eporedia*, a bulwark in the 1C BC against the Salassian Gauls of the Upper Dora. In the Middle Ages its marquises rose to power, and Arduino of Ivrea was crowned King of Italy in 1002. The town has expanded as an industrial centre since the Olivetti typewriter factories were founded here in 1908.

The Ponte Vecchio, or old bridge, was built across the Dora Baltea in 1716 on older foundations. In the upper part of the town, approached by steep lanes, is the **Cathedral**, of which two apsidal towers and the crypt date from the 11C. Look in the raised ambulatory for a row of columns taken from older buildings. The sacristy contains two paintings by Defendente Ferrari.

The *Castle was built by Aymon de Challant (1358) for Amedeo VI, with four tall angle towers, one of which was partially destroyed by an explosion in 1676. It was used as a prison from 1700 to 1970 and has since been restored. The bishop's palace has Roman and medieval fragments in its loggia, and a small diocescan museum occupies San Nicola da Tolentino. The municipal museum, in the Neo-classical Piazza Ottinetti (1843), has Oriental and archaeological collections.

In the public park by the river, below the Dora bridges, is the Romanesque bell tower (1041) of Santo Stefano. The extensive **Olivetti** works, built between 1898 and 1971, extend beyond the railway station. They incorporate the late Gothic convent of San Bernardino with an interesting fresco cycle by Giovanni Martino Spanzotti (late 15C).

The Canavese is a subalpine district extending from the level moraine ridge of the Serra d'Ivrea, to the east, up to the foot of the Gran Paradiso. It has a number of interesting castles, some of them recently opened to the public.

The *Castello di Masino, one of the best preserved castles in Piedmont, stands on an isolated wooded hill south of Ivrea, surrounded by a *borgo*. It was purchased in 1988 by the *FAI (Fondo per l'Ambiente Italiano)*, and has been beautifully restored by them (open Tues–Sun, Feb–Sep 10.00–13.00, 14.00–18.00; Oct–Dec 10.00–13.00, 14.00–17.00; guided visits every hour). It occupies the site of an 11C castle, but was rebuilt in the following centuries. Its present appearance dates largely from the 18C, when it was the residence of Carlo Francesco II, viceroy of Sardinia, and his brother Tommaso Valperga, abbot of Caluso. At this time the double ramp up to the entrance was constructed, and many of the rooms were furnished. These include the print room with French etchings, the library, the Spanish ambassador's bedroom, and a gallery lined with family portraits. Tommaso Valperga, a friend of the poet Vittorio Alfieri, designed the decoration in the poets' gallery.

The medieval northeast tower was adapted in 1730 as a ballroom. The rectangular keep has a lower room, frescoed in the 1690s with coats of arms, and an upper hall, with numerous 18C portraits of the royal house of Savoy. The remains of King Arduino (brought here in the 18C from the castle of Agliè) are preserved in the little family chapel. The stable block has a collection of carriages, open at weekends. The castle is surrounded by an attractive formal garden (a flower show is held on the first weekend in May), the design of which survives in part from the 17C and 18C, and a large park (open Feb–Dec, Tues–Sun 10.00–17.00 or 18.00), laid out in 1840.

A short way south is **Borgomasino**, with another castle (open by appointment, ☎ 0125 770181), on the site of an 11C building, which was also once the property of the Masino. It was largely rebuilt in the 19C.

Further south, across the Dora Baltea, is **Mazzè**, with two castles in a park. They were first built in the 12C but reconstructed in the late 19C. The interior of one (open Mar–Sep on Sun afternoon) is furnished in the Gothic style.

The castle of Pavone Canavese, first built in the 11C, reconstructed in the 16C, and well restored in 1885 rises on a hill east of Ivrea; it is now a restaurant and congress centre. The **Castello di Parella**, on a hill to the west, is a 17C building on medieval foundations, surrounded by a park. It has pretty courtyards, and rooms with fine ceilings and frescoes. Privately owned, it can be visited by appointment (☎ 0125 76288).

The Valle dell'Orco, the chief valley of the Canavese, extends southeast of Ivrea. **Valperga**, in the upper part of the valley near Cuorgnè, has a restored castle and a charming little 15C church (frescoes). Above rises the Santuario di Belmonte, founded by King Arduino of Ivrea, but rebuilt in the 14C. The 12C Castello Ducale at **Agliè** (open for guided visits: summer, Thur–Sun 10.00–12.30, 14.00–18.30; winter, 10.00–12.30, 14.00–17.30) was rebuilt as a ducal palace in 1646, reconstructed by the Savoy in 1763—when the park was laid out—and again by Carlo Felice in 1825. The interior has 19C decorations and Roman sculptures. To the southeast is the castle of San Giorgio, a 14C fortress rebuilt c 1726 with contemporary decorations, surrounded by a park. The Castello Malgrà at Rivarolo dates from the 14C–15C but was heavily restored in 1884–1926. To the west is the medieval Castello di Rivara, with a villa in the Baroque style.

At **Chivasso**, where the Orco meets the Po, the 15C church contains a painting by Defendente Ferrari (1470–1535), who was born in the town. San Benigno has remains of the abbey of Fruttuaria, where King Arduino died, a monk, in 1013.

Cuneo and the Langhe

This and the following chapter deal with southern Piedmont. This is a curious area, famous among Italians but virtually unknown among foreigners. The basis of its reputation is its cuisine—considered by many to be the best in the country—and indeed most visitors to the region come here to eat rather than to look at monuments and museums. There are grounds for arguing that the restaurants (of which there are thousands) could form the substance of a tour of the region, rather than a mere appendix—not just because they are unusually good (which they are), but because each valley and each village has its own, peculiar culinary tradition.

The province of Cuneo, which forms the substance of this chapter, lies in the southwest corner of Piedmont, between the Alps, the source of the river Po and its plain, and the low hills known as the Langhe. The main towns are Saluzzo, below the splendid mountain peak of Monviso and at the head of the Po Valley, Cuneo with its Alpine valleys, Alba and Bra in the Langhe and Roero districts, and Mondovì.

In addition to its food, the province is famous for its **wines** (notably the prestigious *Barolo*) and has numerous small ski resorts. Last but not least, there is a special attraction for train buffs. The spectacular **railway line** through the mountains between Cuneo and Ventimiglia is a remarkable feat of engineering skill, with numerous tunnels and viaducts. Inaugurated in 1928 it was finally reopened in 1979, having been put out of action in the Second World War. Between Limone Piemonte and Ventimiglia it traverses 46km of French territory. The 96km ride takes just under 2 hours.

Practical information

Getting there and getting around
By air

Cuneo Levaldigi Airport, c 50km from the city, has daily flights to/from Rome. Otherwise the airports nearest Cuneo and the Langhe are at Turin (Caselle) and Genoa (Cristoforo Colombo). Both have regional and international flights. Turin is a little closer (112 vs 130km).

By road

The quickest route to Cuneo from Turin is by the A6 and 20, leaving the city via Moncalieri; from Genoa, by A10 and A16 to Montezemolo, then 28 (to Mondovì) and 564; from Milan, by A7, A21 and A6 to Carmagnola, then 20. To Alba from Turin, take 29, again leaving the city via Moncalieri; from Genoa, A7 and A21 to Asti Est, then 231; from Milan, A7 and A21 to Asti Est and 231.

Buses run several times daily from Turin to Cuneo via Saluzzo in c 2hrs 30mins; also from Cuneo to Limone.

By rail

The main rail line serving Cuneo and its province is the Turin–Savona; slow local *Regionali*, *Interregionali* and *Diretti* make the 90km run from Turin to Cuneo in c.1hr 15mins; The trip from Savona to Cuneo takes about the same time (Genoa–Savona is c 20min more). Branch lines connect Cuneo to Saluzzo, Mondovì and Ventimiglia. Alba is served by another branch line, between Asti, Bra and Cavallermaggiore, where you can change for Cuneo.

Information offices

CUNEO Corso Nizza 17, ☎ 0171 693258.
ALBA Piazza Medford, ☎ 0173 35833.
MONDOVÌ Viale Vittorio Veneto 17, ☎ 0174 40389.
SALUZZO Via Griselda 6, ☎ 0175 46710.

Where to stay

CUNEO *Principe*, Piazza Galimberti 5, ☎ 0171 693355, fax 0171 67562; distinguished and well located, in the heart of town; moderate.
Royal Superga, Via Pascal 3, ☎ 0171 693223, fax 0172 699101; comfortable family-run establishment around the corner from the Principe; inexpensive.
ALBA *Savona*, Via Roma 1, ☎ 0173 440440, fax 0173 364312; a friendly, family-run place with in-house pasticceria; inexpensive.
BRA *Elizabeth*, Piazza Giolitti 8, ☎ 0172 422486, fax 0172 412214; central, comfortable; inexpensive.
Giardini, Piazza XX Settembre 28, ☎ 0172 412866, fax 0172 432661; in a renovated townhouse; inexpensive.
LIMONE PIEMONTE *Le Ginestre*, Via Nizza 68 (1km south), ☎ 0171 927596, fax 0171 927597; modern with a lovely garden and good views of the valley; open Dec–Easter and Jul–Sep; moderate.
MONDOVÌ *Park*, Via Delvecchio 2 , ☎ 0174 46666, fax 0174 47771; quietly elegant, in a park; inexpensive.
SALUZZO *Astor*, Piazza Garibaldi 39, ☎ 0175 45506, fax 0175 47450; centrally located and recently renovated; inexpensive.
Griselda, Corso XXVII Aprile 13, ☎ 0175 47484, fax 0175 47489; modern and comfortable; moderate.
SANTA VITTORIA D'ALBA (ALBA) *Castello di Santa Vittoria*, ☎ 0172 478198, fax 0172 478465; a particularly tranquil place, in a former castle, with a good restaurant; open Mar–Dec, inexpensive.
VERDUNO (ALBA) *Real Castello*, Via Umberto I 9, ☎ 0172 470125, fax 0172 470298; another quiet old castle, this time a Savoy residence dating from the 18C; open Mar–Nov, moderate.

Many of the eating places listed below also have rooms.

Eating out
CUNEO *Le Plat d'Etain*, Corso Giolitti 18, ☎ 0171 681918; restaurant specialising in French cuisine; closed Sun; moderate. *Ligure*, Via Savigliano 11, ☎ 0174 681942; restaurant (with rooms) known for its traditional cooking; closed Sun evening and Jan.

Osteria della Chiocciola, Via Fossano 1, ☎ 0171 66277; excellent restaurant and wine bar offering creative and traditional dishes using local ingredients; closed Sun and Aug; inexpensive.

ALBA *Il Vicoletto*, Via Bertero 6, ☎ 0173 363196; excellent renditions of traditional local dishes; closed Mon and Jul–Aug; moderate.

Lalibera, Via Pertinace 24a, ☎ 0173 293155; traditional *osteria*; closed Sun and midday Mon, Jan–Feb; inexpensive.

Osteria dell'Arco, Piazza Savona 5, ☎ 0173 363974; restaurant renowned for its warm friendly atmosphere and excellent regional cuisine; closed Sun, midday Mon, Jul and Jan; inexpensive.

Osteria Italia, Frazione San Rocco Seno d'Elvio, ☎ 0173 441547; traditional *osteria* 5km outside of Alba; closed Wed (except in Oct) and Jan–Feb; inexpensive.

Non Solo Vino, Corso Vittorio Emanuele 31, is a good wine shop with a bar serving snacks.

Umberto has Alba's best **cakes and coffee**, and you can find all sorts of sweets (including chocolate *torrone*) at *Io, Tu e i Dolci*, Piazza Savona 12. For **wines** of the Langhe, try *Enoteca Fracchia*, Via Vernazza 9; *Grandi Vini*, Via Vittorio Emanuele 1a; and *'L Crotin*, Via Cuneo 3.

ALBARETTO DELLA TORRE (ALBA) *Dei Cacciatori da Cesare*, Via Umberto 9, ☎ 0173 520141; restaurant renowned for its creative cuisine using local ingredients; closed Tues–Wed, Jan and Aug; expensive.

BARBARESCO *Antica Torre*, Via Torino 8, ☎ 0173 635170; good traditional restaurant; closed Sun evening, Mon and Aug; moderate.

BAROLO *La Cantinella*, Via Acquagelata 4a, ☎ 0173 56267; traditional **osteria-trattoria**; closed Mon evening, Tues (except in autumn) and Aug; moderate. *Locanda nel Borgo Antico*, Piazza del Municipio 2, ☎ 0173 56355; family osteria serving good local fare; closed Wed, Feb and Jul–Aug; inexpensive.

BOVES *Al Rododendro*, Frazione San Giacomo, ☎ 0171 380372; restaurant serving outstanding creative and traditional dishes using local ingredients; closed Sun evening, Mon and Jun; expensive.

Da Politano, Via Santuario 125, Località Fontanelle, ☎ 0171 380383; traditional restaurant (with rooms); closed Mon evening, Tues and Jan; inexpensive.

Osteria degli Amici, Frazione Rivoira, ☎ 0171 388781; traditional osteria; open midday only, closed Tues; inexpensive.

Trattoria della Pace, Via Santuario 97, ☎ 0171 380398; another place renowned for its original twists on old recipes; closed Sun evening, Mon and Jan; moderate.

BRA Coffee and pastries at *Converso*. *Battaglino*, Piazza Roma 18, ☎ 0172 412509; trattoria serving mainly traditional dishes; closed Mon and Aug; moderate. *Boccondivino*, Via Mendicità Istruita 14, ☎ 0172 425674; excellent traditional *osteria*, closed Sun, midday Mon and Jul–Aug; inexpensive.

BRIAGLIA *Marsupino*, Via Roma 20, ☎ 0174 563888; traditional trattoria known for its fine food and excellent wines; closed Wed, Jan and Sep; moderate.

CARRÙ *Moderno*, Via Misericordia 12, ☎ 0173 75493; very traditional restau-

rant, with a remarkable wine list; closed Mon evening, Tues and Aug; moderate. Carrù is famous for its smoked ox, *bue di Carrù*, available at most grocers' shops.
CERVERE *Antica Corona Reale–da Renzo*, Via Fossano 13, ☎ 0172 474132; great *trattoria* offering local delicacies such as frogs and snails; closed Tues evening, Wed, Mar and Sep; moderate.
CHERASCO *Osteria della Rosa Rossa*, Via San Pietro 31, ☎ 0172 488133; warm, friendly trattoria serving excellent food and wines; closed Tues and Wed, Jan and Aug; inexpensive.
CISSONE *Locanda dell'Arco*, Piazza dell'Olmo 1, ☎ 0173 748200; delicious traditional fare and excellent wines in a warm, quiet restaurant; closed Tues and Jan; moderate.
CRAVANZANA *Da Maurizio–Trattoria del Mercato*, Via San Rocco 16, ☎ 0173 855019; excellent trattoria (with rooms) specialising in regional food and wines; closed Wed, Jan and Jun; moderate.
DIANO D'ALBA *Antica Trattoria del Centro*, Via Alba-Cortemilia 91, at Ricca, ☎ 0173 612018; traditional *trattoria* closed Mon evening, Tues, Jan and Jul–Aug; inexpensive.
FEISOGLIO *Cascina Knec*, Via Roatta Soprana 79 (the Bossolasco road), ☎ 0173 831137; farm offering bed and breakfast accommodation and good country meals; open all year, Nov–Feb by reservation only.
GRINZANE CAVOUR *Nonna Genia*, Località Borzone, ☎ 0173 262410; good *trattoria* in an old house in the hills; closed Wed, Jan and Jul; inexpensive.
LA MORRA *Fratelli Revello*, Frazione Annunziata 103, ☎ 0173 50276; wine estate offering delicious country meals; closed Jan–Feb; inexpensive.
LIMONE PIEMONTE *Lu Taz di Matlas*, Via San Maurizio 13, ☎ 0171 929061; restaurant specialising in local mountain dishes; closed Mon, Jun and Oct; moderate.

MONDOVÌ *Croce d'Oro*, Via Sant'Anna Avagnina 83, ☎ 0174 681464; trattoria just outside the town, serving delicious local fare with a personal touch; closed Mon, Jan and Jul–Aug; moderate.
Mezzavia, Via Villanova 38, ☎ 0174 40363; restaurant offering good regional cuisine; closed Wed and Jul; moderate.
MONFORTE D'ALBA *Giardino-da Felicin*, Via Vallada 18, ☎ 0173 78225; restaurant (with rooms) serving outstanding traditional dishes, on a panoramic terrace in summer; closed evenings Mon–Fri, Jan–Feb and Jul; expensive.
Trattoria della Posta, Piazza XX Settembre 9, ☎ 0173 78120; traditional trattoria with a good wine list; closed Thur and Jul–Aug; moderate.
MONTELUPO ALBESE *Ca' del Lupo*, Via Ballerina 15, ☎ 0173 617249; restaurant with pool, panorama and particularly light cuisine; closed Wed and weekdays at midday, Jan and Feb; moderate.
Vecchia Langa, Via Umberto 23, ☎ 0173 617143; country trattoria on the village square; closed Mon and Jan; inexpensive.
MONTEROSSO GRANA *Locanda dell'Angelo*, Via del Castello 15, ☎ 0171 988115; warm, friendly restaurant, by the castle; closed at midday (except Sun and holidays) and Tues; moderate.
PAGNO *Locanda del Centro*, Via Martiri della Liberazione 2, ☎ 0175 76140; restaurant offering creative interpretations of dishes of the Valle Bronda; closed Wed, inexpensive.
PIOBESI D'ALBA *Locanda le Clivie*, Via Canoreto 1, ☎ 0173 619261; restaurant (with rooms) renowned for its carefully prepared local dishes; closed Sun evening (except Oct) and Mon; moderate.
ROBILANTE *Leon d'Oro*, Piazza Olivero 10, ☎ 0171 78679; old-fashioned trat-

toria offering dishes from Piedmont and Sardinia; closed Wed and Jan–Feb; inexpensive.

ROCCABRUNA (CUNEO) *La Pineta*, Località Sant'Anna (3km north), ☎ 0171 905856, fax 0171 916622; traditional restaurant (with rooms); closed Mon evening and Tues (except Jul and Aug) and Jan–Feb; inexpensive.

SALUZZO *La Gargotta del Pellico*, Piazzetta Mondagli 5, ☎ 0175 46833; traditional restaurant; closed Tues and midday Wed; moderate.

La Taverna di Porti Scür, Via Volta 14, ☎ 0175 41961; trattoria known for its creative interpretations of traditional recipes; closed Mon and midday Tues; moderate.

L'Ostü dij Baloss, Via Gualtieri 38, ☎ 0175 248618; excellent traditional restaurant in a beautiful 17C setting; closed Sun and midday Mon, Jan and Jul–Aug.

For a selection of fine cheeses, try *La Casa del Parmigiano*, Corso Italia 112; or the factory outlet at *Caseificio San Martino*, Corso Piemonte 129.

SERRAVALLE LANGHE *La Coccinella*, Via Provinciale 5, ☎ 0173 748220; traditional *trattoria*; closed Mon, Jan and Jun; inexpensive.

STROPPO *L'Ortica*, Frazione Bassura di Stroppo 58, ☎ 0171 999202; *osteria* with good local cooking and wines; closed Tues and Oct–Jun weekdays; inexpensive.

Lou Sarvanot, Frazione Bassura di Stroppo 64, ☎ 0171 999159; excellent country restaurant (with rooms); closed Mon (and Tues in winter), midday weekdays (except Aug), Jan–Feb and Sep; moderate.

TREISO *La Ciau del Tornavento*, Piazza Baracco 7, ☎ 0173 638333; restaurant specialising in traditional local cuisine with a personal twist; closed Wed, midday Thur and Jan; moderate.

Osteria dell'Unione, Via Alba 1, ☎ 0173 638303; *osteria* offering delicious seasonal menus; closed Sun evening, Mon and Aug; moderate.

VERZUOLO *San Bernardo*, Via San Bernardo 63, ☎ 0175 85882; old-fashioned *trattoria* with garden seating in summer and no written menu; closed Tues, midday Wed and Jan; moderate.

 Shopping

ALBA The town is the **truffle** capital of Italy, as the many signs around town ('*tartuffi*') announce. Among the better-known truffle vendors are *Martino*, Corso Cortemila 43; *Morra*, Piazza Pertinace 2; and Ponzio, Via Vittorio Emanuele 26. In autumn (Oct–Dec) there is a Saturday-morning truffle market at the Maddalena, on Via Vittorio Emanuele.

BAROLO Estate-grown **wines** in the environs.

Sports

Skiing in the Valle Varaita. **Walking** in the mountains above Cuneo and in the Langhe.

CUNEO AND ENVIRONS

Cuneo, approached by a monumental viaduct over the Stura, is a pleasant provincial capital (population 55,000) deriving its name from the 'wedge' of land at the confluence of the Gesso and the Stura. The huge arcaded piazza, the cathedral, and the public buildings were mostly rebuilt after a destructive but unsuccessful siege in 1744. A large market is held in the main square on Tuesdays. Via Roma, with heavy arcades, is the main street of the old town. **San Francesco**, a secularised church of 1227, with a good portal (1481), houses a small museum. Magnificent boulevards have replaced the former ramparts. Cuneo is the gateway to the southern Cottian Alps, approached by the Val Maira and the Val Varaita.

In the valley of the Gesso are the Terme di Valdieri (975m)—rebuilt in 1952–53—with hot sulphur springs. Monte Matto (3088m) and Cima di Argentera (3297m), the highest peak of the Maritime Alps, lie within the **Parco dell'Argentera**, a protected area once part of the royal hunting reserve of Valdieri-Entracque. The Col du Clapier is now thought by some scholars to have been Hannibal's route across the Alps.

At the head of the wooded **Valle Stura**, with hot sulphur springs at Terme di Vinadio (1274m), is the Colle della Maddalena (1991m), an easy pass with meadows noted for their varied flowers, and free from snow between mid-May and mid-October. Francis I passed this way on his invasion of Italy in 1515, and Napoleon decreed that 'the imperial road from Spain to Italy' should be carried over the pass. The descent leads to Barcelonnette (see *Blue Guide Provence and the Côte d'Azur*).

The Palanfrè park in the upper **Val Vermenagna** has remarkable beechwoods and interesting wildlife. **Limone Piemonte** (998m) is a large village among open pastures, one of the older ski resorts in Italy, with a 12C–14C church. The French frontier is quite nearby, on the Colle di Tenda (1909m); but this is a relatively new development. The districts of Tende and La Brigue, although parts of the County of Nice, were given to Italy in the Franco-Italian treaty of 1860, by courtesy of Napoleon III, because a great part of the territory was a favourite hunting-ground of Vittorio Emanuele II. In 1947 they were rejoined to the rest of the county by treaty, an act which was confirmed a month later by a local plebiscite resulting in a large majority in favour of France.

Mondovì grew up in the Middle Ages and by the 16C probably had more inhabitants than any other city in Piedmont. The architect Francesco Gallo (1672–1750), a native, designed numerous buildings in the town. It was the birthplace of Giovanni Giolitti (1842–1928), who was five times prime minister from 1892 to 1921 and introduced universal suffrage into Italy. In the upper town of Mondovì Piazza, with an attractive large piazza, is the elaborate **Chiesa della Missione** (1678), with a *trompe-l'oeil* vault-painting by Andrea Pozzo. The cathedral was built by Gallo in 1743–63. From the garden of the Belvedere there is a fine view.

Southwest of Mondovì is Lurisia, a spa with radioactive springs, developed since 1928. Frabosa Soprana is a summer and winter resort near Artesina and Prato Nevoso, ski resorts in the eastern group of the Maritime Alps. **Bossea** in the Val Corsaglia has stalactite *caves, among the most interesting in Italy (guided tours 10.00–12.00, 14.00–18.00). A skeleton of the gigantic extinct cave bear (*Ursus spelaeus*), found here, is on display.

Vicoforte, to the east of Mondovì, is known for its huge domed pilgrimage church, begun in 1596 by Ascanio Vitozzi, continued after 1728 by Francesco Gallo, and completed in 1890. Casotto Castle (1090m), on the site of an 11C Carthusian monastery, was built in 1835 by Carlo Alberto and used as a summer residence by Vittorio Emanuele II. **Ormea** is another pleasant hill-resort, with a ruined castle and Gothic frescoes of 1397 in the parish church.

THE LANGHE
● ● ● ● ● ● ● ● ● ● ● ● ●

The Langhe and the neighbouring distric of Roero, in the northeast corner of the province of Cuneo, are crossed by the River Tanaro. The rolling low hills are famous for their vineyards, which produce excellent wines—including *Barolo*, *Dolceto*, *Nebbiolo*, *Barbera*, *Barbaresco*, *Roero*, *Roero Arneis*, *Pelaverga* and *Moscato*. Many of the estates with vineyards welcome visitors. The territory includes numerous chestnut, pine and oak woods, particularly beautiful in the autumn. The main towns are Alba and Bra, and there are good restaurants in the area, many of them specialising in truffles (found locally).

Bra is a pleasant town with a small archaeological museum in the 15C Palazzo Traversa, containing finds from the Roman *Pollentia* (now Pollenzo). The Rococo church of Santa Chiara was built by Bernardo Antonio Vittone in 1742. Nearby is a natural history museum founded in 1843. South of Bra are **Pollenzo**, where the church contains fine 15C stalls brought from Staffarda, and **Cherasco**, of Roman origins. The latter has a Visconti castle of 1348, a 13C church, 17C palaces, and the Museo Adriani (good coins and medals).

At **Alba** the historic centre has preserved its polygonal plan from Roman days, and some tall medieval brick tower-houses and decorated house fronts survive. The **duomo**, over-restored in the 19C, contains fine carved and inlaid stalls by Bernardino da Fossato (1512). In the town hall is a painting of the *Madonna and Child*, one of the better works by the 16C artist Macrino d'Alba, and a *Concert* attributed to Mattia Preti (17C). The deconsecrated church of the Maddalena (rebuilt in 1749) contains the **Museo Federico Eusebio** (closed at the time of writing), with local neolithic finds, Roman material, and natural history and ethnographic sections. San Giovanni contains a *Madonna* by Barnaba da Modena (1377) and two more paintings by Macrino. **San Domenico** has 14C and 15C frescoes.

Southwest of Alba is the castle of **Grinzane Cavour**, which may date from the 13C (although it was enlarged in the 17C). Cavour spent part of his childhood

here, and it now houses a wine cellar open to the public.

At **Santo Stefano Belbo** is the birthplace (open at weekends) of the writer Cesare Pavese (1908–50). There is also a study centre (badly damaged in a flood of 1994) devoted to him.

Saluzzo is the historic seat of a line of marquises famous in the 15C and 16C; the upper town is particularly attractive. The large cathedral was built in 1481–1511. The ancient streets of the upper town lead up to the castle (turned into a prison in

The castle of Grinzane Cavour

1821). Just below it is the church of ***San Giovanni**, erected in 1330, with a choir extension of 1480 containing finely crafted stalls and the tomb of Marquess Lodovico II (d. 1503) by Benedetto Briosco. On the north side are the cloister and chapter house, the latter with a monument of 1528 to Galeazzo Cavassa.

Further along Via San Giovanni is the charming 15C–16C **Casa Cavassa** (open Wed–Sun 09.00–12.00, 15.00–18.00), once the residence of Galeazzo. Restored in 1883, it is interesting for its architecture and furniture; the marble portal was added in the early 16C by Matteo Sanmicheli. Since 1891 it has housed the municipal museum, illustrating the history of the marquisate. There is also a section devoted to Silvio Pellico (1789–1854), the patriot author who was born in the town.

The **Castello della Manta** (open Feb–Dec, Tues–Sun 10.00–13.00, 14.00–17.00 or 18.00), to the south, was donated to the *FAI* (*Fondo per l'Ambiente Italiano*) in 1984. This medieval castle was rebuilt by the Saluzzo della Manta family at the beginning of the 15C, later modified and 'reconstructed' in 1860. The church contains early-15C frescoes and the late-16C funerary chapel of Michelantonio di Saluzzo. In the Palazzo di Michelantonio, with a Mannerist staircase, one of the rooms (1563) has a ceiling decorated with painted grotesques and stuccoes. The **Castello di Valerano** has remarkable *frescoes (c 1420; restored in 1989), in the International Gothic style, attributed to the 'Maestro della Manta'. The frescoes show 18 historical heroes and heroines in contemporary costume, and allegorical scenes of the Fountain of Eternal Youth. They form one of the more interesting secular fresco cycles of this period. The park is open Feb–Dec Tues–Sun 10.00–18.00.

Southwest of Saluzzo is **Castellar**, where the 14C castle (reconstructed in the 19C and after the last war) contains the Museo Aliberti (open daily 14.00–18.00), devoted to the uniforms of the Italian army from the Unification to the Second World War.

West of Saluzzo is **Revello** where, next to the town hall, the Cappella Marchionale, with 15C–16C frescoes, is all that remains of the summer palace built by Marquess Lodovico II.

Savigliano, east of Saluzzo, is the birthplace of the astronomer Giovanni SchiaparelliSchiaparelli, Giovanni (1835–1910). Near the central Piazza Santarosa are the Museo Civico and a gipsoteca with works by the sculptor Davide Calandra (1856–1915), the church of San Pietro with a polyptych by Gandolfino di Roveto (1510), and the Teatro Civico (1834–36).

At **Racconigi**, north of Savigliano, is a castle (open Tues–Sun 09.00–13.00, 14.00–17.00), built 1676–1842 by the Savoy kings and owned by the state since 1980. The main façade is by Giovanni Battista Borra (1755) and the front over-

The castle at Racconigi

looking the park is by Guarino Guarini (1676). Umberto of Savoy was born here in 1904 (the ex-king died in exile in 1983). The large park can be visited in summer on Sun 14.00–19.00 or by appointment.

Fossano, south of Savigliano, has a castle of the Acaia family (1324–32), now the seat of the municipal library (opened by request on weekdays), and 17C and 18C palaces and churches, including the Santissima Trinità by Francesco Gallo (1730).

North of Saluzzo near the Po is **Staffarda**, with a fine *Cistercian abbey founded in 1135 and well restored. Since 1750 the abbey has been owned by the Order of Santi Maurizio e Lazzaro. It contains a polyptych by Oddone Pascale (1531) and an altar by Agostino Nigra (1525).

The source of the Po is at Pian del Re (2050m) in the upper Valle Po, in an area interesting for its flora. The first 235km of the banks of the Po, the largest river in Italy, are now protected as a park by the Region of Piedmont.

The splendid mountain of **Monviso** (3841m) was climbed by Quintino Sella, founder of the Club Alpino Italiano, in 1863. Beneath the Colle delle Traversette (2950m) is a tunnel built by Marquis Lodovico II in 1480 for the use of merchants trading with Dauphiny. It leads into the French valley of the Guil and Abriès (see *Blue Guide France*). This pass is thought by some scholars to have been Hannibal's route over the Alps.

In the Valle Varaita (skiing), on the southern slopes of Monviso, is **Casteldelfino** (1295m), a village named from a castle founded in 1336, once the centre of the Dauphins' Cisalpine territory. The Col Agnel (2699m) pass on the French frontier was often used by invading armies: it was crossed by the French hero Bayard in 1515 and by Philip, Duke of Parma, in 1743.

Asti, Alessandria and the southeast

This is the second of our chapters for gourmets (see above). Once again, you're likely to find the menus in southeastern Piedmont more memorable than the art and architecture. On sunny days the landscape, too, can be quite striking—especially in spring, when the meadows come alive with wildflowers, or in autumn, when the grape-leaves turn bright red. As in Cuneo and its province, here, too, the excellent local cuisine is accompanied by fine wines—particularly the whites of Canelli, near Asti, and the Monferrato reds.

The two provinces of Asti and Alessandria were severely damaged in a disastrous flood in 1994 when 70 people lost their lives, and some 4000 became homeless. The banks of the Tanaro overflowed after several days of torrential rain, also causing much damage to agriculture and industry in the area. Reconstruction is still in progress, and you'll probably see signs of it here and there.

Practical information

Getting there and getting around
By air

Asti is c 80km from Turin Caselle Airport and 110km from Genoa Cristoforo Colombo; Alessandria is c 80km from Genova Cristoforo Colombo and 110km from Torino Caselle. Both airports have domestic and international flights.

By road

The quickest route to southeastern Piedmont from Turin is by Autostrade A6 and A21; from Milan and Genoa, A7 and A21; from Bologna, A1 and A21. Several companies offer country bus services between the main towns. For information, ☎ 166 845010, or contact *ARFEA* (☎ 0131 225810), *Franchini SATA* (☎ 0141 593673), *ATAV Vigo* (☎ 011 854853) or *SATTI* (☎ 011 57641). Car parking in marked areas in most towns. In Alessandria, on Piazza Garibaldi and Piazza Libertà, there is a minibus service to the city centre.

By rail

Asti and Alessandria are served by the main Turin–Genoa rail line, and fast *Eurostar* and *Intercity* trains stop in both cities. From Turin to Asti, 56km in c 30mins, to Alessandria 91km in c 50mins (the line continues Via Piacenza to Bologna); from Genoa to Asti, 113km in c 1hr 10mins, to Alessandria 79km in c 50min. You can get from Asti to Alessandria by train in c 20mins. Branch lines run from Asti to Acqui Terme, and Via Alba and Bra to Cavallermaggiore, where there are connections to Cuneo.

Information offices

ASTI Piazza Alfieri 34, ☎ 0141 530357.
Informagioivani, Piazza Alfieri 33, ☎

0141 433315.
ALESSANDRIA Via Savona 26, ☎ 0131 445711; www:alexala.com.
ACQUI TERME Corsi Bagni 8, ☎ 0144 3221420.
CASALE MONFERRATO Via Marchino 2, ☎ 0142 70243.

Where to stay

ASTI *Aleramo*, Via Emanuele Filiberto 13, ☎ 0141 595661, fax 0141 30039; modern and central; moderate.
Reale, Piazza Alfieri 6, ☎ 0141 530240, fax 0141 34357; a traditional place with a long list of eminent guests; moderate.
ALESSANDRIA *Alli Due Buoi Rossi*, Via Cavour 32, ☎ 0131 445252, fax 0131 445255; a fine, family-run establishment with a good restaurant; closed Aug; moderate.
Europa, Via Palestro 1, ☎ 0131 236226, fax 0131 252498; modern and comfortable; inexpensive.
AGLIANO *San Giacomo*, Via Arullani 4, ☎ 0141 954178; a small, cosy place with 6 rooms; closed Jan, Feb and Aug; moderate.
Fons Salutis, Via alle Fonti 125, ☎ 0141 954018, fax 0141 954554; calm and quiet, with a nice garden and its own spa; inexpensive.
CIOCCARO DI PENANGO *Locanda del Sant'Uffizio*, ☎ 0141 916292, fax 0141 916068; a renovated country house with park and pool; closed Jan and Aug; moderate.
MONTEGROSSO D'ASTI *Locanda del Boscogrande*, Via Boscogrande 47, ☎ 0141 956390, fax 0141 956390; a lovely renovated farmhouse with 7 rooms; moderate.
NOVI LIGURE *Relais Villa Pomela*, Via Serravalle 69, ☎ 0143 329910, fax 0143 329912; a stately villa with park 2km outside the town; moderate.

Eating out

ASTI *Pasticceria Giordanino*, Corso Alfieri 254 , for pastries.

Barolo & Co., Via Cesare Battisti 14, ☎ 0141 592059; old-fashioned restaurant with good wholesome food and down-home style; closed Sun evening, Mon and Aug; inexpensive.

Da Aldo, Frazione Castiglione 22 (8km east), ☎ 0141 206008; friendly family-run restaurant with good local cooking; closed Wed and Jan; moderate.

L'Altra Campana, Via Quintino Sella 2, ☎ 0141 437083; simple trattoria; closed Tues and Jan; inexpensive.

Gener Neuv, lungo Tanaro 4, ☎ 0141 557270; excellent restaurant devoted to local tradition; closed Sun evening (all day Sun in summer), Mon, Aug, Dec or Jan; expensive.

ALESSANDRIA *Bistrot*, Via Piacenza 90, ☎ 0131 234321; simple osteria specialising in Tuscan cooking; open evenings only, closed Mon, Tues and Aug; inexpensive.

Cappelverde, Via San Pio V at Via Plana, ☎ 0131 251265; warm, friendly *trattoria*; open evenings only; closed Tues; inexpensive.

ACQUI TERME *Da Bigât*, Via Mazzini 30–32, ☎ 0144 324283; traditional osteria; closed Wed; inexpensive.

San Guido, Piazza San Guido 5, ☎ 0144 320420; another old-fashioned osteria; closed Sat and Aug; inexpensive.

CALAMANDRANA *Osteria dei Puciu*, Regione Quartino, Casina Lacqua, ☎ 0141 75122; osteria in an old farmhouse near Canelli; closed Tues and Jan; inexpensive.

Violetta, Viale San Giovanni 1 (2km north), ☎ 0141 75151; traditional restaurant in an old farmhouse; closed Sun evening, Wed and Jan; moderate.

CAMAGNA *Taverna di Campagna dal 1997*, Vicolo Gallina 20, ☎ 0142 925645; rustic farmhouse with good country cooking; open midday week-

days, all day on weekends; closed Mon and Jan; inexpensive.

CANELLI *Al Grappolo d'Oro*, Via Risorgimento 59–61, ☎ 0141 823812; restaurant (with rooms) known for its good local dishes; closed Mon; moderate.

Piccolo San Remo dal Baròn, Via Alba 179, ☎ 0141 823944; trattoria specialising in regional cuisine; closed Sun evening and Mon, Aug and Jan; inexpensive.

San Marco, Via Alba 36, ☎ 0141 823544; restaurant famous for its great regional delicacies and fabulous wines; closed Tues evening, Wed and Jul–Aug; moderate.

CANIGLIE (ASTI) *Da Dirce*, Via Valleversa 53, ☎ 0141 272949; excellent trattoria with delicate food and great wines; closed Mon and midday Tues, Aug and Jan; moderate.

CASALE MONFERRATO *La Torre*, Via Garoglio 3, ☎ 0142 70295; traditional restaurant with garden and views; closed Wed, Dec–Jan and Aug; moderate.

CASTELLAZO BORMIDA *Lo Spiedo*, Via Acqui 25, ☎ 0131 278184; traditional *trattoria* serving strictly local fare; open evenings Tues–Fri, all day Sun and holidays; closed Aug; inexpensive.

CASTELNUOVO CALCEA *Il Boschetto di Vignole*, Via Marconi 16, ☎ 0141 957434; well-known traditional trattoria; closed Mon evening, Tues and Jul; inexpensive.

CASTIGLIONE TINELLA *Da Palmira*, Piazza XX Settembre 18, ☎ 0141 855176; trattoria offering excellent regional dishes; closed Mon evening, Tues, and Jul–Aug; moderate.

CAVATORE *Cascina Camolin*, Via Valle Prati 17, ☎ 0144 322673; farm serving excellent lunches using fresh, home-grown and home-made ingredients; open evenings and midday Sun; inexpensive.

COAZZOLO *Da Linet*, Via Neive 1, ☎ 0141 870161; traditional trattoria;

closed Tues and Aug; moderate.

CORTANZE *Antichi Sapori*, Via
Marchesi di Roero 22, ☎ 0141
901050; simple but good trattoria,
somewhat off the beaten track; closed
Tues and Jan; inexpensive.

COSSANO BELBO *Trattoria della
Posta da Camulin*, Via Negro 3, ☎
0141 88126; classic Piedmontese cuisine; closed Sun, Mon and Jul–Aug;
moderate. *Universo*, Via Caduti 6, ☎
0141 88167; trattoria with simple but
delicious regional food; closed Mon–Wed
and Jun–Jul; moderate.

COSTIGLIONE D'ASTI *Da Guido*,
Piazza Umberto I 27, ☎ 0141 966012;
outstanding local and regional cuisine
accompanied by excellent wines; closed
midday, Sun and holidays, Dec–Jan and
Aug; expensive.

GAVI *Cantine del Gavi*, Via Mameli 69,
☎ 0143 642458; excellent traditional
restaurant, in a historic building; closed
Mon, Jan and Jul; moderate.

ISOLA D'ASTI *Il Cascinale Nuovo*, on
the 231 (2km wouthwest), ☎ 0141
958166; excellent country restaurant
(with rooms and pool); closed Sun
evening, Mon, midday in summer, Jan
and Aug; expensive.

MASIO *Losanna*, Via San Rocco 36, ☎
0131 799525; an old post stage in the
countryside, now a trattoria serving
regional fare; closed Mon and Aug;
moderate.

MONTALDO SCARAMPI *Il
Campagnin*, Via Binello 77, ☎ 0141
953676; trattoria combining tradition
and imagination in delicious lunches;
closed evenings, Sun and Tues; moderate.

MONTECHIARO D'AQUI *Antica
Osteria di Nonno Carlo*, Via delle
Scuole 1, ☎ 0144 92366; traditional
osteria; closed Wed; moderate.

MONTECHIARO D'ASTI *Tre Colli*,
Piazza del Mercato 5, ☎ 0141 901027;
warm, friendly *trattoria* with a good
wine list; closed Mon, Jan and Jul–Aug;
moderate.

MONTEGROSSO D'ASTI *Da Elvira*, Vi
Santo Stefano 75, ☎ 0141 956138;
farm serving delicious country meals
(try the warm vegetable tarts), closed
Sun evening, Mon and Aug; moderate.

NIZZA MONFERRATO *Le Due
Lanterne*, Piazza Garibaldi 52, ☎ 0141
702480; restaurant offering classic
Piedmontese food and good wines;
closed Mon evening, Tues and Aug;
moderate.

PASTURANA *Locanda San
Martino*, Via Roma 26, ☎ 0143 58444;
restaurant renowned for its creative
interpretations of traditional recipes;
closed Mon evening, Tues and Jan; moderate.

PONZONE *Diana*, Località Abasse 245,
☎ 0144 70227; restaurant known for
its seasonal specialities; closed Mon, Feb
and Jun–Jul; moderate.

PRIOCCA *Il Centro*, Via Umberto I 5,
☎ 0173 611612; another restaurant
famous for its seasonal specialities, with
an excellent wine list; closed Tues;
moderate.

ROCCAVERANO *Aurora*, Via Bruno 1,
☎ 0144 93023; old-fashioned restaurant (with rooms) serving good country
meals; closed Dec–Mar; moderate.

SAN MARZANO OLIVETO *Del Belbo
da Bardon*, Via Valle Asinari 25, ☎
0141 831340; restaurant serving excellent food and wine of the region; closed
Wed evening, Thur and Dec–Jan; moderate.

La Viranda, regione Corte 69, ☎ 0141
856671; delicious country meals on a
farm set amid orchards and vineyards;
closed Mon, Jan and Aug; inexpensive.

SAN MARZANOTTO (ASTI) *Fratelli
Rovero*, Località Valdonata, ☎ 0141
530102; wine estate (*Barbera* and
Grignolino) offering great farm lunches;
closed Sun evening and Mon, Dec–Jan,
Jul–Aug; inexpensive.

SANTO STEFANO BELBO *Club di
Bacco*, Via Cesare Pavese 18, ☎ 0141
843379; refined regional cuisine in the

house where writer Cesare Pavese was born; closed Mon, midday Tues–Fri and Jan; inexpensive.

SEROLE *Trattoria delle Langhe*, Via Concentrico 1, ☎ 0144 94108; good traditional trattoria in an otherwise desolate village; closed Tues, Fri and Nov–Dec; moderate.

TIGLIOLE D'ASTI *Vittoria*, Via Roma 14, ☎ 0141 667123; restaurant offering great food and fine views; closed Sun evening, Mon, Jan and Aug; moderate.

VALLE SAN BARTOLOMEO (ALESSANDRIA) *Da Pietro*, Piazza Dossena 1, ☎ 0131 59124; old-fashioned trattoria popular with locals; closed Wed and Aug; inexpensive.

VIGNALE MONFERRATO *Gabriella Trisoglio*, Ca' Ravino, San Lorenzo, ☎ 0142 933378; farm serving country meals, with a strong local following; closed Mon–Tues; moderate.

Villa San Secondo Per Bacco, Via Montechiaro 26, ☎ 0141 905525; wine bar and *osteria* especially popular on weekends; open evenings only, closed Tues; inexpensive.

Entertainment
Live music and **dancing** at Asti, Canelli, Cisterna, Isola d'Asti, Valfenera and Vigliano d'Asti.

Special events
ASTI The ancient *Palio d'Asti*, a pageant and horse race similar to that of Siena, takes place in early Sep, when there is also a wine fair.

CANELLI The *Assedio di Canelli* (Siege of Canelli) is re-enacted annually in Jun, with mock skirmishes, tableaux of daily life in 1613, and a huge public dinner.

Sports
Walking and, especially, **cycling** and **horse-riding** in the nature reserves of Rocchetta Tanaro, Val Sarmassa, Valle Andona and Valle Botto, and elsewhere in the hills around Asti and Alessandria.

ASTI AND ENVIRONS

Asti, an old Piedmontese city (population 74,000) and provincial capital, was founded by the Romans. It was particularly important in the 13C and became a possession of the house of Savoy after 1532. The main street is the long Corso Vittorio Alfieri, extending the whole length of the town. The Torre San Secondo, a Romanesque tower on a Roman base, serves as bell tower for the church of Santa Caterina (1773). The early 18C Palazzo Alfieri, birthplace of the poet Vittorio Alfieri (1749–1803), has collections devoted to his work. Beneath the adjoining school is the 8C crypt of the destroyed church of Sant'Anastasio, with fine capitals and an interesting lapidary collection.

The **Cathedral** is a Gothic building of 1309–54, with a bell tower of 1266 and a florid south porch of c 1470; the east end was extended in 1764–69. It contains stoups and a font with Roman elements, 18C stalls, and frescoes by Carlo Carlone and Francesco Fabbrica. Near the cloister is the small church of San Giovanni, covering a 7C or 8C crypt, perhaps the original baptistery.

The 18C **Palazzo Mazzetti** houses a small picture gallery, closed for restoration at the time of writing. In Piazza Medici is the ***Torre Troya**, the finest medieval tower in the city. The large Gothic church of **San Secondo** contains a fine polyptych by Gaudenzio Ferrari. At the extreme east end of the Corso is the church and cloister of **San Pietro in Consavia** (1467), which now contains a small local geological and archaeological collection (open Tues–Fri 09.00–13.00, 15.00–17.00; Sat 10.00–13.00, 15.00–18.00; Sun 10.00–13.00). It is adjoined by a circular 10C *baptistery.

Around Asti are several points of interest. There are fine Romanesque churches at Viatosto, Montechiaro and Cortazzone (northwest of Asti), for instance; and the hill-village of Castelnuovo Don Bosco, on the western border of the province, is the home of St John Bosco. He was born at Becchi, where a large Salesian pilgrimage church has been erected. Further north is Albugnano with the Benedictine *Abbey of Vezzolano** (open 09.00–13.00, 14.00–17.00 or 18.00), the finest group of Romanesque buildings in Piedmont, with remarkable sculptures, especially on the façade and the unusual rood-screen. The complex dates from 1095–1189.

Moncalvo, north of Asti, has a 14C Gothic church with paintings by the local artist, Guglielmo Caccia, called 'Moncalvo'. The local wines are renowned.

Roccaverano, in the southern corner of the province, is a typical cheese-making village of the Langhe, with a church (1509–16) in a Bramantesque style and the tall round tower (1204) of its ruined castle.

ALESSANDRIA AND ITS PROVINCE

Alessandria, a cheerful town (population 91,000) and capital of an interesting province, is important for its position, almost equidistant from Turin, Milan and Genoa. It was founded by seven castellans of the Monferrato who rebelled against Frederick Barbarossa in 1168 and named their new city after Pope Alexander III. Most of its buildings date from the 18C–19C. The **Palazzo della Prefettura** (1733), by Benedetto Alfieri, in the central Piazza della Libertà, is the best of the city's mansions. The 14C–15C church of **Santa Maria di Castello** incorporates remains of an earlier 6C church.

To the south of Alessandria is the battlefield of Marengo, where Napoleon defeated the Austrians on 14 June 1800, in a battle that he regarded as the most brilliant of his career. There is a small museum in the villa. The remarkable church of **Santa Croce** at **Bosco Marengo** was erected in 1567 by Pius V (d. 1572), a native of the village, as his mausoleum. His splendid tomb remains empty, however, as he is buried in Rome. The paintings include works by Giorgio Vasari.

The remains of the Roman town of **Libarna**, with traces of its *decumanus maximus*, amphitheatre and theatre, lie near Serravalle Scrivia. The communal cemetery at Arquata Scrivia contains 94 Second World War graves of British soldiers.

Nearby **Gavi** is an ancient little town with a 13C church. Above it towers a huge castle (open Tues–Sun May–Oct) reconstructed by the Genoese in 1626, surrounded by imposing bastions. **Voltaggio** is a summer resort in the upper Lemme valley, with a pinacoteca (art gallery) and local ethnographical museum. In the southern corner of Piedmont is the Capanne di Marcarolo nature reserve.

To the east of Alessandria, across the Scrivia, is the industrial town of **Tortona**. The church of Santa Maria Canale here may date from the 9C or 10C; it was altered in the 13C–14C. The **Museo Civico** (closed at the time of writing), in the 15C Palazzo Guidobono, contains relics of ancient Dertona, including the sarcophagus of Elio Sabino (3C AD), medieval works of art, and a 16C terracotta *Pietà*.

Acqui Terùe, southwest of Alessandria, is the Roman *Aquae Statiellae*, well known for its sulphurous waters and mud baths. The thermal waters (75°C) bubble up beneath a little pavilion in the middle of the town, known as **La Bollente** (1870), designed by the local architect Giovanni Ceruti. The Romanesque **Cathedral**, with a fine portal beneath a 17C loggia, still has its triple apse of the 11C, a campanile completed in the 13C, and a 15C Catalan triptych. In the public gardens are remains of the Paleologi family **castle**, with an archaeological museum (open Tues–Sat 16.00–19.00; Sun and holidays 10.00–12.00). The church of **San Pietro** has a fine 11C apse and octagonal campanile. On the other side of the River Bormida are four arches of a Roman aqueduct.

Nearby Ovada was the birthplace of St Paul of the Cross (Paolo Danei; 1694–1775), founder of the Passionist Order.

Casale Monferrato lies north of Alessandria, on the south bank of the Po. It is the chief town of the old duchy of Monferrato, whose princes of the Paleologi family held a famous court here from 1319 to 1533. In 1873 the first Italian Portland cement was made here, and the town was noted for its production of cement and artificial stone up to the Second World War. Excellent wines are produced in the vineyards of the Monferrato, including the red *Barbera* and *Grignolino*.

The **Cathedral**, consecrated in 1107, was over-restored in the 19C, but it preserves a remarkable narthex. Inside is a Romanesque sculpted crucifix. **San Domenico** is a late-Gothic church with a fine Renaissance portal of 1505. Via Mameli has a number of fine buildings, including Palazzo Treville by Giovanni Battista Scapitta (1725; Rococo atrium and courtyard), the 18C Palazzo Sannazzaro, Palazzo Gozani di San Giorgio (now the town hall, built in 1775 and still with its late 18C furnishings) and the church of San Paolo (1586). In Via Cavour the cloister of Santa Croce houses the municipal museum with sculptures by Leonardo Bistolfi (1859–1933) and late 16C paintings by Matteo da Verona, Moncalvo, etc.

The **Synagogue** (1595) contains an important **Museo Ebraico** (open Sun and holidays 10.00–12.00, 15.00–17.00, otherwise by appointment, ☎ 0142 71807). The huge Piazza Castello to the west, on the Po, surrounds the 14C castle (radically remodelled in the 19C); the church of Santa Caterina here is by Scapitta (c 1725). The Teatro Municipale is a very fine building (recently restored) dating from 1791.

To the west of Casale Monferrato, in a protected park, is the **Santuario di Crea**, founded in 1590 on the site of the refuge of St Eusebius, Bishop of Vercelli (340–70). The church (13C, altered 1608–12) has frescoes by Macrino d' Alba (1503) and a triptych of 1474. The 23 chapels of the Sacro Monte host late-15C sculptures by Tabacchetti and paintings by Moncalvo. The highest chapel, restored in 1995, contains frescoes attributed to Giorgio Albertini and remarkable terracotta statues by Tabacchetti hanging from the ceiling. It has a good view over the Monferrato.

To the north, on the Po, surrounded by a fine park, is the picturesque Castello di Camino (privately owned), the finest of a number of castles in the Monferrato. First built in the 11C and enlarged in the 15C, it was restored at the end of the 19C.

The northeast

Northeastern Piedmont includes the renowned ski areas of Monte Rosa and Monte Cervino (the Matterhorn), as well the romantic summer resorts of Lake Orta and Lake Maggiore. Economic life revolves around the textile trade (centred in Biella) and around large-scale farming, the chief product being the famous *arboreo* rice from which *risotto* is made.

Practical information

Getting there
By air

Milan Malpensa Airport, with domestic, European and intercontinental flights, lies just across the Ticino from northeastern Piedmont.

By road

Novara is located on the A4, 51km from Milan and 97km from Turin. The quickest way to Vercelli from Milan is by A4 and A26 and 11; from Turin, A4, A26 and 455. To reach Biella from Milan take the A4 to Carisio, then 230, 143 and local roads; from Turin, the A4 to Santhia then 143. The easiest route to Orta San Giulio from Milan is by the A8, A26, 142, 229 and local roads; from Turin, by the A4, A26, 229 and local roads. There is pay parking in the centre of Novara (free parking at Allea di San Luca) and at the entrance to Orta San Giulio, off the Via Panoramica ('Diania' and 'Prarondo'). Only cars with special permission are allowed into the centre of Orta.

By rail

The main rail line from Milan to Geneva, Bern and Basel passes through Domodossola and the Val d'Ossola; fast *Cisalpina*, *Eurocity* and *Intercity* trains make the 125km run from Milan to Domodossola with just one stop (at Stresa) in 1hr 10mins.

Novara and Vercelli are on the main Milan–Turin line; from Milan to

Novara, 46km in 30mins; to Vercelli, 68km in 45mins. From Turin to Vercelli, 79km in 40mins; to Novara, 95km in 50mins. Slower commuter services between Milan and Novara are operated by the Ferrovia Nord Milano (station at Corso Vittorio 15).

Secondary lines link Novara with Varallo Sesia, Arona, Luino, Alessandria, Biella (51km in 50mins; or from Turin, Via Santhià in 30mins) and Domodossola (90km in 2hrs10mins). Along the latter line, 44km (50mins) from Novara, is Orta-Masino Station, with some buses to the lakeside.

Getting around
By bus

Biella, Novara and Vercelli are connected to minor towns; the tourist information offices have up-to-date information on all routes.

By boat

Lake Orta boat services run from Easter to Oct to the Isola San Giulio (5mins) and Pella (20mins). A less frequent service runs from Orta via the Isola San Giulio and Pettenasco to Omegna (in 1hr 15mins). Information from *Navigazione Lago d'Orta*, ☎ 0322 844862. There is also a regular cheap motorboat service (c every 20mins) throughout the year from Piazza Motta to the Isola San Giulio.

Information offices

BIELLA Piazza Vittorio Veneto 3, ☎ 015 351128.

BOGNANCO Piazzale Giannini 5, ☎ 0324 234127.

NOVARA Via Dominioni 4, ☎ 0321 394059.

OSSOLA Corso Ferraris 49, ☎ 0324 481308.

ORTA SAN GIULIO Via Olina 9–11, ☎ 0322 911937. In summer there is another information office open on the approach road (Via Panoramica).

VARZO (PARCO NATURALE ALPE VEGLIA) Piazza Castelli 2, ☎ 0324 72572.

VERCELLI Viale Garibaldi 90, ☎ 0161 64631.

Where to stay

BIELLA *Astoria*, Via Roma 9, ☎ 015 402750, fax 015 849 1691; elegant and efficient, closed Aug; moderate.

Augustus, Via Orfanotrofio 6, tel. 015 27554, fax 015 29257; central and quiet; moderate.

Michelangelo, Piazza Adua 5, ☎ 015 849 2362, fax 015 849 2649; a small place, with courteous staff; moderate.

BOGNANCO *Villa Elda*, Via Marconi, ☎ 0324 234127, fax 0324 46975; small and comfortable, near the springs; open Easter–Sep, inexpensive.

DOMODOSSOLA *Corona*, Via Maroni 8, ☎ 0324 242114, fax 0324 242842; small, quiet and comfortable; inexpensive.

FORMAZZA *Pernice Bianca-Schneehendli*, Piano Cascata del Toce (5km north), ☎ 0324 63200, fax 0324 63200; small (6 rooms) and cosy, at 1700m with views of the mountains and cascades; inexpensive.

MACUGNAGA (VALLE ANZASCA) *Alpi*, Frazione Borca, ☎ 0324 65135, fax 0324 65135; a small, seasonal inn, open Dec–Apr and Jun–Sep; inexpensive.

Girasole, Via Monte Rosa 72, Frazione Staffa; another small, cosy Alpine inn;

inexpensive.

NOVARA *Italia*, Via Solaroli 10, ☎ 0321 399316, fax 0321 399310; modern and comfortable, if a bit austere; moderate.

Croce di Malta, Via Biglieri 2a, ☎ 0321 32032, fax 0321 623475; small and conveniently located, a short walk from the castle and cathedral; closed Aug; inexpensive.

Garden, Corso Garibaldi 25, ☎ 0321 625094, fax 0321 613320; quiet and convenient, across from the train station; inexpensive.

OROPA *Croce Bianca*, Via Santuario di Oropa 480, ☎ 015 245 5923, fax 015 245 5963; in the guest house of the sanctuary, with a good restaurant; inexpensive.

ORTA SAN GIULIO *Leon d'Oro*, Piazza Motta 1, ☎ 0322 90253, fax 0322 905646; in a fine old building with good views of Isola San Giulio; open Apr–Oct, moderate. *San Rocco*, Via Gippini 11, ☎ 0322 911977, fax 0322 911964; elegant and quiet, in a former convent with a lakefront terrace and pool; expensive.

SAN DOMENICO (VARZO) *Cuccini*, ☎ 0324 7061, fax 0324 7061; a delightful little mountain lodge; open Dec–Apr and Jun–Sep; inexpensive.

VARALLO (VALSESIA) *Sacro Monte*, at Sacro Monte (4km north), ☎ 0163 54254, fax 0163 51189; quiet and comfortable, open Mar–Dec; inexpensive.

VIVERONE *Marina*, ☎ 0161 987577, fax 0161 98689; simple but nice, with a lakefront garden; moderate.

VIZZOLA TICINO (27km northeast of Novara) *Villa Malpensa*, Via Sacconago 1, ☎ 0331 230944, fax 0331 230950; a lovely renovated villa with park and pool; moderate.

Eating out

BIELLA *Orso Poeta*, Via Orfanotrofio 7, ☎ 015 21252; restaurant offering great local atmosphere and cuisine; closed midday, Wed and Jan; moderate.

Prinz Grill, Via Torino 14, ☎ 015 53876; another restaurant offering good local dishes; closed Sun, Jan and Aug; moderate.

Good coffee and pastries at *Caffè Ferrua*, Via San Filippo 1.

BORGOMANERO *Pinocchio*, Via Matteotti 147, ☎ 0322 82273; restaurant renowned for its delicious personal interpretations of traditional recipes; closed Mon, Aug and Dec; expensive.

DOMODOSSOLA *Sciolla*, Piazza Convenzione 5, ☎ 0324 242633; trattoria with good local dishes; closed Wed, Jan and Aug–Sep; inexpensive.

MACUGNAGA (VALLE ANZASCA) *Chez Felice*, Frazione Staffa, ☎ 0324 65229, fax 0324 65037; typical mountain restaurant (with rooms); open Dec–Apr and Jun–Sep; moderate.

MAGNANO *La Bessa*, Frazione San Sudario 30, ☎ 015 679186; simple but satisfying trattoria; closed Thur and Nov; inexpensive.

NOVARA *Monte Ariolo*, Vicolo Monte Ariolo 2a, ☎ 0321 623394; restaurant serving traditional regional cuisine; closed midday Sat, Sun and Aug; moderate.

La Famiglia, Via Solaroli 8, ☎ 0321 399316; trattoria (with rooms) offering creative interpretations of traditional recipes; closed Fri and Aug; moderate.

ORTA SAN GIULIO *Taverna Antico Agnello*, Via Olina 18, ☎ 0322 90259; traditional osteria; closed Tues (except in Aug), Nov and Jan–Feb; moderate.

Villa Crespi, Via Fava 18 (1km east), ☎ 0322 911902, fax 0322 911919; excellent traditional restaurant (with rooms) in a Moorish folly with park on the outskirts of the town; closed Jan; moderate.

Sandwich bar: *L'Edera*, 11 Via Bersani. There are also a café and restaurant on the hill of Sacro Monte. Good places to picnic include the Passeggiata del Movero (on the lakeside, beyond Villa

Motta) and on the Sacro Monte.

PIODE (VALSESIA) *Giardini*, Via Umberto I 9, ☎ 0163 71135; small, refined restaurant with good wines; closed Mon and Sep; moderate. *Toma* and other local cheeses from *Caseificio Alta Val Sesia*, Via Varallo 5.

QUINTO VERCELLESE *Bivio*, Via Bivio 2, ☎ 0161 274131; good local restaurant with an outstanding wine list, 8km (5 Roman miles) north of Vercelli; closed Mon, Aug and Jan; moderate.

ROMAGNANO SESIA (VALSESIA) *Alla Torre*, Via I Maggio 75, ☎ 0163 826411; restaurant in the old village watchtower, offering traditional dishes with a creative twist; closed Mon; moderate.

Try also *Gelateria Corradini*, Via Grassi 8, for ice-cream; and *Pasticceria Costantino*, Via dei Martiri 9, for pralines, biscuits and the delicious signature cake, 'torta Costantino'.

SORISO *Al Soriso*, Via Roma 18, ☎ 0322 983228; restaurant (with rooms) offering truly memorable, creative cuisine; closed Mon, midday Tues, Jan and Aug; expensive.

VERCELLI *Il Giardinetto*, Via Sereno 3, ☎ 0161 257230, fax 0161 259311; restaurant (with rooms) known for its good regional cooking; closed Mon and Aug; inexpensive.

Entertainment
NOVARA *Teatro Coccia*, with a theatre and music season.

Special events
LAGO D'ORTA Annual *festival of early music* in Jun on the Isola San Giulio. The steps up to the parish church in Orta San Giulio are covered with flowers in Apr and May.

NOVARA Annual *festival of San Gaudenzio*, 22 Jan.

Sports
Golf (18 holes) near Biella at Magnano

(*Le Betulle*, open Apr–Nov, Tues–Sun, ☎ 015 679151). **Sailing** on the lake. **Skiing** in all the Alpine valleys, especially the Valle Anzasca. **Walking** in the hills around Lago d'Orta, in theParco naturale Alpe Veglia and in the Alpine valleys.

Vercelli

Vercelli (population 48,000) was a Roman municipium founded in 49 BC. It was noted in the 16C for its school of painters, including Giovanni Martino Spanzotti, Sodoma, Gaudenzio Ferrari and Bernardino Lanino. It is now the largest rice-producing centre in Europe.

Piazza Cavour is the old market square, with attractive arcades and the battlemented Torre dell'Angelo rising above the roofs. In Via Gioberti is the tall, square **Torre di Città**, dating from the 13C. **Corso Libertà** is the main street of the old town. **Palazzo Centoris** (no. 204) has a delightful interior *courtyard with frescoes and arcades in three tiers (1496). In Via Cagna is **San Cristoforo**, with crowded scenes frescoed by Gaudenzio Ferrari (1529–34), and the *Madonna of the Pomegranate* (1529), considered his masterpiece. The church of San Paolo (begun c 1260) has a Madonna by Bernardino Lanino.

The *Civico Museo Borgona** (open Tues–Fri 14.30–17.00 or 15.00–17.30; Sat–Sun 09.30–12.30) preserves the most important collection of paintings in Piedmont after the Galleria Sabauda in Turin. Founded by Antonio Borgogna (1822–1906), it was donated to the city by him together with the handsome Neo-classical palace and first opened to the public in 1907. It is especially representative of the Piedmontese schools. Highlights include the original Borgogna collection (works by Antonio da Viterbo, Francesco Francia, Marco Palmezzano, Bergognone and Bernardino Luini); a *Deposition*, a replica by Titian of his painting in the Louvre; early-16C *altarpieces by Defendente Ferrari and Lanino; 18C and 19C works by Angelica Kauffmann, Girolamo Induno, Filippo Palizzi and others; Flemish paintings, notably a 16C *Madonna and Child* by Hans Baldung Grien and works by Jan Brueghel the Elder, a *Holy Family* attributed to Andrea del Sarto and a collection of Meissen, Doccia and Ginori porcelain.

Nearby **San Francesco** is a restored church of 1292 containing a *St Ambrose* by Girolamo Giovenone (1535).

The **Museo Leone** (open Tues and Thur 15.00–17.30; Sun and holidays 10.00–12.00; closed Jan–Feb) is an unusual museum housing the collection of Camillo Leone (1830–1907), first opened to the public in 1910. The entrance is through the lovely courtyard of the 15C **Casa degli Alciati**, which has early-16C frescoes and wood ceilings. Rooms built in 1939 to connect the house with the Baroque Palazzo Langosco have a didactic display illustrating the history of Vercelli, interesting for its arrangement dating from the Fascist period. The 18C **Palazzo Langosco**, once the residence of Leone, retains part of its original decorations. There are also some mementoes of the *Risorgimento*.

In front of the station is the basilica of *Sant'Andrea** (1219–27), a largely Romanesque church showing Cistercian Gothic elements at a very early date for Italy. It was founded by Cardinal Guala Bicchieri with the revenues of the Abbey of St Andrew at Chesterton (Cambridgeshire) bestowed on him by his young ward, Henry III of England. The fine façade is flanked by two tall towers connected by a double arcade, and the cupola is topped by a third tower. The two lunettes hold sculptures by the school of Antelami. The detached campanile dates from 1407. Inside, the pointed arcades are carried on slender clustered piers, with shafts carried up unbroken to the springing of the vaults. The crossing and cupola are particularly fine. At the east end are intarsia stalls of 1514. The remains of the Cistercian abbey include a lovely cloister and chapterhouse.

Via Bicheri leads to the huge **Cathedral**, begun in 1572 to a design of Pellegrino Tibaldi, but preserving the Romanesque campanile of an older church. The octagonal chapel—built in 1698 and decorated in 1759—of the Blessed Amedeo IX of Savoy (who died in the castle 1472) contains his tomb and that of his successor Charles I (d. 1490). The chapter library includes the 4C *Evangelistary of St Eusebius* (in a 12C binding); some Anglo-Saxon poems (11C); the *Laws of the Lombards* (8C); and other early manuscripts, perhaps relics of the *Studium*, or early university, which flourished here from 1228 for about a century.

Around Vercelli: the Valsesia

The Valsesia is a lovely valley famous for its lace. Here is **Valduggia**, the birthplace of Gaudenzio Ferrari (1471–1546); the church of San Giorgio has a *Nativity* by him, and a *Madonna* by Bernardino Luini. **Varallo**, the capital of the upper Valsesia, is famous for its *****Sacro Monte**, the ascent to which begins at the church of Madonna delle Grazie, with *frescoed scenes of the life of Christ by Ferrari (1513). The sanctuary (608m; reached on foot in 20mins or by cable railway or road), was founded c 1486 by the Blessed Bernardino Caimi, a Friar Minor. The 45 chapels, completed in the late 17C, recall various holy sites in Jerusalem and are decorated by local artists—Ferrari, Giovanni Tabacchetti, Giovanni d'Errico and Morazzone. Tabacchetti's best chapels are the *Temptation* (no. 38; with a *Crucifixion* by Ferrari) and *Adam and Eve* (no. 1); d'Errico's is the *Vision of St Joseph* (no. 5). The Basilica dell'Assunta, dating from 1641–49, has a façade of 1896.

Rimella (1180m), north of Varallo in the picturesque **Val Mastallone**, retains many traces in its dialect of the German-speaking colony from the Valais that migrated here in the 14C.

Above Varallo the Valsesia is known as *Valgrande*. **Alagna Valsesia** (1183m) is a fashionable summer and winter resort. The Museo Walser occupies a characteristic wooden house here. The Funivia di Monte Rosa, a cableway in three stages, rises to Punta Indren (3260m), another resort. The Regina Margherita CAI Refuge observatory (4559m), on the site of a hut built here in 1893 and inaugurated by Queen Margherita, is the highest refuge in Europe.

Biella and its province

Biella, on the River Cervo, is the capital (population 48,000) of a small province. A funicular railway connects the lower town, site of a 10C *****baptistery** and the Renaissance church of San Sebastiano, with the upper town and its 15C–16C mansions. The Villa Sella (open by appointment, ☎ 015 23778) was the home of the photographer, alpinist, and explorer Vittorio Sella (1859–1943). The Istituto Nazionale di Fotografia Alpina Vittorio Sella here conserves his remarkable collection of negatives made during mountain expeditions in Europe, Asia, Africa and Alaska, as well as his photographic equipment.

Northwest of Biella is **Pollone** with the **Parco della Burcina**, created in 1849 by Giovanni Piacenza. It has fine trees and flowers, and is noted especially for its rhododendrons, in flower May–June. Beyond is the sanctuary of **Oropa** (1181m), the most popular pilgrimage resort in Piedmont and one of the more famous in Italy. Said to have been founded by St Eusebius in 369, it consists of a large hospice of three quadrangles that can house hundreds of visitors, a modest church by Filippo Juvarra, and a grander church, with a large dome, begun in 1885 to a design by Ignazio Galletti (1774) and completed in 1960.

South of Biella is **Gaglianico**, which has a splendid castle, mainly 16C, with a well-decorated courtyard. **Candelo** has a remarkable *Ricetto*, or communal fortress and storehouse, built in the 14C as a refuge for the townsfolk.

A panoramic road in the northern part of the province, built by Count Ermenegildo Zegna in 1939, leads west from Trivero through Caulera (1080m), with lovely woods of rhododendrons and fine views north to Monte Rosa.

Novara

Novara, a Roman town, was occupied in 569 by the Lombards and became a free city-state in 1116. Important battles were fought here throughout the town's history. Lodovico il Moro, Duke of Milan, was taken prisoner by the French after one of them, in 1500. The last famous battle, in 1849, resulted in the defeat of the Piedmontese by Radetzky's Austrians. Carlo Alberto of Savoy abdicated in favour of his son, Vittorio Emanuele II, in the town that same evening, marking the beginning of the *Risorgimento* movement in Italy.

Today Novara is an extremely pleasant and well-kept provincial capital (population 102,000). Its streets are paved in granite and porphyry, quarried locally, and it has particularly good 19C architecture.

In the arcaded Via Fratelli Rosselli is the **Duomo**, rebuilt by Alessandro Antonelli in 1865–69 with a Neo-classical colonnade. Six Brussels tapestries (1565) by Jan de Buck hang in the gloomy interior. Behind the huge orange stucco columns, on the south side, are a 14C carved wooden crucifix, an altarpiece by Gaudenzio Ferrari (c 1525–30), and works by Bernardino Lanino. The chapel of San Siro, which survives from the earlier church, contains damaged late 12C frescoes; the *Crucifixion* dates from the 14C. The adjoining 18C room contains frescoes by Bernardino Lanino (1546–53) from the old cathedral, and paintings by Gaudenzio Ferrari and Callisto Piazza da Lodi.

Remarkable black-and-white mosaic panels from the old cathedral, dating from the 12C, with symbols of the Evangelists, Adam and Eve, and other biblical subjects, are displayed in the sacristy. The Neo-classical high altar is by Antonelli and Thorvaldsen. On the north side are a reliquary bust of St Bernardo of Aosta (1424) and an altarpiece by Giuseppe Nuvolone. The 16C **chiostro della canonica** has an interesting lapidary collection founded in 1813.

The **baptistery** is a centrally planned octagonal building of the late 4C, with 1C Classical columns and an 11C cupola. High up above the windows are very worn 11C frescoes of the Apocalypse, one of them covered with a 15C *Last Judgement*. The funerary monument of Umbrena Polla (1C AD) was once used as a font.

Opposite the duomo is the entrance to the finely paved courtyard of the **Broletto**, a medley of buildings dating from the 13C and 15C with terracotta windows and remains of frescoes above Gothic arches. The third side dates from the 18C. Here is the entrance to the **Museo Civico** (open Tues–Sat 09.00–12.00, 15.00–18.00), founded in 1874–90. Inside are terracotta statuettes, 17C–18C paintings, an archaeological collection including finds dating from the Golasecca culture (9C–8C BC) and the Roman period, and medieval ceramics and sculpture.

Via Fratelli Rosselli, with porticoes, leads east to the arcaded Piazza delle Erbe, the old centre of the town. In the other direction, Classical colonnades continue past a statue of Carlo Emanuele III (by Pompeo Marchesi, 1837) to Piazza Martiri della Libertà, with an equestrian statue of Vittorio Emanule II by Ambrogio Borghi (1881). Here are the handsome Neo-classical buildings of the huge **Teatro Coccia** (1888) and **Palazzo del Mercato** (1817–44). You can see some remains of the Sforza castle on the south side of the piazza. In Via Dominioni is the yellow building of the former **Collegio Gallarini** (restored as a music conservatory), with remarkable late-19C terracotta decoration and a coloured roof. There are also stretches of Roman walls here, in a little park.

Leave the courtyard of the Broletto by Corso Italia. Via San Gaudenzio, on your left, continues north to the church of **San Gaudenzio**, built 1577–1690 on a design by Pellegrino Tibaldi. The church has a fine brick exterior. The *cupola, crowned by an elaborate spire 121m high, is by Alessandro Antonelli (1844–80). The campanile (92m) is another exceptionally original work by Benedetto Alfieri (1753–86). Within, on the south side, are works by Morazzone, Fiammenghino and Gaudenzio Ferrari. The Baroque chapel of San Gaudenzio opens off the south transept. On the north side are works by Ferrari (a polyptych of 1514 in a beautiful frame), Paolo Camillo Landriani, Tanzio da Varallo and Giacinto Brandi.

In the nearby Via Ferrari, **Palazzo Faraggiana** is being restored as the seat of the natural history, ethnographical and music museums. In Via Negroni is the church of **San Marco** (1607), with good woodwork and a painting by Daniele Crespi (1626).

Via Fratelli Rosselli is continued east by Via Canobio, in which are two fine old palaces—Palazzo Natta-Isola, attributed to Pellegrino Tibaldi, and the Casa dei Medici by Seregni.

To the west of the town, on the River Sesia, is the abbey of **San Nazzaro Sesia**, with remains of a fortified Benedictine abbey, including a 15C church and cloister. To the north is **Oleggio**, where the Romanesque church of San Michele has frescoes of the 11C and 13C. Further north is **Agrate Conturbia**, with a nature reserve and an interesting baptistery in front of the church.

LAGO D'ORTA

Lago d'Orta is a beautiful little lake 13km long and about 1km wide, surrounded by mountains. It lies at the northern end of the province of Novara, just west of the much more famous Lake Maggiore. The most attractive place on the lake is

Orta San Giulio, with the little Isola San Giulio just offshore. Sailing regattas are held here in the summer. The lake, also called Cusio (from the Roman *Cusius*), has been admired by numerous travellers over the centuries, including Honoré de Balzac and Friedrich Nietzsche. Its only outlet is the little River Nigoglia, which flows northwards from Omegna (all the other subalpine Italian lakes have southern outflows). The waters of the lake were polluted in the first half of this century by acid effluents from a few factories, but they were cleaned in 1989–90 when the lake surface was spread with a finely powdered natural limestone (a technique known as liming).

*Orta San Giulio is a charming lakeside village with elegant buildings, well equipped with pleasant hotels and restaurants. It has a remarkably peaceful atmosphere, with picturesque narrow old streets and cobbled lanes leading down to the lake, and a splendid view of the Isola San Giulio. It has many attractive houses, most of them built from the 16C to 18C, and some grand villas on the outskirts.

In Piazza Motta, which opens onto the lake, is the lovely little **Palazzo della Comunità**, the former town hall, built in 1582. Nearby, a wide thoroughfare with steps, known as La Motta, leads up past a number of handsome palaces—including the Neo-classical Palazzo Fortis Penotti opposite the 16C frescoed Palazzo Gemelli—to the **parish church**, with a decorative façade (1941) and an 11C doorway. The Baroque interior has interesting frescoes and works by Carlo Beretta, Giulio Cesare Procaccini, Morazzone and Fermo Stella.

A lane to the right of the church (Via Gemelli) continues uphill for 20 minutes past the cemetery (with an 18C wrought-iron gate) to an avenue (left) that ends at the monumental gateway of the *Sacro Monte (you can also get there by car from the Via Panoramica). On this low wooded hill (396m), now a park with some rare plants (including palm trees), are 20 pretty little chapels dedicated to St Francis of Assisi. Most of them were built between 1592 and 1670, and they contain remarkable groups of life-size terracotta figures illustrating scenes from the life of the saint, as well as frescoes.

A path beyond the gateway (usually kept unlocked 09.30–16.00; otherwise enquire at the Capuchin monastery at the top of the hill) continues straight uphill, with good views over the lake, and then leads through the woods past the chapels. Most of these were designed by Padre Cleto (1556–1619), and each has a different ground plan, usually with a pretty loggia or porch. There are notices in each chapel describing the works of art. Carved wooden or wrought-iron screens protect the sculptures from visitors; the best are the earliest (1607–17) by Cristoforo Prestinari (chapels I–VI, XI and XV). The other sculptures are by Giovanni and Melchiorre d'Enrico (1624–34), Dionigi Bussola, Bernardo Falcone, Giuseppe Rusnati (all late-17C), and Carlo Beretta (mid-18C). The 17C frescoes are by Giacomo Filippo Monti, the della Rovere brothers, Antonio Maria Crespi, Il Rocca, Carlo Francesco and Giuseppe Nuvolone, Morazzone, Giacomo Filippo Monti, Giovanni Battista and Girolamo Grandi, Federico Bianchi, Federico Ferrari, Stefano Maria Legnani, and Antonio Busca.

A gravel lane at the northern end of the town, beyond the Hotel San Rocco, leads past a few villas and ends at the wrought-iron gate in front of the pink **Villa Motta**, built in the late 19C in Venetian style and surrounded by a pretty garden (which you can visit by appointment Mar–Dec, ☎ 024 800 9161). First laid out in 1880, it has camellias, rhododendrons and azaleas, and some fine trees. A delightful path, called the **Passeggiata del Movero**, continues to the left round the headland, following the water's edge past more villas with their boathouses (including an eccentric Art Nouveau villa) and lawns.

Outside the town, on the Via Panoramica, is **Villa Crespi** (now a hotel), a remarkable building in the Arab style.

Isola San Giulio, a picturesque little island just offshore, is especially beautiful from a distance (the best view, which changes constantly according to the light, is from Orta San Giulio). With a perimeter of just 650m, it has no cars and hardly any shops.

Isola San Giulio

There is only one lane, which circles round the island past a few villas. The huge former seminary building, with an overgrown garden, is now a Benedictine convent. The 30 nuns (closed order) run a restoration centre here and offer hospitality for retreats.

Boats dock in front of the basilica of **San Giulio**, traditionally thought to have been founded by St Julius. This saint is supposed to have purged the island of serpents and other dangerous beasts in 390—though the first written document testifying to his cult dates from 590 (Paolo Diacono). The interior of the church is Baroque, but there are 14C–16C frescoes. The *pulpit, or *ambone*, in dark Oira marble, dates from the 11C–12C, and the sombre carvings show German influence.The white marble sarcophagus with Roman carvings now serves as an almsbox. Some of the chapels are decorated with 15C Lombard frescoes, one of which is attributed to Gaudenzio Ferrari.

In 962 the island was defended by Willa, wife of Berengar II of Lombardy, against the incursions of the Emperor Otho the Great: the charter of Otho giving thanks for his eventual capture of the island is preserved in the sacristy. The whale's vertebra here is supposed to be a bone of one of the serpents destroyed by St Julius. Fragments of exquisite marble intarsia panels of the 4C–5C, from the cenotaph of the saint (formerly in the apse, destroyed in 1697), are displayed in a room off the crypt. The body of St Julius, and a Greek marble panel incised with the palm, peacock and Cross (6C–7C), also are preserved here.

On the other side of the lake is **Pella**, with a little port. The terraced hills above the town hold some small villages and the sanctuary of the **Madonna del Sasso**, built in 1748 on a granite spur overlooking the lake (panoramic view).

Vacciago lies between Orta San Giulio and Gozzan, to the south. A handsome collection of modern art (open mid-May–mid-Oct, Tues–Sun 10.00–12.00, 15.00–18.00) is displayed in the former home of the painter Antonio Calderara (1903–78), a 17C villa built in Renaissance-revival style. At the southern end of the lake is a hill crowned by the tall (24m) Torre di Buccione, a Lombard watch-tower.

Omegna, a small manufacturing town at the north end of the lake, retains a few old houses, a medieval bridge, and an ancient town gate. It lies at the foot of the Valstrona, a narrow winding glen that descends from the Laghetto di Capezzone (2104m), a lovely tarn beneath the Cima di Capezzone (2420m).

A by-road leads from Omegna to **Quarna Sotto**, where wind instruments have been made since the early 19C. The Forni manufactory was succeeded here by the Rampone company at the end of the century. A small museum (open Jul–Aug, 16.00–19.00) illustrates the history of the craft of making woodwind and brass instruments and preserves a collection of clarinets, oboes, saxophones, flutes and brasses. Another section is devoted to farm life in the valley.

The Val d'Ossola

This Alpine district in the northernmost corner of Piedmont is bordered on three sides by Switzerland. Formerly in the province of Novara, it has recently become part of the new province of Verbania. The main town is Domodossola, at the entrance to Italy from the Simplon Pass and railway tunnel, and it has seven beautiful Alpine valleys, including the Valle Anzasca beneath Monte Rosa. Many of these have scenic hiking trails and are also visited by skiiers and climbers.

Domodossola became important as a halting place for travellers after the opening of the road over the Simplon Pass by Napoleon in 1805 and the construction of the railway tunnel through the Alps in 1906. It is still an important rail junction and preserves its grand station, built in 1906. Of Roman origin, it is the main town in the Val d'Ossola and has expanded in a disorderly way around its tiny old centre. The inhabitants played an important part in the Resistance movement in 1944.

Corso Ferraris leads from the station to the old part of the town. Beyond Piazza Cinque Vie is the pretty arcaded Piazza Mercato, with 15C–16C houses, some with balconies and loggias. A market is held here on Saturday. Just off the Piazza is the handsome grey-and-white Teatro Municipale Galletti.

Via Paletta leads from Piazza Mercato to Piazza della Chiesa and the church of **Santi Gervaso e Protasio**, which has a façade rebuilt in 1953 but retains an old porch with 15C frescoes. **Palazzo Silva** is a handsome building, begun in 1519 and enlarged in 1640, with a frieze, pretty windows and a spiral staircase. It houses the **Museo Galletti** (open for guided visits, Wed 15.00–18.00, Sat–Sun 10.00–12.00 and 15.00–18.00), which includes a room illustrating the construction of the Simplon tunnel, material relating to the flight of Georges Chavez (the Peruvian airman who was killed in his fall near Domodossola after having made the first flight over the Alps, 29 September 1910), a small *pinacoteca* (art gallery) and a natural history collection. Via Carina is an attractive old street with wooden balconies and water channelled beneath the paving stones. To the north, on Via Monte Grappa, is an old medieval tower.

To the west of the town in a protected park is an interesting **Via Crucis**, with a view from the top. The 14 chapels, built from the 17C to the 19C, each on a different design, contain life-size sculptures of the *Passion of Christ* by Dionisio Bussola, Giuseppe Rusnati and others, as well as frescoes.

The **Val Divedro**, northwest of Domodossola, leads to the Simplon Pass. The **Parco Naturale di Alpe Veglia** (1753m), below Monte Leone (3552m), has beautiful scenery, with meadows and larch woods laced with hiking trails. Excavations here in 1990 uncovered a mesolithic site.

Two ways across the Alps

Whether you travel by rail or by car, Domodossola is the traditional gateway between Piedmont and Switzerland.

The **Simplon Railway Tunnel** is the longest rail tunnel in the world (19.8km); its first gallery was constructed in 1898–1905. It is also the lowest of the great Alpine tunnels, with a maximum elevation of only 705m—which means there are 2134m of mountain overhead where the main ridge is pierced.

The **Simplon Pass** (2009m; *Passo del Sempione*) is wholly on Swiss soil. It became important when Napoleon chose it, after the battle of Marengo, as the route for the Simplon road connecting the Rhône valley with the northern Italian plain (182km from Geneva to Sesto Calende). It was begun on the Italian side in 1800, on the Swiss side a year later, and was completed in 1805. About 1km below the summit on the south side is the Simplon Hospice (2001m), built by Napoleon as barracks in 1811 and acquired by the monks of St Bernard in 1825.

The upper **Val d'Ossola**, with spectacular scenery, vineyards, fig trees, and chestnut woods, extends north to Switzerland. The Alpe Devero (1640m) is in the centre of a park with fine scenery and Alpine lakes. The beautiful Val Formazza is an interesting region colonised in the Middle Ages by German-speaking families from the Valais. The *Cascata della Frua (1675m) is one of the great waterfalls of the Alps (viewable on Sun Jun–Sep). The road ends at the Passo di San Giacomo (2315m).

The **Val Vigezzo**, followed by a spectacular railway line to Locarno opened in 1923, has been visited by artists since the 19C. Santa Maria Maggiore has a little museum illustrating the work of chimneysweeps.

In the Valle d'Antrona is the beautiful little *Lago d'Antrona (1083m), formed in 1642 by a landslip from the Cima di Pozzoli (2546m) to the north.

The **Valle Anzasca** also has spectacular mountain scenery, beneath Monte Rosa (Dufourspitze, 4638m); Macugnaga (1326m) is its most important resort.

LOMBARDY

Lombardy, with Milan—the largest city in northern Italy—as its capital, has played an important part in the making of Italy. The region includes areas of remarkable diversity within its boundaries, extending as it does from the summits of the central Alps to the low-lying fertile plain of the Po. Some of the lovelier scenery in the country surrounds the great Italian Lakes (all of which, except Orta, are wholly or partly in Lombardy). The Lombard provinces are Bergamo, Brescia, Como, Cremona, Lecco, Lodi, Mantua, Milan, Pavia, Sondrio and Varese.

In Roman times the centre of Cisalpine Gaul, Lombardy takes its present name from the Lombards, one of the barbarian tribes that invaded Italy in the 6C. They settled in various parts of the peninsula and founded several states; that which centred roughly round Milan became the most important and retained the founders' name.

The association of Lombardy with transalpine powers dates from the time of Charlemagne, and Lombardy, though actually under the control of the Bishops of Milan, remained nominally a part of the Germanic Empire until the 12C. At this time the more important Lombard cities, having freed themselves of the temporal power of the bishops, formed the Lombard League, which defeated the Emperor Frederick Barbarossa at Legnano in 1176. In the following two centuries local dynasties held despotic power, the richest of which also encouraged the arts within their dominions: these included the Torriani, Visconti and Sforza at Milan, Pavia, Cremona, and Bergamo; the Suardi and Colleoni at Bergamo; the Pallavicini, Torriani, Scaligeri and Visconti at Brescia; and the Bonacolsi and Gonzaga at Mantua.

The Venetian Republic encroached on the eastern part of the region after the fall of the powerful Visconti rulers at the beginning of the 15C. Lombard territory was invaded by the kings of France in the 16C, and in 1535 the Duchy of Milan became a dependency of the Spanish Habsburgs, though Ticino and the Valtellina in the north were incorporated into the Swiss Confederation. With the extinction of the Habsburg line in Spain, Lombardy was transferred to the Austrian dominion and, with the brief intervention of the Napoleonic Cisalpine Republic and the French kingdoms of Lombardy and of Italy (1797–1814), it remained a subject-province of Austria, the Valtellina being detached from Switzerland in 1797. National aspirations were repressed by the Austrian military governors of the 19C until the victory of the allied French and Piedmontese brought Lombardy beneath the Italian flag in 1859.

> ### Lombardy and the poets
>
> Lombardy has always been celebrated for its beauty and fertility. The first to term it 'Italy's garden' was, perhaps, Shakespeare: in *The Taming of the Shrew* (c 1593–4) Lucentio speaks of 'fruitfull *Lumbardie*, / The pleasant garden of great *Italy*'. The Bard was soon seconded, in this judgement, by others—for example, the 17th-century traveller Thomas Coryate, who wrote: 'Surely such is the fertility of this country, that I thinke no Region or Province under the Sunne may compare with it. For it is passing plentifully furnished with all things, tending both to pleasure and profit, being the very Paradise, and Canaan of Christendome. For if Italy is the garden of the world, so is Lombardy the garden of Italy.'
>
> From the Euganian Hills (now in the neighbouring Veneto) Percy Bysshe Shelley observed, in 1818: 'Beneath is spread like a green sea / The waveless plain of Lombardy / Bounded by the vaporous air / Islanded by cities fair'. His metaphor of Lombard cities as islands in a sea of green was reworked and re-employed by countless other writers in his century—you can hear it echo, for instance, in this description penned by J.A. Symonds, author of *Sketches and Studies in Italy and Greece*, in 1874: 'The cities of Lombardy are all like large country houses: walking out of their gates you seem to be stepping from a door or window that opens on a trim and beautiful garden, where mulberry tree is married to mulberry by festoons of vines, and where the maize and sunflower stand together in rows between patches of flax and hemp'. Visit Lombardy today in late spring or early summer, and you'll find the garden metaphor still rings true.

Milan and environs

Milan, in Italian *Milano*, is the principal commercial and industrial centre of the country. It is also the second largest city in Italy (population 1,304,000). It has the appearance and characteristics of a busy modern city, with excellent shops, theatres and restaurants. At the same time it is a place of great historical and artistic interest, with magnificent art collections (notably the Brera Gallery), a remarkable Gothic cathedral and many important churches, including Santa Maria delle Grazie, home to the famous fresco of *The Last Supper* by Leonardo da Vinci. It has the most efficient public transport system of any town in Italy, featuring a wide network of trams as well as underground railway lines and buses. The Scala opera house is still world-famous. Many of the large palaces of Milan have handsome courtyards; some of the more interesting are to be found on Via Borgonuovo and Via Brera (most of them are marked with yellow signs). Huge 19C residential blocks with numerous apartments arranged around pretty interior courtyards are characteristic of the city. The northern skyline is punctuated by skyscrapers, and Milan is a good place to study 19C and 20C Italian architecture.

Rapid industrial and residential development have all but eliminated the beautiful meadows and tall poplar forests that once surrounded Milan. Today the most interesting place in the environs is Monza, an affluent town with a fine old cathedral and grand royal villa, just 15km northeast of the city centre. Lodi, some 31km distance to the southeast, also has some noteworthy sights.

Practical information

Getting there
By air

Milan is served by two airports: Malpensa, 45km northwest, for most international and domestic flights, and Linate, 7km east, for a few international and domestic flights and the shuttle to Rome. **Bus 73** runs to Linate from Piazza San Babila (**Map II, 8**) every 10mins (the bus stop is near the underground station of San Babila on line 1). There are also airport express buses from the central station (Piazza Luigi di Savoia; **Map I, 4**) to both airports every 20–30mins. When using a Milanese airport as your Italian gateway bear in mind that there is a long-term plan to move all traffic except the Milan–Rome shuttle from Linate to Malpensa. For information on both airports, ☎ 02 7485 2200.

By road

Northern Italy's major *autostrade* all converge on the *tangenziale*, or ring road, around Milan. These include the A9 from Switzerland, the A4 from Venice and Turin, the A1 from Rome, the A7 from Genoa and the A8 from Varese and Lake Maggiore. To drive from Milan to Lodi , take the A1 or 9 (Via Emilia); you'll find parking in Lodi in Viale Dalmazia.To Monza, the A4 or 36. There is a bus from Milan (Via Jacini, near Nord station; or Piazza 4 Novembre, beside the central station) in 20mins.

A comprehensive network of **country buses** run by the *Trasporti Regione Lombardia* serves western Milan and the province of Varese, southern Milan and the province of Pavia, and the Brianza in the north. The *autostradali* from Piazza Castello run to the main towns in northern Italy.

By rail

Milan has several railway stations. The most important by far is *Centrale* (**Map I, 4**), Piazzale Duca d'Aosta, northeast of the centre, for all main services of the *FS* (☎ 02 675001). Some international expresses stop only at *Lambrate* (on the east side of the city, beyond **Map I, 4**). *Nord* (**Map II, 5**) handles services of the Nord–Milano railway (for Como, Novara, etc.). *Porta Genova* (**Map I, 13**) has trains for Alessandria (with connections to Genoa). Subsidiary stations include *Porta Vittoria* (beyond **Map I, 3**). *FS Lost Property Office*, 108 Via Sammartini (☎ 02 67712667).

There are trains from Milan (Stazione Centrale) to Lodi roughly hourly throughout the day (more frequent at rush hours). Travel time is c 45mins. Frequent train service from Milan (Porta Garibaldi station) to Monza in 10–15mins. Inaugurated in 1840, this was the second line to be opened in Italy.

Getting around
By car

Traffic is heavy in the centre of Milan and parking is restricted at all times. If you are travelling by car, you are strongly advised make the most of the excellent public transport system. There are free car parks by the underground stations of Pagano (on Line 1) and Lambrate (Line 2), and fee-paying car parks at Rogoredo (Line 3) and Romolo (Line 2). Car Pound, Piazza Beccaria (city police station, ☎ 02 77271).

By public transport

The underground lines, buses and trams run by *ATM* are very efficient. Information offices (with a map of the system) in the underground station of Piazza Duomo and at the central railway station (☎ 02 89010797). Tickets (which can be used on buses, trams or the underground) are valid for 1hr 15mins (flat rate fare). They are sold at *ATM* offices, automatic machines at bus stops, and news-stands and tobacconists, and must be stamped on board. Tickets valid for 24 or 48 hours can also be purchased at *ATM* offices or news-stands.

Some of the tram and bus lines most useful to the visitor are the following. **Trams: 1** Milano Centrale railway station—Piazza Cavour—Piazza Scala—Largo Cairoli (for the Castello Sforzesco)—Milano Nord railway station—Corso Sempione. **4** Piazza Repubblica—Via Manzoni—Piazza Scala—Via Legnano—Via Farini. **24** Via Mazzini—Corso Magenta (Santa Maria delle Grazie, for *The Last Supper*). **19** Corso Sempione—Milano Nord railway station—Via Broletto—Via Orefici (for the duomo)—Via Torino.

Buses: 50, **54** Largo Augusto (Duomo)—Corso Magenta—Via Carducci (for Sant'Ambrogio)—Via San Vittore. **61** Corso Matteotti—Piazza Scala—Via Brera—Via Solferino (for San Marco). **65** Milano Centrale railway station—Via San Gregorio—Corso Buenos Aires—Corso Venezia—Piazza Fontana—Via Larga—Corso Italia—Porta Lodovico.

Underground (Metro: M): Three lines are now open: **Line 1** (red) from Sesto railway station to Bisceglie and Molino Dorino. The central section runs from Loreto Via Lima, Porta Venezia, Palestro, San Babila, Duomo, Cordusio, Cairoli (for Castello Sforzesco) to Cadorna (for Milan Nord station). **Line 2** (green) from Gessate and Cologno Nord to Famagosta in its central section links the railway stations of Lambrate, Centrale, Garibaldi, Milano Nord (Cadorna) and (by way of Sant'Ambrogio) Porta Genova. **Line 3** (yellow) from Sondrio to San Donato links the central station Via Repubblica, Turati and Monte Napoleone with the Duomo and continues along Corso di Porta Romana to southern Milan.

Taxis: various companies run taxi services, and as in the rest of Italy there are no cruising taxis. ☎ 02 5353; 02 6767; 02 8585, etc.

Information offices

MILAN Via Marconi 1 (Piazza Duomo; **Map II, 11**), ☎ 02 7252 4300; Stazione Centrale (**Map 1, 4**), ☎ 02 7252 4360. Available at most hotels is the tourist board's free a booklet on Milan, *Milano Mese*, with a map of the city and a summary of current events. See your concierge for details. *Informagiovani*, Corso di Porta Ticinese 106, ☎ 02 6208 5215, is a special office for students.
LODI Piazza Broletto 4, ☎ 0371 421391.
MONZA Palazzo Comunale, ☎ 039 323222.

Where to stay

There are nearly 400 hotels in Milan, but very few nice ones (and most of these are at the high end). A brief selection follows. Bear in mind that it is difficult to find accommodation when big international trade fairs are in progress (Feb–Mar and Sep–Nov).
MILAN *Adriatico*, Via Conca del Naviglio 20, ☎ 02 5810 4141, fax 02 8940 1012; comfortable and centrally located, between Sant'Ambrogio and San Lorenzo; moderate.

Antica Locanda Solferino, Via Castelfidardo 2, ☎ 02 657 0129, fax 02 657 1361; in the heart of the Brera district, Milan's 'left bank', with a wide following of return clients; inexpensive (book well in advance).

Brunelleschi, 12 Via Baracchini, ☎ 02 8843, fax 02 804 924; an elegant Postmodern creation in the heart of the historic centre; expensive.

Carlton Baglioni, Via Senato 5, ☎ 02 77077, fax 02 78330; modern and comfortable, on the edge of the historic city centre; expensive.

De la Ville, Via Hoepli 6, ☎ 02 867651, fax 02 866609; comfortable and strategically located between the Cathedral, La Scala and the shopping district; expensive.

Four Seasons, Via Gesù 8, ☎ 02 77088, fax 02 7708 5000; the usual high standard of luxury offered by this international group, in a beautifully restored convent in the shopping district; expensive.

Gran Duca di York, Via Moneta 1a, ☎ 02 874863, fax 02 869 0344; a comfortable hotel in a carefully restored early 19C townhouse; moderate.

Grand Hotel et de Milan, Via Manzoni 29, ☎ 02 723141, fax 02 8646 0861; Milan's finest for over 130 years, in a centrally located, tastefully renovated patrician palace; expensive.

Manin, Via Manin 7, ☎ 02 659 6511, fax 02 655 2160; central, quiet and comfortable, overlooking the public gardens; expensive.

Manzoni, Via Santo Spirito 20, ☎ 02 7600 5700, fax 02 784212; quiet, comfortable and popular, in the heart of the shopping district; moderate (book in advance).

Pierre Milano, Via De Amicis 32, ☎ 02 7200 0581, fax 02 805 2157; quiet and atmospheric, in the historic city centre; expensive.

Principe di Savoia, Piazza della Repubblica 17, ☎ 02 62301, fax 02 659 5838; a luxury hotel popular with Americans, in a shady square midway between the Stazione Centrale and the historic city centre; expensive.

Sir Edward, Via Mazzini 4, ☎ 02 877877, fax 02 877844; a refined establishment with 38 rooms, on the edge of the shopping district; expensive.

Youth hostel, Via Salmoiraghi 2, ☎ 02 39267095.

LODI *Europa*, Viale Pavia 5, Lodi, ☎ 0371 35215, fax 0371 36281; classic small-town hotel, simple but comfortable; closed Aug and Dec–Jan; inexpensive.

MONZA *De la Ville*, Viale Regina Margherita 15, ☎ 039 382581, fax 039 367647; a fine old place (recently renovated) near the Villa Reale; closed Aug and Dec–Jan; expensive.

Della Regione, Via Elvezia 4, ☎ 039 387205, fax 039 380254; modern and business-like; moderate.

Eating out

MILAN *Aimo e Nadia*, Via Montecuccoli 6, ☎ 02 416886, is generally considered Milan's finest restaurant, offering traditional and innovative cuisine; closed midday Sat and Sun, Aug and Jan; expensive.

Alfredo Gran San Bernardo, Via Borgese 14, ☎ 02 331 9000; restaurant known especially for its risotti; closed Sun, Aug and Dec–Jan; expensive.

Al Girarrosto da Cesarina, Corso Venezia 31, ☎ 02 7600 0481; restaurant specialising in Tuscan cuisine; closed Sat, midday Sun, Aug and Dec–Jan; moderate.

Alla Collina Pistoiese, Via Amedei 1, near Piazza Missori (**Map II, 11**), ☎ 02 877248; old-fashioned trattoria with a Tuscan flair; closed Fri, midday Sat, Easter, Aug and Dec–Jan; moderate.

Al Pont de Ferr, Ripa di Porta Ticinese 55, ☎ 02 8940 6277; traditional osteria overlooking the iron bridge on the Naviglio; closed Sun, Aug and Dec–Jan; moderate.

Al Porto, Piazzale Generale Cantore (**Map I, 13, 14**), ☎ 02 8940 7425; restaurant specialising in fish; closed Sun, midday Mon, Aug and Dec–Jan; expensive.

Bice, Via Borgospesso 12, off Via Monte Napoleone (**Map II, 8**), ☎ 02 7600 2572; restaurant serving traditional Milanese cuisine; closed Mon, midday Tues and Aug; expensive.

Bottiglieria da Pino, Via Cerva 14, ☎ 02 7600 0532; a simple, cosy trattoria open for lunch only; closed Sun and Aug; inexpensive.

Calajunco, Via Stoppani 5, ☎ 02 204 6003; restaurant specialising in Sicilian cuisine from the Aeolian Islands; closed midday, Sun, Aug and Dec–Jan; expensive.

Da Abele, Via Temeranza 5, ☎ 02 261 3855; trattoria known for its risotti, open evenings only; closed Mon and mid-Jul–mid-Sep; inexpensive.

Da Francesca, Viale Argonne 32, ☎ 02 730608; small, cosy trattoria serving traditional Lombard fare; closed Sun and Aug; moderate.

Da Giacomo, Via Cellini at Via Sottocorno, ☎ 02 7602 3313; trattoria specialising in fish; closed Mon, Aug and Dec–Jan; moderate.

Da Gianni e Dorina, Via Pepe 38, ☎ 02 606340; restaurant offering specialities of the Lunigiana region of Tuscany; closed midday Sat, Sun, Aug–Sep and Dec–Jan; expensive.

Don Carlos, Via Manzoni 29, ☎ 02 7231 4640; restaurant of the *Grand Hotel et de Milan*, specialising in fish; open evenings only, expensive.

Grand Hotel, Via Ascanio Sforza 75, ☎ 02 8951 1586; osteria serving northern Italian cuisine in an informal atmosphere; open evenings only, closed Mon and Aug; moderate.

Il Sambuco, Via Messina 10, ☎ 02 3361 0333; restaurant of the *Hotel Hermitage*, specialising in fish; closed midday Sat, Sun, Aug and Dec–Jan; expensive.

Joia, Via Panfilo Castaldi 18, ☎ 02 2952 2124; restaurant known for its fine vegetarian cuisine; closed midday Sat, Sun, Easter, Aug and Dec–Jan; moderate.

La Brisa, Via Brisa 15 (**Map II, 6, 10**), ☎ 02 8645 0521; traditional trattoria with a pleasant garden; closed Sat, midday Sun, Aug and Dec–Jan; moderate.

La Libera, Via Palermo 21 (also for pizza) (**Map I, 6, 7**); moderate.

L'Altra Farmacia, Via Antonio Rosmini 3, ☎ 02 345 1300; osteria serving specialities of the Trentino and Veneto regions; closed Sun, Aug and Dec–Jan; inexpensive.

L'Ami Berton, Via Nullo 14 at Via Goldoni, ☎ 02 7012 3476; restaurant serving creative fish dishes; closed midday Sat, Sun, Aug and Jan; expensive.

La Madonnina, Via Gentilino 6, ☎ 02 8940 9089; trattoria in a busy working-class neighbourhood; closed Sun and Aug; inexpensive.

L'Angolo d'Abruzzo da Giannino, Via Rosolino Pilo 20, ☎ 02 2940 6526; trattoria serving specialities of the Abruzzo region; closed Mon and Aug; inexpensive.

La Piola, Viale Abruzzi 23, ☎ 02 2953 1271; trattoria serving traditional Lombard dishes; closed Sun, Aug and Dec–Jan; moderate.

La Veneta, Via Giusti 14, ☎ 02 342881; Venetian-style trattoria; closed Mon and Aug; moderate.

Le Vigne, Ripa di Porta Ticinese 61, ☎ 02 837 5617; bohemian osteria in the Navigli area; closed Sun, Mon evening and Aug; inexpensive.

L'Osteria, Alzaia Naviglio Grande 46, ☎ 02 837 3426; wine bar on the Naviglio Grande, open for lunch and dinner, year round except 25 Dec and 1 Jan; inexpensive.

L'Osteria del Treno, Via San Gregorio 46–48, ☎ 02 670 0479; still the railway workers' favourite lunch spot, with Liberty-style dining room and much more; closed Sat, midday Sun and two weeks in Aug; moderate.

New Bar Pascone, Viale Montenero 57, ☎ 02 551 0259; trattoria (despite the name) known for its fresh, home-made pasta; closed Sun and two weeks in Aug; inexpensive.

Olivia, Viale D'Annunzio 7–9, ☎ 02 8940 6052; restaurant with a vegetarian bias; closed midday Sat and Sun, Aug and Dec–Jan; moderate.

Osteria di Via Pré, Via Casale 4, ☎ 02 837 3869; trattoria serving specialities of Liguria; closed Mon and Aug; moderate.

Sadler, Via Troilio 14, at Via Cocchetta, ☎ 02 5810 4451; restaurant serving creative variations on traditional recipes; open evenings only, closed Sun, Aug and Jan; expensive.

Savini, Galleria Vittorio Emanuele II, ☎ 02 7200 3433; traditional restaurant in a historic setting; closed midday Sat, Sun, Aug and Jan; expensive.

Tagiura, Via Tagiura 5, ☎ 02 4895 0613; friendly, informal osteria; open midday and evenings by reservation, closed Sun and Aug; inexpensive.

Taverna Visconti, Via Marziale 11, ☎ 02 795821; wine bar in a quiet central sidestreet, with restaurant in the former cellar; closed Sun; inexpensive.

Torre di Pisa, Via Fiori Chiari 21 (**Map II, 2**), ☎ 02 874877; trattoria serving Tuscan specialities; closed midday Sat, Sun and Aug; moderate.

Trattoria all'Antica, Via Montevideo 4, ☎ 02 837 2849, 02 5810 4860; simple trattoria in the Porta Genova-Navigli area; closed Sat and midday Sun, Aug and Dec–Jan; moderate.

Trattoria del Pescatore, Via Vannucci 5, ☎ 02 5832 0452; excellent, popular trattoria specialising in fish (reserve in advance); closed Sun, Aug and Dec–Jan; moderate.

Trattoria Milanese, Via Santa Marta 11, ☎ 02 8645 1991; trattoria run by the same family since 1913, serving classic Milanese fare; closed Tues, Aug and Dec–Jan; moderate. Restaurant in

the department store of **Rinascente**, Piazza del Duomo (**Map II, 11**); inexpensive.

Cafés, confectioners, ice-cream and pastry shops

No Italian city has contributed so much to the culture of the *aperitivo* as Milan, the home of Campari, Zucca and Fernet Branca. For over a century animated discussions of social, cultural and political issues have enlivened the pre-dinner hour in the city's cafés, especially on Sunday, when the Milanese take their traditional downtown stroll; and the *trani*, or wine bars of the working-class neighbourhoods, have been a Milanese institution for as long as anyone can remember.

Cafés, of course, come and go as their popularity rises and falls. Today the most fashionable include:

Bar Metro, Via dei Martinitt 3 (open 07.00–21.00, closed Sun and Aug).

Bee Tee's, Via Santa Croce 21 (open 10.00–01.00, closed Mon and Aug).

Bell'Aurore, Via Castelmorrone at Via Abamonti (open 08.00–02.00, closed Sun and Aug).

Cantina Isola, Via Sarpi 30 (open 09.30–21.30; closed Mon, except in summer, and Aug).

Jamaica, Via Brera 32 (open 09.00–02.00, closed Sun).

La Cantina di Manuela, Via Cadore 30 (open 07.30–01.00, closed Sun and Aug).

Le Terre di Marengo, Viale Gorizia 34 (open 07.00–20.30, closed Sat afternoon and Sun).

Luca's, Corso di Porta Ticinese 51b, at San Lorenzo (open 07.00–01.00, closed Sun and Aug).

Lucky Bar, Via Tito Livio 2, at Viale Umbria (open 08.00–02.00, closed Sun and Aug).

Tango, Via Casale 7 (open 18.00–02.00, closed Mon, except in summer, and Jan).

Milan's best pastries are to be found at: *Marchesi*, Corso Magenta 13.

Panarello, Via Speronari 3 (Corso di Porta Romana).
Ranieri, Via della Moscova.
San Carlo, Via Bandello 1 (near Santa Maria delle Grazie).
Supino, Via Cesare de Sesto.
Taveggia, Via Visconti di Modrone 2 (with Liberty-style interior).
For ice-creams, try:
Buonarroti, Via Buonarroti 9.
Marghera, Via Marghera 3l.
For unusual flavours (sesame-honey, date), *Gelateria Ecologica Artigiana*, Corso Porta Ticinese 40.

Other special food shops

Casa del Formaggio, Via Speronari 3, features cheeses from all parts of Italy and Europe.
Casa del Fungo e del Tartufo, Via Anfossi 14, offers a vast assortment of fresh and preserved mushrooms and truffles.
Cremeria D'Angelo, Via Galiani 4, also has fine cheeses and dairy products.
Enoteca Ronchi, Via San Vincenzo 12, stocks great wines and liqueurs.
Focaccerie Genovesi, Via Plinio 5, makes focaccia bread with olives, cheese, onions, etc.
Friggitoria Vomero, Via Cimarosa 44, excellent *arancini*, potato croquettes, pizzas and pasties.
Guida, Via dei Mille 46, delicious sandwiches, cheeses, cold meats, roasts, ice cream, etc.
Il Girasole, Via Vincenzo Monti 32, is the place to go for organic foods.
La Fungheria di Angelo Bernardi, Viale Abruzzi 93, for fresh, dried and canned porcini mushrooms and truffles.
L'Altro Vino, Via Piave 9, has over 900 Italian and foreign wines, liqueurs, jams, patés, etc.
La Baita del Formaggio, the best of Lombard cheeses.
Peck, Via Spadari 9, is probably the city's most famous delicatessen, with a wide selection of cheeses, cold meats, and a well-stocked wine collection. If

you're in the shopping district, try Milan's other spectacular deli, *Il Salumaio*, Via Montenapoleone 12; the same people have a fine pastry shop at Via San Gregorio 1.

Picnic places in Parco Sempione, in the Giardini Pubblici off Via Palestro, and in the Giardini della Guastalla, Via Francesco Sforza (near the university). At the central station there is a supermarket open every day and all night.

Outside Milan

LODI *La Quinta*, Piazza della Vittoria 20, ☎ 0371 424232; restaurant, closed Sun evening, Mon and Aug; moderate.
Tre Gigli all'Incoronata, Piazza Vittoria 47, ☎ 0371 421404; restaurant, closed Mon and Aug; inexpensive.
MONZA *La Riserva*, Via Borgazzi 12, ☎ 039 386612; restaurant serving Piedmontese specialities, closed Fri, midday Sat, Aug and Dec–Jan; moderate.

Entertainment

Information on theatre performances and concerts is carried in *Milano Mese*, published free every month. It is available at most hotels, or from the tourist information offices.

La Scala, Piazza della Scala, is Italy's most famous **opera** house. The opera season opens on 7 Dec; ballet and concerts run Sep–Nov. **Theatres**, offering avant-garde and traditional performances, include the *Piccolo Teatro*, Largo Greppi; Teatro Manzoni, Via Manzoni 42; *Lirico*, Via Larga 14; *Nuovo*, Piazza San Babila; *Nazionale*, Piazzale Piemonte 12; *Carcano*, Corso di Porta Romana 66. Tickets can be purchased at the theatres or at various agencies, including *La Biglietteria*, 81 Corso Garibaldi (☎ 02 6590188).
Musica e Poesia a San Maurizio, with **classical music** concerts in Milanese churches, throughout the year; ☎ 02 7600 5500. Live **jazz** at *Il Capolinea*, Via Ludovico il Moro 119 and *Il Bolgia*

Umana, Via Santa Maria Segreta 7.
Disco dancing at Ca' Bianca, Via
Ludovico il Moro 117; **Alcatra 2**, Via
Valtellina 21; *De Sade*, Via Valtellina;
and *Propaganda*, Via Castelbarco 11.

Shopping

Milan is the centre of Italian
fashion. The most important
Italian fashion designers have shops
between Via Montenapoleone, Via Spiga,
Via Sant'Andrea and Via Santo Spirito.
These include *Moschino*, Via
Sant'Andrea 12; *Giorgio Armani*, Via
Sant'Andrea 9 (for children at Via
Durini 27); *Krizia*, Via della Spiga 23
(for women) and Via A. Manin 17 (for
men); *Trussardi*, Via Sant'Andrea 5;
Valentino, Via Santo Spirito 3 (women)
and Via Montenapoleone 3 (for men);
Gianni Versace, Via Montenapoleone
2; *Romeo Gigli*, Corso Venezia 11 and
Via Palermo 115; *Gianfranco
Ferré*,Via della Spiga 11 and 13.

Biffi Boutique, Corso Genova 6 and
Via Fabio Filzi 45, stocks clothes by
important international fashion designers (as well as shoes and handbags).
Prada, Galleria Vittorio Emanuele II 11,
Via della Spiga 1 and Via Sant'Andrea
21, is well-known for its handbags and
shoes. Other boutiques include *Marisa*,
Via Sant'Andrea 10A (avant-garde
womens' clothes); *Brigatti*, Corso
Venezia 15 and *Bardelli*, Corso
Magenta 13 (both specialising in classic
clothes for men); *Pupi Solari*, Piazza
Tommaseo 2 (classic clothes for women
and children including cashmere);
Corso Como 10, Corso Como 10
(avant-garde design); *Lisa Corti
Hometextiles*, Via Conchetta 6
(redesigned Indian fabrics).

Well-known elegant shoe shops
include: *Henry Beguelyn*, Via
Caminadella 7; *Sergio Rossi*, Via
Montenapoleone 6a; *Fausto Santini*,
Via Montenapoleone 1; *Diego della
Valle*, Via XX Settembre 12.

Fiorucci, Galleria Passarella 1, is a
large store with reasonably priced and
trendy clothes that are particularly popular with the young. Department stores
for good inexpensive but fashionable
clothes include *La Rinascente*, Piazza
Duomo; *Coin* (the biggest branch is at
Piazza V Giornate 1A), and *Standa*
(numerous branches, including Piazza
San Babila).

For **food and wine**, respectively, try
Gastronomia Peck, Via Spadari 9, and
Enoteca Cotti, Via Solferino 42. Milan's
famous Christmas cake, the tall, dome-
like *panettone* (made with bread dough,
eggs, sugar, nuts and candied fruit), is
available in bakeries throughout the city.

A very different kind of shopping is
offered by Milan's many **markets**. The
Fiera di Senigallia, a large flea market, is
held on Sat morning in Viale
d'Annunzio. Antiques are sold along the
Naviglio on Sun morning (except
Jul–Aug). Open-air markets in Viale
Papiniano (Tues and Sat), Piazza
Mirabello (Mon and Thur), and Largo
Quinto Alpini (Fri).

Special events

MILAN 7 and 8 Dec, Festival
of St Ambrose (patron saint of
Milan): *Oh Bei! Oh Bei!* street fair near
Sant'Ambrogio. *Corteo dei Re Magi*, a
procession with elaborate costumes, animals, bands and majorettes (!), 6 Jan.
Stramilano in Apr, a marathon race in
which some 50,000 people take part.
An open-air art exhibition is held in Via
Bagutta in Oct and Apr. The
Associazione Dimore Storiche Italiane
(☎ 02 9547311) organise the opening
of some historic courtyards in the city
(*Cortili Aperti*) for a week in May. On
Jun evenings the *Festa del Naviglio*
takes place around the Naviglio Grande
(street fairs, musical events, restaurants
on boats, etc.).

LODI Festival of San Bassiano (patron
saint), 19 Jan; *Palio dei Rioni* on 1

Oct; fair and market around 13 Dec (Santa Lucia).

Sports

Milan is by far the best place in northern Italy for spectator sports. The city's two professional **soccer** teams, *Milan* and *Inter*, play at San Siro Stadium—which you might want to visit just for its architecture. Formula 1 **motor racing** has made the track at Monza, just north of Milan, famous the world over. The big event is in Jul. **Cycling** fans should come in Jun, when the *Giro d'Italia* passes through the city to a downtown finishing line (the course of the race changes each year).

There are **golf** courses in the environs at Almenno San Bartolomeo (*Golf Club Bergamo L'Albenza*); Birago di Camnago (*Barlassina Country Club*); Bubbiano (*Golf Culb Ambrosiano*); Carimate (*Golf Club Carimate*); Cernusco sul Naviglio (*Molinetto Country Club*); Lainate (*Green Club Golf*); Monza (*Golf Club Milano*); Noverasco di Opera (*Golf Club Le Rovedine*); Pieve Emanuele (*Castello di Tolcinasco Golf & Country Club*); Tribiano (*Golf Club Zoate*); Usmate Velate (*Golf Club della Brianza*).

Downhill skiing near Sondrio and Bergamo.

History

Milan has been an important place for quite some time. The city's ancient predecessor, *Mediolanum* ('middle of the plain'), was a Celtic settlement which came under Roman control in 222 BC. Occupying a key position on trade routes between Rome and northern Europe, by the 4C AD it had a population of nearly 100,000 and rivalled Rome in importance. Constantine the Great officially recognised the Christian religion by a famous edict made here in 313, and in the years that followed this momentous event the city became a major centre of Christianity. Among the more influential Church fathers who lived and worked here was the great bishop of Milan, St Ambrose (340–397), the friend and mentor of St Augustine.

Though devastated by the barbarian invasions, Milan survived to become a typical Italian city-state, governed by an assembly of free citizens who cast off their feudal obligations and advanced one of Europe's earlier claims to self-determination. Annoyed by this example of republican home-rule, Holy Roman Emperor Frederick Barbarossa sacked Milan in 1158 and 1162, but was beaten at Legnano in 1176 by the survivors and their allies, who came together to form the *Lega Lombarda* (Lombard League). In recent years the name and example of this medieval alliance have been taken up by a separatist movement whose declared goal is to free Lombardy once again—this time from lawmakers in Rome.

In the late Middle Ages Milan was ruled by a succession of powerful families, including the Torriani, who took control of the city around 1260. They were overthrown in 1277 by the Visconti, who held power in Milan until 1447. The city had a period of particular splendour under Gian Galeazzo Visconti (1385–1402), who founded what is still the city's most impressive monument, the Cathedral, in 1386. After a republican interlude of three years, Francesco Sforza, the famous mercenary general and defender of Milan against Venice, who had married Bianca, daughter of the last Visconti, proclaimed himself duke. He was succeeded by his son Galeazzo Maria, and then by his infant grandson Gian Galeazzo, under the regency of his mother.

The infant duke's power was usurped by his uncle Lodovico il Moro, who, despite his low opinion of rule by law (or perhaps because of it), was a great patron of the arts, and under whose rule the city flourished.

A succession of invasions, which would bring Milan under foreign rule for nearly four centuries, began with the expedition in 1494 of Charles VIII of France. Between 1499 and 1535 the dukedom was contested by the French and the Spanish, and under the Spanish emperor Charles V Milan became capital of a province of the Holy Roman Empire. In 1713 the city passed to Austria under the Treaty of Utrecht, which marked the end of the Wars of the Spanish Succession. In 1796 it was seized by Napoleon, who three years later made it capital of his Cisalpine Republic, and, after a brief occupation by the Austrians and Russians, capital of the Italian Republic (1802) and of the Kingdom of Italy (1805). After the fall of Napoleon (1814) the Austrians returned, but the Milanese tenaciously opposed this final, intolerable imposition of foreign rule. After three decades of passive resistance the populace rose up in the rebellion known as the *Cinque Giornate* (18–22 March 1848). When the troops of Victor Emmanuel II and Napoleon III defeated the Austrian forces at the battle of Magenta in 1859, the city declared its allegiance to the nascent Kingdom of Italy.

With the industrial development of the city at the end of the 19C, Milan expanded to absorb a huge influx of immigrant workers from all over Italy. The city was bombed 15 times in the Second World War; the worst air raids were in August 1943, when a great part of the city centre burned for several days. The years of reconstruction were followed by a period of economic boom when sprawling new suburbs were built. Since 1974 the population has been in decline.

Art and architecture

If Florence is the city of *disegno* ('line' or 'drawing'), Venice the home of painterly light and colour, and Rome a place of sculptural exuberance, Milan is primarily an architect's city, where ideas are transposed with singular grace and skill from the two-dimensional surface of the drawing table to the three-dimensional volumes of real space. Here one can trace the history of Italian architecture from antiquity right up to the present day. And although all periods are represented by buildings of some merit, the very old and the very new are those that draw the greatest attention. This is not to say that the other arts have been neglected in Milan; it is just that architecture has always been important here. Even in the domestic sphere today, most Italians will agree that the most beautiful homes are in Milan.

In the early Middle Ages Milan's church builders gave rise to a style that scholars today call the **Lombard Romanesque**. The distinctive characteristic of this style is the mixture of Roman architectural devices such as round arches and cylindrical columns, common to all Romanesque religious architecture, with elements inherited from the Byzantine tradition, such as the extended forecourt or narthex. The most important example of this style is the magnificent basilica of Sant'Ambrogio.

The Cathedral, practically the only **Gothic** building in Milan, is one of the more splendid Gothic cathedrals in the country. Its flamboyant tracery rivals the best examples of this genre in France and northern Europe.

The wealthy and cultured court of the Sforzas attracted many great artists of the Renaissance, including the architects Filarete, Michelozzo, and Bramante, the sculptor Amadeo, and the painters Bergognone and Foppa. Milanese art, however, was completely transformed by the arrival from Tuscany in 1483 of Leonardo da Vinci. This great artist and the city he adopted were the centre of an artistic and humanistic flowering that ended with the fall of Lodovico il Moro in 1499. Leonardo's many pupils and disciples who carried on his tradition of painting in Milan included Boltaffio, Cesare da Sesto, Marco d'Oggiono, Giampietrino, and Andrea Solario. His pupils Luini and Gaudenzio Ferrari formed schools of their own. The sculptors Bambaia and Cristoforo Solari also felt his influence.

Towards the end of the 16C Camillo and Giulio Procaccini introduced a new, **Baroque** style of painting from Bologna, and Galeazzo Alessi imported Baroque ideas from Rome into architecture. The **Neo-classical** buildings of Luigi Cagnola and Luigi Canonica (both born in 1762) reflect the tastes of the Napoleonic period, and a number of districts of the city were built at the turn of the century in a distinctive Art Nouveau style, called **Liberty** after the London shop that played so large a part in the dessemination of this decorative Modernist style.

In the early 20C, bustling, industrial Milan was one of the centres of **Futurism**, Italy's great contribution to the Modern movement, which hailed the new world of mechanical forces and denounced all attachment to the past. 'A roaring motorcar, its hood adorned with pipes like serpents with explosive breath... is more beautiful than the Winged Victory of Samothrace', declared Futurist theorist Filippo Tommaso Marinetti. The original members of the movement were the painters Umberto Boccioni, Carlo Carrà, Luigi Russolo, Giacomo Balla and Gino Severini, and the architect Antonio Sant'Elia. They were later joined by many others. The Futurists aspired to bring art into closer contact with life, which they conceived as force and movement. Like the French Cubists, they held that movement and light destroy the static materiality of objects. The Futurist doctrine of simultaneity, by which movement was to be rendered by simultaneous presentation of successive aspects of form in motion, was similar to the Cubist notion of the simultaneous presentation of multiple views of a single object; but the Futurist idea differed from the more exclusively visual simultaneity put forward by Apollinaire, in his theory of Cubism, in 1911, in that the Futurists spoke of simultaneity of plastic states of the soul in artistic creation. The Futurists were also the first to advocate a new conception of picture space whereby the observer would be situated at the centre of the picture.

The most important artistic event of the 1920s in Italy was the formation, in Milan, of the group that exhibited together in 1924 under the name **Novecento**. The name, coined by the theoretician of the movement, Margherita Sarfatti, means 'Twentieth Century' *par excellence*. Its leading figure, the former Futurist painter Carrà, called for a return to a quieter figurative style based on traditional values. But to find a common denominator for all the artists associated with Novecento is difficult. Even Sarfatti was vague in describing the goals of her artists: she cited 'clarity of form and dignity of conception, nothing magical, nothing eccentric, an increasing closure toward the arbitrary and the obscure'. Thus one finds in Novecento such painters as Mario Sironi, who captured the movement of modernity with expressionistic force, as well as subtly melancholy artists such as Piero Marussig. The movement was much loved by the Fascists because of its emphasis on tradition and national identity.

In the 1920s the Modernist movement in Italian architecture gave rise to the functionalist trend known as **Rationalism**, which made an appeal to ideals of logic and order but claimed also a definitive break with the past. Though initially apolitical, the movement later won the support of the Fascist regime, by this time in full power and needful of a cultural trademark. The protagonists of the movement were Giuseppe Terragni and Mario Pagano, but many other architects—including Ponti, Sartoris, and Gardella in Milan—expressed Rationalist ideals in their buildings and objects.

Faced with the rise of the new Rationalist language, conservative architects of this period proposed yet another return to Classical models. A new traditionalist orientation, called **Novecento** to underscore its bonds to the conservative trend in painting, developed throughout Italy and particularly in Milan, where growth was most rapid and where the Neo-classical tradition of the early 19C offered inspiration and continuity with the past. The leading figure of this movement was Marcello Piacentini, promotor of a supposedly balanced and dignified, spiritual and expressive classicism.

After the Second World War Milan became the undisputed centre of contemporary culture in Italy, asserting its primacy in painting, sculpture and architecture as well as in industrial design and fashion. Lucio Fontana, the painter, and Piero Manzoni, the precursor of Conceptual Art, both lived and worked here.

The first clearly identifiable architectural style of the postwar period was **Neorealism**. This trend, like Neorealism in Italian cinema, arose in reaction to Fascist triumphalism, to which it opposed simpler, more organic forms. It clearly reflected the desire, of a generation of architects compromised by association with the regime, to atone for past sins; but it was also brought about by the arrival in Italy of ideas originating in the United States and northern Europe and expressed in the work of figures such as Frank Lloyd Wright and Alvar Aalto.

By the early fifties Italy was well on the way to attaining the status of a modern industrial democracy. Here, as elsewhere in Europe and in North America, the dominant architectural trend became the **International Style**, a functionalist rereading of the teachings of the great masters of the Modern movement that advocated the adoption of common standards in all buildings, regardless of location. Giò Ponti and Pier Luigi Nervi's Pirelli Building, in front of the Stazione Centrale, is a good example of the International Style. In more recent times this trend has been followed, in Milan as elsewhere, by a **Post-Modern** reaction, embodied in a new eclecticism combining Classical elements (such as arches and columns) with forms derived from vernacular architecture. You'll see a lot of this in Milanese interiors—shops, cafés, hotels and restaurants.

The 1950s, of course, marked the beginning of Italy's economic miracle: the standard of living increased astronomically, creating an enormous demand for high-quality consumer goods. Industry responded by increasing production and by involving some of the country's great creative talents in product **design**, giving rise to that distinctive look for which Italian products are rightly famous. Today the creations of Milanese designers such as Alessandro Mendini, Ettore Sottsass and Aldo Rossi grace homes and workplaces throughout the developed world.

The city centre

Unlike, say, London or New York, where the city centre has shifted over the centuries, the centre of modern Milan corresponds to the centre of the Roman and medieval town. The Roman forum was on the site of Piazza San Sepulcro (**Map II, 11**), and the medieval seat of government stood where the Palazzo Reale rises today—right next to the Cathedral, the city's religious centre. Over time Milan has developed in a series of concentric circles—once marked by *navigli* (canals) or *bastioni* (fortifications), now simply traced by boulevards. In late antiquity the city was just over 1km in diametre. This means that the four early Christian basilicas—*Basilica Virginum* (San Simpliciano), *Basilica Martyrum* (later named after St Ambrose), *Basilica Palatina* (San Lorenzo), and *Basilica Apostolorum* (San Nazaro)—around which the city subsequently grew up, were all outside the walls. Our visit begins at the centre of the inner ring, with the buildings on or around the cathedral square; later we move outward, arranging our wanderings as the Milanese arranged their city: around the four great basilicas.

The Cathedral and its square
Piazza del Duomo, the cathedral square (**Map II; 11**), is the centre of the life of Milan. It is closed to traffic (except for the west end) and is dominated by the splendid Cathedral. The crowded Portici Settentrionali (1873), along the north side, are characteristic of the bustling atmosphere of the city. The equestrian statue of Vittorio Emanuele II is by Ercole Rosa (1896).

The ****Duomo** (**Map II; 11**) is a magnificent late-Gothic building, the only Gothic cathedral in Italy and one of the largest churches in the world (second only to Rome's St Peter's in Italy). The name comes from *domus dei*, 'house of god' in Latin. The remarkable exterior, with numerous flying buttresses, is decorated with some 2000 sculptures, and the roof has a forest of pinnacles and spires. It has a superb tower over the crossing and a remarkable 16C façade in the Gothic style. It was particularly admired in the Romantic Age.

On the site of Santa Maria Maggiore (revealed through excavations), it was begun in 1386 under Gian Galeazzo Visconti, who presented it with a marble quarry at Candoglia which still belongs to the cathedral chapter. The design is attributed to the Lombard masters Simone da Orsenigo and Giovanni Grassi, who were assisted by French, German, and Flemish craftsmen. Filippino degli Organi was appointed master mason in 1400, and he was succeeded by Giovanni Solari and his son Guiniforte, and Giovanni Antonio Amadeo. In 1567 St Charles Borromeo appointed Pellegrino Tibaldi as architect, and under him the church was dedicated. The tower over the crossing was completed in 1762, and the statue of the Virgin placed on its summit in 1774. The façade, begun in the 17C, was completed in 1805. The 'Veneranda Fabbrica del Duomo' has looked after the cathedral for centuries, and is

MILAN I

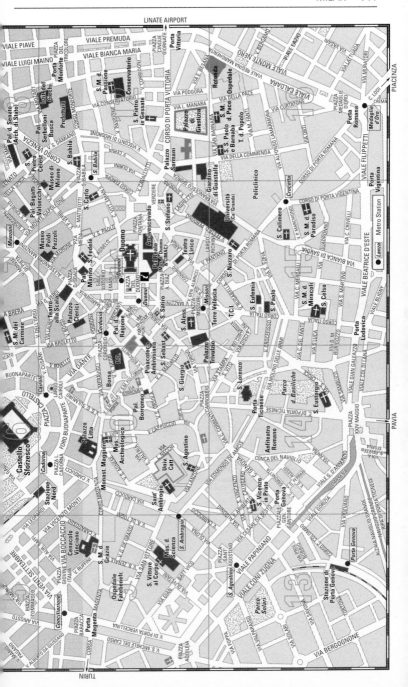

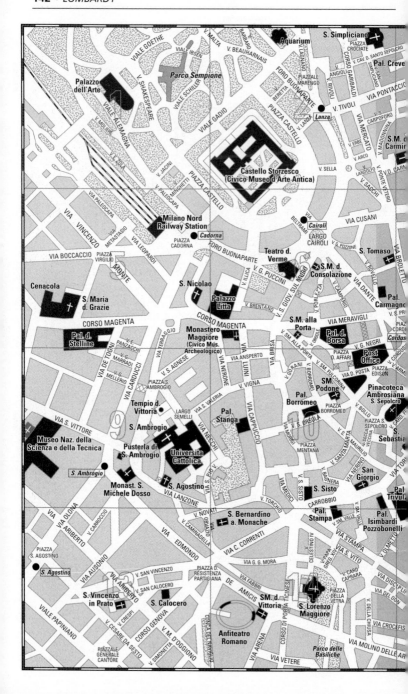

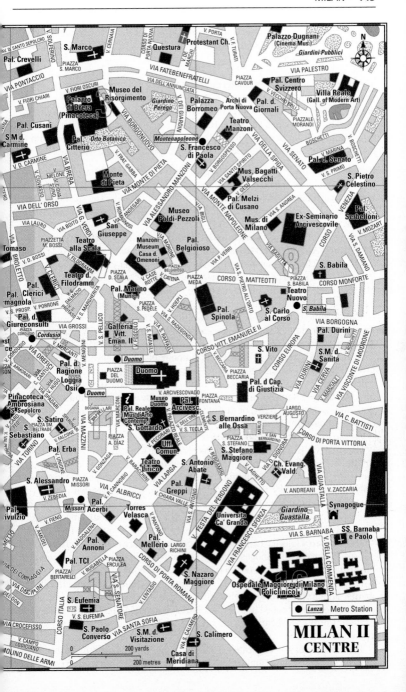

> responsible for the conservation of its numerous delicate sculptural works.
> The famous choir school of the cathedral was directed by Franchino Gaffurio
> from 1484 to 1522.

The *façade was begun by Pellegrino Tibaldi in the 16C on a Classical design but was considerably altered by Carlo Buzzi (1645) and Francesco Castelli, who adopted a Gothic style. It was completed in 1805 by Carlo Amati using Buzzi's design. The doors date from 1906 (Lodovico Pogliaghi), 1948 (Arrigo Minerbi), 1950, and 1960 (Luciano Minguzzi). The best view of the exterior is from the courtyard of Palazzo Reale. The splendid apse has three huge windows.

Interior The huge cruciform *interior, with double-aisled nave, single-aisled transepts and a pentagonal apse, has a forest of 52 tall columns, most of which bear circles of figures in canopied niches instead of capitals. The splendid effect is heightened by the stained glass of the windows. The classical pavement is by Tibaldi.

The visit starts in the **south aisle**. Above the plain granite sarcophagus of Archbishop Aribert (d. 1045) is a stained-glass window by Cristoforo de' Mottis (1473–77). The red-marble sarcophagus on pillars is of Archbishop Ottone Visconti (d. 1295). The next three windows have 16C stained glass. The tomb of Marco Carelli is by Filippino degli Organi (1406). Beyond a relief with a design for the façade by Giuseppe Brentano (1886) is the small monument of Canon Giovanni Vimercati (d. 1548), with two fine portraits and a damaged *Pietà* by Bambaia. The stained glass (1470–75) shows the influence of Vincenzo Foppa. The glass above the sixth altar is by Nicolò da Varallo (1480–89).

In the **south transept** is the *monument of Gian Giacomo Medici, with bronze statues, by Leone Leoni (1560–63). The stained glass in the two transept windows is by Corrado de' Mocchis (1554–64). In the transept apse is the monumental altar of San Giovanni Bono (1763). On the altar with a marble relief by Bambaia, is a statue (right) of St Catherine, by Cristoforo Lombardo. The statue of St Bartholomew flayed and carrying his skin is by Marco d'Agrate (1562).

On the impressive **tiburio**, or tower over the crossing, are medallions (on the pendentives) with 15C busts of the Doctors of the Church, and some 60 statues (on the arches). The four piers had to be reinforced in 1984 in order to consolidate the structure of the building. The *presbytery (usually open to worshippers only) was designed by Pellegrino Tibaldi (1567). It contains two pulpits (supported by bronze figures by Francesco Brambilla), and a large bronze ciborium, also by Tibaldi. High above the altar hangs a paschal candlestick by Lorenzo da Civate (1447).

The **treasury** (closed 12.30–14.30) contains a silver reliquary box of the late 4C; a 13C dove with Limoges enamels; three ivory diptychs (5C–11C); an ivory bucket of 979–80; the pax of Pio IV, attributed to Leone Leoni; the evangelistary cover of Archbishop Aribert (11C) decorated with enamels; and church vestments. The crypt, decorated with stucco reliefs by Galeazzo Alessi and Tibaldi, contains the richly-robed body of St Charles Borromeo, the leading spirit of the Catholic Counter-Reformation, made Cardinal Archbishop of Milan in 1560 and canonised in 1610.

The ambulatory is separated from the choir by a beautiful marble screen designed by Pellegrino Tibaldi (1567). The sacristy doorways date from the late

14C. The sacristy contains a statue of Christ at the column by Cristoforo Solari. Beyond (high up) is a statue of Martin V, the pope who consecrated the high altar in 1418, by Jacopino da Tradate (1424), and the black marble tomb of Cardinal Caracciolo (d. 1538), by Bambaia. The large embroidered standard dates from the late 16C.

In the middle of the **north transept** is the Trivulzio *candelabrum, a seven-branched bronze candlestick nearly 5m high, of French or German workmanship (13C or 14C). The stained-glass window above the sculptured altarpiece of the Crucifix (1605) is by Nicolò da Varallo (1479). The altar in the transept apse dates from 1768. The Gothic altar of St Catherine has two statues attributed to Cristoforo Solari.

In the **north aisle**, the eighth altarpiece is by Federico Barocci. The next four stained-glass windows date from the 16C. On the sixth altar is the crucifix carried by St Charles Borromeo during the plague of 1576; at the third altar, the tomb of three archbishops of the Arcimboldi family, attributed to Galeazzo Alessi; in the second bay, late-12C marble reliefs of apostles. Opposite is the font, a porphyry urn thought to date from Roman times, covered with a canopy by Tibaldi.

The excavations beneath the church (open Tues–Sun 09.00–12.00, 14.30–18.00) are entered from the west end. Here you can see a 4C octagonal baptistery where St Ambrose baptised St Augustine in 387; remains of the basilica of Santa Tecla (begun in the 4C); and Roman baths of the 1C BC.

The roof The entrance to the roof (open 09.00–17.45, winter 09.00–16.15; also lift, entered from outside the north or south transept) is a small door in the corner of the south transept, near the Medici tomb. The *ascent provides a superb view of the sculptural detail of the exterior and is highly recommended. 158 steps lead up to the roof of the transept, from which you can see numerous pinnacles and flying buttresses. From the walkways across the roof you can examine the details of the carving, and beyond are magnificent views of the city. The Carelli spire, the oldest pinnacle, is at the angle facing the corso. From above the west front it is possible to walk along the spine of the nave roof to the base of the crossing, by Amadeo (1490–1500), who also planned the four turrets but finished only the one at the northeast angle. Stairs lead up from the southwest turret to the platform of the crossing. From here another staircase, in the northeast turret, ascends to the topmost gallery at the base of the central spire, surmounted by the Madonnina (108m from the ground), a statue of gilded copper, nearly 4m high. From this height there is a magnificent *view of the city, the Lombard plain, the Alps from Monte Viso to the Ortler (with the prominent peaks of the Matterhorn, Monte Rosa, the two Grigne, and Monte Resegone), and the Apennines.

An interesting series of 52 paintings illustrating the life and miracles of St Charles Borromeo are hung in a double row between the nave and transept pillars 1 November–6 January every year. Known as the Quadroni di San Carlo, they were commissioned in 1602 by Cardinal Federico Borromeo to honour the memory of his cousin Charles. Above are hung the scenes from his life (1602–04) and below the scenes of his miracles (1609–10): the best ones are by Il Cerano and Giulio Cesare Procaccini (others are by Morazzone, Carlo Buzzi, Duchino, Fiammenghino, and Domenico Pellegrini). The last eight were painted in 1660–1740 to complete the series which survives intact.

Some 'expert' opinions

On the cathedral...

How glorious that Cathedral is! worthy almost of standing face to face with the snow Alps; and itself a sort of snow dream by an artist architect, taken asleep in a glacier!
Elizabeth Barrett Browning, letter, 1851

The Cathedral is an awful failure. Outside the design is monstrous and inartistic. The over-elaborated details stuck high up where no one can see them; everything is vile in it; it is, however, imposing and gigantic as a failure, through its great size and elaborate execution.
Oscar Wilde, letter to his mother, 25 June 1875

... the beautiful city with its dominant frost-crystalline Duomo...
John Ruskin, Praeterita, 1885–9

... and the view from the roof:
The Territory of Lombardy which I contemplated round about from this Tower, was so pleasant an object to mine eyes, being replenished with such unspeakable variety of all things, both for profit and pleasure, that it seemeth to me to be the very Elysian fields, so much decanted and celebrated by the verses of Poets, or the Temple or Paradise of the world. For it is the fairest plain, extended about some two hundred miles in length that ever I saw, or ever shall if I should travell over the whole habitable world: insomuch that I said to myself that this country was fitter to be an habitation for the immortal Gods than for mortall men.
Thomas Coryate, Crudities, 1611.

Palazzo Reale

The former Palazzo Reale (**Map II, 11**) stands to the south of the cathedral, on the site of the 13C town hall. It was rebuilt in Neo-classical style in 1772–78 for the Austrian grand dukes by Giuseppe Piermarini (and altered again in the 19C, and restored after bomb damage in 1943). It now belongs to the municipality, and there are long-term plans to restore it and open it to the public. At present important exhibitions are held here.

Opposite the south transept of the Cathedral is the entrance to the **Museo del Duomo** (Map II, 11; open Tues–Sun 09.30–12.30, 15.00–18.00). The collection is well labelled. Beyond the ticket office is room **2** with statues by Giorgio Solari and Bernardo da Venezia (1392). Room **3**, an 18C Neo-classical vaulted hall by Piermarini, has a fine display of sculpture from the Visconti period from the exterior of the cathedral, and 14C–15C stained glass. Room **5** is entered below a cast of the arms of Gian Galeazzo used as a centrepiece for the apse window. Room **6** has 15C statues; room **7**, a crucifix in beaten copper (c 1040) from Archbishop Aribert's tomb in the duomo, and a painting attributed to Michelino da Besozzo (1418). Room **8** contains late 15C sculpture. The St Agnes is attributed to Benedetto Briosco. Works by Cristoforo Solari include a statue of Job.

Room **9** contains sculptures attributed to Giovanni Antonio Amadeo and Andrea Fusina, and a 15C Flemish tapestry of the *Passion*. Room **10** has an altar frontal of St Charles Borromeo (1610) and drawings by Il Cerano. Room **11**: tapestries made in Ferrara c 1540, probably on cartoons by Giulio Romano, and *The Infant Christ among the Doctors*, an early work by Jacopo Tintoretto. Room

12 displays numerous sculptures from the Duomo from the end of the 16C and beginning of the 17C, including works by Francesco Brambilla.

Room **13** (right): models by Giuseppe Perego for the Madonnina which crowns the central spire of the duomo, and the original armature. Room **14** contains 19C sculptures from the façade (Camillo Pacetti, Pompeo Marchesi, etc.). The gallery (room **15**) displays plans illustrating the history of the Duomo. Room **16** contains a splendid wooden *model of the duomo constructed by Bernardino Zenale da Treviglio in 1519, and later models. Room **17** is dedicated to the five 20C doors of the duomo (bozzetti, etc.). Rooms **18** and **19** illustrate the remarkable restoration work carried out on the four pillars of the crossing in 1981–84 in order to consolidate the structure of the building (during which much of the stone was replaced). Off room 12 is room **20** with a fine display of church vestments (and statuettes by Francesco Messina).

The second floor of Palazzo Reale (entered through the main courtyard) hosts the **Civico Museo d'Arte Contemporanea**, known as CIMAC (**Map II, 11**; open Tues–Sun 09.30–17.30). This fairly representative collection of 20C Italian art, in a stark temporary arrangement, is divided into two parts: works up to 1950 in the rooms on the left, later works and the Jucker collection in the right-hand rooms. The rooms on the left (**1–23**) contain paintings by the Futurists Umberto Boccioni, Giacomo Balla and Gino Severini; by Novecento artists Pietro Marussig, Carlo Carrà and Mario Sironi; and by Modern masters such as Amedeo Modigliani, Giorgio De Chirico, Arturo Martini, Giorgio Morandi, Felice Casorati, Massimo Campigli, Filippo De Pisis, and the ubiquitous Picasso. The rooms on the right of the entrance include the Jucker Collection, with works by Balla, Severini, Sironi, De Pisis, Carrà, Morandi, Braque, Matisse and Picasso.

Around the cathedral square

The Arengario, on Via Marconi, is an interesting modern building (1939–56) designed by Giovanni Muzio, with reliefs by Arturo Martini. It is now the headquarters of the tourist board.

The church of San Gottardo (**Map II, 11**), formerly the palace chapel, lies beyond the courtyard of the Palazzo Reale. It is entered from Via Pecorari. The exterior and beautiful campanile are attributed to Francesco Pecorari (1330–36), and the Neo-classical interior has stuccoes by Giocondo Albertolli. It contains a very damaged 14C fresco of the Crucifixion showing the influence of Giotto, who is known to have been in the city in 1335. The monument to Azzone Visconti is by Giovanni di Balduccio.

The archbishops' palace is mainly the work of Tibaldi (1570 et seq), with a façade by Giuseppe Piermarini (1784–1801) on Piazza Fontana (**Map II, 11**). This square is associated with one of the more disquieting episodes in recent Italian history: a terrorist bomb killed 16 people here (and wounded 88) in 1969.

The north side of Piazza del Duomo is connected with Piazza della Scala by the colossal **Galleria Vittorio Emanuele II** (**Map II, 7**). This huge glass-roofed shopping arcade, with cafés and restaurants, was designed in 1865 by Giuseppe Mengoni, who fell from the top and was killed a few days before the inauguration ceremony in 1878. Mengoni's design combines a severely classical style with a remarkable sensitivity for new materials such as iron. The gallery was part of a grandiose project to renovate Piazza del Duomo, and its success led to the construction of numerous imitations in other Italian cities, notably the Galleria

Mazzini in Genoa, the Galleria Principe in Naples and the Galleria Sciarra in Rome.

On the west side of Piazza del Duomo, Via Mercanti leads past (right) Palazzo dei Giureconsulti (1560–64), recently restored and now used for exhibitions. The fine **Palazzo della Ragione** (Map II, 11; right), erected in 1228–33, has an upper storey added in 1771, and remains of 13C frescoes inside. A remarkable equestrian relief of 1233 adorns its rear wall in the peaceful Piazza Mercanti. In this old square are the Gothic Loggia degli Osii (1316) and the Baroque Palazzo delle Scuole Palatine (1645).

La Scala

Piazza della Scala, reached from Piazza Duomo by the Galleria Vittorio Emanuele, has a monument to Leonardo da Vinci (by Pietro Magni, 1872), surrounded by figures of his pupils, Boltraffio, Salaino, Cesare da Sesto and Marco d'Oggiono. The square takes its name from the **Teatro alla Scala** (**Map II, 7**), Italy's most famous opera house. It was built for Empress Maria Theresa of Austria, in 1776, by Giuseppe Piermarini on the site of the church of Santa Maria della Scala after the destruction by fire of the Regio Ducale Teatro. It opened in 1778 with *Europa Riconosciuta* by Antonio Salieri and Mattia Verazi. Works by Rossini, Donizetti, Bellini, Verdi and Puccini were first acclaimed here. From the beginning of this century its reputation was upheld by the legendary figure of Toscanini (who led the orchestra again in 1946 when the building was reopened after serious war damage).

Under the portico to the left of the theatre is the **Museo Teatrale alla Scala** (open Tues–Sun 09.00–12.00, 14.00–17.00; closed Sun Nov–Apr), with a valuable collection relating to theatrical and operatic history. The theatre can be visited from the museum.

*Palazzo Marino** (Map II, 7), the town hall, stands opposite La Scala. It has a fine façade on Piazza San Fedele by Galeazzo Alessi (1553–58), who also designed the splendid Mannerist courtyard. The façade on Piazza Scala was completed by Luca Beltrami (1886–92). Behind the Palazzo, in Piazza San Fedele, are a statue of Manzoni and the church of San Fedele, begun by Tibaldi (1569) for St Charles Borromeo and completed by Martino Basi and Francesco Maria Richini. It has an elaborate pulpit.

The Museo Poldi Pezzoli

The busy and fashionable Via Manzoni (**Map II, 7**) leads northeast from La Scala towards Piazza Cavour; no. 29, the Grand Hotel et de Milan (founded in 1865), still the most elegant hotel in Milan, is where Giuseppe Verdi died in 1901.

At no. 12 is the entrance to the *Museo Poldi-Pezzoli (**Map II, 7**), once the private residence of Gian Giacomo Poldi-Pezzoli. It was bequeathed by him, with his art collection, to the city in 1879, and opened to the public in 1881. It is now a delightful, well-run museum (open Tues–Sun 09.30–12.30, 14.30–18.00; Sat 14.30–19.30; Apr–Sept closed on Sun afternoon).

In the entrance hall with the ticket office is a portrait of Poldi-Pezzoli by Italy's foremost Romantic painter, Francesco Hayez. A delightful elliptical staircase, with a baroque fountain and landscapes by Alessandro Magnasco, ascends to the main picture gallery on the first floor. To the left are the three little **Salette dei Lombardi**, with *Madonnas* by Vincenzo Foppa and Ambrogio Bergognone; a portrait by Vincenzo Foppa; *The Rest on the Flight* (with a charming landscape) by Andrea Solario; a *Madonna* by Boltraffio; and works by Luini and the Lombard school.

Beyond the vestibule is the **Sala degli Stranieri** (or antechamber) with paintings by Cranach, including portraits of Luther and his wife. The Saletta degli Stucchi contains porcelain from Meissen, Doccia and Capodimonte. The Salone Dorato has the masterpieces of the collection: a *Madonna and Child* and *Portrait of a Man* by Mantegna; a *Pietà* by Giovanni Bellini; a *Pietà* and *Madonna* by Botticelli; *St Nicholas of Tolentino* by Piero della Francesca; and a famous *Portrait of a Lady* by Antonio Pollaiolo or his brother Piero.

The three rooms beyond contain the Emilio Visconti Venosta collection, including a portrait of Cardinal Ascanio Sforza by the Lombard school (c 1490) and a small cross painted on both sides attributed to Raphael. Also the Bruno Falck donation of antique clocks and scientific instruments, and a series of portraits, mostly by Vittore Ghislandi of Bergamo (1655–1743).

Beyond the Salone Dorato and the Saletta degli Stucchi (right) is the **Sala Nera**, so-called from its decoration (partly preserved) in ivory and ebony. It contains a Florentine table in *pietre dure* and a statue of *Faith* by Lorenzo Bartolini. The beautiful painting of *Artemesia* is attributed to the 'Maestro di Griselda' (recently attributed also to Luca Signorelli). Works by Bergognone and Sassoferrato, and a 16C Flemish triptych, are also here. The **Sala dei Vetri Antichi di Murano** contains 17C–19C miniatures as well as examples of glass (15C–19C) from Murano. The **Saletta di Dante** is an interesting room decorated at the end of the 19C in the Gothic-revival style. The marble bust of Rosa Poldi Pezzoli is by Lorenzo Bartolini.

The **Sala del Palma**, with a portrait of a courtesan by Palma il Vecchio and a small painting by Giovanni Battista Moroni, is entered from the Sala Nera. Also displayed here is the Portaluppi collection of some 200 sundials of the 16C–19C. Beyond are the two **Sale Trivulzio**. The first has paintings by Bernardo Strozzi, Alessandro Magnasco, and Jusepe Ribera, as well as Islamic bronzes (14C–16C). The second, the **Sala dei Bronzetti**, has small Renaissance bronzes, and a Hellenistic head of the young Bacchus (2C BC).

Beyond the Sala del Palma is the **Gabinetti degli Ori**, which contains a precious collection of ancient jewellery and goldsmiths' work, and medieval religious bronzes and Limoges enamels. The **Sala del Settecento Veneto** has works by Guardi (*Gondolas on the Venetian Lagoon*), Rosalba Carriera, and Gian Battista Tiepolo. The **Sala del Perugino** features works by Cima da Conegliano, Francesco Morone, Andrea Previtali, Mariotto Albertinelli (a tiny portable *altar*), Perugino, Biagio di Antonio di Firenze, and Lorenzo Lotto. The **Saletta dei Trecenteschi** contains 14C works by Jacopo Bellini, Carlo Crivelli, Cosmè Tura, Lazzaro Bastiani, and Bernardo Daddi.

On the ground floor is the Sala dell'Affresco, named after its ceiling fresco by Carlo Innocenzo Carloni. A splendid Persian *carpet with hunting scenes, signed and dated 1542–43, is displayed here, together with other precious carpets and tapestries shown on a rotating basis. The **Sala dei Tessuti** is being arranged to contain the Bertini collection of textiles, which has 268 examples from the 14C to the 19C. Some of these will be displayed in rotation, and there will be access to the rest of the collection by a computer installed here. On the other side of the Sala dell'Affresco is the lace collection (displayed in cupboards), which includes examples of Italian and Flemish work from the 16C–19C, and a library (which includes books printed in 1495–1515 by Aldo Manuzio). Another room off the entrance hall displays the armoury, with 14C–19C arms and armour.

Via Morone (Map II, 7) is a characteristic 19C street. At no. 1 is the **Museo Manzoniano** (open daily except Sat, Mon and holidays 09.30–12.00, 14.00–16.00), in the house where Alessandro Manzoni (1785–1873), author of *I Promessi Sposi* (The Betrothed), lived from 1814 until his death. It contains mementoes of Italy's most famous novelist, who met Balzac here in 1837. In Piazza Belgioioso is the huge Palazzo Belgioioso by Giuseppe Piermarini (1772). In Via Omenoni (right), the house of the sculptor Leone Leoni is decorated with caryatids.

The Museo Bagatti Valsecchi

Further along Via Manzoni, Via Monte Napoleone, another interesting 19C street, with fashionable shops, diverges right. At Via Gesù 5 is the entrance to the *Museo Bagatti Valsecchi (Map II, 4; open Tues–Sun 13.00–17.00). The palace was built by the brothers Fausto and Giuseppe Bagatti Valsecchi in 1876–87 in the style of the Lombard Renaissance and furnished by them with 16C works of art or excellent 19C imitations by Lombard craftsmen. It was the family home until 1974, when the Bagatti Valsecchi established a foundation and sold the palace to the regional government of Lombardy. Its main façade is in Via Santo Spirito (opposite another fine palace in red brick, also built by the brothers in 1895 in 15C style). The palace and its contents represent an extremely interesting and well-preserved example of the eclectic taste of 19C collectors. It was opened to the public in 1994 as a delightful private museum, carefully looked after by volunteer custodians. All the works are well labelled, also in English.

The two brothers lived in separate apartments in the palace on either side of the drawing room, gallery of arms, and dining room, which they shared. The rooms are richly decorated with carved ceilings, fireplaces, doorways, floors and wall hangings, and filled with a miscellany of furniture and works of art, some of it Renaissance and some exquisitely made 19C imitations commissioned by the brothers to fit the rooms.

The main staircase leads up to a vestibule, beyond which a marble portal carved in 1884 in Renaissance style gives access to the **Sala dell'Affresco**, with a fresco by Antonio Boselli (1496). The **Sala Bevilacqua** takes its name from a painting by Ambrogio Bevilacqua. Beyond the panelled library, with a collection of 17C sundials, is Fausto's bedroom with an intricately carved 16C bed and two paintings by Giampietrino. Beyond the dressing room and bathroom, with ingenious plumbing masked by Renaissance carvings, is the Galleria della Cupola, interesting for its architecture and containing a collection of ceramics.

The three rooms of Giuseppe's apartment have a magnificent old stove, a late-15C Venetian painting of the *Blessed Lorenzo Giustiniani*, a painting attributed to Giovanni Bellini, and an early 17C Sicilian bed. The largest room in the house is the **drawing room**, with a 19C fireplace (made up of 16C fragments) and red wall hangings. The long **Galleria delle Armi** was created to display the collection of 16C and 17C armour. The dining room has a pair of sideboards, one 16C and one a 19C copy. The walls are covered with 16C tapestries. The cupboards contain 16C Murano glass and Faenza ceramics. Beyond the study a staircase leads down to the Via Santo Spirito entrance.

The Pinacoteca di Brera

Via Verdi and Via Brera lead north from La Scala to the **Palazzo di Brera** (Map II, 3). The building was begun by Francesco Maria Richini in 1651 on the site of the medieval church of Santa Maria di Brera, the nave of which survives. The main portal is by Giuseppe Piermarini (1780). In the monumental courtyard, by Richini, is a heroic statue in bronze of Napoleon I by Antonio Canova (1809; the marble version of the statue is in Apsley House, London). The Brera is a centre of the arts and sciences in Lombardy: in addition to the picture gallery, it contains the Accademia di Belle Arti, the Biblioteca Nazionale (with some 1,000,000 volumes, including 2357 incunabula and 2000 manuscripts), the Astronomical Observatory and the Institute of Science and Letters.

The *Pinacoteca di Brera is one of the more famous art galleries in Italy. It contains the finest existing collection of Northern Italian painting. The collection is extremely well displayed: the arrangement proceeds chronologically and by schools. There are long-term plans to open the adjacent Palazzo Citterio in Via Brera as an extension to the gallery to exhibit the 19C and 20C works and the Jesi collection.

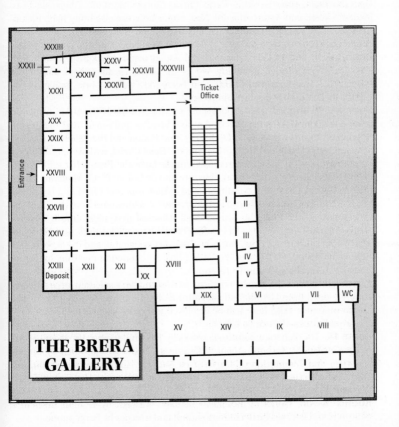

THE BRERA GALLERY

The gallery was founded in the 18C by the Accademia di Belle Arti, and was enlarged through acquisitions and paintings from Lombard and Venetian churches before it was officially inaugurated in 1809. The collection has continued to grow in this century with numerous donations. It is never shown in its entirety. Some rooms are closed when there is a shortage of custodians; scholars can sometimes ask for special permission to see them.

• The gallery is open Tues–Sat 09.00–17.00; Sun and holidays 09.00–12.15. All the rooms are clearly numbered in Roman numerals and the pictures are well labelled. The standard of the paintings is exceptionally high, and only some have been mentioned in the description below.

Stairs lead up from the far side of the courtyard to the loggia on the **first floor**, off which is the entrance to the gallery with the ticket office.

Room I Beyond a small room with the self-portrait of Francesco Hayez, the long gallery (room I) temporarily displays early 20C works (particularly the Futurists) from the Jesi collection, including works by Umberto Boccioni, Mario Sironi, Giacomo Balla, Gino Severini, Carlo Carrà, Giorgio Morandi, Filippo de Pisis, Medardo Rosso and Arturo Martini. New acquisitions are also hung here, including a work by Massimo Campigli. In a little room off the gallery, the Mocchirolo chapel, frescoed by a close follower of Giovanni da Milano, has been reconstructed.

Rooms II, III and IV The chronological display begins in rooms II and III with 13C Italian paintings, including works by Giovanni da Milano, Ambrogio Lorenzetti (*Madonna and Child*), and Bernardo Daddi. A fine *polyptych by Gentile da Fabriano is displayed in room IV.

Rooms V, VI and VII These rooms contain works of the 15C and 16C Venetian school. In room V is a polyptych by Antonio Vivarini and Giovanni d'Alemagna. Room VI contains works by 15C painters from Padua and the Veneto, including some masterpieces by Mantegna: his famous *Dead Christ*, with remarkable foreshortening, and a *polyptych representing *St Luke the Evangelist* with saints (1453). Also three exquisite works by Giovanni Bellini: a *Pietà, *Madonna Greca* (one of his most beautiful paintings), and a *Madonna and Child* in a landscape (1510). Vittore Carpaccio is also well represented, with scenes from the life of the Virgin, two works from the Scuola degli Albanesi in Venice, and *St Stephen Disputing with the Doctors* (1514). *St Peter Martyr with Saints, and *Madonna and Child Enthroned* are two works by Cima da Conegliano, and the *St Sebastian* here is by Liberale da Verona. Room VII has 16C Venetian portraits by Titian, Lorenzo Lotto, Torbido, and Tintoretto.

Room VIII Here is *St Mark Preaching in Alexandria*, a splendid large painting commissioned from Gentile and Giovanni Bellini by the Scuola Grande di San Marco in Venice. Also here will be displayed works by Michele da Verona, and Giovanni Battista Martini da Udine.

Room IX 16C Venetian paintings: works by Jacopo Bassano; Veronese, *Agony in the Garden*, *St Anthony Abbot with Saints*, *Supper in the House of Simon*, *Baptism and Temptation of Christ*, *Last Supper*; Tintoretto, *Deposition, and Saints beneath the Cross*; *Finding of the Body of St Mark at Alexandria*; Titian, *St Jerome*; Lorenzo Lotto, *Pietà* (1545).

Rooms X–XIII Works by Bonifacio Bembo; *frescoes by Donato Bramante; paintings and frescoes by Bernardino Luini; and frescoes by Bergognone.

Room XIV 16C Venetian school: works by Palma Vecchio; Paris Bordone (*Baptism of Christ*), Bonifacio Veronese, Giovanni Cariani, Giovanni Battista Moroni and Gerolamo Savoldo. Room XV (15C–16C Lombard paintings and frescoes): works by Marco d'Oggiono and Bergognone. The *Pala Sforzesca* (Madonna enthroned with doctors of the Church and the family of Lodovico il Moro) is by an unknown Lombard painter (c 1490–1520), known from this painting as the 'Maestro della Pala Sforzesca'. Also here are works by Vincenzo Foppa (*polyptych), Bramantino (Bartolomeo Suardi), and Gaudenzio Ferrari.

Room XVIII The collection continues in room XVIII (16C Lombard paintings): works by Callisto Piazza (*Baptism of Christ*), Giulio Campi, Boccaccino, Bernardino Campi, Giovan Paolo Lomazzo and Antonio Campi, and a portrait of *Alda Gambara* by Altobello Melone. Room XIX contains a very fine collection of paintings by followers of Leonardo da Vinci. Portraits by Giovanni Ambrogio de Predis, Andrea Solario, and Giovanni Antonio Boltraffio (*Gerolamo Casio*), and works by Bartolomeo Veneto, Giampietrino, Cesare da Sesto, Bernardino Luini (*Madonna del Roseto*), and Ambrogio Bergognone.

Room XX 15C Ferrarese and Emilian schools: Francesco del Cossa, *St John the Baptist*, *St Peter*; works by Lorenzo Costa, Gian Francesco Maineri, Marco Palmezzano, Francesco Zaganelli, and Filippo Mazzola.

Room XXI Polyptychs by 15C painters from the Marches, and a delightful group of works by Carlo Crivelli: *Crucifixion*, *Madonna 'della Candeletta*, *Coronation of the Virgin and Pietà* (1483), and a *triptych painted for the Duomo of Camerino. **Room XXII** (15C–16C Ferrarese and Emilian schools): Francesco and Bernardo Zaganelli, Nicolò Rondinelli, Ercole de' Roberti, and Giovanni Luteri.

Room XXIII This room has two works by Correggio.

Room XXIV Here are the two most famous works in the collection: Raphael's *Marriage of the Virgin* (the *Sposalizio*, 1504), the masterpiece of his Umbrian period, with a remarkable circular temple in the background; and Piero della Francesca's *Montefeltro altarpiece*, with the Madonna surrounded by angels and saints, in the presence of Federigo, Duke of Montefeltro. This is Piero's last known work and has a highly refined architectural setting. Also displayed here is a processional standard, an early work by Luca Signorelli, painted on both sides with the *Flagellation and Madonna and Child*, and *Christ at the Column* (from Chiaravalle), the only known panel painting by Donato Bramante.

Room XXVII The collection continues in Room XXVII (central Italian paintings of the 15C–16C): works by Gerolamo Genga, Luca Signorelli, Francesco Salviati, Giovanni Antonio Sogliani and Agnolo Bronzino.

Room XXVIII Works of the 17C Bolognese school: Federico Barocci (*Martyrdom of St Vitale*), Ludovico Carracci, Annibale Carracci (*Samaritan at the Well*), Guercino, Guido Reni (*Saints Peter and Paul*).

Room XXIX Caravaggio and his followers: works by Caravaggio (*Supper at Emmaus*), Mattia Preti, Jusepe de Ribera, Giovanni Battista Caracciolo, and Orazio Gentileschi (*Three Martyrs*).

Room XXX Works by the 17C Lombard school: Giulio Cesare Procaccini, Daniele Crespi, Giovanni Battista Crespi, Morazzone and Tanzio.

Rooms XXXI and XXXII Flemish and Italian 17C paintings: Pietro da Cortona, Bernardo Strozzi, Evaristo Baschenis, Rubens, van Dyck. Room XXXII displays16C and 17C Flemish and Dutch paintings including works by the 'Maestro di

Anversa' (1518), a triptych by Jan de Beer, and *St Francis* by El Greco.
Room XXXIII Portraits by Rembrandt (of his sister) and van Dyck, and works by Brueghel the Elder.
Room XXXIV 17C works by Pierre Subleyras, Giuseppe Maria Crespi (*Crucifixion)*, Sebastiano Ricci, Luca Giordano (*Ecce Homo*), and Giovanni Battista Tiepolo.
Rooms XXXV and XXXVI 18C paintings on either side of a corridor, with portraits by Sir Joshua Reynolds and Anton Raphael Mengs. Room XXXV has Venetian works by Giovanni Battista Tiepolo, Francesco Guardi, Francesco Zugno, Bernardo Bellotto, Canaletto, Giovanni Battista Piazzetta, and Rosalba Carriera. In Room XXXVI are genre scenes by Giacomo Ceruti and portraits by Vittore Ghislandi.
Rooms XXXVII and XXXVIII 19C Italian works by Giovanni Fattori, Silvestro Lega (the *Pergolato*), Zandomeneghi, Prud'hon, and portraits by Francesco Hayez, Andrea Appiani and Sir Thomas Lawrence. A version of Giuseppe Pellizza da Volpedo's famous painting entitled *Quarto Stato* and Boccioni's self-portrait are displayed in room XXXVIII.

In Via Brera, in the little piazza beside the gallery, stands a monument to the painter Francesco Hayez, by Francesco Barzaghi (1898). The 18C Palazzo Citterio has been restored as an extension of the Brera Academy; it conceals botanical gardens founded in 1783 (admission by special permission from the biology department of the university). Palazzo Cusani, by Giovanni Ruggeri (1719), at Via Brera 15, is now a local military headquarters. The adjacent Via del Carmine leads to the 15C church of Santa Maria del Carmine (**Map II, 2**), with a façade completed in 1879 and a fine Baroque chapel decorated by Camillo Procaccini.

Via Borgonuovo with a series of fine palaces and interesting courtyards, lies directly behind the Brera. You can get there by taking Via Fiori Scuri, named after the dark-haired women who sold their services in the houses here (blondes, or *fiori chiari*, worked on the block west of Via Brera). Palazzo Moriggia, at Via Borgonuovo 23, was rebuilt in the 18C by Piermarini. Today it houses the **Museo del Risorgimento** (Map II, 3; open Tues–Sun 09.00–13.00, 14.00–18.00); the exhibits (arranged chronologically in 14 rooms) include material dating from the arrival of Napoleon in Lombardy in 1796 up to the taking of Rome in 1870. There is also a good library.
    Via Borgonuovo ends at the Montenapoleone Metro station, in a small square adjoining Via Manzoni. Turn right here to return to Piazza del Duomo.

On Milan and the Milanese

Milan is striking—the Cathedral superb—the city altogether reminds me of Seville—but a little inferior.
Lord Byron, letter to John Murray, 15 October 1816

Milanese... a vagrant tribe, whose industry and enterprise carry them from the Lake of Como to the remotest regions of the earth. They are seen in all countries; even in Lapland.
E.D. Clarke, *Travels in Various Countries*, 4th ed., 1816

> *The people here, though inoffensive enough, seem both in body and soul a miserable race. The men are hardly men; they look like a tribe of stupid and shrivelled slaves, and I do not think that I have seen a gleam of intelligence in the countenance of man since I passed the Alps. The women in enslaved countries are always better than the men; but they have tight-laced figures, and figures and mien which express (O how unlike the French!) a mixture of coquette and prude which reminds me of the worst characteristics of the English. Everything but humanity is in much greater perfection here than in France.*
> Percy Bysshe Shelley, letter to Thomas Love Peacock, 20 April 1818.
>
> *Milan was entered by us with anticipations the most gracious; which, contrary to ordinary experience, were surpassed by the events. The very name of this city, as I write it, awakens feelings which the impartiality of veracious narrative should distrust.*
> Lady Morgan, *Italy*, 1820.
>
> *Milan always affected my imagination as representing the splendour and wealth of the middle age.*
> Matthew Arnold, letter to his wife, 25 June 1863
>
> *Milan... has seemed prosaic and winterish as if it were on the wrong side of the Alps.*
> Henry James, letter to Mrs Fanny Kemble, 24 March 1881
>
> *Milan is a giant, nightmare city. The snow & rain had just ceased before we arrived—a day or two before. The immensely long, wide streets, which run the entire length of the city, or seem to, were bakingly hot & dusty, clanking with great, packed, racing trams, buzzing with little toy motor bikes.*
> Dylan Thomas, letter to his parents, 11 April 1947
>
> *Italy's answer to Birmingham.*
> Anon.

Around San Simpliciano

During the Middle Ages Milan's northern quarters grew up around the basilica of San Sempliciano. Although this early Christian church remains the area's oldest monument, it has long ceased to be the most conspicuous. Today northern Milan is dominated by the huge fortified complex of the Castello Sforzesco and the shady green Parco Sempione, behind it. But there are several other fine monuments in the area, too.

The walk described below begins a few paces north of the Pinacoteca di Brera. This part of the city can be reached easily from Piazza del Duomo on the underground (**Line 1**) in two stops (Cairoli station), or from Piazza della Scala by **Tram 1**.

San Marco
The church of San Marco (**Map II, 3**), north of the Palazzo di Brera, dates from 1254, but the interior was altered in the Baroque period. On the mock-Gothic façade (1873) the doorway and three statuettes date from the 14C. Verdi's *Requiem* received its first performance here.

Inside, the nave is exceptionally long. The first chapel of the south aisle has frescoes and an altarpiece by Gian Paolo Lomazzo (1571). At the end of the aisle is a *Nativity* by Legnanino. In the south transept stands the tomb of the Blessed Lanfranco da Settala (d. 1264), ascribed to Giovanni di Balduccio, and mid-14C frescoes. The presbytery has a vault and apse frescoed in the early 17C by Il Genovesino (who also painted the two paintings in the choir), and paintings by Camillo Procaccini and Cerano. The altar dates from 1816. The north transept has paintings by Legnanino. In the north aisle are altarpieces by Legnanino, Camillo Procaccini, and Giulio Cesare Procaccini. The third chapel features an interesting *grisaille* fresco by a painter of Leonardo's school. A room contains frescoes of the late 13C Lombard school which have been detached from the campanile.

To the north, in Via Moscova, is the 16C church of Sant'Angelo (**Map I,7**), with paintings and frescoes by Camillo Procaccini (in poor condition).

San Simpliciano

The northernmost of Milan's early Christian basilicas, to the west (**Map II, 2**), is dedicated to the successor of St Ambrose in the episcopal chair. It was probably founded by St Ambrose himself in the 4C and, despite the alterations of the 12C, stands largely in its original form. Eighteen huge window embrasures were revealed after 1945. The interior contains the *Coronation of the Virgin*, a fine fresco by Bergognone, in the restored Romanesque apse, masked by the towering altar. Frescoes of Saints by Aurelio Luini are at the entrance to the presbytery, beneath the organs.

The Castello Sforzesco

The spacious Foro Buonaparte, Largo Cairoli (with a monument to Garibaldi by Ettore Ximenes, 1895), and Piazza Castello, with its trees, were all designed in a huge hemicycle in 1884 in front of the *Castello Sforzesco (**Map II, 1, 2**). This was the stronghold built for Francesco Sforza in 1451–66 on the site of a 14C castle of the Visconti. After a long period of use as barracks, it was restored by Luca Beltrami (1893–1904). Badly damaged by bombing in 1943, when two-thirds of the archives and many other treasures were lost, it was again carefully restored. It now contains important art collections and cultural institutions, and various projects for the reutilisation and restoration of parts of the castle have been under discussion for years.

The fortress is square in plan; on the façade are three towers, of which the central one is the Filarete tower, destroyed by an explosion of powder in 1521 and rebuilt by Beltrami following the supposed design of the original. The entrance to the castle from Largo Cairoli is beneath the tower that gives access to the huge Piazza d'Armi, the main courtyard. Almost in the centre of the far side is the 15C Torre di Bona di Savoia, beyond which to the left is the Rocchetta, with a courtyard, which served as a keep. On the right is the Corte Ducale, the residential part of the castle, with a charming courtyard.

Here is the entrance to the Museo d'Arte Antica and the Pinacoteca (open Tues–Sun 09.00–17.40). The large collections of sculpture, paintings, furniture, musical instruments, and decorative arts are beautifully arranged and well labelled: only a few of the works are mentioned here.

Museo d'Arte Antica

Sculpture is displayed on the **ground floor**. Highlights from the first four rooms include fragments from ancient churches and other Byzantine and Romanesque

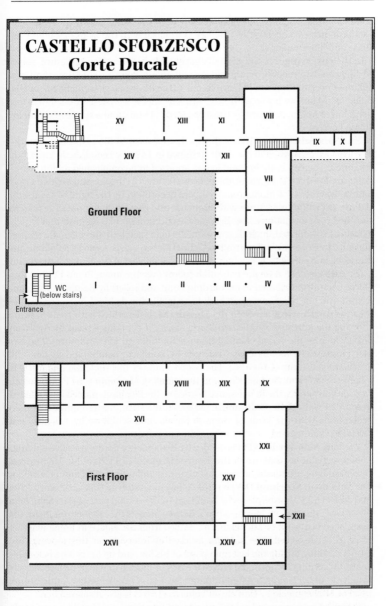

remains, including a 6C marble portrait head supposedly of the Empress Theodora; Visconti tombs by Bonino da Campione (1363); remains of the façade of Santa Maria di Brera and statues from the east gate of the city, by Giovanni di Balduccio of Pisa; a 14C pavement tomb with an effigy thought to be that of

Bona di Savoia; and a *sepulchral monument of the Rusca family by a late 14C Lombard master. The vault of room **IV** is frescoed with the arms of Philip II of Spain and Mary Tudor.

·In the **east wing**, beyond a small chapel with 14C Venetian sculpture, room **VI** contains 12C reliefs from the old Porta Romana, showing the triumph of the Milanese over Barbarossa (1176). Room **VII**, with frescoed escutcheons of the Dukes of Milan, is hung with 17C Brussels tapestries. Here is displayed the Gonfalon of Milan, designed by Giuseppe Meda (1566), and a statue of *Adam* by Stoldo Lorenzi.

The *Sala delle Asse (**VIII**), at the northeast corner of the castle, has remarkable frescoed decoration in the vault, designed in 1498 by Leonardo da Vinci, but repainted. The ilex branches and leaves are used in a complicated architectural structure in which the form of the octagon recurs. On the far wall are two fascinating *fragments of monchrome tempera decoration by the hand of Leonardo (1498), depicting tree trunks with branches and roots growing out of cracks in stratified rock formations. The Belgioioso collection of 17C Flemish and Dutch paintings is exhibited, including a monochrome sketch of three female figures and putti by Rubens, a self-portrait by Gabriel Metsu, a river scene by Solomon van Ruysdael, and portraits by Joachim Wetwael, is exhibited in the centre of the room.

Off the Sala delle Asse are two small rooms over the moat. Room **IX** contains Sforza portraits attributed to Bernardino Luini and reliefs by Bambaia. In Room **X** is an oval low relief carved on both faces by Pierino da Vinci.

In the **north wing**, the **Sala dei Ducali (XI)** is decorated with coats of arms showing the ancestry of Galeazzo Maria Sforza. It contains a relief by Agostino di Duccio from the Tempio Malatestiano at Rimini, and 15C sculptures. The former chapel (**XII**) has frescoes (restored) by Bonifacio Bembo and Stefano de' Fedeliand assistants (1466–76). The seated statue of the *Madonna and Child* is a Lombard work of the late 15C, and the standing *Madonna* is by Pietro Solari. Outside you can see the Renaissance Portico of the Elephant, named after a faded fresco. The **Sala delle Colombine (XIII)**, on the right, has red-and-gold fresco decorations with the arms of Bona di Savoia, and sculpture by Amadeo and Cristoforo Mantegazza.

The long **Sala Verde (XIV)** is divided by Renaissance doorways salvaged from Milanese palaces: that from the Banco Mediceo (1455) is by Michelozzo. Displayed here are tombs, armorial sculptures, and a fine collection of armour. The **Sala degli Scarlioni (XV)** has the *effigy of Gaston de Foix and *reliefs from his tomb (1525), masterpieces by Bambaia. In the second part of the room, on a lower level, uncomfortably placed on a Roman altar, is the *Rondanini Pietà*, the unfinished last work of Michelangelo, named from the palace in Rome where it used to be displayed. The sculptor worked at intervals on this moving, but pathetic, statue during the last nine years of his life, and up to six days before his death. According to Vasari, he reused a block of marble in which he had already roughed out a *Pietà* on a different design and on a smaller scale. A fine bronze head of Michelangelo by Daniele da Volterra (1564) is also displayed here.

From the corner a wooden bridge leads out into the Corte Ducale across a subterranean court with a 16C fountain. On the left stairs lead up to the first floor (rooms **XVI–XIX**) which contains the splendid collection of *furniture arranged to give a progressive chronological impression of Lombard interiors of the 15C–18C.

Pinacoteca

Steps lead up from room XIX to the Pinacoteca (rooms XX–XXVI).

Room XX In the vaulted tower (room XX) are some beautiful paintings: a recently acquired painting of *St Benedict* by Antonello da Messina; the *Pala Trivulzio* by Mantegna (1497); a polyptych signed and dated 1462 by Benedetto Bembo; a superb *Madonna and Child* by Giovanni Bellini; and a very unusual work (the *Madonna of Humility*) by Filippo Lippi.

Room XXI This room contains Lombard Renaissance works by Vincenzo Foppa, Bergognone and Bramantino; works by followers of Leonardo, including Boltraffio and Cesare da Sesto; and paintings by Il Sodoma and Correggio.

Rooms XXII, XXIII, XXIV The little room XXII has a small *Crucifixion* attributed to Marcello Venusti. Room XXIII displays Lombard works by Nuvolone, Cerano and Morazzone, and room XXIV late 16C and early 17C northern Italian schools (including Moncalvo).

Room XXV contains a magnificent display of portraits by Giovanni Bellini, Correggio, Giovanni Antonio Boltraffio (*Lady in Red*), Baldassarre d'Este, Lorenzo Lotto (*Boy Holding a Book*), Agnolo Allori, Giovanni Battista Moroni, Tintoretto and Titian. A fine portrait of *Henrietta Maria of France* by van Dyck hangs at the end of the room on the right wall.

Room XXVI The long rooom XXVI contains 17C and 18C Lombard, Neapolitan, and Venetian works (Daniele Crespi, Cerano, Morazzone, Giacomo Ceruti, Bernardino Strozzi, Jusepe Ribera, Alessandro Magnasco, Sebastiano Ricci, Giovanni Battista Tiepolo, Francesco Guardi and Canaletto).

Rochetta

It is now necessary to return downstairs to the entrance (room **I**). From here stairs lead up to the first floor of the Rocchetta, where the *decorative arts are displayed. Room **XXXVI** contains a splendid large collection of musical instruments, with lutes, an outstanding group of wind instruments, a clavichord of 1503, a spinet played by the 14-year-old Mozart, and a *fortepiano* by Muzio Clementi. There is also a rich collection of musical manuscripts and autographs. The ball court (room **XXXVII**), hung with tapestries of the *Months* from designs by Bramantino (c 1503), has more musical instruments.

From here return to room XXXIII and go upstairs to the second floor. Room **XXVIII** contains wrought-iron work. Rooms **XXIX** and **XXX** contain a large collection of *ceramics, both Italian and foreign. Off room **XXX** is an interesting collection (formed in 1858) of pre-Columbian works from Peru and Argentina, dating from the 2C BC to the 16C. Stairs lead up to a mezzanine above room **XXX** with a collection of costumes from the 1920s and 1930s (including some gorgeous evening gowns). Room **XXXI**, overlooking the ball court (see above) has a display of European 18C and 19C porcelain. Room **XXXII** contains goldsmiths' work, enamels, *ivories, church silver and small bronzes. Return to room **XXVII**, from where stairs descend to the exit.

Three sections of the **Civico Museo Archeologico** are also displayed in the castle. From the Corte Ducale you descend to a basement room with the epigraphic section. This includes 101 Roman inscriptions from Milan arranged in four series: those concerning public life; religious inscriptions; community affairs (merchants, artisans and tradesmen); and private family life.

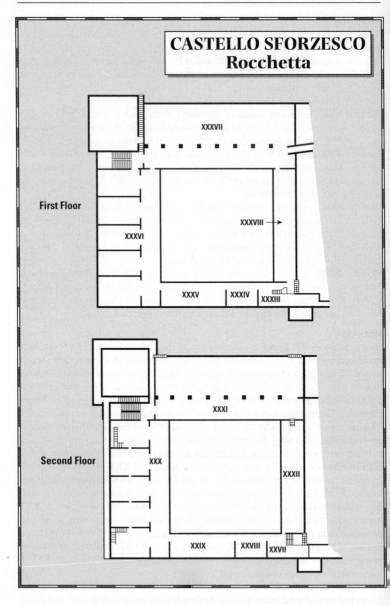

In the arcaded *courtyard of the Rocchetta, in the design of which both Filarete and Bramante had a hand, is the entrance to the Egyptian section, also arranged in the basement. It contains a small collection of objects dating from the Old Kingdom to the age of Ptolemy, illustrating the funerary cult of ancient

Egypt, with sarcophagi, mummies and books of the dead (papyri), and household and personal objects, canopic vases, jewellery, funerary masks, *stelae*, etc.

Also off the courtyard is the entrance to the prehistoric section, which includes a room containing material from Lombardy dating from the late Bronze Age to the Roman period, with the Golasecca culture (9C–5C BC) particularly well represented.

Elsewhere in the castle (admission to scholars) are the Archivio Storico Civico, the Biblioteca Trivulziana (with an Oriental art centre), a medal collection, and the Bertarelli collection of prints and maps.

Parco Sempione

The Parco Sempione (**Map II, 1**), a large park of 47h laid out by Emilio Alemagna in 1893 on the site of a 15C ducal park, begins on the far side of the castle. It contains a fountain by Giorgio de Chirico. The Palazzo dell'Arte (**Map I, 6**), built in 1931–33 by Giovanni Muzio, has recently been restored as an important exhibition centre. The **Aquarium** (**Map I, 6**) in a fine Art Nouveau building of 1906 (open Tues–Sun 09.30–17.30), with delightful 'aquatic' decorations on the exterior, has marine and freshwater fish, and important study collections. The arena (**Map I, 6**) was first built by Luigi Canonica in 1806–07. The high tower (110m), made of aluminium, was erected in 1933 by Giò Ponti and Cesare Chiodi. The fine equestrian monument to Napoleon III is by Francesco Barzaghi (1881). At the far end of the park is the **Arco della Pace** (**Map I, 5**), a triumphal arch modelled on the Arch of Severus in Rome, built by Luigi Cagnola in 1807–38. It was begun in honour of Napoleon I, but was dedicated to Peace by Ferdinand I of Austria on its completion. It marks the beginning of the Corso Sempione (**Map I, 1**), part of the 182km-long historic Simplon Road, constructed by order of Napoleon from Geneva to Sesto Calende across the Simplon Pass (1800–05).

Around Sant'Ambrogio

This area, due west of the duomo, is probably the most expensive residential neighbourhood in Italy. The stately old flats, many in period-revival buildings, overlook shady boulevards and wide, elegant streets. The district can be reached from central Milan (Via Mazzini) by bus **54**. Sant'Ambrogio station is on Metro **Line 1**.

Sant'Ambrogio

**Sant'Ambrogio (Map II, 9; closed 12.00–14.30), the most interesting church in Milan, was the prototype of the Lombard basilica. Founded by St Ambrose, Bishop of Milan, it was built in 379–86, beside a Christian cemetery, and enlarged in the 9C and again after 1080. The present building is the result of numerous careful restorations, and the dating of the various parts of the building is still uncertain. After a radical restoration in the 19C, it had to be repaired again after serious war damage in 1943.

The splendid atrium in front of the church, on an early Christian plan, was probably built in 1088–99, but was reconstructed in 1150. The austere façade consists of a five-bayed narthex below, with five arches above, graduated to fit the gable with decorative arcading. The south, or monks', campanile dates from the

9C; the higher canons' campanile on the north is a fine Lombard tower of 1128–44, crowned with a loggia of 1889. The great doorway has wood imposts made up of fragments from the 8C and 10C (heavily restored in the 18C); the bronze doors date from the 11C–12C.

The beautiful interior has a low rib-vaulted nave divided from the side aisles by wide arcades supported by massive pillars beneath a matroneum. There are no transepts, and beyond the tower over the crossing, with its magnificent ciborium, are three deep apses, the centre one raised above the crypt.

On the right is a statue of Pius IX (1880). On the left, beyond a column with a bronze serpent of the 10C, is the **pulpit, reconstituted from fragments of the 11C and early 12C saved after the vault collapsed in 1196 and one of the most remarkable Romanesque monuments known. Beneath it is a Roman palaeo-christian *sarcophagus (4C).

In the south aisle, the first chapel has a fresco attributed to Gaudenzio Ferrari and Giovanni Battista della Cerva. The second chapel has an altarpiece by Gaudenzio Ferrari, and two detached frescoes by Giovanni Battista Tiepolo. In the sixth chapel is a *Legend of St George* by Bernardino Lanino. The last chapel in this aisle dates from the 18C, with an altarpiece by Andrea Lanzani. To the left, beyond a fine 18C wrought-iron screen, is another 18C chapel with frescoes by Ferdinando Porta. At the end is the Sacello di San Vittore in Ciel d'Oro, a sepul-chral chapel built in a Christian cemetery in the 4C and altered later. Its name refers to the splendid 5C *mosaics, with a golden dome and six panels represent-ing saints (including St Ambrose) on the walls. At the end of the south aisle is a 6C sarcophagus.

The north aisle (first chapel) has a fresco of the *Redeemer* (with very unusual iconography) by Bergognone, and (in the third chapel) a tondo attributed to Bernardino Luini.

In the sanctuary, under the dome (which was rebuilt in the 13C and restored in the 19C), is the great *ciborium, thought to date from the 9C. The shafts of the columns, however, are probably of the time of St Ambrose. The four sides of the baldacchino are decorated with reliefs in coloured stucco in the Byzantine style (mid-10C). The *altar has a magnificent and justly celebrated casing presented in 835 by Archbishop Angilberto II, made of gold and silver plates sculptured in relief, with enamel and gems, the work of Volvinius, and representing scenes from the lives of Christ and St Ambrose. In the apse are mosaics of the 4C or 8C reset in the 18C and restored after the Second World War, and the 9C marble bishop's throne. The crypt contains the bodies of Saints Ambrose, Gervase and Protasius in a shrine of 1897.

From the east end of the north aisle a door admits to the Portico della Canonica, with columns carved in imitation of tree trunks, which was left unfin-ished by Bramante in 1499 (and reconstructed after the Second World War). A second side was added in 1955. The upper part houses the **Museo di Sant'Ambrogio** (open 10.00–12.00, 15.00–17.00; Sat and holidays 15.00–17.00; closed Tues and Aug). This contains textiles, including the Dalmatic of St Ambrose (protected by a curtain); early Christian mosaic frag-ments; 4C and 9C wood fragments from the old doors of the basilica; medieval capitals; a triptych by Bernardino Zenale; frescoes by Bergognone and Bernardino Luini; a 15C embroidered altar frontal; and two 17C Flemish tapes-tries. The illuminated manuscripts (10C–18C; removed), include a missal of Gian

Galeazzo Visconti (1395). The church treasury includes a 12C Cross and the early-15C *Reliquary of the Innocents*. Most of the frescoes of the 15C *Oratorio della Passione* by the school of Bernardino Luini were detached in 1869 and sold to the Victoria and Albert Museum in London.

To the north of the church is a war memorial erected in 1928 by Giovanni Muzio. The **Università Cattolica**, founded in 1921 and of extremely high academic standing, fronts the piazza here. It is housed in the former monastery of Sant'Ambrogio, which includes two fine cloisters designed by Bramante: the Ionic cloister was finished by Cristoforo Solari in 1513, and the Doric cloister in 1620–30. Roman remains have come to light here during work to enlarge the buildings.

At the beginning of Via San Vittore the Pusterla di Sant'Ambrogio, a gate in the medieval city walls, was reconstructed in 1939. Nearby in Via Carducci is a castellated palace built in 1910 by Adolfo Coppedè. Just off Via San Vittore to the right is **San Vittore al Corpo** (Map I, 9), in part by Galeazzo Alessi. The dark interior contains important early 17C works, including frescoes and paintings by Camillo Procaccini and Ambrogio Figino. The cupola is frescoed by Moncalvo and Daniele Crespi, and the beautifully carved choir stalls date from around 1583. In the north aisle are frescoes and paintings by Daniele Crespi, an altarpiece by Pompeo Batoni, and paintings by Pierre Subleyras.

The Museo Nazionale di Scienza e Tecnica

The old Olivetan convent (1507), which still contains a collection of frescoes by Bernardino Luini, was rebuilt in 1949–53 after war damage to house the huge *Museo Nazionale di Scienza e Tecnica (Map I, 9). Open Tues–Fri 09.30–16.50; Sat–Sun and holidays 09.30–18.20, the museum is much enjoyed by children.

The vestibule contains frescoes of the 15C Lombard school. To the right in the first cloister are displayed ancient carriages and velocipedes. To the left is the library, with the cinema beyond.

Staircases take you up to the **first floor**. On the right is the Sala della Bifora (kept locked) with the Mauro collection of goldsmiths' work and precious stones. The gallery is devoted to cinematography. Rooms to the right demonstrate the evolution of the graphic arts (printing, typewriters, etc.). At the end of the gallery, to the right, is the long **Leonardo Gallery**, which extends the entire length of the first and second cloisters. Here are exhibited *models of machines and apparatus invented by Leonardo da Vinci, of the greatest interest.

The rooms (right) which border the first cloister are devoted to time measurement and sound, including musical instruments and the reproduction of a lute-maker's shop. In the middle of the Leonardo Gallery are detached frescoes, and (right), the Sala delle Colonne, formerly the conventual library, used for exhibitions. Three galleries round the second cloister illustrate the science of physics, including electricity, acoustics and nuclear reaction. Beyond the astronomy gallery are rooms devoted to optics and to radio and telecommunications (with mementoes of Marconi).

At the end of the Leonardo Gallery stairs (right) lead down to the **lower floor**, devoted to metallurgy, petrochemical industries and transport, with a fine gallery of early motor cars. An external pavilion, in the form of a 19C railway station, contains railway locomotives and rolling stock. Another huge external pavilion illustrates air and sea transport, with a splendid display of airplanes, along with relics of aeronautical history, and ships, including a naval training ship.

On the ground floor is the Civico Museo Navale Didattico, founded in 1922, with navigational instruments and models of ships.

Santa Maria delle Grazie and the Cenacolo

A church of brick and terracotta with a very beautiful exterior, **Santa Maria delle Grazie** (Map I, 9) was erected in 1466–90 to the design of Guiniforte Solari. In 1492 Ludovico il Moro ordered the striking new choir and unusual domed crossing, and this has for long been attributed to Bramante, although it is now uncertain how much he was directly involved. The fine west portal is also usually attributed to Bramante.

Inside, the nave vault and aisles have fine frescoed decoration of c 1482–85 (restored in 1937). In the aisles, between the chapels, are frescoes of Dominican saints attributed to Bernardo Butinone. The first chapel in the south aisle has a fine tomb of the Della Torre family; in the third chapel are lunette frescoes attributed to Aurelio and Gian Piero Luini. The fourth chapel has frescoes by Gaudenzio Ferrari (1542), and in the fifth are stucco bas-reliefs (late 16C) of angels. The seventh has an altarpiece by Marco d'Oggiono.

The lovely light *tribuna, or domed crossing, designed by Bramante, has very unusual bright graffiti decoration. The choir also has graffiti decoration and fine stalls of carved and inlaid wood. A door leads out to the *chiostrino, also traditionally attributed to Bramante, with a delightful little garden. Off it is the old sacristy (only open for concerts), which marked a significant step in the development of Renaissance architecture.

At the end of the north aisle is the elaborate entrance (with 17C stuccoes and a lunette painting by Cerano to the chapel of the **Madonna delle Grazie**, containing a highly venerated 15C painting of the *Madonna* beneath a vault with restored 15C frescoes. The sixth chapel has a small *Holy Family* by Paris Bordone, and the second chapel has a funerary monument with sculptures attributed to Bambaia. The first chapel has frescoes by Giovanni Donato Montorfano.

In the **cenacolo** or refectory of the adjoining Dominican convent (entrance on the left of the façade; open Tues–Sun 08.00–13.45; reservations recommended, ☎ 199 199100) is the world-famous *Last Supper* by Leonardo da Vinci, painted in 1494–97. In order to protect the painting from dust and lessen the effects of pollution, visitors (only 15 or 20 at a time) go through a series of glass 'cubicles', installed with air-filtering systems, from which there is a good view of the main cloister and exterior of Santa Maria delle Grazie. The vault and right wall of the refectory were rebuilt after they were destroyed by a bomb in 1943.

This extraordinary painting, which was to have a lasting effect on generations of painters, depicts the moment when Christ announces Judas's betrayal at the Last Supper. The monumental Classical figures of the Apostles are shown in a stark room in perfect perspective, an extension of the refectory itself. The light enters through the real windows on the left and the painted windows in the background which look out over a landscape, and the wonderful colours culminate in the blue and red robe of Christ. On the side walls Leonardo painted tapestries decorated with bunches of flowers. Fascinating details of the objects on the table have recently been revealed, including the colour of the Apostles' robes reflected in the pewter plates and the transparent glass carafes. Above are lunettes with garlands of fruit and flowers around the coats of arms of the Sforza family. There is no evidence that Leonardo made use of a cartoon while working on this masterpiece.

The fresco decoration on the long wall is attributed to Bernardino de' Rossi. On the wall opposite the *Last Supper* is a large *Crucifixion* by Donato Montorfano (1495), the fine preservation of which is a vindication of the lasting quality of true fresco-painting. At the bottom of the fresco, at either side, are the kneeling figures, now nearly effaced, of Ludovico il Moro and his wife Beatrice d'Este and their two children, added by Leonardo before 1498.

Notes on Leonardo's technique

The *Last Supper* is painted with a technique peculiar to Leonardo, in tempera with the addition of later oil varnishes, on a prepared surface in two layers on the plastered wall. It is therefore not a fresco, and errors in the preparation of the plaster, together with the dampness of the wall, have caused great damage to the painted surface, which had already considerably deteriorated by the beginning of the 16C. Since that time it has been restored repeatedly, and was twice repainted (in oils) in the 18C. Careful work (begun in 1978 and completed in 1999) has been carried out to eliminate the false restorations of the past and to expose the original work of Leonardo as far as possible. The restoration, like that of Michelangelo's Sistine Ceiling in Rome, has sparked considerable controversy.

Corso Magenta (**Map II, 5**) leads back towards the centre of the city. At no. 24, Palazzo Litta, built by Francesco Maria Ricchino (1648), has a Rococo façade added in 1752–63.

Opposite is the former Monastero maggiore, to which belonged the church of **San Maurizio** (**Map II, 5**) begun in 1503, perhaps by Gian Giacomo Dolcebuono, with a façade of 1574–81. The harmonious *interior is divided by a wall into two parts. The western portion, originally for lay worshippers, has small chapels below and a graceful loggia above and contains numerous *frescoes by Bernardino Luini and his sons Aurelio and Giovan Pietro (1522–29), and other members of his school. A long and careful restoration project has been in progress here since 1980. In the loggia are frescoed medallions by Giovanni Antonio Boltraffio (1505–10).

The cloisters now form the entrance to the **Civico Museo Archeologico** (**Map II, 5**; Corso Magenta 5; open Tues–Sun 09.30–17.30), with Greek, Etruscan and Roman material relating to the history of Milan. In the cloisters are Roman sculpture and a large incised stone from Valle Camonica dating from the late Bronze Age.

The highlight of the ground floor exhibits is the famous *Coppa Trivulzio*, dating from the early 4C AD, a double coloured glass drinking cup of intricate workmanship with the inscription 'Drink and live many years!' It was found in a sarcophagus near Novara in 1675 and was acquired by Abbot Carlo Trivulzio in 1777 (and published by the German scholar Winckelmann in 1779). The silver *Parabiago Patera*, with Attis and Cybele and other fine figures in relief, a Roman work of the late 4C AD, is also displayed here. Other exhibits include a fine collection of antique vases; Roman sculpture (including a colossal torso of Hercules); mosaics found in the city; portrait busts (1C BC–4C AD); finds from Caesarea in the

Holy Land and 6C–7C jewellery from Nocera Umbra and Milan.

In the basement are (left) Etruscan material (*bucchero* vases, etc.) and (right) Indian Gandhara sculpture (2C–3C AD). The hall beyond has a fine display (chronological and topographical) of Greek ceramics (including Attic red- and black-figure vases). At the end of the room you can see the base of a stretch of Roman wall, part of the city walls.

The garden contains the **Torre di Ansperto**, an octagonal tower of Roman origin, with interesting traces of 13C frescoes, and a Roman sarcophagus of the 3C AD.

Via Santa Maria alla Porta, on the right further on, and Via Borromei (right) lead to Palazzo Borromeo (**Map II, 10**), a reconstructed 15C building. In an office (admission on request) off the second courtyard, are interesting frescoes depicting card games, etc. by a painter of the early 15C in the International Gothic style. The Pinacoteca Ambrosiana is a short way to the east.

The Pinacoteca Ambrosiana

The Palazzo dell'Ambrosiana (**Map II, 10**) contains the famous library and Pinacoteca founded by Cardinal Federico Borromeo at the beginning of the 17C. The palace was begun for the Cardinal by Lelio Buzzi in 1603–09 and later enlarged. The *Pinacoteca Ambrosiana (open Tues–Sun 10.00–17.30), entered from the left side of the courtyard, contains a superb collection of paintings. It has recently reopened after nearly a decade of restoration and rearrangement. Remains of Roman paving came to light during work on the foundations.

The Pinacoteca contains works by Botticelli (tondo of the *Madonna and Child*), Ghirlandaio, Pinturicchio, Bartolomeo Vivarini, Timoteo Viti, Bergognone (*Enthroned Madonna*), Marco Basaiti, Bernardino Zenale, Baldassarre Estense, Bambaia (*fragments of the tomb of Gaston de Foix*), Bernart van Orley, Hans Muhlich, Jan Soreau, Jan Brueghel the Younger, Hendrik Averkamp, Giorgione (attributed), Antonio Solario, Bramantino, Bernardino Luini (*Holy Family with St Anne and the Young St John*, from a cartoon by Leonardo, and portraits of the confraternity of Santa Corona, 1521), Giampietrino, Antonio Salaino, Leonardo da Vinci (*Portrait of a Musician*, thought to be Franchino Gaffurio, c 1485), Ambrogio de Predis (*Profile of a Young Lady*, often identified as Beatrice d'Este), Marco d'Oggiono, Il Sodoma and Bachiacca. Venetian painters represented include Giovanni Battista Moroni, Bonifacio Veronese and Jacopo Bassano (*Rest on the Flight into Egypt*). Paintings by Titian include the *Deposition*, *Sacred Conversation*, *Adoration of the Magi* (painted, with assistants, for Henri II and Diane de Poitiers in 1560, and still in its original frame), and a portrait of an old man in armour.

A darkened chamber provides a fit setting for Raphael's *cartoon for the School of Athens*, the only remaining cartoon of the fresco cycle in the Vatican, purchased by Cardinal Borromeo in 1626. The copy of Leonardo's *Last Supper* was made in 1612–16 by order of Cardinal Borromeo by Andrea Bianchi (Il Vespino).

There are also later works by Giulio Romano, Pellegrino Tibaldi, Barocci, Caravaggio (*Basket of Fruit*), Gian Domenico Tiepolo, Thorvaldsen, Canova and Andrea Appiani.

The library contains about 750,000 volumes, including 3000 incunabula and 35,000 manuscripts. Among the more precious works are Arabic and Syriac manuscripts; a *Divine Comedy* (1353); Petrarch's *Virgil* illuminated by Simone Martini; the *Codice Atlantico*, a collection of Leonardo's drawings on scientific and artistic subjects; a printed *Virgil* (Venice, 1470); and a Boccaccio (1471).

To the north, centring on Piazza Edison (**Map II, 10**) and Piazza degli Affari is the main business district of Milan, with the Stock Exchange and a number of banks, most of them built at the beginning of the century. Piazza Cordusio (**Map II, 6**) was laid out in 1889–1901 as the financial centre of the city. Beyond Piazza Cordusio, on Via Clerici, is **Palazzo Clerici** (**Map II; 6, 7**), in the hall of which is a magnificent ceiling painting by Gian Battista Tiepolo (1740).

San Satiro

Via Spadari (with luxury food shops) leads from the Pinocoteca Ambrosiana to the busy Via Torino, across which is the church of *San Satiro (**Map II, 10**). You can see the beautiful exterior, with a campanile of the mid-11C and the Cappella della Pietà, from Via Falcone. The church was rebuilt by Bramante from 1478, with the exception of the façade. This was begun by Giovanni Antonio Amadeo in 1486 to Bramante's design, but finished by Giuseppe Vandoni (1871). The T-shaped interior, by a clever perspective device and the skilful use of stucco, is given the appearance of a Greek cross; the rear wall is actually almost flat. On the high altar is a 13C votive fresco. The Cappella della Pietà, dating from the time of Archbishop Ansperto (868–81), was altered during the Renaissance with an attractive plan and large capitals. The terracotta Pietà is by Agostino de Fondutis. The eight-sided baptistery is a beautiful Renaissance work, with terracottas by Fondutis on a design by Bramante.

Off Via Torino, at Via Unione 5, is the fine 16C Palazzo Erba Odescalchi (**Map II, 11**), now a police station, with a good courtyard and a remarkable elliptical spiral staircase that is attributed by some scholars to Bramante.

Via Unione ends in Piazza Missori, with **Sant'Alessandro** (Map II, 10), the best Baroque church in the city. It contains elaborate marquetry and inlaid confessionals, as well as a striking Rococo high altar of *pietre dure*, inlaid gems and gilt bronze. The adjacent Palazzo Trivulzio (1707–13) is attributed to Giovanni Ruggeri and contains, in its courtyard, a doorway from a destroyed house attributed to Bramante.

Via Torino continues towards the Carrobbio past the round church of San Sebastiano (**Map II, 10**), dating from 1577, and San Giorgio al Palazzo, a church with a chapel decorated by Bernardino Luini.

Around San Lorenzo

The best way to reach the neighbourhood of San Lorenzo from the city centre is on foot or by taxi. From Piazza del Duomo, take Via Torino to the southwest, then Corso di Porta Ticinese southwards. In the ex-church of San Sisto, at Via San Sisto 4, is a museum of the works of Francesco Messina, open Tues–Sun 09.30–17.30, with many sculptures and drawings by this sculptor (1900–95). Further on, on the left, are 16 Corinthian *columns*, the remains of a Roman portico erected in the 4C, restored in the Middle Ages and again in 1954–55.

San Lorenzo and Sant'Eustorgio

Behind this striking colonnade rises the basilica of *San Lorenzo Maggiore (Map I, 14), founded in the 4C. It was rebuilt after the collapse of the vault in 1103, and again in 1574–88 by Martino Bassi (who preserved the original octagonal form and much of the original masonry) and has four heavy square towers. The façade dates from 1894.

The spacious domed *interior, built of grey stone, is of great architectural interest; it is surrounded by an ambulatory beneath a gallery. The *Chapel of Sant'Aquilino was built in the 4C, probably as an imperial mausoleum. In the vestibule (light on right) are fragments of 5C mosaics and early-14C frescoes. The door jambs (1C–3C AD) were brought from a Roman building. The octagonal hall (light on right), a remarkable Roman room, contains an early Christian sarcophagus and two lunettes with 5C *mosaics. Beyond is a 17C silver urn with the relics of St Aquilino, beneath a little vault frescoed by Carlo Urbini. Steps behind it (light on the stairs) lead down to an undercroft with Roman masonry of the imperial period, probably once part of an amphitheatre.

Corso di Porta Ticinese continues south from San Lorenzo, passing through the arches of the medieval Porta Ticinese (c 1330; with a tabernacle by the workshop of Balduccio) at Via Mulino delle Armi. The street is paralleled to the east by the quiet, green Parco delle Basiliche, which links San Lorenzo with the area's other great medieval church, Sant'Eustorgio, and provides an alternative walking route between the two monuments.

*Sant'Eustorgio (Map I, 14) is also of ancient foundation. The 11C church was rebuilt, except for the apse, in the 12C–13C, and the façade was reconstructed in 1863–65. The three 15C chapels on the south side, the apse, the slender campanile (1297–1309), and the graceful Portinari chapel are easy to see from the outside. To the left of the façade is a 16C open-air pulpit.

The long, low interior, with aisles and apse, is typical of the Lombard basilicas, but an important series of chapels was added on the south side from the 13C to 16C. The first *chapel (light on right) dates from 1484, and has good sculptural detail. It contains the tomb of Giovanni Brivio by Tommaso Cazzaniga and Benedetto Briosco (1486), and an *altarpiece by Bergognone. In the second chapel is the tomb of Pietro Torelli (d. 1412), and in the fourth chapel the tomb of Stefano Visconti (d. 1327), probably by Giovanni di Balduccio, and a 14C painted crucifix. In the sixth chapel is the tomb of Uberto Visconti (14C). In the south transept is the tomb of the Magi, where the relics of the Magi were preserved until their transfer to Cologne in 1164 (some were returned to Milan in 1903). It contains a huge Roman sarcophagus that held the relics, and on the altar are reliefs of 1347. On the high altar is a finely carved 14C dossal.

Cross the confessio, with nine slender monolithic columns (above early Christian foundations), beneath the raised apse, to reach the *Cappella Portinari (1462–68), a beautiful Renaissance chapel built for Pigello Portinari and dedicated to St Peter Martyr. A graceful choir of angels with festoons, in coloured stucco, plays over the drum of the dome. The frescoed scenes of the life of St Peter Martyr, by Vincenzo Foppa (1466–68), comprise the most important Renaissance fresco cycle in the city (unfortunately, they are in very poor condition). In the centre is the *tomb, borne by eight Virtues, of St Peter Martyr (Pietro da Verona, the inquisitor, murdered in 1252), by Giovanni di Balduccio (1339).

The sacristy shows the early Christian cemetery beneath the nave, with tombs dating from the 1C–4C AD and some inscriptions, and the old sacristy where the church treasury and vestments are carefully preserved in 16C cupboards.

Just south of Sant'Eustorgio is the huge Piazza XXIV Maggio (**Map I, 14**), with the handsome Neo-classical Porta Ticinese, an Ionic gateway by Luigi Cagnola (1801–14), in the centre. To the west is the Darsena, once the port of Milan. It was connected to an extensive system of rivers and canals, and was particularly busy in the 19C and early 20C. The **Naviglio Grande** (Map I, 13, 14), the most important of Milan's canals, once linked the Darsena to the River Ticino, 50km away. It was begun in the 12C and was navigable as far as Milan by the 13C. It used to carry commodities to and from the city, and there was a regular passenger navigation service along it from the beginning of the 19C. The nearby **Naviglio Pavese** was begun as an irrigation canal from Milan to Pavia by Gian Galeazzo Visconti in the 14C. In this area, known as the **Navigli**, once a neglected part of the city, many of the characteristic houses and courtyards have recently been restored. Now you'll find numerous architects' and designers' studios as well as a selection of fine restaurants. The neighbourhood is particularly lively at night (with restaurants, cafés, snack bars, nightclubs, etc. open till late) and there is a festival here in June when restaurants are opened on boats, etc.

Around San Nazaro

The area around the church of San Nazaro Maggiore, which lies along the old road to Rome, the Corso di Porta Romana, is studded with buildings of great historical significance but little visual interest. The area is within easy walking distance of the cathedral.

Just a couple of blocks southeast of Piazza del Duomo, beyond Via Larga, is the deconsecrated church of Santo Stefano Maggiore (**Map II, 12**), a Baroque building (1584–95) with a later campanile, outside the predecessor of which Galeazzo Maria Sforza was murdered in 1476. In the same piazza is the church of San Bernardino alle Osse, with an ossuary chapel frescoed by Sebastiano Ricci.

Fronting Via Festa del Perdono is the huge building of the former Ospedale Maggiore or **Ca'Granda** (**Map II, 16**), which has been the headquarters of the University of Milan since 1958. The hospital was founded by Francesco Sforza in 1456. One of the larger buildings in the city, it was designed by Filarete with two matching wings, one for men and one for women, each laid out around four courtyards which were separated by a larger central courtyard, off which was the church. Filarete completed only the right wing (towards the church of San Nazaro). The work was continued by Guiniforte Solari after 1465, and taken up again by Francesco Maria Ricchino and others in the 17C. The hospital was moved in 1939, and the buildings were badly damaged in the war. Restoration and renovation have been in progress since 1953.

The long façade on Via Festa del Perdono preserves the 15C wing at the right-hand end, with terracotta decorations thought to have been designed by Guiniforte Solari. The left-hand end, in Neo-classical style, dates from 1797–1804. Beyond the central 17C portal is the huge main *courtyard designed by Francesco Maria Ricchino following Filarete's design. The other courtyards can usually be visited on request. The huge collection of paintings that belonged to the hospital includes portraits of benefactors from 1602 onwards by the best-known artists of the day. There are long-term plans to move it to the Abbazia di Mirasole. The Natural Science schools of the University (founded in 1924) and other important educational institutions are in the Città degli Studi, laid out in 1927, about 2km east of Porta Venezia (**Map I, 8**).

Opposite the Ospedale you can see the 12C campanile of Sant'Antonio Abate (**Map II, 11, 12**), a church of 1582 with good 17C stalls. Adjoining (Via Sant'Antonio 5) is a charming cloister of the early 16C.

San Nazaro Maggiore

In Largo Richini, at the southwest end of the Ca' Grande, is a colossal bust of Dr Andrea Verga (d. 1895) by Giulia Branca. San Nazaro Maggiore (**Map II, 15**), a basilica consecrated in 386, lies just beyond. The easternmost of the four churches founded by St Ambrose outside the walls, it was reconstructed after a fire of 1075, altered c 1578, and restored in the 20C after war damage.

The entrance on Corso di Porta Romana is preceded by the hexagonal Trivulzio Chapel, begun in 1512 by Bramantino and continued by Cristoforo Lombardo. It has an elegant plain interior with uniform family tombs in niches high up on the walls.

The interior of the church preserves in part the plan of the early Christian church (and some of its masonry). In the nave are paintings by Camillo Procaccini and Daniele Crespi. The architecture of the crossing is particularly fine. In the south transept is a *Last Supper* by Bernardino Lanino. In the sanctuary is the reconstructed dedication stone (with two original fragments), and off the south side the little 10C Chapel of St Lino (restored in 1948). In the north transept you can see a 16C carved-wood Gothic tabernacle with the *Nativity* (light on right), very well preserved; a reconstructed funerary epitaph (435); and a painting by Bernardino Luini. The Chapel of St Catherine has frescoes by Bernardino Luini.

Off the busy Corso di Porta Romana (**Map II, 15**) rises the **Torre Velasca**, built in 1956–58 and one of the more important Modern buildings in the city.

Via Lentasio and Via Sant'Eufemia connect Corso di Porta Romana with Corso Italia to the southwest. Here are the churches of Sant'Eufemia, rebuilt in a Lombard Gothic-revival style in 1870, and **San Paolo Converso** (**Map II, 15**), an attractive building of 1549–80 (now used by a cultural society), containing frescoes by Giulio and Antonio Campi. At Corso Italia 10 is the headquarters of the *Touring Club Italiano*, famous for the production of excellent maps and guides, with a statue of its founder Luigi Vittorio Bertarelli (1927).

Further south along Corso Italia, *Santa Maria dei Miracoli* or Santa Maria presso San Celso (**Map I, 15**) stands next to a pretty little garden in front of San Celso (with a façade reconstructed in 1851–54 and a graceful campanile). Santa Maria was begun by Gian Giacomo Dolcebuono in 1490 with a façade by Galeazzo Alessi and Martino Bassi (1572). The fine atrium is by Cesare Cesariano.

The pictures in the dark interior are difficult to see. At the end of the south aisle is a *Holy Family* by Paris Bordone; statues by Annibale Fontana and Stoldo Lorenzi adorn the dome piers. The inlaid choir stalls are by Galeazzo Alessi, and the ambulatory has altarpieces by Gaudenzio Ferrari and Moretto. In the north aisle is an altarpiece by Bergognone. The Romanesque church of San Celso (normally kept closed), entered from the south aisle, dates from the 10C. It has a well-restored interior with fine capitals and a 14C fresco.

The districts to the east

Milan's eastern and northeastern quarters developed relatively late and hence are devoid of monuments of the late antique and early medieval periods. Instead, they are graced with lush, cool gardens and fine examples of early Modern architecture. To reach the area from the city centre, take Metro **Line 3** from the Duomo to Repubblica station, or walk along Via Manzoni (15min).

Porta Nuova

At the end of Via Manzoni are the Archi di Porta Nuova (**Map II, 4**), a gate reconstructed in 1171, with sculptures by a follower of Giovanni di Balduccio (14C). On Piazza Cavour, outside the gate, by a monument to Cavour by Odoardo Tabacchi (1865) stands the **Palazzo dei Giornali**, by Giovanni Muzio (1937–42), with external reliefs by Mario Sironi and a mosaic by him inside.

On the north side of the piazza is the entrance to the **Giardini Pubblici** (**Map II, 4**), notable for fine trees. The gardens contain monuments to distinguished citizens.

Palazzo Dugnani (**Map I, 7, 8**), on Via Manin, has *frescoes by Giovanni Battista Tiepolo (1731) and a Museo del Cinema (open Tues–Fri 15.00–18.00). The Neo-classical Planetarium, by Piero Portalupi, stands on the farther side of the gardens (entered from Corso Venezia 57). Nearby, facing Corso Venezia, is the **Museo di Storia Naturale** (**Map I, 8**; open Tues–Sun 09.30–18.00, Sat–Sun and holidays 09.30–18.30), founded in 1838 and the most important collection of its kind in Italy. The museum building was erected in 1893, but was badly damaged in the Second World War. The mineral collection includes the largest sulphur crystal in the world and a topaz weighing 40kg. The extensive zoological section contains reptiles, giant dinosaurs, etc. There are also a good library and study collections.

The Galleria d'Arte Moderna

On the other side of Via Palestro, which borders the southern side of the park, is the Villa Belgioioso or **Villa Reale** (**Map II, 4**), built by Leopold Pollack for the influential Belgioioso family in 1790. It was once occupied by the Regent Eugène Beauharnais and by Marshal Radetzky, who died here in 1858. Its attractive garden *all'inglese* was laid out in 1790 (open as a public park). The villa now contains the Galleria d'Arte Moderna (open Tues–Sun 09.30–17.30).

On the **first floor**, in the state rooms overlooking the garden, are 19C Lombard paintings, including the large *Quarto Stato*, a well-known work by Giuseppe Pellizza da Volpeda. Other artists represented include Andrea Appiani, Antonio Canova, and Italy's most celebrated Romantic painter, Francesco Hayez (good portraits).

Stairs lead up to the **second floor**, where the large Carlo Grassi bequest of 19C French and Italian works is displayed (Corot, Millet, Zandomeneghi, Domenico Morelli, Giovanni Fattori, Silvestro Lega, Telemaco Signorini, Giovanni Boldini, and especially good works by Giuseppe De Nittis).

The section dedicated to French painting is represented by Eugène Boudin, Alfred Sisley, Gauguin, Manet and van Gogh. There are also graphic works by Corot and Toulouse-Lautrec. In the last group of rooms are Italian paintings of the late 19C and early 20C by Armando Spadini, Giovanni Segantini, Antonio Mancini, Umberto Boccioni, Giacomo Balla, Giorgio Morandi, Renato Guttuso, and Filippo De Pisis. The last gallery has a display of carpets from Anatolia.

On the first floor (on the other side of the stairs) is a section dedicated to Marino Marini, with drawings and sculptures. Next door, the **Padiglione d'Arte Contemporanea** (PAC), which was added to the museum in 1955 to display contemporary works, has recently reopened after extensive renovation.

Around Piazza della Repubblica

From Piazza Cavour, Via Filippo Turati and Via Vittor Pisani lead towards the central station. In Via Turati the Montecatini office buildings, built in 1926–36 by Giò Ponti and others, face the Novecento-style apartment house known as **Ca' Brutta** (1923) by Giovanni Muzio. The huge Piazza della Repubblica (**Map I, 3, 7**) has skyscrapers, including the first to be built in the city (1936, by Mario Baciocchi) at no. 27, and more houses (nos 7–9) by Giovanni Muzio.

The regularly built Via Pisani leads up to the monumental **Stazione Centrale** (**Map I, 4**), the largest in Italy, designed in an eclectic Art Nouveau style by Ulisse Stacchini and built in 1925–31. In the piazza is the **Pirelli Building**, built in reinforced concrete in 1955–59 by Giò Ponti and Pier Luigi Nervi (127m), one of the best modern buildings in the city. Built on the site of the first Pirelli factory, it is now the seat of the Lombard regional government. The area to the west around Via Galvani, known as the Centro Direzionale, has numerous skyscrapers built in the 1960s.

From the Giardini Pubblici (see above), Via Marina leads southwest to **Palazzo del Senato**, now the State Archives (**Map II, 4**), a fine Baroque building by Fabio Mangone and Francesco Maria Ricchino. To the south, at Via Mozart 12 (**Map II, 8**), is the Collezione Alighiero de' Micheli, left to the FAI (*Fondo per l'Ambiente Italiano*) in 1995 (open by appointment on the first Sat of the month, except Jul–Aug, 10.30–17.00, ☎ 02 4815556). It contains 18C furniture and works of art.

Via Sant'Andrea, opposite the Palazzo del Senato, leads back towards the centre. At no. 6 in this street the 18C Palazzo Morando (**Map II, 8**) houses, on the upper floor, the **Museo di Milano** (open Tues–Sun 09.00–13.00, 14.00–18.00), with an interesting collection of paintings, drawings, prints, etc., depicting the changing face of Milan from the mid-16C onwards. On the ground floor is the Museo di Storia Contemporanea (open as above), with material related to the two World Wars.

Via Sant'Andrea ends in Via Monte Napoleone, with its fashionable shops, which leads (right) to Via Manzoni.

Around San Babila

From behind the Duomo, Corso Vittorio Emanuele (**Map II, 8**), a pedestrian street with numerous shops and shopping arcades as well as theatres and hotels, leads through a modern area. On the left is the classic portico of the round church of San Carlo al Corso (1839–47), modelled on the Pantheon, and on the right, at the beginning of Corso Venezia (**Map II, 8**), is San Babila, a 12C church over-restored at the end of the 19C. The 17C column outside bears the Lion of St Mark. At Corso Venezia 11 is the monumental gateway of the former seminary (1564), with huge caryatids; opposite is Casa Fontana, now Silvestri (no. 10), with interesting terracotta work of c 1475. The corso, with fine mansions of the 18C–19C, including the Neo-classical Palazzo Serbelloni (no. 16) by Simone Cantoni (1793), Palazzo Castiglioni (no. 47; 1900–04), a famous Art Nouveau palace, and Palazzo Saporiti (no. 40), built in 1812, goes on to the Giardini Pubblici, Piazzale Oberdan and the modern area east of the station.

Santa Maria della Passione

Corso Monforte continues east from San Babila to the Prefettura and **Palazzo Isimbardi**, seat of the provincial administration, which has a fresco by Giovanni Battista Tiepolo. Via Conservatorio leads right to reach the huge church of Santa Maria della Passione (**Map I, 12**), founded c 1485, with an octagonal dome by Cristoforo Lombardi (1530–50), and a façade by Giuseppe Rusnati (1692).

Inside, in the nave are hung a fine series of portraits of popes and monks (in matching frames), some by Daniele Crespi. The vault is frescoed by Martino Bassi. The chapels in the south aisle have Lombard frescoes and altarpieces of the 16C–17C. In the crossing, beneath the fine dome, is another series of paintings (in their original frames) of the *Passion*, one by Daniele Crespi. The organ on the right by Antegnati (1558) has doors painted by Carlo Urbini, and the one on the left (1613) has doors painted by Crespi. Beneath the organ on the right is the funerary monument of the founder of the church, Archbishop Daniele Birago, by Andrea Fusina (1495). The beautiful choir stalls are attributed to Cristoforo Solari.

In the south and north transepts are altarpieces by Bernardino Luini, Gaudenzio Ferrari and Giulio Campi. The chapels in the north aisle have more 16C–17C works, including one by Daniele Crespi.

Various rooms of the former convent and the museum can usually be visited on request. Beyond the old sacristy is the *chapter house, decorated c 1510 by Bergognone, including nine paintings of Christ and the apostles opposite frescoes of saints and doctors of the church. Beyond is a gallery with 17C Lombard paintings, and a room with the church treasury in 17C cupboards, vestments, and a large painting, *Daniel in the Lions' Den*, by Giuseppe Vermiglio.

Entered from Via Chiossetto, a turning off Via Corridoni, further south, is **San Pietro in Gessate** (**Map I, 12**), a Gothic church built c 1475. In the last chapel in the south aisle is a very damaged detached fresco of the *Funeral of St Martin* by Bergognone. The **Cappella Grifo** has interesting remains of frescoes depicting the life of St Ambrose by Bernardino Butinone and Bernardino Zenale (1490–93), the best-preserved part of which is the vault with delightful angels. The tomb effigy of Ambrogio Grifo (with two portrait medallions) was carved by Benedetto Briosco c 1490. In the south transept is an unusual painting of the *Madonna and Child* by a follower of Leonardo. In chapels in the north aisle are works by Giovanni Donato Montorfano.

Opposite San Pietro, in the Corso di Porta Vittoria, is the huge Palazzo di

Giustizia (1932–40) by Marcello Piacentini. At the east end of the corso is a monument by Giuseppe Grandi (1883–91), commemorating those who died during the Cinque Giornate of March 1848, and a little to the south of that is the Rotonda (**Map I,16**), the old mortuary of the Ospedale Maggiore, locally known as 'Foppone', now a children's garden and exhibition centre. The church was built by Attilio Arrigoni in 1713, and the portico by Francesco Raffagno.

MONZA
• • • • • • • • •

Situated so close to Milan that it is now a suburb, Monza is the most important town in the province and the third largest town in Lombardy. It is a wealthy industrial city, internationally known to motor-racing enthusiasts for its Formula 1 racetrack. It was important under the Lombard Queen Theodolinda in the 7C, and it has a cathedral of great interest.

The **Duomo** is a 13C–14C building on the site of a church founded by Theodolinda around 595. The fine parti-coloured marble *façade by Matteo da Campione (1370–96; restored) is flanked by a brick campanile of 1606 by Pellegrino Tibaldi.

The interior contains more work by Matteo da Campione, including the organ gallery in the nave and the relief of an imperial coronation. The chapel of Queen Theodolinda contains her tomb and is decorated with frescoes (being restored) by the Zavattari family (1444). Enclosed in the altar is the famous *iron crown of Lombardy (shown with the contents of the treasury, see below), used at the coronation of the Holy Roman Emperors since 1311 and containing a strip of iron said to have been hammered from one of the nails used at the Crucifixion. The last emperors crowned with it were Charles V (at Bologna), Napoleon and Ferdinand I (at Milan). The Rococo chapel of the Corpus Domini has frescoes by Mattia Bortoloni (1742).

The *Museo del Duomo** (open Tues–Sun 09.00–11.30, 15.00–17.30) houses the rich treasury. Here are the personal relics of Theodolinda, including her silver-gilt *hen and chickens, supposed to represent Lombardy and its seven provinces (possibly dating from the 4C and 7C), her votive cross and crown, and a book cover with a dedicatory inscription. Also here are three ivory diptychs (4C–9C). Sixteen phials from Palestine, illustrated with biblical scenes, are rare works dating from the 6C. The silk embroideries date from the 6C–7C. The processional cross was given to Theodolinda by St Gregory (altered in the 15C and 17C). There is also a collection of 26 glass phials from Rome (5C–6C), and 16C tapestries made in Milan.

In Piazza Roma is the **Arengario**, the brick town hall of 1293, with a tall battlemented tower and a balcony for public announcements.

Just to the north of the old city is the huge decaying **Villa Reale** (closed at the time of writing), a Neo-classical masterpiece by Giuseppe Piermarini (1777–80), built as a residence for Archduke Ferdinand of Austria, son of Empress Maria Theresa, and presented by the king to the State in 1919. This remarkable palace is in urgent need of restoration, and the state rooms and royal apartments are all closed indefinitely (although Umberto I's apartment has been restored). The ownership of the palace has been contested for years between the State and the Comune of Monza and Milan. The Pinacoteca Civica, with a collection of 19C paintings, has been closed since 1983. There are long-term plans to open a Neo-classical museum in the villa. In the garden is a rotunda with delightful frescoes by Andrea Appiani (1789).

The huge park (7 sq km), traversed by the Lambro river, with fine trees, was created in 1805–10 by Luigi Canonica and Luigi Villoresi. It now contains the famous **autodromo**, a motor-racing circuit built in 1922 (plans to extend it have so far been suppressed) and an 18-hole golf course. From behind the villa an avenue leads to the expiatory chapel, by Giuseppe Sacconi, erected by Vittorio Emanuele III on the spot where his father Umberto I was assassinated on 29 July 1900 by the anarchist Gaetano Bresci.

North of Monza is **Agliate**, with a remarkable 10C–11C ˚church and baptistery traditionally thought to have been founded in 881 by Ansperto, Bishop of Milan. Restored by Luca Beltrami in 1895, they contain remains of 10C frescoes. Southeast of Monza is **Gorgonzola**, which gave its name to an excellent creamy veined cheese which is produced in the district (as well as Bel Paese cheese).

LODI

• • • • •

Lodi, 31km southeast of Milan, is an important provincial capital (population 42,000) and a centre for dairy produce on the right bank of the Adda, in the fertile and well-irrigated district known as the Lodigiano.

History

An ancient town, Lodi was refounded in 1158 by Frederick Barbarossa and became the capital of the new Province of Lodi in 1995. The Piazza family of painters were born here in the 16C, and works by Callisto, Alberto and Scipione Piazza are preserved in churches in the town and province. Lodi was known for its ceramics in the 17C and 18C (and several small ceramics factories still operate here, including *Franchi* in Via Sant'Angelo). At the famous Battle of Lodi in 1796, on the bridge over the river, Napoleon defeated the Austrians.

The town was founded on this higher site after the destruction of Lodi Vecchio (described below) by the Milanese in 1158. Mary Hadfield Cosway (1759–1838), the painter and educationalist, founded a college for girls (the Collegio delle Dame Inglese) here in 1812 which flourished up until 1948 (and was attended by Alessandro Manzoni's daughter). Mary was the wife of the court miniaturist Richard Cosway, and the supposed lover of Thomas Jefferson. The college was at Via Paolo Gorini 6, next to the church of Santa Maria delle Grazie, where Mary is buried (plaque on the wall).

In the centre of the town is the large arcaded Piazza della Vittoria. Here is the 18C façade of the **Broletto** (town hall), and the **Duomo**, with a 12C façade including a fine portal bearing the carved figures of Adam and Eve on the door jambs, attributed to sculptors from Piacenza. The interior was well restored in the 1960s in the Romanesque style. In the first south chapel (lights) is a triptych of the *Crowning of the Virgin* by Alberto Piazza, and a polyptych with the *Massacre of the Innocents* by Callisto Piazza, both in their original frames. The tomb of Andrea Fusina dates from 1510. In the nave is a 13C gilt statue of San Bassiano. The choir has intarsia *panels set into modern stalls, exquisite works by Fra Giovanni da Verona (1523). By the entrance to the crypt is a Romanesque relief of the *Last Supper* above fresco fragments. In the crypt, where the body of St Bassiano is preserved, is a well-preserved wooden *Deposition* group by a local 16C sculptor. The Diocesan Museum (usually closed) contains vestments and church silver.

Piazza Broletto, on the north side of the duomo, has remains of the 13C part of the Broletto and the Romanesque font from the cathedral used as a fountain. From here a passageway leads into Piazza Mercato (markets on Tues, Thur, Sat and Sun).

Via dell'Incoronata leads from Piazza della Vittoria to the inconspicuous entrance to the church of the *Incoronata, built in 1488–94 by Giovanni Battagio and Gian Giacomo Dolcebuono. The octagonal interior is totally covered with 16C paintings, frescoes, and gilded decoration, on a design by Callisto Piazza. In the first chapel on the right, the altarpiece of the Conversion of St Paul, a late work (1580) by Callisto, is flanked by four exquisite *panels by Bergognone. The chapels on either side of the main altar also have altarpieces by Callisto, with the intervention of his son Fulvio, and his brother Scipione. In the last chapel is a polyptych of 1519 by Alberto Piazza in its original frame, and four small paintings by Scipione. The original 16C organ survives. Over the west door was an *Adoration of the Magi*, the only signed and dated work by Scipione Piazza (1562); it is now in the Museo Civico. The charming frescoed decoration on the pilasters, etc. is also by Scipione Piazza. A gonfalon, painted on silk by Alberto Piazza, and Rococo carved stalls can be seen behind the high altar. The 18C sacristy preserves its cupboards and pretty vault. A small museum with 15C–16C church silver and vestments is usually kept closed.

Corso Umberto leads out of Piazza della Vittoria to the **Museo Civico** (open Sat–Sun 15.00–18.00), with a fine collection of local ceramics on the ground floor, including works with floral decorations in the 'Vecchia Lodi' style produced by the Ferretti family in the late 18C. There is also an archaeological section, a collection of paintings and a museum dedicated to the Risorgimento.

From the other side of Piazza della Vittoria, Via Marsala leads to **Sant'Agnese** (left), a 15C church with terracotta decoration on the façade, and a polyptych by Alberto Piazza. From here Via XX Settembre, with the fine 15C **Palazzo Mozzanica** (no. 51; now Varesi), with a good portal and terracotta friezes, leads east to **San Francesco** (1289), a church with an unusual façade. The interior has numerous 14C–15C frescoes, the most interesting on the nave pillars, in the third chapel on the south, and in the aisles and south transept. The hospital in the piazza has a charming little 15C cloister with a double loggia decorated with terracotta.

Lodi Vecchio

The *Lodigiano*, or territory of Lodi, was an unhealthy, marshy area before the local monastic communities constructed canals, many of which still survive. In the well-irrigated countryside there are numerous dairy farms which produce *mascarpone* and a cheese known locally as *raspadura*, a type of unmatured Parmesan served as an hors d'oeuvre which you eat with your fingers. Near the

River Adda, which borders the eastern side of the province, are itineraries recommended for cyclists (for information and guides, enquire at the information office in Lodi; there are also various places where bicycles can be hired).

Lodi Vecchio is 5km west of Lodi. The Roman *Laus Pompeia* was a constant rival of Milan until its total destruction in 1158. Only the church of **San Bassiano** was left standing, and it is now in an isolated position outside the village of Lodi Vecchio. Of ancient foundation, it was rebuilt in Gothic style in the early 14C, with a fine exterior. High up on the façade is a ceramic statue of the 4C bishop St Bassiano.

The interior is interesting for its delightful early-14C frescoed *decoration (restored in the early 1960s) in the nave vaults and apse, with colourful geometric designs and flowers, and including one bay with very unusual rustic scenes of four carts drawn by oxen (the frescoes were financed by a local farming corporation in 1323), and *Christ Pantocrator* in the apse. Votive frescoes include a scene of St Eligius blessing a horse. At the end of the north aisle (high up) is a relief with bulls and a man on a horse dated 1323. The 11C capitals are also interesting, and in the south aisle is a series of 17C paintings. The site of the Roman city was identified in 1987 by aerial photography, and excavations are in progress near the village.

Places of interest around Lodi include **Sant'Angelo Lodigiano** to the southwest (on the Pavia road), where the restored 14C Visconti Castle may be visited (Sun and holidays, Mar–July, Sep–Oct, 14.30–17.00). It has 17C–18C furniture, a fine armoury, an agricultural section, etc.

Codogno, south of Lodi, is an agricultural centre. In the 16C church of San Biagio are an *Assumption* by Callisto Piazza, *Madonna and Child between St Francis and Charles Borromeo* by Daniele Crespi, and 16C works by Cesare Magni.

At **Ospedaletto Lodigiano**, west of Codogno, is an abbey founded in 1433, with a 16C church containing paintings (formerly part of a triptych) by Giampietrino. Part of the 16C cloister survives. At **Borghetto Lodigiano** the town hall occupies Palazzo Rho (c 1490).

East of Lodi is **Abbadia Cerreto**, where there is a Cistercian Lombard church built in the 12C, with a fine exterior and an altarpiece by Callisto Piazza.

Pavia and its province

Pavia is an old provincial capital (population 75,000) of Roman origin on the Ticino. It has one of the more ancient universities in Europe, still very much at the centre of the life of the town. On 24 February 1525 the famous Battle of Pavia was fought here, in which the French king Francis I was defeated and taken prisoner by Emperor Charles V—a decisive moment in European history.

Although virtually nothing remains of the Roman city, Pavia has a number of fine medieval churches and palaces in its cobbled streets, and interesting well arranged art collections in the Castello Visconteo. There are some exceptionally fine sights also in the province of Pavia. The beautiful 15C–16C Certosa di Pavia, one of the more important buildings in Italy, is a few kilometres north of the town; and the lovely main square of Vigevano is one of the great achievements of Italian Renaissance town planning.

Practical information

 ### Getting there
By air

The airports nearest Pavia are Milano Malpensa (85km northwest) and Linate (58km north).
By road

Pavia can be reached by A7 (exit at Bereguardo-Groppello) or 35 from Milan; A7 from Genoa; A21 from Turin (exit at Casteggio-Stradella).
By rail

Pavia is on the main Milan–Genoa line. Fast *Intercity* trains make the run from Milan in c 30min; from Genoa in c 70mins. There is also a slow local service from Codogno (on the Milan–Piacenza line) and from Stradella (on the Alessandria–Piacenza line).

 ### Getting around
By road

Traffic is limited in the centre of Pavia. You can park free on Piazza Petrarca and Piazzale Libertà, and there are pay car parks on Viale Matteotti, Viale II Febbraio and Piazzale Cairoli. **Bus 3** runs from the railway station to the centre of the town along Corso Cavour and Corso Mazzini. Pavia's bus station, with buses to places in the province, is on Via Trieste.

 ### Information offices
PAVIA Via Fabio Filzi 2, tel. 0382 22156.
CERTOSA DI PAVIA At the entrance to the monastery (closed in winter).
VIGEVANO Corso Vittorio Emanuele 29, tel. 0381 299282.

 ### Where to stay
PAVIA *Moderno*, Viale Vittorio Emanuele 41, ☎ 0382 303401, fax 0382 25225; modest but comfortable, a stone's throw from the train station; closed Dec–Jan, moderate.
CERVESINA (6km outside Voghera) *Castello di San Gaudenzio*, Via Mulino 1, ☎ 0383 3331, fax 0383 333409; 14C castle with a lovely park and an excellent restaurant; moderate.
SALICE TERME *President Terme*, Via Enrico Fermi 5, ☎ 0383 91941, fax 0383 92342; a large, modern spa, closed Dec–Jan; moderate.
Roby, Via Cesare Battisti 15, ☎/fax 0383 91323; a small, pleasant place open Apr–Oct only; inexpensive.
VIGEVANO *Europa*, Via Trivulzio 8, ☎ 0381 9085, fax 0381 87054; modern and friendly, closed Dec–Jan; moderate.
VOGHERA Youth hostel, Viale Repubblica 25.

 ### Eating out
PAVIA *Antica Osteria del Previ*, Via Milazzo 65, ☎ 0382 26203; traditional trattoria on the banks of the Ticino; closed Wed and midday in summer; moderate.
Demetrio, Via Guidi 33; pastry shop with great cakes.
Locanda Vecchia Pavia, Via Cardinal Riboldi 2, ☎ 0382 304132; restaurant featuring seasonal dishes based on fresh ingredients; closed Mon, midday Wed, Jan and Aug; expensive.
Osteria della Madonna de Peo, Via dei Liguri 28, ☎ 0382 302833; traditional osteria popular with the locals; closed

Sun and Aug; moderate.
Osteria del Naviglio, Via Alzaia 39, ☎ 0382 460392; wine bar, good for bruschette, cheese and salads; open evenings only, closed Mon and Jul; inexpensive.
Vignoni, Strada Nuova 110; pastry shop where the city's signature cake, *torta paradiso*, was invented.
CERTOSA DI PAVIA *Vecchio Mulino*, Via al Monumento 5, ☎ 0382 925894; restaurant offering excellent regional cuisine; closed Sun evening, Mon and Jan; moderate.
Chalet della Certosa, Viale Monumento 1, ☎ 0382 934935; restaurant in a pleasant garden, serving good country cuisine; closed Mon and Jan; moderate.
MORTARA *La Gambarina*, Strada Milanese 2260, ☎ 0384 98399; farm serving country lunches made from home-grown ingredients; closed Mon–Wed, except holidays; moderate.
MONTALTO PAVESE *Trattoria del Povero Nando*, Piazza Vittorio Veneto 15, ☎ 0383 870119; trattoria known for its large portions of wholesome country fare; closed Tues–Wed, Aug and Jan; moderate.
MONTECALVO VERSIGGIA *Prato Gaio*, località Versa, ☎ 0385 99726; restaurant serving traditional recipes of the Valle Versa; closed Mon evening, Tues and Jan; moderate.
SALICE TERME *Ca' Vegia*, Via Diviani 23, ☎ 0383 93248; restaurant specialising in fish, with garden seating in summer; closed Mon; moderate.
SAN MARTINO SICCOMARIO (3km from Pavia) *Da Giannino*, Via Turati 18, ☎ 0382 559627; hotel restaurant serving traditional regional cuisine; closed Mon; inexpensive.
VIGEVANO *I Castagni*, Via Ottobiano 8/20 (2km south), ☎ 0381 42860; restaurant with excellent regional cuisine, closed Sun evening, Mon, Aug and Jan; moderate. *Da Maria*, Via Bellaria

5, ☎ 0381 347429; another fine regional restaurant, closed Wed, Aug and Dec–Jan; moderate.

Entertainment
PAVIA Music and theatre at *Teatro Fraschini*, Strada Nuova.

Shopping
Pavia has an **antiques** market (first Sun of the month, except Jan and Aug). Elsewhere, there are antiques markets at Broni (second Sun of the month), Stradella (second Sat), Vigevano (third Sat), Voghera (fourth Sun), Belgioioso (week before Easter). Presentation and sale of new wine, Canneto Pavese (first and second weekends in Mar), Rovescala (all Mar weekends). Plants and flowers (plus farm machinery and more), Belgioioso (Easter weekend); other events at Belgioioso include a paperback book fair (late Apr); *Officinalia*, natural food and medicine fair, (early May); *Amicolibro*, children's book fair (last weekend in Oct). *Festa dell'Uva*, vintage feast and wine fair, Broni (third Sun in Sep). Black truffle fair, Menconico (third Sun in Sep). Forest fair, with truffles, mushrooms, honey and other forest products, Casteggio (late Oct).

Special events
Any occasion is good for a *festa* in most villages. Highlights of the year's events include colourful Carnival celebrations at Menconico, Santa Margherita Staffora, Santa Maria della Versa, Varzi. *Scarpe d'Oro* amateur footrace at Vigevano (Easter Mon); extemporaneous painting competitions at Montesegale (last Sun in Jun) and Salice Terme (second Sun); *Città di Stradella* chamber-music competition, Stradella (late Jun–early Jul); horse show, Salice Terme (Sep); historic procession, Vigevano (first Sun in Oct); *Festa di San Martino*, with roasted

chesnuts and *vin brulé*, Canneto (second sun in Oct); *Capodanno Anticipato*, New Year's Eve for early birds, Borgo Priolo (29 Dec).

Sports

Golf at Vigevano (*Golf Club Vigevano Santa Martretta*) and Chignolo Po (*Croce di Malta Golf & Country Club*).

PAVIA
● ● ● ● ● ●

Pavia came in first, in 1999, in the 'most liveable city' competition sponsored by the Italian environmentalist organisation, *Legambiente*. It won the award not just because of the peaceful—and relatively clean—atmosphere of its old historic centre (maintained despite the town's development as an important industrial and agricultural centre, which has led to indiscriminate new building outside the limits of the historic centre) but also because of the civic-mindedness of its inhabitants, leaders in the fields of waste management, air and water quality management, etc.

History

The Roman *Ticinum* was founded on this site about 220 BC. In the 6C the town became the capital of the Lombards, who called it *Papia*. Here the Lombards crowned their sovereigns: the church of San Michele hosted the coronations of Charlemagne (774), Berengar, the first king of Italy (888), Berengar II (950) and Frederick Barbarossa (1155).

The commune of Pavia took the Ghibelline side against Milan and Lodi, afterwards passed to the Counts of Monferrato and, from 1359 onwards, to the Visconti. After the failure of the French to win control of Pavia from the Spaniards in the decisive battle fought here in 1525, Francis I wrote to his mother: *Madame, tout est perdu hors l'honneur* ('All is lost save honour'). The ramparts which still surround part of the city were built by the Spanish in the 17C. Pavia was the birthplace of Lanfranc (1005–89), the first Norman archbishop of Canterbury. The name of the Piazza Petrarca recalls Petrarch's visits to his son-in-law here.

The town centre

Pavia's two straight main streets, the Strada Nuova and Corso Cavour-Corso Mazzini, intersect in the centre of the town in true Roman style near the huge arcaded Piazza Vittoria, its market now relegated below ground. At the southern end of the piazza rises the **Broletto** (12C; restored in the 19C), with a double loggia of 1563.

Next to the town hall is the **Duomo**, begun in 1488 from designs by Cristoforo Rocchi and Giovanni Antonio Amadeo, and afterwards modified by Bramante (with, possibly, also the intervention of Leonardo da Vinci). The immense cupola, the third largest in Italy, was not added until 1884–85, and the façade was completed in 1933. The rest of the exterior remains unfinished. The impressive, centrally planned interior has a very pronounced cornice above the capitals. On the west wall are paintings by Cerano, Daniele Crespi and Moncalvo. In the transepts are altarpieces by Carlo Sacchi and Bernardino Gatti, and the 17C *Madonna di Piazza Grande*.

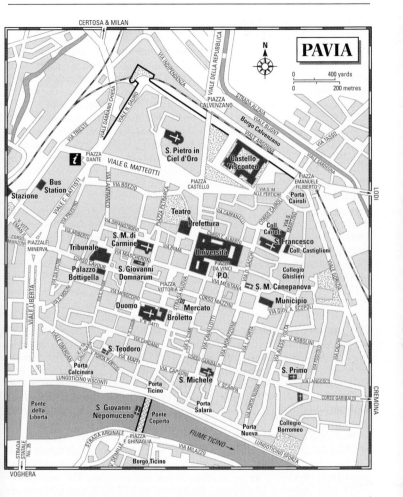

Several palaces with porticoes, including the handsome Palazzo Vescovile (1577), line the piazza. The equestrian statue by Francesco Messina (1937) recalls the gilded bronze Roman statue that stood here from the 11C until its destruction in 1796. Next to the duomo are the neglected ruins of the **Torre Civica**, the campanile of two demolished Romanesque churches, with a bell-chamber by Pellegrino Tibaldi (1583) that collapsed without warning in 1989, killing four people and wounding 15. Discussions continue about whether it should be reconstructed.

Via dei Liguri leads downhill out of the piazza and Via Maffi continues right to the 12C church of **San Teodoro**, with its octagonal cupola-tower and 16C lantern. Inside, the remarkable 15C–16C frescoes include a view of Pavia with its numerous towers (west wall) in 1522, by Bernardino Lanzani, and the *Lives of St Theodore* (north transept) and *St Agnes* (south transept), attributed to

Lanzani. The short, broad crypt lies beneath the sanctuary.

Below the church, Via Porta Pertusi continues to the picturesque **Ponte Coperto**, a covered bridge across the Ticino, still used by cars. The original bridge, built in 1351–54 on Roman foundations and roofed in 1583, collapsed in 1947 after bomb damage. The present one, a few metres further east, is to a different design, as is the chapel replacing the 18C bridge-chapel. In the suburb across the bridge is the 12C church of Santa Maria in Betlemme, which has a façade decorated with faience plaques and a plain Romanesque interior.

The Strada Nuova leads uphill from the bridge back towards the centre of the town. Via Capsoni leads right to *****San Michele**, the finest church in Pavia, consecrated in 1155, with an octagonal cupola. The elaborately ornamented front has profusely decorated triple portals and sculptured friezes, but the sandstone in which they are carved has been almost totally worn away, despite restoration in 1967. The portals of the transept and the galleried apse also have interesting carving. The lower part of the campanile, decorated with terracotta tiles, dates from c 1000. The interior is similar to that of San Pietro in Ciel d'Oro (see below), whereas the gallery above the nave recalls that of Sant'Ambrogio in Milan. There is fine sculptural detail in many parts of the interior, particularly on the *capitals. The rood above the crossing is 15C. In the crypt is the tomb of Martino Salimbeni (d. 1463), by the school of Amadeo.

Opposite the church, behind a railing and surrounded by a garden, is Palazzo Corti (or Arnaboldi), an 18C building altered in 1875 by Ercole Balossi.

The university quarter

Via San Michele and Via Cavalotti lead uphill to the north. Across Corso Mazzini, Via Galliano continues past the post office to Piazza Leonardo da Vinci, where three ancient **tower-houses** survive, built by the noble families of Pavia (the town was once called the 'city of a hundred towers', and some 80 of them survived up to the 19C). Under cover are remains of the 12C **crypt of Sant'Eusebio** (open by appointment at the Castello Visconteo), with restored early-13C frescoes.

Here is the **University of Pavia**—one of the oldest in Europe—the successor of a famous school of law, the ancient Studio where Lanfranc is said to have studied. The school was made a university in 1361 by Galeazzo II Visconti, and is now particularly renowned for its faculties of law and medicine. The buildings of 1533 were extended by Giuseppe Piermarini in 1771–79, and by Leopoldo Pollack in 1783–95. The Aula Magna was begun in 1827.

Off Corso Carlo Alberto and the Strada Nuova are numerous attractive courtyards, all of which are open to the public. From the one with a war memorial you enter the **Museo per la Storia dell'Università di Pavia** (Mon 15.30–17.00 and Fri 09.30–12.00, or by appointment, ☎ 0382 29724), with interesting collections relating to the history of medicine and physics in an old-fashioned arrangement (the showcases survive from the 18C). The collections include mementoes of the most distinguished alumni, including Alessandro Volta, whose statue is in the central courtyard. The Teatro Fisico and the anatomical theatre (named after Antonio Scarpa) were both designed by Leopoldo Pollack (1787). The adjoining courts of the former Ospedale di San Matteo (1499), to the east, are also part of the university.

Via Roma leads left from the Strada Nuova to the large red brick church of

Santa Maria del Carmine, begun in 1373. It has an attractive façade adorned with terracotta statues and an elaborate rose window. On some of the nave pillars and in the transept are frescoes by local 15C painters. The charming lavabo in the sacristy (south transept) is by Giovanni Antonio Amadeo.

In Piazza Petrarca, reached by Via XX Settembre, is the Biblioteca Civica in **Palazzo Malaspina**, built for the Malaspina collection (now displayed in the Castello Visconteo). The collection was opened to the public here in 1838 by Luigi Malaspina for the enjoyment of scholars, students and townspeople. To the west, in Via San Felice, is **San Felice**, with an interesting Lombard crypt (9C; restored), and a Renaissance cloister.

The Castello Visconteo

Strada Nuova continues north past the Teatro Fraschini, built in 1771–73 by Antonio Galli, to the Castello Visconteo, surrounded by public gardens. The great fortress was built in 1360–65 by Galeazzo II Visconti, who here housed his important collections of literature and art. A huge park (with a perimeter wall of some 22km) extended north from the ducal residence as far as the Certosa di Pavia. The famous Battle of Pavia took place in this park in 1525; two years later, in revenge for their defeat in battle, the French destroyed the northern wing of the castle and two of its corner turrets. The restored interior (entrance on the west side; open Tues–Sun 09.00–13.30; Sun 09.00–13.00) with a splendid *courtyard, now houses the civic collections of art and antiquities.

Ground floor On the ground floor (rooms **I–VI**) is the **archaeological collection**, which includes Roman finds with good glass and sculpture, and exhibits from the Lombard period when Pavia was capital of the Lombard court (sculptures and inscriptions from the royal tombs, 572–774). The museum's collection of Lombard jewellery was not on display at time of writing.

On the other side of one of the castle's entrance gates is the **Romanesque collection** (rooms **VII–X**) with architectural fragments, capitals, friezes and portals from the Romanesque cathedrals (8C–12C). In room **X** are the best Romanesque sculptures from San Giovanni in Borgo, with finely carved capitals. The last wing (room **XI**) contains mosaic pavements.

The **Renaissance collection** is displayed in rooms **XII–XIV**. It includes sculpture and a 16C fresco, detached in 1895, sold in 1945 to the Philadelphia Museum of Art, and generously given to this museum in 1994. More sculpture is arranged beneath the portico.

First floor Steps ascend to the first floor. From the end of the east loggia you enter the **Pinacoteca Malaspina**. The collection was formed by Luigi Malaspina di Sannazzaro (1754–1835) and is interesting as an example of a private collection of this time. It is arranged in fine rooms with 16C vault frescoes. Room **1**: *Madonna and Saints* by Vincenzo Foppa, 1478 (the *Pala Bottigella* from the monastery of San Tommaso); portrait of a *Condottiere* by Antonello da Messina, and early works by Hugo van der Goes and Giovanni Bellini. The painting of *Christ Carrying the Cross* by Bergognone shows a procession of Carthusian monks in front of the Certosa di Pavia (with the façade still under construction, c 1494).

Room **2**: local ceramics; carved wood dossals (1470); gilded wood relief of the *Nativity* (late 15C; from the Certosa); paintings by Correggio, Bartolomeo Montagna, Giampietrino and Boltraffio (portrait of a *Lady*); and a fresco by Bernardino Luini.

In the corner room is a remarkable wooden *model of the duomo, a master-piece by Gian Pietro Fugazza (1493–1502). Beyond is a huge hall with 17C and 18C paintings, including works by Camillo Procaccini, Nuvolone, Daniele Crespi, Orsola Maddalena Caccia (the daughter of Moncalvo), Carlone, Alessandro Magnasco and Gian Domenico Tiepolo, and 18C ceramics.

On the second floor is a gallery of plaster casts (opened on request). The Museo del Risorgimento, with relics of the Pavese Cairoli brothers, is to be reopened here.

Elsewhere around town

Via Liutprando leads northwest from Piazza Castello to the quiet square in front of the Lombard church of *San Pietro in Ciel d'Oro, consecrated in 1132. The church's name comes from its former gilded vault, mentioned by Dante in his *Paradiso* (X, 128; quoted on the façade). The single portal in the handsome façade is asymmetrically placed, and the buttress on the right is made broader than that on the left in order to contain a stairway.

The fine Romanesque interior, restored in 1875–99, has 'bestiary' capitals. The altarpiece is the *Arca di Sant'Agostino, a masterpiece of Italian sculpture. It was executed c 1362 by Campionese masters (from Campione d'Italia on Lago di Lugano), whom scholars say were influenced by the Pisan Giovanni di Balduccio. It has a galaxy of statuettes, and bas-reliefs illustrating the story of the saint (the details are difficult to see from a distance). It is supposed to contain the relics of St Augustine (d. 430), removed from Carthage during the Arian persecutions. The large crypt contains the remains of the Roman poet and states-man Boëthius (476–524), executed by Theodoric on a charge of treason.

Churches of interest in the eastern part of the city include **San Francesco d'Assisi**, a late-Romanesque edifice (1238–98) with a restored Gothic façade. Also on Corso Cairoli is a Renaissance building readapted to its original purpose when the Collegio Cairoli was founded in 1948. Further east, in Via San Martino (no. 18), is the Collegio Castiglione-Brugnatelli (for women), which occupies a 15C building. The college chapel (shown on request) has restored 15C frescoes by the school of Bonifacio Bembo. A bronze statue of Pope Pius V by Francesco Nuvolone (1692) faces the Collegio Ghislieri, which the pope established in 1567. The square is closed by the façade of San Francesco di Paola by Giovanni Antonio Veneroni, beyond which are the **Botanical Gardens**, with roses, aquatic plants, conifers, etc.

Via Scopoli returns towards the centre of the town past **Santa Maria delle Cacce**, rebuilt in 1629, with frescoes of the life of St Theodoric and an 8C crypt, and (right) Palazzo Mezzabarba, a Baroque building by Giovanni Veneroni (1730), now the town hall. The church of **Santa Maria Canepanova**, at the corner of Via Sacchi and Via Negri, is a graceful octagonal building begun by Giovanni Antonio Amadeo in 1507, probably on a design by Bramante; it has a pretty little cloister.

In the southern part of the town, near Corso Garibaldi, is the much altered Lombard church of **San Primo**. Further south, reached by Via San Giovanni, is the Collegio Borromeo, founded by St Charles Borromeo in 1561 and built in 1564–92 largely by Pellegrino Tibaldi; the river façade was added in 1808–20, to a design by Leopoldo Pollack.

In the western part of the town, off Corso Cavour, is the 11C Lombard campanile of **San Giovanni Domnarum**. The crypt and its frescoes go back to the 11C. Corso Cavour is distinguished by a 15C tower (at no. 17) and the Bramantesque Palazzo Bottigella (no. 30), with fine brick decorations. Corso Manzoni prolongs Corso Cavour to the railway, beyond which is (5 minutes) the church of **San Salvatore**, reconstructed in 1467–1511 with frescoes by Bernardino Lanzani. A further 10mins walk brings you to **San Lanfranco**, a 13C building containing the fine cenotaph (by Amadeo; 1498) of the beatified Lanfranc—actually buried at Canterbury—and traces of 13C frescoes on the right wall of the nave, including one showing the murder of St Thomas Becket at Canterbury. One of the cloisters retains some terracotta decoration, also by Amadeo.

THE PROVINCE OF PAVIA

The province of Pavia abounds in interesting sights, but you'll need a car to see most of them. In all seasons but summer the roads are subject to heavy fog, and cautious driving is necessary.

The Certosa di Pavia

Certainly the most important place in the province is the Certosa di Pavia, 8km north of the city. It is difficult to reach by public transport. Buses run every 30mins from the bus station in Pavia, but from the bus stop it is an unpleasant walk of at least 20mins along a busy road; from the train station, on the other side of the Certosa, the walk is even longer. If you come by car or taxi, glance out the window from time to time: you will notice the Milan road from Pavia is skirted by the Naviglio di Pavia, an irrigation and transportation canal begun by Galeazzo Visconti, lined with abandoned locks and lock-houses.

The **Certosa di Pavia, a Carthusian monastery, was founded by Gian Galeazzo Visconti in 1396 as a family mausoleum. Its construction was entrusted to the Lombard masons of Milan cathedral and the builders of the castle of Pavia. The monastery proper was finished in 1452 and the church in 1472, under the Sforzas. The façade was completed in the 16C.

- The Certosa, now occupied by ten Cistercian monks, is open 09.00–11.30 and 14.30–16.30, 17.00 or 18.00 (closed Mon and major national holidays).

From the entrance, facing west, a vestibule with frescoed saints by Bernardino Luini leads through to the great garden-court in front of the church. On the left are the old pharmacy and food and wine stores; on the right the prior's quarters and the so-called Palazzo Ducale, rebuilt by Francesco Maria Richini (1620–25) to house distinguished visitors and now containing a museum (described below).

Exterior The sculptural and polychrome marble decoration of the **west front** of the church, of almost superabundant richness, marks the height of the artistic achievement of the Quattrocento in Lombardy; it was begun in 1473 and worked on up to 1499 by Cristoforo and Antonio Mantegazza and Giovanni Antonio Amadeo. In the 16C Cristoforo Lombardo continued the upper part in simplified form, but it was never completed. The attribution of the various parts is still under discussion. On the lowest order of the façade are medallions of Roman emperors; above, statues and reliefs of prophets, apostles and saints by the Mantegazza; and scenes from the Life of Christ by Amadeo. The *great portal* was probably designed by Gian Cristoforo Romano (also attributed to Gian Giacomo Dolcebuono and Amadeo) and executed by Benedetto Briosco, the sculptor also of the bas-reliefs representing the *Life of the Virgin* and of four large reliefs: the *Foundation of the Carthusian Order*, 1084; *Laying the First Stone of the Certosa*, 27 August 1396; *Translation to the Certosa of the Body of Gian Galeazzo*, 1 March 1474; *Consecration of the Church*, 3 May 1497. On each side are two very rich *windows by Amadeo. The upper part, by Cristoforo Lombardo (1540–60), is decorated with 70 statues of the 16C by Lombard masters. The rest of the exterior is best seen from the northeast.

Interior The *interior is purely Gothic in plan, but Renaissance decorative motives were introduced towards the east end; the chapels opening off the aisle were expensively redecorated and provided with handsome Baroque grilles in the 17C–18C, and only traces remain of their original frescoes and glass. As the grilles are kept locked, the works of art in the chapels are extremely difficult to see.

In the south aisle, the first chapel is a Baroque work by Camillo Procaccini with a lavabo by the Mantegazza. The altarpiece of the second chapel incorporates panels by Macrino d'Alba and Bergognone. In the fourth chapel is a *Crucifixion* by Bergognone, and in the fifth chapel an altarpiece of *St Syrus*, first bishop of Pavia, by Bergognone, and unrestored ceiling frescoes by Jacopo de' Mottis (1491).

In the north aisle, the first chapel has a lavabo by the Mantegazza (c 1470). The altarpiece in the second chapel is made up from a painting representing *God the Father* by Perugino, flanked by *Doctors of the Church* by Bergognone, and—below—17C copies of panels by Perugino (1499), now in the National Gallery, London. In the fourth chapel, the *Massacre of the Innocents* by Dionigi Bussola is the best of the Baroque altar reliefs. The altarpiece in the sixth chapel, of *St Ambrose and Saints*, is by Bergognone (1492).

In the centre of the **north transept** are *tomb statues of Lodovico il Moro and Beatrice d'Este by Cristoforo Solari (1497), brought from Santa Maria delle Grazie in Milan in 1564. The frescoes include *Ecce Homo* (over the small west door) and *Crowning of the Virgin*, with the kneeling figures of Francesco Sforza and Lodovico il Moro (north apse), both by Bergognone. The two *angels on either side of the window above are attributed to Bramante. The two *candelabra are by Annibale Fontana.

The **south transept** holds the *tomb of Gian Galeazzo Visconti by Gian Cristoforo Romano (1493–97; the *Madonna* is by Benedetto Briosco, the sarcophagus by Galeazzo Alessi, the figures of *Fame* and *Victory* by Bernardino da Novate). The lunette fresco in the south apse by Bergognone depicts Gian Galeazzo, with his children, presenting a model of the church to the Virgin; higher up are two angels attributed to Bramante. Over the altar is an *Enthroned Madonna* enthroned with St Charles and St Bruno, by Cerano. The fresco over the small west door depicting the *Madonna* is by Bergognone.

Off the south transept, a pretty *door by Amadeo, with profile-portraits of the Duchesses of Milan, leads into the lavatorium, which contains a finely-carved lavabo by Alberto Maffiolo of Carrara, and, on the left, a charming fresco of the *Madonna* by Bernardino Luini. A matching doorway by Amadeo, with medallions of the Dukes of Milan, in the north transept, leads into the old sacristy, with a good vault. It contains fine 17C presses. The remarkable ivory *altarpiece, with nearly 100 statuettes, attributed to Baldassarre degli Embriachi, was made in the early 15C.

The choir contains carved and inlaid *stalls (1498), frescoes by Daniele Crespi (1629), and a sumptuous late 16C altar.

From the south transept a pretty doorway by the Mantegazza leads into the *small cloister, with a garden, and embellished by terracotta decorations in the Cremonese style by Rinaldo de Stauris (1465), and a terracotta lavabo. The beautiful little *doorway into the church, with a *Madonna*, is by Amadeo (1466). There is a good view of the southern flank of the church. Off this cloister is the new sacristy (only open for services), with an altarpiece of the *Assumption* by Andrea Solari (completed by Bernardino Campi) and 16C illuminated choir-books. The refectory has ceiling frescoes by Ambrogio and Bernardo Bergognone, a reader's pulpit, and a little fresco of the *Madonna* by the Zavattari or Bergognone (1450).

A passage leads from the small cloister into the *great cloister, with 122 arches and more terracotta decoration by de Stauris (1478). Above the porticoes on three sides you can make out 24 identical monks' cells, each with its chimney. Entered by a decorative doorway, they have two rooms, with a little garden below, and a bedroom and loggia above.

The chapter house (no admission), entered through a charming little court, perhaps the work of Bramante, has reliefs by the Mantegazza and in the style of Amadeo.

The **museum** in the Palazzo Ducale, on the garden-court in front of the church, has recently reopened after years of closure. The collection is displayed in two frescoed rooms by Fiammenghino and Giovanni Battista Pozzo (attributed). The paintings include works by Bartolomeo Montagna, Bergognone, Bernardino Luini, Giuseppe Vermiglio, and Vincenzo and Bernardino Campi. The portrait of Pope Paul V is a copy by Gerolamo Ciocca of a work by Caravaggio. There are also sculptures by Bambaia, Mantegazza and Cristoforo Solari. A gallery of plaster casts occupies the ground floor, where the arms from the tomb of Gian Galeazzo Visconti are also preserved. The 15C and 16C illuminated choirbooks are displayed in the library.

Northeast of the Certosa, near Landriano, is the **Oasi di Sant'Alessio** (open mid-March–Oct, Sat and holidays 10.30–18.30), a bird sanctuary founded in 1973, used as a breeding ground for storks, ibis, flamingo, heron, etc. East of Pavia is **Belgioioso**, with the well-preserved medieval castle (open Apr–Sept, 14.00–dusk), where Francis I was imprisoned immediately after the battle of Pavia.

Vigevano and the west

The western part of the province of Pavia is known as the *Lomellina*. Rice has been grown since the 16C on this cultivated plain between the Ticino, Sesia and Po rivers. A number of castles survive in the area. The ancient capital of the region is **Lomello**, 32km west of Pavia, interesting for its medieval monuments, including Santa Maria Maggiore (11C) and its baptistery (5C; upper part rebuilt in the 8C), but the chief town is now Mortara, of little interest. A local speciality is salami made from goose meat. Nearby is Cilavegna, known for its asparagus.

Northeast of Mortara near the Ticino is **Vigevano**, an ancient town which grew to prominence in the 14C under the Visconti. Lodovico il Moro and Francesco Il Sforza were born here. It has been famous for the manufacture of shoes since the end of the 19C, and the modern city expanded rapidly in the 1950s. In 1492–94 buildings were demolished to create space for the *Piazza **Ducale** (138 x 48m), a beautiful rectangular Renaissance square built by order of Lodovico il Moro. It is surrounded on three sides by uniform graceful arcades, and its classical design may have been made with the help of Bramante (or even Leonardo da Vinci). The other end was closed in 1680 when the unusual curved façade of the **Duomo** was added to give the cathedral prominence. The cathedral interior (1532–1612) is interesting for its paintings by the 16C Lombard school. A **museum** (open Sun and holidays 15.00–18.00; closed mid-Dec–mid-Jan) houses the rich treasury, which includes Flemish and local tapestries, illuminated codexes, and goldsmiths' work.

A tall Lombard **tower** (probably redesigned by Bramante; open on request) belongs to the huge **Castle** (open Tues–Sun 8.30–13.30; Sat and holidays guided visits at 14.30 and 18.30; closed mid-Dec–mid-Jan), begun by Lucchino Visconti in the mid-14C. On a raised site, this was connected to the piazza by a monumental entrance (destroyed) beneath the tower. The castle was transformed by Lodovico il Moro (with the help of Bramante) into a very grand ducal palace. It has remarkable stables and a beautiful loggia. The raised covered way built by Lucchino Visconti to connect the castle with the Rocca Vecchia survives.

Palazzo Crespi, in Corso Cavour on the outskirts of the old town, houses a museum illustrating the history of footwear, including a collection of shoes (some dating from the 15C), and the Museo Civico (closed at the time of writing), with an archaeological collection and picture gallery.

Southeast of Vigevano is the large Sforzesca, a model farm designed by Guglielmo da Camino for Lodovico il Moro in 1486.

Vigevano is in the centre of the large **Parco Regionale della Valle del Ticino**, instituted in 1974 as a protected area on either side of the Ticino river from Sesto Calende to Pavia (90,000 hectares). Where cars are banned, the trails can be followed on foot or by bicycle to see the wildlife in an interesting landscape. Information from the park office in Magenta (☎ 02 9794401).

The Oltrepò Pavese

The southern part of the province of Pavia, beyond the Po, is known as the Oltrepò Pavese. It is well known for its wines (particularly *Pinot Nero*). Here is **Voghera**, an important industrial centre and railway junction, with a 12C church (Santi Flavio e Giorgio, a cavalry memorial chapel), a Visconti castle, and a museum of fossils.

A road ascends the Val di Staffora to the southeast passing Salice Terme, a little spa with iodine waters (season May–Oct). Just beyond Ponte Nizza, a by-road (left) leads to the **Abbazia di Sant'Alberto di Butrio**, founded in the 11C. Three Romanesque churches here have 15C frescoes. The road continues through Varzi, noted for its salami, and up over the Passo del Penice (1149m; with skiing facilities). Here you can visit the **Giardino Alpino di Pietra Corva** (950m; open May–Sep, Tues–Sun 09.00–12.00, 15.00–19.00), a little botanical garden planted in 1967.

East of Voghera is **Montebello della Battaglia**, where a monument marks the site of two important battles: the victory of the French over the Austrians in 1800, and the Franco-Italian success of 1859, the first battle of the second War of Independence. Nearby is **Casteggio**, where the 18C Palazzo della Certosa contains the Museo Storico Archeologico dell'Oltrepò Pavese (open by appointment, ☎ 0383 83941), with material from the Roman *Clastidium*. East of Casteggio is Stradella, where another museum contains fossils found near the Po and archaeological material.

Lago Maggiore

Lago Maggiore, covering some 121 sq km, is the second largest lake in Italy (the largest is Lake Garda). Its west bank has belonged to Piedmont since 1743, but its east bank lies in Lombardy. The north end (about one-fifth of its area), including Locarno, is in Swiss territory.

Surrounded by picturesque snow-capped mountains, Lago Maggiore became well known at the beginning of the 19C as a European resort, visited for its romantic scenery and good climate. The Simplon highway, constructed by Napoleon in 1800–05 from Geneva to Milan, skirts its southwest shore. A mild climate and high rainfall account for the luxuriant vegetation on its banks. Among its famous gardens, open from spring to autumn, are those on the Isola Madre and the Isola Bella, and at the Villa Taranto. The central part of the lake, around Stresa, is particularly interesting, and the northern reach has the best scenery. Since the 15C the Italian family of Borromeo have held important possessions on the lake, notably the Borromean Islands and the castle of Angera. There is a road around the shore of the lake and public boat services (inaugurated in the 19C) linking all the main towns on its shores. The lake is often called Verbano, from the Latin *Lacus Verbanus*, a name derived from the vervain (verbena) which grows abundantly on its shores.

The total length of the lake, from Magadino to Sesto Calende, is 64.3km, and its greatest breadth 4.8km between Baveno and Laveno; its greatest depth, off Ghiffa, is 372m. The chief affluent is the Ticino, which flows in at Madagino and out at Sesto Calende. Other important feeders are the Maggia, which enters the lake at Locarno; the Toce or Tosa, which flows into the gulf of Pallanza, and is joined just before its inflow by the Strona, fed by the waters of the Lago d'Orta; and on the east side the Tresa, which drains the Lago Lugano and enters Lago Maggiore at Luino.

Practical information

Getting there
By air

The nearest airport in Italy is Milan Malpensa (c 20km south); in Switzerland, Lugano (c 20km east). Both have regional and international flights.

By road

The quickest route to Lake Maggiore from Milan is usually the A8. On Fri and Sun evenings, when traffic is thick with escaping/returning *milanesi*, 33 offers a viable alternative. To reach the lake from Turin, take A4 and A26 to Stresa. From Bellinzona (Switzerland), follow 13 west to Locarno, Ascona and Brissago.

The main road from the Simplon Pass to Milan (33) touches the lake at Sesto Calende and follows the west bank to Baveno. The upper part of the west bank is followed by a good road from Bavena to Bellinzona (Swiss route 13, Italian 34). Another road (combining 394, 629 and local roads) follows the east bank.

By rail

The main rail line from Milan to Geneva, Bern and Basel via Domodossola and the Simplon Tunnel passes along the west shore of the lake. Fast *Cisalpina*, *Eurocity* and *Intercity* trains stop at Arona and/or Stresa (both c 50mins from Milan). The stations of Baveno, Stresa, Belgirate, Lesa, Meina, and Arona, built by Luigi Boffi, date from the turn of the century, when the line was opened. The east shore of the lake is served by a minor line from Milan to Bellinzona via Luino (c 90 mins), with a change of trains sometimes necessary at Gallarate. Laveno has a second station serving the Nord railway for Varese and Milan.

Getting around
By boat

Information from *Navigazione Lago Maggiore*, Arona, ☎ 0322 46651.

There are frequent services between Stresa and Intra, calling at Isola Bella, Isola dei Pescatori, Baveno, Isola Madre, Pallanza and Villa Taranto. There is also a frequent service between Arona, Angera and Belgirate. In summer the route from Arona to Locarno, calling at the main ports, is served once a day by a hydrofoil (2hrs) and a boat (3hrs 30 mins). There are also services linking Cannero, Luino and Cannobio. There is a car ferry every 20mins between Intra and Laveno (10 mins). The timetable changes for each of the four seasons.

By cable car

Cableways connect Laveno, San Domenico di Varzo, Stresa, Alagna Valsesia (Bonda) and Neggio Magliasco with sites in the hills.

By bus

There are local bus services between the main towns; information from *Autoservizi Nerini*, ☎ 0323 401526.

Information offices
ARONA Piazzale Duca d'Aosta, ☎ 0322 243601.
BAVENO Corso Garibaldi 16, ☎ 0323 924632.
LAVENO Palazzo Municipale, ☎ 0332 666666.
LUINO Via Piero Chiara 1, ☎ 0332 530019.
STRESA Via Canonica 8, ☎ 0323 31308, the main office for the west (Piedmontese) side of the lake.
VARESE Via Carrobio 2, ☎ 0332 283604. Viale Ippodromo 9, ☎ 0332 284624, for the east (Lombard) side of the lake; branch offices at Laveno and Luino.
VERBANIA Corso Zanitello 8, Pallanza, ☎ 0323 503249.

Where to stay

There are numerous hotels of all categories in all the main resorts, but many are open only Easter–Oct. The latter are marked in the text; those without a specific mention of season are open all year round.

ANGERA *Dei Tigli*, Via Paletta 20, ☎ 0331 930836, fax 0331 960333; simple and friendly, on the lake; inexpensive.

ASCONA *Ascona*, Via Colina, ☎ 093 351135, fax 093 361748; a pleasant place with garden and views; moderate. *Castello del Sole*, Via Muraccio (1km northeast), ☎ 093 350202, fax 093 361118; a fine garden hotel, recently renovated; expensive. *Eden Roc*, Via Albarelle, tel. 093 350171, fax 351571; grand hotel in a lakeside garden; open Apr–Dec, expensive. *Europe au Lac*, Via Albarelle, ☎ 093 352881, fax 093 361809; another big lakefront establishment; open Apr–Oct, expensive.

BAVENO *Grand Hotel Dino*, Via Garibaldi 20, ☎ 0323 922201, fax 0323 924515; large, modern hotel in a beautiful park with views of the Isole Boromee; expensive. *Lido Palace Baveno*, Via Sempione 30, ☎ 0323 924444, fax 0323 924744; a large 19C establishment with luxuriant gardens, overlooking the Isole Boromee; moderate. *Rigoli*, Via Piave 48, ☎ 0323 924756, fax 925156; simple, family-run establishment on the lake, also with views of the Isole Boromee; open Apr–Oct, inexpensive.

BELGIRATE *Villa Carlotta*, Via Sempione 121/125, ☎ 0322 76461, fax 0322 76705; on the lake with a beautiful park and fine restaurant; moderate.

CANNOBIO *Antica Stallera*, Via Zaccheo 3, ☎ 0323 71595, fax 0323 72201; an old stage-halt, with a pleasant garden; open Mar–Dec, inexpensive. *Pironi*, Via Marconi 35, ☎ 0323 70624, fax 0323 72184; small and intimate, in a 15C convent with frescoed rooms; open Mar–Nov, moderate.

GHIFFA *Park Hotel Paradiso*, Via Marconi 20, ☎ 0323 59548; small (15 rooms) and quiet, in a Liberty-style villa with garden; moderate.

ISPRA *Europa*, Via Berbano 19, ☎ 0332 780184, fax 0332 782058; a cordial, family-run place in a lovely park; moderate.

LOCARNO *Grand Hotel Locarno*, Via Sempione 17, ☎ 093 330282, fax 093 333013; calm and quiet, in a verdant garden; moderate. *Orselina*, località Orselina (2km north); likewise restful, in a tropical garden with views over the lake and mountains; open Mar–Nov, moderate.

LUINO *Camin Luino*, Viale Dante 35, ☎ 0332 530118, fax 0332 537226; warm and comfortable, a 19C villa in a lakefront park, with Liberty furniture and 13 rooms; open Mar–Dec, moderate.

SESTO CALENDE *David*, Via Roma 56, ☎ 0331 920182, fax 0331 913939; an old townhouse, with garden, in the historic centre; closed Dec–Jan, inexpensive. *Tre Re*, Piazza Garibaldi 25, ☎ 0331 924229, fax 0331 913023; an old locanda, simple but comfortable; open Mar–Nov, inexpensive.

STRESA *Ariston*, Corso Italia 60, ☎ 0323 31195, fax 0323 31195; a small (11 rooms), friendly place, open Mar–Nov; inexpensive. *Des Iles Borromées*, Lungolago Umberto I 67, ☎ 0323 938938, fax 0323 32405; a fine luxury hotel with a lovely park and views of the Isole Boromee; expensive. *Du Parc*, Via Gignous 1, ☎ 0323 30335, fax 0323 33596, also with a shady garden, open Easter–Oct, moderate. *Verbano*, ☎ 0323 30408, fax 0323 33129; on the charming Isola dei Pescatori; moderate.

VERBANIA *Majestic*, Via Vittorio Veneto 32, ☎ 0323 504305, fax 0323 556379; elegant 19C establishment on the lake-

front, open Easter–Oct; moderate.
San Gottardo, Vale delle Magnolie 4, ☎ 0323 504465, fax 0323 504466; recently renovated early-20C villa on the lakefront, managed by the same people who run the adjacent Belvedere; open Mar–Oct, inexpensive.
Villa Azalea, Salita San Remigio 4, ☎ 0323 556692; small and simple, in a Liberty-style villa; open Easter–Oct, inexpensive.

Eating out

ARONA *Campania* , Via Vergante 12, ☎ 0322 57294; trattoria serving creative and traditional dishes using local ingredients; closed Mon evening (in winter), Tues, Jul and Nov; moderate.
Taverna del Pittore, Piazza del Popolo 39, ☎ 0322 243366; closed Mon, Jun and Nov; restaurant widely known for its salt- and fresh-water fish dishes; expensive.
ASCONA *Da Ivo*, Via Collegio 7, ☎093 351031; traditional restaurant with garden; closed Mon, Tues and Jan–Mar; moderate.
Giardino, ☎ 093 350101; excellent restaurant of the equally impressive *Hotel Giardino*, on the northeastern outskirts of the city; open Mar–Nov, closed midday Mon and Tues; moderate.
CANNOBIO *Del Lago*, Via Nazionale 2, località Carmine on the Swiss border; ☎ 0323 70595; restaurant offering innovative variations on old regional recipes; closed Tues, midday Wed, Feb and Nov; expensive.
LAVENO *Il Porticciolo* (with rooms), Via Fortino 40, ☎ 0332 667257; restaurant specialising in fresh- and saltwater fish; closed Tues (midday only in Jul–Aug) and Jan–Feb; moderate.
LESA *L'Antico Maniero*, Via alla Campagna 1, ☎ 0322 7411; restaurant in a 19C villa with park (reservations necessary); open evenings only (except Sun), closed Mon, Nov and Jan; expensive.

LOCARNO *Centenario Perriard*, Lungolago Motta 17, ☎ 093 338222; fine international cuisine; closed Sun, Mon, Feb and Jul; expensive.
RANCO (near Ispra) **Il Sole di Ranco**, Piazza Venezia 5, ☎ 0331 976507; restaurant (with rooms) famous for its lake fish and seafood; closed Mon evening (except May–Sep), Tues and Dec–Jan; expensive.
SESTO CALENDE *Da Mosè*, Via Ponzello 14, ☎ 0331 977240; restaurant serving traditional dishes with a special flair; open evenings only (except weekends and holidays), closed Mon, Tues and Jan–Feb; moderate.
San Pietro, Via Crocera 38, località Lisanza; ☎ 0331 977197; trattoria serving traditional local dishes; closed Wed and Jan; inexpensive.
STRESA *Il Piemontese*, Via Mazzini 25, ☎ 0323 30235; restaurant in a 17C building with private garden, known for its fine regional cuisine; closed Mon and Dec–Jan; moderate. **L'Emiliano**, Corso Italia 50, ☎ 0323 31396; restaurant serving innovative fish dishes, wide selection of local cheeses; closed Tues, midday Wed and Nov–Dec, expensive.
VERBANIA *Osteria dell'Angolo*, Piazza Garibaldi 35, ☎ 0323 556362; restaurant known for its lake fish and other local specialities; closed Mon; inexpensive.

Entertainment

STRESA Classical music at **Villa Francesca**, May–Oct. Live pop, rock and jazz at clubs around Lago Maggiore in summer.

Shopping

Sweets are the main things to buy, especially *Margheritine di Stresa* and *Baci di Stresa*. Traditional markets at Baveno, Mon; Arona, Tues; Luino, Wed; Omegna, Thur; Stresa and Pallanza, Fri; Intra, Sat; Cannobio, Sun.

Special events
Food, music and pageantry accompany patron-saints' days in most towns. In addition, several interesting fairs and events are held annually at Stresa; among the more important are the *Camellia Show*, Apr; *International Philatelic Exhibition*, *Youth Music Competition* and *Piedmont Wine Show*, Jun; *Premio Stresa* narrative literary prize, Oct; *Settimane Musicali*, international music festival, Aug–Sep.

 Sports
There is really no end to the possibilities here. You'll find **golf courses** and **tennis courts** in or near Stresa; **swimming**, **sailing** and **water-skiing** on the lake; **walking** in the hills, especially on Monte Mottarone and in the Parco Nazionale della Val Grande (information and maps from the tourist information office in Varese and the Parco Nazionale della Val Grande, ☎ 0323 557960); **horse-riding** at Fondotoce; **downhill skiing** on Monte Mottarone and at Macugnaga (Val d'Ossola) in winter, or on Monte Rosa year-round.

The west side of the lake

From Sesto Calende, at the southern tip of the lake, the Napoleonic road (33) winds northwest. **Arona** is an ancient town looking across the lake to Angera. The Palazzo Podestà dates from the 15C. In the upper town, the church of **Santa Maria** contains an *altarpiece by Gaudenzio Ferrari (1511) in its Borromeo chapel. The lunette over the main door has a charming 15C relief of the Holy Family. The nearby church of the Santi Martiri has an altarpiece by Bergognone. The church of the Madonna di Piazza (1592) is attributed to Pellegrino Tibaldi. To the north, above the road, stands San Carlone, a colossal copper statue of St Charles Borromeo (1538–84), Archbishop of Milan and an important figure of the Counter-Reformation. He was born in the castle that now lies in ruins above the town. The statue, 23m high, standing on a pedestal 12m high, was commissioned by a relative of the saint from Giovanni Battista Crespi (Il Cerano) and finished in 1697. It can be climbed by steps and an internal stair.

At **Lesa**, the novelist Alessandro Manzoni often stayed at Palazzo Stampa. **Belgirate** is a pretty hamlet with a good view of the lake and some old houses surviving in its highest part. The road follows the course of the Simplon Highway built by Napoleon in 1800–05.

Stresa and the Isole Borromee

The most important place on the west side of the lake is **Stresa**, nestled in a charming position on the south shore of the gulf of Pallanza. It became fashionable as a European resort in the mid-19C, but is now somewhat in decline. On the lake front, with pleasant gardens, is the orange-and-grey **Villa Ducale**, an 18C edifice that once belonged to the philosopher Antonio Rosmini (1797–1855). It is now a study centre devoted to Rosmini, who founded an order of charity in 1852 (the Rosminian college is above the town). Beyond the Regina Palace Hotel, opened in 1908, at the bend of the road, is the huge monumental **Hotel des Iles Borromées**, which has had many famous guests since it opened in 1863. Frederick Henry in Hemingway's *Farewell to Arms* also stayed here. South of the pier is the **Villa Pallavicino**, built in 1855 with a small formal garden at the

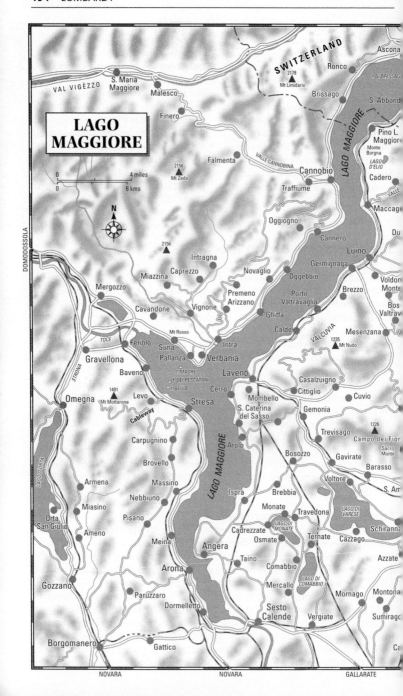

LAGO MAGGIORE

0 —— 4 miles
0 —— 6 kms

N

SWITZERLAND

VAL VIGÈZZO

S. Maria Maggiore
Malesco
Finero

Ascona
Ronco
Mt Limidario 2178
Brissago
S. Abbond
I. DI BRISSAG

Falmenta
Mt Zeda 2156
VALLE CANNOBINA
Cannobio
Traffiume
Pino L. Maggior
Monte Borgna
LAGO D'ELIO
Cadero
VALLE
Maccag
Du

2156
Intragna
Caprezzo
Miazzina
Novaglio
Oggiogno
Cannero
Luino
Germignaga
Oggebbio
Voldor
Monte
Bos
Valtrav

Mergozzo
Cavandone
Premeno Arizzano
Vignone
Porto Valtravaglia
Brezzo

Mt Rosso
Ghiffa
Calde

DOMODOSSOLA

TOCE
Feriolo
Suna
Pallanza
Intra
Verbania
Mesenzana
VALCUVIA
Mt Nudo 1235

Gravellona
Baveno
I. MADRE
I. DEI PESCATORI
I. BELLA
Laveno
Casalzuigno
Cittiglio
Cuvio

STRONA

Omegna
Levo
Mt Mottarone 1491
Stresa
Cerro
Mombello
S. Caterina del Sasso
Gemonia

Cableway
Carpugnino
Arolo
Trevisago
Campo dei Fior
Sacro Monte

Brovello
Bosozzo
Gavirate
Barasso
S. An

LAGO D'ORTA

Armena
Massino
Voltore
Schiranna

Miasino
Nebbiuno
Ispra
Brebbia
LAGO DI VARESE

Orta San Giulio
Ameno
Pisano
Monate
Travedona
Cazzago
Azzate

Meina
Cadrezzate
Osmate
LAGO DI MONATE
Ternate

Angera
Taino
Comabbio
LAGO DI COMABBIO
Mercallo
Mornago
Montona

Arona
Sesto Calende
Vergiate
Sumirag
Co

Gozzano
Paruzzaro
Dormelletto

Borgomanero
Gattico

LAGO MAGGIORE

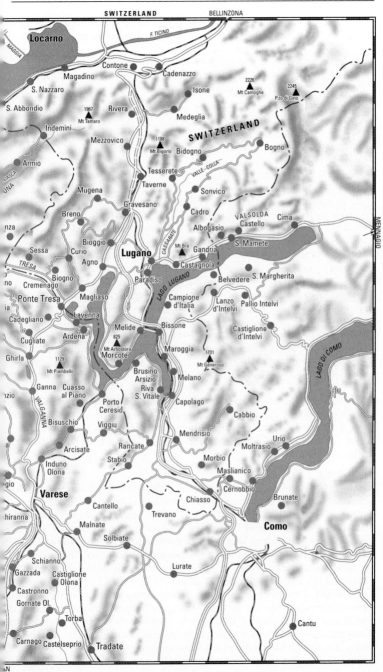

front of the house. It is surrounded by a fine wooded park (open Mar–Oct, 09.00–18.00) planted with palms, magnolias and cedars, with a zoological garden.

Lago Maggiore at the turn of the 19th century

The English author Hilaire Belloc, who visited Lago Maggiore in 1902, left this impression of a beauty so intense as to seem almost immoral:

The Italian lakes have that in them and their air which removes them from common living. Their beauty is not the beauty which each of us sees for himself in the world; it is rather the beauty of a special creation; the expression of some mind. To eyes innocent, and freshly noting our great temporal inheritance—I mean to the eyes of a boy and girl just entered upon the estate of this glorious earth, and thinking themselves immortal, this shrine of Europe might remain for ever in the memory; an enchanted experience, in which the single sense of sight had almost touched the boundary of music. They would remember these lakes as the central emotion of their youth. To mean men also, who, in spite of years and of a full foreknowlege of death, yet attempt nothing but the satisfaction of sense, and pride themselves upon the taste and fineness with which they achieve this satisfaction, the Italian lakes would seem a place for habitation, and there such a man might build his house contentedly. But to ordinary Christians I am sure there is something unnatural in this beauty of theirs, and they find it in either a paradise only to be won by a much longer road or a bait and veil of sorcery, behind which lies great peril. Now, for all we know, beauty beyond the world may not wear this double aspect; but to us on earth—if we are ordinary men—beauty of this kind has something evil. Have you not read in books how men when they see even divine visions are terrified? So as I looked at Lake Major in its halo I also was afraid, and I was glad to cross the ridge and crest of the hill and to shut out that picture framed all round with glory.

In the lake close to Strasa lie the ***Isole Boromee**, a group of beautiful little islands named after the Italian Borromeo family, who still own the Isola Madre, Isola Bella and Isola San Giovanni. There are regular daily boat services (see above) for Isola Bella, Isola dei Pescatori and Isola Madre from Stresa, Baveno, Pallanza, and Intra.

Isola Bella

The most famous of the islands is the *Isola Bella, which was a barren rock with a small church and a few cottages before it was almost totally occupied by a huge palace with terraced gardens built in 1631–71 by Angelo Crivelli for Count Carlo III Borromeo, in honour of his wife, from whom it takes its name. The island measures just 320 x 180m, and there is a tiny hamlet by the pier outside the garden gates, with tourist shops and a few restaurants and cafés. The palace and gardens (combined ticket) are open only from late Mar–late Oct (daily 09.00–12.00, 13.30–17.30; Oct–17.00).

To the left of the pier is the vast grey palace, entered from an open courtyard behind four palm trees. On the right of the courtyard (seen through a grille) is the chapel, which contains three family *tombs with elaborate carvings by Giovanni Antonio Amadeo and Bambaia, brought from demolished churches in Milan. On the left of the courtyard is the entrance to the palace. Twenty-five rooms on the piano nobile, decorated with Murano chandeliers and Venetian mosaic floors, can be visited (the three floors above are the private apartments of the Borromeo family). The English historian Edward Gibbon stayed here as a guest of the Borromeo in 1764.

The octagonal blue-and-white Sala dei Concerti was built in 1948–51 in Baroque style following the original plans. There is a view of the Isola dei Pescatori and (right) the Isola Madre. The Sala di Musica has musical instruments, two Florentine cabinets in ebony and semi-precious stone (17C–18C), and paintings by Jacopo Bassano and Tempesta. In 1935 a conference took place here between Mussolini and the French and British governments in an attempt to guarantee the peace of Europe. Napoleon stayed in the next room in 1797. The library preserves, besides its books, some paintings by Carnevalis. Another room has paintings by Luca Giordano, and beyond a room with views of the Borromeo properties, by Zuccarelli, is the ballroom.

Stairs lead down to the grottoes built on the lake in the 18C. Beyond a room with 18C–20C puppets (once used in puppet shows held in the 'amphitheatre' in the garden) are six grottoes encrusted with shells, pebbles, marbles, etc. Displayed here are statues by Gaetano Matteo Monti, remains of an ancient boat found in the lake off Angera, archaeological material and bridles. A spiral staircase in an old tower that pre-dates the palace leads up to a short corridor of mirrors and from there to the anticamera, with a ceiling tondo attributed to Giovanni Battista Tiepolo and two paintings by Daniele Crespi. Beyond the chapel of St Charles Borromeo is the gallery of tapestries, with a splendid collection of 16C Flemish *tapestries commissioned by St Charles Borromeo. The painting of *St Jerome* is by Moretto.

A door leads out to the famous *gardens, inhabited by white peacocks. The terraces are built out into the lake, and soil for the plants had to be brought from the mainland. A double staircase leads up onto a terrace with a huge camphor tree, camellias, bamboos, breadfruit, sugar cane, tapioca and tea and coffee plants. Beyond is the 'amphitheatre', an elaborate Baroque construction with statues, niches, pinnacles and stairs, crowned by a unicorn (the family crest). The terrace at the top looks straight to Stresa, and below is the Italianate garden with box hedges and yew, and ten terraces planted with roses, oleanders and pomegranates descending to the lake. Other parts of the garden are laid out in the 'English style', with beds of tulips and forget-me-nots in spring and geraniums in summer. Below the terraces are rhododendrons and orange trees (protected in winter). The azaleas are at their best during April and May. The second exit leads out of the gardens through the delightful old-fashioned greenhouse.

Near Isola Bella are a tiny islet inhabited by cormorants in winter and the **Isola dei Pescatori**, or Isola Superiore, not owned by the Borromeo. It is occupied by a pretty little fishing village, and has a hotel and restaurant.

Isola Madre

The *Isola Madre (330 x 220m) is nearer to Pallanza than to Stresa. It is entirely occupied by a Borromeo villa and ***botanical garden** (open late Mar–end Oct, daily 09.00–12.00, 13.30–17.30; Oct, 09.30–12.30, 13.30–17.00), and inhabited only by a custodian. It has one restaurant (otherwise you can bring a sandwich). The landscaped gardens, at their best in April, are laid out in the English manner and were replanted in the 1950s by Henry Cocker. The particularly mild climate allows a great number of exotic and tropical plants to flourish here (most of the plants are labelled), and white peacocks and white pheasants inhabit the gardens. Viale Africa, with the warmest exposure, is lined with a variety of plants, including citrus fruits. The camellia terrace has numerous species of camellia and mimosa. Beyond a wisteria-covered arboured walk is the Mediterranean garden, with rosemary, lavender, etc. and a rock garden. The cylindrical tower was once used as an ice house; beyond it are ferns. From the little port with its boat house (and an 18C boat suspended from the roof) is a view of Pallanza. Nearby is the oldest camellia on the island (thought to be some 150 years old). On a lawn is a group of taxodium trees, with their roots sticking up out of the ground—an odd sight—and beyond are banks of azaleas, rhododendrons, camphor trees and ancient magnolias. Beside steps up to the villa, by a remarkable Kashmir cypress—said to be 200 years old—is an aviary with parrots that nest in the cedar of Lebanon here. Near the villa are ornamental banana trees and the Art Nouveau family chapel. The terrace near the villa is planted with tall palm trees, including a majestic Chilean palm, planted in 1858, which bears miniature edible coconuts. The steps nearby are covered with a trellis of kiwi fruit.

The 18C villa is also open to the public. It contains 17C and 18C furnishings from Borromeo properties and servants' livery, as well as a collection of porcelain, puppets and dolls (19C French and German), and paintings by Pitocchetto. The little theatre dates from 1778.

The **Isola San Giovanni** is not open to the public. The villa on the island was once the summer home of Toscanini.

Above Stresa is **Monte Mottarone** (1491m), reached by a cableway (which replaces a funicular inaugurated in 1911), or by road. The road (20km) passes a 9-hole golf course at Vezzo. The local industry of umbrella-making at Gignese is recorded in the umbrella museum here, founded in 1939, which has a collection of umbrellas and parasols dating from 1840 to 1940. At Alpino is the **Giardino Alpinia** (605m), a botanical garden founded in 1933, with some 544 species of Alpine plants. It is open Apr–mid-Oct, Tues–Sun 09.00–18.00. Here a private toll-road, owned by the Borromeo since 1623 (9km; always open), continues through the meadows and woods of the **Parco del Mottarone** on the slopes of Monte Mottarone, with a view of the whole chain of the Alps from Monte Viso in the west to the Ortler and Adamello in the east, and the Monte Rosa group especially conspicuous to the northwest. Below, on a clear day you can make out seven lakes and the wide Po Valley. The mountain has been visited by skiers since the beginning of the century, and there are spectacular walks in the area.

North of Stresa

Baveno, northwest of Stresa, is in a fine position on the south shore of the gulf of Pallanza opposite the Borromean Islands. Quieter than Stresa, it preserves a pleasant little square with a Renaissance baptistery (frescoes) and a church with an early façade and campanile. The landing stage is a pretty Art Nouveau building, and the delightful shore road to Stresa, with a good view of the Borromean Islands, is flanked by villas and hotels built in the 19C when the town was well known as a resort. Among these is the Castello Branca (formerly Villa Clara), built in 1844, where Queen Victoria spent the spring of 1879. To the northwest of Baveno rises Monte Camoscio (890m), with quarries of pink granite for which Baveno is famous.

Across the lake from Baveno is **Verbania**, which includes the towns of Pallanza and Intra on either side of the promontory of the Punta della Castagnola. In a charming position in full view of the Borromean Islands and below Monte Rossa (618m), it has a mild climate which makes the flora particularly luxuriant; the lake front is planted with magnolias. The Hotel Majestic was opened here in 1870. Near the pier is the mausoleum, by Marcello Piacentini of Marshal Cadorna (1850–1928), a native of Pallanza; and just inland is the market-place, with the town hall and the church of San Leonardo (16C; modernised in the 19C), the tall tower of which was completed by Pellegrino Tibaldi in 1589. In the Baroque Palazzo Dugnani is a small local museum (open Tues–Sun 09.00–12.00, 15.00–18.00), founded in 1914 and containing 19C landscapes of the lake, as well as sculptures by Paolo Troubetzkoy and Arturo Martini. The Villa Kursaal (1882), surrounded by gardens, is open to the public.

The narrow Via Cavour leads north from the market-place. Some way beyond is the fine domed church of the Madonna di Campagna, which was begun in 1519 and contains contemporary decorations (notably works attributed to Carlo Urbini, Aurelio Luini and Gerolamo Lanino).

On the **Punta della Castagnola**, a promontory on the lake, is the **Villa San Remigio**, built in 1903 (now the seat of the administrative offices of the Regional government; open only by previous appointment, ☎ 0323 504401). The formal gardens, when they were laid out in 1905 by Sophie Browne, an Irish painter, and Silvio della Valle di Casanova, were among the best in northern Italy, with topiary terraces, fountains, and statues by Orazio Marinali. The plants include yellow and white banksia roses, wisteria, camellias, myrtle, conifers and palm trees.

Next to Villa San Remigio on the slopes of the Punta della Castagnola is the 19C **Villa Taranto**, with famous *botanical gardens (open Apr–Oct, 08.30–19.30, no entry after 18.30) much visited by tourists—the villa has a landing stage served by regular boat services. The huge estate was bought by Captain Neil McEacharn (1884–1964) in 1930. Together with Henry Cocker, he created a garden with an outstanding collection of exotic plants from all over the world, which he later donated to the Italian State. The plants include magnolias (at their best at the beginning of April), superb camellias (which flower in Apr), rhododendrons (which flower May–Jun), azaleas and paulownias (best in May). The herbaceous borders and dahlias (over 300 varieties) are at their best in July and August. Birches, maples and conifers distinguish the woodlands. The statues include a bronze fisher-boy by Vincenzo Gemito.

Above Verbania is the **Parco Nazionale della Val Grande**, a protected mountainous area with fine walks.

Intra is the most important commercial centre on Lago Maggiore, with a car ferry (every 20mins) across the lake to Laveno on the opposite shore. To the north, close to the lake, are the beautiful private gardens of the Villa Poss and Villa Ada. Roads lead up to Miazzina (719m) at the foot of Monte Zeda (2188m), and Premeno (802m), a winter and summer resort, above which is Pian di Sole (949m), with a 9-hole golf course.

The road skirts the lake to Ghiffa, a scattered village, with the castle of Frino. The little 13C church of Novaglio, above the road, is built in a mixture of Lombard and Gothic styles. Above Oggebbio, in chestnut groves, is the little oratory of Cadessino, with 15C–16C frescoes. Ahead, across the lake, Luino comes into view, as, beneath Oggiogno high up on its rock, the road passes the villa of the statesman Massimo d'Azeglio (1798–1866), where he wrote most of his memoirs. Cannero Riviera is a resort lying in a sheltered and sunny position at the foot of Monte Carza (1118m). Off the coast are two rocky islets on which stood the castles of Malpaga, demolished by the Visconti in 1414. One island is now occupied by the picturesque ruins of a castle built by Ludovico Borromeo in 1519–21. On the hill above the town is the 14C–15C church of Carmine Superiore, built on the summit of a precipice. It has some ceiling paintings and a triptych of the 14C Lombard school. The road rounds Punta d'Amore opposite Maccagno.

Cannobio has ancient origins and preserves some medieval buildings. Near the pier is the **Santuario della Pietà** (reconstructed in 1583–1601), with a fine altarpiece by Gaudenzio Ferrari. The town hall, called Il Parrasio, is a 13C building with 17C alterations.

Inland, in the Val Cannobina is the Orrido di Sant'Anna, a romantic gorge with a waterfall. Just beyond Cannobio is the frontier with Switzerland. The road goes on Via Brissago to **Ascona** and **Locarno** which are famous for their climate and views.

The east side of the lake

The road re-enters Italy at Zenna and winds southwards, with good views over the water to the east.

Luino is the most important centre on the Lombard side of the lake. A small industrial town, it lies a little north of the junction of the Tresa and Margorabbia, which unite to flow into the lake at Germignaga. Near the landing stage is a statue of Garibaldi, commemorating his attempt, on 14 Aug 1848, to renew the struggle against Austria with only 1500 men, after the armistice which followed the defeat of Custozza. The town hall occupies an 18C palazzo by Felice Soave. An *Adoration of the Magi*, attributed to Bernardino Luini, who was probably born here, decorates the cemetery church of San Pietro, and the Madonna del Carmine has frescoes by his pupils (1540). The little Museo Civico Archeologico Paleontologico (open by appointment, ☎ 0332 532057) has local antiquities, minerals and fossils, and a small painting collection. A market has been held in the town on Wed since 1541. On the landward side of the town is the railway station where the Swiss line from Bellinzona meets the Italian line from Novara and Milan. This was an important frontier station (with custom-house) on the St Gotthard line.

Laveno, now part of the municipality of Mombello, is in a fine position on the lake, with good views of the Punta della Castagnola and the Isola Madre in the distance. Its small port serves the car ferry to Intra. The old-fashioned railway station of the Milano-Nord line for Varese and Milan (one of two stations in Laveno) adjoins the ferry station. The town was once noted for its ceramics, and there is a **ceramics museum** (open Tues–Thur 14.30–17.30; Fri–Sun also 10.00–12.00) in the adjacent village of Cerro. A monument in the piazza by the waterside commemorates the *garibaldini* who fell in an attempt to capture the town from the Austrians in 1859 (the Austrian fort was on the Punta di San Michele).

An excursion from Laveno

A cableway (closed on Mon and in bad weather) mounts to **Poggio Sant'Elsa** with a view north to Monte Rosa, the Mischabel group and the Fletschhorn group. From the cableway station here it is 30mins on foot to the Sasso del Ferro (1062m), the beautiful hill to the east. The panorama is still better from Monte Nudo (1235m).

Along the shore

The road follows the shore of the lake past the ceramics museum at Cerro (see above) and Leggiuno, where the Oratory of Santi Primo e Feliciano (9C) has Roman foundations. The solitary convent of **Santa Caterina del Sasso** (reached in 10mins by a steep path which descends from the main road, or by boat from Laveno or Stresa in summer) was founded in the 13C and reinhabited by Dominicans in 1986. Open daily 09.30–12.00 and 14.00 or 15.00–17.00 or 18.00, it is built into a sheer rock face directly above the lake (there is an 18m drop to the water). The picturesque Romanesque buildings, particularly attractive when seen from the water, were restored in 1624 and have a good view of the gulf of Pallanza and the Borromean Islands. They contain 15C and 16C frescoes and a 17C *Last Supper*.

Ispra is the seat of *Euratom*, the first centre in Italy for nuclear studies. **Angera** has a pleasant spacious waterfront planted with horse chestnuts. A road (signposted) leads up to the ***Rocca Borromea** (open Mar–Oct, 09.30–12.30, 16.00–18.00). Formerly a castle of the Visconti, it passed to the Borromeo in 1449 and is still owned by them. It was extensively restored in the 16C–17C. The fine gateway leads into a charming courtyard with a pergola open to the south end of the lake. Off the second courtyard is a wine press dating from 1745. The Sala di Giustizia has interesting 14C Gothic frescoes commissioned by Giovanni Visconti, Bishop of Milan, with signs of the zodiac and episodes from the battles of Archbishop Ottone Visconti. In other rooms are displayed paintings, Roman altars, and detached frescoes from Palazzo Borromeo in Milan. It also has a doll museum, and you can climb the 13C Torre Castellana. In Via Mazzini, for grappa lovers, is a distillery dating from 1850. And at nearby **Ranco** is an interesting transport museum (open Tues–Sun 10.00–12.00, 15.00–18.00), mostly displayed in the open air. It illustrates the history of transport from horse-drawn carriages to steam engines, electric tramways, funicular railways, etc. There are quite a few original vehicles and reconstructions of several stations.

Sesto Calende is the southernmost town on the east bank of the lake. It is said to derive its name from its market day in Roman times—the sixth day before the Calends. A small **Museo Civico** (open Tues–Sat 14.30–16.30; Sun and holidays 10.00–12.00, 15.00–19.00) houses archaeological finds from tombs of the local Golasecca culture (800–450 BC).

Varese and environs

The town of Varese has only a few monuments worth visiting, but there are various places of interest nearby, notably Castiglione Olona with its Renaissance works of art and frescoes by Masolino. The province is situated between Lago Maggiore and Lago di Lugano and has numerous minor lakes, but the countryside has been ruined in many places by new building. The Sacro Monte above Varese has beautiful 17C chapels, and Castelseprio, south of the town, is one of the more important Lombard sites in Italy. There are many villas in the province with particularly beautiful gardens open to the public. These include the Villa Porta Bozzolo at Casalzuigno, Villa Cicogna Mozzoni at Bisuschio, and the Palazzo Estense in Varese.

Practical information

Getting there
By air

Milan's Malpensa airport is in this area, at Gallarate, c 35km south of Varese (and 50km northwest of Milan). If faced with the prospect of staying at the airport hotel, you might want to try one of the places listed below instead.

By road

The A8 takes you directly from Milan, where it starts, to Varese, where it ends (be careful not to take the A26 link road westwards for Lago Maggiore). 233, the shortest route in terms of distance, is the longest in terms of time, due to heavy local traffic. From Turin, take A4 east to A26, A26 north and east to A8 and A8 north to Varese. From Switzerland you can cross the border at Ponte Tresa and take 233 south, or cut over from Como on 342.

By rail

There is a frequent commuter service from Milan to Varese in just over 1hr. The two train stations (one for the State railways and one for the Nord–Milano line) are only a few metres apart.

Getting around

This is Milan's industrial hinterland, and traffic can be quite intense on local roads. Lorries are a special problem. From Varese, **Bus C** every 15mins to Sacro Monte and Campo dei Fiori; **Bus A** to Biumo Superiore. **Country buses** to towns in the province, Lago Maggiore, Lago di Lugano, Como, etc.

Information offices
VARESE Via Carrobbio 1, ☎ 0332 283604; website: www.hcs.it/varese
ANGERA Piazza Garibaldi 19, ☎ 0331 960207.
CASTIGLIONE OLONA Piazza Garibaldi, ☎ 0331 858048.
LAVENO MOMBELLO Piazza Italia 1, ☎ 0332 666666
LUINO Via Piero Chiara 1, ☎ 0332 530019
MACCAGNO Via Garibaldi 1, ☎ 0332 561200.

Where to stay
VARESE *Crystal*, Via Speroni 10, ☎ 0332 231145, fax 0332 237181; modern and functional, moderate.
Palace, Via Manara 11, at Colle Campigli, ☎ 0332 327100, fax 0332 312870; another villa with garden;

moderate.

Bologna, Via Broggi 7, ☎ 0332 234362, fax 0332 287500; small (14 rooms) and friendly; closed Aug; inexpensive.

AZZATE ***Locanda dei Mai Intees***, Via Nobile Claudio Riva 2, ☎ 0332 457233, fax 0332 459339; small (7 rooms) and intimate, in a 15C building, with a good restaurant; closed Jan; moderate.

CANTELLO ***Madonnina***, Largo Lanfranco 1, località Ligurno, ☎ 0332 417731, fax 0332 418403; another small place, with 12 lovely rooms in a patrician villa and an excellent restaurant; moderate.

INDUNO OLONA ***Villa Castiglioni***, Via Castiglioni 1, ☎ 0332 200201, fax 0332 201269; 19C villa set in a beautiful garden, also with good restaurant; moderate.

SACRO MONTE ***Colonne***, Via Fincarà 37, ☎ 0332 244633, fax 0332 821593; cosy (8 rooms), with great views of the valley and a restaurant with summer seating outside; moderate.

 ### Eating out

VARESE ***Da Annetta***, Via Fè 25 at Capolago, ☎ 0332 490230; restaurant representing the best of local traditiion; closed Tues evening, Wed and Aug; moderate.

Lago Maggiore, Via Carrobbio 19, ☎ 0332 231183; restaurant serving tradional regional dishes prepared with great care; reservations required, closed Sun, midday Mon and Jul; expensive.

CERRO MAGGIORE (LEGNANO) ***Tana del Lupo***, Via Risorgimento 8, località Cantalupo, ☎ 0331 535148; restaurant serving traditional regional dishes; closed Tues evening, Wed and Jul–Aug; moderate.

OLGIATE-OLONA ***Ma.Ri.Na.***, Piazza San Gregorio 11, ☎ 0331 640483; restaurant specialising in fish; open evenings only (except Sun and holidays), closed Wed and Aug; expensive.

TRADATE ***L'Enoteca***, Corso Bernacchi 97, ☎ 0331 844584; wine bar with good hot sandwiches; open daily until 20.30, 24.00 on weekends; closed Mon, Aug and Jan; inexpensive.

TERNATE ***Locanda del Lago***, Via Motta, ☎ 0332 960864; restaurant specialising in lake fish; closed Mon; moderate.

TRAVEDONA MONATE ***Ristorante del Torchio***, Via Cavour 1, ☎ 0332 977436; restaurant serving traditional Lombard dishes, notably game and lake fish; closed Mon, Feb and Aug; inexpensive.

 ### Entertainment

Theatre in Varese at ***Cinema-Teatro Impero***, Via Bernasconi.

 ### Shopping

Antiques markets in Varese, first Sun of the month; Angera, second Sun of the month; Azzate, fourth Sun; Castiglione Olona, first Sun; Gallarate, third Sun; Sesto Calende, second Sat.

 ### Special events

Falò di Sant'Antonio, patron saint's feast in Varese, 16 Jan; ***Estate Varesina***, open-air cinema, theatre and music, summer.

 ### Sports

Golf at Luvinate (***Golf Club Varese***), Solbiate Olona (***Le Robinie Golf Club***) and Travedona Monate (***Golf Club dei Laghi***). **Downhill skiing** at Brinzio, Cunardo and Alpe Forcora. **Back-country skiing** at Brinzio.

VARESE
• • • • • • • • •

A flourishing industrial town of 91,000 inhabitants and one of the richer places in Italy, Varese has a typically Lombard character. The rapid increase in its population in the 20C resulted in much indiscriminate new building and sprawling suburbs, but a few attractive streets of old houses with fine courtyards have survived in the centre. After the opening of the State and Nord Milano railway lines to Milan (only 50km away) in 1865 and 1886, many Milanese built their summer homes in the environs, and some Art Nouveau villas survive.

The city centre

The attractive, arcaded Corso Matteotti leads to Piazza del Podestà, separated from the church square by a war memorial arcade. **San Vittore** was built in 1580–1625, probably on designs by Pellegrino Pellegrini. It has a Neo-classical façade by Leopoldo Pollack (1788–91). The detached campanile is by the local architect Giuseppe Bernasconi (1617). In the interior are paintings by Il Cerano, Morazzone and Pietro Antonio Magatti, and magnificent 17C carved wooden pulpits and choir galleries. The **baptistery** behind (unlocked on request by the sacristan) dates from the 12C. It has an interesting plan and 14C Lombard frescoes on the right wall. The unfinished 13C font has been raised to reveal the earlier 8C font.

At the southern end of Corso Matteotti is Piazza Monte Grappa, laid out in 1927–35 and brimming with Fascist architectural rhetoric. Via Marcobi and Via Sacco lead to the huge, monumental **Palazzo Estense** (now the town hall), built by Francesco III d'Este, Duke of Modena, in 1766–72 as the seat of his imperial court. Called by Stendhal the Versailles of Milan, it is one of the more interesting palaces of its period in Italy. The attractive garden façade overlooks the spacious **gardens** (open daily), laid out by Giuseppe Bianchi in imitation of the imperial gardens of Schönbrunn in Vienna. Paths lead up past a grotto to terraces with a good view of the Alps, and a little children's playground in a wood.

On the hill is the eccentric 18C–19C **Villa Mirabello** with a tall tower, surrounded by a garden in the English style. The villa houses the **Musei Civici** (open Tues–Sat, 09.30–12.30, 14.00–17.30; Sun and holidays 09.30–12.30), with prehistoric finds from Lombardy, Roman and medieval material, and the mummy of a boy dating from 1645. Another room has a display of butterflies and birds.

North of the centre of Varese, on a low hill, is the residential district of **Biumo Superiore**. Here is the 18C Villa Litta, which was donated to the *FAI* (*Fondo per l'Ambiente Italiano*) in 1996 by Giuseppe Panza, together with 133 works from his collection of 20C American art (most of which was sold, and partially donated, to the Museum of Contemporary Art in Los Angeles and the Guggenheim Museum of New York). The villa (which will be opened to the public; ☎ 02 467615) also contains furniture and African and pre-Columbian sculpture, and is surrounded by a park. Also in this district is the Villa Andrea Ponti, a vast 19C pile by Giuseppe Balzaretto, with a park, adjoining another 19C Villa Ponti.

The immediate environs

On the northern outskirts of the town rises the **Sacro Monte**, one of the more important of the numerous shrines known as Sacri Monti erected during the Counter-Reformation in the 17C in Piedmont and Lombardy in honour of the Madonna, and consisting of a series of chapels illustrating the Mysteries of the

Rosary. The 14 pretty chapels, lining a broad winding path some 2km long up the steep hillside, were designed to be seen by pilgrims on their way up the hill (a walk of about an hour). The first chapel can be reached from the centre of Varese by car or bus along Via Veratti and Viale Aguggiari. The road climbs up through the residential district of Sant'Ambrogio with numerous Art Nouveau villas and their gardens, to end at an archway near the first chapel.

A less strenuous way of visiting the chapels is to continue up a by-road from the first chapel under the old stone arches of a funicular railway (no longer in operation) with a view of the hill of Campo dei Fiori. At the top of the Sacro Monte is a small village (880m) with a few Art Nouveau houses huddled around the sanctuary church of Santa Maria del Monte. The view (on a clear day) takes in Como with the mountains beyond and the plain towards Milan, and in the opposite direction the Lago di Varese. The bronze monument to Paul VI dates from 1984.

The church dates mostly from 1472. On the high altar of 1662 is the venerated 14C image of the Madonna. Outside the west door is a terrace with a view of five lakes: Lago di Varese in the foreground, Comabbio and Biandronno on the left, and Monate beyond. On the right you can just make out the tip of Lago Maggiore. The hill of Campo dei Fiori is prominent on the right with a huge abandoned Art Nouveau hotel.

From the terrace a cobbled passageway leads down to the broad cobbled path that descends past a statue of Moses and a the **Museo Pogliaghi** (open Apr–Sep, 10.00–12.00, 14.30–17.30), surrounded by a garden, in the villa that belonged to the sculptor Lodovico Pogliaghi (1857–1950). It contains his eclectic collection of works of art, archaeological material, and some of his own sculptures, including the model for the bronze doors of the duomo of Milan.

The path leads downhill to the 14th (last) chapel. The monumental *chapels, all of them of different design, are excellent works by the local architect Giuseppe Bernasconi (Il Mancino) from 1604 onwards. They are all kept locked but you can see the interiors (push-button lights) through the windows. They contain lifesize terracotta groups representing the *Mysteries of the Rosary* by Francesco Silva, Cristoforo Prestinari and Dionigi Bussola. The frescoes are by Carlo Francesco Nuvolone, Giovanni Battista and Giovan Paolo Recchi, and Morazzone. Outside the chapel of the Nativity is a 20C fresco by Renato Guttuso depicting the *Flight into Egypt*. From the hillside there are views of Como to the left and of Lago di Varese on the right.

A road continues up from the Sacro Monte to **Monte delle Tre Croci** (1033m), which has a wonderful view (and an observatory). The road deteriorates into a track to cross the **Campo dei Fiori** (1227m), a protected area with an even wider panorama. Here in 1908–12 Giuseppe Sommaruga built a huge hotel, restaurant and funicular station, all fine Art Nouveau buildings that have been abandoned since 1953.

In the western outskirts of Varese is the **Castello di Masnago** (open Tues–Sun 15.00–19.00) owned by the municipality, a 15C building which incorporates a 12C tower. It is adorned with frescoes of court life, dating from 1450. The painting collection contains works by Jacopo Bassano, Innocenza da Imola, Carlo Francesco Nuvolone, Camillo Procaccini and Giacomo Ceruti (Il Pitocchetto), as well as a wood model of the campanile of San Vittore (c 1677). The 19C works include paintings by Carlo Bossoli, Mosè Bianchi, Giuseppe Pellizza da Volpedo and Giacomo Balla, and busts by Vincenzo Vela and Lorenzo Bartoliniano. There is also a small museum of contemporary art. The park is open to the public daily.

In the southern outskirts of the town, in the locality of **Bizzozero**, is a Romanesque cemetery church on 7C–8C foundations, containing interesting frescoes (14C–16C), including some by Galdino da Varese (1498), and an 11C frescoed altar.

AROUND VARESE
● ● ● ● ● ● ● ● ● ● ● ● ● ● ● ● ● ● ●

The most interesting place to visit near Varese is **Castiglione Olona**, off the road to Saronno (poorly signposted), which was practically rebuilt by Cardinal Branda Castiglione (1350–1443) when he returned from a stay in Florence, bringing with him Masolino da Panicale. The works of art he commissioned to adorn the little town take their inspiration from the Florentine Renaissance. There are now a number of antiquarian bookshops in the little town, and an antiques and bric-à-brac fair is held in the streets on the first Sunday of the month.

*Palazzo Branda Castiglione** (open Tues–Sun 09.00–12.00, 14.30–17.30; holidays 10.30–12.30, 15.00–18.00) is where the cardinal was born and died. The little courtyard has an interesting exterior, and the chapel has frescoes attributed to Vecchietta. Stairs lead up to a loggia (enclosed in the 19C) with a wooden coffered ceiling and traces of frescoes. Low down on the wall is a frescoed still life with jars, attributed to Paolo Schiavo. The main hall has a Renaissance fireplace with Baroque stucco decoration on the upper part and family portraits on the walls. The bedroom has very unusual allegorical frescoes; dated 1423 and thought to be by Michelino da Besozzo, they show ten trees and white putti. In the study are frescoes attributed to Masolino of the Hungarian city of Veszprem, where Castiglione served as bishop in 1412–24, with strange rocky landscapes.

Opposite the palace, preceded by a courtyard, is the *Chiesa di Villa**, with an unusual dome, built and decorated in 1431–44 by local masons and sculptors in the style of Brunelleschi. It has a handsome exterior, and two colossal carved saints flank the fine portal. In the lovely, simple interior, with a dome and apse, are six stone and terracotta statues (including a polychrome *Annunciatory Angel* and *Madonna* that have been attributed to Vecchietta) high up on corbels. In the apse are a small fresco of the *Resurrection of Christ* and a delightful frescoed frieze of red-and-white flowers below. Beneath the altar is a 15C stone statue of the *Dead Christ*.

The road continues uphill past the 19C **town hall**, which incorporates a school building founded by the Cardinal in 1423 to teach grammar and music. Above the door is a bust of the Cardinal dating from 1503, and on the left is a fresco from the early 15C. The courtyard dates from the 18C.

A cobbled lane leads up to the top of the hill where the **Collegiata** was built in 1422–25, replacing the Castiglione family's feudal castle. Above the portal is a lunette of the *Madonna with Saints and the Cardinal*, dating from 1428. The church is entered through a side door off the garden (open Tues–Sun, Apr–Sept 10.00–12.00, 15.00–19.00; Oct–Mar 10.00–12.00, 13.30–17.30). The well-proportioned and luminous interior has Gothic Revival decoration in the side aisles. In the sanctuary is the funerary monument (1443) of the Cardinal with his effigy supported by four statues of the *Virtues*. On the vault are six frescoed *scenes from the life of the Virgin signed by Masolino. In the lunettes below and above the windows are scenes from the lives of Saints Stephen and Lawrence by Paolo Schiavo and Vecchietta. In the apse is a painting of the *Crucifixion* attributed to Neri di Bicci. The 15C bronze candelabra showing *St George and the Dragon* was made in Flanders.

Across the garden, in a former tower of the castle, is the entrance to the family chapel, later used as a baptistery and museum. The *baptistery is a beautiful little building dating from 1435. The *frescoes of the life of St John the Baptist are Masolino's masterpiece, executed on his return to the town in 1435. On the right wall is the *Banquet of Herod* with a long loggia, and in the sanctuary, the *Baptism of Christ*, with a splendid group of nude figures on the right and the river disappearing into the distance. In the vault are the symbols of the Evangelists, and in the vault of the sanctuary, *God the Father* with angels and doctors of the Church on the arch. The other frescoes (including a view of Rome on the entrance wall) are very damaged. The font is a 15C Venetian work.

Opposite the baptistery a small room serves as a **museum** with a miscellany of objects that have survived from the rich treasury (pillaged over the centuries) that the cardinal donated to the church. They include reliquaries, and a small painting of the *Annunciation* by Paolo Schiavo and frescoes of the same subject by Masolino.

Castelseprio, south of Castiglione, on a plateau in a wood above the Olona valley, is an extensive archaeological area (open Tues–Sun 09.00–18.00 or 19.00, holidays 09.00–17.30), beautifully kept by the State since 1950, when excavations were begun here. On the site of a late Bronze Age settlement, it includes the ruins of the late Roman *castrum* of *Sibrium*, occupied throughout the Lombard period (568–771 AD). A fortified *borgo* grew up around the camp, but this was destroyed by Milan in 1287. The site is well labelled and includes the remains of two churches, an octagonal baptistery, defensive walls, towers, medieval houses, and cisterns and wells. A custodian accompanies you to unlock the most important church, **Santa Maria Foris Portas**, a short distance away from the *castrum*, which has a remarkable plan with lateral apses and windows in the corners of the nave. The building dates from somewhere between the 7C and the 9C; it was restored and partly reconstructed in the 1940s, when the frescoes were discovered, and remains of its black-and-white marble floor survive. In the apse are extraordinary *mural paintings with scenes from the apocryphal Gospels illustrating the infancy of Christ, including the *Nativity* with the reclining figure of the Madonna, and the *Journey to Bethlehem* (with a graceful donkey). They are in an Oriental (Alexandrian) style and are thought to date from the 8C.

Part of the camp of *Sibrium* extended across the Olona to the site later occupied by the **Monastero di Torba** (open Tues–Sun 10.00–13.00, 14.00–17.00; Feb–Sep 10.00–18.00), which is reached by a path down through woods (c 200m, but temporarily impassable) or—much longer—by a (signposted) road from Gornate Olona. Part of the ruined defensive walls have been exposed, and the massive corner tower survives, both dating from the 5C. A Benedictine nunnery was established here in the late Lombard period (8C), and the monastic buildings were occupied up until 1480. In a pretty position at the foot of a wooded hill, they were donated to the *FAI* (*Fondo per l'Ambiente Italiano*) in 1976 and have been beautifully maintained since their restoration in 1986. The early medieval church has an 8C crypt and a 13C apse. Opposite is a 15C farmhouse built above the ancient defensive walls, which incorporates the refectory, a splendid old room with a fireplace. The corner tower, on 5C–6C foundations, was also occupied by the nuns in the 8C. Steps lead up past an oven, which may date from the 12C, to the first floor and a room used as a burial place (with an 8C fresco of a nun named Aliberga). The room above functioned as an oratory, and it contains fascinating Carolingian (late 8C) frescoes of female saints and nuns (uncovered in the 20C).

Lago di Varese

West of Varese is the Lago di Varese, 8.5km long, a lake admired for its scenery by the English painter and nonsense poet Edward Lear. It used to have an abundance of fish, but is now polluted. Voltorre, on the shore of the lake, has an old monastery with an interesting Romanesque brick cloister where concerts are held in June. From Biandronno (yellow signposts), boats can be hired for the little **Isola Virginia**, an island on which is the Museo Preistorico di Villa Ponti (open Jun–Sep), which contains objects found in prehistoric lake dwellings here (Neolithic to Bronze Age). In May–Oct guided visits to the island are organised by the Musei Civici of Varese (☎ 0331 281590). At Gavirate, at the north end of the lake, is a pipe museum (open on request), with some 20,000 pipes from all over the world and of all periods.

Northwards to Switzerland

A road leads north from Varese through the **Valganna**, the narrow valley of the Olona. At the beginning of the valley, near Induno Olona, is the Moretti (now Tuborg) brewery, in a remarkable Art Nouveau factory building. The road passes the little Laghetto di Ganna, and the **Abbey of San Gemolo**, founded in 1095 and Benedictine until 1556. It has a 12C church and a five-sided cloister. The **Lago di Ghirla** (used for swimming in summer) has a nice Art Nouveau tram station. At Ghirla the Lugano road branches right and descends to **Ponte Tresa** on the frontier with Switzerland. This consists of an Italian and a Swiss village separated by the River Tresa, which here marks the frontier, entering a little landlocked bay of the Lago di Lugano. Beyond Ghirla is **Cunardo**, known since Roman times for the production of ceramics. The interesting old 18C pottery of Ibis, with its conspicuous tall furnace, is still in use and family run. It produces traditional 18C blue-and-white ware, and visitors are welcome.

From Cunardo a road leads west into the **Valcuvia**, with hills of chestnut woods and an open landscape extending towards Lago Maggiore. Here is Casalzuigno, a hamlet, with the splendid ***Villa Porta-Bozzolo**, formerly Ca' Porta (the garden is open daily 10.00–18.00). It was left to the *FAI* (*Fondo per l'Ambiente Italiano*) in 1989 and is beautifully maintained. The villa dates from the 16C, when it was in the centre of a huge estate purchased by the Porta family, and silkworms were bred in the farm buildings. Additions were made to the house in the 17C, and the splendid ***garden** was laid out in the French style on the hillside at the beginning of the 18C by Gian Angelo III Porta. Beyond the parterre are four stone terraces with balustrades and statues on either side of steps, up to a green lawn surrounded by cypresses and in front of a fountain. A cypress avenue climbs the wooded hillside behind. There is another little garden to the right of the parterre on a line with the façade of the villa, approached by a gate with statues of the *Four Seasons* and with an avenue of oak trees leading to a little Rococo frescoed garden house. The villa preserves elaborate frescoes by Pietro Antonio Magatti (1687–1768).

Above the villa a narrow road winds up to **Arcumeggia**, a tiny hamlet in the hills. Since 1956 the exterior of many of the houses have been frescoed by contemporary artists, including Aligi Sassù.

To Lago di Como via Lugano

Another road (344) leads northeast from Varese to Porto Ceresio on Lago di Lugano. It passes Bisuschio, where the 16C *Villa Cicogna Mozzoni, frescoed by the school of the Campi brothers and with 17C and 18C furnishings, stands surrounded by a classical Renaissance garden and fine park. The greenhouses protect a good collection of orchids. The villa and gardens are open Apr–Oct on Sun and holidays 09.00–12.00, 15.00–19.00.

Porto Ceresio is situated at the foot of Monte Pravello on a wide bend in **Lago di Lugano** (270m, 52 sq km), a little more than half of which belongs to Switzerland; only the northeast arm, the southwest shore between Ponte Tresa and Porto Ceresio, and the enclave of Campione, nearly opposite Lugano, belong to Italy. The scenery of the shores, except for the bay of Lugano, is far wilder than on the greater lakes. There are regular boat services between all the main places along the shore.

Lugano, the main place on the lake, and the largest town of the Swiss Canton Ticino, is Italian in character. In the centre of the lake is the small Italian enclave of **Campione d'Italia**, in the province of Como, which uses Swiss money and postal services. It has long been noted for its sculptors and architects; the chapel of St Peter (1327) is a good example of their work. In the parish church are some 15C reliefs, and here is kept the key to the cemetery chapel of **Santa Maria dei Ghirli**, with frescoes outside (*Last Judgement*, 1400) and in the interior (14C). The village is famous for its casino.

At the head of the northeast arm of the lake, also in the province of Como, is **Porlezza**, where the church of San Vittorio contains beautiful 18C stuccowork. In the Valsolda, above the northern shore of the lake, is the picturesque village of **San Mamette**, with a 12C campanile. On the road which descends to Lake Como is the attractive Lago del Piano (279m).

Backroads to Milan

A road traverses the southwest corner of the province from Sesto Calende on Lago Maggiore to Milan, passing Somma Lombardo, with its Visconti castle (privately owned). Nearby, at **Arsago Seprio**, are the ancient basilica of San Vittore and its 12C baptistery, and an archaeological museum (open Sat 15.00–18.00, Sun 10.00–12.00, 15.00–18.00). Another road leads from Somma Lombardo to Golasecca, with its Iron Age necropolis.

Gallarate is the first of three large industrial towns (the others are Busto Arsizio and Legnano) near the Olona River northwest of Milan, noted in the 19C for their cotton-spinning works. They are now important manufacturing towns. In the centre of Gallarate are the 12C church of San Pietro and the small Civica Galleria d'Arte Moderna (Viale Milano 21; open Tues–Sun 09.00–12.00, 15.00–18.00). At **Busto Arsizio** is the church of Santa Maria di Piazza (1517–27; restored in 1992) with a polyptych by Gaudenzio Ferrari (1541). The octagonal cupola is frescoed by Giovan Pietro Crespi (1531). The **Museo di Palazzo Bandera**, Via Andrea Costa 29 (open Tues–Sat 09.30–12.00, 15.00–18.30), has holdings of Italian and international contemporary art; the **Civico Museo Storico Artistico**, Piazza Vittorio Emanuele II (open daily 16.00–19.00), old-master paintings, sculpture, ceramics and drawings.

East of Busto Arsizio is **Saronno**, an industrial town noted for its macaroons, the famous *amaretti*. The sanctuary of the **Madonna dei Miracoli** here was begun in 1498 perhaps by Giovanni Antonio Amadeo, who designed the cupola in 1505. It was enlarged after 1556 by Vincenzo Seregni. The façade is by Pellegrino Tibaldi (1596). It contains beautiful, brightly coloured *frescoes by Bernardino Luini (1525 and 1531), including the *Presentation in the Temple* and *Adoration of the Magi*, admired by Stendhal in his diary. They were well restored in 1992. The large fresco in the cupola of the *Virgin in Paradise*, with a concert of angels, was painted after Luini's death by Gaudenzio Ferrari, and is usually considered his masterpiece. The remarkable group of lifesize polychrome wood figures representing the *Last Supper* by Andrea da Milano (c 1548–52) have recently been restored. They are apparently a copy of Leonardo's famous painting in Milan.

Saronno also has an interesting **Collezione di Ceramiche e Maioliche** (Via Carcano 9, open Tues, Thur and Sat 15.00–18.00 or 19.00), featuring Asian and Meissen porcelain and Italian and European majolica.

Lago di Como

Lago di Como is a beautiful large lake, some 50km long, surrounded by wooded hills below the Alpine foothills. Many of the small towns on its shores, originally fishing villages, became resorts in the 19C. The lake was visited by the English Romantic poets, including Shelley and Byron, and Wordsworth lived here in 1790. Numerous villas surrounded by lovely gardens were built on its steep banks in the 18C and 19C, but in more recent times its shores have been disfigured in places by unattractive holiday houses, many of them built by the Milanese. There is an efficient regular service of boats, hydrofoils and car ferries throughout the year between all the main towns, used by residents as well as visitors. Como, at its southern end, is the most important town on the lake: Roman in origin, it has an interesting plan and a splendid cathedral. The most beautiful part of the lake is in the centre, at Bellagio. You can see spectacular natural scenery at the Villa Serbelloni, the Villa del Balbianello and the Isola Comacina. Villas with famous gardens open to the public include Villa Carlotta at Tremezzo, Villa Melzi at Bellagio, and Villa Olmo at Como. The most pleasant resorts, with good old-established hotels, include Bellagio, Menaggio, Varenna, Cernobbio and Tremezzo.

Lago di Como is 199m above sea level. Virgil called it *Lacus Larius*, and it is still often known as Lario. The lake is formed of three long, narrow arms which meet at Bellagio, one stretching southwest to Como, another southeast to Lecco, the third north to Colico. Its greatest breadth is 4.4km just north of Bellagio, its greatest depth 410m off Argegno, and its area is 145 sq km. The chief feeder is the Adda, which flows in at Colico and out at Lecco. The lake is subject to frequent floods (last in 1997, when Como was inundated), and is swept regularly by two winds, the *tivano* (north to south), and the *breva* (south to north) in the afternoon.

Practical information

Getting there
By air

Como is c 45mins by car from Milan Malpensa airport and 30mins from Lugano airport. Milano Linate and Bergamo Orio Al Serio are also nearby. All have direct service to/from Italian and other European cities. Malpensa also has intercontinental flights, and there is bus service from Malpensa to Como.

By road

From Milan you can take the A9 (or 35, leaving the city by Via Carlo Farini) to Como and then follow one of the shore roads northwards. 583 winds its way along the lake's eastern shore to Bellagio; 340 hugs the west shore to Cadenabbia, Menaggio and points north. If you are bound for Bellagio but don't like narrow, winding roads, take 340 to Cadenabbia and cross to Bellagio on the ferry. If you love winding roads and stunning views, take the local roads from Como to Bellagio via Erba.

By rail

Como and Lecco are easily reached by frequent train services from Milan, and there is a railway line that skirts the eastern shore of the lake from Lecco to Colico. From Milan to Como by the main St-Gotthard line, 46km in 35–55min; fast *Cisalpina* and *Intercity* trains depart from the Stazione Centrale; slower trains from Porta Garibaldi station. Beyond Como the international trains go on to the frontier at Chiasso, for Lugano and the north. When planning your journey bear in mind that Como has two train stations: San Giovanni for the State Railway line to Milan, Lecco, and to Lugano and the rest of Switzerland; and Como–Lago (on the lakeside; the most convenient station for visitors) for trains on the Nord–Milano line to Milan via Saronno. From Milan to Lecco, 50km in 50–65mins; to Varenna in 1hr 15mins; to Colico in 1hr 40mins. Trains continue on to Sondrio and Tirano in the Valtellina (see p 233).

Getting around
By boat and hydrofoil

An efficient service of boats and hydrofoils is maintained throughout the year between Como and Colico, calling at numerous places of interest on the way. It is run by the *Navigazione Lago di Como*, Via per Cernobbio 18, Como, ☎ 031 579211. Tickets valid for 24hrs or several days can be purchased. The timetable changes according to season. Most of the boats run between Como and Bellano (boats in c 2hrs 30mins, hydrofoils in c 1hr), while most of the hydrofoils continue to Colico (Como to Colico in c 1hr 30mins). There is a less frequent service between Bellagio and Lecco in summer (only on holidays for the rest of the year). In the central part of the lake a service runs between Bellano (or Varenna) and Lenno. A car ferry runs frequently between Bellagio and Varenna (in 15mins), Bellagio and Cadenabbia (in 10mins), and Cadenabbia and Varenna (in 30mins). Fewer services in winter.

Private boats for hire at Bellagio, *Barindelli*, ☎ 031 950834 and 0368 3677844; *Gilardoni*, ☎ 031 950201; *Venini*, ☎ 031 951376. Como, *Tasell*, ☎ 031 304084; Lezzeno, *Mostes*, ☎ 031 914621; Moltrazio, *Aquilini*, ☎ 031 376120 and 0368 3671533; Sala Comacina, *Boat Service*, ☎ 031 821955 and 0337 384572; Tremezzo, ☎, tel. 0344 40151.

By bus

There are bus services between all the main centres around the lake, run by *Trasporti Regione Lombardia* (information offices in Lecco: ☎ 0341 367244; Como: ☎ 031 247111). Buses leave from Piazza Matteotti for towns on the lake, and in the province.

Car parks in Como (with an hourly tariff or time limit) in Piazza Roma, Piazza Volta, Lungo Lario Trento, Via Recchi, Viale Varese. Elsewhere mainly on the waterfront.

Information offices

BELLAGIO Piazza della Chiesa 14, ☎ 031 950204.
CERNOBBIO Via Regina 33b, ☎ 031 510198.
COMO Piazza Cavour 16, ☎ 031 269712, Stazione San Giovanni, ☎ 031 267214.
LANZO D'INTELVI Piazza Novi (Palazzo Comunale), ☎ 031 840143.
LECCO Via Nazario Sauro 6, ☎ 0341 362360.
MENAGGIO. Piazza Garibaldi 7, ☎

0334 32924.
TREMEZZO Piazzale Trieste (May–Oct), ☎ 0344 40493.

Where to stay

BELLAGIO *Florence*, Piazza Mazzini 46, ☎ 031 950342, fax 031 951722; on Bellagio's lakefront square, charming and elegant with a fabulous café and restaurant (seating on the water in summer); some rooms have terraces, others overlook the gardens of Villa Serbelloni; open Apr–Nov, moderate.
Grand Hotel Villa Serbelloni, Via Roma 1, ☎ 031 950216, fax 031 951529; ideally situated in a former villa of the Serbelloni family, on the headland of Bellagio with stunning views, lakeside pool and excellent restaurant; lakefront rooms are fabulous, rooms on the back are not; open Easter–Oct; expensive.
Silvio, Via Cercano 12, località Loppia, ☎ 031 950322, fax 031 950912; a quiet, restful place on the lake within walking distance of Bellagio; closed Dec–Jan, inexpensive.
CERNOBBIO *Centrale*, Via Regina 39, ☎ 031 511411, fax 031 341900; small but comfortable, with a shady terrace on Cernobbio's main street; moderate.
Miralago, Piazza Risorgimento 1, ☎ 031 510125, fax 031 342088; facing the lake, on the square where the boats land; open Mar–Nov, moderate.
Villa d'Este, Via Regina 40, ☎ 031 3481, fax 031 348844; a historic property on the lake, with National Landmark park, excellent restaurant and Lombardy's friendliest bartender; only suites and junior suites have lake views; open Mar–Nov; expensive.
COMO *Barchetta Excelsior*, Piazza Cavour 1, ☎ 031 3221, fax 031 302622; on Como's lakefront square; moderate.
Como, Via Mentana 28, ☎ 031 266173, fax 031 266020; on the south side of the town, with a rooftop terrace

and pool; moderate.

Metropole Suisse, Piazza Cavour 19, ☎ 031 269444, fax 031 300808; also on the waterfront in downtown Como; open Feb–Nov; moderate.

Terminus, Lungo Lario Trieste 14, ☎ 031 329111, fax 031 302550; in a Liberty-style building on the water, with good views of the lake and mountains; expensive. *Villa Flori*, Via per Cernobbio 12, ☎ 031 573105, fax 031 570379; a favourite place of Garibaldi, on the lake just outside Como, on the road to Cernobbio; open Feb–Nov; expensive. **Youth hostel**, Via Bellinzona, ☎ 031 573800.

LANZO D'INTELVI *Belvedere*, Via Poletti 27, ☎ 031 840122, fax 031 842976; an extremely friendly and comfortable family-run establishment in a charming village; closed Nov–Dec; moderate.

MALGRATE *Il Griso*, Via Provinciale 51, ☎ 0341 202040, fax 0341 202248; in a lovely garden with good views over the lake and mounains, and an excellent restaurant; closed Dec–Jan; moderate.

MARGNO (above Bellano) *Baitock*, Via Sciatori 8, ☎ 034 803042, fax 803042; a small (15 rooms) mountain inn popular with hikers and skiers; inexpensive.

VARENNA *Du Lac*, ☎ 0341 830238, fax 034 831081; small and intimate, in a former lake house; open Mar–Nov; moderate.

Royal Victoria, Piazza San Giorgio 5, ☎ 034 815111, fax 0341 830722; also in a 19C villa, with garden; moderate.

Eating out

BELLAGIO *Caffè Roma*, on the waterfront, has an original Liberty-style interior and a distinctive local flavour in a town crowded with outsiders.

La Barchetta, Salita Mella 13, ☎ 031 951389; restaurant offering innovative variations on traditional recipes; closed Tues (except Jun–Sep) and Nov–Mar.

Mella, Via Jacopo Rezia 1, at San Giovanni (just beyond the Villa Melzi gardens), ☎ 031 950205; restaurant specialising in lake fish, with good views over the lake; inexpensive.

CERNOBBIO *Terzo Croto*, ☎ 031 512304; restaurant (with rooms) serving outstanding interpretations of local recipes; moderate.

COMO *Croto del Lupo*, Via Pisani Dossi 17, at Cardina, ☎ 031 570881; traditional restaurant with garden; closed Mon and Aug; moderate.

Sant'Anna 1907, Via Turati 3, at Camerlata, ☎ 031 505266; restaurant serving innovative variations on traditional recipes; closed Fri, midday Sat and Aug; moderate.

Terrazo Perlasca, Piazza De Gasperi 8, ☎ 031 303936; old regional dishes served with a special flair; closed Mon and Aug; moderate.

LECCO *Al Porticciolo 84*, Via Valsecchi 5/7, ☎ 0341 498103; restaurant speciallising in grilled fish and meats; closed Mon, Jan and Aug; moderate.

Antica Osteria Casa di Lucia, Via Lucia 27, ☎ 0341 494594; osteria and wine bar with a wide selection of cheese and good local dishes; closed midday Sat, Sun and Aug; inexpensive.

Nuova Casa del Formaggio, Via Roma 81, and *Spaccio del Parmigiano*, Via Roma 13, have delicious local cheeses.

Panificio Enoteca Negri, Corso Matteotti 65, sells excellent focaccia bread and wine to drink with it.

Taverna ai Poggi, Via ai Poggi 14, ☎ 0341 497126; osteria serving wholesome regional cuisine; closed Mon; inexpensive.

Trattoria di Montalbano, Via Montalbano 30, ☎ 0341 496707; trattoria just outside town, with good local cooking and outside seating in summer; closed Tues (except in Aug) and Jan–Feb; inexpensive.

LENNO *Oleificio Vanini*, Via Pellico 10, has extra virgin olive oil made from olives grown on the lakeshore.
Santo Stefano, Piazza XI Febbraio 3, ☎ 0344 55434; trattoria specialising in fish; closed Mon and Oct–Nov; inexpensive.
LIERNA *La Breva*, Via Imbarcadero 3, ☎ 0341 741490; traditional restaurant with lakeside seating in summer; closed Mon evening, Tues (except Jun–Sep), Nov and Jan; moderate.
MANDELLO DEL LARIO (near Lecco) *Ricciolo*, Via Provinciale 165, at Olcio, ☎ 0341 732546; restaurant offering delicious lake-fish recipes; closed Sun evening, Mon, Sept and Dec–Jan.
ORIMENTO (above San Fedele Intelvi) *Baita di Orimento*, ☎ 031 817068 or 830412, 0335 6380242; mountain hut (with rooms) on the high pastures between Lakes Como and Lugano serving the best country lunches in the area—all local specialities lovingly prepared; open daily Jun–Sep, weekends May and Oct; inexpensive.
ROGARO DI TREMEZZO *Al Veluu*, ☎ 0344 40510; restaurant serving exquisitely prepared local dishes; closed Tues and Nov–Mar; moderate.
TORNO *Belvedere*, at the boat landing, ☎ 031 419100; trattoria offering deliciously prepared home cooking and great lake views; inexpensive.
TREMEZZO *La Fagurida*, Via San Martino 17, ☎ 0344 40676; good local cuisine, especially polenta; closed Mon, inexpensive.
Rusall, Via San Martino 2, at Rogaro; ☎ 0344 40408; family-managed place in the hotel of the same name, also offering wholesome local cuisine; closed Wed and Jan–Mar; moderate.
VARENNA *Vecchia Varenna*, Contrada Scoscesa 10, ☎ 0341 830793; restaurant with summer service on a terrace overlooking the port; closed Mon, Tues (in Feb–Mar) and Jan; inexpensive.

Entertainment

Como has a *Teatro Sociale* with a **music** season Sep–Nov. There is live music at cafés and clubs in Como, Albavilla, Bellagio, Bosisio, Cantù, Capiago, Cermenate, Erba, Gravedona, Maslianico, Menaggio, Merone, Tavernerio, Torno, Vertemate and Villaguardia. **Disco dancing** at Como, Bizzarone, Cadenabbia, Cantù, Castelmarte, Dongo, Erbga, Fino Mornasco, Lanzo d'Intenvi, Lipomo, Menaggio, Novedrate, Porlezza, San Fedele Intelvi and Valbrona. **Night clubs** in Como, Brienno, Monguzzo and Porlezza.

Shopping

COMO is famous for its **silk**, and the major mills all have outlets in or near the town. Those in town include *Mensitieri*, Viale Cavallotti 3; *Binda*, Viale Geno 6; Mantero, Via Volta 68; *Martinetti*, Via Torriani 4; *Ratti*, Via per Cernobbio 19; *Ricci*, Via Scalabrini 85; *Gift Shop* of the Museo Didattico della Seta, Via Valleggio 3. In the environs, *Emporio della Seta*, Via Canturina 190, Albate; *In Seta*, Via Paoli 43, *Camerlata*; Albisetti, Via Nazionale 3, Vertemate con Minoprio; *Ratti*, Via Madonna/C. 30, Guanzate; *Seta Shop*, Via Carducci 13, Montano Lucino. *Factory's Store*, Via per Bregnano, Vertemate con Minoprio, is an Armani outlet. Hours vary, but most are open Tues–Fri or Sat 10.00–12.00 and 15.00–18.00. Street markets are held Tues and Thur mornings, and all day Sat.
BELLAGIO, too, has a tradition of silk-making and several good shops.

Special events

COMO *Fiera di Pasqua*, with a flea market by the walls from Maundy Thur–Easter Mon. *St Abbondio*, the patron saint, is celebrated 31 Aug with a livestock fair. *Il*

Canto delle Pietre, music festival, May–Jun. *Palio del Baradello*, historical pageant, late Aug–early Sep; *Autunno Musicale*, concert series, Sep–Dec.

Sports

Golf at Annone Brianza (*Golf Club Lecco*), Appiano Gentile (*La Pinetina Golf Club*), Carimate (*Country Club Carimate*), Grandola ed Uniti (*Golf Club Menaggio &* *Cadenabbia*), Lanzo d'Intelvi (*Golf Club Lanzo*), Monticello Cassina Rizzardi (*Golf Club Monticello*), Montorfano (*Golf Club Villa d'Este*). **Downhill skiing** at Monte San Primo and Monte Crocione. **Back-country skiing** at Pian del Tivano and Lanzo d'Intelvi. **Swimming** in summer at Como, Villa Geno, on the eastern shore, beyond the funicular station, and at the little public beaches elsewhere on the lake.

COMO
• • • • • • •

The town of Como lies in a fine position on the southern shore of Lake Como. It has preserved its Roman plan, within high walls, to a marked degree. The southern and western stretches of the walls have survived. The city has a particularly attractive old centre with long, straight, narrow streets, many of their houses with pretty courtyards. The cathedral is a splendid Gothic building with remarkable sculptures inside and out. A delightful path, shaded by huge old trees, skirts the lake as far as the public gardens of Villa Olmo, passing charming villas with gardens and boathouses on the waterfront. The traditional local industry of silk-weaving survives here in several large factories (and silk products can be purchased all over the town). As a provincial capital and manufacturing town with a population of 84,000, Como's economy has developed rapidly in this century.

History

Originally a town of the Insubrian Gauls—the same people who founded Milan—Como was captured and colonised by the Romans in the 2C BC. The town was a city-state by the 11C, but in 1127 it was destroyed by the Milanese. Frederick Barbarossa rebuilt it in 1155, and Como secured its future independence by the Peace of Constance (1183). In the struggles between the Torriani and the Visconti, Como fell to the latter in 1335 and became a fief of Milan. From then on it followed the vicissitudes of the Lombard capital. In March 1848 a popular rising compelled the surrender of the Austrian garrison, and the city was finally liberated by Garibaldi on 27 May 1859.

Among famous natives are two Roman authors, the Elder and the Younger Pliny (23–79 AD and 62–120 AD), uncle and nephew. The Younger Pliny often mentions Como and its surroundings in his *Letters*, and he endowed a library and school here. Physicist Alessandro Volta (see below) was also born here. The English author Walter Savage Landor lived in Como in 1815–18, where he was unjustly suspected of spying on Queen Caroline, who was staying at Cernobbio.

The city centre

The centre of the life of Como is **Piazza Cavour**, open to the lake and adjoining

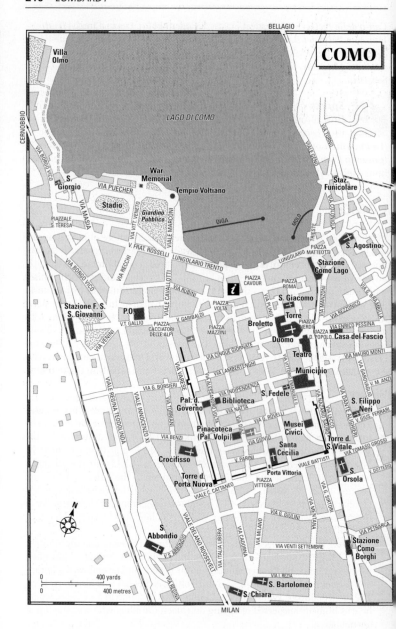

COMO

LAGO DI COMO

BELLAGIO

Villa Olmo

CERNOBBIO

S. Giorgio

VIA PUECHER

War Memorial

Tempio Voltiano

Staz. Funicolare

VIA TORNO

VIALE GENO

Stadio

Giardino Pubblico

VIA VITT. VENETO

VIALE MARCONI

DIGA

PIAZZALE S. TERESA

VIA MASIA

VIA BORGO VICO

VIA RECCHI

V. FRAT. ROSSELLI

LUNGOLARIO TRENTO

PIAZZA CAVOUR

S. Agostino

Stazione Como Lago

LUNGOLARIO MATTEOTTI

PIAZZA MATTEOTTI

PIAZZA ROMA

VIA MANZONI

VIA COLONOLA

TRIESTE

MOLO

VIA BORGO VICO

Stazione F. S. S. Giovanni

P.O.

VIA VENINI

VIA T. GALLIO

PIAZZALE CACCIATORI DELLE ALPI

VIA CAVALLOTTI

VIA RUBINI

PIAZZA VOLTA

VIA PLINIO

i

S. Giacomo

Torre

Broletto

Duomo

PIAZZA VERDI

PIAZZA D. POPOLO

Casa del Fascio

VIA REZZONICO

VIA G. RASIMBLIA

VIA ENRICO PESSINA

VIA GARIBALDI

PIAZZA MAZZINI

VIA CINQUE GIORNATE

Teatro

Municipio

VIA MAURO MONTI

VIA GARIVAGLIO

V. M. ANZI

VIA LAMBERTENGHI

VIA VARESE

VIA G. BORSIERI

VIA ALESSANDRO VOLTA

VIA INDIPENDENZA

S. Fedele

S. Filippo Neri

V. GIUS. FERRARI

VIA DANTE ALIGHIERI

VIA GIOVIO

Pal. d. Governo

Biblioteca

VIA NATTA

Pinacoteca (Pal. Volpi)

VIA G. ROVELLI

Musei Civici

Santa Cecilia

Torre d. S. Vitale

VIA TOMASO GROSSI

VIALE INNOCENZO XI

VIALE REGINA TEODOLINDA

VIA BENZI

V. PARINI

Crocifisso

Torre d. Porta Nuova

Porta Vittoria

PIAZZA VITTORIA

VIALE BATTISTI

S. Orsola

VIA DOTTESIO

VIALE C. CATTANEO

VIA G. SIRTORI

VIA G. GIULINI

VIA MENTANA

VIA PETRARCA

N

S. Abbondio

V. S. ABBONDIO

VIALE DELANO ROOSEVELT

VIA ITALIA LIBERA

VIA CADORNA

VIA MILANO

VIA VENTI SETTEMBRE

VIA REGINA

Stazione Como Borghi

VIA I. REZIA

0   400 yards

0   400 metres

S. Bartolomeo

S. Chiara

MILAN

the quay. It was created in 1887 by filling in the old harbour. The piazza has a splendid view with the Tempio Voltiano on the left and beyond it the large Villa Olmo; straight ahead amidst trees is the Villa Flori, and in the distance the town of Cernobbio climbing the hillside above the lake. On the right bank you can see Villa Geno and the line of the funicular up to Brunate. An avenue of lime trees skirts the lake to the **public gardens** with the **Tempio Voltiano** (open daily 10.00–12.00 and 14.00 or 15.00–16.00 or 18.00), erected in 1927 as a memorial to the physicist Alessandro Volta (1745–1827). The Neo-classical rotunda contains his scientific instruments, charmingly displayed in old-fashioned show cases. The conspicuous **war memorial** was designed by the Futurish architect Antonio Sant'Elia, a native of Como, himself killed in 1916. It is his only constructed work.

Beyond the stadium, Via Puecher leads past a naval club and a hangar for sea planes, beyond which a very pleasant **lakeside path** continues past a number of lovely private villas with their gardens and boathouses and decorative gazebos. Beyond Villa Pallavicino, with statues on the façade and stuccoes inside by Piermarini and Giocondo Albertolli, is the Villa Resta Pallavicini (called 'La Rotonda') with a semicircular Neo-classical rotunda in the centre of its façade. The path ends at **Villa Olmo**, built for the Odescalchi by Simone Cantoni (1782–95; altered in 1883). It is preceded by an attractive formal garden (open daily as public gardens) with topiary, statues and a charming fountain, and behind are remains of its large park. The villa is used for exhibitions.

From Piazza Cavour (see above) the short Via Plinio leads away from the lake to Piazza del Duomo, with the **Broletto** (1215; the old town hall), built in alternate courses of black and white marble, with a few red patches, and the **Torre del Comune** of the same period, used as a campanile since the addition of the top storey in 1435 (partly rebuilt in 1927).

The Cathedral and central Como
The *Cathedral (Santa Maria Maggiore), built entirely of marble, dates mainly from the late 14C, when it replaced an 11C basilica. Its appearance, a union of Renaissance and Gothic architectural motives, is remarkably homogeneous. The rebuilding, financed mainly by public subscription, was entrusted first to Lorenzo degli Spazzi who, like his many successors, worked under the patronage of the Milanese court. Many of the works of art were restored in 1988–92.

West front The west front (1460–90), designed by Fiorino da Bontà and executed by Luchino Scarabota of Milan, is in a Gothic style with a fine rose window, though the three doorways are unexpectedly round-arched. The twenty 15C statues framing the two large windows between the central doorway and the rose window are still Gothic in conception, whereas the numerous other reliefs and statues from the workshop of Tommaso and Jacopo Rodari (local sculptors from Maroggia), dating from c 1500, show a new Renaissance style. The delightful seated figures of the two Plinys on either side of the main doorway are probably by Amuzio da Lurago. The two lateral doorways, also decorated by the Rodari, are wonderful examples of detailed carving. The work of rebuilding continued through the 16C (choir) and 17C (transepts), and ended with completion of the dome in 1770 by Filippo Juvarra.

Interior Inside the aisled nave of five bays is covered with a groined vault and hung with tapestries (1598). On the west wall are brightly coloured stained-glass windows by Giuseppe Bertini (1850). The two stoups supported by lions are survivals from the ancient basilica. A graceful little rotunda (1590) serves as a baptistery. In the south aisle the first altar has a wooden ancona (altarpiece) dating from 1482. Beyond a Neo-classical funerary monument by Agliati is another *ancona by Tommaso Rodari (1492) and more stained-glass windows. Past the south door (also well carved) is the tomb of Bishop Bonifacio da Modena (1347). The *Altar of Sant'Abbondio* (coin-operated light) is finely decorated with gilded woodcarving (1514), and three marble panels below. The *Virgin and Child* with four saints and the donor, Canon Raimondi, and a beautiful angel-musician in front, is a masterpiece of Bernardino Luini. The two paintings above are attributed to Francesco del Cairo and Simone Peterzano. Opposite, beneath the organ, is a standard attributed to Giovanni Pietro Malacrida (c 1515).

The Baroque altar in the south transept was designed by Francesco Richini (begun c 1641). In the sanctuary are five stained-glass windows (1861–78) and an altar (1674) with a crucifix of the late 15C, and 16C polychrome wooden statues. The Gothic high altar dates from 1317.

On the fourth altar of the north aisle is a carved *Deposition* group by Tommaso Rodari (1498) and opposite, hanging in the nave, a painted and embroidered *standard of the Confraternity of Sant'Abbondio by Morazzone (1608–10). On either side of the third Neo-classical altar are paintings by Bernardino Luini and Gaudenzio Ferrari. By the side door is the sarcophagus of Giovanni degli Avogadri (d. 1293), with primitive carvings. On the second altar, between busts of Innocent XI and Bishop Rovelli, is a lovely carved ancona by Tommaso Rodari, and on the first altar a painting by Andrea Passeri di Tomo (1502).

The yellow bishop's palace and the church of San Giacomo, with an unusual yellow-and-red façade, overlook Piazza Grimoldi, to the north of the cathedral. The church has Romanesque elements (columns, brickwork in aisles, apse and dome).

Behind the fine east end of the cathedral is the ruined Palazzo Pantera, the **Teatro Sociale**, built in 1811 by Giuseppe Cusi with a Neo-classical façade, and—across the Nord–Milano railway line—the white **Casa del Fascio** (now a police station), built in 1932–36 to a design by Giuseppe Terragni and an important example of the architecture of this period.

The Musei Civici and the Pinacoteca

Via Vittorio Emanuele leads south from the cathedral to the 17C town hall, opposite which is the five-sided apse of **San Fedele**, a 12C church that at one time served as the cathedral. The angular northeast doorway, with remarkable bas-reliefs, shows Byzantine influences. The church is entered from the delightful piazza behind. The interior, partly under restoration, has an unusual plan. It contains a fresco signed by G.A. Magistris (1504), and a little painted and stuccoed 17C vault.

In the piazza and on Via Natta are several old houses with wooden eaves and brickwork. Further along Via Vittorio Emanuele two palaces house the **Musei Civici** (open Tues–Sat 09.30–12.30, 14.00–17.00, Sun and holidays 10.00–13.00). The old-fashioned arrangement of the archaeological section is in the course of renovation. The interesting material includes Neolithic, Bronze Age and Iron Age finds, a stele of the 5C BC, Roman finds and medieval fragments. There are also 19C American artefacts, a natural history section, an Egyptian collection, a good Risorgimento museum and material relating to the First and Second World Wars. There are wooden models of the Duomo and casts of the

Pliny statues on the façade. A small organ dates from 1795, and there is a local ethnographical collection with 18C costumes.

To the west, at Via Diaz 84, the **Pinacoteca** (open as above) has been arranged in the modernised Palazzo Volpi (1610–30), which is also used for exhibitions. On the ground floor, beyond an 11C arch salvaged from a monastery in the town, are sculptural fragments, including capitals, from the Carolingian and Romanesque periods; and frescoes, including charming scenes from the lives of Sts Liberata and Faustina. Upstairs are 16C–17C paintings and a *Madonna Annunciate* attributed to the 15C Sicilian artist Antonello da Messina (not exhibited at the time of writing).

Other sights in town

The second turning on the left off Via Giovio leads to the church of **Santa Cecilia**, the front of which incorporates some Roman columns. It has a Baroque interior. Next door was the school where Volta once taught; there is a fragment of the Roman wall in the courtyard. The **Porta Vittoria** is surmounted by a tower of 1192 with many windows. It is named in memory of the surrender of the Austrian garrison (1848) in the barracks immediately opposite. The Garibaldi monument by Vincenzo Vela, in Piazza Vittoria, was erected in 1889.

Outside the gate, beyond a busy road and 500m to the southwest, is the fine Romanesque basilica of *Sant'Abbondio, isolated amid industrial buildings near the railway. On the site of an early Christian building, the present church dates from the 11C and is dedicated to St Abondius, bishop of Como. The exterior has two graceful campanili and a finely decorated apse. The interior has five tall aisles, despite its comparatively small size, and a deep presbytery. The apse is entirely frescoed with scenes from the life of Christ by mid-14C Lombard artists. The statue of *St Abondius* is attributed to Cristoforo Solari (1490).

On Viale Varese, which skirts the walls and gardens, is the sanctuary of the **Crocifisso**, a huge 16C building with a façade of 1864 by Luigi Fontana and Baroque decorations inside. In Via Alessandro Volta, inside the walls, is the house where the scientist lived and died (plaque).

An interesting **Museo Didattico della Seta**, documenting Como's main industry, has been set up on the outskirts of the town, at Via Valleggio 3 (open Tues–Fri 09.00–12.00, 15.00–18.00). Changing exhibitions of fine and applied art are mounted at the **Museo Tessile e Fondazione Ratti**, Lungo Lario Trento 9 (open for exhibitions or by appointment, ☎ 031 233411).

Environs of Como

From Piazza Cavour (see above), Lungo Lario Trieste leads past several large hotels, the old-fashioned station of the Nord–Milano line, and a small port, to the funicular station for **Brunate** (713m; services every 15mins, taking 7mins). Brunate can also be reached from Via Grossi by road or by path. In a fine position overlooking the lake, it became a resort at the end of the19C. The funicular climbs steeply up the hillside through a tunnel and then traverses woods and the gardens of some fine villas. From the upper station a 10mins walk (signposted 'panoramic view') leads gently uphill past huge, elaborate 19C and 20C villas and their gardens, beneath an archway to emerge high above the lake and the

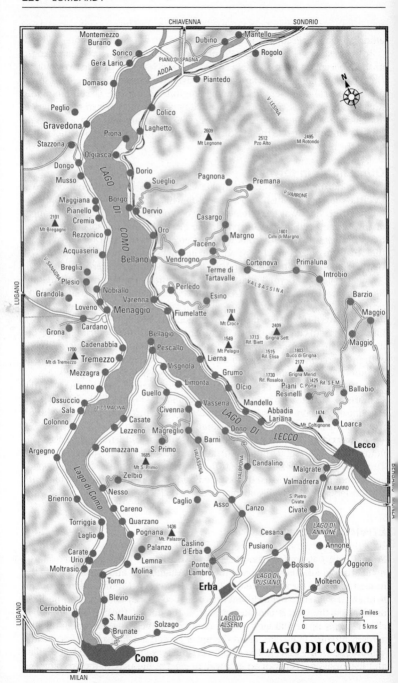

LAGO DI COMO

Breggia River. The fine view takes in the boatyard of the Villa Lariana on the left, and to the right is Cernobbio with the huge Villa d'Este on the lakeside.

At the highest point of the village, near the funicular station (the mechanism of which you can see in the engine room), is the church of **Sant'Andrea**. It has 19C and 20C frescoes inside, as well as a charming 15C fresco of a certain St Guglielma, thought to have been an English princess who married King Theodoric of Hungary in the 8C. Her cult has been known in Brunate since before the 15C, and her feast day is celebrated here on the fourth Sunday in April. Steps lead down the other side of the hill, away from the lake to the centre of the village (pedestrians only). At **San Maurizio** (871m), 2km higher, is the Faro Voltiano, a monument to Alessandro Volta (1927).

A walk above the lake

For walkers there is a good circular excursion from Como, through the woodlands on the mountainside along the lake's eastern shore. The ascent from Como is made by the Brunate funicular; you then walk along the contour of the mountain before descending, by the 1200 steps of an old mule path, to Torno. From this quiet little village there are frequent boats back to Como. The walk is easy, except for the final descent of c 400m.

From the funicular station at Brunate, walk left on cobblestones and then right on asphalt, toward San Maurizio. After 100m the road forks; follow the blue-and-white blaze left (Via Niorino). After 5mins the road forks again. Go downhill left to the end of the pavement, at the soccer field, then follow the blue-and-white blaze downhill right, into the forest. Twenty minutes later you reach a wooden cross and switchback; proceed straight. After 25mins more you come to a farm; follow the arrow for Montepiatto (straight, not downhill). After just 5mins you come to **Montepiatto**, a village that can only be reached on foot. Go right at the fork (yellow tourist sign). After 25mins a group of houses on a hill comes into sight and the trail intersects a stepped path. Proceed downhill left. Twenty minutes (and c 1000 steps) later, you come upon a tabernacle with the Christ Child and the Archangel Gabriel (?). Turn downhill left. Ten minutes later you come to the first houses of **Torno**, a delightful little village of terraced walkways, on the water. Continue straight downhill, then left (follow the red arrow). Cross the highway and continue down the steps to the waterfront. The landing with the boat back to Como is on your right.

South of Como, above the suburb of Camerlata, is the 11C–12C church of **San Carpoforo** with the supposed tomb of St Felix in its crypt. Monte Baradello above the church, with a good view of the lake, is crowned by the conspicuous tower of the **Castello Baradello** (open Thur, Sat–Sun and holidays 10.00–12.00, 14.00–17.00), the solitary remnant of a stronghold reconstructed by Barbarossa c 1158 and destroyed by Charles V's Spaniards in 1527. In 1277 Napo Torriani and other members of his family were exposed here in cages after their defeat by the Visconti.

The road goes on to **Cantù**, a pleasant town with lace and furniture industries. The parish church has a remarkably slender Romanesque campanile, and San Teodoro has a fine apse in the same style. At **Galliano**, to the east, are the 10C–11C basilica and baptistery of San Vincenzo. The church has a *fresco cycle of 1007. The fertile Brianza region here, once covered by vast forests, used to have many imposing country houses built by the Milanese. At Inverigo is the fine Villa La Rotonda, built by Luigi Cagnola (1813–33), now a children's home (open by appointment). At Alzate Brianza the 17C Villa Odescalchi is now a hotel. Erba, on the road which links Como with Lecco, is a scattered community with an open-air theatre (the *Licinium*) built in 1926. There is an archaeological museum at Crevenna.

FROM COMO TO COLICO BY WATER
●●

The frequent boats that connect Como with Colico all year round offer a calm, convenient way of touring the lake. After leaving Como the boats cross to the west shore and the red Villa Lariana, surrounded by poplars on the delightful Breggia river. Beyond is a modern congress centre in the gardens of the Villa Erba. **Cernobbio** is a resort at the foot of Monte Bisbino (1325m). It has a pleasant waterfront with boats pulled up on the quay and an attractive Liberty-style landing stage. Beyond is the huge white Villa d'Este hotel, which occupies a villa built in 1568 by Cardinal Tolomeo Gallio (1527–1607), a native of Cernobbio. In 1816–17 it was the home of the future Queen Caroline of England, who had the park landscaped in the English style. On the headland amidst trees is the Villa Il Pizzo, with cypresses in its park and a garden gazebo, and low down on the waterfront is the yellow Villa Fontanella. Lovely parks can also be seen at Villa Il Pizzo (open for guided visits Apr–Oct, except Aug, Fri 14.00–17.00 and 09.30–12.30) and Villa Erba (open May–Oct, Sat 14.00–18.00, Sun 10.00– 18.00; closed during fairs and conventions).

Moltrasio, with a Romanesque church, is less pretty. Here at the Villa Salterio in 1831 Bellini composed the opera *Norma*. On the bay on the east bank beyond Torno is the **Villa Pliniana** (1570; open May–Oct by appointment). In the garden is the famous intermittent spring described in detail by the Younger Pliny in his *Letters*, and also studied by Leonardo da Vinci. The abundant flow of water is channelled from a grotto down the cliff into the lake. Ugo Foscolo, Percy Bysshe Shelley, Stendhal and Rossini (who composed *Tancredi* here in 1813) were among the illustrious visitors to the villa in the 19C. The 18C Villa Passalacqua was built by Felice Soave and has an Italianate garden. Bellini composed *La Sonnambula* here.

On the west bank beyond Moltrasio are the yellow Villa Angelina, behind cypresses and a garden, and the twin villages of Carate Urio; Urio has a tall Lombard campanile, but a lot of unattractive new building spoils Carate. Laglio, beyond, has another tall church tower. A mountain torrent enters the lake in a waterfall between two hills near the green and white Villa Annetta. At the narrowest reach of the lake is Torriggia, with the small Villa Pia and its garden on the point. Beyond the churches of Sant'Anna and Brienno is **Argegno**, where the high mountain ranges northeast of the lake come into view.

Argegno lies at the foot of the beautiful, fertile **Val d'Intelvi**, also reached by a road to Lanzo d'Intelvi above Lago di Lugano. At Castiglione d'Intelvi the medieval Casa del Capitano has a room with 14C frescoes. At San Fedele a scenic road branches right, climbing through Laino and Ponna before descending to Porlezza on Lago di Lugano. The Lanzo d'Intelvi road continues to Pellio and Scaria, which has a diocesan museum with works by Ercole Ferrata and other local sculptors, before reaching the charming old resort of Lanzo d'Intelvi (907m). Campione d'Italia, beyond on Lago di Lugano, is described on p 209.

Walking from lake to lake

The highlands around the Val d'Intelvi are popular with walkers, who make the trek from Lake Lugano to Lake Como, usually in two days, staying overnight at Lanzo d'Intelvi.

The moderately challenging point-to-point excursion, beginning at Lugano and ending at Tremezzo, takes a minimum of 12hrs, with a boat and cog-railway transfer at the outset and a short road transfer on the morning of the second day. Altitude gains are: Day 1 -600m; Day 2 +600m. A more challenging (and rewarding) alternative begins on Day 2 at Pelio d'Intelvi, ascends to the Rifugio Boffalora (1252m), then descends to join the trail described below to Tremezzo.

Depart by boat from **Lugano Castagnola** landing stage; at Capolago, continue by train to the terminus of the **Monte Generoso** railway (timetables and tickets from *Navigazione Lugano*, ☎ 091 971 5223, fax 971 2793). From the train terminal continue south, keeping the café on your left. About 300m later turn downhill left (do not take the first turn to the left). This turn is marked by a yellow arrow; the path is rough at first but gets better. Continue downhill for about half an hour; you'll pass some old houses and the trail will widen and pass through a gate. Follow the contours of the mountain until you reach **Orimento**, where you'll find a delicious lunch at the *Baita* (or if you prefer, there are good picnic places just before and just after the hamlet).

After lunch continue downhill on the road, then the footpath, which has been marked by the *CAI* (*Club Alpino Italiano*), turning left at the yellow bullet-ridden sign to the ski hut. After c 2hrs you reach an asphalt road. Turn left on road and follow it for about 10–15min, then turn right onto a smaller asphalt road and follow it to its end. At the intersection turn right onto the main road, and 300m later turn left into **Lanzo d'Intelvi**.

From Lanzo, transfer by road to the village church at Croce (your hotel staff will help you do this). Take the paved suburban road from the church uphill right to the entrance to the golf course, then turn left into the forest. After 30mins you reach a church by a small clearing, the Madonna delle Grazie di Paulo. Here you can pause for a cappuccino and a slice of pie (follow the signs right to the café-restaurant; closed Mon) before proceeding uphill left to the summit (2hrs) of Monte Nava. The trail (marked) winds steeply uphill for an hour and a half, first through forest, then across a broad meadow with stunning views over Lake Como. The farmers and shepherds in the area have paved the first part of the trail with grooved cement, so they can get up and down in their 4WDs. Don't worry: the cement ends at a certain point, and you walk on soft and relatively level terrain, through woods and meadows and past medieval farmhouses, now largely abandoned.

Choose a picnic lunch spot on the grassy hills overlooking the lake. After lunch, proceed downhill at a farm complex (marked) onto a gravel trail that winds down the mountainside to Rogaro. Here you emerge on an asphalt road, which you take right; at the intersection just beyond the *Ristorante Al Veluu*, you turn left and descend to the lakeshore at Tremezzo.

On Lake Como, opposite Sala Comacina, is the **Isola Comacina**, a pretty little wooded island with a trattoria open March to October but no permanent residents. The regular boat services call here, and a ferry service operates from Sala Comacina.

The island was used as a hiding place by political refugees during the disturbed medieval history of Lombardy, and it was captured and raided by Como in 1169. In 1917 it passed by inheritance to Albert, King of the Belgians, but was later given to the Accademia delle Belle Arti of Milan, who built three houses here as artists' retreats. Paths lead along the shore of the lake and over the top of the island through wild vegetation past the ruins of its six medieval churches.

Two remarkable gardens

The boats skirt the wooded headland called the Punta del Balbianello with an excellent view of the ***Villa del Balbianello**, the garden and loggia of which can be visited Apr–Oct (open Tues, Thur–Sun 10.00–12.30, 15.30–18.30). It can only be reached by water (regular boat service every 30mins from Sala Comacina to coincide with the opening hours) or on foot (only Apr–Oct, on the last Sunday of the month) by a signposted path of roughly 800m, which starts from the church square in Lenno. The villa is surrounded by plane trees, magnolias, ilexes and cypresses. Silvio Pellico, author of *Le Mie Prigioni*, stayed here in 1819. It was left to the *FAI* (*Fondo per l'Ambiente Italiano*) in 1988 by the explorer Guido Monzino, who was the first Italian to climb Everest (in 1973), and who reached the North Pole in 1971.

A steep flight of steps lead up from the dock to the villa, built by Cardinal Angelo Maria Durini in 1787 and incorporating the scant remains of a Franciscan convent (the façade of the church and its twin campanili survive). In the small formal garden above the villa, with laurel and box hedges, wisteria, azaleas and rhododendrons, is a delightful garden loggia with fine views. It incorporates a library and map room with Monzino's collections relating to the polar regions and mountaineering. The villa (not open to the public at the time of writing) contains more of Monzino's collections from his explorations, and 18C and 19C English and French furniture.

At **Lenno** the shore is flatter at the mouth of the Acquafredda, at the south end of the Tremezzina (see below). The parish church has an 11C–12C crypt and an 11C octagonal baptistery adjoining. Here on the shore was the site of Pliny's villa 'Comedia' (his other villa, called 'Tragedia', was at Bellagio). Mussolini was shot by partisans at nearby Giulino in 1945. Beyond Lenno the boats follow the attractive Tremezzina, the fertile green shore dotted with villas and gardens, which extends along the foot of Monte di Tremezzo as far as La Maiolica, north of Cadenabbia.

Tremezzo and **Cadenabbia** are both elegant resorts with numerous hotels and some fine villas. On the busy road between them is the prominent ***Villa Carlotta** (open Apr–Sep, 09.00–18.00; Mar and Oct, 09.00–11.30, 14.00–16.30), built at the beginning of the 18C by Marchese Giorgio Clerici. The interior was altered after 1795 by the Marchese Giambattista Sommariva, and the opening scenes of *La Chartreuse de Parme* (1839) recall Stendhal's stay here as Sommariva's guest in 1818. The villa was bought in 1843 by Princess Albrecht of Prussia, who gave it to her daughter Carlotta on her marriage to the Crown Prince of Saxe-Meiningen. The magnificent wooded park was laid out by Princess Carlotta in the Romantic style. It has always been much admired by the English, and has beautiful camellias, rhododendrons and azaleas in spring.

You enter by the Neo-classical funerary chapel of the Sommariva. The **villa** is interesting for its early 19C decorations, including Neo-classical works and Empire-style French furniture, and for its lovely painted ceilings dating from the 18C. In the main room is Thorvaldsen's frieze of the *Triumphal Entry of Alexander into Babylon*, cast in plaster for Napoleon in 1811–12 and intended for the throne-room at the Quirinal. Also here are works by Canova (*Cupid and Psyche*, *The Repentant Magdalen*, and *Palamedes*), and *Mars and Venus* by Luigi Acquisti. In other rooms on the ground floor are three Gobelin tapestries (1767–73), fine frescoes by Andrea Appiani, paintings by Francesco Hayez and Giovanni Battista Wicar, and plaster models by Canova and Acquisti.

The upper floor has good views of the gardens, fine painted-wood 18C ceilings and Empire-style French furniture. The view from the terrace extends across the lake to San Giovanni with its church, just to the left of which is Villa Melzi, and further left on the hill the Villa Serbelloni, with Bellagio and its church below. Beyond Bellagio the Lecco arm of the lake can just be seen.

In front of the house is a formal Italianate garden reached by a theatrical flight of steps that descend to the entrance gate on the lake. The **park** is of great botanical interest (all the plants are labelled), and is very well cared-for. A path leads past rhododendrons and tropical plants to a hillside planted with azaleas. Beyond a rock garden is a plantation of palms and cacti. A valley watered by a stream has a splendid variety of tree ferns. Beyond, a straight path leads past banks of azaleas, and higher up the hillside are conifers, camphor trees and beech trees. Behind the villa is a hedge of azaleas, and a bridge leads across a stream to a smaller garden on the other side of the villa, with tropical plants, plane trees, monkey-puzzle trees, Japanese maples and palms.

At the Villa Margherita on the shore just north of Cadenabbia, while staying with his publisher Ricordi, Verdi composed Act II of *La Traviata* in 1853.

The Centro Lago

The Centro Lago, where the Como and Lecco arms meet, is the most beautiful part of the lake. In a lovely, quiet position on a headland at the division of the lake is the famous resort of **Bellagio**, which retains much of the picturesque aspect of an old Lombard town. It has local industries of silk-weaving and olive-wood carving. To the left of the car ferry station is an attractive arcaded piazza with the boat and hydrofoil pier. Stepped streets lead up to the church of **San Giacomo**, with a 12C apse. It contains a reconstructed primitive pulpit with symbols of the Evangelists, a painted triptych by the late 15C Lombard school, a 19C copy of a *Deposition* by Perugino, and a 16C wooden *Dead Christ* (a Spanish work). In the apse is a gilded tabernacle (16C and 18C).

In the old tower opposite is the Tourist Information Office and, on the floor above, the ticket office for the ***Villa Serbelloni** (the park is shown Apr–Oct at 11.00 and 16.00 to a maximum of 30 people on a guided tour of about 1hr 30mins, except Mon and when raining). The entrance gate is behind San

Giacomo. The villa and grounds were left to the Rockefeller Foundation of New York in 1959 by Ella Walker Della Torre Tasso to be used as a study centre for students (who come here on scholarships for one month) from all over the world. The younger Pliny's villa 'Tragedia' is thought to have occupied this site. Stendhal stayed here in 1825.

The magnificent **park** on the spectacular high promontory overlooking the lake was laid out at the end of the 18C by Alessandro Serbelloni. A gravel road leads up past a delightful little pavilion used as a student's study, and just before the villa there is a good view of Cadenabbia. In front of the villa, which incorporates a Romanesque tower, is a formal garden with topiary and olive, cypress and fruit trees. From here there is a view of the Lecco branch of the lake, with the little fishing village of Pescallo and a 17C monastery. On the hill in front is the Villa Belmonte, below which you can see a Gothic-Revival building that was once the English church and is now a private villa. A path continues through the park past artificial grottoes created in the 19C up to the highest point on the promontory with remains of a ruined castle and an 11C chapel. The splendid view takes in Varenna with the Villa Cipressi and the Villa Monastero (separated by a prominent square boathouse), and to the north are the high mountains beyond Colico. Another path returns to the villa, from which steps continue down to the exit in the little town of Bellagio.

From the car ferry station it is a 5–10mins walk along the road to Loppia to **Villa Melzi** (the grounds are open Mar–Oct 09.00–18.30), standing in a fine park with an interesting garden. The villa, chapel and greenhouse were built in 1808–10 by Giocondo Albertolli as a summer residence for Francesco Melzi d'Eril. Franz Liszt, the composer and pianist, stayed here (his daughter Cosima was born at the Casa Lillia in Bellagio in 1837). From the entrance a path leads past a little Japanese garden and a circular pavilion on the lake to an avenue of plane trees which leads to the villa. On the left is the former orangery, which contains a small museum. The two statues in front of the villa of Meleager and Apollo are 16C works by Guglielmo della Porta. The park contains beautiful trees and shrubs (most of which are labelled), including rhododendrons and azaleas. Beyond the villa at the end of the gardens is the chapel with particularly fine Neo-classical family tombs.

The road continues to **Loppia** with a half-ruined church in a romantic site beside a great grove of cypresses. At San Giovanni the church contains an altarpiece by Gaudenzio Ferrari. Further on is Villa Trotti with fine gardens (no admission).

Lago di Como and the Romantics

As you might imagine, this area was particularly popular with the Romantics and their literary heirs. Here are a few things they said:

More pleased, my foot the hidden margin roves
Of Como, bosomed deep in chestnut groves.
William Wordsworth, *Descriptive Sketches*, 1791–2, published 1793

And Como! thou, a treasure whom the earth
Keeps to herself, confined as in a depth
of Abyssinian privacy. I spake of thee
Of thee, thy chestnut woods, and garden plots
Of Indian corn tended by dark-eyed maids;

> *Thy lofty steeps, and pathways roofed with vines,*
> *Winding from house to house, from town to town,*
> *Sole link that binds them to each other; walks,*
> *League after league, and cloistral avenues,*
> *Where silence dwells if music be not there:...*
>   *...ye have left*
> *Your beauty with me, a serene accord*
> *Of forms and colours, passive, yet endowed*
> *In their submissiveness with power as sweet*
> *And gracious almost, might I dare to say,*
> *As virtue is, or goodness; sweet as love.*
> William Wordsworth, *The Prelude*, 1805 (text of 1850)

> *This lake exceeds any thing I ever beheld in beauty, with the exception of the arbutus islands of Killarney. It is long and narrow, and has the appearance of a mighty river, winding among the mountains and the forests...*
>
> *This shore of the lake is one continued village, and the Milanese nobility have their villas here. The union of culture and the untameable profusion and loveliness of nature is here so close, that the line where they are divided can hardly be discovered.*
> Percy Bysshe Shelley, letter to Thomas Love Peacock, 20 April 1818

> *The day has been spent on the lake, and so much exquisite pleasure I never had on water. The tour or rather excursion we have been making surpasses certainly all I have ever seen, and Wordsworth asserts the same.... But the pleasure can hardly be recorded, it consisting in the contemplation of scenes absolutely indescribable by words, and in sensations for which no words have ever been invented.*
> Henry Crabb Robinson, *Diary*, 29 August 1820

> *As I sit writing in the garden under a magnolia I look across to Varenna in the sun... and the grand jagged line of mountains that bound the lake towards Colico, almost snowless in August, stand glittering now like the Oberland range. You never saw anything so calculated to make you drunk.*
> Matthew Arnold, letter to Walter Arnold, 5 May 1873

A road leads south from Bellagio to Asso Via Civenna, with a fine panorama of the lake. Beyond Guello a road on the right ascends to the foot of Monte San Primo (1686m). At the edge of the town of **Civenna** by the cemetery is a small park with spectacular views of the lake from Gravedona in the north to Lecco in the south. From the small church of Madonna del Ghisallo (754m; with votive offerings from champion cyclists), the highest point of the road, there is a *view of the lake (left) with the two Grigne beyond, and of Bellagio behind. The road descends the steep **Vallassina** to **Asso** with remains of a medieval castle. Here the graceful 17C church of San Giovanni Battista has an elaborate gilded-wood Baroque altar and an *Annunciation* by Giulio Cesare Campi. Almost continuous with Asso is **Canzo**, the centre of valley life. Another road from Bellagio, with magnificent views, goes along the west bank of the Lecco arm of the lake, Via Limonta, Vassena and Onno, and ascends the Valbrona to Asso.

Walking on the Bellagio peninsula

There are a number of great walks in the hills above Bellagio. The following is a moderately challenging circular excursion of about 6hrs, including picnic lunch. Altitude gain: +300m.

Leave Bellagio by the waterfront, walking through or around the Villa Melzi gardens to the main road to San Giovanni and Como. Cross a stream, turn left and climb steeply to Perlo (the road is marked Via al Perlo). After about 15mins the way to Perlo diverges left: don't miss the turn. Ten minutes later you reach the hamlet of Perlo and cross a cascading stream: at the main road, then turn uphill right. The road winds upward in endless switchbacks. After c 10mins leave the pavement at a forest road with an iron bar, which you'll spot on the left, and after 10mins more leave the forest road by a marked trail on the left. Above, to the right, you will see two farmhouses, one of which is just a ruin. Beyond a cabin marked 'El Casel ...' climb the woods at the red flash marked 'Limonta'. Keep to the marked trail. After roughly 15mins you come to a good picnic spot, a grassy meadow overlooking the Lago di Lecco.

Continue south after lunch. After 5–10mins you'll pass a ruined stone hut: ignore the flash and trail on the left; continue uphill right. Twenty minutes later you emerge in the hamlet of Chevrio.

Walk through Chevrio, then proceed (right) along the road. At the edge of the village turn right for 'Belvedere-Macalle'. Proceed uphill on a paved, then dirt road. After 20mins you come to the Belvedere, a scenic viewpoint overlooking Bellagio and the lake. Ten minutes later, the road ends. Turn right on the marked trail (#27) for Limonta. After 100m the trail forks; you go left and follow the blazes downhill. After 15mins of steep descent, rejoin the trail you took near the ruined farmhouses. From here, you can return to Bellagio the way you came, or follow the main road right to enter the town by the Villa Serbelloni gardens. A third route branches left from the main road after c 10min: the 'blaze' is a trail of little white feet painted on the pavement.

The upper lake

The next place of importance on the west bank of the lake is **Menaggio**, a pleasant little town. Beyond the pier and the Grand Hotel the busy main road can be followed on foot for a few minutes to the pretty piazza on the waterfront. Roads lead uphill behind the church to the narrow cobbled lanes which traverse the area of the castle, with some fine large villas and a 17C wall fountain. Beyond the Sangra river is **Loveno**; near its church is Villa Vigoni (now owned by the German State; open by appointment), with a garden pavilion containing sculptures by Thorvaldsen. The Villa Calabi was the home of Massimo d'Azeglio (1798–1865), patriot and writer. There are several fine walks in the area beneath the beautiful Monte Bregagno (2107m). Acquaseria lies at the foot of the Cima la Grona; to the south rises the Sasso Rancio. Further north is Rezzonico, with a castle, the home of the powerful family which bore its name and numbered Pope Clement XIII among its famous members. The old church of San Vito has a fine *Madonna and Angels* attributed to Bergognone.

From Menaggio the boat crosses to the eastern shore of the lake, offering spectacular views of both southern stretches with Bellagio on its headland in the middle.

Varenna is a delightful little town whose port can be reached only on foot, by narrow stepped streets. It has a good view across the lake of the promontory of Bellagio with the park of Villa Serbelloni. On the main road are the piazza with plane trees, the Royal Victoria Hotel and four churches. **San Giorgio** has a 14C fresco on its façade. It contains a pavement and altar made of the local black marble and a 15C polyptych by the local artist Pietro Brentani. The 11C church of **San Giovanni** has a fine apse and remains of frescoes. The spring of **Fiumelatte**, active from May to Oct, can be reached from the piazza by a pretty path (c 1km) via the cemetery. Although it has been studied by numerous experts (including Leonardo da Vinci), it is still not known why the water is intermittent.

Just out of the piazza, on the main road to Lecco is the entrance to **Villa Cipressi** (garden open daily Apr–Oct), an annexe of the Royal Victoria, with a 19C–20C interior. The villa takes its name from its numerous cypresses, 60 of which had to be felled after a tornado in 1967. The well-maintained garden, with a venerable wisteria, descends in steep terraces down to the lakeside. It has a good view of Villa Monastero, which it adjoins, beyond an attractive little boathouse and private dock.

A few metres further along the main road towards Lecco is the entrance to the **Villa Monastero** (open as Villa Cipressi). The monastery here founded in 1208 was closed down in the 16C by St Charles Borromeo, and the villa is now owned by a science research centre (CNR) and administered by the province as a centre for scientific conventions. The garden is laid out on a long, narrow terrace on the lakeside with 19C statuary, fine cypresses, palms, roses and cineraria, and one huge old magnolia tree. The enormous greenhouse protects orange and lime trees. The gloomy villa, with elaborately carved furniture, yellow and black marble, and Art Nouveau decorations, is in urgent need of repair.

The old stepped streets of Varenna lead down from the piazza (see above) to the picturesque little port, with an arcaded street on the waterfront where the workers who prepared the black marble and green lumachella, or shell-marble, from the neighbouring quarries for shipping used to have their workshops. A walkway built in 1982 continues above the lake (with wonderful sunsets across the water in Oct) round to the car ferry pier. There is an **ornithological museum** in the upper town.

Walking on the Lago di Lecco...

The old *Strada dei Viandanti*, an ancient bridlepath that links the villages on the east bank of the lake south of Varenna, has recently been cleared (enquire at the information office in Lecco for details). The route begins at Madonna di Val Pozzo and ends just over 6km north of Lecco at the church of San Martino (Abbadia Lariana). Some 36km long, it is largely paved with cobblestones and can be walked in 10–12hrs.

... and driving the Grigne

Another road from Varenna follows the right bank of the Esino inland through Perledo, with the medieval Vezio castle, to **Esino** (907m, with a fine view), with the Museo della Grigna (ask at the town hall for the key). The road ends at Cainallo (1245m) beneath Monte Grigna Settentrionale (2410m), a dolomitic peak.

Back on the lake shore, **Bellano** is a town with silk and cotton mills at the mouth of the Pioverna. The deep **Pioverna Gorge** can be viewed from stairs and walk ways (Easter–Sep, Thur–Tues 09.30–12.30, 13.30–17.30). The restored church of Santi Nazaro e Celso is a good example of the 14C Lombard style. From Bellano a road runs to Premana (with a local ethnographical museum).

Dervio has a ruined castle and an old campanile at the foot of Monte Legnone (2601m). Just beyond Dorio a cobbled road (signposted for Piona) diverges left and traverses woods for c 2km to end at the Benedictine **Abbey of Piona** in a peaceful spot on the lake. The simple church has two large stoups borne by Romanesque lions, and behind it is the ruined apse of an earlier church. The irregular cloister has a variety of 12C capitals. There is a ferry station here open in summer.

The boat crosses back to the west shore. The village of **Pianello del Lario** has a 12C church and a small museum of lake boats (open Jul–Sep, daily 14.30–18.30; Apr–Nov, Sat–Sun 10.30–12.30). At **Calozzo** is a museum with a col lection of boats used on the lake (open Easter–Nov, Sun and holidays; guided tours 14.30–17.30). **Musso** is overlooked by the almost impregnable Rocca di Musso, the stronghold in 1525–32 of the piratical Gian Giacomo Medici, who levied tribute from the traders of the lake and the neighbouring valleys.

Dongo, with Gravedona and Sorico, formed the independent Republic of the Three Parishes (Tre Pievi), which survived until the Spanish occupation of Lombardy. Mussolini was captured by partisans at Dongo in the spring of 1945. The 12C church of Santa Maria in the adjacent hamlet of Martinico preserves an interesting doorway.

Gravedona is the principal village of the upper lake. The great square Villa Gallio with four turrets at the north end of the village, was built c 1586 by Pellegrino Tibaldi for Cardinal Tolomeo Gallio. Surrounded by a garden where there is a giant rhododendron, it is now used for exhibitions. Nearer the boat station are the very scant remains of the ivy-covered castle with its clock tower.

Beyond several piazze with hotels and restaurants the main road can be fol lowed on foot for 5mins to two churches, side by side, on the lake in a less attractive part of the town. *Santa Maria del Tiglio is a little 12C building with an eccentric west tower, square in its lower storeys and octagonal higher up, and a very unusual plan with one eastern and two transverse apses. It con tains columns and capitals, as well as frescoes and a fragment of mosaic pave ment. The fine wooden crucifix dates from the 12C. Beside it is the large church of San Vincenzo, with a very ancient crypt which can be visited by descending steps outside Santa Maria. There are a number of other churches of interest in and around Gravedona.

Beyond **Domaso**, at the mouth of the Livo, at the extreme north end of the lake where the Mera flows in, are the villages of Gera and Sorico. The boat con tinues to Colico, an uninteresting town on a plain near the mouth of the Adda at the junction of the routes over the Splügen and Stelvio passes.

THE LECCO REACH OF THE LAKE

Boats ply several times daily from Bellagio to Lecco, May to October, in just over an hour. From Colico an old road skirts the lake with good views, and a new *superstrada* (36) traverses numerous tunnels beneath the mountains a short distance inland (with exits only at Bellano and Fuentes). The two roads join after Mandello, and the last six kilometres are dual carriageway.

The most interesting town on this reach of the lake is on the west shore, reached from Lecco by the Ponte nuovo. This is **Malgrate**, a pleasant little lakeside resort with good views of Lecco backed by mountains. The huge old red silk mill on the waterfront has been restored as a conference centre.

Lecco

Lecco is an unattractive town (population 45,000) with a diminishing population, which became the capital of a new province in 1991. Its old metalworks have been demolished and numerous ugly new buildings have taken their place. Lecco is, however, in a fine position at the southeast end of the Lago di Como (known locally as the Lago di Lecco) at the outflow of the Adda. Above it rise high mountains—the Grigna group to the north with San Martino on the lake, and the Resegone to the south. The town is well known in Italy for its associations with the novelist Alessandro Manzoni (1785–1873), who lived here as a boy and whose famous novel *I Promessi Sposi* (The Betrothed) is set in and around Lecco. The most important buildings in the town are by the local architect Giuseppe Bovara (1781–1873).

The Lungolago leads to the large arcaded Piazza XX Settembre, just off the lakefront, where a market is held on Wed and Sat. At one corner is the 14C Torre Viscontea. Steps lead up to the basilica of **San Nicolò**, a Neo-classical building by Bovara with an eccentric and unusually tall campanile (96m) built in 1904 on a medieval base. Via Mascari crosses Via Bovara, in which (uphill to the left) is the Palazzo del Governatore Spagnolo and a short stretch of 16C walls. Beyond Via Bovara is the little church of Santa Marta with an 18C façade in the Baroque style. Via Mascari crosses Via Cavour (the main street of the town) and leads right to Piazza Garibaldi, with a statue of the hero by Francesco Confalonieri and the theatre by Bovara (1840). Via Roma leads into Piazza Manzoni, with a bronze seated statue of the novelist, also by Confalonieri.

Beyond the railway is **Villa Manzoni** (open Tues–Sun 09.30–14.00), a gloomy, austere house, bought by Manzoni's ancestors before 1621, where Manzoni lived as a boy. It contains a small museum of memorabilia and a collection of local paintings. To the north (800m) is **Palazzo Belgioioso**, an 18C palace surrounded by public gardens containing a natural history museum, with minerals and fossils found locally.

The river Adda is crossed by four bridges, including the **Ponte Vecchio**, built by Azzone Visconti in 1336–38 and later altered and enlarged. This, the 'old bridge', was the only road bridge before 1956. Nearby is the little (privately owned) Isola Viscontea.

Around Lecco

In the southern suburbs, beyond the railway bridge, is **Pescarenico**, a fishermen's hamlet also associated with Manzoni, with narrow streets and an attractive little piazza on the waterfront (paved in the 17C). Here you can sometimes seen the flat-bottomed covered *lucie*, characteristic fishing boats once used all over the lake (and named after Lucia in *I Promessi Sposi*). Across the main road is the church, interesting for its eccentric triangular campanile of 1472 and a 16C ancona (altarpiece) with little polychrome scenes in papier mâché and wax. In front of the church is a tabernacle with friars' skulls, a reminder of the plague.

To the south of Lecco the Adda expands to form the **Lago di Garlate** beneath Monte Barro. Garlate town has a Romanesque church and a silk museum in the old Abegg factory. The **Monte di Brianza** (or San Genesio; 800m), interesting for its vegetation, is crossed by numerous marked trails. Further south, at **Brivio** on the Adda, is another old silk mill (restored and used for exhibitions). In the environs is an unusual sanctuary with an 18C outside staircase. From Brivio a pretty path follows the river all the way downstream to Trezzo sull'Adda. At **Imbersago** you can cross the River Adda to Villa d'Adda on a car ferry whose design—it is a barge operated by hand, using the river current and an overhead cable—was first developed by Leonardo da Vinci.

From the end of the road to Malnago a cableway leads part way up the saw-shaped **Monte Resegone** (1875m), which dominates Lecco from the east.

The **Valsassina**, the valley of the Pioverna, northeast of Lecco has skiing facilities. Its principal village, Introbio, is known for its cheeses. A road leads northeast from Lecco through Ballabio, a rock-climbing centre, past a by-road for the ski resort of Piani Resinelli (1276m), with the wooded **Parco Valentino** (way-marked trails and a museum dedicated to the Grigne group) overlooking the lake. At the Colle di Balisio the road divides: the right-hand branch leads to the resorts of Moggio and Barzio (with skiing facilities), and the left-hand branch traverses the Valsassina.

To the west of Lecco is the **Lago d'Annone**. From Civate a footpath leads in 1–1.5hrs up to the sanctuary of *San Pietro al Monte, with the partly ruined church of San Pietro dating from the 10C; it has lateral apses, 11C–12C mural paintings, and a remarkable baldacchino (canopy) above the main altar. The tri-apsidal oratory of San Benedetto was also built in the 10C. On the other side of the lake are **Annone**, where the church has a magnificent carved wooden altar-piece of the 16C (removed), and **Oggiono**, which has a polyptych by Marco d'Oggiono in its church, and a Romanesque baptistery. Further east is the Lago di Pusiano with its poplar-grown islet.

The Valtellina and Valchiavenna

This chapter covers the province of Sondrio, a mountainous area in the north-ernmost part of Lombardy on the borders with Switzerland.

The **Valtellina**, the upper valley of the Adda, is famous for its numerous ski resorts, including Bormio. It also produces good wines (*Grumello*, *Sassella*, etc.) from vines trained to grow on frames on the steep hillsides. The valley has had a chequered history, but has a high cultural tradition. In the 14C it came under the control of Milan, but in 1512 it was united to the Grisons in Switzerland. The Reformation took a firm hold here, and on 19 July 1620, at the instigation of the Spanish governor of Milan, the Catholic inhabitants of the valley ruthlessly massacred the Protestants (the 'Sacro Macello'). Twenty years of warfare followed, but in 1639 the valley was regained by the Grisons, who held it until Napoleon's partition of 1797. The area has for long been subject to disastrous landslides and flooding, particularly in the 1980s as a result of uncontrolled new building, deforestation and changes in the traditional methods of cultivation. In some places, notably in the area around Sant'Antonio Morignone south of Bormio, landslides have interrupted the course of the Adda and changed the geological formation of the valley.

The **Valchiavenna** is in fact the valley of the River Mera (or Maira)—the same valley in which St Moritz, in Switzerland, is located. It takes its name from the main Italian centre, the delightful medieval town of Chiavenna. Near Chiavenna the Mera is joined by the Liro, which cascades down the steep Valle San Giacomo from the scenic Splügen (Ital. *Spluga*) pass (2116m).

Practical information

Getting there
By air
The airports nearest the Valtellina are at Milan (Malpensa, Linate) and Bergamo (Orio di Serio).

By road
From Milan Linate, take the *tangenziale* to Monza, 41 to Vimarcate, then 36 to Lecco and Colico. At Colico turn onto 38, which ascends the Valtellina Via Sondrio and Bormio, or continue on 36 to Chiavenna and its valley. **Country buses** operated by *STPS* (☎ 0342 213170) from Sondrio (Via Tonale) to Aprica, Valralenco, Teglio and most other towns in the area.

By rail
There are trains from Milano Centrale or Porta Garibaldi stations to (130km) Sondrio in 2–3hrs, with connecting light railway or bus in 30mins to Tirano and bus only (1hr15min) to Bormio. Railroad from Colico to Chiavenna, 27km in 30mins.

Information offices
Valtellina
APRICA Corso Roma 150, ☎ 0342 746113.
BORMIO Via Roma 131b, ☎ 0342 903300.
MARBEGNO Piazza Bossi 7/8, ☎ 0342 610015.
SONDRIO Via Cesare Battisti 12, ☎ 0342 512500. *Comunità Montana Valtellina di Sondrio* (for ski and hiking trails), 33 Via Nazario Sauro, ☎ 0342 210331. *Informagiovani*, Piazza Bertacchi 33, ☎ 0342 211672.

Valchiavenna
CHIAVENNA Corso Vittorio Emanuele II 2, ☎ 0343 36384.

Where to stay
Valtellina
APRICA *Larice Bianco*, ☎ 0342 746275, fax 0342 745454; small and comfortable, open Dec–Apr and Jun–Sep; inexpensive.

BORMIO *Genzianella*, Via Zandila 6, ☎ 0342 904746, fax 0342 904158; a simple but warm family-run establishment; open Dec–Apr and Jun–Sep; inexpensive.
Palace, Via Milano 54, ☎ 0342 903131, fax 0342 903366; modern and functional, with a small garden; closed May, Oct and Nov; expensive.
SONDRIO *Della Posta*, Piazza Garibaldi 19, ☎ 0342 510404, fax 0342 510210; centrally located in a 19C building; moderate.
TEGLIO *Combolo*, Via Roma 5, ☎ 0342 780083, fax 0342 781190; simple but nice, with a garden terrace, in the centre of town; inexpensive.

Valchiavenna

CHIAVENNA *Aurora*, Via Rezia 73, località Campedello (1km east), ☎ 0343 32708, fax 0343 35145; comfortable and efficient; inexpensive.
MADESIMO (VALCHIAVENNA) *Emet*, Via Carducci 29, ☎ 0343 53395, fax 0343 53303; warm and cosy; open Dec–Apr and Jul–Aug, inexpensive.

 Eating out

Valtellina

BORMIO Try *Guanella*, Via Roma 37, for *bresaola* and other cold meats.
Pozzi, Via Roma 39, for sausage, mushrooms, jams and honey.
Taulà, Via Dante 6, ☎ 0342 904585; restaurant offering traditional regional cuisine; closed midday Tues and midday Wed in low season, May and Nov; moderate.
Vecchio Combo, Via Sant'Antonio 6, località Combo; ☎ 0342 901568; trattoria with simple, wholesome local dishes; closed Sun (except in summer); inexpensive.
GROSIO *Sassella*, Via Roma 2, ☎ 0342 847272; restaurant with rooms, serving great game and regional dishes; closed Mon (except Jun–Sep); moderate.
MORBEGNO *Osteria del Crotto*, Via

Pedemontana 22/24, località Madonna, ☎ 0342 614800; trattoria in a *crotto*, or mountain farmhouse, with wood-panelled interiors, majolica wood stove and other rustic amenities in winter, garden seating in summer; closed Sun and Aug–Sep; moderate.
Vecchio Ristorante Fiume, località Cima alle Case, ☎ 0342 610248; trattoria in a historic building, serving excellent local fare; closed Tues evening and Wed; moderate.
PONTE IN VALTELLINA *Cerere*, Via Guiccardi 7, ☎ 0342 482294; traditional restaurant, in an old historic house, serving local delicacies such as air-dried venison and *sciatt* ('toads'); closed Wed (except Aug) and Jul; moderate.
Osteria del Sole, Via Sant'Ignazio 11, ☎ 0342 482298; trattoria serving great game and local delicacies such as *sciatt*, wholewheat fritters made with grappa, and local cheese; closed Tues and Sept; inexpensive.
SONDRIO *Amici Vecchie Cantine*, Via Parravicini 6, ☎ 0342 512590; osteria and wine bar, the place to go for Valtellina wines and snacks (and, perhaps, a game of cards); open 10.00–21.00, closed Sun; inexpensive.
Mossini, località Mossini, ☎ 0342 514040; trattoria with good local food; closed Mon and Jul; inexpensive.
Motta, Piazza Rusconi 4; delicatessen with good bresaola and cold meats.
Sozzani, Piazza Garibaldi 19, ☎ 0342 510404; restaurant of the *Hotel della Posta*, in a historic building with garden; closed Sun and Jul–Aug; moderate.
Tornolina, Via Beccarià 4; delicatessen with *bitto* and other local cheeses.
TIRANO *Bernina*, Via Roma 24–28, ☎ 0342 701302; restaurant with rooms, specialising in local and regional cuisine; closed Mon (except Jun–Nov) and Jan; moderate.

Valchiavenna

CHIAVENNA *Enoteca Marino*, Via

Dolzino 66, offers a wide selection of Valtellina wines and grappas.
Passerini, Via Dolzino 128, ☎ 0343 36166; the town's finest restaurant, serving traditional dishes with an original twist; closed Mon and Jul; moderate.
MESE (CHIAVENNA) *Crotasc*, Via Don Lucchinetti 63, ☎ 0343 41003; trattoria offering good local specialities; closed Mon–Tues; inexpensive.

Entertainment
At Sondrio there is a classical music season at *Teatro Pedretti*, Nov–Apr. Live music and dancing at bars and discos throughout the region, especially during ski season.

Shopping
Some of Lombardy's best **red wines** are made in the upper reaches of the Valtellina (the others come from the Oltrepò Pavese and Garda Bresciano). The Valtellina dinner wines all share the general appellation, *Valtellina Superiore*, which encompasses five types: *Fracia*, *Gumello*, *Inferno*, *Sassella* and *Valgella*. The strong (15 per cent) *Sfursat della Valtellina*, made from dried grapes, is drunk as a dessert wine or with game. Most of the vintners of the Valtellina sell wine directly from the estate. The best known is Nino Negri, with vineyards here and there in the valley and cellars at Chiuro (Sondrio).

Also famous are the kitchen utensils and other household objects made from the smooth local grey stone known as *pietra ollare*.

Special events
Valtellina
ALBOSAGGIA *Rally Internazionale delle Orobie*, amateur back-country skiing competition, Jan–Feb.
BORMIO *Trofeo Vita Walter Fontana*, Italian alpine and nordic ski and snow-board championship, Jan. *Palio delle Contrade*, intramural downhill and cross-country ski race, Jan–Feb.
Penthatlon del Boscaiolo, lumberjack skill competition, Aug.
CASTIONE *El Ciapel d'Oro*, summer wine festival, with presentation and tasting of Valtellina wines, Jul.
CHIESA IN VALMALENCO *Stagione Musicale Estiva*, concert serçies, Jul–Aug.
CHIURO *Il Grappolo d'Oro*. Vintage festival with presentation and tasting of Valtellina wines, Sep.
MORBEGNO *Stagione Musicale*, classical music concerts, Apr–May.
Festenal, ethnic music festival.
PIURO *Canto delle Pietre*, medieval music festival, with concerts in churches, castles, etc.
PONTE IN VALTELLINA *Ponte in Fiore*, culture and folklore festival.
SONDALO *Rally Valle di Rezzalo*, international alpine skiing competition, Jan–Feb.
SONDRIO *Omaggio al Santuario della Sassella*, concert series, Jun.
Valtellina Jazz Festival, Aug. *Fiera Città di Sondrio*, food and wine fair, Sep. *Michelangelo Abbado International Violin Competition*, Sep. *Sondrio Festival*, international festival of documentary films on nature and parks, Oct.
TARTANO *Rally Edelweiss*, international alpine skiing competition, Jan–Feb.
VALFURVA *Ortles-Cevedale* international alpine ski-fest, Apr.
VAL MASINO *Trofeo Kima*, high-altitude foot race, Aug.
VALTELLINA (start at Chiuro a Piateda) *Italian Rafting Championship*, along the River Adda, Jun. *Valtellina Basket Circuit*, pre-season basketball tournament among professional teams training in the Valtellina, summer. *Stagione Musicale*, concert series, Oct–Apr.

Valchiavenna
CHIAVENNA (VALCHIAVENNA) *Le Chiavi d'Argento*, choral music festival, May.

Elsewhere
Carnival celebrations, patron saints' feasts and seasonal festivities (especially 'rites of spring') in most towns and villages.

 Sports
Golf at Bormio (*Golf Club Bormio*) and Ponte di Legno (*Golf Club Ponte di Legno*). **Horse-riding**, **paragliding**, and **sports fishing** in the Valtellina. **Downhill** and **back-country skiing** in both valleys; the most renowned downhill slopes are at Valmarenco, Aprica, Teglio, Bormio, Santa Caterina, Velgerola and Malesimo. **Walking**, **mountain-biking** and **climbing** everywhere, especially in the Parco Nazionale dello Stelvio (for information, *CAI* ☎ 0342 214300).

THE VALTELLINA

From the north end of Lake Como the Valtellina road winds its way eastward amid increasingly dramatic scenery, passing several little resorts on the way to **Sondrio**, a pleasant little town (population 22,000), capital of the valley and of the province. Here a museum of the Valtellina (open Tues–Sat 10.00–12.00, 15.00–18.00) displays archaeological collections, 18C paintings by the Ligari family, furniture, etc. To the north is the Val Malenco—frequented for winter sports—beneath the central massif of the Bernina, a great mountain rising to 4068m, that marks the frontier with Switzerland.

A few kilometres east of Sondrio, above Montagna in Valtellina, are the ruins of **Castel Grumello** (open 10.00–15.00, 17.00–24.00 except Sun afternoon and Mon). Situated on a rocky ridge, the castle consists of two fortresses built in the late 13C to early 14C by Corrado de Piro. One was used for defensive purposes, the other as a residence; both were destroyed in 1526. The castle commands a splendid view towards the Adamello mountain range and is surrounded by terraced vineyards.

At **Ponte in Valtellina**, east of Sondrio, the 14C–16C church has a fresco by Bernardino Luini and a bronze ciborium of 1578. A monument commemorates the astronomer Giuseppe Piazzi (1746–1826), a native of the town, who discovered the first asteroid.

West of Sondrio is the industrial town of **Morbegno**, at the end of the Bitto valley, with skiing facilities. The church of San Lorenzo (the Santuario dell'Assunta), east of the village, was begun in 1418. There is also a small natural history museum here. Palazzo Malacrida, with an interesting garden, was finished in 1762 by Pietro Solari. At the head of the western arm of the valley rises the Pizzo dei Tre Signori (2554m), so-called from its position on the boundaries of the old lordships of Milan, Venice and the Grisons. On the other side of the Adda is the Val Masino, with a number of climbing centres and, at the head of the valley, the spa town of Bagni di Masino (1171m), whose curative waters have been known since ancient times.

Tirano and Bormio

Tirano is another important town in the Valtellina. It has an old district on the left bank of the Adda, with the historic mansions of the Visconti, Pallavicini and Salis families. The late 16C Palazzo Salis (still owned by the family), with a garden, is open Apr–Nov (10.00–12.00, 14.00–16.00). Many of the Protestant inhabitants of the town were massacred in 1620 (see above). The Bernina and Valtellina railways terminate here. To the north is the pilgrimage church of the **Madonna di Tirano**, begun in 1505, in the style of Bramante, with a fine doorway by Alessandro della Scala. The richly stuccoed interior has a large organ of 1617; outside is a painted fountain of 1780. The convent buildings house a local ethnographical museum. North of Tirano is the Swiss border: the road continues over the Bernina pass to St Moritz.

South of Tirano, at Tresenda, a road ascends steeply over the Passo dell'Aprica (1181m). The village of Aprica is a scattered summer and winter resort. On the other side of the Adda is **Teglio** (776m), once the principal place in the valley, to which it gave its name (*Vallis Tellina*). Here the **Palazzo Besta**, rebuilt in the 16C, is open to the public for guided tours (Tues–Sun 09.00/10.00/ 11.00/ 12.00/13.00; May–Sep also 14.30/15.30/16.30). It has a 16C frescoed courtyard and a museum of local antiquities. The late-15C church of Santa Eufemia is also of interest. The chapel of San Pietro has an 11C campanile.

North of Tirano on the Adda is **Mazzo di Valtellina**, where the church of Santo Stefano has a portal carved by Bernardino Torigi (1508), and the Casa Lavizzari contains frescoes by Cipriano Valorsa (see below). Nearby is **Grosotto**, with its 15C houses, and the Santuario della Madonna, erected in the 17C as a thanks-offering for the defeat of the Swiss Protestants in 1620, with a good choir.

The most important place on the main road between Tirano and Bormio is **Grosio**, a large village with 15C–16C houses, including a mansion owned by the Venosta (restored as the seat of the Museo Civico). It was the birthplace of Cipriano Valorsa (1514/17–1604), 'the Raphael of the Valtellina', whose paintings adorn nearly every church in the valley. In the chestnut woods above the road are the ruins of two Venosta castles, one dating from the 12C with the Romanesque campanile of the church of Santi Faustino e Giovita, and the other from the 14C with fine battlements. Here in 1966 were discovered thousands of **rock carvings** (including human figures) dating from the Neolithic period to the Iron Age, the most interesting of which are on the Rupe Magna. The park is shown on request (☎ 0342 847454). Yellow signs indicate the paths through the park from near the huge electric power station (1917–22) beside the main road.

Bormio (920m), backed by a magnificent circle of mountain peaks, is an ancient town whose many ruined towers and picturesque old houses with carved doorways and painted façades recall its once-prosperous transit trade between Venice and the Grisons. It is now well equipped for a long season of winter sports. In 1985 much new building took place when the world ski championships were held here, and new ski slopes were created to the detriment of the natural beauty of the area. Valdisotto and Valdidentro are also now ski resorts.

The most interesting church is the **Crocifisso**, on the south side of the Frodolfo, which is decorated with 15C and 16C frescoes. The painting of the *Crucifixion* by Agostino Ferrari dates from 1376. The **Castello de Simoni** (now the town hall), reconstructed in the 17C, contains a small museum of local art and ethnology (open Mon–Wed, Fri 15.00–19.00; Thur 08.30–12.30, 15.30–18.30; Sat 15.30–18.30). Bormio is the administrative centre of the Stelvio National Park, described on p 332.

Above Bormio on the Stelvio road are the Bagni di Bormio, a well known spa with warm springs. Some remains of the Roman baths are visible, but the 19C baths were demolished in 1977. To the east of Bormio is the Valfurva, with the ski resort of Santa Caterina (1718m).

The Valdidentro
A remarkable road ascends the Valdidentro, west of Bormio, to the Italian frontier station at Passo di Foscagno (2291m), beyond which lies the duty-free zone of the Valle di Livigno, watered by the Spöl (good trout fishing) and one of the few parts of Italian territory north of the Alpine watershed. It has recently been developed as a winter sports centre. **Livigno** is a long, straggling village (1816m), with characteristic wooden houses built at a set distance one from the other to lessen the risk of fire. The church contains 18C wood carving. It is connected by road with the Bernina pass in Switzerland. East of Livigno is the source of the Adda on the Alpisella pass (2285m).

The Stelvio Pass road
A road leads north from Bormio past Rovinaccio, where the botanical garden of **Rezia** (open in summer, and particularly beautiful in Jul–Aug; ☎ 0342 927370) has c 1000 species of flora from the Parco Nazionale dello Stelvio (see p 332). The Adda valley comes in from the left and the road ascends steeply up the Val Braulio, rarely altogether free from snow, to the **Stelvio Pass** (2758m), the second highest road pass in the Alps (generally open only Jun–Oct) and the gateway between Lombardy and the Alto Adige.

THE VALCHIAVENNA
••••••••••••••••••••••

This centre of community life in this remote part of Lombardy is **Chiavenna**, the Roman *Clavenna*, perhaps so named because it was the key (*clavis*) of the Splügen, September and Julier passes. It is a small town in a charming position in the fertile valley of the Mera. Above the turreted 15C Palazzo Balbiani rises the Paradiso (view), a rock with botanic gardens and an archaeological collection on its slopes. The church of **San Lorenzo** dates from the 16C, and has a massive detached campanile. The octagonal baptistery contains a font with reliefs of 1156, and in the treasury is a gold *pax (osculatory) by a 12C German artist.

In the wide valley to the south of Chiavenna is Samolaco, which indicates by its name (*summus lacus*) the point to which Lago di Como extended in Roman times. The Lago di Mezzola is separated from Lago di Como by the silt brought down by the Adda.

Towards St Moritz and Splügen

The **Val Bregaglia** is the fertile upper valley of the Mera, which has traces of a Roman road. The road soon enters Switzerland and continues across the Maloja pass to St Moritz.

North of Chiavenna are the resorts of **Campodolcino** (1103m), beneath the snowfields of Motta (1725m), and, in the sunless valley of Pianazzo, **Madesimo** (1533m), an old-established climbing centre beneath the frontier peaks of Pizzo d'Emet (3211m) and Pizzo Spadolazzo (2948m). The Val di Lei is the only part of Italy where the waters flow into the Rhine.

The **Splügen Pass** (2118m) lies on the narrow frontier-ridge with Switzerland, between the Pizzo Tambò (3274m) and the Surettahorn. The pass was known to the Romans, and the route from Clavenna (Chiavenna) to Curia (Coire) is mentioned in the Antonine itinerary. In 1800, between 26 November and 6 December, Marshal Macdonald, despite stormy weather and bad snow conditions, succeeded in conveying an army of infantry, cavalry and artillery from Splügen to Chiavenna to guard the left flank of Napoleon's Army of Italy, losing 100 men and over 100 horses in the snow. The pass is usually closed November to May. The road descends steeply to Splügen.

Bergamo and the Bergamasco

A beautiful and interesting city (population 117,000), Bergamo is divided into two sharply distinguished parts. The pleasant Città Bassa, laid out on a spacious plan at the end of the 19C and the beginning of the 20C with numerous squares between wide streets, has the station and nearly all the hotels and the principal shops. The Città Alta (366m), the lovely old town, has a varied and attractive skyline crowning a steep hill and peaceful narrow streets. The Città Bassa and Città Alta have been connected since 1887 by an efficient funicular railway. Bergamo stands just below the first foothills of the Alps, between the valleys of the Brembo and the Serio.

The Bergamasco, the traditional territory of Bergamo, consists of two main valleys, the Valle Brembana and the Valle Seriana, in the mountains north of Bergamo. The lower reaches of the valleys are now industrial with unattractive buildings, but the higher regions are prettier with small ski resorts. The interesting churches in these two valleys, and the castle of Malpaga on the plain south of Bergamo, are best reached in a day from Bergamo—preferably by car, as they are not well served by bus.

Practical information

Getting there
By air

Bergamo's Orio di Serio airport, 3km south of the city, has direct flights to/from domestic and European cities; an airport bus runs to the city centre every 30mins. Other convenient airports are Milan Malpensa and Linate, and Brescia Montichiari.

By road

The A4 from Milan or Venice to Bergamo. Bus from Milan (Piazza Castello) every 30min, taking 1hr. To explore the Bergamasco requires a good deal of driving. 470 traverses the Val Brembana. The Val Seriana is served by local roads. 42 provides access to the area east of the city, continuing on Via Lago d'Iseo and Ponte di Legno to the Trentino Malpaga castle is off 498; Treviglio and Caravaggio are reached by 42 and 11. Long-distance buses depart from the bus station in front of the railway station for the Bergamasque valleys and places in the province (SAB), and for Milan (Piazza Castello).

By rail

Trains from Milan Centrale, Porta Garibaldi or Lambrate stations to Bergamo, c 50km in 1hr via Treviglio Ovest; or 1hr 15mins via Monza and Carnate-Usmate, where a change is usually necessary. Branch lines from Lecco, 30km in 40mins; from Brescia, 50km in 50mins (connecting with *Intercity* and *Eurostar* trains on the main Venice–Milan line); from Cremona, 87km in c 90mins. Railway station at Piazza Marconi in the lower town.

Getting around
Funicular railway

From the end of Viale Vittorio Emanuele II to the upper town in Bergamo every 10–15mins (in connection with **Bus no. 1** to and from the railway station: same ticket), used by residents as well as visitors.

By bus

Buses. No. 1: from Bergamo station along Viale Papa Giovanni through Piazza Matteotti (the centre of the lower town), Viale Roma and Viale Vittorio Emanuele II to the funicular station for the upper town (same ticket). **3**: through the lower town to the funicular station and through the upper town to Colle Aperto.

Country buses from the bus station in Piazza Marconi to Milan, Como, Cremona, Lodi and points throughout the province.

Car parking

In the upper town (except on Sun afternoon, when the upper town is totally closed to cars) in Piazza Mercato del Fieno. In the lower town, Piazzale della Malpensata, otherwise numerous pay car parks.

Information offices

BERGAMO In the upper town, Vicolo Aquila Nera 2, ☎ 035 232730; in the lower town, Piazza Marconi 7, ☎ 035 242226. *Informagiovani*: Via Paleocapa 2, ☎ 035 238187.

Valle Brembana
SAN PELLEGRINO TERME Via Papa Giovanni XXIII 18, ☎ 0345 21020.

Where to stay

BERGAMO *Radisson SAS Hotel Bergamo*, Via Borgo Palazzo 154, ☎ 035 308111, fax 035 308308; conveniently located for exploring the region by car, just outside the town to the east; moderate.
In the lower town: *Excelsior San Marco*, Piazzale Repubblica 6, ☎ 035

366111, fax 035 223201; modern and efficient, with a roof garden; expensive.
Arli, Largo Porta Nuova 12, ☎ 035 222014, fax 035 239732; simple but comfortable; moderate.

In the upper town: *Agnello d Oro*, Via Gombito 22, ☎ 035 249883, fax 035 235612; in a historic 17C building; inexpensive.

Youth hostel in the Monterosso district (**Bus 14** from largo Porta Nuova).
Youth hostel, Via Galileo Ferraris, ☎ 035 361724, fax 035 343038.

Valle Brembana
FOPPOLO *Des Alpes*, Via Cortivo 9, ☎ 0345 74037, fax 0345 74078; a seasonal place popular with skiers and hikers; open Dec–Apr and Jul–Aug; moderate.
SAN PELLEGRINO TERME *Ruspinella*, Via De' Medici 47, ☎ 0345 21333, fax 0345 21333; small, warm and friendly, on the outskirts of the town; closed Sep; inexpensive.
Terme, Via Villa 26, ☎ 0345 21125, fax 0345 21306; a quiet, restful place with a large garden; open May–Oct; moderate.

Valle Seriana
CLUSONE *Erica*, Viale Vittorio Emanuele II, ☎ 0346 21667, fax 0346 25268; small and cosy; closed Feb–Mar; inexpensive.

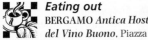

Eating out
BERGAMO *Antica Hosteria del Vino Buono*, Piazza Mercato delle Scarpe at Via Donizetti; ☎ 035 247993; osteria serving Bergamasque delicacies; closed Mon (except in summer); inexpensive.
Antica Trattoria della Colombina, Via Borgo Canale 12, ☎ 035 261402; traditional trattoria with Liberty-style dining room and summer seating outside; closed Mon; inexpensive.
Da Ornella, Via Gombito 15, ☎ 035 232736; trattoria serving dishes from

the Val Brembana; closed Thur and midday Fri, Jul and Dec; inexpensive.
Da Vittorio, Viale Papa Giovanni XXIII 23, ☎ 035 21860; specialising in fish; closed Wed and Aug; expensive.
Dell'Angelo–Taverna del Colleoni, Piazza Vecchia 7, ☎ 035 231991; restaurant in a historic building, serving regional dishes with an innovative twist; closed Mon and Aug; moderate.
Il Gourmet, Via San Vigilio 1, ☎ 035 437 3004; restaurant with rooms, on the hill of San Vigilio outside the upper gate; closed Tues and Dec–Jan; moderate.
Il Pianone, Vicolo al Pianone, ☎ 035 216016; traditional restaurant with summer seating on a panoramic terrace; closed Wed, midday Thur and Jan–Feb; moderate.
La Cantina, Via Ghislanzoni 3, ☎ 035 237146; osteria offering the best of Bergamasque cuisine; closed Sun; inexpensive.
Lio Pellegrini, Via San Tommaso 47, ☎ 035 247813; restaurant offering creative cuisine; closed Mon, midday Tues, Jan and Aug; expensive.
Ol Formager, Piazzale Oberdan 2, for *taleggio, formmai de mut* and other local cheeses.

Cafés
In the upper town: *Cavour*, Via Colleoni; *Caffè del Tasso*, Piazza Vecchia; and *Donizetti*, Via Gombito 17a, a wine bar serving good light lunches.
In the lower town: *Balzer*, in front of the Teatro Donizetti. Marrons glacés at *Pasticceria Jean Paul*, Via Moroni 361. Great ice-cream at *La Marianna*, Via Colle Aperto 4.

Valle Brembana
ALMÈ *Frosio*, Piazza Unità 1, ☎ 035 541633; excellent fish restaurant in a historic palace with garden; closed Wed and Aug; moderate.
COSTA DI SERINA (GAZZO) *La Peta*, Via Peta 3, ☎ 0345 97955; farm serv-

ing delicious country lunches and giving a part of revenues to charity; closed Mon–Thur (except in summer) and Jan. Don't leave without sampling their olive oil, aromatic vinegars, honey, jams and vegetable preserves.

PONTIDA *Hosteria La Marina*, Via Bonanomi 7, ☎ 035 795063; osteria offering good home-made *foiade* and risotti as well as other traditional dishes; closed Tues, Aug and Sep; inexpensive.

VILLA D'ALMÉ *Franco*, Via Ca' dell'Orto 5, ☎ 035 638343; trattoria serving specialities of Liguria; closed Wed; inexpensive.

Osteria della Brughiera, Via Brughiera 49, ☎ 035 638008, fax 035 638008; excellent fish and regional delicacies prepared with skill and imagination; closed Mon, midday Tues, Jan and Aug.

Valle Seriana

ALBINO (ABBAZIA) *Il Beccofino*, Via Mazzini 200, ☎ 035 773900; traditional restaurant known for its vegetable terrines, stuffed quail and beef stew with Cabernet; closed Sun evening, Mon, Aug and Jan; moderate.

Trattoria della Civetta, Via Lunga 89–91, ☎ 035 770797; trattoria offering outstanding mushroom dishes in season; closed Tues; inexpensive.

Elsewhere in the Bergamasco

MOZZO *La Caprese*, Via Crocette 38, ☎ 035 611148; trattoria offering excellent fish and seafood; closed Sun evening, Mon, Dec and Aug; moderate.

PALAZZAGO (BURLIGO) *Burligo*, Via Burligo 12, ☎ 035 550456; simple country trattoria in the woods, serving hearty dishes made with fresh local produce; closed Mon–Tues and Jan; inexpensive.

PALAZZOLO SULL'OGLIO *Osteria della Viletta*, Via Marconi 104, ☎ 030 7401899; osteria serving excellent traditional fare; closed Mon–Tues, Aug and Jan; moderate.

TRESCORE BALNEARIO *Conca Verde*,

Via Croce 3, ☎ 035 940290; trattoria known for its cheese-and-walnut crêpes, pappardelle with rabbit sauce, potato tortelli and other fine pasta dishes; closed midday Sat, Mon and Tues evening, Aug–Sep and Jan; inexpensive.

Della Torre, Piazza Cavour 26, ☎ 035 941365; restaurant with rooms, serving regional specialities; moderate.

TREVIGLIO *L'Usteria*, Via dei Mille 3, ☎ 0363 41686; traditional trattoria; open for lunch only (dinner by reservation Fri–Sat), closed Sun and Aug; inexpensive.

Entertainment

BERGAMO *Teatro Donizetti* in the lower town, with an opera season in Sep–Oct and important musical events throughout the year, including concerts given by the Bergamo symphony orchestra. A Donizetti festival is held every autumn. *Arturo Benedetti Michelangeli International Piano Festival* held jointly with Brescia, May. Concerts are also often held in the basilica of Santa Maria Maggiore (season of Baroque music in Oct).

Drama is performed at *Teatro Prova*, Via Fratelli Calvi; *Teatro San Giorgio*, Via San Giorgio; *Sezione Aurea*, Via Quarenghi; and *Teatro Tascabile*, Via Colleoni.

Shopping

BERGAMO **Antiques** market in Piazza Cittadella, third Sun of the month. **Book** fair, Quadriportico del Sentierone, Apr–May.

Special events

BERGAMO *Celebrazioni di Mezza Quaresima*, annual festival in the middle of Lent with a bonfire, etc. *Bergamo Film Meeting*, Mar. *Immagini - Appuntamento con la Danza*, dance festival, Teatro Donizetti, Feb–Apr. *International Folklore*

Festival, Aug. *Sonavan le Vie d'Intorno*, street theatre festival, Bergamo Alta, Sep. Music festivals, see above. *Bergamo International Marathon*, Sep. In summer (Jun–Sep) guided visits are organised to the lesser-known parts of the city. Summer courses in the Italian language for foreigners at the university.

Valle Brembana
CARONA (VALLE BREMBANA) *Parravicini Alpine Ski Trophy*, Apr.
SAN PELLEGRINO TERME *San Pellegrino Terme National Poetry Prize*, Jul.
PONTIDA *Giuramento di Pontida*, re-enactment in costume of the foundation of the Lombard League, Jun.

Valle Seriana
CLUSONE and neighbouring towns, *Clusone Jazz*, jazz festival, Sep.
MARTINENGO *International Sacred Music Festival*, Chiesa di Santa Maria Incoronata, Sep.

Elsewhere
TRESCORE and MONASTEROLO *Trescore in Blues*, blues festival, Jun. Carnival celebrations, with processions, pageantry, etc., in towns and villages throughout the province. Organ music concerts throughout the Bergamasco,

May–Sep. *Andar per Musica*, music series in towns and villages throughout the province, Jun–Sep. *A Scena Aperta*, open-air theatre around the province, Jul–Aug. *Musiche di Natale*, Christmas concerts in Bergamo and throughout the province, Dec. *Il Canto delle Pietre*, sacred and secular medieval music festival in towns throughout the province, May–Oct. *Gli Organi Storici della Lombardia*, organ music series in churches throughout the province, May–Oct.

Sports
Golf at Almenno San Bartolomeo (*Golf Club Bergamo L'Albenza*), Bergamo (*Golf Club Parco dei Colli*) and Chiuduno (*Golf Club La Rossera*). **Hang-gliding** in Valbrembo. **Horse-riding** at Circolo Ippico Bergamo Brusaporto. **Ice-skating** at Palazzo del Ghiaccio, Bergamo. **Downhill skiing** at numerous resorts, including Valtorta, Piani di Bobbio, Cusio, Monte Avaro, Piazzatorre, San Simone a Valleve, Foppolo, Carona, Val Canale, Ardesio, Lizzola, Valbondione, Presolana, Monte Pora, Castione della Presolana and Colere and Schilpario. **Walking** in the Alpine resorts.

BERGAMO
• • • • • • • • • •

Bergamo is one of the richer towns in Italy, with a booming economy (clothes manufactures, metalworks, etc.), and much new building has taken place on the outskirts in recent years. The town has its own newspaper and symphony orchestra, and its elegant tree-lined streets and many fine shops attest to a long-standing tradition of affluence.

History

Bergamo has been split in two since Roman times, when the *civitas* stood on the hill, the *suburbia* on the plain below. The centre of a Lombard duchy in the early Middle Ages and seat of a bishop in the 10C, it emerged as a free commune in the 12C. In the 14C the Visconti and the Torriani disputed possession of the city, and in 1408–19 Pandolfo Malatesta was its overlord. Another period of Visconti rule ended in 1428, when Venice took the town. Bergamo remained a Venetian possession until the fall of the Republic in 1797, then until 1859 it was part of the Austrian dominion. The Bergamasques played a prominent part in the Risorgimento and contributed the largest contingent to Garibaldi's 'Thousand'. Its most famous citizens were Bartolomeo Colleoni, the 15C mercenary general, and Gaetano Donizetti (1797–1848), the composer. The painters Giovanni Battista Moroni (c 1525–78) and Palma Vecchio (c 1480–1528) were born in the neighbourhood. Another native, the explorer Costantino Beltrami (1779–1855), found the source of the Mississippi in 1823.

The lower town

The Città Bassa, or lower town, was laid out at the foot of the hill on which the old city was built, in the area between the medieval borghi, successors of the Roman *suburbia*. The broad avenues and pleasant squares, which were planned by Marcello Piacentini in the first decades of the 20C, give it a remarkable air of spaciousness. The principal thoroughfare consists of Viale Giovanni XXIII and its continuation, Viale Vittorio Emanuele II. Beyond the **Porta Nuova** with its two little Doric 'temples', opened in 1837 as the monumental entrance to the new city, Viale Giovanni XXIII crosses the huge Piazza Matteotti, with the **Palazzo del Comune (Municipio)** to the left, begun in 1836 by Rodolfo Vantini. In front is a monument to the Calvi brothers (1933) with bas-reliefs by Giacomo Manzù, and a monument to Cavour by Leonardo Bistolfi (1913). Next to the town hall is a bank in a building of 1909 decorated by Luca Beltrami. Adjoining Piazza Matteotti to the north is the arcaded Piazza Vittorio Veneto, designed by Piacentini (1929), with the Torre dei Caduti (1924) as a war memorial. The monument to the Partisans is by Giacomo Manzù.

The wide promenade known as the '*sentierone*', opened in 1762, leads (right) past the **Teatro Donizetti** with a façade of 1897 by Pietro Via and a late 18C interior, to Piazza Cavour, with gardens surrounding a monument to Donizetti by Francesco Jerace (1897). Opposite is the church of **San Bartolomeo**, with a large but poorly lit *altarpiece by Lorenzo Lotto (1516) and fine intarsia choir stalls.

Via Torquato Tasso continues past the Palazzo della Prefettura e Provincia (1870) to the church of **Santo Spirito** with a good interior of 1521. It contains paintings by Lorenzo Lotto, Andrea Pevitali and Bergognone, and in the sacristy is a monument to Bishop Luigi Tasso (1524).

Via Pignolo, which leads left through Borgo Pignolo, is the street with the greatest number of noble houses in Bergamo, dating from the 16C–19C. No. 80 once belonged to Tasso's family, and the 17C Palazzo Agliardi (no. 86) has a *salone* frescoed by Carlo Carloni. On the corner of Via San Giovanni is the church of **San Bernardino** (if closed ring at the door on the left of the façade), which contains a particularly beautiful *altarpiece by Lorenzo Lotto, painted in 1521 (and restored in 1993). Further on is **Sant'Alessandro della Croce** (being restored) with small paintings in the sacristy by Lorenzo Lotto, Lorenzo Costa and Andrea Previtali. Via San Tommaso continues uphill to the Accademia Carrara (see below).

Beyond Borgo Pignolo is the old Borgo Santa Caterina and, across the railway, the huge **cemetery** with a monumental entrance by Ernesto Pirovano

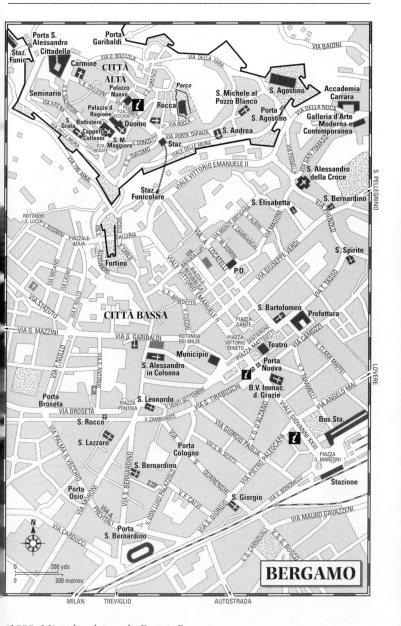

BERGAMO

N

| 0 | 200 yds |
| 0 | 200 metres |

MILAN   TREVIGLIO   AUTOSTRADA

(1900–13) and sculptures by Ernesto Bazzaro.

To the west of Piazza Matteotti, reached by Via XX Settembre, a shopping street, is the old district of **Borgo Sant'Alessandro** (or Borgo San Leonardo).

Here Piazza Pontida is still the commercial centre of the city. The interesting old Via Sant'Alessandro runs north from the Piazza past the church of **Sant'Alessandro in Colonna**. Outside is a column erected in 1618 made up from Roman fragments. The paintings in the interior include works by Leandro Bassano, Lorenzo Lotto and Francesco Zucco. Via Sant'Alessandro winds northwards around an old fort before entering the upper town by a stone bridge built in 1780 through the Porta San Giacomo, a splendid 16C gateway in the Venetian walls.

The upper town

Higher up Viale Vittorio Emanuele II is the lower station of the funicular, which tunnels through the Venetian walls to the Città Alta. By far the quickest and most convenient way of reaching the upper town, it has been in operation since 1887 (and was last restored in 1987). The well-preserved upper town is no less prosperous than the lower town, and contains the most important monuments. Its quiet, narrow streets, attractively paved in a herringbone pattern, have many large mansions, handsome shop fronts, and some old-fashioned cafés. The University of Bergamo was founded here in 1970.

The upper station of the funicular is on Piazza Mercato delle Scarpe, paved with small cubes of porphyry, where seven roads meet. The fountain covers a cistern built in 1486. The narrow old Via Gombito, with pretty old-style shop fronts, climbs up past a little piazza with a 16C fountain and the church of **San Pancrazio**, its Gothic portal decorated with 14C statues and a 15C fresco.

Beyond the 12C **Torre di Gombito** (52m high) the road ends in the spacious Piazza Vecchia, the centre of the old town, with a pretty fountain (1780). On the right is **Palazzo Nuovo** (designed by Vincenzo Scamozzi in 1611, but unfinished until the 20C), opposite which rises **Palazzo della Ragione**, rebuilt in 1538–43, bearing a modern Lion of St Mark and with a meridian of 1789 beneath the portico. The massive 12C **Torre Civica** (or Torre del Campanone, open May–Sep 10.00–20.00 or 22.00; Sep–Apr 09.30 or 10.00–12.30 and 14.00–18.00 or 19.00) can be climbed (the lift is out of action). From the top, beside the three bells, the view north takes in the green fields within the walls with an old ammunition store, the hill of San Vigilio and, nearer at hand, the Colleoni chapel, Santa Maria Maggiore and the cathedral. Beyond Piazza Vecchia rises the square, medieval Torre di Gombito and the Rocca on its hill.

Piazza Vecchia

Beyond the arcades of Palazzo della Ragione lies the small Piazza del Duomo, crowded with fine buildings. The **Cathedral**, altered in 1689, has a 19C west front. Its interesting history is summarised in an inscription on the southwest pier of the crossing. The St Benedict altarpiece on the first south altar is by Andrea Previtali (1524). In the south transept are an altar by Filippo Juvarra and a painting by Sebastiano Ricci. Opposite is a painting by Giovanni Battista Cignaroli. The 18C paintings in the apse include one by Giovanni Battista Tiepolo. The carved panels in the north transept are by Andrea Fantoni. On the second north altar is a statue of St Charles Borromeo by Giacomo Manzù. The altarpiece on the first north altar is by Giovanni Battista Moroni

The charming little **baptistery**, opposite, by Giovanni da Campione (1340), originally stood inside Santa Maria Maggiore. It is open by appointment only (☎ 035 210223).

Between the cathedral and the baptistery rises the church of Santa Maria Maggiore (described below), against the south wall of which—behind a railing of 1912—is the colourful *Colleoni Chapel. The famous mercenary general Bartolomeo Colleoni, having ordered the demolition of the sacristy, commissioned Giovanni Antonio Amadeo in 1472 to erect his funerary chapel on this site. It is one of the more important High Renaissance works in Lombardy, although the over-lavish decorations are unconnected with the architectural forms. The elaborate carving celebrates the brilliant captain-general (who served both the Visconti and the Venetian Republic) by means of complicated allegories combining classical and biblical allusions. The charming exterior details include copies of cannon shafts (which Colleoni used for the first time in pitched battle) in the eccentric windows. The 12 statues are to be replaced by copies.

The **interior** contains the tomb of Colleoni (d. 1476) and the *tomb of his young daughter Medea (d. 1470), both by Giovanni Antonio Amadeo. The equestrian statue in gilded wood is by Leon and Sisto Siry (c 1493). The tomb of Medea was transferred in 1842 from the country church of Basella, on the Crema road. The three altar statues are by Pietro Lombardo (1490). The remaining decoration of the chapel is 18C work, including some excellent marquetry seats, ceiling frescoes by Giovanni Battista Tiepolo, and a *Holy Family* by Angelica Kauffmann.

*Santa Maria Maggiore, a Romanesque church begun by a certain Maestro Fredo in 1137, has a beautiful exterior. Next to the Colleoni Chapel is the *north porch of 1353 by Giovanni da Campione. Above the delightful arch, borne by two red marble lions, is a tabernacle with three statues of saints, including an equestrian statue of St Alexander. Above is another tabernacle with the *Madonna and Child and Saints* sculpted by Andreolo de' Bianchi (1398). The door itself is surrounded by more carving. To the left you can see the exterior of the apses, the Gothic sacristy door (northeast), also Campionese, and the exterior of the polygonal new sacristy (1485–91). Steps lead up beside the fine apse and campanile (1436) and a lane goes round to the south porch, also by Giovanni da Campione (1360) above which is a little tabernacle with statues by Hans von Fernach (1401).

The centrally planned interior is decorated with splendid 16C stuccoes, and late-16C and 17C frescoes and paintings in the vault. At the west, north and south ends are three large paintings in elaborate frames, and on the walls are hung fine tapestries, most of them Florentine works dating from 1583–86 to designs by Alessandro Allori. At the west end the well-preserved Flemish tapestry of the *Crucifixion* dates from 1696–98. Above it is a painting by Luca Giordano. The monument to Donizetti is by Vincenzo Vela. The elaborate confessional was carved by Andrea Fantoni in 1705, and the funerary monument of Cardinal Longhi is attributed to Ugo da Campione (1330).

In the south transept is a fresco of the *Tree of Life* dating from 1347, a large painting of the *Flood* by Pietro Liberi, and an altarpiece of the *Last Supper* by Francesco Bassano; and in the north transept are interesting 14C frescoes (including a scene in a smithy and a *Last Supper*). The two side cantorials are decorated with paintings by the local painters Il Talpino and Gian Paolo Cavagna (1595 and 1593). In the chapel to the right of the choir are four more tapestries and an altarpiece by Antonio Boselli (1514).

At the entrance to the sanctuary are six 16C bronze candelabra and two 16C pulpits with fine bronze railings. A wooden crucifix hangs above. The choir screen has four splendid large intarsia *panels (kept covered except on holidays, but shown on request by the custodian) designed by Lorenzo Lotto, showing the *Crossing of the Red Sea*, the *Flood*, *Judith and Holofernes* and *David and Goliath*. There are also beautiful intarsia choir stalls in the sanctuary, and in the apse is a large curving painting of the *Assumption* by Camillo Procaccini.

Just behind the cathedral and Santa Maria Maggiore is a building dating from 1769, which was adapted in the early 19C as the seat of an academy known as the Ateneo (it is now in very poor repair).

Between the Colleoni chapel and the baptistery, steps lead up to a passageway through the ground floor of the **Curia Vescovile**. It has a fine arch and frescoes of the 13C–14C. Beyond is the centrally planned Tempietto di Santa Croce (probably dating from the 11C, but altered in the 16C). Steps lead down to the south porch of Santa Maria Maggiore. On the right is the pretty, cobbled Via Arena, which leads uphill past the interesting monastery wall of Santa Grata (with traces of frescoes) and an eccentric portal opposite the Istituto Musicale Donizetti (no. 9). Here is a **Donizetti Museum** (open Tues–Fri 10.00–13.00, Sat–Sun 10.00–13.00, 14.30–17.00 or by appointment, ☎ 035 244483), founded in 1903. In a large room, decorated at the beginning of the 19C, are manuscripts, documents, wind instruments, portraits, mementoes, etc. Also here is the piano at which the composer worked. Via Arena ends at the huge seminary building (1965); Via Salvecchio leads right to Via Salvatore (left), which continues downhill past high walls and gardens into Piazza della Cittadella (see below).

From Piazza Vecchia (see above) Via Colleoni, with attractive shops and cafés, is a continuation of Via Gombito. It passes (left) the **Teatro Sociale**, designed by Leopoldo Pollack (1803–07), and (right; no. 9) the **Luogo Pio Colleoni** (open May–Sep, Sat 10.00–13.00, Sun 15.00–18.00), beside a little garden bequeathed by the *condottiere* to a charitable institution founded by him in 1466. On the ground floor are 15C detached frescoes (two of them depicting Colleoni), and a pretty vault dating from the late 15C. Upstairs a room contains a few mementoes and a portrait of Colleoni by Giovanni Battista Moroni.

Via Colleoni next passes the church of the **Carmine**, rebuilt in the 15C and again in 1730. It contains a painting by Andrea Previtali, and a finely carved 15C Venetian wooden ancona. The road ends in Piazza della Cittadella, with a

14C portico and two museums. The **Museo di Storia Naturale** (open Apr–Oct, Tues–Fri 09.00–12.30, 14.30–18.00; Sat, Sun and holidays 09.00–19.30; Nov–Mar, Tues–Sun 09.00–12.30, 14.30–17.30) contains a well arranged collection, including a section devoted to the explorer Costantino Beltrami (see above). The **Museo Archeologico** (open Tues–Sun 09.00–12.30, 14.30–18.00), which originated in a collection formed by the town council in 1561, is also well arranged and has locally found material from prehistoric times to the early Christian and Lombard era. The Roman section includes epigraphs, funerary monuments, statues, mosaics, and frescoes from a house in Via Arena.

Beyond the courtyard is the Torre di Adalberto, a tower probably dating from the 12C, beside a little walled public garden. Outside the gateway is **Colle Aperto**, usually busy with cars and buses, with an esplanade overlooking fields that stretch to the northwest corner of the walled city (the powder store was built in the 16C by the Venetians). Here is the well-preserved **Porta Sant' Alessandro**.

Just outside the gate is the station of the funicular railway (open 10.00–20.00, every 15mins, taking 3mins; longer hours in summer) to San Vigilio (461m). Opened in 1912, closed in 1976, but rebuilt in 1991, it runs along the walls of the Forte di San Marco. **San Vigilio** is a quiet little resort with several restaurants and a hotel. On the right of the upper station a cobbled lane (with a view of the Città Alta) leads uphill: by an Art Nouveau house, steps continue up left to a little public garden on the site of the **castle** (511m; open 09.00 or 10.00–dusk) with remains of a 16C–17C Venetian fortress on a mound with views on every side. A number of pleasant walks can be taken in the surrounding hills (Monte Bastia and San Sebastiano); or the Città Alta can be reached on foot by descending, from the church of San Vigilio, the stepped Via dello Scorlazzone and (left) Via Sudorno.

Also outside Porta Sant'Alessandro, on the hillside at Via Borgo Canale 14, is **Donizetti's birthplace** (open by appointment only, ☎ 035 244483).

From Colle Aperto, Via Costantino Beltrami continues uphill to a traffic light: on the left is a signpost for the botanical garden. Beyond a powder store with a conical roof, built by the Venetians in 1582, steps continue up to the little **botanical garden** (open Mar–Oct 09.00–12.00, 14.00–17.00 or 18.00; open all day Sat–Sun and holidays), opened in 1972, from which there is a good view of the two towns below. The plants (600 species), in an area of only 1357 sq m, are well labelled.

From Piazza Mercato delle Scarpe (see above) a road is signposted uphill for the **Rocca** (open Tues–Sat, 09.00, 09.30 or 10.00–dusk), the remains of a castle built by the Visconti in 1331 and reinforced by the Venetians in the 15C (restored in 1925). It contains a Risorgimento museum (closed indefinitely) and incorporates the little church of Sant'Eufemia, documented from 1006. Outside the walls is a public park, with conifers, cypresses and a few palm trees, laid out as a war memorial with cannon used in the First World War, tanks, etc. There is a path right round the castle and the fine view takes in Santa Caterina and the lower town and a hillside with the orchard and terraced gardens of Palazzo Moroni, while to the west there is a splendid panorama of the upper city, with its towers and domes.

Via Donizetti leads steeply uphill out of Piazza Mercato delle Scarpe past (no.

3) the **Casa dell'Arciprete**, a Renaissance mansion of c 1520 attributed to the local architect Pietro Isabello, with an elegant marble façade and delicate windows. It contains a small diocesan museum (open by appointment only).

From Via Gombito, just out of Piazza Mercato delle Scarpe, Via Solata leads to Piazza Mercato del Fieno, with two medieval towers and the former **Convent of San Francesco**, dating from the end of the 13C, with two fine cloisters and 14C frescoes. Inside is a small museum of local history, open 09.30–13.00, 14.00–17.30.

Via Porta Dipinta (for centuries the main approach to the town) descends from Piazza Mercato delle Scarpe. At no. 12 is the 17C **Palazzo Moroni** (still owned by the family but usually opened at weekends mid-April to mid-July: enquire at the information office) with good windows and a handsome portal and a grotto in the courtyard. It has a very large garden behind, which covers about a twelfth of the entire area of the Città Alta. The interior has 17C frescoes by Gian Giacomo Barbelli on the staircase and on the ceilings of the *piano nobile*. The furnished rooms have 15C–19C paintings, including three by Giovanni Battista Moroni, and works by Previtali, Fra Galgario and Hayez. Opposite the palace is a little garden with a view of the lower town. The Neo-classical church of **Sant'Andrea** (open Sun morning) has an *Enthroned Madonna* by Moretto. Further on is **San Michele al Pozzo Bianco** with a fine interior, having 12C–14C frescoes in the nave and, in the chapel on the left of the sanctuary, a fresco cycle of the life of the Virgin by Lorenzo Lotto.

The road now skirts the Prato della Fara, a pleasant green with an attractive row of houses. At the end is the former church of **Sant'Agostino** (which has been undergoing restoration for years) with a Gothic façade. It has a green-and-red vault dating from the 15C and numerous interesting fresco fragments.

From the church, Viale della Fara leads above the northern stretch of walls, overlooking open country, in which you can see defence banks. Via San Lorenzo leads away from the walls to the church of San Lorenzo, next to which is the **Fontana del Lantro** (opened by a group of volunteers who restored it in 1992; enquire at the information office). This 16C cistern, fed by two springs, was built at the same time as the city walls. The water source was already known by 928, and the name is thought to come from *atrium* or from *later*, referring to the milky colour of the water as it gushes out of the spring. There is a walkway with a view of the cistern with its 16C vault pierced by holes through which buckets were drawn up. A second cistern dates from the 17C.

Beside the church of Sant'Agostino is the **Porta Sant'Agostino** near a little public garden. There is a good view of the Venetian walls (begun 1561–88), which still encircle the upper town. Off Via Vittorio Emanuele is the entrance to the **Cannoniera di San Michele** (open on special occasions and by appointment, ☎ 035 251233). One of about 27 such defences in the walls, this protected the Porta Sant'Agostino. A tunnel leads down to a hall, used by the soldiers, which still contains cannon balls. You can see the two holes (now blocked) used for positioning the cannon, as well as a passageway—high enough for a horse—which leads outside the walls. The limestone has formed into stalactites.

The Galleria dell'Accademia Carrara

From outside the Porta Sant'Agostino (see above), Via della Noca (left; pedestrians only) leads downhill; it is the most pleasant (and easiest) way of reaching the Galleria dell'Accademia Carrara from the upper town.

The *Galleria dell'Accademia Carrara (open Wed–Mon 09.30–12.30, 14.30–17.30) was founded, together with the academy, in 1780 by Count Giacomo Carrara, and the splendid collection of paintings has since been augmented (notably with the Guglielmo Lochis and Giovanni Morelli collections). The Venetian school is particularly well represented. There are long-term plans to re-hang the works by collections rather than chronologically. In the courtyard is a sculpture by Giacomo Manzù. The building was purchased by Carrara for his gallery and academy, and was enlarged in 1807–10 by Simone Elia.

Second floor The main collection is exhibited on the second floor. Room **1**: works by Bonifacio Bembo, Antonio Vivarini and Jacopo Bellini (*Madonna and Child*). Room **2**: works by Alesso Baldovinetti (*Self-portrait* in fresco), Sandro Botticelli (including a portrait of *Giuliano de' Medici*, one of several versions of this subject), Donatello (a relief), Francesco Botticini, Francesco Pesellino, Benedetto da Maiano, Fra' Angelico (and his school), Pisanello (portrait of *Lionello d'Este*) and Lorenzo Monaco. Room **3**: works by Jacobello di Antonello (a copy of 1480 of a lost painting by the father of Antonello da Messina), Bartolomeo Vivarini, Pietro de Saliba, Giovanni Bellini (*Pietà*, *Madonna Lochis*, *Madonna di Alzano*, portrait of a *Young Man*), Marco Basaiti, Andrea Mantegna (*Madonna and Child*), Vincenzo Catena, Lorenzo Lotto, Carlo Crivelli (*Madonna and Child*), and small works by Gentile Bellini and Lazzaro Bastiani. Room **4**: Lorenzo Costa, Gian Francesco Bembo and Bergognone. Room **5**: Andrea Previtali and Marco Basaiti. Room **6**: Lorenzo Lotto (*Mystic Marriage of St Catherine*, *Holy Family with St Catherine*, 1533), Giovanni Cariani (portrait of *Giovanni Benedetto Caravaggi*), Palma Vecchio and Titian. Room **7**: El Greco (attributed), Jacopo Bassano, and Gaudenzio Ferrari. Room **8**: portraits by the Florentine school, Marco Basaiti and Pier Francesco Foschi. Room **9** contains a fine series of portraits by Giovanni Battista Moroni, including an *Old Man with a Book*. Room **10**: Dürer 'Master of the St Ursula Legend', Jean Clouet (*Portrait of Louis of Clèves*).

From the top of the stairs outside room 1 is the entrance to room **11**, with portraits by the local painter Carlo Ceresa and works by Guercino and Sassoferrato. In room **12** are portraits by the local painter Fra' Galgario, and beyond are three small rooms with 19C works by Il Piccio, Giuseppe Pelliza da Volpedo (allegorical portrait of a *Woman*) and Francesco Hayez. Room **13**: Flemish and Dutch paintings, including one by Rubens, and a portrait by Velasquez. Room **14**: Francesco Zuccarelli, Piero Longhi and Piazzetta. Room **15**: the Venetian school, including Francesco Guardi, Giovanni Battista Tiepolo and Canaletto.

The fine collection of prints and drawings, especially important for the Lombard and Venetian schools, is open to scholars by special request.

The seven rooms on the first floor (usually closed, but opened with special permission) contain more 15C–17C paintings (Lombard and Veneto masters). Across the road, a 14C monastery which was transformed into the Camozzi barracks has been partially restored by Vittorio Gregotti as an exhibition centre. Another part of the building is to be used to display the permanent collection of 20C works.

The nearby **Galleria d'Arte Moderna e Contemporanea** (entrance at Via San Tommaso 53; open Mon, Wed, Thur 10.00–22.30, Sun and holidays 10.00–19.00) hosts a small but beautiful collection of modern Italian art and temporary exhibitions of 19C and 20C art.

The centre of the lower town is reached from the Accademia by descending Via San Tomaso, Via Pignolo and Via Torquato Tasso (all described above).

THE BERGAMASCO

Bergamo's diverse province extends from the alpine Valle Brembana and Valle Seriana, on the north, to the foggy flatlands of the Po River basin south and east of the city. They are most easily explored by car.

The Valle Brembana

The lower part of this verdant valley north of Bergamo runs through part of the Parco Regionale dei Colli di Bergamo, an area of some 8500 hectares protected since 1977. Here the village of **Ponteranica** has a fine parish church containing a polyptych by Lorenzo Lotto. *Valcalepio* wine is produced in the hills of the Valle Imagna, which branches west.

Almenno San Bartolomeo and **Almenno San Salvatore** are two neighbouring municipalities. In the latter is the **Pieve di San Salvatore** (or Madonna del Castello), marked by a tall campanile, above the River Brembo (in which you can see a few remains of a large Roman bridge destroyed in a flood). This is the oldest church in Almenno and is thought to have been founded c 755. The interior (key at the priest's house next door), altered in the 12C, has a fine 12C pulpit in sandstone with the symbols of the Evangelists. The sanctuary has Ionic capitals and frescoes (c 1150). The ancient columns in the crypt date from before the 11C. The church adjoins the 16C **Santuario della Madonna del Castello**, which has a delightful early-16C ciborium over the high altar, with paintings of sibyls attributed to Andrea Previtali, and an altarpiece by Gian Paolo Cavagna.

Close by (5mins walk) is the large 12C **Basilica di San Giorgio**, with a good exterior. The whale bone hanging in the nave, dating from the Pliocene era, was found nearby. The most interesting frescoes are those high up—and difficult to see—on the inside of the nave arches (on the right): they date from the late 13C or early 14C.

Also outside Almenno San Salvatore is the church of **San Nicola** (or Santa Maria della Consolazione), next to the former convent of the Agostiniani, founded in 1486. It has an attractive interior, with stone vaulting supporting a painted wood roof, and side chapels beneath a matroneum. It contains 16C frescoes by Antonio Boselli, and an altarpiece of the Trinity by Andrea Previtali.

Outside Almenno San Bartolomeo is the little circular church of ***San Tomé**, one of the more interesting Romanesque buildings in Lombardy. It is usually open at weekends spring–Oct; otherwise the key is kept at a house nearby (no. 21). Excavations in the area have revealed remains of tombs dating from the 1C and the 9C, but the date of the church is still under discussion. It is now generally thought to be an 11C building, although the apse and presbytery may have been added later. The nun's door connected the church to a fortified convent. It was restored in 1892. The beautiful interior has an ambulatory and above it a matroneum (which can be reached by stairs) beneath a delightful cupola and lantern lit by four windows. The capitals are decorated with sirens, eagles, etc.

In Almenno San Bartolomeo is the Museo del Falegname, a private museum dedicated to the work of carpenters, with a collection of tools (from the 17C), reconstructed artisans' workshops, bicycles and puppets.

A road leads west to **Pontida**, with a Benedictine abbey (open Mon–Fri 09.00–12.00, 16.00–18.00; Sunday 16.00–18.00), the upper cloister of which is a fine work, probably by Pietro Isabello (c 1510). On the other side of Monte Canto, Sotto il Monte Giovanni XXIII has taken the papal name of Angelo Roncalli, born here in 1881, and Pope 1958–63.

Zogno is the chief place in the lower Val Brembana, and it has a local museum. **Serina**, visited for cross-country skiing, was the birthplace of Palma il Vecchio (polyptych in the sacristy of the church).

San Pellegrino Terme has famous mineral water springs. The elegant spa town was laid out at the beginning of this century: the grand Art Nouveau buildings include the Palazzo della Fonte and the former Casinò Municipale. The Val Taleggio is noted for its cheese. In the main valley is the remarkable medieval village of **Cornello**, which was the 14C home of the Tasso family, who are supposed to have run a European postal service from here. **Piazza Brembana** is a summer resort and a base for climbs in the mountains. Above Piazza the valley divides, both branches giving access to numerous little climbing and winter-sports resorts, the most important of which is **Foppolo** (1545m).

The Valle Seriana

This is the principal valley in the Bergamesque Alps, and is mainly industrial, with many silk and cotton mills and cement works, but the upper reaches are unspoilt. The churches have some fine works by the Fantoni family of sculptors and carvers, who lived and worked in the valley in the 15C–19C.

Alzano Lombardo is noted for its wool workers. The basilica of **San Martino** was rebuilt in 1670 and has a splendid interior designed by Girolomo Quadrio, with coupled marble columns and stuccoes by Angelo Sala. It has a pulpit by Andrea Fantoni and a painting by Andrea Appiani. The three *sacristies have superb carvings and intarsia work, beautifully restored in 1992. The first sacristy has Baroque walnut cupboards carved by Grazioso Fantoni (1679–80), while the second sacristy (1691–93) has even better carving in walnut and box wood by his son Andrea Fantoni and his three brothers. Above are statuettes showing the martyrdom of saints and apostles, and in the ovals the story of Moses and scenes from the New Testament. The seated statues represent the *Virtues*; the prie-dieu has a *Deposition*, also by Fantoni; and the stuccoes are by Girolamo Sala. The intarsia in the third sacristy is partly by Giovanni Battista Caniana (1700–17); the barrel vault has more stuccoes by Sala.

At **Olera** the parish church contains a polyptych by Cima da Conegliano. **Albino**, an industrial village, has a *Crucifixion* by Giovanni Battista Moroni (born nearby at Bondo Petello) in the church of San Giuliano.

Gandino, an ancient little town noted for its carpets, was the birthplace of the sculptor Bartolomeo Bon the Elder. The basilica of *Santa Maria Assunta* was rebuilt in 1623–30 and has a very fine interior on an interesting central plan.

The dome was finished in 1640 and the *trompe l'oeil* fresco added in 1680. The bronze balustrade dates from 1590. Giacomo Ceruti painted the spandrels above the arches, and the organ was built by Adeodato Bossi in 1868 (in an earlier case by Andrea Fantoni). Outside the church a little baptistery was erected in 1967, and beside it is the Museo della Basilica, first opened in 1928 (now open by appointment, ☎ 035 745425). It contains two series of Flemish tapestries (1580), a silver altar (begun in 1609 and finished in the 19C) and an organ made by Perolini in 1755. On the first floor are vestments, church silver, a 16C German sculpture of *Christ on the Cross* (with movable arms) and ancient textiles.

Vertova has a prominent 17C parish church surrounded by a portico. On the wooded hillside above you can see the sanctuary of **San Patrizio**, a 16C building with an earlier crypt. The valley now becomes prettier.

Clusone is a small resort in the Valle Seriana. The medieval town hall has a remarkable astronomical clock made by Pietro Fanzago in 1583, and numerous remains of frescoes. Above is the grand basilica of **Santa Maria Assunta**, built in 1688–1716 by Giovanni Battista Quadrio, preceded by an impressive terrace with statues added at the end of the 19C. The high altar has sculptures by Andrea Fantoni (who also designed the pulpit) and an *Assumption* by Sebastiano Ricci. The altarpieces are by Domenico Carpinoni, Gaspare Diziani, Giambettino Cignaroli and Gian Paolo Cavagna. Above the west door is a large painting by the local painter Lattanzio Querena.

To the left is the **Oratorio dei Disciplini** with a remarkable *fresco on the exterior depicting the *Dance and Triumph of Death* (1485), fascinating for its iconography. Inside (unlocked by the sacristan of the church) are well-preserved frescoes showing small, colourful scenes of the *Passion*, dating from 1480. Over the choir arch is a fresco of the *Crucifixion* (1471). The life-size polychrome wood group of the *Deposition* is attributed to the school of Fantoni.

Further downhill are the grand Palazzo Fogaccia, built in the early 18C by Giovanni Battista Quadrio, with a garden; and the church of Sant'Anna, with 15C and 16C frescoes inside and out and a fine altarpiece by Domenico Carpinoni, in a lovely frame.

Just outside Clusone is **Rovetta**, where the house and workshop of the Fantoni family of sculptors, who were born here, is now a little museum, and the church has an early altarpiece by Giovanni Battista Tiepolo. The **Passo della Presolana** (1286m) is a ski resort, and there are more resorts in the upper Valle Seriana.

On the plain

East of Bergamo is **Trescore Balneario**, a small spa with sulphur and mud baths. A chapel (shown on request) in the park of the Suardi villa at Novale contains frescoes by Lorenzo Lotto (1524). At **Credaro** the church of San Giorgio has another chapel, with more frescoes carried out a year later by Lotto.

South of Bergamo, the *Castle of Malpaga** (open for guided tours on holidays 14.30–dusk; otherwise by appointment; ☎ 035 840003) is approached by a road bordered on either side by narrow canals regulated by locks connected to the Serio River. It is set in the centre of an agricultural estate, surrounded by farm buildings with double loggias. The 14C castle, on the extreme western limit of the land owned by the Venetian Republic, was bought as a residence by

Bartolomeo Colleoni in 1456, the year after he became Captain of the Venetian army. He heightened the castle in order to protect it against firearms (you can see the castellations of the first castle in the walls) and built the pretty loggias. There also used to be two moats.

The castle is particularly interesting for its frescoes, carried out at the time of Colleoni and in the following century. The main entrance has 16C frescoes of courtiers, and the courtyard has frescoes commissioned by Colleoni's grandchildren in the early 16C to illustrate his achievements in battle: the siege of Bergamo in 1437 includes a good view of the Città Alta, and under the loggia is a scene of the great soldier's last battle in 1497 (Colleoni is shown in a red hat). The Sala dei Banchetti contains more 16C frescoes, here showing the visit of King Christian I of Denmark to the castle in 1474 on his way to Rome (the soldiers in white-and-red uniform are those of Colleoni). The reception room upstairs retains its original 15C frescoes (in poor condition), with courtly scenes in the International Gothic style. Colleoni died at the age of 80, in the bedroom that has a 15C Madonna and Child with Saints in a niche.

At **Treviglio**, an agricultural and industrial centre, the Gothic church of San Martino contains a beautiful polyptych by Bernardino Zenale and Bernardino Butinone (1485). Santa Maria delle Lacrime is a Renaissance building with another triptych by Butinone. Here in 1915, while in hospital with jaundice, Mussolini was married (probably bigamously) to Donna Rachele.

Caravaggio was the probable birthplace of the painter Michelangelo Merisi, known as Caravaggio (1571–1610). An avenue leads to a large sanctuary dedicated to the Madonna, who is said to have appeared to a peasant woman here in 1432 on the site of a miraculous spring. The domed church was enlarged by Pellegrino Tibaldi in 1575 and is visited by thousands of pilgrims every year (festival on 26 May). The little Museo Navale is open Sat (except Aug) 15.00–18.00.

On the other side of the Serio River is **Romano di Lombardia**, with an interesting urban plan. The medieval Palazzo della Comunità was altered in later centuries. The church of **Santa Maria Assunta**, reconstructed in the 18C by Giovanni Battista Caniana, contains a *Last Supper* by Giovanni Battista Moroni, and intarsia by Caniana. Above the Neo-classical Palazzo Rubini is the 13C Visconti castle.

Brescia, Lago d'Iseo and the Val Camonica

Brescia (population 190,000) is the second most important industrial town in Lombardy after Milan, and has a flourishing economy based on the service industries and the manufacture of iron and steel (it has long been known for its production of arms, cutlery, etc.). Situated at the mouth of the Val Trompia, it has always enjoyed an abundance of water and still has numerous fountains. It has interesting Roman remains (including a reconstructed temple and an exceptionally fine bronze statue), important Lombard relics in the huge, once-powerful monastery of Santa Giulia, founded by the Lombard king Desiderius in 753, a beautiful Renaissance building known as the Loggia, and numerous churches with paintings by the early 16C local artist Moretto. However, it is not usually visited for its artistic treasures (except by tour groups on day trips from the Lago di Garda) and is poorly provided with hotels in the centre of the city.

The province of Brescia is exceptionally large and includes the Valle Camonica in the north, famous for its prehistoric rock carvings, the Lago d'Iseo, the smaller Lago d'Idro, the Franciacorta winemaking district, and several mountain valleys with ski resorts. The western side of the Lago di Garda, also within the province, is described on p 350.

Practical information

Getting there and getting around
By air

Brescia's Gabriele d'Annunzio Airport, with daily flights to Italian and European cities, is located at Montichiari, 30km from the city centre. You can also reach Brescia via Milan (Malpensa, Linate), Bergamo (Orio di Serio) and Verona (Caselle di Sommacampagna). There are shuttles to Brescia from all airports.

By road

Brescia lies at the junction between the busy A4 from Venice to Milan, and the A21 from Turin, Piacenza and Cremona. Parking at the railroad station, the Autosilo (Via Vittorio Emanuele 11) and in car parks around the city.

There is a comprehensive network of **country buses**, with services to/from Bergamo, Milan, Lake Como, Cremona, Mantua and places of interest in the province (information, ☎ 035 3774237 or 030 44915). In Brescia buses arrive at or depart from the bus station (Via Solferino 6) or the railway station. **City bus D** runs from the station to Corso Zanardelli.

By rail

Brescia is on the main line (FS) from Turin to Venice and Trieste. Trains from Rome and central Italy connect via Milan or Verona. Fast *Intercity* trains make the run from Milan in 50mins, from Verona in 25mins. There are also trains from Lecco (63km in 1hr 20min), Cremona (51km in 35–50mins), Parma (92km in 1hr 25mins) and Edolo (103km in 2hrs 2mins)—the latter following the east bank of the Lago d'Iseo to Pisogne and then plying a very scenic route through the Valle Camonica. Brescia is also served by commuter trains from Milan (operated by FNME).

By boat

Boat services connect the main towns on Lago d'Iseo: Pisogne, Lovere, Castro, Riva di Solto, Marone, Tavernola, Siviano, Paradiso, Carzano, Sale Marasino, Sulzano, Sensole, Peschiera, Predore, Clusane, Paratico and Sarnico.

Information offices
BRESCIA Corso Zanardelli 34–38, ☎ 030 43418, and Piazza Loggia 6, ☎ 030 240 0357; website: www: bresciaholiday.com. A seasonal kiosk operates at the Brescia-Centro *autostrada* exit.
Informagiovani, Piazza Vittoria 5a, ☎. 030 375 3004.

Lago d'Iseo
ISEO Lungolago Marconi 2, ☎ 030 980209.

SARNICO Via Piccinelli 18, ☎ /fax 035 919000.

Val Camonica
BOARIO TERME Piazza Autostazione, ☎ 0364 531609.
BRENO Comunità Montana di Valle Camonica (for foot- and ski-trails), Via Aldo Moro.
EDOLO Piazza Martiri della Libertà 2, ☎ 0364 71065.
PONTE DI LEGNO Corso Milano 41, ☎ 0364 91122.

Lago d'Idro
IDRO Località Pieve, ☎ 0365 83224.
Valle Trompia
COLLIO VAL TROMPIA Piazza Zanardelli, ☎ 030 927330.

Where to stay
BRESCIA The only real possibility in this very business-minded city is the elegant but comfortable late Liberty-style *Vittoria*, Via X Giornate 20, ☎ 030 280061, fax 030 280065; expensive.
Outside Brescia, at Via Cappuccini 54, Cologne, ☎ 030 7157254, fax 030 7157257, is the *Cappuccini*, in a former 16C convent, with a good restaurant; moderate.

Franciacorta
BELLAVISTA (ERBUSCO) *L'Albereta Locanda in Franciacorta*, Via Vittorio Emanuele 11; ☎ 030 7760550, fax 030 7760573; in a beautifully restored 19C villa, with a renowned restaurant (closed Sun evening, Mon and Jan); expensive.

Lago d'Iseo
INVINO (ISEO) *I Due Roccoli*, Via Silvio Bonomelli, ☎ 030 982 2977, fax 030 982 2980; a lovely country house amid woods and meadows, with wonderful views over the lake; closed Jan; moderate.
ISEO *Ambra*, Porto Rosa 2, ☎ 030 980130, fax 030 982 1361; warm and hospitable; inexpensive.

LOVERE *Moderno*, Piazza 13 Martiri 21, ☎ 035 960607, fax 035 961451; a cordial, family-run place at the north end of the lake; inexpensive.

Valle Camonica
BOARIO TERME *Brescia*, Via Zanardelli 6, ☎ 0364 531409, fax 0364 532969; small, central and comfortable; inexpensive. *Rizzi*, Via Carducci 5/11, ☎ 0364 531617, fax 0364 532969; a homelike, family-managed establishment, with a nice garden; inexpensive.
PASSO DEL TONALE *La Mirandola*, Via Tonale 115, ☎ 0364 903933; simple and peaceful, but difficult access in winter; open Dec–Apr and Jun–Sep; moderate.
PONTE DI LEGNO *Mirella*, Via Roma 21, ☎ 0364 900500, fax 0364 900530; modern and efficient, amid woods and meadows; moderate.
VILLA DALEGNO (PONTE DI LEGNO) *Sorriso*, Via Plaza 6, ☎ 0364 900488, fax 0364 91538; a sober but elegant place with a good restaurant; moderate.

Eating out
BRESCIA *Hosteria*, Via 28 Marzo 2a, at Sant'Eufemia, ☎ 030 360605; trattoria serving traditional local dishes, outside the city centre; closed Tues and Aug; inexpensive.
Il Ciacco, Via Indipendenza 23b, ☎ 030 361797; good traditional restaurant in a neighbourhood known locally as 'Food Valley' for its many osterie; closed Mon, Jan and Aug; moderate.
Il Lorenzaccio, Via Cipro 78, ☎ 030 220457; restauant specialising in Tuscan dishes, across the railway from the city centre; closed Sun (and Sat, Jun–Jul), Dec and Aug; moderate.
La Piazzetta, Via Indipendenza 87c, at Sant'Eufemia, ☎ 030 362668; good fish restaurant outside the city centre; closed midday Sat, Sun, Jan and Aug; moderate.
La Sosta, Via San Martino della Battaglia 20, ☎ 030 295603; fine

regional cuisine in a historic building with garden; closed Sun evening, Mon, Jan and Aug; expensive.

La Vineria, Via X Giornate 4, ☎ 030 280477; wine bar serving great *risotti* and other warm dishes; closed Mon and Aug; inexpensive.

Cafés

The best coffee and pastries in town are at: *Pasticceria San Carlo*, on the corner of Corso Zanardelli and Via 10 Giornate.

Bar Impero, Piazza Vittoria.

Capuzzi, Via Pia Marta.

G.A. Porteri, Via Trento 52, ☎ 030 380947, is a warm, friendly osteria run by the people who have the (excellent) delicatessen next door; closed Sun evening, Mon and Aug; moderate.

Franciacorta

PIÈ DEL DOSSO (GUSSAGO)

L'Artigliere, Via Forcella 6, ☎ 030 277 0373; traditional trattoria where tourists are all but unknown; closed Mon and Tues evening, Aug and Jan; inexpensive.

Lago d'Iseo

ISEO *Al Porto*, Piazza Porto, ☎ 030 989014, Clusane (Iseo); traditional osteria specialising in lake fish; closed Wed evening (except in summer); moderate.

Cinema Teatro Eden, wine shop taking its name from the theatre that used to occupy the building; excellent wines as well as pastas, jams, etc.

Il Castello, Via Mirolte 43, ☎ 030 981285; traditional trattoria with garden; moderate.

Il Volto, Via Mirolte 33, ☎ 030 981462; osteria serving excellent regional dishes; closed Wed, midday Thur and Jul; moderate.

La Fenice, Via Fenice 21, ☎ 030 981565; simple restaurant specialising in lake fish; closed Thur and Aug; moderate.

Val Camonica

DARFO *Gatti*, has a wide selection of local salami and cold meats ideal for picnics.

PEZZO (PONTE DI LEGNO) *Da Giusy*, Via Ercavallo 39, ☎ 0364 92153; trattoria, simple but good; closed Tues (except Jul–Aug) and weekdays Oct–Nov; inexpensive.

RIVA DEI BALTI (ARTOGNE) *Le Fise*, Via Pieve 2, ☎ 0364 598298; a mountain cabin (with rooms) surrouned by flowers and orchards, serving delicious farm meals made with genuine home-grown ingredients; open all year, Fri–Sun; inexpensive.

Entertainment

BRESCIA *Teatro Grande*, opera season Sep–Nov, concerts Oct–Mar, drama Nov–Apr; *Teatro di Santa Chiara* and *Teatro Sancarlino*, drama. Music and dancing at roughly a dozen clubs and discos around town.

Special events

BRESCIA *Arturo Benedetti Michelangeli International Piano Festival*, Apr–Jun. Organ concerts from mid-Sep–mid-Oct in various churches in the city. Choral music is performed in various churches Apr–Jun. In summer, music is performed in the gardens of palaces, etc (information from your concierge or the information office). The *Mille Miglia* is a veteran car race held in May (the three-day course of 1000 miles—1600km—runs from Brescia via Ferrara to Rome and back to Brescia).

Lago d'Iseo

LOVERE *Stagione dei Concerti*, concert season, Accademia Tadini, Apr–Jun.

SARNICO *World Music Festival*, Jul.

Sports

Golf at Nicoline di Corte Franca (*Franciacorta Golf Club*) and Soiano del Lago (*Gardagolf Country Club*). **Skiing**, **horse-riding** and **hiking** in the Alpine resorts. **Swimming** and **watersports** on the lakes.

BRESCIA
• • • • • • • • •

Modern Brescia extends in a haphazard manner around the historic city centre, dominated by the old castle on its little knoll.

History

Just who founded Brescia is a mystery. Legend speaks—or rather, whispers—of the Ligurians; historians point to Gaulish Celts. Certainly, by the 3C BC the city had come under Roman influence, and you can still see traces of the crisscross Roman street plan in the old city centre. Reduced to rubble by Goths and Visigoths, the Roman colony of *Brixia* re-emerged into prominence under the 8C Lombard king Desiderius, who was born in the neighbourhood. The city was a member of the Lombard League, but in 1258 it was captured by the tyrant Ezzelino da Romano. Later it was contested by the Lombard Torriani and Visconti, the Veronese Scaligeri, and Pandolfo Malatesta; but from 1426 to 1797 it prospered under Venetian suzerainty. Between 1509 and 1516 it was twice captured by the French under Gaston de Foix. In March 1849 it out for ten days against the Austrian general, Haynau (nicknamed the 'hyena of Brescia'), but in the 20C it was severely damaged in the Second World War.

The city centre

The wide, arcaded Corso Zanardelli, together with the adjoining Corso Palestro and Via delle X Giornate, can be regarded as the centre of the town. Here is the **Teatro Grande** (entered from Via Paganora), founded in 1709 and rebuilt in 1863, but with a façade of 1782. The arcades continue north along Via delle X Giornate.

Just to the west is Piazza della Vittoria, designed by Marcello Piacentini and finished in 1932. It is built in grey marble and white stone and presents an interesting example of the kind of rhetorical Modernism that was dear to the Fascist regime. The red marble Arengario, a rostrum for public speaking, has bas-reliefs by Antonio Maraini. At the north end is the striped post office.

Near the latter, but hidden by a war memorial, is the church of **Sant'Agata**, built c 1438–72. In the attractive interior is an apse fresco of the *Crucifixion* (1475; attributed to Andrea Bembo). The nave frescoes (1683) are by Pietro Antonio Sorisene and Pompeo Ghitti. In the 18C chapel of the Sacrament (right) are two oval paintings by Giovanni Antonio Pellegrini.

An archway under the **Monte di Pietà** (with a loggia of 1484 and an addition of 1597), behind the post office, leads to the harmonious Piazza della Loggia. On the left rises the *****Loggia**, or Palazzo Pubblico, a beautiful Renaissance building with exquisite sculptural detail. The ground floor was built between 1492 and 1508, the upper storey between 1554 and 1574. The architect is unknown, although Lodovico Beretta, Jacopo Sansovino, Galeazzo Alessi and Andrea Palladio are all thought to have been involved. It was restored in 1914. On the right of the Loggia is a fine 16C portal.

Above the northeast of the square rises the **Porta Bruciata**, a fragment of the oldest city wall. The arcade at the east end was the scene in 1974 of one of the

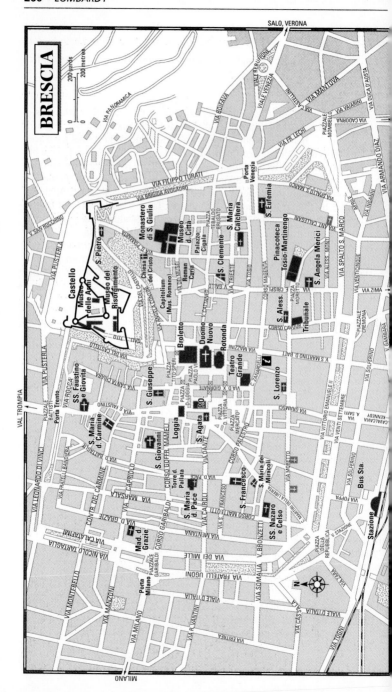

more brutal political murders in modern Italian history when a bomb exploded; eight people lost their lives and over a hundred were injured. The memorial is by Carlo Scarpa.

The new and old cathedrals

Beneath the **Torre dell'Orologio** (c 1547) a passageway leads to Piazza Paolo VI (right; formerly Piazza del Duomo), with a delightful row of buildings lining its east side. The local inhabitants gravitate here in summer when it is the coolest place in the town; for the rest of the year it remains comparatively deserted.

The **Duomo Nuovo** (New Cathedral), begun in 1604 by the local architect Giovanni Battista Lantana on the site of the old 'summer cathedral' of San Pietro de Dom, was completed only in 1914. The cupola, built in 1825, is 82m high. The bust of Cardinal Querini over the main entrance is by Antonio Calegari. The elaborate white marble interior contains a wooden 15C crucifix, and the fine tomb (1504) of the bishop Saint Apollonius with beautiful carving attributed to Maffeo Olivieri. The Mannerist Zorzi Chapel has an altarpiece by Palma il Giovane, and above a monument to Pope Paul VI are four panels by Gerolamo Romanino.

The Romanesque *****Rotonda** or **Duomo Vecchio** (Old Cathedral) is sometimes closed in winter; ask at the duomo nuovo to be let in. This is an extremely interesting circular building of the 11C or early 12C with a central rotunda supported on eight pillars (the transepts and choir, at the east end, were added in the 15C). The church was built above a 6C basilica of Santa Maria Maggiore, remains of which have survived here and there.

Inside, in front of the entrance, is the red-marble *sarcophagus of Bishop Berardo Maggi (d. 1308) by a Lombard sculptor. In the ambulatory (right) is a chapel with a fine marble altar and an altarpiece of the *Guardian Angel* by Bernardino Gandino. Beside it (above) is the wall monument of Bishop Balduino Lambertini by Bonino da Campione. Two stairways lead down to the Romanesque crypt of San Filastrio, which preserves columns of various periods (Roman–11C) and traces of frescoes. Stairs lead up from the crypt to the east end.

In the south transept is an elaborate painting by Francesco Maffei, the *Translation of the Patron Saints from the Castle to the Cathedral*. Above the altar opposite is a curious 15C fresco of the *Flagellation*. Glass panels in the pavement show remains of the presbytery of the earlier church and walls and mosaic pavement thought to belong to Roman baths of the republican era, excavated in 1975. The vault of the ancient presbytery of Santa Maria Maggiore preserves some fresco fragments including, on the entrance arch, a tondo with the Virgin between angels and the sun and the moon. The organ, in a 16C case, was built by Giangiacomo Antegnati in 1536 (restored by Serassi in 1826).

In the presbytery are two paintings by Moretto, and over the high altar is an *****Assumption**, also by him. Three more works by Moretto decorate the north transept. The contents of the treasury here are displayed only on the last Friday in March and on 14 September. They include a Byzantine cross-reliquary (with a base by Bernardino delle Croci, 1487) and the *Croce del Campo*, a cruxifix dating from the 12C. Protected by glass in the pavement is a mosaic fragment of the apse of the 8C Basilica di San Filastrio, burned down in 1097 with the exception of the crypt. You can see other fragments of the mosaic pavement beneath the floor on the west side of the rotunda. In the ambulatory of the rotunda is the tomb of Bishop De Dominicis (d. 1478). The ancient stairs which led up to the campanile (destroyed in 1708) survive.

Around the cathedral square

At Via Mazzini 3, behind the new cathedral, is the **Biblioteca Queriniana**, founded by Cardinal Querini in 1750. Among its treasures are a 6C evangelistary with silver letters on purple vellum, and a *Concordance of the Gospels* by Eusebius (11C).

On the left of the duomo nuovo is the **Broletto**, a fine Lombard town hall of 1187–1230, now serving as the prefecture. The exterior preserves its original appearance; in the courtyard one loggia is a Baroque addition. Frescoes attributed to Gentile da Fabriano were found in the Cappella Ducale here in 1986. Beyond the sturdy, battlemented **Torre del Popolo** (11C), the north part of the Broletto incorporates the little church of **Sant'Agostino**, the west front of which has early 15C terracotta ornamentation with two lion gargoyles.

At the top of Vicolo Sant'Agostino is the little secluded Piazza Tito Speri, with a public garden. Steps (signposted) lead steeply uphill from here in 15 minutes to the castle hill (described below, from Via Piamarta). Via dei Musei leads east from the piazza to the imposing *Capitolium, a Roman temple erected by Vespasian (AD 73) which stands on a high stylobate approached by steps, 15 of which are original, and has a hexastyle pronaos of Corinthian columns with, behind, a colonnade of three columns on each side. The three cellae were probably dedicated to the Capitoline Trinity (Jupiter, Juno and Minerva). The temple was excavated in 1823–26 and reconstructed in brick in 1939–50. Beneath it is a republican sanctuary (open only by special permission), dating from after 89 BC, with mosaics of small uncoloured tesserae.

The temple stood at the north end of the **Roman forum**, of which remains of porticoes can be seen in the piazza, beside a stretch of the paved *decumanus maximus*. On the right of the temple are the neglected remains of a Roman **amphitheatre**.

The **Museo Romano** (closed at the time of writing), founded in 1826, is arranged in the cellae of the temple and in a building behind it. In the cellae are inscriptions and mosaics. Stairs lead up to room 1, with a Greek amphora (c 510 BC), Gaulish silver horse-trappings (3C BC), an Italic bronze helmet and a marble head of an athlete (5C BC). Room 2 has Roman terracottas and glass, and in room 3 are Lombard arms and bronzes. Room 4 displays the remarkable *Winged Victory*, a splendid bronze statue nearly 2m high, probably the chief figure of a chariot group from the roof of the Capitol. It appears to be a Venus of the Augustan age (of the Venus of Capua type) remodelled as a Victory under Vespasian. Also displayed here is a gilded bronze statuette of a captive (2C AD?) and six bronze heads, all from the same group, discovered at the same time as the statue in 1826.

Santa Giulia

Further on, on the corner of Via dei Musei and Via Piamarta, is the monastery of **Santa Giulia**, a huge group of buildings with three Renaissance cloisters and several churches. Formerly called San Salvatore, the monastery was founded by the Lombard king Desiderius in 753 on the site of a Roman edifice. Ermengarde, the daughter of Lothair I, and many other royal and noble ladies were sisters in the original Benedictine nunnery, which survived here until it was suppressed in 1798. Part of the complex houses the **Museo della Città** (open Tues–Sun 10.00–18.00), with displays covering all periods of the city's history; special exhibitions are held frequently in the church of Santa Giulia, in rooms near the entrance to the monastery, and in the lower part of Santa Maria in Solario.

Guided tours of the monastery are given every half-hour. The first area visited is a **Roman house** (seen from a walkway), with remains of rooms round a peristyle with black-and-white mosaic floors and traces of wall paintings. Beyond is the atrium of the church of **San Salvatore**, where Lombard sculptural fragments (8C) are displayed. A walkway continues (above excavations of various periods from the Roman era to the 9C) to the church proper, founded c 753. Here you can see 13 Roman columns in the nave, all with beautiful capitals (only some of them Roman; the others date from the 8C); chapels frescoed in the 15C; and traces of Carolingian frescoes, above the nave arches. The southwest chapel has frescoes by Gerolamo Romanino. Below is the crypt, dating from 760–63 (enlarged in the 12C), with 42 columns of varying origins and capitals by the school of Antelami.

The square undercroft below Santa Maria in Solario, with a cippus for a central column, is used for exhibitions. The building beyond is to exhibit the Renaissance collections. The upper church of **Santa Maria in Solario**, built in the 12C, is covered with early-16C frescoes by Floriano Ferramola and his workshop. Three showcases here contain the rich treasury of San Salvatore. The so-called *Cross of Desiderius* (late 8C–early 9C) is made of wood overlaid with silver gilt and set with over 200 gems (dating from the Roman period to the 9C). It incorporates cameos, miniatures (9C–15C), a 16C crucifix and, on the lower arm, a remarkable triple portrait painted on gilded glass in the 4C. Another case has early *ivories, including the Querini diptych (5C), with Paris and Helen (?) on each leaf; the consular diptych of Manlius Boethius (5C), and a leaf of the diptych of the Lampadii, with circus scenes (late 5C). The last case displays an exquisite *ivory coffer with scriptural scenes in relief dating from the 4C.

The former church of **Santa Giulia** (1599), which has handsome 16C frescoes by Floriano Ferramola, is only open for exhibitions. Other items in the collection which are not at present on display include Lombard gold jewellery; 13C–14C ivories; Renaissance medals; Murano glass; Limoges enamels; majolica; and works by Maffeo Olivieri, Alessandro Vittoria, Antonio Canova, Francesco Hayez, Telemaco Signorini and Silvestro Lega.

The castle

Via Piamarta, a deserted old cobbled street between high walls, ascends towards the castle: on the left is the Chiesa del Cristo, with 15C terracotta decoration. Paths lead through pleasant public gardens on the side of the hill up to the main gateway into the **castle**, a huge edifice on the Cydnean hill (mentioned by Catullus, and now pierced by a road-tunnel), which was rebuilt by the Visconti in the 14C. Its extensive walls now enclose gardens, various museums and an observatory. At the highest point of the hill is the **Museo delle Armi 'Luigi Marzoli'** (open Tues–Sun, Jun–Sep 10.00–17.00, Oct–May 09.30–13.00, 14.30–17.00). Beyond a drawbridge, a path leads up through a fort to the cylindrical Torre della Mirabella on a lawn with wide views. The museum was opened in 1988 in a fine

14C building with traces of painted decoration inside, and the collection of 15C–18C arms and armour is excellently displayed on two floors. Many of the arms and firearms were made in Brescia, which was renowned for its weapons production. In one room there are remains of the steps of a Roman temple.

Downhill to the right is the **Museo del Risorgimento** (open Tues–Sun, Jun–Sep 10.00–17.00, Oct–May 09.30–13.00, 14.30–17.00), founded in 1887 and arranged on two floors of a large 16C grain store. The interesting collection illustrates Italian history from the last years of the 18C up to Unification, with prints, arms, uniforms, mementoes, etc.

The best way of reaching the centre of the town from the castle hill is by descending the steps below the public gardens to Piazza Speri, just to the north of the duomo.

From the Capitolium (see above), Via Gallo leads south past the site (Piazza Labus 3) of the Roman curia, fragments of which can be seen below ground level and on the façade of the house. Further on, Vicolo San Clemente (left) leads to the church of **San Clemente**, containing paintings by Romanino, Moretto (who is buried here) and Callisto Piazza.

The Pinacoteca Tosio-Martinengo

Via Crispi leads across Corso Magenta to Piazza Moretto. On the left is the Pinacoteca Tosio-Martinengo (open Tues–Sun, Jun–Sep 10.00–17.00, Oct–May 09.30–13.00, 14.30–17.00), a large collection of paintings and frescoes in which the local schools are well represented. It was opened to the public in 1908 to display the two collections of Paolo Tosio (1844) and Francesco Leopardo Martinengo (1884), and more works have since been added.

Stairs lead up to the first floor. In room **1** are portraits of Tosio and Martinengo, the two principal benefactors of the museum. Room **2** contains the treasures of the Tosio collection: portraits by the circle of François Clouet, and Romanino; Moretto, *Salome*; Raphael, *Angel and Risen Christ* (two fragments); a copy of a Raphael *Madonna* by an early 16C painter; and works by Andrea Appiani and Cavalier di Arpino. Rooms **3** and **4** contain 13C–14C frescoes and a charming painting of *St George and the Dragon* by a Lombard master (c 1460–70). Rooms **5**, **6** and **7**: Vincenzo Foppa, Vincenzo Civerchio and Moretto; early 16C works by Marco Palmezzano and Floriano Ferramola; *Christ and the Adulterer* by a painter close to Titian.

Room **9** contains a beautiful painting of the *Nativity* by Lorenzo Lotto and another painting of the same subject by Savoldo. Room **10** displays 16C portraits by Giovanni Battista Moroni, Sofonisba Anguissola, Moretto and Savoldo (*Boy with a Flute*). Room **11** contains large Renaissance paintings and frescoes by Moretto, Romanino and others, and a lectern with intarsia by Raffaello da Marone (1520). Room **12**: detached *frescoes by Moretto from Palazzo Ugoni (c 1525). Room **13** has late-16C works by Giulio and Antonio Campi, and room **14** works by Luca Mombello. Room **15** has works by 17C artists including Lo Spadarino, and room **16** paintings by Giacomo Ceruti and Antonio Cifrondi. Room **17** has preserved its original decoration from the late 18C and beginning of the 19C. Rooms **18–23** contain 17C and 18C paintings. Room **24**, the 'galleria', has works by Sassoferrato, Luca Giordano and Francesco Albani. Room 25 has 17C works.

Outstanding in the fine collection of drawings (shown only with special permission) is a *Deposition* by Giovanni Bellini. On the ground floor is an exhibition of 15C illuminated manuscripts from San Francesco and the duomo (also shown only with special permission), and the Print Room, with works by Jacopo Filippo d'Argento and others.

Elsewhere around town

Sant'Angela Merici (formerly Sant'Afra), just to the south of the Pinacoteca, has a *Transfiguration* by Jacopo Tintoretto in the apse and works by Francesco Bassano and Giulio Cesare Procaccini, among others.

From the Pinacoteca Via Moretto leads back towards the centre of the town, passing (right) the church of **Sant'Alessandro**, with a pleasant fountain outside. It contains a beautiful painting of the *Annunciation* by Jacopo Bellini, and works by Vincenzo Civerchio and Lattanzio Gambara.

On the left is the 17C Palazzo Martinengo-Colleoni. Via San Martino della Battaglia leads right to Corso Zanardelli (described above), and Corso Palestro continues west to the church of **San Francesco**, built in 1254–65, with a handsome façade. Inside, the south aisle contains an altarpiece by Moretto; a Giottesque fresco of the *Entombment* (with a scene of monks above, dating from the mid-14C); and 14C frescoes including a charming frieze of angels. The high altarpiece is by Romanino, in a frame of rich workmanship by Stefano Lamberti (1502). In the north aisle are an elaborately decorated chapel (15C–18C), a 14C cross, and an altarpiece by Francesco Prato. The fine cloister dates from 1394.

Just to the south, in Corso Martiri, is Santa **Maria dei Miracoli**, rebuilt since the war but preserving intact an elaborately carved Renaissance façade of 1488–1560. It contains *St Nicholas of Bari with his Pupils*, taken to be a copy of a work by Moretto (now in the Pinacoteca). The paintings (1590–94) in the presbytery are by the local artists Tommaso Bona, Pietro Bagnadore, Grazio Cossali and Pietro Marone.

In Via Fratelli Bronzetti, on the right, is the 16C side doorway of the church of **Santi Nazaro e Celso** (if closed, ask for admission at Santa Maria dei Miracoli), an 18C building with the *Averoldi polyptych—a superb early work by Titian (1522)—and paintings by Moretto (including the *Crowning of the Virgin*), Giovanni Battista Pittoni and Antonio Zanchi, and monuments by Maffeo Olivieri.

From San Francesco, Via della Pace leads north to the massive 13C Torre della Pallata. Nearby is **San Giovanni Evangelista**, which contains handsome paintings (1521) by Moretto and Romanino in the Corpus Domini chapel, an altarpiece of the *Madonna and Saints* by Moretto, and works by Bernardino Zenale and Francesco Francia (*Holy Trinity*).

Further north **Santa Maria del Carmine**, a 15C building with a fine façade and portal, contains paintings by Vincenzo Foppa. At the west end of Via Capriolo is the *Madonna delle Grazie* by Lodovico Barcella (1522). The delightful Rococo *interior (1617) has an exuberance of stucco reliefs and frescoes. A 16C courtyard gives access to a venerated sanctuary, rebuilt in the 19C and covered with charming ex-votos.

From Via Turati the Strada Panoramica leads up to **Monte Maddalena** (875m), a noted viewpoint.

Franciacorta

The fertile foothills south of the Lago d'Iseo, with numerous vineyards, are known as the **Franciacorta**, a pretty region with a number of villas built by the noble families of Brescia in the 18C. It has long been known for its excellent red and white wines (and since the 1960s for the *spumante Franciacorta*, produced with *Chardonnay*, *Pinot Bianco* and *Pinot Nero* grapes). Numerous cellars in the area welcome visitors, and at the Villa Evelina at Capriolo there is a private agricultural museum.

At **Rodengo** is the Abbazia di San Nicola, a Cluniac foundation, inhabited by Olivetan monks since 1446. It contains three cloisters, frescoes by Romanino and Lattanzio Gambara, a painting by Moretto, and fine intarsia stalls by Cristoforo Rocchi (1480). Outside **Passirano** is an interesting castle, and at **Provaglio d'Iseo** the Romanesque church of San Pietro in Lamosa.

Lago d'Iseo

The pretty Lago d'Iseo, an expansion of the Oglio River, surrounded by mountains, has a perimeter of 60km and an average width of 2.4km; its maximum depth is 251m. It was the *Lacus Sebinus* of the Romans. In the centre is the island of Monte Isola, the largest island of any European lake. Lovere, Iseo and Pisogne are holiday resorts on its banks, which have suffered less from modern development than those of the more famous lakes. It is much visited for sailing.

Iseo is a pleasant resort on the south bank of the lake. The church tower was built by Count Giacomo Oldofredi (1325), whose tomb is built into the façade alongside. Inside is a painting of *St Michael* by Francesco Hayez. On the southern edge of the lake is a marshy area known as the Torbiere d'Iseo, a large peat bog surrounded by reeds, of great interest to naturalists. Waterlilies grow here in abundance, and it is a sanctuary for aquatic birds. Traces of Bronze Age pile-dwellings were found here.

On the east bank are **Sulzano**, a sailing centre and port for Monte Isola, and **Sale Marasino**, another port for the island, with a conspicuous church by Giovanni Battista Caniana (1737–54), and the 16C Villa Martinengo.

The wooded island of **Monte Isola**, 3.2km long, where all the boats call, is also well served by ferries from the eastern shore (see above). It is closed to private cars (although there is a bus service from the fishing village of Peschiera Maraglio), and it can be visited on foot in c 3 hours. The hill in the centre is covered with chestnut woods and broom. There is a large tourist development on the west side of the island, north of Menzino.

Marone is a large village beneath Monte Guglielmo (1949m), the highest point of the mountain range between the lake and the Valle Trompia. A road winds up to a zone in chestnut woods, of geological interest for its erosion pyramids surmounted by granite boulders, caused by the erosion of the moraine deposits. At the northeast end of the lake is the little town of **Pisogne**, where the church of Santa Maria della Neve contains splendid *frescoes of the Passion of Christ* by Romanino (1532–34).

On the Bergamo side of the lake is **Lovere**, the principal tourist resort on its shores. To the north of the town is the church of Santa Maria in Valvendra

(1473–83), which contains organ-shutters decorated outside by Ferramola and inside by Moretto (1518). To the south, on the shore of the lake, is the **Galleria dell'Accademia Tadini** (open May–Oct, daily 15.00–18.00; Sun and holidays 10.00–12.00, 15.00–18.00), founded in this Neo-classical building in 1828 by Luigi Tadini. It contains a collection of paintings including works by Jacopo Bellini, Magnasco and Vincenzo Civerchio, as well as porcelain, arms and bronzes. In the garden, the cenotaph of Faustino Tadini (d. 1799) is by Antonio Canova. There is a path above the town to the Altipiano di Lovere (990m), with some attractive country villas, and to Bossico, among meadows and pine woods.

A road follows the west side of the lake through Riva di Solto, whose quarries provided the black marble for the columns of the basilica of San Marco in Venice, with two little bays displaying unusual rock strata. On the western side of the lake, beneath the barren slopes of Monte Brenzone (1333m), is **Sarnico**, at the outflow of the Oglio, well known to motor-boat racing enthusiasts. It has a number of Art Nouveau villas built at the beginning of the century by Giuseppe Sommaruga.

The Val Camonica

To the north of Pisogne and the Lago d'Iseo is the lovely, fertile **Val Camonica**, the upper course of the Oglio. It is famous for the remarkable prehistoric rock carvings of the Camuni, which you can see throughout the valley, especially in the two parks at Capo di Ponte and Darfo-Boario Terme, and at Cimbergo, Ossimo and Sellero. The chestnut woods were once an important source of wealth, as both nuts and timber were exported. The inhabitants of the valley (and especially of Boario) are excellent woodcarvers. Ironworks were established here in the Middle Ages, and the valley now has generating stations for hydroelectric power. The cheeses and salt meats locally produced are of excellent quality. The extreme upper end, below the Tonale Pass, was the scene of many dramatic battles in the First World War.

Regardless of whether you are travelling by road or rail, the first village of importance in the valley is **Darfo**, where the parish church has an *Entombment* attributed to Palma Giovane. At **Montecchio** the little church of the Oratorio contains 15C frescoes. **Boario Terme** is the main town in the valley and an important mineral spa. It is noted for its cabinetmakers. Over 10,000 rock carvings may be seen here in the **Parco delle Luine** (open Tues–Sun 09.00–12.00, 14.00–18.00). Most of them date from 2200–1800 BC, but some are even earlier—the oldest so far found in the valley. You can see the rock known as Corni Freschi, with its rock carvings, on a country road just outside the town near the *superstrada* for Edolo.

From Boario a road ascends the **Val di Scalve** past Gorzone, dominated by a castle of the Federici first built in the 12C (privately owned), through Angolo Terme, a small spa with a very fine view of the triple-peaked Pizzo della Presolana. Further on the road enters the gorge of the Dezzo, a narrow chasm with overhanging cliffs. Unfortunately, the torrent and its falls have almost been dried up by hydroelectric works.

Just north of Boario is **Erbanno**, unusual for its plan consisting of parallel straight streets along the hillside and a piazza on two levels. The main road continues to **Esine**, with the church of Santa Maria Assunta containing frescoes by Giovan Pietro da Cemmo (1491–93). **Cividate Camuno** is the site of *Civitas Camunnorum*, the ancient Roman capital of the valley. It preserves a few ancient remains and a much more conspicuous medieval tower. Roman finds are displayed in an archaeological museum.

A winding road ascends west via **Ossimo** (where prehistoric statue-stele dating from 3200–2000 BC have been found) to **Borno**, a resort among pine woods in the Trobiolo valley, beneath the Corna di San Fermo (2326m). The Santuario dell'Annunciata, with a fine view of the valley, has two 15C cloisters.

Breno, an important town in the valley, is dominated by the ruins of its medieval castle (9C and later). The parish church has a granite campanile and frescoes by Giovan Pietro da Cemmo and Girolamo Romanino.

A mountain road leads east towards the Lago d'Idro via **Bienno**, a medieval village with 17C and 18C palaces, one of the more interesting places in the valley. Several old forges are still operating here, worked by channelled water. The church of Santa Maria degli Orti has frescoes by Girolamo Romanino.

Above Breno the dolomitic peaks of the Concarena (2549m) rise on the left and the Pizzo Badile (2435m) on the right. The villages are mostly high up on the slopes of the foothills on either side, and include **Cerveno** with a remarkable 18C *Via Crucis* that has nearly 200 life-size statues.

    Capo di Ponte came to prominence with the discovery in the Permian sandstone of tens of thousands of rock engravings dating from Neolithic to Roman times, a span of some 8000 years. These are the feature of the *Parco Nazionale delle Incisioni Rupestri di Naquane* (open Tues–Sun 09.00–17.00 or 19.00), one of the more important prehistoric sites in the world. It can be visited on foot in c 2hrs. So far some 180,000 engravings made by the Camuni, a remarkable Alpine civilisation, depicting hunting scenes, everyday life, religious symbols, etc., have been catalogued here on the wooded hill of Naquane. The largest rock has 900 figures carved in the Iron Age. Other prehistoric carvings have been found in the localities of Ceto, Cimbergo and Paspardo, on a secondary road to the south, and above Sellero to the north. There is a research centre (the Centro Camuno di Studi Preistorici) at Capo di Ponte.

    Just outside Capo di Ponte, in woods to the north, is **San Salvatore**, a Lombard church of the early 12C. Across the river in Cemmo is the church of *San Siro*, dating from the 11C, probably on the site of a Lombard church. The road continues to **Pescarzo**, a pretty little village with interesting peasant houses.

    Cedegolo, with a church entirely frescoed by Antonio Cappello (17C), stands at the foot of the lovely Val Saviore, below Monte Adamello (3555m). **Edolo**, surrounded by beautiful scenery, is the main place in the upper Valle Camonica, and the terminus of the railway. It stands on the road from Switzerland and Tirano in the Valtellina via the Aprica pass to Tonale and the Tyrol. The Oglio is on the edge of two large protected areas, the Parco Nazionale dello Stelvio and the Parco dell'Adamello. **Ponte di Legno** (1260m) is the main resort of the region in a wide-open mountain basin, beneath the Adamello and Presanella mountains. To the north a road, one of the highest in Europe, ascends the Val di Pezzo and crosses the Passo Gavia (2652m) to Bormio. The **Tonale Pass** (1884m), in the Presanella foothills, is on the former Austro-Italian frontier, separating Lombardy from the Trentino. There are ski slopes on Presena and Monte Tonale.

Other sights around Brescia

The **Lago d'Idro**, the Roman *Lacus Eridius*, 9.5km long and 2km wide, is surrounded by steep, rugged mountains. Its waters are utilised for hydroelectric power, and it is renowned for its trout. It is frequented by sailors and windsurfers. On the west bank are **Anfo** with an old castle, founded by the Venetians in 1486 but largely rebuilt, and **Sant'Antonio**, where the church has a 15C fresco cycle. **Bagolino** is a mountain village in a good position on the Caffaro (visited by skiers, and famous for its carnival). **Ponte Caffaro**, beyond the head of the lake, marks the old international frontier.

To the south of Brescia is **Montirone**, where the beautiful Palazzo Lechi (1738–46), by Antonio Turbino, is very well preserved and has magnificent *stables of c 1754. It contains paintings by Carlo Carloni (his best work), and was visited by Mozart in 1773 and Napoleon in 1805. At **Verolanuova** the church contains two large paintings by Giovanni Battista Tiepolo, in excellent condition. **Gottolengo** was the main residence, in 1746–56, of Lady Mary Wortley Montagu, who often visited the Lago d'Iseo.

The road from Brescia to Crema passes the suburban church of **Chiesanuova**, with a charming *Nativity* by Foppa, and crosses the plain to **Orzinuovi**, with imposing remains of the Venetian ramparts designed by Michele Sanmicheli.

On the road to Milan is **Chiari**, with a small Pinacoteca founded in 1854 by Pietro Repossi, and a library founded by Antonio Morcelli in 1817.

Cremona and its province

Cremona, a busy, cheerful city (population 72,000), has a world-wide reputation for its stringed instrument makers and restorers. It was the home in the 16C–18C of the most famous violin-makers of all time, including Andrea and Nicolò Amati, Giuseppe Guarneri and Antonio Stradivari (some of whose more precious instruments are preserved here). Cremona's many ancient brick buildings are survivals of the age of the Lombard city-states, and it has a beautiful Romanesque cathedral. Its churches are particularly noteworthy for their 16C frescoes, many of them by the Campi brothers, a gifted Cremonese family of painters, some of whose best work you can see in San Sigismondo. Cremona is an important agricultural market for southern Lombardy.

The small province of Cremona is bordered to the south by the Adda and Po rivers, on the north by the Oglio, and at Crema it is crossed by the Serio. The abundance of water and the rich alluvial soil make it ideal for farming, and in fact the area's agricultural vocation can be seen and felt everwhere. The countryside is studded with huge cascinali, rural building complexes in which hay-barns, stables, granaries and peasant labourers' quarters rise side by side; and most of the towns and villages still bear the imprint of the country market centre, with lovely central squares often surrounded by arcaded walks.

Practical information

Getting there
By air
The airports nearest Cremona are at Brescia (Montichiari), Bergamo (Orio di Serio) and Milan (Malpensa, Linate). All offer domestic and international flights; Malpensa also has inter-continental flights.

By road
To Cremona from Milan, A1 to Piacenza, then A21 north; or 415. The latter is slower, but allows you to visit Crema on the way. From Verona and points west, A4 to Brescia, then A21 south. From Parma and points south, A1, A21dir and A21.

By rail
From Milan, 86km in c 1hr 15mins. The line follows the Via Emilia via Lodi to Casalpusterlengo, then branches at Codogno, where a change is sometimes necessary. Another line via Treviglio to Cremona (99km) takes longer but serves Crema in 1hr 15min–2hr; Crema to Cremona in 1hr more. Branch lines serve Cremona from Piacenza (30min), Fidenza (30min), Bergamo (1hr 15min) and Brescia (30–40min).

Getting around
Car parking in Cremona, in Via Villa Glori, Via Dante (by the bus station), ex Foro Boario–Piazzale Libertà. **Bus no. 1** from the station to the centre of the town. Buses from Via Dante next to the railway station for places in the province. Brescia, Bergamo and Milan are best reached by train.

Information offices
CREMONA Piazza del Comune 5, ☎ 0372 21722, freephone 800 655511. *Informagiovani*, Via Palestro 11a, ☎ 0372 407950

Where to stay
CREMA *Palace*, Via Cresmiero 10, ☎ 0373 81487, fax 0373 86876; central, quiet and comfortable; closed Aug; moderate.
CREMONA *Continental*, Piazza della Libertà 26, ☎ 0372 434141, fax 0372 454873; large (57 rooms), comfortable and fairly central; moderate.

Eating out
Here in the Lombard heartland the farmers and their friends know a thing or two about fine food, and to the vigilant eye the menus say nearly as much about local history and tradition as the museums. Restaurants, osterie and trattorie abound, but some patience and plenty of petrol may be needed to find the best.
CREMONA *Alba*, Via Persico 40, ☎ 0372 433700, a traditional trattoria, 15mins walk from the town centre; closed Sun, Mon and Aug; inexpensive.
Ceresole, Via Ceresole 4, ☎ 0372 23322; restaurant offering brilliant interpretations of traditional recipes; closed Sun evening, Mon, Jan and Aug; moderate.
La Sosta, Via Sicardo 9, ☎ 0372 456656; modern décor and old-fashioned cuisine in a 15C building near the Palazzo del Comune; closed Mon and Aug; moderate.

Mellini, Via Bossolati 105, ☎ 0372 30535; trattoria known for its fresh, home-made pasta and fine wines; closed Sun evening, Mon and Jul; moderate.
Porta Mosa, Via Santa Maria in Betlem 11; ☎ 0372 411803; simple but delicious trattoria where wine is served in the traditional bowls called *pauline*; closed Sun, Aug–Sep and Dec–Jan.

Cafés

Cremona is absolutely brimming with cafés and pastry shops. The adventure begins as soon as you arrive: just outside the station, to the right, is *Dondeo*, one of the favourite cafés of the Cremonese.
The author's favourite is opposite the north flank of the cathedral: at *Pasticceria Duomo* (Via Bocaccino 6) you can sip cappuccino, sample delightful cakes or savoury pastries and admire the finest brickwork in Lombardy, all at once.
Other handsome places are *Lanfranchi*, Via Solferino 30, and *Ebli*, Via Cavallotti 5.
You can find good sandwiches and light lunches in town at *Lo Snack Italia '68*, Via Anguissola 4; *Rio Bar*, Piazza Pace 2; *Paninoteca No. 1*, Via Cavallotti 21. And there are at least two good *salumerie* in Cremona: *Saronni*, Corso Mazzini 38, which makes an explosive garlic salame; and *Barbieri*, on route 10 just beyond the bridge over the Po, with good cold meats and cheeses.

Beyond Cremona

CALVISANO *Gambero*, Via Roma 11, ☎ 030 968009; restaurant featuring outstanding regional cuisine; closed Wed, Jan and Aug; moderate.
CASALETTO CEREDANO (10km from Crema) *Antica Locanda del Ponte*, Via al Porto 19, at Ca' de Vagni; ☎ 0373 262474; simple trattoria serving traditional local dishes; closed Tues evening, Wed and Aug; moderate.
CASALBUTTANO *La Granda*, Via Jacini

51, ☎. 0374 362406; osteria in a traditional *cascinotta* with central courtyard; closed Wed, Jan and Aug; inexpensive.
CASTELLEONE *Tre Rose*, Via Maltraversa 1, ☎ 0374 57021; traditional trattoria in a restored farmhouse; closed Wed and midday Sat; moderate.
CICOGNOLO (14km east of Cremona) *Osteria de l'Umbreleèr*, Via Mazzini 13, ☎ 0372 830509; osteria serving local delicacies and fine wines; closed Tues evening and Wed, Aug and Feb.
CORTE DE' CORTESI *Il Gabbiano*, Piazza Vittorio Veneto 10, ☎ 0372 95108; trattoria, likewise specialising in local delicacies and great wines; closed Thur and Jul; inexpensive.
CREMA Fine wines and good snacks at *Circolo Enoteca*, Piazza Trento e Trieste 14 (closed Sun). *Gobbato*, Via Podgora 2, ☎ 0373 80891, is a good blue-collar trattoria much loved by railway workers; closed Mon (except Jul and Aug); inexpensive.
MOSCAZZANO (near 415 between Cremona and Crema) *Hosteria San Carlo*, at Colombare, ☎ 0373 66190; trattoria in an old farmhouse, serving hearty peasant dishes; closed Mon evening, Tues, Jan and Aug; moderate.
PRALBOINO *Leon d'Oro*, Via Gambara 6, ☎ 030 954156; restaurant known for its *lumacche* (snails) and other regional delicacies; closed Sun evening, Mon, Jan and Aug; expensive.
RIPALTA CREMASCA (8km southwest of Crema) *Via Vai*, Via Libertà 18, ☎ 0373 268232; country trattoria combining excellent local cuisine with great wines; closed Tues–Wed; moderate.
SCANDOLARA RIPA D'OGLIO (15km northwest of Cremona) *Al Caminetto*, Via Umberto I 26, ☎ 0372 89589; restaurant serving outstanding seasonal dishes; closed Mon–Tues, Jan and Aug; moderate.
TORRE DE' PICENARDI (20km east of Cremona on 10) *Italia*, Via Garibaldi 1, ☎ 0375 94108; on the Mantua

road, delicious creative interpretations of traditional regional dishes; closed Sun evening, Mon, Jan, Jul or Aug; inexpensive.

TRESCORE CREMASCO (18km north-west of Cremona) *Bistek*, Viale De Gasperi 31, tel. 0373 273046; good traditional restaurant, upstairs from an unimpressive birreria on the Crema–Treviglio road; closed Tues evening, Wed, Jul–Aug and Jan; moderate.

Il Fulmine, Via Carioni 12, ☎ 0373 273103; good innovative renditions of traditional dishes; closed Sun evening, Mon, Jan and Aug; moderate.

VHO DI PIADENA (31km east of Cremona on 10) *Trattoria dell'Alba*, Via del Popolo 31; trattoria on the road to Mantua serving great local cuisine; closed Sat, Mon evening and Aug; inexpensive.

Entertainment

Theatre and concerts in Cremona (*Teatro Ponchielli*, Corso Vittorio Emanuele 52; *Teatro Monteverdi*, Via Vecchio Passeggio 1; *Filo*, Piazza Filodrammatici 1), Casalbuttano (*Teatro Bellini*, Via Jacini), Casalmaggiore (*Teatro Comunale*, Via Cairoli), Romanengo (*Teatro Galilei*, Via Guaiarini) and Soresina (*Teatro Sociale*, Via Verdi 23). Live-music bars and discos in Cremona, Bagnolo Cremasco, Casaletto di Sopra, Castelleone, Calvatone, Crema, Gussola, Offanengo, Ostiano, Pianengo, San Giovanni in Croce, San Marino and Soncino.

Shopping

The Cremona area is known for its **flea markets** and **antiques** fairs: in Cremona, the *Mercatino d'Antiquariato*, Piazza Cavour, third Sun of the month except Jul–Aug; Piadena, *Mercatino delle Pulci*, Piazza Garibaldi, second Sat of the month except Aug; Castelleone,

Mostra-Mercato dell'Antiquariato e dell'Artigianato, in the historic centre, second Sun of the month except Aug; Pandino, *Cose d'Altri Tempi*, Castello Visconteo, first Sun of the month except Jan, Jul–Aug.

Cremona's most distinctive products are, of course, **stringed instruments**; but the city is known also for its *mostarda*, *torrone*, salame and aged cheeses.

Special events

Progetto Jazz, jazz concert season in Cremona, Casalbuttano, Casalmaggiore, Soresina and Romanengo, Feb–May.

Antiche Accademie Musicali, chamber-music series in Cremona, Mar.

Spazionovecento, concert series, Cremona, Apr.

Ponchielli Woodwind Competition, Cremona, May.

Organi Storici Cremonesi, organ concerts at Casalmaggiore, Castelverde, Annicco, Pizzighettone, May.

Omaggio a Cremona, stringed-instrument festival, Cremona, spring.

Festival di Cremona, classical music for strings, Cremona, May–Jun.

Selezione Internazionale 'Mario Basiola', opera-singing competition, Crema, Jun.

Appuntamento con gli Organi Antichi, organ concerts in the churches of Cremona, Jun.

Il Canto delle Pietre, sacred music concert series, Cremona and province, Jun–Oct.

La Danza, dance festival, Cremona, Jul.

Estate in Festa, open-air concert series, Cremona, Jul–Sep.

Burattini d'Estate, puppet-theatre festival, Cremona, Jul–Aug.

An Piasa dal Dom and *Cinema in Piazza*, open-air theatre and cinema series in Piazza Duomo, Crema, Jul–Aug.

Celtic Music Festival, Ostiano, Aug–Sep.

Festival degli Ottoni, brass-instrument festival and master classes, Vescovato, Sep.

Rassegna di Teatro Amatoriale, amateur theatre series, Soresina, Sep.

Premio Nazionale Tognazzi – Città di Cremona, cabaret competition, Cremona, Sep–Nov.

Rassegna Nazionale Pianistica Ghislandi, piano competition, Crema, Nov.

Organi Storici della Lombardia, organ-music series, Cremona and province, Nov–Dec.

Oh, Che Armonico Fracasso, opera music, Vescovato, Nov–Dec.

Food, music and pageantry accompany patron-saints' days in most towns.

Sports
Golf at Cremona (*Golf Club Cremona* and *Il Torrazzo*) and Crema (*Golf Crema*); **boating**, **bocce**, **swimming** and **tennis** in Cremona. *Kiss* **aquapark** for children, Ostiano.

CREMONA

Cremona has a lively, friendly atmosphere that combines a history of artistic distinction with a genuine love of life.

History

Founded by the Romans as a colony in 218 BC, Cremona became an important fortress and road junction on the Via Postumia. Its decline after a siege and sacking in AD 69 ended in destruction by the Lombards in 603. Cremona re-emerged as a free commune in 1098, at war with its neighbours, Milan, Brescia and Piacenza. In 1334 it was taken by Azzone Visconti of Milan, and from then on remained under Milanese domination. It enjoyed a century of patronage and prosperity after it was given in dowry to Bianca Maria Visconti on her marriage to Francesco Sforza in 1441.

The Campi family of painters were born here, and you can see many of their works in the town. Cremona is also celebrated for its terracotta sculpture work. Andrea Amati was the founder here in the 16C of a school of stringed-instrument makers that is still renowned. His grandson Nicolò Amati (1596–1684) was his most famous follower. Two later famous Cremonese families of instrument-makers were headed by Antonio Stradivari (Stradivarius, 1644–1737) and Giuseppe Guarneri (c 1660–1740), and his son Giuseppe Guarneri del Gesù (1698–1744). The composer Claudio Monteverdi (1567–1643) is another famous native.

The city centre

The beautifully paved *Piazza del Comune is the centre of the life of Cremona and has its most important buildings. The Romanesque ***Torrazzo** (open Apr–Nov, 10.30–12.00, 15.00–18.00) is one of the higher medieval towers in Europe (112m). It was completed in 1250–67 and crowned with a Gothic lantern in 1287–1300, probably by the local sculptor Francesco Pecorari. 502 steps lead up past a room with an astronomical clock, made in 1583 by the Divizioli, still with its original mechanism (it is wound by hand every day).

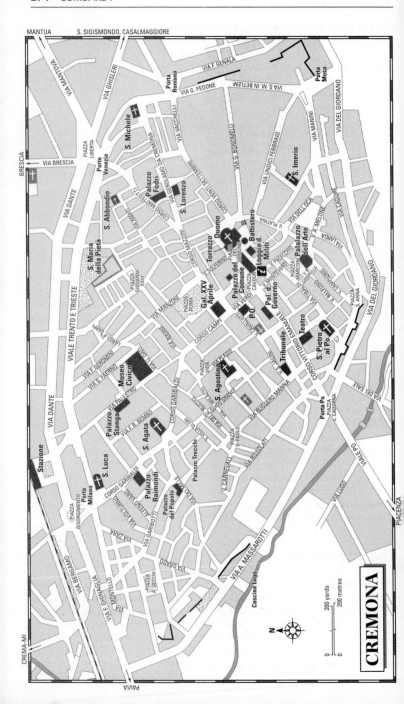

MANTUA
S. SIGISMONDO, CASALMAGGIORE

VIA MANTOVA
VIA GHISLERI
VIA F. GENALA
VIA S. M. IN BETLEM
Porta Mosa
Porta Romana
VIA G. PEDONE
Porta Romana
VIA MANINI
VIA DEL GIORDANO

S. Michele
PIAZZA LIBERTA
Porta Venezia
VIA GIROLAMO DA CREMONA
VIA VACCHELLI
VIA G. BONOMELLI
VIA UNDICI FEBBRAIO
S. Imerio

BRESCIA → VIA BRESCIA

VIA DANTE
VIA G. VERDI VIA XX SETTEMBRE
CORSO MATTEOTTI
Palazzo Fodri
S. Lorenzo
VIA DELLOCA
VIA PLATINA
VIA MELONE
VIALARGA
VIA CADORE

S. Abbondio
CORSO MAZZINI
Duomo
Battistero
Loggia d. Militi
Palazzo dell'Arte

S. Maria della Pietà
PIAZZA GIOVANNI XXIII
Torrazzo
Palazzo del Comune
Loggia d.
V. MONTEVERDI
V. PATECCHIO
PIAZZA S. ANNA

VIALE TRENTO E TRIESTE
VIA MANZONI
PIAZZA ROMA
VIA SOLFERINO
Gal. XXV Aprile
PIAZZA CAVOUR
Pal. d. Governo
PIAZZA MARCONI
VIA BELLISIO
VIA TIBALDI
VIA CAPORALO

VIA GEROMINI
VIA T. FAERNO
CORSO CAMPI
VIA VERDI
P.O.
VIA SALVATERINO
Tribunale
Teatro
S. Pietro al Po
VIA DEL SALE

Museo Civico
VIA PALESTRO
CORSO GARIBALDI
S. Agostino
PIAZZA VIDA
VIA GUIDO GRANDI
VIA RUGGERO MANNA
CORSO VITTORIO EMANUELE
Porta Po
PIAZZA C. CADORNA
PIACENZA

Palazzo Stanga
VIA F.F. BEMBO
S. Agata
VIA BRISTO
PIAZZA S. PAOLO
Palazzo Trecchi
VIA RISORGIMENTO

Stazione
PIAZZA RISORGIMENTO
Porta Milano
S. Luca
CORSO GARIBALDI
Palazzo Raimondi
VIA DEL VECCHIO
Palazzo del Popolo
VIA CARNEVALI

VIA F. GHINAGLIA
VIA BERGAMO
VIA ZARA
VIA LUBRIO
VIA VOLTURNO
VIA GARIBOTTI
PIAZZA LUBECCHI
VIA A. MASSARUTTI
Cascina Lugo
VIALE PO
VIA LUGO

CREMA-MI

PAVIA

N

200 yards
200 metres

CREMONA

A double loggia, known as the Bertazzola, stretches across the front of the cathedral. It was built in 1497–1525 and beneath its arcades are the sarcophagus of Folchino Schizzi (d. 1357), by Bonino da Campione, and that of Andrea Ala (1513), by Giovanni Gaspare Pedoni.

The Duomo

The *Duomo is a splendid Romanesque basilica of 1107, consecrated in 1190 and finished considerably later. It has a particularly fine exterior. The west front (1274–1606) has a rose window of 1274 and a tabernacle above the main door with three large statues of the **Madonna and Child** and the patron saints Imerio and Omobono. These unusual works, influenced by the French Gothic style, are now thought to be by Marco Romano (c 1310). The lions date from 1285, and the marble frieze of the **Months** from 1220–30. The later transepts, which altered the basilican plan of the church to a Latin cross, have splendid brick façades: the north transept dates from 1288, with a fine porch (the **Annunciation** is attributed to Wiligelmus, and **Christ and the Apostles** dates from the 12C), and the south transept from 1342. The beautiful apse faces the piazza behind.

Interior The interior is remarkable, especially for the *frescoes (1514–29; extremely difficult to see without strong light; being restored) on the walls of the nave and apse, by Boccaccino, Gian Francesco Bembo, Altobello Melone, Gerolamo Romanino, Pordenone and Bernardino Gatti. On the west wall is a *Deposition, beneath a **Crucifixion**, both by Pordenone. In the south aisle, the first altarpiece is by Pordenone, the second by Alessandro Arrighi (1650), and the third by Luca Cattapane. In the south transept (high up, looking back towards the nave) is a huge painting by Giulio Campi. The Sagrestia dei Canonici has a ceiling painted by Antonio Bibiena and an **Assumption** by Giulio Campi. The unusual funerary monument of Cardinal Sfondrati is by Giovanni Battista Cambi. Outside the 17C Cappella del Sacramento stairs lead down to the crypt, with the beautifully carved tomb of Sts Peter and Marcellius (1506). On a nave pillar by the crypt steps is a marble triptych of 1495, and (protected by glass) a high relief by Amadeo (1482), showing the *Charity of St Imerio.

The chapel of the **Madonna del Popolo** is beautifully decorated with stuccoes by Carlo Natali (1654) and paintings by Bernardino and Giulio Campi. In the north transept is an altarpiece by Giulio Campi, and a splendid silver *cross, nearly 2m high, with

The Duomo, Cremona

numerous tabernacles and statuettes. The work of Ambrogio Pozzi and Agostino Sacchi, it was completed in 1478 (the base was added in 1774). Also here are a *Deposition* by Antonio Campi, four marble reliefs by Giovanni Antonio Amadeo, and high up, looking back towards the nave, a large painting by Sante Legnani (1815). Twelve Brussels tapestries, which illustrate the story of Samson (1629, by Jas Raes), were not on view at the time of writing.

The octagonal ***baptistery**, a plain Lombard building dating from 1167 and partially faced with marble, has been closed for many years for restoration.

The **Loggia dei Militi** is a fine Gothic Lombard building of 1292 (with handsome three-light windows), restored as a war memorial. The ***Palazzo del Comune** (open Tues–Sat 08.30–18.30, Sun and holidays 10.00–18.00) was built in 1206–45 but has an older tower. It was enlarged in 1245 and altered in the 16C and 19C. On the first-floor landing is a 16C doorway designed by Francesco Dattaro. The grand rooms of the palace contain paintings by Francesco Boccaccino, Luca Cattapane and Il Genovesino, and a marble chimneypiece by Giovan Gaspare Pedoni (1502).

The **Room of the Violins** contains five famous ***violins** made in Cremona. The one by Andrea Amati is thought to have been commissioned by Charles IX of France in 1566; the *Hammerle* of 1658 is by Nicolò Amati, Andrea's grandson. The others are a violin made by Giuseppe Guarneri in 1689, the *Cremonese* made in 1715 by Antonio Stradivari, and the *Guarneri del Gesù* by Giuseppe Guarneri del Gesù (1734). A recording of the instruments is provided, but it is also possible, by appointment, to hear them being played by a violinist who comes here regularly to keep them in tune.

Via Solferino leads out of the piazza, and Corso Mazzini continues right. It leads into Corso Matteotti, with many fine old mansions. Notice especially **Palazzo Fodri** (no. 17), dating from c 1500, decorated with a terracotta frieze and with a lovely courtyard. A road on the other side of the corso leads to the church of **Sant'Abbondio**, with an interesting 16C interior. The vault frescoes are by Orazio Sammacchini. In the sanctuary are paintings by Malosso and Giulio Campi. The Loreto chapel dates from 1624, and there is a Renaissance cloister.

On the other side of the corso, narrow roads lead to Via Gerolamo da Cremona, which continues east to the church of **San Michele**, near remains of the walls. Lombard in origin (7C), it is the oldest church in Cremona. It was reconstructed in the 11C and 12C (the exterior of the apse dates from this time) and contains 12C columns in the nave with fine leafy capitals as well as noteworthy fresco fragments, including one by Benedetto Bembo. The paintings are by Bernardino Campi, Alessandro Pampurino and Antonio della Corna (attributed), among others.

The museums

Corso Mazzini leads back towards the centre of the town and Piazza Roma, a public garden. Here are a statue of the native composer Amilcare Ponchielli (1834–86) and the tombstone of Stradivarius. The latter was salvaged from the church of San Domenico, which stood on this site but was demolished in 1878. Just off the square, a monumental arcade beneath a building of 1935 leads into Corso Campi, which continues right, changing its name to Via Palestro, to Via Ugolani Dati. Here, at no. 4, is the **Museo Civico** (open Tues–Sun 08.30–18.30, Sun and holidays 10.00–18.00), housed in the huge Palazzo Affaitati built in

1561 by Francesco Dattaro, with a good staircase by Antonio Arrighi (1769). The collection of Count Sigismondo Ala Ponzone, left to the city in 1842, was transferred here in 1928. The arrangement is provisional, so don't be surprised if something has moved.

The visit begins in the **Pinacoteca**. In the first room are 15C paintings by Benedetto and Bonifacio Bembo, and works by Boccaccio Boccaccino. The central hall contains ten wooden high *reliefs by Giacomo Bertesi (1643–1710), and works by Bernardino Campi, Bernardino Gatti and Camillo Boccaccino. Beyond are paintings by Antonio Campi, Giuseppe Arcimboldo (*Scherzo con Ortaggi*, a well-known portrait), L'Ortolano, Panfilo Nuvolone, Il Genovesino and Caravaggio (*St Francis in Meditation*). On the right is a large room with 16C–17C works by the Cremonese school. Stairs lead up to a display of small icons.

The section dedicated to the **decorative arts** contains 16C Limoges enamels, ivories, wrought-iron work, etc. The collection of 18C–19C porcelain includes Viennese, Wedgwood, Meissen and Ginori (Doccia) ware. There are also Italian majolicas and 16C–18C Cremonese ceramics.

From the central hall another flight of stairs leads up to a room with 15C–17C Flemish paintings, including a *Madonna* by Jan Provost. Beyond are three rooms with 19C paintings including portraits by Il Piccio, and works by Luigi Sabatelli and Giuseppe Dotti.

Off the courtyard is the extensive archaeological collection, with exhibits from the prehistoric era (including a sword of the 9C BC), Attic craters and a good Roman section: helmets, fine geometric mosaic pavements (1C–3C AD), coins, epigraphs, portrait heads and the front of a legionary's strongbox. The cache of at least 650 amphorae was found in the centre of Cremona in 1993, in an area once probably part of the Roman port on the Po. The medieval finds include wrought-iron work and sculpture.

At Via Palestro 17 is the **Stradivarius Museum** (open Tues–Sun 08.30–18.30, Sun and holidays 10.00–18.00), founded in 1893 and including the Salabue bequest of 1920. In the well-arranged gallery are models made by Stradivarius in wood and paper, his tools, drawings, etc., as well as a fine collection of stringed instruments (17C–20C). Palazzo Stanga, at Via Palestro 36, has a Rococo front rebuilt in the 19C and a handsome courtyard, probably by Pietro da Rho.

Elsewhere in town

In Corso Garibaldi, which branches off to the left from Corso Campi, is the conspicuous Neo-classical façade of **Sant'Agata**, built in 1848 by Luigi Voghera. The campanile is Romanesque. Inside, on the right, is the Trecchi tomb by Giovanni Cristoforo Romano (1502–05), with beautifully carved bas-reliefs. The painting of the life of St Agatha (painted on both sides) is by a northern Italian master of the 13C. The handsome frescoes on the sanctuary walls are by Giulio Campi (1536).

Across the Corso is the **Palazzo del Popolo** or Palazzo Cittanova (1256), with a ground-floor portico, the headquarters of the popular—or Guelf—party in the days of the free city-state of Cremona. It is adjoined by **Palazzo Trecchi** with a Gothic-revival façade of 1843–44. Nearby, in Via Grandi, is the little church of **Santa Margherita** (1547), in an extremely ruinous state. The frescoes inside (now almost invisible) are the best work of Giulio Campi. Not far off, at Via Milazzo

16, is a remarkable Art Nouveau house façade with floral motifs and leaves.

On the left of Corso Garibaldi (no. 178) is the fine **Palazzo Raimondi** (1496; by Bernardino de Lera), with damaged frescoes on its curved cornice. It is the seat of the international **Scuola di Liuteria** and the centre of musical activity in Cremona. This school for violin-makers continues a tradition for which the city has been famous since the 16C. Beyond on the right is the church of **San Luca**, with a 15C façade in poor repair adorned with the terracotta ornament typical of Cremona; adjoining is the little octagonal Renaissance chapel of Cristo Risorto (1503), attributed to Bernardino de Lera.

From Sant'Agata (see above), Via Trecchi and Via Guido Grandi lead southwest to *Sant'Agostino, a 14C church with a handsome tower and terracotta ornamentation on the façade. In the interior are frescoes by Bonifacio Bembo, a stoup with reliefs by Bonino da Campione (1357), an *Annunciation* by Antonio Campi, and a *Madonna and Saints* by Perugino.

Via Plasio leads south to the church of **Santi Marcellino e Pietro**, with elaborate marble and stucco decorations in the interior (1602–20; being restored). Further south is Corso Vittorio Emanuele with (right) the **Teatro Ponchielli** by Luigi Canonica (1808). Behind the theatre is the monastic church of **San Pietro al Po**, sumptuously decorated with 16C paintings and stuccoes by Malosso, Antonio Campi, Gian Francesco Bembo, Bernardino Gatti and others. The cloister at Via Cesari 14 is by Cristoforo Solari (1509).

On the outskirts

On the outskirts of the town (on the Casalmaggiore road; **bus no. 2** for the hospital) is the important church of *San Sigismondo, where Francesco Sforza was married to Bianca Visconti in 1441. The present building was started in 1463 in celebration of the event; it is a fine Lombard Renaissance work. The interior contains splendid painted decoration carried out between 1535 and 1570, much of it by the local artists Camillo Boccaccino, Bernardino Gatti and the Campi family. The nave vault was decorated by Bernardino and Giulio Campi and Bernardino Gatti. In the south aisle, the first chapel contains a niche in which two glass carafes are preserved; these were found in 1963 on a brick dated 1492 at the base of the façade (they were filled with oil and wine to commemorate the beginning of its construction). The fifth chapel has a vault exquisitely decorated by Bernardino Campi and an altarpiece by Giulio Campi, and the sixth chapel has an altarpiece by Bernardino Campi.

The transept vaults were painted by Giulio Campi; the choir stalls by Domenico and Gabriele Capra (1590–1603) are partially in restoration; and the Menarini organ has recently been restored. The dome bears a fresco of *Paradise* by Bernardino Campi. The presbytery and apse have fine *frescoes by Camillo Boccaccino, and the high altarpiece, in a beautiful contemporary wooden frame, is by Giulio Campi (1540). Behind the high altar is the foundation stone of the church. In the north aisle, the fifth *chapel is entirely decorated with paintings, frescoes and stuccoes by Antonio Campi, and the third chapel has fine works by Bernardino Campi. Off the **cloister**, a Renaissance work finished in 1505, are works by Paolo and Giuseppe Sacca (1536) and the refectory, with a *Last Supper* by Tommaso Aleni (1508).

THE PROVINCE OF CREMONA
••••••••••••••••••••••••••••••••

Crema

The most important town in the province after Cremona is Crema, on the west bank of the Serio. It was under Venetian rule from 1454 to 1797 and was the birthplace of the composer Francesco Cavalli (1600–76). The **Cathedral**, in the Campionese style (1284–1341), has a fine tower and contains one of the last works of Guido Reni. The piazza in front of it is surrounded by Renaissance buildings, including the 16C Palazzo Pretorio with an archway leading to the main street.

The ex-convent of Sant'Agostino houses the library and **Museo Civico** (open Mon 14.30–18.30; Tues–Fri 09.00–12.00, 14.30–18.30; Sat–Sun and holidays 10.00–12.00, 16.00–19.00), which has burial armour from Lombard tombs. The refectory, restored as a concert hall, has frescoes attributed to Giovanni Pietro da Cemmo (1498–1505). **Santa Maria della Croce**, north of the town, is a handsome centrally planned church (1490–1500) in the style of Bramante, by Giovanni Battagio. It contains altarpieces by Benedetto Diana and the Campi brothers.

West of Crema

Pandino has an impressive castle (open Mon–Tues 8.30–12.30, 14.30–18.00, Wed 15.00–19.00, Fri 14.00–18.00, Sat 10.00–12.00, Sun 10.30–12.00, 14.30–18.00) begun by the Visconti in 1379. At **Palazzo Pignano** excavations beneath the 12C Pieve di San Martino revealed remains of an early Christian basilica. The church contains 15C frescoes and a 15C terracotta **Pietà**. Behind the church remains of a late-Roman villa have been found. **Rivolta d'Adda** has a handsome basilica of 1088–99, with interesting carvings. A park here (open Mar–Nov 09.00–dusk) displays lifesize models of prehistoric animals.

East of Crema

East of Crema is **Soncino**. The *Castle here (open Apr–Oct, Tues–Sat 10.00–12.00, Sun and holidays 10.00–12.30, 14.30–19.00; Nov–Mar, Tues–Sat 10.00–12.00; Sun and holidays 10.00–12.30, 14.30–18.00) was rebuilt by Galeazzo Maria Sforza and is among the best preserved in Lombardy. It was restored in 1886 by Luca Beltrami, the *enfant terrible* of Milanese architecture at the turn of the 19C. Ezzelino da Romano died here after his defeat in the battle of Cassano d'Adda. The splendid town *walls (13C–15C) are nearly 2km in circumference. Five watermills survive in or near the town, one of which is still in operation, and the town preserves a 13C drainage system.

The wide main street descends from the site of the south gate past the 15C Palazzo Azzanelli, with terracotta decoration, to the main square with the 11C Torre Civica and the church of **San Giacomo**, which has a curious seven-sided tower (1350) and a cloister. It contains two stained-glass windows by Ambrogio da Tormoli (1490) and a late 15C terracotta Pietà. Nearby is the **Casa degli Stampatori** (open as the Castle, above), a medieval tower house that may be on the site of the first printing works founded in the town in 1480. The press was set up by the Jewish family Nathan, who were allowed by the Sforza (in return for cash loans) to take up residence here, having been forced to leave Germany. They adopted the name of the town for their press and, in the decade in which they lived and worked here, they printed their first book (in 1483) and the first complete Hebrew bible (in 1488). There is a little museum, and a reproduction press is still in operation.

The *pieve* of **Santa Maria Assunta** was reconstructed in the 17C–19C on the site of a much older church. On the outskirts of the little town is the church of **Santa Maria delle Grazie** (ring for admission at the convent), begun in 1492 and consecrated in 1528, splendidly decorated with terracotta friezes and *frescoes, many of them by Giulio Campi (including the triumphal arch and sanctuary vault).

South of Soncino is **Soresina**, where the church of San Siro contains altarpieces by Malosso and Il Genovesino, and the church of San Francesco a wooden crucifix by Giacomo Bertesi. The delightful theatre (restored in 1991) was built to a design by Carlo Visioli in 1840. A large market is held in the town on Mon.

West of Soresina is **Castelleone**, where the Museo Civico (open daily 16.00–19.00) displays local archaeological finds (prehistoric and Lombard), and the church of Santa Maria di Bressanoro, built in 1460–65, has terracotta decorations and interesting frescoes.

Pizzighettone, west of Cremona, is an old town divided in two by the Adda. Significant remains of its fortifications are preserved, including the circuit of *walls (last strengthened in 1585), the passageways and battlements of which can be visited; and the Torrione, where Francis I was imprisoned after the battle of Pavia (1525). The church of San Bassiano dates from the 12C, but has been greatly altered. Inside is a frescoed *Crucifixion* by Bernardino Campi, and three carved 14C panels.

East of Cremona
In the southeast corner of the province is the town of **Piadena**. A small archaeological museum (open Wed–Thur 09.30–12.00, Sun and holidays 17.00–20.00 in summer, 14.00–17.00 in winter) includes finds from the supposed site of *Bedriacum*, scene of a battle in AD 69 in which the generals of Vitellius defeated Otho. West of the town is **Torre de' Picenardi**, with the 18C Villa Sommi-Picenardi surrounded by a moat in the centre of a park. At **San Giovanni in Croce**, the Villa Medici del Vascello is a castle of 1407 remodelled with a graceful loggia in the 16C and surrounded by a Romantic park. **Casalmaggiore** has impressive embankments along the Po, which is crossed on a long bridge. It has a theatre dating from 1783.

Mantua and Sabbioneta

Mantua, in Italian *Mantova*, is a charming old town (population 50,000) famous for its associations with the Gonzaga, under whose rule it flourished as a brilliant centre of art and civilisation in the 15C and 16C, when Mantegna, Leon Battista Alberti and Giulio Romano created some of their more important works here. It is in the extreme southeastern corner of Lombardy and has much in common with neighbouring towns in Emilia Romagna and the Veneto. Mantua's feeling of isolation is emphasised by the practical difficulties of reaching it by public transport. In the centre of the town, with its quiet old cobbled streets and piazzas, is the huge Palazzo Ducale of the Gonzaga, celebrated for its Camera degli Sposi, frescoed by Mantegna. The dukes' summer villa, the suburban Palazzo Te, is the masterpiece of Giulio Romano.

Mantua is the unofficial capital of this corner of Lombardy—a flat, fertile area possessing a certain bucolic charm, and studded with architectural jewels like the little theatre at Sabbioneta. Nevertheless, it is not a region for everyone. Aldous Huxley found the whole place—the city and its territory—perfectly dreadful: over no city, he commented, 'did there brood so profound a melancholy as over Mantua; none seemed so dead or so utterly bereft of glory.... And not in Mantua alone. For wherever the Gonzaga lived, they left behind them the same pathetic emptiness, the same pregnant desolation, the same echoes, the same ghosts of splendour' (*Along the Road*, 1925).

Practical information

Getting there
By air

The airports nearest Mantua are at Verona (Valerio Catullo, 35km northeast), Brescia (Montichiari), Bergamo (Orio di Serio) and Milan (Malpensa, Linate). All handle domestic and international flights; Malpensa also has intercontinental flights.

By road

To Mantua from Milan, take the A4 east to Verona, then A22 south; from Bologna, A1 to Modena, then A22 north; from Cremona, 10 east. From Mantua to Sabbioneta, 420 southwest. Sabbioneta is conveniently reached also from Parma, by taking 343 north.

By rail

To Mantua from Milan, 149km in 2hrs–2hrs 30mins via Codogno, where a change is sometimes necessary; from Verona, 37km in 35mins; from Modena, 62km in 1hr 15mins; from Monselice (see p 487), 85km in 1hr 45mins. From Cremona 53km in 1hr via Piadena, where the line is met by trains from Brescia and Parma. The Parma stretch also serves Castelmaggiore, from where there are buses to (5km) Sabbionetta.

Getting around
By bus

Buses run by *APAM* (☎ 0376 230338), from Mantua to Sabbioneta-Parma, Brescia, Sirmione (Lago di Garda), San Benedetto Po and Ostiglia; bus station at Via Mutilati e Caduti del Lavoro 4 (Piazza Mondadori).

By bicycle

Can be rented for the day from *La Rigola*, Lungolago Gonzaga, ☎ 0335 605 4958.

Car parking

In Mantua, Lungolago dei Gonzaga (near Palazzo Ducale), Lungolago di Mezzo, Via Trieste, Via Mazzini, Piazzale Mondadori, Piazza d'Arco and around Palazzo Te.

Information offices

MANTUA Piazza Mantegna 6, ☎ 0376 328253. *Informagiovani*, Via Chiassi 18, ☎ 0376 364233.

SABBIONETA Via Vespasiano Gonzaga, ☎ 0375 52039. The office is open Oct–Mar, Tues–Sun 09.00–12.00, 14.30–17.00 or 18.00; Apr–Sep daily 09.00–12.00, 13.30 or 14.30–18.00 or

19.00. It is necessary to book here (and purchase a ticket) for a guided tour of the monuments of the town (the theatre, the Palazzo Ducale, the church of the Incoronata, Palazzo del Giardino and the Galleria), otherwise they can only be seen from the outside. A separate ticket has to be purchased here for the tour of the synagogue.

Where to stay

MANTUA *Mantegna*, Via Filzi 10, ☎ 0376 328019, fax 0376 368564; simple but adequate, halfway between the Palazzo Ducale and Palazzo Te; closed Dec–Jan, inexpensive.

Rechigi, Via Calvi 30, ☎ 0376 320781, fax 0376 220291; centrally located, with a small contemporary art collection; moderate.

San Lorenzo, Piazza Concordia 14, ☎ 0376 220500, fax 0376 327194; elegant and refined, with genuine antiques and a rooftop terrace with magnificent views over the city; expensive.

VIADANA *Europa*, Vicolo Ginnasio 9, ☎ 0375 780404, fax 0375 780404; small (17 rooms) but comfortable, with an excellent restaurant; inexpensive.

Eating out

MANTUA *Aquila Nigra*, Vicolo Bonacolsi 4, ☎ 0376 327180, fax 0376 226490, offers the finest regional dishes prepared with a special touch; closed Mon, Sun evening in Apr–May and Sep–Oct, all day Sun at other times, and Jan; moderate.

Due Cavallini, Via Salnitro 5, ☎ 0376 322084; trattoria serving the best traditional Mantuan cuisine; closed Tues and Jul–Aug; inexpensive.

Grifone Bianco, Piazza Erbe 6, ☎ 0376 365423; excellent Mantuan cuisine (expecially first courses) and pleasant ambience in the heart of the old town; closed Tues and Jul; moderate.

Il Portichetto, Via Portichetto 14, ☎ 0376 360747; osteria famous for its

freshwater fish dishes; closed Sun evening, Mon and Aug; moderate.

L'Ochina Bianca, Via Finzi 2, ☎ 0376 323700; warm, friendly osteria with a strong local following; closed Mon, midday Tues and Jan; inexpensive.

San Gervasio, Via San Gervasio 13, ☎ 0376 350504; restaurant, traditional regional cuisine; closed Wed and Aug; moderate.

Cafés

For good coffee and cakes, try *Caffè Caravatti*, Piazza delle Erbe; for something stronger, *Buca della Torre*, Via Cavour 98.

If you like *tortelli di zucca* (and other Mantuan pastas and breads), try *Panificio Freddi*, Piazza Cavallotti 7. You can get Mantua's famous (infamous?) garlic salame at *Salumeria Carra*, Via Tassoni 1.

Beyond Mantua

ACQUANEGRA SUL CHIESE *Al Ponte*, Via del Ponte Oglio 1312, ☎ 0376 727182; trattoria known for its freshwater fish; closed Tues, Jul–Aug and Feb; moderate.

CANNETO SULL'OGLIO *Dal Pescatore*, Via Runate 13, ☎ 0376 723001; restaurant famous for its highly refined renditions of traditional Mantuan dishes; expensive.

CASTEL D'ARIO *Castello*, Via di là dell'Acqua 8 (off the Cremona road); ☎ 0376 660259; trattoria famous for its risotti; closed Wed–Thur, Aug and Dec; inexpensive.

CASTEL GOFFREDO *Villa*, at Villa, ☎ 0376 770395; trattoria clebrated for its tortelli; closed Mon, Jan and Aug; inexpensive.

CASTIGLIONE DELLE STIVIERE *Hosteria Viola*, Via Verdi 32, at Fontane, ☎ 0376 638277; restaurant specialising in regional dishes, near the Brescia–Mantua road; closed Mon and Jul–Aug; moderate.

CURTATONE *Viator*, Via Livorno 3, at

Montanara, ☎ 0376 49737; restaurant offering traditional Mantuan cooking with a modern twist; closed Sun; inexpensive.

DOSOLO *Corte Brandelli*, Via Argine Destro 11a, ☎ 0325 89497; traditional restaurant famous for its creative interpretations of traditional recipes; closed Thur evening, Sun, Dec and Jul–Aug; moderate.

Nizzoli, Via Garibaldi 8, at Villastrada; another good traditional restaurant— try the *risotto di zucca* and the fried snails in Parmesan sauce; closed Wed and Dec–Jan; moderate.

GOITO *Adami*, at Massimbona,☎ 0376 60020; osteria serving strictly local fare (tortelli, risotto, freshwater fish); open evenings only, closed Mon; inexpensive.

Al Bersagliere, Strada Statale Goitese 260, ☎ 0376 688399; on the Mincio, restaurant renowned for its masterful interpretations of old Mantuan recipes; closed Mon, midday Tues and Dec–Jan; expensive.

MARMIROLO *Ancilla*, Via Ponte 3, at Pozzolo; ☎ 0376 460007; restaurant serving freshwater fish especially with pasta and rice; closed Mon evening and Tues; moderate.

MONZAMBANO *La Dispensa*, Via Castello 21, at Castellaro Lagusello; wine bar serving simple but delicious local specialities; open Fri and Sat evenings, Sun all day, closed Mon–Thur, Jul–Aug; inexpensive.

QUISTELLO *Ambasciata*, Via Martiri di Belfiore 33, ☎ 0376 619169; another fine traditional restaurant; closed Wed, midday Thur and Aug; expensive.

POMPONESCO *Il Leone*, Via 4 Martiri 2, ☎ 0375 86077; a family-run restaurant with rooms, offering good local fare; closed Sun evening, Mon and Dec–Jan; moderate.

Saltini, Piazza XXIII Aprile 10, ☎ 0375 86017; traditional trattoria on the vil-lage square; closed Mon and Jul–Aug; inexpensive.

VIADANA *Caol Ila*, Vicolo Quartierino 10, ☎ 0375 830381; wine bar with good risotti and other hot lunch offerings; closed Sun and Aug; inexpensive.

Entertainment

Mantua's four theatres, the *Sociale, Ariston, Bibiena* and *Teatreno*, offer music and drama series as well as children's programmes. More classical music is offered Nov–Apr by the Mantua Youth Orchestra, Conservatory and Chamber Orchestra. At Sabbioneta, concerts are held in May–Jun in the Theatre; organ recitals take place in Sep in the Incoronata. There is live music and dancing in Mantua (*Masseria*, Piazza Broletto) and in the environs.

Shopping

Gourmets shouldn't leave Mantua without trying the *tortelli di zucca* (pumpkin tortelli), *insaccati di maiale* (pork salame) and *torta sbrisolona* (low, crisp shortbread cake).

Special events

People in these parts love to dress up—for religious festivals such as Mantua's *Sacri Vasi* (Good Friday procession) and saint's day (18 Mar), or secular occasions like the *Invito a Corte* (Gonzaga-era costumes) at Mantua, *Re Gnocco* (historic carnival celebration) at Castel Goffredo (Feb) and *Rievocazione Storica Aloisiana* (Renaissance costume) at Castiglione delle Stiviere (Jun).

Sports

Golf at Corte Bersaglio (*Migliaretto*). **Walking** and **canoeing** on the Lago Inferiore.

MANTUA
• • • • • • • • • •

Somewhat like a landlocked Venice, Mantua is surrounded on three sides by the River Mincio, which widens out to form a lake of three reaches, Lago Superiore, Lago di Mezzo and Lago Inferiore. The presence of so much water, which cools the air more in winter, it would seem, than in summer, gives the town its rather chill atmosphere.

History

Virgil was born on Mantuan territory about 70 BC, and some of the town's earliest recorded history is due to the poet's interest in his birthplace. Mantua became a free commune about 1126 and was afterwards dominated by the Bonacolsi and Gonzaga families. Under Gonzaga rule from 1328 the town was a famous centre of art and learning, especially in the reigns of Ludovico II (1444–78), Francesco II (1484–1519), husband of Isabella d'Este, the greatest patron of her time (who died in Mantua in 1539), and their son Federico II (1519–40).

The city was sacked by imperial troops in 1630, and many of the best Gonzaga paintings were sold to Charles I of England. The duchy was extinguished in 1708 by the Austrians, who fortified the town as the southwest corner of their 'quadrilateral'. It held out against Napoleon for eight months in 1796–97, and was retaken by the French in 1799. The town was again under Austrian rule in 1814–66. It was damaged by bombs in 1944.

Among the artists who flourished at the court of the Gonzagas were Leon Battista Alberti, Luca Fancelli and Pisanello. Andrea Mantegna was court artist from 1460 until his death in 1506. Giulio Romano, architect and painter, was called to Mantua in 1524 by Federico II, and worked there under the duke's patronage until his death in 1546, leaving numerous monuments in the city. Titian often visited the city, and it was here he first saw the works of Giulio Romano. Alari Bonacolsi, nicknamed 'L'Antico', was born in Mantua, and he was commissioned by the Gonzaga to make bronze copies of Classical statues. Rubens worked at the court from 1600 to 1606. The success of Monteverdi's *Orfeo* at court in 1607 was the first landmark in the history of opera. The popularity of Verdi's *Rigoletto* has endowed several Mantuan localities with spurious associations.

The Palazzo Ducale

The whole of the upper side of the large, cobbled Piazza Sordello is occupied by the famous •Palazzo Ducale, a huge fortress-palace that remains a fitting emblem of the hospitality of the Gonzaga princes, who were especially famous as patrons of the arts (see above).

The vast rambling palace is divided into three main parts, all connected by corridors and courtyards: the original 14C Bonacolsi palace, known as the Corte Vecchia, on Piazza Sordello, which was adapted by the Gonzaga rulers; the castle added by the Gonzaga in the 15C to defend the approach to the city from the lake (and once connected to the palace by drawbridges only); and the Corte Nuova wing, mainly planned by Giulio Romano in the 16C. Architects who worked on the palace included Luca Fancelli in the 15C and,

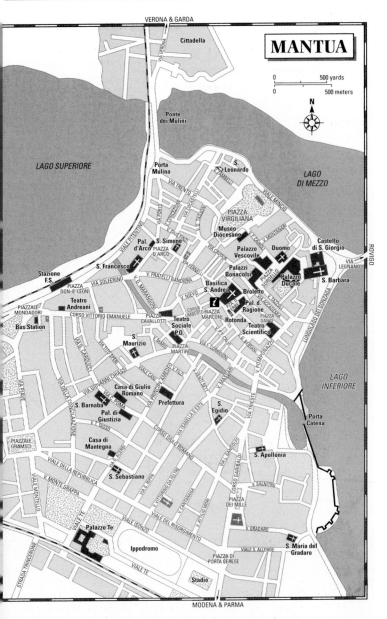

MANTUA

0   500 yards
0   500 meters

N

VERONA & GARDA

Cittadella

Ponte
dei Mulini

LAGO SUPERIORE

LAGO
DI MEZZO

Porta
Mulina

S.
Leonardo

PIAZZA
VIRGILIANA

Museo
Diocesano

Pal.
d'Arco   S. Simone
PIAZZA
D'ARCO

Palazzo
Vescovile   Duomo

Castello
di S. Giorgio

ROVIGO

VIA
LEGNANO

S. Francesco

Stazione
F.S.

PIAZZA
DON E. LEONI

Palazzi
Bonacolsi

Palazzo
Ducale

S. Barbara

Basilica
S. Andrea

Broletto

PIAZZALE
MONDADORI

Teatro
Andreani

CORSO VITTORIO EMANUELE

PIAZZA
CAVALLOTTI

Pal. d.
Ragione

Rotonda

Bus Station

Teatro
Sociale
P.O.

PIAZZA
MARCONI

Teatro
Scientifico

S.
Maurizio

PIAZZA
MARTIRI

LAGO
INFERIORE

Casa di Giulio
Romano

Prefettura

S.
Egidio

Porta
Catena

S. Barnaba

Pal. di
Giustizia

PIAZZALE
GRAMSCI

Casa di
Mantegna

S. Apollonia

S. Sebastiano

PIAZZA
DEI MILLE

Palazzo Te

Ippodromo

S. Maria del
Gradaro

PIAZZA DI
PORTA CERESE

Stadio

MODENA & PARMA

in the 16C and early 17C, Giulio Romano, Giovanni Battista Bertani and
Antonio Maria Viani. The palace is now chiefly remarkable for its decorations, including the famous Camera degli Sposi in the castle. Most of the great

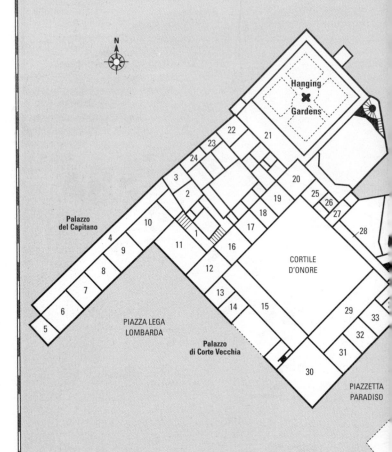

PALAZZO DUCALE

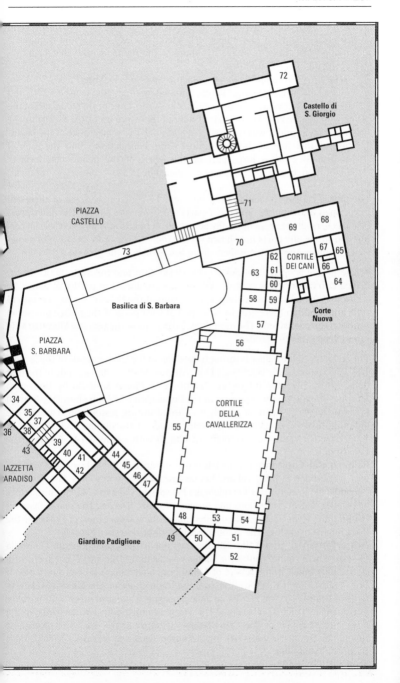

PIAZZA
CASTELLO

Castello di
S. Giorgio

72

71

73

70

69

68

67

65

66

64

62

61

60

63

CORTILE
DEI CANI

58

59

Corte
Nuova

Basilica di S. Barbara

57

56

PIAZZA
S. BARBARA

55

CORTILE
DELLA
CAVALLERIZZA

34

35

37

36

38

43

39

40

41

42

44

45

46

47

48

53

54

49

50

51

52

IAZZETTA
ARADISO

Giardino Padiglione

Gonzaga art collections begun by Isabella d'Este, wife of Francesco II, and enriched in the 16C, have been dispersed; Charles I of England acquired a large part of them in 1627–30. Many of the rooms of the palace contain excellent Classical sculpture.

The Corte Vecchia, or ducal palace proper, overlooking Piazza Sordello, consists of the low Domus Magna, founded by Guido Bonacolsi c 1290, and the higher Palazzo del Capitano, built a few years later by the Bonacolsi at the expense of the city. The Austrians altered the windows of the façade in the Gothic style, and it was restored to its original 15C appearance at the beginning of this century by the Samuel Kress Foundation. After the sack of Mantua in 1630 a large part of the fabric of the palace deteriorated. Restoration, begun in 1902, was completed in 1934.

The palace consists of some 700 rooms and 15 courtyards. Some of these are never open to the public, and other parts are sometimes closed. The description below covers all the areas normally accessible: scholars may be given special permission to see any parts not shown on the tour. As the order of the visit sometimes changes, the room numbers given below refer to the plan on p 286–287.

- The palace is open Tues–Sat 09.00–19.00, Sun and holidays 09.00–14.00 (last entry 1hr before closing). Visitors are conducted in parties of about 30 (there is usually no more than 15mins wait at the ticket office for a group to form), although there are plans to open at least parts of the palace to visitors not on the guided tour. The most crowded periods of the year are March to May and September to October.

The entrance to the palace is through the door on the left-hand side of the façade. The 17C Scalone delle Duchesse (1) by Antonio Maria Viani ascends to the first floor. Notice here the interesting *painting of *Piazza Sordello* by Domenico Morone, illustrating the expulsion of the Bonacolsi in 1328. It shows the front of Palazzo Ducale (a detail of which was useful during restoration work on the building in this century) and the Gothic façade of the duomo (pulled down in 1761). On the right are two rooms (2 and 3) with a ruined 14C fresco of the *Crucifixion*.

Palazzo del Capitano On the left is the entrance to the Palazzo del Capitano, with a collection of medieval and Renaissance sculpture in rooms 4–9. The long Corridoio del Passerino, or Corridoio del Palazzo del Capitano (4), has interesting late-Gothic mural decorations and numerous coats of arms. The seated figure of *Virgil* dates from c 1220, and the stemma of the *podestà* Ginori (1494) is by the Della Robbia workshop. The mantelpiece is attributed to Luca Fancelli.

Appartamento Guastalla Off the corridor is the Appartamento Guastalla (5–10). These rooms contain a lapidary collection; a group of five terracotta statues attributed to the school of Mantegna; a terracotta bust of Francesco II Gonzaga by Gian Cristoforo Romano; the tomb effigy of Margherita Malatesta (wife of Francesco I) by Pier Paolo dalle Masegne; a classical relief of Philoctetes attributed to Tullio Lombardo; a 16C sleeping cupid with two serpents; and a large ruined fresco of the *Crucifixion* attributed to the 14C–15C Bolognese school. In the last room (10) are displayed detached frescoes (1303) and a Byzantine *Madonna*.

Sala del Pisanello The Sala del Pisanello or Sala dei Principi (11) contains a splendid fragment of a mural *painting discovered in the 1960s showing a battle tournament. The unfinished but vivacious composition is one of the master-pieces of Pisanello. Forming a border along the top of the painting is a beautiful frieze incorporating the Lancastrian 'SS' collar entwined with marigold flowers, the emblem of the Gonzaga—it was Henry VI who granted the Gonzaga the con-cession to use the heraldic crest of the House of Lancaster. On the other wall are *sinopie* (underdrawings) of Arthurian scenes by Pisanello. The adjoining room (**12**) displays the *sinopia* of the battle tournament.

Salette dell'Alcove The Salette dell'Alcove (**13** and **14**) are not always open. They contain 18C works including *St Thomas with Angels* by Giuseppe Bazzani. The Galleria Nuova (**15**; closed at the time of writing) displays 17C paintings including works by Carlo Bononi and Giuseppe Maria Crespi.

Appartamento degli Arazzi The next four rooms form the Appartamento degli Arazzi (**16–19**), overlooking the Cortile d'Onore, with Neo-classical deco-ration by Paolo Pozzo (1779). The Brussels *tapestries here, designed after Raphael's cartoons of the *Acts of the Apostles* (now in the Victoria and Albert Museum, London), are the most important replica of the Vatican series. They were acquired by Ercole Gonzaga. Some of the other rooms have false painted 'tapestries'. The ceiling of the Sala dello Zodiaco (**20**) has delightful frescoes by Lorenzo Costa the Younger (1580).

Sala dei Fiumi To the left is the Sala dei Fiumi (**21**), decorated in 1775 by Giorgio Anselmi, with allegories of river gods, two stucco 'grottoes' and a 16C table of *pietre dure* made in Florence. It overlooks the Giardino Pensile, a hanging garden off which is a 'Kaffeehaus' with ceilings decorated in the 18C by Antonio Bibiena.

Appartamento dell'Impertrice Three rooms near here (**22–24**), known as the Appartamento dell'Imperatrice, with Empire-style furniture dating from the early 19C, are usually closed.

Sala dei Falconi Beyond the Sala dello Zodiaco is the Sala dei Falconi (**25**), named after a ceiling painting of hawks, attributed to Ippolito Andreasi.

Saletta dei Mori The Saletta dei Mori (**26**) has a fine gilded-wood ceiling and 16C and 17C paintings. Beyond the Loggetta dei Mori (**27**) is the narrow Corridoio dei Mori (**28**; with a view of the handsome 16C campanile of the Palatine Basilica of Santa Barbara), decorated in the early 17C.

Appartamento di Eleonoara Medici Gonzaga In the Domus Nova (closed) are the Appartamento di Eleonora Medici Gonzaga (**39–42**), wife of Vincenzo II, designed by Viani, and the Scala del Paradiso (**43**).

Appartamento dei Nani On a mezzanine floor, the so-called Appartamento dei Nani (also closed), once thought to have been for the Court dwarfs, is in fact a miniature reproduction of the Scala Santa in Rome made by Viani for Ferdinando Gonzaga c 1620, and used for religious functions.

Appartamento delle Metamorfosi The Appartamento delle Metamorfosi (**44–47**), with ceilings by Viani and his school, and Roman busts and reliefs, looks out onto the *Giardino del Padiglione, with a view of the Domus Nova by Luca Fancelli. The Appartamento Estivale (**48–54**), redecorated by Bertani and Viani, is closed.

Galleria della Mostra The *Galleria della Mostra (**55**), with a magnificent ceil-ing, was built by Viani for the display of the most important part of the ducal col-lection: it now contains original busts of Roman emperors. There is a view of the splendid Cortile del Cavalerizza by Giulio Romano and Bertani, and the lake beyond.

Sala di Troia Beyond the Galleria dei Mesi (**56**), built as a loggia by Giulio Romano and now holding a large antique relief brought by Rome by the architect and painter, is the Sala di Troia (**57**), with frescoes of the Trojan War designed by Giulio Romano and executed by his pupils. Beyond is the pretty Sala di Giove or delle Teste (**58**).

The next series of small rooms (**59–62**) are closed. These include the Stanza dei Cesari (**59**), the Camerino di Ganimede (**60**), and the Loggetta dei Cani (**61**), which opens on to the Giardino dei Cani. The Camerino degli Uccelli (**62**) has a pretty ceiling and contains a statuette of *Aphrodite*, a Roman copy of a 3C BC original.

Sala dei Cavalli Next to the Sala di Giove is the Sala dei Cavalli (**63**), which takes its name from paintings of horses by Giulio Romano, which formerly hung here. It has a fine wooden coffered ceiling. The classical sculpture includes two circular altars.

The rooms (**64–69**) on the opposite side of the Giardino dei Cani are closed. They include the Sala dei Duchi (**64**), and the Appartamento del Tasso (**65** and **66**), where the Gonzaga are supposed to have received Torquato Tasso on his flight from Ferrara. It contains more classical sculpture.

Stanza di Apollo The Stanza di Apollo (**67**) has beautiful decoration traditionally attributed to Francesco Primaticcio (from a previous building).

Sala dei Marchesi The Sala dei Marchesi (**68**) has fine allegorical figures and busts in stucco by Francesco Segala. The beautiful Greek sculpture here includes the stele of a male figure and child (4C BC), and an Attic lute player.

Sala dei Capitani The Sala dei Capitani (**69**) has a fine Hellenistic *torso of Aphrodite*. The handsome Salone di Manto (**70**) contains more good Classical sculpture, including a *Caryatid* of the 5C BC and the *Mantua Apollo*. It has a beautiful coffered ceiling.

The Camera degli Sposi

The Scalone di Enea (**71**) and the spiral Scala dei Cavalli lead into the Castello di San Giorgio, a keep built in 1395–1406 with an interesting exterior (formerly covered with frescoes). The design of the loggia of the courtyard, built by Luca Fancelli, is attributed to Mantegna. A spiral ramp leads up to a series of rooms beyond which is the famous *Camera degli Sposi* (**72**), formerly known as the Camera Picta, one of the more celebrated works of the Renaissance. The magnificent paintings by Mantegna were commissioned by Ludovico, the second Marquis of Mantova, and carried out in 1465–74. Beautifully restored in 1984–86, they illustrate the life of Lodovico and his wife Barbara of Brandenburg. The painted decoration of the room, with a remarkable use of light, was immediately recognised as a masterpiece and was of fundamental importance to later Renaissance artists. It is now known that only part of the work was executed as a true fresco. The room appears to have been used by Ludovico as a bedroom, as well as an office and as a place for receiving visiting dignitaries.

On the **north wall**, above the fireplace, the marquis and his wife are shown seated, surrounded by their family, courtiers and messengers. Between the husband and wife is their son Gianfrancesco with his hands on the shoulders of a younger son, Lodovico, and a daughter, Paola, shown holding an apple. Rodolfo stands behind his mother, and to the right is his pretty sister Barbara (with her nurse behind and a dwarf in front). Beneath Lodovico's chair is his old dog

Rubino, who died in 1467. On the right is a group of courtiers dressed in the Gonzaga livery.

On the **west wall** are three scenes presumed to represent the meeting in 1462 at Bozzolo between the marquis, on his way to Milan, and his son Francesco, the first member of the Gonzaga family to be nominated cardinal, travelling back from Milan. On the left are servants in the Gonzaga livery with hounds and a horse—the Gonzaga were famous as horse breeders and dog lovers. Above the door is a dedicatory inscription, supported by winged putti, signed and dated 1474, by Mantegna. In the right-hand section is the scene of the meeting: the first full figure in profile is the marquis, dressed in grey with a sword at his side, talking to Francesco, in cardinal's robes; the children are also members of the Gonzaga family. The group to the right is thought to include Holy Roman Emperor Frederick III (in profile) and, dressed in red in the background, Christian I of Denmark. The landscape in the background of all three scenes is particularly beautiful and includes classical monuments (derived from buildings in Rome and Verona) and an imaginary city. In the frieze on the pilaster to the right of the door is Mantegna's self-portrait.

The vaulted ceiling, also by Mantegna, has a *trompe l'oeil* oculus in the centre, one of the first examples of aerial perspective in painting. The curious, inventive scene shows a circular stone balustrade on which winged putti are playing; and peering over the top of it are five courtly female figures, a peacock and more putti, and balanced on the edge is a plant in a tub. The vault, with a background of painted mosaic, is divided by *trompe l'oeil* ribs into eight sections with medallions containing the portraits of the first Roman emperors and, below (damaged) mythological scenes.

The last two walls were decorated with painted gold damask (now very damaged), and the lower part of the walls has painted marble intarsia.

The exit from the Camera degli Sposi is usually along the long Corridoio Bertani (**73**), with modern copies of the stucco portraits of the Gonzaga in the Palazzo Ducale of Sabbioneta, and down to the Cortile d'Onore.

Pinacoteca From the vestibule, with a small café and bookshop, a stairway on the right ascends to the Pinacoteca (heated in winter). The first room, the Salone degli Arcieri (**30**), has an unusual frescoed frieze of horses behind curtains. Here are hung some of the more important paintings in the palace. The *Gonzaga Family in Adoration of the Trinity* by Rubens was cut into pieces during the French occupation; two other fragments of the same painting are exhibited here. Three works by Domenico Fetti include a monochrome lunette showing Vianipresenting a model of the church of Sant'Orsola to Margherita Gonzaga d'Este, and a lunette with the Miracle of the Loaves and Fishes. There are also two paintings by Antonio Maria Viani. A door by the monochrome lunette leads to the 18C Neo-classical Galleria degli Specchi (**29**) with a 17C frescoed ceiling.

Appartamento Ducale The Appartamento Ducale (**31–38**) was arranged by Vincenzo I shortly after 1600. The Sala di Giuditta (**31**) has fabulous nocturnal scenes telling the *Story of Judith* by the Neapolitan painter Pietro Mango, and paintings of *Apostles and Saints* by Domenico Fetti. The Sala del Labirinto (**32**), named after the labyrinth carved in the wood ceiling, was rearranged in 1995 with sculptures and paintings from the palace of the Pico at Mirandola. The episodes from the story of *Psyche* are by Sante Peranda, and the two marble busts by Lorenzo Ottoni are portraits of **Beatrice d'Este Pico** (with lace) and **Maria Cybo Pico** (with a veil), both duchesses of Mirandola. High up on the walls are paintings by Sante Peranda and Palma Giovane. The ceiling of room 33 has the gold crucible motif, Vincenzo's emblem, and more Pico portraits, including *Alfonso and Giulia d'Este* by Sante Peranda. Beyond are small Neo-classical rooms (**34–38**).

Appartamento di Isabella d'Este The *Appartamento di Isabella d'Este, off the Cortile d'Onore, is sometimes opened on request. Her *studiolo*, for which she commissioned paintings from Mantegna, Perugino, Lorenzo Costa and Correggio (all of them now in the Louvre) has a door by Gian Cristoforo Romano. Her grotto contains intarsie by the Della Mola brothers. Both rooms have fine gilded wood ceilings.

The palatine basilica of **Santa Barbara** (closed) was built for Duke Guglielmo by Giovanni Battista Bertani in 1562–65.

The city centre

On the opposite side of Piazza Sordello are two grim, battlemented **Bonacolsi Palaces**, belonging to the family who ruled Mantua before the Gonzaga. Above the first rises the Torre della Gabbia, from which (seen from Via Cavour) an iron cage protrudes where condemned prisoners were exposed. The second, Palazzo Castiglioni, dates from the 13C. Beyond is the Rococo Palazzo Bianchi, now the bishop's palace.

At the end of the piazza is the **Duomo**. The late Gothic building burned down in 1545 (although part of the south side of this church survives), and the unsuccessful façade was built in 1756 next to the broad brick campanile.

The light *interior was designed by Giulio Romano (after 1545) in imitation of an early Christian basilica. It is covered with exquisite stucco decoration. In the south aisle is a 6C Christian sarophagus, and the baptistery with remains of 14C and 15C frescoes. The *Cappella dell'Incoronata, a charming work in the style of Alberti, is reached by a corridor off the north aisle. The octagonal Cappella del Sacramento at the end of the north aisle has two altarpieces by Domenico Brusasorci and Paolo Farinati.

At the opposite end of the piazza an archway leads into Piazza del Broletto, where a small daily market is held. On the **Broletto** (1227), with its four corner towers, is a quaint figure of Virgil sculpted in the 13C, showing the poet at a rostrum wearing his doctor's hat. At no. 9 is the entrance to a small museum (open Mar, Nov and Dec, Sat–Sun 10.00–13.00, 15.30–18.30; Apr–Oct, daily except Mon and Thur 10.00–13.00, 15.30–18.30), dedicated to Tazio Nuvolari (1892–1953), the famous motor-racing champion, who was born in Mantua. Connected to the Broletto by an archway is the **Arengario**, a little 13C building with a loggia. A restaurant beneath the archway occupies a Gonzaga office with an early 14C fresco of the city, and the arms of Gianfrancesco, the first marquis. **Palazzo Andreasi**, with a portico, has an interesting first floor, now used by a shop (entered from 79 Via Cavour), with handsome wood ceilings.

On the other side of the Broletto is Piazza delle Erbe, a charming square with a delightful row of houses at the far end. A long portico faces **Palazzo della**

Ragione, dating partly from the early 13C but with 14C–15C additions, including a conspicuous clock-tower (1473) by Luca Fancelli with an astrological clock by Bartolomeo Manfredi (1473), in perfect working order since its restoration in 1990. Next to it is the **Rotonda di San Lorenzo**, a small round church founded in 1082 and restored in 1908. The domed interior has two orders of columns and a matroneum. There is a small daily market in the square, and a large general market is held here on Thursday.

Sant'Andrea

In the adjoining Piazza Mantegna is the basilica of *Sant'Andrea, a very important Renaissance building commissioned from Leon Battista Alberti by Lodovico II Gonzaga in 1470 as a fit setting to display the precious relic of the Holy Blood. Although it was built after Alberti's death by Luca Fancelli (1472–94), then enlarged in 1530 under the direction of Giulio Romano, and the dome was added by Filippo Juvarra in 1732, it remains the most complete architectural work by Alberti. The brick campanile of 1413 is a survival from the 11C monastery on this site.

The remarkable **façade**, with giant pilasters, is classical in inspiration. In the barrel-vaulted vestibule, a beautiful marble frieze with animals and birds surrounds the west door.

Interior The huge *interior, on a longitudinal plan, has a spacious barrel-vaulted nave without columns or aisles. The rectangular side chapels, also with barrel vaults, are preceded by giant paired pilasters raised on pedestals. Between them are small, lower domed chapels. The transepts, with the same proportions, are also rectangular. The nave chapels were decorated in the 16C, partly by pupils of Giulio Romano, and the rest of the church in the 18C.

Begin your visit in the **south aisle**. You can appreciate Alberti's architecture in the first little chapel (the baptistery), whose walls are bare. Detached frescoes by Correggio have been placed here, but they do not interfer with the overall effect. In the next chapel are 16C frescoes attributed to Benedetto Pagni, and the pretty little third chapel is frescoed by Rinaldo Mantovano (1534). In the fourth chapel is a 16C wood ancona. The sixth chapel has a fine altarpiece, a 16C copy of the original by Giulio Romano (now in the Louvre); the frescoes, designed by Romano, were executed by Rinaldo Mantovano.

In the **south transept**, in the chapel to the right, are 16C funerary monuments, including that of Cantelmi (1534), with a painting attributed to Francesco Borgani. On the end wall of the transept is the fine Andreasi tomb by Prospero Clementi (1549), possibly on a design by Giulio Romano. The chapel of the Holy Sacrament has two paintings by Felice Campi.

The **dome** and **apse** are frescoed by Giorgio Anselmi (1782). On the left of the high altar is a statue of Guglielmo Gonzaga in prayer (1572). Beneath the dome is an octagonal balustrade marking the crypt, which contains the precious reliquary of the Holy Blood. Inside the balustrade is a black-marble plaque by Giovanni Bellavite and marble tondi by Gaetano Muttoni. The crypt is opened on request.

In the **north transept** is a door that leads out to a piazza, from where you can see the exterior of the church and a walk of the Gothic cloister of the monastery that stood on this site. The transept chapel contains 16C and 17C funerary monuments including that of Pietro Strozzi, an ingenious work of 1529 with four caryatids, designed by Giulio Romano. On the north side, the sixth chapel has an altarpiece of the *Crucifix* by Fermo Ghisoni, a pupil of Giulio Romano. The third chapel has an early 17C wooden ancona, and in the second chapel there is a beautiful altarpiece by Lorenzo Costa (1525).

The first little chapel, the *Cappella del Mantegna (unlocked on request by the sacristan), was chosen by Mantegna in 1504 as his funerary chapel. It contains his tomb with his *bust in bronze, possibly his self-portrait. The charming *panel of the *Holy Family and the Family of St John the Baptist* is almost certainly by Mantegna. Above is his coat of arms. The terracotta decoration and frescoes on the walls and dome, including the symbols of the Evangelists, were designed by Mantegna and probably executed by his son Francesco. The painting of the *Baptism of Christ*, probably on a design by Mantegna, is also the work of Francesco.

Palazzo Te

On the southern edge of the old town (see **Map**), about 1.5km from Piazza Sordello, surrounded by a public garden is *Palazzo Te (open Mon 13.00–18.00, Tues–Sun 09.00–18.00), one of the more important Mannerist edifices in Italy. This delightful suburban villa, on the site of the Gonzaga stables, was used in the summer by Federico II Gonzaga. Begun in 1525 and built of brick and stucco with bold rustication and numerous classical elements, it is Giulio Romano's most famous work, inspired by the great villas of Rome. The low building is spaciously laid out around a courtyard with symmetrical loggias and has a large walled garden beyond two fishponds. Here Federico held splendid entertainments and, in 1530, received Charles , when he was granted the Dukedom of Mantua by the emperor. The name is probably derived from *Teieto*, the name of the locality.

The architect and painter Giulio Romano was called 'that rare Italian master' by Shakespeare in *The Winter's Tale*. In the decorative design of Palazzo Te he was helped by his pupils, including Primaticcio, who executed some of the stucco work. The rooms of the palace, bare of furniture, are of interest for their painted and stuccoed decoration: they have been beautifully maintained after a careful restoration in 1979–89.

The entrance is through the west loggia, beyond which you can see the beautiful Cortile d'Onore. The Camera di Ovidio has a red Verona marble fireplace and landscapes by Anselmo Guazzi and Agostino di Mozzanega. The **Camera del Sole** has a fine ceiling with stuccoes by Primaticcio and a painting of the *Sun and Moon* by Giulio Romano. On the walls are casts of ancient reliefs put here in the Neo-classical era. Across the Loggia delle Muse is the *Sala dei Cavalli*, with frescoed portraits of horses from the Gonzaga stables by Rinaldo Mantovano (on a design by Giulio Romano) and a carved ceiling by Gasparo Amigoni (1528).

The **Sala di Psiche** has splendid *frescoes by Giulio Romano illustrating the story of Psyche as told by Apuleius. The next room, the Sala dei Venti, was the studio of Federico II. It has a ceiling with signs of the zodiac and tondi illustrating horoscopes, together with a fine stucco frieze and fireplace. The Camera di Fetonte or Camera delle Aquile has a fresco of the *Fall of Phaëthon* in the centre, and stuccoes including four eagles.

The fine **Loggia di Davide** (or Loggia d'Onore), with biblical frescoes, opens onto two fishponds and the gardens beyond. The Sala degli Stucchi was the last work executed by Primaticcio before his departure for France. The two classical friezes, in imitation of a Roman triumphal column, are thought to have been executed in honour of Charles V's visit. The Sala dei Cesari has a *trompe l'oeil* frieze of putti and Roman historical scenes in the vault.

The famous **Sala dei Giganti**, in which painting and architecture are united in a theatrical *trompe l'oeil*, is the work of Rinaldo Mantovano, Fermo da Caravaggio and Luca da Faenza (1532–34), on designs by Giulio Romano. It represents the *Fall of the Giants*, crushed by the thunderbolts of Jupiter hurled from Mount Olympus. The pavement was originally concave and was made up of large stones in imitation of a river bed. The room has strange acoustical properties.

The three Camerini a Grottesche were painted with grotesques in 1533–34 by Luca da Faenza and Gerolamo da Pontremoli. Beyond are three more rooms, the Camere dell'Ala Meridionale, with coffered ceilings and friezes of 1527–28, and Neo-classical stuccoes on the lower part of the walls.

The **garden**, beyond the fishponds, is closed at the end by an exedra (seated arcade), added c 1651, probably by Nicolò Sebregondi. The huge **Frutteria** to the right is now used for important exhibitions. On the left is the little **Casino della Grotta**, a secret apartment with more charming stuccoes by Giulio Romano and Primaticcio. There are long-term plans to reconstruct the gardens to the north of the villa.

The upper floor of Palazzo Te contains collections from the **Museo Civico**. These include the Egyptian collection of Giuseppe Acerbi; the Gonzaga collection of weights and measures; a numismatic collection; and a gallery of modern art including works by Federico Zandomeneghi and Armando Spadini.

Viale Te leads back towards the centre of the town: across Piazzale Vittorio Veneto and the Porta Pusterla, Largo XXIV Maggio leads to the ducal church of **San Sebastiano** (1460), designed by Alberti on a Greek-cross plan. This unusual building, with a beautiful raised vestibule, a side portico and a ground-level crypt, has been brutally altered over the centuries. The interior (open by appointment; apply at Palazzo Te) now contains the sarcophagus of the 'Martyrs of Belfiore' (Italian patriots shot by the Austrians in 1851–52), and the crypt serves as a war memorial.

Opposite is the plain brick **house of Mantegna** (open Tues–Fri 10.00–12.30; when used for exhibitions, Tues–Sun 10.00–12.30, 15.00–18.00). It was built to Mantegna's design in 1466–74 as a studio and private museum and has a remarkable circular courtyard. The artist lived here until 1502 when he donated it to Francesco II Gonzaga. A painting by Titian of Mantegna (or Giulio Romano) is exhibited here.

Via Giovanni Acerbi continues north to Via Carlo Poma. On this street is the **Palazzo Guerrieri**, now the courthouse (no. 7), with bizarre monster caryatids attributed to Viani. On the other side of the road (no. 18) is **Giulio Romano's house** (not open), which he purchased in 1538 when it was on the outskirts of the town. He transformed it in the 1540s, and it was enlarged in the 19C. The huge domed church of **San Barnaba** contains works by Lorenzo Costa the Younger (16C) and Giuseppe Bazzani (18C), and a fine high altar in *pietre dure*.

The Museo Diocesano and Palazzo d'Arco

From Piazza Sordello, Via Fratelli Cairoli leads west to the spacious Piazza Virgiliana, laid out in the Napoleonic period at the beginning of the 19C, with fine trees and a grandiose monument to Virgil. At no. 55 is the **Museo Diocesano**

Francesco Gonzaga (open Apr–Jun and Sept–Oct Tues-Sun 09.30–12.00, 14.30–17.00; Nov–Mar only on Sun and holidays, and Jul and Aug only on Thur, Sat and Sun), which contains a large miscellany of works of art in a provisional arrangement. It is entered through a pleasant courtyard with four large lime trees.

In the corridor is a Greek marble female head dating from the 1C AD (from the campanile of the duomo). In the large hall are paintings, including a tondo of the *Ascension* attributed to Mantegna (with its *sinopia*). The church silver includes processional crosses of the 14C and 15C. Also here are paintings by Francesco Borgani, Girolamo Mazzola Bedoli, Giuseppe Bazzani and Domenico Fetti. The second part of the room displays a bronze crucifix by Pietro Tacca; more paintings by Bazzani; a *collection of Limoges enamels (mostly 16C–19C); a 17C oval relief in silver; and the missal of Barbara of Brandenburg illuminated by Belbello da Pavia, Girolamo da Cremona and others.

At the end is a small room that displays ivories, a German jewel pendant that belonged to Duke Guglielmo Gonzaga, and a large *reliquary chest made of rock crystal (Venetian, c 1600).

Another section of the museum displays the splendid suits of *armour (some of them 15C) found on the life-size ex-voto statues in the sanctuary of Santa Maria delle Grazie. A marble statue by the Dalle Masegne family (1401) is also displayed here.

Beyond the other side of Piazza Sordello, reached by Via Zambelli, is the church of **San Leonardo**, with a high altarpiece attributed to Francesco Francia and a fresco attributed to Lorenzo Costa the Elder.

From the south end of the piazza, Via Virgilio, Via Cavour (right) and Via Finzi lead to Piazza Carlo d'Arco with the Neo-classical **Palazzo d'Arco** (open Mar–Oct, Tues–Sun 10.00–12.30, 14.30–18.00; Nov–Feb, Sun and holidays 10.00–17.00, Sat 10.00–14.30, 14.00–17.00). Built by Antonio Colonna in 1784 and decorated and furnished by the d'Arco counts, it was recently left to a foundation by Giovanna d'Arco. A large number of rooms in the palace are on show, with their 18C and 19C furniture. A room dedicated to Andreas Hofer, the Tyrolese patriot who was tried by a Napoleonic court here in 1810 before being shot outside the walls, is decorated with wallpaper of 1823 painted with *grisaille* views of Italy. Other rooms contain a collection of musical instruments, including a spinet, and many paintings, including works by Lorenzo Lotto (attrib.), Giuseppe Bazzani, Pietro Muttoni, Sante Peranda, Fra Semplice da Verona and Alessandro Magnasco. The library and the kitchen (with a good collection of pewter) are not usually shown.

In the garden are the remains of a 15C palace, where the *Sala dello Zodiaco has remarkable painted decoration attributed to Giovanni Maria Falconetto (c 1520). The frieze around the top of the walls, decorated with gilded wax, illustrates classical myths. Below are 12 lunettes with the signs of the zodiac over elaborate representations of classical myths against landscapes with Roman or Byzantine buildings (derived from monuments in Rome, Ravenna and Verona). Below each scene is a panel in *grisaille*.

Nearby is the Gothic church of **San Francesco** (1304; rebuilt in 1954), which contains a chapel where the first Gonzaga were buried with their wives, with frescoes (very worn) by Tommaso da Modena.

Frozen in time?

In winter, Mantua is one is the colder spots on the planet, due to its high relative humidity and the biting wind that blows down the Mincio. But it is a 'frozen' city in more ways than one: compare these descriptions, penned years ago, with what you see as you walk around town.

The Citie is marveilous strong, and walled round with faire bricke wals, wherein there are eight gates, and is thought to be foure miles in compasse: the buildings both publique and private are very sumptuous and magnificent: their streets straite and very spacious. Also I saw many stately Pallaces of a goodly height: it is most sweetly seated in respect of the marvailous sweete ayre thereof, the abundance of goodly meadows, pastures, vineyards, orchards, and gardens about it. For they have such store of gardens about the Citie, that I thinke London whch both for frequencie of people, and multitude of howses doth thrise exceed it, is not better furnished with gardens.
Thomas Coryate, *Crutidies*, 1611

The country... presents one continued grove of dwarfish mulberries, among which start up innumerable barren hills. Now and then a knot of poplars diversify their craggy summits, and sometimes a miserable shed. Mantua itself rises out of a morass formed by the Mincio, whose course, in most places is so choked up with reeds, as to be scarcely discernible. It requires creative imagination to discover any charms in such a prospect, and a strong prepossession not to be disgusted with the scene where Virgil was born... I abandoned poetry and entered the city in despair.
William Beckford, *Dreams, Waking Thoughts and Incidents*, 1783

Retrospect of Mantua, with its dome, & spires & towers; the first spires I have seen in Italy—a long line just above the waters of its lake—more like a Dutch town than any other.
Samuel Rogers, *Italian Journal*, 8 April 1815

If ever a man were suited to his place of residence, and his place of residence to him, the lean apothecary and Mantua came together in a perfect fitness of things. It may have been more stirring then, perhaps. If so, the Apothecary was a man in advance of his time, and knew what Mantua would be, in eighteen hundred and forty-four. He fasted much, and that assisted him in his foreknowledge.
Charles Dickens, *Pictures from Italy*, 1846

Back to the city centre

From Piazza d'Arco Via Fernelli leads back towards the centre past Piazza Canossa with the large **Palazzo Canossa** (with an interesting long façade and a handsome staircase), a little 18C chapel (two paintings by Bazzani have been removed from the interior), a fountain and a cast-iron kiosk. In Via Fratelli Bandiera is an interesting palace (no. 17) with remains of frescoed decoration and a handsome doorway.

Via Verdi continues back to the church of Sant'Andrea (described above), to the south of which Corso Umberto I, with its dark, heavy porticoes, widens out as it reaches Piazza Cavallotti. The latter is overlooked by the handsome **Teatro Sociale**, built in 1822 to a design by Luigi Canonica. Corso della Libertà leads east to Piazza Martiri di Belfiore, beside which, below a little park on the river is a **fish market** with a rusticated portico, built by Giulio Romano in 1546.

Just north of Piazza Broletto, Via Accademia leads to Piazza Dante with the **Accademia Virgiliana**, built by Piermarini in 1767. Here you can visit the ***Teatro Accademico Bibiena** by Antonio Bibiena (open Tues–Sun 09.30–12.30, 15.00–18.00), where Mozart gave the inaugural concert in 1770 at the age of 13, during his first visit to Italy. It is still sometimes used for concerts. In Via Pomponazzo are several palaces with handsome courtyards (nos 31, 27, and 23).

In a remote part of the town to the southeast (see **Map**) is the restored Romanesque church of **Santa Maria di Gradaro**, with a handsome Gothic portal of 1295 and Gothic frescoes in the presbytery.

In recent years naturalists have taken an interest in the birdlife and flora of the marshlands surrounding lakes, where lotus flowers introduced from China in 1921 grow in abundance. The valley of the Mincio is now a protected area. Boat excursions can be arranged by appointment (at the information office).

SABBIONETA

Sabbioneta, southwest of Mantua, was planned in 1556 by Vespasiano Gonzaga (1531–91) as an ideal fortified city, with regular streets within hexagonal walls and some beautiful buildings, including two palaces, a gallery and a theatre, all of which reflect his admiration for the classical world of Rome. Now a quiet little village, it is extremely well preserved, with fields reaching up to its walls and no ugly buildings on the outskirts. Vespasiano, who received the Dukedom of Sabbioneta from the Holy Roman Emperor in 1577, was a cultivated man, as well as a *condottiere*, and he spent many years at the court of Philip II of Spain. Besides its splendid 16C monuments, many of them recently restored, the town—which probably had a population of some 2000 at its height—preserves pretty streets of simple houses with a number of walled gardens.

History

Even with Vespasiano Gonzaga's comprehensive plans, the town was not built *ex novo*. Roman remains have been found in the area, and there was a *castrum* on this site in the Lombard period. There was already a castle here when Vespasiano chose the site for his new town in 1556. Many of the more important buildings were erected from 1578 to 1591, the date of Vespasiano's death, after which the town declined in importance. Because of its low position, it has often been subject to flooding from the River Po (especially in 1595, 1705 and 1951).

At the entrance to the town is the huge Piazza d'Armi, on the site of a 14C castle (only the foundations of two towers remain) that occupied this part of the town until it was demolished at the end of the 18C. The Corinthian **Roman column**, which supports a Roman statue of Athena, was set up here by Duke Vespasiano. Also here are the Palazzo del Giardino and the Galleria (both described below), and a monumental school building erected in 1930, as well as the tourist office.

Just off Via Vespasiano Gonzaga is the ***Teatro all'Antica**, by Vincenzo

Scamozzi, the last building erected for the duke (1588–90). This is the first example of a theatre built as an independent structure (not within a larger building) and provided with a foyer, separate entrances for the public and artists, changing rooms, etc. It has a handsome exterior with an inscription dedicated to Rome, and a charming interior (which can hold 200). The peristyle has stucco statues and busts of the Greek gods, and monochrome painted figures of Roman emperors. Above is a frescoed loggia with painted spectactors and musicians, by a Venetian artist. On the two side walls are large frescoes of the Campidoglio and Hadrian's mausoleum in Rome. The fixed backdrop, which represented a piazza and streets, was destroyed in the 18C (although there are plans to reconstruct it). The ceiling, which is lower than the original ship's keel roof, also dates from the 18C.

The **Porta Vittoria** (1567) was the main gate of the town. From outside there is a good view of the walls. The **Convent of the Servi di Maria** incorporates the octagonal church of the Incoronata, built in 1586–88 and modelled on the Incoronata of Lodi. It was beautifully decorated with frescoes in the 18C. The late 17C mechanical organ has its original pipes (concerts are given here in Sep). The monument to Vespasiano, with numerous rare marbles, was erected by Giovanni Battista della Porta in 1592 and incorporates his bronze statue by Leone Leoni (1588). He is buried in the crypt below.

In the delightful Piazza Ducale is **Palazzo Ducale**, the first important building built by the duke and his official residence. On the first floor the Salone delle Aquile has frescoes with festoons of fruit, and four wooden equestrian *statues representing Vespasiano, two of his ancestors, and a captain. They were made in 1589 by a Venetian sculptor and were part of a group of ten (the others six perished in a fire in the early 19C, except for the five busts exhibited here). The Sala degli Imperatori has a panelled oak ceiling and a frieze of fruit and vegetables including peppers and maize (which Vespasiano must have seen in Spain as they were not grown in Italy in the 16C). The Galleria degli Antenati, probably used as a studio, has *reliefs in stucco of Vespasiano's ancestors by Alberto Cavalli, and a barrel-vaulted ceiling with stuccoes and paintings. Other rooms on this floor have a painted frieze of elephants, a ceiling of carved cedar, and frescoes with views of Constantinople and Genoa.

On the ground floor are rooms with *grotteschi*, gilded wood ceilings and a monumental fireplace.

Also in the piazza is the church of **Santa Maria Assunta** (open for services on holidays), built in 1582. The chapel of the Holy Sacrament was added by Antono Bibiena in 1768 and has a delightful double perforated dome in stucco and wood and two marble reliquary 'cupboards'. The **Museo d'Arte Sacra** (open 10.00–12.00, 15.00–18.00; closed Mon, Fri morning, Nov–Mar and Aug) has two paintings by Bernardino Campi. The *Teson d'Oro* ('Golden Fleece') was the gold medal presented to Vespasiano in 1585 by Philip II of Spain when he was made a knight of the Order; it was found in his tomb in the Incoronata. Also exhibited here are a portable 16C organ, 17C–18C vestments, and church silver.

In Piazza d'Armi is the ***Palazzo del Giardino**, which was Vespasiano's summer villa built in 1578–88, with an oak cornice on the exterior. The atrium on the ground floor has a pretty vault, while the adjoining room has another charming vault with birds attributed to Bernardino Campi, and a lovely fireplace. From here you can see the remains of the walled garden with three *nymphaeums*. The first floor has a delightful series of *rooms with stuccoes and frescoes by

Campi and his pupils. They depict the Circus Maximus and Circus of Flaminius in Rome; myths from Ovid; Gonzaga personal devices (imprese); scenes from the Aeneid; and exotic animals (some of them probably seen by Vespasiano on his travels in Africa). The original polychrome marble floors are preserved. Another room (once decorated with Venetian mirrors) has painted landscapes.

Beyond a little room with grotesques is the entrance to the *Galleria, built in 1583–84. This remarkable gallery, 96m long, was built to display the duke's superb collection of Classical busts, statues and bas-reliefs (most of them taken to the Palazzo Ducale in Mantua in 1774). Decorated with frescoes and *trompe l'oeil* perspectives at the two ends, it has a handsome brick exterior and an open, well ventilated loggia below.

The **synagogue** (for admission enquire at the tourist office) is on the top floor of a house in Via Barnardino Campi. It has a fine interior by Carlo Vizioli (1824). There was a Jewish community in the town from 1436.

Outside Sabbioneta is the church of **Villa Pasquali** (if closed, ring at no. 1), built in 1765 by Antonio Bibiena. The second tower on the handsome brick façade was never completed. The interior is especially remarkable for the beautiful perforated double ceiling of the dome and three apses in terracotta. The various treasures of the church are carefully preserved.

Southeastern Lombardy

Southeast of Mantua is **Pietole**, a village usually regarded as the birthplace of Virgil. At Bagnalo San Vito is the furst Etruscan site (5C BC) discovered north of the Po and the most ancient site in Lombardy. The road crosses the Po, and there is a good view from the bridge of the pretty landscape on its banks.

San Benedetto Polirone

On the right bank is San Benedetto Po, which grew up round the important Benedictine abbey of *San Benedetto Polirone, founded in 1007 and protected by Countess Matilda of Canossa (1046–1115), who was buried here. United to the abbey of Cluny until the 13C, it was suppressed by Napoleon in 1797.

The extensive abbey buildings, mostly dating from the 15C, are in the large central piazza of the little town. The fine **church** was rebuilt by Giulio Romano in 1540–44 and is one of his more interesting works. It contains 33 terracotta statues by Antonio Begarelli and his school, including St Benedict (in the ambulatory). Here and there you can also see altarpieces by Francesco Bonsignori and Fermo Ghisoni (on the north side), handsome 18C wrought-iron work, 16C stalls, a Neo-classical altarpiece by Giovanni Battista Bottani and an 18C organ.

Off the ambulatory is the Romanesque church of **Santa Maria**, with a pretty interior. The fine mosaic pavement of 1151, with figures of animals, the Cardinal Virtues, etc. is well preserved at the east end (and there is another fragment in the nave). The altarpiece is by Fermo Ghisoni. In the sacristy, with frescoes by the school of Giulio Romano and fine wooden cupboards, is an equestrian portrait of *Matilda of Canossa* by Orazio Farinati: her empty tomb is just outside (her remains were sold by the abbot to Pope Urban VIII in 1633 when Bernini was commissioned to provide a monument in St Peter's).

To the right of the church is the entrance to a cloister, off which a Baroque staircase by Giovanni Battista Barberini (1674) leads up to the **Museo della Cultura Popolare Padana** (open summer, Tues–Sun 09.00–12.30, 14.00–17.30; by appointment in winter), a large, interesting ethnographical museum focusing on the region along the banks of the Po. Displays are arranged around the upper floor of the cloister of San Simeone, in the grand abbot's apartments and the simpler monks cells, and in the late-18C library, a Neo-classical space designed by Giovanni Battista Marconi. The lower walk of the 15C **Cloister of San Simeone** has 16C frescoes and a garden that has been replanted following its 16C design.

Across the piazza, on the other side of the church, is the former **refectory** (open at weekends or by appointment) built in 1478, with a museum of sculptural fragments and ceramics, and a *Madonna* by Begarelli. The huge *fresco, discovered in 1984, and attributed as an early work (1514) to Correggio, provided the architectural setting for a *Last Supper* by Girolamo Bonsignori, now in the Museo Civico of Badia Polesine and replaced here by a photograph. Two sides of the 15C cloister of St Benedict survive in the piazza, and the huge 16C infirmary behind the refectory is to be restored.

Along the Po

On the Po, further downstream, is **Ostiglia**, where the marshes have been declared a bird sanctuary. A short distance further down the river is the Isola Boschina, its woods a rare survival of the vegetation that was once typical of the Po landscape. There are plans to make the island into a nature reserve. On the south bank of the river is **Revere**, where there is a palace of Lodovico Gonzaga with a charming courtyard and portal by Luca Fancelli, and an 18C parish church with paintings by Giuseppe Bazzani. Here the Museo del Po has archaeological and historical material relating to the river. The Romanesque *pieve* of **Coriano** was founded c 1085.

South of Mantua, on the north bank of the Po, is **Borgoforte**, with an 18C castle and a parish church containing works by Giuseppe Bazzani. On the south bank of the river at **Motteggiana** is the Ghirardina, a 15C fortified villa attributed to Luca Fancelli. Southeast of here is Gonzaga, a pretty little town which was the ancestral home of the famous ducal family.

West of Mantua

West of Mantua on the Cremona road is the unusual church of *Santa Maria delle Grazie*, founded by Francesco Gonzaga in 1399. The nave has two tiers of lifesize statues in various materials set up as ex-votos—an astonishing sight. Some of the figures were clad in the armour now exhibited in the Museo Diocesano in Mantua. Also here is the tomb of Baldassarre Castiglione (d. 1529), probably by Giulio Romano. From **Rivalta**, to the north, boat excursions can be taken on the Mincio.

Canneto sull'Oglio, west of Mantua, preserves a massive tower belonging to its former castle. The Museo Civico (open Sun 10.00–12.30, 14.30–18.00 or 15.00–19.00; Mar–Oct also Sat 14.00–18.00 or 15.00–19.00) is dedicated to life on the River Oglio and also has a collection of dolls, which have been manufactured in the town since 1870. Nearby are **Asola**, which preserves its old walls, and **Bozzolo**, with its 14C tower and a palace of the Gonzaga.

North of Mantua

In the northern part of the province is **Castiglione di Stiviere**, which was once a fief of the Gonzaga. The Museo Storico Aloisiano in the Collegio delle Nobili Vergini (open Tues–Sun 09.00–11.00, 15.00–17.00 or 18.00) has mementoes of St Luigi Gonzaga, born here in 1568; paintings by Francesco Bassano, Federico Barocci, Giulio Carpioni and Giambettino Cignaroli; and collections of glass, ironwork and furniture. The Museo Internazionale della Croce Rossa (open Tues–Sun 09.00–12.00 and 14.00–17.30, Oct–March, or 15.00–19.00, April–Sept) commemorates the Red Cross, which was founded after the famous battle that took place at **Solferino** to the southeast, in which Napoleon III—in alliance with Vittorio Emanuele—defeated the Austrians in 1859. There is a memorial here to Jean Henri Dunant who, horrified by the sufferings of the wounded in this battle, took the first steps to found the international relief organisation. The tower of Solferino was erected on a hill probably by the Scaligers in 1022; it contains a Risorgimento museum. At the foot of the hill is Piazza Castello, a remarkably well preserved rectangular piazza on the site of the 11C–16C castle, whose domed watchtower survives. The attractive houses surround the 17C church.

TRENTINO-ALTO ADIGE

Trentino-Alto Adige, the mountain territory of the upper Adige Valley and South Tyrol, incorporates the modern provinces of Bolzano and Trento. It is a semi-autonomous region: it has a special administrative order, much like that of the Valle d'Aosta, that reflects its multi-cultural (Germanic, Italian and pre-Italian Latin, or Ladin) make-up. Most characteristic among the mountains of this region are the fantastic pinnacles of the Dolomites, the strangely shaped mountains disposed in irregular groups between the Adige and Piave valleys.

Strictly speaking, the Dolomites are a sub-range of the Eastern Alps. But anyone who has seen them knows that they are much more than that. 'The Dolomites... recall quaint Eastern architecture, whose daring pinnacles derive their charm from a studied defiance of the sober principles of stability.... The Dolomites are strange adventurous experiments, which one can scarcely believe to be formed of ordinary rock. They would have been fit background for the garden of Kubla Khan', wrote Leslie Stephen in *The Playground of Europe* (1871). This region, the 'Playground of Europe', has attracted visitors for centuries. Only recently (in the last ten years or so) have large areas of its unique landscape come under special tutelage. The major nature reserves of the Dolomites are dealt with at length in this section. So, too, are the region's main cities, Trento and Bolzano, each of which has its own, distinctive charm.

The region of Trento is almost entirely Italian-speaking, while in that of Bolzano (the Alto Adige) the native language of Ladin has, except in the more remote valleys, been overlaid by the official language of the ruling power: German until 1918 and, since then, Italian or German. The two provinces represent respectively the old ecclesiastic principalities of Trento and Bressanone (or Brixen), both of which in the Middle Ages paid nominal allegiance to the Holy Roman Empire. In the 14C–15C the prince-bishops held the balance between the rising power of Venice on the south and the Counts of Tyrol on the north, while in the 16C, under the bishops Clesio of Trento and Madruzzo of Bressanone, the valleys were practically independent.

The decay of local powers prevailed here as elsewhere in the 17C–18C, and the Trentino and southern Tyrol became more closely attached to the empire. During Napoleon's campaigns the region was transferred first to Austria, then (in 1803) to Bavaria; the insurrection of Andreas Hofer in 1809 led to a return to Austria in 1814. Austrian misgovernment in the 19C caused great discontent in the Trentino, and a movement for absorption into the Veneto. The successful outcome of the First World War brought the Trentino under Italian power, and the extension of the frontier northward to the strategic line of the Brenner was an inevitable consequence, though the mountain warfare in the region produced little result for either side. In the Second World War the road and railway over the Brenner Pass, the main channel of communication between Italy and Germany, was heavily attacked from the air.

Trento and its territory

The gateway to the eastern Alps is the valley of the River Adige, the southern entrance to which is guided by Trento and its sister city, Rovereto. To the east and west lie some some of the finest country in the Italian Alps, including the soaring Adamello-Brenta group with the lovely Non and Sole valleys; and the peaks known as the Pale di San Martino, with the long, beautiful Val di Fiemme and Val di Fassa. There are marvellous parks in the high-mountain areas, and numerous summer and winter resorts in the valleys.

Practical information

 Getting there and getting around
By air

The international airports nearest Trento are at Verona and Bolzano in Italy, and Innsbruck in Austria. Bolzano has daily flights to Rome and Frankfurt; the others to cities throughout Europe.

By road

The area is reached from Verona or Innsbruck by the A22 and 12. A long but scenic road (38) connects Lombardy with Bolzano via the Stelvio Pass, and a series of beautiful but tiring mountain roads link Trieste, Venice, Padua and Vicenza with Trento and Bressanone. **Parking** at the railway station and in marked lots (some underground) in Trento and Rovereto. Frequent **bus services** (operated by *SAD*, ☎. 0471 450111 or freephone 1678 46047; and *Atesina*, ☎ 0464 434299) connect Trento to Rovereto, Verona, Bolzano, Bressanone and most towns and resorts in the Dolomites.

By rail

Trento is on the main rail line from Verona to Innsbruck, with direct through service to Munich, Munster, Dortmund, Berlin and Vienna; or in the other direction, to Florence, Rome and Naples.

 Information offices
TRENTO Corso III Novembre 134, ☎. 0461 914444; Via Alfieri 4, ☎ 0461 983880.
ROVERETO Via Dante 63,☎ 0464 430363.

Parks

PARCO NATURALE ADAMELLO-BRENTA *Direzione* (park offices), Via Nazionale 12, Strembo (Val Rendena), ☎ 0465 804637; *Centro Visitatori* (Visitors' Centre), Lago di Tovel, Tuenno, Valle di Non, ☎ 0463 451033.
PARCO NATURALE PANEVEGGIO-PALE DI SAN MARTINO *Sede* (park offices), Via Roma 19, 38054 Tonadico, ☎ 0439 64854; *Centro Visitatori* (Visitors' Centres), Paneveggio-Predazzo, ☎ 0462 576283; San Martino di Castrozza, ☎ 0439 768859; *Azienda Promozione Turistica di San Martino di Castrozza e Primiro*, Via Passo Rolle 165, ☎ 0439 768867. *Parco Naturale Adamello-Brenta*, Corso III Novembre 134, Trento, ☎ 0461 914444. Madonna di Campiglio, Via Pradalago 4, ☎ 0465 442000. Pinzolo, Via al Sole, ☎ 0465 501007.

Resorts

VALLE DI FIEMME Via Fratelli Bronzetti 60, Cavalese, ☎ 0462 241111.
VAL DI NON Piazza San Giovanni 14 , Fondo, ☎ 0463 830133.
VALLE DI SOLE Viale Marconi 7, Malè,

☎ 0463 901280. Madonna di Campiglio, Via Pradalago 4, tel. 0465 442000.

SAN MARTINO DI CASTROZZA Via Passo Rolle 165, ☎ 0439 768867.

 ### Where to stay
Most of the hotels in the Trentino are open during the winter and summer holiday seasons, Dec–Apr and Jun–Sep. Hotels in the city of Trento are open all year round, unless otherwise marked.

TRENTO Because it is not a resort (notwithstanding its many natural and cultural assets), Trento is somewhat short on good hotels. Three comfortable, moderately priced places are:

America, Via Torre Verde 50, ☎ 0461 983010, fax 0461 230603; situated between the castle and the cathedral.

Aquila d'Oro, Via Belenzani 76, ☎ 0461 986282, fax 0461 986282 (closed Christmas week); adjoining the cathedral square.

Buonconsiglio, Via Romagnosi 16–18, ☎ 0461 980089, fax 0461 980038 (closed for a few days in Aug); between the train station and the castle.

Villa Madruzzo, Ponte Alto 26, ☎ 0461 986220, fax 0461 986361; a fine hotel and restaurant in a tranquil 19C villa with park, situated in a panoramic position above the city; moderate.

Parks

PARCO NATURALE PANEVEGGIO-PALE DI SAN MARTINO San Martino di Castrozza, physically in the centre of the park but outside the park boundaries, has several fine hotels:

Colfosco, Via Passo Rolle 8, ☎ 0439 68319, fax 0439 68427.

Cristallo, Via Passo Rolle 51, ☎/fax 0439 68134.

Des Alpes, Via Passo Rolle 118, ☎ 0439 769 069, fax 0439 769068.

Letizia, Via Colbricon 8, ☎ 0439 768615, fax 0439 762386.

Regina, Via Passo Rolle 154, ☎ 0439 68017, fax 0439 68017.

San Martino, Via Passo Rolle 277, ☎ 0439 68011, fax 0439 68841.

Stalon, Via Pez Gaiard 21, ☎ 0439 68126, fax 0439 768738.

All are warm, comfortable and moderately priced places enjoying views of the forests and mountains.

Try also at TONADICO, *Chalet Pierini*, ☎ 0439 62348, fax 0439 64792; a cosy chalet where the owner is an expert chef and alpine guide; inexpensive.

PARCO NATURALE ADAMELLO-BRENTA is best reached from Madonna di Campiglio, likewise surrounded on three sides by the nature reserve. Here are: *Bertelli*, Via Cima Tosa 80, ☎ 0465 441013, fax 0465 440564; comfortable and close to the lifts; moderate.

Grifone, Via Vallesinella 7, ☎ 0465 442002, fax 0465 440540; richly decorated with wood; moderate.

Hermitage, Via Castelletto Inferiore 69, ☎ 0465 441558, fax 0465 441618; a very pleasant place in a panoramic position on the outskirts of the town; inexpensive.

La Baita, Piazza Brenta Alta 17, ☎ 0465 441066, fax 0465 440750; small, cosy and centrally located; inexpensive.

Lorenzetti, Viale Dolomiti di Brenta 119, ☎ 0465 441404, fax 0465 440644; tasteful and restful, on the outskirts; moderate. *Oberosler*, Via Monte Spinale 2, ☎ 0465 441136, fax 0465 443220; a delightful, comfortable chalet with a good restaurant; moderate.

Spinale Club Hotel, Via Monte Spinale 39, ☎ 0465 441116, fax 0465 442189; centrally located and especially child-friendly; moderate.

Above the town at Campo Carlo Magno: *Golf Hotel*, Via Cima Tosa 3, ☎ 0465 441003, fax 0465 440294; the former mountain lodge of the Austrian emperors; expensive.

Carlo Magno-Zeledria, Via Cima Tosa 26, ☎ 0465 441010, fax 0465

440550; ideally located next to the golf course and ski slopes; moderate.

Try also at **PINZOLO**:

Corona, Corso Trento, ☎ 0465 501030, fax 0465 503853.

Ferrari, Via Matteotti 36, ☎ 0465 502624, fax 0465 502624; both comfortable; moderate.

Resorts

VAL DI FIEMME *Park Hotel Azalea*, Via Cesure 1, Cavalese, ☎ 0462 340109, fax 0462 231200; on the outskirts of the town, surrounded by a large park; inexpensive.

Ancora, Via IX Novembre 1, Predazzo, ☎ 0462 501651, fax 0462 502745; warm, well managed and comfortable; moderate.

Sporthotel Sass Maor, Via Marconi 4, Predazzo, ☎ 0462 501538, fax 0462 501538; central, friendly and full of light; moderate.

Zirmerhof, Redagno (Radein), ☎ 0471 887215, fax 0471 887225; a lovely, quiet place in an old farmhouse surrounded by woods and meadows; open Dec–Mar and May–Nov; moderate.

VAL DI FASSA *La Perla*, Via Pareda 26, Canazei, ☎ 0462 602453, fax 0462 602501; modern and comfortable, not far from the ski-lifts.

Tyrol, Viale Cascata 2, Canazei, ☎ 0462 601156, fax 0462 602354; family run, good views, great cuisine; inexpensive.

Alle Alpi, Via Moene 47, Moena, ☎ 0462 573194, fax 0462 574412; rustic but modern, with fitness centre; moderate.

Catinaccio/Rosengarten, Via Someda 6, Moena, ☎ 0462 573235, fax 0462 574474; a lovely alpine hotel looking over the town square to the mountains; moderate.

Post, Piazza Italia 10, Moena, ☎ 0462 573760, fax 0462 573281; central and comfortable, with a famous restaurant ('*Tyrol*'); moderate.

Patrizia, Via Rif 2, Moena, ☎ 0462 573185, fax 0462 574087; traditional family-run establishment, enjoying good views over the mountains; inexpensive.

Park Hotel Corona, Via Dolomiti 8, Vigo di Fassa, ☎ 0462 764211, fax 0462 764777; a traditional old hotel, all wood and fireplaces, with an excellent *pasticceria*; moderate.

VAL DI NON *Maria*, Piazza Centrale 2, Andalo, ☎ 0461 585828, fax 0461 585815; wooden balconies, rooms, central yet quiet; moderate.

Cles, Piazza Navarrino 7, Cles, ☎ 0463 421300, fax 0463 424342; a cordial and comfortable family-run place; inexpensive.

Lady Maria, Via Garibaldi 20, Fondo, ☎ 0463 830380, fax 0463 831013; in a carefully renovated old building in the town centre; inexpensive.

Alexander/Cima Tosa, Piazza Scuole 7, Molveno, ☎ 0461 586928, fax 0461 586950; central and elegant, with good views over the mountains and lake; inexpensive.

Ischia Dolomiti, Via Lungolago 8, Molveno, ☎ 0461 586057, fax 0461 586985; in a lovely lakeshore garden; inexpensive.

VAL DI SOLE *Henriette*, Via Trento 36, Malè; ☎ 0463 902110, fax 0463 902114; warm and comfortable, with lots of wood; sauna and pool; inexpensive.

Kristiana, Via Sant'Antonio 18, Pejo (Cògolo), ☎ 0463 754157, fax 0463 754400; modern-traditional architecture, good rooms and extensive health and beauty facilities; moderate.

Cevedale, Via Roma 33, Pejo, ☎ 0463 754067, fax 0463 754544; a traditional alpine hotel with cosy rooms and friendly staff; inexpensive.

 Eating out

TRENTO *Chiesa*, Parco San Marco, ☎ 0461 238766; fine local cuisine and ambience; closed Sun, Wed evening and Aug; moderate.

Le Due Spade, Via Don Rizzi 11, ☎ 0461 234343; osteria established in

1545, offering creative interpretations of traditional recipes and regional, Italian and imported wines; closed Sun, Mon morning and Aug; moderate. **PERGINE VALSUGANA**, 12km east of Trento, *Al Castello* (with rooms), ☎ 0461 531158; an excellent restaurant and small hotel in a 10C castle enjoying marvellous views over the surrounding countryside; closed some Mons and Oct–May.
VEZZANO, 4km from Lake Toblino, *Fior di Roccia*, Località Lon, ☎ 0461 864029; has a reputation for exquisite cuisine served with a flair; closed Sun evening and Mon; moderate.
ROVERETO *Al Borgo*, Via Garibaldi 13, ☎ 0464 436300; restaurant famous for its fish dishes and its wine cellar (which you can visit); closed Sun evening (all day Sun in summer), Dec–Jan and Jul–Aug; expensive.
At nearby Nogaredo, *Le Stie*, Piazza Centrale 10, ☎ 0464 412220, is a wonderful osteria with a good wine list, in the medieval Vallagarina; open evenings only, closed Mon and Jul–Aug; inexpensive.

Parks

PARCO NATURALE PANEVEGGIO-PALE DI SAN MARTINO After a brisk walk, stop in at *Malga Ces*, at Ces, 3km west of San Martino, ☎ 0439 68145; an elegant and inexpensive restaurant in a magnificent position, serving traditional Tyrolean fare with regional and Italian wines; closed May–Jun and Oct–Nov; inexpensive. *Tressane*, Via Roma 30, Tonadico, ☎ 0439 62415; another traditional place in splendid natural surroundings; moderate.
PARCO NATURALE ADAMELLO-BRENTA *La Trisa*, Via Manzoni 50, Giustino,
☎ 0465 501665; on a dairy farm, serving great cheeses and other local delicacies; open evenings only, closed Jun, Oct–Nov; inexpensive.
Mezzosoldo, Via Nazionale 196, Spiazzo (Mortaso), ☎ 0465 801067; a

hotel restaurant famous among locals for its exquisitely prepared regional dishes; closed Thur (except in summer), Oct–Nov and Apr–June; moderate.

Resorts

VAL DI FIEMME *Al Cantuccio*, Via Unterberger 14, Cavalese, ☎ 0462 340140; a family-managed place offering creative interpretations of traditional recipes; closed Mon evening, Tues (except in high season), late autumn and late spring; moderate. *Alla Chiusa*, Via Chiusa, 1 (the Cavalese-Lavazé road), Varena, ☎ 0462 340626; a simple trattoria with fixed menu (always delicious); closedd weekdays in low season; inexpensive.
VAL DI FASSA *Ja Navalge*, Via dei Colli 4, Moena, ☎ 0462 573930; exquisite game, mushrooms and other local delicacies; closed Sun evening and Mon in low season, and Jun and Nov; moderate. *Malga Panna*, Via Costalunga 29, Moena, ☎ 0462 573489; delicious country cooking, with outside seating and great views in fair weather; closed Mon (except Jul–Aug) and in low season; moderate.
Da Bocol, Via Avisio 10, Pozza di Fassa, ☎ 0462 763752; good wine, great local cuisine, beautiful location; closed Thur and Sun in low season; moderate.
Fuchiade, Località Fuchiade, Soraga (Passo di San Pellegrino), ☎ 0462 574281; another place for exquisite traditional food, an alpine hut (with rooms) accessible by foot or 4WD in summer, on skis or snowcat in winter (telephone ahead to reserve a ride); open Jun–Oct and Dec–Apr; moderate.
VAL DI NON *El Filò*, Piazza Scuole 3, Molveno, ☎ 0461 586151; good country osteria in the heart of the village; closed weekends in low season, and Nov; inexpensive.
VAL DI SOLE *Conte Ramponi*, Piazza San Marco 38, Malè, ☎ 0463 901989; excellent traditional fare and atmosphere to match, in a 16C building with plenty

of wood and old ceramic stoves; closed Mon (except in high season), Jun and Nov; moderate. *Mangiasa*, Località Mangiasa, Malè, ☎ 0463 902123; characteristic local cuisine on a flower farm; open Fri–Sun, evenings only, closed May–Jun; inexpensive.

Apple, aromatic-herb and wine ice-cream at *Gelateria Roby*, Piazza Garibaldi 5, Malè.

Entertainment

The favourite evening activity in the mountainous Trentino is to have a few drinks with friends at the local tavern (and then drive home, possibly on snow). Having said this, there are any number of other 'events' in the villages and resorts, either handed down by tradition or invented *ad hoc* for outsiders like ourselves, which fill the long summer evenings and dark winter nights. Many involve live music, theatre, pageantry, etc. Trento is a university town, which means there is music, film, and so on, during the academic year. In ski season après-ski clubs in and around the major resorts offer live folk and rock music well into the night. Check with the local information office, or with your hotel concierge, for details.

Shopping

The area around Trento and Rovereto is renowned for its wines, both red (*Marzemino, Merlot, Cabernet*) and white (*Nosiola, Pinot Grigio, Moscato*); the best growing district is the Vallagarina.

There are antiques fairs in Rovereto (*Mercato d'Altri Tempi*, first Sat of the month) and at Villa Lagarina.

Judging from the shop windows in Trento, there appears to be an extraordinary interest in sexy lingerie and scruptuous cakes—commodities that would seem to be incompatible with each other and with the city's chief claim to historical fame, as the home of the Counter-Reformation. But then again, this is Italy.

Special events

TRENTO *Mostra dei Vini del Trentino*, regional wine fair, Apr; *Festival Internazionale del Film della Montagna, dell'Esplorazione e dell'Avventura*, International Festival of Mountain, Exploration, and Adventure Films, Apr–May; *Feste Vigiliane*, with the *Palio dell'Oca*, popular feast and pageant, Jun; *Mostra Micologica*, mushroom fair, Sep; *Autunno Trentino*, classical music, Sep–Oct).

ROVERETO *Torneo Internazionale di Tiro con l'Arco*, international archery tournament, Sep. *Fiera di Santa Caterina*, local folk fair with food, drink and street theatre, Nov. *Rassegna Jazz*, international jazz festival, Nov.

Sports

There is no end to what you can do in this department—from **hiking**, **horse-riding** and **swimming** in summer, to **downhill**, **cross-country** and **back-country skiing** in winter. The Val di Sole is on the world championship **snowboard** circuit, and the ski-slopes of Madonna di Campiglio, Val di Fiemme and Val di Fassa are renowned throughout Europe. For details and discounts on lodging, ski passes, etc., contact the information offices listed above.

TRENTO
• • • • • • • • •

Trento is a cheerful town (population 101,000), capital of its province and of the autonomous region of Trentino-Alto Adige. It is encircled by spectacular mountain ranges. Though it remained in Austrian hands until 1918, it is a typically northern Italian city and entirely Italian speaking. It has a number of fine palaces and churches as well as the Castello di Buonconsiglio, famous seat of the prince-bishops of Trento.

History

A pre-Roman Raetian settlement in which traces of Celtic influence have been found, Trento was Romanised in the course of the 1C BC and became a *municipium* and an honorary colony (called *Tridentum*) in the Antonine period. Laid out on a regular plan around the Capitolium, which stood on the Doss Trento, the lone hill that rises above the left bank of the Adige, it was later extended along the left bank of the Adige. During the Middle Ages Trento owed its importance to its position on the main road from the Germany to Italy. Invaded by the Goths, Lombards and Franks, it became an episcopal fief in 1027, its bishops acquiring the temporal power that they held almost without interruption until 1802. Early in the 15C the citizens rebelled against the overwhelming power of the bishops, but local unrest came to an end with the threat of a Venetian invasion, Venice having secured control of the Val Lagarina as far up as Rovereto (1416). The Tridentines (as the inhabitants of Trento are known) asked for help from the Count of Tyrol, the Venetians were defeated in 1487, and in 1511 Austria established a protectorate over the Trentino. In the 16C the city rose to prominence under Bishop Bernardo Clesio and Bishop Cristoforo Madruzzo, and during the episcopate of the latter the famous Council of Trent met here (1545–63). The last prince-bishop escaped from the French in 1796, and the Austrians took possession of the town in 1813, holding it until 1918 through a century of great unrest.

The city centre

Piazza del Duomo is the monumental centre of the city. It is an extraordinarily handsome square, with an 18C Neptune fountain standing in the shadow of the 13C **Palazzo Pretorio** and **Torre Civica** (in front of which some Roman ruins have been excavated), and the 16C **Case Cazuffi**, adorned with frescoes by Marcello Fogolino and preceded by the small Fontana dell'Aquila.

On the south side of the square extends the austere left flank of the **Cathedral** of San Vigilio, a Romanesque-Gothic building of the 12C–13C with a powerful 16C campanile and a Romanesque-revival dome. Faced entirely in marble, it has magnificent decorative detailing and a beautiful apse against which stands the 13C Castelletto, with mullioned windows and crenellated roof.

The **interior** has three tall aisles with compound piers, a small clerestory in the nave, and cross vaults. Arcaded staircases ascend the west wall, amid 16C tomb monuments, to the galleries. The large Cappella del Crocifisso, in the south aisle, preserves a 16C wooden crucifix before which the decrees of the Council of Trent were promulgated. In the transepts are remains of 13C and 15C frescoes, and at the end of the north aisle, a 13C stone statue known as the *Madonna degli*

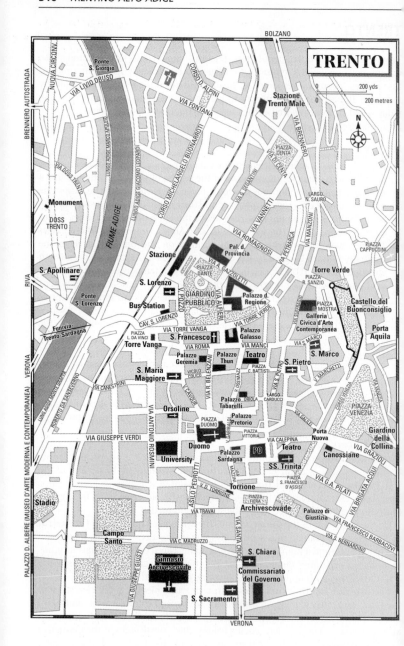

Annegati (Madonna of the Drowned), at the foot of which people drowned in the Adige were identified. It used to stand in a niche outside. The baldachin (canopy) over the high altar makes deliberate reference to that of St Peter's in Rome. Beneath the church are some masonry, remains of a mosaic pavement, and sculptural fragments from the 6C early-Christian basilica, which was rebuilt in the 11C and replaced by the present building two centuries later.

Inside the **Castelletto**, clusters of tall columns carry the arcades, surmounted by a diminutive clerestory, and unusual arcaded staircases lead up to the galleries. It contains numerous tombs of bishops, 13C–14C frescoes (some attributed to Tommaso da Modena), paintings by Carlo Loth, a 13C statue of the Madonna, and two 13C marble reliefs of St Stephen. The crucifix, before which the decrees of the Council of Trent were promulgated, is the work of Sixtus Frei of Nuremberg (1510–12).

The **Museo Diocesano** (open Mon–Sat 09.30–12.30, 14.30–18.00) occupies the Palazzo Pretorio, once the bishops' palace. It has a wonderful and beautifully displayed collection of paintings and sculpture from local churches and the most valuable objects from the cathedral treasury. These include the 13C treasure of Bishop Federico Vanga, the 15C crosier of Bishop Giorgio Hack, and a fine series of 16C Flemish *tapestries by Pieter van Aelst.

The 18C Palazzo Sardagna houses the **Museo Tridentino di Scienze Naturali** (open Tues–Sun 10.00–12.30, 14.30–18.00), with interesting natural history collections. Near the charming Renaissance Palazzo Tabarelli is the picturesque Cantone, once the chief crossroads in the town.

Via Belenzani, the city's elegant shopping street, is flanked by Renaissance palaces showing a strong Venetian influence, some—like the 16C **Palazzo Geremia** (no. 19), with charming frescoes of the early 16C showing the Emperor Maximilian, who stayed here in 1508–09, and members of his court; and **Palazzo Alberti-Colico** (no. 32)—with painted façades. Across the street stands **Palazzo Thun**, today the town hall, with frescoes by Brusasorci in the Sala della Giunta. At the corner here Vicolo Colico leads left to **Santa Maria Maggiore**, a Renaissance church of 1520–24 with a remarkable doorway and a fine campanile. Several sessions of the Council of Trent were held here, including the last one. The great portal of the façade dates from 1535; on the south side is a 16C Lombardesque portal. The *Assumption* over the high altar is by Pietro Ricchi, a pupil of Guido Reni; the marble organ gallery of 1534 is a masterpiece of the Vicentine sculptors Vincenzo and Gian Gerolamo Grandi.

Via Belenzani ends before the church of **San Francesco Saverio**, a fine example of local Baroque architecture; take Via Manci to the right. Here, too, are some interesting 16C and early-17C houses, notably no. 63, the baroque **Palazzo Galasso**, built by the banker Georg Fugger in 1602; no. 57, **Palazzo Pedrotti**, with a small museum of mountain-climbing; and, at the corner of Via del Suffragio, **Palazzo del Monte**, with a fine door and frescoes depicting the Labours of Hercules, executed around 1540.

The Castello del Buonconsiglio

Via San Marco, the continuation of Via Manci, ends at the foot of the Castello del Buonconsiglio, once the stronghold of the bishop-princes. It has two main parts. The crenellated Castelvecchio on the north was built in the 13C and altered in 1475. The Magno Palazzo on the south is a Renaissance edifice built in 1528–36

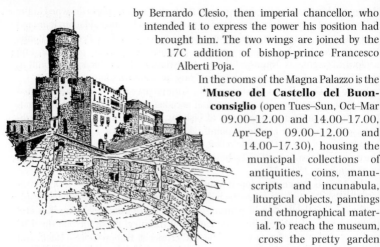

by Bernardo Clesio, then imperial chancellor, who intended it to express the power his position had brought him. The two wings are joined by the 17C addition of bishop-prince Francesco Alberti Poja.

In the rooms of the Magna Palazzo is the *Museo del Castello del Buonconsiglio (open Tues–Sun, Oct–Mar 09.00–12.00 and 14.00–17.00, Apr–Sep 09.00–12.00 and 14.00–17.30), housing the municipal collections of antiquities, coins, manuscripts and incunabula, liturgical objects, paintings and ethnographical material. To reach the museum, cross the pretty garden courtyard to the open stairway, built under

Castello del Buonconsiglio

bishop-prince Johannes Hinderbach (1465–86), whose coat of arms (the unicorn and flames) appears together with those of the principality of Trento (the eagle) and of the religious authority of the bishop (the pastoral staff and mitre) on the capitals of the columns here.

The stairs are frescoed by Marcello Fogolino, who painted the Renaissance decorative motives and historical potraits (Charlemagne with dignitaries and soldiers, and the early bishops of Trento) on a commission from Clesio. At the top the lovely **Loggia Veneziana**, with Venetian-style trilobate arches, overlooks the city in its amphitheatre of mountains. Through the former apartment of the bishop you reach the **private chapel**, adorned with the arms of Clesio (on the doorposts) and Hinderbach (on the ceiling) and figures of the evangelists, doctors of the Church (seated) and bishop-princes (standing).

First floor Now return to the first floor, where the state rooms are located. At the centre of the ceiling in the entrance hall is the Clesio coat of arms surrounded by a garland. The lunette frescoes of Greek mythological figures were painted in 1531–32 by Dosso Dossi and his brother Battista and make reference to the prince's humanistic political platform. The **Cappella Clesiana** or *Domus Orationis* was the state chapel; it has niches in the vault containing terracotta figures (of apostles, evangelists and four doctors of the Church) by Zaccharia Zacchi, a painted leather paliotto (altar frontal) and a 16C Veronese *Madonna*. The lovely **Cortile dei Leoni**—named after the two stone lions that are all that remain of a 16C fountain—follows. On its west side, a suite of magnificent rooms used by Bishop Clesio have ceilings frescoed in 1531–32 by the Dossi, Romanino and Fogolino, and plaster and terracotta decoration by Zaccaria Zacchi. In the **Camera delle Udienze** you can see Emperor Charles V speaking to his brother Ferdinand I and, above the entrance, Clesio with his secretary—together with lunettes in which eminent Hapsburgs are compared to Roman emperors. The **Stua delle Figure** has terracotta detailing by Zacchi and frescoes by Dosso and

Battista Dossi, who also worked together on the rich decorative programme of the **Camera del Camin Nero** or 'Camara di Stucchi' (in the paintings, cardinal virtues, arms of Pope Clement VII and Emperor Charles V, the liberal arts and their ancient epitomes, and medallions of Roman emperors); the **Sala del Tribunale**, formerly Stua de la Famea, was the dining room of the bishop's 'family', or court, before coming to host a court of a different kind (it was here that Italian patriot Cesare Battisti was condemned to death in the First World War).

Returning to the Cortile dei Leoni, you immediately come to the monumental **Loggia** that encloses its south side: on the ceiling is an ambitious cycle of mythological figures, allegories of night and day, and other humanistic subjects, frescoed in 1531–32 by Gerolamo Romanino. On the east the cortile overlooks the **Fossa dei Martiri**, where Cesare Battisti and his fellow patriots Damiano Chiesa and Fabio Filzi were executed by the Austrians in 1916.

Second floor Stairs at the west end of the loggia lead to the **second floor** and (straight ahead) the **Sala Grande**, where state ceremonies were held. The frieze, painted by Dosso and Battista Dossi in 1532, shows playful putti, letters of Clesio's Christian name, Berenardt, and elements of the Clesio arms mixed with symbols of ecclesiastic and temporal power. On the walls are the emblems of Charles V and Ferdinand I, bishop Francesco Felice Alberti d'Enno and the bishopric of Trento. The gilt coffered ceiling dates from 1531; the marble fireplace, by Vincenzo Grandi, from 1532. At the south end of the hall (left of the entrance) is the **Sala degli Specchi**, the room of mirrors, in the circular Torion de Sora. At the north (far) end a doorway leads into four more handsome rooms.

The first is the **Stua Grande**, where the frescoes, executed by the Dossi brothers in 1532, were destroyed and replaced in 1759 by the ones you see today, representing the Creation, the planets, the constellations, the zodiac and mythological scenes from Ovid's *Metamorphoses*. The large majolica stove, decorated with Old Testament scenes and grottesques, was part of the original 16C furnishings. From the Stua grande you can visit the **Camera degli Scarlatti**, named after the scarlet tapestries that once adorned its walls (gone today, though the complementary frescoes by the Dossi survive); and the rooms of the Giunta Altertiana, with fabulous carved wooden ceilings.

Return through the Sala Grande and past the stairs to enter the **private apartments** of the bishop, consisting of the **Stua del Signor**, the bishop-prince's bedchamber (frescoed by Romanino with busts of Roman emperors and other motives capable of reminding Clesio of his status even as he slept), the **Stua de la Libraria**, and the large, luminous **library**, with original wood ceiling (you recognise the arms by now) and 18C mural decorations. In the ceiling coffers paintings by Dosso Dossi reflect the prince's humanistic aspirations: pagan and Christian sages, orators, poets, and philosophers, all look down over a *faux* parapet to ensure their tradition is carried on.

The custodian stationed at the top of the stairs takes groups of visitors into the towers to see two more frescoed rooms and a part of the old fortifications. Make sure you do this, as it is the highlight of the visit to the castle. On a commission from Clesio the **Torre del Falco** was decorated after 1530 by an anonymous German painter, with a delightful series of *hunting scenes. Here you can learn all you need to know about falconing, hunting big game (bear, deer, chamois, boar), capturing birds and even angling; the city in the background is Salzburg,

Austria. In the **Torre dell'Aquila** are the castle's most famous ˚frescoes, com-missioined probably from a Bohemian artist by bishop-prince Giorgio di Liechtenstein, c 1400. Known as the *Cycle of the Months*, they are a perfect com-pendium of farming in the Sud Tyrol. In eleven handsome frames (March, unfor-tunately, has been destroyed) they show seasonal agricultural activities in the minutest detail. Harvests are plentiful and life is good—or almost: in winter while the peasants prepare for the spring planting, the nobles frolic in the snow...

The castle complex also houses the **Museo Civico del Risorgimento e della Lotta per la Libertà** (open as the Museo del Castello) with memorablia mainly of the Irredentist movement, of the First World War, and of the Resistance. In nearby Via Suffragio is the **Galleria Civica d'Arte Contemporanea** (entrance at Via del Suffragio 35; open Tues–Sun 10.00–18.00), offering an outstanding exhibition programme, mainly of contemporary painting and sculpture.

Other sights

The 14C church of **Sant'Apollinare**, with a doorway and rose window in Veronese red porphyry, a distinctive pointed roof and polygonal apse, lies on the right bank of the Adige. Behind it rises the **Doss Trento**, crowned by the mau-soleum of Cesare Battisti, from which there is a fine view over the city. Nearby are the remains of an early-Christian basilica and, to the south, the Museo Storico delle Truppe Alpine, tracing the history of the famous Italian Alpine Corps.

Returning to the left bank and walking southwards, you eventually come to Palazzo delle Albere, a square suburban villa encircled by a moat, built around 1535 for Bishop-Prince Cristoforo Madruzzo. Decorated with frescoes of which only traces remain today, it is home to the Trentine section of the **Museo d'Arte Moderna e Contemporanea di Trento e Rovereto** (open Tues–Sun 10.00–18.00), with works by Depero, Marinetti, Balla, Cangiullo, Prampolini, and other artists of the Futurist area; and exhibitions of contemporary art.

Around Trento

Monte Bondone, cloaked in forests, overlooks the city from the southwest. It is known for its alpine flora (it produces herbs used in baths in special establish-ments) and as a ski resort. The Conca delle Viotte, set beneath the peaks of the massif (Palon, 2090m; Doss d'Abramo, 2140m); and Monte Cornetto (2180m) hosts the **Giardino Botanico Alpino** (open Jun–Sep, 09.00–12.00, 14.30–18.00), with over 2000 plant species from the Trentino and the principal mountains of the world.

The **Lago di Toblino**, lying amid rocky mountains in the valley of the Sarca, 16km west of the city, is overlooked by a medieval castle. The lake is joined by an isthmus to the Lago di Santa Mazsenza, surrounded by olive trees. The modern **Museo Aeronautico Gianni Caproni** (open Tues–Sun 09.00–13.00, 14.00–18.00), at Mattarello, near the airport, has 18 antique planes and various exhibits regarding the history of flight in Italy.

The **Castel Beseno** (open Apr–Oct, Tues–Sun 09.00–12.00, 14.00–17.00; Jul–Sep 09.00–18.00), which controlled the valley south of Trento, is near Calliano. The hill was inhabited in the Iron Age, as well as in the Roman and

Lombard periods. The castle dates from the 12C and was owned by the Castelbarco from 1303 until the 15C, when it was given to the Trapp family, who donated it to the province in 1973. It has recently been restored and includes two large courtyards within its impressive walls. A room of the castle preserves 16C frescoes of the Months.

Rovereto

The most important town in the environs of Trento is Rovereto, a city possibly of Roman origin, spread out at the foot of a 14C castle. There are grand plans to open a museum and library complex in the historic centre of the city; the **Polo Culturale e Museale di Rovereto**, under construction at the time of writing in Corso Bettini, will combine facilities of the Biblioteca Civica and the Museo d'Arte Moderna e Contemporanea di Trento e Rovereto. The complex, designed by Mario Botta and Giulio Andreolli, is scheduled for completion in autumn 2000.

The castle is now home to the **Museo Storico Italiano della Guerra** (open Jul–Sept, Tues–Sun 08.30–18.30, Oct–May Tues–Sun 08.30–12.30, 14.00–18.00), with some 30 roooms devoted to the First World War. The war is commemorated also by the Sacrario (1936) and the Campana dei Caduti, the largest bell in Italy, which tolls every evening for the fallen of all nations. The front line of 1916–18 was in the valley south of the town.

The 15C **Palazzo del Municipio** has remains of façade frescoes attributed to Fogolino, and the contemporary Palazzo della Cassa di Risparmio shows Venetian influence. The **Museo Civico** (open Tues–Sat 09.00–12.00, 15.00–18.00; Jul–Oct, Fri 20.00–22.00), first opened to the public in 1855, houses the collections of the archaeologist Paolo Orsi (1849–1925), who was a native of the town, a planetarium and a natural history section. The Accademia degli Agiati was founded in 1750. Roverato is also the birthplace of Fortunato Depero, the Futurist painter (1892–1960), whose works can be seen at the **Museo Fortunato Depero**, Via della Terra 53 (open Tues–Sun 09.00–12.00, 14.30–18.00). The tapestries, furniture, mosaics, paintings and graphic works were all produced here in Depero's 'Casa d'Arte' between 1920 and 1942. Temporary exhibitions of early 20C art are held at the **Archivio del Novecento**, 58 Corso Risimini (open Tues–Sun 09.00–12.00, 14.30–18.00).

Castello di Sabbionara d'Avio

Around Rovereto

The picturesque **Castello di Sabbionara d'Avio**, the home of the Counts of Castelbarco since the 14C, lies to the south of Rovereto in a fine position on a hillside with woods and cultivated terraces above the Adige. It was the first monument in Italy to be donated (in 1977) to the *FAI* (*Fondo per l'Ambiente Italiano*) who restored it (open Feb–Dec, Tues–Sun 10.00–13.00, 14.00–17.00 or 18.00). The **Casa delle Guardie** has remarkable frescoes (1345–60) of battle scenes. The well-preserved keep, which dominates the fortress, dates from the 11C–12C. The **Stanza d'Amore**, on the fourth floor, preserves fragments of 14C frescoes with courtly scenes. In front of the tower is the Palazzo Baronale with remains of its chapel.

The Adamello-Brenta Group

The west flank of the Adige Valley, opposite Trento, is formed by the Presanella and Brenta mountain groups which, together with the east flank of Monte Adamello (3539m), constitute a protected area rich in sights of natural and historic interest.

In the Valli Giudicarie, between Stenico and Tione, is the ***Gola della Scaletta**, a narrow winding gorge of the Sarca. **Stenico** castle (open Tues–Sun 09.00–12.00, 14.00–17.00), dating from the 12C, was a stronghold of the prince-bishops of Trento. It is now owned by the province and has been restored. Inside are frescoes including battle scenes and female allegorical figures, as well as arms, furniture and archaeological material. To the north of Stenico is the lovely peaceful ***Lago di Molveno**, 6.5km long, lying under the lee of the Brenta mountains. Spectacular walks can be taken in the area.

The lovely ***Val di Non**, with its woods and ruined castles, is known for its apples: the landscape is particularly beautiful in spring, when the trees are in blossom. A scenic branch railway line runs through the valley, connecting Trento to Malè. The most important place along the way is **Cles**, whose castle was the ancestral home of the famous episcopal Clesio family, rebuilt in the 16C. Standing at the foot of Monte Peller (2319m), the northern peak of the Brenta group, it has a good Renaissance church and old houses. Also pleasant is **Sanzeno**, a village with a large 15C church built on the site of the martyrdom in 397 of Sisinio, Martirio and Alessandro from Capodoccia. The **Museo Retico** in Piazza Fontana (open daily, Jul–Aug 10.00–12.00, 16.00–19.00), has an interesting collection of archaeological material ranging from the Neolithic to the late Bronze Age. Above the village is the sanctuary of ***San Romedio**, a pilgrim shrine on a steep rock.

To the northwest of Cles is the **Val di Sole**, the upper glen of the Noce (now used for canoeing and rafting). **Malè**, the main village in the valley, has a local ethnographical museum (Museo della Civiltà Solandra).

Madonna di Campiglio (1522m) is a famous winter and summer resort in a wooded basin in the upper valley of the Sarca, below the Brenta mountains. It has excellent ski facilities. The Brenta mountains, an isolated Dolomitic group between Madonna di Campiglio and the Adige valley, are for expert climbers only, but there are many easier walks (marked by coloured signs) in their foothills. A path (or chair-lift) ascends Monte Spinale (2104m), from which there is a splendid circular view of the Brenta, Adamello, Presanella and Ortler mountains. To the south is the magnificent **Val Brenta**.

Pinzolo, another ski resort and climbing centre, is in a splendid position at the junction of the two main upper valleys of the Sarca.The church of ***San Vigilio** has a remarkable external fresco of the *Dance of Death* by Simone Baschenis (1539). A similar painting (1519) by the same artist decorates the exterior of the church of Santo Stefano, which also contains frescoes by him inside.

The **Val di Genova** is a magnificent valley, thickly wooded in parts and with several waterfalls, which is the main approach to the Presanella and Adamello groups from the east. The Presanella (3556m) was first ascended by the English alpinist Douglas Freshfield (d. 1929) in 1864.

Riserva Naturale Adamello-Brenta

The largest protected area in the Trentino (618sq km) lies a stone's throw from Trento. The Adamello-Brenta nature reserve extends from the Dolomiti di Brenta on the east to the Adamello and Presanella massifs on the west, encompassing a total of 618sq km. It forms a sort of natural bridge between the limestone-like Dolomites and the granite massifs of the Central Alps, presenting visitors with majestic glaciers, secluded high-mountain lakes and a variety of flora and fauna.

The flora of the reserve reads like an encyclopaedia of southern alpine plantlife, with splendid forests—consisting mainly of red and white firs, larches and Scots pines at higher altitudes, and oaks, maples, sorbs, hazels, alders and cornels below—growing to an altitude of c 2000m, and colonies of mugo pine, dwarf willow and rhododendron reaching to 2500m. As elsewhere in the Alps, thousands of years of human presence have left their mark: not only is settlement intense in valley areas (especially on the hillsides, at a safe distance from the 'bad air' or *malaria*, which made the valley floor uninhabitable); seasonal grazing has reduced the extent of the autoctonous high-altitude plants, turning many of the areas above the treeline into pasture. These high meadows have, in their turn, been colonised by innumerable species of Alpine flowers—notably gentians, anenomes, arnicas, Alpine poppies, edelweiss and several kinds of lily.

The reserve is the last refuge in Italy of the Alpine brown bear, who shares the woodlands with numerous deer, chamois, roe deer, marmots and rare birds. As a rule the bear are too few and too secluded (they live largely on the wild northeast slopes of the Brenta) to be sighted, but chamois are quite common: there were over 6000 at last count, nearly half the population of the Trentino. These and the park's 5000 deer can best be seen at dawn and dusk. Marmots abound above the tree line, and the forests abound with squirrel, weasel, hare and other small animals. Birdlife includes white partridge, wood grouse, woodpeckers, owls, cuckoos, hawks and eagles.

The Val di Fiemme and Val di Fassa

Cavalese is the main village in the Val di Fiemme, the middle course of the Avisio. Like many of the valleys of the Pyrenees, this glen has preserved something of its medieval independence, and the 'Magnifica Comunità', installed in the ancient palace of the bishops of Trento, still administers the valuable communal lands. The palace contains a museum (open Jul–Aug and at Christmas, daily 16.30–19.30), illustrating the history of the valley.

Predazzo (1018m) has an interesting collection of local geological specimens in the Museo Civico (open Mon–Fri 15.00–18.00; also 10.00–12.00 in summer).

The Ladin-speaking Val di Fassa is in the heart of the Dolomites; between Pozza di Fassa and Canazei it forms part of the Strada dei Dolomiti. The main village is **Vigo di Fassa** (1382m), a winter sports resort, where the Museo Ladino (being moved to new quarters at the time of writing) records the history of the fascinating Ladin cultural-linguistic minority, which inhabits the area around the Sella massif (Val di Fassa, Val Badia, Val Gradena, and parts of the Livinallongo-Ampezzano, Comelico and Canton Grison in Switzerland). The fantastic **Torri del Vaiolet** is typical of the Dolomitic mountains.

Parco Naturale Paneveggio-Pale di San Martino

The marvellous peaks of the Pale di San Martino and the vast national forest of Paneveggio, to the east of Predazzo, comprise the most spectacular nature reserve in the province of Trento, opened in 1987. It is an area of extraordinary beauty, marred only by the presence of ski slopes around the popular resort of **San Martino di Castrozza** which, though surrounded by the park, does not fall under its protection.

Getting there

To reach the Parco Naturale Paneveggio-Pale di San Martino from Trento, take the A22 north to the Egna-Ora exit, then 48 to Predazzo and 50 to Paneveggio. To reach the park from the east, take 47 from Bassano del Grappa to Primolano, then 50 to San Martino di Castrozza. By train, take the branch line from Padua to Feltre and proceed to San Martino by bus. Maps: Kompass 1:25,000, *Parco Naturale Paneveggio-Pale di San Martino*.

The park covers an area of 190sq km, the geology of which varies considerably from place to place. The northwestern region is characterised by porphyritic rock of volcanic origin and by areas of sandstone and marl; the southwest by Palaeozoic metamorphic rock, and the southeast (the Pale di San Martino area) by Triassic Dolomite, of which the highest mountains—the Cima della Vezzana (3192m) and the Cimon de la Pala (3184m)—are made.

The great green mantle of the **Foresta di Paneveggio**, which occupies the upper valley of the Travignolo, includes 2690h of conifers and 1300h of active pastures. Although it suffered extensive damage during the First World War, it remains an example (rare in Italy) of correct forest management, where a century-old tradition, inaugurated during the Austro-Hungarian period, has been carefully preserved. Here you'll find red and white firs, larches, cembra pines, yews and various deciduous trees, including beeches, oaks and aspens. At higher altitudes the ground is covered with scrub pine and rhododendron, whortleberry and heather.

The flora of the park presents a wide variety of alpine species, among which are edelweiss, dwarf rhododenron, the indigenous bellflower *Campanula moret-*

tiana, poppies, gentians and arnicae. The most interesting area is the Val Venegia, where you can find over 500 species, among them rare endemisms such as *Saxifraga facchinii, Primula tyrolensis, Juncus arcticus* and *Dactilorhiza cruenta*.

The park's fauna includes hundreds of chamois and roe dear, and numerous deer, which were extinct in the area until they were reintroduced in the 1960s. Also present in good numbers are marmot, squirrel, hare, ermine, weasel, marten and fox. Among the more interesting birds are the royal eagle, dwarf owl, white partridge and black woodpecker.

Walking in the Val Venegia

This easy (though long) walk departs from Passo Rolle (1980m), on route 50; to do it all will take you around 7 hours. In addition to interesting fauna and flora (the Paneveggio Forest), it offers a textbook tour of the Dolomites' chief geological formations, ranging from the crystalline calcium magnesium carbonate that gives the mountains their name, to magmatic porphyry, to sedimentary Werfen strata.

From the curve just east of the Passo Rolle take a dirt road that climbs northwards to the **Capanna Cervino** (2082m) and, beyond the Passo Costazza, to the **Rifugio Segantini** (2174m), amidst stunning scenery. From the shelter, a dirt track descends into the stupendous Val Venegia beneath the steep walls of the **Cimon della Pala** (3184m), the **Vezzana** (3192m) and the **Bureloni** (3130m). At an altitude of 1884m turn right on Trail 749, which climbs through the vast pastures of the Buse dei Laibi to the **Forcella Venegia** (2217m), where it joins the Dolomite High Trail no. 2. Heading northwest, you soon reach the **Passo Vallès** (2032m), with its shelter, ☎ 0437 50270. From here you descend on the dirt road to **Malga Vallazza** (1935m), where you pick up, heading south, an old military mule track that crosses the **Paneveggio Forest**, passes near the **Malga Juribrutto** (1912m) and descends to Paneveggio. From here you can return to the Passo Rolle on foot or by bus.

Bolzano and environs

This chapter focuses on the main city and provincial capital of the Alto Adige, Bolzano. It also deals with a portion of the Dolomites and with the Central Alps between Lombardy and the Adige. The pale rock towers of the Dolomites rise to the east of Bolzano; the dark-grey granite peaks of Central Alps to the west. The difference in atmosphere between the two areas is remarkable. Though the Dolomites are more picturesque, the Central Alps are more imposing. They are also the higher of the two ranges and are covered with snow much of the year. There are magnificent nature reserves in both areas—the most accessible, the Parco Naturale dello Sciliar, is just a stone's throw from the city—and summer and winter resorts abound.

Practical information

Getting there and getting around
By air

Bolzano has a small regional airport with flights to and from Rome and Frankfurt, Germany. The international airports nearest Bolzano and the central Dolomites are at Verona in Italy, and Innsbruck in Austria. Both have daily flights to cities throughout Europe.

By road

The area is reached from Verona or Innsbruck by the A22 and 12. A long but scenic road (38) connects Lombardy with Bolzano via the Stelvio Pass, and a series of beautiful but tiring mountain roads link Trieste, Venice, Padua and Vicenza with Trento and Bressanone. Frequent bus services (operated by SAD, ☎ 0471 450111 or freephone ☎ 1678 46047; VVB, ☎ 0473 448209) connect Trento, Bolzano and Bressanone to most towns and resorts.

By rail

Bolzano is on the main rail line from Verona to Innsbruck, with direct through service to Munich, Munster, Dortmund, Berlin and Vienna; or in the other direction, to Florence, Rome and Naples. Merano has a rail service to and from Verona, Milan, Florence, Rome, Innsbruck and Munich. A secondary rail-and-bus line runs from Padua to Cortina d'Ampezzo via Castelfranco, Feltre and Belluno, with connections for the Val Pusteria, Bressanone and Bolzano.

Information offices
BOLZANO Piazza Walther 8, ☎ 0471 307000.
MERANO Corso della Libertà 35, ☎ 0473 235223.

Parks

PARCO NATURALE DELLO SCILIAR
Ufficio Parchi, Provincia Autonoma di Bolzano, Via Cesare Batisti 21, ☎ 0471 994300; Ufficio Provinciale per il Turismo dell'Alto Adige, Servizio Informazioni Alpine, Piazza Walther 8, 39100 Bolzano, ☎ 0471 993809.
PARCO NAZIONALE DELLO STELVIO
The administrative centre of the park is now at Bormio in Lombardy (Via Roma 26, ☎ 0342 901654, fax 0342 919357). There are seasonal information centres at Prato allo Stelvio and Cogolo.

Resorts

BOLZANO has a **central information office** for all the resorts in its province at Piazza Parrocchia 11, Bolzano, ☎ 0471 993808, fax 0471 993889, www:provincia.bz.it.turismo. *Hotel reservation service,* ☎ 0471 222220, fax 0471 222221. *Snow bulletin,* ☎ 0471 200198, fax 0471 201157. *Walking and climbing bulletin,* ☎ 0471 993809.

Where to stay

Most of the hotels in the environs of Bolzano are open during the winter and summer holiday seasons, Dec–Apl and Jun–Sep. Hotels in the city are open all year round unless otherwise marked.
BOLZANO *Alpi,* Via Alto Adige 35, ☎ 0471 970535, fax 0471 400156; a modern place conveniently located near the train station; moderate.
Greif, Piazza Walther 7, ☎ 0471 318000, fax 0471 318148, www.greif.it; established in the 16C and managed since the early 19C by the same family, it was recently renovated in a beautiful contemporary Viennese style; it is located across the square from the cathedral; moderate.
Luna-Mondschein, Via Piave 15, ☎ 0471 975642, fax 0471 975577; featuring a pleasant garden where meals can be taken in summer and a traditional

stube for colder weather; moderate.
Magdalenerhof, Via Rencio 48a, ☎
0471 978267, fax 0471 981076; a
carefully appointed place with Tyrolean
ambience, set amid vineyards on the
outskirts of town; inexpensive.
Park Hotel Laurin, Via Laurin 4, ☎
0471 311000, fax 0471 311148;
named after the mythical dwarf-king of
the Dolomitesa great historic hotel in a
lovely park a stone's throw from the
train station and from Piazza Walther;
expensive.
Scala-Stiegl, Via Brennero 11, ☎ 0471
976222, fax 0471 976222; a fully renovated turn-of-the-20C home with spacious rooms and garden restaurant;
inexpensive.
RENON *Kemten*, at Caminata, ☎ 0471
356356, fax 0471 356363 (closed mid-
Nov–mid-Dec and mid-Jan–early Feb); a
particularly tranquil place in a lovely
park with great views of the Dolomites
and a very good restaurant; moderate.
Lichtenstern, at
Costalovara/Wolfsgruben, ☎ 0471
345147 fax 0471 345635; set in an
immense park with walking paths and a
playground; moderate.

Parks

PARCO NATURALE DELLO SCILIAR
Good places to stay in and around the
park (all moderately priced) are:
Cavallino d'Oro-Goldenes Rössl, on
the main square of Castelrotto/
Kastelruth, ☎ 0471 706337, fax 0471
707172; dating back to the 14C and
offering the most distinctive Tyrolean
atmosphere, including two fine *stuben*;
closed Nov–Dec.
Emmy, at Fie' allo Sciliar, ☎ 0471
725006, fax 0471 725484; in a fine
position surrounded by meadows, with
views of the forests and mountains;
closed Nov–Mar.
Schlosshotel Mirabell, 1km north of
Siusi, ☎ 0471 706134, fax 0471
706249; in a tastefully renovated
villa; closed mid-Apr–May and mid-

Oct–mid-Dec.
Sporthotel Floralpina, Saltria 50, Alpe
di Siusi, ☎ 0471 727907, fax 0471
727803; in a picturesque location with
views of the mountains and forests;
closed mid-Apr–mid-Jun, mid-Oct–Dec.
Steger Dellai, ☎ 0471 727964, fax
0471 727848; with swimming in a
nearby lake; closed Oct–Nov and May.
Thurm, Piazza della Chiesa 9, Fiè allo
Sciliar, ☎ 0471 25014, fax 0471 25474;
was a medieval prison but is now a
refined, comfortable hotel with an excellent restaurant; closed Nov–Dec, moderate. Simpler and less expensive is the
Waldrast, Via Hauenstein 25, Siusi, ☎
0471 706117, fax 0471 707062;
closed Oct–Dec and late Apr–early May.
PARCO NAZIONALE DELLO STELVIO
The park straddles the boundary
between Lombardy and the Alto Adige;
accommodation on the west (Lombard)
slope can be found in and around
Bormio (see p 237). The gateway to the
east slope is the Val Venosta, listed
under 'resorts', below.

Resorts

MERANO *Park Hotel Mignon*, Via
Grabmayr 5, ☎ 0473 230353, fax
0473 230644; centrally located, with
heated pool and sauna; closed Nov–Mar;
expensive.
Meranerhof, Via Manzoni 1, ☎ 0473
230230, fax 0473 233312; also comfortable, with heated pool in the garden;
moderate.
Kurhotel Schloss Rundegg, Via Scena
2, ☎ 0473 234100, fax 0473 237200;
probably the most interesting place to
stay in town, a 12C building enlarged in
the 16C, immersed in a lush garden;
closed Jan; moderate.
Villa Tivoli, Via Verdi 72, ☎ 0473
446282, fax 0473 446849; family-
managed, with a sunny breakfast terrace and exotic garden; closed Nov–Mar;
moderate.
Aurora, Passeggiata Lungo Passirio 38,
☎ 0473 211800, fax 0473 211113;

quiet and elegant, in the pedestrian area; closed Dec–Mar; moderate.

Schloss Labers, Via Labers 25, ☎ 0473 234484, fax 0473 234146; another old (13C) castle, surrounded by vineyards, with garden restaurant in summer; closed Nov–Mar; moderate. **Isabella**, Via Piave 58, ☎ 0473 234700, fax 0473 211360; comfortable and relaxed—ask for a rooftop suite; closed Nov–Mar; inexpensive.

VAL VENOSTA Ludwigshof, Breitofenweg 9a, Lagundo/Algund, ☎ 0473 220355, fax 0473 220420; small and cosy, with a nice garden; closed Nov–Mar; inexpensive.

Pünthof, Via Steinagh 25, Lagundo/Algund, ☎ 0473 448553, fax 0473 449919; a tastefully renovated farmhouse with fine restaurant, tavern, orchard and pond; closed Nov–Mar; moderate.

Lindenhof, Via della Chiesa 2, Naturno/Naturns, ☎ 0473 666242, fax 0473 668298; nice rooms, good restaurant, covered pool; closed Nov–Mar; moderate.

Sunnwies, Via Kleeberg 7, Naturno/Naturns, Tyrolean decor, pleasant atmosphere; closed Nov–Mar; moderate.

VAL SENALES Rosa d'Oro, at Certosa/Karthaus, ☎ 0473 679130, fax 0473 679115; a small, tasteful and comfortable family-managed establishment; inexpensive.

 ### Eating out

BOLZANO The large, comfortable bar at the *Hotel Laurin* is frescoed with the legend of King Laurin, and is a good place to spend an evening with friends (summer seating on the open veranda), even if you don't stay there.

The **Belle Epoque** restaurant (☎ 0473 311000), one of the finest in the city, serves traditional local dishes prepared with great care, accompanied by a wide selection of regional, Italian and imported wines; its prices are surprisingly moderate, given the setting, and excellent value.

Elegantly decorated interiors and summer garden service go hand-in-hand with skilfuly prepared traditional dishes to make **Da Abramo**, Piazza Gries 16, ☎ 0471 280141; one of the favorite restaurants of Bolzanini; here, too, you'll find an interesting wine list and moderate prices; closed Sun and a few days in Aug.

Try also **Amadè**, Vicolo Cà dè Bezzi 8, ☎ 0471 971278; offering traditional cuisine with a personal twist; closed Sun and Aug; inexpensive.

Cavallino Bianco/Weisses Rössl, Via Bottai 6, ☎ 0471 973267; a favourite old-fashioned osteria, always crowded, with delicious local food; closed Sat evening and Sun; inexpensive.

Da Cesare, Via Perathoner 15, ☎ 0471 976638; a friendly, centrally located establishment where fresh pasta and grilled meats are specialties; closed Mon; inexpensive.

Rastbichler, Via Cadorna 1, ☎ 0471 261131; a well-known place with a nice garden for the warmer months, offering periodic 'gourmet weeks'; closed Sat morning and Sun, Jan and Jul; inexpensive.

On the Renon/Ritten highland, try **Patscheiderhof**, Località Signato/Signat 178, ☎ 0471 365267; a farm, famous among Bolzanini but unknown to outsiders, serving delicious country meals; closed Tues and Jul; moderate.

Parks and resorts

PARCO NATURALE DELLO SCILIAR
Heubad (with rooms), Via Sciliar 13, Fie', ☎ 0471 725020; a family-run restaurant in a historic building, now a hotel with pool and garden, in a good position.

Tschafon (with rooms), ☎ 0471 725024; a small, cosy restaurant offering refined, creative interpretations of regional and French cuisine; closed Mon, Jan and Nov. Both are inexpensive.

MERANO *Sissi*, Via Galilei 44, ☎ 0473 231062; a family restaurant offering good traditional cuisine; closed Mon and Jul; moderate.

Home-made beers at *Greiterhof*, on the Stradina di Castel Verruca, near Avelengo.

VAL VENOSTA/VAL SENALES/PARCO NAZIONALE DELLO STELVIO The best restaurant in this area is *Steghof* at Naturno/Naturns, ☎ 0473 668224; featuring authentic medieval ambience and delicious cuisine; open evenings only, closed Sun, Mon and Jan–Feb: inexpensive.

Moserspeck, Via Stein 17, Naturno/Naturns, has good locally-made speck and salami.

Reinhold Messner lives in the castle just above *Schlosswirt Juval*, Località Juval-Stava Venosta, Castelbello Ciardes/Kastelbell Tschars, ☎ 0473 668238; a *buschenhschanki*, or old farmhouse serving traditional Tyrolean fare and wines from the estate of the climber; closed Wed, Dec–Easter and Jul; inexpensive.

Another old farmhouse with cosy *stuben* is *Oberlechnerhof*, Località Velloi 7, Lagundo/Algund, ☎ 0473 222557; serving local food and wines; closed Wed and Jan; inexpensive.

The *Latteria Sociale* at Lagundo is a dairy-farmers' co-op selling fresh and aged local cheese. At San Leonardo in Passiria/Sankt Leonard in Passeier, is Jägerhof, Via Passo del Giovo 80, Vàltina/Walten, a friendly family-run place (with rooms) offering delicacies of the Val Passiria; closed Mon and Nov; inexpensive.

Entertainment

As in the Trentino, the favourite evening activity in Bolzano and environs is social drinking: especially in the villages, the local bars can get noisy, crowded and smoky after 20.00. In high season there are also *feste* in the resorts, often involving live music, theatre, pageantry, etc. In ski season après-ski clubs in and around the major resorts offer live folk and rock music well into the night. Check with the local information office, or with your hotel concierge, for details.

Shopping

For vacationing Italians, Austrians and Germans, Bolzano seems to be *the* place in the Dolomites to shop. As a result, the shops are filled with beautiful merchandise, from clothing to Italian designer housewares. Unfortunately, high demand tends also to drive up prices.

Throughout the region farms sell local products, ranging from herbal teas, grappa, honey and fruit preserves, to handmade pillows and slippers.

Special events

BOLZANO *Atelier dell'Artigianato Artistico Altoatesino*, local crafts fair in Piazza Walther, Apr. *Concerto di Pasqua*, traditional music and costume at San Genesio, Easter Sunday; *Festa dei Fiori*, flower show in Piazza Walther, May. *Mostra Assaggio Internazionale di Vini*, wine fair and tasting at Castel Mareccio, May. *Musica in Piazza Walther*, outdoor concert series, Apr–May. *Festa dello Speck*, feast of local dishes, featuring the famous smoked ham, May. *Festival Internazionale di Scacchi*, international chess tournament, Jun. *Campionato Europeo di Scherma*, European fencing championships, Jun. *Bolzano Danza*, dance festival, Jul; *Passeggiata Gastronomica a San Genesio*, food fair, Jul; *Giro Cicloturistico delle Dolomiti*, bike tour of the Dolomites, Jul; *Festival Internazionale delle Orchestre Giovanili*, youth orchestra festival, Aug. *Concorso Pianistico Internazionale E. Busoni*, international piano competition, Aug–Sep. *Cabarena*, cabaret festival, Aug–Sep. *Mambo*, mountain-bike meeting, Aug. *Jazz Festival*, Sep. *Alla Corte di Re Laurino*, folk fair with local farm and craft products, food and drink, Sep. *Climbo*, free-climbing championship, Sep. *Mercatino di Natale*, folk fair with Christmas-tree ornaments, *vin brulé*, Christmas pastries and live music, Nov–Dec. *Boclassic*, amateur footrace, Dec. *World Cup Speed Skating Championships*, Renon/Collalbo, Feb.

Resorts

MERANO AND ENVIRONS *Meranflora*, flower show, Merano, Apr–May. *International Wine Festival*, Merano, Nov. *Mercatino di Natale*, market of Christmas ornaments and sweets, Merano, Nov–Dec. *Ballo di San Silvestro*, Boxing Day ball, Merano, Dec. ROSENGARTEN-LATEMAR *Coppa Europa di Sci Maschile—Super G and Slalom*, Men's European Cup ski championships, Obereggen, Dec. *Coppa Europa di Sci Femminile—Slalom Gigante e Speciale*, Women's European Cup ski championships, Passo Carezza, Dec. *Festa Sulla Neve 'Re Laurino'*, winter snow festival, Passo Carezza, Feb. VAL GARDENA-ALPE DI SIUSI *Settimane del Bambino*, children's week with special kids' activities, Jun–Jul. *Settimane Musicali Gardenesi*, classical music festival at Selva, Santa Cristina and Castel Gardena, Jul–Aug. *Gardena Starbike* and *Starbike Light*, amateur mountain-bike marathons, Jul. *International Masterclasses*, music courses in Italian, German, English and French, with internationally recognised masters, Jul. *Festa del Folclore Gardenese* and *Corteo Storico*, folk festival and historic procession, Aug. *Coppa del Mondo di Sci Maschile—Discesa Libera*, Men's World Cup ski championships, Dec. *Concorso di Sculture di Neve*, snow-sculpture competition, Selva Gardena, Feb. *Snow Countdown*, après-ski festival, Mar. *Matrimonio Contadino*, historic pageant, Castelrotto, Jan. *Come Sciavano i Nostri Nonni*, old-fashioned ski festival, Sciliar Plateau, Mar.

September is the month of grape-harvest feasts in wine districts, and the month in which the cows are brought down from the high pastures, amidst great celebration and pageantry, in mountain villages. The shepherds of the Val Senales celebrate the *transumanza*, or driving of the (3000) sheep over the Giogo passes to their summer pastures in the Vent Valley in Austria, in Jun and Sep. Exact dates vary, of course, with the weather.

Sports

Downhill, **back-country** and **cross-country skiing**; **snow-shoeing**, **ice-skating** and **sledding**; **walking**, **hiking** and **climbing**; **swimming** and **rafting**, **mountain-biking** and **horse-riding** throughout the region. Major downhill areas: Dolomiti (Alta Badia, Val Gardena-Alpe di Siusi, Rosengarten-Latemar), Val Venosta (Alta Val Venosta, Watles, Zona dell'Ortles, Laces), Merano (Val Senales, Merano 2000-Monte San Vigilio, Plan-Val d'Ultimo/Malga Guazza) and Bolzano (San Martino-Corno del Renon). Year-round back-country skiing at the Giogo and Stelvio passes. Children's sledding runs at Solda and Trafoi (Val Venosta); other children's activities organised seasonally in most resorts.

Golf at Merano (*Golf Club Lana*) and in the Val Gardena (*Golf Club Ortisei*).

An alpine picnic

A basic ingredient of any picnic is bread—which people in Italy's Eastern Alps make *con i fiocchi* ('with ribbons and bows'), as the saying goes. Wheat (*frumento*), rye (*segale*), barley (*orzo*) and oats (*avena*) have been used in local recipes for ages, partly because they were among the few products of the field that could easily be cultivated on the steep slopes of the Alps. The region's breads are high in nutritional value because they are made with healthy wholegrain flours and without preservatives.

In this neck of the woods bread is often eaten with speck, a delicacy born of the necessity to preserve freshly slaughtered pork. Farmers realised that by hanging a ham in the chimney of their hearths and then exposing it to the cool, dry air of the forests, they could preserve it for a long time. Over the years both the conservation and the flavour of the meat were improved by salting it before smoking it; and as knowledge of herbs and spices increased, the curing mixture was enriched with new aromas and the smoking was refined by the addition of juniper branches.

And of course, one can't talk about alpine cuisine without mentioning cheese. The Trentino-Alto Adige, with its abundant valleys, rivers, streams and lakes, has hundreds of microclimates that, together with the particular composition of the soil, influence both the variety of alpine flora and its flavour, giving the grass of the pastures (during the summer grazing period) and the hay of the valley floors (during the winter) particular characteristics that make their way into the region's cheeses, with flavours and aromas typical of each 'form'. In bygone days, before the advent of cheese-making on an 'industrial' scale, every *malga* (shepherds's hut) had its own cheese, its unique characteristics deriving from the characteristics of the feed and the skill of the farmer—a secret skill that was often handed down from father to son. Now there are cheese 'factories' that process the milk of an entire valley. This has led to the disappearance of many small producers. If you look hard enough, however, you can still find great local cheeses. Try *spressa*, a low-fat, flavourful cheese typical of the Val Rendena; or the famous *puzzone di Moena*, from the Val di Fassa, whose curious name ('stinker') doesn't do justice to its flavour and aroma. On the other side of the Passo Rolle, at Primiero, is the homeland of fresh *tosella*, eaten with polenta accompanied by the wild yellow mushrooms known as *finferli*.

Finally, the forests of the Trentino-Alto Adige produce red and black whortleberries, wild strawberries, raspberries, gooseberries, redcurrants and rose hips—all important elements of the very special tradition of this area. These fruits initially provided subsistence-level food and drink, their use improving when it was noticed that they could be preserved over a longer time in sweets. A slice of cheescake or buckwheat cake with wild fruit topping is a very satisfying experience indeed, almost a meal in itself.

BOLZANO
• • • • • • • • • • •

Bolzano, in German *Bozen* (population 98,000), is the largest town in the upper basin of the Adige and has been the capital of the (mainly German-speaking) province of Bolzano-Alto Adige since 1927. It has the character of a German rather than Italian town, although its population is now mainly Italian-speaking. The old town, with its low-pitched Tyrolean arcades and Gothic architecture, has a distinctly medieval appearance. Lovely walks can be taken in the neighbourhood, though in summer the heat can be oppressive.

History

Mentioned for the first time (as *Bauzanum*) by Paulus Diaconus in his medieval history of the Lombards, Bolzano formed part of the episcopal principality of Trento in the 11C and was joined to the Tyrol in the 16C. The oldest part of the city grew up around the little Romanesque church of San Giovanni in Villa (12C), but the greatest building activity was that of the Gothic period, when Bolzano became a major mercantile centre. Long a possession of the bishop-princes of Trento, it eventually passed to the Counts of the Tyrol, who were succeeded by the Dukes of Carinthia and, after 1363, the Dukes of Austria. The Habsburgs held the city until 1918, except during the Napoleonic period, when it was briefly united first to Bavaria and then to the Napoleonic Kingdom of Italy. In the late 19C the old city, having remained substantially unchanged over the centuries, grew to include the elegant suburb of Gries. In the 1930s industrial development gave rise to a number of new factories and working-class neighborhoods towards the west and south, which also changed the city's predominantly German ethnic composition by attracting large numbers of labourers from southern Italy.

The city centre

The centre of the city is the busy, spacious **Piazza Walther**. It takes its name from a monument erected in the 19C to the medieval German poet Walther von der Vogelweide, thought to have been a native of the region. The **Cathedral**, a Gothic church of the 14C and 15C (restored after 1945) with an elegant apse, a steep tile roof and a fretwork spire, overlooks the square from the south. Fine doorways and reliefs adorn the exterior, and the three-aisled interior has frescoes of the 14C to the 16C, a fine pulpit with reliefs, of 1514, and a great Baroque altar.

The **Chiesa dei Domenicani**, one block west, is the old church of the Italian community in Bolzano. It too was damaged in the war and has subsequently been rebuilt. The interior preserves remains of 14C and 15C frescoes. Over the last north altar is a restored altarpiece by Guercino (1655), and adjoining the apse, the Cappella di San Giovanni, with fine frescoes by followers of Giotto (c.1340). More frescoes, dating from the 14C to the 16C, are in the Gothic cloister (entrance at no. 19A), the Chapter House and the Cappella di Santa Caterina.

Piazza Domenicani ends on the west at the corner of Via Sernesi, where an obtrusive iron palissade marks the entrance to the **Museion-Museum für Moderne Kunst** (open Tues–Sun 10.00–12.00, 15.00–19.00), with a small permanent collection of modern and contemporary art and an excellent programme of temporary exhibitions.

Returning to the church, turn left at the east end of the square to reach Piazza Erbe, the site of a colourful fruit-and-vegetable market. This lively square, at the crossing of two major pedestrian streets, is flanked by fine old houses and adorned, on one side, by the 18C Fontana del Nettuno, with a bronze statue by Giorgio Mayr, a local artist. To the east stretches the straight, narrow **Via dei Portici**, the oldest thoroughfare in the city and now also its main shopping street. It is flanked by handsome porticoed houses dating from the 15C–18C, with distinctive bay windows; at no. 39 (the main façade is in Via Argentieri) is the Baroque **Palazzo Mercantile** (1708), by the Veronese architect Francesco Pedrotti.

From Piazza Erbe, Via dei Francescani winds northwards to the 14C Gothic **Chiesa dei Francescani**, with a richly carved high altar (1500) and a graceful 14C cloister with fragmentary frescoes. At the next corner Via Vinfler leads right to the **Museo Provinciale di Scienze Naturali** (open Tues–Sun 09.00–17.00), devoted to the landscape and ecosystems of the upper valley of the Adige. Continuing along Via Hofer you take your first left, first right, and first left again to reach **San Giovanni in Villa**, the oldest church in Bolzano, built in the 13C and enlarged in the early 14th. It has a powerful Romanesque-Gothic campanile and 14C frescoes.

Via del Museo, also with elegant shops (and cafés serving unforgettable cakes and pastries) leads west from Piazza Erbe to the **Museo Civico** (open Tues–Sun 09.00–12.30, 14.30–17.30), in the former Hullach mansion at the corner of Via Cassa di Risparmio. It contains ethnographic material (notably a collection of costumes, household articles and reconstructions of *stuben* from old farm-houses), and a Pinacoteca with works by local artists of the 15C (including numerous shuttered altars and wood sculptures). Across the street, in Via Museo, the **Museo Archeologico dell'Alto-Adige** (open May–Sep, Tues–Sun 10.00–18.00, Thur 10.00–20.00; Oct–Apr, Tues–Sun 09.00–17.00, Thur 09.00–20.00) displays antiquities from the Mesolithic to the Roman age. The most outstanding (and disquieting) exhibit of the museum is ****Ötzi**, the 5000-year-old traveller found mummified beneath the ice of the Similaun Glacier, pre-served here in a special refrigerated cell. Numerous well-mounted displays show his garments and tools and explain (the pictures are sufficiently clear if you don't read Italian or German, and recorded tours are available) his life and times.

The Ponte Tàlvera crosses the river to the **Monumento della Vittoria**, a huge triumphal arch erected to a design by the Roman architect Marcello Piacentini in 1928. The monument, seen as a provocation by ethnic Germans, has been the object of several terrorist attacks and is now inaccessible. On the river banks are a park with beautiful promenades. That on the east bank leads northwards to join the Passeggiata Sant'Osvaldo, which climbs the slopes of the Renon hill, offering splendid views back over the town and valley. At the foot of the hill the promenade passes the medieval Castel Maréccio, now a convention centre.

West of the Tàlvera, Corso Libertà leads through the Rationalist neighbour-hoods of the early 20C extension of the city to the garden suburb of Gries. On the main square are the **Abbazia dei Benedittini**, whose late-Baroque church (1771) has frescoes and altarpieces by the Tyrolean painter Martin Knoller, and a little museum displaying antique and modern Christmas cribs. A little further on is the old Gothic parish church, with a carved and painted altarpiece by Michael Pacher (1475).

Bolzano walks

One of the characteristic features of Bolzano is the amazing number of walks you can take in the immediate environs of the city. The **Passeggiata del Gùncina** winds up the hill behind the parish church in Gries to the Castel Gùncina (476 m), with great views over Bolzano and the Dolomites. The path, cut out of a porphyry wall, is planted with Mediterranean flora. The **Passeggiata Sant'Osvaldo-Santa Maddalena** ascends the hill of Santa Maddalena, with a Romanesque church of Mary Magdalen in a picturesque setting amidst vineyards. It can be followed from Via Sant'Osvaldo to the Lungotàlvera and vice versa. A cableway (lower station in Via Sarentino) climbs the 1087m to **San Genesio Altesino**, a busy summer and winter resort on the Altopiano del Salto, with splendid views over the Val Sarentina and the Dolomites. Another cableway starts from Via Renon (near the station) and mounts to **Soprabolzano/Oberbozen**, on the *Renon Highland north of the city. Near **Collalbo**, the main town of the plateau and an excellent starting point for walks and climbs, are the earth-pillars of Longomoso, the most dramatic of the many examples of this curious erosion phenomenon in the area; the path continues to the Rifugio Corno di Renon (2259m, a 3hr ascent), commanding a magnificent view.

A short drive away

You need a car to reach **Castel Ròncolo/Schloss Runkelstein**, a 13C castle on a clifftop at the mouth of the Val Sarentina. Inside are frescoes (shown on a guided tour Mar–Nov, Tues–Sat 10.00–17.00) of late-medieval court life and stories of Tristan and Isolde (in the Palazzo Occidentale, Stua da Bagno and Sala del Torneo), 16C scenes of chivalry (in the Casa d'Estate) and a martyrdom of St Catherine (in the 13C chapel).

On the other side of the Adige is the ruined ***castle of Appiano**, founded in the 12C, which retains a Romanesque chapel with murals (open Apr–Oct, Wed–Mon). **Terlano/Terlan**, 10km northwest on the road to Merano, is the centre of a wine-growing district. It has a Gothic parish church with a 15C fresco of St Christopher on the façade, and two campanili. **Appiano sulla Strada del Vino** has several fine 17C–18C houses in a Renaissance style peculiar to the district. At **Caldaro**, on the Lago di Caldaro, there is a wine museum.

The Parco Naturale dello Sciliar

The Parco Naturale dello Sciliar, established in 1974, combines the rocky walls, cliffs and the ledges of the Sciliar Massif with the verdant pastures of the Alpe di Siusi, where traditional human activities are allowed, but new building (including ski-lifts) is strictly limited and the circulation of motor vehicles is forbidden.

The geological history of the Sciliar can be read clearly by following the succession of rock layers from the lowest altitudes (where the oldest formations are to be found) up. Above the dark-red quartziferous porphyry of the Adige valley are the sandstones of the Val Gardena which, because of their high iron content, colour the soil of the fields red. Higher up, covered by forests, are rocks that were formed just 65 million years ago, in the Permian and lower Triassic eras. There follow layers of sedimentary and vulcanic rock—a clear sign that the coral reefs of the ancient Mediterranean (which over time would become the pink stone of the Sciliar) were periodically submerged beneath layers of lava and ash (to which the soil of the Alpe di Siusi, by the way, owes its fertility).

The fact that it was spared by the glaciers of the Pleistocene era and is consituted by a variety of rocks of diverse origin has allowed the Sciliar to accommodate an extraordinary variety of plant species. In addition to the common alpine flowers (gentians, primroses, crocuses, anemones) you'll find numerous saxifrages (*S. oppositifolia*, *S. caesia*, *S. squarrosa*), the so-called '*strega dello Sciliar*' (*Armeria alpina*), edelweiss, alpine poppies, streaked daphnae, and many, many more. In the forests, keep an eye out for chamois, roe dear, hare and ermine; sparrow hawks and various owls; grouse, white partridges, alpine crows, black woodpeckers, and numerous sparrows.

The park is reached via **Siusi/Seis am Schlern**, a summer and winter resort with a pleasant main square, or **Castelrotto/Kastelruth**, a fairytale village huddled around a massive (and loud) 18C bell-tower and taking its name from the medieval castle, set on a wooded knoll a short way from the village square. **Tiers** and **San Cipriano** are the gateways to the wild Val Ciamin and the adjacent Catinaccio/Rosengarten group, the mythical lair of the dwarf-king Laurin. At **Fiè a Sciliar** is the 13C **Castel Presule Colonna**, rebuilt in 1517 (open Apr–Oct, Sun–Fri at 11.00, 14.00 and 15.00).

Walk to the Rifugio Alpe di Tires

The departure point for this moderately difficult walk (6–7hrs) is Malga Ciamin/Tschaminschwaige (1184m), reached from Tires Via San Cipriano and the road (left) for Bagni di Lavina Bianca

From the car park at the Rifugio Tschaminschwaige cross the bridge over the Rio di Ciamin and follow the mule track (Trail 3) that climbs in switchbacks through fir woods to reach a forest road. By this road and another mule track (marked) ascend the forested Valle di Ciamin and, beyond a *malga* (shepherds's hut), climb left to the base of the rocky walls of the gorge known as the Buco dell'Orso. After crossing the stream at an altitude of 1890m, leave on your right Trail 3a, which leads to the Rifugio Bergamo, and climb left over stony ground dotted with scrub pine to the steep walls of the Buco dell'Orso. The trail, fitted with a steel cable that you'll want to grasp tightly in the narrower stretches, climbs the rocks on the right of the gorge and comes out on the pastures dominated by the Cima di Terrarossa (2655m), where you are joined by Trail 4 from the Rifugio Bolzano. Turning right, in just a few minutes you comfortably reach the **Rifugio Alpe di Tures** (*Tierser Alpe*, 2441m, ☎ 0471 727958), beneath the imposing bastions of the Denti di Terrarossa. The return can be made along the same route, or if you want to avoid the Buco dell'Orso, by taking the trail that, climbing southwards over the **Passo di Molignon** (2598m) and the **Passo Principe** (2400m), leads to the **Rifugio Bergamo** (2134m), from which it is easy to descend to the Val Ciamin. This route will take at least an hour longer.

The Val Gardena

The *Val Gardena is a Ladin-speaking valley reached via **Ponte Gardena/ Waidbruck**, north of Bolzano on the Brenner road. Wedged between the steep walls of the Val d'Isarco, Ponte Gardena is a rather dark place nestled around the **Castel Forte Trostburg**, a 12C castle of the Wolkenstein, with a 16C hall (open Easter–Oct, Tues–Sat at 10.00, 11.00, 14.00, 15.00 and 16.00).

The Val Gardena road winds up and out of the Isarco Valley, through verdant forests and farmland, to **Ortisei/St Ulrich** (1234m), a small resort. The 18C church here contains good examples of woodcarving, for which Ortisei is noted. The **Museo della Val Gardena** (open Jul–Aug, Tues–Sun 10.00–12.00 and 15.00–19.00, Jun and Sep, Tues–Fri 15.00–19.00) has art, craft and natural history collections of local interest.

The road continues to climb, offering a series of changing views over the Sciliar and Puez-Odle peaks. **Selva di Val Gardena/Wolkenstein in Groden** (1563m), stands at the foot of the Vallunga, which penetrates the heart of the Puez and Gardenaccia mountains to the northeast. The valley ends at the *Passo Sella (2213m), beyond which lies the Val Badia (see p 343). The pass has a splendid view, perhaps the finest in all the Dolomites, which takes in the Sasso Lungo (northwest), Sella (northeast) and Marmolada (southeast).

Beyond Ponte Gardena (see above) the Brenner road passes the ancient small town of **Chiusa/Klausen**. The chapel of the Madonna di Loreto contains a precious treasury. The fine *Castel Velturno, built in 1577–87, is now owned by the province (shown on guided tours Mar–Nov, Tues–Sun at 10.00, 11.00, 14.30 and 15.30).

Merano

Merano, in German *Meran*, is famous as a climatic resort and spa, and also a climbing centre and ski resort. Together with **Maia Alta/Obermais** and **Maia Bassa/Untermais** on the opposite bank of the torrent, it consists mainly of monumental hotels and villas, many of them built at the turn of the century by Austrian architects, surrounded by luxuriant gardens in a sheltered valley. Spring and autumn are the fashionable seasons for visiting Merano. The inhabitants are mainly German-speaking.

History

Although it is probable the area was already inhabited in Roman times, the name *Mairania* appears for the first time in 857. After the town came into the possession of the Counts of Venosta in the 13C it gradually assumed importance, and by 1317 it had been designated a municipality. After 1836, under Austrian rule, its good climate began to attract visitors and it developed into one of the more celebrated climatic resorts in Italy. The thermal centre here uses radioactive springs.

The old main street of the medieval town is the dark, narrow **Via dei Portici**. Beneath its low arcades are excellent shops and the town hall (1930). Behind this is **Castello Principesco** (open 09.30–12.00, 14.00–18.00; Sat 09.00–12.00; closed

Sun and holidays), one of the better-preserved castles in the region, built by Archduke Sigismund in 1445–80 and containing contemporary furnishings. The arms of Scotland alongside those of Austria recall the marriage of Sigismund with Eleanor, daughter of James I of Scotland. Also in Via Galilei is the **Museo Civico** (open Tues–Sat 10.00–12.00, 15.00–18.00; closed holidays), with local collections.

At the end of Via dei Portici is the **Duomo**, a Gothic church of the 14C–15C with a curious battlemented façade, a tall tower (83m), and 14C–16C tomb-reliefs. Inside are two 15C altarpieces by Martin Knoller. Along the River Passirio extend gardens and promenades laid out at the turn of the century. The cheerful **Corso Libertà**, with the most fashionable shops, was laid out before the First World War. It passes the Kursaal (1914), the Neo-classical theatre, and several elaborate hotels.

In Maia Bassa is the Hippodrome (1935), run in conjunction with a famous national lottery.

Around Merano

Tirolo to the north, a village given over to tourism, is especially favoured by Germans on walking holidays. Ezra Pound stayed in the **Castel Fontana** (reconstructed in 1904), which contains mementoes of the poet as well as a local ethnographical museum (open Apr–Nov, Wed–Mon 09.30–12.00, 14.00–17.00). On the opposite side of a ravine, in a superb position, is *Castel Tirolo (open Mar–Nov, Tues–Sun 10.00–17.00), the 12C castle of the counts of Tyrol which gave its name to the region. With the abdication of Margaret Maultasch, the 'ugly duchess', in 1363, the castle and province passed to the Habsburgs. Damaged by a landslip in 1680, the castle was restored in 1904.

The castle of **Scena**, on the hill northeast of Maia Alta, is a 14C building, restored by the Count of Liechtenstein in 1700. It is privately owned but shown to visitors (open Easter–Nov, Mon–Sat at 10.30, 11.30, 14.00, 15.00, 16.00 and 17.00). There is an armoury, and rooms with Renaissance furniture.

In the pastoral **Val Passiria** is **Maso della Rena**, the birthplace of Andreas Hofer (1767–1810). Hofer was the Tyrolese patriot who led the successful insurrection of 1809 against Bavaria; his house (now a hotel) contains a little private museum.

The Val Venosta

The Val Venosta (*Vinschga*) is the wide and fertile upper valley of the Adige to the west of Merano, near the Austrian and Swiss borders. It has numerous small summer and winter resorts and fine mountain scenery. Part of the valley lies in the Parco Nazionale dello Stelvio (see below).

The summer resort of **Naturno/Naturns** has a little Romanesque church, San Procolo, with remarkable 8C mural paintings. From here a minor road winds northwards up the long **Val Senales**, dominated by the great pyramid of the Similaun (3597m), on the Austrian frontier. *Ötzi* (see p 327) was found in the glacier on the saddle between the Val Senales and the Venter Tal in Austria. The **Val di Fosse** is a beautiful side valley in front of Monte Tessa, a protected area (33,000h), with deer and other wildlife.

A turning on the south, from the Val Venosta, ascends the **Val Martello**, which is in the Parco Nazionale dello Stelvio. The little village of **Morter** has a Romanesque church with three lovely apses and an aviary for falcons.

The main place in the Val Venosta is **Silandro/Schlanders**, with the valley's highest vineyards (722m). The Val Venosta turns to the north beyond **Spondigna/Spondinig**, gaining in altitude as it approaches the source of the Adige.

The **Castel Coira/Churburg**, above Sluderno, is the 13C castle of the bishops of Coire. It was restored in the 16C by the Counts Trapp. **Glorenza**, to the west, is a typical old Tyrolean town with medieval and 16C ramparts and three gates. It is particularly well preserved and draws quite a few visitors. In the **Val Monastero** (*Münster-Tal*), which extends to the west of Glorenza, is the Calven Gorge: here in 1499 the Swiss defeated the Austrians and won their practical independence of the empire. **Tubre/Taufers** (1240m), on the Swiss border, has a Romanesque church with good 13C frescoes.

Malles Venosta (1051m) is an old mountain town with its churches rebuilt in the Gothic style. **San Benedetto** dates from the 9C or earlier; it has an important Carolingian fresco cycle. Other medieval remains include the ruined **Castel Frölich** (near the parish church), the **Torre Dross** (near the Casa della Cultura), and the Preschgenegg (in Via Winkel), Lichtenegg (in the main square), Goldegg, Pracassan and Malsegg (in Via General Verdross) houses. The large Benedictine abbey of **Monte Maria**, outside the town, mainly rebuilt in the 17C–19C, preserves frescoes of c 1160.

At the north end of the Lago di Resia, below the source of the Adige, stands **Resia** (1525m), with a splendid view down the valley of the Ortler group. It was rebuilt when its original site was submerged. The Austrian frontier lies just beyond the **Passo di Resia** (1507m).

The Parco Nazionale dello Stelvio

At Spondigna the Stelvio Pass road diverges to the southwest, leaving the Val Venosta to enter the Parco Nazionale dello Stelvio. This immense nature reserve, stradling the boundary between the Trentino-Alto Adige and Lombardy, is the largest national park in Italy (135,000h) and one of the oldest, established in 1935. It encompasses the magnificent mountain group of the Ortles-Cavedale, with peaks well over 3000m, and is one of the two designated wilderness areas of northern Italy (the other is the Parco Nazionale del Gran Paradiso in Piedmont, see p 71). Unlike the other parks of the Trentino-Alto Adige, where an effort is made to safeguard the human as well as the natural landscape, here logging, mining, farming and grazing are discouraged, with a view to allowing the area to return as nearly as possible to a 'natural' (though by no means 'original' or 'virgin') state.

Although several roads penetrate the park, providing access from the valleys of Lombardy and the Trentino-Alto Adige, there is only one through-road (38, the Stelvio Pass road). The park authorities maintain a significant number of well-marked trails for environmentally compatible summer sports (hiking, climbing) and winter sports (cross-country and back-country skiing, snow-shoeing). In the last few decades the beauty of the park has been threatened, especially in the area within the Province of Bolzano: hunting has been allowed, as well as the building of roads, hotels, ski-lifts, etc.

At Gomagoi (1266m) a minor road ascends the **Val di Solda**, a lovely side valley inside the park boundaries. Its main village, **Solda** (1907m), is one of the more important climbing centres in the upper Adige and a holiday resort. Above rise Monte Cevedale (3769m) and the *Ortles (*Ortler*, 3905m), a magnificent peak, defended by the Austrians throughout the First World War.

Trafoi (1543m) is a summer and winter resort with a magnificent panorama of the Ortles massif. Beyond Trafoi begins the long, winding ascent to the **Passo dello Stelvio/Stilfserjoch** (2758m). This is the second highest road-pass in the Alps (12m lower than the Col d'Iseran). Generally open only Jun–Oct, it is visited for summer skiing (chair-lift to 3174m). It was the meeting-place of the frontiers of Italy, Switzerland and Austria until 1918. There is a good view from the Pizzo Garibaldi (2838m), in German called *Dreisprachenspitze* ('Three Languages Peak') from the meeting of the districts where Italian, Romansch and German are spoken. A minor road winds over the **Giogo di Santa Maria** (2502m) to Switzerland.

The Strada delle Dolomiti

The famous *Strada delle Dolomiti (route 241) runs from Bolzano, on the west side of the Dolomites, to Cortina d'Ampezzo on the east. It is one of the more beautiful roads in the Alps, as well as a magnificent feat of engineering.

From Bolzano the road enters the wild and romantic gorge of the Val d' Ega, passing the *Ponte della Cascata. It then passes the resorts of Nova Levante/Welschnofen (1182m), and Carezza al Lago (1609m), dominated by the two most typical Dolomite mountain groups with their characteristic battle-mented skyline, the **Látemar** (2842m) and the **Catinaccio** (2981m). The latter is especially famous for its marvellous colouring at sunrise, from which it takes the German name *Rosengarten* ('Rose Garden').

The road summit is reached at the **Passo di Costalunga** (1745m), with a splendid view ahead of the Val di Fassa and the Marmolada and San Martino mountains. The **Marmolada** (3342m), the largest and highest group of mountain peaks in the Dolomites, is approached from the Avisio and Contrin valleys by cableways and chair-lifts.

A winding descent through high pastures into the province of Belluno, in the Veneto, brings the road into the Val Cordevole, with the villages of Arabba (1601m) and Pieve di Livinallongo (1475m). The Val Pettorina is the main approach to the east side of the Marmolada. The Cortina road beyond Pieve leaves the Val Cordevole and begins a long ascent beneath the ruined castle of Andraz. The **Passo di Falzarego** (2105m) was a hotly contested strongpoint in the First World War. The road descends to Cortina d'Ampezzo (see p 416).

Bressanone and the Eastern Alps

This chapter deals with the northernmost part of the Alto Adige, with particular emphasis on Bressanone, the former political and cultural capital of the Sudtyrol. Attention is also given to the fabulous parks of the north-central Dolomites—the Vedrette di Ries, Fanes-Sennes-Braies and Dolomiti di Sesto nature reserves—as well as to the many summer and winter resorts of the verdant valleys.

Practical information

Getting there and getting around
By air

Bolzano has a small regional airport with flights to and from Rome and Frankfurt, Germany. The international airports nearest Bressanone and the eastern Alps are at Verona and Venice in Italy, and at Innsbruck in Austria. Both have daily flights to cities throughout Europe.

By road

Bressanone is reached from Verona or Innsbruck by the A22 and 12. A long but scenic road (38) connects Lombardy with Bolzano via the Stelvio Pass, and a series of beautiful but tiring mountain roads link Trieste, Venice, Padua and Vicenza with Trento and Bressanone. Frequent **bus services** (operated by *SAD*, ☎ 0471 450111 or freephone 800 846047) connect Bressanone to towns and resorts throughout the northern Dolomites, as well as to Bolzano and Innsbruck. To explore the Val Pusteria, follow 49 north and east from Bressanone.

By rail

Bressanone is on the main rail line from Verona to Innsbruck, with direct through service to Munich, Munster, Dortmund, Berlin and Vienna; or in the other direction, to Florence, Rome and Naples. A secondary rail-and-bus line runs from Padua to Cortina d'Ampezzo via Castelfranco, Feltre and Belluno, with connections for the Val Pusteria, Bressanone and Bolzano.

Information offices
BRESSANONE/BRIXEN Viale Stazione 9, ☎ 0472 836401.
BRUNICO/BRUNECK Via Europa 24, ☎ 0474 555722.
VIPITENO/STERZING Piazza Città 3, ☎ 0472 765325.

Parks

PARCHI NATURALI DELLE VEDRETTE DI RIES, DI FANES-SENNES-BRAIES, DELLE DOLOMITI DI SESTO *Ufficio Parchi, Provincia Autonoma di Bolzano,* Via Cesare Batisti 21, ☎ 0471 994300; *Ufficio Provinciale per il Turismo dell'Alto-Adige, Servizio Informazioni Alpine,* Piazza Walther 8, 39100 Bolzano, ☎ 0471 993809.

Resorts

BOLZANO has a **central information office** for all the resorts in its province, at Piazza Parrocchia 11, ☎ 0471 993808, fax 0471 993889, website www.provincia.bz.it.turismo. *Hotel reservation service,* ☎ 0471 222220, fax 0471 222221. *Snow bulletin,* ☎ 0471 200198, fax 0471 201157. *Walking and climbing bulletin,* ☎ 0471 993809.

Where to stay
BRESSANONE/BRIXEN This is the best place to stay if you wish to explore the peaks and valleys of the northern Dolomites without changing hotels. Among the better hotels are: *Dominik*, Via Terzo di Sotto 13, ☎ 0472 830144, fax 0472 836554; an extremely refined, comfortable place in a quiet, secluded position amid trees and lawns yet within walking distance of the cathedral; it has an excellent restaurant, with table service under an arbour in warm weather; closed Jan–Mar; moderate.
Elefante, Via Rio Bianco 4 , ☎ 0472 832750, fax 0472 836579; a 16C building with antique furniture, a large garden, and the city's most renowned restaurant; closed Nov–Christmas and Jan–Mar; expensive.
Grüner Baum, Via Stufles 11, ☎ 0472 832732, fax 0472 832607; offers a cordial, homely atmosphere in an elegant old house on the left bank of the Isarco, near the *Dominik*; closed late Nov–early Dec; moderate.
Gasser, Via Giardini 19, ☎ 0472 832732, fax 0472 832697; situated in the oldest part of town, near the Parco Rapp; guests use the pool and other facilities of the *Grüner Baum*, which is under the same management; closed late Nov–early Dec; inexpensive. At Cleran/Klerant, 5km south, is the *Fischer*, ☎ 0472 852075, fax 0472 852060; in a magnificent position overlooking Bressanone and the Valle d'Isarco; closed Nov; inexpensive.

Parks
PARCO NATURALE FANES-SENNES-BRAIES See Val Badia, Brunico and Upper Val Pusteria.
PARCO NATURALE DELLE VEDRETTE DI RIES See Brunico and Upper Val Pusteria.
PARCO NATURALE DOLOMITI DI SESTO See Upper Val Pusteria.

Resorts
UPPER VAL D'ISARCO *Aquila*

Nera/Schwarzer Adler, Piazza Città 1, Vipiteno/Sterzing, ☎ 0472 764064, fax 0472 766522; the traditional place to stay (and to eat) in Vipiteno, dating back to the 16C; closed Jun–Jul and Nov–Dec; moderate.
VAL BADIA *Sassongher*, Strada Sassongher 45, Corvara, ☎ 0471 836085, fax 0471 836542; an elegant place in the heart of the Alta Badia ski area; closed May and Oct–Nov; expensive.
La Perla, Strada Col Alt 105, Corvara, ☎ 0471 836132, fax 0471 836568; another upmarket establishment with heated pool and stunning views; closed May and Oct–Nov; expensive.
Lech da Sompunt, 3km southwest of Pedraces, ☎ 0471 847015, fax 0471 847464; in a fine position by a pond; closed May and Oct–Nov; moderate.
Rosa Alpina, Via Centro 31, San Cassiano, ☎ 0471 841111, fax 0471 849377; very comfortable indeed, with spa facilities and an excellent restaurant; closed May and Nov; expensive.
Armentarola, 2km southeast of San Cassiano on the road to Cortina, ☎ 0471 849522, fax 0471 849389; in an early-20C lodge by the ski slopes; closed May and Nov; moderate.
Ciasa Salares, 2km southeast of San Cassiano on the road to Cortina, ☎ 0471 849445, fax 0471 849369; also by the ski slopes, with an excellent restaurant; closed May and Oct–Nov; moderate.
Gran Ancëi, 2km southeast of San Cassiano, ☎ 0471 849540, fax 0471 849210; warm and comfortable, by Armentorola and Ciasa Salares; closed May and Oct–Nov; inexpensive.
Monte Sella, at San Vigilio di Marebbe, ☎ 0474 501034, fax 0474 501714; a delightful Jugendstil villa built for the Austrian aristocracy at the turn of the century and tastefully renovated; within walking distcance of the ski-lifts and recently provided with a beautiful top-floor health centre; closed Apr–May and

Oct–Dec; moderate.

BRUNICO/BRUNECK On the Riscone highland, 3km southeast of the city, is the *Royal Hotel Hinterhuber*, ☎ 0474 548221, fax 0474 548048; a fine old Tyrolean farm complex renovated to the highest modern standards, in truly splendid surroundings; closed Easter–May and Oct–Dec; moderate.

UPPER VAL PUSTERIA *Posta/Post*, Vicolo della Chiesa 6, Valdàora di Sopra/Oberolang, ☎ 0474 046127, fax 0474 48019; beautiful position, comfortable rooms; horse-riding on request; closed Apr–May and Oct–Dec; moderate. *Messnerwirt*, Vicolo della Chiesa 7, Valdàora di Sopra/Oberoland, ☎ 0474 046178, fax 0474 48087; cosy and distinctive; closed Nov–Dec; inexpensive. At Sorafurcia (1360m), above Valdàora, *Berghotel Zirm*, ☎ 0474 592054, fax 0474 592051; a warm, friendly place in a truly magnificent position; closed Apr–May and Nov–Dec; inexpensive. At Monguelfo/Welsberg: *Chalet Olympia*, ☎ 0474 944079, fax 0474 944650; closed May–Jun and Nov; and *Alpenhof*, ☎ 0474 944212, fax 0474 994775; closed mid-Apr–mid-May and mid-Oct–mid-Dec; are inexpensive and perfectly comfortable.

In a class of its own is *Ansitz Heufler*, at Rasun di Sopra in the Valle d'Anterselva, ☎ 0474 498582, fax 0474 498047; an impeccably renovated 16C castle with fairytale rooms and an outstanding restaurant; closed Apr and Nov; moderate.

Park Hotel Sole Paradiso/ Sonnenparadies at San Candido/Innichen, ☎ 0474 73120, fax 0474 73193; offers warm atmosphere, good location, and a great restaurant; closed Apr–May and Oct–Nov; moderate.

Sport e Kurhotel Bad Moos at Moso/Moos, ☎ 0474 70365, fax 0474 70509; a modern establishment incorporating 15C and 16C *stuben*, in a fine

location; closed Nov–Dec and Easter–May; expensive

Dolomiti-Dolomitenhof, at Campo Fiscalino/Fischleinboden, 4km south of Sesto/Sexten, ☎ 0474 70364, fax 0474 70131; a starting point for most excursions in the Val Fiscalino and Tre Cime areas of the park as well as a marvellous place to stay; closed May and Nov; moderate.

If you're looking for seclusion, try the *Alpino Monte Rota-Alpen Ratsberg*, at Monte Rota/Radsberg (1650m), 5km northwest of Dobbiaco/Toblach, ☎ 0474 72213, fax 0474 72916 (chair lift); fresh air, magnificent surroundings, and a view you won't soon forget more than compensate for the trouble of getting there; closed Apr–May and Nov–Dec; inexpensive.

Eating out

Most of the hotels in Bressanone and the northern Dolomites have very satisfactory restaurants, and some of the restaurants listed below have rooms.

BRESSANONE/BRIXEN *Fink*, Via Portici Minori 4, ☎ 0472 834883; a simple place established in 1896, serving local specialties, especially meats and cheeses (*Zieger*, *Graukaese*, *Lista*); closed Tues evening except Jul–Oct, Wed and two weeks in Jul; inexpensive.

Grappolo d'Uva, Via Portici Minori, ☎ 0472 834731; good international cuisine and excellent wines, coupled with pleasant ambience and friendly service; moderate.

Oste Scuro/Finsterwirt, Vicolo del Duomo 3, ☎ 0472 835343; a characteristic Tyrolean restaurant (with rooms on separate premises) established in 1879, with a lovely garden for the warm months, an innovative twist on traditional recipes, and a good selection of regional and Italian wines; closed Sun evening, Mon, and a few days in Jan and Jun; moderate.

Parks

PARCO NATURALE FANES-SENNES-BRAIES See Val Badia, Brunico and Upper Val Pusteria.

PARCO NATURALE DELLE VEDRETTE DI RIES See Brunico and the Upper Val Pusteria.

PARCO NATURALE DOLOMITI DI SESTO. See Upper Val Pusteria.

Resorts

UPPER VAL D'ISARCO *Caffè Konditorei Prenn*, Altstadt 17, Vipiteno/Sterzing, is a café serving truly memorable cakes and pastries.

Pretzhof, Località Tulve/Tulfer, Vipiteno/Sterzing, ☎. 0472 764455; fine local food and ambience; closed Mon–Tues, Dec, Jan and Jun–Jul; moderate.

LOWER VAL PUSTERIA *Pichler*, Rio di Pusteria/Mühlbach, ☎ 0472 849458; known for its creative interpretations of traditional Tyrolean specialities, as well as for its ambience and wines; closed Mon, midday Tues and Jul; moderate.

Strasshoff, Località Spinga/Spinges 2, Rio di Pusteria/Mühlbach, ☎ 0472 849798; an 11C castle entirely dedicated to the preservation of local culinary traditions; closed Wed, midday Thur and Jan–Feb; moderate.

BRUNICO/BRUNECK *Agnello Bianco/Weisses Lamm*, Via Stuck 5, ☎ 0474 411350; good regional food and wines on the first floor of a historic building in the pedestrian district; closed Sun and Jun; moderate.

Oberraut, Località Ameto/Amaten 1, ☎ 0474 559977; is a *maso* or mountain farm (with rooms) above Brunico; outstanding local fare, good wines, friendly people, fabulous views; moderate.

Speck and other delicacies in Brunico at *Gasgtronomia Bernardi*, wines at *Enoteca Schondörf*, home-made jams at *Willy Horvat*, all in Via Centrale.

VAL BADIA *La Gran Ciasa*, Pieve di Marebbe, ☎ 0474 501511; Ladin country cooking in the beautiful *stuben* of an original 16C Gothic mansion; telephone to reserve table; inexpensive.

UPPER VAL PUSTERIA *Gratschwirt* (with rooms), 1km southwest of Dobbiaco/Toblach, ☎ 0474 72293; offering regional specialities prepared with care; closed Tues, Easter–May and Oct–Dec; inexpensive.

Durnwald, Località Planca di Sotto/Unterplanken, in the sinuous Valle di Casies/Gsies, ☎ 0474 746920; offers a perfect combination of local delicacies and regional wines; closed Mon and Jun; inexpensive.

Kupferdachl, San Candido/Innichen, ☎ 0474 913711; friendly ambience and excellent regional cuisine that appeals to locals as well as to travellers; closed Thur, Jun and Nov; inexpensive.

Uhrmacher's Weinstube, Via Tintori 1, San Candido/Innichen, ☎ 0474 913158; wine bar serving excellent regional wines and cheeses; closed Wed (except in summer) and Jun; inexpensive.

Reidere, Via San Giuseppe 27, Moso/Moos, ☎ 0474 710304; a fine old restaurant with a beautiful little *stube* and traditional menu; closed Tues, Jan and Jun; moderate.

For great *Graukäse, Beregkäse, Zieger* and other Val Pusteria cheeses (but no wine), try the **Latteria Sociale di San Candido**, Via Castello 1, San Candido/Innichen.

 Entertainment

As elsewhere in the eastern Alps, the favourite evening activity in Bressanone and the northern Dolomites is social drinking. In Bressanone the most popular spot to meet for a beer or a grappa is the *Grappolo d'Oro*, mentioned above as an eating place. In high season there are also *feste* in the villages and resorts, often involving live music, theatre, pageantry, etc. Check with the local information office, or with your hotel concierge, for details.

Shopping
BRUNICO/BRUNECK
Mercatino Natalizio Brunicense, folk fair with local farm and craft products, food and drink, Nov–Dec. **Mercatino Pasquale Brunicense**, ditto, Easter.

Special events
BRESSANONE **Mercatino di Natale**, market of Christmas ornaments and sweets, Nov–Jan. **Trofeo Fila Sprint**, international children's ski competition, Plose, Dec. **Grande Festa di San Silvestro**, Boxing Day folk festival, Dec. **Häppi Plose**, carnival ski festival, Plose, Feb.

Resorts

UPPER VAL ISARCO **Corteo di San Nicolò** and **Corteo di Natale**, folk processions, Vipiteno, Dec. **Biathlon Champions Night**, night biathlon competition, Ridanna, Jan. **Gran Fondo della Val di Vizze**, cross-country ski race, Val di Vizze, Jan. **Gran Fondo della Val Ridanna**, cross-country ski race, Ridanna, Mar. **Settimana della Buona Cucina**, regional cuisine week, Alta Val d'Isarco, Mar.

VAL BADIA **Coppa del Mondo di Sci Maschile—Slalom Gigante**, Men's World Cup ski championships, La Villa, Dec–Feb. **Horse-Drawn Sleigh Races**, La Villa, Jan–Feb. **Haysled Races**, Colfosco, Jan–Mar; **New Year's Eve celebration** with fireworks, candlelight procession and concert, Corvara, Jan. **Festival Internazionale delle Sculture di Neve**, international snow-sculpture competition, San Vigilio di Marebbe, San Candido and Sesto, Jan. **Bikemarathon Transalp Challenge**, world's longest and toughest bike race (550km, 15,000m altitude gain), San Vigilio di Marebbe, Jul. **Olimpiadi dei Bambini**, children's Olympics, San Vigilio di Marebbe, Jul–Aug. **Simposio Internazionale di Sculture in Legno**, woodcarving competition, San Vigilio di Marebbe, Sep.

BRUNICO/BRUNECK **Aria di Jazz**, jazz festival, Brunico, Jul. **Accademia Internazionale Estiva di Belle Arti**, visual arts courses, Brunico, Jul. **Concerti Estivi Brunicensi**, chamber music concerts, Brunico, Jul–Aug. **Incontri con l'Autore**, book signings, Brunico, Aug.

UPPER VAL PUSTERIA **Festival Nazionale di Canto Corale**, chorus festival, Alta Pusteria (Sesto, San Candido, Dobbiaco, Villabassa, Braies), Jul. **Settimana Musicale Gustav Mahler**, classical musical festival, Dobbiaco, Jul. **Estate Culturale di Anterselva**, visual and performing arts, seminars and round-tables, Valle d'Anterselva, Jul–Sep. **Degustazione Estiva dei Vini**, summer tasting of Alto-Adige wines, Valdaora, Aug. **Men's and Women's World-Cup Cross-Country Ski Championships**, Dobbiaco, Dec. **Men's and Women's World Cup Cross-Country Ski Championships**, Val Casies, Dec. **Maratona dei Canederli**, amateur cross-country ski marathon, Val Casies, Jan. **Pustertaler Skimarathon**, amateur cross-country ski marathon, Valle d'Anterselva-Dobbiaco, Jan. **Alpitrail**, dogsled races, Sesto, Jan. **Festival Internazionale delle Sculture di Neve**, international snow-sculpture competition, San Candido, Sesto and San Vigilio di Marebbe, Jan. **Coppa del Mondo di Biathlon**, World-Cup biathlon, Valle d'Anterselva, Jan–Feb. **Gran Fondo della Val Casies**, Tyrol Trophy free-style cross-country ski marathon, Val Casies, Feb. **Gran Fondo Dobbiaco-Cortina**, Tyrol Trophy free-style cross-country ski marathon, Feb. **Gran Premio Valle d'Anterselva**, Italian championship dogsled races, Feb. **FIS Snowboard World Cup Finals**, Plan de Corones (Valdaora), Mar. **Locknfest—Festa delle Pozze**, wild party on the last day of the downhill-skiing season; participants negotiate a steep run in or on beds, bathtubs, wheelless cars, frying pans, etc., then dive into a frozen pond while spectators look on; prizes for most original vehicle and bathing costume; live music and roasted würstel; Plan de Corones (Valdaora), Apr.

September is the month for harvest feasts, as well as the month in which the cows are brought down from the high pastures, amidst great celebration and pageantry in many villages. Exact dates vary, of course, with the weather.

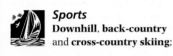

Sports
Downhill, **back-country** and **cross-country skiing**; **snow-shoeing**, **ice-skating** and **sledding**; **walking**, **hiking** and **climbing**; **swimming** and **rafting**, **mountainbiking** and **horse-riding** throughout the region. Major downhill areas: Dolomiti (Alta Badia, Val Gardena-Ape di Siusi, Rosengarten-Latemar); Val Pusteria (Plan de Corones, Alta Pusteria, Valle di Tures and Valle Aurina) and Valle Isarco (Maranza-Plose-Valles, Alta Val d'Isarco). Dolomiti Superski pass gives access to 484km of lifts, 1180km of runs. Children's activities organised seasonally.
Golf at Corvara (*Golf Club Alta Badia*).

BRESSANONE

Bressanone, in German *Brixen*, stands at the meeting-point of two Alpine streams, the Isarco and the Rienza, and of two important old roads, from the Val Pusteria and the eastern Tyrol, and from Brennero and Austria. Situated in a lovely open landscape of cultivated hills between steep mountain peaks and green forests and meadows, the city conserves the austere mark of its history as a centre of a vast ecclesiastical principality. The power of its bishop-princes in fact lasted 800 years, from 1027 to 1803. The Germanic quality of its architecture, monuments and artworks, which embody the full variety of styles from the Romanesque to the Baroque (it is the largest art centre of the Alto-Adige), carries the singular inflexions of a site on a cultural frontier.

The city centre

The **Cathedral**, built in the 9C, enlarged in the 13C, and completely rebuilt in baroque forms in 1745–90, dominates the shady **Piazza del Duomo**. The beautifully preserved interior is adorned with ceiling frescoes by the Austrian artist Paul Troger, and fine carvings. In the adjacent Romanesque cloister are 14C and 15C frescoes of Old and New Testament scenes and the entrance to the 11C baptistery, which hosted the famous council called in 1080 to depose Pope Gregory VII (Hildebrand) and elect the Antipope Clement III.

The **Palazzo dei Principi Vescovi** is a fortified building, preceded by a moat, rising in the nearby Piazza del Palazzo. Built in the early 13C by the bishop-prince Bruno de Kirchberg, it was several times enlarged and then rebuilt as a Renaissance château, after 1595, for Cardinal Andrea of Austria. Rendered in Baroque forms after 1710, it remained the residence of the bishop-princes and the administrative centre of their feudality until 1803. It has an elegant façade and an imposing courtyard with 24 life-size terracotta statues representing members of the Habsburg family.

The interior hosts the *****Museo Diocesano** (open Tue–Sat 10.00–17.00, Sun 10.00–13.00) with one of the larger art collections in northeastern Italy. It includes sculptures, paintings, and medieval decorative arts from area churches;

original furnishings of the bishop's residence; objects from the cathedral treasury dating from the 12C to the 16C; manuscripts and incunabula, old fabrics, embroideries and vestments; diplomas and seals of the bishop-princes and of the aristocracy; and last but not least, an extraordinary collection of *presepi*, or Christmas crêches, ranging in date from the 18C to the 20C. In the adjacent garden, flowers and kitchen vegetables are grown together in surprisingly harmonious beds.

Adjoining Piazza del Duomo on the north, Piazza della Parrocchia takes its name from the 15C Gothic parish church of **San Michele**, with a spired campanile called the Torre Bianca. Inside are 18C frescoes by the Viennese painter Josef Hautzinger. On the north of the church stands the Renaissance **Casa Pfaundler** (1581, a medley of Nordic and Italian elements. From here Via dei Portici Maggiori, a lovely old street full of shops, leads westward, flanked by houses of the 16C and 17C, many with crenellated roofs and bay windows. The old **town hall** at no. 14, has a painting of the *Judgement of Solomon* in the courtyard.

Around Bressanone

To explore the lovely environs of Bressanone you don't necessarily need a car. The **Rifugio Città di Bressanone/Plosehütte**, an alpine shelter in an incomparable setting at 2447m, can be reached by cableway, or by 23km of scenic highway in the Valle d'Eores. In the latter case you drive as far as Valcroce/Kreuztal, 2050m, then continue the ascent on foot (1hr 30mins) or by chairlift. The shelter is on the southern crest of the Cima della Plose, 2504m, a massif frequented as much for its spectacular views over the Dolomites and the Alpi Aurine as for its excellent skiing.

Surrounded by meadows and vineyards 3km north on the main road to Brennero and the Val Pusteria (12) is the **Abbazia di Novacella/Neustift**, a vast complex of monastic buildings ranging in date from the 12C–18C. The church and cloister are open all day, but the library and pinacoteca are only shown on guided tours at 11.00 and 15.00 (or by appointment). Three beautiful marked trails starting near the little Chiesa dell'Angelo Custode in Bressanone make walking to the abbey easy, and you really should make an effort to go this way—as many of the townsfolk do on a warm, sunny Sunday.

The abbey was founded in 1141–42 and now belongs to priests of the Augustinian order. Among the older structures are the circular chapel of San Michele (12C, fortified in the 16C); the campanile (12C–13C); the cloister, rebuilt at the end of the 14C, with frescoes of the same period; the Romanesque chapel of San Vittore, with frescoes of the early 14C; and the monastery church (Santa Maria Assunta), a Romanesque foundation rebuilt in Bavarian Baroque form in the 18C and adorned with exuberant frescoes by Matthäus Gündter of Augsburg, a disciple of Tiepolo. Also noteworthy is the library by Antonio Giuseppe Sartori (1773), with stuccoes by Hans Mussack. It preserves some 75,000 volumes and 14C and 15C paintings by local artists.

On a steep rock southwest of Bressanone is the **Monastero di Sabiona**, an episcopal seat under the patriarch of Aquileia (see p 526) from the 6C–10C. Destroyed in the 16C and rebuilt in the 17C, it preserves parts of its ancient walls.

Interesting castles in the area include **Castello di Velturno/Schloss Ziernberg**, 3km southwest, the Renaissance summer residence of the bishops of Bressanone, with frescoes inside.

The Puez-Odle Nature Reserve

The Puez-Odle Nature Reserve is situated just south of Bressanone, in the western Dolomites on the watershed between the upper Val di Funes and the Val Badia. Occupying an area of 9400h, it includes the towering peaks of the Puez Group and Sasso Putia, as well as the dramatically beautiful Vallunga and Val di Longiarù. The easiest way to reach the park is from Bressanone, via the Val di Funes to Zanser Alm, where there are restrooms, refreshments and parking.

The mountains of the park are classic Dolomites, dating from the Mesozoic and Tertiary period and altered in the Quarternary. On the Côl dela Soné and Côl de Montijela are more recent strata, dating from the Jurassic and Cretaceous periods and rich in fossiliferous sediments. There is a high-mountain lake, the Lago di Crespeina, and Dolomitic pinnacles dominate the landscape around the Passo Cir. Glacial erosion created the U-shaped Vallunga.

As in all the nature reserves of the Alto-Adige, traditional farming and grazing have been allowed to continue in the low-lying areas and on the high pastures, whereas the mountain slopes in between are heavily wooded. The most common essences are stone pine, red fir (especially beautiful on the Putia) and larch (around Halsl). Vast expanses of mugo pine and rhododendron carpet the western slopes of the Putia, and heathers, cranberries and blueberries are not uncommon on the forest floor. In May and June the high pastures, especially Zanser Alm and Gampen Alm, explode with crocuses, soldanellas, pasque flowers, primulas and anenomes. These are followed, in July, by monkshood, hellebore, gentians, and other late bloomers. Various lilies (Turks cap) grow here and there, and a large colony of dwarf rhododendron thrives in the Vallunga. In late Jun–Jul you can expect to find bellflowers and edelweiss around the Rifugio Genova. Deer and chamois abound, marmots whistle among the rocks in the more remote areas, and wood grouse live on the slopes of the Putia.

Walk from Zanser Alm to Rifugio Genova

Though by no means easy (there is an altitude gain of c 500m), this is undoubtedly the most popular walk in the park. Breathtaking scenery more than compensates for the effort made, and the lunch served by the farmers at Gampen Alm alone is worth the trip—roughly 6hrs up and back.

From the parking lot at Zanser Alm (1689m), follow the trail (no. 32) leading uphill along the brook behind the little log cabin (refreshments, restrooms). It's a steep climb, but there's no need to rush it. After a while the trail levels off somewhat, and you reach a wooden footbridge across the brook, the Rio Casedì (a longer, steeper alternative trail continues straight up the mountain to Rifugio Genova via the Malga Busa). After crossing the bridge you enter a lush meadow and the trail again climbs steeply, this time in steps. Halfway up the trail curves left and the Odle group suddenly appears before you in all its glory. As you climb the view becomes more and more open, allowing you to see all the way down the verdant Val di Funes and across the Val d'Isarco to the imposing peaks of the Central Alps.

At the farm at Gampen Alm you can enjoy a truly memorable meal at cut-rate prices. From here you may either return to your starting point by a forest road and woodland path (Trails 33 and 32), or continue onward and upward to the Rifugio Genova (2297m), clearly visible on the saddle above you. If you do go to the Alpine hut (and in fair weather there is no reason not to, having come this far), allow some time to explore a few hundred metres of the *Alta Via dei Dolomiti* (Trail 3), the High Trail of the Dolomites, which follows the contour of the mountain. The views eastward over the Val Badia and the Fanes-Sennes-Braies highlands, and back over the Val di Funes, are unforgettable. The easiest way down from the hut is by the access road, rather than the steep, winding path you came up on; at Gampen Alm pick up the forest road (Trail 33/35) and follow the signs back (via Trail 32) to Zanser Alm.

The upper Val d'Isarco

North of Bressanone the Upper Val d'Isarco has beautiful scenery and spectacular views of the mountains. Followed by both the railway and the *autostrada*, the valley gives access via the Brenner Pass to Austria. For many centuries this has been one of the more important routes over the Alps. Imposing fortifications defend the way. The most modern are the bleak Austrian structure of Fortezza/Franzensfeste (1833–38), which is still used by the Italian Alpine Corps (and, hence, closed to the public); the earliest, **Castel Tasso/Reifenstein** (open Easter–Nov, Sat–Thur at 09.30, 10.30, 14.00 and 15.00), dating from the 12C–16C, with late-Gothic decorations.

Vipiteno/Sterzing takes its Italian name from a Roman post established here. The town owed its importance to the mines that were worked in the side-valleys until the 18C. The Palazzo comunale is an attractive building of 1468–73, and around the tall Torre di Città are 15C–16C *mansions, many with battlements, built by the old mine-owning families. The Casa dell'Ordine Teutonico, with the **Museo Civico** and **Museo Multscher** (open May–Oct, Mon–Sat 10.00–12.00, 14.00–17.00) contains maps, prints, artisans' products, and paintings by Hans Multscher (1458). The 15C Palazzo Jochelsthurn houses the **Museo Provinciale delle Miniere** (open Apr–Oct, Tues–Sat 10.00–12.00, 14.00–17.00), which illustrates the history of mining in the area.

North of Vipiteno the valley narrows and its higher slopes are covered with pine forests. **Colle Isarco/Gossensass** (1098m) is a resort at the foot of the wooded Val di Fléres, once famous for its silver mines.

Brennero/Brenner (1375m) is the last Italian village, just south of the stone pillar (1921 that marks the Austrian frontier on the **Brenner Pass** (Passo di Brennero; 1375m). This is the lowest of the great Alpine passes, and the flat broad saddle of the Brenner, first mentioned with the crossing of Augustus in 13 BC, was the main route of the medieval invaders of Italy. From here to Innsbruck, see *Blue Guide Austria*.

The lower Val Pusteria

The Val Pusteria, the valley of the Rienza, is one of the more beautiful districts in the South Tyrol. In the attractive, brightly coloured villages many of the churches have bulbous steeples and contain good local woodcarvings. The breadth of the valley allows splendid views of the mountains at the head of the side-glens on either side. In the main valley German has replaced Ladin as the language of the inhabitants, but in one side-valley (the lovely Val Badia) the old language has been preserved. The Val Pusteria now has good facilities for cross-country as well as downhill skiing. There are numerous small family-run hotels in the valley, and bed and breakfasts scattered through the countryside.

The entrance to the valley is guarded by handsome castles. **Castello di Rodengo/Schloss Rodeneck** (868m), a 12C fortress overlooking the valley of the Rienza near the ski resort of Rio di Pusterìa/Mühlback (open May–Oct, Tues–Sun at 10.00, 11.00 and 15.00), is a well-preserved fortress dating from 1140 (but altered in the 16C). It contains secular frescoes of c 1200. **Casteldarne/Ehrenburg** has a fine Baroque 16C castle (open in summer, not Sun and holidays, on guided tours). The convent of **Castel Badia/Sonnenburg** (in part restored as a hotel), with a 12C chapel, can be seen on the left on the approach to **San Lorenzo di Sebato**, a village on the site of the larger Roman *Sebatum* (partly excavated: you can see the walls). The 13C church here contains good carvings; a covered bridge still marks the original approach to the village from the Val Pusteria road.

The Val Badia and the Parco Naturale Fanes-Sennes-Braies

South of San Lorenzo a winding road, built by Russian prisoners for the Austrians at the turn of the 19C, leads through a steep, narrow gorge to the Val Badia. This Ladin-speaking valley, one of the more secluded and spectacular of the Dolomites, is widely renowned for its natural beauty and has a number of summer and winter resorts. The most charming of these is **San Vigilio di Marebbe/Sankt Vigil im Enneberg/La Plan**, a Brigadoon-like spot at the foot of the Fanes highlands. **San Cassiano/Sankt Kassian** has a small museum (open Tues–Sun 16.00–19.00) with collections illustrating the valley's natural history and Ladin ethnography.

Established in 1980, the **Parco Naturale Fanes-Sennes-Braies** covers 25,680hs. Situated between the Val Pusteria on the north and the Val Badia on the west, the park extends eastwards to the Val di Landro and the Parco delle Dolomiti di Sesto, whereas on the south it joins with the Parco Regionale delle Dolomiti d'Ampezzo.

The three parks form an immense reserve that is unique in the world. The central nucleus of the protected area is formed by the limestone plateaus of Fanes and Sennes, separated by the deep furrow of the Val dai Tàmersc and dominated on the north by the Dolomiti di Braies with the **Croda Rossa** (3148m, the highest peak of the park), the **Picco di Vallandro** (2839m) and the **Croda del**

Becco (2810m), at the foot of which lies the marvellous ***Lago di Braies** (1493m), a vividly green mountain lake in a remarkable position surrounded by pine woods.

Imposing stratifications of sedimentary dolomite form the geological underpinnings of these mountains. Over these lie deposits of Jurassic limestone (Piccola and Grande Alpe di Fanes, Alpe di Sennes, Croda del Becco, Croda Rosso), often marked by dolinas, furrows, etc., caused by water erosion of the porous stone. Here surface waters vanish rapidly in the subsoil, leaving on the plateaus, especially those of Sennes and Fosses, a fairly arid environment where streams flow only during summer storms and spring thaw.

This fact determines a marked contrast between the high central areas, with scarse plant cover, and the lower regions, on the mountainsides and in the valleys, where the waters re-emerge: these are covered by dense forests of red fir, alternating, at the higher altitudes, with larch and cembra pine. Further up, beyond the low growths of scrub pine, rhododendron, and whortleberry, the alpine meadows, rocks and rubble are populated by a rich alpine flora that includes the *papavero retico*, *linaiola alpina*, certain saxifrages, *androsace*, *raponzolo chiomoso*, *semprevivo delle Dolomiti*, edelweiss, *orecchia d'orso*, and many other species.

The park's fauna includes roe deer, chamois and small colonies of ibex in the area of the Croda del Becco, where they were introduced in the 1960s. There are also the classic alpine mammals (marmots, hare, ermine, weasel), amphibians (*rana temporaria*, *tritone alpino*) and a wide variety of birds (royal eagle, kestrel, owls, crows, grouse, white partridge, red woodpecker, *picchio muraiolo*, *crociere*, alpine finches, *spioncello*, *fiorancino*, *cinca dal ciuffo*, etc.)

Walk to Monte Vallon Bianco (2687m)

This is a moderately strenuous walk along the First World War military trail now known as the Via della Pace. It begins at the Rifugio Pederù (1545m), reached from San Vigilio di Marebbe via the long Valle di Tamores. Time required is 8–9hrs.

From the Rifugio Pederù climb by a dirt track (Trail 7) that ascends the Valle di Rudo beneath by the steep walls of the Furcia dai Fers on the right, and of the Croda Ciamin on the left, to reach in c 2hrs the Malga Fanes Piccola and the shelters of **La Varella** (2042m, ☎ 0474 501092) and **Fanes** (2060m, ☎ 0474 501097). If you want to shorten the walk you can take one of the jeeps that ferry visitors back and forth from the Rifugio Pederù. From the Rifugio Fanes you climb in a southeasterly direction by a mule track (Trails 10, 11 and 17), which leads to the **Passo di Limo** (2172m) and to the little lake of the same name, overlooking the broad basin of the Alpe di Fanes Grande. From here you descend to the **Malga di Fanes Grande** (2104m), then continue southwards (Trail 17) to the fork where Via della Pace begins on the left. This is an Austrian military trail from the First World War, recently restored, which, passing beneath the Cime di Furcia Rossa, climbs with a last steep tract to the crest of the Furcia Rossa, near the **Bivacco Baccon-Baborka** (2665m), overlooking the deep Val Travenanzes and the Tofane massif. From here, on the ridge top, you reach the panoramic peak of **Monte Vallon Bianco** (2687m). The return follows the same course.

Brunico and the Parco Naturale delle Vedrette di Ries

Brunico/Bruneck is the picturesque capital of the Val Pusteria. It stands in a small upland plain with fir trees and is overlooked by the castle of Bruno, the 13C bishop of Bressanone who is traditionally credited with founding it. Brunico is the native town of Micheal Pacher (c 1430–98), whose sculpted wooden crucifixes can be found in the churches of the region. The main **Via di Città** is lined with pretty alpine houses with bay windows and fanciful gables; many of the shops have old (or old-fashioned) wrought-iron signs. The **castle**, on a hill, was built in the 13C and 14C and altered in the 15C and 16C. In the courtyard are frescoed coats of arms. In the suburb of Teodone (*Dietenheim*), on the Mair am Hof farm is an interesting museum of local agricultural methods and folk customs, the **Museo Provinciale degli Usi e Costumi** (open Apr–Oct, Tues–Sat 09.30–17.30, Sun and holidays 14.00–18.00).

North of Brunico the Val di Tures provides access to a group of thickly wooded mountain glens lying beneath the peaks and glaciers of the Alpi Aurine on the Austrian frontier. **Campo Tures/Sand in Taufers** is the main centre in these valleys, visited by climbers and skiers. It is dominated by the 13C–15C castle (shown on guided tours) of the barons of Tures. In the Valle Aurina is the peak of the **Vetta d'Italia** (2912m), the northernmost point in Italy. The Picco dei Tre Signori (3498m) further east, marked the junction of the counties of Tyrol, Salzburg and Gorizia.

Established in 1989, the **Parco Naturale delle Vedrette di Ries** covers a surface of 21,850h between the Val Pusteria and the Valle di Anterselva on the south, the Val di Tures on the west, the Valle Aurina on the north and the Austrian border on the east. In addition to the crystalline Riesenferner Group, the park includes the southwest slopes of the Durreck Massif. These mountains constitute a small subgroup of the chain of the Alti Tauri (*Hohne Tauren*); nevertheless they include a dozen peaks over 3000m and some fine glaciers on the northern slopes—the Vedrette di Ries and the Schneebiger Nock, Gelttal and Althaus.

The rocks that form much of the Riesenferner group are gneiss and schist extant in the Palaeozoic era, which were subjected to metamorphosis during the orogenesis of the Alps. On the wooded northern slopes of the Durreck massif you find schist belonging to the so-called *finestra dei Tauri*, while the main chain of the Riesenferner, which includes the **Collalto** (*Hochgall*, 3436m), the highest peak, is composed of a powerful mass of solid tonalite inserted among more fragile schist and gneiss.

The glaciers of the Pleistocene have deeply moulded these mountains, transforming the heads of the valleys into glacial cirques, carving grooves in the mountain walls, accumulating moraines along their path and hollowing in the rock the niches now occupied by numerous high-mountain lakes, found mainly between 2200 and 2500m. Lower down, the streams have formed spectacular gorges and cascades like the Cascate di Riva, near Campo Tures. Among the geological peculiarities of the park are the erosion pyramids (*Platten*) on the right orographic side of the Val Pusteria. At the head of the Valle di Anterselva is one of the larger lakes of the Alto Adige, the **Lago di Anterselva**, formed by the alluvial cones that descend the southern slope of the Collalto and the Rotwand.

At the entrance to the same valley, but outside the borders of the park, is the **biotope of Rasun**, a wetland frequented by migratory birds.

A continental climate and the siliceous nature of the soil are the main influences that have shaped plant life in the Riesenferner group. The most common tree in the forests is the red fir, in the shadow of which rhododendron and whortleberry form a sort of underwood. On the sunnier slopes, larches also grow. Deciduous trees are few and far between, with the notable exception of a local variety of sorb. The treeline reaches a maximum of 2200m, but a few isolated cembra pines can be found as high up as 2465m on the Tristennöckl, at the foot of the Vedretta di Tristen (*Tristenkees*). The most beautiful flowers in the park—which include arnica, bellflowers, anemones, dwarf primrose, edelweiss, dwarf gentian, saxifrages and artemisia—grow in the high-mountain meadows and amid the rocks and rubble at the foot of the peaks.

The forests are populated by numerous roe deer and deer, as well as by badgers, fox, marten, squirrels and several native species of birds (*crociere*, *nocciolaia*, etc.). It is also possible to spot royal eagles, grouse, owls, marmots, chamois, white partridges, ermine, crows and the alpine finch. The invertebrate population includes some beautiful butterflies.

> ### Walk to the Cascate di Riva
>
> This is an easy one which anyone can do. The departure point is Winkel (860m), near Campo Tures; the time required is 1hr 30mins–2hrs 30mins (round trip).
>
> Near the bridge at Winkel, signs mark the beginning of the trail to the waterfall, a mule track that enters the forest toward the east. After about 200m, a sign indicates on the left the turning for the first, spectacular cascade on the **Torrente di Riva**. From here climb through the forest to rejoin the mule track, which you follow uphill as far as a rock on the left in the woods. Here leave it again, following the signs for the second and third cascade. After passing a dizzying overlook on the second cascade, the path climbs again and, after skirting the edge of the ravine, reaches the third waterfall, which ends in a narrow gorge crossed by a small iron bridge. Beyond the bridge clamber up steep steps through the woods to a fork where, on the left, you can climb in 5mins to the *Ristorante Toblhof* and the paved road, or on the right, follow a brook and a steep climb to the ruins of the 12C **Castello di Tobl**. From here you can return to Winkel by the same route or reach the road and return to Campo Tures by bus.

The upper Val Pusteria

The Val Pusteria opens out at Rasun and the three interlocking villages of **Valdaora** (Valdaora di Sotto, di Mezzo and di Sopra), each with a church. In the lovely **Val Casies** are the picturesque 12C castle of Monguelfo, with a tall tower, and **Tesido**, a pretty village on the lower sunny slopes of the hillside with two delightful churches, one Baroque, with a pink exterior, and the other—older—with a large external fresco of St Christopher.

Dobbiaco/Toblach (1256m) has a large church and a castle built in 1500 for the Emperor Maximilian I. Gustav Mahler stayed here in 1908–10 (small

The village of Valdaora

museum open in summer, ☎ 0474 972132).

San Candido/Innichen (1175m) is a lovely little summer and winter resort, with a Baroque parish church. The 13C *****Collegiata** (tower 1326) is dedicated to St Candidus and St Corbinian, who are depicted in the fresco above the south door by Michael Pacher. It is the most important Romanesque monument in the Alto-Adige, with interesting sculptural details. The 15C atrium protects the main portal with Romanesque carvings. In the interior is a splendid *Crucifixion* group above the high altar (c 1200). The remarkable frescoes in the cupola date from about 1280. The crypt has handsome columns, and there is a small museum open in summer.

East of San Candido the Dolimiti di Sesto take their name from the village of **Sesto/Sexten**, a small summer and winter resort with a Baroque parish church (San Vito), frescoed houses, and a small museum with works by local painter Rudolf Stolz (1874–1960). Beyond Sesto the road continues via the Passo di Monte Croce (1636m) to Tolmezzo and Udine (see p 511). San Candido is 7km from the Austrian frontier on the road to Lienz (see *Blue Guide Austria*).

The Parco Naturale delle Dolomiti di Sesto

The Parco Naturale delle Dolomiti di Sesto was established in 1981 and extends over 11,650h. Seen from the Val Pusteria, the landscape here is indescribably dramatic. In the foreground are the subgroups of the Baranci and the Tre Scarperi, among which open two parallel valleys (Val di Dentro and Val Fiscalina) closed at their upper ends by the spectacular vertical walls of the **Tre Cime di Lavaredo** (2999m), **Paterno** (2744m), and **Cima Dodici** (3094m).

The oldest rocks of this last northeastern bastion of the Dolomites are conglomerates of porphyry and sandstone, buried beneath layers of black limestone, dolomite and gray marl. Werfen layers reach altitudes of nearly 2000m, but they are largely concealed by dense forests. The spectacular dolomitic peaks were formed in the Middle and Upper Triassic periods—65–1.8 million years ago. During the Ice Age the region was almost completely buried beneath a gigantic glacier, which has left clear signs of its presence—particularly in the Valle del Rio Alto Fiscalina, where you can see moraines and streaked and round-backed rocks formed by the retreating ice. Today the glaciers have practically disappeared.

The forests here (which reach a maximum altitude of 1900m), are composed mainly of red fir mixed with larch and a few rare white firs and cembra pines. Sylvan pine grows in groups in the Val di Landro on the more arid slopes. Above the treeline scrub pine and rhododendron abound. Interesting semi-natural environments are the *prati a larice* ('larch meadows') of the Val Fiscalina and Val Campo di Dentro. The flora includes several species of gentians (for example, *G. punctata* and *G. asclepiadea*), saxifrages (*S. squarrosa*, *S. oppositifolia*, *S. caesia*), edelweiss and alpine poppies, just to mention a few.

There is quite a variety of fauna, too, including chamois, roe deer, deer, marmots, hare, fox, badgers, marten, weasels and ermine. Other mammals include the alpine bat (*Hypsugo savii*), which is found in the forests and even above the treeline. Among the numerous species of birds are royal eagles, sparrowhawks, goshawks, falcons, owls, grouse, white partridges, the black woodpecker, and some 70 songbirds.

Walk from Rifugio Zsigmondy-Comici to Rifugio Locatelli

This is one of the more popular hikes in the Dolomites. Moderately strenuous, it starts out at *Hotel Dolomitenhof* (1454m) in Val Fiscalina, near Sesto, and takes 6hrs 30mins–7hrs 30mins.

From the car park of the *Hotel Dolomitenhof* set out along the valley floor through meadows and pine woods, reaching in roughly half an hour the Rifugio Fondovalle (*Talschlusshütte*, 1526m). From here you continue along Trail 102–103 in the Valle di Sasso Vecchio (*Altsteiner Tal*) to a fork where you take the trail on the left (no. 103) which, passng beneath the rocks of **Cima Uno** (2698m) climbs to the **Rifugio Zsigmondy-Comici** (2224m, ☎ 0474 70358). From the shelter follow Trail 101 in a westerly direction, climbing steeply to the Passo Fiscalino and then more gently to the **Rifugio Pian di Cengia** (*Büllele Joch Hütte*, 2528m, ☎ 0474 70258), among clear signs of the First World War. From the shelter, again on Trail 101 descend to the slopes of **Monte Paterno** (2744m) and then, after a short climb, reach the **Rifugio Locatelli** (*Drei Zinnen Hütte*, 2405m, ☎ 0474 72002), from which you have a spectacular view over the **Tre Cime di Lavaredo** (2999m). From the shelter, Trail 102 descends to Val di Sasso Vecchio by way of the Laghi dei Piani, and returns to the Val Fiscalina.

THE VENETO

The Veneto includes the provinces of Belluno, Padua, Rovigo, Treviso, Venice, Verona and Vicenza. It has a rich and varied past, the ramifications of which go well beyond the history of Venice, from which the region receives its name.

In the 12C Verona, Padua, Vicenza and Treviso formed the Veronese League in imitation of the Lombard League, as a means of containing the power of the Holy Roman Emperor. In the following century important families—such as the Scaligeri in Verona and Vicenza, and the Carraresi in Padua and Vicenza—held courts that developed a reputation throughout Europe for their generous support of the arts. When the maritime expansion of Venice in the east was checked by the rising power of the Turkish Empire and the Venetians turned their interests to the terraferma, Treviso, Padua and numerous other cities willingly joined the Most Serene Republic. By 1420 the whole territory, from Verona to Udine and from Belluno to Padua, was under the banner of a larger and more compact Republic of Venice. Further extensions of the doges' dominion, to Bergamo in the west, Rimini in the south, and Fiume in the east, provoked the jealousy of the powers beyond the Alps, and the League of Cambrai (1508) put an end to Venice's imperial ambitions. But the Venetian dominions in Italy remained united for 300 years.

The Napoleonic invasion of Italy saw the dismemberment of the Veneto; in 1797 Venice itself and the area east of the Adige was ceded to Austria, who also took control of areas in the west in 1814, after a brief union with the Cisalpine Republic. In 1859 an armistice stopped the progress of Vittorio Emanuele at the Lombard frontier, and it was not until the Austrian defeat by the Prussians in 1866 that the Veneto was able by plebiscite to join the Piedmontese kingdom. The region was attacked from the air in the Second World War, and much destruction was caused by the Germans at Verona. The Allies reached Udine on the last day of the fighting in Italy (1 May 1945).

Since the Second World War the Veneto has become the centre of what Italians call the 'Miracle of the Northeast'. This is the wealthiest region of the country and its fastest-growing industrial district. But it is also the area where economic development has most successfully adapted itself to ideas of ecological and historical preservation. Thanks to a prevalence of small, flexible and clean industries, affluence has made a 'soft landing' in the area, whose stunning natural and artistic assets remain relatively unspoilt. As a result, the Veneto has become one of Europe's more successful 'post-industrial' experiments—a fascinating place to visit, but also a wonderful place in which to live.

Lago di Garda

*Lago di Garda is the largest and perhaps the most beautiful of the northern Italian lakes. The west bank is in Lombardy (the province of Brescia), the east bank in the Veneto (the province of Verona), and the northern tip in the Trentino region. The lake's mild climate permits the cultivation of olives and lemon trees, and the vegetation of its shores is characterised by numerous cypresses in thick woods. Before the lake was developed as a resort at the beginning of the 20C, the local economy was based on the production of olive oil (particularly on the east bank) and the cultivation of lemons (the lake was the northernmost locality in the world where citrus fruits could be grown commercially).

Practical information

Getting there
By air

Airports at Milan (Malpensa, Linate), Bergamo (Orio di Serio), Brescia (Montichiari) Verona (Caselle di Sommacampagna) and Venice (Marco Polo). Malpensa handles intercontinental and European flights; all others domestic and European flights only.

By road

Lago di Garda is on Italy's main east–west *autostrada*, the A4, from Venice to Milan. All exits for the lakes (Peschiera del Garda, Sirmione and Desenzano del Garda) are clearly marked. Lago di Garda can also be reached from Innsbruck (Austria) and the Passo del Brennero via A22 and 12; the *autostrada* intersects the A4 near Verona, then continues south to Modena. A secondary road (240; leave the A22 at Rovereto Sud) connects Rovereto, on the latter route, to Riva del Garda, at the north end of the lake.

By rail

The Venice–Milan line serves Peschiera del Garda, Desenzano del Garda–Sirmione and Lonato, from which there are frequent country bus services to outlying points. Regional trains connect the lake stations to Verona or Brescia in

less than 30mins; fast *Intercity* trains stop at Desenzano–Sirmione only, making the run in c 20mins. *Intercity*, *Eurocity* and *Eurostar* trains connect Verona with Venice, Trieste, Milan, Turin and Genoa; Bologna, Florence and Rome; and Trento, Bolzano and Bressanone. There are direct through services to and from Basel, Berlin, Bern, Dortmund, Geneva, Lugano, Munich, Munster, Nice, Paris, Vienna and Zurich.

Getting around
By bus

Bus services run several times daily by the roads on the west and east banks from Peschiera and Desenzano to Riva. Frequent service from Verona via Lazise and Garda to Riva, and from Brescia to Desenzano, Sirmione, Peschiera and Verona, and between Salò and Desenzano, and Desenzano, Salò and Riva.

By boat

Boat services (including two modernised paddle-steamers built in 1902 and 1903) are run by **Navigazione sul Lago di Garda**, Piazza Matteotti, Desenzano, ☎ 030 914 1321, from around mid-Mar–beginning Nov (the timetable changes three times a year). A

daily boat service runs between
Desenzano and Riva in 4hrs 30mins,
calling at ports on the west bank and
Malcesine. Hydrofoils run twice daily in
2hrs (with fewer stops). More frequent
boats between Desenzano and Maderno
(in 1hr 50mins). Services also run
between Peschiera, Lazise, Bardolino
and Garda, and between Malcesine,
Limone, Torbole and Riva. A boat or
hydrofoil runs c every hour between
Desenzano and Sirmione. All year round
a car ferry operates between Maderno
and Torri di Benaco in 30mins (every
30mins, but less frequently in winter).
Tickets are available allowing free circulation on the lake services for a day.
Tours of the lake in the afternoons in
summer are also organised. Ask the
information offices listed below for
timetables and fares.

Information offices
BRESCIA Corso Zanardelli
34–38, ☎ 030 45053.
DESENZANO DEL GARDA Piazza
Matteotti 27, ☎ 030 914 1510.
GARDA Lungolago Regina Adelaide, ☎
045 725 5194
GARDONE RIVIERA Corso della
Repubblica 35, ☎ 0365 403657.
LAZISE Via Francesca Fontana 14, ☎
0457 758 0114.
MALCESINE Via Capitanato 6, ☎ 045
740 0044.
RIVA DEL GARDA Giardini di Porta
Orientale 35, tel. 0464 554444.
SALÒ Lungolago Zanardelli 39, ☎
0365 21423.
SIRMIONE Viale Marconi 2, ☎ 030
916 114.
VERONA Via Leoncino 61, ☎ 045 806
8680, fax 045 800 3638, and Piazza
delle Erbe 42, ☎ 045 803 0086 (sum-
mer only).

Where to stay
Most of the places on Lago di
Garda are open during the

summer season only, Apr/May–Oct.
FASANO DEL GARDA (near Gardone
Riviera) *Fasano e Villa Principe*, ☎
0365 290220, fax 0365 290221; a former hunting lodge of the emperors of
Austria set in a lovely park with garden
terrace overlooking the lake; expensive.
Villa del Sogno, ☎ 0365 290181, fax
0365 290230; another villa in a
romantic garden with an immense terrace on the lake; expensive.
GARDA *Locanda San Vigilio*, Località
San Vigilio, ☎ 045 725 6688, fax 045
725 6551; small and on the lakefront,
with a good restaurant and garden;
expensive.
GARGNANO *Villa Giulia*, Viale
Rimembranza 20, ☎ 0365 71128; fax
0365 72012; a lakeside villa with lovely
garden; closed Jan–Mar; moderate.
LIMONE SUL GARDA *Capo Reamolo*,
Via IV Novembre 92, ☎ 0365 954040,
fax 0365 954262; park, pool, and
everything from Oriental medicine to
windsurfing; moderate.
MALCESINE *Park Hotel Querceto*,
Località Campiano 17/19, ☎ 045 740
0344, fax 045 740 0848; small (19
rooms) and relaxed, with restaurant service outside in summer; moderate.
RIVA DEL GARDA *Du Lac et du Parc*,
Viale Rovereto 44, ☎ 0464 551500, fax
0464 555200; a luxurious establishment
in a large park, offering peace and quiet,
elegance and refinement; expensive.
Grand Hotel di Riva, Piazza Garibaldi
10, ☎ 0464 521800, fax 0464
552293; another classic hotel with a
quiet park, frequented also for its roof-
garden restaurant; moderate.
ROCOLINO (above Gargano) Roccolino,
☎ 0365 71443, fax 0365 72059; 10
rooms, with fine views of the lake and
mountains; closed Jan–Feb; moderate.
SALÒ *Barbarano al Lago*, Località
Barbarano, ☎ 0365 20324; a small (16
rooms), tranquil hotel with a pleasant
garden; closed Oct–May; inexpensive.
SIRMIONE *Ideal*, Via Catullo 31, ☎

030 990 4245, fax 030 990 4245; one
of the finest settings on the peninsula, a
tranquil olive grove overlooking the lake
and the Grotte di Catullo; moderate.

Palace Hotel Villa Cortine, Via Grotte
12, ☎ 030 990 5890, fax 030 916
390; luxury accomodation in a 19C
villa with large park, on the lake shore;
expensive.

TORRI DEL BENACO *Europa*, ☎ 045
722 5086, fax 045 722 5065; a small
establishment (18 rooms) in a renovated
villa with a pleasant garden, enjoying
splendid views over the lake and mountains; closed Nov–Mar; inexpensive.

TREMOSINE (Campi-Voltino) *Le Balze*,
☎ 0365 917179, fax 0365 917033;
small and comfortable, with good views;
closed Nov–Mar, inexpensive.

Pineta Campi, ☎ 0365 917158, fax
0365 917015, as above; closed
Nov–Mar; inexpensive.

Youth hostel: *Villa Pariani*, Località
Val di Sogno, Malcesine.

Eating out
DESENZANO DEL GARDA
Cavallino, Via Gherla 30, ☎
030 912 0217; good seasonal dishes
made with the freshest ingredients;
closed Mon, midday Tues, Jan and midday Aug; inexpensive.

Esplanade, Via Lario 10 ☎ 030
9143361; fresh seasonal cuisine with
summer seating in a garden overlooking
the lake; closed Wed; inexpensive.

GARDONE RIVIERA *Villa Fiordaliso*
(with rooms), ☎ 0365 20158; in business since 1890 in an old villa in a small
park with summer seating on a terrace
overlooking the lake; closed Mon and
Jan–Feb; moderate.

GARGNANO *La Tortuga*, by the harbour, ☎ 0365 71251; a gourmet's
delight, known for its *charlotte di melan-
zane, spaghettini di pasta fresca al pesce
di lago, filetti di persico croccanti in bat-
tuta di rosmarino, sella di coniglio al profumo di timo* and *torte di pere con salsa*

di fragole, and its excellent selection of
regional, Italian and imported wines;
closed Mon evening (except Jun–Sep),
Tues and Jan; expensive.

LUGANA (5km southeast of Sirmione)
Vecchia Lugana, ☎ 030 919012; summer seating on a terrace overlooking the
lake and creative interpretations of local
specialties, with special attention to seasonal dishes; closed Mon evening, Tues
and Jan–Feb; moderate.

PESCHIERA DEL GARDA *Papa* (with
rooms), Via Bella Italia 40, ☎ 045 755
0476; good local food and wine; closed
Wed and Nov–Dec; inexpensive.

TORRI DEL BENACO *Al Calval* (with
rooms), ☎ 045 722 5666; hearty local
cuisine and regional wines; closed Mon,
Jan–Feb and Nov–Dec; moderate.

Special events
RIVA DEL GARDA *Intervela*,
international sailing week, Jul;
Musica Riva, international conference
of young musicians, Jul; *Bikemarathon
Transalp Challenge*, world's longest and
toughest bike race (550km, 15,000m
altitude gain), from Mittenwald, Baveria
(Germany) to Riva di Garda, Jul.

Flicorno d'Oro, international band
competition, Aug; *Mostra
Internazionale di Musica Leggera Vela
d'Oro*, pop music festival, Sep.

SALÒ Music festival, Jul.

Sports
Golf at Marciaga,
Costermano, Sommacam-
pagna (18 holes), Soiano and Toscolano
Maderno (9 holes).

Swimming at beaches all around the
lake.

Walks along marked trails can be taken
on Monte Baldo on the eastern bank,
and in the Parco Alto Garda Bresciano
(in the territory of Valvestino,
Tremosine and Tignale) above Salò,
Toscolano Maderno and Limone on the
western bank. Information and maps

from the *Comunità Montana del Baldo* (☎ 045 7241600) and the *Comunità Montana Parco Alto Garda Bresciano* (☎ 0365 71449), and local information offices.

THE LAKE

Lago di Garda is 51km long and 369sq km in area; its maximum depth is 346m. The only important stream flowing into it is the Sarca, descending from the Trentino; the outlet is the Mincio. The predominant winds (which can swell into violent storms) are the *sover*, from the north, in the morning, and the *ora*, from the south, in the afternoon.

History

Sirmione, in a spectacular position on a narrow peninsula on the south shore, has been known since Roman times as a resort on Lacus Benacus (from the Celtic, meaning 'horned'). The little resorts of Salò, Desenzano and Gardone on the west shore were first developed as such in the 1920s and 1930s, although some grand hotels had already been built at the end of the 19C for Austrian and German clients who came to the mild western shore, many of them to cure respiratory disorders. In 1931 the road was continued north from Gargnano to Limone (previously accessible only by boat) by cutting tunnels through the sheer rock face that drops straight into the lake and provides some of its most dramatic scenery. The east side, beneath the conspicuous Monte Baldo, has been developed as a holiday area only since the Second World War.

Lago di Garda has traditionally been popular with writers, perhaps because of its inspiring beauty. Goethe visited the lake at the start of his Italian journey in 1786 and saw his first olive trees here. He sailed down the lake from Torbole past Limone, where he admired the lemon gardens, and was forced to land for a night at Malcesine because of unfavourable winds. While sketching the castle there he was almost arrested as an Austrian spy. The next day he docked at Bardolino, where he mounted a mule to cross into the Adige Valley for Verona. Byron stayed at Desenzano in 1816, and Tennyson visited the lake in 1880. D.H. Lawrence lived on its shores in 1912 and 1913, and he describes the lemon gardens in *Twilight in Italy*. Winston Churchill wintered at the Grand Hotel in Gardone Riviera in 1949.

Citrus cultivation around the lake dates from at least the 16C and reached a height in commercial production in the early 19C. A few of the characteristic monumental pavilions, with tall stone pilasters covered with wooden slats and glass in winter, where lemons and citrons were cultivated in the 19C, still survive at Gargnano and Torri del Benaco. These shelters, unique to Garda, were designed for maximum protection from the cold. Duck and swans flourish on the lake, and fishing is still practised in a few localities (the *salmo carpio*, a kind of large trout, is found only in Garda; other fish include pike, trout and eel).

Remains of two of the more important Roman villas in northern Italy are to be found on the shores of Garda at Sirmione and Desenzano. There are fine Scaliger castles open to the public at Sirmione, Malcesine and Torri del

Bernaco. The most curious sight on the lake is the famous 'Vittoriale', the last home of the eccentric poet Gabriele D'Annunzio.

The best time to visit Lago di Garda is May to June: in August it is very crowded and can be extremely hot. Garda is now visited mostly by German tourists. The breezier upper part of the lake, where the water is deepest, is much used for sailing and windsurfing (boats can be hired), and there are sailing regattas in summer. A purifying plant near Peschiera has successfully cleaned the waters of the lake, which is now considered the cleanest of the big Italian lakes, and swimming is permitted (the best places include the peninsula of Sirmione, the Isola dei Conigli off Moniga, the Baia del Vento between Salò and Desenzano, and the Isola San Biagio).

Sirmione

Sirmione stands at the tip of a narrow promontory 3.5km long and in places only 119m wide, in the centre of the southern shore of the lake. It was a Roman station on the Via Gallica, halfway between Brescia and Verona. Now it is a famous resort with numerous hotels and is usually crowded with tourists in the season (though deserted in winter). There are many enjoyable walks on the peninsula, and you can swim in the lake on the east side.

The picturesque 13C ***Rocca Scaligera** (open daily 09.00–13.00; summer 09.00–18.00), where Dante is said to have stayed, marks the entrance to the town. Completely surrounded by water, it was a stronghold of the Scaliger family, lords of Verona. The massive central tower, 29m high, has a good view.

Via Vittorio Emanuele (closed to cars) leads north from the castle through the scenic little town towards the Grotte di Catullo at the end of the peninsula. A road on the right leads to the 15C church of **Santa Maria Maggiore**, which preserves some antique columns. At the end of Via Vittorio Emanuele is a spa with a hotel that uses warm sulphur springs rising in the lake. Via Catullo continues, passing close to **San Pietro in Mavino**, a Romanesque church of 8C foundation with early frescoes.

Rocca Scaligera

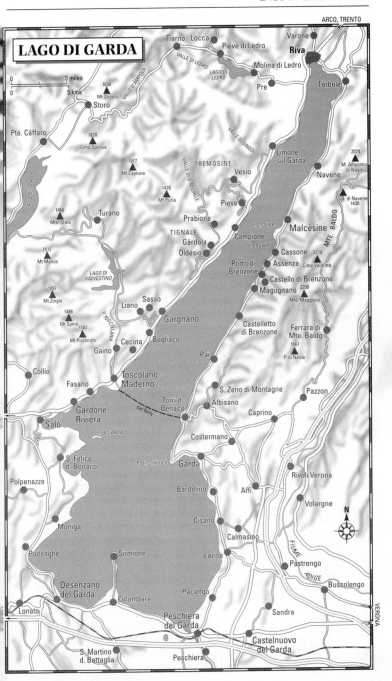

At the end of the road is the entrance to the so-called ***Grotte di Catullo** (open Tues–Sun 09.00–dusk), really the romantic ruins of a large Roman villa. This is the most important example of Roman imperial domestic architecture in northern Italy. It is set amid olive groves on the end of the headland, with splendid views out over the lake and of the rocks beneath the clear shallow water. The most beautiful spot on the lake, the site is very well maintained and planted with trees. The vast ruins belong to a country house of the 1C BC (abandoned by the 4C) that may have belonged to the family of Valerii Catulli. Many wealthy Romans came to Sirmione for the summer, and Catullus—who is known to have had a villa here—speaks of '*Paene peninsularum, Sirmio, insularumque ocelle*' ('Sirmione, gem of all peninsulas and islands'). Though the ruins have been known for many centuries, excavations took place here only in the 19C and the beginning of the 20C. Near the entrance is a small antiquarium, with exquisite fragments of frescoes dating from the 1C BC.

The most conspicuous remains are the vast substructures and vaults built to sustain the main buildings of the villa, which occupied an area over 150m long and 100m wide on the top of the hill: virtually nothing is left of the villa itself, as it was used as a quarry for building stones over the centuries, and its site is now covered by an olive grove. An earlier edifice of the 1C BC has been discovered here. You can see a number of huge cisterns, as well as thermal buildings and a long colonnaded terrace with a covered walkway below.

A little way inland

The road along the shore of the lake leads west. From Rivoltella, halfway between Sirmione and Desenzano, a by-road leads away from the lake up to the tower (74m high) of **San Martino della Battaglia**, which commemorates Vittorio Emanuele II's victory over the right flank of the Austrian army on 24 June 1859. The interior contains sculptures and paintings relating to the campaign. At Solferino (in the province of Mantua, see p 280), Napoleon III, in alliance with Vittorio Emanuele, defeated the rest of the Austrian army on the same day. The low moraine hills south of the lake, formed by the ancient glacier of the Adige, have been the theatre of many battles: during Prince Eugène's campaign in the War of the Spanish Succession (1701–06), during Napoleon's enterprises (1796–1814), and during the Wars of Italian Independence (1848–49, 1859 and 1866).

Desenzano and the west bank

Desenzano del Garda is a pleasant little resort, well equipped with hotels. From the quay a bridge crosses a tiny picturesque inlet used as a harbour for small boats. Behind is the main piazza, with pretty arcades and a monument to St Angela Merici (1474–1540), foundress of the Ursuline order, who was born here. Just out of the piazza is the **parish church** with a ***Last Supper** by Giovanni Battista Tiepolo.

Nearby is the entrance to the excavations of a **Roman villa** (open Tues–Sun 09.00–dusk), mostly dating from the 4C AD but on the site of an earlier edifice of the 1C AD. The various building stages are still unclear. It is the most important late Roman villa in northern Italy, of great interest for its colourful 4C mosaics.

The grandiose design of the reception rooms of the main villa includes an octagonal hall, a peristyle, an atrium with two apses, and a triclinium with three apses, all with mosaics. Other, less grand rooms to the south may have been baths. An antiquarium (beneath which a Roman edifice of the 1C AD, with an underfloor heating system, was discovered) has finds from the site, including remains of wall paintings. Separate excavations to the north have revealed a residential area, with part of an apsidal hall and baths, to the east. The villa was discovered in 1921, and excavations have continued even though the site is in the centre of the town.

Lonato has a 15C castle built by the Visconti, which was the scene of French victories over the Austrians in 1509, 1706 and 1796, the last an early success of Napoleon. The castle (open Easter–Sep 09.00–20.00) was reconstructed in its 15C form by Antonio Tagliaferri at the beginning of the 20C and houses a small museum and a fine library (50,000 volumes, with 411 incunabula). Nearby, at **Fornace dei Gorghi**, excavations in 1988 revealed a number of Roman brick ovens of the 1C–2C AD, near the largest of which is a small antiquarium.

North of Lonato

North of Lonato the road leaves the lake, with many camping sites, and crosses the hilly district of **Valtenesi**, noted for its olive oil and wine. A by-road leads to the **Rocca di Manerba**, a headland once crowned by a castle. The Pieve of Santa Maria (or San Rocco) dates from the 11C–12C, with remains of frescoes, and is one of a number of Romanesque country churches in the Valtenesi. Further north there is a narrow channel between the romantic headland of Punta San Fermo and the **Isola di Garda**, on which is the Villa Borghese Cavazza, built c 1900 in the Venetian-Gothic style on the ruins of a Franciscan convent. The lovely gardens are open by previous appointment in April–June, and September–Octer.

Back on the lake shore

Salò, the Roman *Salodium*, is perhaps the most appealing town on the western shore, with a slightly old-fashioned atmosphere. It has two gates, one surmounted by a lion, the other by a clock.

It was the birthplace of Gaspare Bertolotti (also known as Gaspare da Salò, 1540–1609), generally considered to be the first maker of violins, and gave its name to Mussolini's short-lived puppet republic (the Repubblica Sociale Italiana, or Repubblica di Salò). Mussolini returned here, in a last attempt to re-establish the Fascist government of Italy, a few months after his release from prison and his escape to Germany in 1943. Salò was an ideal place for the re-establishment of Fascist authority, as the borders of the Reich had reached Limone, only 20km north, with the annexation of the Trentino-Alto Adige, and the many huge hotels and villas by the lake were easily adapted as ministries. The Republic of Salò ended with the Liberation in 1945 and Mussolini's execution a few days later.

Near the waterfront is the **Cathedral**, a fine building in a late-Gothic style built at the end of the 15C, with a good Renaissance portal (1509). It contains paintings by Zenon Veronese and Romanino, and a carved 15C tabernacle. **Palazzo Fantoni** is the seat of the Biblioteca Ateneo, which has its origins in the

Accademia degli Unanimi founded by Giovanni Maione in 1560. The library has over 25,000 volumes, many of great historical interest. There is also a small museum relating to the Republic of Salò. Villa Laurin (now a hotel), built in 1905, has a fresco by Angelo Landi.

The village of **Barbarano**, just north of Salò, is known for the huge Palazzo Martinengo (not open), connected by a bridge across the road with its garden, which has numerous fountains. The palace was built in 1577 by the Marchese Sforza Pallavicino, the Venetian general.

Gardone Riviera was once famous as a winter resort. It has a sheltered position and used to enjoy a particularly mild winter climate—its parks and gardens are planted with rare trees. On the left of the highway here is the **Vittoriale degli Italiani** (open daily 09.00–12.30 and 14.00 or 14.30–18.00 or 18.30; villa closed on Mon), the famous residence of Gabriele D'Annunzio (1863–1938) designed for him in the last years of his life by Gian Carlo Maroni. It takes its name from the Italian victory over Austria in 1918. D'Annunzio donated the Vittoriale to the Italian State 15 years before his death here in 1938, and it is a remarkable monument to the eccentric martial poet, who had a great influence on Italian poetry in this century.

From the gate a path leads up past the amphitheatre (used for theatre and music performances in summer), built by Maroni, to the 18C **villa** (shown in a 30mins tour to a maximum of 6–10 people by appointment at the ticket office). It has been preserved, with its elaborate and gloomy décor, as a museum. Off the dark hallway is a reception room with an inscription that D'Annunzio made Mussolini read on his visit here: 'Remember that you are made of glass and I of steel.' Other rooms are crammed full of eclectic items: Art Nouveau *objets d'art*, chinoiserie, mementoes, sacred objects, Indian works of art, and even an organ. The Art Deco dining room was designed by Maroni.

The private **garden** in front of the villa harbours such items as odd statuary and columns surmounted by projectiles. A path leads down through the pretty woods of the Acquapazza Valley towards the main road. Behind the villa, Viale di Aligi leads up past a building that houses D'Annunzio's motorboat to his grand mausoleum at the top of the hill, where he and his architect are buried. Another path leads through woods to the prow of the ship *Puglia*, reconstructed here as a monument. His private plane is also exhibited. The Fondazione del Vittoriale promotes the study of D'Annunzio's works.

Downhill, on the other side of the road, are the small privately owned **botanical gardens** (open Mar–Oct, 09.00–dusk), laid out by Arturo Hruska in 1940–71, with narrow paths through luxuriant vegetation. Nearer the lake is the conspicuous Neo-classical **Villa Alba**, now a conference centre with a fine large public park. Claretta Petacci, Mussolini's mistress, lived in Villa Fiordaliso (now a restaurant) during the Republic of Salò.

Toscolano-Maderno is another resort, with a little port. In Maderno the 12C church of **Sant'Andrea** on the waterfront shows remains of Roman and Byzantine architecture, especially in the decoration of the pillar capitals, doors and windows; an older church seems to have been incorporated in the building. Across the Toscolano River, in Toscolano, is the church of **Santi Pietro e Paolo** (unlocked on request at the house on the right). It has paintings by Celesti and early-20C stained glass. The **Santuario della Madonna di Benaco**, behind it on the lake, has a barrel vault and numerous 15C frescoes. Four Roman columns stand in front of the church. Nearby, opposite a large paper mill, is an enclosure with scant remains (under a roof) of a Roman villa of the 1C–2C AD with mosaics. Toscolano, called *Benacum*, was the chief Roman settlement on the west shore of the lake.

A pretty road ascends from Toscolano (just after the bridge) to **Gaino** in a valley that was a centre of paper-making from the 15C to the early 20C. Another road (just before the bridge) leads up to Monte Maderno and Monte Pizzocolo, with fine walks (marked paths).

Beyond Toscolano the landscape becomes prettier, with green hills and few buildings. At **Bogliaco**, on the right of the road, is the huge 18C Villa Bettoni (not open) with a collection of 17C–18C works of art; its lovely garden is on the left of the road. This was the seat of the Prime Minister of Mussolini's Republic of Salò.

Gargnano is a very attractive little port. Several large stone pavilions where lemon trees were once cultivated seem to march up the hillside in terraces. San Francesco is a 13C church with a cloister. An inland road from Gargnano to Limone has spectacular views: it passes the hill sanctuary of **Madonna di Monte Castello**, which has the finest view of the whole lake. Mussolini lived at Villa Feltrinelli (1892) here from 1943 until three days before his death.

Campione stands on the delta of a torrent and has a large cotton mill. A very fine road ascends, with many tunnels, viaducts and sharp curves, to **Pieve di Tremosine**, a village on a steep cliff descending into the lake, with a good view. This is in the Parco Regionale Alto Garda Bresciano, a protected area with marked hiking trails.

Limone sul Garda takes its name from its lemon plantations, said to be the first in Europe. Up until the beginning of this century it was surrounded by terraced lemon and citron gardens, but now only two pavilions survive; one of them, in Via Orti, was bought by the town council in 1995 in order to preserve it. Limone was accessible only by boat before the road along the shore from Gargnano was built in 1931, and its unattractive buildings and numerous hotels date from its development as a resort in the 1950s and 1960s. There are some nice walks in the district.

Riva del Garda

Riva del Garda, the Roman *Ripa*, is an agreeable, lively little town and the most important place on the lake. Sheltered by Monte Rochetta to the west, it became a fashionable winter resort at the turn of the century and remained in Austrian territory until 1918. The centre of the old town is **Piazza 3 Novembre** overlooking the little port. Here are the 13C **Torre Apponale**, the 14C **Palazzo Pretorio**, the 15C **Palazzo Comunale** and some medieval porticoes. The **Rocca**, a 14C castle encircled by water, has been heavily restored over the centuries. The **Museo Civico** here (open daily, Sep–Jun 09.30–17.30; Jul–Aug 16.00–22.00) has an archaeological section including finds from the lake dwellings of the Lago di Ledro; there is also a collection of armour, and locally printed works, including a Talmud of 1558. On the road to Arco is the church of the **Inviolata**, begun in 1603 by an unknown Portuguese architect. It has a graceful Baroque interior.

In the valley of the Sarca is the little health resort of **Arco**, particularly fashionable before the First World War. The **Collegiata** is a handsome 17C church by Giovanni Maria Filippi. The former palace of the counts, to the left, is a handsome 16C building. A monument by Bistolfi to the painter Giovanni Segantini (1858–99), who was born here, adorns the public garden. To the west is the **Parco Arciducale** with remains of the villa of Archduke Albert of Austria. Near Via dei Capitelli are several large 19C buildings including the former casino (now a public library). The **castle** of the counts of Arco, on a rocky eminence, provides a fine view of the valley of the Sarca and the lake.

The turquoise-blue **Lago di Tenno** extends beyond the waterfall known as *Cascata del Varone*. At the mouth of the Vale di Ledro, a valley of great botanical interest, is the **Lago di Ledro**, nearly 3km long, with the little resort of Pieve di Ledro. When the water is low you can see some of the c 15,000 wooden stakes from lake dwellings of the early Bronze Age, discovered in 1929, on the east side of the lake near **Molina**. There is a small museum (open daily 09.00–12.00, 13.00–18.00), and a Bronze Age hut has been reconstructed on the lakeside.

The east bank

Torbole, a summer resort near the mouth of the Sarca, played a part in the war of 1439 between the Visconti and the Venetians, when fleets of warships were dragged overland by teams of oxen and launched into the lake here. Goethe stayed at Torbole in 1786, before embarking on a boat down the lake on his way to Verona.

The east side of Lago di Garda is bounded by the cliff of Monte Altissimo di Nago (2079m). This is the northern peak of **Monte Baldo**, which lines the shore as far as Torri del Benaco. A region of great interest for its flora and fauna, part of it is a protected area. It was once known as *Hortus europae* from its remarkable vegetation, which varies from lemon trees and olives on its lower slopes to beech woods and Alpine flowers on the summit. The highest peaks are Cima Valdritta (2218m) and Punta Telegrafo (2290m). There are numerous marked hiking trails on the slopes of Monte Baldo, some of them starting from Navene and Malcesine (information and excellent guide from the *Comunità Montana del Baldo*, ☎ 045 7241600). There is a botanical garden at Novezzina.

Malcesine is a likeable resort (much visited by Germans) with a little port. It was the seat of the Veronese Captains of the Lake in the 16C–17C, and their old palace is now used as the town hall. The little garden on the lake is open to the public. Narrow roads lead up to the 13C–14C castle of the Scaligeri, restored by Venice in the 17C. Very well maintained and open daily, it has various small museums in separate buildings, including one dedicated to Goethe, who here had his run-in with the law (see above), and another with finds from a Venetian galley salvaged from the lake off Lazise after 1990; it was probably used in the battle of 1439. The tower, with a fine view, can be climbed. Concerts are often held in the castle. A cableway mounts to ski-slopes on Monte Baldo (1748m), and there are pleasant walks in the area. You can see a little island (privately owned) just offshore from Malcesine.

To the south the coast becomes less wild. At **Cassone** a stream only 175m long enters the lake, and at **Brenzone** there is another small island offshore. Further on, the road passes a cemetery and the early-12C church of **San Zeno**, and at Pai there is a magnificent view of the opposite shore of the lake. The coast here is known as the *Riviera degli Olivi*, from its many olive trees.

Torri del Benaco, the Roman *Castrum Turrium* and the chief town of the Gardesana after the 13C, has a pretty **port** (with a duck house). The fine **castle** of the Scaligeri dates from 1383 and is open daily. It contains a small local museum that illustrates the history of fishing on the lake and the production of olive oil. There is a also a section dedicated to the rock carvings found in the district, the oldest dating from 1500 BC. A splendid pavilion of 1760, which protects a plantation of huge old lemon trees—as well as citrons, mandarins and oranges—against its south wall, can also be visited. This is one of very few such structures to survive on the lake where once lemons were cultivated in abundance. On the other side of the castle is a tiny botanical garden illustrating the main plants which grow on the shores of the lake. There are 15C frescoes in the church. Benaco is locally famous for its red-and-yellow marble. A car ferry crosses from here to Maderno.

The headland of *****Punta Di San Vigilio** (parking on the main road) is the most romantic and secluded place on the lake. A cypress avenue ends at Villa Guarienti (1540), possibly by Sanmicheli, and a path continues downhill on the left, past a walled lemon garden, to a hotel in a lovely old building next to the church of San Vigilio, among cypresses. A stone gate leads out to a picturesque miniature port, with reeds and a few old fig trees.

The resort of **Garda** was developed after the Second World War at the head of a deep bay. It was famous in the Roman and Lombard periods, and was later a fortified town; it still retains some interesting old houses.

The hills become lower and the landscape duller as the broad basin at the foot of the lake opens out. **Bardolino**, another ancient place retaining some commercial importance, is well known for its wine; there is a private wine museum in the Cantina Guerrieri Rizzanti. A tower and two gates remain from an old **castle** of the Scaligeri. On the left of the main road, in a little courtyard, is the tiny Carolingian church of **San Zeno**, which retains its 9C form with a tower above the crossing and ancient paving stones. It has four old capitals and fragments of frescoes. The 12C church of **San Severo**, with contemporary frescoes, is also on the road.

Lazise retains part of its medieval wall and a castle of the Scaligeri, with Venetian additions. The 16C Venetian customs house on the lakefront attests to its former importance. San Nicolò is a 12C church with 16C additions and 14C frescoes.

Peschiera del Garda, an ancient fortress and one of the four corners of the Austrian 'quadrilateral' (the other three are Verona, Mantua and Legnago), stands at the outflow of the Mincio from Lago di Garda. The impressive fortifications, begun by the Venetians in 1553, were strengthened by Napoleon and again by the Austrians. **Gardaland**, the most famous children's theme park in Italy, is nearby (free bus service from the station; open daily Apr–Sept, and weekends in Mar and Oct). With reconstructions of a pirates' ship, a town in the American Wild West and a castle, as well as a fun fair, cinemas and other entertainments, it is especially attractive to children under ten.

Verona and environs

Prosperous, busy Verona (population 253,000) is one of the more attractive places in northern Italy. The wide pavements of its pleasant streets, made out of huge blocks of red Verona marble, give the town an air of opulence. The birthplace of Catullus and perhaps Vitruvius in the 1C BC, Verona has impressive Roman remains including the famous amphitheatre known as the Arena, a theatre, and the gateway that provided the entrance to the Roman town. Its numerous fine Romanesque and Gothic churches, including the beautiful basilica of San Zeno, contain interesting sculptures and paintings by local artists. Shakespeare's *Romeo and Juliet* was set in Verona. The Scaligeri family who ruled the town from the late 13C for over a century are commemorated by their sumptuous tombs and their castle, Castelvecchio, with its bridge over the Adige. The river is an important feature of the town, and Piazza dei Signori and the adjoining Piazza delle Erbe are two of the finer squares in Italy.

Verona is well equipped to receive hundreds of thousands of visitors every year, and is it especially crowded during the famous opera season at the Arena in Jul–Aug. Its modern commercial activity is in great part due to its position at the junction of two main arteries of transport: from Germany and Austria to central Italy, and from Turin and Milan to Venice and Trieste.

The environs of Verona are famous among Italians for their excellent winemaking districts, Soave and Valpollicella, and for the beautiful scenery of the Alpine foothills known as the Monti Lessini.

Practical information

Getting there
By air

Verona's Valerio Catullo Airport, at Caselle di Sommacampagna, has daily flights to Rome, Bari, Palermo, Catania, Naples, Olbia and Cagliari in Italy; and international flights to London, Frankfurt, Munich, Paris, Vienna, Madrid and Barcelona. Buses run every 20mins from the station

By road

Verona is on Italy's main east–west *autostrada*, the A4, from Venice to Milan. It can also be reached from Innsbruck in Austria and the Passo del Brennero via the A22 and 12; the *autostrada* continues south to Modena.

By rail

Verona stands at the junction of two of Italy's most important rail lines. The principal trains connect with Venice, Trieste, Milan, Turin and Genoa; Bologna, Florence and Rome; and Trento, Bolzano and Bressanone. There are direct through services to and from Basel, Berlin, Bern, Dortmund, Geneva, Lugano, Munich, Munster, Nice, Paris, Vienna and Zurich.

Getting around

Verona has two underground **car parks**: *Arena* (open 24hrs), Via Bentegodi (close to Piazza Brà) and *Cittadella*, Piazza Cittadella. Free parking near the station, around the walls, at the *gasometro* (near the cemetery), and near the *arsenale* (Lungadige Cangrande).

Town buses

Connect Porta Nuova railway station

with the Arena (**nos 11, 12** and **13**); with the Castelvecchio (**nos 21, 22, 23** and **24**); and with Piazza Erbe (**no. 70**). From the Castelvecchio to San Zeno take **nos 31, 32** or **33**. From the station to the Roman theatre, **nos 70** or **72**.

Country buses

Run by *APT* depart from Porta Nuova station (☎ 045 800 4129) for Lago di Garda and other points in the province. If you are exploring Verona's environs by **car**, take 11 north to reach the Monti Lessini; 11 and A4 east to reach Soave (which has its own exit), and 12 northwest to the Valpolicella.

Information offices

VERONA Scavi Scaligeri, Cortile del Tribunale, ☎ 045 806 8680, and Stazione Porta Nuova, ☎ 045 800 0861.

MONTI LESSINI Piazza della Chiesa 34, Bosco Chiesanuova, ☎ 045 7050088.

Where to stay

VERONA Given its position—midway between Vicenza and Lago di Garda—and its considerable architectural and artistic heritage, Verona is an ideal place to stay. Among the many offerings are:

Accademia, Via Scala 12 , ☎ 045 596222, fax 045 596222; occupying the former Academy of Fine Arts, not far from the Arena; moderate.

Cavour, Vicolo Chiodo 4, ☎ 045 590508, fax 045 590508; a small place (17 rooms) in a renovated old building near the Castelvecchio; inexpensive.

Due Torri Baglioni, Piazza Sant'Anastasia 4, ☎ 045 595 044, fax 045 800 4130; a 17C inn transformed into a luxurious hotel with rooms furnished in different styles using genuine antiques (the restaurant, *L'Aquila*, is also warm and refined); expensive.

Gabbia d'Oro, Corso Borsari 4a, ☎ 045 800 3060, fax 045 590293; a small hotel (27 rooms) known for its genteel,

cosy atmosphere, situated in the very centre of the old town; expensive.

Giulietta e Romeo, Via Tre Marchetti 3 , ☎ 045 800 3554, fax 045 801 0862; a well-known establishment situated in the pedestrian area near the Arena; moderate.

Grand, Corso Porta Nuova 105, ☎ 045 595600, fax 045 596385; near the train station, with antique furniture, old paintings and a small garden with fountain; moderate.

Montresor Giberti, Via Giberti 7, ☎ 045 810 1444, fax 045 810 0523; in a quiet street, also not far from the station; moderate.

Torcolo, Vicolo Listone 3, ☎ 045 800 7512, fax 045 800 4058; a warm, cosy hotel in a small square near the Arena but off the beaten track, with restaurant service outside during summer; closed Jan; inexpensive.

Victoria, Via Adua 8, ☎ 045 590566, fax 045 590155; occupying a tastefully restored historic building and hosting a small display of Roman archaeology (near the Ponte della Vittoria, halfway between the cathedral and the Castelvecchio); moderate.

Youth hostel: Salita Fontana del Ferro 15; *Casa della Giovane*, Via Pigna 7 (women only).

VALPOLICELLA *Villa Quaranta*, Via Brennero 65, Località Ospadaletto, Pescantina, ☎ 045 676 7300, fax 045 676 7301; an 18C villa in a lovely old park; moderate. *Villa del Quar*, Via Quar 12, Località Pedemonte, San Pietro in Cariano, ☎ 045 680 0681, fax 045 680 0604; 18 rooms in another splended villa; closed Jan–Feb, expensive.

Eating out

VERONA The Veronese love good food, and consequently Verona has some of the finest restaurants in Italy (unfortunately, few are inexpensive). Recommended ones are:

Arche, Via Arche Scaligere 6, ☎ 045

800 7415; a seafood restaurant near Sant'Anastasia, in business since 1879; closed Sun, Mon morning and Jan; expensive.

Bottega del Vino, Via Scudo di Francia 3, ☎ 045 800 4535; a very traditional Veronese restaurant in a quiet lane off Via Mazzini; closed Tues and Feb; moderate.

Dodici Apostoli, Vicolo San Marco 3, ☎ 045 596999; an elegant restaurant located in a historic building in the heart of the city centre, serving traditional Veronese dishes since 1750; closed Sun evening, Mon, Jan and Jun; expensive.

Il Desco, Via Dietro San Sebastiano 7, ☎ 045 595358; near the Adige on the east side of the city centre, features innovative cuisine; closed Sun, Jan and Jun; expensive.

Maffei, Piazza delle Erbe 38, ☎ 045 801 0015; with pavement seating in Verona's most colourful square in summer; closed Sun, Mon in Jul and Aug; moderate. At Lavagno (12km east on 11),

Il Busòlo, Località Vago, ☎ 045 982146; warm, friendly osteria with a good wine list; closed Thur, inexpensive.

Cafés and pastry shops: *Dante*, 2 Piazza dei Signori; *Mattei*, Vicolo Crocioni (off Via Cappello); *Cordioli*, Via Cappello; *Flego*, Corso Portoni Borsari.

Picnic places: there are good picnic places in the park near San Giorgio in Braida, in the Giusti gardens, in the small public garden off Piazza dei Signori, in the Teatro Romano, and in the gardens on the far side of Ponte Scaligero.

SOAVE *Alpone*, Via Pergola 51, Costalunga, Montecchia di Crosara (9km north), ☎ 045 617 5387; restaurant offering delicious local food and home-grown wine; closed Sun evening, Tues, Jan and Aug; moderate.

VALPOLICELLA *Alla Ruota*, Via Proale 6, Località Mazzano, Negrar, ☎ 045 752 5605; carefully prepared local specialities, served on a large scenic terrace in summer; closed Mon evening and Tues (except in summer); inexpensive.

Dalla Rosa Alda, Strada Garibaldi 4, frazione San Giorgio di Valpolicella, Sant'Ambrogio di Valpolicella, ☎ 045 770 1018; a simple, genuine trattoria with a great wine list; closed Sun evening (except in summer), Mon, Jan and Jun; moderate. *Enoteca della Valpolicella*, Via Osan 45, Fumane, ☎ 045 683 9146; not (as the name might suggest) merely a wine bar, but a fine country restaurant in a 15C farm complex; closed Mon and midday Sat; moderate.

 ## Entertainment

VERONA Music and drama at the *Teatro Nuovo*, *Teatro Filippini* and *Teatro Laroratorio*. *Stagione Sinfonica*, classical concerts and opera at the *Teatro Filarmonico*, Feb–Apr. Live music at bars and clubs in Verona and throughout the province, especially in summer.

 ## Shopping

VERONA There are markets daily in Piazza Erbe; Tues and Fri in Piazza San Zeno; Tues in Piazza Isolo (near the Roman theatre); Wed and Fri in Piazza Santa Toscana (Porta Vescovo); Fri in Piazza degli Arditi (Volto San Luca). A market with bric-à-brac and artisans' ware is held on the third Sat of the month at San Zeno.

 ## Special events

VERONA *Settimana Cinematografica Internazionale*, film festival, Apr; *Estate Teatrale*, drama at the Roman theatre, Jun–Aug; *Stagione Lirica*, opera at the Arena, Jul–Aug.

Annual festivals include the *Festa di Santa Lucia*, with a street market in Piazza Brà and Via Roma from around 10–12 Dec. Carnival celebrations, which have been held in the town since the 16C, culminate on the Fri before Shrove Tuesday (*Venerdì Gnocolar*). 12 Apr is the festival of the patron saint, Zeno.

An entrance ticket for the most important churches has been introduced (cumulative ticket available) so that they can be kept open all day.

Sports

Golf at Sommacampagna (*Golf Club Verona*).

Walking, cycling and **downhill** and **cross-country skiing** in the Monti Lessini.

VERONA

● ● ● ● ● ● ● ● ●

Verona is probably the only authentic large city in the Veneto, as Venice is now predominantly geared to tourists.

History

Archaeologists have found evidence of lake dwellings on this site dating back to the Bronze Age. From the 7C BC there was a centre of Atestine culture here, and the Cenomane Goths seem to have entered the area in the 4C BC. Contacts with Rome began in the 3C, and Verona became a Roman colony in 89 BC. The seat of various medieval monarchies (Ostrogoths, Lombards and Franks), in the 11C it became an independent commune. In the 13C and 14C it was a seigniory, first of Ezzelino da Romano, then of the Della Scala (or Scaligeri), and finally of the Milanese Visconti.

By far the most important of these dynasties was the Scaligeri. Mastino della Scala, the *podestà* (or elected head of communal government), established his position as overlord of Verona in 1260, and his family held power in the city until 1387. This was the most brilliant period of Veronese history. Dante found a refuge in the Ghibelline city under Bartolomeo (nephew of Mastino) in 1301–04, and in the reign of Cangrande I (1311–29) Verona reached its greatest period of magnificence. Gian Galeazzo Visconti became tyrant of the city after the decline of the Scaligeri.

Verona chose to become part of the Venetian Republic in 1405. John Evelyn, who visited the city in 1646, called it 'one of the delightfulest places that ever I came in'. In 1796 it was occupied by the French. Armed protest against the invaders (the 'Pasque Veronesi', 1797) was avenged by the destruction of much of the city, and Verona was several times exchanged between France and Austria by the treaties of the early 19C, until it was finally given to Austria in 1814. During the Wars of Independence it formed the strongest point of the Austrian 'quadrilateral' (together with Peschiera, Mantua and Legnago), but in 1866 it was united with the Italian kingdom. During the Second World War the city suffered considerably from bombing, and the bridges were all blown up. In the Castelvecchio in 1944, Mussolini's puppet Republican government staged the trial of Count Galeazzo Ciano, Mussolini's son-in-law, who had been a Fascist minister but later became a leading opponent of the Duce.

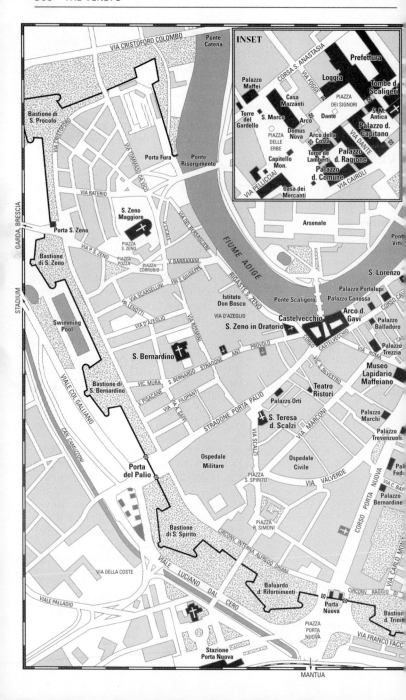

VIA CRISTOFORO COLOMBO

Ponte Catena

INSET

CORSA S. ANASTASIA

VIA FOGGE

Prefettura

Palazzo Maffei

Loggia

Tombe d. Scaligeri

Casa Mazzanti

PIAZZA DEI SIGNORI

Torre del Gardello

S. Marco

Arco

Dante

S. M. Antica

Domus Nova

Arco della Costa

Palazzo d. Capitano

PIAZZA DELLE ERBE

Capitello Mon.

Torre de Lamberti

Palazzo d. Ragione

VIA DANTE

Palazzo d. Comune

VIA PELLICCIAI

Casa dei Mercanti

VIA CAIROLI

Bastione di S. Procolo

VIA CRISTOFORO

Porta Fura

Ponte Risorgimento

Arsenale

Ponte Vitt

GARDA, BRESCIA

VIA RATERIO

VIA OMBRASO PA VICI

S. Zeno Maggiore

PIAZZA S. ZENO

V. CICALE

VIA DEL BERSAGLIERE

FIUME ADIGE

S. Lorenzo

Palazzo Portalupi

Palazzo Canossa

CORSO CA

Porta S. Zeno

VIA P. S. ZENO

PIAZZA POZZA

V. BARBARANI

PIAZZA CORRUBIO

VIA S. GIUSEPPE

VIA SCARSELLINI

RIGASTE S. ZENO

Ponte Scaligero

Castelvecchio

Arco d. Gavi

Palazzo Balladoro

Bastione di S. Zeno

STADIUM

Istituto Don Bosco

VIA D'AZEGLIO

S. Zeno in Oratorio

CORSO CASTELVECCHIO

VIC. S. SILVESTRO

VIA ROMA

Palazzo Trezzia

Swimming Pool

VIA LENOTTI

VIA D'AZEGLIO

VIA ROSMINI

STRADONE ANT. PROVOLO

Museo Lapidario Maffeiano

S. Bernardino

VIC. MURA

S. BERNARDO

V. PISACANE

STRADONE PORTA PALIO

Teatro Ristori

Bastione di S. Bernardino

VIA FILOPANTI

VIA SAFFI

Palazzo Orti

VIA MARCONI

Palazzo Marchi

VIALE COL GALLIANO

CAV. CAMUZZONI

S. Teresa d. Scalzi

Palazzo Trevenzuoli

Porta del Palio

VIA SCALZI

CORSO PORTA NUOVA

Pal Fed

VIA C. BA

Ospedale Militare

PIAZZA S. SPIRITO

Ospedale Civile

VIA VALVERDE

Palazzo Bernardine

Bastione di S. Spirito

PIAZZA R. SIMONI

VIA CARLO MONT

VIA DELLA COSTE

CIRCONV. INTERNA ALFREDO ORIANI

VIALE PALLADIO

VIALE LUCIANO DAL CERO

Baluardo d. Rifornimenti

CIRCONV. RAGGIO

Porta Nuova

Bastion d. Trini

PIAZZA PORTA NUOVA

VIA FRANCO FACC

Stazione Porta Nuova

MANTUA

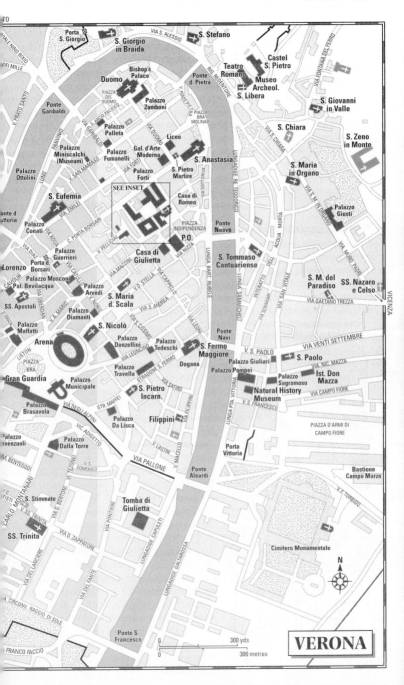

VERONA

Art and architecture

Verona is one of the more beautiful and fascinating cities of northeastern Italy, and the richest artistic centre after Venice. The handsome church of San Zeno marks Verona as a centre of architecture in the Romanesque period. Sculpture at Verona is best represented by Pisanello, the medallist, and by Fra Giovanni da Verona, the woodcarver. In the early 15C the painters Altichiero and Jacopo di Avanzo, and their followers, were active in Verona. Giovanni Badile, Stefano da Zevio and Pisanello also were important Veronese painters. Among their successors were Francesco Bonsignori, Domenico and Francesco Morone, Girolamo dai Libri (a skilful illuminator), Liberale, Francesco Torbido, Bonifazio Veronese, Antonio Badile and, most famous of all, Paolo Caliari, called 'Il Veronese' (1528–88). There are numerous works in the city by the Veronese architect Michele Sanmicheli (1486–1559), including beautiful palaces, sculptural work and fortifications.

The city centre: Piazza Brà to Piazza delle Erbe

This visit begins on the outskirts of the old city centre, amid the shady gardens and swank sidewalk cafés of **Piazza Brà** (at the centre of the **Map**). Once a suburban meadow (*braida*), this huge square is the undisputed centre of modern Verona. From the station, Corso Porta Nuova enters it by a double archway known as the Portoni di Brà (1389), which once carried a covered passage joining the Scaligeri fortress of Castelvecchio to the Visconti citadel. A pentagonal tower of the latter can still be seen as you arrive, to the right of the arches.

The south side of the square is dominated by the immense Doric façade of the **Gran Guardia**, begun in 1609 by Domenico Curtoni (using stones taken from the Arena) and completed some two centuries later. Originally built as a military parade-ground, it is now used as a venue for exhibitions. Further along on this side stands the Neo-classical **Gran Guardia Nuova**, or **Palazzo Municipale** (1838). On the other side of the Portoni di Brà is the Accademia Filarmonica, a concert hall with a majestic Ionic porch designed by Curtoni (1604) in the courtyard. Here is the **Museo Lapidario Maffeiano** (open Tues–Sun 08.00–18.30), one of the older public museums in Italy (est. 1716), with a collection that includes some 100 Greek inscriptions ranging in date from 5C BC–5C AD, as well as Etruscan, Roman, early-Christian and medieval material from sites throughout the Veneto. Steps ascend to the walkway over the Portoni di Brà, from which there is a fine view. On the northwest side of the square extends the lively promenade known as the *Listón*, lined with fashionable cafés and restaurants and backed by patrician palaces.

The Arena

By far the most remarkable monument on the piazza is the great elliptical **Arena** (open Tues–Sun 08.00–dusk; during the opera season, Jul–Aug, 08.00–13.00). This is one of the larger extant Roman amphitheatres, third in order of size after the Colosseum in Rome and the amphiteatre of Capua. It was built in the 1C AD using limestone quarried in the nearby Valpolicella. The most famous of Verona's ancient buildings, it retains only four of the triple archways of its outer walls, but the second circuit of 74 double arcades is intact. The interior, 139m long, 110m wide and 30m high, has a *cavea* of 44 tiers (restored), capable of holding 22,000 spectators, surrounding the *platea*. The Arena hosts a famous opera festival in Jul–Aug, and if you are in town at this time be sure to ask your hotel staff to obtain tickets. The performances are truly spectacular.

Via Mazzini (commonly called Via Nuova), Verona's elegant shopping street, leads from the northwest corner of Piazza Brà towards Piazza delle Erbe, described below. Turn right at the end of Via Mazzini to reach what is commonly called the **House of Juliet** (Via Cappello 21–23; open Tues–Sun 08.00–18.30), a 13C Gothic townhouse with a balcony of questionable authenticity and a bronze statue of the fictional heroine (touching her breast will supposedly bring one a new lover). Shakespeare's play of *Romeo and Juliet*, set in Verona, tells the story of Juliet Capulet (the Anglicisation of Cappelletti) and Romeo Montague (Montecchi), an adaptation of a tale by the 16C novelist Luigi da Porto. The legend of a feud between the two families is apocryphal; in fact, it is probable that the clans were in close alliance. Although there is nothing here that relates concretely to Juliet, the painted walls and finely crafted ceilings of the interior merit a glance.

If you continue to walk to the end of Via Cappello you come to the Roman **Porta dei Leoni**, built in the 1C AD, with a great arch, fluted columns, pedimented windows, loggia and niches.

Just outside the gate is one of Verona's great medieval monuments, **San Fermo Maggiore**, a complex of two superimposed churches, the lower one of 1065–1143, the upper of 1313–20. It has a fine façade featuring a broad Romanesque doorway with deep splay, a gallery of small arches, tall ogival windows, and a central mullioned window. On the north side is another doorway (the usual entrance) of 1363, beneath an attached porch.

The interior, a single vast aisle covered by a wooden ship's-keel roof of 1314, holds a number of important artworks. In the lunette over the doorway is a *Crucifixion* attributed to Turone; on the south side, next to the ambo with its baldachin and pointed spire, a fragment of a detached fresco of *Angels* by Stefano da Verona. Halfway along the north side is the Baroque Cappella della Madonna, with unimpressive 17C paintings and a *Madonna and Saints* by Gian Francesco Caroto (1528). Over the first north altar is a *St Nicholas with Saints* by Battista dal Moro and, in the corner, the *Brenzoni Tomb* by the Florentine Nanni di Bartolo (1427–39). This is framed by a famous fresco of the *Annunciation* by Pisanello. From the right transept you can enter the old Romanesque cloister and from here descend to to the lower church, with fragmentary frescoes of the 11C to the 13C and, behind the high altar, a 14C wooden crucifix.

Retrace your steps to the end of Via Mazzini. The long, rectangular **Piazza delle Erbe** stands over the ancient Roman forum. Today, as in the Middle Ages, it is the site of a colourful market, in the midst of whose hustle and bustle you can make out some medieval sculptures: the 15C Colonna del Mercato (with a Gothic stone lion), the 16C Berlina or Capitello (where the city's rulers took office), the 14C Fontana di Madonna Verona (incorporating a Roman statue) and the 16C Colonna di San Marco (with a Venetian lion).

The square is bounded on the southwest by the 14C **Casa dei Mercanti**, or merchants' hall, now the chamber of commerce; its mullioned windows and crenellated roof are all that remains of the original building, extensively altered in the 17C. The monument in the small piazzetta here commemorates the victims of an Austrian bomb that fell nearby during the First World War. At the narrow northwest end of the piazza are the 14C Torre del Gardello (or Torre delle Ore) and the **Palazzo Maffei**, a Baroque building of 1668 crowned by statues. The northeast side is bounded by the frescoed **Case Mazzanti**, begun in the 14C as a residence of the Scaligeri but radically altered in the 16C; the **Domus Nova** (or Palazzo dei Giudici), a 17C reconstruction of the 14C residence of the podestà; and the Palazzo della Ragione and Palazzo del Comune, begun in the late 12C but modified in the 16C and again in the 19C, when the Neo-classical façade on this side was added.

Piazza dei Signori and environs

By the 15C **Arco della Costa**—which takes its name from a whale's rib hung beneath the vault, ready to fall, the legend says, on the first honest person to walk beneath it—you enter **Piazza dei Signori**, a small, handsome square with monumental buildings surrounding a central monument to Dante. This was the seat of city government in the Middle Ages. The **Palazzo della Ragione**, here seen in its earlier form, has a splendid Romanesque courtyard encircled by a portico on piers and occupied in part by a fine external Gothic-Renaissance staircase. Above it rises the symbol of civic power, the 84m **Torre dei Lamberti**, begun in 1172 and completed in the mid-15C. Stairs and a lift go to the top (84m; open Wed–Sun 09.30–13.30; Sat 09.30–18.30), from which there is a splendid view over the city and its surroundings.

The **Palazzo del Capitanio**, now the courthouse, stands on the other side of the narrow Via Dante. It is a 14C building with a crenellated tower and a doorway by Michele Sanmicheli (1531). It has another, rather unusual doorway by Giuseppe Miglioranzi (1687) in the courtyard. The **Palazzo della Prefettura** (formerly Palazzo del Governo) rises at the end of the square. Built in the 14C, it was restored to its original appearance in 1929–30; the doorway of 1533 is by Sanmicheli. Dante and Giotto stayed here as guests of the Scaligeri.

The adjoining **Loggia del Consiglio**, built in the late 15C as the seat of the city council, is the first significant expression of the Veronese Renaissance. It consists of an elegant portico and an order of mullioned windows flanked by small pilasters; the coloured-marble facing and the sculptural decoration (by Alberto da Milano, 1493) give it a sense both of vivacity and of delicate harmony. An arch surmounted by a 16C statue joins the loggia to the **Casa della Pietà**, built in 1490. On the side facing Piazza delle Erbe the square terminates in the ornate façade of the Domus Nova.

The passage on the right of the Palazzo della Prefettura leads into the little **Piazzaletto delle Arche**, which takes its name from the monumental *arche*, or tombs of the Scaligeri, executed in the 14C by Bonino da Campione and his followers. At the centre of a stone-and-iron enclosure bearing the family emblem, the ladder (in Italian, scala), stands the graceful Romanesque church of **Santa Maria Antica** (1185, several times restored), its doorway surmounted by the tomb of Cangrande I (d. 1329), with a copy of the equestrian statue now in the Museo del Castelvecchio (described below). Inside the enclosure are, against the wall of the church, the simple tomb of Mastino I, the first of the dynasty, assassinated in 1277 in Piazza dei Signori; on the left of the entrance, the tomb of the Mastino II (d. 1351); in the opposite corner, that of Cansignorio (d. 1375); and at the rear, the tomb of Giovanni della Scala (d. 1359)—all in the form of aedicules surmounted by rich Gothic baldachins and adorned with statues. Also part of the complex are the profusely carved sarcophagi of Bartolomeo (1304), Alboino (1311), Cangrande II (1359) and Alberto (1301) Della Scala. The Gothic house at the corner of Via delle Arche Scaligere is thought to be the home of Romeo, though on what grounds nobody seems to know.

Across the river

Now walk back to Piazza dei Signori through the courtyard of Palazzo del Capitanio, and along the wooded left flank of the post office. You'll come out at the foot of the Ponte Nuovo, which crosses the Adige with good views (left) of the Roman theatre and the hill of San Pietro (see below).

On the other side of the river Via Carducci leads past the 15C church of San Tommaso Cantuariense to the Giardini di Palazzo Giusti (Via Giardino Giusti 2; open daily 09.00–18.30), a famous and beautiful formal garden with terraces, a boxwood labyrinth and a *belvedere*, or scenic overlook. This green hillside oasis, laid out in the 16C with the contemporary Palazzo Giusti, was one of Goethe's favourite spots in Italy.

One block northwest is **Santa Maria in Organo**, founded on this site in the 7C but dating in its present form from 1481. Michele Sanmicheli is probably the author of the white-marble façade (1546) on the otherwise Gothic west front. The elegant interior is entirely covered with frescoes, by Nicolò Giolfino (south side), Gian Francesco Caroto (north side), Domenico Brusasorci (north transept and sacristy) and Francesco Morone (sacristy), among others. The choir and sacristy have extraordinary inlaid woodwork executed in the late 15C by Fra' Giovanni da Verona. In the three-aisled crypt are traces of the primitive church (7C or 8C) and remains of the Roman walls. A large Renaissance cloister of the Olivetan convent adjoins the church on the north.

To the northwest, in a lovely position on the hill of San Pietro, is the **Roman theatre** (open Tues–Sun 08.00–13.30; during the summer drama season 08.00–13.30). This extraordinary complex, of which the *scena*, the semicircular *cavea*, and the two entrances survive, was built in the early 1C AD and later enlarged. It was brought to light in the 18C, in one of the first archaeological excavations conducted to modern scientific standards. The ruins of the *cavea* end on one side in the small church of Santi Siro e Libera, founded in the 9C and altred in the 14C, and on the other in the arcades that once marked the perimeter of the edifice. Plays and ballet are staged in the theatre in summer.

Above the theatre (lift), the Renaissance cloister of the former convent of San Girolamo houses a **Museo Archeologico** with glass, sculpture and mosaics from Roman Verona, and Greek and Etruscan material. The views from the windows and terraces over the theatre, the river and the city are themselves worth the climb. The church has a fine ceiling and frescoes by Gian Francesco Caroto and others; over the altar is a Renaissance triptych by an anonymous Veronese artist. High up on the hill is the Castel San Pietro, built by the Visconti, destroyed by the French and rebuilt by the Austrians.

At the foot of the hill the **Ponte della Pietra**, part-Roman and part-medieval, leads back across the Adige. Its five arches were destroyed in the Second World War and rebuilt in 1957–59, after dredging the original stones from the river. The bridge enjoys a superb view over the city and the San Pietro hill.

Sant'Anastasia and the cathedral

Turn left as soon as you set foot on the right bank to reach the Gothic church of **Sant'Anastasia**, whose polygonal apses and spired campanile have been visible from the river. The largest church in Verona, it was erected by the Dominicans between 1291 and 1323 and reworked in 1423–81. The unfinished façade has a superb 14C doorway with coloured marbles and carvings. Inside, the 16C *Acquasantiere dei Gobbi* take their name from the crouching figures (*gobbi* means 'hunchbacks') in their bases. The first altar on the south side, incorporating the *Fregoso Tomb*, was designed by Sanmicheli in 1565. The third altar on this side is surrounded by frescoes attributed to Liberale and Benaglio da Verona. Over the altar in the south transept is a painting of the *Madonna and SS Thomas Aquinas and Augustine* by Girolamo dai Libri. The first south apsidal chapel has a large fresco depicting the *Cavalli Family Presented to the Virgin*, by Altichiero (1390–95); and the second south apsidal chapel, two Gothic tombs and 24 terracotta reliefs with stories from the life of Christ by Michele da Firenze (1435). In the sanctuary are a large 14C fresco of the *Last Judgement* by a painter called the 'Master of the Last Judgement', and the *Tomb of General Cortesia Serego*, attributed to the Florentine Nanni di Bartolo (1424–29). From the north transept, with an altarpiece by Francesco Morone, a Gothic doorway leads into the sacristy, with a delightful detached fresco of *St George and the Dragon* by Pisanello, the church's chief claim to fame. Here too are 15C stalls and stained glass, and the banner of the Millers' and Bakers' Guild.

Beyond the Gothic tomb of Guglielmo Castelbarco (d. 1320), above the former convent-gate, rises the little 14C church of **San Pietro Martire**, now used for exhibitions. It contains a large frescoed lunette of the *Annunciation*, a very unusual allegorical composition by Giovanni Maria Falconetto, with symbolic animals and idealised views of Verona. The two German knights who commissioned the fresco are shown kneeling. Exhibitions are held in the nearby Palazzo Forti, where Napoleon lodged in 1796–97, now the **Galleria d'Arte Moderna** (open Tues–Sun 09.00–19.00; entrance at Via Forti 1).

Via Duomo leads northwest from Sant'Anastasia. The **Cathedral of Santa Maria Matricolare**, dominating the secluded **Piazza del Duomo**, is a 12C Romanesque building with Gothic and Renaissance additions. The front has a monumental two-storied porch adorned with column-bearing lions and reliefs by Maestro Nicolò (1139); another Romanesque porch is on the south side. The campanile, Romanesque on the bottom and 16C above, was completed in the 20C. The overall design is by Sanmicheli. The 12C semicircular tufa apse, a pure expression of the Veronese Romanesque style, is adorned with pilasters and a fine classical frieze. The entrance is by a door in the south flank, also with a good porch.

The Gothic **interior** has broad arches on tall compound piers. The walls of the west bays are decorated with architectural frescoes by Gian Maria Falconetto (c 1503). More frescoes, by Francesco Torbido after cartoons by Giulio Romano, adorn the sanctuary, which is enclosed by a fine curved choir screen by Sanmicheli, incorporating a *Crucifixion with the Virgin and St John* by Giambattista da Verona (1534). The second south chapel has a painting of the *Adoration of the Magi* by Liberale da Verona, and the first north chapel an *Assumption* by Titian, in a frame by Jacopo Sansovino. The Nichesola tomb here is also by Sansovino.

From the north side entrance is gained to the church of **San Giovanni in Fonte** (1123), the former Romanesque baptistery, a three-aisled apsidal building with fine 9C capitals and an octagonal *baptismal decorated with attributed to Brioloto (c 1200). The fragmentary frescoes date from the 13C–14C: on the left of the entrance is a *Baptism of Christ* by Paolo Farinati (1568). The same vestibule gives entrance to the little church of **Sant'Elena**, also of the 9C, rebuilt in the 12C and preserving part of its early Christian structures. Excavations here have revealed 6C mosaic pavements and the tombs of two early bishops. The finely carved narrow stalls date from the 16C. The altarpiece is by Brusasorci.

Opposite the south door of the cathedral, a seated 14C figure of St Peter surmounts the doorway of San Pietro in Archivolto. In Piazza Vescovile, where you can see the cathedral's beautiful *apse, the **Bishop's Palace** has an unusual façade of 1502 with Venetian crenellations and a portal decorated with statues, including a delightful *Madonna and Child* attributed to Fra Giovanni da Verona. The attractive courtyard, with curious Romanesque capitals, is dominated by the Torrione di Ognibene (1172). Next to the palace is the flank of San Giovanni in Fonte (described above), and opposite is an ancient wall (now propped up) with a gate into a neglected garden. Nearby, the Ponte Pietra crosses over the Adige, guarded by a medieval gateway.

A passageway to the left of the façade of the duomo leads past the exterior portico of Sant'Elena and (opposite) the charming Romanesque **cloister** (with a double arcade on one side), also partly on the site of the 5C basilica, with remains in two places of a 6C mosaic pavement (one of which is coloured).

The **Chapter Library**, at Piazza Duomo 21, was founded by the archdeacon Pacificus (778–846). It contains many precious texts and illuminated choirbooks (c 1368) attributed to Turone, the artist of the *Last Judgement* at Sant'Anastasia.

Stradone Arcidiacono Pacifico extends from the cathedral square past **Palazzo Paletta** (no. 6; with a finely carved portal) to Via Garibaldi, which you follow to the left. Turn right at the next corner and, after a few paces, look right to see the monumental Neo-classical façade of Palazzo Miniscalchi. The present entrance to the palace is in Via San Mamaso, where the beautiful *side façade can be seen. This one-family townhouse was built in the mid-15C by the Miniscalchi and has handsome marble windows and doorways. The painted decoration was carried out c 1580 by Michelangelo Aliprandi and Tullio India il Vecchio. It is one the last vestiges of what was once a common tradition (numerous palaces in Verona once had painted façades). The **Museo Miniscalchi-Erizzo** (open Tues–Sat 16.00–19.00; Sun and holidays 10.30–12.30, 16.00–19.00) was opened here in 1990, after the last descendant of the family had left the house and collections to a foundation in 1955. It contains a miscellany of objects, all well labelled and spaciously arranged.

The **ground floor** is used for exhibitions of the decorative arts. The permanent collections include ivories, 16C–18C furniture, family portraits by Alessandro Longhi and Sebastiano Bombelli, 16C–18C majolica, a plate decorated in 1519 which belonged to Isabella d'Este, 16C ceramics from Urbino, Venetian bronzes, Murano glass, a fireplace decorated in majolica from Faenza (17C–18C), a good collection of 16C–17C drawings (mostly by Venetian masters), an armoury, 17C wooden soldiers, and curios that belonged to Ludovico Moscardo (1611–81).

To the Castelvecchio

Return to Piazza delle Erbe. From the southwest corner of the square Corso Porta Bórsari follows the straight line of the Roman *decumanus maximus* to the 1C **Porta dei Bórsari**, which takes its name from the episcopal tax collectors, or *bursari*, whose offices were located here. Outside the gate Corso Cavour continues along the path of the *decumanus*. Set back from the street on the south are the campanile and flank of the Romanesque church of the **Santissimi Apostoli**, from the sacristy of which you can enter the small, semi-interred church of Santi Tosca e Teuteria, which supposedly dates back to the 5C. Across the street is the beautiful Romanesque church of **San Lorenzo** (1110), in alternating bands of tufa and brick, with a narrow façade flanked by towers. No. 19 (left) is the spectacular **Palazzo Bevilacqua**, Sanichele's masterpiece, with rusticated ground floor, balcony, loggia with spiral columns, and a fine cornice. Sanmichele also designed the **Palazzo Canossa** (no. 44), with a splendid atrium and courtyard. At the end of the street, in a little garden on the right, is the **Arco dei Gavi**, a Roman arch erected in the 1C AD in honour of the family of the Gavii, demolished in 1805, and reconstructed from the fragments in 1932.

The **Castelvecchio**, the main monument of medieval civil architecture in Verona, dominates the busy square here. It was built by Cangrande II Della Scala as his home and fortress in 1354–57, and was completed with the addition of the keep in 1375. It has been restored many times, most recently between 1958 and 1964 by Carlo Scarpa. The imposing brick fortress consists of two main blocks divided by the crenellated **Ponte Scaligero**, which extends to the north bank of the Adige, and the tall tower of the keep. The rectangular east block surrounds a large courtyard, formerly a parade ground; the trapezoidal west block has a double circuit of walls with two courtyards and drawbidges.

(the original fortified residence of Cangrande) has a double circuit of walls with two courtyards and drawbidges.

Inside the castle is the **Civico Museo d'Arte** (open Tues–Sun 08.00–18.30), famous for its holdings of Veronese art from the 14C to the 18C. Here are works by the primitives Turone (*Trinity*), Altichiero, Stefano da Verona (*Madonna del Roseto*) and Pisanello (*Madonna della Quaglia*); the 15C painters Francesco Morone, Liberale da Verona, Paolo Cavazzola and Gian Francesco Caroto (*Boy with Drawing*); and the 16C masters Paolo Veronese

Equestrian statue of Cangrande I (*Bevilacqua-Lazise Altarpiece, Deposition*)

and Paolo Farinati. Among the Venetian artists are Andrea Mantegna (*Holy Family*), Jacopo Bellini (*St Jerome*, *Crucifix*), Giovanni Bellini (two *Madonnas*), Carlo Crivelli (*Madonna della Passione*), Bartolomeo Montagna, Alvise Vivarini (*Madonna*), Bernardo Strozzi (*Male Portrait*), Jacopo Tintoretto (*Concert of the Muses* and *Adoration of the Shepherds*) Gian Battista Tiepolo (*Heliodorus and the Treasure of the Temple*; sketch for a ceiling painting), and Francesco Guardi (two *Capricci*). Also present are Tommaso da Modena and several Flemish artists. The museum contains some important antiquities and artefacts— notably early Christian glass, 7C gold, the so-called *Tesoretto di Isola Razza*, including 4C devotional spoons—fabrics and silks from the Arca di Cangrande I and miniatures by Liberale and by Girolamo dai Libri. An outstanding collection of arms and armour ranges from the Lombard period to the 17C. The focal point of the collection of 14C Veronese sculpture is the dramatically displayed *Equestrian Statue of Cangrande I*, from the Arche Scaligere.

San Zeno Maggiore

Regaste San Zeno runs along the Adige, offering good views back over the Castelvecchio and its bridge. At the end of the street and to the right is the basilica of San Zeno Maggiore, Verona's most distinctive religious building and one of the more important Romanesque churches of northern Italy. Tickets, required for admission (open Mon–Sat 08.30–18.30, Sun and holidays 13.00–18.00) are sold on the left, as you enter the square.

Erected in the 5C and rebuilt in the 9C as the church of the Benedictine monastery, of which one stout battlemented tower remains (to the north of the façade as you face the church), San Zeno was reconstructed in 1120–38 and completed in the 13C. The polygonal apse, with Gothic ogival windows and engaged buttresses, dates from 1385–98. The warm-hued tufa façade is divided horizontally by pilaster strips and vertically by a gallery with mullioned windows, and pierced by a large rose window (representing the *Wheel of Fortune*) and a fine doorway of 1138. The latter, with an attached porch, carved arch, lunette, column-bearing lions and two splendid bands of reliefs representing biblical and allegorical scenes, was executed by Maestro Nicolò and his pupil Guglielmo around 1135. Equally splendid are the 12C doors, with bronze relief panels depicting Old and New Testament stories and the lives of Sts Zeno and Michael. The south flank presents the red-and-white marble bands typical of Veronese churches. The tall, detached campanile (1045–1140) terminates in a two-tiered belfry with mullioned windows.

From the north side you enter the noble **interior**, with three aisles on piers and columns, wooden ship's-keel roof and split-level east end—sanctuary above, crypt below. Fine 13C statues decorate the choir screen. On the west wall is a *Crucifixion* by Lorenzo Veneziano, painted around 1360; at the beginning of the south aisle, an octagonal **baptistery** of the late 12C. The walls of the nave and sanctuary are decorated with fragments of Romanesque-Gothic frescoes; over the high altar is the splendid triptych of the *Madonna and Saints* by Andrea Mantegna (1457–59), one of the key works of Renaissance painting in Verona. The wooden choir stalls date from the 15C. The 13C crypt, with antique columns, holds a modern sarcophagus containing the remains of the saint, Verona's first bishop (d. 380), and the tombs of other saints and bishops. In the north apse is a curious 13C or 14C polychrome statue of St Zeno laughing. From the north aisle you go out into the fine Romanesque cloister (with small double columns of red marble, dating from the 12C, 13C and 14C), left over from the abbey. Beneath the portico are tombs and sepulchral monuments. A doorway on the left leads to the **Oratorio di San Benedetto**, a 13C chapel displaying columns and piers with 'recycled' capitals, some dating as far back as the 6C.

Walking southwards through streets with a distinctly suburban atmosphere, you come to the **Porta del Palio** (1552–57), through which the *palio* horse race passed. Mentioned by Dante, it is the most harmonious of the four city gates designed by Sanmicheli—the others are the Porta San Giorgio, 1525; Porta Nuova, 1533–46; and Porta San Zeno, 1541–42. Skirting the outside of the walls, the design and construction of which were probably Sanmicheli's greatest single commission, you soon reach the Porta Nuova, from which Corso Porta Nuova returns to Piazza Brà.

Impressions of Verona

Verona has left its mark on literary minds. Here are a few of their remarks:

Romeo: *There is no world withoutVerona walles,*
But Purgatorie, Torture, hell itselfe:
Hence banished, is banisht from the world,
And world's exile in death.
William Shakespeare, *Romeo and Juliet*, c 1594–95

This most faire City is built in the forme of a Lute.... It hath a pure aire, and is enno-bled by the civility and auncient Nobility of the Citizens, who are inbued with a chearfull countenance, magnificent mindes, and much inclined to all good literature.
Fynes Moryson, *An Itinerary*, 1617

Certainly this Citty deserv'd all those Elogies Scaliger has honour'd it with, for in my opinion, tis situated in one of the most delightfullst places that ever I came in, so sweetly mixed with risings, & Vallies, so Elegantly planted with Trees, on which Bacchus seems riding as it were in Triumph every Autumn, for the Vines reach from tree to tree; & here of all places I have travell'd in Italy would I fix preferable to any other, so as well has that learned Man given it the name of the very Eye of the World.
John Evelyn, *Diary*, May 1646

I have been over Verone.... Of the truth of Juliet's story, they seem tenacious to a degree, insisting on the fact—giving a date (1303), and showing a tomb. It is a plain, open, and partly decayed sarcophagus, with withered leaves in it, in a wild and desolate conventual garden, once a cemetery, now ruined to the very graves. The situation struck me as being very appropriate to the legend, being blighted as their love. I have brought away a few pieces of the granite, to give to my daughter and my nieces.
Lord Byron, letter to Augusta Leigh, 7 November 1816

It was natural enough to go straight from the Market-place, to the House of the Capulets, now degenerated into a most miserable little inn. Noisy vetturini and muddy market-carts were disputing possession of the yard, which was ankle-deep in dirt, with a brook of splashed and bespattered geese; and there was a grim-vis-aged dog, viciously panting in a doorway, who would certainly have had Romeo by

the leg, the moment he put it over the wall, if he had existed, and been at large in these times.... The house is a distrustful jealous-looking house as one would desire to see, though of a very moderate size.
Charles Dickens, *Pictures from Italy*, 1846

I must not say more of Verona, than that, though truly Rouen, Geneva and Pisa have been the centres of thought and teaching to me, Verona has given the colouring to all they taught. She has virtually represented the fate and beauty of Italy to me; and whatever concerning Italy I have felt, or been able with any charm or force to say, has been dealt with more deeply, and said more earnestly for her sake.
John Ruskin, *Praeterita*, 1885–59

Juliet's home-town, I suppose some would call it. The phrase takes the edge off romance, and I designed it to do so, determined as I am somehow to vent my rage at being shown Juliet's house, a picturesque and untidy tenement, with balconies certainly too high for love, unless Juliet was a trapeze acrobat, accustomed to hanging downwards by her toes.
   This was not Juliet's house, for the sufficient reason that so far as authentic history knows, there never was any Juliet.
Arnold Bennett, *Journal 1929*, 1930

At Verona, an American in Auden's compartment said to his companion, "Hey, didn't Shakespeare live here?" at which Auden observed loudly, "Surely it was Bacon."
Charles Osborne of 5 September 1951, *W.H. Auden*, 1980

ENVIRONS OF VERONA

The road from Verona to Soave passes the sanctuary of the *Madonna di Campagna, at San Michele Extra, a round church with a peristyle, designed by Michele Sanmicheli (1484–1559), who was born in the village, and Caldiero, which has hot springs (perhaps the Roman *Fontes Junonis*—two of the thermal pools are Roman).

Soave is a pleasant little town famous for its white wine, for which the district has been known for many centuries. Probably the best-known Italian white wine, it is made from *Garganega* grapes in vineyards in a limited geographical area around the town (the estates with wine cellars welcome visitors). A wine festival is held here in September. The impressive battlemented **walls**, extremely well preserved, were built by the Scaligeri before 1375. In the central Piazza Antenna (named after a mast from which the flag of St Mark was flown) are Palazzo Cavalli, a Venetian Gothic palace of 1411, and Palazzo di Giustizia (1375).

A paved path leads up from the piazza to the medieval **castle** (also reached by road), enlarged by the Scaligeri in 1369. The keep is defended by three courtyards, each on a different level. Privately owned (open Tues–Sun 09.00–12.00, 15.00–18.30), it was restored and partly reconstructed in 1892. The residence has an armoury on the ground floor, and above are rooms with Gothic Revival painted decorations and imitation furniture. There is a fine view from the battlements.

South of Soave is **San Bonifacio** with the Romanesque abbey of San Pietro Apostolo (1131–39), recently restored.

The Monti Lessini

To the north of Verona are the Monti Lessini, with the valleys of the '*tredici comuni*', a high-lying district occupied by the descendants of Germanic settlers who migrated here in the 13C. Their dialect has practically died out. This pleasant remote area, part of which has been protected since 1990 as a regional park, with cherry trees and woods of chestnut and beech, has been visited for holidays by the Veronese since the begining of the century. The highest areas (around 1700m) have winter-sports facilities. The flint outcrops in the limestone hills were used in the Palaeolithic era for making tools, and remarkable fossils have been found in the volcanic and sedimentary rocks. Some of the houses still have characteristic roofs made out of slabs of stone quarried locally. This stone is also sometimes used to form drystone walls around fields. **Bosco Chiesanuova**, the main resort, has a museum illustrating the history of Lessinia—as the region as a whole is known.

In the central Val Pantena are **Santa Maria in Stelle**, with a Roman hypogeum (underground chamber), **Grezzana** (Romanesque campanile) and **Stallavena**. Near here the Riparo Tagliente, a shelter used by Palaeolithic hunters, has revealed numerous interesting finds.

In the easternmost valley are **Roncà**, with a fossil museum, and **Bolca**, with another museum, famous for its fossilised tropical fish found in the area. The neighbouring Val d'Illasi is known for its wrought-iron craftsmen. Beyond **Illasi**, with two grand 18C villas and a fresco by Stefano da Zevio in the church, is **Cogollo**, with pretty, locally made street lights and a well-known wrought-iron workshop. At the head of the valley is **Giazza**, where a German dialect is still spoken. It has a local ethnographical museum.

In a neighbouring valley **Velo Veronese** has interesting stone columns in its church. **Campo Silvano** has a tiny geological museum housing a collection of fossils and an interesting underground limestone cavern, the roof of which has collapsed (admission to both on request).

The Valpolicella

The Valpolicella, in the westernmost part of Lessinia, is a hilly district near a bend in the Adige, famous for its red wine (grown in a specific geographical area). The chief village, San Pietro in Cariano, preserves the old Vicariate, the seat of the Venetian district magistrates.

Sant'Ambrogio has quarries of 'rosso di Verona' marble. The church of *San Giorgio* dates from the 7C and has a 13C cloister. At Volargne the 15C **Villa del Bene** (open Tues–Sun 09.00–12.00, 15.00–18.00) has frescoes by Domenico Brusasorci, Giovanni Francesco Caroto and Bernardino India.

At Negrar is the 15C Villa Bertoldi. The valley is planted with cherry trees, which blossom in May. To the north are **Sant'Anna d'Alfaedo**, with a museum of prehistory including flints, arrowheads found locally, and fossils (among them a shark 6m long), and Fosse, both good walking centres. On the northeast side of the Corno d'Aquilio (1545m), above Fosse, is the Spluga della Preta, a remarkable pothole in the limestone, which was first descended in 1925. Speleologists have reached a depth of about 1000m.

At **Molina** there is a lovely park with numerous waterfalls and interesting vegetation (open 08.00–dusk; apply in the village at the visitors' centre or the trattoria *Du Scalini*). The visit, along marked trails, takes about 2hrs. The botanical museum in the village is to be reopened.

Around the province

South of Verona, **Villafranca di Verona** preserves a castle of the Scaligeri (1202), now home to a *Risorgimento* museum (open Sat–Sun 15.30–18.30). The armistice of Villafranca was concluded here on 11 July 1859 between Napoleon III and Austrian Emperor Francis Joseph. To the west is **Valeggio sul Mincio** with another Scaligeri castle (not open) and, nearby, the ruins of the fortified Ponte Visconteo (1393) over the Mincio. On the Verona road is the unusual **Parco-Giardino Sigurtà** (open Mar–Nov, Thur, Sat–Sun and holidays 09.00–19.00), a park of some 50h with gardens accessible only by car (7km of drives, with parking areas near footpaths).

Vicenza and environs

Vicenza is a thriving provincial capital (population 107,000) in a pleasant geographical position at the confluence of two mountain torrents, the Retrone and the Bacchiglione, at the foot of the Colli Berici. It was a palaeo-Venetic settlement and a Roman *municipium*. After the barbarian invasions and a period of relative independence, it flourished under Venetian rule, which began in 1404. Although it did not achieve the greatness of its neighbours, Verona and Padua, during the 16C it experienced a period of splendor that was reflected in a vast building programme. The many fine buildings by the town's favourite son, architect Andrea Palladio, have given the city centre a noble, Classical aspect. The high standard of life is reflected today in the constant maintenance of the old palaces and monuments, which contributes to the unusual stylistic coherence and unmistakable elegance of the historic city centre.

The environs of Vicenza are studded with magnificent Renaissance villas, many of which were designed by Palladio. There are also charming towns, such as Bassano del Grappa, Marostica, Schio and Asiago, in the foothills of the Alps.

Practical information

Getting there
By air
Vicenza is served by Verona Valerio Catullo airport at Caselle di Sommacampagna, with daily flights to domestic and European destinations.

Buses run every 20mins from Vicenza station.
By road
Vicenza has two exits (*Vicenza Est* and *Vicenza Ovest*) on Italy's main east–west *autostrada*, the A4, from Venice to

Milan. The city can also be reached easily from Trento or Modena via Verona on the A22. A fast, scenic approach from Rovereto and points north is by 46 and local roads to Thiene, then A31 south.

To reach Bassano del Grappa, Marostica and the Altopiano dei Setti Comuni, take 248 north from Vicenza.

By rail

All trains on the main Venice–Milan line stop at Vicenza, from which there are frequent country bus services to outlying points. The principal trains connect with Venice, Trieste, Milan, Turin and Genoa; Bologna, Florence and Rome; and Trento, Bolzano and Bressanone. From Verona there are direct through services to and from Basel, Berlin, Bern, Dortmund, Geneva, Lugano, Munich, Munster, Nice, Paris, Vienna and Zurich.

There are branch railways from Vicenza to Schio, Bassano del Grappa (via Cittadella) and Treviso (via Cittadella and Castelfranco Veneto). At Castelfranco you can connect to Belluno, Pieve di Cadore and Cortina d'Ampezzo; and from Bassano del Grappa to Trento.

Getting around

Vicenza has large **car parks** (with a minibus service for the historical centre) near the wholesale fruit market (north of the Verona road) and beyond the stadium. Limited space (with hourly tariff) is available in the centre of the town, off Viale Roma and Piazza Matteotti.

City buses

The Santuario di Monte Berico can be reached by a bus (*IUM*) from Viale Roma, near the train station. The Villa Valmarana is reached in c 15mins by bus **no. 8** from Viale Roma (direction Noventa Vicentina) to Borgo Berga (request stop at Via Tiepolo, 500m below the villa); it continues along the

Viale Riviera Berica to another request stop at the foot of Via della Rotonda, 200m below Villa Rotonda. If you intend to visit both villas (and not the basilica) it is best to take bus **no. 8** to the stop below Villa Rotonda, and from there walk back to Villa Valmarana.

Country buses

These are run by *FTV* (*Ferrovie e Tramvie Vicentine*, ☎ 0444 223115) and *AIM* (*Aziende Industriali Municipali*, ☎ 0444 394909) for places in the province, as well as for Padova, Montagnana, Gazzo Padovano, Piazzola Sul Brenta, Jesolo, San Donà di Pieve, Caorle, Bibione and Lavarone.

Information offices

VICENZA Piazza Duomo 5, ☎ 0444 544122; Piazza Matteotti 12, ☎ 0444 320854. Web: www.ascom.vi.it/aptvicenza. *Informagiovani*, Via Levà degli Angeli 9, ☎ 0444 222045.
ASIAGO Via Stazione 5, ☎ 0424 462221.
BASSANO DEL GRAPPA Largo Corona d'Italia 35, ☎ 0424 524351.
MAROSTICA Piazza Castello, ☎ 0424 72127.
RECOARO TERME Via Roma 25, ☎ 0445 75070.

Where to stay

VICENZA *Campo Marzio*, Viale Roma 21, ☎ 0444 545 700, fax 0444 329495; a quiet place in the large public garden between the train station and Corso Palladio; moderate.
Cristina, Corso Santi Felice e Fortunato 32, ☎ 0444 323751, fax 0444 543656; a family-run hotel at the edge of the historic city centre, just outside Porta Giusti; closed Dec–Jan; inexpensive.
Youth hostel: *Olimpico*, Viale Giuriolo 7–9, ☎ 0444 540222, fax 0444 547762.
ASIAGO *La Baitina*, Località Kaberlaba, ☎ 0424 462149, fax 0424

463677; a small, modern place near the ski slopes; closed Nov; inexpensive.
MUSSOLENTE *Villa Palma*, Via Chemin Palma 30, ☎ 0424 577407, fax 0424 87687; a lovely villa (20 rooms), with an excellent restaurant; moderate. *Volpara*, ☎ 0423 567766, fax 0424 968841; small and quiet, also with good restaurant; inexpensive.

Eating out
VICENZA *Antica Trattoria Trevisi*, Contrà Porti 6, ☎ 0444 324868; trattoria in an aristocratic palace of the 15C, one block north of Corso Palladio, serving Vicentine specialties with regional and Italian wines; closed Sun evening, Mon and Jul; moderate.
Cinzia e Valerio, Piazzetta Porta Padova 65/67 (across the Bacchiglione from the city centre), ☎ 0444 505213; a seafood restaurant generally considered the best place in town; closed Mon, Jan and Aug; expensive.
Da Remo, Via Caimpenta 14, Caimpenta (2km east), ☎ 0444 911007; a converted farmhouse with garden seating in summer, serving regional dishes; closed Sun evening, Mon, Aug and Dec–Jan; inexpensive.
Scudo di Francia, Contrà Piancoli 4, ☎ 0444 323322; just a few steps from the Basilica, also offers classical Vicentine cuisine; closed Sun evening, Mon, Dec–Jan and Aug; moderate.
Tinello, Corso Padova 181, ☎ 0444 500325; a renovated train station provides the setting for a popular restaurant serving local delicacies with regional and Italian wines; closed Sun evening, Mon and Aug; inexpensive.
Wine bars: Vicenza's best wine bar is *Bere Alto* in Contrà San Biagio; there are numerous others including one on the corner of Contrà Battisti Fontana and one in Contrà Lioy (near Piazza Gualdi).
For **coffee and pastries**, try

Pasticceria Sorarù, Piazza dei Signori and *Offelleria della Meneghina*, Contrà Cavour.
Good **picnic places** are the Giardino Salvi and Parco Querini.
ALTISSIMO (19km southeast of Recoaro Terme) *Casin del Gamba*, Strada per Castelvecchio, ☎ 0444 687709; regional cuisine and wines well worth the trip; closed Sun evening, Mon, Jan and Aug; moderate.
ARZIGANO (20km west of Vicenza) *Principe*, Via Caboto 16, ☎ 0444 675131; restaurant (with rooms) renowned for its seasonal specialties; closed Sun and Aug; moderate.
BASSANO DEL GRAPPA Cafés and **wine bars**: *Nardini* and *Taverna degli Alpini* at either end of the Ponte Vecchio, and *Danieli* by the Museo Civico.
MAROSTICA Wine bar: *Osteria alla Madonnetta*, Piazza Castello.
Café: *Centrale*, Piazza Castello.
MUSSOLENTE *Volpara*, Via Volpara 3, ☎ 0424 577019; simple Venetian cooking with fresh local ingredients; inexpensive.
TORREBELVICINO (Pievebelvicino, 4km from Schio) *Alla Sorgente*, Via Tenaglia 4, ☎ 0445 661233; trattoria offering delicious, highly personal cuisine, including breads baked on the premises; closed Mon evening and Tues; inexpensive.

Entertainment
VICENZA abounds in theatres, which offer a combination of music, drama and cinema. The main ones are: *Teatro Olimpico*, *Astra*, *San Marco*, *Roma*, *Maddalene* and *Zuccato*. The season usually runs Nov–May. There are special theatre programs at the *Teatro San Giuseppe* (*Theatroforum*), Nov–Mar, and *San Marco* (*Festival Nazionale Maschera d'Oro*), Feb–Mar. Chamber-music concerts are organised Oct–Jun by the *Società del Quartetto* and *Amici della Musica* at various sites around the city.

Live music in summer at clubs and bars throughout the area.

BASSANO DEL GRAPPA Drama at the *Teatro Astra*, Oct–Apr.

LONIGO Drama at the *Teatro Comunale*, Nov–Apr.

NOVENTA VICENTINA Drama at the *Teatro Modernissimo*, Nov–Mar.

THIENE Drama at the *Teatro Comunale*, Oct–Apr.

Shopping

Once again, food and wine are the main things to buy. Keep an eye open for *Bassano* grappa, *Marostica* cherries, and *Colli Berici* extra-virgin olive oil and DOC wines. There is also interesting jewellery, and ceramics from Bassano are locally renowned.

VICENZA Markets in Piazza dei Signori and Piazza Duomo on Thur.

BASSANO DEL GRAPPA Thur and Sat in the two piazzas.

Special events

VICENZA *Incontri Culturali*, art and theatre talks and workshops, Apr. *Viva il Cabaret*, cararet festival, Apr–May. *Il Suono dell'Olimpico*, classical music at the *Teatro Olimpico*, May–Jun. *Premio Faber Teatro*, performance by Maschera d'Oro prize winners, May. *Estate Show*, open-air music, dance, theatre and cinema at sites throughout the city, Jun–Sep. *Teatro delle Regioni*, amateur theatre festival, Jul–Aug. *Festival d'Autunno*, classical theatre festival at the *Teatro Olimpico*, Sep. *Vicenza Danza*, dance festival with performances at various sites around the town, Oct–Dec. Special exhibitions are held throughout the year at the basilica.

BASSANO DEL GRAPPA *Incontri Culturali di Primavera*, featuring music, lectures, poetry, history, art and photography, Mar–Apr. *Rido Ergo Sum*, contemporary comedy theatre festival,

Mar–Apr. *Meeting Internazionale Volo Libero*, international hang-gliding and super-light competition, Apr. *Concerti di Pasqua*, classical music, Easter. *Minimondo*, collectibles fair, May. *Alpine Choral Festival*, May. *Sei Giorni* and *Bassano-Montegrappa* amateur bicycle races, Jul. *Opera Estate Festival*, music, dance, drama and folk festival, Jul–Aug. *Organ Music Festival*, Oct. *Rally Città di Bassano*, international road rally, Oct. *Fiera d'Autunno*, autumn fair on the weekend after the first Thur of Oct. *Opera Festival*, Nov–Dec.

BREGANZE *Wine Festival*, with presentation and tasting of new wines, May. *Teatro in Corte*, theatre festival, Jun–Jul.

CARTIGLIANO *Primavera Musicale in Villa*, Villa Cappello, Mar–Apr.

GAMBELLARA *Festa dell'Uva e del Recioto*, vintage feast and wine fair, Sep.

LONIGO *Horse Show*, Aug.

MAROSTICA *Umoristi a Marostica*, comic-strip and cartoon exhibition, Apr–May. *Cherry Fair*, May. *Partita a Scacchi*, early Sep.

RECOARO TERME *Poetando Insieme*, national poetry prize, Apr. *Grand Fondo Recoaro Terme*, international men's and women's bicycle race, Apr.

ROMANO D'EZZELINO *Antique Car Race*, Sep.

SOSSANO *Festa degli Aquiloni*, national kite-flying prize, Apr.

THIENE *Amateur Theatre Festival*, Mar–Apr. *Thienedanza*, dance festival, Apr. *Cabaret Festival*, Nov–Feb.

TONEZZA DEL CIMONE *Tonezza Estate*, music, dance and theatre, Jun–Sep.

ELSEWHERE *Carnival* celebrations and patron saints' feast days with processions and festivities throughout the area. *Cantine Aperte*, weekend of wine-tastings at area estates, May. *Concerti in Villa*, classical music concerts in many of the Vicentine villas, Jun–Jul.

Sports

The countryside around Vicenza offers excellent opportunities for participatory sports: for instance, **walking**, **cycling** and **horse-riding** in the Colli Berici and in the area around Bassano del Grappa, Thiene and Marostica.

Golf at Brendola (*Golf Club Colli Beric*) and Creazzo (*Golf Club Creazzo*).

VICENZA

Vicenza's ancient Roman street plan is clearly recognisable, structured along the monumental Corso Palladio (the Roman *decumanus maximus*) and around Piazza dei Signori (probably the ancient forum), both of which are now distinguished by the 16C Classical creations of Palladio. Central Vicenza is really quite small, and can be visited comfortably in a couple of hours.

Corso Palladio and the Cathedral

The 11C Porta Castello, the west gate of the city, is the most conspicuous remainder of the town walls. It is adjoined by a shady garden, with a 16C loggia on a small canal. Just inside the gate, in Piazza Castello, stand the **Palazzo Piovini** (1656–58) and **Palazzo Porto Breganze**, begun by Vicenzo Scamozzi to a design by Palladio (c 1600) and never finished.

Here begins the magnificent **Corso Andrea Palladio**, the main street of the city centre, lined with monumental palaces and churches dating from the 14C to the 18C. The corner house, **Palazzo Bonin Thiene** (no. 13), was designed by Palladio, continued by Vincenzo Scamozzi and, like the Palazzo Porto Breganze, left incomplete; the Renaissance **Palazzo Capra-Clementi** (no. 45) dates from the late 15C. Nos 47 and 67 are 15C Venetian Gothic houses.

The first important cross street, Corso Fogazzaro, is flanked by more fine palaces: on the right, (no. 16) the splendid **Palazzo Valmarana-Braga** (1566), a remodelling by Palladio of an earlier building; and further on, the **Palazzo Repeta**, now the *Banca d'Italia*, by Francesco Muttoni (1711). The latter fronts onto **Piazza San Lorenzo**, which takes its name from the simple Franciscan church erected in the 13C. The single-gabled façade has an elaborately carved doorway of 1344 set against a tall blind arcade and flanked by monumental tombs. The three-aisled interior with polygonal apses is entirely Gothic in flavor and contains the *Poiana Altar*, with a delicate relief (1474), a detached fresco of the *Beheading of St Paul* by Bartolomeo Montagna, and the cenotaph of architect Vincenzo Scamozzi (d. 1616). In the north aisle is the door to the cloister (1492), where some sculptural fragments are displayed.

Retracing your steps and crossing over Corso Palladio, you soon come to the **Cathedral**, dating from the 14C, 15C and 16C. It has a coloured-marble façade designed in 1467 by Domenico da Venezia, a stout Romanesque campanile on a Roman foundation, a Gothic lateral doorway, another attributed to Palladio, and a large Renaissance tribune begun in 1482 and finished nearly a century later. The interior, a single broad aisle with tall lancet arches and high, vaulted ceiling, contains a number of fine artworks, notably Lorenzo Veneziano's polyptych of the *Dormitio Virginis* (fifth south altar, 1356), a gold-ground altarpiece of considerable primitive charm showing the sleeping Virgin. There are also an *Adoration of the Magi* by Francesco Maffei (third south altar), and a *Madonna*

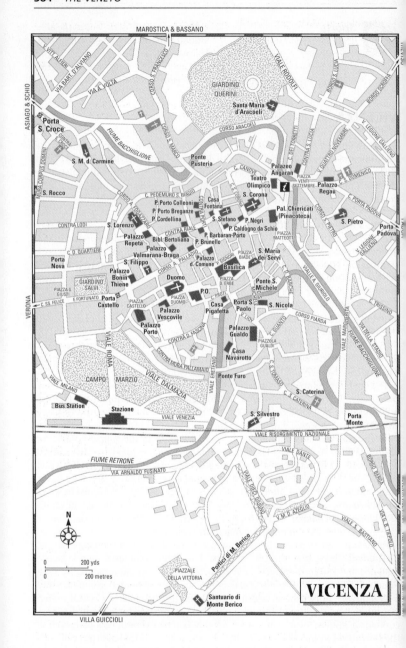

MAROSTICA & BASSANO

VIALE RODOLFI

VIA VITT. ALFIERI

VIA BART. D'ALVIANO

VIA A. VOLTA

CORSO S. FRANCESCO

ASIAGO & SCHIO

GIARDINO
QUERINI

BORGO S. LUCIA

BORGO SCROFEA

Porta
S. Croce

CONTRA
S. CROCE

Santa Maria
d'Aracoeli

FIUME BACCHIGLIONE

CORSO S. MARCO

CORSO Aracoeli

V. DEI TORRETTI

CONTRA S. LUCIA

VIA QUATTRO NOVEMBRE

MURA CORPUS DOMINI

S. M. d. Carmine

S. Rocco

Ponte
Pusteria

C. CANOVE

Palazzeo
Angaran

PIAZZA
VENTI
SETTEMBRE

V. LEGIONE GALLIENO

S. DOMENICO

Teatro
Olimpico

CORSO A. PALLADIO

CONTRA PORTI

C. S. CORONA

C. PEDEMURO S. BIAGIO

C. S. STEFANO

Casa
Fontana

S. Corona

Palazzeo
Regau

CORSO LODI

CONTRA LODI

P. Porto Colleoni
P. Porto Breganze
P. Cordellina

S. Lorenzo

S. Stefano

P. Negri

Pal. Chiericati
(Pinacoteca)

S. Pietro

PORTA PADOVA

Palazzo
Repeta

Bibl. Bertoliana

CONTRA RIALE

P. Caldogno da Schio
P. Barbaran-Porto
P. Brunello

PIAZZA
MATTEOTTI

Porta
Padova

C. D. QUARTIERE

Palazzo
Valmarana-Braga

CORSO A. FOGAZZARO

S. Maria
dei Servi

V. LEGIONE
GALLIENO

Porta
Nova

S. Filippo

Palazzo
d. Comune

PIAZZA
BIADE

PIAZZA
DEI SIGNORI

Basilica

Ponte S.
Michele

C. D. BERCHE

C. TRISSINO

PIAZZA G
GIUSTI

GIARDINO
SALVI

Palazzo
Bonin
Thiene

Duomo

PIAZZA
D'ERBE

C. PROTI

S. Nicola

CORSO PIARDA

VIALE MARGHERITA

FIUME BACCHIGLIONE

VIALE DELLA STADIO

VERONA

E FORTUNATO

Porta
Castello

PIAZZA
CASTELLO

P.O.

Casa
Pigafetta

Porta S.
Paolo

C. S. PAOLO

S. TOMASO

C. GUANTO

V. C. SS. FELICE

PIAZZA
DUOMO

Palazzo
Vescovile

Palazzo
Porto

CONTRA D. FASCINA

Palazzo
Gualdo

PIAZZOLA
GUALDI

VIALE ROMA

VIALE MILANO

CAMPO MARZIO

CONTRA MURA PALLAMAIO

VIALE DALMAZIA

Casa
Navarotto

VIALE ERETENIO

Ponte Furo

C. S. TOMASO

S. Caterina

C. S. CATERINA

Porta
Monte

Bus Station

Stazione

VIALE VENEZIA

S. Silvestro

VIALE RISORGIMENTO NAZIONALE

FIUME RETRONE

VIA ARNALDO FUSINATO

VIALE DANTE

VIALE DIEGO RUGGIO

BORGO BERGA

VIALE S. BASTIANO

VIALE B. TIEPOLO

N

0   200 yds
0   200 metres

V. M. D'AZEGLIO

Portici di M. Berico

PIAZZALE
DELLA VITTORIA

Santuario di
Monte Berico

VICENZA

VILLA GUICCIOLI

by Bartolomeo Montagna (fourth north altar). The adjoining Neo-classical bishop's palace has a splendid Renaissance portico, known as the **Loggia Zeno**, in the courtyard. On the south side of the square, beside the *APT*, is the entrance to the **Criptoportico Romano** (open Wed, Sat 10.00–11.30, or by appointment, ☎ 0444 321716), probably part of a Roman house of the 1C AD.

Back in Corso Palladio, the **Galleria d'Arte Municipale**, displaying canvases by local painters of the 16C and 17C, occupies the restored 16C church of Santi Giacomo e Filippo, set back somewhat from the street. Vincenzo Scamozzi's masterpiece is no. 98, the **Palazzo del Comune**, originally a private palace (designed 1592, completed 1662), with a doorway flanked by Ionic columns and a large arched window at the centre of the middle floor. Four symmetrical atria lead into the solemn rectangular courtyard; within are rooms with 17C and 18C decorations.

Piazza dei Signori

Turning right at the corner, you immediately reach Piazza dei Signori, the centre of civic life. The south side of the square is occupied by the **Basilica**, or Palazzo della Ragione, Vicenza's most important monument and one of the finer buildings of the Venetian Renaissance, created by Palladio after 1549. What he made here is in essence a transparent involucre that encircles a pre-existent Gothic construction designed by Domenico da Venezia and built in the latter half of the 15C. A double order of porticoes and logge, carried by Tuscan Doric columns on the ground floor and Ionic columns on the floor above, frames rounded arches and is crowned by a balustrade with statues. The huge interior hall (today used for temporary exhibitions; open Tues–Sat 09.30–12.00, 14.15–17.00; Sun and holidays 09.00–12.30) is covered by a ship's-keel vault and lighted by 24 ogival windows opening onto the logge.

The basilica

Across the square stands the **Loggia del Capitaniato** (or Loggia Bernarda), which Palladio designed in 1571, when construction on the Basilica was well underway. Once the residence of the military commander, it has immense, engaged Corinthian columns rising from the pavement to the attic level and framing the tall arches of the ground-floor portico as well as the windows and balconies of the floor above. The roofline is marked by a trabeation and balcony, behind which the discreetly low, set-back attic can be glimpsed. On the same side of the square, across the street from the Loggia, is the Renaissance

Monte di Pietà (1499). It incorporates the church of San Vincenzo, which was built a century and a quarter later than the palace proper and shows a lively Baroque face with two tiers of arcades and locally-made sculptures. The complex stands in the shadow of the **Torre di Piazza**, a slender campanile begun in the 12C and completed in the 14C, rising 82m above the pavement and ending in a fine Gothic belfry with mullioned windows and dome. Below, two columns, surmounted by the Lion of St Mark and Christ the Redeemer, and respectively dating from 1520 and 1640, separate Piazza dei Signori from the adjoining Piazza delle Biade, where the 15C church of Santa Maria dei Servi presents a curious façade of 1710 incorporating the original Renaissance doorway. Inside is an *Enthroned Madonna* by Benedetto Montagna.

South to the Retrone

The square on the south side of the Basilica, the narrow Piazza delle Erbe, is considerably less monumental than Piazza dei Signori and, as its name suggests, less noble in function. It is a marketplace, packed with colourful stalls and thronged with shoppers on weekday mornings. As though to assure that the difference in symbolic value of the two squares is understood, the humble Piazza delle Erbe lies on a lower level than its ostentatious counterpart. The outstanding buildings here are the medieval Torre del Girone or ('del Tormento'), and the late-15C Arco del Registro.

Continuing southwards, just before the bridge over the River Retrone you come to the birthplace (Via Pigafetta 9) of Antonio Pigafetta, the navigator, who accompanied Magellan on his first trip around the world (1519–22). It is a graceful Gothic mansion with a small façade delicately adorned with spiral columns. On the other side of the Retrone, here little more than a creek, stands **San Nicola da Tolentino**, a 17C oratory interesting for its elaborate stuccoes framing canvases by Francesco Maffei (who also did the *Trinity* over the altar), Giulio Carpioni, Antonio Zanchi, and others. The **Ponte San Michele**, of 1623, offers a good view over the city centre.

North to Santa Corona

Return to Piazza dei Signori, walk north between the Loggia del Capitaniato and the Monte di Pieta, and continue across Corso Palladio to reach Contrà Porti, another street flanked by superb palaces. Here are: at no. 6–10, **Palazzo Cavalloni-Thiene**, a 15C Venetian Gothic building; at no. 11, the majestic **Palazzo Barbaran-Porto**, by Palladio (1571), awaiting a new 'Museo Palladiano'; at no. 12 **Palazzo Thiene**, with a main façade and terracotta doorway attributed to Lorenzo da Bologna (1489), and a courtyard and rear façade (1550–58) designed by Palladio; at no. 14 the Gothic **Palazzo Trissino-Sperotti** (1450–60); at no. 17 the **Palazzo Porto-Breganze**, a Venetian Gothic building of 1481 with a fine Renaissance doorway and porticoed courtyard; at no. 16 the Renaissance **Palazzo Porto-Fontana**; at no. 19 the magnificent, early-14C **Palazzo Porto-Colleoni**, the oldest Venetian Gothic house on the street; and at no. 21 the unfinished **Palazzo Iseppo da Porto**, by Palladio (1552).

Now go around the block to the east and return by Contrà Zanella. No. 2 is the **Casa Fontana** (formerly Secco-Zen); its large, mullioned windows are unusual in Vicentine Gothic architecture. No. 1, at the corner of Piazzetta Santo Stefano, is the crenellated **Palazzo Negri De Salvi**, a 15C Renaissance mansion. Beyond the Baroque church of **Santo Stefano** (where there is a *Madonna and Child with Saints* by Palma Vecchio in the north transept), is Palladio's rear façade of Palazzo Thienne.

Back in Corso Palladio you soon reach the **Palazzo Caldogno da Schio** (no. 147), also called Ca' d'Oro, a gem of Venetian Gothic architecture with fine mullioned windows and round-arched Renaissance doorway. Its design is attributed to Lorenzo da Bologna, author of the Casa Valmarana Bertolini; in the atrium are architectural fragments and antique inscriptions. No. 165–67 is the **Casa Cogollo**, a house once attributed to Palladio, with late-Renaissance façade of 1559–62, possibly by Giovanni Antonio Fasolo.

The most magnificent religious building in town is the Dominican monastic church of **Santa Corona**, built in the 13C, given a new transept and apse in the 15C, and further refined over the following centuries. The single-gabled façade has Gothic windows, including a large rose window. Inside, the sense of space is Romanesque; the verticality, Gothic; and the harmony of the easternmost areas, Renaissance. The deep, raised Renaissance sanctuary was laid out in 1489 by Lorenzo da Bologna. The crypt is entered through the Cappella Valmarana, designed by Palladio. Above, the 17C high altar and 15C choir stalls bear beautiful inlay work. Among the many altarpieces are two genuine masterpieces: Paolo Veronese's *Adoration of the Magi* (1573; third south altar) and Giovanni Bellini's magnificent *Baptism of Christ* (c 1502; fifth north altar), the latter set in a monumental architectural frame of 1501. The third altar on this side has a *St Anthony* by Leandro Bassano; the second, a *Magdalen and Saints* by Bartolomeo Montagna. The church takes its name from a thorn of the Crown of Christ, donated by St Louis of France and shown on Good Friday.

The adjoining cloister has a small **Museo Naturalistico** illustrating the geology, vegetation and zoology of the *Colli Berici*, and a **Museo Archeologico**, with prehistoric, Roman and Lombard antiquities. Both are open Tues–Sat 09.00–12.30, 14.15–17.00; Sun and holidays 09.00–12.30. Particularly interesting are the square-mouthed Neolithic vases and the Palaeo-Venetic figured votive laminettes of the 4C and 3C BC.

On the other side of Contrà Santa Corona is **Palazzo Leoni Montanari** (open Apr–Oct, Sat 10.00–12.00, 16.00–19.00), now owned by a bank which has carefully restored it. The building was begun in the late 17C and has interesting architectural elements (some of which were added in 1808). The interior, with 18C decorations (frescoes by Giuseppe Alberti and Lodovico Dorigny), and Neoclassical elements, includes the elaborate Baroque Galleria della Verità and a loggia profusely decorated with stuccoes. In one room are displayed seven paintings by Pietro Longhi (and seven by his school) from the 19C collection of Giuseppe Salom.

Piazza Matteotti: Palladian highlights

Corso Palladio ends in Piazza Matteotti, a broad, open space planted as a garden, at the northeastern end of the pedestrian zone. On the north side of the square, in a garden surmounted by a crenellated medieval tower, stands the **Teatro Olimpico**, Palladio's last work (1580, completed in 1584 by Scamozzi; open Mon–Sat 09.00–12.30, 14.15–17.00; Sund and holidays 09.00–12.30). It was built for the Accademia Olimpica, founded in 1555, of which Palladio was a member and which produced numerous plays. The opening play, given in 1585, was Sophocles' *Oedipus Rex*.

A corridor leads from the entrance to the Odeon, the meeting place of the Accademia degli Olimpici, realised by Scamozzi in 1608, with a magnificent wooden ceiling and walls frescoed by Francesco Maffei. The Antiodeon, also with a wooden ceiling, follows; from here you enter the theatre proper. The latter, made of wood and stucco, takes up the forms of the theatres of classical antiquity described by Vitruvius. It has a *cavea* of 13 semielliptical tiers ending in a Corinthian colonnade crowned by an attic. The classical *frons scenae*, built in wood and stucco, its architecture derived from ancient Roman buildings, has niches with statues of academicians by Agostino Rubini, Domenico Fontana and others, and reliefs of the Labours of Hercules. Scamozzi designed the magnificent, two-storied fixed backdrop, populated by statues (95 in all) and presenting spectacular architectural views of seven streets, supposedly of the ancient city of Thebes.

The majestic **Palazzo Chiericati**, designed by Palladio in 1550–57, stands alone on the west side of the square, without the spatial limitations of adjoining buildings—which left the architect free to design a double portico, Doric below and Ionic above, closed in the central part of the upper level by a wall with rectangular windows. The luminous, elegant solution of the façade finds an ideal complement in the spatial definition of the courtyard and of the ground floor rooms, decorated with frescoes by Domenico Brusasorci and Giovan Battista Zelotti, and with stuccoes by Bartolomeo Ridolfi.

The building is home to the **Pinacoteca**, open Tues–Sat 09.00–12.30, 14.15–17.00; Sun and holidays 09.00–12.30), established in 1855. The ground floor hosts the contemporary paintings of the Raccolta Neri Pozza, recently donated to the museum. In the courtyard is a small but valuable selection of Renaissance sculptures. On the first floor is the picture gallery, displaying mainly Venetian painting of the 16C–18C, by Cima da Conegliano, Bartolomeo Montagna (*Madonna and Child with Saints*), Paolo Veronese (*Madonna and Child with Saints*), Jacopo Tintoretto, Jacopo Bassano, Francesco Maffei, Sebastiano and Marco Ricci, Pietro della Vecchia, Giuseppe Zais, Giovan Battista Tiepolo (*Time Revealing Truth*) and G.B. Piazzetta. Among the artists of other schools are Memling (*Crucifixion*), van Dyck (*The Three Ages of Man*) and Sansovino. The museum also possesses a precious collection of drawings by Andrea Palladio.

Just across the bridge over the Bacchiglione are two fine 15C palazzi: **Palazzo Angarano**, in Piazza XX Settembre, and the Gothic **Palazzo Regaù**, in Contrà XX Settembre. The 14C church of **San Pietro**, with a 15C brick cloister, is visible to the right. North of Piazza XX Settembre, at the end of Contrà Torretti, is the eliptical Baroque church of **Santa Maria d'Aracoeli**, possibly based on designs by Guarino Guarini (1675–80). It stands on the edge of the **Parco Querini**, pretty public gardens (open daily).

Out of town

In the immediate environs of Vicenza are two or three outstanding sights easily reached on foot. A point of pilgrimage is the **Santuario di Monte Berico**, in a panoramic position south of the city centre, to which it is connected by a long portico (Viale X Giugno) designed by the 18C architect Francesco Muttoni. The church (1668–1703), the work of Carlo Borella, has three symmetrical Baroque façades with 42 statues by Orazio Marinali; the stout campanile dates from the early 19C.

The Greek-cross interior (closed 12.30–15.30) conserves, in its eastern part, the primitive sanctuary of 1428, which legend holds was traced out by the Virgin Mary who appeared to a woman of the people. Among the votive decorations are a venerated statue of the *Virgin*, of 1430, and a splendid painting of the *Pietà* by Bartolomeo Montagna. A 15C cloister precedes the refectory, in which is set the large painting of the **Supper of St Gregory the Great* by Veronese (1572).

Piazzale della Vittoria beside the church, built as a memorial of the First World War, commands a magnificent view of Vicenza and of the mountains that once marked the front line. Viale X Giugno continues beyond the basilica to the **Villa Guiccioli**, built at the end of the 18C by Gianantonio Selva, with a beautiful park (open Tues–Sun 09.00–17.30 or 18.00) and a **Museo del Risorgimento e della Resistenza** (open Tues–Sat 09.30–12.00, 14.15–17.00; Sun and holidays 09.00–12.00).

From the great bend in Viale X Giugno, Viale d'Azeglio and Via San Bastiano wind southeast to two spectacular villas. The **Villa Valmarana ai Nani** (open Mar–Nov, Wed–Thur, Sat–Sun 10.00–12.00 and all afternoons except Mon, Mar–Apr 14.30–17.30, May–Sep 15.00–18.00; Oct–Nov 14.00–17.00), attributed to Antonio Muttoni, has a panoramic terrace overlooking the sanctuary of Monte Berico. Five rooms of the villa are decorated with frescoes by Giovanni Battista Tiepolo (1757), inspired by classical poems (*Iliad, Aeneid, Orlando Furioso, Gerusalemme Liberata*); the guest house is frescoed with scenes of country life by Gian Domenico Tiepolo, Giovanni Battista's son.

The stony path (Stradella Valmarana) on the right beyond the villa continues downhill to the equally famous Villa Almerico, better known as **La Rotonda** (open Mar–Nov: admission to the garden on Tues–Thur 10.00–12.00, 15.00–18.00; other days usually on request; to the interior, Wed only, 10.00–12.00, 15.00–18.00; always closed Mon; ☎ 0444 321793). Built as a *belvedere* for Paolo Almerico on a charming hilltop site, it has a central plan consisting of a circular core within a cube. The four classical porticoes complete its symmetry. Crowned with a remarkable low dome, its design is reminiscent of the Pantheon in Rome. Begun c 1551 by Palladio, it was taken over at his death by Vincenzo Scamozzi and finished in 1606 for the Capra family. The Villa Rotonda had a profound influence on the history of architecture and was copied in numerous buildings, including Chiswick House, London. The domed central hall was frescoed at the end of the 17C by Lodovico Dorigny, and the *piano nobile* was painted by Anselmo Canera, Bernardino India and Alessandro Maganza. The *barchessa* (working wing) was designed by Vincenzo Scamozzi.

Palladio and the music of architecture

The 16C architect Andrea di Pietro della Gondola, better known as Palladio, designed villas, palaces and churches throughout the Veneto in a Classical style that would profoundly change the face of the region and inspire numerous imitations. His *Quattro Libri*, or *Four Books on Architecture*, became a manual for later architects, especially in England and the United

States. In the engraved illustrations for this treatise, Palladio noted the significant dimensions of his buildings, linking together their plan, section and elevation in a series of proportional relationships. The seemingly easy elegance that distinguishes Palladio's designs was, in fact, the result of his careful calculation of such proportional relationships. In applying these systems of numerical progression, which were often associated with contemporary musical harmonic theory, to the spatial relationships of a building, Palladio succeeded in creating pleasing the visual harmonies that characterise his architecture.

The return may be made by following Via Rotonda to the bottom of the hill (200m), where **bus no. 8** can be taken back to the centre of Vicenza. From Villa Valmarana, Via Giovanni Battista Tiepolo descends to the Porta Monte, just above which is a charming little arch attributed to Palladio and dated 1595. **Bus no. 8** runs back along the main road into Vicenza.

The Ville Vicentine

The province of Vicenza is particularly rich in villas of the famous *ville venete* type. These were built from the 15C onwards by rich noble Venetian families who were anxious to invest in land on the terraferma and contribute to its fertility by the construction of canals and irrigation systems. In the early 16C Palladio invented an architecture peculiarly fitted to these prestigious villas, which he also saw as places of repose and as working farms. He derived their design in part from the villas of the ancient Romans and used Classical features in their construction. He took particular care in the siting of his villas, sometimes on low hills or near canals, and almost always surrounded by gardens and farmland. The outbuildings, known as *barchesse*, were often porticoed.

Numerous villas by Palladio survive in the province (some of them with frescoes and stuccoes by Giovanni Antonio Fasolo, Giovanni Battista Zelotti and Bartolomeo Ridolfi). In the 17C and 18C many more villas were constructed, some of these particularly interesting for their interiors and frescoes (including some by Giovanni Battista Tiepolo and his son Gian Domenico). Architects of importance who succeeded Palladio include Vincenzo Scamozzi, Antonio Pizzocaro, Francesco Muttoni and Giorgio Massari. Orazio Marinali was responsible for the statuary in the gardens of many of the villas.

Finding the villas

The names of the villas change with each new owner, but they generally also carry the name of the original proprietor. They are scattered widely over the province, often in remote areas outside small towns (the name of the comune as well as the locality has been given in the description below to help with their location, as signposting is generally poor). The villas are often privately owned, and many of the interiors are closed to the public (except with special permission), but the exteriors and gardens are often their most important features. Opening times change frequently and accessibility varies; it is therefore advisable to consult the information office in Vicenza (see p 379) before starting a tour, or to ring the villa for confirmation of opening times. Concerts are organised in some of the villas in July.

The most important villas (but by no means all of them) are described below by geographical areas: the outskirts of Vicenza (including those within the municipal limits); those south and west of Vicenza; and those to the north of the town. The villas in the environs of Bassano del Grappa are described on p 395. Other villas in the provinces of Padua, Venezia, Treviso, Verona, Rovigo and Belluno, are also described).

The outskirts of Vicenza

The suburban **Villa Trissino Rigo** (1532–37) at Cricoli was designed by Palladio's first patron, Gian Giorgio Trissino. Palladio probably worked here as a young artist in the workshop of Giovanni da Pedemuro. The exterior can be viewed by appointment (☎ 0444 922122). At Anconetta is the **Villa Imperiali Lampertico**, built in 1681, surrounded by a garden. At Bertisina are **Villa Gazzotti Curti**, built by Palladio in 1542–43; **Villa Negri Ceroni**, built in 1709 (perhaps by Carlo Borella) in Palladian style, with a park and garden; and **Villa Chiericati Ghislanzoni**, dating from 1764.

East of Vicenza

East of Vicenza, at Monticello Conte Otto, is the **Villa Valmarana Bressan**, begun in 1541 by Palladio, an austere building with a typical Palladian entrance. It is open Mon–Fri 09.00–12.00, 14.00–18.00; Sat, Sun and holidays by appointment (☎ 0444 596242). The **Villa Thiene**, owned by the town of Quinto Vicentino, is another work by Palladio (c 1546), left unfinished. It is open Mon–Fri 10.00–12.30; Tues and Thur also 18.00–19.00; ☎ 0444 357009. At Bolzano Vicentino (Località Lisiera) is the **Villa Valmarana Zen**, on a Palladian design, with numerous statues in the garden and a pretty little chapel.

South and west of Vicenza

South and west of Vicenza, at Altavilla Vicentina, the **Villa Valmarana-Morosini** was built by Francesco Muttoni in 1724. It has been restored by the university (open Wed–Thur, 14.30–17.30; ☎ 0444 572499). Near Monteviale is the **Villa Loschi Zileri dal Verme**, attributed to Francesco Muttoni, surrounded by a fine park with exotic trees. It contains the earliest frescoes by Giovanni Battista Tiepolo (1734) outside Venice: the allegorical scenes decorate the staircase and the salone (open by advance appointment, ☎ 0444 566146). At Costabissari to the west, **Villa Bissari Curti** (reconstructed in the 19C) has a loggia attributed to Ottone Calderari, and a garden with antique fragments and an amphitheatre.

The picturesque village of **Montecchio Maggiore,** a legendary stronghold of the 'Montagues' of Romeo and Juliet, has two restored Scaligeri castles. Just outside is the **Villa Cordellina Lombardi**, by Giorgio Massari (1735), owned by the province of Vicenza and used for conferences, courses, etc. (open Apr–Oct, Tues–Fri 09.00–13.00; Sat, Sun and holidays 09.00–13.00, 15.00–18.00; ☎ 0444 399111). It has very fine *frescoes (1743) by Giovanni Battista Tiepolo in the central hall (restored in 1984). To the north of Montecchio is Trissino, with the **Villa Trissino Marzotto**, whose delightful park is open by advance appointment (☎ 0445 962029). At nearby Castelgomberto the **Villa Piovene da Schio** was built in 1666, probably by Antonio Pizzocaro (chapel of 1614); it has 18C additions and is surrounded by a garden with statues by the workshop of Marinali. Inside are three early works by Giovanni Battista Tiepolo. The exterior can be viewed by appointment, Jun–Sep, Sat 10.00–12.00 (☎ 0445 940052). To the west of Montecchio is Montorso Vicentino with the **Villa da Porto Barbaran**, dating from 1724 with an Ionic pronaos and a pretty Ionic *barchessa*. Nearby, at Arzignano, are two more 18C villas.

At Sarego is the **Villa da Porto 'La Favorita'**, by Francesco Muttoni (1714–15). The little town of Lonigo, at the foot of the Monti Berici, has its town hall in Palazzo Pisani, a very grand mansion of 1557. On the outskirts stands the Rocca, or **Villa Pisani** (1576), a charming work by Vincenzo Scamozzi (recalling Palladio's Villa Rotonda) on the site of an old castle, with a park (open by appointment, ☎ 049 875 7462). Outside Lonigo, at Bagnolo, is the beautiful **Villa Pisani Ferri**, one of Palladio's earlier villas, built in 1542. The main entrance has rusticated arches beneath a pediment, and the villa is surrounded by farm buildings. It is open 1 Apr–4 Nov, Wed, Fri and Sun 10.00–12.00, 15.00–18.00, or by appointment, ☎ 0444 831104.

At Orgiano is the **Villa Fracanzan Piovene**, built in 1710 and attributed to Francesco Muttoni, with an interesting garden (and *barchessa*). Open 1 Mar–30 Nov on holiday afternoons; otherwise by appointment (☎ 0444 874589). At Noventa Vicentina the town hall occupies **Villa Barbarigo** (early 17C; open Mon–Sat 8.30–12.30, or by appointment, ☎ 0444 760360). Nearby, on the road to Agugliaro is the *****Villa Saraceno**, begun by Palladio between 1545 and 1555, and surrounded by farm buildings. Acquired by the Landmark Trust of Great Britain, it was beautifully restored in 1988–94, and is open 1 Apr–31 Oct on Wed at 14.00–16.00; at other times by previous appointment only (☎ 0444 891371).

On the main road at Pojana Maggiore is the **Villa Pojana**, built in 1540 by Palladio, with a typical Palladian arch over the entrance. It is in very poor condition, but has contemporary frescoes by Bernardino India and Anselmo Canera and stuccoes by Bartolomeo Ridolfi. The frescoes in the atrium are attributed to Giovanni Battista Zelotti.

At Mossano is the Villa Pigafetta Camerini, a charming late-17C building attributed to Antonio Pizzocaro. The *barchesse* and chapel may be by Francesco Muttoni. Open May–Oct, Sat–Sun and holidays 09.00–13.00, 14.00–18.00, or by appointment (☎ 0444 886838). At Longare are two villas: **Villa Trento-Carli**, built in 1645, is attributed to Antonio Pizzocaro (open by appointment only); the **Ville da Schio**, with three buildings on a hillside, is surrounded by a lovely garden with sculptures by Orazio Marinali. The Villino Garzadori here, built into the hillside in 1690, has frescoes by Lodovico Dorigny. The park is open Tues–Sun 09.30–12.30, 15.00–19.00.

Near Grumolo delle Abbadesse, at Vancimuglio, is the **Villa Da Porto Rigo** or Villa Chiericati (1554), almost certainly by Palladio (but left unfinished), with an Ionic portico with statues on the pediment, and in Grisignano di Zocco is the **Villa Ferramosca-Beggiato**, by Gian Domenico Scamozzi (c 1560).

On either side of the Bacchiglione River are Montegalda and Montegaldella. In **Montegalda** are the **Castello Grimani Sorlini**, a 12C castle adapted as a villa in the 18C (with a fine park), **Villa Chiericati Fogazzaro**, rebuilt in 1846 by

Caregaro Negrin, with a garden, and—at Colzè—**Villa Colzè Feriani**, rebuilt in the 17C, with a chapel containing sculptures by Orazio Marinali. In **Montegaldella** is the 17C **Villa Conti Campagnolo**, called 'La Deliziosa' (altered in the 19C), its garden decorated with statues by Orazio Marinali.

North of Vicenza

North of Vicenza, at Caldogno, is the **Villa Caldogno-Nordera** (owned by the town; open 1 Apr–30 Oct, Tues and Sat 09.00–12.00, Thur 15.00–18.00; ☎ 0444 585756), built in 1570 and attributed to Palladio. It is decorated with frescoes by Giovanni Fasolo, Gian Battista Zelotti and Giulio Carpioni. Villaverla has two fine villas: the **Villa Verlato** (1576 by Vincenzo Scamozzi), with frescoes by Girolamo Pisano and Giovanni Battista Maganza, and **Villa Ghellini** (1664–79) by Antonio Pizzocaro (now owned by the town; the exterior and park are open to visitors Mon–Sat 10.00–12.00, 15.00 or 16.00–17.00 or 18.00).

At **Thiene** is the **Castello Porto-Colleoni Thiene**, a late-Gothic Venetian castle perhaps begun by Domenico da Venezia and completed in 1476. It has frescoes by Giovanni Antonio Fasolo and Giovanni Battista Zelotti, a charming contemporary chapel, and a stable block attributed to Antonio Muttoni (open Mar–Nov on Sun and holidays at 15.00, 16.00 and 17.00, or by appointment, ☎ 041 5289274). The **Villa Beregan Cunico**, with a long, low façade and portal attributed to Antonio Pizzocaro, is open to visitors Wed and Sat 09.00–12.30, 15.00–17.00 (☎ 0445 380944). At Sarcedo is the **Villa Capra** (1764; open by appointment, ☎ 0424 511833).

Beyond the Astico is **Lonedo di Lugo** (in the *comune* of Lonedo di Lugo). Here the **Villa Godi Valmarana**, now Malinverni (open Tues, Sat and Sun 15.00–19.00, winter 14.00–18.00; closed Dec–mid-Feb), is one of the earliest known works by Palladio (1540–42). The *piano nobile* was frescoed in the 16C by Battista del Moro and Giovanni Battista Zelotti. A wing of the palace has a representative collection of 19C Italian paintings, including works by Francesco Hayez, Tranquillo Cremona, the Indunno brothers, Segantini, De Nittis, Domenico Morelli, the 'Macchiaioli' painters, Giovanni Boldoni and Pietro Annigoni. A fossil museum has local exhibits including a palm tree 5m high. The **Villa Piovene**, close by (open 14.30–19.30 or by appointment, ☎ 0445 860613), has a Palladian core, altered in the 18C by Francesco Muttoni. It is surrounded by a park designed by Antonio Piovene.

Breganze has several villas, including the **Villa Diedo Basso** (1664–84, with additions) with a garden. Breganze is known for its wines (including the red *Maculan*) which can be purchased at the *Cantina Sociale San Bartolomeo*.

At **Dueville** are the **Villa Da Porto Casarotto**, by Ottone Calderari (1770–76; exterior only open to visitors, 09.30–11.30, 15.30–18.30), and the **Villa Da Porto del Conte**, at Vivaro, on a Palladian design (remodelled in 1855. The town hall of Dueville occupies **Villa Monza**, built in 1715, probably by Francesco Muttoni (open Mon and Wed 09.30–13.00; Thur 09.30–13.00, 16.00–18.00; ☎ 0444 594060).

At Sandrigo, the **Villa Sesso Schiavo Nardone** (open by appointment, ☎ 0444 659344) was built by a follower of Palladio in 1570 and has contemporary frescoes. At Longa di Schiavon, the **Villa Chiericati Lambert** was built in 1590 (and altered in the 19C); it contains 16C frescoes attributed to Ludovico Pozzoserrato.

Bassano del Grappa

Situated where the Brenta River emerges from the hills, Bassano is a pleasant town of arcaded streets and old houses, many of which have frescoed façades. First documented in the 10C, it was united with Venice in 1402. It was home to a family of well-known painters—the Da Ponte, called Bassano after this, their birthplace. The Austrians were defeated here by Napoleon in 1796, and by the Italians in 1917–18. The city suffered severe damage in the latter campaign, which was fought on nearby Monte Grappa; but this and the recent flourishing of small industries have done little to mar the integrity of the city centre, which is still one of the finest in the region. Shoppers will be pleased to know that there is a strong tradition here in wrought iron and ceramics. Bassano is known also for its produce, especially asparagus and porcini mushrooms, and of course for its grappa, the best in Italy.

The town centre

The northernmost part of the historic centre, including the 15C **Cathedral** (with paintings by the Bassano), stands inside the walled complex of the **Castello Superiore**, which dates as far back as 900–950 but was enlarged and fortified in the 13C, 14C and subsequent centuries. A tower of the old fortress serves as the base of the campanile. The area to the south of this, occupied in part by the 14C **Castello Inferiore**, develops around three adjacent squares, Piazza Garibaldi, Piazza Libertà, and Piazzetta Monte Vecchio.

In **Piazza Garibaldi** stands the former Franciscan church of **San Francesco**, a Romanesque-Gothic building with an elegant vestibule of 1306 and a graceful campanile. It conserves remains of 15C frescoes and, in the apse, a painted wooden crucifix of the 14C.

A door on the right of the porch leads to the **Museo Civico** (open Tues–Sat 09.00–18.30, Sun and holidays 15.30–18.30), housed in the monastic buildings. In the beautiful 17C cloister (partly rebuilt) are a collection of Roman and medieval inscriptions and another of ceramics. The archeological section includes protohistoric material of the Angarano culture (11C BC); Greek, Italiot and Roman finds; and antique coins. The print and drawing cabinet (with works by Vittore Carpaccio, Lorenzo Lotto, Gian Lorenzo Bernini, Giovanni Battista Tiepolo, Francesco Guardi and Antonio Canova) is famous for the Remondini collection of 17C–19C popular prints.

On the **first floor** is the picture gallery, with paintings by Jacopo Bassano (*Flight into Egypt*; *Baptism of St Lucilla, St Martin and the Beggar*), Francesco and Leandro Bassano, Michele Giambono and Guariento; and numerous works from the 17C and 18C, by Francesco Maffei, Marco Ricci, Giovanni Battista Tiepolo, Pietro Longhi and Alessandro Magnasco. The last rooms are dedicated to Antonio Canova (casts and models); to painters of the 19C; and to Tito Gobbi (1913–84), the great baritone, who was born in Bassano.

In the neighbouring **Piazza Libertà** are the **Loggia del Commune** (1582) with a fresco of *St Christopher* ascribed to Jacopo Bassano, and two 18C buildings, the Palazzo del Municipio and the church of San Giovanni Battista.

Piazzetta Monte Vecchio, which was the main square of the city in the Middle Ages, is lined with fine old frescoed palaces, most notably the 15C **Palazzetto del Monte di Pietà**, with inscriptions and coats of arms on the façade. The square

Ponte Vecchio

leads down to the *****Ponte Vecchio** or Ponte degli Alpini, a famous covered wooden bridge across the picturesque River Brenta, which retains the form designed for it by Palladio in 1569. The river is subject to sudden floods, and the bridge has had to be rebuilt many times: it has been proved over the centuries that only a wooden structure (rather than stone) can survive the force of the water. There is a lovely view of the mountains upstream from the bridge, and the houses on the riverfront are well preserved. Beside the bridge is a characteristic little wine bar, with a grappa distillery of 1769 (there is a private museum in the nearby Poli distillery illustrating the production of grappa, open daily except Mon morning, 09.00–13.00, 14.30–19.30). The bridge is named after the Alpini regiment, which crossed the bridge numerous times during the campaigns on Monte Grappa and above Asiago in the First World War, and which was responsible for its reconstruction after the last war (small museum in the Taverna al Ponte, Via Angarano 2, open Tues–Sun 08.00–20.00; possible lunch break in winter, 13.00–15.00). The best view of the bridge is from the other side, from a lane which leads left beside a little garden on the banks of the river.

Also on the river (south bank) is the lovely 18C **Palazzo Sturm**, where the **Museo della Ceramica** (part of the Museo Civico) has recently been arranged (open Apr–Oct, Tues–Sat 09.00–12.30, Sun and holidays 15.30–18.30; Jun–Sep, Sun 10.00–12.30; Nov–Mar, Fri 09.00–12.30, Sat–Sun 15.30– 18.30). The entrance is through the attractive Neo-classical courtyard overlooking the river. The entrance hall (1765) has frescoes by Giorgio Anselmi. The collection of ceramics illustrates the production of local manufactures, including Manardi ware, made here in the 17C, and later pieces from Nove and Faenza. Beyond a *belvedere* (now enclosed) overlooking the river is the delightful little *boudoir, which preserves its original Rococo decoration intact (after careful restoration), including very fine stuccowork.

Villas in the environs of Bassano

On the outskirts of Bassano, at Sant'Eusebio, is the **Villa Bianchi Michiel**, built in the late 17C by Domenico Margutti, perhaps on a design by Longhena. It has two wings with Doric porticoes (open by appointment only).

A road leads northeast out of Bassano to Romano d'Ezzelino, where the 17C **Villa Corner**, with an orangery by Vincenzo Scamozzi, may be visited by appointment. Nearby is Mussolente, with the **Villa Negri Piovene** on a low hill approached by a flight of steps from the Asolo road, and flanked by two porticoes. It was built in 1763 by Antonio Gaidon.

To the south of Bassano is the **Villa Rezzonico**, reminiscent of a medieval castle, built in the early 18C and attributed as an early work to Longhena. It contains stuccoes by Andrea Brustolon, and has a fine park and garden (☎ 0424

524217). At Rosà, the park of the late-17C **Villa Dolfin-Boldù** may be visited by previous appointment. Rossano Veneto has two 18C villas. On the Brenta at Cartigliano is the eccentric **Villa Morosini Cappello** (now the town hall). It was begun in 1560 probably by Francesco Zamberlan, but was left unfinished. The remarkable Ionic loggia which surrounds the building may have been added in the 17C. It is open Mon–Fri 09.00–13.00; Sat 09.00–12.00; Wed 16.30–18.30 (☎ 0424 590234). In the parish church, the Chapel of the Rosary is decorated with frescoes (1575) by Jacopo Bassano and his son Francesco, and has an altarpiece by Bartolomeo Montagna.

Monte Grappa

This infamous mountain (1775m), north of Bassano, was the scene of heavy fighting between Austrians and Italians in 1917–18, in three historic battles which ended in the loss of 12,615 Italian soldiers (only 2283 of whom could be identified). On the summit is a monumental cemetery built in 1935 by Giovanni Greppi, with a votive chapel dedicated to the Madonnina del Grappa. Nearby is the Austro-Hungarian cemetery with the remains of 10,295 soldiers (only 295 of whom were identified). A small museum (open daily 09.00–12.00 and 13.00 or 14.00–16.00 or 17.00) documents the fighting.

Marostica and the Altopiano dei Sette Comuni

Marostica, a stronghold of the Ezzelini in the 12C–13C, was rebuilt in 1311–86 by the Scaligeri. It came under Venetian control in 1404 and remained faithful to the republic from then onwards. Today it is a charming old fortified townlet preserving its medieval *ramparts, which connect the lower castle on the piazza with the upper castle on the green hillside above. The biennial chess game with human combatants has become a famous spectacle. Marostica has a particularly pleasant climate, and excellent cherries are grown in the surroundings.

The town centre

The delightful **Piazza Castello**, with a stone chessboard on which the chess game is played, has a superb view of the ramparts climbing the green hillside to the upper castle. The battlemented **Castello da Basso** in the piazza was built by the Scaligeri in the early 14C (restored in 1935). It can be visited on request at the information office. There are a beautiful well and an ancient ivy in the courtyard; stairs lead up to the loggia with a catapult reconstructed in 1923. The Sala del Consiglio was frescoed in the 17C.

Chessboards are provided for the public at the other end of the piazza, in a loggia beneath a bank building (matches are often played here at weekends).

The Partita

A chess game (*Partita a Scacchi*), in which the whole town participates, takes place every two years (even years) on a Fri, Sat and Sun evening in early Sep in Piazza Castello. The match was introduced in the 20C to commemorate and reproduce a 'duel' fought in 1454 between Rinaldo d'Angarano (black) and Vieri da Vallonara (white) for the hand of Lionora, daughter of Taddeo

Parisio, the local Venetian governor. The herald's announcements are made in Venetian dialect. At the end of the game the wedding takes place, with some 500 participants in 15C costume—flag-throwers, etc. Each year a particular 'historic' chess game is chosen to be re-enacted. The game is held at 21.00 (also at 17.00 on the last day) and tickets should be bought by Jun. In odd years, when the 'players' are sent abroad to perform the game, an international chess festival is held in the town.

Via Sant'Antonio leads past the church of **Sant'Antonio**, which contains an altarpiece by Jacopo Bassano and his son Francesco (1574), to the 17C church of the Carmine. A path leads up the green hillside to the **Castello Superiore**, also built by the Scaligeri, but ruined by the Venetians in the 16C (it can also be reached by road).

Near Marostica at **San Luca di Crosara**, the parish church has an early work (c 1537) by Jacopo Bassano. South of the town is **Nove**, known for its ceramics. The Antonibon family were active here from 1727 producing majolica and porcelain, examples of which you can see in the **Museo Civico** in Palazzo De Fabris, open Tues–Thur 16.00–18.00 (15.00–17.00 in winter); Fri–Sun 10.00–12.30, 16.00–19.00 (winter 15.00–18.00). The collection is particularly representative of ceramics from the Veneto from the 18C onwards. There is also a ceramics museum in the **Istituto Statale d'Arte per la Ceramica** (founded in 1875), with a chronological display of ceramics produced in Nove from the beginning of the 18C to the present day.

Bassano and Marostica lie at the foot of the **Altopiano dei Sette Comuni**—a plateau c 1000m above sea level that takes its name from seven townships (Asiago, Enego, Foza, Gallio, Lusiana, Roana and Rotzo), united from 1310–1807 in an autonomous federation. The inhabitants of the plateau are of Germanic origin (the '*Cimbri*') and the area, which has a good climate, has been developed as a winter and summer resort since the 1960s.

Asiago, near the centre of the plateau, was the scene of bitter fighting in the First World War (1916–18); a monumental war cemetery (1932–38) has the remains of 33,086 Italian and 18,505 Austro-Hungarian dead. Nearby is a museum illustrating the history of the battles. In the battle of 15–16 June 1918, the British XIV Corps was heavily engaged, and the dead are buried in five cemeteries: Barenthal, Granezza, Cavalletto, Boscon and Magnaboschi. Near Asiago is an important astrophysical observatory, administered by Padua University, which includes the largest telescope in Italy (built in 1973). The pretty old railway line (closed down in 1958) from Asiago south to Cogollo can be followed on foot. Asiago is the centre of the area producing the cheese to which it gives its name.

Recoaro Terme is a spa with ferruginous springs discovered in 1689 (beneficial to liver, intestine and kidney complaints), with hotels of all categories. A cable car ascends to the ski resort of Recoaro Mille (1021m).

Valdagno has been known since the beginning of the century for its woollen mills. Here the late 17C **Villa Valle** (now the town hall) is open to visitors Mon–Fri 14.30–19.00; Sat 14.30–18.00 (☎ 0445 401887).

Monte Pasubio (2235m) was hotly contested in 1916–18, and a ring of boundary-stones defines the 'Zona Sacra', dedicated to those who died here. On the Pian delle Fugazzem (1159m) is the Sacello del Pasubio, another war memorial with a battle museum.

On the other side of the lovely Valle del Posina is **Tonezza del Cimone**, a mountainous plateau (1000–1500m) with fine walks. Monte Cimone, also fought over in the First World War, has a war memorial and cemetery.

Schio, in a pretty position, was once important for its wool manufacturies. It has a cathedral begun in 1740, a good 15C–16C church (San Francesco) and an ossuary-cloister on the Asiago road, with 5000 graves of soldiers who fell in 1915–18.

Treviso and the northern Veneto

North of Venice begin the *prealpi*, the foothills of the Alps, sprinkled with beautiful old towns and imposing villa and castles where Venetian notables like Caterina Cornaro and Cardinal Bembo sought respite from the summer heat. The first thing you'll notice here is the air—crisp and fragrant with mountain breezes in spring and autumn, but noticeably 'lighter' than that of Venice, even in the warm summer months. The cultural and economic capital of the area is Treviso, a lively town whose nearness to Venice (less than half an hour by train) causes most visitors to overlook it—a genuine shame. Further north are the almost unbearably pleasant towns of Castelfranco and Asolo, and the distinctly alpine centres of Feltre and Belluno, backed by one of the Eastern Alps' fabulous nature reserves. Everywhere in the region the countryside is extremely attractive.

Practical information

Getting there and getting around
By air

Treviso is served by Venice's Marco Polo International Airport, on the Venetian lagoon 25km south. Domestic flights connect with Milan, Naples, Palermo, Rome and Turin; international flights with Amsteram, Barcelona, Brussels, Copenhagen, Düsseldorf, Frankfurt, London, Lugano, Montpellier, Moscow, Munich, New York, Nice, Paris, Stüttgart, Vienna and Zurich. Treviso's little San Giuseppe Airport takes occa-sional charter flights.

By road

Treviso, Conegliano and Vittorio Veneto are located on the A27, which runs from Mestre (Venice) to Belluno, closely followed by 13 and 51. 50 connects Belluno with Feltre; 47, Feltre with Bassano del Grappa and Padua via Cittadella; 248, Bassano with Asolo; and 53, Cittadella with Castelfranco and Treviso. Acess to the area east of Treviso (Eraclea and Caorle) is provided by 53, 62, 14, 54 and 42. To reach the Parco Naturale delle Dolomiti Bellunesi take the A27 and 51 and 50 from Venice and Treviso to Belluno (north area); or 348 and 50 from Treviso to Feltre (southern area).

Buses

Run from Treviso station to Piazza Indipendenza. **Country buses** to Mestre and Venice, and to points throughout the province (information from *Dolomitibus*, ☎ 0437 941167; *Zani*, ☎ 0345 21022; *Brusutti*, ☎ 041 929333).

By rail

Treviso is on the main rail line from Venice to Udine and Tarvisio (with a through service to Vienna and Prague); from here secondary lines connect with Castelfranco, Bassano, Feltre and Belluno. There are also direct trains from Vicenza to Castelfranco and Treviso; from Padua to Castelfranco, Fanzolo, Feltre and Belluno (continuing on to Cortina d'Ampezzo).

Information offices

TREVISO Via Toniolo 41, ☎ 0422 547632.

ASOLO Piazza D'Annunzio 2, ☎ 0423 529046. Via Santa Caterina 258, ☎ 0423 529046/524192.

BELLUNO Piazza dei Martiri 27e, tel. 940083. *Informagiovani*, Piazza Duomo, ☎ 0437 913255.

CASTELFRANCO VENETO Via Francesco Maria Preti 39, ☎ 0423 495000.

CONEGLIANO Via Colombo 45, ☎ 0438 21230.

CORTINA D'AMPEZZO Piazzetta San Francesco 8, ☎ 0436 3231.

FELTRE Piazza Trento e Trieste 9, ☎ 0439 2540.

PARCO NATURALE DELLE DOLOMITI BELLUNESI Piazza Trento e Trieste 9, Feltre, ☎ 0439 2540; Via Pesaro 21, 32100 Belluno, ☎ 0437 940083.

VITTORIO VENETO Piazza del Popolo, ☎ 0438 57243.

Where to stay

TREVISO *Al Foghèr*, Viale della Repubblica 10, ☎ 0422 432950, fax 0422 430391; in a nicely renovated building with a renowned restaurant, outside the city centre on the road to Padua; moderate.

Campeol, Piazza Ancilotto 11, ☎ 0422 56601, fax 0422 540871; a small (14 rooms), family-run establishment with a good restaurant, a stone's throw from Piazza dei Signori; inexpensive.

Scala, Viale Felissent 1, ☎ 0422 307600, fax 0422 305048; another small hotel (20 rooms) in a patrician home next to the gardens of Villa Manfrin, on the road to Conegliano; inexpensive.

ASOLO *Al Sole*, Via Collegio 33, ☎ 0423 528111, fax 0423 528399; a lovely old palace, recently restored, in the heart of Asolo; moderate. *Duse*, Via Robert Browning 190, ☎ 0423 55241, fax 0423 950404; a small (12 rooms), comfortable and centrally located hotel; moderate.

Villa Cipriani, Via Canova 298, ☎ 0423 952166, fax 0423 952166; surely one of the more charming (and restful) hotels in the region, occupying a 16C villa with splended views over the hills of Asolo; expensive.

BASSANO DEL GRAPPA *Belvedere*, Piazzale Generale Giardino 14, ☎ 0424 529845, fax 0424 529849; pleasant, with a renowned restaurant; moderate.

Brennero, Via Torino 7, ☎ 0424 228544, fax 0424 227021; comfortable; inexpensive.

Palladio, Via Gramsci 2, ☎ 0424 523777, fax 0424 524050; modern and efficient; moderate.

Victoria, Viale Diaz 33, ☎ 0424 503620, fax 0424 503130; small and comfortable; inexpensive.

BELLUNO *Alle Dolomiti*, Via Carrera 46, ☎ 0437 941660, fax 0437 941436; modern, comfortable and centrally located; inexpensive.

Astor, Piazza dei Martiri 26e, ☎ 0437 942094, fax 0437 942493; on a lovely square in the city centre; inexpensive.
Delle Alpi, Via Jacopo Tasso 13, ☎ 0437 940545, fax 0437 940565; a comfortable place with a good restaurant, in a house midway between the train station and the cathedral; moderate.
Villa Carpenada, Via Mier 158, ☎ 0437 948343, fax 0437 948345; a calm, relaxing hotel in an 18C villa with park, 2km west of the city centre; moderate.
CASTELFRANCO VENETO *Alla Torre*, Piazzetta Trento e Trieste 7, ☎ 0423 498707, fax 0423 498737; in a tastefully renovated old home conveniently located in the heart of the historic city centre; moderate.
Al Moretto, Via San Pio X 10, ☎ 0423 721313, fax 0423 721066; another renovated old home, this time dating from the 17C, managed by the same family for three generations; inexpensive.
Roma, Via F. Filzi 39, ☎ 0423 721616, fax 0423 721515; overlooking Piazza Giorgione and the town walls, a comfortable hotel with private parking; inexpensive.
At Salvarosa, 3km northeast, are *Fior*, Via dei Carpani 18, ☎ 0423 721212, fax 0423 498771; a very comfortable place in an old patrician home with garden; moderate.
Ca' delle Rose, Circonvallazione Est 33a, ☎ 0423 490232, fax 0423 490261; yet another tastefully restored old building, with warm, comfortable rooms and modern facilities; inexpensive.
FELTRE *Doriguzzi*, Viale Piave 2, ☎ 0439 2902, fax 0439 83660; centrally located; moderate. *Nuovo*, Vicolo Fornere Pazze 5, ☎ 0439 2110, fax 0439 89241; modern and efficient; inexpensive.
MUSSOLENTE *Villa Palma*, Via Chemin Palma 30, ☎ 0424 577407, fax 0424 87687; a lovely villa (20 rooms), with an excellent restaurant;

moderate.
Volpara, ☎ 0423 567766, fax 0424 968841; small and quiet, also with good restaurant; inexpensive.

 ## Eating out

TREVISO *Al Bersagliere*, Via Barberia 21, ☎ 0422 541988; offering traditional Trevisan dishes with a personal twist—the building dates from the 13C; closed midday Sat, Sun, Jan and Aug; inexpensive.
Alfredo-Relais el Toulà, Via Collalto 26, ☎ 0422 540275; an elegant restaurant in a historic building, serving regional specialties and classic Italian dishes with a wide selection of regional, Italian and imported wines; closed Sun evening, Mon and Aug; moderate.
All'Antico Torre, Via Inferiore 55, ☎ 0422 53694; also in a historic building in the old city, specialising in regional and seafood dishes; closed Sun and Aug; moderate. At Preganziol (4km south), *Ombre Rosse*, Via Franchetti 78, Località San Trovaso, ☎ 0422 490037; osteria and wine bar in an old farmhouse; closed Sun, Jan and Aug; inexpensive. At Quinto di Treviso (5km west), *Da Righetto*, Via Ciardi 2, ☎ 0422 379101; trattoria (with rooms) renowned for its eel dishes; closed Mon and Jan; inexpensive.
ASOLO *Charley's One*, Via Roma 55, ☎ 0423 952201; wholesome, straightforward regional cuisine in a warm atmosphere with wood panelling and antique furniture; closed Wed evening, Thur, Jan and Feb; moderate.
Due Mori, Piazza D'Annunzio 5, ☎ 0423 952256; restaurant with rooms, offering delicious regional dishes on a panoramic terrace in summer; closed Wed; moderate.
Tavernetta, Via Schiavonesca 45, ☎ 0423 952273; an old tavern at once rustic and refined; closed Tues and Jul; inexpensive.
At Pagnano, 2km west, *Bacco e*

Tabacco, Via Ponte Pagnano 3, ☎ 0423 529475; dedicated, as the name suggests, to wine and tobacco and offering a limited but delicious menu; closed Mon, midday Tues and Aug; moderate. *La Trave*, Via Bernardi 5, ☎ 0423 952292; small, traditional, trattoria; closed Mon, Feb and Aug; inexpensive.

BASSANO DEL GRAPPA *Al Ponte-da Renzo*, Via Volpato 60, tel. 0424 503055; honest local food and wine; closed Mon evening, Tues and Jan; moderate.

Bauto, Via Trozzetti 27 , ☎ 0424 34696; an inexpensive place with a great deal of rustic charm, run by the same family since 1917; closed Sun and Aug.

San Bassiano, Viale dei Martiri 36, ☎ 0424 521453; renowned for its selection of regional dishes, prepared with skill and care, for its fine local cheeses and for its extensive list of regional, Italian and imported wines; closed Sun and Aug; expensive.

Wine bar: *Breda*, Vicolo Iacopo da Ponte 3.

BELLUNO *Al Borgo*, Via Anconetta 8, ☎ 0437 926755; traditional fare and regional, Italian and imported wines in an 18C villa with gardens; closed Mon evening, Tues, Jan and Jul; inexpensive. At San Gregorio nelle Alpi, 16km southwest near the road to Feltre,

Locanda a l'Arte, Via Belvedere 43 , ☎ 0437 800124; another family-run establishment with garden (and fine views), serving personalised versions of traditional regional cuisine; closed Mon and midday Tues; inexpensive. At Pieve d'Alpago, 17km east, near the road to Treviso,

Dolada (with rooms), ☎ 0437 479141; a more elegant (and somewhat more expensive) garden restaurant showing an innovative approach to traditional regional recipes; closed midday Mon and Tues except Jul–Aug, and Feb; moderate.

CASTELFRANCO VENETO *Alle Mura*, Via Preti 69, ☎ 0423 498098; an elegant place set against the medieval town walls and specialising in seafood; closed Thur, Jan and Aug; moderate.

Al Teatro, Via Garibaldi 17, ☎ 0423 721425; situated across from the Teatro Accademico, traditional and dependable; closed Mon and Aug; inexpensive.

Osteria ai Due Mori, Vicolo Montebelluna 24 , ☎ 0423 497174; small but excellent selection of refined, innovative dishes, especially made with game and with mushrooms; closed Wed, midday Thur and Sep; moderate.

At Cison di Valmarino (15km west), *Ad Andreetta*, Via Enotria 5–7, Località Rolle, ☎ 0438 85761; good country restaurant famous among locals for its panoramic terrace; closed Wed and Aug–Sep; inexpensive. At Salvarosa (4km northeast), in the *Cà delle Rose* hotel, *Barbesin*, ☎ 0423 490446, menu especially rich in vegetables and regional and Italian wines; closed Wed evening and Thur, Dec–Jan and Aug.

CAVASO DEL TOMBA (9km north of Asolo) *Al Ringraziamento*, Via San Pio X 107, ☎ 0423 543271; restaurant famous for its delicious seasonal dishes; closed Mon, midday Tues and Aug; moderate.

CONEGLIANO *Al Salisà*, Via XX Settembre 2, ☎ 0438 24288; an elegant restaurant in an old building with garden, awarded the Accademia Italiana della Cucina's *Diploma Cucina Eccellente* in 1995; closed Tues evening, Wed and Aug; moderate. *Tre Panoce*, Via Vecchia Trevigiana 50, ☎ 0438 60071; impeccably prepared regional dishes plus extraordinary ambience in an 18C villa with gardens; closed Sun evening, Mon, Jan and Aug; moderate.

Wine bar: *Due Spade*, Via Beato Ongaro 69. At Colfosco, 9km southwest, *All'Antica Trattoria da Checco*, Via San Daniele 56, ☎ 0438 781386; simple osteria on a hill overlooking the

Piave; closed Mon evening, Tues and Jan; inexpensive.

CROCETTA DEL MONTELLO *Casa Brusanda*, Via Erizzo 117, ☎ 0423 86614;

traditional trattoria in a house with a story; closed Sun evening and Mon, Jan, Aug and Sep.

FELTRE Although just about any place in town will be satisfactory, there are a couple of real musts out in the hills. At Miane, 32km southeast, is the area's finest restaurant,

Da Gigetto, ☎ 0438 960020; where regional dishes are served with an original twist, the wine list is endless, and there is summer service in the garden; closed Mon evening, Tues, Jan and Aug; expensive.

At Cavaso del Tomba, 26km southwest, is *Al Ringraziamento*, Via San Pio X 107, ☎ 0423 543271; where traditional regional specialities are prepared with skill and imagination; closed Mon, Tues morning and Aug; moderate.

Entertainment

TREVISO *Teatro Comunale*, classical concert season, Oct–Jan.

ASOLO *Annual Chamber Music Festival*, Sep.

BELLUNO Classical music at sites around the town throughout the year. Jazz and ethnic or antique music, in city squares and at Centro Giovanni XXIII, Jun–Sep.

ELSEWHERE Live music in clubs and bars, and dancing at discotheques throughout the area.

Shopping

Here as elsewhere in the Veneto, the name of the game is **fine foods**. Especially good are local farm cheeses, grappas (some flavoured with blueberries, mugo pine, juniper or other essences), herbal liqueurs, honey, mushrooms, etc. There is an **antiques** fair in Belluno, Jun–Sep (fourth Sun of the month). Strong local **crafts** are woodcarving and wrought-iron work.

Special events

TREVISO *Treviso in Fior*, flower show, May–Sep; *Concorso Internazionale Cantanti Lirici*, opera competition, Jun; *Autunno Musicale Trevigiano*, classical music, Oct–Dec; *Concorso Nazionale di Esecuzione Pianistica*, classical piano competition, Dec.

BELLUNO *Oltre le Vette*, cinema, round tables and exhibitions on mountaineering, Oct.

FELTRE *Palio della Città*, historic pageant, first weekend in Aug.

Sports

BELLUNO Professional **soccer** (*Belluno Ponte*) at Baldenich Stadium. **Golf** at Pian del Cansiglio (*Golf Club Cansiglio*). **Horse-riding** at La Costa and Cirvoi. **Ice-skating** at Palaghiaccio. **Mountain-biking** (on World Cup trials) and **downhill skiing** at Nevegal.

PARCO NATURALE DELLE DOLOMITI BELLUNESI Hiking, **climbing**, **swimming**, **cross-country** and **back-country skiing** in many park locations.

ELSEWHERE Excellent, challenging **cycling** throughout the area.

TREVISO

· · · · · · · · ·

A city of porticoed streets and fine old houses situated at the confluence of two rivers, Treviso (population 83,000) is known for its medieval atmosphere and for the picturesque canals that flow through and around the old centre, giving the town its nickname, 'Little Venice'. Gardens are everywhere, and are particularly lush. A flourishing manufacturing and agricultural centre, Treviso is home to a number of leading Italian entrepreneurs, and its high standard of living is clearly evident.

History

Although a palaeo-Venetic settlement and a Roman *municipium*, called *Tarvisium*, existed on more or less the same area the old city occupies today, Treviso reached its greatest prosperity in the Middle Ages. It was the centre of a Lombard duchy, then the capital of a Carolingian *marca*, or frontier buffer zone, a free commune, a seignory and, after 1389, a component of the Venetian Republic. Old prints showning Treviso as a fortified city bear witness to the importance that Venetian military planners gave to its strategic location, on the northwestern border of their republic. The town walls were considered impenetrable, and their impression of fortitude was enhanced by the fact that they were pierced by just three gates: Porta Altinia, Porta Santi Quaranta and Porta San Tomaso. Only the 18C agricultural revolution and the consequent construction of patrician residences in the countryside to the north, brought expansion outside the walls.

In the Middle Ages, Treviso was well known for its hospitality to poets and artists, especially under the dominion of the Da Camino family (1283–1312). Today the city has the best works of Tommaso da Modena, a brilliant follower of Giotto. Unfortunately, little else remains of its medieval past: during both world wars it suffered severely from air raids, notably on Good Friday 1944, when half the city was destroyed in a few minutes.

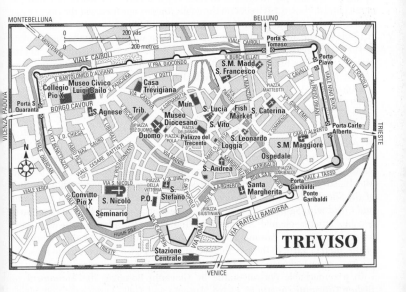

Piazza dei Signori

Since Roman times, the political and social centre of the city has been the beautiful Piazza dei Signori, with palaces built in the 13C on the site of the Roman forum. The most important of these is the **Palazzo dei Trecento**, named after the 300 members of the Greater Council. It was built on the east side of the square in 1210 and has a ground-floor loggia of 1552 on the main façade. An external staircase and another 16C loggia grace the flank facing Piazza Independenza. On the north side of the square is the **Palazzo del Podestà** (now the Prefecture), surmounted by the Torre Civica, which the Trevisans call *Il Campanon* ('The Big Bell'). Both were rebuilt in the 19C in a Gothic-revival style. Next door is the **Palazzo Pretorio**, with a rusticated façade of the 17C.

In a little square behind these buildings is the **Monte di Pietà** (open Fri 09.00–12.00), which incorporates the 16C Cappella dei Rettori, a small chapel with gilt-leather wall coverings of the 17C, frescoes and canvases, and a fine ceiling. On your right as you return are **Santa Lucia** and **San Vito**, two adjoining churches of medieval origin. The more interesting is Santa Lucia, a 14C building containing frescoes by Tommaso da Modena and his school (*Madonna delle Carceri*), and 14C and 15C sculptures, notably busts of Saints on the balustrade. San Vito, built in the 11C and 12C and rebuilt in 1568, conserves a Byzantine-Romanesque fresco of the 12C or 13C depicting *Christ among the Apostles*.

The Cathedral

Views of considerable charm are offered along the **Via Calmaggiore**, the street that joins Piazza dei Signori with Piazza del Duomo. The street is lined with 15C and 16C townhouses, many with porticoes and frescoed façades. Just before meeting Piazza del Duomo it passes (left) the church of **San Giovanni**, or baptistery, a Romanesque building of the late 11C and early 12C with pilaster strips, small blind arches, a 14C relief on the gable, Roman-age friezes at the sides of the doorway and, within, some fresco fragments of the 12C–14C in the apses. Behind rises the massive 11C and 12C campanile, unfinished at the top.

The **Cathedral** of San Pietro was founded in the late 12C or early 13C, but its present form has little in common with the original church. The apses were rebuilt in the 15C and 16C to a design by Pietro Lombardo, the central structure was altered in the 18C, and the façade with its Ionic hexastyle porch was added in 1836.

The three-aisled **interior**, covered by seven lead-and-copper domes, contains an *Adoration of the Shepherds* by Paris Bordone, a statue of *St John the Baptist* by Alessandro Vittoria and a marble relief of the *Annunciation* by Lorenzo Bregno (or Antonio Lombardo). The Cappella dell'Annunziata, at the end of the south aisle, was built to a design by Martino Lombardo in 1519 for the Malchiostro family. In the vestibule are several sculptures, notably an *Adoration of the Shepherds* and *St Lawrence and Saints* by Paris Bordone and a *Madonna and Child with Saints* (the 'Madonna of the Flower') by Girolamo da Treviso il Vecchio. Titian's splendid *Annunciation* hangs over the altar, and the walls have frescoes by Giovanni Antonio Pordenone and assistants, notably the *Adoration of the Magi* (1520). In the sanctuary, designed by Pietro Lombardo and his sons, are frescoes by Lodovico Seitz (1880); the tomb of Pope Alexander VIII (d. 1691), with a remarkable portrait-statue by Giovanni Bonazza; the *Monument to Bishop Giovanni Zanetto* by Pietro, Antonio and Tullio Lombardo; and, above the altar, the **Urn of Sts Teonisto, Tabra and Tabrata**, with carved portraits attributed to Tullio Lombardo. In the Cappella del Santissimo Sacramento (on the north; 1513) are more Renaissance sculptures, by Pietro and Tullio Lombardo and Lorenzo Bregno. Beneath the sanctuary extends the 12C and 13C Romanesque crypt, with mosaic pavement fragments and remains of frescoes. The capitals on the columns were taken from earlier buildings.

Treviso museums

Flanking the cathedral is the Bishop's Palace, built in the 12C and 13C and later altered, with a large hall frescoed by Benedetto Calieri. From Piazza Duomo, Via Canoniche leads under an arch to a circular Roman mosaic, an early-Christian work of the early 4C AD, probably belonging to a baptistery.

The **Museo Diocesano di Arte Sacra** (Via Canoniche 9, open Mon–Thur 09.00–12.00; Sat 09.00–12.00, 15.00–18.00), located in the recently restored Canoniche Vecchie, displays paintings, sculpture, and liturgical items. Highlights include the **Arca del Beato Enrico**, acquired by the commune in 1315; several marble reliefs from the cathedral (notably a 13C **Enthroned Christ**); a detached fresco by Tommaso da Modena, and tapestries and objects from the cathedral treasury.

The continuation of Via Calmaggiore, Via Canova, leads over a small canal and past a pleasant garden to the **Museo della Casa Trevigiana** (no. 38). Occupying the Casa da Noal, a 15C Gothic mansion, it contains medieval and Renaissance marbles and terracottas, wood sculptures of the 15C–18C, furniture, ceramics, wrought iron, weapons, and antique prints and musical instruments, shown on a rotating basis. Next door (no. 40) is the Casa Robegan, a Renaissance townhouse decorated with faded 16C frescoes. More old homes, some with 15C and 16C frescoes, stand in the nearby Via Riccati.

Continuing westward, you soon reach the **Museo Civico Luigi Bailo** (open Tues–Sat 09.00–12.00, 14.00–17.00, Sun and holidays 09.00–12.00), which displays the municipal collections of art and archaeology. In the **archaeological section** are Copper, Bronze and Iron Age objects (axes, fibulae and swords), Roman material (sarcophagi, tablets, sculpture, portraits and small bronzes) and early Christian and Byzantine sculpture. In the **picture gallery** are paintings, frescoes, and statues of the 12C–20C, with works by Giovanni Bellini (**Madonna**), Cima da Conegliano, Girolamo da Treviso, Girolamo da Santacroce, Titian (**Portrait of Sperone Speroni**), Lorenzo Lotto (the famous *Portrait of a Dominican*), Jacopo Bassano (**Crucifixion**), Govanni Antonio da Pordenone, Francesco Guardi (**View of the Isle of San Giorgio**), Gian Domenico Tiepolo, Pietro Longhi and Rosalba Carriera (three portraits). There are also 19C works by Francesco Hayez and Antonio Canova, and sculptures and drawings by the 20C Trevisan artist Arturo Martini. A section of the museum housed in the former Gothic church of Santa Caterina dei Servi contains an important cycle of detached frescoes by Tommaso da Modena and a fragmentary **Madonna** by Gentile da Fabriano. The museum also owns the prisms with which Newton made his experiments with the refraction of light, and which passed into the hands of his disciple Count Algarotti.

At the end of the street is **Porta Santi Quaranta**, a town gate of 1517. To the north is the most interesting stretch of city wall, built by Fra Giocondo and others in 1509–18, the top of which has been laid out as a pleasant walk almost as far as Porta San Tomaso, another fine gateway. The wall itself is better seen from the gardens outside.

The southern quarters

From the Museo Bailo it is a short walk southwards to the 14C Dominican church of **San Nicolò**, with a fine rose window and doorway on the façade, slender windows on the flanks and three tall polygonal apses. The vast three-aisled **interior**, with a beautiful ship's-keel ceiling, has frescoes by Tommaso da Modena and his school on the columns and other paintings ranging from the 16C to the 18C. In the south chapels are a finely carved altar of Lombardesque workmanship, a large fresco of *St Christopher* attributed to Antonio da Treviso (1410), and a 16C organ by Gaetano Callido with shutters painted by Antonio Palma. In the apse are a *Sacra Conversazione* begun by Fra' Marco Pensaben and completed by Giovan Gerolamo Savoldo (1521), a 17C *Memorial to St Benedict XI* (Nicolò Bocassino, 1240–1303, born in Treviso and the founder of the church) and (left) the 16C *Tomb of Agostino Onigo*, incorporating a fresco of *Pages* attributed to Lorenzo Lotto.

Next to the church is the former convent of San Nicolò, now the **Seminario Vescovile** (open 08.00–12.30, 15.30–17.30 or 19.00). The complex is connected by cloisters to the 14C chapter house, which is decorated with charmingly realistic frescoes (1352) of 40 eminent Dominicans by Tommaso da Modena. The Abbot of Cluny wears on his nose the first pictorially documented pair of eyeglasses. The complex also houses two small museums, the Museo Etnografico Dino Grossa, displaying articles from the Venezuelan Amazon; and the Museo Zoologico Giuseppe Scarpa, with Italian fauna and exotic reptiles.

The northern quarters

In Via Martiri della Libertà, leading northeast from the Corso dei Popolo, is the **Loggia dei Cavalieri**, a Romanesque building of 1195. Near San Leonardo, beyond remains of an old watermill beneath a modern building, is the picturesque **fish market** on an island in the Cagnan. Via San Parisio continues left to **San Francesco**, a large brick church of the 13C. In the floor near the south door is the tomb slab of Francesca, daughter of Petrarch, who died in childbirth in 1384; in the north transept that of Pietro Alighieri (d. 1364), the son of Dante; and in the chapel to the left of the high altar is a fresco by Tommaso da Modena (1351).

The deconsecrated church of **Santa Caterina** (open Fri–Sun 09.00–12.00, 15.30–18.30) stands a little to the east of the fish market. It contains fine frescoes by Tommaso da Modena, including some detached in 1882 from a church before its demolition (*Virgin Annunciate* and *Story of the Life of St Ursula*).

Via Carlo Alberto leads to **Santa Maria Maggiore**, a church of 1474 containing a tomb by Bambaia and a much-venerated *Madonna* originally frescoed by Tommaso da Modena. The delightful Riviera Garibaldi (reminiscent of Amsterdam), alongside the Sile, returns towards the centre.

The Valley of the Piave

East of the city, San Donà di Piave is on the Piave, a river famous as the line of Italian resistance after the retreat from Caporetto in 1917–18. At Fossalta di Piave, Ernest Hemingway, as a member of the US Red Cross, was wounded in

1918 at the age of 19 (the episode is described in *A Farewell to Arms*). A memorial stele was set up here in 1979.

Eraclea, a modern village on the Piave, has taken the name of the ancient *Heraclea* (called after Emperor Heraclius), the episcopal and administrative centre of the Venetian lagoon in the 7C–8C after the sack of Oderzo by the Lombards. The site of the ancient city, near Cittànova, has been identified by aerial photography. It was formerly surrounded by a lagoon, and it recalls Venice in plan, with a central canal and many smaller canals. From 750 onwards the inhabitants migrated to the safer islands of Malamocco and Rialto, and a leader from Heraclea is thought to have become the first Doge of Venice. Heraclea rapidly declined as its lagoon silted up and Venice grew in importance.

Caorle is an ancient fishing village and now a seaside resort near the mouth of the Livenza. Founded by refugees from Concordia (see p 532), it was a bishop's see for 12 centuries and has a cathedral of 1048 with a celebrated Venetian pala of gilded silver. The beautiful lagoon to the north (Valle Vecchia, etc.), with its fishing huts and interesting wildlife, may become a nature reserve.

Castelfranco Veneto

Castelfranco Veneto is west of Treviso. A medieval chronicle narrates that those who settled in this *castello* were freed (*affrancati*) of all fiscal obligations. The town was founded by the commune of Treviso in 1199 to defend its western frontier, and a rectangular fortification with five towers and brick walls and doorways, encircled by a moat (the **castello** proper), still encloses its centre. Throughout the town are small porticoed palaces, some of them frescoed. The sky, the clouds, and green fields of the environs are those of Giorgione (1477/78–1510) who was born and began to paint here.

The **Cathedral** (San Liberale) was erected in 1723–45 to plans by Francesco Maria Preti, in a Palladian style. Inside, in the south apsidal chapel, is Giorgione's famous altarpiece of the ***Madonna and Child with Sts Francis and Liberale*** (c 1505) and, in the sacristy, works by Palma Giovane and Jacopo Bassano and early frescoes by Paolo Veronese (***Allegorical Figures***, 1551) brought from the destroyed Villa Soranza; the campanile of the church is one of the towers of the defensive walls.

Adjoining the piazza, on the east, is the 15C **Casa di Giorgione** (or Casa Pellizzari), where Giorgione lived and worked (he painted the chiaroscuro decorative band, with symbols of the liberal and mechanical arts, in one room). Inside are reproductions of works by the painter, a small picture gallery, and collections of prehistoric and Roman antiquities, Venetian objects, minerals and medals. Also noteworthy is the **Teatro Accademico**, in the nearby Via Garibaldi. Designed by Francesco Maria Preti in 1754, it has a brick façade and four-tiered stuccoed interior.

Outside the walls are the old market square (now Piazza Giorgione), lined with 16C–18C townhouses, some with frescoed façades; the church of **Santa Maria della Pieve** (founded in the 11C, but rebuilt 1821–25, with a Corinthian porch; and the Villa Revedin-Bolasco (built in 1607 by Vincenzo Scamozzi, but remodelled in the 19C), surrounded by a large park with an open amphitheatre decorated with statues by Orazio Marinali.

The area around Castelfranco abounds with magnificent villas. At Istrana, on the Treviso road, the 18C **Villa Lattes**, now part of the Museo Civico of Treviso (open Mar–Nov, Tues and Fri 09.00–12.00; Sat–Sun and holidays 09.00–12.00, 15.00–18.00), has a collection of furniture, Oriental art, musical boxes and 19C dolls. At Sant'Andrea, the **Villa Corner** (now Chiminelli; open by appointment, ☎ 0424 525103) has frescoes of the school of Veronese. Fanzolo di Vedelago, a small farm town 8km northeast, is known for the splendid **Villa Emo** (c 1564), one of Palladio's masterpieces. The central building, preceded by a wide, stepped ramp, has a monumental porch with seven Doric columns surmounted by triangular pediments. At the sides are two long, symmetrical *barchesse* terminating in the little towers of the dovecotes. The interior is frescoed with mythological scenes by G.B. Zelotti, possibly with the help of Paolo Veronese (open in daylight-savings time months, daily 15.00–19.00, Sun and holidays also 10.00–12.30; in standard time months, Sat–Sun and holidays 14.00–18.00). Another villa by Palladio, the Villa Cornaro (1560–70), is at Piombino Dese, 10km southeast. At nearby Treville are remains of the Villa Priuli Gran Can (1530) and Villa Priuli San Felice, by Vincenzo Scamozzi.

ASOLO

• • • • • • •

Called 'City of a Hundred Horizons' and 'Pearl of the Veneto', Asolo is a charming little town with numerous private villas surrounded by luxuriant gardens and picturesque old streets with miniature arcades and a number of fountains. A bus ascends to the centre of the little town from the main road (bus stop) and car park.

The town was presented by Venice to Queen Caterina Cornaro in exchange for her dominions of Cyprus, and she lived in the castle here from 1489 to 1509. From the name of this town Cardinal Bembo (who frequented Queen Catherine's court) coined the term '*asolare*' (to gambol, amuse oneself at random), from which is derived 'Asolando', the name chosen by Robert Browning 'for love of the place' for his last volume of poems (1899). Browning's first visit to Asolo was in 1836, and it is the scene of 'Pippa Passes', published five years later. The actress Eleonora Duse (1850–1924), and Browning's son Pen (1849–1912) are both buried at Asolo in the cemetery of Sant'Anna. Dame Freya Stark (1893–1993), the traveller and writer, lived here for most of her life. Asolo's other eminent visitors include writers Giosuè Carducci, Henry James and Ernest Hemingway; composers Gian Francesco Malipiero and Arnold Schönberg; and architect Carlo Scarpa.

Exploring the town

By the entrance gate nearest the car park is **La Mura**, a palace where Browning stayed on his second visit to the town, and where Eleonora Duse later lived. **Villa Freia**, where Freya Stark lived, is on the right, preceded by a little garden (the house is now owned by the province). Nearby is a weaving school founded in 1840 and later run by Freya Stark's mother (usually open Mon–Sat 08.00–12.00, 16.00–19.00).

Via Browning, with delightful little arcades along one side, continues from the gate past another house where Browning stayed (plaque) to **Piazza Brugnoli**, overlooked by the grandiose **Villa Scotti**, with its impressive terraced garden.

Below the piazza is the **Duomo**, rebuilt in 1747 on remains of Roman baths. It contains a copy of Titian's *Martyrdom of St Laurence*, a baptismal font by Francesco Graziolo donated to the church by Caterina Cornaro, two angels by Torretti, and two paintings of the *Assumption*, by Jacopo Bassano (1549) and Lorenzo Lotto (1506; with an interesting predella).

In the central **Piazza Maggiore** (officially Piazza Garibaldi) is the 15C **Loggia del Capitano** with a fine portico and frescoed façade of 1560. Once the seat of municipal government, today it hosts the **Museo Civico** (closed at the time of writing), with palaeontological and archaeological collections, historical memorabilia, and 15C to 20C paintings and sculpture.

Impressions of Asolo

I assure you that, even though I have knowledge of and have seen with my own eyes the most beautiful panoramas in Italy and elsewhere, I have found nothing quite like the view one can enjoy from the tower of the Queen's palace.
Robert Browning

I love Asolo because it is so beautiful and peaceful, a town full of fine lace and poetry.
Eleonora Duse

Neither San Gimignano, Siena, nor Volterra takes my breath away as does Asolo, a town that from my very first visit has ruled my emotions and made me its slave.
Gian Francesco Malipiero

Standing atop the rocca, you feel as if you are perched on a diamond, one whose every facet sparkles with incomparable brilliance.
Giovanni Comisso

Just out of the piazza are the remains of the **castle** where Caterina Cornaro lived (before she moved downhill to the larger Barco at Attivole). It incorporates the **Teatro Duse**, which was sold to America at the beginning of this century but is now being reconstructed. At present only the battlements of the castle may be visited. Part of the large garden that surrounded the castle was purchased by Browning (despite local opposition) so that he could construct here the Villa La Torricella (in Via Sottocastello) for his son Pen.

The empty **rocca**, above the town, is open on weekends: there are fine views from the ramparts. It can be reached by a pleasant path that follows the walls from Porta Colmarion (or by car from Via Rocca).

The imposing **Palazzo Beltramini** is now the town hall; Eleonora Duse's home is in the Contrada Canova (marked), near Porta Santa Caterina. Eleonora Duse and Freya Stark are buried in the cemetery by the church of Sant'Anna; and Carlo Scarpa's Brion tomb (a 'cult' piece among modern architects) is in the cemetery of San Vito di Altivole, 5km southeast of the town. On the hills surrounding Asolo are some pretty villas with lovely gardens, including Villa Armena.

Around Asolo ~ Villa Barbaro

The countryside around Asolo—a harmonious ensemble of handsome farms and vineyards—is enchanting, and it is dotted with fine old villas, such as the 18C **Villa Falier**, on the outskirts of the town, visited for its lovely park; or the 17C **Villa Rinaldi Barbini** at Casella, an exuberant Baroque creation decorated by Andrea Celesti and Pietro Liberi.

At **Maser** in a lovely setting at the foot of the hills of Asolo, is the *****Villa Barbaro** (now Villa Luling Buschetti), built by Palladio in the late 1550s for Daniele Barbaro, patriarch of Aquileia. This villa is one of the architect's higher achievements: following the traditional plan of the Venetian Renaissance farm, it has a central manor house with engaged Ionic columns and carved tympanum, and symmetrical porticoed *barchesse*. The interior (open Mar–Oct, Tues, Sat–Sun and holidays 15.00–18.00; Nov–Feb, Sat–Sun and holidays 14.30–17.00) contains beautiful *frescoes (1560–62) by Veronese (see the cover of this Blue Guide) and stuccoes by Alessandro Vittoria. In the grounds are a nymphaeum and a carriage museum. The little **tempietto**, a private chapel built on a centralised plan, was one of Palladio's last works (1580).

Montebelluna, near Maser, has local archaeological and natural history exhibits in the **Museo Civico Bellona** (open summer, Tues–Sun 09.00–12.30, 15.30–18.00 or 19.00; winter 09.00–12.30 and 14.30–17.30 or 19.00) and a unique collection of hiking boots at the **Museo dello Scarpone** (open Mon–Sat 09.00–12.00, 15.00–18.00; Sun and holidays until 19.00). Both museums are housed in lovely villas.

Possagno, northwest of Asolo, was the birthplace of the sculptor Antonio Canova (1757–1822). His house and a museum of models and plaster casts of his works are open Tues–Sun 09.00–12.00, 14.00 or 15.00–17.00 or 18.00. The **Tempio**, now the parish church, was designed by Canova as his burial place.

Conegliano Veneto and Vittorio Veneto

The wine-growing town of Conegliano Veneto, noted also as the birthplace of the painter Giovanni Battista Cima (c 1459–1518), has many attractive 16C–18C houses, especially in the central Via XX Settembre. The **Casa di Cima** (Via Cima 24; open Sat–Sun 16.00 or 17.00–18.00 or 19.00) has an archive dedicated to the painter. The **Cathedral** (14C–15C) contains a fine altarpiece by Cima (1492); the adjacent guildhall ('Scuola dei Battuti'; open Thur–Tues 09.00–12.00, 15.00–19.00) is covered with 16C frescoes attributed to Pozzoserrato, and inside are frescoes by Andrea Previtali, Jacopo da Montagnana, Francesco da Milano and Gerolamo da Treviso. In the main piazza is the Neo-classical **theatre** (1846–68). Above rises the ruined **castle**, with a museum in one tower (open Tues–Sun 08.00 or 09.00–12.00, 14.00 or 15.30–17.30 or 19.00), and the Oratorio di Sant'Orsola.

Vittorio Veneto was, by a twist of fate, the site of the final victory of the Italians over the Austrians in October 1918. It was created in 1866 by merging the lower (now industrial) district of Ceneda with the old walled town of *Serravalle. Ceneda has a museum relating to the battle (open daily except Mon and Fri, 10.00–12.00, 15.00 or 16.00–17.00 or 18.00) in the former town hall. In the fine main piazza of Serravalle is the **Loggia di Serravalle** (1462), the old town hall. The **Museo del Canedese**, here, contains local archaeological finds, paintings, frescoes, etc. (open 15.00–18.00; in winter 09.00–12.00; Sat–Sun and holidays 09.00–12.00, 15.00–17.30). The 14C **Cathedral**, rebuilt in 1776, contains a fine altarpiece by Titian (1547). **San Giovanni Battista** (1357) has 15C frescoes (some attributed to Jacobello del Fiore) and **Santa Giustina**, the tomb (1336–40) of Rizzardo IV da Camino.

Above Vittorio Veneto is the **Bosco del Cansiglio**, a high-lying plateau with forests of beech and fir (1120m) to the east. There is a natural history museum here (open in summer). The village of Oderzo was the Roman *Opitergium*, finds from which are exhibited in the Museo Civico. The cathedral, founded in the 10C, was rebuilt in Gothic style in the 14C.

Feltre

The northern Veneto, where the Dolomites merge with the white limestone peaks of the eastern Alps, is renowned above all for its ski resorts, the most famous of which is Cortina d'Ampezzo. But there are also a number of places you can visit out of season, where natural beauty goes hand-in-hand with historical heritage.

History

Feltre was a Roman centre, probably a *municipium*, and before that it may have been a Raetian community on the Via Opitergium–Tridentum. In the Middle Ages it was a free commune and a seignory of various families before coming under Venice in 1404. The Venetian heads of state dated their dispatches *ex cineribus Feltri*, 'from the ashes of Feltre', after forces of the Holy Roman Empire sacked the city twice (in 1509 and 1510) during the War of the Cambrai League. The architectural uniformity of the city centre, Feltre's most distinctive asset, is a direct consequence of this double debacle and of the ambitious programme of reconstruction that followed it.

The city centre

The old walled city has numerous 16C buildings with projecting roofs and façades bearing frescoes or graffiti. Almost all the city gates date from the Renaissance. The porticoed Via Mezzaterra begins at the 16C Porta Imperiale, or Castaldi, and runs uphill through the old city to the Renaissance **Piazza Maggiore**. This is laid out on several levels. On the north side stands the church of San Rocco (1599); the fine fountain is attributed to Tullio Lombardo (1520). On the west is the 19C Gothic-revival Palazzo Guarnieri; and on the south, the unusual **Palazzo della Ragione** or Palazzo del Municipio, actually two buildings meeting at the corner—the one with the rusticated arcade (1558) is the former Palazzo dei Rettori Veneti, attributed to Palladio. Inside is a small wooden theatre of 1802. Above

Piazza Maggiore

the square rises the **castello** with its square keep, a Roman watchtower rebuilt in the Middle Ages.

The continuation of Via Mezzaterra, called **Via Luzzo**, is lined with interesting houses. Note especially no. 3, Palazzo Banchieri, with a graffitied façade; no. 13, Palazzo Pasole, and no. 23, Palazzo Villabruna, a Venetian-Gothic-revival building now home to the **Museo Civico** (open Tues–Sun, Apr–Oct 10.00–13.00, 16.00–19.00; Nov–Mar 10.00–13.00, 15.00–18.00). The museum has an archeological section with palaeo-Venetic and Roman antiquities; a historical section with memorabilia; and a picture gallery with a small portrait by Gentile Bellini, a triptych by Cima da Conegliano, a *Resurrection of Lazarus* by Palma Giovane and four views by Marco Ricci. There are also works by the native artists Pietro Mariscalchi and Morto da Feltre. Outside the walls at the northeast end of the town is the 15C church of the **Ognissanti**, with a 9C or 10C campanile, fragmentary frescoes on the outside and a *Madonna with Sts Victor and Nicholas of Bari* by Tintoretto within.

From Piazza Maggiore, Via del Paradiso leads past the elaborately decorated Monte di Pietà to the **Galleria d'Arte Moderna Carlo Rizzarda** (Via del Paradiso 8; open Jun–Oct, Tues–Sun 10.00–13.00, 16.00–19.00, Nov–Apr on request, ☎ 0439 2540), situated in the 16C Palazzo Cumano. This is less interesting for the wrought-iron works of the founder, Carlo Rizzarda, than for its 19C and 20C Italian paintings and sculpture by Giovanni Fattori, Francesco Paolo Michetti, Carlo Carrà and Arturo Tosi.

Outside the walls, to the south, is the **Cathedral** of San Pietro. Its present appearance dates from the 16C, notwithstanding the 14C Gothic apse and campanile. The three-aisled interior, with its 9C crypt, conserves paintings of the *Adoration of the Shepherds* and *St John the Baptist* by Pietro Mariscalchi, the *Tomb of Andrea Bellati* by Tullio Lombardo (in the sanctuary), the 13C *Throne of Bishop Vilata* (at the end of the north aisle), a fine Byzantine crucifix of 542 (in the Archivio Capitolare), and other interesting artworks. Steps behind the cathedral ascend to the **baptistery** of San Lorenzo, with a 15C apse, a 17C doorway on the façade and a Renaissance doorway on the side. Inside are a baptismal font of 1399 with a Baroque wooden cover, and paintings by Leandro Bassano and other artists of the 16C and 17C. Remains of an early-Christian baptistery have been found nearby; the excavations are open Mar–Sep 10.00–13.00, 15.30–18.30.

The environs

A pleasant excursion can be made to the sanctuary of **Santi Vittore e Corona**, 4km southeast of Feltre. This is a Byzantine-Romanesque church of 1096–1101 with a narrow façade adorned with chiaroscuro frescoes. The three-aisled interior has 13C–15C frescoes (some of which are thought to be by the school of Giotto) and 11C sculptures. The adjoining convent of 1494 has more frescoes in the cloister. Other points of interest in the environs are the 15C church of **Santa Maria Assunta** at **Lentiai**, with coffered ceiling and paintings by Palma Vecchio; and the **Villas Bovio**, **Martini e Moro** and **Mauro**, dating from the 17C and 18C, at **Soranzen**. **Pedavena**, north of Feltre, noted for its beer, is a climbing centre. The 17C **Villa Pasole** here has an interesting little garden (open Sun 10.00–17.00 by appointment).

Belluno

The old town of Belluno (population 35,000) stands on a rocky eminence at the point where the River Ardo flows into the Piave—a position that protected it over the centuries both from foreign incursions and from seasonal flood waters. Here you immediately feel the nearness of the Alps (the Dolomiti Bellunesi, the most southerly of the Dolomite ranges, rise just to the west), and of the forests that have long been the city's principal asset. From Belluno, in fact, came the piles on which Venice is built; and something of the deep greens and browns of the Alpine woodlands can be seen in the paintings of Sebastiano Ricci and his nephew Marco, who were born here in 1659 and 1679, respectively. The wood-sculptor Andrea Brustolon was also a native.

History

Founded in palaeo-Venetic times (the place name *Belunum* seems to be of Celtic origin), Belluno was a Roman *municipium*, the residence of a civil and military functionary called a *sculdascio* in the Lombard period, and the seat of a count in Carolingian times. As early as the 9C temporal power over the city was held by its bishops, who retained control until the formation of the commune, after 1200. In the 13C and 14C the city lost its independence, first to the Trevisan seignories, then to the dukes of Austria and the Visconti. The beginning of Venetian rule in 1404 brought renewed security and a vast building programme that spared only a few medieval monuments.

The city centre

The spacious, park-like **Piazza dei Martiri**, dedicated to the victims of a Nazi massacre of 1944, is the centre of city life. It stands on the north edge of the old town, just a few blocks from the religious and civic buildings lining Piazza del Duomo.

The **Cathedral** is a 16C edifice designed by Tullio Lombardo, with an unfinished façade and a detached campanile by the Baroque architect Filippo Juvarra (1743). The luminous interior has paintings by Jacopo Bassano (third south altar) and Palma Giovane (fourth south altar). The two small marble statuettes in the first north chapel are attributed to Tullio Lombardo. The **baptistery**, also called Santa Maria delle Grazie, dates from the 16C.

A closer-than-usual relationship between civil and religious power might explain the location, on the north side of Piazza del Duomo, of the 19C town hall and of its historic predecessor, the **Palazzo dei Rettori** (now the prefecture), a Venetian Renaissance building of 1491 with porticoed façade, mullioned windows, central logge, and an imposing clock tower (1549) over the eastern corner. The former palace of the bishop-counts (1190), opposite, has been completely rebuilt, the Torre Civica being the only vestige of the original structure.

One block east of the cathedral, at Via Duomo 16, is the **Museo Civico** (open Apr–Oct, Tues–Sat 10.00–12.00, 16.00–19.00, Sun 10.30–12.30; Nov–Mar, Mon and Sat 10.00–12.00, Tues–Fri 15.00–18.00), arranged in the 17C Palazzo dei Giuristi. Here you can see the usual pre-Roman and Roman antiquities, as well as a picture gallery with works by Bartolomeo Montagna, Palma Giovane and Sebastiano and Marco Ricci, coins and seals, jewellery and prints.

The street continues to **Piazza Erbe** or Piazza del Mercato, on the site of the

Roman forum. It has a fountain of 1410 at the centre and porticoed Renaissance buildings all around, the finest of which is the **Monte di Pietà** (1531), adorned with coats of arms and inscriptions. Here you have a choice: continuing north along Via Rialto and, beyond the ancient Porta Doiona, Via Roma, you come to the late Gothic church of **Santo Stefano** (1468), with a large 15C doorway on the side. The Cappella Cesa, within, has frescoes by Jacopo da Montagna (c 1487) and painted wood statues of Matteo, Antonio, and Francesco Cesa by Andrea Brustolon, over the altar. To the south, **Via Mezzaterra**—the main thoroughfare of the city, lined with Venetian-style townhouses—and Vicolo San Pietro lead to the Gregorian church of **San Pietro**, a 14C edifice rebuilt in 1750, with a bare façade and, inside, paintings by Sebastiano Ricci (over the high altar) and Andrea Schiavone (former organ shutters), and two wooden altar panels carved by Andrea Brustolon. The adjacent seminary encloses two cloisters, of which the oldest (15C–16C) has a frescoed lunette attributed to Jacopo da Montagnana. Via Santa Maria Battuti, which flanks the seminary, continues south to the medieval Porta Rugo, which affords a magnificent view of the Dolomites and the Piave valley.

The environs
To the east of Belluno is the hilly region of Alpago with a number of small resorts, including **Tambre** on the edge of the Cansiglio forest. The **Alpe del Nevegal** (1030m), south of Belluno, is a ski resort (chair-lift to the Rifugio Brigata Alpina Cadore, 1600m), with a botanical garden nearby. Northwest of Belluno is the **Lago di Mis** at the foot of the wild and rugged **Canale del Mis**, in an area of the Dolomites which may one day become part of the Parco Naturale delle Dolomiti Bellunesi (described below). **Longarone**, north of Belluno, has been reconstructed after it was almost totally wiped out by a disastrous flood in 1963, when a landslide from Monte Toc (1921m) into the basin of the Vaiont Dam caused a huge water displacement to sweep through the Piave valley, destroying five villages and killing 1908 people. A definitive sentence in 1997 found the hydroelectric company guilty and responsible for damages of over 55 billion lire. The parish church (1966–76) was designed by Giovanni Michelucci.

The Parco Naturale delle Dolomiti Bellunesi

The Parco Naturale delle Dolomiti Bellunesi was established in 1990 by joining eight existing nature reserves. Extending over 29,000h, the park includes the last southern ramifications of the Dolomites, including the great limestone massifs of the Talvena (2542m), the Schiara (2565m), the Monti del Sole (2240m) and the Alpi Feltrine (Sas de Mura, 2550m). These mountains join typically alpine landscapes, characterised by bold peaks and powerful vertical walls, with the grassy meadows and shady forests and valleys of the *prealpi*. Their geological history is linked to mountain-building processes that raised the sea floors of the Mesozoic and Tertiary periods (some 65 million years ago), whose sediments compose most of the rock here. Over time, glaciers carved cirques (deep, steep-walled basins shaped like half a bowl) and grooves or furrows on the mountain walls, and the waters dug dolinas and caverns in the limestone, some as deep as 960m. The incessant action of the mountain streams has created immense waterfalls.

The vegetation of the park is made up of magnificent beech woods and broad-leafed deciduous forests, which yield at higher altitudes to firs and larches, and above the treeline to scrub pine and rhododendron. The flora, which counts over 1500 species and is one of the prime assets of the park, includes numerous native species and rarities such as *Delphinium dubium*, *Sempervivum dolomiticum*, *Alyssum ovirense*, *Geranium argenteum*, *Astragalus sempervirens* and *Cortusa matthioli*. Along with the classic Alpine flowers—edelweiss, gentian, rhododendron, and so forth—the southern slopes support thermophile species which, in particularly favourable positions, grow at altitudes much higher than might be expected. Such is the case, for instance, of the striking *Iris cengialti*, which in some areas of the Alpi Feltrine can be found as high up as 1700m.

The fauna of the Dolomiti Bellunesi includes large colonies of chamois, deer and roe deer. Hunters have stocked the area with mouflon, which in addition to damaging the forests have entered into competition in the food cycle with these native animals. The royal eagle, various owls, kestrel, grouse, and white partridge inhabit vast areas of the park. Reptiles include the alpine asp and the common salamander. Among the numerous insects are certain native species of coleoptera, such as *Orotrechus pavionis*, *Orotrechus theresiae* and *Neobathyscia dalpiazi*. Less endemic but much more bothersome are ticks (*Ixodes ricinus* and *Ixodes dammini*), which show a particular predilection for hikers in shorts.

Walking in the park

There are a number of great walks in the park. The following is a moderately strenuous circular excursion of 6–7hrs, including picnic lunch.

The trailhead is the Albergo Alpino Boz (660m) in Val Canzoi, reached via Soranzen, north of Feltre. From the Albergo Boz a road (closed to vehicular traffic) climbs steeply to the dam on the Lago de la Stua (696m) and follows the left bank of the lake until it crosses the affluent, the Torrente Caorame. Soon after, on the right, you join the mule path for the Piani Eterni (Trail 802), which climbs first through beech woods and then crosses a glen. At 1417m you encounter a fork in the trail: continue right along the mule path, which continues to climb in a southeasterly direction to the slopes of the **Pala del Lenzuoletto** (1797m), where it turns northwards in a broad curve to reach the highland known as the **Piani Eterni** (Eternal Plains), at an altitude of 1755m. On this limestone plateau, covered with meadows and low bushes, are numerous dolinas, caverns and abysses, some of which reach a depth of several hundred metres. Continuing northwards on Trail 802, you reach the Casera Erera (1708m) and just beyond, the Casera Brendol. From here descend along the Val Porzil along another trail that returns to the mule path at the fork at 1417m.

The Venetian Dolomites

The **Cadore** is the mountainous district surrounding the upper valley of the Piave and its western tributaries. Here the mountain peaks of Marmarole (2932m), Sorapiss (3205m), Antelao (3263m) and Monte Cristallo (3221m) are among the more impressive of the Dolomites. Until 1918 only the southeastern half of the district was Italian territory, and there was heavy mountain fighting during the First World War on the old frontier line. It now borders to the north on Trentino-Alto Adige and Austria. The Cadorini still speak Ladino, a Romance language, with Ladino-Venetian dialects in the lower valleys; but German is understood everywhere from Cortina northwards. The area is much visited for skiing and mountaineering.

Pieve di Cadore (878m), the chief town of the Cadore, is now a summer and winter resort beneath the southern foothills of the Marmarole. The **Palazzo della Magnifica Comunità Cadorina** (open in summer 09.00–12.00, 15.00–19.00), rebuilt in 1525, contains a small archaeological museum. Outside is a statue by Antonio Dal Zotto (1880) of the painter Titian, who was born here c 1488. His modest birthplace has a small museum (open in summer 09.00–12.00, 15.00 or 16.00–19.00; closed Mon; ring in winter). In the parish church there is a *Madonna with Saints* by Titian. The 'Casa di Babbo Natale' on the hillside of Montericco receives Italian mail addressed to Father Christmas.

Cortina d'Ampezzo (1210m at the church), a summer and winter resort once frequented by the best society, is now definitely *demodé*. It lies in a sunny upland basin, and the view of the mountains on all sides is magnificent. It has a parish church with a wooden tabernacle carved by Andrea Brustolon and an altarpiece painted by Antonio Zanchi; a small geological museum; and a pinacoteca containing works by Filippo De Pisis (1896–1956), who often stayed in Cortina, and other modern Italian painters. Aldous Huxley wrote much of *Point Counter Point* here in 1926–27. The spectacular road across the Dolomites to Canazei and Bolzano was built by the Austrians in 1901–09. The **Lago di Misurina** (1737m), northeast of Cortina, is one of the more beautifully situated lakes in the Dolomites.

Venice

Venice, in Italian *Venezia*, stands on an archipelago of 117 islets or shoals, roughly 3km from the mainland and 2km from the open sea, whose force is broken by the natural breakwater of the Lido. The buildings are supported on piles of Istrian pine, driven down beneath the water to a solid bed of compressed sand and clay, on foundations of Istrian limestone which withstand the corrosion of the sea. The official population (334,000) includes the mainland community of Mestre; that of the historic centre is now only 70,000, compared with 200,000 when the republic was at its zenith, in the 15c and 16C. A unique position, the grace of her buildings, the changing colours of the lagoon, and not least the total absence of wheeled transport make Venice the most charming and poetic city in the world. For a full description of the city, see *Blue Guide Venice*.

A quick geography lesson

The irregular plan of Venice is traversed by some 100 canals of which the **Grand Canal** divides the city into two unequal parts. The other canals, called *rii* (singular, *rio*), with the exception of the Cannaregio, have an average breadth of 4–5 metres and are spanned by c 400 bridges, mostly of brick or stone. The streets, nearly all very narrow, are called *calli*, the more important thoroughfares, usually shopping streets, are known as *calle larga, ruga,* or *salizzada*. Smaller alleys are called *caletta* or *ramo*. A street alongside a canal is called a *fondamenta*; a *rio terra* is a street on the course of a filled-in *rio*. A *sottoportico* or *sottoportego* passes beneath buildings. The only piazza is that of St Mark; there are two piazzette, one in front of the Doges' Palace, the other the Piazzetta dei Leoncini (now Giovanni XXIII). Other open spaces are called *campo* or *campiello*, according to their size. Names of streets and canals are written up on the walls in the Venetian dialect. Houses are numbered consecutively throughout each of the six *sestieri* (neighbourhoods) into which the city is divided (San Marco, Castello, Dorsoduro, San Polo, Santa Croce, and Cannaregio).

How to be an amphibian

Venice is subject to periodic flooding (*acqua alta*) from exceptionally high tides. A special law was passed in 1973, and renewed in 1984, by the Italian government to safeguard the city, but measures to prevent the flood tides and clean the polluted lagoon were still at an experimental stage. Meanwhile, committees funded from various countries have been working in conjunction with the Italian authorities for many years on the restoration of buildings damaged by 'high water'.

For visitors, *acqua alta* can be a memorable experience, to say the least. Contrary to what one might think, the lagoon and canals rarely rise above the level of their quays. More often, their waters invade the sewer system and bubble up from the drains in the pavement. Special squads then lay out the kilometres of elevated walkways that ordinarily lie stacked here and there around the city. As these may not get you to your doorstep, keep your feet dry by carrying two tightly folded plastic trash bags and two robust rubber bands in purse or pocket. In an emergency (and all it takes is a sudden downpour) the bags can be pulled on over your shoes and fastened at the calf with the rubber bands.

Venice and the poets

Venice has left a lasting impression on innumerable travellers down through the centuries. Here are a few of their more poetic remarks.

Once did she hold the gorgeous East in fee;
> *And was the safeguard of the West: the worth*
> *Of Venice did not fall below her birth,*
Venice, the eldest Child of Liberty.
She was a maiden City, bright and free;
> *No guile seduced, no force could violate;*
> *And, when she took unto herself a mate,*

She must espouse the everlasting Sea.
And what if she had seen those glories fade,
>*Those titles vanish, and that strength decay;*
>*Yet shall some tribute of regret be paid*
>*When her long life hath reach'd its final day:*
Men are we, and must grieve when even the Shade
>*Of that which once was great is pass'd away.*
William Wordsworth, *On the Extinction of the Venetian Republic*, 1802

Venice ... is my head, or rather my heart-quarters.
Lord Byron, Letter to Thomas Moore, 11 Apr 1817

She looks a sea Cybele, fresh from ocean,
Rising with her tiara of proud towers
At airy distance, with majestic motion,
A ruler of the waters and their powers:
And such she was ...

States fall, arts fade—but Nature doth not die,
Nor yet forget how Venice once was dear,
The pleasant place of all festivity,
The revel of the earth, the masque of Italy!
Lord Byron, *Childe Harold's Pilgrimage*, Canto the Fourth, 1816

Underneath day's azure eyes
Ocean's nursling, Venice lies
A peopled labyrinth of walls,
Amphitrite's destined halls,
Which her hoary sire now paves
With his blue and beaming waves ...
Sun-girt city, though hast been
ocean's child, and then his queen
Now is come a darker day
And thou soon must be his prey,
If the power that raised thee here
Hallow so thy watery bier.
...
Those who alone thy towers behold
Quivering through aerial gold,
As I now behold them here,
Would imagine not they were
Sepulchres, where human forms,
Like pollution-nourished worms
To the corpse of greatness cling,
Murdered, and now mouldering.
Percy Bysshe Shelley, *Lines Written among the Euganian Hills*, Oct 1818

Mourn not for Venice; though her fall
>*Be awful, as if Ocean's wave*
Swept o'er her, she deserves it all,

> *And Justice triumphs o'er her grave.*
> *Thus perish ev'ry King and State,*
> *That run the guildy race she ran,*
> *Strong but in ill, and only great*
> *By outrage against God and man!*
> Thomas Moore, *Rhymes of the Road*, 1819

Practical information

Getting there
By air

Venice's **Marco Polo International Airport** is located on the mainland 13km north of the city. Domestic flights connect with Milan, Naples, Palermo, Rome and Turin; international flights with Amsteram, Barcelona, Brussels, Copenhagen, Düsseldorf, Frankfurt, London, Lugano, Montpellier, Moscow, Munich, New York, Nice, Paris, Stüttgart, Vienna and Zurich. Airport buses run to and from the terminal and the car park at Piazzale Roma, and there are regular boat connections between the airport, San Marco (Giardinetti landing stage) and the Lido. If you are carrying a lot of baggage, you might want to consider a water taxi, which will take you directly to the landing nearest your hotel.

By road

You can reach Venice from Padua and the west by A4 or 11; from Treviso and the north by A27 and 13 (the latter is faster from central Treviso); and from Trieste and the east by A4 or 14. All roads from the mainland terminate at Piazzale Roma, on the Tronchetto land fill.

Car parks and bus station. Motorists approaching the city have to leave their vehicles in a multi-storey garage or an open-air car park (charges according to the size of the vehicle; the rates are per day, and space is very limited, especially in summer). The most convenient multi-storey garages are at Piazzale Roma, garages and huge open-air car parks also at Isola del Tronchetto. Frequent vaporetto services (see below) serve all of these. In summer, at Easter, and Carnival time open air car parking is usually available also at San Giuliano and Fusina (with vaporetto services). The bus station is at Piazzale Roma.

By rail

Venice **Santa Lucia Station** is located on the Fondamenta Santa Lucia, at the west end of the Grand Canal. The principal trains connect with Verona, Milan, Turin and Genoa; Bologna, Florence and Rome; and Trieste. There are direct through services to and from Basel, Bern, Geneva, Lugano, Munich, Nice, Paris, Vienna and Zurich. Water-buses, motor-boat taxis, and gondolas operate from the quay outside.

Getting around

There are only two ways to get around Venice—by land and by water—and neither of them is very fast. If you manage to go from your starting point to your destination without making a wrong turn, walking is probably the most practical means of locomotion. The trouble is, Venice's maze-like street plan prevents out-of-towners like you and me from getting from here to there on the first try. If you wish to walk through Venice without carrying luggage, shopping bags, or other encumberances, you can hire a *portabagagli* (porter), to do the work for you; details from your hotel.

By vaporetto

The *vaporetto* (water bus) is the most convenient way of getting around town, but it is painfully slow and, in the season (May–Oct), jam-packed with passengers.

1 *accelerato*, calling at all stops on the line: Piazzale Roma–Ferrovia (the train station)–Rialto–San Marco–Lido and vice versa

52 *diretto*, an express service calling at selected stops on the line: Lido–San Zaccaria–Piazzale Roma–Ferrovia-Fondamenta Nuove–Murano–Fundamenta Nuove–San Zaccaria–Piazzale Roma and vice versa

82 another *diretto* calling at selected stops on the line: San Marco–Rialto–Casinò–Ferrovia–Piazzale Roma–Tronchetto–Santa Marta–Saccafisola–Zattere–Giudecca-San Giorgio-San Zaccaria and vice versa

6 *diretto*, a fast motor boat that runs from San Marco to the Lido and back

12 and **14** serving the northern lagoon: San Zaccaria–Lido–San Nicolò–Punta Sabbioni–Treporti–Burano–Torcello–Burano–Mazzorbo–Murano–Fundamenta Nuove and vice-versa

Timetables are posted at most landing stages and published monthly in the tourist board's helpful booklet, *Un Ospite di Venezia* (see *Information offices*, below). Tickets can be bought during working hours at most landing stages and from shops displaying municipal transport logo, ACTV, or on board after hours. There are discounts for round-trip, 24-hour and 3-day tickets. There is also a sort of frequent-flyers card, called Carta Venezia, which entitles holders to substantial discounts on all lines; enquire at the ACTV offices in Corte dell'Albero (near the Sant'Angelo landing on the Grand Canal), or on Piazzale Roma.

By motoscafo

Motoscafi (water taxis) are the fastest and most exclusive vehicles in Venice. Point-to-point service in town is metred, and there are fixed rates (published *in Un Ospite di Venezia*) for the most common destinations outside the city centre. Taxi-stands on the quays in front of the Station, Piazzale Roma, Rialto, San Marco, etc.

By gondola

Gondole can be hired for a leisurely tour of the city, at standard rates or on a custom-service basis. In the latter case be sure to agree upon the duration and price of your ride before setting out. Gondola stands at the station, Piazzale Roma, Calle Vallaresso (San Marco), Riva degli Schiavoni, etc.

By traghetto

Traghetti (gondola ferries) offer a handy way of getting across the Grand Canal without walking all the way to one of the bridges (there are only three: at the train station, Rialto and the Accademia). You'll see yellow signs marked Traghetto with a gondola here and there as you wander the city. They are extremely cheap and quite a lot of fun, for in all but the roughest weather you ride standing up. Most operate from early morning until late afternoon. Furthermore, some vaporetti operate as traghetti on short, single-stop trips: cases in which a traghetto fare applies will appear on the tariff list at the ticket booth.

Information offices

Azienda Promozione Turistica, Castello 4421, ☎ 041 529 8711, fax 041 523 0399. Branch offices at the train station, ☎ 041 719 078; Giardini di San Marco, ☎ 041 522 6356, Lido di Venezia, Gran Viale Santa Maria Elisabetta, ☎ 041 526 5721. Ask your concierge for the valuable (free) publication, *Un Ospite di Venezia*, listing everything you need to know to get around, including current events and emergency numbers.

Where to stay

There are no street addresses in Venice. Mail is delivered by neighbourhood and number (for instance, San Marco 1243), but that's not much help if you're wandering the streets in search of a hotel. For this reason, you'll find two addresses, below, for hotels and restaurants: first the postal address, then the (approximate) street location, in parentheses.

Most of Venice's luxury hotels are arranged in a neat row along the waterfront on either side of San Marco. Moderately priced hotels can be found throughout the city, but good ones are few and far between. The level of comfort and service in inexpensive hotels can be downright disappointing—as is to be expected in a town, like Venice, subject to excessive demand. If you're looking for an adequate place to stay but are short on cash, bear in mind that several of the city's religious communities open their convents to visitors during high season, offering very good accommodation at remarkably low prices. Details from the APT.

Accademia, Dorsoduro 1058 (Fondamenta Bollani), ☎ 041 523 7846, fax 041 523 9152; near the Accademia, with a shady garden; moderate.

Cipriani, Isola della Giudecca 10, ☎ 041 520 7744, fax 041 520 3930; surely one of the world's finest hotels, also Venice's most exclusive, with luxuriously appointed rooms, a stunning garden and views that are hard to forget (its position at the tip of the Isle of the Giudecca, however, makes getting into the centre rather a bother); closed Nov–Mar; expensive.

Danieli, Castello 4196 (Riva degli Schiavoni), ☎ 041 522 6480, fax 041 520 0208; the most famous of the city's

other luxury hotels, where Marcel Proust stayed (breakfast is served on the roof terrace overlooking the lagoon, the Isle of San Giorgio and the Grand Canal, weather permitting); expensive.

Europa & Regina, San Marco 2159 (Calle Larga 22 Marzo), ☎ 041 520 0477, fax 041 523 1533; difficult to find by land, but with a private dock the Grand Canal, on which it fronts; expensive.

Falier, Santa Croce 130 (Salizzada San Pantalon), ☎ 041 522 8882, fax 041 520 6554; simple but quite good (especially the top-floor rooms with private terrace); moderate.

Flora, San Marco 2283a (Calle dei Bergamaschi), ☎ 041 520 5844, fax 041 522 8217, nicely situated between the Luna and the Gritti, with a beautiful small garden; moderate.

Gritti Palace, San Marco 2467 (Campo Santa Maria del Giglio), ☎ 041 794611, fax 041 520 0942; rich in Venetian atmosphere, with summer dining on the Grand Canal; expensive.

La Calcina, Dorsoduro 780 (Zattere), ☎ 041 520 6466, fax 041 522 7045; where Ruskin stayed: the rooms overlooking the Giudecca are among the city's most charming; moderate.

La Fenice et des Artistes, San Marco 1936 (Campiello de la Fenice), ☎ 041 523 2333, fax 041 520 3721; it really is frequented by artists (there are some original works by 20C masters in the lobby); moderate.

Londra Palace, Castello 4171 (Riva degli Schiavoni), ☎ 041 520 0533, fax 041 522 5032; near but less ostentatious than the Danieli: still in the luxury class, it offers marvellously appointed rooms and an equally impressive roof terrace; expensive.

Luna Baglioni, San Marco 1243 (Calle Larga del 'Ascensione), ☎ 041 5289840, fax 041 528 7160; quieter and more secluded than the other grand hotels; expensive.

Quattro Fontane, Via Fontane 16, ☎ 041

526 0227, fax 041 526 0726; on the Lido, with a pleasant garden; moderate.

 Eating out
Restaurants in Venice can be entertaining in their own right, especially in the warmer months when most offer table service outside. Unlike Rome or Florence, Venice is traffic free, which makes eating outside and watching the boats—or crowds—go by remarkably like dinner theatre.

Restaurants

VENICE *Al Bacareto*, San Marco 3447 (at San Samuele), ☎ 041 528 9336; osteria dating back a hundred years, known for its wholesome Venetian fare, including *ombre* and *cicheti*; closed Sat evening, Sun and Aug; moderate.

Al Graspo de Ua, San Marco 5094 (Calle dei Bombaseri), ☎ 041 520 0150; an authentic Venetian tavern; closed Mon, Tue, late Dec–early Jan and two weeks in Aug; moderate.

Al Mascaron, Castello 5525 (Calle Lunga Santa Maria Formosa), ☎ 041 522 5995; a very well-known place, serving the best of traditional Venetian cuisine; closed Sun and winter; moderate.

Alle Testiere, Castello 5801 (Calle del Mondo Novo), ☎ 041 522 7220; a tiny (four tables), friendly place serving good Venetian dishes; closed Aug and winter; moderate.

Ai Gondolieri, Dorsoduro 366 (Fondamenta San Vio), ☎ 041 528 6396; small and refined, near Peggy Guggenheim's house; closed Tues; moderate.

Bentigodi da Andrea, Cannaregio 1423–24 (Calesele Cannaregio), ☎ 041 716269; a good place for simple food and wine, near the Ghetto; closed Sun, inexpensive.

Cip's, Giudecca 10 (near the Zitelle), ☎ 041 240 8575; the newest addition to the Cipriani family, offering various menus from pizza, up; moderate.

Corte Sconta, Castello 3886 (Calle del Pestrin), ☎ 041 522 7024; serving Venetian specialties, especially seafood, in a rustic interior and a pleasant garden court; closed Sun, Mon, a few days in Jan–Feb and mid-Jul–mid-Aug; inexpensive.

Fiaschetteria Toscana, at San Giovanni Crisostomo, ☎ 041 528 5281; truly delicious cuisine (Tuscan as well as Venetian) and excellent wines, with outside seating in summer; closed Tue and Jul–Aug; moderate.

Harry's Bar, on the Grand Canal near San Marco, at San Marco 1323 (Calle Vallaresso), ☎ 041 528 5777, draws three kinds of clientele: the people-watchers, who like to sit downstairs and watch the artists, musicians and movie stars walk in; the romantics, who prefer a table upstairs, by the window, where they can gaze out over the water; and of course the *divi*, particularly abundant during the Biennali. Founded many years ago by legendary hotelier Harry Cipriani, this is still one of Venice's finest restaurants (specialities: *risotto alle seppioline, scampi alla Thermidor con riso pilaf* and a remarkable selection of desserts)—and one of its most expensive; closed Mon.

Harry's Dolci, Giudecca 773, ☎ 041 522 4844; the same impeccable level of cuisine and service as Harry's Bar, but less formal, with tables on the water in summer; closed Tues; moderate.

La Caravella, San Marco 2397, (Calle Larga 22 Marzo), ☎ 041 520 8901; excellent restaurant (specialities: *antipasto Tiziano con granseola, Bigoli in salsa, filetto di branzino alle erbe*) with a distinctive maritime decor and extensive list of regional, Italian and imported wines; closed Wed, except from Jun to Sep; expensive.

Osteria da Fiore, San Polo 2202a (Calle del Scaleter), ☎ 041 721308; serving very good seafood; closed Sun, Mon, a few days around Christmas and in Aug; moderate.

Taverna la Fenice (Campiello de la Fenice), ☎ 041 522 3856; serving skilfully prepared regional specialities and great wines, with tables in the *campiello* in fair weather; closed Sun, Mon morning and a few days in Jan; moderate.

MURANO *Ai Frati*, ☎ 041 736694; a well-known seafood restaurant; closed Thu and Feb; moderate.

BURANO *Al Gatto Nero-da Ruggero*, ☎ 041 730 120; serving Venetian specialities such as *spaghetti al nero di seppia*, *pesce in umido* and *biscotti di Burano* accompanied by regional wines; closed Mon and a few days in Feb and Nov; moderate.

Antica Trattoria alla Maddalena, Mazzorbo 7C, ☎ 041 730151; the place to go for old-fashioned lagoon food—try the *selvadego de vale* (wild fowl) and *castraure* (baby artichokes); closed Thur and Dec–Jan; inexpensive.

TORCELLO *Locanda Cipriani*, ☎ 041 730 150, fax 041 735 433; known for its *insalatina novella con scampi al sesamo*, *tagliatelle nere con ragout di vongole e capesante*, *sorpresa di mare in crosta* and *semifreddo alla Grappa di Picolit*; closed Tue and Nov–Mar; expensive.

Osteria al Ponte del Diavolo, ☎ 041 730 401; house specialities include *polipetti caldi*, *filetti di sogliola in salsa di zucchine*, *seppioline fritte* and *crespelle alla crema della casa*; closed Thur and all evenings except Sat, as well as Jan–Feb; moderate.

Cafés and wine bars

Venice's best pastries, ice-cream and hot chocolate are to be had at *Rosa Salva*, in historic old rooms on Campo Santi Giovanni and Paolo.

Two other cafés known for their antique décor are *Florian* and *Quadri*, located across St Mark's square from each other. You can find delicious sweets (but no coffee) at *Marchini* on Calle del Spezier between Campo Santo Stefano and Campo San Maurizio.

A truly Venetian experience is to go for **ombre** and **cicheti**. An *ombra* (literally, 'shadow') is a glass of wine and *cicheti*, finger-food. Good places to *ombreggiare* and *chichetare* are: *Alla Frasca*, Cannaregio 5176 (Campiello della Carità, near the church of the Gesuiti), a time-honoured establishment in historic quarters (Titian stored his paints and canvas here) pleasantly situated in an out-of-the-way part of town; *Vino Vino*, San Marco 2007A (Calle del Cafetier), a newer and trendier place, between San Marco and the Teatro della Fenice; and *La Mascareta*, Castello 5183 (Calle Lunga Santa Maria Formosa), one of the few places in town open after midnight.

Entertainment

The *Teatro La Fenice* traditionally hosts opera in winter and classical music in spring, summer and autumn; but it was recently damaged by fire, and at the time of writing events are held in a large tent in a rather out-of-the-way position on the Tronchetto. There is good drama at the *Teatro del Ridotto* and *Teatro Goldoni*; and there is usually at least one major exhibition of art or architecture going on at the Fondazione Cini, Palazzo Grassi, Museo Correr, or one of the other major venues in the city.

Concerts are often given in churches, and organ recitals are held in St Mark's in summer.

The **Casinò** is open in summer at the Lido, with gaming rooms. In winter it operates at Palazzo Vendramin on the Grand Canal.

Shopping

Probably everyone knows that the thing to buy in Venice is **glass**. The best value for your money is to be found on Murano, where much of the glass is made; but there are also many shops in Venice offering excellent craftsmanship at only slightly higher prices. Mass demand for Burano **lace** has led to a decline in quality.

Special events

La Biennale di Venezia organises biennial historical and documentary exhibitions in five areas: visual arts, cinema, theatre, music and architecture. These events, which draw immense international crowds, usually take place in odd years, between June and September. Also important are the Mostra Internazionale del Cinema, on the Lido (annual, Sep) and the Premio Letterario Campiello (Sep).

Surviving from past ages are the popular *Festa della Sensa* (late spring), culminating in a ceremony recalling the traditional marriage between the Doge and the Sea; the great gondola race known as the *Regata Storica* in the Grand Canal (first Sun in Sep); the *Festa del Redentore* (third week in Sep), with ceremonial boat processions and fireworks; and many other feasts in the towns and islands of the lagoon. Last but by no means least, *Carnevale* draws merry-makers from all parts of the world, many in fancy dress and masks.

Sports

Swimming and other water sports at the Lido.

EXPLORING THE CITY

Venice is also unique in Europe in that its historic centre practically coincides with the entire area of the city. The principal neighbourhoods, or *sestieri,* are San Marco, Dorsoduro, Santa Croce, San Polo, Canareggio and Castello.

History

Venice was founded in the wetlands between the mouths of the Piave and the Brenta rivers by fugitives from the barbarian invasions inland, around AD 450, and its population grew as a result of the Lombard invasion of 568–69. In the 9C the centre was the *Civitas Rivoalti*—the modern zone of the Rialto, San Marco and Castello. The city was first governed by *tribuni* named by the Byzantine exarch of Ravenna, and subsequently by a duke (*doge* in Venetian) who, by playing the interests of the Eastern Empire against those of the Germanic Holy Roman Empire to the north, attained first a relative independence, and then complete sovereignty, in the 11C. As the power of its maritime republic increased, the city grew in size, gradually extending over more than 100 islands. Later, after winning a war with Genoa for the control of the Eastern Mediterranean, it extended its dominions on the mainland.

The Turkish expansion and the development of the European powers, however, caused a gradual waning of Venice's political and economic importance—an effect that was compounded by the discovery of the New World and the establishment of alternative trade routes. Conquered by Napoleon in 1797 and annexed to Austria, it was joined to Italy in 1866.

Today Venice is threatened by another kind of peril: the degradation caused by the gradual sinking of the lagoon floor, which, together with the continuous flight of its population and the pollution caused by the industries of the mainland, is posing serious problems of conservation. What the future holds, lamentably, is anyone's guess.

Venetian painting

Painting was the preferred medium in this city of reflected light. By the mid-15C, the Bellini family (Jacopo and his sons, Gentile and Giovanni) were capturing the luminescence of the atmosphere of Venice in their beautifully rendered altarpieces. Giovanni's *Madonna and Child with Saints* in the church of San Zaccaria is a masterpiece of the brilliant colouration and subtle light effects that have come to characterise Venetian painting. The Bellini inspired a number of other painters, most notably Giorgione, whose enigmatic *Tempest* (now in the Accademia) continues to haunt the viewer with the mysterious atmosphere of an approaching storm; Titian, whose works in the church of the Frari are radiant examples of lustrous Venetian colourism; and Paolo Veronese, who mixed illusionistic perspectives with sacred and profane themes. Tintoretto left hundreds of paintings in the churches of Venice, working very quickly and impressionistically, sharply focusing his dramatic light effects. The era of the great Venetian painters closes in the age of the Grand Tour, when the *vedutisti,* such as Canaletto, painted lyrical images of the city which capture most poetically the unique atmosphere of Venice.

The Grand Canal

The Grand Canal is the main thoroughfare of Venice and possibly its most famous sight. In terms of beauty and sheer dramatic impact, it rivals the boulevards of the great European capitals, most of which, it should be remembered, were constructed much later and with a clear master-plan in mind. Strictly speaking, the Grand Canal has more in common with midtown Manhattan than with the Champs-Elysées—for it was the Venetian spirit of individualism which led each patrician family to build a mansion larger and more magnificent than its neighbour, or to lavish more money on its parish church. It is important to remember that at the time these buildings were constructed, direct contact was the only means of commercial communication. Foreign clients would be entertained and business would be conducted in the sumptuous rooms behind these grand façades, and on Sunday clients would be ushered off to Mass in churches that were as magnificent as human imagination allowed.

The Grand Canal weaves through the city from northwest to southeast, forming a reversed 'S' some 4km long, 6m deep and 40–130m wide. The best way to see its extraordinary architectural parade—indeed, the only way to see it in its entirety—is from the water. Whether you choose a gondola, water-taxi or vaporetto (the slow no. 1 from Piazzale Roma or the train station is ideal), make sure you have a good view to both sides.

VENICE

La Giudecca

REDENTORE

0   200 yards
0   200 metres

Cimitero
ISOLA DI S. MICHELE

SACCA DELLA MISERICORDIA

S. Caterina
Gesuiti
Oratorio d. Crociferi
P. Serriman

SS. Apostoli
Valmarana
S. Canciano
a da losto
S.M. dei Miracoli
P. Sanudo
Scuola di S. Marco
SS. Giovanni e Paolo
S. Giov. Crisostomo
Teatro Malibran
L'Ospedaletto
BARBARIA D. TOLE
S. Francesco d. Vigna

P.O.
CAMPO S. BARTOLOMEO
S. Bart
S. Lio
S.M. Formosa
S. Lorenzo
P. Manin
S. Salvatore
S.M. d. Fava
Palazzo Grimani
MERCERIA
S. Giuliano
Palazzo Querini Stampalia
Questura
S. Giorgio d. Schiavoni
S. Giov. Nuovo
S. Antonio
Palazzo Trevisan
S. Giorgio dei Greci
Torre d. Orologio
Palazzo Patriarcato
Procur. Vecchie
C. S. PROVOLO
S. Zaccaria
S. Martino
S. Marco
PIAZZA S. MARCO
Campanile
Museo Diocesano
CAMPO BANDIERA E. MORO
Mus. Correr
Prigioni
S. Giov. in Bragora
Procur. Nuova
Palazzo Ducale
Ponte d. Sospiri
S. M. d. Visitazione
P.O.
Libreria Vecchia
DEGLI
SCHIAVONI
Moise
Zecca
MOLO
RIVA
Museo Navale
Giardinetti
Cap. di Porto
P. Giustinian
RIVA CA DI DIO
VIA GARIBALDI
P. Treves de'Bonfili
ANAL GRANDE
RIVA DEI 7 MARTIRI
PUNTA DELLA DOGANA
Dogana di Mare

DARSENA GRANDE

ISOLA DI S. PIETRO

CANALE DI S. MARCO

S. Giorgio Maggiore
BACINO
Fondazione Giorgio Cini

CANALE DELLA GRAZIA

Teatro Verde
ISOLA DI S. GIORGIO MAGGIORE

From **Santa Lucia Station**, built in 1954 to replace the city's original 19C terminal, the boat enters the Grand Canal leaving on the right the church of San Simeone Piccolo, with its tall green dome and Corinthian portico. The church of the **Scalzi**, adjoining the station quay, is a Baroque edifice designed by Baldassare Longhena for a Carmelite community in the mid-17C. The modern bridge here is one of the three that span the Grand Canal.

The first building of note that comes into sight is the 18C church of **San Geremia**, on the left bank opposite the Riva di Biasio landing stage. Its façade faces the Canale di Cannaregio, the largest in the city after the Grand Canal. An inscription on the wall announces that the church contains the relics of St Lucy, martyred in Syracuse in AD 304. Her body was stolen from Constantinople in 1204, when the Venetians sacked the imperial capital during the Fourth Crusade.

On the right bank, opposite the San Marcuola landing stage, is one of the better-known buildings of the Veneto-Byzantine type, the **Fondaco dei Turchi**, unfortunately somewhat carelessly restored in 1858–69. A Turkish warehouse from 1621 to 1838 and now the Natural History Museum, it is recognisable by the tall towers on either side of its colonnade. Among the several sarcophagi beneath its portico is one which once held the remains of Doge Marin Falier, beheaded for treason in 1355.

Across the Rio del Megio is the plain crenellated façade of the 15C Granaries of the Republic, flanked by the Palazzo Belloni Battaglia, a 17C palace by Baldassarre Longhena with an elaborate water-gate and fine first-floor loggia. The magnificent house on the left bank here is the Palazzo Vendramin Calergi, begun by Mauro Codussi and completed by Pietro Lombardo and his assistants (1509). Now the winter home of Venice's Casinò, its Renaissance façade, with a delicately carved cornice and frieze, is faced with white Istrian limestone. The German composer Richard Wagner died here in 1883.

At the next landing are the church of **San Stae**, with a Baroque façade by Domenico Rissi (1709) and (left of the façade) the charming little Scuola dei Battiloro e Tiraoro, once the seat of the confraternity of goldsmiths. The next important building on this side of the canal is the exuberant **Ca' Pesaro**, a Baroque masterpiece begun by Baldassarre Longhena in 1628 and completed by Giacomo Gaspari in 1710. The palace houses the city's Galleria d'Arte Moderna and Museo Orientale. On the left bank, overlooking the broad Rio di Noale, is Palazzo Gussoni, a handsome 16C mansion attributed to the Veronese architect Michele Sanmicheli and once decorated with frescoes by Tintoretto. These were erased long ago by sun, wind and rain. **Ca' Corner della Regina**, a Classical edifice by Domenico Rossi (1724) on the right bank, belonged to the family of Caterina Cornaro, Queen of Cyprus, who was born on this site in 1454. It now holds the archives of the Venice Biennale.

At the next landing stage is the superb **Ca' d'Oro**, possibly the most beautiful Gothic mansion in Venice. In the 15C, when it was built, the carved details of the façade were gilt and much of the remaining surface was painted deep red or bright blue. The palace now houses the Galleria Giorgio Franchetti, with a fine collection of Venetian painting and sculpture. Three more important houses follow: the **Palazzo Michiel dalle Colonne**, rebuilt in the late 17C, with a ground-floor colonnade and elegant logge; Palazzo Mangilli-Valmarana, designed by Antonio Visentini for the English consul Joseph Smith (1682–1779), patron of Canaletto; and the Veneto-Byzantine Ca' da Mosto (birthplace in of the explorer Alvise Da

Mosto, 1432–88), one of the older houses on the Grand Canal and another fine example of the Veneto-Byzantine style.

On the right bank, on a projecting quay, is the **Pescheria**, a Gothic-revival edifice built in 1907 on the site of the 14C fish market. Here begin the Rialto markets, which include the arcaded Fabbriche Nuove, built in 1554–56 by the Florentine architect and sculptor Jacopo Sansovino, the Fabbriche Vecchie, built by Scarpagnino in 1522, and the Erberia, an open-air fruit and vegetable market. This is followed closely by the **Palazzo dei Camerlenghi**, an elegant Renaissance building of 1528 with two storeys of arcades, now leaning conspicuously to one side (like many Venetian buildings) due the gradual subsidence of the piles on which it is built. On the left as the boat turns to approach the Ponte di Rialto is the **Fondaco dei Tedeschi**, once the most important of the trading centres established by the Venetians for foreign merchants. In *The Merchant of Venice* Shakespeare alludes to the business relations between Venice and the various German states in a remark made by Shylock concerning a diamond purchased in Frankfurt; the Fondaco dei Tedeschi was where these Northern European traders were obliged to live and conduct their affairs. The building was reconstructed after a fire in 1505–08 by Scarpagnino to plans by Girolamo Tedesco, and the exterior was adorned with frescoes by Giorgione and Titian (these paintings, too, have disappeared, but detached fragments are displayed in the Ca' d'Oro). It now houses the main post office.

The sudden appearance of the **Ponte di Rialto** invariably draws an expression of surprise and wonder from first-time visitors to Venice. What is without a doubt the most photographed bridge in the world was built in 1588–92 by Antonio da Ponte, whose design was chosen by the Venetian Senate over those of several more famous architects, including Michelangelo, Palladio and Sansovino. Its single arch, 28 metres across and 7.5 metres high, carries three parallel walkways divided by two rows of shops. The reliefs of St Mark and St Theodore are by Tiziano Aspetti; the *Annunciation* on the downstream side is by Agostino Righi.

Near the Rialto landing stage the Renaissance Palazzo Dolfin Manin, designed by Jacopo Sansovino (1536–75), is now the Banca d'Italia. During office hours you can see its beautiful atrium and courtyard. **Palazzo Loredan** and **Ca' Farsetti**, both Veneto-Byzantine buildings of the 12C and 13C, together constitute the town hall. They have nearly identical logge and arcades. Palazzo Loredan is the more ornate of the two, with statues beneath Gothic canopies and the arms of the famous Corner family. Elena Corner Piscopia (1646–84), who lived here, was the first woman to receive a university degree (in philosophy, from Padua University). The Renaissance **Palazzo Grimani**, on the left bank adjoining the Rio di San Luca, was designed by Sanmicheli shortly before his death in 1559 and built by Giangiacomo dei Grigi. Behind its stately three-storey Renaissance façade, with broad arches on pilaster strips and columns, is the modern Court of Appeal.

On the right bank here are Palazzo Papadopoli, a sumptuous 16C house with two broad logge; Palazzo Bernardo, a refined 15C Gothic palace with delicate tracery on its front; and Palazzo Grimani-Marcello, an early 16C building in the Renaissance style called Lombardesque, after the prominent sculptor and architect Pietro Lombardo and his family, who worked extensively in and around Venice. On the opposite bank is **Palazzo Corner Spinelli**, another fine

Renaissance building designed by Mauro Codussi (1490–1510), with a rusticated ground floor and large mullioned windows above. Across the Grand Canal from the Sant'Angelo landing stage are Palazzo Pisani-Moretta, an early 15C Gothic palace with two fine logge; Palazzo Giustinian-Persico, a 16C Renaissance building; and, adjoining the San Tomà stop, Palazzo Marcello dei Leoni, named after the two Romanesque lions beside the door. The Palazzi Mocenigo, on the left bank, appear as one building with a long, symmetrical façade. Here Byron wrote the beginning of *Don Juan* and entertained Irish poet Thomas Moore.

On the right bank, as the canal swings sharply to the left, are Palazzo Balbi, a large building of Classical aspect attributed to Alessandro Vittoria, and the late Gothic **Ca' Foscari** (1452), commissioned by Doge Francesco Foscari, displaying handsome columns, fine tracery and a frieze of putti bearing the Foscari arms. It is now part of the university. There follow the Palazzi Giustinian, elegant Gothic buildings of the late 15C where Wagner composed the second act of his opera, *Tristan and Isolde* (1858–59); and the magnificent Baroque **Ca' Rezzonico**, designed by Longhena (1649) and completed by Massari (c 1750), now home to the city's collection of 18C art. On the left bank, the large, white **Palazzo Grassi** was begun in 1748 by Giorgio Massari. It is now a venue for exhibitions. The campo and landing stage here receive their names from San Samuele, an 11C church rebuilt in 1685.

Further on, on the right bank, rises the 15C Palazzo Loredan dell' Ambasciatore, a late Gothic building with shield-bearing youths in niches on the façade. Just beyond the Rio San Trovaso stands Palazzo Contarini degli Scrigni, made up of two buildings—one late Gothic, the other designed by Vincenzo Scamozzi in 1609. On the left bank is Palazzo Giustinian Lolin, a Baroque palace by Baldassarre Longhena (c 1630) with two levels of tall logge. The Galleria dell'Accademia, in the former convent of Santa Maria della Carità, comes into sight on the right bank.

You are now approaching the last of the canal's three bridges, the **Ponte dell' Accademia**, a 1986 replica of a 1930s reconstruction, in wood, of a 19C iron bridge. On the left bank amid gardens, just beyond the bridge, is Palazzo Cavalli Franchetti, a 15C palace renovated and enlarged in the late 19C. Across the narrow Rio dell'Orso are the two Palazzi Barbaro, of which the one on the left is 15C Gothic and the other, 17C. The older one was bought in the 19C by the Curtis family of Boston, whose guests included writers Robert Browning and Henry James (who wrote *The Aspern Papers* during his stay and described the palace in *The Wings of the Dove*), and painters John Singer Sargent, James Whistler and Claude Monet.

On the right bank is Palazzo Contarini Dal Zaffo, a fine example of the Lombardesque architectural style, and on the narrow Campo San Vio, Palazzo Da Mula, a late Gothic building of the 15C with three orders of quadrifoil logge. Past the latter, again on the right, is the **Palazzo Venier dei Leoni**, begun in 1749 but abandoned after just one storey had been built (there is a tale that the powerful Corner family, fearing that their palace across the Grand Canal would be overshadowed by what promised to be a more magnificent building, drove the owners to bankruptcy). Peggy Guggenheim lived here from 1949 until her death in 1979; now owned by the Solomon R. Guggenheim Foundation, which also administers the Guggenheim Museum in New York, the building displays her collection of modern art. Also on this side is the leaning Palazzo Dario, built in 1487 (possibly to a design by Pietro Lombardo) and recognisable by its multi-coloured marble façade and its many chimneys.

The magnificent building on the left bank of the canal is **Palazzo Corner della Ca' Grande**, by Jacopo Sansovino (c 1545), with three-storey High Renaissance façade, now the Prefecture. Beyond the landing stage of Santa Maria del Giglio, squeezed tightly by its neighbours, is the 15C Palazzo Contarini-Fasan, with just three windows on the piano nobile and two on the floor above; here legend places the home of Desdemona, heroine of Shakespeare's *Othello*. On the right bank, before the canal broadens into the expanse facing San Marco, is Longhena's magnificent basilica of **Santa Maria della Salute**.

As the boat makes its final crossing of the Grand Canal before stopping at San Marco, you pass (left) the Classical façade of the 17C Palazzo Treves de' Bonfili; and another Ca' Giustinian, a late Gothic building (1474) with three orders of windows and logge. It is occupied by the offices of the tourist bureau and the Venice Biennale. The right bank ends at the **Dogana di Mare**, or customs house, a Doric edifice by Giuseppe Benone (1676–82) dramatically marking the entrance to the San Marco basin and terminating—appropriately—in a golden globe and a revolving weathervane of Fortune.

San Marco

Venice life circulates around the incomparable setting of ***Piazza San Marco**, for more than a thousand years the symbol of the city and the centre of its public life. The product of a long process of adaptation to the functional and symbolic needs of the Venetian Republic, today it appears as an immense open space flanked on three sides by porticoed buildings, with St Mark's Basilica and its tall, free-standing campanile closing the east end of the piazza. At all hours one of the world's more spectacular squares (Napoleon called it the finest drawing room in Europe), Piazza San Marco is most beautiful in the subdued light of early morning and late evening when the mosaics of the church come alive and the buildings take on a warm, golden glow. This is also the best time to avoid the crowds, which in high season can make serious sightseeing impossible.

The basilica
The focal point of the square and the fulcrum of religious life in the city is the *Basilica of San Marco, built in the 9C to enshrine the relics of the Evangelist Mark, stolen from Alexandria, Egypt, in 828. Originally the chapel of the doges (and only since 1897 the cathedral of Venice), it has substantially maintained its early form and appearance despite alterations of the 11C, 14C and 16C. Ruskin described it as 'a multitude of pillars and white domes, clustered into a long low pyramid of coloured light; a treasure heap'; his American contemporary Mark Twain called it 'a vast warty bug taking a meditative walk'. Whatever the case may be, San Marco is unique.

- The church is open all day, but tourists are asked to visit the interior between 09.30 and 17.00, in order not to disturb religious services. The Treasury and Pala d'Oro may be seen 09.30–16.30 (Sun & holidays 14.00– 16.30). The loggia on the façade and the Museo Marciano are open 09.30– 17.00, Sun & holidays 14.00–16.30).

Exterior Its architecture is inspired by the church of the Twelve Apostles in Constantinople (no longer extant) and resembles the slightly later church of St Front at Perigueux in France. Built in the form of a Greek cross, with a large central dome over the crossing and smaller domes over the aisles and transepts, it is adorned with marbles and mosaics combining Romanesque, Byzantine and Gothic influences. The façade has two superimposed orders of five arches, of which the one in the middle is the widest, and five doorways separated by groups of columns with capitals of Middle Eastern inspiration (these date from 12C and 13C). The arches springing from the balcony have imaginative Gothic aedicules, pinnacles, tracery and sculpture, added in the 14C and 15C; the tabernacles at the ends contain an *Annunciation* (on one side, the Archangel Gabriel, on the other, the Virgin Mary) attributed to the Florentine sculptor Jacopo della Quercia. On the balcony itself are copies of the four bronze horses brought in 1204 from Constantinople and now in the cathedral museum for safe-keeping (see below).

The **narthex**, or vestibule leading into the nave of the church, is an ecclesiastical adaptation of the Roman triumphal arch, using columns rather than statues and mosics rather than reliefs to animate its front. The north door incorporates the *Arrival of the Body of St Mark in Venice* (1260–70), the oldest mosaic on the façade, containing the earliest known image of the church. The other lunette mosaics date from the 17C to the 19C. The central doorway is carved with 13C reliefs which, read from the inside outwards, represent allegories of the months, personifications of virtues and Christ and the prophets. Within, the narthex has a marble mosaic pavement of the 11C and 12C, and its walls, vaults and domes are covered with extraordinary gold-ground mosaics, of Veneto-Byzantine workmanship. These tell Old Testament stories. Particularly interesting are the 13C *Stories of Genesis* in the dome above the bronze Porta di San Clemente (11C, from Constantinople) and the 11C and 12C figures of the *Evangelists*, in the bay in front of the main door. In the south flank of the church are the door of the baptistery, preceded by two finely carved free-standing columns, possibly of 5C or 6C Syrian workmanship, and in a corner, two 4C porphyry reliefs known as the *Tetrarchs*, believed to represent Diocletian and three other Roman emperors. They may be Egyptian works of the 4C.

Interior The dazzling interior is an epitome of Byzantine decorative craftsmanship. The 12C floor has a richly decorative design of marble, porphyry and other stones, which is fully uncovered only in late July and early August: the ripple effect is due to the settling of the building over the centuries. Each arm of the cross has three aisles separated by colonnades, above which runs the matroneum—a gallery for women in the Greek Orthodox rite, here also an ingenious device for masking the buttresses that support the five great domes. The sanctuary is raised above the crypt and set off from the rest of the church by an elaborate screen. An immense Byzantine chandelier hangs at the centre of the nave.

Visitors are directed through the church in a circuit that begins on the south side and ends on the north. The upper walls and ceiling vaults are completely covered with **mosaics**. Most are by Byzantine and Venetian artists of 12C and 13C, though some—recognisable by their greater naturalism—were done over in 16C and 17C to designs by Titian, Tintoretto, Veronese and other Venetian painters. The mosaics celebrate the triumph of Christ and His Church. As is customary in Byzantine iconography, *Christ Pantocrator* (The All-Powerful) is enthroned in the apse; he sits above four protectors of Venice, Sts Nicholas, Peter, Mark and Hermagorus. The cupola above the high altar is devoted to the *Prophets*, who heralded the coming of Christ. The central cupola shows the *Ascension* over figures of *Virtues*; the arch between this and the west dome, scenes from the Passion of Christ. The dome above the nave, where the congregation gathered, represents *Pentecost*. On the west wall, Christ seated between the Virgin and St Mark looks towards the high altar. Higher up are scenes from the Apocalypse, and the barrel vault over the narthex bears a representation of the *Last Judgement* (from a design by Tintoretto). Minor mosaics are arranged around these. The cupolas in the transepts represent action and meditation in the service of the Church: the south cupola has figures of Sts Nicholas, Clement, Blaise, Leonard and, in the squinches, Erasmus, Euphemia, Dorothy and Tecla, all of them martyrs; the north cupola has scenes from the life of St John the Evangelist supported by the Doctors of the Western Church in the squinches. All around are scenes from the life of Christ.

From the south aisle of the nave you enter the **baptistery** (1343–54), built by closing off a portion of the narthex. Here are a baptismal font designed by Jacopo Sansovino (1545) and the tombs of several doges—including that of Andrea Dandolo, the friend of Petrarch who commissioned the 14C mosaics of the life of St John the Baptist and the early life of Christ. The baptistery altar incorporates a granite slab on which Christ is said to have rested; it was brought from Tyre in the 13C. Pius X, honoured by a statue above the altar, was Patriarch of Venice before becoming pope in 1903. Reached by a door at the west end of the baptistery is the burial chapel of Cardinal Giovanni Battista Zen (d. 1501), with a bronze statue of the *Madonna* (called the Madonna of the Shoe) by Antonio Lombardo, a fine doorway to the narthex and late 13C vault mosaics, all of which merit a glance.

The **Treasury of San Marco**, one of the richer ensembles of religious art in Italy, is reached from the end of the south transept. Here you can see a very interesting display of liturgical objects by Eastern craftsmen (including chalices, icons, reliquaries, prayer books and altar frontals mainly from the 12C and 13C), many of which were brought back in 1204 from Constantinople. All reveal the medieval preoccupation with symbolism, and many show the distinctively Byzantine concern for richness, colour and texture. Highlights include an Islamic rock-crystal ewer carved with rliefs of two seated lions; a black glass bowl decorated in enamel with nude figures and Classical busts, a work of the 11C Byzantine 'Renaissance'; and the so-called crown of Leo VI, decorated with enamal medallions of saints and an emperor, made in Constantinople between 886 and 912. When viewing these pieces it is important to remember that in Byzantium, as in China, there was no division between the major and minor arts.

The highest civil and religious ceremonies of the republic took place in the **sanctuary**, which is raised over the crypt and enclosed by a marble iconostasis crowned by a silver and bronze crucifix by Jacopo di Marco Bennato and statues of the Virgin, St Mark and the Apostles by Pier Paolo and Jacobello Dalle Masegne (1394). Two ambones constructed in the 14C out of earlier materials adjoin the ends of the screen: from that on the left the Epistle and the Gospel were read; from that on the right the newly elected doges showed themselves to the people. The high altar, which rises over the body of St Mark, is supported by four historiated (New Testament scenes) alabaster columns with 12C capitals and surmounted by a ciborium decorated with six 13C statues. Behind it is the famous *Pala d'Oro*, a remarkable gold altarpiece encrusted with enamels and gems, made by Byzantine and Venetian goldsmiths between the 10C and 14C. Among the precious stones that adorn the work are emeralds, rubies, amethysts, sapphires, topaz and pearls. In the apse are an altar with six tall columns, a gilt tabernacle by Jacopo Sansovino, and statues by Lorenzo Bregno; and the bronze door of the sacristy, Sansovino's last work (1546–69). Beneath the sanctuary are the beautiful crypt and the little 15C church of San Teodoro, with an *Adoration of the Child* painted by Tiepolo in 1732.

The 12C Byzantine icon of the *Madonna Nicopeia* ('bringer of victory'), set in a magnificent enamel frame, gives its name to the chapel at the beginning of the north transept. This is the most venerated image in the cathedral, considered the protectress of Venice. It bears the epithet nicopeia because it was carried into battle by the Byzantine emperors before being 'captured' in Constantinople in 1204. Placed in the basilica in 1234, it has never been removed, except in 1968 when a radical cleaning removed many of the additions that had been made over the centuries and revealed the glittering, enamel-like colours of the original, restoring life to a primitive image that exudes all the mysterious fascination of the Orient but is, at the same time, intensely human.

There are two chapels at the end of this transept. The larger is dedicated to St Isidore, who evangelised the island of Chios and was martyred there in 250. His remains were brought from Chios to Venice in 1125 but hidden until the mid-14C, when Doge Andrea Dandolo had this chapel prepared to enshrine them. The mosaics on the walls and vault tell the story of the saint, whose statue is in a niche behind the altar. The smaller is the chapel of the Madonna dei Mascoli, which once belonged to a confraternity of laymen (*mascoli* is male in Venetian dialect). It has a *Virgin and Child between Sts Mark and James* over the altar and mosaics of the Life of the Virgin on the vault. The latter were carried out under the direction of Michele Giambono using cartoons attributed to Andrea del Castagno, Jacopo Bellini and Andrea Mantegna—all pioneers of Renaissance art in Venice.

A winding staircase reached from the narthex leads up to the **Museo Marciano**, arranged on the upper floor of the cathedral. It includes illuminated manuscripts, fragments of mosaics from the basilica, paintings, tapestries and antique Persian silk-pile carpets. Here, too, are the splendid Hellenistic Greek bronze **Horses* brought to Venice from Constantinople in 1204 and beautifully restored in 1978–81 to reveal their original gilding. The horses were looted a second time by Napoleon, who swept them off (with, among other Italian artworks, 506 paintings) to Paris for display on the Arc du Carousel. Other exhibits include the cover for the Pala d'Oro painted in 1345 by Paolo Veneziano and vestments adorned with delicate Venetian lace. The fine view of the piazza from the loggia alone justifies a visit to the museum.

About mosaics

An heir to Byzantium, Venice long held onto the traditions of the East in her rich mosaic art. At San Marco, mosaics glitter in the low light of the basilica, revealing abstract, almost icon-like figures. The earliest mosaics at San Marco, dating from the 11C through the 14C, cling most strongly stylistically to their Byzantine cousins. In these early mosaics (seen in the apse, the domes and the narthex of the church), individual cubes of coloured glass, stone, and enamels, called *tesserae*, were set into a plaster bed at different depths and at different angles. This irregular setting catches as much light as possible, intensifying the brilliant, sparkling glow of the mosaic. Early mosaic technique also had a limited range of *tessera* colours, which encouraged a rather non-naturalistic pictorial style with attention focused on line and simplified colour definition. By the mid-15C, however, Venice saw the arrival of Florentine painters who designed mosaics with *tesserae* laid as smoothly as possible, minimising surface irregularity and eliminating the fantastic light effects of earlier mosaics. These artists also developed a range of tile colours that could produce delicate gradations of tonal values. With these innovations, mosaics lost the stylisation of earlier works and gained a painterly naturalism in the depiction of form, becoming, in essence, 'paintings in stone'.

Around the square

Look right as you come out of the basilica and you'll see the **Torre dell'Orologio**, a delightful construction built by Mauro Codussi in 1496–99. The *orologio* in question is a very handsome astronomical clock on top of which two bronze Moors (1497) strike the hours on a great bell. The event is worth waiting for, but to see it you must step back at least to the centre of the square.

Beyond the Torre dell'Orologio extends the former residence and offices of the Procurators of St Mark known as the **Procuratie Vecchie**, with a double portico built in the 12C and remodelled in the 16C under the direction of Jacopo Sansovino, who added the third floor after 1532. On the opposite side of the square stretches its near twin, the **Procuratie Nuove**, begun in 1582 by the Vicentine architect Vincenzo Scamozzi to a plan by Sansovino and completed in 1640 by Baldassarre Longhena. Napoleon made this building his royal palace and demolished the church of San Geminiano, which had stood at the western end of the piazza, to build the Neo-classical **Ala Napoleonica** (or Procuratie Nuovissime) in 1809.

Beneath the porticoes of the Procuratie Nuove, about half way along, is the 18C *Caffè Florian*, the most famous in the city, with a richly decorated interior and an orchestra outside on summer evenings. During the Austrian occupation this was the watering-place of Italian patriots, and its orchestra often engaged in battles to the last note with that of the philo-Austrian *Caffè Quadri*, on the other side of the square. Both are good (though pricey) places to take a break.

The area between the basilica and the waterfront is known as **Piazzetta San Marco**. At the far end, against the magnificent backdrop of the Isle of San Giorgio, are two Syrian granite columns erected in 1180 and topped by Venice's two historic patrons: St Theodore, patron of the original republic, who perches with his crocodile, and the saint who displaced him, Mark, represented by his traditional symbol as a winged lion. Public executions took place in the area between the columns.

Opposite the southwest corner of the basilica, at the corner of the Procuratie Nuove, rises the **Campanile**, erected in the 12C, altered in 1511 and completely rebuilt after collapsing (fortunately without claiming victims) on the morning of 14 July 1902. At the bottom is the elegant marble **Loggetta** (1537–49), with an ornate façade with three arches with sculptures and, inside, a terracotta *Madonna and Child*, all by Jacopo Sansovino. Initially a meeting place of the Venetian patricians, the Loggetta later housed the honour guard when the Great Council was in session. A lift ascends to the top (open daily 09.00–19.30; Jul & Aug 09.00–21.00), nearly 100m above the square.

Palazzo Ducale

Extending from the basilica to the water is the Palazzo Ducale, the residence of the doge and the seat of the highest magistrature of the Venetian Republic. Although it has stood on this site since the 9C, its present appearance is the product of a late Gothic reconstruction (c 1340–1420), the general design of which is attributed to the sculptor and architect Filippo Calendario. With its vast walls of white Istrian limestone and pink Verona marble, fine portico, delicate loggia, magnificent balconies (by Pier Paolo and Jacobello Dalle Masegne) and crenellated roof, it is by far the highest expression of Venetian Gothic architecture. Well preserved medieval carvings (as well as some good 19C copies) adorn the 36 capitals of the lower colonnade, representing the months, animals and foliage. Of special note are the marble reliefs of moral exemplars high up on the corners: on the northwest (nearest the basilica), the *Judgement of Solomon* with the archangel Gabriel; on the southwest (facing the lagoon), *Adam and Eve* with the archangel Michael; and on the southeast, the *Drunkenness of Noah* with the archangel Raphael—all of uncertain 14C attribution.

The palace is joined to San Marco by the **Porta della Carta** (1438), which forms the main entrance to the courtyard. The Paper Door is possibly so called because placards displayed here once decreed the republic's ordinances. This splendid gateway, a masterpiece of Venetian Gothic architecture and sculpture, was executed in 1438–42 by Giovanni and Bartolomeo Bon and their assistants. Its theme is a celebration of Justice (personified in the figure enthroned at the top) as the highest principle of government, accompanied by Temperance, Fortitude, Prudence and Charity. Doge Francesco Foscarini, who commisioned the work, is shown kneeling before the lion of St Mark in the lower part. His statue is an 1885 reproduction of the original smashed in 1797.

The Porta della Carta takes you into the palazzo's magnificent courtyard, probably the best part of the palace interior and the only part that can be viewed without charge. Here the unitary architectural image of the exterior gives way to a medley of styles united only by a desire for impressive magnificence. The Renaissance classicism of Antonio Rizzo's east façade (1485), decorated by Pietro, Antonio and Tullio Lombardo, predominates over the Gothic west and south sides. The **Scala dei Giganti**, a monumental staircase overlooked by colossal statues of *Mars* and *Neptune*—by Sansovino, who finished them in the mid-16C—leads up to the first-floor loggia. At its top doges were crowned after a religious service in San Marco; and from this landing they subsequently received important visitors.

Interior Before passing the ticket office and entering the palace (open daily 09.00–19.00), bear in mind that the building caught fire in 1577, destroying a remarkable collection of Renaissance paintings by Giovanni Bellini, Titian, Gentile da Fabriano and Pisanello, for which the Tintoretto and Veronese school pieces that now adorn the interior are very weak replacements. If the palace is crowded and there is a wait to get in, you are better off spending your time elsewhere.

If you do go in, take the staircase beneath the southeast side of the portico up to the Gothic loggia. From here the Scala d'Oro—designed by Sansovino in 1554 and bearing gilt stuccoes by Alessandro Vittoria in the ceiling—ascends to a succession of 16C rooms, many of which have carved, gilt ceilings and fine Renaissance chimney-pieces. The best are the **Sala degli Scarlatti**, decorated by Pietro Lombardo, with a marble bas-relief and blue and gold ceiling; the **Cappella Privata del Doge**, which has a *St Christopher* frescoed on the outside by Titian; the **Sala delle Quattro Porte**, named after the monumental doors decorated with statues and columns and containing Titian's *Doge Antonio Grimani Kneeling before Faith*; the **Sala dell'Anticollegio**, with *Tintoretto's Vulcan's Forge, Mercury and the Graces, Bacchus and Ariadne*, and *Minerva and Mars*, and a *Rape of Europa* by Veronese; the **Sala del Collegio**, designed by Antonio Palladio, with canvases on the walls by Tintoretto (each showing a doge among the saints) and Veronese (*Sebastiano Venier Thanking God for the Victory of Lepanto*) and a carved ceiling with more opulent paintings by Veronese; the **Sala del Consiglio dei Dieci**, with paintings by Veronese in the carved and gilt ceiling; the **Sala dell'Armamento**, with what is left of the magnificent fresco of *Paradise* by Guariento (1365–67, ruined in the fire of 1577) and, in the adjoining loggia, the statues of *Adam and Eve* carved by Antonio Rizzo in 1468 for the Arco Foscari in the courtyard; and the **Sala del Maggior Consiglio**, or Great Council Chamber, a vast (53 x 24m) hall whose decoration, like that of the adjacent Sala dello Scrutinio, was executed after the fire. On the walls is the huge *Paradise* painted by Tintoretto and assistants in place of Guariento's (reputedly the largest oil painting in the world). The frieze is decorated with portraits of doges (that of Marin Falier, beheaded in 1355 for treason, has been replaced by a black curtain) and the ceiling holds Veronese's great *Apotheosis of Venice*, surrounded by paintings by Tintoretto and Palma Giovane.

The palace is connected to the 17C prison by the famous **Ponte dei Sospiri** (Bridge of Sighs,1602), over which the condemned were led, often never to emerge alive. The best exterior view of the bridge is from the beautiful 15C Ponte della Paglia, on the quayside.

The Libreria Sansoviniana and Museo Correr

The piazzetta is bordered on the west by the *****Libreria Sansoviniana**, a masterpiece of 16C Venetian architecture begun by Sansovino and completed after the architect's death by Scamozzi. The solemnly Classical building, with its portico and loggia, Ionic columns and rooftop balustrade, was built to house the Biblioteca Marciana, the Library of St Mark established by Cardinal Bessarione in 1468, but is now used as a venue for exhibitions. A monumental staircase ascends to the vestibule, with a ceiling frescoed by Titian (Wisdom), and to the magnificent main hall, with paintings of philosophers by Veronese, Tintoretto and Andrea Schiavone. The adjoining rooms of the Procuratie Nuove house the

Museo Archeologico (open daily 09.00–19.00). It has an important collection of Greek and Roman sculpture, including a series of Greek statues of women dating from the 5C and 4C BC (*Demeter, Hera, Athena*); three *Gallic Wariors* (copies of a group presented by Attalus of Pergamum to Athens, 3C BC), the *Grimani Altar*, of Hellenistic workmanship; portrait busts of *Trajan* and *Vitellius;* and the Hellenistic *Zulian Cammeo*. There are also marbles, inscriptions and a collection of Roman coins.

Next door to the Libreria is the Palazzo della Zecca, or Mint, likewise designed by Jacopo Sansovino and built between 1537 and 1566. It is the modern home of the Biblioteca Marciana (open daily 09.00–19.00), possessing numerous rare books and manuscripts, notably the splendid *Breviario Grimani*, a masterpiece of 15C illumination.

A monumental staircase beneath the arches of the Ala Napoleonica leads up to the **Museo Correr** (open daily 09.00–19.00), with collections illustrating Venetian art and history from the 13C to the 16C. Highlights include works by Jacopo Bellini (*Crucifixion*) and his sons Gentile (*Portrait of Doge Mocenigo*) and Giovanni (*Crucifixion, Transfiguration* and *Pietà*); Vittore Carpaccio (*Two Venetian Ladies*), Antonello da Messina (*Pietà*), Lorenzo Lotto (*Portrait*), Lucas Cranach and Hugo Van der Goes. The same building houses a small museum of the Risorgimento with documents and memorabilia ranging from the late 18C to the incorporation of the city into the Kingdom of Italy (1866).

A masterpiece at the Correr

One of the more significant works in the Correr is Giovanni Bellini's *Pietà*, ascribed to the period between 1445 and 1455. Unknown to critics until a few decades ago, this painting is important because it was done at the beginning of the artist's career, possibly during his sojourn in Padua, where the Florentine sculptor Donatello was working at the same time. In fact, whereas the cityscape in the background suggests the archaeological accuracy of Mantegna (who, incidentally, was Bellini's brother-in-law), the angels holding up the dead Christ recall the bronze angels that Donatello made for the famous altar in Sant'Antonio. In addition to this evidence of early influences you can see traces of that use of colour which was to become the hallmark of Bellini's work—for instance, in the way the artist uses thin layers of paint to create atmospheric effects both in the distant landscape and in the foreground figures of Christ and the angels. This specific characteristic of Bellini's artistic language, indicative of a new interest in naturalism, is one of the first signs of the arrival of the Renaissance in Venetian painting.

West of Piazza San Marco

To explore the *sestiere* of San Marco, pass beneath the arch of the Ala Napoleonica and take the broad Salizzada San Moisè, which takes you past the church of the same name, a soot-blackened operatic, self-indulgent and spectacular building interesting above all for its façade, a stage-set where you must search determinedly for any trace of religious imagery. From here the broad Calle Larga XXIII Marzo leads westwards, running parallel to the Grand Canal amid luxury hotels and expensive shops. A few steps along, Calle del Sartor da Veste diverges right to Campo San Fantin, a picturesque old square surrounded by elegant white façades; the well-heads date from the 15C. Here stands the **Teatro La Fenice**, an 18C building destroyed by fire in 1837 and again in 1996, and presently under reconstruction. Across from the theatre is the Renaissance church of **San Fantin**, begun by Scarpagnino. The beautiful apse was added by Jacopo Sansovino, who probably also did the marble cantoria inside. On the left is the former Scuola di San Fantin, seat since 1812 of a literary-scientific academy founded by Napoleon.

Return to Calle Larga and follow it to its end. Left, right and over the bridge is **Santa Maria del Giglio** (or Santa Maria Zobenigo, 1683), another example of Baroque decorative exuberance with a façade by Giuseppe Sardi. Here, too, the secular character of the design overwhelms any latent religious content: the financial patron stands above the door (in a position usually reserved for the patron saint), between figures of Honour and Virtue, while four relatives peer down on passersby; detailed low reliefs of the fortresses the family commanded appear at the bottom of the façade. The interior has several fine paintings: on the south, in the Cappella Molin, a *Madonna and Child with the Young St John*, by Peter Paul Rubens; on the third south altar, a *Visitation* by Palma Giovane; behind the high altar, an *Addolorata* by Sebastiano Ricci and *Evangelists* by Jacopo Tintoretto, who also did the painting of *Christ and Saints* over the third north altar.

The street ends in Campo Santo Stefano (or Campo Morosini), at an important crossroads. The statue in the middle represents Niccolò Tommaseo, a 19C patriot. **Santo Stefano** (right) is a church of the 14C and 15C, with a 15C façade displaying mullioned windows and a white marble Gothic doorway somewhat darkened by soot. The vast interior has three aisles and a polygonal apse, a fine ship's-keel roof and tomb monuments of various epochs. The best of these are the tombs of Giacomo Surian on the west wall, and of the jurisconsult G.B. Ferretti in the chapel on the north of the sanctuary. Both were made in the Renaissance; the Ferretti tomb has been attributed to Michele Sanmicheli. The church's most valuable artworks, however, are in the sacristy; here you can see a crucifix by Paolo Veneziano (c 1348), a polyptych by Bartolomeo Vivarini, a *Holy Family* by Palma Vecchio and three large canvases (*Last Supper, Washing of the Feet* and *Agony in the Garden*) by Tintoretto. A door in the left aisle leads to the interesting 16C cloister, with an Ionic colonnade attributed to Scarpagnino. At the beginning of the same aisle is the entrance to the Cappella del Battista, with a *Baptism of Christ* by Pomponio Amalteo over the altar and the funerary stele of a member of the Falier faily, by Antonio Canova, on the wall.

Go right as you leave Santo Stefano. Walk around the side of the church and over the bridge to Campo Sant'Angelo (where the composer Domenico Cimarosa lived: his house is marked by a plaque). Cross the square and descend the steps in the left-hand corner to Calle dei Avocati, take your first right and cross another little bridge. On your right will be **Palazzo Fortuny**, a 15C palace whose Gothic façade overlooks the little Campo San Beneto. Here is the house-museum (closed for restoration at the time of writing) of the Spanish painter and designer Mariano Fortuny y Madrazo (1861–1949), whose fashions and textiles were the rage of *fin-de-siècle* Europe. Fortuny himself furnished and decorated the rooms, which now contain a number of his designs, together with curios and memorabilia.

With your back to the little church of San Beneto, walk to the end of Salizzada de la Chiesa and take Calle de la Mandorla left. You'll come out in Campo Manin.

A narrow alley on the right here (marked) winds its way eventually to the **Scala del Bovolo**, in the garden court of Palazzo Contarini. This splendid late 15C spiralling stair (*bovolo* means spiral in Venetian) allowed external access to the upper floors of the palace. Although you can buy a ticket and climb to the top (open daily 10.00–18.00), there's not much reason to do so: the best viewpoint is from the pavement just outside the garden.

Back in Campo Manin, walk diagonally across the square and bear left to reach the Grand Canal; the **Ponte di Rialto** appears quite suddenly on your right, at the end of a pleasant quay. This and the quay on the opposite bank—both of which are lined with small restaurants and cafés—are among the few places in Venice where you can actually walk along the canal. On the corner of Calle del Carbon is a commemorative plaque to Elena Lucrezia Cornaro Piscopia, born in this house in 1646. The plaque recalls that she was graduated from Padua University on 25 June 1678—making her the first woman in history to receive a degree. A little further on is Sansovino's Palazzo Dolfin Manin (now the Banca d'Italia).

Just a few steps south of the Rialto Bridge, Campo San Bartolomio stands at the crossroads of streets coming from Piazza San Marco and the train station. The monument at the centre commemorates playwright Carlo Goldoni (1707–93), a native. South of the square begins the lively succession of shopping streets known as the Mercerie. From this corner the white Baroque façade of the 16C church of **San Salvador** overlooks the campo to which it gives its name. Inside are sculptures by Sansovino and two late paintings by Titian: the *Annunciation* over an altar in the south aisle and the *Transfiguration*, over the high altar. South of the church is the former convent, with two 16C cloisters.

On the Mercerie dell'Orologio are the campo and church of **San Zulian**, a very old foundation rebuilt in its present form by Jacopo Sansovino in 1553–55. Some believe Sansovino also made the bronze statue of the patron, the physician Tommaso Rangone, above the doorway. Inside are works by Paolo Veronese (*Pietà*, first south altar) and Palma Giovane (*Glory of St Julian*, on the wooden ceiling; *Assumption*, second south altar; *Resurrection*, in the arch of the chapel north of the sanctuary. From here it is a very short walk down the Mercerie and through the Torre dell'Orologio to Piazza San Marco.

Dorsoduro

The sound of voices over water and the rumble of the vaporetto become noticeably clearer as you make your way from Campo Santo Stefano to the great wooden arch of the **Ponte dell'Accademia**, first built by the Austrians in order to move troops quickly from one part of the city to another. The view of the Grand Canal from the top is inspiring: on one side are the Bacino di San Marco, with the church of Santa Maria della Salute and the Punta della Dogana on the right; on the other, the great, wide bend called Volta del Canal.

Galleria dell'Accademia
Just beyond the bridge is the *Galleria dell'Accademia, one of the great museums of Europe. The entrance is through the Neo-classical doorway of the former Scuola Grande della Carità, which dates from 1765.

- Open Sun 09.00–19.00, Mon 08.30–14.00, Tues–Sat 08.30–19.30. As the queue at the Accademia can be quite long during high season (only a few visitors are admitted at a time), plan to arrive at least 20 minutes before opening time. If you are not a morning person, the last hour before closing is also a good time.

The collection here ranges over five centuries of Venetian painting, with 14C works varying between Byzantine-style paintings and the Gothic works of Paolo Veneziano, 15C painting represented by the early Renaissance works of the Bellini family and Carpaccio, and 16C works ranging from the powerful paintings of Giorgione and Titian to the late mannerism of Bassano, Tintoretto and Veronese. The theatrical 17C is represented by the works of foreign artists visiting the city and by the baroque works of Maffei; while the 18C collection ranges from the great Rococo decorators Ricci, Pellegrini, Tiepolo and Antonio Guardi, to the more naturalistic works of Longhi, Canaletto and Francesco Guardi. The collection is arranged chronologically, and the works are well labelled.

A brief guide to the Accademia

Paolo Veneziano (active 1310–62), *Coronation of the Virgin*. Paolo Veneziano is the first great master of Venetian painting for whom we have a name, and this polyptych, from the church of Santa Chiara, is his masterpiece. The most striking feature of the work is its complexity, which suggests it was done toward the end of the artist's career, when he was assisted by his sons Luca and Giovanni (c 1358). Within the imposing original frame, the large central panel showing Jesus crowning his Mother is flanked by some 20 smaller panels telling stories of Christ, St Francis and St Claire, with the Four Evangelists on either side. The fascination of this work is partly due to the fact that it so clearly reveals the two formal traditions on which Paolo drew—Byzantine in the side panels and Gothic in the large central panel. The fine decoration of the flowing robes of Christ and the Virgin recalls the rich gold brocades that adorned Venetian garments of 14C and 15C; and the delicate tones used in portraying the angel-musicians foreshadow that intense interest in colour which was to become the hallmark of Venetian art.

Giovanni Bellini (c 1430–1516), *Camerlenghi Madonna*. This painting takes its name from the Rialto palazzo where it originally hung. It reflects the 'primitive' style of the two earlier Madonnas alongside it, which were painted by Giovanni's father Jacopo Bellini. The chiaroscuro is reminiscent of Mantegna, with whom the young artist studied in Padua; and the incisive line, used to create large fields of colour, recalls the style of the Florentine Filippo Lippi, who was also working in Padua. This clear reference to the style of other, more established painters may date the masterpiece to the early part of the artist's career. Nevertheless, in the facial expressions of the Mother and Child, one glimpses Giovanni's own very personal, almost moody humanity—a consequence, perhaps, of the continuing fascination exercised by Byzantine icons.

Gentile Bellini (1429–1507), *Procession of the Reliquary of the True Cross in Piazza San Marco*. The appearance of the city in 1496 is recreated in this large scene, one of a cycle of paintings (there are two others by Gentile Bellini, two by Mansueti, one each by Bastiani and Diana, and one by Carpaccio) that hang in the same room. The subject of the cycle is the legend of the True Cross, which had been discovered in Palestine by St Helen. It was published in Venice, in Jacopo da Varagine's *Golden Legend*, in 1475. At the time, Gentile Bellini was Master Artist of the Scuola di San Giovanni Evangelista, and this painting gave him an ideal opportunity to attempt a narrative work using the theatrical techniques adopted in sacred pageants. The painter spices up his narrative by adding the anecdote of the miraculous healing of the son of Jacopo de Solis (portrayed in red, kneeling near the centre of the procession); to the left, the three figures in the red robes of the Confraternity of San Giovanni Evangelista are portraits of the artist, his father Jacopo and his brother Giovanni. The painting is particularly interesting because of what it shows of Piazza San Marco. The Procuratie Vecchie are visible on the left; the Procuratie Nuove have yet to be built. On the façade of San Marco appear the lost lunette mosaics of the narthex and, on the loggia, the four great gilt-bronze horses flanked by the original mosaics representing scenes from the life of Christ. Some scholars see proto-Renaissance features in these mosaics which they attribute to the influence of early 15C Tuscan art, brought to Venice by Paolo Uccello and Andrea Castagno.

Vittore Carpaccio (c 1465–1526?), *The Dream of St Ursula.* The story Carpaccio chose for the cycle of paintings commissioned by the Loredan family for the (destroyed) Scuoletta di Sant'Orsola and painted between 1490 and 1500, was the poetic tale—also told in Jacopo da Varagine's *Golden Legend*—of a Catholic princess from Brittany, whose hand is asked in marriage by the English prince Etherius, a pagan. Ursula tells the prince's ambassadors that if he truly wants her he will have to convert to Catholicism and accompany her to Rome to be married by the pope. During the pilgrimage an angel appears to Ursula in a dream and tells her of her imminent martyrdom, which occurs during the return journey, at Cologne, under siege by the Huns. In *The Dream of St Ursula* the perfect perspective of the composition contributes to the creation of an atmosphere typical of Carpaccio's style—a marvellous medley of deep spirituality and meticulous attention to detail, which serves to make this supernatural event totally credible. The scene is set in the serene light of dawn, the luminescent colour veiled by particles of gold that seem to settle calmly on all the objects—especially on the bedside table and its prayerbooks, on the soft bed and on the windowsill with its potted myrtle and carnations, symbols of faith and chastity.

Giorgione (1476–1510), *The Tempest.* Despite the brevity of his active life (he died of plague at the age of 34), Giorgione managed to impose a new style that his contemporary Giorgio Vasari described as 'without drawing'. In this sense he was one of the pioneers of Venetian Renaissance painting, in which colour and paint are paramount. The theme of *La Tempesta* (as the work has been known since the 19C) seems designed to force the curiosity of the observer towards an area of mystery (which the incessant efforts of critics have made no easier to penetrate). No one knows exactly what Giorgione was intending to represent when he painted this evocative image. Certainly the claim that it is a portrait of the painter's family can be discounted—biographers make no mention of the artist having either a wife or a child. It seems most likely that the true meaning of *The Tempest* is an esoteric one. The key to the work may in fact be Francesco Colonna's poem *The Dream of Polyphilus,* published by the famous Venetian printer Aldus Manutius in 1499, which contains a description of Venus feeding

Love while the poet-shepherd Polyphilus looks on and the sky becomes heavy with an impending storm. Whatever the correct reading—and some have argued there is no reading at all, that this is the first modern landscape painting—*The Tempest* remains one of the more forceful images in the history of painting. The air of mystery in the picture is underscored by the colours—from the soft greens of the grass, to the pale glow of the nude against the white cloak and the silvery light of the towers and city walls, which seem to glow beneath the dark sky. A dramatic and visionary scene, in poetic contrast with the apparent indifference of the figures occupying it.

Titian (Tiziano Vecellio, 1480?–1576), *Presentation of the Virgin in the Temple*. This splendid picture was painted for the room in which it hangs—the *albergo* (chapter room) of the former Scuola della Carità. The composition, executed around 1559, makes ample use of details in the work of contemporary architects who were deeply influenced by Roman antiquity. The work's rigorous perspective gives it a marked theatrical quality, underscored by the stunning richness of colour in the scene and by the narrative realism of the rendering, which seem to draw the viewer into the event depicted. The theme of the Virgin's affirmation of religious faith was a reference to one of the principal functions of the Scuola della Carità, which once a year, in this room, gathered together a number of poor but virtuous girls to secure them the dowry that would enable them to marry. The widowed Titian made the painting as his own daughter Lavinia was reaching womanhood, and it may not be coincidental that there is something particularly intimate and personal about the figure of the fair-haired Mary in her blue gown, suffused by a supernatural light. At the bottom of the steps leading up to the temple Titian has portrayed a chorus of witnesses, composed of patrician ladies and gentlemen dressed in the ceremonial robes of the scuola.

Lorenzo Lotto (c 1480–1556), *Portrait of a Melancholic Young Man*. Lorenzo Lotto was at times seen as the 'alternative' to Titian, though he never encouraged direct comparison. He began his career just after the encounter in Venice of the Bellini, Antonello da Messina and Albrecht Dürer, and he used this convergence of influences to good effect in his early works. Later, as a result of a long period in Rome alongside Raphael and Michelangelo, Lotto would be drawn towards Mannerism, which better suited his elegant draughtsmanship and unusual palette. His period in the Marches and in the Bergamo area then brought him into contact with patrons whose high expectations were the result of their familiarity with the work of the Lombard and Rome schools. Though Lotto never enjoyed unbridled success—his modesty itself was against him—he was highly esteemed, particularly in the provinces, where his sophistication compared well to the less advanced styles of regional artists. The *Portrait of a Melancholic Young Man* dates from the late 1520s or early 1530s. Its 'dark' atmosphere is heightened by details that would seem to indicate a solitary existence—such as the letter and crumpled petals, which perhaps indicate some past love. An acute and sensitive psychologist, Lotto has been called the most 'modern' of 16C Venetian painters. Emphasis has been placed on the way his pictures would seem to suggest a very reserved character—and indeed, as he retreated further and further into himself, Lotto's work became more and more intensely religious. He died in 1556 or 1557 in the monastery of the Santa Casa di Loreto, where he had lived for years, painting his last tormented pictures.

Jacopo Tintoretto (1519–94), *Miracle of St Mark Freeing the Slave*. In April 1548 Pietro Aretino, one of the more famous and feared writers of his day, wrote a letter to Jacopo Tintoretto that was destined to become famous. After extensive praise, the noted critic concluded with the observation that 'blessed would be your name if you reduced the speed with which you have done in patience in doing'. The letter should be seen in the context of the debate over the relative merits of the 'rational' figurative tradition of Rome and Florence and the reckless improvisation of Venetian painters—in other words, of the fine draughtsmanship of Michelangelo and Raphael as opposed to the virtuoso brushwork of Titian and Tintoretto.

In that same year, 1548, Tintoretto completed a painting that would seem to justify Aretino's remarks—the *Miracle of St Mark Freeing the Slave*, which was destined for the large central hall of the Scuola di San Marco. The story concerns the slave of a landowner in Provence who left his owner's estate to journey to Venice to venerate the relics of St Mark. Recaptured, he was condemned to death; but the saint intervened to save him. In Tintoretto's interpretation the crowd flees in terror, the slave's shackles break open, and the torturers' instruments fall apart in their hands. Giorgio Vasari gives an idea of the public reaction to this scene when he describes Tintoretto as 'the most terrible mind that ever dedicated itself to painting'. But while there may be some truth in the rumour he reports— that the officials of the scuola who had commissioned the painting were left dumbfounded by such vehement images—the work is not as shocking as it once was. This is the real Tintoretto, at the height of his youthful vigour and daring inventiveness. As if to confirm his creative genius, the painter includes a number of portraits in the picture: the bearded gentleman on the left is Marco Episcopi, Grand Guardian of the Scuola and the artist's future father-in-law; the black-robed figure among the columns of the palace is a self-portrait. Completed before he was 30 years of age, this work is an open declaration of the distinguishing characteristics of Tintoretto's art: stunning realism, strong religious devotion and intense feeling.

Paolo Veronese (1528–88), *The Mystic Marriage of St Catherine*. The original site of this painting was the church of Santa Caterina in Cannaregio—a very humble setting for one of Veronese's more sumptuous works, a symphony of gold and silver silks and brocades beneath a chorus of heavenly voices accompanied by two lutes. As if in deliberate contrast to the setting, Veronese used the whole range of his palette to create an unforgettable feast of colour. In the words of the 17C poet and essayist Marco Boschini, 'One could say that the Painter / to achieve these effects / Had mixed gold, pearls and rubies / and emeralds and sapphires beyond fineness / and pure and perfect diamonds.' The work seems to draw on the magnificence of aristocratic life in the city: the saint's gown seems exactly like that of a Venetian noblewoman, who is tentatively approaching a ceremony she does not fully understand. As always, there is a sort of aristocratic detachment in the way Veronese follows through the ideas inspired by light and colour. 'I paint figures', he was to say to the judges of the Inquisition who, in this same period, called him before them to justify the religious coldness and decorative excess in his work. Here, once again, you can see this master of the sumptuous palette betting everything on the inevitable triumph of colour.

Jacopo Bassano (c 1510–92), *St Jerome the Hermit*. In the glorious triumvirate of Venetian painting of the second half of the 16C—formed by Tintoretto, Veronese and Jacopo Bassano—the latter was the champion of a naturalistic poetics inspired by the world of concrete objects. Bassano had little interest in the pomp of this Golden Age and seems to have chosen his models from among humble farming folk. Painted around 1565, his *St Jerome the Hermit* appears to be a robust woodsman caught resting after a hard day's work. Around him are a few objects—a crucifix, a skull, an hourglass and some books—chosen to indicate his saintly vocation. None of these objects, however, seems out of place; their very simplicity makes them credible. Bassano was most at ease when depicting scenes of popular life—all of which are described with ingenuous faith; yet his works are painted in a manner that reveals the artist to be capable of the most complex, refined effects.

Bernardo Bellotto (1720–80), *The Scuola di San Marco at San Giovanni e Paolo*, and **Francesco Guardi** (1712–93), *Fire at San Marcuola*. The works of the *vedutisti*, or view painters, had a special appeal for those numerous foreign visitors who were passionately interested in the buildings, squares and canals of Venice. Bernardo Bellotto, like his uncle and teacher, Canaletto, belonged to the realist school of view painting, which sought 'objective' accuracy in the rendering of places and events. The *Scuola di San Marco at San Giovanni e Paolo* is a sharply painted image in which the reflections of sky and architecture are rendered with meticulous care. The patches of colour are enlivened with the merest touch of paint, applied with the very point of the brush to achieve an effect of surprising naturalism. Other view painters preferred a more 'impressionistic' approach—suggesting rather than representing the scene before them. This group included the striking colourist Francesco Guardi. Whereas Bellotto represented the real world in the spirit of Enlightenment Rationalism, Guardi was much more a painter of the imagination and of individual sensibility. His works seem to anticipate romanticism, or even impressionism. *Fire at San Marcuola* was inspired by a real event—the fire in Venice's oil warehouses on 28 December 1789—but even here Guardi takes great liberties with his subject, creating a composition that is built around vibrant lines and dramatic atmospheric effects.

Ca' Rezzonico

Hop on a vaporetto to reach Ca' Rezzonico, one stop up the Grand Canal on the left; or if you like, take your chances on getting lost in the maze of calli and bridges (actually quite pleasant) north and west of the Accademia. This powerful Baroque palazzo on the Grand Canal, begun in 1649 by Baldassare Longhena and completed after 1750 by Giorgio Massari, is a refined example of an 18C patrician home. It was the last home of Robert Browning, who died in 1889 in a small apartment (not open) on the first floor. Today it hosts the **Museo del Settecento Veneziano** (open Sat–Thur 10.00–16.00), which, in sumptuous rooms (some with ceilings frescoed by Tiepolo and his pupils) creates a vivid image of Venetian life and culture in the 18C, drawing on tapestries, furniture, lacquer work, costumes and paintings. Among the latter are a fine series of small canvases with scenes of family life and rustic idylls by Pietro Longhi (1701–85), who occupies a very special place among the 'realist' painters of the second half of the 18C. His work marks the introduction into Venetian art of the 'conversation piece' painting—a European genre that was being popularised in France by Watteau and in England by Hogarth.

Ca' Rezzonico also has a room hung with the pastel portraits of Rosalba Carriera (1675–1752), one of Europe's first internationally acclaimed women artists. Admired and courted by many of the ruling families of Europe, she used an eminently naturalistic artistic language which made her talents respected by all. She was a significant influence on the great French pastel artists Quentin de la Tour and Chardin.

Pietro Longhi at Ca' Rezzonico

One of the more subtle and fascinating of Pietro Longhi's works at Ca' Rezzonico—which are all of more or less the same small size—is *The Moor and the Letter*. In this depiction of a Moorish slave delivering a secret letter to a young Venetian patrician, the workroom in which the lady sits with her maids is depicted in far too intimate a way to be 'merely' realistic. And, perhaps, the Zuccarelli painting recognisable on the wall of the room—a sensual vision of arcadia—is too clear an allusion to a moment of pleasure enjoyed by the letter's unknown writer. Longhi's works sometimes suggest that the artist was a bit of a rebel—especially when he charges his paintings with repressed eroticism (visits paid by important personages, little *tete-à-tete* suppers with English lords, procuresses offering saucy girls). It is even said that the Inquisition was keeping its eye on him. Even without giving credence to these unsubstantiated rumours, there is no doubt that Longhi belonged to that intellectual bourgeoisie which was becoming increasingly critical of the *veneta nobiltà*.

A scuola and its neighbourhood

Down the little canal from Ca' Rezzonico (fruit and vegetables are sold from boats here on weekday mornings) and to the right is Campo Santa Margherita, a charming working-class square and marketplace, surrounded by old houses. At the west end of the square, flanked by its church, stands the 17C **Scuola Grande dei Carmini**. This was one of Venice's six *scuole grandi*, or philanthropic confraternities (the others are the Scuola Grande dei Greci, della Misericordia, di San Giovanni Evangelista, di San Marco and di San Rocco), which engaged in charitable activities throughout the republic. *Scuole* were formed by laymen involved in the same trade, who often shared a common national ancestry and were committed to a particular religious cult. These confraternities are of particular artistic interest, since their participants' annual membership fees decorated the headquarters, often supporting the more prominent Venetian artists of the day. This building's design is attributed to Baldassare Longhena.

The rooms of the **interior** (open Mon–Sat 09.00–18.00, Sun 09.00–16.00) are decorated with stuccoes, wooden benches and 17C and 18C paintings. In the great upper hall, or Salone, is a fine ceiling with nine paintings by Giovanni Battista Tiepolo (1739–44) centring around a depiction of the *Virgin Presenting St Simon Stock with the Scapular of the Carmelite Order*, a work of the artist's later years. The Sala dell'Archivio has a beautiful carved wooden ceiling with paintings by Balestra, and the passage contains a *Judith and Holofernes* by Piazzetta.

The conventual church of **Santa Maria del Carmine** (or I Carmini), built in 1348, preserves a 14C doorway and porch on the north flank. The Renaissance façade with its arched gable was added in the early 16C. The interior, with three aisles on monolithic columns (faced with carmine-red damask at Christmas and Easter) and a Gothic polygonal apse, has a magnificent 17C/18C wooden decoration in the nave incorporating statues of *Prophets* and *Saints* between the arches and a continuous frieze of paintings above. These illustrate the history of the Carmelite Order and are by minor artists. Over the second south altar is an *Adoration of the Shepherds* by Cima da Conegliano; the chapel on the south of the sanctuary holds bronze relief of the *Deposition* by Francesco di Giorgio Martini and a charming little *Sacra Famiglia* by Veronese with a particularly playful young St John. Lorenzo Lotto's moody painting of *St Nicholas in Glory* hangs over the second north altar. Adjoining the church is the entrance to the former monastery (now a school), with a fine 16C cloister.

Upon leaving the church turn left, then left again along canals to reach **San Sebastiano**, rebuilt in 1504–48 in elegant Renaissance forms. It is famous for the impressive *decorative scheme created between 1555 and 1565 by Paolo Veronese, who was buried here in 1588. The splendid complex of canvas and frescoes covers the ceiling, the walls of the nave and sanctuary, the sacristy and the nuns' choir. Particularly noteworthy are the three canvases of the nave ceiling (*Stories of Esther*), the organ shutters (*Purification of the Virgin* outside and *Pool of Bethesda* inside) the large canvases with stories of St Sebastian in the sanctuary; the *Virgin in Glory with Sts Sebastian, Peter, Catherine and Francis*, over the high altar; and the ceiling compartments of the sacristy *(Coronation of the Virgin, Evangelists)*, the artist's first work in Venice. Among the other works of art preserved in the church are a beautiful marble group of the *Madonna and Child with the Young Saint John* by Tullio Lombardo, over the second south altar; the tomb of Livio Podocattaro by Sansovino after the third south chapel; and a *St Nicholas* by Titian over the altar of the vestibule. The former convent, rebuilt in 1851, now hosts a part of the university.

Le Zattere

Le Zattere is the name of the pleasant quay along the wide Canale della Giudecca, which separates the city from the long Isle of the Giudecca. *Zattere* in Venetian means 'lighters', and the fondamenta is named after the large, flat-bottomed barges that used to unload wood here. Almost 2km long, it is divided into four parts, which take their name from their most distinctive element: Zattere al Ponte Lungo, ai Gesuati, allo Spirito Santo, ai Saloni. As you cross the first little canal (Rio de San Trovaso), look left and you'll see one of Venice's last remaining *squeri*, the boatyards where gondolas are made and repaired. Further on, roughly halfway along the quay, stands the 18C church of the **Gesuati**, which holds works by Tiepolo (over the first south altar and ceiling fresco), Piazzetta (third south altar) and Tintoretto (third north altar).

The Punta della Dogana, the promontory separating the Grand Canal from the Canale della Giudecca, projects into the Bacino di San Marco towards the Isle of San Giorgio. It receives its name from the long, low building known as the **Dogana da Mar**, the Maritime Customs House, built over an earlier edifice by Giuseppe Benoni in 1677. The spectacular construction, designed to resemble an arcaded ship's prow, terminates in a triangular piazza offering unforgettable views over the city and the lagoon. From here you can imagine what it must have been like to arrive in Venice by sea. Sailing ships moored at the Molo di San Marco, at the foot of the Palazzo Ducale, where foreign visitors were immediately confronted by the highest symbols of political and religious power. Above the Doric façade of the Dogana di Mare rises Bernardo Falcone's sculptural composition of atlantes carrying a golden globe, topped by a weathervane in the shape of that most fickle of influences, Fortune.

Back to the Grand Canal

Just around the point, on the Grand Canal, is **Santa Maria della Salute**, a masterpiece of Venetian Baroque architecture. It was built to a design by Baldassare Longhena to commemorate the end of a terrible plague that swept the city in 1630. The church is designed in the shape of a crown, possibly in reference to the invocations to the Queen of Heaven in the Venetian litany that was recited in times of plague, or to the mention in Revelation of 'a woman clothed in the sun, and the moon under her feet, and upon her head a crown of twelve stars'. A statue of the Virgin with these attributes stands atop the cupola. At a lower level, on huge scrolls, are statues of the Apostles—the twelve stars in Longhena's 'crown'.

The **interior** of the church is a spacious octagon with an ambulatory, a lofty dome and a second, smaller dome over the sanctuary. An inscription in the centre of the pavement—*unde origo inde salus* (whence the origin, thence the salvation and health)—alludes to the legend that Venice was founded under the protection of the Virgin. Around the church are a number of important artworks: the high altar, designed by Longhena with sculptures by Josse Le Court, holds a venerated Byzantine icon; on the left is the Sagrestia Grande, over the altar of which is *St Mark Enthroned between Sts Cosmas, Damian, Roch and Sebastian*, an early work of Titian painted to commemorate the plague of 1510. Titian also painted the three fine paintings on the ceiling *(Sacrifice of Abraham, David and Goliath, Cain and Abel)* originally for the church of Santo Spirito. On the wall to the south of the altar is the *Marriage at Cana*, a large painting by Tintoretto.

At the foot of the church extends the Campo della Salute, one of the few Venetian squares facing the Grand Canal. It offers a fine view over the Bacino di San Marco. West of the church, high above the steps, is the Seminario Patriarcale, a severe building by Baldassare Longhena (1671) organised around a cloister and a monumental staircase. Here is the small **Pinacoteca Manfrediniana**, with paintings by 15C to 18C artists, notably Giorgione, Cima da Conegliano, Filippino Lippi and Domenico Beccafumi; and sculpture, including two Renaissance reliefs by Tullio Lombardo and a terracotta bust by Antonio Canova.

You leave Campo della Salute by the apse of the little Gothic church of San Gregorio (now a conservation laboratory), then follow the signs through the narrow calli to the ivy-clad entrance of the **Peggy Guggenheim Collection** (open Wed–Mon 10.00–18.00; Sat 10.00–22.00). This fascinating group of works of the European and American avant-gardes is arranged in the 18C Palazzo Venier dei Leoni, on the Grand Canal, where the spirited American heiress and patron of the arts lived from 1949 until her death in 1979. Artists represented in the collection include Piet Mondrian, Paul Klee, Giacomo Balla, Gino Severini, Max

Ernst, Joan Miró, Giorgio De Chirico, Pablo Picasso and Jackson Pollock. There is also a cool, shady garden and a sun-baked terrace on the canal where weary feet may be rested. To the surprise of many, the Guggenheim Collection is the second most visited museum after the Accademia, so in high season come a few minutes before opening time or just before closing for quieter viewing. When you leave the Guggenheim walk west (right), and you'll soon come out at the Accademia.

San Polo and Santa Croce

Campo San Giacomo di Rialto, formerly the centre of the city's financial life and now the centre of a colourful fruit and vegetable market, lies at the foot of the Rialto Bridge on the side farthest from San Marco. Flanked by the porticoes of the Fabbriche Vecchie, it is overlooked by the 15C façade of San Giacomo di Rialto (San Giacometto), built in the 12C and rebuilt in 1531 and 1601. From the Campo Ruga degli Orefici ('Goldsmiths' Row') leads into Ruga degli Speziali ('Apothecaries'). Meandering along in a more or less northwesterly direction you eventually come to the 17C church of San Cassiano, on the north side of its campo. An old foundation several times altered, it has a 13C brick campanile and some paintings by Tintoretto.

From here you must carefully follow the signs for the Ferrovia and the Galleria d'Arte Moderna to reach **Ca' Pesaro**, one of the more magnificent Venetian palaces on the Grand Canal. Entrance to the palazzo is by a modest door on the garden side; the vast courtyard has a large well attributed to Jacopo Sansovino.

On the first floor is the **Galleria d'Arte Moderna** (Tues–Sun 10.00–16.00), with a vast but undistinguished collection of works by the principal Italian and foreign artists of the 20C. The list includes most of the stars in the firmament of Modernism—Hans Arp, Umberto Boccioni, Joseph Calder, Carlo Carrà, Felice Casorati, Marc Chagall, Giorgio De Chirico, Filippo De Pisis, Raoul Dufy, Max Ernst, Emilio Greco, Vasily Kandinsky, Paul Klee, Gustav Klimt, Arturo Martini, Henri Matisse, Joan Miró, Henry Moore, Giorgio Morandi, Arnaldo and Giò Pomodoro, Ottone Rosai, Alberto Savinio and Mario Sironi. There are also some 19C paintings by Pierre Bonnard, Camille Corot, Giuseppe De Nittis, Giovanni Fattori, Francesco Hayez and Giuseppe Pellizza da Volpedo.

On the third floor is the **Museo d'Arte Orientale** (open Tues–Sun 09.00–14.00), which has a splendid collection of Japanese paintings, sculpture, porcelain, lacquer work, ivories and costumes of the Edo period (1614–1868), in addition to more modest holdings of Chinese porcelain and jades and Indonesian weapons, fabrics and shadow-theatre figures.

Leave the museum and go straight over the bridge, then down a covered portico and over another bridge. You'll come out on the Grand Canal, in front of **San Stae**, a church with a late Baroque façade by Domenico Rossi. The interior, now used for concerts and exhibitions, has 18C paintings by Giovanni Battista Tiepolo, Sebastiano Ricci and Giovanni Battista Piazzetta—the latter's *Capture of St James* is a masterpiece. The Salizzada San Stae, on the south side of the church, leads past **Palazzo Mocenigo**, where there is a small museum of 18C frescoes, paintings and furniture (open Tues–Sun 10.00–17.00).

Turn right in Calle del Tentor, then left at the bridge. Almost due south, in one of the few wooded spaces in the heart of the city, is **San Giacomo dell'Orio**.

This is one of the older churches of Venice, built in 1225 and altered between the 14C and the 17C; the extant elements of the original, 13C building are the central apse and brick campanile. The Latin-cross interior, with a 14C wooden ship's-keel roof, preserves several fine works of art: in the nave, a 13C holy-water stoup and a Lombardesque pulpit; beneath the arch of the sanctuary, a wooden crucifix by Paolo Veneziano; in the sanctuary, a *Madonna and Saints* by Lorenzo Lotto in the north transept, *Sts Jerome, Lawrence and Prosperus* by Paolo Veronese; and in the old sacristy, a cycle of paintings by Palma Giovane.

The church of the Frari

From the apse of San Giacomo continue southwards via Calle del Tentor to reach Santa Maria Gloriosa dei Frari, which rivals Santi Giovanni e Paolo as the most important church in Venice after San Marco. Built by the Franciscans between 1340 and 1443, it is a brick edifice with a lively exterior design, magnificent apses and a slightly leaning campanile of 1361–69 (the tallest after that of San Marco). The vast façade, crowned by stone pinnacles, is pierced by a marble doorway bearing sculptures by Bartolomeo Bon and Pietro Lamberti, and by Alessandro Vittoria (who did the *Resurrected Christ* at the top).

Interior The church is entered by the doorway in the north flank (open Mon–Sat 09.00–12.00 and 14.30–18.00, Sun & holidays 15.00–18.00), also faced in marble. A vast, solemn space with three aisles separated by tall pointed arches, it has numerous tombs of doges and other illustrious Venetians of the 14C to the 19C, as well as some major works of art. At the centre of the nave is the late Gothic-early Renaissance monks' choir, with a marble enclosure by Pietro Lombardo and carved and inlaid stalls.

Now walk to the west end of the church. In the second bay of the **south aisle** is an 1852 monument to Titian; over the third altar, a statue of *St Jerome*, by Alessandro Vittoria, considered one of his better sculptures. High up in the south transept, on the right, is Pietro Lombardo's tomb of Jacopo Marcello, with the statue of the deceased on the sarcophagus supported by three caryatides. The tomb of Beato Pacifico, on the adjoining wall, was made by 15C Florentine masters. Above the door to the sacristy is the tomb of Benedetto Pesaro, by Lorenzo Bregno.

In the **sacristy** are fine reliquaries displayed in an elaborate Baroque showcase; on the altar, an enchanting triptych by Giovanni Bellini showing the *Madonna and Child with Saints Nicholas, Peter, Paul and Benedict* (signed and dated 1488), commissioned for this location and still surrounded by its original gilt wood frame. The perspective effect is truly remarkable and may distract your attention from the two angel-musicians at the bottom of the throne, which are not to be missed. Paolo Veneziano's 1339 *Madonna and Child with Sts Francis and Elisabeth* has been placed at the opposite end of the sacristy.

The south apsidal chapels hold various Gothic tombs of the 14C. In the third (the first as you come out of the sacristy) is a *Madonna and Child* by Bartolomeo Vivarini; in the first, Donatello's powerful wooden *St John the Baptist*, carved around 1450 but repainted in the 19C.

The **sanctuary** has a beautiful apse with large mullioned windows, before which rises Titian's magnificent *Assumption of the Virgin*. An inscription in the marble frame records that the work was commissioned in 1516 by Friar Germano, Superior of the Franciscan Monastery; the finished altarpiece was installed on 20 May 1518, in an elaborate public ceremony. This is probably the most famous painting of the Venetian Renaissance. At the time it was made, the painter's unorthodox approach to his subject—such a shapely Virgin and excited Apostles had never been seen before—was seen as scandalous; but the stir soon mellowed into praise, and by 1548 critic Paolo Pino could claim, 'If Titian and Michelangelo were one person; that is, if the draughtsmanship of Michelangelo went together with the colour of Titian, one could call that person the god of painting.' So much for religious orthodoxy.

On the south wall here is the tomb of Doge Francesco Foscari, a late Gothic-early Renaissance monument by Antonio and Paolo Bregno. On the north wall, the marble facing with the tomb of Doge Niccolò Tron, by Antonio Rizzo and assistants, is one of the outstanding funerary monuments of the Venetian Renaissance. The first north apsidal chapal contains an altarpiece by Bernardino Licinio, who also did the Franciscan martyrs on the north wall; in the third is the *St Ambrose Altarpiece* by Alvise Vivarini and Marco Basaiti; the fourth has a triptych by Bartolomeo Vivarini over the altar and a statue of *St John* by Jacopo Sansovino on the baptismal font.

Over the second altar of the **north aisle** is Titian's *Pesaro Altarpiece*, commissioned in 1519 by Bishop Jacopo Pesaro, former admiral of the Venetian fleet, who appears at the bottom left with a soldier in armour leading a Turkish prisoner. In the opposite corner of the painting is Senator Francesco Pesaro with two other brothers, Antonio and Giovanni, and Antonio's young sons Leonardo and Niccolò. St Peter and the family patron saints Francis and Anthony stand above, forming the sides of an ideal triangle culminating in the image of the Virgin and Child. The two powerful columns, whose upper ends are lost above the top of the painting, represent the Gates of Heaven.

The lateral doorway is framed by the colossal funerary composition created by Baldassarre Longhena for Doge Giovanni Pesaro (1669). The last bay on this side contains the monument to Antonio Canova, in the form of a pyramid, executed by his pupils using designs by Canova himself for a tomb of Titian. Remains of the Franciscan convent include a few rooms and the cloisters, renovated between the 16C and 18C.

The Scuola Grande di San Rocco

Opposite the apse of the Frari is the *Scuola Grande di San Rocco (open daily 09.00–17.30), begun in 1516 to an initial design by Bartolomeo Bon and completed in 1560 under the direction of Sante Lombardo and Scarpagnino. Scarpagnino is responsible for the magnificent façade, on which High Renaissance elements (on the ground floor) are tied together with foreshadowings of the Baroque taste (above). Inside, the large halls are decorated with a magnificent cycle of large paintings executed over a period of 23 years (1564–87) by Jacopo Tintoretto.

The visit begins on the upper floor, which is reached by Scarpagnino's grand staircase. Antonio Zanchi's 1666 *Plague of 1630* lines the walls. In the **Sala dell'Albergo** (where the chapter met) is Tintoretto's vast *Crucifixion* of 1565, universally considered his masterpiece, a work so profoundly moving that it left even the eloquent Ruskin speechless ('I must leave this picture to work its will on the spectator, for it is beyond all analysis and above all praise'). The other paintings represent scenes of the Passion (**Christ Before Pilate, Christ Carrying the**

Cross and *Ecce Homo*). The famous—or infamous—*Triumph of St Roche* shines down from the great oval in the middle of the ceiling. Set on easels are two small paintings brought here from the church of San Rocco for safekeeping: *Ecce Homo*, an early work of Titian, and *Christ Carrying the Cross*, which some ascribe to Titian and others, to Giorgione.

Tintoretto at San Rocco

The Scuola Grande di San Rocco could be described as a veritable monument to Tintoretto's art, and the adventurous (and probably true) story behind the painting here casts light on the artist's bizarre character. Soon after the completion of the building, the Confraternity of St Roche called a competition for the decoration of the interior, inviting four leading Venetian artists of the day (Federico Zuccari, Giuseppe Salviati, Paolo Veronese and Tintoretto) to submit proposals. The competition design had to be an oval painting of *The Triumph of St Roche*. On 31 May 1564 the committee met to judge the entries. Zuccari, Salviati and Veronese showed up with drawings and sketches; but Tintoretto—with the help of the custodian of the building—arranged for the judges to find a finished picture, whipped together with characteristic impetuosity, already installed in the oval space of the ceiling. He offered this work as a gift to the confraternity and promised to paint the rest of the ceiling at no extra cost—provided he was commissioned to do the entire decorative scheme for the scuola. Over the protests of the other artists and of a few members of the confraternity, who accused him of cheating, he won the commission.

In the large **Sala Maggiore** the ceiling is occupied by stories drawn from the Old Testament (*Moses Drawing Water from the Rock* in the first large frame, surrounded by *Adam and Eve, God Appearing to Moses, The Pillar of Fire and Jonah and the Whale; The Brazen Serpent*, flanked by the *Vision of Ezekiel and Jacob's Ladder*; and the *Gathering of Manna*, surrounded by the *Sacrifice of Isaac, Elijah Fed by the Angel, Elisha Multiplying the Loves* and the *Passover Feast*). On the walls are *Sts Roche and Sebastian* (by the windows) and New Testament stories (*Adoration of the Shepherds, Baptism of Christ, Resurrection, Agony in the Garden, Last Supper, Miracle of the Loaves and Fishes, Resurrection of Lazarus, Ascension, Pool of Bethesda* and *Temptation*). The artist executed the cycle in just five years, between 1576 and 1581, adding the altarpiece of the *Vision of St Roche* in 1588. On the sides of the altar, on easels, are an *Annunciation* by Titian and a *Visitation* and *Self-portrait* by Tintoretto, and *Abraham Visited by the Angels and Agar Rescued by the Angels* by Giovanni Battista Tiepolo. In the ground floor hall are eight large canvases that Tintoretto painted in 1583–87. the *Annunciation, Flight into Egypt, St Mary Magdalen* and *St Mary of Egypt* are particularly beautiful. The statue of *St Roche* over the altar was carved by Girolamo Campagna in 1587.

Across the way is the church of **San Rocco**, with an elegant façade of 1760 decorated with sculptures by Giovanni Marchiori and the Austrian G.M. Morlaiter. The 18C interior has more paintings by Tintoretto, two of which are particularly significant. The powerful handling of the nudes in *St Roche in Prison*, on the south wall, is a reminder that Tintoretto originally painted his great *Crucifixion* with naked figures, to which he later added draperies. The privileged position of *St Roche*

Ministering to the Plague-Stricken—in the sanctuary—recalls that St Roche's miraculous ability to heal those afflicted with plague was intimately tied to the enormous prestige his scuola enjoyed in Venice. The church also holds paintings by Sebastiano Ricci and Giovanni Antonio da Pordenone, and (by the main door) elegant Rococo statues of *David* and *St Cecily* by Giovanni Marchiori.

San Polo and its square

Now cross back over the Rio dei Frari, then cross over the Rio di San Polo and follow the signs for San Marco to reach the old church of San Polo, a Byzantine foundation several times altered, which you enter by a large 15C Gothic doorway on the south flank. The interior, which still retains a marked medieval feeling, has three aisles of columns with a wooden ship's-keel roof and paintings by Tintoretto (west wall and first south altar), Tiepolo (second north altar) and Palma Giovane (on the walls). The organ dates from 1763.

The large square behind the church, where popular feasts were once held, is overlooked by several patrician palaces, all of which have their more elaborate façades on the water. Baron Corvo stayed at the Palazzo Corner Mocenigo, (no. 2128a) while writing his last book, *The Desire and Pursuit of the Whole;* nos 2169 and 2171 are Gothic palaces with finely decorated windows and balconies; next to them rises the 18C Palazzo Tiepolo (whose aristocratic owners were no relation to the painter). Continue walking northeast, past the churches of Sant' Aponal and San Giovanni Elemosinario. In just a few minutes you'll come to the Rio degli Orefici and the Rialto Bridge.

CASTELLO, SAN GIORGIO AND THE GIUDECCA

Looking at the crowded quay that stretches eastwards from the Palazzo Ducale to the Giardini di Castello, you'd never guess that one of the quieter and more relaxed areas of Venice lies just behind San Marco. Oddly enough, the throngs stick to the waterfront, notwithstanding the presence just a few paces inland of some of the more delightful and magnificent achievements of Venetian art and architecture.

From Piazza San Marco, take the Mercerie (beneath the clock tower) to the church of San Zulian, then Calle delle Bande right to Campo Santa Maria Formosa. Among the livelier Venetian of campi, formerly used for open-air theatre, this pleasant square is surrounded by fine palaces: no. 5866, Palazzo Ruzzini, of 1580; nos 6121 and 6125–26, three Palazzi Donà—the first late 16C, the others 15C Gothic. At no. 5246 is Palazzo Vittturi, an unusual example of Veneto-Byzantine architecture of the 13C; no. 5250 is Palazzo Malipiero, a 16C house remodelled in the 19C.

The church of **Santa Maria Formosa**, erected according to tradition in 639 following a miraculous apparition of the Virgin Mary in the form of a beautiful (*formosa*) maiden, was rebuilt in 1482 by Mauro Codussi in Renaissance forms. In the 16C it received its two Classical façades, and in the 17C its Baroque campanile.

The **interior**, whose Greek-cross plan may be a carry-over from the earlier church, combines the elegance of Renaissance ornament with the spatial values of Byzantine architecture. It preserves a *Madonna of Mercy* by Bartolomeo Vivarini, signed and dated 1473; and a polyptych with *St Barbara and Four Saints* by Palma Vecchio. St Barbara was the patron of the artillerymen who had their chapel in this church, and her valiant, resolute bearing in Palma's painting caused George Eliot to describe her as 'an almost unique presentation of a hero-woman, standing in calm preparation for martyrdom, without the slightest air of pietism, yet the expression of a mind filled with serious conviction'.

Walk all the way around the church and then south to reach Campiello Querini Stampalia, along the Rio Santa Maria Formosa. Here, in a palace of 1528, stands the **Fondazione Querini Stampalia**, with an important library and picture gallery (open Tues, Wed, Thur and Sun 10.00–13.00 and 15.00–18.00, Fri and Sat 10.00–13.00 and 15.00–22.00). The building was renovated in the 1960s to a design by Carlo Scarpa, the most prominent Italian architect of the time, and the collection was completely rearranged to meet state-of-the-art museological standards in 1995–96. The works reflect the personal taste of the founder, Count Giovanni Querini, whose interest focused on the social portraits, conversation pieces and rich furnishings of 18C Venice.

A Portrait by Tiepolo

The real surprise in this collection is Giovanni Battista Tiepolo's *Portrait of the Procurator Dolfin*, painted between 1750 and 1755. Tiepolo rarely showed much interest in portraiture; his imagination was attracted more by mythological or historical subjects. The sitter has only tentatively been identified as Daniele Dolfin IV (1656–1723), a captain in the Venetian navy and Procurator of the Republic for whose palace the young Tiepolo had painted a series of Roman generals. The cruel energy in the gloved hand, and the sinisterly spectral white wig, are perfectly in keeping with the prestige of such a position. The daring perspective and the theatrically billowing draperies give the painting an expressive power so strong that it verges on caricature.

Santi Giovanni e Paolo

Return to Santa Maria Formosa and walk north to reach Campo Santi Giovanni e Paolo ('San Zanipolo' in dialect). Opening around the imposing Dominican church of Santi Giovanni e Paolo and the small marble façade of the Scuola di San Marco, it is the most monumental of Venetian squares after Piazza San Marco. Near the corner of the church stands the bronze equestrian monument to mercenary general *Bartolommeo Colleoni, the last and grandest work of the Florentine sculptor Andrea Verrocchio.

The story of the statue offers an interesting anecdote. Colleoni, who had commanded the land forces of the Venetian Republic, died in 1475, leaving a considerable sum of money to erect a bronze equestrian monument in his honour. The legacy stipulated that the statue should be set up in Piazza San Marco. The authorities had no intention of glorifying a single individual in the city's main public square, however, and destined the statue for a less important site, in front of the Scuola of San Marco—thus, in a sense, fulfilling the terms of the will.

Verrocchio received the commission in 1479 and completed a full-scale clay model by 1483, but died before it was cast. This work was eventually done by a

Venetian bronze-founder, Alessandro Leopardi, who also designed the base on which the monument was set in 1496. In keeping with the new interests of his period, Verrocchio has abandoned the static concept of equestrian statuary expressed by Donatello in the Gattamelata monument in Padua. The horse is strong and unruly, its veins swollen, its muscles tense. Erect in the stirrups, his torso twisted against the movement of the horse's head, the general frowns down with fierce pride, in full command of his nervous charger. Never was there a more convincing portrait of power and command than this, Verrocchio's last work. 'I do not believe that there is a more glorious work of sculpture existing in the world', remarked Ruskin of this monument.

Santi Giovanni e Paolo is the second largest Gothic church in Venice, almost on a par with the Frari. It was begun in the mid-14C. The apses and transept had been completed by 1368, and the church was consecrated in 1430. The austere façade, in striking contrast with the extremely ornate front of the adjacent Scuola di San Marco, has a delicately designed roofline, above, and a large marble doorway by Bartolomeo Bon and assistants flanked by tall arches bearing sarcophagi, below. The right flank and polygonal apses are also quite handsome.

The **interior** is a feast of Venetian sculpture and painting. From the 15C on, San Zanipolo was the traditional site of the doges' funerals, and splendid Gothic and Renaissance monuments to 25 of the republic's leaders line the walls. The most impressive of these is Pietro Lombardo's 1476 monument to Pietro Mocenigo, whose family occupies the entire west wall. Two paintings are of special note: Giovanni Bellini's gentle, sensual triptych of *St Vincent Ferrer* flanked by Sts Christopher and Sebastian (near the Lombardo tomb, in the south aisle) and Lorenzo Lotto's warm, sensitive *St Anthony Giving Alms*, in the south wing of the transept. Here also is the last surviving example of the large painted glass windows that were a specialty of Murano glassmakers, the *Window of Warrior Saints* (1515), based on designs by Bartolomeo Vivarini and Gerolamo Mocetto. The Cappella del Rosario, reached from the north transept, contains ceiling paintings by Paolo Veronese. Back on the south side, the Cappella di San Domenico, adjoining the south transept, has paintings by Piazzetta in the ceiling and low reliefs of the saint's life on the walls by Giuseppe Mazza and Giambattista Alberghetti. The Cappella della Madonna della Pace, in the south aisle, has fine paintings by Leandro Bassano, stuccoes and a Byzantine icon of rare beauty over the altar.

On the piazza's north side is the **Scuola Grande di San Marco**, now the city hospital. The palace, largely a work of the early Renaissance, was begun by Pietro and Tullio Lombardo, continued by Mauro Codussi and completed by Jacopo Sansovino. The splendid coloured-marble façade has sophisticated trompe-l'œil reliefs in which a marvellous sense of depth is obtained from an essentially two-dimentional surface. The roofline presents arched pediments of various size and the main doorway has a porch with lunette by Bartolomeo Bon. From the ground floor hall you can enter the former Dominican convent of Santi Giovanni e Paolo, rebuilt by Baldassarre Longhena in 1660–75 on a 13C plan around two cloisters and a courtyard.

San Zaccaria

Winding southwards towards the Riva degli Schiavoni you eventually come to the quiet, sheltered Campo San Zaccaria, overlooked by the façade of its church. San Zaccaria was founded in the 9C, and there are still traces (in the crypt) of the original building, where eight of the first doges were buried. The church you see today was begun during the 15C in Gothic forms and completed in 1480–1515 by Mauro Codussi, who gave it its multi-level white stone façade, one of the first Renaissance church façades in the city. Despite the Classical trabeation, columns and round-headed arches, its vertical thrust is still distinctly Gothic.

The **interior** is tall, vaulted and three-aisled; its ambulatory with radial chapels lit by tall windows is unique in Venice. Along the walls are numerous paintings, the most important of which is Giovanni Bellini's *Madonna and Saints* over the second north altar, signed and dated 1505. Executed when the painter was in his seventies, this is considered a pivotal work in Venetian painting's progress towards the mastery of light and colour. Off the south aisle is the late Renaissance Cappella di Sant'Atanasio, which holds paintings by Tintoretto (*Birth of the Baptist*) and Tiepolo, and inlaid choir stalls of 1455–64. From the adjoining Cappella dell'Addolorata you enter the **Cappella di San Tarasio**, formerly part of the apse of the church, where there are three carved and gilt Gothic polyptychs jointly painted by Antonio Vivarini, Giovanni d'Alemagna and Stefano da Sant'Agnese (1443). Perhaps the most impressive of these is the *Madonna of the Rosary*, with saints by Vivarini, decorative panels by d'Alemagna and a *Madonna* by Sant'Agnese set in a massive wooden frame of carved niches, turrets and pinnacles. On the walls are Andrea del Castagno's *Church Fathers*, executed by the Florentine artist in 1442 with the help of Francesco da Faenza. Andrea, who had been Masaccio's first pupil, was 19 years old when he brought the Tuscan Renaissance style to Venice in these paintings.

Back in the campo, a 16C doorway (no. 4693) marks the entrance to the former Benedictine convent, once the wealthiest and wildest in Venice. Here the city's aristocratic families sent young girls against their will, to save the expense of dowries. The more rebellious naturally refused to renounce the luxury and extravagance of patrician life, with results that can easily be imagined. There is a painting by Francesco Guardi in the museum at Ca' Rezzonico (*The Parlour of the Nuns of San Zaccaria*) which shows the notoriously libertine atmosphere that prevailed in the convent, with dancing, theatre and novices making doughnuts. By a peculiar twist of fate, the convent is now a police station.

Where the Eastern merchants lived

Walk away from the church and turn right in the triangular Campo San Provolo, then follow the Fondamenta Osmarin and cross over the narrow Rio di Greci. Here, in a shady garden on the right, is **San Giorgio dei Greci**, a 16C church built to a design by Sante Lombardo for the Greek Orthodox community. The most important foreign church in Renaissance Venice, it has a magnificently decorated interior divided by a marble iconostasis with late Byzantine gold-ground paintings. On the north, in the rooms of the former Scuola dei Greci (now the Istituto Ellenico), is the **Museo dei Dipinti Sacri Bizantini** (open daily 09.00–12.30 and 13.30–16.30, Sun & holidays 10.00–17.00), which preserves some 80 Byzantine and post-Byzantine icons and various liturgical objects. One of the highlights here is a hieratic icon of *St Anastasius* by the 16C painter Michele Damaskinos, who is credited with having encouraged a young artist from Crete who was in Venice at the time—Domenico Theotocopoulos—to absorb all he could from Tintoretto's work and then move on to Spain, where he would establish a reputation under the name of El Greco.

The **Scuola di San Giorgio degli Schiavoni** (open Tues–Sat 09.30–12.30 and 15.30–18.30; Sun 09.30–12.30), one block north along the canal and to the right, was erected in the early 16C by the Dalmation confraternity, whose members were mainly merchants involved in trade with the East. The beautiful painting cycle on its ground-floor walls is one of the artistic jewels of Venice and should not be missed. Executed by Vittore Carpaccio, who worked in Venice between 1490 and 1523, the richly fantastic scenes portray episodes from the lives of three protectors of Dalmatia, Sts George, Jerome and Tryphon.

Carpaccio tended to work on commissions that allowed him to indulge in his natural vocation for simple and apparently ingenuous narrative art, which in many ways recalls the *sacre rappresentazioni* that were the most widespread form of popular theatre of the time. These works, with their entrancing atmospheric power, mark the high point of his career. Most poetic of all, perhaps, is the *Study of St Augustine* (right), which depicts a scene described in the *Golden Legend*: alone in his study, the Bishop of Hippo hears the voice of his friend St Jerome (then absent in Antioch) announcing that he has died. The room is flooded with a sudden light and all movement comes to a halt (even the saint's fluffy dog is silent and still) as St Augustine interrupts his writing. The vanishing point of the perspective scheme has been shifted from the centre to the right of the painting, to coincide with the saint's pen, suspended above the page. Carpaccio never again achieved such expressive force, nor created an effect as magical as that achieved here. The painted wood ceiling and inlaid benches of the scuola are also noteworthy.

Towards the Arsenal

Now go down the rio, over the bridge, through a charming passageway with a tabernacle of the Madonna, then right to Salizzada San Francesco, which leads under an imposing portico to **San Francesco della Vigna**. This large 16C church, built to a design by Jacopo Sansovino, has a noble Classical façade by Andrea Palladio based on a complex arrangement of superimposed temple fronts. The vast Latin-cross interior contains numerous masterpieces. Over the first altar of the south transept is the one work that can be attributed with certainty to Fra' Antonio da Negroponte, a *Madonna Adoring the Child* painted in the 1450s in a curious retro style; in the sanctuary are monuments to Doge Andrea Gritti and his circle, possibly by Sansovino; in the chapel on the north of the sanctuary, an outstanding ensemble of sculptures by Pietro Lombardo and pupils (1495–1510) with a fine illusionistic floor; in the Cappella Santa, entered from the north transept, *Madonna and Child with Saints* by Giovanni Bellini (signed and dated 1507); and in the fifth north chapel, another Madonna and Saints, the *Giustinian Altarpiece* by Paolo Veronese, the earliest of his masterpieces to be seen in Venice (1551).

In Campo Bandiera e Moro, almost due south near the Riva degli Schiavoni, is the late Gothic church of **San Giovanni in Bràgora**, with a distinctive linear brick façade and a low, cosy interior. Here are more masterpieces of Gothic and

Renaissance painting: a *Resurrected Christ, Madonna with Sts Andrew and John the Baptist, Praying Madonna and Child* and a small panel with the *Head of the Redeemer* by Alvise Vivarini; *Sts Andrew, Jerome and Martin* by Francesco Bissolo; *Constantine and St Helen* and *Baptism of Christ* by Cima da Conegliano; and a *Last Supper* by Paris Bordone. The stuccoed vault of the sanctuary is the work of Alessandro Vittoria.

Continuing eastwards you soon come to the **Arsenale**, once the greatest shipyard in the world. From here, after 1155, came the Venetian galleys, the basis of the republic's economic and political power. From here, also, comes the modern European word 'arsenal'—a corruption of the Arabic *darsina'a*, workshop. Dante described this once-bustling dockyard in the *Inferno* (xxi), comparing the pitch in which he placed barterers of public offices to that boiled in the arsenal for caulking the damaged hulls of Venetian ships. The complex is usually closed to the public, except when the *corderie*—huge, long buildings originally designed for the storage of rigging—are being used for an exhibition. Part of the complex can be seen, however, from vaporetto no. 52, which runs along the canal inside. The land entrance is marked by a doorway of 1460, considered the first work of the Venetian Renaissance, surmounted by an attic with a large lion of St Mark attributed to Bartolomeo Bon. In 1692–94 the doorway was given a terraced porch adorned with Baroque allegorical statues; at the sides of this are two stone lions brought here from Greece (the one on the left comes from the harbour of Pireus). Further right are two smaller lions, one from the Isle of Delos.

Walk down the Rio dell'Arsenale to reach the waterfront. You'll pass two sections of the **Museo Storico Navale** (open daily 08.45–13.30, Thur 08.45–13.30 and 14.30–17.00, closed Sun & holidays)—one with historic ships, in the Officina Remi (just outside the Arsenale); the other with a beautiful model collection of typical Adriatic galleys, Venetian gondolas and other vessels—including the famed Bucintoro, the doges' ceremonial barge—in the former republican granary on the wharf at the end of the canal. When on display there is also an interesting model of the system of wooden piles on which Venice is built.

Riva degli Schiavoni, the broad, lively quay along the basin of San Marco, takes its name from the merchants of Schiavonia or Slavonia (modern Dalmatia), who anchored their ships and carried on their business here. You saw their scuola a few minutes ago. From Rio dell'Arsenale follow the riva along the waterfront past the church of the Pietà (where Vivaldi was choir master) to reach the landing stage of vaporetto no. 9, which plies across the San Marco basin to San Giorgio and the Giudecca.

The Isle of San Giorgio

Henry James called the island of San Giorgio 'a success beyond all reason', attributing its fortune to its position, to the immense detached campanile, which seems to pin the buildings to their magnificent background, and above all to its colour. 'I do not know whether it is beacause San Giorgio is so grandly conspicuous, with a great deal of worn, faded-looking brickwork', he wrote, 'but for many persons, the whole place has a kind of suffusion of rosiness'.

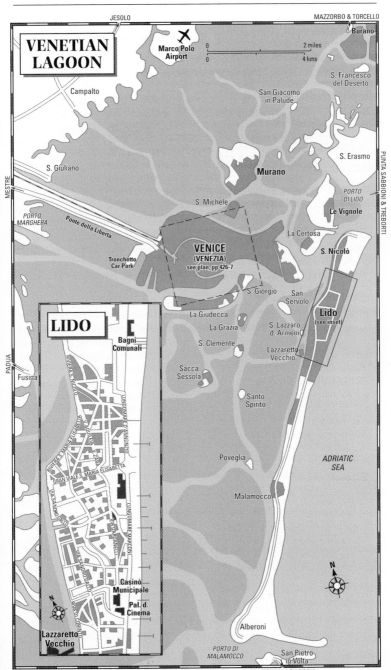

VENETIAN LAGOON

JESOLO

MAZZORBO & TORCELLO

Burano

Marco Polo Airport

0 — 2 miles
0 — 4 kms

Campalto

S. Francesco del Deserto

San Giacomo in Palude

MESTRE

S. Giuliano

S. Erasmo

PUNTA SABBIONI & TREBORTI

Murano

PORTO DI LIDO

Le Vignole

PORTO MARGHERA

Ponte della Libertà

S. Michele

La Certosa

VENICE (VENEZIA) see plan, pp 426-7

S. Nicolò

Tronchetto Car Park

S. Giorgio

San Servolo

Lido (see inset)

PADUA

Fusina

La Giudecca

La Grazia

S. Lazzaro d. Armeni

S. Clemente

Lazzaretto Vecchio

Sacca Sessola

Santo Spirito

ADRIATIC SEA

Poveglia

Malamocco

Alberoni

PORTO DI MALAMOCCO

San Pietro in Volta

PELLESTRINA, CHIOGGIA

N

LIDO

Bagni Comunali

RIVIERA S. NICOLÒ

RIVIERA S. MARIA ELISABETTA

LUNGOMARE D'ANNUNZIO

GRAN VIALE S. MARIA ELISABETTA

VIA SANDRO

LUNGOMARE MARCONI

VIA NEGROPONTE

VIA S. GALLO

VIA LEPANTO

Casinò Municipale

Pal. d. Cinema

RIVA DI CORINTO

N

Lazzaretto Vecchio

The most striking building on the island is Palladio's church of **San Giorgio Maggiore** (open daily 09.30–12.30 and 14.30–18.00), built between 1565 and 1580 over the remains of earlier churches dating back as far as the 8C. On the right you can see a group of low red edifices, the convent, built by Baldassare Longhena in the 17C.

The island of San Giorgio Maggiore

The campanile is a later construction, as its Neo-classical detailing suggests. It was erected in 1792 to replace an earlier one that had collapsed. The little harbour, with its twin lighthouses, was added in the early 19C.

Palladio and his contemporaries were convinced that a harmony like that of music underlay the great buildings of the past, and that the secrets of that harmony could be unravelled by a careful study of mathematical proportions. You can see this belief at work on the façade of San Giorgio, where the triangle ideally formed by the lateral pediments reaches its apex at base of the central pediment—an ingenious expedient that prepares the visitor, visually, for the aisled church within. Palladio's most complex church-front design, San Giorgio's Classical façade was completed after the architect's death, in the early 17C.

The **interior** of the church impresses more by virtue of its luminosity and spaciousness than for the complexity of its design, although it is the latter that gives rise to the former. Its remarkable sculptural quality is based on a sustained opposition between flat and rounded forms—walls, arches and vaults, engaged columns and giant pilasters—and decoration is almost totally eliminated. Its art treasures include two works by Tintoretto, the *Last Supper* and the *Gathering of Manna*, on the walls around the high altar (1594). The gift of manna to the Israelites in the wilderness provided the Old Testament parallel to the institution of the Eurcharist, and the paintings were designed to be most effective when seen by the communicant from the altar rails. In the monks' choir are stalls carved with stories from the life of St Benedict; over the altar of the winter choir is a *St George and the Dragon* by Vittore Carpaccio.

The **monastery of San Giorgio Maggiore**, seat of the Fondazione Giorgio Cini, is a fine complex arranged around two cloisters. Palladio designed the refectory, where there is a *Marriage of the Virgin* by Jacopo Tintoretto; and a monumental staircase by Baldassarre Longhena ascends to the first floor, where the Library, also by Longhena, has 17C inlaid bookcases with over 100,000 books on the history of art. In the park is the Teatro Verde, for open-air theatre. The complex is open to the public only for special events. The campanile, reached by a lift, is 60m high and offers unsurpassed views of the city and the lagoon.

The Giudecca

The Giudecca is a long, narrow island delightfully off the beaten track. Originally known as *Spinalonga* (long spine) because of its shape, its present name probably derives from the Jewish community that lived here in the 13C. By the 16C it had become a place of green quietude, abounding with lush gardens, aristocratic homes and tranquil convents. Following the decline of the Venetian aristocracy and the suppression of the convents, the island was gradually given over to barracks, prisons and factories. Today its simple houses are home to many of Venice's boatmen. The quay, along the inner, southern side of the island, takes different names as it goes along, offering splendid views of the Giudecca Canal, San Marco and the Riva degli Schiavoni. The entire section from the Rio di San Biagio canal, on the island's western tip, to the church of the Zitelle, on the east, is almost tourist-free and gives a sense of a simpler, original Venice.

The boat stops fist at the church and convent of Santa Maria della Presentazione, usually known as **Le Zitelle** (The Virgins), where the nuns once made excellent Venetian lace. Its design is attributed to Palladio, though it was not built until after his death. From here it is a short walk to the main monument on the Giudecca, the church of the **Redentore**, designed by Palladio in 1577 and completed after the architect's death by Antonio da Ponte. This church, which was erected as a thank-offering after an outbreak of plague that killed more than one-third of the population, is another of Palladio's masterpieces. Its façade is a development of that of San Francesco della Vigna, which he had designed some ten years earlier, with pediments over the door and central bay and the end sections of a hidden pediment emerging on either side of the main block. As at San Francesco della Vigna (and again at San Giorgio Maggiore), the overall scheme is regulated by a complicated system of proportions. In past centuries the doge paid an annual visit to this church, crossing the canal from the Zattere on a bridge of boats—and the tradition is still kept up today, with fireworks and other events on the third Saturday in July.

In the **interior**, Palladio appears to have paid more attention to the visual effects than he did at San Giorgio Maggiore: there is a more harmonious relationship between the various parts, and a much better climax in the semi-circular colonnade behind the high altar. From the door the church appears as a simple rectangular basilica with an apse; but as you approach the high altar, the curves of the dome and arms gradually reveal themselves, giving a sense of elation and expansion rarely achieved by purely architectural means. Over the altars are paintings by 16C and 17C painters, notably a *Nativity* by Francesco Bassano, a *Deposition* by Palma Giovane, a *Resurrection* by Francesco Bassano and an *Ascension* by Jacopo Tintoretto and assistants. Over the Baroque high altar (which Palladio certainly didn't anticipate) is a crucifix between 16C bronze statues of **St Mark** and **St Francis**. In the sacristy are a *Madonna and Child with Angels* by Alvise Vivarini, a *Madonna and Saints* attributed to Francesco Bissolo and a *Baptism of Christ* by Paolo Veronese.

Further west rises the church of Sant'Eufemia, originally of the 11C, and at the end of the fondamenta beyond a metal bridge, the imposing Gothic-revival mass of the Mulino Stucky, presently undergoing a face-lift.

Beyond the Giudecca are the island of **San Lazzaro degli Armeni**, seat of an Armenian monastery founded in the 18C by a group of monks who fled the Orient (open for guided tours, daily 15.20–17.00); and the **Lido di Venezia**, a busy suburban neighbourhood and bathing beach the island separating the Adriatic sea from the lagoon. Noteworthy buildings include the *Grand Hotel des Bains* (1900), the setting of Thomas Mann's *Death in Venice*, and the *Grand Hotel Excelsior* (1898–1908), in a Moorish style.

Cannaregio

The church of Santa Maria di Nazareth, usually known simply as **Gli Scalzi** (literally, 'the Barefoot') was built by Baldassarre Longhena after 1654 for a community of Carmelite monks who moved here from Rome, and its design and interior décor in fact recall those of Roman Baroque churches. Giuseppe Sardi added the white marble façade in 1680. The second south and first north chapels have vault frescoes by Tiepolo, who also painted the ceiling of the nave. This painting was destroyed by Austrian bombs in 1915, and the modern replacement dates from 1934.

The Ghetto and environs

The crowded Lista di Spagna leads northeastwards, crossing the broad Canale di Cannaregio by the Ponte delle Guglie. Once across the canal you turn left then immediately right through the Sottoportico del Ghetto. The street leads past a synagogue with beautifully carved doors, and over a bridge to the **Ghetto Nuovo**. Set aside from 1516 to 1797 for the city's Jewish population, this tiny, water-ringed neighbourhood is the oldest historically documented ghetto in the world. The site was originally occupied by a foundry—in Venetian dialect, *getto*—and this term was subsequently taken to describe the Jewish quarter in cities everywhere.

On the whole the Venetian Jews enjoyed a relatively relaxed relationship with the republic: though they were obliged to follow certain rules that limited their social and economic activities, they maintained their religious freedom and, except for a brief period of expulsion between 1527 and 1533, they remained within the city, in this neighbourhood, until Napoleon demolished the gates of the ghetto in 1797. After this time they were allowed to live where they pleased. As the area of the ghetto was limited, the Jews were forced to build tenements that, without violating the city's height limitations, would accommodate many families. Several of the houses therefore have very low ceilings.

The **Museo d'Arte Ebraica** (open daily 10.00–19.00; closed Sat & Jewish holidays), in Campo Ghetto Nuovo, offers guided tours of the ghetto and of three of its synagogues, also called 'scuole' by virtue of the mixed purposes they served. The most sumptuous is the Scuola Levantina, in the Ghetto Vecchio, established in 1538 and remodelled in the 17C, possibly to a design by Baldassarre Longhena. The museum's collections include liturgical objects and other interesting examples of Venetian Jewish art of the 17C to the 19C, and text boards describing the plight of Venetian Jews during the holocaust.

Away from the crowds

Cross the Campo di Ghetto Nuovo to the Fondamenta degli Ormesini and turn right. This is one of the quieter parts of the city, almost untouched by tourists. Most of the alleys on the left will lead you eventually to the beautiful Gothic church of **Madonna dell'Orto**, founded in the 14C and rebuilt in the 15C to hold a miraculous image of the Virgin discovered in a nearby garden (*orto* in Italian). This was the parish church of Tintoretto, who was buried in the chapel on the south side of the sanctuary in 1594. Inside are several of his works: the *Presentation of the Virgin in the Temple* at the end of the south aisle, the *Last Judgement and Worship of the Golden Calf* in the choir, and the *Vision of the Cross to St Peter* and *Beheading of St Paul* in the apse. The latter are hung around an *Annunciation* by Palma Giovane, and a *St John the Baptist and Saints* by Cima da Conegliano stands over the first south altar. There is also a fine 15C cloister.

It takes some fancy footwork, down the busy Rio di Noale towards the Grand Canal and up the other side almost to the Fondamenta Nuove to reach **I Gesuiti**, the church of Venice's Jesuit community. This is an early 18C edifice with a lively Baroque façade based on Roman models. Like so many Jesuit churches in Italy, it has an elaborately decorated interior—in this case an extraordinary work of *trompe-l'œil* with green and white inlaid marbles imitating damask wall hangings and white and gold stuccoes. Over the first north altar is Titian's *Martyrdom of St Lawrence*, and in the transept on this side is an *Assumption* by Jacopo Tintoretto. Palma Giovane decorated the nearby Oratorio dei Crociferi, founded in the 13C and renovated in the late 16C (open Fri, Sat and Sun 10.00–13.30). If it strikes you as odd that the seat of such an important order should be located so far from the mainstream of city life, you have not yet begun to understand Venetian psychology: the senate managed to keep the powerful Jesuits out of the city for a long time, and when the order finally was allowed to establish itself, it was kept as far from the centres of political and economic affairs as topography would allow.

Towards Rialto

From Campo dei Gesuiti cross the Rio Santa Caterina and follow the calli southwards to their end, near the church and campo of Santi Apostoli. Now turn left, cross the Rio Santi Apostoli and bear slightly left again. **Santa Maria dei Miracoli**, a lonely little church in the narrow Campo dei Miracoli, is one of the higher achievements of the early Venetian Renaissance. Constructed between 1481 and 1489 to enshrine a miraculous image of the Virgin, it is covered with coloured marble panels whose ingeniously complex design makes the church appear larger than it really is without disturbing the overall effect, which is undoubtedly one of harmonious tranquility. The church is the work of Pietro Lombardo, who was assisted here by his sons Antonio and Tullio. The interior also has exquisite Lombardesque marblework and a delightful *Madonna*, over the high altar, by Nicolò di Pietro Paradisi. The figures of *Saints* in the coffered ceiling were painted by Pier Maria Pennacchi (1528). The choir loft above the entrance bears a *Madonna and Child* by Palma Giovane.

The pleasant red and white church of **San Giovanni Crisostomo** almost fills its small campo. The last work of Mauro Codussi, it, too, is a masterpiece of Venetian Renaissance architecture. The Greek-cross interior preserves two important paintings—Giovanni Bellini's *St Jerome with St Christopher and St Augustine* (over the first south altar), the high altarpiece of *St John Chrysostom and Six Saints* by Sebastiano del Piombo—and an extraordinarily powerful, classically serene marble relief of the *Coronation of the Virgin* (over the second north altar) by Tullio Lombardo, who also decorated the pilasters in the chapel.

At the eastern end of the Strada Nuova, a broad thoroughfare cut in 1871 to connect Rialto with the train station, stands the plain brick church of Santi Apostoli, built in 1575 possibly to a design by Alessandro Vittoria. Some way down the Strada Nuova, but before the first bridge, Calle della Ca' d'Oro leads left to the land entrance of the **Ca' d'Oro**, the fine Gothic palace designed by Giovanni and Bartolomeo Bon and Matteo Raverti (1420–34), named the Golden House after the splendid gilt decoration that used to adorn the façade on the Grand Canal. The palace is now a museum (open daily 09.00–14.00) displaying the outstanding art collection of its former owner, Baron Giorgio Franchetti. Here you can see Italian and foreign paintings and Venetian marbles, bronzes and ceramics of the 15C to the 18C. Highlights include Antonio Vivarini's remarkable *Polyptych with Passion Scenes* (1476–84) and Andrea Mantegna's *St Sebastian*, a splendid masterpiece of the early Renaissance; a double portrait by Tullio Lombardo and fresco fragments by Giorgione and Titian from the exterior of the Fondaco dei Tedeschi. From the ground-floor atrium, take a stroll outside, in the small secret garden and stunning canal-front portico, before leaving.

Mantegna's Saint Sebastian

The subject of St Sebastian seems to have held some mysterious fascination for Andrea Mantegna, who painted at least three other versions (now at the Accademia, in Paris and in Vienna); but the most powerful treatment of the theme is to be found in this Ca' d'Oro painting. The style is certainly that of the his later years (1490–1500), filled with symbolic nuance: the tortured line of the drapery accentuates the idea of Christian suffering in the name of faith, and the ample use of purple-grey 'bruise' tones emphasises the saint's human agony. The perspective rendering of anatomy (notice the foot that steps out of the frame at the bottom of the painting) is as sophisticated as that of the artist's most famous painting, the *Dead Christ* in Milan.

Murano, Burano and Torcello

To see Murano, Burano and Torcello—the three inhabited islands in the lagoon between Venice and the mainland—requires a long morning or afternoon, but it is well worth the time and trouble. Murano and Burano are known for their glass and lace, respectively. Torcello, now a romantic place with a little village counting fewer than 50 souls, is famous for its great cathedral, whose sheer splendour alone justifies the journey. Take vaporetto **no. 12** from Fondamenta Nuove, easily reached by the **no. 52** from San Marco or on foot from the church of the Gesuiti. Remember to check schedules when you arrive on the islands, and to give yourself at least an hour to go to and from Venice.

Shortly after leaving the Fondamenta Nuove the boat passes the walled island of **San Michele**, the cemetery of Venice and site of the city's oldest Renaissance church—the chapel of San Michele in Isola, designed by Mauro Codussi in 1469. Between Murano and Burano you'll be able to spot the cypress-girt Franciscan hermitage of San Francesco del Deserto, on a solitary little island to the southwest. The monks do allow visits, and you can hire a boat from Burano to get there if you wish.

Murano

The Venetian glass factories were moved to Murano as a safety measure in 1291 (the idea was to remove the risk of fire from the city), and the town has been synonymous with exquisite craftsmanship ever since. The Venetians rediscovered this lost art in the 10C, when merchants brought the secrets of the trade from the East, and the making of clear 'crystal' glass remained a well-kept secret until the 16C. After a period of decline the making of artistic glass was revived at the end of the 19C, and today the many glass factories all welcome visitors. In the 16C Murano became a favourite retreat of Venetian intellectuals, many of whom had splendid houses and luxuriant gardens on the island. Few of these remain, however, and it is difficult today to imagine this aspect of the island's past.

The small Grand Canal that runs betwen the town's shops and houses takes you to the **Museo dell'Arte Vetraria** (Glass Museum; open Thur–Tues 10.00–17.00) located in the 17C Palazzo Giustinian. Here, on the ground floor, are examples of antique glass ranging in date from the 2C BC to the 2C AD, largely from the necropolis of Enona. Venetian glass of the 15C to the 18C is displayed on the upper floor; among the earliest surviving pieces is a dark blue marriage cup of 1470–80 with portraits of the bride and groom and allegorical devices in coloured enamel, ascribed to the workshop of Angelo Barovier. There are also examples of foreign glass. Modern and contemporary glass is displayed in an annex to the museum (one ticket gives admission to both) on Rio dei Vetrai.

Murano's main architectural monument is **Santi Maria e Donato**, a splendid example of Veneto-Byzantine church type founded in the 7C but rebuilt in the 12C. It was originally dedicated to the Virgin Mary; St Donato's name was added when his relics were brought here from Cephalonia, in Greece, together with the bones of a dragon he supposedly slew (four of which, for sceptics, hang behind the altar). The church is known above all for its magnificent Romanesque mosaic pavement (1141), although the capitals of the columns, the Byzantine mosaic of the Virgin in the apse and the colourful wooden ancona by Paolo Veneziano in the north aisle, are also quite beautiful.

Burano

Burano, about half an hour away from Venice, is a charming little fishing village resplendent with colour, a delightful place just to wander without any precise goal, though there are a few paintings—by Girolamo da Santacroce, Giovanni Battista Tiepolo and Giovanni Mansueti—in the parish church. In past centuries the island was a favourite haunt of painters, who were drawn by the maritime atmosphere of water, sky and sails, as well as by the colour of its walls and by the picturesque quality of its *merlettaie*, or lace-makers, who used to pursue their minute craft outside, in the sunlight as Canaletto shows them. Lace-making in fact has been a mainstay of the island's economy since the early 16C, and lace is still made and sold on the island. If you plan to buy some, however, be sure to get genuine the Venetian variety, which you'll learn to recognise in the lace museum at the **Scuola di Merlietti** (open Wed–Mon 10.00–17.00). And don't leave Burano without strolling over to its small sister-island, **Mazzorbo**, whose pretty little canal is still lined with fishing-nets spread out to dry in the sun. Here too is some of the best contemporary architecture in Venice, G. De Carlo's 1986 housing project built in full respect of local vernacular forms and colours.

Torcello

Ruskin tells the early history of Torcello with uncommon poetic skill: 'Thirteen hundred years ago, the grey moorland looked as it does this day, and the purple mountains stood as radiantly in the deep distances of evening; but on the line of the horizon there were strange fires mixed with the light of sunset, and the lament of many human voices mixed with the fretting of the waves on their ridges of sand. The flames rose from the ruins of Altinum; the lament from the multitudes of its people, seeking, like Israel of old, a refuge from the sword in the paths of the sea'. In more prosaic terms it can be said that Torcello flourished between the 7C and the 13C, when it was the insular stronghold of refugees driven from mainland Altinum by the Lombard invasions. At one time it counted as many as 20,000 inhabitants, but by the 15C rivalry with Venice and chronic malaria had eroded its prestige and decimated its population. Now it is little more than a small group of houses in a lonely part of the lagoon, huddled in the shadow of one of the more singular and impressive churches in Venice.

The **Cathedral of Santa Maria Assunta** is a 10 minute walk from the landing stage, down a lonely canal amid fields and a few houses. This great church (open daily 10.00–12.30 and 14.00–17.00) was founded in 639, rebuilt in 864 and again in 1008. Before it are remains of the baptistery and by a narthex enlarged in the 14C and 15C. The tall detached campanile, as you will have seen from the boat, is a conspicuous landmark in the lagoon.

The stunningly beautiful *interior is among the higher achievements of Christian religious architecture. Eighteen Greek marble columns with finely carved capitals separate the aisles and nave, and a superb 11C mosaic pavement covers the floor. Four elaborately carved screens, of Byzantine inspiration, mark the entrance to the sanctuary, surmounted by 15C paintings of the *Virgin and Apostles*. The relics of St Heliodorus, first bishop of Altinum, are preserved in a Roman sarcophagus beneath the 7C high altar. Set into the wall north of the altar is an inscription commemorating the foundation of the church (639), considered the oldest document of Venetian history.

The most striking feature of the church, however, is the important cycle of mosaics, almost certainly fully completed by the time the mosaicists set to work on San Marco in 1156. The *Virgin and Child with Apostles* in the apse represents a break with traditional iconography, which ordinarily reserves this position for Christ Pantocrator (as at San Marco); the exception may be justified, in part, by the inscription in the arch, which begins, 'I am God and the flesh of the Mother ...'. The work was probably done by craftsmen from Constantinople. In the chapel to the right of the high altar is a somewhat earlier representation of *Christ between the Archangels Michael and Gabriel with Sts Nicholas, Ambrose, Augustine and Martin*, in which the workmanship is considerably coarser.

The west wall of the church holds a vast mosaic of the *Last Judgement*, thoughtlessly restored in the 19C when many areas were removed and replaced by copies. The most intact sections are those depicting the realm of Hell, with the seven deadly sins (Pride, Lust, Greed, Anger, Envy, Avarice and Sloth). There are many memorable details here: the tremendous energy of the angels as they drive the Proud into hellfire, the smoky burst of flame that envelops the Lustful, the chill bodies of the Greedy depicted engulfed by darkness, the sinister pallor that throws into relief the writhing serpents emerging from the eyes of the Envious.

In front of the basilica and a little to one side is the church of **Santa Fosca**, built in the 11C to enshrine the relics of an early Christian martyr brought to the island in 1011. This is a centrally-planned building with a projecting apse, an arcaded portico and a tiled wooden roof. It is an austere building inside and out, with little decorative detail to distract from its well proportioned forms and space. On the grass outside is a primitive stone seat known as 'Attila's chair'.

The Palazzo del Consiglio, across the lawn, now houses the **Museo dell'Estuario di Torcello** (open Tue–Sun 10.30–17.30, closed holidays), which contains an interesting and well displayed collection of objects tracing the history of the island and its environs. It includes some objects from the cathedral—fragments of 12C mosaics removed from the tympanum of the apse, and all that remains of the 13C silver-gilt altar frontal—as well as archaeological finds and a number of paintings from demolished churches in the area.

Padua and environs

This chapter centres around Padua. Big, busy and dirty, foggy in winter and unbearably muggy in summer, it's a disagreeable place, especially if you're coming from Venice. Once you've overcome its disastrous first impression, however, it becomes almost likeable, for culturally it is an extremely active, rich and stimulating city.

Padua's cultural leadership dates back half a millennium and is closely tied to the presence in the city of one of Europe's oldest and most prestigious universities. Even after the rise of Venice, Padua remained a leading centre of humanist thought, and the best Renaissance artists were called here from Florence and elsewhere to work on important commissions for the city's enlightened patricians. Dante, Petrarch and Galileo all lived in Padua at some point of their respective lives. Here, too, is one of the key monuments of proto-Renaissance art, Giotto's magnificent fresco cycle in the Scrovegni Chapel.

Padua's environs are every bit as beautiful as the city is ugly. Between here and Venice flow the languid waters of the Brenta Canal, to whose green shores the best Venetian society moved en masse in summer. The luxurious villas here and in the hills to the north attest to the tenor of life that was enjoyed during the twilight of the republic. In the gentle southern landscape of the Euganean Hills an earlier aristocracy built its seignories, and the great religious orders constructed vast retreats. All these areas invite leisurely exploration.

Practical information

Getting there
By air

Padua is served principally by Venice's Marco Polo International Airport, 40km northeast. Domestic flights connect with Milan, Naples, Palermo, Rome and Turin; international flights with Amsterdam, Barcelona, Brussels, Copenhagen, Düsseldorf, Frankfurt, London, Lugano, Montpellier, Moscow, Munich, New York, Nice, Paris, Stüttgart, Vienna and Zurich. Airport bus every 30mins Mon–Sat; hourly Sun and holidays. Verona Caselle di Sommacampagna airport (94km west) also has daily flights to domestic and European destinations.

By road

Padua stands at the junction of the A4 (Milan–Venice) and A13 (Bologna–Venice) and is the hub from which many of the region's major highways radiate. 11 runs along the north bank of the Brenta from Padua to Mestre, and 16 skirts the eastern slopes of the Euganean Hills to Monselice. From Monselice 10 runs west to Este and Montagnana. **Country buses** are frequent throughout the area.

By rail

Padua is situated on the main rail lines from Milan and Rome to Venice. There are through services to Slovenia, Croatia, Hungary, Ukraine and Russia (via Villa Opicina), to Vienna and Prague (via Tarvisio), and to Paris, Geneva and Munich. The Euganean Hills are served by the main rail line from Padua to Bologna and Rome (change at Monselice for Este and Montagnana).

Getting around
By road

Town buses nos 8, 12 and **18** run from the railway station to the city centre, every 5mins Mon–Fri, every 15mins Sun and holidays.
Country buses run by *SITA* (☎ 049 8206811) depart from Piazzale Boschetti for Venice (although Venice is best reached from Padua by train); to Rovigo, Monselice-Montagnana and numerous destinations in the Veneto; and to Bologna.

The **Euganean Hills** are best explored by car (routes 11 and 16), but the journey can also be made by train (see above).

The **car parks** in Padua at Prato della Valle and Via Fra Paolo Sarpi have a minibus service to Piazza dei Signori. There is also a large car park near the station.

By boat

The Burchiello motor-launch usually operates Apr–Oct from Padua (Scalinata del Portello) along the **Brenta Canal** to Venice in 8hrs 30mins (on Wed, Fri and Sun) with stops at Strà, Dolo, Mira, Oriago and Malcontena (including visits to the villas at Strà, Mira, and Malcontena). At present it is only operating from Strà (bus from Piazzale Boschetti, Padua to Strà). Bookings at *New Siamic Express*, Via Trieste 42, ☎ 049 660944. Other companies now also arrange trips on the Brenta (details from the information office).

Information offices
PADUA Riviera dei Mugnai 8, ☎ 049 875 0655, fax 049 650794; at the train station, ☎ 049

875 2077. *Informagiovani*, Vicolo Ponte Molino 7, ☎ 049 654328. A **cumulative ticket** for free entrance to the main museums and monuments of Padua can be purchased from these offices (or at the ticket offices of any of the museums). The tourist board also publishes quarterly *Padova Today* with up-to-date information for visitors. The Comune runs an information office for young people at Vicolo Ponte Molino 7.
RIVIERA DEL BRENTA Via Don Minzoni 26, Mira Porte, ☎ 041 424973.
EUGANEAN HILLS Via Pietro d'Abano 18, Abano Terme, ☎ 049 866 9055.

Where to stay

PADUA *Al Fagiano*, Via Locatelli 45, ☎ 049 875 3396, fax 049 875 3396; a simple establishment just off Piazza del Santo; inexpensive.
Donatello, Via del Santo 102, ☎ 049 875 0634, fax 049 875 0829; a comfortable hotel overlooking the Santo; its *Sant'Antonio* restaurant has a pleasant summer terrace; closed Dec–Jan; moderate.
Igea, Via Ospedale Civile 87, ☎ 049 875 0577, fax 049 660865; a warm, homely inn near the Santo; inexpensive.
Leon Bianco, Piazzetta Pedrocchi 12, ☎ 049 875 0814, fax 049 875 6184; a small, quiet place in the heart of the old city, next door to the *Caffè Pedrocchi*; moderate.
Majestic Toscanelli, Via dell'Arco 2, ☎ 049 663244, fax 049 876 0025; an elegant, distinctive establishment situated in a little square near Piazza delle Erbe; moderate.
Youth hostel: Città di Padova, Via Aleardi 30, ☎ 049 8752219, fax 049 654210. The 1-star hotels *Pace* (Via Papafava 3) and *Pavia* (Via Papafava 11) are also used by students.
EUGANEAN HILLS The best place to stay in this area is without a doubt Abano Terme. Hospitality is the only game in town here, and all the hotels (open Apr–Nov as a rule) are comfortable, modern, and restful, though there is not one that is downright luxurious.
Trieste e Victoria, Via Pietro d'Abano 1, ☎ 049 866 8333, fax 049 866 8396; is a well-established, elegant place with lovely gardens and thermal pool; expensive.
Terme Columbia, Via Augure 15, ☎ 049 866 9606, fax 049 866 9430; modern and efficient, with a thermal pool; moderate.

Eating out

PADUA *Ai Porteghi*, Via Battisti 105, ☎ 049 660746; a traditional trattoria located halfway between the Cappella Scrovegni and the Basilica del Santo, serving Paduan specialties; closed Sun, midday Mon and Aug; moderate.
Antico Brolo, Corso Milano 22, ☎ 049 664555; a small, traditional restaurant in a historic building in the city centre; closed midday Sun, Mon and Aug; moderate.
Belle Parti, Via Belle Parti 11, ☎ 049 875 1822; situated near Piazza dei Signori, serving innovative cuisine; closed Sun and Aug; moderate.
Cavalca, Via Manin 8, ☎ 049 876 0061; traditional fare accompanied by regional and Italian wines; closed Tues evening, Wed and Jul; inexpensive.
San Clemente, Corso Vittorio Emanule II 142, ☎ 049 880 3180; probably the city's best, located a few blocks south of the Prato della Valle, in a historic building with a lovely garden; closed Sun evening, midday Mon, Aug and Dec; expensive.
L'Anfora, Via dei Soncin 13, ☎ 049 656629; wine bar and osteria with live jazz at lunch; closed Sun, midday Mon and Aug; inexpensive.
Leonardi, Via Pietro d'Abano 1, ☎ 049 875 0083; wine bar serving soups and simple meals; closed Mon, mid-day Tues,

Feb and Aug; inexpensive.

RUBANO, 8km west on the road to Vicenza, is home to *Le Calandre*, Via Liguria 1, Località Sarmeola, ☎ 049 630303; a favourite haunt of local gourmets, serving original variations on traditional recipes; closed Mon and Aug; moderate.

Cafés and pastry shops. *Pedrocchi*, Via 8 Febbraio; *Pasticceria Brigenti*, Piazza dei Signori.

Picnic places. Giardino dell'Arena (by the Cappella degli Scrovegni) and Prato della Valle (near the Basilica del Santo).

RIVIERA DEL BRENTA *Da Conte*, Via Caltana 133, Località Marano, Mira, ☎ 041 479571; good traditional osteria just a few steps from the station; closed Sun evening, Mon, Jan and Sep; moderate.

Da Nalin, Via Nuovissimo Argine Sinistro 29, Mira, ☎ 041 420083; a fine country restaurant established in 1914, offering Venetian specialities and grilled meat and fish; closed Sun evening, Mon, Aug and Dec–Jan; moderate.

Margherita (with rooms), Via Nazionale 312, Mira, ☎ 041 420879; an elegant restaurant in a garden along the Brenta offering Venetian cuisine, especially grilled meat and fish; closed Tues evening, Wed and Jan; moderate.

EUGANEAN HILLS *Aldo Moro* (with rooms), Via Marconi 27, Montagnana, ☎ 0429 81351; local specialities cooked with care and a good selection of regional and Italian wines; closed Mon, Jan and Aug; moderate.

Al Sasso, Via Ronco 11, Località Castelnuovo, Teolo (12km west of Abano Terme), ☎ 049 992 5073; trattoria serving delicious regional dishes, not far from the Abbazia di Praglia; closed Wed, Jan and Sep; inexpensive.

Casa Vecia, Via Appia 130, Monterosso, ☎ 049 860 0138; a great trattoria offering deliciously prepared local dishes; closed Mon and midday Tues; moderate.

Da Mario, Corso Terme 4, Montegrotto

Terme, ☎ 049 794090; restaurant offering excellent cuisine and wines from the Veneto; closed Tues, Feb and Jul; moderate.

La Torre, Piazza Mazzini 14, Monselice, ☎ 0429 73752; an inexpensive place serving traditional dishes prepared with considerable skill; closed Sun evening, Mon, Jul–Aug and Dec–Jan; moderate. The *Abbazia di Praglia* sells several varieties of honey, as well as liqueurs and herb teas.

Entertainment

PADUA *Teatro Verdi*, Via dei Livello 32, *Teatro Antonianum*, Via Briosco 32, and *Teatro delle Maddalene*, Via S. Giovanni da Verdara 40, for music and drama, and *Auditorium Pollini*, Via Cassan 15, for classical music and opera. The *Orchestra di Padova e del Veneto* have a concert season Oct–Apr at the *Teatro Verdi* and *Auditorium Pollini*. The *Amici della Musica* arrange excellent concerts Oct–Apr in the *Auditorium Pollini*. Classical music concerts are often held also in Paduan churches; rock and pop concerts at *Palasport San Lazzaro*, Strada San Marco, or *Supercinema*, Via Filiberto; and pop and jazz festivals are staged in the *Giardini dell'Arena*, Corso del Popolo.

Shopping

Padua is known among Italians for **food and wine**: *prosciutto di Montagnana*, *Vini dei Colli* DOC wines, *Dolce di Sant'Antonio*, Este **ceramics**, and **leather goods** and **jewellery**. Daily markets open all day in the three central piazzas (Piazza della Frutta, Piazza delle Erbe and Piazza dei Signori). The market in Piazza delle Erbe has good-value produce, while that in Piazza della Frutta also has delicacies. A weekly market is held on Sat in the Prato della Valle.

Special events

PADUA *Festival dei Solisti Veneti*, classical music concerts in Paduan churches; *Villeggiando*, concerts and theatre in villas around Padua; *Notturni d'Arte*, music and theatre in museums—all May–Sep. *Teatro Estate*, theatre festival, Aug. *Stagione Concertistica*, classical music, Oct–Mar. *Rassegna del Jazz Italiano*, jazz festival, Nov–Dec. Annual *festival of St Anthony* on 13 Jun, with processions, pageantry, etc. You can see more pageantry on the first Sun in Oct for the *Padova del Medioevo* celebrations.

EUGANEAN HILLS Monsélice, *Giostra della Rocca*, popular feast in costume, Sep. Este, *Settembre Euganeo*, with folk and cultural events, Sep; *Mostra della Ceramica Estense* (ceramics show, Sep). Montagnana, *Palio dei 10 Comuni* (popular festival, first Sun in Sep, with a horse race outside the walls and celebrations, fairs and markets that last a week). Cittadella, *Fiera Franca*, a fair held on the third Sun in Oct since 1608.

Sport

Golf courses at Valsanzibio, Teolo and Frassanelle.

PADUA

Padua, in Italian *Padova* (population 231,000), is a lively town, crowded with young people in the evenings. The three central piazzas, around Palazzo della Ragione, are filled every day with busy markets. In Italy Padua is known as the place where St Anthony of Padua lived and carried out numerous miracles, and his tomb in the Santo is visited every year by thousands of pilgrims. Although the old town has many pretty arcaded streets, the rest of the city is unattractive.

History

According to the Roman historian Livy (59 BC–18 AD), the most famous native of Padua (born at Teolo, in the Euganean Hills), *Patavium* was founded by the Trojan Antenor. In reality the city was established later—not before the 8C or 7C BC, probably by palaeo-Venetic tribes. It is known to have been an important settlement of the Euganei and Veneti, and it received full Roman franchise in 89 BC. It prospered under Byzantine and Lombard rule, and declared itself an independent republic in 1164. The foundation of the university in 1222 attracted many distinguished teachers to Padua, including Dante and Petrarch, as well as numerous students from England, and the city came to be known as *la Dotta* ('The Learned'). In 1237–54 Ezzelino da Romano was tyrant of Padua, then after the suzerainty of the Carraresi (1318–1405) it was conquered by the Venetians, remaining a faithful ally of Venice until the end of the Venetian Republic.

Art

Giotto's frescoes in the Cappella degli Scrovegni gave rise to a flourishing local school of 'Giottesque' painters (Guariento, Giusto de' Menabuoi, etc). The Veronese Altichiero (c 1330–c 1395), who was active in Padua in the 1380s, was one of the more creative interpreters of Giotto's achievements before Masaccio. Renaissance art was introduced into Padua with the arrival of Donatello in 1443 to work on his equestrian statue of Gattamelata and the high altar of the Santo. He was to have a profound influence on Andrea

Mantegna (1431–1506). The painter Francesco Squarcione (1397–1468) influenced a great number of followers, in particular Mantegna, who produced a superb fresco cycle in the Ovetari chapel in the church of the Eremitani between 1454 and 1457 (almost totally destroyed in the Second World War). In the late 15C Bartolomeo Bellano (1434–96) and Andrea Briosco ('Il Riccio', 1470–1532) created some of the finest small bronze sculpture of the Renaissance.

The city centre

The centre of city life, which gravitates around the university, is **Via VIII Febbraio**, **Piazzetta Pedrocchi** and **Piazza Cavour**, all now rather pretentiously designed pedestrian precincts, lacking in character but free of all motor traffic. The female bronze statue by Emilio Greco dates from 1973; nearby a stele by Giò Pomodoro was set up in 1992 as an unnecessary memorial to Galileo.

The huge ***Caffè Pedrocchi** is one of the more celebrated cafés in Italy and was famous in the 19C as a meeting-place for intellectuals (when it was kept open 24 hours a day). It was founded by Antonio Pedrocchi and built in a triangular shape in Neo-classical style in 1831 by Giuseppe Jappelli. On the piazzetta are two protruding Doric loggias, whose four lions by Giuseppe Petrelli (copies of those at the foot of the Campidoglio in Rome) are irresistible to children. The south façade has another Doric loggia, and the little wing was added by Jappelli in Gothic-revival style in 1837. It was opened to the public in 1836 and was left to the city in 1891. The ground floor has a long white-and-yellow main room, and two smaller red-and-green drawing rooms, all prettily furnished.

The **upper floor** (entered from the piazzetta; open Tues–Sun 09.00–12.30, 15.30–18.00) was opened in 1842 and has recently been beautifully restored. A grand staircase, with a stuccoed apse, leads up to the **Etruscan room**, beyond which is the octagonal Greek room with a fresco by Giovanni Demin (1842). The charming circular **Roman room** has four views of Rome by Ippolito Caffi (1841–42). The **Herculaneum room** was decorated by Pietro Paoletti. The elaborate **ballroom** has a stage for the orchestra. The **Egyptian room** was inspired by Jappelli's friend Belzoni, actor, engineer and famous Egyptologist, and it is decorated with mock porphyry and painted stucco statues attributed to Giuseppe Petrelli and Antonio Gradenigo. Off the ballroom is the little **Moorish room** with good wood carvings, and beyond are the **Renaissance room** and the **Gothic room** (with paintings on glass by Demin).

Opposite the café is the **university**, the second oldest university in Italy (after Bologna), founded in 1222. It was famous as a medical school and flourished in the 15C and 16C, when it was the only university in the Venetian Republic. It was nicknamed 'il Bo' (*bue*, or ox) from the sign of an inn, the most famous in the city, which used to stand on this site.

The older façade dates from 1757, and the tower from 1572; the adjoining building to the right (with the entrance) was reconstructed in 1938–39. The dignified courtyard (1552) is by Andrea Moroni. In the old courtyard (left) you can buy tickets for a guided tour of the university (usually on Tues and Thur at 09.00, 10.00 and 11.00, and on Wed–Fri at 15.00, 16.00 and 17.00). At the foot of the stairs is a statue of Elena Cornaro Piscopia (1646–84), who was the

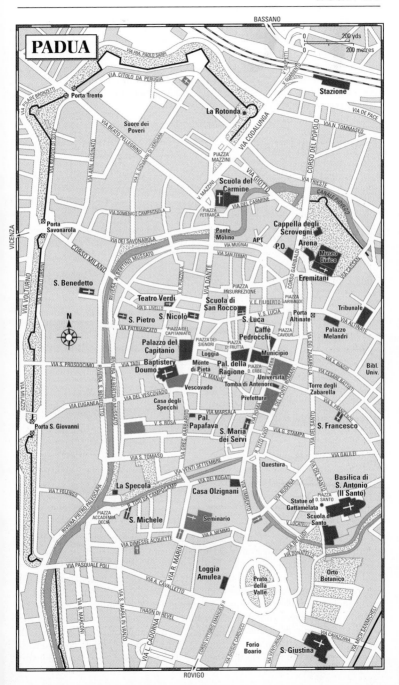

PADUA

0 ___ 200 yds
0 ___ 200 metres

BASSANO

VIA FRA PAOLO SARPI
VIA CITOLO DA PERUGIA
VIA G. GIUSTI
VIA G. GUERENTI
Stazione
VIA DE PACE
Porta Trento
VIA PILADE BRONZETTI
VIA RAGGIO DI TULLO
VIA BEATO PELLEGRINO
VIA ABT. LUGINATO
VIA S. GIOVANNI DI VERDARA
Suore dei
Poveri
La Rotonda
VIA CODALUNGA
VIA N. TOMMASEO
CORSO DEL POPOLO
PIAZZA
MAZZINI
VIA TRIESTE
CANALE PIOVEGO
VICENZA
Porta
Savonarola
VIA DOMENICO CAMPAGNOLA
VIA DEI SAVONAROLA
CORSO MILANO
V. MAZZINI
Scuola del
Carmine
VIA DEL CARMINE
PIAZZA
PETRARCA
Ponte
Molino
APT
VIA MUGNAI
Cappella degli
Scrovegni
P.O.
Arena
Museo
Civico
Eremitani
VIA CASSAN
VIA SAN FERMO
VIA SAVONAROLA
VIA ALBERTINO MUSSATO
RIVIERA ALBERTINO MUSSATO
VIA NICOLÒ ORSINI
VIA VOLTURNO
VIA MILAZZO
S. Benedetto
VIA D. LIVELLO
Teatro Verdi
S. Pietro
VIA PATRIARCATO
S. Nicolò
PIAZZA DEL
CAPITANIATO
Palazzo del
Capitanio
VIA S. PROSDOCIMO
RIVIERA S. BENEDETTO
VIA TADI
Baptistery
Duomo
Monte
di Pietà
VIA D. MANIN
Scuola di
San Rocco
PIAZZA
INSURREZIONE
PIAZZA
DEI
SIGNORI
PIAZZA
DI FRUTTA
Loggia
V. E. FILIBERTO GARIBALDI
CORSO GARIBALDI
S. Luca
Caffè
Pedrocchi
V. S. LUCIA
PIAZZA
CAVOUR
Porta
Altinate
Tribunale
VIA ALTINATE
Palazzo
Melandri
Municipio
Pal. della
Ragione
PIAZZA
D. ERBE
VIA ZABARELLA
Bibl.
Univ.
Università
Tomba di Antenore
VIA S. BIAGIO
VIA CESARE BATTISTI
Torre degli
Zabarella
Vescovado
VIA DEL VESCOVADO
Casa degli
Specchi
Prefettura
VIA S. FRANCESCO
VIA EUGANEO
Porta S. Giovanni
Pal.
Papafava
VIA GREG. BARBARIGO
V. S. ROSA
VIA MARSALA
VIA DEI CONTI
S. Maria
dei Servi
VIA ROMA
S. Francesco
VIA TITO LIVIO
VIA G. STAMPA
VIA GALILEI
VIA S. TOMASO
VIA VENTI SETTEMBRE
La Specola
Questura
Basilica di
S. Antonio
(Il Santo)
VIA DEI ROGATI
Casa Olzignani
VIA UMBERTO I
VIA RUDENA
PIAZZA
D. SANTO
Statue of
Gattamelata
Scuola di
Santo
VIA DEL SANTO
VIA RITO PIERO PALEOCAPA
PIAZZA
ACCADEMIA
DECIA
S. Michele
VIA T. FOLENGO
Seminario
V. LOCATELLI
VIA BELUDI
VIA DONATELLO
Orto
Botanico
VIA DIMESSE ACQUETTE
VIA A. MEMMO
VIA PASQUALE POLI
VIA R. MARIN
VIA A. CAVALLETTO
Loggia
Amulea
Prato
della
Valle
VIA G. MARCONI
VIA CADORNA
THAON DI REVEL
CORSO VITTORIO EMANUELE II
VIA GIOSUE CARDUCCI
VIA S. MARIA IN VANZO
Forio
Boario
S. Giustina
VIA CAVAZANA
VIA VENTURINI
VIA F. SANMICHELI

ROVIGO

first woman to take a doctor's degree, in philosophy. The upper loggia gives entrance to a room where Galileo's wooden '*cattedra*' is preserved. This great teaching desk is supposed to have been made as a sign of affection by his pupils so that they could see him better: the great scientist taught physics here from 1592–1610, a period he looked back on as the best of his life (one of his pupils was Gustavus Adolphus of Sweden). The Aula Magna is covered with the coats of arms of rectors, and 19C frescoes.

On the other side of the courtyard a door leads into a small museum, off which is the most ancient ***anatomical theatre** in Europe (1594). It was built by the surgeon Fabricius, master of William Harvey, who took his degree here in 1602. Thomas Linacre (1492) and John Caius (1539) also qualified here as doctors, and Vesalius (1540) and Fallopius (1561) were among the famous medical professors. Since its restoration the theatre can now only be visited from below (where the dissecting table used to be); the wooden galleries above could accommodate (standing) some 250 students.

The perils of academic life

The University of Padua reached the height of its fame in the 16C, then gradually lost its international standing. Some of the reasons for its decline can be gleaned in these lines:

The scholars here in the night commit many murders against their private adversaries, and too often executed upon the strangers and innocent, and all with gunshot or else with stilettoes.
William Lithgow, *Rare Adventures and Painfull Peregrinations*, 1614–32

The University here, tho' so much supported by the Venetians, that they pay fifty Professors, yet sinks extremely: There are no Men of any great Fame now in it; and the Quarrels among the Students have driven away most of the Strangers that used to come and study here; for it is not safe to stir abroad ... after Sun-set.
Gilbert Burnet, *Some Letters...*, 1687

In thine halls the lamp of learning
Padua, now no more is burning;
Like a meteor, whose wild way
Is lost over the grave of day,
It gleams betrayed, and to betray.
Percy Bysshe Shelley, *Lines Written among the Euganian Hills*, 1818.

Opposite the university, the eastern façade (1928–30) of the **Municipio** disguises a 16C building, by Andrea Moroni, that incorporates a tower of the 13C Palazzo del Podestà (seen from a side road). Behind is **Piazza della Frutta**, a delightful large piazza with a lively daily market overlooked by the splendid ***Palazzo della Ragione**. The latter is entered from the Municipio (on Via VIII Febbraio). The immense roof was reconstructed in 1756 after storm damage. A broad flight of modern stairs in the courtyard of the Municipio leads to the ***salone**, on the upper floor (open Tues–Sun 09.00–18.00 or 19.00), one of the larger and more remarkable halls in Italy. It was built by Fra Giovanni degli Eremitani in 1306–08, and is 79m long, 27m wide and 26m high, covered with a wooden ship's-keel roof. On the walls are 333 frescoes of religious and astrological subjects, divided according to the months of the year, by Nicolò Miretto and Stefano da Ferrara. These were painted shortly after a fire in 1420 that had destroyed paintings carried out by Giotto and his assistants in 1313.

It is not known how closely the frescoes follow the originals by Giotto. Each month is represented by nine scenes in three tiers, representing an allegory of the month, together with its sign of the zodiac, planet and constellation. Other scenes show the labours of the month and astrological illustrations. The hall contains a block of stone that once served as a stool of repentance for debtors, and a giant wooden horse, a copy of Donatello's *Gattamelata*, made for a fête in 1466. From the two terraces there are delightful views of the market squares. The hall is often used for exhibitions: its splendid proportions can only be fully appreciated when it is empty.

The palace separates Piazza della Frutta from **Piazza delle Erbe**, a particularly attractive square with arcaded buildings and a pretty fountain, and another daily market. At the corner of Piazza della Frutta at the Canton delle Busie is **Palazzo Consiglio** (1283) with two Byzantine capitals.

The ground floor of Palazzo della Ragione is also used as a market (with permanent stalls), which extends to a third piazza beyond (reached by Via San Clemente), called **Piazza dei Signori**. This is attractively enclosed by old buildings. The **Loggia della Gran Guardia** is a charming Lombard edifice begun by Annibale Maggi (1496) and finished in 1523. **Palazzo del Capitaniato** (1599–1605) occupies the site of the castle of the Carraresi, of which a 14C portico survives just off Via Accademia (at no. 11). The palace incorporates a tower, adapted in 1532 by Giovanni Maria Falconetto to accommodate an astronomical clock dating from 1344 (the oldest in Italy).

Beyond the Arco dell'Orologio lies the Corte Capitaniato, with the **Liviano**, which houses the arts faculty of the university, built in 1939 by Giò Ponti. The entrance hall was frescoed by Massimo Campigli. The building incorporates the **Sala dei Giganti** with frescoes of famous men by Domenico and Gualtiero Campagnolo, and Stefano dell'Arzere (1539). These were painted over earlier 14C frescoes, including a fragment attributed to Altichiero showing Petrarch reading in his study, possibly drawn from life (Petrarch lived nearby in Arquà in 1368–74).

In Via Accademia is the beautiful **Loggia Carrarese**, seat of the Accademia Patavina di Scienze, Lettere ed Arti. The former chapel here has frescoes of Old Testament scenes by Guariento (c 1360).

From Piazza Capitaniato, with a 16C Loggia and ancient acacias, the Corte Valaresso (fine staircase of 1607) leads under an arch of 1632 to Piazza del Duomo, with the 13C–14C Monte di Pietà, remodelled with a portico by Giovanni Maria Falconetto in 1530.

The **Cathedral** was reconstructed in 1552 by Andrea da Valle and Agostino Righetti to a much-altered design of Michelangelo. The sacristy contains works by Nicolò Semitecolo (1367), Francesco Bassano, Giorgio Schiavone (four *Saints), Gian Domenico Tiepolo, Sassoferrato and Paris Bordone. The treasury includes 12C and 13C illuminated *manuscripts, a Byzantine thurible (censer) of the 11C, a processional cross of 1228, and a large *reliquary of the Cross, of silver gilt with enamels, dating from c 1440.

The **baptistery** (open 09.30–12.30, 15.00–18.00) was built at the end of the

12C. The interior is entirely covered with *frescoes by Giusto de'Menabuoi, his best work. Executed in 1378, this is one of the more interesting medieval fresco cycles in Italy. *Christ Pantocrator* appears in the dome surrounded by a host of angels and the Blessed; scenes from Genesis adorn the drum; the evangelists look down from the pendentives; and scenes from the lives of Christ and St John the Baptist cover the walls. There are scenes from the Apocalypse in the apse, and a polyptych, also by Giusto, on the altar.

To the south of the cathedral is the bishop's palace, housing the **Museo Diocesano d'Arte Sacra**, open Thur–Fri 15.00–19.00, with a frescoed *Annunciation* by Jacopo da Montagnana. At Via del Vescovado 79 is the **Casa degli Specchi**, an early 16C Lombardesque building by Annibale Maggi with tondi of polished marble.

Adjoining Piazzetta Pedrocchi to the north, are Piazza Cavour and Piazza Garibaldi with a Roman column surmounted by the 'Madonna dei Noli' by Antonio Bonazza. On the far side of Piazza Garibaldi opens the **Porta Altinate**, a gateway of the 13C town wall.

The Scrovegni Chapel and Museo Civico agli Eremitani

Two blocks north of Piazza Garibaldi you come to the Giardino dell'Arena, with fragmentary remains of a Roman amphitheatre of the 1C AD. Here stands Padua's loveliest attraction, which is not to be missed.

The ***Cappella degli Scrovegni**, also known as the Arena Chapel, was commissioned by the merchant Enrico degli Scrovegni for his family palace, which was demolished in the 19C. Inside are the magnificent frescoes executed around 1305 by Giotto and his pupils—the only cycle by the master to survive intact and one of the greatest achievements of Italian painting. The frescoes tell the story of Christian redemption through the lives of Mary and Christ—an important theme for Scrovegni, whose father had been a usurer (see Dante, *Inferno*, xvii, 64–75). Their monumental composition, concise representation, and intense sense of drama were revolutionary in their time.

The chapel is part of the immense **Museo Civico agli Eremitani**, which occupies the former Convento degli Eremitani on the south side of the park (open Tues–Sun 09.00–18.00 or 19.00; inclusive ticket). From the entrance hall and gift shop you enter a lovely cloister, on the far side of which a doorway leads out to a little garden. Here are the ruined walls of the Roman amphitheatre and, on the right, the entrance (present your ticket) to the Cappella degli Scrovegni.

A milestone in the history of art

Giotto's influence on all subsequent Italian painting can here be understood to the full: his painting has a new monumentality and sense of volume that had never been achieved in medieval painting. The biblical narrative is given an intensely human significance for the first time. Bernard Berenson pointed out that his figures have remarkable 'tactile values'. The superb colouring (with strong blues) is extremely well preserved. The frescoes were last restored in 1887.

The chapel is small, intended for a congregation of the Scrovegni family and their retainers, and the frescoes themselves are about half lifesize. They are arranged in three superimposed rows of scenes, enclosed in delicately ornamented frames that form a continuous structure, a sort of 'motion-picture' in which it is the viewer who moves from one dramatic incident to the next. The vault is painted the same bright blue as the background of the frescoes—quite naturally, as the vaults and domes of medieval churches were held to be symbolic of Heaven. This one is sprinkled with gold stars, with portraits of Christ and the four Evangelists set in circular medallions.

The wall surfaces are divided into 38 scenes:

Top band The narrative begins on the top band, to the right of the chancel arch. The frames trace the lives of Joachim and Anna, the Virgin's parents (*Expulsion of Joachim from the Temple, Joachim among the Shepherds, Annunciation to Anna, Sacrifice of Joachim, Vision of Joachim, Meeting of Joachim and Anna*) on the south wall, and the life of the Virgin (*Birth, Presentation in the Temple, Presentation of the Rods to Simeon, Watching of the Rods, Betrothal of the Virgin, The Virgin's Return Home*) on the north, ending with the *Annunciation* and (in a frame borrowed from the central order) *Visitation* on either side of the sanctuary and *God the Father Dispatching Gabriel* over the chancel arch.

Second level On the second level the Infancy of Christ (*Nativity, Adoration of the Magi, Presentation in the Temple, Flight into Egypt, Massacre of the Innocents*), on the south wall, leads into His adult life (*Dispute with the Elders, Baptism of Christ, Marriage at Cana, Raising of Lazarus, Entry into Jerusalem, Expulsion from the Temple*), on the north, ending in the *Pact of Judas*, by the arch. On the lowest tier, the Passion of Christ (*Last Supper, Washing of the Feet, Betrayal of Christ, Christ before Caiaphas, Mocking of Christ*) on the south is followed by His Death and Resurrection (*Way to Calvary, Crucifixion, Deposition, Angel at the Empty Tomb* and *Noli me Tangere, Ascension, Pentecost*) on the north. A *faux*-marble dado below is punctuated by chiaroscuro images of the Seven Virtues (on the south side) and the Seven Deadly Sins (on the north).

Entrance wall The drama of human salvation reaches its climax in the *Last Judgement* on the entrance wall. The stories of Mary in the apse were executed later by followers of Giotto; Giusto de'Menabuoi frescoed the two *Madonne del Latte* in the niches at the sides of the altar, and Giovanni Pisano carved the delicate statues of the *Virgin and Angels*. Behind the altar is the tomb of Enrico degli Scrovegni, who died in 1336.

Return to the cloister and turn left to enter the **museum**. Splendidly displayed in recently renovated quarters, the collections include antiquities, paintings and coins.

A steel staircase climbs to the **first floor**. In the **Pinacoteca** are works by Giotto (the *Arena Chapel Crucifix*), Guariento (*Madonna with Angels*), Alvise Vivarini (*Male Portrait*), Jacopo Bellini (*Christ in Limbo*), Paolo Veronese (*Last Supper, *Crucifixion, Martyrdom of St Justina*), Jacopo Tintoretto (*Supper in the House of Simon*), Giovanni Battista Tiepolo, Francesco Guardi, Marco and Sebastiano Ricci, and others.

The **Bottacin Museum** consists of the collection made between 1850 and 1875 by Nicola Bottacin (1805–76). It includes mildly interesting 19C paintings and sculptures, and an extraordinary collection of coins and medals, all well displayed and labelled.

A large vetrine in the continuation of the pinacoteca displays small bronzes by Italian and foreign sculptors of the 14C–17C; northern-Italian masters

(Moderno, Antico, Riccio, Alessandro Vittoria, Tiziano Aspetti) are particularly well represented.

The huge **Emo Capodilista Collection** of 15C–18C paintings was left to the city by Leonardo Emo Capodilista in 1864. Here are works by Venetian and Flemish painters, notably Giorgione's *Leda and the Swan* and *Country Idyll*, and a *Portrait of a Young Senator* by Giovanni Bellini. There are also works by Titian and Luca Giordano, Jan van Scorel (*Portrait of a Man*) and Quentin Metsys (*St John the Evangelist*).

The **archaeological section**, occupying the main cloister and several **ground-floor** rooms, has prehistoric, Roman, Egyptian, Etruscan and early Christian antiquities. Highlights include a Roman *bust of Silenus (2C AD); an imposing aedicular *tomb of the Volumnii family, dating from the Augustan period; and two *statues of the Goddess Sekhmet in black basalt, given to the city by Giovanni Battista Belzoni in 1819. Belzoni (1778–1823), born in Padua, was the first European to enter the tomb of Ramesses II at Abu Simbel, and supplied the British Museum with many of its largest Egyptian statues. Splendid examples of Roman, Islamic and medieval European glass are displayed in vetrines throughout the museum.

The adjacent church of the **Eremitani**, or Santi Filippo e Giacomo, was built in Romanesque-Gothic forms between 1276 and 1306 for the Augustinian monastic order. Damaged by bombs in 1944, it was rebuilt after the war. The lower part of the façade, added in 1360, has a broad doorway and tall, deep arches that continue on the south flank. Here, beneath an attached porch, is a remarkable Renaissance doorway with carvings of the *Months* by the Florentine Niccolò Baroncelli.

The **interior**, a single broad aisle with a ship's-keel roof, contains tombs and sculptures of the 14C–16C and fragmentary frescoes. On the south side, the first chapel has remains of frescoes by Giusto de'Menabuoi; and the fourth chapel, a *Madonna and Child* and *Ecce Homo* by Guariento. At the end of the south aisle stands the **Cappella Ovetari**, once famous for its frescoes by Andrea Mantegna. Their destruction in 1944 was the greatest single loss of Italian art in the war. Of the remaining fragments, the best-preserved scenes are the *Martyrdom of St Christopher* (south wall), the *Assumption* (behind the altar) and the *Martyrdom of St James* (north wall). The terracotta altarpiece of the *Madonna and Child with Saints* was made by a follower of Donatello. There are more 14C frescoes in the sanctuary (*Stories of Sts Augustine, James, and Philip*, by Guariento) and in the other apsidal chapels. In the north aisle are the tombs of Marco Mantova Benavides, a law professor, by Bartolomeo Ammannati; and of Jacopo da Carrara, with Latin verses by Petrarch.

Around the Eremitani

Via Altinate leads east from Piazza Garibaldi past **Palazzo Melandri** (no. 18), with a beautiful four-light window, and **San Gaetano**, a pleasant church by Scamozzi (1586), to **Santa Sofia**, the oldest church in Padua. Founded in the 9C on an earlier structure, it was rebuilt in the 11C–12C in a Romanesque style recalling earlier churches of the Adriatic exarchate. The apse is remarkable.

Via Filiberto leads west from Piazza Garibaldi to the modern Piazza Insurrezione, the centre of a rebuilt business quarter. Here is the **Scuola di San**

Rocco (open Tues–Sun 09.30–12.30, 15.30–19.00), an attractive Renaissance building of 1525, which is interesting for its frescoes illustrating the life of St Roch, attributed to Domenico Campagnola and Girolamo Tessari. They are, however, in very poor condition, and some of them have been detached. The 17C altarpiece is by Alessandro Maganza.

The **Scuola del Carmine** (open 07.00–12.00, 16.00–19.30), dating from 1377, has frescoes attributed to Giulio and Domenico Campagnola, notably the *Meeting of St Anne and St Joachim*.

The statue of Gattemelata

From Via XIII Febbraio, Via San Francesco leads east from the university past the alleged **Tomb of Antenor**, a marble sarcophagus erected in 1233 on short columns; another sarcophagus (1309) was set up here on the 2000th anniversary of Livy's birth. The restored **Torre degli Zabarella** dates from the 13C. Via Cesare Battisti to the north is a pretty road with porticoes, typical of the old town. Via San Francesco continues to the church of **San Francesco**, dating from 1416, which contains the *monument of Pietro Roccabonella, natural philosopher, by Bartolomeo Bellano and Il Riccio (1496–97), while the narrow Via del Santo leads south to the pleasant **Piazza del Santo**.

Statue of Gattamelata by Donatello (1453)

The square is dominated by the great church of Sant'Antonio. First, notice the famous equestrian statue of *Gattamelata, a masterpiece by Donatello (1453) and the first great Renaissance bronze equestrian monument cast in Italy. Gattamelata, or Erasmo da Nardo, was a celebrated Venetian *condottiere* (mercenary general) and protector of the Venetian Republic. He died in 1443 and had a state funeral in Venice: it is known that he desired to be buried in the Santo (see below). On the exceptionally high base are copies of the two reliefs carved by Donatello in 1447.

Just out of the piazza in Via Cesarotti is the pretty **Palazzo Giusti del Giardino**, with a double loggia. It incorporates the *Loggia and Odeo Cornaro (not open) attributed to Giovanni Maria Falconetto and Gaultiero dell'Arzere, built in 1524 for Alvise Cornaro as the seat of a literary society. Derived from classical models, the buildings are decorated with statues attributed to Giovan Maria Mosca, and stuccoes by Tiziano Minio.

The basilica of Sant'Antonio

The Franciscan basilica of Sant'Antonio (open daily 06.30–19.00 or 19.30), familiarly called *Il Santo* by *padovani*, was built between 1232 and the mid-14C to enshrine the body of St Anthony of Padua. St Anthony was born in Lisbon in 1195, but on a missionary journey to Africa he was forced in a storm to land in Italy and settled at Padua, where he preached and carried out miracles under the guidance of St Francis. He was canonised the year after his death in 1231. The church is now one of the great pilgrim shrines of Italy, for St Anthony is one of the best-loved saints in the country (it is estimated that some five million pilgrims visit the church every year).

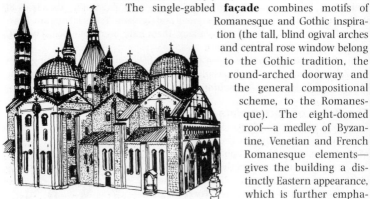

The single-gabled **façade** combines motifs of Romanesque and Gothic inspiration (the tall, blind ogival arches and central rose window belong to the Gothic tradition, the round-arched doorway and the general compositional scheme, to the Romanesque). The eight-domed roof—a medley of Byzantine, Venetian and French Romanesque elements—gives the building a distinctly Eastern appearance, which is further emphasised by the small towers and the two octagonal campanili, seemingly drawn from the *Arabian Nights*.

Basilica del Santo

Interior The magnificent nave is separated from the lateral aisles by great piers and terminates, at the east end, in a profusely decorated ambulatory. The holy-water stoups against the first two piers bear statues of *St John the Baptist* (south) by Tullio Lombardo, and Christ (north) by Tiziano Aspetti. The second north pier holds the tomb of the Venetian general Alessandro Contarini (d. 1553), designed by Michele Sanmicheli and incorporating sculptures by Danese Cattaneo and Alessandro Vittoria. On the opposite side is the tomb of Cardinal Bembo (d. 1547), attributed to Palladio, with a bust by Cattaneo. The first chapel in the south aisle preserves the 15C tombs of Gattamelata, by Bartolomeo Bellano, and his son Giannantonio, by Pietro Lombardo. The 14C *Capella di San Felice, in the south transept, was designed by Andriolo and Giovanni De Santi. It has frescoes representing the *Legend of St James*, the *Crucifixion* and other scenes, by Altichiero.

Behind the bronze doors of the choir (the custodians will unlock these on request) is the *high altar, the second major commission Donatello received during his ten-year sojourn among the 'fogs and frogs' of Padua, as he put it. The altar (1443–50) is decorated with splendid bronze statues and reliefs by the master and his pupils. Their original configuration is unknown, and their present arrangement, devised by Camillo Boito in 1895, has been a matter of controversy among art historians for a full century. Above the predella, with twelve small reliefs of *Angel Musicians* and a *Pietà*, are four larger reliefs (two on the front and two on the back) of *Miracles of St Anthony*, all showing a startlingly bold treatment of architectural space that would profoundly influence Venetian Renaissance painting from Mantegna onwards. Also on this level are a small *Christ in Pietà* and, at the ends, symbols of the evangelists. At the top of the composition are an enthroned *Madonna* in an unusual rising pose between life-size statues of the six patron saints of Padua (*St Louis of Anjou, St Justina, St Francis, St Anthony, St Daniel*, and *St Prosdocimus*), and a splendid bronze *crucifix, probably intended to be placed elsewhere in the church. The placement of the stone *Deposition*, behind the altar, is also questionable. North of the altar stands a magnificent bronze paschal candelabrum by Andrea Briosco, 'Il Riccio' (1507–15). Along the sanctuary walls are twelve bronze reliefs of Old Testament stories, by Bartolomeo Bellano and Andrea Briosco.

Around the sanctuary are the ambulatory and its radiating chapels; the fifth chapel, known as the **Capalla delle Relique** or Cappella del Tesoro, built to a central plan by Filippo Parodi (who also made the statues, in 1689) holds a rich treasury, with remarkable reliquaries (including one for St Anthony's tongue), incense boats, and the wood boxes that once held the remains of the saint. At the north end of the ambulatory is the Chapel of the Madonna Mora, a vestige of the earlier (12C) church of Santa Maria Mater Domini.

The ***Cappella dell'Arca del Santo**, in the north transept, was designed in 1499 by Tullio Lombardo and executed by his assistant, Antonio Minello. The stuccoed ceiling was done by G.M. Falconetto in 1533. On the walls are nine large reliefs with stories of St Anthony, by 16C sculptors including Jacopo Sansovino (4th and 5th from the left), Tullio Lombardo (6th and 7th) and Antonio Lombardo (last). At the centre stands the magnificent altar, designed by Tiziano Aspetti (1593), behind which is St Anthony's tomb. This is still visited by hundred of pilgrims every year, many of whom leave votive offerings. The adjacent Cappella Conti, with the tomb of the Blessed Luca Belludi, St Anthony's companion, is frescoed by Giusto de'Menabuoi.

On the wall of the north aisle of the basilica are the 17C tomb of General Catrino Cornaro, by Juste le Court, and that of Antonio Roselli (d. 1466), by Pietro Lombardo.

To the south of the church are four **cloisters**, built between the 13C and the 15C. In the second, with a Romanesque doorway, a Renaissance loggia and a well of 1492, is a monument to Cornelio Musso by Andrea Briosco. Steps climb from the fourth past the original stone reliefs by Donatello from the Gattamelata monument to the Biblioteca Antoniana, with 85,000 books, manuscripts, and incunabula, including a manuscript of sermons with notes in the hand of St Anthony.

In the **Chiostro del Beato Luca Belludi**, with a magnificent magnolia tree, The **Museo Antoniano** preserves paintings, sculpture, and votive offerings from the basilica, notably the fresco of *Saints Anthony and Bernard Adoring the Monogram of Christ* by Andrea Mantegna, formerly in the lunette of the main doorway. In another cloister, on the north side near the church, a modest slab marks the burial-place of the entrails of Thomas Howard (1586–1646), Earl of Surrey and Arundel, collector of the 'Arundel Marbles'.

The **Scuola di Sant'Antonio** and the **Oratory of San Giorgio** (inclusive ticket; open 09.00–12.30, 14.30–17.00 or 19.00) adjoin the basilica on the southwest. The scuola was begun in 1427, with an upper storey added in 1504. A handsome 18C staircase ascends to the main hall, decorated with *frescoes of the life of the saint by Venetian artists, including Bartolomeo Montagna, Domenico Campagnola, Girolamo del Santo and Titian, who painted the scenes of the *Miracle of the Irascible Son* (considered his first important independent works). The coloured terracotta *Madonna* is by Andrea Briosco. The oratory, once a chapel of the Soranzo family, is entirely covered with *frescoes by Altichiero and his assistants (1379–84). The paintings represent the lives of

Christ and Saints George, Catherine and Lucy, and their arrangement in horizontal bands clearly calls to mind Giotto's decoration for the Scrovegni Chapel.

In the corner of the piazza is a building of 1870–80, with an unusual façade by Camillo Boito, now used for exhibitions.

Prato della Valle and its neighbourhood

The quiet Via Orto Botanico leads out of the piazza across a canal to the *Orto Botanico (open daily except Sun and holidays 09.00–13.00; May–Sep also 15.00–18.00), the most ancient botanical garden in Europe, founded in 1545 and retaining its original form and structure. It is beautifully tended and all the plants are well labelled. The charming circular walled garden, with geometrical beds, is laid out around a pond with tropical water lilies. The various sections include medicinal and aquatic plants, rare species from northern Italy, flora from the Colli Euganei, and poisonous plants. Also here are a tamarisk tree, a ginkgo tree of 1750, a mimosa tree and an ancient magnolia dating from the mid-18C. A palm tree, planted in 1585 and known as 'Goethe's palm' (he visited the garden in 1786) survives in a little greenhouse. Behind this are interesting 19C hothouses, where succulents and carnivorous plants are kept, opposite which is a row of the plants first introduced into Italy in this garden, including the lilac, first cultivated in 1565, the sunflower in 1568, and the potato in 1590. There is also a greenhouse for orchids. Trees in the arboretum surrounding the walled garden include swamp cypresses, magnolias, Chinese palm trees, cedars, pines, a plane tree dating from 1680, and ilexes.

Via Beato Luca Belludi leads past an interesting Art Nouveau house (no. 3) to the pleasant *Prato della Valle, the largest 'piazza' in Italy, surrounded by a miscellany of arcaded buildings. This huge area has been used since Roman times for public spectacles, fairs, etc. (and a large market is held here on Sat). In the centre is the Isola Memmia, encircled by a canal bordered by 18C statues of famous citizens, professors and students of the university. Four bridges lead to the centre, decorated with fountains. On the west side of the Prato is the **Loggia Amulea**, built in 1861 in the Venetian style with two Gothic loggias in brick and marble. The statues of Giotto and Dante are by Vincenzo Vela (1865). On the south side of the square is the monumental entrance to the former Foro Boario, now used as a car park and stadium.

Set back from the southern end of the piazza is Padua's most important 16C monument, the majestic brick basilica of **Santa Giustina** (1532–60), designed by Andrea Briosco and Andrea Moroni. Its plain façade and eight domes, some with metal statues of saints, recalls the exotic appearance of the church of Sant'Antonio.

The large three-aisled interior is a masterpiece of Venetian Baroque architecture, with elaborate detailing and exuberant paintings. In the south transept, the Sacello di San Prosdocimo (burial place of St Prosdocimus, the first bishop of Padua) is a remnant of the original early–Christian basilica. It contains an unusual 6C marble screen and an altar made from a Roman sarcophagus. The 15C Coro Vecchio, reached from the ninth chapel (not always open) has fine inlaid stalls and a statue of St Justina; in the adjoining rooms are a contemporary terracotta of the *Madonna and Child* and the lunette and lintel of a Romanesque doorway, dating from the 11C. The sanctuary contains walnut stalls carved in

1566 by the Norman Riccardo Taurigny, with the help of Vicentine craftsmen; the large altarpiece of the **Martyrdom of St Justina** was painted by Paolo Veronese in 1575. In the north transept is the so-called **Arca di San Luca**, with alabaster reliefs by a Pisan sculptor (1316). The second north chapel holds a painting of **St Gregory the Great Liberating Rome from the Plague**, by Sebastiano Ricci. On the south of the church stands the Benedictine monastery, founded in the 8C, suppressed in the 19C, and now shared by monks and soldiers. From the Prato della Valle, Via Umberto I and Via Roma lead back to the city centre.

Part of the **walls** of Padua survive, built by the Venetians in 1513–44, with a circumference of some 11km. The two gates to the north, the Porta San Giovanni (1528) and the Porta Savonarola (1530) are by Giovanni Maria Falconetto, their design derived from ancient Roman architecture.

North of Padua

In the northern part of the province of Padua is **Cittadella**, built by the Paduans in 1220 as a reply to Castelfranco, fortified by Treviso some 20 years earlier. The old centre is enclosed in medieval *walls, remarkably well preserved with numerous towers and gates. The two main gates, the Porta Padova and Porta Bassano, are painted with the red coat of arms of the Carrarese family. The Porta Bassano and Porta Treviso can both be visited by appointment (made at the Municipio). The Torre Malta, built by Ezzelino III da Romano, is used for exhibitions. The moated fortifications, designed in an unusual elliptical shape, surround a simple and symmetrically planned town, which may follow the plan of a Roman town.

In the central piazza is the Neo-classical **Duomo** (1820–28), by Giuseppe Jappelli, with works by Jacopo Bassano (including the *Supper at Emmaus* in the sacristy). In the same square is the 19C **Municipio**. In Via Indipendenza the Neo-Classical **theatre**, built by Giacomo Bauto in 1828, with a façade by Jappelli, has recently been restored. In Borgo Treviso is the interesting **Palazzo Pretorio**, with a well-carved 16C marble portal and 15C–16C frescoes. The gardens on the outside of the walls, which have a little zoo, can be entered from Porta Padova or Porta Vicenza. A weekly market is held in the town on Mon.

To the northwest, at **Santa Croce Bigolina**, is the church of Santa Lucia di Brenta, frescoed by Jacopo Bassano c 1540 (recently restored).

On the River Brenta north of Padua is the small town of **Piazzola sul Brenta**. Here is the splendid **Villa Contarini** (open Tues–Sun 09.00–12.00, 14.00–18.00; owned by a private foundation), rebuilt in the 17C for Marco Contarini as a summer house. It is preceded by a remarkable long avenue of magnolia trees, and a monumental semicircular portico (only half built), in Palladian style, across two canals and a fountain. The façade is 180m long. The central room is the auditorium, with remarkable acoustics (the gallery in the ceiling is for the orchestra), where concerts are held in May–Jun. Some of the rooms in the vast interior retain their 18C decorations. The carriage entrance to the villa on a lower level has a loggia decorated with shells and pebbles. There is also a small lapidarium, with Greek and Latin inscriptions.

The park of 45h can also be visited: it is surrounded by canals and has fish-ponds, and a huge lake with black and white swans. To the right of the villa is the handsome stable block. A market is held in front of the villa on Friday.

In the northeastern corner of the province is **Piombino Dese**, with the beautiful **Villa Cornaro** (open Sat in May–Sep, 15.30–18.00), built for Giorgio Cornaro by Palladio in 1552. With two storeys, it has a double portico. The rooms are frescoed by Mattia Bortoloni (1716), and have stuccoes of the same date by Bortolo Cabianca. The statues in the main room are by Camillo Mariani (c 1592–94). Set beside the River Dese, it has a small garden.

To the northeast is **Levada** with the Villa Marcello (privately owned), rebuilt in the 18C, with frescoes by Giovanni Battista Crosato. South of Piombino is **Massanzago**, where the town hall in Villa Baglioni has frescoes by Gian Battista Tiepolo.

On the eastern outskirts of Padua is **Noventa Padovana** with the Villa Giovanelli, built in the 17C with a pronaos and steps on the garden front added by Giorgio Massari (1738), and the 18C Villa Valmarana, frescoed by Andrea Urbani, both now owned by institutions.

The Riviera del Brenta

The Venetians built the canal known as the **Naviglio di Brenta** or Brenta Vecchia to facilitate navigation between their city and Padua, diverting the river itself to the north in order to reduce the amount of silt pouring into the lagoon. The magnificent villas for which the area is famous first appeared in the 16C when, the in the face of Turkish expansion in the Eastern Mediterranean, Venetian patricians shifted their investments from foreign trade to real estate. The great farms that grew up here were intended both to generate income and to provide a pleasant escape from the heat and humidity of the lagoon in summer. The principal façades of the houses faced the water, like the palaces on the Grand Canal—and not by chance, for the same festive lifestyle that graced the latter in winter continued in summer in the villas of the riviera. With the approach of the 18C, the idyllic pleasures of country life merged with a taste for the exotic, and the architecture of the noble manors assumed connotations of luxury and extravagance, with spectacular parks, gardens, aviaries, greenhouses and private zoos stocked with exotic animals. Meanwhile patricians of limited means (of whom there were quite a few), adventurers (even more) and the *nouveaux riches* rented lodgings in the towns, in order not to miss the great social events of the Venetian summer.

Those who, for one reason or another, chose not to make the trip up the canal in the family gondola took the *burchiello*, a large riverboat rowed by slaves or pulled by horses—a 'marvellous and comfortable craft', as Goldoni recalls, 'in which one glides along the Brenta sheltered from winter's cold and summer's ardour'. Today a motorised *burchiello* lazily winds its way from Padua to Venice or vice versa for a handsome fee, stopping to visit several of the 50-odd extant villas. The trip can also be made by bicycle (there are marked cycling routes), or by car. Here the villas are listed in the order in which they appear if you depart from Padua.

At **Stra** is the largest villa on the Riviera, the 18C **Villa Pisani** or Villa

Nazionale, named after its original owner, the Venetian doge Alvise Pisani. Purchased by Napoleon in 1807, it was the site of the first meeting between Mussolini and Hitler in 1934. The interior is decorated by 18C Venetian artists, including Giovanni Battista Tiepolo, who frescoed the *Triumph of the Pisani Family* on the ceiling of the ballroom (1762). In the vast park is the labyrinth described by poet Gabriele D'Annunzio in 'Fire'. A little beyond, on the opposite bank of the canal, rises the long front of the **Villa Lazara Pisani**, also called 'la Barbariga', with a Baroque central structure and symmetrical 18C wings.

At **Dolo**, the principal town of the Riviera in the 18C, you can see a mill, a *squero* (or boatyard) and one of the old locks. The **Palazzo Faletti-Mocenigo** (now a school) was designed in 1596 by Vincenzo Scamozzi. In the environs are the **Villa Ferretti Angeli** (1598), also by Scamozzi; the Baroque Villa Grimani Migliorini, with a Doric porch; and the **Villas Andreuzzi Bon** and **Mocenigo Spiga**, both of the 18C.

Next comes the fragmented town of **Mira**, still one of the more pleasant towns on the canal. Here Lord Byron, the English poet, wrote the fourth canto of 'Childe Harold' and first met Margherita Cogni, 'la bella Fornarina'. On the outskirts are the **Villas Pisani Contarini** (or 'dei Leoni'), **Querini Stampalia** and **Valier** (or 'la Chitarra'). A little further, at Riscossa, is the **Villa Seriman**, and at Oriago, the **Villa Widmann-Rezzonico-Foscari**, built in 1719 but remodelled in the French Rococo manner after the middle of the 18C. The most famous of the villas of Mira, it has a two-storey façade with curved tympanum, and frescoed rooms.

After Oriago, on a shady bend of the river, stands the **Villa Foscari** (also known as La Malcontenta), which legend would have the home of a Dame Foscari (the 'malcontent' of the name), exiled here for betraying her husband. It was constructed around 1555–60 for the brothers Nicola and Alvisa Foscari by Andrea Palladio. The exterior is very slightly rusticated; the side towards the river is characterised by a noble seven-columned Ionic porch, which projects outward and is raised on a tall basement with lateral ramps. Within, the rooms are arranged around a large, central Greek-cross salone frescoed by Battista Franco and Giovan Battista Zelotti. Further on, at Fusina, the canal enters the lagoon and you glimpse Venice, 4km away.

THE EUGANEAN HILLS

Although the area to the southwest of Padua offers nothing as magnificent as the Brenta villas, the several small towns huddled in and around the Euganean Hills (Colli Euganei)—a volcanic formation that rises unexpectedly in the midst of the Po River Basin—nevertheless provide a number of sights of considerable interest. The hills themselves (which reach a maximum height of 600m) have been protected as a regional park since 1989. There are a number of marked paths for walkers in the hills, and farms offering accommodation. A good white wine is produced here, and wild mushrooms grow in abundance. The hills have been famous since Roman times for their hot thermal springs (70°–87°C), rich in minerals, and there are four spa towns here, most notably Abano Terme. Petrarch spent the last four years of his life in a little village in the hills, and it was here that Shelley was inspired to compose his *Lines Written among the Euganean Hills*.

The north slope

Abano Terme is one of the leading spas in Europe. Known since Roman times for its hot springs, today it is famous for its mud therapy, which uses special thermophile alghe and is especially helpful in the treatment of rheumatism and arthritis. Abano is an elegant town with a distinctive 19C atmosphere. Though it is virtually deserted in winter, during the season (Mar–Oct) it is thronged with visitors, many of whom return year after year.

The main street is the shady **Viale delle Terme**, where the fancier hotels are located. The most notable of these is the Neo-classical *Hotel Orologio*, designed in 1825 by Giuseppe Jappelli, author of the *Caffè Pedrocchi* in Padua. The **Montirone**, a knoll at the centre of the town planted as a park and the site of Abano's warmest spring (80°C), is adorned with an early 20C Corinthian colonnade and a Doric column of 1825 (also by Jappelli) commemorating a visit of Emperor Francis I of Austria. The cathedral of San Lorenzo is undistinguished.

The **Santuario della Vergine** at **Monteortone**, 3km west of Abano Terme, was begun in 1435 on a site where a miraculous image of the Virgin Mary was reputedly found. It has a simple façade with a Baroque doorway of 1667, and a 15C brick campanile with pointed spire. The three-aisled interior is built in a hybrid Gothic-Renaissance style; it contains frescoes by Jacopo da Montagnana and a fine Renaissance altar in the sanctuary, and a *Crucifixion and Saints* by Palma Giovane in an adjoining chapel. The former Salesian convent, with a lovely Renaissance cloister, is now a hotel.

The **Abbazia di Praglia**, 12km further in the same direction, is approached by a beautiful, tree-lined driveway. It is a Benedictine foundation of 1080 rebuilt in the 15C and 16C. It is shown on a guided tour every 30mins, Tues–Sun, winter 14.30–16.30, summer 15.30–17.30). The church (Santa Maria Assunta) was built between 1490 and 1548, probably to a design by Tullio Lombardo; the Romanesque campanile is a remnant of the original building. The vaulted Latin-cross interior has 16C Venetian paintings, a 14C wooden crucifix over the high altar, and frescoes in the apse by Domenico Campagnola. The abbey is still active, and parts of it are closed to the public; but you can see a 15C *chiostro botanico* or herb-garden cloister (a reminder that the most expert pharmacists, here as elswhere in Europe, were once monks), a *chiostro pensile* of the late 15C and a large refectory with ceiling paintings by Giovanni Battista Zelotti, 18C carved woodwork and a famous *Crucifixion* frescoed by Bartolomeo Montagna (1490–1500).

Montegrotto Terme is another important spa, with extensive remains of Roman baths and a small Roman theatre. Above the town, a lovely park (open to the public) surrounds the Gothic-revival Villa Draghi. Nearby is the curious **Castello del Catajo** (open Tues, Sun and holidays 14.30–18.00; 15.00–19.00 in summer). It was built in 1570 by Andrea della Valle for Pio Enea degli Obizzi, a captain of the Venetian army. In the 19C it became the property of the dukes of Modena. It was altered in the 17C when part of the beautiful garden was created, with numerous fountains. The frescoes (1571–73) by Giovanni Battista Zelotti on the first floor depict the exploits of members of the Obizzi family, including one who accompanied Richard I of England on the Crusades, and another who perhaps fought for Edward III at Neville's Cross.

At **San Pelagio** the castle has a Museo dell'Aria (open Tues–Sun 09.30–12.30, 14.00–17.00). The display is arranged chronologically from the experiments of Leonardo to the era of space travel. The exhibits include material relating to d'Annunzio's flight to Vienna in 1918, planned in the castle; a model of the first helicopter designed by Forlanini in 1877; and planes used in the Second World War.

Battaglia Terme is an attractive small, old-fashioned spa on the Canale della Battaglia, much less grand than the other neighbouring spa towns. A park laid out by Giuseppe Jappelli in the early 19C surrounds the Villa Emo Selvatico, an unusual centrally planned building with four corner towers and a dome dating from 1648. Just outside, on a byroad to Arquà Petrarca, is another Villa Emo, built in 1588 on a design attributed to Vincenzo Scamozzi. The garden (open Sat, Sun and holidays 10.00–19.00) was laid out in the 1960s and has numerous rose beds.

At **Valsanzibio** is the **Villa Barbarigo** (open 09.00–12.00, 14.00–19.00; Sun and holidays 14.00–19.00), built in the mid-17C. The fine ***garden**, probably laid out around 1699, is a maze, and numerous pools, fountains and statues. It is surrounded by a 19C park.

Nearby, in a pretty position in the hills, is **Arquà Petrarca**, a delightful little medieval borgo with numerous gardens, where Petrarch lived from 1370 until his death in 1374. At the top of the village is his house (open Tues–Sun 09.00–12.30 and 14.30 or 15.00–17.30 or 19.00) which contains visitors' books, one with Byron's signature. In the lower part of the village is the church, outside of which is Petrarch's plain marble sarcophagus with an epitaph composed by himself. Numerous *giuggiole* trees grow here, producing an orange fruit in the shape of an olive (*festa* on 1 October).

To the west of Battaglia Terme is another spa town, **Galzignano Terme**. Further north, near Torreglia, is **Luvigliano**, above which is Villa dei Vescovi (open Mon, Wed, Fri and the first Sat of the month, 10.30–12.30, 14.30–18.30), built under the direction of Alvise Cornaro by Giovanni Maria Falconetto in 1532, and continued by Andrea della Valle in 1567. It contains frescoes attributed to the Netherlandish artist Lambert Sustris (1545), and is surrounded by a pretty garden. In the church is an altarpiece by Girolamo Santacroce, signed and dated 1527.

The south slope

Rising on the southeast slopes of the Euganean Hills, **Monselice** was a Roman settlement, a Lombard *gastaldato*, a free commune, a seignory, and finally a Venetian dominion. Today is an active industrial and agricultural centre. It takes its name (literally, 'mountain of flint') from the small mound of debris dug from the quarry that twice served to pave Piazza San Marco in Venice. The castle stands at the top of the hill, the town at the bottom, the monuments along a road and walkway that wind along the slopes.

In the lower town, on the east side of Piazza Mazzini, is the medieval **Torre Civica**, with a fine loggia and crenellated parapet. From the square, Via del Santuario climbs past the 16C Monte di Pietà, with a small loggia, to the **Castello**, a remarkable complex of buildings with an 11C or 12C core, enlarged between the 13C and 16C. The interior (shown on guided tours, summer, Tues–Sun 09.00–12.00, 15.00–18.00; by appointment in winter) houses a collection of paintings, sculpture, weapons, Renaissance furniture, tapestries, and in the Sala del Camino Vecchio, a monumental fireplace shaped like a tower.

Continuing along Via del Santuario you soon come to the 16C and 17C **Villa Nani-Mocenigo**, with a wall decorated with curious 18C statues of dwarfs and a spectacular terraced staircase. Just a little further on is the **Duomo Vecchio**, dedicated to St Justina, a Romanesque-Gothic church of 1256 with a 12C campanile and a three-part façade with a rose window, smaller mullioned windows, and a 15C porch. Within are frescoes and altarpieces by minor 15C Venetian painters. At the end of the avenue stands the **Villa Duodo**, by Vincenzo Scamozzi (1593), enlarged in the 18C, when the monumental staircase to the formal garden was added. It now belongs to the University of Padua. Its grounds include the cypress-shaded **Santuario delle Sette Chiese**, entered from the 18C Piazzale della Rotonda, a scenic overlook behind the Duomo Vecchio. The sanctuary comprises six chapels designed by Scamozzi after 1605, containing paintings by Palma Giovane, and the church of San Giorgio, octagonal outside and elliptical within.

In a panoramic position at the top of the hill stands the ruined **rocca**, built by Holy Roman Emperor Frederick II and enlarged by the Carraresi. Today little more than the keep remains, but there is a fine view. On the east slope of the hill is the old church of San Tommaso, which conserves some 13C frescoes. At Valsanzibio di Galzignano, 8km north, is the Villa Barbarigo, now Pizzoni Ardemagni, with a 17C formal garden and fountains.

Southeast of Monselice is **Bagnoli di Sopra**, where monastic buildings were transformed in the 17C by Baldassarre Longhena into the **Villa Widmann** (privately owned), with 18C frescoes. Carlo Goldoni stayed here with Ludovico Bagnoli in the 18C and put on several performances of his plays. It is surrounded by a fine garden (open Thur 14.00–18.00) decorated with numerous statues by Antonio Bonazza (1742). Also in the piazza is the Palazzetto Widmann (owned by the town) with frescoes by Giovanni Battista Pittoni and Lodovico Dorigny.

Este

At the southern edge of the Colli Euganei is the little town of Este, a centre of the ancient Veneti before it became the Roman *Ateste*. Later it was the stronghold of the Este family, who afterwards became dukes of Ferrara, and from 1405 was under Venetian dominion. The huge battlemented Carrarese **castle** dates mainly from 1339, and its impressive walls enclose a public garden. Here in the 16C Palazzo Mocenigo is the **Museo Nazionale Atestino** (open daily 09.00–13.00, 15.00–19.00), illustrating the culture of the Veneti, who inhabited the Veneto in the pre-Roman period, including a remarkable collection of bronzes. The museum, founded in 1888, was opened here in 1902, and many of the exhibits, arranged chronologically, come from excavations carried out in the 19C near Este. The Roman section, on the ground floor, contains inscriptions, mosaics, architectural fragments, sculpture, glass and medals. The pre-Roman Section, on the first floor, has prehistoric collections that offer a glimpse of ancient Venetic civilisation, notably material of the Aeneolithic and Bronze Ages, and bural artefacts from the early Iron Age. The Benvenuti *situla (c 600 BC) is decorated with bronze reliefs, and the Roman material includes a fine bronze head of *Medusa (1C AD). A *Madonna and Child* by Cima da Conegliano is also displayed here.

Behind the castle (Via Cappuccini) are the fine parks of several villas, including the **Villa Kunkler**, occupied by Byron in 1817–18, where Shelley composed *Lines Written among the Euganean Hills*.

The **Cathedral** of St Tecla, a medieval church rebuilt in 1690–1708 by Antonio Francesco Gaspari, has an 18C campanile built on an 8C base. The elliptical interior abounds with sculptures and paintings, among which the large *St Tecla Freeing Este from the Plague*, by Giovanni Battista Tiepolo (1759), is certainly the most striking.

From here Via Garibaldi and Via Alessi bear southwest to the church of **Santa Maria delle Consolazioni** (or Santa Maria degli Zoccoli, 1504–10), with a campanile of 1598 and a single-aisled interior with a later addition. At the end of this is the Cappella della Vergine, containing a magnificent Roman mosaic pavement excavated nearby. The church possesses a fine Madonna by Cima da Conegliano, on temporary loan to the museum; and the adjoining cloister has 15C capitals.

On the other side of town (about 500m away) are the Romanesque church of **San Martino**, with a campanile of 1293 (leaning since 1618), 18C sculptures and two altarpieces by Antonio Zanchi; and the 15C basilica of **Santa Maria delle Grazie**, rebuilt in the 18C, in the Latin-cross interior of which are marble altars, statues, frescoes from the earlier church and a Byzantine *Madonna* of the early 15C, venerated as miraculous.

Other interesting monuments are the 16C **Palazzo del Principe**, by Vincenzo Scamozzi, who also designed the façade of the church of San Michele; **Villa Cornaro** (now Benvenuti), with a 19C park designed by G. Japelli; the 18C **Villa Contarini**, known also as the 'Vigna Contarena'; the **Palazzo del Municipio**, also dating from the 18C; and the octagonal church of the **Beata Vergine della Salute** (1639), with two octagonal campanili flanking the apse.

Ten kilometres south of Este is the **Abbazia di Càrceri**, dedicated to the Virgin Mary. Founded in the 11C, it includes an octagonal church of 1643 with 15C–18C paintings, remains of a 12C Romanesque cloister and a 16C Renaissance Chiostro Grande and library.

Montagnana

Of prehistoric origin, Montagnana was a Roman vicus (village) and a medieval Lombard centre. The old town—with porticoed streets, a large square, and the lazy atmosphere of the quinessential Venetian farm town—lies within a well-preserved complex of turreted walls built by Ezzelino and the Carraresi between the 12C and the 14C. The walls are pierced by four gates and surrounded by a moat, now a park. During the Venetian period (after 1405), hemp was grown here for use in ships' rigging.

The **walls** surround the entire town, enclosing an area of 24h within a perimeter of almost 2km. The most impressive of the gates are the **Rocca degli Alberi** or Porta Legnano, dating from 1362, with a fortified bridge and tower with *piombatoi*, and the **Porta Padova**, adjoining the Castello di San Zeno, with the tall Torre Ezzelina. The **Castello di San Zeno** was built in 1242; the Venetian wing (and temporarily also the small church of San Giovanni) holds the **Museo Civico**, with Bronze and Iron Age finds (9C–8C BC) from a local prehistoric complex, Roman burial treasures of the 1C AD, Roman inscriptions and medieval ceramics.

Inside the town, on the southwest side of the central Via Carrarese, rises the **Palazzo del Municipio**, an austere building with rusticated portico laid out in 1538 by Michele Sanmicheli and remodelled in the 17C and 18C. Within, the Sala del Consiglio has a coffered ceiling of 1555 by Marcantonio Vannini.

The **Cathedral** of Santa Maria, in the large, central Piazza Vittorio Emanuele, was built in a transitional Gothic-Renaissance style between 1431 and 1502 on the site of an 11C structure of which a few traces remain. The brick façade, with three bell niches, has a doorway shaped like a triumphal arch, attributed to Jacopo Sansovino. Notice also the south flank and large polygonal apse of the south transept. The tall, early Renaissance interior, a single aisle with barrel vaulting, contains a Venetian School gold-ground painting of the *Annunciation*, dating from the 14C; 15C and 16C frescoes; a *Transfiguration* by Paolo Veronese over the high altar; and a large fresco of the *Assumption of the Virgin* in the apse, attributed to Giovanni Buonconsiglio, an early 16C painter, author also of several altarpieces. Other frescoes possibly by his hand are on the west wall of the north transept and on the inside of the façade.

Up against the wall to the south is the church of **San Francesco**, a 14C and 15C edifice altered in the 17C, with a tall campanile of 1429 or 1468. Within are a *Transfiguration* by the school of Paolo Veronese, in the sanctuary, and a *Madonna* by Palma Giovane in the apse.

Just outside the walls, accross the moat from the Porta Padova, stands the **Palazzo Pisani** (now Placco), the central part of which was designed by Andrea Palladio. It was built around 1560. The two main elevations have a double central order of Ionic and Corinthian columns terminating in a pediment. Also noteworthy are the splendid frieze with bucranic metopes and the harmonious ground-floor atrium, with statues of the *Seasons* by Alessandro Vittoria (1577).

Rovigo and the Po Delta

The southeastern Veneto encompasses the lower course of the River Po, a place as rich in natural history as it is in human history. The area represents the last alluvial plain of the great river, which begins in the northwestern corner of Italy and flows toward the Adriatic bearing tonnes of silt from its Alpine sources and depositing them along its way, 'filling in' the sea more and more every year. The delta of the Po is Italy's most extensive and interesting wetland, a permanent home to dozens of animal species (they are detailed below) and a stopping place for migratory birds en route to and from Africa. Rovigo is a prosperous town and provincial capital in the Polesine, the fertile strip of land between the lower Adige and River Po.

Practical information

Getting there
By air

Rovigo is equidistant (85km) from Venice Marco Polo and Bologna Borgo Panigale airports, both of which are served by domestic and European flights.

By road

Rovigo is on the A13 from Padua to Bologna and 16 from Padua to Ferrara. 309 connects Adria and the Po River Delta with Padua to the north, and Ravenna to the south.

By rail

Rovigo is located on the main Bologna–Venice rail line, with fast *Eurostar* and *Intercity* trains from Venice in 55mins, Padua in 25mins and Bologna in 50mins. A branch line connects Rovigo with Adria, Rosolina and Chioggia.

Getting around

The Po River Delta can be reached from Rovigo by **car**, via 443, or by train (see above); road and railway both touch upon Adria. **Boat excursions** are arranged by several companies, including *Marino Cacciatori* (Caparin; ☎ 0426 81508 or 0337 513818), starting from Ca' Tiepolo. **Bicycles** can be hired at Taglio di Po and Ca' Tiepolo.

Information offices
ROVIGO Via Dunant 10, ☎ 0425 361481.

Where to stay
ROVIGO *Villa Regina Margherita*, Viale Regina Margherita 6, ☎ 0425 361540, fax 0425 31301; in an Art-Nouveau building on a wooded boulevard; moderate.
CONTARINA *Villa Carrer*, Piazza Mattgeotti 44, ☎ 0426 632686, fax 0426 632676; a 16C villa in a beautiful park; inexpensive.
ROSOLINA *Golf*, Isola Albarella, ☎ 0426 367811, fax 330628; small and elegant, with a nice garden; closed Oct–Mar; moderate.
TAGLIO DI PO *Tessarin*, Piazza Venezia 4, ☎ 0426 346347, fax 0426 346346; simple but comfortable; inexpensive.
Youth hostel: *Rifugio Parco Delta del Po* (open all year) at Gorino Sullam (with a simple restaurant), where bicycles can be hired.

Eating out
ROVIGO *Tavernetta Dante-Dai Trevisani*, Corso del Popolo 212, ☎ 0425 26386; traditional Trevisan cooking, with outside seating in summer; closed Sun and Aug; moderate. Rovigo upholds with honour the Venetian tradition of sipping a glass of red wine (called an *ombra*, or 'shadow') with finger food (*cicheti*). Good places to do this are the wine bars, *Al Sole*, Via Bedendo 6; *Caffè Conti Silvestri*, Via Silvestri 6; *Caffè San Marco*, Corso del Popolo 186; and *Hosteria la Zestea*, Via X Luglio.
ARIANO POLESINE *Due Leoni*, Corso del Popolo 21, ☎ 0426 372129; traditional restaurant (with rooms), offering delicious local cuisine; closed Mon and July; moderate.
ARQUÀ POLESINE *Trattoria degli Amici*, Via Quirina 4, Località Granze, ☎ 0425 91045; trattoria known especially for its vegetable and chicken dishes; closed Jan; inexpensive.
LOREO *I Cavalli*, Riviera Marconi 69, ☎ 0426 369868; restaurant (with rooms) in the heart of the Polesine, renowned for its risotto and seafood; closed Mon; moderate.
LUSIA (10km west of Rovigo) *Al Ponte*, Località Bormio 5, ☎ 0425 69890; rustic trattoria in an ancient house with

garden, also known for its good local dishes; closed Mon and Aug; inexpensive.

PONTECCHIO POLESINE (6km southeast of Rovigo) *La Vecia*, Località San Pietro, ☎ 0425 492601; family-run trattoria with hearty country fare and local wines; closed Mon, Jan and Aug; moderate.

PORTO TOLLE *Da Brodon*, Località Ca' Dolfin, ☎ 0426 384240; rustic trattoria renowned for its rice and fish dishes; closed Mon and July; moderate.

ROSOLINA *SottoVento*, Località Norge Polesine, ☎ 0426 340138; excellent seafood restaurant; closed Tues, mid-day Sun in summer, and Dec; moderate.

VILLADOSE (9km east of Rovigo) *Da*

Nadae, Via Garibaldi 371, Località Canale, ☎ 0425 476082; trattoria known for its outstanding renditions of traditional local recipes; closed Tues and Aug–Sep; moderate.

Shopping
Fish markets at Donada and Scardovari in the morning, and in the afternoon at Pila.

Sports
Deep-sea fishing in the Adriatic. **Freshwater fishing** in the Po Delta. **Swimming** and **water sports** at the coastal resorts.

ROVIGO
• • • • • • • • •

A walled town in the 12C, Rovigo (population 52,000) was taken by the Venetians in 1482, and they held control of the town until the end of the republic. It still has a Venetian atmosphere. Once, it also a main street paved with water: the 1930s the River Adigetto was covered over to form the Corso del Popolo.

The city centre
Just off the southern corner of the central **Piazza Vittorio Emanuele II** is **Palazzo Roncale**, a fine building by Sanmicheli (1555). In the piazza is the attractive 16C **Palazzo del Municipio**, restored in 1765 with a tower. Beside it the 18C Palazzo Bosi houses the Civic Library and the **Pinacoteca dei Concordi** (open Mon–Fri 09.00.30–12.00, 15.30–19.00; Sat 09.30–12.00; Sun by appointment only; Jul–Aug Mon–Sat 10.00–13.00). The Accademia dei Concordi was founded in 1580, and the origins of the Pinacoteca go back to 1833. The fine collection of paintings is particularly representative of Venetian art from the 15C–18C. It includes a *Madonna by Giovanni Bellini, works by Sebastiano Mazzoni, and *portraits by Alessandro Longhi and Giovanni Battista Tiepolo.

Opposite the Accademia is **Palazzo Roverella**, begun in the 15C on a design attributed to Biagio Rossetti. At the other end of the Piazza is the **Gran Guardia**, built for the Austrians in 1854 by Tommaso Meduna.

Just to the north is **Piazza Garibaldi**, with an equestrian statue of the hero by Ettore Ferrari, and the *Caffè Borsa*. The Camera del Commercio encloses the well-preserved Salone del Grano, built in 1934 with a remarkable glass barrel-vault. The Teatro Sociale has a Neo-classical façade dating from 1819.

Via Silvestri leads out of the square past the church of **San Francesco** (with sculptures by Tullio Lombardo) to Piazza XX Settembre, at the end of which is **La**

Rotonda or Santa Maria del Soccorso, a centrally planned octagonal church surrounded by a portico built in 1594 by Francesco Zamberlan. The campanile was designed by Baldassarre Longhena in the 17C. The interior *decoration, which survives intact from the 17C, consists of a series of paintings celebrating Venetian officials with elaborate allegories: the lower band includes five by Francesco Maffei and others by Pietro Liberi. Above stucco statues (1627) is another cycle of paintings by Antonio Zanchi, Pietro Liberi, Andrea Celesti, and others. The painted dome dates from 1887. The organ by Gaetano Callido (1767) is also decorated with 17C paintings.

On the south side of Corso del Popolo, in Piazza Matteotti, is a little public park around two old towers and part of the old town defences. Nearby is the **Cathedral** of 1696. It contains altarpieces by Andrea Vicentino and Palma Giovane.

The huge convent of **San Bartolomeo**, reached off Corso del Popolo, is being restored, and there are long-term plans to open the Museo Civico delle Civiltà in Polesine here. While work is under way you can glimpse a sample of the collections (Italic and Roman antiquities, Renaissance ceramics) in one room, open Mon–Sat 08.30–13.30.

The Polesine

This flat area west of Rovigo between the Adige and Po rivers is traversed by numerous canals. At **Fratta Polesine**, facing a bridge over a canal, is *Villa **Badoer** (open Tues–Sun 10.00–12.00, 14.00–17.00), built by Palladio in 1556 for the Venetian nobleman Francesco Badoer (and now owned by the province of Rovigo). It is enclosed by an attractive brick wall and preceded by a green lawn with two fountains and two 19C magnolia trees. The outbuildings are linked to the house by curving porticoes, and a wide flight of steps leads up to the villa with an Ionic portico and temple pediment. The empty interior is interesting for its remarkable plan (the service rooms and servants' quarters are on a lower level) and damaged contemporary frescoes by Giallo Fiorentino.

Next door is another fine country house, the **Villa Molin** (Grimani), now owned by the Avezzù (open Sat 15.00–16.00), a fine building in the Palladian style. There are more villas nearby, including (on the canal) the early-18C Villa Cornoldi, the Villa David (Franchin) preceded by two 18C statues, and the late-17C Villa Oroboni.

North of Fratta Polesine is **Lendinara**, with a few fine palaces and, in the duomo, a painting by Domenico Mancini. The campanile, built in 1797, is exceptionally tall (107m). Here is buried Jessie White, wife of Alberto Mario, both important figures in the Italian *Risorgimento*. The Canozzi family of woodcarvers were born here: they produced finely carved choir stalls for a number of churches in Italy during the 15C.

West of Lendinara is **Badia Polesine** with remains of the abbey of Vangadizza, founded in the 10C and enlarged in the 11C. The attractive 12C campanile stands near two 12C tombs and the drum of the domed chapel, all that remains of the church destroyed by Napoleon. The picturesque irregular cloister is used for concerts, and the refectory is being restored. The chapel (opened on request) contains painted decoration attributed to Filippo Zaniberti and interesting stuccoes of the cardinal virtues. The Museo Civico Baruffaldi contains 12C–17C ceramics. The Teatro Sociale dates from 1813.

At **Canda**, on the Bianco canal, is the Villa Nani-Mocenigo (no admission), attributed to Vincenzo Scamozzi (1580–84), enlarged in the 18C.

The town hall of **Fiesso Umbertiano** is in a fine building by Andrea Tirali (1706).

The delta of the Po

The Po is the largest river in Italy (652km), its waters now sadly polluted with chemicals. Its source is at Pian del Re (2050m) in Piedmont, on the French border, and it is joined by numerous tributaries (including the Ticino and the Adda) as it crosses northern Italy from west to east through Lombardy and the Veneto on its way to the Adriatic. The wide-open plain—the largest in Italy—through which it runs and which separates the Alps from the Apennines, is known as the *Pianura Padana*. In the late Middle Ages the Po was navigable and one of the principal waterways of Europe. In 1599 the Venetian Republic carried out major works of canalisation in the delta area in order to deviate the course of the river south to prevent it silting up the Venetian lagoon. It now reaches the sea by seven different channels: the largest (which carries 60 per cent of its waters) is called the 'Po di Venezia'. The delta formed by this operation is the largest area of marshlands in Italy.

The flat open landscape with wide views over the reedy marshes and numerous wetlands (known as *valli*), channels and rivers is remarkably beautiful, whether in typical misty weather or on clear autumnal days. Rice and sugar beet were once intensely cultivated here, and some attractive old farmhouses survive, although most of them have been abandoned. There seems to be a desire on the part of most of the local inhabitants to preserve this remote area from unsightly 'development', although the long-term project to make the Po delta (which falls mostly in the province of Rovigo, but also partly in that of Ferrara) into a national park has still not been approved (a regional park has recently been established in Emilia Romagna); those opposed to the institution of a park include local sportsmen and fishermen.

The marshes are on the migratory bird routes from northern Europe and have extremely interesting birdlife, counting some 350 species, including cormorants, herons, egrets, grebes, blackwinged stilts, wild geese and duck. Despite opposition from the naturalists, the shooting season is still open September to January. Pila and the Po della Pila have important fisheries, and all over the delta area eels, bass, carp, tench, pike and grey mullet are caught. Clams (a new clam was imported into the delta in the early 1980s from the Philippines) and mussels are also cultivated here.

Very few boats (apart from those of the fishermen) venture into the delta area, for many of the channels are only 1–2m deep. A few characteristic bridges of boats and ferries survive (see below). The area is ideal for cyclists.

In the last few decades the delta area has sunk below sea level because of drilling operations for natural gas off the coast and quarrying in the area. In the 19C a flood submerged three-quarters of the Polesine area, and it was devastated by another flood in 1951. Pumping stations help to regulate the waters, and a new canal was built in 1990 between the Po di Venezia and Po della Pila, which saved the area from another disastrous flood in 1994.

Since 1982 a thermo-electrical plant near Porto Tolle (on the island of Polesine Camerini) has been in operation: it is criticised because of the atmospheric pollution it causes. Scientific studies have shown that the river (from its source over 600km away) feeds hundreds of tons of arsenic into the Adriatic every year, and according to European Community regulations, none of its waters should be used for drinking, swimming or irrigation.

Adria, the ancient capital of the Polesine, gave its name to the Adriatic Sea (to which it is now joined only by canal). The **Museo Archeologico** (open daily 09.00–19.00) contains proof of the city's Graeco-Etruscan origins. The earliest finds from the upper Polesine date from the 11C–9C BC. There are also Greek red- and black-figure *ceramics, Roman *glass (1C AD), and gold and amber objects.

Nearby is the 17C church of **Santa Maria Assunta**, which incorporates some Roman masonry. Across the Canal Bianco (near which is the theatre dating from 1930), is the **Cathedral**, which has a little 6C Coptic bas-relief and a crypt with remains of Byzantine frescoes.

A road leads east past **Loreo**, built on a canal with a parish chuch by Baldassarre Longhena, to **Rosolina** on the Via Romea, in parts a post-war revival of the long-decayed Roman *Via Popilia*, which ran down the Adriatic coast from Venice to Ravenna. Following the road north you soon come to **Chioggia**, one of the main fishing ports on the Adriatic (particularly famous for mussels) and the most important town on the Venetian lagoon after Venice. It has a remarkable longitudinal urban structure with three canals and a parallel wide main street (described in *Blue Guide Venice*).

Rosolina is on the edge of a series of typical *valli* or wetlands, which you can see from a pretty but very narrow road leading from Chiesa Moceniga to Portesine. On a narrow peninsula facing the Adriatic, pine woods were planted and a small resort called **Rosolina Mare**, built in the 1950s. At the southern end of the peninsula is a *botanical garden (open Apr–Sep, or on request), opened in 1991. This is one of the very few stretches of Adriatic coast where the vegetation of the dunes (including juniper bushes, oaks and elms) is preserved intact; it can be visited along marked paths and bridges over the marshes. On a clear day from the shore there is a spectacular view of the Alps (swimming is allowed here in summer). Further south is the **Isola di Albarella** (reached by another road from Rosolina along the Po di Levante), a well-run resort (limited access for cars; bicycles are provided) built in 1967, with a port and an 18-hole golf course. The two hotels, and residences, open April to September, are surrounded by parks and woods.

South of Taglio di Po is **San Basilio**, a simple Romanesque church beneath the pavement of which seven ancient tombs have been found. A small museum nearby illustrates the life of the delta.

Porto Tolle is on the **Isola della Donzella**, the largest island on the delta. The island used to have *valli* with fisheries, but was reclaimed after a flood in 1966 (a decision which met with much justified opposition), and now has rice fields. Across the Po della Donzella is Ca' Vendramin, an attractive old pumping station built in 1900–05 with a tall chimney stack. It is now out of use, although the pumps are preserved here and there are plans to turn it into a museum illustrating the history of land reclamation in the delta.

At **Ca' Tiepolo** a privately run car ferry (it carries about 20 cars and operates up to midnight) crosses the Po di Venezia to Ca' Venier; it is soon to be replaced by a bridge under construction a short way downstream. Near the ferry station is the starting point for boat excursions on the delta, including the **Po di Maistra**, the most interesting part of the delta for naturalists, the Po della Pila, and the Po delle Tolle. The southern part of the Isola della Donzella is occupied by the **Sacca di Scardovari**, an attractive lagoon lined with fishermen's huts and boats. Mussels and clams are cultivated here, and it is inhabited by numerous birds. On its shores is a tiny protected area illustrating the typical vegetation of the wetlands that once covered this area. There are characteristic bridges of boats (with tolls) over the Po della Donzella near Santa Giulia, and over the Po di Goro near Gorino Veneto.

The Isola della Donzella is separated by the Po delle Tolle from the **Isola di Polesine Camerini**, with a thermo-electrical plant; its exceptionally tall chimney is about 250m high. Beyond Pila, with a lot of fisheries, is the easternmost island on the delta, the **Isola di Batteria**, which is gradually being engulfed by the sea. It is no longer inhabited and is the only oasis on the delta (run by the Forestry Commission). At the end of the delta is a lighthouse built in 1949 on land only formed some hundred years ago.

The rest of the delta area to the south, in the province of Ferrara, which includes the woods of Mesola with oak and pine trees, is described on p 619.

FRIULI-VENEZIA GIULIA

Friuli-Venezia Giulia, at the northeastern corner of the Adriatic, consists of the provinces of Udine, Trieste, Pordenone and Gorizia. The Friuli (the former county of Udine) was under the patriarchate of Aquileia until 1420 when, with the mountainous country of Carnia to the north and the city of Aquileia itself, it was absorbed into the Venetian Republic. Trieste, as an independent commune under her bishops, remained a rival of Venice for the seaborne trade of the Adriatic. At certain periods, Trieste—with the help of the counts of Gorizia or the dukes of Austria—held the upper hand, but on more than one occasion the Venetians captured the port. Although the Istrian coast for the most part came under Venetian influence, the hinterland and Gorizia belonged to Austria.

The Venetians at first made important conquests in the war against Austria in 1507–16, but outside intervention forced them to withdraw their frontier west of Aquileia. The raids of Liburnian pirates (from modern-day Croatia), nominally subject to Austria, disturbed conditions on the Istrian coast throughout the 16C, and the power of Venice diminished.

The outcome of the Napoleonic Wars here was the short-lived Kingdom of Illyria, which extended from the Isonzo to Croatia but was shattered in 1813–14 by an Austrian army and a British fleet. From 1815 to 1918 the whole region fell under Austro-Hungarian dominion. In the First World War prolonged and fierce fighting took place in the region between the valleys of the Isonzo and the Piave, the Italians ultimately achieving success with the aid of the British and French detachments. The frontier was extended east and south to include the whole of Istria (including Fiume, after much negotiation), with the adjacent isles and Dalmatian Zara.

In 1945 Allied forces met Marshal Tito's Yugoslav forces at Cividale del Friuli and Monfalcone. New Zealanders arrived at Trieste, where the occupying German force surrendered to General Freyberg. Italian and Yugoslav claims to the liberated territory came at once into conflict, and the administration of Trieste, which had been occupied by the Yugoslavs, was taken over by Allied Military Government. All territory east of the so-called 'French Line' was ceded by Italy to Yugoslavia, the ceded areas including the eastern suburbs of Gorizia and all Istria south of Cittanova. The region around Trieste, including the coast from Monfalcone to Cittanova with a portion of the hinterland, was established as a neutral and demilitarised free territory by the Treaty of Paris in 1947. At the same time the province of Udine was transferred from the Veneto to Venezia Giulia and the new region, under the title Friuli-Venezia Giulia, was granted special measures of autonomy. A more rational adjustment of the frontier at Gorizia was made in 1952, and in 1954 Trieste finally returned to Italian rule while the remainder of Istria was incorporated into Yugoslavia (now Slovenia).

Trieste and the east

There is a curious feeling about Trieste and its environs: you really do sense you're in another country—or perhaps more precisely, in no country at all. Trieste itself is an Austrian city inhabited by Italians. 'We are the furthest limit of Latinity,' a recent mayor of the city was quoted as saying, 'the southern extremity of Germanness', and the city's mixed heritage may be responsible for its peculiar lack of identity, the consequence of being an 'outsider' in both cultures. The overall atmosphere of the region, however, is quite pleasant. With the notable exception of the beach resorts, tourist crowds are few and far between—even the roads are less encumbered with traffic. All this notwithstanding the fact that there are some truly memorable things to see.

Practical information

Getting there and getting around
By air

The regional airport serving Friuli-Venezia Giulia is located at Ronchi dei Legionari, 35km northwest of Trieste. There are daily flights to domestic and European destinations; coaches connect with the airport terminal at the Trieste railway station (journey time: 60mins) and with Gorizia.

By road

The A4 runs from Venice to Trieste, not far from the Adriatic shore. Near Palmanova it links up with the A23, which winds northwards via Udine to Austria. 56 connects the A4 at Monfalcone to Gorizia. **Car parking** in the centre of Trieste is particularly difficult; your best bets are on the Rive or on the hill of San Giusto. There is a multi-storey car park ('Sì silos') beside the station.

Country buses depart from Trieste (Piazza Oberdan) to Miramare, Duino, etc; and from the main bus station in Piazza della Libertà to Muggia, Sistiana and Slovenia. Buses from Gorizia (Via IX Agosto) to points throughout the region (information, *APT*, ☎ 0481 593511).

There is a **rack tramway** from Trieste (Piazza Oberdan) to Opicina. To Miramare, **bus no. 36** every 30mins from Piazza Oberdan and the station. To Muggia, **bus no. 20** from the station; Muggia to Muggia Vecchia, **bus no. 37** from the Porto Vecchio.

By rail

There is a direct rail service from Venice to Trieste, some trains continuing on to Slovenia, Croatia, Hungary, Ucraine, and Russia (via Villa Opicina), and from Venice to Udine (continuing on to Vienna and Prague). Branch lines run from Trieste to Udine, and from Udine to Conegliano, Cividale, Palmanova and Cervignano (the latter is also on the Venice–Trieste line), from which buses shuttle passengers to Aquileia and Grado. A branch line runs from Trieste to Gorizia (in c 25mins), continuing on to Udine (c 45mins more)

By boat

There are regular car and passenger ferries to and from Greece (*Anek Lines*, Piazza Tommaseo 4, ☎ 040 364386), and Turkey.

Boat tours of the port and gulf by motor launch are organised in summer from Riva del Mandracchio.

Information offices

TRIESTE Via San Nicolò 20, ☎ 040 679 6111; at the train station, ☎ 040 420182.
GORIZIA Via Diaz, ☎ 0481 386225. *Informagiovani*, Via dei Cappuccini 21, ☎ 0481 537089.
MUGGIA Via Roma 20, ☎ 040 273259 (May–Sep).

Where to stay

TRIESTE *Abbazia*, Via della Geppa 20, ☎ 040 369464, fax 040 369769; near the train station, comfortable and practical; moderate.
Duchi d'Aosta, Via dell'Orologio 2, ☎ 040 7351, fax 040 366092; offering turn-of-the-century Austrian style and ambience, and a restaurant (**Harry's Grill**) among the best in town; both are expensive.
San Giusto, Via C. Belli 3, ☎ 040 762661, fax 040 734477; a bit out of the way (on the landward side of the hill of San Giusto) but very pleasant; moderate.
Youth hostel: *Tergeste*, in a lovely position on the sea at Miramare.
GORIZIA *Nanut*, Via Trieste 253, ☎ 048 120595; a small, family-managed place on the outskirts of the town; inexpensive.
Palace, Corso Italia 63, ☎ 0481 82166, fax 0481 31658; centrally located, modern and comfortable; inexpensive.
MUGGIA *Sole*, Località Lazzaretto, ☎ 040 271106, fax 040 273515; green and flowery with wisteria, a stone's throw from the Slovenian border; inexpensive.

Eating out

TRIESTE *Ai Fiori*, Piazza Hortis 7, ☎ 040 300633; a family-run place with an innovative seafood menu; closed Sun, Mon and Jul; moderate.
Al Bragozzo, Riva Nazario Sauro 22, ☎ 040 303001; a seafood restaurant with nice ambience; closed Sun, Mon and a few days in Jul; moderate.
Al Granzo, Piazza Venezia 7, ☎ 040 306788; another good seafood restaurant, established in 1923 and offering excellent *granseola* (crab) *alla triestina*; closed Wed; moderate.
Allo Squero, Viale Miramare 42, ☎ 040 410884; an inexpensive trattoria drawing a strong local crowd; closed Mon and Feb; moderate.
Antica Trattoria Suban, 2/D Via Comici, ☎ 040 54368, fax 040 57920; an outstanding restaurant established in 1865 and serving traditional regional cuisine; closed Mon, Tues, Jan and Aug; moderate.
Da Giovanni, Via San Lazzaro 14, ☎ 040 639396; simple trattoria with wholesome local food and lots of wood, marble and copper; closed Sun and Aug; inexpensive.
Re di Coppe, Via Geppa 11, ☎ 040 370330; warm, friendly trattoria with good regional fare; closed Sat, Sun and Jul–Aug; inexpensive.
Savron, Strada Devincina 25, Località Prosecco (9km northwest), ☎ 040 225592; country restaurant and wine bar much loved by Triestini; closed Tues–Wed and Feb; moderate.
Picnic places on the hill of San Giusto.
Cafés and pastry shops. The capital of Venezia Giulia imports more coffee than any other Italian city: in some areas of the town the warehouses are so numerous that the aroma of coffee lingers in the air. Naturally, where so many people are in the business you can expect some extraordinary cafés; the city's best are **San Marco**, Via Battisti 18; **Tommaseo**, Riva III Novembre 5; **Degli Specchi**, Piazza dell'Unità; and **Pirona**, Largo Barriera Vecchia 12. There are also some great pastry shops (**Penso**, Via Cadorna; **La Bomboniera**, off Via San Niccolò), where Italian,

Austrian and Slovene traditions are skilfully combined.

GORIZIA *Alla Luna*, Via Oberdan 13, ☎ 0481 530374; a place popular with townsfolk, where local traditions blend with influences from Slovenia and Austria; closed Sun evening, Mon and Aug; inexpensive.

Rosen Bar, Via Duca d'Acaia 96, ☎ 0481 522700; another place with strong local ambience and cross-cultural cuisine; closed Sun and Mon; inexpensive.

For **coffee and cakes**: *Bar Ferigo*, Corso Italia; Bisiach Donaldo, Via Mazzini 15.

CORMÒNS (13km west) *Al Cacciatore*, Località Subida 22, ☎ 0481 60531; restaurant (with rooms) offering creative interpretations of traditional recipes, winner of the Accademia Italiana della Cucina 'Excellent Cuisine' award in 1991; closed Tues, Wed, Feb and Jul; moderate.

Al Giardinetto, Via Matteotti 54, ☎ 0481 60257; restaurant (with rooms) serving outstanding dishes based on local ingredients, including Cormòns ham, and a fine wine list; closed Mon, Tues and Jul; moderate.

Good wines, light snacks and great ambience at *Enoteca di Cormòns*, Piazza XXIV Maggio 21 (closed Tues).

DOLEGNA DEL COLLIO (18km northwest) *Al Castello dell'Aquila d'Oro*, Castello di Trussio, Località Rutars, ☎ 0481 61255; refined regional cuisine in a 13C castle with park and panoramic views (outside seating in summer); closed Wed–Thur; expensive.

The nearby *Antico Mulino Tuzzi* is an old-fashioned mill known for its wholewheat and buckwheat flours and especially for its barley, used to make *fasui e vardi* (bean and barley) soup.

GRADISCA D'ISONZO (12km southwest) *Mulin Vecio*, Via Gorizia 2, ☎ 0481 99783; traditional osteria in an ancient (but working) mill, serving simple country meals; closed Wed–Thur; inexpensive.

MOSSA (6km west) *Blanch*, Via Blanchis 35, ☎ 0481 80020; straightforward, genuine country cooking in an old-fashioned osteria; closed Wed and Aug–Sep; inexpensive.

SAVOGNA D'ISONZO (7km northwest) *Devetak*, Località San Michele del Carso 48, ☎ 0481 882005; excellent food (especially Slovene dishes) and fabulous wines at a trattoria in the same family for nearly 200 years; closed Mon–Tues; moderate.

Entertainment

TRIESTE has three very active theatres: *Teatro Politeama Rossetti*, Viale XX Settembre, *Teatro Comunale Giuseppe Verdi* and *Sala Tripcovich*, Piazza Verdi (opera season in Nov–Mar, concerts in May and Oct, and international operetta festival in summer). There are also open-air theatre performances in the castle, Jul–Aug.

GORIZIA Classical music at *Auditorium della Cultura Friulana* and *Kulturni Dom*, and at the *Sala Convegni dei Musei Provinciali di Borgo Castello*.

ELSEWHERE Live music at bars and clubs throughout the region.

Shopping

Excellent wines are made in the Collio and Isonzo districts, and there is very good locally-made honey. These items are available throughout the region.

TRIESTE The busy Corso Italia is the main street, with elegant shops.

GORIZIA Market on Thur in the public gardens in Corso Giuseppe Verdi; crafts market on the second Sun of the month in Via Ascoli.

Special events

TRIESTE *Festival Internazionale dell'Operetta*, international operetta festival, Jun–Aug.

Light and sound show, Castello di Miramare, Jul–Aug. *Mostra-Mercato dell'Antiquariato*, antiques fair, at the Stazione Marittima, late Oct–early Nov. *Barcolana*, sailing regatta, second Sun in Oct.
CORMONS *Festa dei Popoli della Mitteleuropa*, Central European folk festival, Aug; *Renaissance pageant*, Sept.
GORIZIA *Medieval Music Festival*, Jun;

National Theatre Festival, Jun–Jul; *Folkfest*, ethnic music festival, Jul; *Amidei Film Festival*, Aug. *Comic Theatre Festival*, Sep. *Alpe Adria Puppet Festival*, Sep.

Sports

Golf at San Floriano del Collio (*Golf Club San Floriano*) and at Trieste (*Golf Club Trieste*).

TRIESTE

Trieste (population 229,000) is the capital of the region of Friuli-Venezia Giulia as well as the capital of a small province. In a gulf backed by the low, rolling hills of the Carso, it is the most important seaport of the northern Adriatic, although its commercial traffic has diminished in recent years. For many centuries part of the Austrian empire, it retains something of the old-fashioned atmosphere of a middle-European city. Regular, spacious streets were laid out around the Canal Grande at the end of the 18C, when the city flourished under the enlightened rule of the Habsburg empress Maria Theresa. Its numerous monumental Neo-classical and Art Nouveau buildings date from the 19C and early 20C. Now on the borders of Slovenia, the town is increasingly looking towards eastern Europe for commercial outlets. An icy-cold wind (the *bora*) can blow from the northeast across the Carso plateau through the town in some seasons.

History

The settlement of *Tergeste*, already an important outlet into the Adriatic for the produce of the middle Danube and its tributaries, was absorbed into the Roman dominion early in the 2C BC. The city was ruled by its bishops from the 9C to the 13C. Rivalry with Venice for the commerce of the Adriatic began at the beginning of the 13C, with the rise of the independent Commune of Trieste, and continued for many centuries. In 1382 Trieste came under the protection of the Austrian Emperor Leopold III, and in 1463 the city was saved by Pius II from a Venetian blockade; it was then rebuilt by Frederick III. Charles VI declared Trieste a free port in 1719, and it flourished under the rule of Maria Theresa (1740–80). Despite the increased prosperity brought about by the opening of the Suez Canal (1869), Trieste became the centre of Irredentism. The desire for liberation from Austrian rule was fulfilled when Italian troops entered Trieste in 1918, and the city, together with the Carso and Istria, was ceded to Italy by treaty in 1920. These territories fell in 1945 to Yugoslav forces, and the Carso was incorporated into Yugoslavia. By the Italian peace treaty of 1947 Trieste and Istria were created a Free Territory, with Anglo-American trusteeship of the city and a Yugoslav zone in Istria. In 1954 the existing frontier was agreed at a further four-power conference. Trieste remains a free port.

Literary associations

Trieste was the birthplace or the chosen place of residence of several well-known modern authors. The British traveller and writer Sir Richard Burton was consul here from 1872 until his death in 1890. At the Albergo Obelisco in Villa Opicina he completed the translation of the *Thousand and One Nights*. James Joyce (1882–1941) lived in the city in 1904–15 and 1919–20, with his wife Nora Barnacle, and their two children were born here. They lived at Via Donato Bramante 4 (near Piazza Vico, on the far side of the hill of San Giusto), where Joyce wrote part of *Ulysses*. While here he befriended the native writer Italo Svevo (Aron Hector Schmitz; 1861–1928). The poet Umberto Saba (Umberto Poli; 1883–1957) was also born in Trieste.

The Cittavecchia

The old quarter of the city, commonly called the *Cittavecchia*, lies on the hill of San Giusto, at the top of which stand the cathedral and castle. The **Cathedral**, dedicated to St Justus (a Christian martyr who was thrown into the sea during Diocletian's persecution), is the fruit of a 14C union of two earlier churches, San Giusto (on the south) and Santa Maria Assunta (on the north). The simple façade, with a single, large gable, is graced by a large 14C rose window; the posts of the main doorway incorporate elements of a Roman tomb. Three modern busts of bishops of Trieste (including Pope Pius II) are set above the door. The campanile, also of the 14C, resembles a defensive tower. It stands on the remains of the vestibule of a Roman temple. A Byzantine-Romanesque statue of the patron saint occupies a Gothic aedicule on the south side.

Inside, the cathedral has five asymmetrical aisles divided by columns with fine capitals. The 16C ship's-keel ceiling of the nave was reconstructed in 1905; also modern is the central apse, with a mosaic inspired by fragments of the original. In the south apse you can see original blind arcading, frescoes of the 13C and, on the ceiling, a remarkable late-13C mosaic depicting Christ between Sts Justus and Servulus upon a gold ground with a beautifully decorated border. The old choir-bench and some pretty little Byzantine columns with 6C capitals can be seen below, between very worn early-13C frescoes of the life of St Justus. More worn frescoes and a finely carved 9C pluteus (light wall) with doves are in the little side apse to the right.

In the main nave you can see fragments of the original, old polychrome mosaic pavement. The north apse contains a splendid 12C *mosaic of the Veneto-Ravenna school showing the **Madonna Enthroned between two Archangels above the Apostles**, with another beautifully decorated border. In the side apse to the left is a sculptured wooden group of the *Pietà* (16C). Next to this is the treasury, protected by a fine iron gate (1650), with remains of 15C frescoes. A 13C painting on silk of St Justus, a cross donated to the church in 1383, and precious reliquaries are preserved here.

An inconspicuous door off the north aisle (above which is a *Madonna and Saints* by Benedetto Carpaccio,1540) leads into the **baptistery**, which has a 9C immersion font and five frescoes detached from the south apse, illustrating the life of St Justus (1350), in good condition.

At the foot of the castle stretches the area known as the **Platea Romana**, with remains of the basilica of the Roman forum (2C AD) and of the so-called Tempio

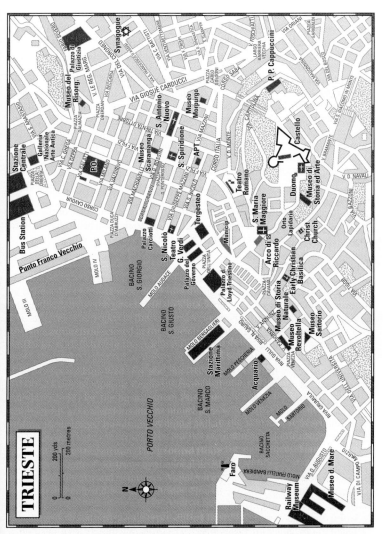

Capitolino (1C AD). The **Castello** (open Tues–Sun 09.00–19.00) as it appears today was constructed between 1470 and 1630 on the site of an earlier Venetian fortress, which in its turn rose on the probable site of a prehistoric fortification. Plays are given in the courtyard in summer. To the right of the atrium is the Cappella di San Giorgio, with a wooden 15C statue of the saint. The castle contains part of the **Museo Civico** (open Tues–Sun 09.00–13.00). A staircase, rebuilt in the 1930s, leads up to the **Sala Veneta**, which is the reconstruction of a 17C room in a private palace with its furniture and 16C Flemish tapestries. The wooden ceiling has a painted *Allegory of Venice* by Andrea Celesti. More stairs lead up to the (covered) battlements with a large collection of arms. The old kitchen and a loggia can also be visited here. From the courtyard near the entrance you can access the walkways above the ramparts, from which there are good views of the entire city.

The tree-lined Via della Cattedrale descends from the steps of the cathedral to the **Museo di Storia ed Arte e Orto Lapidario** (no. 15; open Tues–Sun 09.00–13.00, Wed 09.00–19.00), the most important museum in Trieste. Here antique and medieval sculpture and inscriptions, Egyptian antiquities, prehistoric and protohistoric material, Greek and Italic antiquities (pottery, glass, bronze, jewellery and coins), and drawings and prints are displayed in a pleasant building and a lovely garden. Also here is the cenotaph of the archaeologist J.J. Winckelmann (1717–68), who was murdered at Trieste under the assumed name of 'Signor Giovanni' by a thief whose cupidity he had excited by displaying some ancient gold coins.

The street ends at the **Arco di Riccardo**, a vaulted Roman gate of the 1C AD, dedicated to Augustus. Its name survives from the traditional belief that Richard I was imprisoned here after his return from the Holy Land.

The Borgo Teresiano

The Borgo Teresiano, the quarter developed by Maria Theresa in the 18C, extends along the waterfront north of the San Giusto hill. Its southern limit is marked by the large, dramatic **Piazza dell'Unità d'Italia**, which was created in the 19C by filling in the old Roman harbour. Facing the sea is the eclectic façade of the Palazzo Comunale (1875). To the north stand the Palazzo del Governo, designed in 1904 by the Austrian architect Emil Artmann, and the historic *Caffè degli Specchi*, a good place to take a break. (Coffee is particularly delicious in Trieste, which imports more than any other port in the Mediterranean.) To the south, the seaward side of the square is dominated by the imposing Renaissance-revival Palazzo del Lloyd Triestino, by the Viennese architect Heinrich Ferstel (1880–83), who also designed the two allegorical fountains. Next door stands another Renaissance-revival building, today a hotel, and next to this, the elegant Palazzo Pitteri (1785), in a style somewhere between the Baroque and the Neo-classical.

Triestine trivia

The **harbour** is fronted by the broad quay, or Riva. The name of **Riva Mandracchio** is derived from *mandraki*—in Greek 'sheepfold'—which often denotes an ancient galley port (as at Rhodes, Kos and Hvar). The **Molo Audace** commemorates the name of the destroyer from which the first Italian troops landed on 3 November 1918 to liberate the city from Austrian rule. Salty dogs will be pleased to know that the first screw-propelled steamer in Europe, the **Civetta**, was tested in Trieste's roadstead in 1829.

A short walk northwards along the waterfront brings you past the Teatro Verdi, the city's main concert hall (1801) and the church of San Nicolò dei Greci, built in 1784–87 by the Greek Orthodox community and possessing a composite Neo-classical façade with twin campanili by Matteo Pertsch (1819–21) and a magnificent silver iconostasis.

Keeping the gulf on your left, you soon come to the **Canal Grande**, constructed in 1750–56 to provide a safe harbour for merchant vessels and to allow cargo to be unloaded directly into the warehouses of the Borgo Teresiano. On the southwest corner is Matteo Pertsch's Palazzo Carciotti (1802–05; now the port authority), a Neo-classical

The Canal Grande

building with a hexastyle façade and a balustrade with statues. On the opposite corner stands Palazzo Aedes, a work of the Viennese Secession architect Arduino Berlam (1926–28).

At its far end, the Canal Grande is spectacularly concluded by Pietro Nobile's Neo-classical church of **Sant'Antonio Nuovo** (1827–42). In Piazza Ponterosso, halfway down on the right, the house at no. 3 was the first home of Joyce and his wife Nora, who lived in Trieste from 1904 to 1915 and again in 1919–20. The **Museo Scaramangà di Altomonte** (open Tues and Fri 10.00–12.00), across the canal at 1 Via Filzi, houses a small but important collection documenting the history of art in Trieste.

The area of the Borgo Teresiano between the Canal Grande and the Corso Italia, four blocks south, is a genuine gold mine of **early modern architecture**. If you are fond of this period, or just interested in meeting the grandparents of today's architectural styles, take a look at Romeo Depaoli's Casa Smolars (1906–07), at the corner of Piazza della Repubblica and Via Dante; the Casa Fontana (Via Mazzini 5, at the corner of Via Roma); the bank at Via Roma 9; and the Casa Bartoli (Piazza della Borsa 7B), a mansion designed in the Italian variant of Art Nouveau known as the Liberty style, by Max Fabiani (1905).

Along the Corso Italia are several buildings by major architects of the period between the wars, notably the Casa delle Assicurazioni Generali (nos 1–3) and the Banco di Napoli (no. 5), by Marcello Piacentini (1935–39) and the *grattacielo* ('skyscraper') by Umberto Nordio (1936; in Largo Riborgo), as well as interesting remnants of the old Austro-Hungarian corso—the Neo-classical Casa Steiner (no. 4) by Matteo Pertsch (1824), the Tuscan-revival Casa Ananian (no. 12), by Giorgio Polli (1905) and the building at the corner of Piazza Goldoni (no. 22), with a Liberty gable end, by Romeo Depaoli (1908).

At the foot of the San Giusto hill, just south of Largo Riborgo, excavations in 1938 brought to light remains of a 6000-seat Roman theatre dating from the 2C AD; a small antiquarium displays finds from the excavations. Just one block east, on the site of the former Polish Aschenazi synagogue, is the **Museo della Communità Ebraica** (Via del Monte 7, open Sun 17.00–20.00, Tues 16.00–18.00, Thur 10.00–13.00), created in 1993 to hold the collections of Jewish art and culture of the Triestine community, particularly sacred vessels and vestments from the synagogue.

A Triestine house-museum

A peculiar feature of Trieste is the unusual number of old mansions that have been turned into museums. A stately Eclectic townhouse by Giovanni Berlam (1875), just off Corso Italia at Via Imbriani 5, houses the **Museo M. Morpurgo de Nilma** (open Tues–Sun 09.00–13.00, Wed 09.00–19.00), with furniture, paintings, miniatures, prints, ceramics, porcelain and a library—all in a fascinating *fin-de-siècle* bourgeois setting. The **Civico Museo Teatrale** (open Tues–Sun 09.00–13.00, Wed 09.00–19.00), with an extremely interesting collection and archive including 19C musical instruments and documents relating to the production of operetta, for which Trieste has been famous since the 19C, is provisionally displayed on the first floor. The museum was founded in 1924 in the Teatro Verdi with the collection of Carlo Schmidl.

The northern districts of the city are centred around Piazza Oberdan, laid out in the 1930s. The **Museo del Risorgimento** (open Tues–Sun 09.00–13.00) is arranged in a fine palace by Umberto Nordio (1934), which incorporates the cell of Guglielmo Oberdan, hanged in 1882 by the Austrians in the old barracks on this site. Here also is the station of the Opicina tramway—the line, first opened in 1902, was rebuilt in 1978. **Palazzo di Giustizia**, in the Foro Ulpiano, was built by Enrico Nordio in 1933.

The western districts

Riva Mandracchio leads west along the seafront from Piazza dell'Unità d'Italia. Beyond the Molo dei Bersaglieri, on another jetty, is the **pescheria** (fish market) with its spacious market hall (1913, by Giorgio Polli) open to the sea, and a clock tower. At the side is the entrance to a fine **aquarium** (closed at the time of writing), founded by the municipality in 1933, with fish from the Adriatic and tropics as well as three penguins.

The **Museo Revoltella** (Via Diaz 27; open Mon, Wed, Fri and Sat 10.00–20.00; Thur, Sun and holidays 10.00–23.00) occupies a Renaissance-revival building designed by Friedrich Titzig (1852–58) for the businessman Pasquale Revoltella (1795–1869) as a museum for his art collections and as an art institute. It still has some of its interesting furnishings, handsome ceilings, inlaid wooden floors and enamelled terracotta stoves.

An allegorical fountain by Pietro Magni adorns the atrium. The **ground floor** exhibits include 17C and 18C landscapes, a room of portraits by the local artist Giuseppe Tominz (1790–1866), the panelled library and a statue of *Napoleon as Mars* by Antonio Canova (the model for his colossal statue in Apsley House, London).

On the **first floor** are an elaborate allegorical statuary group representing the *Suez Canal* by Pietro Magni (Revoltella was vice-president of the company responsible for the cutting of the canal), and paintings by Vincenzo Cabianca, Girolamo Induno, Giovanni Fattori, Filippo Palizzi and Francesco Hayez.

The **top floor** holds four more allegorical statues by Magni, and the handsome dining room.

The visit continues in the adjacent building, renovated to plans by Carlo Scarpa in 1960–92. It displays a large collection of modern art acquired through funds set aside for this purpose by Revoltella. The artists represented include Medardo Rosso, Giuseppe de Nittis, Felice Casorati, Giorgio Morandi, Giorgio De Chirico and Lucio Fontana. The large collection of works by local artists includes paintings by Pietro Marussig, who is known internationally. Frequent exhibitions are held on the fifth floor, and there are fine views of Trieste and the port from the sixth floor.

The **Museo Civico di Storia Naturale** (open Tues–Sun 08.30–13.30; Jul–Aug also Wed–Fri 17.00–21.00) is housed in a palazzo designed in 1816 by Pietro Nobile in Piazza Attilio Hortis, with a little public garden. Founded in 1846, it has a very fine and well-displayed natural history collection, particularly rich in material from the Carso and Venezia Giulia. Mammals, fish, shells, insects, an Egyptian mummy and a botanical section (with lovely watercolours of plants that grow in the region) are displayed on the third floor. On the floors below are sections devoted to mineralogy, palaeontology, birds and reptiles. The museum also has extensive study collections and a specialised library.

The **Civico Museo Sartorio** (Largo Papa Giovanni XXIII 1; open Tues–Sun 09.00–13.00) is located in an 18C mansion remodelled in 1820–38 by Nicolò Pertsch. On the ground floor are Italian and European majolicas and porcelains, Triestine ceramics and rooms for temporary exhibitions. The first floor has rooms furnished in the Gothic-revival and Biedermeier styles, and paintings of the 17C–19C (notably by Tiepolo and his followers). On the second floor are rotating exhibitions of paintings from various Triestine collections.

At the end of Riva Grumula, in Via Campo Marzio, is the **Museo del Mare** (open Tues–Sun 08.30–13.30; Jul–Aug also Tues and Thur 17.00–20.00) with sections devoted to harbours, navigation and fishing. The old railway station of Campo Marzio (Via G. Cesare 1) is now home to the **Museo Ferroviario** (open Tues–Sun 09.00–13.00), which illustrates the history of railways in the region and preserves some old locomotives. Beyond is the modern harbour.

A sadly important place is the **Risiera di Santa Saba** (open Tues–Sun 09.00–13.00), in the industrial district south of the city on the Muggia road, at Ratto della Pileria 1. This former rice-hulling plant was the only Nazi death camp in Italy. Some 5000 prisoners are believed to have been executed here between the German invasion of Italy in 1943 and the liberation of Trieste by Tito's Partisans in 1945. It is now a national monument with death and detention cells, a permanent photographic exhibit and a library.

Environs of Trieste

The best of Trieste's house-museums is reached by a short drive or bus ride. The **Castello di Miramare** (open daily 09.00–18.00), situated 8km northwest of the city along 14 and surrounded by a large formal garden, was built to an English Renaissance-revival design by Karl Junker (1855–60) for Archduke Maximilian of Austria.

There are three entrances to the park of Miramare (open as public gardens, Mon–Fri 08.00–19.00, Sat 09.00–21.45, Sun 09.00–19.00). The nearest one to Trieste is on the sea (at a road fork), but from this entrance it is a good 20mins walk to the castle. The entrance closest to the castle is on the main road before the two tunnels that precede Grignano, and the third entrance is by the bus terminus at Grignano, near the Castelletto.

Maximilian lived here until 1864, the year in which he accepted the imperial crown of Mexico; and in 1931–36 the mansion was the home of Amedeo di Savoia. It rises in a splendid position at the end of a promontory and, with its furniture, paintings, porcelains, and ivories, is one of the more remarkable examples of a 19C aristocratic residence. Notices in each room describe the contents; highlights include a painting of celebrations in Venice in honour of Maximilian and his bride, Charlotte of Saxony, by Ippolito Caffi; portraits of Maximilian and Charlotte; and a sculpture of *Daedalo and Icarus* by Innocenzo Fraccaroli. The huge throne room has an elaborate Gothic-revival ceiling.

The **park** has some fine trees and an Italianate garden. The small Castelletto, where Maximilian lived while the castello was being built, houses the Centro di Educazione all'Ambiente Marino di Miramare, with a museum of the marine environment. The sea around the promontory is now a marine reserve. The road to Miramare passes the **Faro della Vittoria** (open daily except Wed 09.00–11.00 and 16.00–18.00), a lighthouse and memorial to seamen who died in the First World War, designed in the 1920s by Arduino Berlam and today a popular viewpoint.

Sistiana, on a delightful bay known to the Romans as *Sextilianum*, is used as a harbour for private boats. A path (known as the Sentiero Rilke) follows the rocky coast from here to Duino for nearly 2km, through interesting vegetation, with fine views.

Duino is a fishing village with a ruined Castello Vecchio. The imposing Castello Nuovo, on a rocky promontory above the sea, was built in the 15C on the ruins of a Roman tower (which has been partly reconstructed). The poet Rainer Maria Rilke stayed here as a guest of Maria von Thurn und Taxis in 1910–14. Since 1964 part of the castle has been occupied by the United World College of the Adriatic, one of eight international schools all over the world for scholarship students between the ages of 16 and 18. The other part of the castle, rebuilt since damage in the First World War, is still owned by the Della Torre Tasso family.

At **San Giovanni al Timavo** is the mouth of the River Timavo, which emerges here from an underground course of over 38km. The six springs here have been sacred since Roman times.

A tramway (5km) and funicular run from Trieste (Piazza Oberdan) to **Villa Opicina**. In the Carsic hills between Opicina and Sistiana a good dark red wine known as *terrano* is produced. Near Opicina is the **Grotta Gigante** (open Tues–Sun, Apr–Sep 09.00–12.00, 14.00–19.00, Oct–Mar 10.00–12.00, 14.30–16.30), the largest single cave yet discovered in the Carso (280m long, 107m high). It was first opened to the public in 1908 and is famous for its stalactitic formations.

From **Monrupino** there is a superb view of the **Carso** (German *Karst*, Slav *Kras*), a curiously eroded limestone plateau, now mostly in Slovenian territory. It was the scene of the most violent struggles in the Austro-Italian campaign during the First World War. Vast trenches and veritable caverns were easily constructed by widening the existing crevasses in its surface; and although large-scale operations were made difficult by the nature of the ground, immense concentrations of artillery were brought up by both sides for the defence of this key position. It was the Duke of Aosta's stand here with the Third Italian Army that averted complete disaster after Caporetto (October 1917). A local ethnographical museum at Rupingrande is open on holidays.

Muggia, across the bay south of Trieste, is a charming little old fishing-port with brightly painted houses, the only Istrian town that has remained within the Italian border. For centuries a faithful ally of the Venetian Republic, it retains a remarkably Venetian atmosphere (the streets are called *calli*, like the streets in Venice). The **harbour**, with its fishing boats, is also used by numerous yachts, and there are several simple fish restaurants here. The 14C **castle** rises above the harbour. Near the inner basin (or *mandracchio*) is the main piazza with the **Duomo**, a 13C foundation with a 15C Venetian Gothic façade and an interesting treasury; the town hall; and the **Palazzo dei Rettori** (rebuilt after a fire in 1933), once a palace of the patriarchs of Aquileia, who controlled the town in the 10C. An archway opposite the town hall leads into Via Dante with interesting old houses. There is a particularly pretty Venetian Gothic palace at Via Oberdan 25.

On the hillside above are the ruins of the Roman and medieval settlement of **Muggia Vecchia**, destroyed in 1356 by the Genoese for having taken the side of Venice in the battle of Chioggia. The basilica here is a 9C building with an ambo of the 10C, transennae in the Byzantine style, and remains of early frescoes.

Gorizia

Gorizia (population 38,000) is a provincial capital standing in an expansion of the Isonzo valley hemmed in by hills on the Slovenian border. It is a particularly pleasant and peaceful little town with numerous public gardens and pretty buildings in Austrian style.

History

After the fall of the independent counts of Gorizia in the 15C, the city remained an Austrian possession almost continuously from 1509 to 1915. In the First World War it was the objective of violent Italian attacks in the Isonzo Valley and was eventually captured on 9 August 1916. Lost again in the autumn of 1917, it was finally taken in November 1918. The Treaty of Paris (1947) brought the Yugoslav frontier to the streets of the town, cutting off its eastern suburbs, but in 1952, and again in 1978–79, more reasonable readjustments were made, including a 16km wide zone in which local inhabitants may circulate freely.

The city centre

The attractive, wide **Corso Italia**, lined with trees and some Art Nouveau villas, leads up from the railway station into the centre of the town. Via Garibaldi diverges right to the **Palazzo Comunale**, built by Nicolò Pacassi in 1740, with a public garden. Via Mazzini continues to the **Cathedral**, a 14C building much restored, with a pleasant interior including galleries and stucco decoration. It contains a pulpit of 1711, a high altarpiece by Giuseppe Tominz, and a precious treasury brought from Aquileia in 1752.

Viale Gabriele d'Annunzio leads uphill to the pleasant, peaceful **Borgo Castello** (approached on foot by steps up through the walls and past a garden).

The castle was built by the Venetians in 1509; the **Musei Provinciali di Borgo Castello** (open Tues–Sun, summer 10.00–19.00, winter 10.00–18.00) are well arranged in two 16C palaces within its wards. Late-19C paintings by local painters, including works by Giuseppe Tominz (1790–1866), are exhibited on the ground floor. A display on the upper floor illustrates the history of silk production in the town from 1725 to 1915, including a wooden 18C twisting machine, looms, samples of silks, and costumes showing Balkan influence.

Another section of the museum has delightful reproductions of local artisans' workshops, and a street of reconstructed shops. Downstairs is the ***Museo della Grande Guerra**, one of the more important museums in Italy dedicated to the First World War, founded in 1924. Excellently displayed in ten rooms, it includes the reconstruction of a trench, material illustrating both the Italian and Austrian fronts in the Carso campaign, and a room dedicated to General Diaz.

The **Museo di Storia e Arte** next door is closed for restoration. The unusual little church of **Santo Spirito**, with the copy of a 16C crucifix outside, dates from 1398. The **castle** (open Tues–Sun 09.30–13.00, 15.00–19.30) was built by the counts of Gorizia and remodelled in 1508. Important exhibitions are held here. The rampart walk commands a good view towards Slovenia, and the interesting interior has some 17C and 18C furniture and paintings. The park on the castle hill is a good place to picnic.

Below the hill, off Viale Gabriele d'Annunzio, the pretty Via Rastello, with arcades along one side and some old shop fronts, leads to **Piazza della Vittoria** (commonly called Piazza Grande). Here are a fountain designed in 1756 by Nicolò Pacassi and the 17C–18C church of **Sant'Ignazio** (1654–1747), with eccentric Oriental domes on its two bell towers.

Beyond the far end of the piazza, Via dell'Arcivescovado and Via Seminario lead to Via San Giovanni, another nice street. Its continuation, Via Ascoli, passes several houses with attractive balconies and windows, including Palazzo Ascoli (with a garden), next to San Giovanni; the church, founded in 1587, is set back from the road behind two cedars of Lebanon. At the end of Via Ascoli is the little yellow **synagogue** (open Mon and Fri 16.00–19.00; Tues and Thur 17.00–19.00), first built in 1756 and restored in the 19C and 20C (the façade dates from 1894). **Palazzo Attems**, beyond on the right, is a fine building by Nicolò Pacassi (1745), with a library and archive.

In Corso Giuseppe Verdi, on the corner of Via Boccaccio, is a pretty market building of 1927. Via Santa Chiara and Viale XX Settembre lead northwest from Corso Garibaldi to the late-18C gateway (removed from Palazzo Attems) at the entrance to **Palazzo Coronini**, left to the city by Guglielmo Coronini Cronberg in 1990. It is surrounded by a fine *park laid out in the 19C, with evergreen trees, statues by Orazio Marinali, and a sculpture of Hecate that may date from the 2C AD. Built in 1597 by Giulio Baldigara, the palace was purchased from Marshall Radetzky in 1820 by the Coronini. Charles X Bourbon of France died here in exile of cholera in 1836. It has a 19C wing and portico, and a 17C family chapel. The 30 rooms are preserved intact and contain 18C furniture, paintings and porcelain. The library has some 15,000 volumes, including illustrated manuscripts and incunabula.

Viale XX Settembre continues to the Isonzo River, across which are the public gardens of the Parco Piuma.

Environs of Gorizia

Across the Isonzo, northwest of Gorizia at **Oslavia**, a 'Gothic' castle (open Tues–Sun, summer 09.00–11.45, 15.00–17.45; winter 08.00–11.45, 14.00–16.45) holds the graves of 57,000 men of the Second Army who fell in 1915–18.

To the north is the hilly area of **Collio**, famous for its excellent wine. **San Floriano del Collio** has a wine museum (open Mon–Fri 08.00–17.00), and the attractive little town of **Cormòns**, an ancient seat of the patriarchs of Aquileia, has a few hotels and good restaurants.

South of Gorizia on the Isonzo is **Gradisca**, an old Venetian fortress still preserving many of its 15C watchtowers and some good Baroque mansions. In the 17C–18C Palazzo Torriani, the Civico Museo Gradiscano (open Tues, Thur and Fri 17.00–19.00) contains Roman material. The county of Gradisca was ceded to Austria in 1511, and in 1615–17 it caused a war between Austria and Venice.

Monte San Michele was a ridge hotly contested in the Carso campaign. At Sagrado a museum (open Tues–Sun 08.00–12.00, 14.00–17.00) commemorates the battle.

Further south is **Redipuglia** with the huge war cemetery of the Third Army, containing over 100,000 graves, including that of the Duke of Aosta (1869–1931), the heroic defender of the Carso. A small museum here is dedicated to the First World War. Nearby is a war cemetery with the graves of 14,550 Austro-Hungarian soldiers. **Ronchi dei Legionari**, with the airport of Trieste, is on the edge of the Carso and the region of the battlefront of 1915–17. Guglielmo Oberdan (1858–82), the patriot, was arrested here by the Austrians in 1882 before his execution, and from here in 1919 the poet and nationalist Gabriele D'Annunzio set out to occupy Fiume.

Udine and the north

The Friuli, Italy's extreme northeastern corner, is one of the country's more beautiful and less-known regions. Most of the tourists you'll find here will be locals—Venetians drying their bones in the crisp Alpine air, or city folk from Trieste looking for a hearty country meal. The exception to this rule is the odd German or Austrian en route to the beach resorts. And yet this area, now the province of Udine, has much to offer. Udine, for instance, is a small treasure chest of Venetian art and architecture, and Cividale has some of the finest vestiges anywhere of Lombard art—a real rarity. Everywhere the landscape—from the verdant hills of the south and east to the white limestone peaks of the Carnic Alps in the north—is unforgettable.

Practical information

Getting there
By air

The regional airport serving Friuli-Venezia Giulia is located at Ronchi dei Legionari, 41km southeast of Udine. There are daily flights to domestic and European destinations; coaches connect with the airport terminal at the Trieste railway station (journey time: 60mins).

By road

The A4 runs from Venice to Trieste, not far from the Adriatic shore. Near Palmanova it links up with the A23, which winds northwards via Udine, Gemona and Tarvisio to Austria. 52 connects the A23 to Tolmezzo (exit at Carnia-Tolmezzo), continuing westward to Pieve di Cadore. Udine and Cividale del Friuli are linked by 54. **Car parking** in Udine in Piazza I Maggio and Piazza XX Settembre.

By rail

There is a direct rail service from Venice to Udine, continuing on to Vienna and Prague via Gemona and Tarvisio; fast *Intercity* trains make the Venice–Udine run in c 90mins. Branch lines run from Trieste to Udine, and from Udine to Conegliano, Cividale (with hourly service taking 15mins), Gorizia, Palmanova and Cervignano.

By bus

Bus no. 1 runs from the train station to the town centre. **Country buses** depart from the bus station at Viale Europa Unita 31 (next to the railway station) to destinations all over the province (for information, ☎ 0432 50694, 0432 503004).

Information offices
UDINE Piazza I Maggio 7, ☎ 0432 295972.

ARTE TERME (Carnia) Via Umberto I 15, ☎ 0433 929290

CIVIDALE DEL FRIULI Largo Bioani 4,

☎ 0432 731461.

TARVISIO Via Roma 10, ☎ 0428 2135.

Where to stay

UDINE *Ambassador Palace*, 46 Via Carducci, ☎ 0432 503777, fax 0432 503711; generally considered the top venue, occupies a historic building midway between the cathedral and the train station; moderate.

Astoria Italia, Piazza XX Settembre 24, ☎ 0432 505091, fax 0432 509070; elegant with a good restaurant, in the heart of the old town; moderate.

Friuli, Viale Ledra 24, ☎ 0432 234351, fax 0432 234354; a comfortable place a few blocks west of the city centre; inexpensive.

Là di Moret, Viale Tricesimo 276, ☎ 0432 545096, fax 0432 545096; an excellent hotel with a renowned restaurant, unfortunately somewhat distant from the city centre and across town from the station; inexpensive.

CIVIDALE DEL FRIULI *Locanda al Castello*, Via del Castello 20, ☎ 0432 733242, fax 0432 700901; a former Jesuit convent with ten rooms, in a quiet, wooded setting; closed Nov; inexpensive.

Roma, Piazza Picco, ☎ 0432 731871, fax 0432 701033; centrally located, comfortable; inexpensive.

SAN DANIELE DEL FRIULI *Alla Torre*, Via del Lago 1, ☎ 0432 954562, fax 0432 954562; simple, pleasant and centrally located; inexpensive.

TARVISIO *Nevada*, Via Kugy 4, ☎ 0428 2332, fax 0428 40566; straightforward and comfortable, with good views; inexpensive.

Eating out

UDINE *Alla Vedova*, Via Tavagnacco 9, ☎ 0432 470291; established in 1887, strong points are game dishes, home-made wine and a distinctive ambience; closed Sun evening, Mon and Aug; moderate.

Alla Colonna, Via Gemona 98, ☎ 0432 510177; traditional trattoria and wine bar; closed Sun; moderate.

Al Lepre, Via Poscollo 27, ☎ 0432 295798; traditional osteria, simple but good; closed Tues and Aug; inexpensive.

Al Passeggio, Viale Volontari della Libertà 49, ☎ 0432 46216; good Friulan food (including fresh-baked bread), though a bit out of the way; closed midday Sat, Sun and Aug; moderate.

Vitello d'Oro, Via Valvason 4, ☎ 0432 508982; a popular trattoria serving local specialities, particularly (despite the name, 'Golden Calf') seafood, around a great fireplace; closed Wed and Jul; moderate.

Wine bars: (where you can join the Udinesi for a *tajut*, or aperitif, usually of white wine) *Ai Piombi*, Via Manin; *Ai Vecchi Parrocchiani*, Via Aquileia 66; *Al Cappello*, Via Sarpi 5; Speziaria Pei Sani, Via Poscolle 13.

Cafés and cake shops: *Cantarena*, Piazza del Comune; *Caucigh*, Via Gemona; *Volpe Pasini*, Via Cangiani; *Sommariva*, Via Rialto. Local **cheeses** from B*ottega del Formaggio*, Via Poscolle 16; and *La Baita dei Formaggi*, Via delle Erbe 1b.

Picnic places on the castle hill.

ENVIRONS OF UDINE

At LAVARIANO, 14km south, *Blasut*, Via Aquileia 7, ☎ 0432 767017; fine regional foods prepared with great care; closed Sun evening, Mon, Jan and Aug; moderate.

At REANA DEL ROIALE, 8km north, *Da Rochet*, ☎ 0432 851090; a country restaurant in a lovely position, with garden seating in the summer; closed Tues–Wed and Jul–Sep; moderate.

At TRICESIMO, 10km north, *Antica Trattoria Boschetti* (with rooms), Piazza Mazzini 10, ☎ 0432 851230; antique (est. 1830), elegant restaurant serving personal variations on local spe-

cialities; closed Sun evening, Mon, Jan and Aug; moderate.

CIVIDALE DEL FRIULI *Al Fortino*, Via Carlo Alberto 46, ☎ 0432 731217; traditional fare accompanied by mainly regional wines, in a setting featuring 14C frescoes and a great fireplace; closed Mon evening, Tues, Jan and Aug; inexpensive.

Alla Frasca, Via de Rubeis 8a, ☎ 0432 731270; a popular trattoria with garden seating in summer; closed Mon and Feb; inexpensive.

Zorutti, Borgo di Ponte 9, ☎ 0432 731100; another good trattoria with cosy rooms and fireplaces, in an 18C building; inexpensive.

RIVE D'ARCANO (RODEANO BASSO) *Antica Bettola-da Marisa*, Via Coseano 1, ☎ 0432 807060; excellent trattoria with menus in Friulan dialect and summer seating outside; closed Thur, Jan and Sep; inexpensive.

SAN DANIELE DEL FRIULI *Ai Binars*, Via Trento e Trieste 63, ☎ 0432 957322; crowded, lively osteria named after the farmhands who commuted seasonally between here and Austria; closed Wed evening, Thur and Jul; inexpensive. *Prosciutto di San Daniele* is famous throughout Italy and beyond; you can pick up some of the best at *Prosciuttificio Prolongo*, Via Trento e Trieste 115.

If you'd like simply to taste some with a glass of wine, try the *Prosciutterie Dok Dall'Ava*, Via Gemona 29.

SAURIS (SAURIS DI SOTTO) *Alla Pace*, Via Roma 38, ☎ 0433 86010; traditional trattoria (with rooms) in the same family since 1804; closed Wed (except in high season), May and Jun; moderate.

STREGNA *Sale e Pepe*, Via Capoluogo 19, ☎ 0432 724118; excellent regional cuisine using only the freshest ingredients; open weekends, weekdays by reservation; inexpensive.

TARCENTO (LONERIACCO) *Da Gaspar*,

Via Gaspar 1, ☎ 0432 785950; traditional trattoria, above Tarcento at the edge of the forest; closed Mon, Tues and Jul; moderate.

TOLMEZZO *Roma* (with rooms), Piazza XX Settembre 14, ☎ 0433 2081; exceptional interpretations of regional specialties; closed Sun evening, Mon, Jun and Nov; moderate.

 ### Entertainment
UDINE Classical music and drama at *Teatro Nuovo Giovanni da Udine* and *Auditorium Zanon*. *Amici della Musica*, classical music series, and *Realtà del Territorio*, drama series, Palamostre, autumn/winter.

 ### Special events
UDINE *Concerto di Capodanno*, New Year's Eve concert by the Filarmonica di Udine, *Teatro Nuovo Giovanni da Udine*, 1 Jan. *Omaggio al Balletto*, dance festival, spring. *Udineincontri Cinema*, film festival, Apr. *Jazz Festival*, Jun. *Friuli D.O.C.*, wine and gastronomic festival, Oct. *Festa di Santa Caterina*, with a fair and market for three days in Piazza I Maggio, 25 Nov.
CICONICCO DI FAGAGNA *Good Friday Procession* and passion play.
CIVIDALE DEL FRIULI *Messa dello Spadone*, historic pageant, Jan. *Mittelfest*, festival of drama, music, dance and puppet theatre from Central Europe, Jul.

PALMANOVA Historic pageant in 16C and 17C costume, Jul.
SAN PIETRO DI ZUGLIO *Zuglio Carnico*, religious pageant celebrating the Ascension, May.
SELLA NEVEA *Coppa Duca d'Aosta*, men's European slalom championship, Jan.
TARVISIO *Trofeo Alpe Adria*, international dogsled race, Jan. *World-Cup Snowboard Championships*, Feb.
ELSEWHERE *Cantine Aperte*, presentation and tasting of new wines on estates throughout the region, May. *Folkfest*, itinerant international ethnic music festival, Jul.

 ### Shopping
Antiques are the most prized commodity for outside visitors to Friuli: there are markets in Udine (first Sun of the month), San Daniele del Friuli (last Sun) and Venzone (second Sun).

 ### Sport
Udine's professional **soccer** team (*Udinese*) plays at the Stadio del Friuli. **Golf** at Lignano Sabbiadoro (*Golf Club Lignano*), Tarvisio (*Golf Club Tarvisio*), Fagagna (*Gulf Club Udine*) and Chiasiellis di Mortegliano (*Country Club Chiasiellis*). Facilities for most summer and winter sports throughout the region; excellent **downhill**, **cross-country** and **back-country skiing** at Tarvisio.

UDINE
• • • • • •

Udine (population 99,000), the historical centre of the Friuli and capital of a large province, is a delightful, lively town. Its attractive old streets, most of them arcaded, fan out round the castle hill. Some splendid examples of Tiepolo's work are preserved here. The streets are often full of soldiers, as there are numerous barracks in or near the town.

History

A Roman station called *Utina* is alleged to have occupied the site of Udine, and a 10C castle here is recorded as part of the domain of the Patriarch of Aquileia. In the 13C Patriarch Berthold of Andrechs moved his residence here from Aquileia, marking the beginning of a period of growth of which few traces remain, but which made Udine an important regional capital. In 1420, after nine years' resistance, Udine surrendered to Venice and from then on remained under her influence. It was occupied by Napoleon's marshals Bernadotte in 1797, and Massena in 1805. In the First World War it was Italian General Headquarters until October 1917, and then was held by the Austrians for a year. In the Second World War, after considerable destruction from air raids, it was entered by South African troops on 1 May 1945, the day before the official end of the campaign. The castle hill was damaged in the 1976 Friuli earthquake and is still partly under restoration.

Piazza della Libertà and the castle hill

The centre of town life is still the Venetian Piazza Nuova, now called *Piazza della Libertà. Set at the foot of the castle hill, this 16C square is considered one of the more beautiful urban complexes in Italy.

The **Loggia del Lionello**, on the southwest side, is the town hall. It was built in 1448–56 by Bartolomeo delle Cisterne to a design by the Udinese goldsmith, Nicolò Lionello, in Venetian Gothic forms. Faced with alternating bands of white and pink stone, it has a first-floor loggia with balustrade, mullioned windows and a niche on one corner holding a 15C statue of the *Madonna* by Bartolomeo Bon.

Piazza della Libertà

Opposite is the Renaissance **Porticato di San Giovanni** (1533), with a chapel that has been converted into a war memorial, and the **Torre dell' Orologio**, by Giovanni da Udine (1527; the *mori* on the clock, which strike the hours, are 19C). In the piazza are a fountain of 1542, two columns with the *Lion of St Mark* and *Justice*, and colossal statues of *Hercules* and *Cacus* (called by the Udinese 'Florean' and 'Venturin') from a demolished 18C palace. The statue of *Peace* (with a sarcastic inscription) commemorates the Treaty of Campo Formio, by which Napoleon ceded Venice to Austria in 1797.

Beyond the **Arco Bollani**, a rusticated triumphal arch designed by Palladio (1556), a road lined with a delightful Gothic portico (1487) and steep steps climbs up the castle hill. The 13C church of **Santa Maria di Castello** (unlocked on request at the museum; often used for weddings at weekends) has been beautifully restored after the 1976 earthquake. The campanile dates from 1540. It has fine 13C frescoes and a seated wooden statue of the *Madonna*. Next to the church is the 15C **Casa della Confraternità**, restored in 1929. The summit of the hill has a green with two wells, from which there is a fine view stretching as far as the Alps on a clear day. The **Casa della Contadinanza**, with a double loggia, was reconstructed in the 20C.

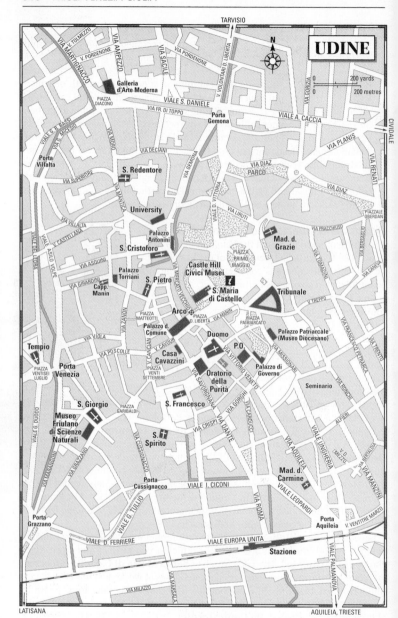

UDINE

N

| 0 | | 200 yards |
| 0 | | 200 metres |

TARVISIO

LATISANA

AQUILEIA, TRIESTE

CIVIDALE

VIA V. TOLMEZZO
VIA MARTIGNACCO
V. PORDENONE
VIA AMPEZZO
VIA SACILE
VIA PORDENONE
VIA VOLONTARI D. LIBERTÀ
VIA GORIZIA
VIA A. CACCIA

Galleria
d'Arte Moderna
PIAZZA
DIACONO
VIALE S. DANIELE
VIA FR. DI TOPPO
Porta
Gemona
VIA DÉCIANI
VIA PLANIS
VIA RENATI

VIALE G. B. BASSI
VIA S. MIGESIO
VIA MORO
VIA GEMONA

Porta
Villalta
VIA SUPERIORE
S. Redentore
VIA D. VITTORIA
VIA DIAZ
PARCO
VIA DIAZ
PIAZZALE
OBERDAN

VIA AMATICA
VIA LIRUTI
VIA PRACCHIUSO

University
VIA VILLALTA
V. CASTELLANA
Palazzo
Antonini
PIAZZA
PRIMO
MAGGIO
Mad. d.
Grazie

VIA ASQUINI
S. Cristoforo
VIA MERCATO VECCHIO
VIA TOMADINI
VIA CANEVA

VIA GIRARDINI
Palazzo
Torriani
Castle Hill
Civici Musei
i
Tribunale

Capp.
Manin
S. Pietro
S. Maria
di Castello
V. TREPPO

VIA DEL TORRE
VIA ASILO V. VOLPE
VIA ZANON
Arco
PIAZZA
MATTEOTTI
PIAZZA
D. LIBERTÀ
VIA MANIN
PIAZZA
PATRIARCATO

Tempio
PIAZZA
VENTISEI
LUGLIO
VIA VIOLA
V. CANCIANI
Palazzo d.
Comune
Duomo
P.O.
Palazzo Patriarcale
(Museo Diocesano)
VIA FRANCESCO PETRARCA

Porta
Venezia
VIA POSCOLLE
V. CAVOUR
Casa
Cavazzini
VIA VITTORIO VENETO
Palazzo di
Governo
VIA MISSIONARI
VIA TRENTI

PIAZZA
VENTI
SETTEMBRE
Oratorio
della
Purità
Seminario
VIA RONCHI

S. Giorgio
PIAZZA
GARIBALDI
S. Francesco
VIA SAVORGNANA
VIA GORGHI
VIA CARDUCCI
ALFIERI
VIALE UNGHERIA

Museo
Friulano
di Scienze
Naturali
VIA CUSSIGNACCO
S.
Spirito
VIA CRISPI
VIA DANTE
V. O.
I. MEZZO
VIA MANZINI

VIA MANGONI
VIA GRAZZANO
Porta
Cussignacco
VIALE I. CICONI
Mad. d.
Carmine
VIALE LEOPARDI

Porta
Grazzano
VIALE G. TULLIO
VIA ROMA
Porta
Aquileia
V. VENTITRE MARZO
VIALE PALMANOVA

VIALE D. FERRIERE
VIALE EUROPA UNITA
Stazione

VIA MILAZZO
VIA MARSALA

The **castle**, built over the ruins of the castle of the patriarchs of Aquileia, was begun in 1517 to a design by Giovanni da Udine, a pupil of Raphael. Today it is home to the **Civici Musei e Gallerie di Storia e Arte** (open Tues–Sat 09.30–12.30, 15.00–18.00, Sun and holidays 09.30–12.00), a complex of several museums and galleries.

The **Galleria d'Arte Antica** has Italian paintings ranging from the late Middle Ages to the 19C, including several works by Tiepolo (*Strength and Wisdom*, *Consilium in Arena*). Particularly interesting are the 14C Friulan primitives, the 15C Scuola Tolmezzina, and the paintings by Vittore Carpaccio (*Christ and the Instruments of the Passion*), Giovanni Antonio da Pordenone (*Madonna della Loggia; Eternal Father*), Palma Giovane (*St Mark Placing Udine under the Protection of St Ermacora*), Caravaggio (*St Francis Receiving the Stigmata*), Luca Carlevaris (*Plan of the City of Udine*), and Marco and Sebastiano Ricci (*Landscape*).

The **Museo Archeologico** presents material assembled over the past 200 years from sites in Udine and its environs, notably finds from the Mesolithic to the Iron Age from Cassacco, from Sammardenchia and from excavations in Via del Mercato Vecchio and on the castle hill in Udine; Roman-age material from excavations in town, from Aquileia and from Sevegliano; Lombard weapons; and local and imported ceramics and glass from the Middle Ages and the Renaissance. There are also extensive collections of coins (50,000 pieces, some very rare, of Roman, Byzantine, barbarian and medieval origin, including the fabulous Collezione Colloredo Mels); Roman ambers, precious stones, glass, perfume vases and gold from Aquileia; and cut gems from the Roman age and the 18C and 19C.

The **Gabinetto dei Disegni e delle Stampe** exhibits, on a rotating basis, a selection from the enormous collection (c 10,000 pieces) of works by Fiulan and Venetian printmakers and Italian and foreign old masters. The first-floor Salone del Parlamento hosts Tiepolo's *Triumph of the Christians over the Turks* and other fine paintings.

Around the duomo

The **Duomo**, located one block south-east of Piazza della Libertà, preserves its original 14C Gothic appearance, particularly in the fine central doorway with its carved lunette, deep splays and sharp cusp, and in the other great doorway on the north flank, by the campanile (1390). A third, Renaissance doorway graces the south flank. The unfinished campanile was begun in the 15C over an octagonal baptistery built a hundred years earlier.

The three-aisled **interior** has paintings by Tiepolo on the south side (*Trinità* in the first chapel; *Sts Hermagoras and Fortunatus* in the second; *Resurrection* and frescoes in the fourth). The stuccoed Baroque complex of the sanctuary and crossing is preceded by two organs with painted parapets; its spectacular tone is maintained by the large marble high altar with statues (1717) and, at the ends of the arms of the transept, the two colossal Manin tombs (18C). The two side altars have dossals attributed to Andrea Brustolon. The vault is frescoed by Lodovico Dorigny, who also decorated the choir with paintings and frescoes. The 18C sacristy contains paintings by Giovanni Antonio da Pordenone, Franz Hals and Giovanni Battista Tiepolo.

A door on the left leads to the **Museo del Duomo**, which includes the 14C

Cappella di San Nicolò, frescoed with episodes from the *Life of St Nicholas* by Vitale da Bologna in 1348-49; panel paintings by the Maestro dei Padiglioni, his pupil; and the old baptistery, beneath the campanile, with a beautiful vaulted ceiling and the sarcophagus of Beato Bertrando, with fine reliefs of the Lombard-Venetian school (1343).

The 18C **Oratorio della Purità**, across the square from the south flank of the cathedral, has an altarpiece and ceiling painting by Giovanni Battista Tiepolo and chiaroscuro mural paintings by his son, Gian Domenico. The cathedral sacristan will open it for you.

Via Lovaria leads east from the cathedral square to **Palazzo Patriarcale**, reconstructed in the early 18C by Domenico Rossi and Giorgio Massari and decorated in 1726 by Giovanni Battista Tiepolo. Since 1995 it has housed the **Museo Diocesano e Gallerie del Tiepolo** (open Wed–Sun 10.00–12.00, 15.30–18.30). On the first floor is an interesting collection of 13C–18C wood sculpture from churches in Friuli, arranged chronologically. A pretty spiral staircase, with a fresco by Nicolò Bambini, leads up to the second floor, or piano nobile, with splendid *frescoes carried out in 1726 by Giovanni Battista Tiepolo for the patriarch Dionisio Delfino. Beyond the blue room, with ceiling frescoes by Giovanni da Udine, the red room contains the *Judgement of Solomon* and four *Prophets* in the lunettes by Giovanni Battista Tiepolo. The *galleria* is entirely frescoed with delightful Old Testament scenes (the stories of Abraham, Isaac and Jacob) by Tiepolo, using remarkable pastel colours. On the stairs is another splendid fresco by him of the *Fall of the Rebel Angels*.

Elsewhere around town

A good place to stop for coffee is the historic *Caffè Contarena*, with Liberty décor and furniture (1925), beneath the portico on Via Cavour, directly behind the Loggia del Lionello. The building, the monumental **Palazzo degli Uffici Municipali**, was designed by Raimondo D'Aronco, in an eclectic Liberty style, in 1911. One block north of Via Cavour is the elegant Via Rialto, today reserved for pedestrians, which runs along what was once the main axis of the medieval *Villa Udin*.

Turning right at the end of the street, you soon come to **Piazza Matteotti** (Piazza San Giacomo for the *udinesi*), perhaps the oldest of the city's squares, with low porticoes on columns and a fountain by Giovanni da Udine (1542). On the west side stands the 14C church of **San Giacomo**, with a lively Lombardesque façade designed by Bernardino da Morcote in the early 16C, and 17C and 18C paintings inside. One block further west (reached by a passageway next to the church) Via Zanon, flanked by one of the characteristic little canals the *udinesi* call *rogge*, is lined with fine palaces mostly of the 18C; at the corner of Via dei Torriani is the **Torre di Santa Maria**, a remnant of the 13C town wall. Behind the tower and beyond the austere façade of Palazzo Torriani (no. 4) is the 18C **Cappella Manin**, a gem of Baroque architecture, whose hexagonal interior has fine sculptures and high reliefs by G. Torretti.

On the northwest corner of Piazza della Libertà begins the handsome **Via Mercatovecchio**, the traditional site of the evening promenade. The city's first marketplace, it is still the main shopping street. Broad and slightly curved, it is flanked by porticoed buildings, notably the monumental **Monte di Pietà**, today a bank, with a façade of 1690 and a chapel, at the centre, with fine wrought-iron work and frescoes by Giulio Quaglio (1694). Continuing north you come to the **Palazzo Antonini** (Via Gemona 3), today the Banca d'Italia, built after 1570 to plans by Palladio. Almost opposite, to the northwest, is the 17C Palazzo Antonini-Cernazai, now occupied by the University Faculty of Languages.

At the northern edge of the city centre stands the **Galleria d'Arte Moderna** (open Tues–Sat 09.30–12.30, 15.00-18.00, Sun and holidays 09.30–12.00), where the holdings focus on Italian artists of the 20C. On the **first floor** are a section devoted to modern and contemporary architecture (including some original drawings by Raimondo D'Aronco); works by the well-known Italian modernists Arturo Martini, Mario Mafai and Felice Casorati; and a small collection of American art of the seventies, notably by Willem De Kooning. The **ground floor** is mainly devoted to the *Astaldi Collection of modern masters, with works by Gino Severini, Giorgio De Chirico, Savinio, Mario Sironi, Giorgio Morandi, Massimo Campigli, Ottone Rosai, Fausto Pirandello and Carlo Carrà.

Behind the Municipio in Piazza Libertà, Via Savorgnana leads south. At no. 5 is the **Casa Cavazzini**, left to the municipality by Dante Cavazzini, with an apartment on the first floor containing murals (1939) by Corrado Cagli and Afro. The large building is to be restored, and the Astaldi collection of modern art, at present displayed in Piazzale Diacono (see below), may be moved here. Further south, in Piazza Venerio, the church of **San Francesco** has been restored to its 13C appearance for use as an auditorium. To the southwest, beyond Piazza Garibaldi, in Palazzo Giacomelli in Via Grazzano, is the **Museo Friulano di Scienze Naturali** (open Tues–Sat 09.00–12.00, 15.00–18.00 or 16.00–19.00; Sun 09.00–12.00), with an important natural history collection.

In Via Vittorio Veneto, which leads south from Piazza Libertà, is **Palazzo Tinghi** (no. 38), first built in 1392 with a wide ground-floor portico. The façade of 1532 has very faded frescoes by Pordenone.

Cividale del Friuli

This pleasant town stands on the banks of the River Natisone, on a site that once marked the meeting-point of Venetic and Celtic cultures. Founded as *Forum Julii*, probably by Julius Caesar, the town gave its name to the Friuli. It became a municipium in the Augustan age, an episcopal seat in the 5C, and an important fortress under the Lombards. In the 8C its name was changed to Civitas Austriae and it became the seat of the patriarch of Aquileia, a position it retained until 1031.

Exploring the town

From the station and the main road from Udine, Viale Libertà leads east to Corso Alberto, which continues south to the pleasant large Piazza Diacono, scene of a daily market, with an old-fashioned café and a house traditionally taken to be on the site of the birthplace of Paul the Deacon (Warnefride; 723–799), historian of the Lombards. The fountain is surmounted by an 18C statue of Diana. **Corso Mazzini**, the main street of the town, leads past **Palazzo Levrini-Stringher**, with remains of 16C frescoes on its façade, to the cathedral square.

Piazza del Duomo stands on the site of the ancient Roman forum, enclosed on one side by the north flank of the **Cathedral**. The church was begun in 1457 in the Venetian Gothic style to plans by Bartolomeo delle Cisterne, but it was rebuilt in the 16C in Renaissance forms by Pietro and Tullio Lombardo, whose design is particularly evident in the interior. It has a simple stone facade with three pointed Gothic doorways (the central one is a work of Jacopo Veneziano, 1465), and is flanked by a Baroque campanile. In the north apsidal chapel are a *Last Supper and Martyrdom of St Stephen* by Palma Giovane. Above the high altar is the gilt-silver *Altarpiece of Patriarch Pellegrino II* (1195–1204), a masterpiece of medieval silversmithing showing the Virgin in the company of Gabriel, Michael, saints, prophets and the patron himself.

The third south bay gives access to the **Museo Cristiano** (entered also from behind the bell tower on Sun; open daily 09.00 or 09.30–12.00, 15.00–18.00 or 19.00), where exhibits include the octagonal aedicule of the 8C *baptistery; the beautiful *altar carved for Ratchis, Duke of Cividale and King of the Lombards (also from the 8C); a marble patriarchal throne of the 11C (the feet were added in the 17C); fragments of a 7C–8C balustrade and ciborium; and detached frescoes from the Tempietto Lombardo (described below).

Facing the cathedral and preceded by a copy of the statue of Julius Caesar in the Campidoglio in Rome, is the 14C **Palazzo Comunale**, with the pointed arches and mullioned windows typical of Gothic public buildings. At the end of the square stands the **Palazzo dei Provveditori Veneti**, built to a design by Andrea Palladio in 1581–96. Inside is the **Museo Archeologico Nazionale** (open Tues–Sat, summer 09.30–19.00; winter 09.30–14.00), with very important collections of prehistoric, Roman and medieval archaeology, jewellery and miniatures.

The best displays on the **ground floor** are the Roman, Byzantine and medieval inscriptions, reliefs and architectural elements; and the fragments of Roman and early Christian mosaic pavements, including a representation of a marine deity (1C–2C AD). The extraordinary *Lombard holdings*, from necropoleis near Cividale and throughout the Friuli, are displayed on the **first floor**. Highlights include the material found in a knight's tomb at Cella (early 7C) including a gold leaf disk showing a mounted knight; a sarcophagus (mid-7C) with its contents, including a fine cross, a signet ring, an enamelled gold fibula, a glass bottle and a tiny *box with polychrome enamels in the shape of a bird; the contents of a warrior's tomb, including his arms, gold and silver ornaments, and ivory chessmen; goldsmiths' work (*Pax of Duke Orso*, with a relief of the Crucifixion in a jewelled silver frame, and *Croce di Invillino*, both from the 8C–9C); weapons, tools and utensils. Also noteworthy are the 8C *Psalter of St Elisabeth of Hungary* with Saxon miniatures, and the late-13C *Veil of Beata Benvenuta Boiani*, embroidered with religious scenes.

Stairs lead up to the **upper floor**, where finds from recent excavations are displayed, including very fine glass (1C–2C AD), and a hoard of 15C ceramics. Stairs from the ground floor lead down to the **basement**, where walkways provide a view of excavations showing various levels from the late-Roman period (3C AD) to the 16C.

A passage on the south side of the museum leads into **Via Monastero Maggiore**, once the main street of the town and attractively paved with cobblestones. This winds through the medieval quarter, passing beneath two gates to reach Cividale's most unusual monument, the Tempietto Longobardo (or Oratorio di Santa Maria in Valle; entrace in Piazzetta San Biagio, open daily 10.00–13.00, 15.30–17.30 or 18.30). Situated on a cliff above the Natisone and reached by a raised walkway above the river, this is one of the more interesting and evocative early-medieval sacred buildings in Italy. Thought to date from the mid-8C, and

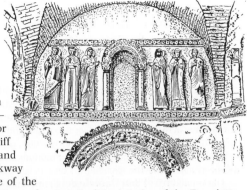

Detail of the interior of the Tempietto Longobardo

damaged over the centuries by earthquakes, it is in a peaceful corner of the town from which only the sound of the river can be heard. The present entrance is through the presbytery of the little church, with an iconostasis consisting of a marble screen and two very unusual columns (5C–6C) beneath three small barrel vaults, the central one of which has 14C frescoes. The beautifully carved stalls also date from the 14C.

The little quadrangular nave preserves remarkable *stucco decoration on the end wall (formerly the entrance wall) with the monumental figures of six female saints and beautifully carved friezes, thought to be by the hand of an artist from the east and contemporary with the building (c 760). The two side walls would have had similar decorations. Fragments of the original frescoes also survive.

Across the square from the Tempietto is the small 15C church of **San Biagio**, with remains of contemporaneous frescoes on its façade and inside. In a private garden at Via Monastero Maggiore 2 is the **Ipogeo Celtico** (key at *Bar Al Ponte*, Corso Aquileia, ☎ 0431 700572), a system of tunnels cut in the rock on the bank of the Natisone, believed to have been the burial place of Celtic chieftans of the 5C–2C BC.

From the cathedral square Corso Ponte d'Aquilea leads down to the **Ponte del Diavolo**, the 'devil's bridge' built to join the high rocky banks of the Natisone in the mid-15C and destroyed and rebuilt during the First World War. The views are extraordinary. On the left bank a flight of steps leads down from the parapet to the river. There is a good view of the bridge from near the church of San Martino.

From Piazza Paolo Diacono (see above), Via Ristori leads to Piazza Diaz where the **theatre**, first built in 1815, is named after the tragedienne Adelaide Ristori (1821–1906), born here, who is also commemorated by a monument in Foro Giulio Cesare. In Piazzetta Terme Romane scant remains of **Roman baths** can be seen below the level of the pavement. Beyond **Porta San Pietro** (used by the Venetians as a store) is the church of **San Pietro**, with a good altarpiece by Palma Giovane.

The Natisone Valley, northeast of Cividale, is Slovene-speaking in its upper reaches. Across the Slovenian border, 30km from Cividale, is Caporetto, memorable for the disaster inflicted on the Italian armies in October 1917.

North of Udine

The road, railway and motorway for Austria lead north from Udine through an area that was the epicentre of an earthquake in May and September 1976. The communes of Gemona, Tarcento, San Daniele, Maiano and many others were devastated. Earth tremors continued for two years, and the final toll was nearly 1000 dead and over 70,000 homeless. Reconstruction, where possible, has now been all but completed, and the most spectacular monument to the skill and determination of the local people is the splendidly reconstructed little town of Venzone.

The small town of **San Daniele del Friuli**, famous for cured ham (celebrated with a festival at the end of August), has been largely rebuilt at the foot of its hill. The former church of Sant'Antonio Abate has *frescoes (1487–1522) by Pellegrino da San Daniele. The duomo was designed by Domenico Rossi (1725). The Guarneriana Library, founded here in the 15C, has some precious incunabula and illuminated manuscripts. There is also a Museo Civico.

Gemona was devastated by the 1976 earthquake, in which over 300 people lost their lives. It has been rebuilt with colourful new buildings and a modern railway station in the plain below (from which it is a 30mins walk uphill to the centre), but it has lost some of its atmosphere since reconstruction.

The fine Romanesque and Gothic *Cathedral has been carefully restored. Its tall 14C campanile had to be entirely reconstructed (the original stones were recovered and reused). The **façade** (redesigned in 1825) bears an inscription (above and to the left of the door) dated 1290 with the name of the architect and sculptor 'Magister Johannes', in charge of work on the building and responsible for the portal. There is a gallery with niches, and statues representing the Epiphany (c 1350) include the delightful seated statues of the weary Magi and a groom holding their three horses. The colossal statue (7m high) of St Christopher dates from 1332, and the superb rose window from 1334.

In the beautiful **interior** the pilasters have been strengthened but left leaning out of line. The choir arch and dome over the sanctuary are particularly beautiful. The 12C font incorporates a Roman altar of the 1C or 2C AD with a delightful relief of a dolphin ridden by a putto. Beneath the sacristy is the shrine of St Michael with 14C frescoes. The church owns a rich treasury including a superb 15C *monstrance made by Nicolò Lionello and eight illuminated choir books (late 13C and early 14C).

The tiny medieval town of *Venzone, nestled on the Tagliamento and enclosed by high hills, was first documented in 1001. It became a free commune in 1381 and part of the Venetian Republic in 1420. It has been exquisitely reconstructed after it was reduced to rubble by the 1976 earthquake. The stones of its monuments were numbered and reused, and its *genius loci* remains. Local limestone and sandstone have been used to pave the streets. The town is surrounded in part by medieval walls. The railway station is 5mins walk from Porta di Sotto (1835), on the site of the 14C town gate. The beautiful *Duomo, consecrated in

1338, was carefully reconstructed in 1988–95. Partly Romanesque and partly Gothic, it appears to have been designed by Magister Johannes, who was also responsible for the sculptural details (inscription with the date 1308 above the north door) and who also worked on the cathedral of Gemona. Above the main door is a bas-relief of the *Crucifixion*, a fine work of the mid-14C. Between two bell towers (one never completed) at the east end is the lovely apse in the Cistercian style. In the beautiful interior is a 14C fresco by the school of Vitale da Bologna showing the consecration of the duomo. Only fragments now remain of the early 15C frescoes in the Cappella del Gonfalone.

In the pretty piazza with a 19C fountain is the Gothic **Palazzo Comunale** (also entirely reconstructed), which dates from 1410. The church of **San Giovanni Battista** has been left as a ruin. The **Torre di Porta San Genesio** is inserted in the 13C double walls (well seen from here, defended by a moat).

Northeast of Venzone is **Tarvisia**, the Valle di Dogna, dominated by the Iôf di Montasio (2754m), the highest peak in a forested area of c 40,000h, a protected park which extends north to the Austrian border and east to the Slovenian border. The Valcanale is a Slovene-speaking region. **Tarvisio** is a ski resort close to the Austrian frontier.

Carnia

Tolmezzo is the chief centre of Carnia. It has a museum of local handicrafts (open Tues–Sun 09.00–12.00, 14.00–18.00). To the west are summer resorts in the Carnic Alps. Nearby is the village of **Zuglio**, the ancient *Iulium Carnicum*, which guarded the Roman road (the Via Iulia Augusta) from Aquileia over the Monte Croce pass. A fortified settlement established here in 50 BC became a Roman colony in the following century. It was important throughout the imperial period and was the seat of a bishop up to the 8C. Excavations were carried out here in the early 19C and in the 1930s: the Roman forum and its basilica, as well as an early-Christian basilica with mosaics, have been exposed. An archaeological museum contains finds from the site. The little church of San Pietro di Carnia is the oldest in the district (possibly 14C).

West of Udine

On the main road between Udine and Pordenone is **Codroipo**, which was the Roman *Quadrivium*, on the Via Postumia. Nearby is **Passariano** with the vast Villa Manin (altered c 1650, perhaps by Giuseppe Benoni, and later by Domenico Rossi). It belonged to Lodovico Manin, last of the Venetian doges. It was restored by the Region and is now a cultural centre and the seat of a restoration school. The interior (open Tues–Sun 09.00–12.30, 15.00–18.00; winter 09.00–12.00, 14.00–17.00) has frescoes by Lodovico Dorigny and Amigoni, a chapel with sculptures by Giuseppe Torretti, a carriage museum and an armoury. The fine **park**, the most important in the region, first laid out in the 18C, is open Easter–Oct at weekends. The villa was occupied by Napoleon in 1797 when he concluded the shameful treaty of Campo Formio, which sacrificed Venice to Austria. The village after which it is named is now called **Campoformido** and is a few kilometres west of Udine.

South of Udine

The area between Udine and Trieste holds little of interest, with the notable exception of **Palmanova**, a marvellously preserved, star-shaped town built in 1593 to defend the eastern frontier of the Venetian Republic. It is one of the few brick-and-mortar examples of that order and symmetry which Renaissance culture considered a fundamental feature of the ideal city. Its centre is the hexagonal Piazza Grande, dominated by the **Cathedral**, whose design has been attributed to Vincenzo Scamozzi. From this hub six streets radiate in a spoke-like pattern, three leading to the city's monumental gates. The town itself is most interesting for its 16C ambience, but there are also two small musems, the **Civico Museo Storico** (Borgo Udine 4), with weapons, documents and memorabilia ranging from the foundation of the city to the First World War; and the **Museo Storico Militare** (in Borgo Cividale, next to the gate), with military uniforms from 1593 to the Second World War. Guided tours of the fortifications (in Italian) are led from the latter.

The Adriatic coast

Although flat, the Adriatic seaboard east of Venice is anything but dull. The marshy lowlands of the coast, in addition to their inherent beauty, are a favourite stopping place of migratory birds. Aquileia is known far and wide for its late-Roman and early-Christian remains, and each of the other cities—beginning with neighbouring Grado—has some notable antiquity. Last but not least, the beach resorts, with their broad sandy beaches and shallow waters, are among the country's most popular—especially with families.

Practical information

Getting there and getting around
By air

The regional airport serving Friuli-Venezia Giulia is located at Ronchi dei Legionari, 15km northeast of Aquileia, 81km southeast of Pordenone. There are daily flights to domestic and European destinations; coaches connect with the airport terminal at the Trieste railway station (journey time: 60mins).

By road

The A4 runs from Venice to Trieste, not far from the Adriatic shore. Near Portogruaro it meets the A28, which runs norhwest to Pordenone. At Cervignano 352 diverges southwards to Aquileia and Grado. Spilimbergo and the valley of the Tagliamento are reached by 251, 13, 403 and local roads. **Bus services** run from Gorizia to Aquileia and from Pordenone to points throughout the province (information from *ATAP*, ☎ 0434 522526, and *Giordani*, ☎ 0434 520821). **Car parking** in Pordenone, Via Coda Fora (beyond the town hall).

By rail

There is a direct rail service from Venice to Pordenone, continuing on to Udine,

Vienna and Prague; fast *Intercity* trains make the Venice–Pordenone run in c 1hr. Branch lines run from Pordenone via Casarsa to Portogruaro, and via Sacile to Gemona. Buses meet trains at Cervignano for Aquileia and Grado.

Information offices

AQUILEIA Piazza Capitolo, ☎ 0431 91087 (summer only).
GRADO Viale Dante Alighieri 72, ☎ 0431 899220.
PORDENONE Corso Vittorio Emanuele 38, ☎ 0434 21912. *Informagiovani*, Piazzetta San Marco, ☎ 0434 392535.

Where to stay

FIUME VENETO (BANNIA) *L'Ultimo Mulino*, Via Molino 45, ☎ 0434 957911, fax 0434 958483; small (7 rooms) and quaint, occupying an ancient mill; moderate.
PASIANO DI PORDENONE (RIVAROTTA) *Villa Lupis*, Via San Martino 34, ☎ 0434 626969, fax 0434 626228; somewhat larger (21 rooms) but equally charming, in a former Benedictine monastery with park and pool; moderate.
PORDENONE *Park*, Via Mazzini 43, ☎ 0434 27901, fax 0434 522353; simple, comfortable, centrally located; moderate. *Villa Ottoboni*, Piazzetta Ottoboni 2, ☎ 0434 208891, fax 0434 208148; elegant and refined, occupying a 16C villa and the adjacent building; moderate.
PORTOBUFFOLE *Villa Giustinian*, Via Giustiniani 11, ☎ 0422 850244, fax 0422 850260; an 18C Venetian villa with gardens; moderate.
Youth hostel: San Vito al Tagliamento, ☎ 0434 842910.

Eating out

ANDREIS (Ponte Molassa, 35km north of Pordenone). *La Molassa*, ☎ 0427 76147; old-fashioned osteria offering fresh local ingredients and great wines; closed Tues and Nov–Easter; inexpensive.
AQUILEIA *La Colombara*, Località la Colombara (on the road to Grado), ☎ 0431 91513; restaurant specialising in seafood, accompanied by regional and Italian wines; closed Mon and Jan; inexpensive.
CAVASSO NUOVO (32km northeast of Pordenone) *Ai Cacciatori*, Via Diaz 4, ☎ 0427 777800; good regional food, wines and views; closed Mon evening and Tues (except in summer); moderate.
GRADO *Tavernetta all'Androna*, Calle Porta Piccola 4, ☎ 0431 80950; traditional dishes prepared with an innovative twist; closed Tues and Dec–Feb; moderate.
PORDENONE *Veccia Osteria del Moro*, Via Castello 2, ☎ 0434 28658; centrally located, in a renovated 14C convent, and renowned throughout the region for its excellent traditional fare (try the *s'ciosi*, snails); closed Sun (and Sat in summer), Jan and Aug; moderate.
CORDENONS (5km east of Pordenone), *Al Curtif*, Via del Cristo 3, ☎ 0434 931038; in an old farmhouse, around a stone court (*curtif* in dialect); closed Mon evening, Tues and Aug; inexpensive.
SAN QUIRINO (9km northeast of Pordenone), *Alle Nazioni*, Via San Rocco 47, ☎ 0434 91005; a more accessible version (under the same management) of *La Primula*; closed Mon (and Sun evening in summer), Jan and Aug; inexpensive.
La Primula, Via San Rocco 47, ☎ 0434 91005; traditional restaurant (with rooms) known for its delicious regional dishes, especially pork; closed Sun evening, Mon, Jan and Jul; moderate.
SPILIMBERGO *Da Afro*, Via Umberto I 14, ☎ 0427 2264; friendly, old-fashioned osteria; closed Tues and Jan; moderate.
La Torre, in the castle, ☎ 0427 50555; traditional restaurant serving good local specialities; closed Sun evening and Mon; moderate.

Entertainment

PORDENONE Theatre and music at *Teatro Auditorium Provinciale Corncordia*.

Shopping

The most distinctive local products are *Grave del Friuli* wines and Pordenone knives. Mosaics are made at Spilimbergo. There is a market in Pordenone (Piazza della Motta) Wed and Sat.

Special events

PORDENONE *Festa della Città*, patron saint's day celebration, with award of the Premi San Marco for distinction in economics, social work and culture, 25 Apr. *Estate in Città*, theatre, music and cinema, summer. *Giostra del Castello*, 15C tournament in costume, Sep. *Le Giornate del Cinema Muto*, annual silent-film festival, Oct. *Incontriamoci a Pordenone*, music and theatre in streets and squares, Oct. *Natale Pordenonese con Presepe Subacqueo*—yes, an underwater Christmas crêche, 24 Dec.
POLCENIGO *Sagra dei Sést*, annual basket fair, Sep.
ROVEREDO IN PIANO *Gioco dei Pindoi*, re-enactment of a medieval game played with stones, last Sun in Aug.

SACILE *Sagra dei Osei*, annual game fair held on 16 Aug since 1274.
SESTO AL REGHENA *Estate Musicale*, music and theatre in a medieval abbey, summer. *Presepe Vivente*, over 100 players form a living Christmas creche, 24 and 26 Dec.
SPILIMBERGO *Spilimbergo Fotografia*, international photography exhibition, Sep.
VALVASONE *Concerti di Musica Antica*, organ music concerts in the cathedral, Sep.
ELSEWHERE *Carnival* celebrations and patron saints' feast days with processions and festivities throughout the area. *Cantine Aperte*, presentation and tasting of new wines on estates throughout the region, May. *Folkfest*, international ethnic music festival, at sites throughout the region, Jul. *Estate a Teatro*, theatre in towns around Pordenone, summer.

Sports

Golf at Castello d'Aviano (*Golf Club Aviano*). **Skiing** and **ice hockey** at Piancavallo (Aviano). **Swimming and water sports** at Grado and other beach resorts.

AQUILEIA

Aquileia preserves magnificent and evocative remains of its great days, both as a Roman city and as an early medieval capital, including some splendid mosaics. One of the last colonies founded by the Romans as a military outpost, it became an important city, and its population is thought to have reached between 70,000 and 100,000 by the end of the Roman empire. It is is now a village of some 3000 souls, in a fertile plain. There are still large areas of the Roman city being excavated.

History

Aquileia was founded as a Roman colony in 181 BC and quickly grew to be the fourth largest city in Italy, capital of one of the Augustan Regions—the ancient equivalent of an English county or an American state. And it is no wonder, for this affluent market town was the departure point for the roads over the Alps to the Danube basin. In 10 BC Augustus was in residence here and received Herod the Great. The 'Emperor' Maximinus was murdered by his troops while besieging the city in 238 AD, and in 340 Constantine II was killed on the banks of the Aussa (a little to the west) by his brother Constans in their struggle for imperial power. The bishopric or patriarchate was founded soon after 313, but civil wars and barbarian incursions, culminating in the Lombard sack of 568, led to the transference of the see to Grado, which had become the foreport of Aquileia. There were two rival patriarchs after 606, but in 1019 the patriarch Poppo united the sees and rebuilt the basilica, and the town had a second period of splendour that lasted up to the 14C. In the following centuries its importance declined because of malaria. The civil power passed to Venice in 1420, and in 1509 Aquileia was seized by the Austrians. The patriarchate was merged in the archbishoprics of Udine and Gorizia in 1751.

The Basilica

The approach road follows the line of the Roman *cardo*. There are car parks off the main road and by the *Basilica. This great church (open daily, summer 08.30–19.00; winter 08.30–12.30, 14.30–17.30), built soon after 313 by the first patriarch Theodore, was the scene of a historic council in 381, attended by Sts Ambrose and Jerome. It was extended soon afterwards and was reconstructed in its present form by the patriarch Poppo in 1021–31.

A portico, probably dating from the beginning of the 9C, extends from the west front to the Chiesa dei Pagani, a rectangular 9C hall for catechumens (Christian converts under instruction) with remains of 13C frescoes (now used as a shop), and to the much-altered remnants of the 5C **baptistery**. Beneath the font, an earlier octagonal font was discovered in 1982 above part of a Roman house. The tall leaning **campanile** (73m) was built by Poppo; the upper part dates from the 14C, the bell-chamber and steeple from the 16C. On a Roman column facing it is a figure of the Capitoline Wolf, presented by Rome in 1919.

The spacious **interior** is built to a Latin-cross plan. The arcades surmounting the fine Romanesque capitals date from the patriarchate of Markward (1365–81), the nave ceiling from 1526. The huge colourful mosaic *pavement (700sq m), discovered at the beginning of the 20C, dates from Theodore's basilica. It is the largest antique mosaic pavement known and one of the more remarkable early Christian monuments in Italy. Its iconographic programme combines Christian images (like the Good Shepherd, fish, and birds in trees) with pagan symbols such as the cock fighting the tortoise, the seasons, and a winged figure of Victory holding a crown and palm branch. Other panels contain the portrait heads of donors and numerous animals and birds, including two waders catching a serpent and frog. At the east end is one large mosaic representing the sea filled with a great variety of fish, with 12 putti fishing from boats and rocks. The story of Jonah is illustrated here in three scenes: the prophet is thrown from a boat into a sea monster's mouth (the praying figure in the boat probably represents him before his martyrdom); the prophet is regurgitated safely on shore by the monster; and Jonah rests after his adventures beneath a pergola. In the centre of the sea is a circular inscription recording Theodore.

In the south aisle is the Gothic chapel of St Ambrose, built by the Torriani in

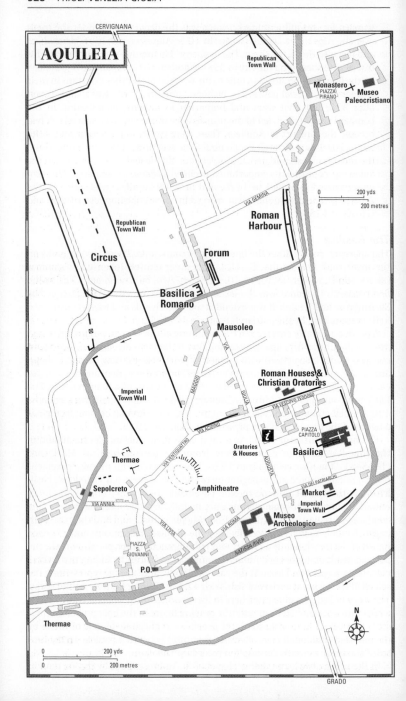

CERVIGNANA

AQUILEIA

Republican
Town Wall

Monastero
PIAZZA
PIRANO
**Museo
Paleocristiano**

VIA GEMINA

**Roman
Harbour**

Republican
Town Wall

0   200 yds
0   200 metres

Circus

Forum

**Basilica
Romano**

Mausoleo

**Roman Houses &
Christian Oratories**

VIA VESCOVO TEODORO

Imperial
Town Wall

PIAZZA
CAPITOLO

MAGGIO

GIULIA

VIA AQUINO

VIA VENTIQUATTRO

Oratories
& Houses

Basilica

AUGUSTA

Thermae

Amphitheatre

Sepolcreto

VIA ANNIA

VIA DEI PATRIARCHI

Market

Imperial
Town Wall

VIA LIVIA

VIA ROMA

**Museo
Archeologico**

PIAZZA
S.
GIOVANNI

NATISSA RIVER

P.O.

Thermae

N

0   200 yds
0   200 metres

GRADO

1298, with family tombs and a polyptych by Pellegrino da San Daniele (1503) in a fine frame. The chapel on the right of the presbytery has a 9C–10C transenna, and frescoes. To the left of the chapel is the sarcophagus of the canonised Pope Mark (14C, Venetian Gothic), and in front of the tomb is a fragment of 5C mosaic pavement (discovered in 1972).

In the presbytery, the central Renaissance tribune and the altar to the right of it, with a *Pietà*, are the work of Bernardino da Bissone. The high altar was carved by Sebastiano and Antonio da Osteno (1498). In Poppo's apse are faded frescoes, with a dedicatory inscription (1031), showing the patriarch (with a model of the church), Emperor Conrad II with Gisela of Swabia, and Prince Henry (later Henry III) before the Madonna and six patron saints. The bishop's throne is probably somewhat earlier. In the chapel to the left of the presbytery are interesting frescoes and (north wall) a bas-relief with Christ between St Peter and St Thomas Becket, sculptured soon after St Thomas's martyrdom at Canterbury in 1170. Outside the chapel is a bust of *Christ* (1916) by Edmondo Furlan. In the north aisle is the **Santo Sepolcro**, an 11C reproduction of the Holy Sepulchre at Jerusalem.

The **Cripta degli Affreschi** (the ticket includes admission to the Cripta degli Scavi), beneath the presbytery, has frescoes of great interest, thought to date from around 1180. They depict scenes from the life of Christ (including a fine *Deposition*) and from that of the Virgin Mary, and scenes relating to Sts Hermagoras and Fortunatus.

The **Cripta degli Scavi** is entered from beside the Santo Sepolcro. It is remarkable for three levels of *mosaics: those of a Roman house of the Augustan period (to the left on entering); the magnificent floor of a second basilica of the time of Theodore, encircling the foundations of Poppo's campanile; and parts of the floor of the late 4C basilica, as well as its column-bases.

The **Museo del Patriarcato**, opposite the Basilica at 7 Via Patriarca Popone, merits a visit if you are interested in learning more about the patriarchate of Aquileia. Unfortunately, it is open only for special events. Highlights include a 14C reliquary bust of *Santa Ermacora*; a 13C painted-wood statue of the *Madonna del Latte*; 12C and 13C reliefs depicting the life of Christ and St Thomas of Canterbury; and an 11C crosier.

Museums and excavations

The ***Museo Archeologico Nazionale** (open Mon 09.00–14.00, Tues–Sun 09.00–19.00) is reached by the main road (Via Giulia Augusta) and Via Roma (right). This is one of Italy's leading museums of Roman antiquities. The well-displayed collections include examples of Roman architecture, sculpture, inscriptions and mosaics; a remarkably well-conserved Roman ship; and many unique specimens of glass, amber and cut stone. Notice especially, on the **first floor**, the golden *flies, ornaments from a lady's veil; and on the second floor, the unusual bronze *relief of a head in profile, a Hellenistic work or a Roman imitation (very well preserved), and the gilded bronze *head of a man dating from the 3C AD. In the hall with the Roman ship (2C AD, recovered from the sea in one of the most successful operations of underwater archaeology in recent years) is an exquisite little *mosaic panel with 20 different fish from the late 1C AD. On the south side of the quadriporticus are more Roman mosaics, including one depicting a *vine branch and a ribbon tied in a bow, dating from the Augustan age.

The *excavations are open daily 09.00–dusk. Near the basilica, across Via dei Patriarchi, are the foundations of late Roman market halls, and, beyond, along the river, the foundations of a stretch of two circuits of the town walls. The inner walls were built c 238 and the outer walls at the end of the 4C.

On the other side of the basilica, reached from Piazza Capitolo, are the remains of **Roman houses and Christian oratories** with superb *mosaic pavements. A path to the east, clearly marked by a noble avenue of cypresses, follows the Natissa stream north. It is lined with architectural fragments of the 1C–4C AD found here. The little Roman harbour has a finely wrought quay that still skirts the greatly diminished waters of the Natissa, once a navigable river as far as Grado.

Across Via Gemina a road leads past a group of modern houses to a quiet little piazza (with a fragment of Roman road) in front of the former Benedictine Monastery of Santa Maria. Here is the **Museo Paleocristiano** (open Sun–Wed 09.00–14.00, Thur–Sat 09.00–19.00), housed in a huge, long early Christian basilica (5C AD). The church has another remarkable *mosaic floor, with polychrome geometrical decorations and Greek and Latin inscriptions. At the west end modern stairs lead up to a balcony on which a good collection of sarcophagi, transennae and mosaic panels is arranged. The three-level display has been designed to show the transition of art from the Classical Roman period to the new Christian era.

Via Gemina leads right to the busy Via Giulia Augusta, which follows the course of the *cardo maximus*, the principal north–south thoroughfare of the ancient city. The street passes several Roman monuments on its way back towards the basilica. On the right you can see a fine stretch of Roman road, and beyond are traces of the circus. On the left of the road, a row of fluted composite columns belongs to the **forum**. The sculptural fragments include a fine Gorgon's head. The west and east porticoes, as well as part of the pavement, have been uncovered, and on the other side of the road are the foundations of the Roman basilica of the forum.

At the road fork is the **grande mausoleo**, an imposing family tomb of the 1C AD, brought here from the outskirts of Aquileia. Further on, on the right of the main road (opposite the church), is a large area still being excavated of Roman houses and early Christian oratories (2C–4C AD) with good pavements (especially near the vineyard). The polychrome mosaic floor, under cover, belonged to an oratory. Via Acidino leads west past (left) the scanty remains of the amphitheatre and (right) the site of the thermae (still being excavated) towards the **sepolcreto** (key at no. 17), a row of five family tombs of the 1C–2C. Via XXIV Maggio returns south to Piazza Giovanni, the village square.

Grado

The road from Aquileia continues towards the sea for just over 4km to Belvedere, at the start of a causeway nearly 7km long that leads across a beautiful lagoon to the island-city of Grado. The tiny old town has been suffocated by a large seaside resort with a very popular sandy beach equipped with thermal and sand baths, holiday flats and numerous hotels (mostly closed in winter). An ugly raised concrete esplanade lines the seafront—only the beaches at the extreme west and east end are free.

Old Grado is a place of narrow lanes and little squares. In ancient times it was the foreport of Aquileia, and many of that city's wealthier citizens had beach houses here. It reached its greatest prosperity after the 6C, when the patriarchate of Aquileia split in two, the second patriarch taking up residence in Grado. The rival sees were eventually reunited and moved to Venice, and by the 15C, when the title was abolished altogether, the town was well into its decline.

In the centre of the old town is the *Cathedral of Sant'Eufemia, built in the 6C on the site of a small 4C or 5C basilica, in the style of the great churches of Ravenna. The campanile, with a distinctive pointed steeple, is crowned by a 15C statue of the archangel Michael. The interior follows the classical basilican plan, with three aisles separated by antique Roman columns with fine capitals, a large apse and a magnificent *mosaic pavement dating from the 6C. This features charming geometrical patterns and stylised waves, connected and interlinked with a knot frieze, incorporating numerous inscriptions of donors. Near the west door is a dedicatory inscription in honour of the prophet Elias. The 11C *ambo has reliefs with symbols of the evangelists and an unusual Moorish dome. The sanctuary is surrounded by a 6C pluteus (light wall); on the high altar is a silver altarpiece of 1372, and in the apse 15C fresco and panel paintings.

Off the right side of the basilica is a rectangular room with another fine mosaic pavement (and inscription of Elias). Here has been placed the cast of the bishop's throne donated to Grado by Emperor Heraclius in 630 (the original was taken to Venice after 1451, and is still there, in the treasury of the Basilica of San Marco).

The lapidarium has Roman sepulchral inscriptions (1C–3C AD), 4C–5C early-Christian fragments, sarcophagi of the 2C–3C AD, architectural fragments (1C–6C), liturgical fragments (8C–9C), and Carolingian reliefs. The **treasury** (only open in summer) contains some splendid works, many of them made by local craftsmen, including little silver reliquary boxes (6C and 7C), a 12C Byzantine evangelistery cover, and the silver reliquary urn of Sts Hermagoras and Fortunatus, an early 14C Venetian work.

North of the basilica is the 6C **baptistery**, an octagonal building with another mosaic pavement, a pretty wooden roof and a hexagonal font; and further north, the small basilica of **Santa Maria delle Grazie**, a 4C or 5C church reworked in the 6C, with a mosaic pavement and a carved transenna of the same period. In the presbytery is a marble intarsia pavement, and excavations have revealed some good 6C floor mosaics (seen below the level of the floor on the right side).

In the small garden of Piazza della Vittoria you can see traces of foundations and remains of the mosaic pavement of another 4C or 5C Christian basilica; nearby are sarcophagi of the same period. On the modern esplanade on the seafront a former school building is being restored as the seat of a **Museum of Underwater Archaeology**, where the *Julia Felix*, a Roman wreck discovered in the sea between Grado and Marano in 1986, is to be exhibited. The ship, built at the end of the 2C or beginning of the 3C AD, and about 16m by 5m, was carrying wine and fish sauce in amphorae, and a wooden barrel full of pieces of broken glass (for recycling). It has been recovered from the sea bed using all the latest scientific methods.

Laguna di Grado

The *Laguna di Grado—a maze of channels, dunes and *mote* (islands) punctuated by *casoni* (straw and cane huts)—provides a winter home to herons, cormorants, swans, teal and swamp hawks. You can visit the islet of **Barbana** by hiring a private boat in Grado (usually available every hour daily in summer, and on weekends in winter; the journey takes c 30 minutes and the boatman will wait while you visit the island). The church here, built in 1593 and rebuilt since 1918, contains a venerated statue of the *Virgin*, and there is an annual procession of boats on the first Sunday in July. Away to the west, on the adjacent Laguna di Marano, is Lignano Sabbiadoro, a huge planned tourist resort with some 400 hotels along a sandy spit. Across the mouth of the Tagliamento is Bibione, another resort.

The coastal plain

The coastal plain north and west of Aquileia is studded with points of historical and artistic interest, mostly dating from the early Christian era and the High Middle Ages. Officially in the Veneto but an important junction on the road to Pordenone, **Portogruaro** is a medieval town with an interesting urban plan. Its two main streets run parallel on either side of the River Lemene, which is still navigable from here to Caorle on the sea. The cathedral, with a Romanesque campanile, was rebuilt in 1793. The handsome 14C **Loggia Municipale** was enlarged in 1512. The arcaded Via Martiri della Libertà is lined with 14C–15C houses. A museum contains finds from the Roman station of *Concordia Sagittaria*, from which the nearby village of **Concordia** (with a 15C cathedral above remains of an earlier church, and a fine 11C baptistery) takes its name. Also near Portogruaro is the Romanesque church of the early Benedictine abbey of **Summaga**.

At **Sesto al Reghena**, on the border with the Veneto, you can visit the former Benedictine abbey church of **Santa Maria in Sylvis** (open daily 08.00–19.00), founded in 762 and fortified and surrounded by a moat in the 9C (the walls were demolished in 1939). Beautifully restored in 1989–92, it has an unusual plan, preceded by a vestibule and large aisled atrium. On the left of the entrance a little loggia has a fragment of a fresco with courtly scenes (12C). On the right, steps lead up to the salone with a fine wooden ceiling and delightful painted decoration in pastel shades in imitation of curtains with flowers above. The fragment of the head of St Michael is the oldest fresco to have survived in the abbey (12C).

The vestibule has frescoes of *Heaven* and (very ruined) *Hell*, traditionally attributed to Antonio da Firenze. The little refectory, on the right, has more fresco fragments. The large atrium has sculptured fragments, a detached lunette of St Benedict, and an unusual scene of three figures on horseback and three coffins, thought to date from 1316.

The **church** has a remarkable *fresco cycle in the presbytery (including scenes from the life of St Benedict) dating from the early 14C by the *bottega* of Giotto. The crypt, rebuilt at the beginning of the 20C, contains the splendid reliquary urn of St Anastasia, adapted in the late Middle Ages from an 8C abbot's throne. Also here is a late 13C sculpted diptych of the *Annunciation* (with a view of the fortified abbey in the background) and a stone 15C *Pietà*. On the lawn outside you can see the foundations of the first Lombard early-Christian church.

To the east of Sesto is the tiny, well-preserved town of **Cordovado**, which was a fortified *borgo* on the southern border of Friuli. The delightful old centre has one street between the two gates and narrow alleys on either side. Opposite Villa Freschi, with a garden with statues, is Villa Marrubini. Outside the walls next to the town hall is the octagonal church of Santa Maria delle Grazie. The spring of Venchiaredo, mentioned by Ippolito Nievo in his *Confessioni di un Italiano* (1867), is nearby.

San Vito al Tagliamento is an interesting little town with a pleasant long piazza in front of its duomo and tall campanile. The cathedral contains some important works by Pomponio Amalteo. Also in the piazza are Palazzo Fancello, with a painted façade and, next to it, the 15C Palazzo Rota (the town hall) with a fine garden (a public park). At the end of the piazza the Torre Raimonda hosts the town library and museum (on the top floor; open Mon–Fri 10.00–12.00, 15.00–18.30). It contains prehistoric and Roman finds from the area, as well as Renaissance ceramics and 15C frescoes. There is also a small museum of farm life (Palazzo Altan, Via Altan 47, open Mon–Sat 09.00–12.30, Thur 15.00–17.00).

PORDENONE

Several kilometres northwest of San Vito in the midst of verdant farmland, Pordenone is a very pleasant provincial capital (population 50,000) with a delightful long corso. Modern buildings, some of them by the prominent 20C architect Gino Valle, have been successfully integrated into the town. There are pretty parks on the banks of the River Noncello.

History

The river used to be navigable down to the Adriatic, and Pordenone was for centuries important as a port. Cotton factories were established here in 1840, and it is still the industrial centre of Friuli. The town was the birthplace of the painter Giovanni Antonio de' Sacchis (c 1483–1539), called 'Il Pordenone', many of whose works survive in the town and province.

Exploring the town

The long, undulating *Corso Vittorio Emanuele begins in the central Piazza Cavour and winds through the old centre. It is lined on either side by arcades and has interesting houses from all periods. Beyond some 13C and 14C palaces is the Neo-classical façade of the former theatre. A side road leads to the Chiesa del Cristo (or Santa Maria degli Angeli), with two fine 16C portals, one by Pilacorte. Back in the corso the monumental Palazzo Gregoris (no. 44), has masques in the Venetian style. No. 52 has faded frescoes attributed to Pordenone, and no. 45, the former Palazzo dei Capitani, has good fresco decoration (also on its side façade in Via Mercato). Palazzo Montereale-Mantica (no. 56) has a fine interior with Baroque stuccoes (recently restored).

Via Castello and Via della Motta lead to Palazzo Mantica, with a fresco attributed to Pordenone. In Piazza della Motta is the **Museo Civico delle Scienze** (open Mon–Fri 09.00–12.00, 15.00–18.00), with an unusual collection, arranged on three floors, some of it in old-fashioned showcases. Opposite, the former church of San Francesco, with damaged 15C frescoes, is used for exhibitions. Also in the piazza are the 18C civic library (with the Lion of St Mark over the door) and the 13C castle (now a prison).

At Corso Vittorio Emanuele 51 is Palazzo Ricchieri, which houses the **Museo Civico d'Arte** (open Tues–Fri at time of writing, 09.30–12.30, 15.00–18.00). The palace dates from the 15C and has fine painted wooden ceilings and some remains of mural paintings. The collection consists mainly of 16C–18C works by regional artists including Giovanni Caroto, Pordenone and Luca Giordano. It also contains a 15C seated wooden *Madonna* attributed to Andrea Bellunello, a wooden crucifix by the circle of Donatello, and an altar frontal in gilded and painted wood of c 1508.

The corso ends in front of the delightful **Palazzo Comunale**, which has a projecting clock tower in a Venetian Renaissance style (16C) at odds with its 13C Emilian Gothic core. Beyond is Piazza San Marco with pretty houses, some with frescoes.

The **Cathedral** has a Romanesque *campanile and good west portal by Pilacorte (1511). In the light interior are altarpieces by Pordenone (*Madonna of the Misericordia*, 1515), Marcello Fogolino and Pomponio Amalteo. The treasury contains 16 precious Gothic reliquaries (not on view at time of writing). The **Museo Diocesano d'Arte Sacra** (Via Revedole 1, open Tues–Fri 09.00–13.00 and 14.30 or 15.00–18.30 or 19.00) displays sculpture, painting and liturgical objects documenting the history of Christianity between the Livenza and the Tagliamento from the 4C to the present day.

At the other end of the corso, beyond Piazza Cavour, is Corso Garibaldi, with two grand palaces in the Venetian style facing each other. A side road leads to the 16C church of **San Giorgio**, with one of the more eccentric bell towers in Italy—a giant Tuscan column (1852).

Around Pordenone

The lovely countryside around Pordenone holds several worthwhile sights.

Spilimbergo, northeast of Pordenone, has a pleasant, spacious green. Along one side is the flank of its large **Cathedral**, with a side door by Zenone da Campione (1376). The organ by Bernardo Vicentino (1515) has doors painted by Pordenone, and the presbytery is covered with 14C frescoes attributed to the school of Vitale da Bologna.

At the end of the piazza is the entrance (across the dry moat, now a garden) to the *castle. Built in the 12C and reconstructed after a fire in 1511, the fortress encloses a pleasant medley of 16C–18C palaces, notably one with restored frescoes on its façade attributed to Bellunello. There is a fine view of the Tagliamento valley, and you can visit the **mosaic school** (one of four in Italy) by appointment (☎ 0427 2155).

North of Spilimbergo are the village churches of **Vacile**, with apse frescoes by Pordenone; **Lestans**, with frescoes by Pomponio Amalteo; and **Valeriano**, where two churches side by side (recently restored) both have frescoes by Pordenone.

South of Spilimbergo, **Provesano** has a church with lovely *frescoes in the sanctuary by Giovanni Francesco da Tolmezzo, and a stoup and font by Pilacorte. Further south is **Valvasone**, where the cathedral has a splendid *organ (recitals in September) dating from 1532 and restored in 1974, with painted doors begun by Pordenone in 1538 and completed by Pomponio Amalteo. Nearby, the church of **San Pietro** has a tiny Venetian 17C organ and frescoes by Pietro da Vicenza. The castle, which encloses an 18C theatre, is in very poor condition. A medieval pagaent is held here in September.

Just to the west of Pordenone is the old town of **Porcia**, which has an interesting old centre. From Sacile, further west, there is a pretty branch railway line which leads northeast and crosses the Tagliamento to Gemona.

LIGURIA

The region of Liguria comprises the narrow strip of land lying between the Mediterranean and the summits of the Maritime Alps and the Apennines from the frontier of France to the borders of Tuscany. It is made up of the provinces of Genoa, Imperia, La Spezia and Savona. Liguria includes two of the more fertile stretches of the Italian coastline, the Riviera di Ponente and the Riviera di Levante, west and east of Genoa, where the mild winter climate encourages a luxuriant growth of vegetation, including palms, oranges and lemons; the cultivation of flowers in early spring is important, too.

The Ligurian people, occupying a territory that has always been easier of access by sea than by land, are noted seafarers, and they have been influenced by immigrations from overseas rather than by landward invasions. Traces of Punic and Greek connections are evident, and Genoa became an important Roman seaport. Liguria was exposed to the attacks of Saracen pirates in the later Middle Ages. The aristocratic republic of Genoa, at the height of its power after its defeat of Pisa in 1290, ruled the destinies of the whole seaboard from the 13C to the days of Napoleon. The Napoleonic campaigns of 1796 and 1799 resulted first in the creation of a Ligurian Republic and then the absorption of the province into the French Empire; but in 1815 Liguria was attached to the kingdom of Piedmont. Genoa played an important part in the history of the Risorgimento, and Ligurian vessels provided transport for Garibaldi's attack on Sicily in 1860. In the Second World War the coastal area, especially Genoa, suffered severely from air attack.

Genoa

Genoa, in Italian Genova (population 654,000), is one of the main cities of Italy and one of the more important ports on the Mediterranean for container traffic. It is built on an unusually awkward site, the irregular seaward slopes of an amphitheatre of hills. It preserves many relics of an ancient, honourable history, including the numerous palaces and magnificent art collections of its great maritime families (many still in private hands). Genoa acquired a powerful maritime empire in the 14C, and even though rivalry with Venice led to the defeat of the Genoese at Chioggia in 1380, the maritime importance of Genoa lasted well into the 17C. The town is famous as the birthplace of Christopher Columbus.

The old city, clustered round the old port, is still a most interesting district, with its tall houses in steep, narrow alleys or *carugi*, some less than 3m wide. There are long-term plans to restore some of these dark streets, with their quaint old-fashioned shops, which have suffered damage from numerous floods as well as from Allied air and sea bombardment in the Second World War, and which have greatly deteriorated in the past few decades. Over half the inhabitants of this area are now immigrants.

The city has expanded rapidly since the Second World War, and the raised motorway running between the old town and the port symbolises the chaotic town planning to which Genoa was subjected in the 1960s. Some important restorations, including that of Palazzo Ducale and Palazzo di San Giorgio, and new buildings (the Carlo Felice opera theatre, and the Aquarium) were completed for the controversial celebrations in 1992, which marked the 500th anniversary of the discovery of America by Columbus. An attempt by the internationally renowned architect Renzo Piano to revitalise the area of the old port has been only partially successful, and the city is now having to face the consequences of industrial decline. The hinterland is covered with tower blocks that sprawl across the hills, and the city limits now extend along the coast in both directions for some 30km between Nervi and Voltri.

Practical information

Getting there
By air
Genoa's Cristoforo Colombo Airport, at Sestri Ponente (6km west of the city), handles domestic and international flights. Airport bus ('*Volabus*') regularly from Brignole Station, with stops in Piazza de' Ferrari (**Map 11**) and at Principe Station (Piazza Acquaverde).

By road
The French and Italian rivieras are connected by excellent motoways. In France the A8 from Nice passes the Principality of Monte Carlo, then crosses into Italy at Menton. The first Italian town on the motorway (in Italy, the A10) is Ventimiglia; the first major city is Genoa. This is the best all-weather route from France to Italy.

Genoa can be reached also by the A6 from Turin and Savona, A26 from Alessandria; A7 from Milan and A12 from Pisa and La Spezia. All these highways, given the nature of the terrain, have plenty of curves, viaducts and tunnels, and commercial traffic can be heavy on weekdays.

By rail
The main rail line from Rome to Paris follows the Tyrrhenian coast to Genoa, then continues via Turin to the French capital. Fast *Eurostar* trains cover the 500km from Rome to Genoa in c 4hrs 15mins; *Intercity* in c 5hrs. Both stop in Liguria at La Spezia and often at Sarzana, Sestri Levante, Chiavari and Rapallo. Genoa is also on the main line to Italy from southern France; from Nice to Genoa takes c 3hrs. The French *TGV* runs as far as Menton, making it possible to reach Genoa from Paris in c 10hrs.

Genoa enjoys frequent connections also to Turin (166km in 1hr 30mins), Milan (154km in 1hr 30mins) and Pisa (165km in 1hr 40mins). There is also one daily *Interegionale* to and from Bologna (4hrs 50mins).

Genoa has two railway stations: **Porta Principe** (**Map 1**) is the most central station, but nearly all trains stop also at **Brignole**.

By sea
The main quay for passenger and car ferries is Ponte Colombo, next to the Stazione Marittima at Ponte Andrea Doria and Ponte dei Mille (**Map 5**).

Regular car ferries to Sardinia, Sicily and Tunis.

Getting around
City transport

Is run by *AMT* (☎ 010 5997414). A ticket valid for one day on any line can be purchased at the *AMT* office at Via D'Annunzio 8.

Buses

The following **buses** serve the outskirts of the city: **1** Piazza Caricamento—Sampierdarena—Pegli—Voltri. **15** Piazza Caricamento—Piazza Tommaseo —Sturla—Quarto—Quinto —Nervi. **33** Piazza Acquaverde—Circonvallazione a Monte—Piazza Manin—Piazza Corvetto —Piazza De Ferrari—Stazione Brignole. **34** Piazzale San Benigno—Piazza Principe—Piazza Nunziata—Piazza Corvetto—Piazza Manin—Cimitero di Staglieno.

Funicular railways

Funicular railways: **F** Fargo della Zecca (**Map 6**)—Righi Via San Nicolò. **H** Piazza Portello (**Map 7**)—Corso Magenta. **Rack railway: (G)** Via del Lagaccio, near Piazza Principe (**Map 1**)—Granarolo. **Lifts: L** Via XX Settembre—Corso Podestà (Ponte Monumentale; **Map 12**). **M** Corso Magenta—Via Crocco. **N** Piazza Portello—Spianata di Castelletto.

Car parking

There is parking space in the area of the old port, near the aquarium (**Map 9, 10**). Multistorey car parks in Piazza Piccapietra (**Map 12**) and Piazza Dante (**Map 11, 12**).

Tours of the harbour

Organised trips round the harbour by motor boat (c 1hr) depart from the Stazione Marittima (Ponte dei Mille, Calata Zingari; **Map 1**). Information from *Cooperativa Battellieri* (☎ 010 265712), and *Alimar* (☎ 010 255975).

Country buses

These depart from the bus station in Piazza della Vittoria; frequent service along the coast in both directions.

Information offices

GENOA Principe Station (☎ 010 246 2633), the airport (☎ 010 601 5247), and in Palazzina Santa Maria, near the aquarium (☎ 010 248711).

Where to stay

GENOA *Agnello d'Oro*, Via Monachette 6, ☎ 010 246 2084, fax 010 462327; a warm, simple, family-run place; moderate.
Alexander, Via Bersaglieri d'Italia 19, ☎ 010 261371, fax 010 265257; near Porta Principe station, with good views over the harbour; moderate.
Bristol Palace, Via XX Settembre 35, ☎ 010 592541, fax 010 561756; 19C ambience; centre of the city; expensive.
City, Via San Sebastiano 6, ☎ 010 5545, fax 010 586301; centrally located, modern and comfortable; expensive.
Metropoli, Vico Migliorini 8 (Piazza Fontane Marose), ☎ 010 246 8888, fax 010 246 8686; between Piazza De Ferrari and Via Garibaldi; moderate.
Youth hostel (*Ostello della gioventù*), 120 Via Costanzi (**bus 35** from Principe station, and **40** from Brignole station).
PEGLI *Torre Cambiaso*, Via Scarpanto 49, ☎ 010 665055, fax 010 697 3022; calm and quiet, in a lovely park with pool; moderate.

Eating out

GENOA *Ferrando*, Via Carli 110, ☎ 010 751925; good Ligurian fare and great views, with garden seating in summer; closed Sun evening, Mon, Wed evening, Jan and Aug; moderate.
Gran Gotto, Viale Brigate Bisagno 69r, ☎ 010 583644; excellent seafood and

an interesting wine list; closed midday Sat, Sun, holidays and Aug; moderate.

Il Pampino Vino e Cucina, Via Ruspoli 31r, ☎ 010 588402; wine bar with simple but delicious hot and cold meals; open evenings only, closed Sun and Aug; inexpensive.

La Bitta nella Pergola, Via Casaregis 52r, ☎ 010 588543; another place known for its excellent fish dishes; closed Sun evening, Mon, Jan and Aug; moderate.

Saint Cyr, Piazza Marsala 8, ☎ 010 886897; good Ligurian food and wines; closed midday Sat, Sun, Dec and Aug; moderate.

Santa Chiara, Via Capo Santa Chiara 69r, Località Boccadasse, ☎ 010 377 0081; personal interpretations of traditional regional dishes and summer seating on a seafront terrace; closed Sun, Dec–Jan and Aug; moderate.

Antica Osteria del Bai, Via Quarto 12, Località Quarto dei Mille, ☎ 010 387478; an outstanding seafood restaurant worth the 7km drive from Genoa; closed Mon, Jan and Aug; moderate.

Genoa is the home of **focaccia**, the delicious soft, low white bread that goes well with just about anything. You can buy focaccia in most bakeries and grocery shops—plain (have it sliced open and stuffed with cold meats, cheeses, sun-dried tomatoes, olive spread, etc. for a truly memorable sandwich) or topped with cheese, onions or potatoes. Equally good but less well known is **farinata**, a type of pizza made with chick-pea flour, extra virgin olive oil, water and salt. A popular food from Nice to Pisa, in Genoa it is sold in modest snack bars called *farinotti*. These include *Sa Pesta*, 16 Via dei Giustiniani; *Sciamadda*, 19 Via Ravecca; and *Spano*, 35 Via Santa Zita.

For a good Ligurian wine to drink with your focaccia or farinata, try *Vinoteca Sola*, Piazza Colombo 13r.

Entertainment

GENOA has several fine theatres: *Carlo Felice*, Piazza De Ferrari (opera season). For prose: *Sala Duse*, 6 Via Bacigalupo (Piazza Corvetto), *Politeama Genovese*, 2 Via Bacigalupo; *Teatro della Corte*, Corte Lambruschini (Via Duca d'Aosta).

Special events

International exhibitions are held at the Fiera Internazionale, Piazzale Kennedy (beyond **Map 14**). A boat show (the *Salone Nautico*) is held annually in Oct, and *Euroflora*, a flower show is held in spring every five years (next in 2001).

Sports

The Genoa professional **soccer** team, Sampdoria, plays at the Ferraris Stadium. There are two major **sailing** events: the *Regata Storica delle Quattro Repubbliche Marinare*, with antique ships from the former maritime republics of Genoa, Venice, Pisa and Amalfi, is in May, while the *Little Ships Transatlantic Regatta* takes place in Spring every four years (next in 2004).

History

The position of Genoa, at the northernmost point of the Tyrrhenian sea and protected by mountains, has given it a lasting maritime importance. The original Ligurian inhabitants of the site established early contact with the first known navigators of the Mediterranean, the Phoenicians and Greeks, and objects excavated have proved the existence of a trading-post here in the 6C BC. In the 3C BC Genoa took up alliance with Rome against the Carthaginians, and when the town was destroyed by the Carthaginians in 205 BC, it was quickly rebuilt under the Roman *praetor* Cassius.

Roman connections were not entirely severed until the arrival of the Lombards in 641. In the succeeding centuries the sailors of Genoa withstood the attacks of Saracen pirates and captured their strongholds of Corsica and Sardinia. Sardinia was taken with the help of Pisa, and its occupation led to two centuries of war, which ended in the final defeat of the Pisans at Meloria (1284). With this success began the acquisition of Genoa's great colonial empire, which extended as far as the Crimea, Syria and North Africa. Important Genoese colonies were established in the Morea (Peloponnese). These advances, and the large profits made during the Crusades, led to a collision with the ambitions of Venice; the subsequent war ended in the defeat of the Genoese at Chioggia (1380).

After the fall of the consuls in 1191, power passed to the *podestà* and the *Capitani del Popolo* (1258–1340), with intervals of submission to Emperor Henry VII (1311–13) and to Robert of Anjou, King of Naples (1318–35). In 1340 came the election of the first Doge, Simone Boccanegra. Petrarch, on a visit in 1358, described the city as 'la superba' (the proud), a name used by numerous subsequent travellers to Genoa. Chaucer was sent to Genoa in 1372–73 by Edward II to arrange a commercial treaty with the maritime republic. The continual strife between the great families (Doria, Spinola and Fieschi) made Genoa an easy victim to the rising military powers, and it had a succession of foreign rulers in the 15C. In 1528 Andrea Doria (1466–1560), the greatest of the Genoese naval leaders, formulated a constitution for Genoa that freed the city from foreign rule, though it established despotic government at home and was followed (1547–48) by the insurrections of Fieschi and Cibo.

The conquests of the Turks in the Middle East, the transfer of overseas trade with America to Atlantic ports, and the domination of Spain, brought about the rapid decline of Genoa in the 17C, and in 1684 Louis XIV entered the town after a bombardment. The Austrian occupation of 50 years later was ended by a popular insurrection in 1746, which was started by the action of a boy, Giovanni Battista Perasso (known as Balilla). In 1768 the Genoese sold to France their rights to their last remaining colony, Corsica. Napoleon entered Genoa in 1796, and four years later the city was attacked by the Austrians on land and the English at sea. The Ligurian Republic, formed in 1802, soon became a French province, but in 1815 Genoa was joined to Piedmont, by the treaty of Vienna, and became a stronghold of the Risorgimento, with Giuseppe Mazzini (born in Genoa) as the leading spirit. He was abetted by Garibaldi (who planned his expedition with the 'Thousand' from here in 1860), the soldier patriot Nino Bixio (1821–73), and Goffredo Mameli (1827–49), the warrior poet. Charles Dickens and his family spent much time in Genoa in 1844, and came 'to have an attachment for the very stones in the streets of Genoa, and to look back upon the city with affection as connected with many hours of happiness and quiet'. He left an interesting description of his stay in *Pictures from Italy*. The most eminent 20C native was poet Eugenio Montale (1896–1981).

Art

The architecture of medieval Genoa is characterised by the black-and-white striped façades of the older churches, and the earliest sculpture came from the workshops of the Pisano family and the Comacini. Galeazzo Alessi, the Perugian architect, worked here during the Renaissance, and the Gaggini family of sculptors were active in the 16C–17C. Through its close commercial links with the Netherlands, the city acquired many Dutch and Flemish paintings. In 1607 Rubens visited Genoa, and in 1621 Van Dyck arrived and stayed in the city for six years on and off. The most productive period of Genoese painting is the 17C, with Bernardo Strozzi, Bernardo and Valerio Castello, Giovanni Battista Castiglione, Domenico Fiasella and the Piola brothers.

The city centre

Piazza De Ferrari (Map 11), where numerous main roads converge, is at the centre of the city. It has a large fountain and, behind Augusto Rivalta's Garibaldi monument (1893), the **Teatro Carlo Felice**, rebuilt on a huge scale by Aldo Rossi in 1987–91. The first theatre, designed by Carlo Barabino in 1828, was gutted by fire in 1944, although its Neo-classical pronaos survives. The new building includes a massive rectangular tower. In front of this is the Neo-classical **Accademia Ligustica di Belle Arti** (1827–31), also by Carlo Barabino. A gallery here (open Mon–Sat except holidays 09.00–13.00) contains paintings by Ligurian artists of the 14C–19C. Between Via XX Settembre and Via Dante, which lead to the newer districts of the city, is the elaborate curved façade of the Borsa (1907–12).

Opposite is the side of Palazzo Ducale, recently repainted, and on the last side of the square is a palace built as offices in 1923 by Cesare Gamba. Behind this, in Piazza Matteotti (**Map 11**), is the Baroque church of **Sant' Ambrogio o del Gesù**, built 1589–1606 by Giuseppe Valeriani. The sumptuous, colourful interior has frescoes by Giovanni Carlone and altarpieces by Guido Reni and Rubens.

Palazzo Ducale (Map 11), a huge building of various periods, surrounds Piazza Matteotti. It was restored in 1975–92 as a cultural centre. The left wing, Palazzo di Alberto Fieschi, was the seat of the Capitano del Popolo in 1272, and from 1294 the meeting place of the comune. It became the residence of the doges from 1340 onwards, and Andrea Vannone carried out radical modifications c 1591–1620, adding the attractive spacious *vestibule with a light courtyard at either end. The palace was reconstructed by Simone Cantoni in 1778–83 and given a Neo-classical façade. On the upper floors are the Salone del Maggior Consiglio and the doges' chapel, frescoed by Giovanni Battista Carlone. Exhibitions are held here, and there are two restaurants.

The Cathedral and the old town

In Via San Lorenzo is the flank of the *Cathedral (San Lorenzo; **Map 11**), a Romanesque-Gothic building consecrated (unfinished) in 1118 and modified in the 13C–14C and during the Renaissance. On the south side are Roman sarcophagi, a 15C Grimaldi family tomb, and the Romanesque portal of San Gottardo. The façade (restored in the 20C) has doorways in the French Gothic style. The campanile on the south side was completed in 1522; the north one is unfinished, with a loggetta of 1447. On the north side are the 12C portal of San Giovanni and many more classical sarcophagi.

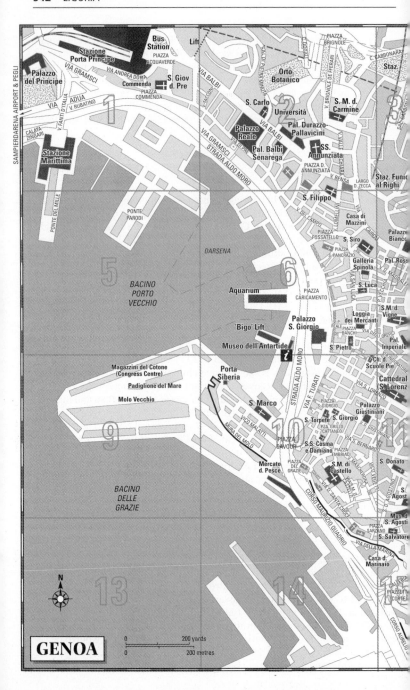

GENOA

0 ____ 200 yards
0 ____ 200 metres

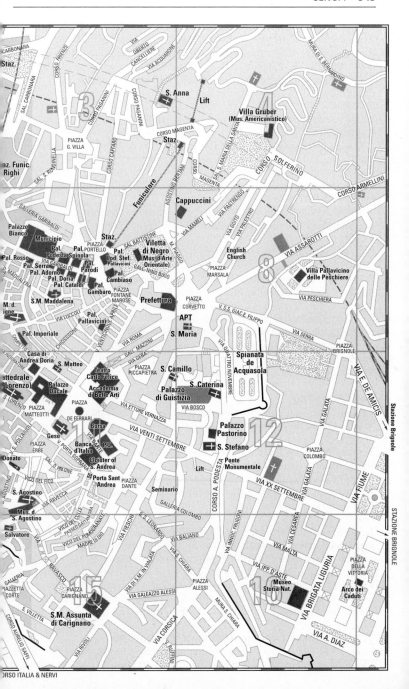

The **interior** is distinguished by its dark Corinthian columns. The proportions were altered when the nave roof was raised in 1550 and the cupola, by Galeazzo Alessi, added in 1567. The pulpit dates from 1526. The lunette over the west door has early 14C frescoes. In the south aisle, beside a British naval shell that damaged the church without exploding in 1941, is a marble relief of the *Crucifixion* of 1443. The chapel to the right of the high altar holds a painting by Federico Barocci. The stalls in the apse date from 1514–64. In the chapel to the left of the high altar are wall and ceiling paintings by Luca Cambiaso and Giovanni Battista Castello.

The great *chapel of St John the Baptist** was designed by Domenico and Elia Gagini (1451–65), with a richly decorated front. It contains statues by Matteo Civitali and Andrea Sansovino (1504), a baldacchino of 1532, and a 13C French shrine for the relics of St John the Baptist. In the adjoining chapel is the tomb of Giorgio Fieschi (d. 1461) by Giovanni Gagini. The *treasury (reopened in 1996) contains ancient glass, copes, the Byzantine *Zaccaria Cross and precious reliquaries in vaults designed in 1956 by Franco Albini.

From Palazzo Ducale the Salita Pollaiuoli descends into the old town with its narrow dark streets, or *carugi*, with tall houses. Some charming portals survive in this district, in white marble or black slate, often bearing reliefs of St George, patron of the city. There are also numerous Baroque tabernacles with religious images on the streets. Via Canneto il Lungo is a typical long street of the old town, with food shops and some good doorways.

The church of **San Donato** (Map 11), probably founded in the early 12C, has a splendid polygonal campanile and a good doorway. In the beautiful basilican interior are a late-14C painting by Nicolò da Voltri and a triptych of the *Adoration of the Magi* by Joos van Cleve.

Sant'Agostino

The Stradone Sant'Agostino leads up past the new building of the faculty of architecture of the university to Piazza Sarzano, once a centre of the old city, but partly derelict since the war. Here is the pink building (1977–84) of the **Museo Di Sant'Agostino** (Map 15; open Tues–Sat 09.00–19.00, Sun and holidays 09.00–12.30), housing the city's collection of architectural fragments, sculptures and detached frescoes. The interior of the museum is built in a pretentious Modern style with much of the structure in black. Highlights of the collection include, on the first floor, fragments of the funerary *monument of Margaret of Brabant (d. 1311), by Giovanni Pisano, a painted *crucifix by Barnaba da Modena, and other sculptures in wood and marble; and on the second floor, 15C black slate *architraves with reliefs of St John the Baptist and St George. There are also carved masks by Taddeo Carlone; detached frescoes by Luca Cambiaso; 16C sculptures (Gian Giacomo Della Porta, Silvio Cosini); paintings by Domenico Piola; and sculptures by Filippo Parodi, Pierre Puget and Antonio Canova, as well as 15C English alabaster carvings. The 13C Gothic church of Sant'Agostino, with a graceful campanile and spire, has been restored for use as an auditorium.

Santa Maria di Castello and its neighbourhood

From below Piazza San Donato, Via San Bernardo leads left. Some way along, Vico dei Giustiniani diverges left to Piazza Embriaci (**Map 11**), where steps lead up to the Doric portal (by Giovanni Battista Orsolino) of the Casa Brignole Sale (no. 5), restored in 1538. On the right, the steep-stepped Salita, passing the 12C Torre degli Embriaci, restored and completed in 1923, ascends to *Santa Maria di Castello (Map 10), a Romanesque church with 15C Gothic additions. It occupies the site of the Roman *castrum* and preserves some Roman columns.

Inside, on the west wall, is a late-15C fresco by Lorenzo Fasolo; in the south aisle, altarpieces by Aurelio Lomi, Pier Francesco Sacchi and Bernardo Castello. Next to the new altar is a wooden crucifix (c 1100, the *Black Christ*); in the sanctuary, a marble group of the *Assumption of the Virgin* by Antonio Domenico Parodi; and in the chapel to the left of the sanctuary, St Rosa di Lima by Domenico Piola. The baptistery contains a 15C polyptych, some ruined 15C frescoes and a Roman sarcophagus. The sacristy has a beautifully carved portal (inner face) by Giovanni Gagini and Leonardo Riccomanno (1452).

The Dominican convent (1445–1513) has pretty frescoes in the loggia of the second cloister, possibly by 'Iustus de Alemania', the German painter who signed and dated (1451) the *Annunciation* on the wall. In the upper loggia (view of the port), with Roman and medieval capitals, is a *tabernacle of the Trinity by Domenico Gagini, and a detached *fresco in monochrome of the vision of St Dominic, attributed to Braccesco. The old library has a polyptych of the *Annunciation* by Giovanni Mazone (1470; one of only two works known by this local artist). The museum (opened on request) contains the *Coronation of the Virgin*, a painting showing Flemish influence, signed and dated 1513 by Ludovico Brea.

Via San Bernardo continues past several fine doorways to Piazza Grillo Cattaneo, where a portal by Tamagnino survives at no. 6, surrounded by dilapidated buildings. Vico Dietro il Coro di San Cosimo leads past the east end of the 11C church of Santi Cosma e Damiano (Map 10). Piazza San Giorgio (Map 10), an important market square in the Middle Ages, has two attractive, domed and centrally planned churches: San Giorgio, documented as early as 964 and reconstructed in 1695, and San Torpete, rebuilt with an elliptical cupola after 1730, on a design by Giovanni Antonio Ricca. In Piazza dei Giustiniani busts and reliefs decorate the portico of the 17C Palazzo Giustiniani (no. 6).

From Piazza San Giorgio, Via Canneto il Curto, another typical street of the old town, leads back up to Via San Lorenzo and the cathedral.

Around Piazza San Matteo

Between Palazzo Ducale and the cathedral is Via Reggio, which skirts the left wing of Palazzo Ducale and the Torre del Popolo (1307), known as the 'Grimaldina'. At no. 12 is the cloister of San Lorenzo (c 1180).

Piazza San Matteo, reached along Salita allo Arcivescovato, was created in the 12C when it was surrounded by the mansions and church of the Doria family, with striped black-and-white façades. *San Matteo (Map 11), founded in 1125 but rebuilt by the Doria in 1278, has a striped black-and-white Gothic façade with inscriptions recounting the glorious deeds of the Dorias.

The interior was transformed in 1543–47 for Andrea Doria by Giovanni Angelo Montorsoli. The sanctuary is an interesting sculptural work by Montorsoli (with the help of Silvio Cosini). The nave was decorated with stuccoes and frescoes by Giovanni Battista Castello (Il Bergamasco) and Luca Cambiaso. The wood group of the *Deposition* is by Anton Maria Maragliano. The *crypt and staircase, decorated with marbles and stuccoes, were designed by Montorsoli for the tomb of Andrea Doria. An archway on the left of the church leads to the cloister (1308–10) by Magister Marcus Venetus.

Of paupers and princesses

Here are a few of the impressions Genoa left on those who visited before you:

The Genoese manner... is exceedingly animated and pantomimic; so that two friends of the lower class conversing pleasantly in the street, always seem on the eve of stabbing each other forthwith. And a stranger is immensely astonished at their not doing it.
Charles Dickens, letter to John Forster, 20 July 1844

The people here live in the heaviest, highest, broadest, darkest, solidest houses one can imagine. Each one might "laugh a siege to scorn". A hundred feet front and a hundred high is about the style, and you go up three flights of stairs before you begin to come upon signs of occupancy. Everything is stone, and stone of the heaviest—floors, stairways, mantels, benches, everything. The walls are four to five feet thick. The streets generally are four to five to eight feet wide, and as crooked as a corkscrew. You go along one of these gloomy cracks and look up and behold the sky like a mere ribbon of light, far above your head, where the tops of the tall houses on either side of the street bend almost together. You feel as if you were at the bottom of some tremendous abyss, with all the world far above you. You wind in and out, and here and there, in the most mysterious way, and have no more idea of the points of the compass than if you were a blind man. You can never persuade yourself that these are actually streets, and the frowning, dingy, monstrous houses dwellings, till you see one of these beautiful, prettily dressed women emerge from them—see her emerge from a dark, dreary looking den that looks dungeon all over, from the ground away halfway up to heaven. And then you wonder that such a charming moth could come from such a forbidding shell as that.... There may be prettier women in Europe, but I doubt it.
Mark Twain, *The Innocents Abroad*, 1869

Genoa is the crookedest and most incoherent of cities; tossed about on the sides and crests of a dozen hills, it is seamed with gullies and ravines that bristle with those innumerable palaces for which we have heard from our earliest years that the place is celebrated. These great edifices, with their mottled and faded complexions, lift their big ornamental cornices to a tremendous height in the air, where, in a certain indescribably forlorn and desolate fashion, overtopping each other, they seem to reflect the twinkle and glitter of the warm Mediterranean. Down about the basements, in the little, dim, close alleys, the people are for ever moving to and fro, or standing in their cavernous doorways or their dusky, crowded shops, calling, chattering, laughing, scrambling, living their lives in the conversational Italian fashion. For a long time I had not received such an impression of human agglomeration. I had not for a long time seen people elbowing each other so closely, or swarming so thickly out of populous hives.
Henry James, 'Italy Revisited', 1877, in *Portraits of Places*, 1883

The dock-front of Genoa is marvellous. Such heat and colours and dirt & noise and loud wicked alleys with all the washing of the world hanging from the high windows.
Dylan Thomas, letter to his parents, 5 May 1947

Opposite the church is the **Casa di Lamba Doria** (no. 15), built in the 13C with a portico. The **Casa di Andrea Doria** (no. 17) was built for Lazzaro Doria in 1468 and presented to the famous admiral by his native city in 1528. No. 14 is the **Casa di Branca Doria**, with a charming relief over the portal.

Off Via Chiossone, in which no. 1 is another Doria house with a marble portal by Pace Gaggini, the ancient Vico della Casana, a busy lane, leads to the left. The animated Via Luccoli (left again), with many good shops and attractive street lighting, crosses Piazza Soziglia (with a café founded in 1828) to reach the Campetto (Map 7). **Palazzo Imperiale** (1560; no. 8) is a sumptuous building by Giovanni Battista Castello. The upper part of the curved façade is decorated with paintings and stuccoes by Ottavio Semino.

On the other side of Via degli Orefici, a short road leads to **Santa Maria delle Vigne** (Map 7), a church redesigned in 1640 by Daniele Casella (good Baroque interior), with a façade of 1842. You can see parts of its 10C and 12C Romanesque predecessors from the lane on the left side, together with an interesting 14C tomb incorporating the front of a 2C sarcophagus. Inside is the tomb slab of the goldsmiths' corporation, with a fine relief of St Eligius (1459).

From the piazza in front, Vico dei Greci leads west to Vico Mele with some interesting houses.

In the crooked and busy Via degli Orefici (see above) are more carved reliefs. At the end of the street is Piazza Banchi which, until the end of the 18C, was where the money-changers had their tables (*banchi*). Here is the **Loggia dei Mercanti**, designed in 1589–95 by Vannone and restored in the 19C, when it became an exchange, the first of its kind in Italy (now used for exhibitions). The restored, centrally planned church of **San Pietro in Banchi** was designed by Bernardino Cantone and built by Giovanni Ponzello and Vannone (1581). Via Ponte Reale leads down to the quays, past the house where Daniel O'Connell—'the Liberator'—died in 1847 (plaque). The arcaded Portici di Sottoripa, with numerous snack bars, are characteristic of the old port area.

The southern waterfront

Piazza Caricamento (Map 6) faces the Porto Vecchio, Genoa's old harbour. Here is the Gothic **Palazzo di San Giorgio** (restored in 1992), begun c 1260 and extended towards the sea in 1570. The façade facing the harbour was frescoed by Lazzaro Tavarone in 1606–08. Once the palace of the Capitani del Popolo, it became in 1408 the seat of the famous Banco di San Giorgio, which was largely responsible for the prosperity of the city from the mid-15C onwards. Here citizens could lend money for compound interest, and the idea of cheques was introduced. It is now occupied by the Harbour Board (open Sat 10.00–18.00).

Across the road and under the *sopraelevata* (or Strada Aldo Moro), an ugly raised motorway (1965) that distributes traffic from the western suburbs to the city, is the **Molo Vecchio** (Map 9). The quay was begun in 1257 by the Cistercian friars Oliverio and Filippo; the imposing **Porta Siberia**, designed by Galeazzo Alessi, dates from 1553. The area was redesigned by Renzo Piano in 1992: he converted the old cotton warehouses into a congress centre (which can hold 1600 people), and created an open-air space on the quay for spectacles and fairs, next to the *bigo*, an unusual metal structure that serves as a 'crane' for a lift from which there is a panoramic view. In this area are two new museums: the

Museo dell'Antartide (open Tues–Sat 09.45–18.15, Sun and holidays 10.00–19.00) documenting Italian scientific expeditioins to Antarctica and giving visitors an experience of conditions there; and the **Padiglione del Mare e della Navigazione** (open Tues–Fri 10.30–17.30; Sat–Sun and holidays 10.30–18.00), a maritime museum with models and reconstructions of ships and life at sea in various historical periods.

The Aquarium

The Aquarium (Map 6; open Tues–Wed and Fri 09.30–19.00; Thur, Sat and Sun 09.30–20.30), also designed by Piano in 1992, is the largest in Europe (much visited by school parties), with 50 huge tanks that can be viewed both from an underwater level and from above. The natural habitat of the Red Sea and the Caribbean coral reef have been reconstructed; and you can admire some 20,000 creatures, including dolphins, seals and sharks, and tropical fish. The redesigning of the rest of the area has still to be completed.

Palazzo Spinola and its neighbourhood

Leave the waterfront by Via Ponte Reale, at the northeast corner of Palazzo San Giorgio. From Piazza Banchi, Via San Luca (**Map 7**) leads north. This was the main street of the city from the Middle Ages to the 18C, when it was the principal place of residence of the great Genoese families. It is now a commercial street, full of shops and offices. The little church of **San Luca**, to the right, rebuilt in 1626, is a fine example of Genoese Baroque architecture, with an interior frescoed by Domenico Piola. It contains sculptures by Filippo Parodi and an altarpiece by Grechetto.

Beyond, Vico Pellicceria leads right to Piazza Pellicceria, with Spinola family townhouses. No. 1 is now the **Galleria Nazionale di Palazzo Spinola** (Map 7; open Tues–Sat 09.00–19.00; Mon 09.00–13.00; Sun and holidays 14.00–19.00). This 16C mansion became the property of the Spinola in the early 18C when the collection of paintings was formed. It was left by the family, with the contents, to the Italian state in 1958, and is a particularly interesting example of a patrician Genoese residence that preserves more or less intact its 17C–18C decorations, as well as its furniture and paintings. The first two floors have been restored as far as possible to their original state under the Spinola, while the third floor is occupied by the Galleria Nazionale della Liguria, with restored works from churches, and an important porcelain collection.

The **first-floor Salone** has a vault frescoed by Lazzaro Tavarone c 1615, and bronzes by Ferdinando Tacca. The **Primo Salotto** contains works by Stefano Magnasco, Baciccio, and Giovanni Battista Carlone. The **Secondo Salotto** contains a portrait of *Ansaldo Pallavicino* by van Dyck, another of him with his father by Domenico Fiasella (who also painted him as doge: this portrait is in the dining room), and a portrait of a lady by Bernardo Strozzi. The kitchen has been reconstructed on the mezzanine floor.

The **second floor** was decorated for Maddalena Doria (wife of Nicolò Spinola) in 1734. The **Salone**, with another ceiling fresco by Tavarone, completed by Giovanni Battista Natali in the 18C, who also painted the walls as a setting for paintings by Domenico Piola, Gregorio de Ferrari, Luca Giordano and Bernardo Strozzi. The **Primo Salotto** still has its 18C decorations and furniture. The **Secondo Salotto** displays paintings by Guido Reni, Luca Cambiaso, Valerio

Castello and Bernardo Strozzi. The *Four Evangelists* are by van Dyck. The **Terzo Salotto** has works by Carlo Maratta, Bernardo Castello, Giulio Cesare Procaccini and Francesco Vanni. The *Virgin in Prayer* is by Joos van Cleve, who stayed in Genoa in 1515–20 and again in 1525–28. The charming **Galleria degli Specchi** (1736) was probably designed by Lorenzo de Ferrari, who painted the vault fresco. The **Quinto Salotto** has paintings by Marcantonio Franceschini, a portrait of *Paolo Spinola* by Angelica Kauffmann, and 18C furniture.

The **Mezzanine** has a collection of Spinola engravings and 19C silver. On the stairs is a statue by Filippo Parodi.

The National Gallery's collections of paintings and sculpture are displayed on the **third floor**. Highlights include an *Ecce Homo by Antonello da Messina, an equestrian *portrait of Gio Carlo Doria by Rubens, a portrait of a *Lady with a Child* by van Dyck, a statue of *Justice*, part of the funerary monument of Margaret of Brabant by Giovanni Pisano, a portrait of Scipione Clausone by Tintoretto, saints by Carlo Braccesco, and bronzes by Giambologna. The two small female portraits by Mignard are in exquisite 17C frames (one by Filippo Parodi).

On the **top floor** are a fine display of European and Asian porcelain that belonged to the Spinola, and a collection of antique textiles. A spiral staircase leads up from here to a little terrace with a delightful view of the city.

Vico della Scienza leads east from Piazza Pellicceria into Via della Posta Vecchia, with several good portals. Via San Luca (see above) continues to **San Siro** (Map 7), a large church rebuilt by Andrea Ceresola and Daniele Casella (1586–1613), with a façade of 1821. Its predecessor was the cathedral of Genoa before the 9C. It contains frescoes by Giovanni Battista Carlone and paintings by Pomerancio and Fiasella.

From Via San Luca, the pretty Via della Maddalena (**Map 7**) leads east past a palace (no. 29, with a delightful courtyard) that belonged to Simone Boccanegra, elected first doge of Genoa in 1340, to the church of **Santa Maria Maddalena** (**Map 7**), rebuilt in 1588 by Andrea Ceresola. The richly decorated interior contains paintings and frescoes by Bernardo Castello and Giovanni Battista Parodi, and five beautiful *statuettes of the *Virtues*, attributed to Giovanni Pisano. From here numerous alleyways lead up to Via Garibaldi.

Some patrician palaces

***Via Garibaldi** (Map 7), formerly known as the Strada Nuova, was laid out in 1558 by Bernardino Cantone, pupil of Galeazzo Alessi. In the following decade the leading Genoese patrician families built their magnificent mansions here, making it one of the more handsome streets in Europe. Narrow lanes lead down from the street into the old city.

Palazzo Bianco

Built for the Grimaldi c 1565 and enlarged after 1711 by Giacomo Viano for Maria Durazzo, widow of Giovanni Francesco Brignole Sale, *Palazzo Bianco (no. 11; open Tues, Thur–Fri and Sun 09.00–13.00; Wed and Sat 09.00–19.00) was presented to the municipality in 1884 by Maria Brignole Sale, the Duchess of Galliera. The palace contains part of her collection of paintings, together with later acquisitions, with some particularly beautiful Flemish and Dutch paintings.

The gallery was excellently rearranged and modernised in 1950 by Franco Albini. Only the outstanding pieces are on view.

The exhibits begin on the **first floor**. Room **1** (beyond Room 2) has 13C Byzantine works; the *Madonna of the Goldfinch* by Barnaba da Modena; and works by the Brea family (late 15–16C). Room **2** is devoted to Luca Cambiaso.

On the **second floor**, Room **3** (south loggia) displays paintings by two very diverse Florentine artists, Filippino Lippi and Giorgio Vasari. Room **4** contains the masterpieces of the collection: Master of St John the Evangelist (Flemish, late 15C), four *Scenes from the Life of the Saint*; Hans Memling (*Christ Blessing*); *Madonnas* by Joos van Cleve and Gerard David; Jan Provost (*St Peter*, *Annunciation*, *St Elizabeth*). Room **5**: Jan Matsys and Jan van Scorel. Room **6**: Cornelis de Wael and Jan Wildens.

Room **7**: van Dyck, Jan Roos and Rubens. Room **8**: Flemish and Dutch 17C genre paintings by David Teniers the Younger, Jan Steen, Jacob Ruysdael and Aelbert Cuyp. Room **9** displays Italian paintings from the 16C to early 17C (Veronese and Palma il Giovane; Procaccini, Cerano, Morazzone, Paggi and Salimbeni). Room **10** (north loggia): Caravaggio (*Ecce Homo*), Simon Vouet and Matthias Stomer. Room **11**: Works of the Spanish school, including Murillo and Francesco Zurbaran.

Rooms **12–15** contain interesting paintings of the 17C–18C Genoese school, by Bernardo Strozzi; Anton Maria Vassallo, Antonio Travi, Giovanni Battista Carlone and Sinibaldo Scorza; Domenico Fiasella, Giovanni Andrea Ansaldo and Giovanni Andrea de Ferrari; Gioacchino Assereto and Silvestro Chiesa. The local collection is continued on the ground floor (across the courtyard) in Rooms **16–20** (Domenico Piola, Gregorio de Ferrari, Bartolomeo Guidobono, Il Baciccio, Valerio Castello, Giovanni Benedetto Castiglione and Alessandro Magnasco).

Palazzo Rosso

Almost opposite Palazzo Bianco is *Palazzo Rosso (**Map 7**; open as Palazzo Bianco), a magnificent building of 1671–77 erected for Ridolfo and Gio Francesco Brignole Sale by Pier Antonio Corradi and decorated in 1687–89 by Gregorio De Ferrari, Domenico Piola and others. Like Palazzo Bianco it was bequeathed to the city (in 1874) by the Duchess of Galliera, together with her magnificent art collection, which includes fine portraits of the Brignole family by van Dyck. It was likewise well restored after damage in the war, in 1953–61 by Franco Albini.

First floor. Room **2**: works by Giambono, Veronese, Dürer and Palma Vecchio. Room **3**: portraits by Paris Bordone. Room **4**: works by Giulio Cesare Procaccini and Lodovico Carracci. Room **5**: Guido Reni and Guercino. Room **6**: Mattia Preti and Ribera. Rooms **7–10**: Bernardo Strozzi, Giovanni Benedetto Castiglione and Bartolomeo Guidobono.

Second floor. Room **12**, the Salone, has frescoes by Antonio and Enrico Haffner. Rooms **13 and 14** have vault frescoes by Gregorio de Ferrari; portraits by van Dyck: Geronima Sale Brignole with her daughter Aurelia; Frederick, Prince of Orange; a Genoese patrician; *Pucci the goldsmith and his son*; Anton Giulio Brignole Sale and his wife Paolina. Rooms **15–16** have vaults decorated by Domenico Piola. Room **15**. Brignole portraits by Yacinthe Rigaud. The **loggia** has a good view of the striped campanile of the duomo, the campanile of Santa

Maria delle Vigne, and the Torre degli Embriaci. Rooms **18** and **19** are frescoed by Giovanni Andrea Carlone. Room **22** has frescoes by Parodi and Guidobono.

Immediately beyond Palazzo Rosso, on the left, is *****Palazzo Dorio Tursi** (the town hall), flanked by raised gardens. It was begun in 1568 for Nicolò Grimaldi by the Ponzello brothers, and the loggias were added in 1597 around the magnificent courtyard. It is open Mon–Thur 09.00–12.00, 13.00–16.00, Fri 09.00–12.00, 13.00–15.00, and contains the Guarneri violin (1742) that belonged to Genoa-born Nicolò Paganini (1784–1840), the violinist and composer, as well as three letters from Columbus.

Most of the other mansions in this street can be admired only from the outside, though the courtyards are usually accessible. No. 12 is the late-16C Palazzo Serra. **Palazzo Podestà** (no. 7) was begun by Giovanni Battista Castello and Bernardino Cantone in 1563, and has a good stuccoed vestibule and a Rococo grotto and fountain in the courtyard. **Palazzo Spinola** (no. 5) has frescoes in the atrium and vestibule (the fine courtyard has been enclosed for use as a banking hall). **Palazzo Doria** (no. 6) of 1563 was remodelled in 1684, with a charming little courtyard. **Palazzo Carrega Cataldi** (no. 4) is by Giovanni Battista Castello and Bernardino Cantone (1558–60), and has a splendid hall of mirrors (opened on request). **Palazzo Lercari Parodi** (no. 3), attributed to Galeazzo Alessi (1571–78), has a portal with two atlantes (male figures) by Taddeo Carlone (1581). **Palazzo Gambaro** (no.2) is by Bernardo Spazio (1558–64), and Palazzo Cambiaso (no. 1) is by Bernardino Cantone (1558–60).

In the irregular Piazza Fontane Marose (**Map 7**) are Palazzo Pallavicini (no. 2), begun 1565; Palazzo Negrone (no. 4), altered c 1750; and the 15C **Palazzo Spinola dei Marmi** (no. 6), with a coloured-marble façade and statues of the Spinola family.

Beyond the western end of Via Garibaldi is Via Cairoli (**Map 7**), where **Palazzo Balbi** (no. 18) has an ingenious staircase by Gregorio Petondi (1780). In Largo della Zecca is the entrance to the Galleria Garibaldi, a road-tunnel of 1927.

Via Bensa continues to Piazza della Nunziata, dominated by the19C Neo-classical pronaos of **Santissima Annunziata** (**Map 2**), a church rebuilt 1591–1620. The elaborate 17C interior has frescoes by Giovanni Battista and Giovanni Carlone in the nave vault, and by Andrea Ansaldo and Gregorio de Ferrari in the dome. The fine altarpieces by the 17C Genoese school include numerous works by Giovanni Battista Carlone, Domenico Piola, Pierre Puget and Anton Maria Maragliano.

From here the narrow Via Balbi (**Map 2**) continues uphill towards Principe Station, past many dignified old mansions. On the right is **Palazzo Durazzo-Pallavicini** (no. 1; now Giustiniani Adorno), by Bartolomeo Bianco, with a later double loggia. It contains a remarkable private collection (not open to the public) including the best works by van Dyck in the city. **Palazzo Balbi-Senarega**, opposite (no. 4; used by the university), is also by Bianco. Since 1803 the **University** has occupied the palace at no. 5, built in 1634–36 as a Jesuit college by Bartolomeo Bianco. It has an imposing court, and statues and reliefs by Giambologna (1579) in the Aula Magna. The Botanical Garden (**Map 2**) was founded in 1803.

Opposite (no. 10) is the former **Palazzo Reale** (or Palazzo Balbi-Durazzo; **Map 2**), designed c 1650 for the Balbi family by Michele Moncino and Pier Francesco Cantone and remodelled in 1705 for the Durazzo by Carlo Fontana. From 1842 to 1922 it was the royal seat in Genoa, and it contains several suites of sumptuously decorated 18C rooms (open daily 09.00–14.00; in Jul–Sep, Tues–Sat 09.00–19.00); a *Crucifixion* by van Dyck; and works by Luca Giordano, Domenico Parodi, Bartolomeo Guidobono and Bernardo Strozzi.

The northern waterfront

Via Balbi ends in Piazza Acquaverde, with a monument (1862) to Columbus in front of **Principe Railway Station**, an impressive building of 1854. Downhill to the left is the church of San Giovanni di Prè (**Map 1**), founded in 1180, with a severe interior (often restored); the church has been turned round and a false apse created at the west end, the entrance being in the original apse. An upper and lower church adjoin the **Commenda** (**Map 1**), the Commandery of the Knights Hospitaller of St John, built at the same time as a convent and hospice for crusaders. On Piazza Commenda is the fine five-spired campanile and flank of the church (with Gothic windows), next to the beautiful triple loggia of the Commenda, altered in the Renaissance (restored in 1992).

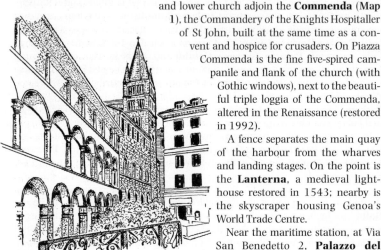

A fence separates the main quay of the harbour from the wharves and landing stages. On the point is the **Lanterna**, a medieval lighthouse restored in 1543; nearby is the skyscraper housing Genoa's World Trade Centre.

Near the maritime station, at Via San Benedetto 2, **Palazzo del Principe** (**Map 1**) has recently been opened to the public (Sat 15.00–

San Giovanni di Prè

18.00; Sun 10.00–13.00; closed Aug). Two buildings here were acquired by Andrea Doria in 1521 and were made into one by Domenico Caranca (1529); Montorsoli may have added the loggia (1543–47), facing the garden. Charles V and Napoleon were entertained here in 1533 and 1805 respectively, and the composer Verdi wintered here from 1877. Still owned by the Doria Pamphili family, the palace contains frescoes by Perin del Vaga and stuccoes by Luzio Romano and Guglielmo della Porta in the vestibule and on the stairs, as well as portraits of Andrea Doria (by Sebastiano del Piombo) and Giannettino Doria (attributed to Bronzino).

From San Giovanni di Prè, the long and dilapidated Via di Prè (**Map 2**) leads back towards the centre parallel to the sea. It passes the circular Neo-classical church of San Sisto (1827), behind Palazzo Reale, and ends at Porta dei Vacca, a Gothic arch dating from 1155. Beyond the arch is Via del Campo (**Map 6**) which has some good portals, and ends at Piazza Fossatello. From here Via Lomellini leads left to the church of **San Filippo Neri**, with a fine 18C interior decorated by Antonio Maria Haffner and a painted *Deposition* group by Anton Maria Maragliano. The **oratory** next door (no. 10; if closed ask at the Casa Mazzini) has an *interior of 1749 (used for concerts), with a statue of the *Immacolata* by Pierre Puget. The **Casa Mazzini**, at no. 11 Via Lomellini (open 09.00–13.00 except Mon and Wed), where Giuseppe Mazzini (1805–72) was born, contains an excellent museum of the Risorgimento. Narrow roads lead back up to Via Cairoli (see above).

The modern town

From Piazza De Ferrari, Via Roma leads northeast to Piazza Corvetto (**Map 8**). The Vittorio Emanuele II monument here is by Francesco Barzaghi (1886). Behind the Mazzini monument (by Pietro Costa, 1882) is the hillside garden of the **Villetta di Negro** (**Map 8**). A fine building (1971, by Mario Labò) houses the *Museo d'Arte Orientale Edoardo Chiossone** (open 09.00–13.00 except Mon and Wed). This splendid collection of Japanese, Chinese and Thai art was left to the municipality of Genoa by the painter Edoardo Chiossone (1832–98) and has been augmented during this century. It is especially notable for its Japanese works, including large sculptures (10C–18C) and arms and armour.

From Piazza Corvetto the long, straight Via Assarotti leads northeast to Piazza Manin, passing the sumptuous church of the **Immacolata** (1864–73). On the hill opposite is the beautiful **Villa Pallavicino delle Peschiere** (by Galeazzo Alessi), where Dickens stayed in 1845.

From Piazza Manin you soon reach the **Mura Nuove**, the 17C walls which extend as far as Forte Sperone. On Via Cesare Cabella is the **Castello Mackenzie**. Derived from Tuscan Gothic buildings, it was commissioned at the end of the 19C from Gino Coppedè by a Scottish insurance broker, Evan Mackenzie. Partly restored by the Wolfsonian Foundation as a museum of Italian decorative arts from the period 1885–1945, it was donated to the city in 1996.

At Piazza Manin begin the avenues known as the *Circonvallazione a Monte** (**Map 2, 3, 7** and **8**), over 4km long, which provide an interesting view of the city. **Bus 33** follows them from beginning to end, and lifts and funicular railways serve as intermediate approaches. The most important monuments on the first segment are the 17C Villa Gruber, the seat of the **Museo Americanistico Federico Lunardi** (**Map 4**; open Tues–Sat 09.30–12.00, 15.00–17.30; Sun and holidays 15.00–17.30), with archaeological and ethnographical material from North and South America; the Gothic-revival **Castello Bruzzo**, by Gino Coppedè; and the 16C church of San Nicola da Tolentino, with statues by Taddeo Carlone. Nearby is a station on the funicular that mounts to **Righi**, where there are good views of the city and its fortifications. The huge **Albergo dei Poveri** was founded by the Brignole family in 1656 as one of the first poorhouses of its kind, and built to a functional design by Stefano Scaniglia and Giovanni Battista Ghiso. The magnificent **Castello d'Albertis** is a 19C reconstruction of a medieval Ligurian castle on the old bastion of Monte Galletto. The interior, with an ethnographical museum (pre-Columbian art), is closed for restoration.

From Piazza De Ferrari, the wide, arcaded Via XX Settembre leads southeast past the church of **Santo Stefano** (**Map 2**), with a colourful front of the 13C–14C and a 10C crypt. The choir-gallery of 1499 is the work of Donato Benti and Benedetto da Rovezzano. On the south wall is a painting by Giulio Romano. A lift ascends to the Ponte Monumentale (**Map 2**) which crosses Via XX Settembre. Above are the **Acquasola Gardens**, with fine trees, and **Santa Caterina**, a church largely rebuilt from 1556, with a portal of 1521 by Pier Antonio Piuma, and containing good 16C Genoese paintings, including works by Giovanni Battista Castello.

Via XX Settembre continues past the church of **Santa Maria della Consolazione**, by Pier Antonio Corradi (1684–1706), with a dome by Simone Cantone (1769) and a front of 1864. The street ends at the gardens of Piazza Verdi in front of Brignole station, and Piazza della Vittoria, with a triumphal arch erected as a war memorial by Marcello Piacentini in 1931. In Via Brigata Liguria, in a building of 1905–12, is the **Museo di Storia Naturale** (open 09.00–12.00, 15.00–17.30 except Mon and Fri), founded in 1867 with the zoo-logical collections of Giacomo Doria.

In Corso Buenos Aires are the glass skyscrapers of **Corte Lambruschini** (which incorporate the Teatro della Corte), built in the 1980s by Piero Gambacciani. In Piazza Tommaseo is a monument to General Manuel Belgrano (1770–1820), liberator of the Argentine Republic, by Arnaldo Zocchi (1927). The interesting 19C district of **Foce** extends to the south as far as the seafront.

From Piazza De Ferrari the short, broad Via Dante runs southeast. On the right, beside a little house reconstructed in the 18C and called the **House of Columbus**, is a garden with the reconstructed 12C **Cloister of Sant'Andrea**. Above rises **Porta Soprana** (**Map 11**), a tall gateway of 1155.

Across Piazza Dante, with skyscrapers built in the 1930s, is Via Fieschi, which ascends to the classical church of **Santa Maria Assunta di Carignano** (**Map 15**), one of the best works of Galeazzo Alessi (begun in 1552). The sculptures on the façade are by Claude David, and inside on the dome-piers are statues (1662–90) by Pierre Puget, Filippo Parodi and Claude David. Via Nino Bixio and Via Ruffini lead southeast to **Villa Croce**, with a contemporary art museum (open Tues–Sat 09.00–19.00; Sun and holidays 09.00–12.30), and a library. Nearby, on the seafront are the buildings of the **Fiera Internazionale**, where big international exhibitions are held.

Around Genoa

The *****Staglieno Cemetery** (open daily 08.00–17.00) was laid out, with exten-sive gardens, in 1844–51 and has intriguing 19C funerary sculpture. The con-spicuous colossal statue of *Faith* is by Santo Varni, and near the upper gallery, in a clump of trees, is the simple tomb of Mazzini, surrounded by memorials to members of Garibaldi's 'Thousand'. To the left of the Pantheon and the main enclosure—on the third terrace, planted with oak trees—is the Protestant temple and cemetery: Constance Mary Lloyd, the wife of Oscar Wilde, is buried here. From the viale a long staircase ascends to the English cemetery designed by Gino Coppedè in 1902. This includes the British military cemetery from both world wars.

A single-track **railway** line (29km) built in 1929 winds up the Val Bisagno, the Valpolcevera and the Valle Scrivi from Piazza Manin, to end at Casella. It has splendid views.

West of Principe Station and the harbour is the port of Sampierdarena, known for its old-established engineering and metallurgical works: the first Italian loco-motive was built at the Ansaldo works here in 1854. The airport of Genoa, built out into the sea on reclaimed land, is at Sestri Ponente.

Pegli, now at the western limit of the city, was once a popular weekend resort of the Genoese. It still has a few fine villas backed by pine woods. The **Villa Doria**, a pleasant public park with a 16C mansion (containing frescoes by Lazzaro Tavarone), houses the **Naval and Maritime Museum** (open Tues–Thur 09.00–13.00, Fri–Sat 09.00–19.00; first and third Sun of the month 09.00–13.00; closed Mon). This illustrates the history of the great Genoese maritime republic and includes a portrait of Columbus attributed to Ridolfo Ghirlandaio. The splendid, luxuriant garden of *Villa Durazzo-Pallavicini (open Tues–Sun, Apr–Sep 09.00–19.00; Nov–Mar 10.00–17.00), created in the 1840s, includes a partly underground lake and a 'Chinese' temple. The villa of 1837 houses the **Museo di Archeologia Ligure** (open Tues–Thur 09.00–19.00, Fri–Sat 09.00–13.00, second and fourth Sun of the month 09.00–13.00; closed Mon), notable for prehistoric finds from Ligurian cave-dwellings, and pre-Roman necropolis finds from the city of Genoa.

The eastern districts of the city include **Albaro**, which has numerous villas. From Piazza Vittoria, Corso Buenos Aires leads east to Piazza Tommaseo, where steps mount to Via Pozzo, rising below the **Villa Saluzzo Bombrini**, known as Villa Paradiso, with its beautiful garden. Built by Andrea Vannone in the 16C, it is one of the better preserved of the villas in the district of Albaro. Via Pozzo ends at Via Albaro, with **Villa Saluzzo Mongiordino** (no. 1), where Byron lived in 1822. Further on to the left, the Faculty of Engineering of the university occupies the splendid **Villa Giustiniani Cambiaso** (1548, on a design by Galeazzo Alessi), with another garden. The little church of San Giuliano d'Albaro, built in 1240, was enlarged in the 15C. In Via San Nazaro, the **Villa Bagnerello** (plaque), was where Dickens lived in 1844 before moving into Genoa: 'I was set down in a rank, dull, weedy courtyard, attached to a kind of pink jail; and was told I lived there.'

A short way east is the tiny old fishing port of **Boccadasse**, well preserved, still with its old gas lamp standards. It has good fish restaurants and a popular ice-cream shop. Above it is a mock medieval castle by Gino Coppedè.

Further east is **Quarto**, where a monument marks the starting-point of Garibaldi and the 'Thousand' (*I Mille*) on their expedition to Sicily (5 May 1860). The expedition was the first major campaign in the five-year war that united the many city-states of Italy under the rule of a single king, Victor Emanuel of Savoy. In Villa Spinola, where Garibaldi stayed while planning the expedition with his friend Candido Augusto Vecchi, is a small Garibaldi Museum (open Thur–Tues 09.00–12.00, 14.30–18.00).

Nervi, 11km east of the centre of Genoa, is now included in its municipal lim-its. It became the earliest winter resort of the Riviera di Levante in 1863. The Passeggiata Anita Garibaldi extends for nearly 2km between the railway and the rock-bound shore. The **Parco Municipale** incorporates the gardens of Villa Gropallo, Villa Serra and Villa Grimaldi. In Villa Serra is a Galleria d'Arte Moderna (not at present open). **Villa Grimaldi** is home to the Frugone collection of 19C and 20C art (open Tues–Sat 09.00–19.00, Sun and holidays 09.00–13.00). Further east is the charming park of the **Villa Luxoro** (open Tues–Sat 09.00–13.00), with a small museum of furniture, lace, paintings, etc.

The Riviera di Ponente

This part of the Ligurian coast, west of Genoa, has a mild climate, numerous winter resorts and luxuriant vegetation with palms, bougainvillaea and exotic plants. Now usually known as the 'Riviera dei Fiori', it has been important for its cut flower industry (especially roses and carnations) since the beginning of the century. In the tract nearest to Genoa chaotic new building has ruined much of the coast since the last war, although the interesting town of Albenga is still well preserved.

Practical information

 Getting there and getting around

By air

Genoa's Cristoforo Colombo Airport, at Sestri Ponente (6km west of the city) handles domestic and international flights, but if you are flying from Britain or North America you may find Nice-Côte d'Azur (59km from San Remo) equally convenient.

By road

The French and Italian rivieras are connected by excellent motoways. In France the A8 from Nice passes the Principality of Monte Carlo, then crosses into Italy at Menton (queues at weekends). The first Italian town on the motorway (in Italy, the A10) is Ventimiglia; other exits serving the Riviera di Ponente are at Bordighiera, San Remo, Arma di Taggia, Imperia, San Bartolomeo, Albenga, Pietra Ligure, Finale Ligure, Sportona, Savona, Albisola, Arenzano and Voltri. Route 1 hugs the coast all the way from Ventimiglia to Genoa; it is more scenic, but considerably slower.

The area can be reached via Savona by the A6 from Turin, or via Genoa by A26 from Alessandria; A7 from Milan and A12 from Pisa and La Spezia. All these roads, given the nature of the terrain, have plenty of curves, viaducts and tunnels, and commercial traffic can be heavy on weekdays.

There are **local bus services** between the main towns; for information and schedules contact *Riviera Trasporti*, ☎ 0184 502030. **Car parks** (some underground or in silos) around the historic centres of most towns.

By rail

The main rail line from Italy to southern France runs the length of the Riviera di Ponente; from Genoa to Nice takes c 3hrs. The French *TGV* runs as far as Menton, making it possible to reach the area from Paris in c 8hrs. Genoa enjoys frequent connections to Turin (166km in 1hr 30mins), Milan (154km in 1hr 30mins) and Pisa (165km in 1hr 40mins). There is also one daily *Interegionale* to and from Bologna (4hrs 50mins). Slow trains serve Savona from Turin and Alessandria (connection to Milan); and there is a scenic mountain railway from Cuneo to Ventimiglia (96km in 1hr 50mins).

 ## Information offices
ALASSIO Via Mazzini 62, ☎ 0182 647027.
ARENZANO Via Cambiaso 2, ☎ 010 9127581.
ALBISSOLA MARINA Via dell'Oratorio 2, ☎ 019 481648.
CELLE LIGURE Via Boagno (Palazzo Comunale), ☎ 019 990021.
DIANO MARINA Piazza Martiri della Libertà 1, ☎ 0183 496956.
FINALE LIGURE Via San Pietro 14, ☎ 019 692581.
IMPERIA Viale Matteotti 54a, ☎ 0183 24947.
LOANO Corso Europa 19, ☎ 019 668044.
SAN REMO Largo Nuovoloni 1, ☎ 0184 571571. *Informagiovani*, Piazza Colombo, ☎ 0184 505002.
SAVONA Piazza del Popolo, ☎ 019 820522.
VARAZZE Viale Nazioni Unite (Palazzo Municipio), ☎ 019 96315.
VENTIMIGLIA Via Cavour 59, ☎ 0184 351183.

 ## Where to stay
There are numerous hotels of all categories in all the main resorts, but few are distinctive and many are open only from spring to early autumn. The latter are marked in the text; those without a specific mention of season are open all year round.
ALASSIO *Dei Fiori*, Viale Marconi 78, ☎ 0182 640519, fax 0182 644116; warm and friendly, in a renovated townhouse; inexpensive. *Grand Hotel*

Diana, Via Garibaldi 110, ☎ 0182 642701, fax 0182 640304; by the sea, with a lovely garden terrace; closed Nov–Jan; moderate. *Regina*, Viale Hanbury 220, ☎ 0182 640215, fax 0182 660092; a comfortable place on the seafront promenade; closed Nov–Mar; moderate.
CENOVA *Negro*, Via Canada 10, ☎ 0183 34089, fax 0183 324991; in the hills above Alassio, a calm, quiet place with 12 rooms; inexpensive.
FINALE LIGURE *Punta Est*, Via Aurelia 1, ☎ 019 600611, fax 019 600611; an 18C villa in a shady park overlooking the sea; closed Nov–Apr; moderate.
GARLENDA *La Meridiana*, Via ai Castelli, ☎ 0182 580271, fax 0182 580150; near the golf course, a renovated country house with nearly as many suites (15) as rooms (18), and an excellent restaurant; closed Dec–Feb; moderate.
SAN REMO *Royal*, Corso Imperatrice 80, ☎ 0184 5391, fax 0184 661445; a fine luxury hotel with luxuriant gardens, heated pool, and outside restaurant seating in fair weather; closed Nov–Dec; expensive.

 ## Eating out
ALASSIO *Il Palma*, Via Cavour 5, ☎ 0182 640314; delicious creative interpretations of traditional Ligurian recipes, in a historic building in the heart of town; closed Wed and Dec–Feb; expensive.
ALBISOLA MARINA *Da Mario*, Corso Bigliati 70, ☎ 019 481640; traditional fish restaurant, with outside seating in summer; closed Wed and Sep; moderate.
ALBISOLA SUPERIORE *Trattoria del Molino*, Piazza Cairoli 2, Località Ellera, ☎ 019 49043; country trattoria with good local food and outstanding views; closed Tues; inexpensive.
APRICALE *La Favorita*, Località Richelmo, ☎ 0184 208186; restaurant (with rooms) offering good

regional cuisine; closed Wed, Jun and Nov; inexpensive.

ARMA DI TAGGIA *La Conchiglia*, Lungomare 33, ☎ 0184 43169; outstanding regional cuisine, especially fish; closed Wed (open Wed evening in Jul–Aug), Jun and Nov–Dec; moderate.

BERGEGGI *Claudio*, Via XXV Aprile 37, ☎ 019 859750; superior traditional restaurant (with rooms) on a clifftop above the sea; closed Mon, midday Tues and Jan; expensive.

BORDIGHERA *Carletto*, Via Vittorio Emanuele 339, ☎ 0184 261725; another truly outstanding fish restaurant; closed Wed, Jun–Jul and Nov–Dec; moderate.

La Via Romana, Via Romana 57, ☎ 0184 266681; excellent traditional fish restaurant; closed Wed and midday Thur; moderate.

Magiargè, Piazza Giacomo Viale, ☎ 0184 262946; simple osteria offering delicious local cooking and good wines; closed Thur; inexpensive.

BORGO VEREIZZI *Da Casetta*, Piazza San Pietro 12, ☎ 019 610166; a warm family-run place in a historic building, serving regional specialties; closed midday (except Sun and holidays), Tues and Nov; moderate.

D.O.C., Via Vittorio Veneto 1, ☎ 019 611477; delicious Ligurian food in an elegant villa setting; closed Mon (midday only in summer); moderate.

CELLE LIGURE *Mosè*, Via Colla 30, ☎ 019 991560; traditional Ligurian cuisine, prepared with care; closed Wed and Oct–Dec; moderate.

IMPERIA *Lanterna Blu*, Via Scarincio 32, Località Porto Marizio, Borgo Marina,
☎ 0183 650178; truly outstanding seafood and excellent French and Italian wines, by the harbour; closed Wed, Oct and Dec; moderate.

Pane e Vino, Via Des Geneys 52, ☎ 0183 290044; wine bar with great soups, sandwiches and fondue; closed

Wed, midday holidays, and Jul–Aug; inexpensive.

MELE (near Voltri) *Osteria dell'Acquasanta*, Via Acquasanta 281, Località Acquasanta, ☎ 010 638035; osteria offering traditional dishes from Liguria and northern Italy and good wines; closed Mon; moderate.

NOLI *Lilliput*, Regione Zuglieno 49, ☎ 019 748009; traditional Ligurian cuisine with an innovative twist (Accademia Italiana della Cucina Excellence Award 1994); closed midday (except weekends), Mon, Jan–Feb and Nov; moderate.

SAN REMO *Da Giannino*, Lungomare Trento e Trieste 23, ☎ 0184 504014; one of the region's better restaurants, serving delicious local specialities, especially fish; closed Sun evening, Mon and Oct; expensive.

Il Bagatto, Via Matteotti 145, ☎ 0184 531925; restaurant serving personal interpretations of traditional recipes; closed Sun and Jun–Jul; moderate.

La Pignese, Piazza Sardi 7, ☎ 0184 501929; traditional trattoria, serving good local dishes; closed Mon and Jun; moderate.

Osteria del Marinaio, Via Gaudio 28, ☎ 0184 501919; good seafood and other local specialties; closed Mon and Oct–Dec; moderate.

Paolo e Barbara, Via Roma 47, ☎ 0184 531653; outstanding Ligurian cuisine with a personal twist; closed Wed and midday Thur, Dec–Jan and Jun–July; expensive.

Try **Enoteca Marone**, Via San Francesco 61, for Ligurian wine and extra virgin olive oil.

SAVONA *A Spurcacciuna*, Via Nizza 89r, ☎ 019 264065; restaurant of the *Hotel Mare*, offering especially good seafood; closed Wed and Dec–Jan; moderate.

Bosco delle Ninfe, Via Ranco 10, ☎ 019 823976; an old-fashioned osteria known for good seafood; closed Mon; inexpensive.

VALLECROSIA *Giappun*, Via Maonaira 7, ☎ 0184 250560; more excellent seafood served with a flair; closed Wed, Jul and Nov; moderate.

VARIGOTTI *Muraglia-Conchiglia d'Oro*, Via Aurelia 133, ☎ 019 698015; outstanding fish and other regional dishes; closed Wed (and Tues, Oct–Mar), Jan–Feb; moderate.

VENTIMIGLIA *Baia Beniamin*, Corso Europa 63, Località Grimaldi Inferiore, ☎ 0184 38002; exquisite seafood restaurant (with rooms), on a luxuriant little bay; closed Sun evening and Mon (Mon only in summer), Apr and Nov; expensive.

Balzi Rossi, Ponte San Ludovico 11, ☎ 0184 38132; another very fine regional restaurant with outside seating in summer and beautiful views of sea and coast; closed Mon, midday Tues (and midday Sun in summer), Mar and Nov–Dec; expensive.

Entertainment

SAN REMO *Casino Municipale*, with gambling in all shapes and forms well into the night. *Orchestra Sinfonica della Città di San Remo*, with summer and winter concert series.

ELSEWHERE Live rock, pop and jazz and clubs and bars in most resorts.

Shopping

Interesting traditional markets include:

ALASSIO *Collezionismo d'Antiquariato*, antiques, days vary.

ALBENGA *Mercato dell'Antiquaritato e del Curioso*, antiques and curiosities, mid-Jul and mid-Aug.

ARMA DI TAGGIA *Collezionismo Sotto i Portici*, collectables, third Sat of the month.

DOLCEACQUA *Mercatino Biologico, dell'Articianato e dell'Antiquariato*, mixing antiques, crafts and organic foods, last Sun of the month.

FINALE LIGURE *Mercato dell'Antiquariato*, antiques, first Sat and Sun of the month.

PIETRA LIGURE *Mercato dell'Antiquariato e dell'Artigianato*, antiques and crafts, last Sat and Sun of the month.

SAVONA *Mercato dell'Antiquariato*, antiques, first Sat and Sun of the month.

VENTIMIGLIA *Mercatino Brocante*, crafts, antiques and flowers, first three Sats and last Sun of the month.

Special events

CERVO *International Chamber Music Festival*, Aug. **IMPERIA** *World Cup Swimming Championship*, Mar; *Rally delle Palme*, car race, Apr; *Infiorata del Corpus Domini*, flower festival (also at Diano Marina and Cervo), Jun; *International Chess Festival*, Aug–Sep; *Raduno di Vele d'Epoca*, biennial antique sailboat show, in even years, Sep.

RIVA LIGURE *Fiori d'Estate*, floral composition contest in the historic town centre, Jul.

SAN BARTOLOMEO AL MARE *Premio Rovere d'Oro*, international vocal and instrumental music competition, Jul–Aug.

SAN REMO *Concorso Internazionale di Arte Floreale Città di San Remo*, international flower show, and *San Remoinfiore*, flower display along the Corso, Jan. *Festival della Canzone Italiana*, annual pop music festival, Feb. *Esposizione Internazionale Felina*, international cat show, and *Milano–San Remo Ciclisica*, professional bicycle race and *Sulle Strade della San Remo*, amateur bicycle race, Mar. *Criterium Preolimpico di Primavera* and *Campionato del Mediterraneo*, sailing, Mar–Apr. *Esposizione Internazionale Canina*, international dog show, and *San Remo Rally Storico 'Coppa dei Fiori'*, antique car rally, Apr.

International Women's Volleyball Tournament and International San Remo Yacht Meeting, May; Gran Fondo Internaziionale di Cicloturismo Milano–San Remo, bicycle race, May–Jun; Festival internazionale del Film e del Video Musicale, film and music video festival, Regata della Giraglia, regatta, and Concorso Ippico Nazionale, horse show, Jun; Campionato Mondiale dei Fuochi d'Artificio, world fireworks championship, International Beach Volley Festival and European Under-14 Tennis Championship, Jul; San Remo Immagine Jazz-San Remo Blues, jazz-blues festival, Jul–Aug. Rally San Remo-Rally d'Italia, car races, Sep; Festival della Lirica, young opera-singers' competition, Oct; Mini Open Riviera dei Fiori, Nov, and Pro-Am Ritorno a San Remo, golf tournaments, Dec.

TAGGIA La Luna e i Suoi Raggi, street-theatre festival, Jul–Aug.

VILLA FARALDI Theatre Festival, Jul–Aug.

ELSEWHERE Festa di Primavera, concerts, art and flower shows throughout the Riviera dei Fiori, Mar.

 Sports

Bungee-jumping at Ponte di Loreto-Triora. Golf courses at Garlenda and San Remo. Diving, fencing, horse-riding, hang-gliding and surfing at San Remo. Hiking, swimming, water-skiing and sailing at or around most resorts.

Savona and its coast

Albisola Superiore, the first town of any importance west of Genoa, was the birthplace of Pope Julius II (Giuliano della Rovere, 1443–1513). It has been famous since the 16C for its ceramics, examples of which are displayed in a museum in Villa Faraggiana.

Savona, a provincial capital (population 64,000) with a conspicuous thermo-electrical plant, was a maritime power and rival of Genoa up until the 16C. Its old district, overlooking the inner harbour, is surrounded by the regular streets of the new town. In recent years its industries of iron founding and shipbreaking have declined.

In the main arcaded Via Paleocapa is the 16C church of **San Giovanni Battista**, with 18C paintings. The theatre (1850–53) is named after the native lyric poet Gabriello Chiabrera (1553–1638), the 'Italian Ronsard'. Near a terrace of pretty Art Nouveau houses overlooking the harbour is the 14C **Torre Pancaldo**, named after Leon Pancaldo of Savona, Magellan's 'Genoese' pilot.

Via Pia, with stone doorways, leads into the old town. The **Cathedral** was built in 1589–1605 (façade 1886). It contains an altarpiece by Albertino Piazza, a Romanesque font, and choir stalls of 1500. A little diocesan museum contains works by Lodovico Brea and the 'Maestro di Hoogstraten', and the 17C oratory of **Santa Maria di Castello** holds a polyptych by Vincenzo Foppa and Lodovico Brea (1490). Facing the cathedral is **Palazzo Della Rovere**, begun by Giuliano da Sangallo for Julius II but never finished.

On the right of the cathedral is the **Cappella Sistina**, erected by Sixtus IV in memory of his parents and given a harmonious Baroque interior in 1764. It contains a fine marble tomb, by Michele and Giovanni de Aria, with figures of the two Della Rovere popes, Sixtus IV and Julius II. In Piazza del Mercato are two 12C towers. The small **Pinacoteca Civica** (open Mon–Sat except holidays,

08.30–12.30) contains works by Donato de Bardi, Vincenzo Foppa and Giovanni Battista Carlone.

The **Fortezza del Priamar**, on a hill on the southern seafront by the public gardens, was erected by the Genoese in 1542. Mazzini was imprisoned here in 1830–31. It contains an archaeological museum and a museum of works of art (including paintings by Filippo De Pisis and Mario Sironi) donated by the former Italian president Sandro Pertini.

On the coast road west of Savona is **Zinola**, with a British Military Cemetery containing 104 graves, mostly from the wreck of the *Transylvania*, torpedoed off Savona in 1917. Beyond the headland of Bergeggi, with its islet offshore, is **Spotorno** with a fine sandy beach, but much ugly new building has taken place here since D.H. Lawrence's sojourn in 1926, when he wrote *Lady Chatterley's Lover*.

Noli, an important port in the Middle Ages, preserves its walls and three tall towers of brick, as well as some old houses and an 11C church.

The old village of **Finalborgo**, 2km inland from **Finale Marina**, has a church with a fine octagonal campanile (13C). It contains a 16C tomb of the Del Carretto family, whose ruined castle is nearby. In the cloister of Santa Caterina is the Civico Museo del Finale (open Tues–Sun 09.00–12.00, 14.30–16.30; summer 10.00–12.00, 15.00–18.00; Sun and holidays 09.00–12.00; closed Jan) with finds from the many local limestone caves in which prehistoric remains have been discovered. On the old Roman road further inland are about a dozen Roman bridges (1C AD), five of them intact.

Pietra Ligure has a church by Fantone (1791). **Loano**, an old seaside town with palm groves, has a town hall in the Palazzo Doria (1578), which contains a 3C mosaic pavement. Via Cavour 32 was the birthplace of Rosa Raimondi, Garibaldi's mother. Inland is the **Grotta di Toirano**, a remarkable stalactite cavern, with the only footprints of Mousterian man (probably Neanderthal) so far discovered, and a museum of local prehistory.

Albenga

Albenga was the Roman port *Albium Ingaunum*, but is now over a kilometre from the sea, as the course of the Centa River was altered in the 13C. It still has most of its medieval walls (on foundations of the 1C BC) and three 17C gates; also about a dozen 12C–14C brick tower-houses, mostly well restored. The town has expanded towards the sea since the 19C.

The **Cathedral**, on late-4C or early-5C foundations, with an elegant campanile of 1391, was reconstructed in its medieval form in 1967. The **Palazzo Vecchio del Comune** (1387 and 1421), incorporating a tall tower of c 1300, houses the Civico Museo Ingauno (open Tues–Sun 10.00–12.00, 15.00–18.00) with prehistoric, Roman and medieval remains. The 5C *baptistery, ten-sided without and octagonal within, preserves a fine Byzantine mosaic of the 5C or 6C in its principal apse and 8C transennae.

The charming Piazzetta dei Leoni has three Renaissance lions brought from Rome in 1608. The former **bishop's palace** has external frescoes (15C). The little diocesan museum inside contains finds from the cathedral and paintings by Guido Reni and Domenico Piola. Via Bernardo Ricci (the Roman *decumanus*) crosses Via delle Medaglie (the *cardo maximus*) at the 13C Loggia dei Quattro Canti.

In Piazza San Michele is the **Museo Navale Romano** (open Tues–Sun

10.00–12.00, 15.00–18.00), containing more than 100 wine amphorae and marine fittings salvaged since 1950 from a Roman vessel sunk offshore in 100–90 BC. This is the largest Roman transport ship yet found in the Mediterranean; it was carrying more than 10,000 amphorae of wine (700 of which were recovered) from Campania to southern France and Spain. Attached to the museum is an important centre for underwater archaeology. In a fine 18C hall there is a collection of Albisola pharmacy jars. You can see scanty remains of the Roman city along the River Centa.

Alassio, one of the more popular Ligurian coastal resorts, has an exceptionally mild winter climate and an excellent sandy beach. It is at the head of a wide, beautiful bay, facing nearly east. It was well known to the English by the end of the 19C—they built the church of St John's here—and is famed for the luxuriance of its gardens. While wintering here in 1904 Elgar composed his overture *In the South (Alassio)*. Carlo Levi, the writer and painter, spent much time in Alassio, and a collection of his paintings is to be exhibited in the town.

Offshore is the **Isola Gallinara**, or Gallinaria (boat trips from the *porto turistico* or from Loano). Little remains of the once powerful Benedictine monastery founded here in the 8C, which at one time owned most of the Riviera di Ponente. St Martin of Tours took refuge from his Arian persecutors here in 356–360. The island is now privately owned; it has been a protected area since 1989, with lovely vegetation and grottoes, and interesting birdlife.

A short way west of Alassio is **Laigueglia**, a resort with an 18C church by Gian Domenico Baguti. Inland is **Andora Castle**, the finest medieval building on the Riviera del Ponente. Circular walls enclose a ruined castle and a late 13C church. A medieval bridge crosses the Merula.

Continuing westward, you soon reach **Cervo**, a very well-preserved medieval *borgo*, with a rich Baroque church by Giovanni Battista Marvaldi (1686) and a small ethnographic museum (open daily 09.00–12.30, 15.00–18.30 or 21.00–23.00). **Diano Marina**, another olive-growing town, with a sandy beach, is a summer and winter resort.

Imperia is a provincial capital (population 41,000) created in 1923 by the fusion of Porto Maurizio, Oneglia and adjoining villages. In **Porto Maurizio**, with an old district of stepped streets, is a large church (1781–1832). **Oneglia** is at the mouth of the Impero Torrent, from which the province takes its name. It is an important centre of the olive-oil trade, and has a large pasta factory on the seafront. The town hall, built in 1932, is between the two towns. Grock (Adrien Wettach), the great Swiss clown, died in 1959 in the eclectic Villa Grock. The **Museo Navale Internazionale del Ponente Ligure**, in Piazza Duomo (open Wed and Sat, summer 21.00–23.00, winter 15.30–19.00) has ship models, dioramas and other exhibits about sailing; the **Museo dell'Olivo**, Via Garessio 13 (open Wed–Mon 09.00–12.00 and 15.00–18.30) offers displays regarding olive oil, its production and uses, and a rebuilt Roman ship. The exhibits at the **Istituto Storico della Resistenza e dell'Età Contemporanea** (open Mon–Fri 09.00–13.00 except Aug) document the Ligurian resistance in the Second World War.

San Remo and the road to France

San Remo is the largest summer and winter resort on the Italian Riviera, visited since the mid-19C for its superb climate. Its villas and gardens lie in an amphitheatre in a wide bay, although the sea is separated from the town by the old railway line. Edward Lear (1812–88) spent his last years at San Remo, and built the Villa Emily (now Villa Verde) and Villa Tennyson (both named after Tennyson's wife). He died at the latter and was buried in San Remo. Alfred Nobel (1833–96) also died here, and here in 1878 Tchaikovsky finished his *Fourth Symphony* and *Eugene Onegin*. The empress of Russia, Maria Alexandrovna, consort of Alexander II, lived here, surrounded after 1874 by a large Russian colony. The town is famous for its annual festivals, especially the *International Song Contest*.

Via Roma and the parallel Via Matteotti are the main streets of the modern town. In the latter, at no. 143, is the early-16C **Palazzo Borea d'Olmo**, which houses a small museum with an archaeological collection and Pinacoteca (open Tues–Sat 09.00–12.30, 15.00–18.30). To the southwest, surrounded by gardens, in an Art Nouveau building by Eugenio Ferret (1904–06), is the **Casinò Municipale** (always open), with celebrated gaming rooms.

> ### The smile of San Remo
> At San Remo, as the Italian coast draws to a close it gathers up on its lovely bosom the scattered elements of its beauty and heart-broken at ceasing to be that land of lands, it exhales towards the blind insensate heavens a rapturous smile, more poignant than any reproach. There is something hideous in having at such a place to get back into one's carriage.
> Henry James, letter to Henry James Sr, 18 January 1870

The **Corso dell'Imperatrice*, lined with magnificent palm trees, leads past the delightful Russian church (San Basilio) to the Parco Marsaglia, in which is a monument to Garibaldi by Leonardo Bistolfi (1908). The English Church (All Saints) is in Corso Matuzia.

Along the shore in the other direction, Via Nino Bixio leads to the Genoese fort of **Santa Tecla** (1755) and the mole of the old harbour. Corso Trento e Trieste continues along the waterfront, past the harbour for private boats, to the public gardens. The old district of La Pigna has quaint narrow streets. The duomo here is a 13C building enlarged in the 17C.

Nearby **Taggia** is an interesting old village in a pretty position. The 15C Gothic church of **San Domenico** contains works by Lodovico Brea; the convent houses a small museum (open daily 09.00–12.00, 15.00–17.00 or 18.00) displaying paintings, sculpture, manuscripts, miniatures and prints ranging in date from the 14C to the 18C. In the old walled town is a palace attributed to Gian Lorenzo Bernini and the parish church, perhaps designed by him. A 16C **bridge** (on Romanesque foundations) of 16 arches crosses the Argentina.

At the head of the pretty Valle Argentina is **Triora**, with remains of its fortifications, a painting by Taddeo di Bartolo in the Collegiata, and a museum of witches and witchcraft (open Mon–Sat 15.00–18.30, Sun and holidays 10.00–12.30 and 15.00–18.30.

Ospedaletti, on a sheltered bay, is a horticultural centre, and has fine palms and eucalyptus trees.

Bordighera is another winter resort with a mild climate. It became known in Britain after 1855, when *Doctor Antonio* by Giovanni Ruffini, set in the town, was translated, and became a best-seller. By the end of the 19C a large English colony had been established here. It is also a centre for the cultivation of cut flowers (a market was built here in 1898), and has numerous palm trees.

Several buildings in the town were built in the 1870s by the Frenchman Charles Garnier. In Via Romana, the villa in which Queen Margherita di Savoia (widow of Umberto I) died in 1926, faces the **Museo Bicknell** (open Mon–Fri 09.30–13.00, 13.30–17.00), founded by the Englishman Clarence Bicknell in 1888, with good local natural history and archaeological collections. Here, too, is the Istituto Internazionale di Studi Liguri. The International Library, at Via Romana 30, was also founded by Bicknell. Northeast of the town is a British Military Cemetery, with 72 graves.

Ventimiglia is divided by the Roia into an old medieval town on a hill to the west and a new town on the coastal plain between the railway and the Via Aurelia. At the east end of the latter is the site of the Roman *Albintimilium* where Agricola spent his boyhood. Since its decline in the 13C Ventimiglia has had all the characteristics of a frontier town. In the old town is the 11C–12C **Cathedral** with a portal of 1222; its apse adjoins the 11C **baptistery**. In **San Michele** (open Sun only, 10.30–12.00), rebuilt c 1100, the stoups are made up from Roman milestones, and the Romanesque crypt is interesting. The Forte dell'Annunziata in Via Verdi houses the **Museo Archeologico Girolamo Rossi** (open Tues–Sat 09.00–12.30, 15.00–17.00; Sun and holidays 10.00–12.30), founded in 1900 by Sir Thomas Hanbury. It contains finds from the Roman *municipium*.

The lower town expanded after 1872 when it became an important station on the railway line to France. The excavations (begun in 1876) of the Roman town, which include a theatre of the 2C AD, and baths, are now isolated by modern buildings and the railway; you can see them from a viaduct on the Aurelia.

A road runs west to **La Mortola**, where the upper road (right) leads to a wooded cape with the ***Giardino Hanbury** (open Thur–Tues 09.00–19.00; winter 10.00–17.00), a remarkable botanic garden founded in 1867 by Sir Thomas Hanbury and his brother Daniel, a botanist. The splendid garden was famous in the late 19C. It was acquired by the Italian State from the Hanbury family in 1960, and since 1983 has been run by Genoa University, who are now trying to rescue it from the grave state of abandon in which it had been left after 1979. Hanbury collected exotic plants from all over the world—particularly from Asia and Africa. There are also woods of umbrella pines and cypresses, carob trees and palms, as well as medicinal plants, citrus fruits, etc. A section of the Roman Via Aurelia was exposed here by Hanbury, and a plaque recalls famous travellers who passed along this route (including Dante, Machiavelli and Pius VII).

On the beach below the frontier village of **Grimaldi**, at the **Balzi Rossi**, are several caves where relics of Palaeolithic man were discovered in 1892. Some of these are exhibited in the **Museo Nazionale Preistorico** (open Tues–Sun 09.00–19.00), founded here in 1898 by Sir Thomas Hanbury. Ponte San Luigi is on the French frontier (see *Blue Guide France*).

In the flowery **Val Nervia**, inland from Ventimiglia, is the pretty village of **Dolceacqua** beneath its splendid castle, first built in the 10C–11C and transformed in the 15C and 16C by the Doria. It is now empty and in urgent need of restoration. Below the village is a single-arched 15C bridge. **Pigna** is another delightful little village (with late 15C works by Giovanni Canavesio); built on an interesting plan, it stands in a picturesque position opposite the fortified village of **Castel Vittorio**.

The Riviera di Levante

The coastal strip east of Genoa known as the Riviera di Levante has numerous resorts, including Rapallo and Santa Margherita Ligure on the gulf of Tigullio. Although the beauty of the landscape, with olive groves and luxuriant gardens, has been threatened by indiscriminate new building, its character is as tenacious as that of its inhabitants. The best-preserved part is the lovely peninsula of Portofino. Further to the east and south are the Cinque Terre, five tiny villages huddled on a dramatic, rocky coast, popular with walkers. At the eastern tip of Liguria lies the Gulf of La Spezia, ringed with lovely villages—notably Porto Venere—and home to the Italian navy's largest base.

Practical information

Getting there
By air
Genoa's Cristoforo Colombo Airport (at Sestri Ponente, 6km west of the city) and Pisa's Galileo Galilei Airport both handle domestic and international flights. Check flight and train schedules to see which is more convenient.

By road
The French *Autoroute* A8 crosses into Italy at Menton, becoming the A10 in Italy. It runs as far as Genoa, where you take the A7 to the A12 and the Riviera di Levante. Genoa can be reached also by the A6 from Turin and Savona, A26 from Alessandria, and A7 from Milan. All these roads, given the nature of the terrain, have plenty of curves, viaducts and tunnels, and commercial traffic can be heavy on weekdays.

If you are arriving from the south, take the A1 from Rome to Firenze Nord, the A11 to Lucca, the A11/12 to Viareggio, and finally the A12 to your destination. From Pisa take the A12; from the Tuscan coast, 1 (Aurelia) to Livorno, then the A12. In Liguria 1 hugs the coast from Sestri Levante to Genoa; though more scenic, it is considerably slower.

By rail
The main rail line from Rome to Paris follows the Tyrrhenian coast to Genoa, then continues via Turin to the French capital. Fast *Eurostar* trains cover the 500km from Rome to Genoa (Brigole Station) in c 4hrs 15mins; *Intercities* in c 5hrs. Both stop in Liguria at La Spezia and often at Sarzana, Sestri Levante,

Chiavari and Rapallo. There is one *Intercity* daily from Florence to Genoa, stopping at Sarzana (1hr 40mins), La Spezia (1hr 50mins), Sestri Levante (2hrs 20mins), Chiavari (2hrs 30mins) and Rapallo (2hrs 40mins). Commuter trains run up and down the coast at frequent (c 30mins) intervals throughout the day.

Getting around
Boats

In summer from Rapallo and Santa Margherita Ligure every 30mins for Portofino and San Fruttuoso. In winter, 3 or 4 services daily. Information from *Servizio Marittimo del Tigullio* (☎ 0185 284670). Regular services also from Camogli every hour in summer to San Fruttuoso; from La Spezia and Lerici in the Gulf of La Spezia, and (Jun–Sep) from Monterosso al Mare for the Cinque Terre. Information from *Navigazione Golfo dei Poeti* (☎ 0187 732987).

Buses and trains

There are local **bus services** between the main towns or the riviera, and **trains** between Sestri Levante and La Spezia at c hourly intervals, with stops at Monterosso al Mare, Vernazza, Corniglia, Manarola and Riomaggiore (the Cinque Terre). Village-to-village journey time is c 10mins.

Information offices

CAMOGLI Via 20 Settembre 33r, ☎ 0185 771066.
CHIAVARI Corso Assarotti 1, ☎ 0185 325198.
LA SPEZIA Viale Mazzini 47, ☎ 0187 770900. *Informagiovani*, Via Pietro Micca 3, ☎ 0187 727247.
LERICI Via Biagini 6, ☎ 0187 967346.
LEVANTO Piazza Cavour 12, ☎ 0187 808125.
MONTEROSSO AL MARE Via del Molo, ☎ 0187 817204.

PORTOFINO Via Roma 35, ☎ 0185 269024.
RAPALLO Via Diaz 9, ☎ 0185 230346.
SANTA MARGHERITA LIGURE Via XXV Aprile 2b, ☎ 0185 287485.
SESTRI LEVANTE Viale 20 Settembre 33, ☎ 0185 457011.

Where to stay

There are numerous hotels of all categories in all the main resorts, but few are distinctive and many are open only from spring to early autumn. The latter are marked in the text; those without a specific mention of season are open all year round.
AMEGLIA *Garden*, Via Fabricotti 162, Località Bocca di Magra, ☎ 0187 65613; small (10 rooms) and secluded, on the sea at the mouth of the River Magra; inexpensive.
Il Gabbiano, Via della Pace 2, Località Montemarcello, ☎ 0187 600066; small (10 rooms) and comfortable, with good views and outside restaurant seating in summer; closed Oct–May, inexpensive.
CAMOGLI *Cenobio dei Dogi*, Via Cuneo 34, ☎ 0185 7241, fax 0185 772796; an elegant old place with terraced park overlooking the sea; moderate.
CHIAVARI *Mignon*, Via Salietti 7, ☎ 0185 324977, fax 0185 309420; small and pleasant, not far from the waterfront; closed Nov; inexpensive.
DEIVA MARINA *Caravella*, Via Colombo 1, ☎ 0187 815833, fax 0187 825551;
a renovated railway station on the waterfront; inexpensive.
Clelia, Corso Italia 23, ☎ 0187 815827, fax 0187 816234; near the sea, small and comfortable; closed Jan–Feb and Nov–Dec; moderate.
LA SPEZIA *Firenze e Continentale*, Via Paleocapa 7, ☎ 0187 713210, fax 0187 714930; provincial elegance in an early-20C townhouse; closed Dec; moderate. *Genova*, Via Fratelli Rosselli 84, ☎/fax 0187 15777; simple but comfort-

able, near the cathedral; moderate.
LERICI *Byron*, Via Carpanini 1, ☎ 0187 967104, fax 0187 967409; a simple place, on the sea with great views; inexpensive.
Doria Park, Via Doria 2, ☎ 0187 967124, fax 0187 966459; quiet and restful, with good sea views; closed Dec–Jan; moderate.
Europa, Via Carpanini 1, ☎ 0187 967800, fax 0187 965957; high up in the hills, surrounded by trees, with good views of the gulf; moderate.
Il Nido, Via Fiascherino 75, Località Fiascherino, ☎ 0187 967286, fax 0187 964225; in the olive groves 4km outside town; closed Nov–Mar; moderate.
Shelley e Delle Palme, Lungomare Biaggini 5, ☎ 0187 968205, fax 0187 964271; on the waterfront, with good views of the gulf; moderate.
Villa Maria Grazia, Via Fiascherino 7, Località Fiascherino, ☎ 0187 967507; small (9 rooms) and secluded, near the sea 4km from Lerici; closed Nov–Feb; inexpensive.
LEVANTO *Stella Maris*, Via Marconi 4, ☎ 0187 808251, fax 0187 897351; small (8 rooms) and cosy, near the waterfront; closed Nov; moderate.
MANAROLA *Ca' d'Andrean*, Via Discovolo 101, ☎ 0187 920040, fax 0187 920452; 10 rooms in a renovated oil- and wine-press; closed Nov; inexpensive. **Youth hostel**: Via Riccobaldi 21, ☎ 0187 920215, fax 0187 920218.
MONTEROSSO AL MARE *Palme*, Via IV Novembre 18, ☎ 0187 817541, fax 0187 818265; modern and comfortable, with a small garden; closed Nov–Mar; moderate.
Porto Roca, Via Corone 1, ☎ 0187 817502, fax 0187 817692; on a rock above the town, overlooking the sea; closed Nov–Feb; moderate.
PORTOFINO *Eden*, Vico Dritto 18, ☎ 0185 269091, fax 0185 269047; small (12 rooms) and pleasant, with garden

restaurant seating in summer; moderate. *Nazionale*, Via Roma 8, ☎ 0185 269575, fax 0185 269578; quiet elegance, excellent location; closed Dec–Feb; expensive.
Piccolo, ☎ 0185 269015, fax 0185 269621; a cosy little place with pleasant garden and good sea views; closed Nov; moderate.
Splendido, Salita Baratta 16, ☎ 0185 269551, fax 0185 269614; one of the top European luxury hotels, above the town with magnificent views in all directions; closed Jan–Mar; expensive.
PORTOVENERE *Belvedere*, Via Garibaldi 26, ☎ 0187 900608, fax 0187 901469; what the youngest captain in the Italian Navy did when he retired: a warm, family-run place with sea views and good restaurant; closed Nov–Dec; moderate.
Paradiso, Via Garibaldi 34, ☎ 0187 900612, fax 0187 902582; another pleasant family-run establishment, with comfortable rooms and good views of the gulf; moderate.
RAPALLO *Astoria*, Via Gramsci 4, ☎ 0185 273533, fax 0185 62793; a tastefully renovated Art Nouveau villa on the sea; closed Dec–Jan; moderate.
Grand Hotel Bristol, Via Aurelia Orientale 369, ☎ 0185 273313, fax 0185 55800; another Art Nouveau villa in a shady park, with roof-garden restaurant and great views of the gulf; closed Jan–Feb; moderate.
Rosabianca, Lungomare Vittorio Veneto 42, ☎ 0185 50390, fax 0185 65035; small (16 rooms) and central, on the waterfront; moderate.
Riviera, Piazza IV Novembre 2, ☎ 0185 50248, fax 0185 65668; yet another Art Nouveau villa, by the park, with sea views; closed Nov–Dec; moderate.
Stella, Via Aurelia Ponente 6, ☎ 0185 50367, fax 0185 272837; simple but adequate, one block in from the harbour; closed Jan–Feb; inexpensive.
RIOMAGGIORE *Due Gemelli*, Località

Campi, ☎ 0187 731320, fax 0187
732320; small (13 rooms) and secluded
(amid the vineyards and pine woods by
the sea, 9km from the town), with good
views; inexpensive.

SANTA MARGHERITA LIGURE *Conte
Verde*, Via Zara 1, ☎ 0185 283580, fax
0185 284211; simple but adequate, in
a central location not far from the sea;
closed Mar and Nov–Dec; inexpensive.

Continental, Via Pagana 8, ☎ 0185
286512, fax 0185 284463; elegant and
refined, in a palm-and pine-shaded garden by the sea; moderate.

Fasce, Via Bozzo 3, ☎ 0185 286435,
fax 0185 283580; small and cosy;
closed Jan–Feb; inexpensive.

Grand Hotel Miramare, Lungomare
Milite Ignoto 30, ☎ 0185 287013; fax
0185 284651; an old-fashioned riviera
hotel, on the sea with park and pool;
expensive.

Imperial Palace, Via Pagana 19, ☎
0185 288991, fax 0185 284223;
another place from another century,
with park and pool by the sea; closed
Dec–Feb; expensive.

Jolanda, Via Costa 6, ☎ 0185 287513,
fax 0185 284763; not in the best location (noisy), but warm and friendly with
a good restaurant; moderate.

Minerva, Via Maragliano 34d, ☎ 0185
286073, fax 0185 281697; centrally
located and adequately comfortable;
moderate.

SESTRI LEVANTE *Due Mari*, Vico del
Coro 18, ☎ 0185 42695, fax 0185
42698; a renovated patrician villa with
garden; closed Nov–Dec, moderate.

Grand Hotel dei Castelli, Via alla
Penisola 26, ☎ 0185 485780, fax
0185 44767; a Gothic-revival castle in
a shady park; closed Oct–Apr; moderate.

Grand Hotel Villa Balbi, Viale
Rimembranza 1, ☎ 0185 42941, fax
0185 482459; occupying a luxurious
17C villa and out buildings, with large
park and heated pool; closed Nov–Mar;
moderate.

Miramare, Via Cappellini 9, ☎ 0185
480855, fax 0185 41055; calm and
comfortable, with a garden on the bay;
moderate.

Sereno, Via Val di Canepa 96, ☎ 0185
43303, fax 0185 457301; a small (10
rooms), quiet, family-run establishment;
inexpensive.

Vis a Vis, Via della Chiusa 28, ☎ 0185
42661, fax 0185 48053; on a headland
amid olive groves, with good views over
the town and sea; closed Dec; moderate.

 Eating out

AMEGLIA *Dai Pironcelli*, Via
delle Mura 45, Località
Montemarcello, ☎ 0187 601252; simple trattoria with good local food and
excellent wines; open evenings only (all
day Sun), closed Jun and Nov; moderate.

Locanda delle Tamerici, Via Litoranea
106, località Fiumaretta,
☎ 0187 64262; restaurant (with
rooms) serving truly outstanding
seafood, with outside seating in summer; closed Tues and midday Wed
(except in summeer); moderate.

Paracucchi-Locanda dell'Angelo, Via
XXV Aprile, località Ca' di Sgabello, ☎
0187 64391; restaurant (with rooms)
offering innovative fish dishes; closed
Mon (except in summer) and Jan; moderate.

CASTELNUOVO MAGRA *Mulino del
Cibus*, Via Canale 46, località Canale,
☎ 0187 676102; wine bar serving
good hot and cold meals; open evenings
only; closed Mon; inexpensive.

CHIAVARI.*Ca' Peo*, Via dei Caduti
(Strada Panoramica) 80, località Leivi,
☎ 0185 319696; restaurant (with
rooms) offering outstanding Ligurian
mountain and seafood dishes; closed
Mon and midday Tues; expensive.

Lord Nelson, Corso Valparaiso 27, ☎
0185 302595; a well-known seafood
restaurant (with rooms); closed Wed
(except in Aug) and Nov–Dec; moderate.

LA SPEZIA *Al Negrao*, Via Genova 430,

☎ 0187 701564; traditional trattoria offering simple regional dishes; closed Mon, Dec–Jan and Sep; inexpensive.

Nettare e Ambrosia, Via Fazio 85, ☎ 0187 737252; wine bar serving good hot and cold dishes; closed Sun and Aug; inexpensive.

Parodi, Viale Amendola 212, ☎ 0187 715777; good traditioal restaurant specialising in fish; closed Sun; moderate.

Good **cakes and pastries** at *Conca d'Oro*, Via Veneto 183, and *Fiorini*, Piazza Verdi 25.

Ice-cream at *Conca d'Oro* and *Sorbetto*, Corso Cavour 232.

LERICI *Conchiglia*, Piazza del Molo 3, ☎ 0187 967334; good traditional seafood restaurant, with outside seating in fair weather; closed Wed (except in summer), Nov and Feb; moderate.

Sandwiches and wine at *Bar-Enoteca da Franco*, Via Militare 72, località Solaro.

LEVANTO *Hostaria da Franco*, Via Olivi 8, ☎ 0187 808647; trattoria offering creative interpretations of traditional regional recipes and outside seating in summer; closed Mon (except in summer) and Nov; moderate.

MONEGLIA *La Ruota*, Via per Lemeglio 6, località Lemeglio, ☎ 0185 49565; good views and creative cuisine, mainly fish; closed Wed and Nov; moderate.

NE (above Lavagna) *Garibaldi*, Via Caminata 106a, località Caminata, ☎ 0185 337615; delicious local food, especially fresh pastas and vegetable dishes; closed Thur and in winter; moderate.

La Brinca, Via Campo di Ne 58, località Campo di Ne; another country trattoria offering great Ligurian food and wines; closed Mon; moderate.

PORTOFINO *Da Puny*, Piazza Martiri dell'Olivetta 5–7, ☎ 0185 269037; traditional seafood restaurant, with good views of the town and its bay; closed Thur and Dec–Feb; moderate.

PORTOVENERE *Da Iseo*, Calata Doria 9, ☎ 0187 900610; simple seafood restaurant with outside seating in summer; closed Wed and Dec–Jan; moderate.

Taverna del Corsaro, Calata Doria 102, ☎ 0187 790622; excellent fish and good wine list; closed Tues and Nov–Dec; moderate.

La Marina-da Antonio, Piazza Marina 6, ☎ 0187 790686; traditional trattoria specialising in fish; closed Thur and Mar; moderate.

Ice-cream at *Bar Lamia*, Calata Doria; **focacce**, **pizzas** and **farinata** at *La Pizzaccia*, Via Cappellini 96.

RAPALLO *Da Monique*, Lungomare Vittorio Veneto 6, ☎ 0185 50541; another traditional restaurant with good seafood and nice views; closed Tues and Jan–Feb; moderate.

Ü Gianco, Via San Massimo 78, Località San Massimo, ☎ 0185 261212; creative interpretations of traditional Ligurian recipes, in a scenic location; closed midday (except weekends), Wed evening, Jan–Feb, Jun–Jul, Sept–Dec (!); moderate.

RECCO *Da Vittorio*, Via Roma 160, ☎ 0185 74029; traditional trattoria (with rooms) serving hearty regional dishes; closed Thur and Nov–Dec; moderate.

Manuelina, Via Roma 278, ☎ 0185 74128; traditional restaurant with excellent regional fare, garden and pool; closed Wed and Jan; moderate.

Vitturin, Via dei Giustiniani 48, ☎ 0185 720225; another traditional trattoria, 1km north of the town; closed Mon; moderate.

SANTA MARGHERITA LIGURE *Cesarina*, Via Mameli 2c, ☎ 0185 286059; traditional trattoria specialising in fish; closed Tues, Nov and Mar; moderate.

L'Approdo, Via Cairoli 26, ☎ 0185 281789; another good seafood restaurant, in the historic centre; closed Mon, Dec and Mar; moderate.

SARZANA *Il Cantinone*, Via Fiasella 59, ☎ 0187 627952; simple trattoria in an ancient wine-cellar in the heart of the old town; closed Mon, Mar and Sep; inexpensive.

SESTRI LEVANTE *Bottega del Vino*, Via Nazionale 530, ☎ 0185 43349; wine bar with good bruschette, cheeses etc.; open evenings only, closed Thur; inexpensive.

El Pescador, Via Queirolo 1, ☎ 0185 42888; delicious seafood on the harbour; closed Tues and Dec–Mar; moderate.

Fiammenghilla Fieschi, Via Pestella 6, località Trigoso, ☎ 0185 481041; truly outstanding regional cuisine served with a flair; closed midday (except Sun and holidays), Mon, Jan–Feb and Nov; moderate.

Polpo Mario, Via XXV Aptile 163, ☎ 0185 480203; 'Mario the Octopus' could only mean creative seafood dishes; closed Mon and Jan–Feb; moderate.

TELLARO *Miranda*, Via Fiascherino 92, ☎ 0187 968130; a simple but excellent restaurant (with rooms), in a quiet village on a headland; closed Jan–Feb, moderate.

VERNAZZA *Gianni Franzi*, Piazza Marconi 5, ☎ 0187 812228; creative interpretations of traditional Ligurian recipes; closed Wed (except in summer) and Jan–Mar; moderate.

Entertainment

LA SPEZIA Classical music and theatre at the *Teatro Astra*.

Special events

CAMOGLI *Blessing of the Fish*, second Sun in May, and *Stella Maris* procession of boats to the Punta della Chiappa, first Sun in Aug.

DEIVA MARINA Classical music in the church of Sant'Antonio Abate, Easter. *Cantamaggio*, traditional music festival, May.

LA SPEZIA *Grande Estate Spezina* music festival, summer.

SARZANA *National Antiques Show*, Aug.

VARESE LIGURE *Allestimento dell'Opera Lirica*, open-air opera performances, Aug.

Sports

Golf at Rapallo and at Lerici (*Golf Club Villa Marigola*).

Swimming, **diving**, **sailing**, **windsurfing**, **kayaking**, **fishing**, **rafting**, **canoeing**, **walking**, **cycling**, **mountain-biking**, **bocce**, **horse-riding**, **free-climbing** and **hang-gliding** at resorts all along the coast.

Portofino and its peninsula

The delightful Penisola di Portofino is of great botanic interest for its characteristic Mediterranean *macchia* (scrub forest) mixed with thick vegetation more typical of central Europe. A scenic road (one of several on the peninsula) skirts its east short to **Portofino**, a romantic fishing village with pretty houses, now an exclusive resort in a beautiful position, partly on a small wooded headland, and partly in a little bay which has offered a safe anchorage to boats since Roman times. Portofino was much visited by the English in the 19C. Up to the 1970s important sailing regattas were organised here by the *Yacht Club Italiano*, and it is now the haunt of rich yachtsmen and Italian VIPs, many of whom own grand villas here. High above the village, towards the Punta del Capo, is the little church of **San Giorgio**, which is reputed to contain the relics of St George, brought by Crusaders from the Holy Land. In front of the church is the 16C **Castello Brown** (reconstructed in the 18C; open Tues–Sun 10.00–19.00, closed Jan).

Portofino

Portofino walks

Delightful walks can be taken in the Portofino area. The local visitor information office hands out free maps, and trails are generally clearly marked and well maintained.

The quickest and easiest walk takes you over the hill of San Giorgio to the *Punta del Capo** (15mins) with a lighthouse and a small café serving refreshments (including home-made ice-cream) in summer.

Another easy walk of c 1hr takes you to **Santa Margherita** (described below), passing the tiny sandy bay of Paraggi, at the mouth of a wooded glen.

A bridlepath involving some stiff climbs leads in 1hr 30mins to **Portofino Vetta**, in a large park beneath *Monte di Portofino** (610m). This has been a protected area since 1935 because of its natural beauty, although long-term plans to designate the area a national park have still not been settled. From the summit there is a wonderful view, and there are beautiful short walks throughout the area.

A very popular walk (1hr 30mins–2hrs; moderately strenuous) leads via Case del Prato to *San Fruttuoso di Capodimonte**, a picturesque little hamlet on the sea in a rocky inlet of a lovely bay surrounded by wooded hills. It can only be reached by boat (from Camogli, Portofino, Santa Margherita Ligure and Rapallo) or on foot. San Fruttuoso is owned by the *FAI*, and visitors are admitted Tues–Sun, May–Sep 10.00–18.00; Oct and Mar–Apr 10.00–16.00; Dec–Feb weekends only 10.00–16.00; closed Nov.

An abbey was founded here beside an abundant spring before the 10C and was of great importance in the 11C and 12C. It was reconstructed by the Doria in the 13C, but deserted by the Benedictines in 1467. It survived under Doria patronage until 1885, after which the buildings were taken over by fishermen and severely damaged by the sea in 1915. They were donated by the Doria Pamphili family to the *FAI* in 1983, and restoration work began in 1989.

The abbey and church are supported on large vaulted arches. The upper cloister was built in the 12C and restored in the 16C (it includes Roman and medieval capitals). In the 13C part of the abbey you can see 13C and 14C ceramics found during excavations. The lower cloister and church, with an unusual dome, date in part from the 10C. The 13C crypt contains Doria tombs in white marble and grey stone. The grey square Torre Doria was erected on the point in 1561 as a defence against pirates. A bronze statue of Christ, by Guido Galletti (1954), stands offshore, eight fathoms down, as protector of all those who work beneath the sea.

Camogli, on the west side of the peninsula, is a picturesque little fishing port descending steeply to a rocky shore. It was famous for its merchant ships in the days of sail, its fleet having played a prominent part in the naval wars of Napoleon, of Louis-Philippe, and in the Crimea. It is interesting for its architecture, with unusually tall houses lining the seafront. The Dragonara castle has an aquarium (open 10.00–12.00, 15.00–19.00; winter Fri–Sun only). The Museo Marinaro (open Mon, Thur–Fri 09.00–11.40; Wed, Sat–Sun also 15.00–17.40) has models of ships, ex-votos, navigational instruments, etc. There is also a local archaeological museum here.

Camogli walks

A pretty walk leads south from Camogli to San Rocco, the Romanesque church of San Nicolò, and (1hr 15 mins) **Punta Chiappa**, a fishing hamlet, where the view is remarkable for the ever-changing colours of the sea. A rough-hewn altar on the point reproduces in mosaic a graffito found at San Nicolò.

Other trails lead to **Monte di Portofino** (1hr 30mins; challenging) and **San Fruttuoso** (2hrs; moderately challenging): take the high trail to San Fruttuoso, as the low one involves some dangerous rock-climbing.

West of Camogli is **Recco**, a little port noted for its hardy seamen in the Middle Ages and for clockmaking today. Its church (1960) contains 17C Genoese paintings.

Gulfo di Tigullio

On the east side of the peninsula, on the broad bay between Portofino and Sestri Levante known as the Gulfo di Tigullio, is **Santa Margherita Ligure**, a fishing village that became a seaside resort at the turn of the century. It is still one of the more popular resorts of the Riviera, with numerous hotels. The lovely park of the 16C Villa Durazzo is open daily in summer. In the church of the Cappuccini is a fine 13C statue of the Madonna enthroned.

On the road south to Portofino is the former 14C monastery of **La Cervara**, where Francis I of France was held prisoner after the Battle of Pavia (1525), and where Gregory XI rested on the return of the papacy from Avignon to Rome (1377).

The pretty road from Santa Margherita to Rapallo passes **San Michele di Pagana**, where the church contains a fine *Crucifixion* by van Dyck. Nearby, in a large garden, is the Villa Spinola, where the Italo-Yugoslav Treaty of Rapallo was signed in 1920. The church of San Lorenzo della Costa has a triptych by Quentin Matsys (1499).

Rapallo, in a sheltered position at the head of its gulf, was much visited by the English in the 19C and 20C. It is the best known holiday resort on the Riviera di

Levante and is popular both in summer and winter. There is an 18-hole golf course at Sant'Anna, north of the town.

The lovely surroundings, which used to be the main attraction of Rapallo, were spoilt by new buildings in the 1960s and 1970s, and the mole of the new port for private boats has blocked the view out to sea. In the town are the Collegiate church (1606), and the restored castle in the harbour (open for exhibitions). In the 19C **Villa Tigullio**, surrounded by a public park, is a museum illustrating the local handicraft of lace-making. The Villino Chiaro, on the coast road, was the home of writer Max Beerbohm (1872–1956) from 1910. Ezra Pound also spent much time in Rapallo after 1959. A winding road ascends inland through woods to the sanctuary of **Montallegro**, where the 16C church contains frescoes by Nicolò Barabino and a Byzantine painting.

Chiavari is a shipbuilding town with an arcaded old main street and a sandy beach and port for small boats at the mouth of the Entella. Here Garibaldi, on his arrival in exile from the south, was arrested on 6 Sept 1849 'in the most polite and friendly manner possible', since his forebears came from the town. Chiavari was also the family home of two other prominent Risorgimento patriots, Nino Bixio and Giuseppe Mazzini. A large necropolis dating from the 8C–7C BC has been excavated here; the interesting finds are exhibited in the little archaeological museum in the 17C–18C **Palazzo Rocca**. On the second floor of the palace are 16C–17C paintings, representative of the Genoese school, including the Torreglia collection.

Inland, on Monte Caucaso, is Monteghirfo, an isolated hamlet amid chestnut woods with a local ethnographical museum; and in the Sturla Valley is Terrarossa, popularly thought to be the home of Columbus' grandparents. In a side valley (reached from Borzonasca) is the lovely abbey of **Borzone**, with a church of c 1244.

Lavagna, a resort separated from Chiavari by the Entella bridge, has a long sandy beach and is famous for its slate quarries. A pretty road leads up the valley to the early Gothic **Basilica dei Fieschi**, founded by Innocent IV (Sinibaldo Fieschi, d.1254), who was born in Lavagna.

Sestri Levante, in a delightful position at the base of the peninsula of Isola (once an island), is a summer resort, spoilt since the 1950s by new buildings. From Piazza Matteotti, with the 17C parish church, a street ascends past the restored Romanesque church of San Nicolò to the Grand Hotel dei Castelli, rebuilt with antique materials (1925) on Genoese foundations, with a magnificent park, at the end of the peninsula. Marconi carried out his first experiments in short-wave radio transmission from the Torretta here. The **Galleria Rizzi**, with a modest collection of local paintings, is open May–Sep (Thur, Sat–Sun and holidays 16.00–18.00).

The Cinque Terre

The *Cinque Terre are five delightful little medieval villages—Riomaggiore, Manarola, Corniglia, Vernazza and Monterosso al Mare—on a beautiful unspoilt stretch of rocky coast. These were remote fishing hamlets accessible only by sea before the advent in 1874 of the railway, which tunnels through the high cliffs between the railway stations. The Cinque Terre are now famous, having remained relatively isolated and been largely preserved from new building, as no coastal road has ever been built here; by car they can only be reached along winding, steep inland roads.

Walking the Cinque Terre

Although swift local trains connect the five villages at brief, regular intervals, they are best visited along the network of steep *footpaths on the edge of the cliffs between Levanto and Porto Venere (marked; maps available from the information offices or at news-stands). If you get tired, or the weather suddenly turns bad, the walk can be combined with a short train journey between any of the villages. Each walk between the villages takes several hours, while the train (through tunnels) takes only a few minutes. In summer the villages are also connected by boat services. They are noted for their white wine: the vines are trained on wires across gorges and up the cliffs. The terrain is subject to landslides and, although methods are being studied to prevent these, the villages are suffering from depopulation. Some of the footpaths between the villages have also been damaged by landslides. The best seasons are May–Jun and Sep–Oct. Summer is unbearably hot.

The approach from Sestri is made via Bonassola, a village in beautiful surroundings. A sea grotto here has been turned into a marine study centre. **Levanto**, on the coast to the south, once a secluded bathing resort in a little bay, has recently been developed for tourism. It has lovely gardens, and a good sandy beach, and preserves remains of its old walls along with a 13C–15C church.

A steep, winding inland road (or an equally steep and winding coastal trail) leads from here to **Monterosso al Mare**, the northernmost and largest of the Cinque Terre. It has a good church of 1300 and, higher up, the church of San Francesco with a *Crucifixion* attributed to van Dyck. The poet Eugenio Montale spent much of his youth at Monterosso. It now has some incongruous new buildings, and the sandy beach is crowded in summer.

Vernazza is a charming port, interesting for its architecture—the cylindrical tower is one of Italy's oldest lighthouses (torches were burned at the top). It also has a Gothic church (on two levels) and pleasant cafés on the harbour.

Corniglia, the highest of the five villages, lies above the sea, surrounded by orchards and vineyards (it has been known for its excellent wine since Roman times). It has a Gothic church.

Manarola has an equally spectacular position with splendid views.

Riomaggiore, connected to La Spezia by road, has an interesting layout on the steep cliffside. The fishermen have to pull their boats up on shore (and further up into the streets in rough weather).The village came under the control of the Genoese Republic in 1276. The 14C parish church contains a 15C triptych and a painting by Domenico Fiasella. The 19C post-Impressionist landscape painter Telemaco Signorini often stayed here.

In the Val di Vara, inland from the Cinque Terre, is **Varese Ligure** with a 15C castle of the Fieschi (well restored). A steep road leads up from here to the spectacular **Passo di Cento Croci** (1053m) on the border with Emilia.

Beyond Riomaggiore, if you're walking, you join the lofty Cinque Terre high trail, which bears you across (3hrs; challenging) the wild, rocky peninsula of Portovenere. Excursion boats from the Cinque Terre follow the same route, affording truly memorable views of the sea and coast. The land route (by car, or by train to La Spezia, then by bus) is considerably less interesting.

Portovenere and the Gulf of La Spezia

Portovenere, the ancient *Portus Veneris*, a dependency of Genoa since 1113, is a charming fortified village built on the sloping shore of the Bocchette, the narrow strait (114m wide) separating the Isola Palmaria from the mainland. On a rocky promontory at the southern end of the village, the restored 6C and 13C church of **San Pietro** commands a splendid view of Palmaria and the lofty cliffs of the Cinque Terre. The Grotto Arpaia, formerly beneath it, collapsed in 1932. It was known as 'Byron's Cave', for it was from here that the poet started his swim across the gulf to San Terenzo to visit Shelley at Casa Magni, in 1822 (see below).

In the upper part of the village is the beautiful 12C church of **San Lorenzo**, above which (steep climb) towers the 16C castello (open daily 10.00–12.00, 14.00–18.00; winter 15.00–17.00). Below the church, steps descend to the characteristic **'Calata Doria'**, where tall houses rise from the sea.

The rugged island of **Palmaria**, with numerous caves, can be visited by boat (daily service) from Portovenere. The island has been purchased by a developer and is in danger of being turned into a tourist resort. On the northern point is the old Torre della Scuola, built by the Genoese in 1606 and blown up by the English fleet in 1800. The island is noted for the gold-veined black 'portoro' marble. The Isola del Tino (owned by the navy and off-limits to the general public) has remains of the 8C monastery of Santa Venerio.

On the opposite (northern) shore of the gulf is the Bay of Lerici, with the fishing village of **San Terenzo**. On a small cape is **Casa Magni**, the 'white house with arches', the last home of Shelley (1822).

Shelley's last days

Mary Shelley wrote: 'I am convinced that the few months we passed there were the happiest he had ever known. He was never better than when I last saw him, full of spirits and joy, embark for Leghorn, that he might there welcome Leigh Hunt to Italy.' On that fatal voyage to Livorno, on 8 July 1822, Shelley and his friend Lieutenant Williams were drowned when their little schooner sank. Their bodies were recovered on the beach near Viareggio, where they were cremated in the presence of Shelley's friends Trelawney, Byron and Leigh Hunt. Byron probably visited Shelley at Casa Magni on his boat *Bolivar* while he was staying at Montenero near Livorno. The Casa Magni Shelley Museum was created here in 1972, but when the house was sold in 1979 the contents were moved back to Boscombe Manor in England.

Lerici is a resort with a splendid 13C–16C castle (opened by appointment with the custodian, ☎ 0187 965108). Tuscan coaches were embarked here by *felucca* for Genoa before the modern Via Aurelia was built.

A coast road, roughly paralleled by a beautiful trail, goes on above the charming little bay of Fiascherino, where D.H. Lawrence lived in 1913–14, to **Tellaro**, a medieval village that rises sheer from the sea—and that has suffered damage due to the instability of the rocks here. A higher by-road from Lerici continues around the wooded peninsula up to **Montemarcello**, a pretty village of red and pink houses surrounded by olives, with fine views of Tellaro and of the Gulf of La Spezia. A path leads to Punta Corno with a bird's-eye view of the coast. The road descends through lovely woods to Ameglia (see below).

La Spezia

La Spezia, at the head of its fine gulf, has been one of the chief naval ports of Italy since a naval arsenal was built here in 1861. A provincial capital (population 98,000), the town—which was laid out in the late 19C—forms a rectilinear L round a prominent hill.

The main Corso Cavour passes the **Museo Civico** (open Tues–Sun 08.30–13.00, 14.00–19.00) with an archaeological section that contains interesting Ligurian statue-stelae of the Bronze- and Iron-Age Lunigiana cult found on the bed of the River Magra, and Roman remains from Luni. **Santa Maria Assunta**, the cathedral until 1975, was founded in 1271 but later rebuilt. It contains a large coloured terracotta by Andrea della Robbia. At the seaward end of Corso Cavour are fine public gardens. The Naval Arsenal, the most important in Italy, was built by Domenico Chiodo in 1861–69. Next door is the *Museo Tecnico Navale** (open Tues, Wed–Thur and Sat 09.00–12.00, 14.00–18.00; Mon and Fri 14.00–18.00; Sun 08.30–13.15), where models and relics collected since 1571 illustrate the marine history of Savoy and Italy. The 13C **Castello di San Giorgio** is undergoing restoration. The **Museo Amedeo Lia** (open Tues–Sun 10.00–18.00), opened in 1996, contains an important collection (made since the 1940s) of 13C–15C paintings (Coppo di Marcovaldo, Pietro Lorenzetti, Bernardo Daddi, Sassetta, Giovanni Bellini), as well as later works, decorative arts, illuminated manuscripts, small bronzes, etc.

Sarzana and the Lunigiana

The last Ligurian city you encounter before entering Tuscany, **Sarzana** is an ancient fortified town, once of great strategic importance. It was the southeastern outpost of the Genoese Republic. The **Cittadella**, a rectangular fort with six circular bastions, was rebuilt for the Florentine Lorenzo de' Medici in 1487 by Francesco di Giovanni (Il Francione). For years used as a prison, it is now empty and awaiting restoration. On the main Via Mazzini is the **Cathedral** (the see of the Bishop of Luni was transferred here in 1204). It contains a panel painting of the *Crucifixion*, signed and dated 1138 by a certain Guglielmus, and 15C marble reliefs by Leonardo Riccomanni of Pietrasanta. Some of the paintings are by Domenico Fiasella, who was born here in 1589. Nearby is **Sant'Andrea**, the oldest monument in the town, probably dating from the 11C. The 16C portal has pagan caryatids. The church of **San Francesco**, north of the town, contains the tomb by Giovanni di Balduccio of Guarnerio degli Antelminelli, son of Castruccio Castracani, who died as a child in 1322. A market is held in Piazza Matteotti on Thur.

On a hill to the east is the **Fortezza di Sarzanello** (open by appointment, ☎ 0187 623025), known as the Fortezza of Castruccio Castracani, restored by the Florentines in 1493 to designs by Il Francione and Luca Caprina.

Across the wide river Magra is **Ameglia**, dominated by a 10C castle, with picturesque houses and fishing boats. The old port of Luni and a necropolis have been excavated here.

A road leads back across the river to the site of the important Roman colony of **Luni**. It was founded in 177 BC beside the sea on the site of a prehistoric settlement famous for its statue-stelae, displayed in La Spezia and in the museum of Pontremoli (see *Blue Guide Tuscany*). Of great commercial and strategic importance in the 2C AD, Luni was well known for its marble. A bishopric by the 5C and still thriving in the Middle Ages, it was important enough to lend its name to the whole district, the **Lunigiana**. Its fame was recorded by Dante (*Il Paradiso*, xvi, 73–78). By the 13C, partly because of the flooding of the river Magra, and malaria, the town had disappeared. Excavations are still in progress. The walled city has a typical Roman plan, with remains of the forum and capitolium (150 BC) dedicated to Jove, Juno and Minerva, as well as two houses and another large temple. The **Museo Archeologico Nazionale** (open daily 09.00–19.00), in the centre of the excavated area, contains interesting finds from here and the surrounding territory (Ortonovo, Ameglia, etc.), including marble sculptures, bronzes and mosaics. An honorific inscription is dedicated to M. Acilius Glabrio, who defeated Antiochus III at Thermopylae in 191 BC. To the east, outside the walls, is the *amphitheatre dating from the 2C AD, which could hold 5000 spectactors.

A road leads inland from Luni to the pretty, old village of **Castelnuovo Magra**. In the church are a painting of the *Crucifixion* attributed to van Dyck and a large *Calvary* by Brueghel the Younger. The old 13C Malaspina castle here has associations with Dante.

The rest of the Magra valley, with Aulla and Pontremoli, the most important centre of the Lunigiana, lies in Tuscany (see *Blue Guide Tuscany*).

EMILIA ROMAGNA

Emilia Romagna, as the name of a district, dates only from the Risorgimento (c 1860), but its use is derived from the Via Emilia, the great Roman road built in 187 BC, by M. Aemilius Lepidus, as a military thoroughfare from which to guard the newly conquered lands of Cisalpine Gaul. Emilia occupies the region between the middle and lower Po, the Apennines and the Adriatic. The modern provinces are those of Bologna, Ferrara, Forlì, Modena, Parma, Piacenza, Rimini, Ravenna and Reggio Emilia; Bologna is the chief town. The eastern and southern part of the region, coinciding roughly with the modern provinces of Ravenna, Forlì and Rimini, is known as Romagna, whereas the western and northern part, including Bologna, Ferrara, Modena, Reggio Emilia, Parma and Piacenza, forms Emilia.

All the principal towns except Ferrara and Ravenna lie along the line of the Via Emilia at the foot of the Apennines. The climate here is subject to extremes, and the summers are often unpleasantly hot.

Ravenna was the capital of the western Roman Empire from 402, after the fall of Rome, until it was taken by Odoacer who, like his successor Theodoric, made it capital of a short-lived Gothic Empire. It was conquered by the Byzantines in 540 and was governed by Exarchs of the Eastern Empire for two centuries. In 757 Romagna came into possession of the popes, who maintained at least a nominal suzerainty here until 1860; in the 13C–15C, however, the effective rule of the Da Polenta clan gave Ravenna a pre-eminent position in the world of learning. Parts of historic Romagna are now included in the modern regions of Tuscany and the Marches.

Emilia was invaded in the 5C–8C by the Goths, Lombards and Franks. In the early Middle Ages Guelfs and Ghibellines struggled for power in the region, and Piacenza and Parma came under the influence of Milan. The dominion of the Este family at Ferrara in the 13C extended over Modena and Reggio, while the Pepoli and Bentivoglio at Bologna, the Ordelaffi at Forlì, and the Malatesta at Rimini held temporary rule before the 16C. Papal power was later firmly established in Romagna and at Ferrara and Bologna, whereas the Farnese family, descended from the son of Pope Paul III, made Modena the capital of a new duchy and the centre of a court of some pretensions. The ex-empress Marie Louise (wife of Napoleon) became Duchess of Parma, with Piacenza and Lucca, in Tuscany, also subject to her rule; the rest of Emilia went to Austria, as successor of the Este dynasty, and Romagna remained papal land. In 1860 Emila and Romagna were united with Piedmont. Emilia, and especially Romagna, played an important part in the Second World War: the Romagnole partisans were particularly active in 1945.

Bologna

Bologna (population 404,000) is the capital of Emilia and one of the older cities of Italy, the seat of a famous university. The old town, built almost exclusively of red brick, has attractive porticoes on each side of almost every street. With numerous Romanesque and Gothic churches, and interesting civic museums, Bologna is one of the more beautiful cities in northern Italy, often unjustly left out of the usual tourists' itinerary. The important Bolognese school of painting is well represented in the Pinacoteca Nazionale. The city stands at the southern edge of the plain of the Po, at the northeastern foot of the slopes of the Apennines.

Practical information

Getting there
By air

Bologna's Guilelmo Marconi Airport, at Borgo Panigale (7km northwest), handles daily flights to and from domestic and international destinations. **Airport buses**: no. 91 to and from the station at 41mins past the hour; *Aerobus* every 30mins to and from the airport; stops in Via Ugo Bassi and Via dell'Indipendenza, at the station and at the trade-fair ground.

By road

Bologna lies at the junction of the A1 (Autostrada del Sole, from Florence and Milan), A13 (from Padua) and A14 (from Ancona). It is the main place on the ancient Roman Via Emilia, now route 9, connected to Milan via Modena, Regio Emilia, Parma and Piacenza, and to Ancona via Forlì, Rimini and Pesaro. Scenic mountain roads wind their way over the Apennines from Florence (65), Prato (325) and Pistoia (64). The Florence road crosses the beautiful *Futa Pass (Passo della Futa, 903m) and offers a leisurely alternative to the busy Autostrada del Sole (journey time by mountain road 2hr 30mins, by Autostrada 1hr). There are **long-distance bus** services between Bologna and Strasbourg, Metz, Brussels and Amsterdam; Paris and London; Budapest; Barcelona, Madrid, Valencia and Alicante; Cracow and Warsaw; Munich and Frankfurt; Bratislava, Zagreb and other European cities.

By rail

Bologna is Italy's most important rail junction. The main north–south line closely follows the Via Emilia from Milan to Bologna; fast *Eurostar* trains make the 219km journey in 1hr 40mins non-stop. *Intercities* are just a tad slower, stopping at Piacenza, Parma, Reggio Emilia and/or Modena. *Eurostars* and *Intercities* will also take you to Bologna from Florence (1hr), Ancona (2hrs, stopping at Rimini, Forlì and/or Faenza), Venice (via Padua, 1hr 50min) and Verona (1hr 20mins). Commuter trains (*Regionali* and *Interregionali*) serve Ravenna and other centres in the region.

Getting around
Car parks

The centre of the city is closed to traffic (except for those with special permits) every day including holidays 07.00–20.00, and cars are controlled electronically. Access is allowed to hotels by arrangement with the hotel. The large free car park outside the historic centre in Via Tanari has a minibus service every 15mins to the station (from there Piazza Maggiore is reached by **buses 25** and **30**). Car parks in the historic centre (with hourly tariff and limited space) include Piazza Roosevelt and Piazza 8 Agosto (closed Fri–Sat). A map of car parks is published by the comune.

Buses

Buses are run by *ATC* (☎. 051 290290). **Nos 25**, **30**, **37** or **90** from the railway station to Via Ugo Bassi (for Piazza Maggiore). **Bus 30** continues to San Michele in Bosco. **Bus 29** from Via Ugo Bassi for San Mamolo; and **bus 14** for the Certosa. **Bus 20** from Via Indipendenza to Villa Spada (and from there minibus every 30mins to the Madonna di San Luca). **Buses 10**, **35** and **38** from the station to the Quartiere Fieristico (trade fair centre).

The **bus station** at Piazza XX Settembre (**Map 3**, ☎ 051 242150) has excellent services to nearly all places of interest in the region, as well as long-distance coaches to other Italian regions and international services.

 ### Information offices
BOLOGNA Piazza Maggiore 6, ☎. 051 239660, and at the station (☎ 051 346541) and airport (☎ 051 647 2036). *Informagiovani*, Via Pier de' Crescenzi 14, ☎ 525842.

 ### Where to stay
BOLOGNA The city has numerous hotels of all categories, but they are often all full when big trade fairs are being held (especially in spring and autumn).There is a scheme called '*Bologna non solo weekend*' which offers good rates at certain hotels at weekends, and in the summer. Some of the better hotels are:
Baglioni, Via dell'Indipendenza 8, ☎ 051 225445, fax 051 234840; elegant and refined, with a good restaurant; expensive.
Cappello Rosso, Via de' Fusari 9, ☎ 051 261891, fax 051 227179; in business since the 14C; expensive.
Corona d'Oro 1890, Via Oberdan 12, ☎ 051 236456, fax 051 262679; closed Jul–Aug; moderate.
Orologio, Via IV Novembre 10, ☎ 051 231253, fax 051 260552; in an ancient building with views over Piazza Maggiore; moderate.
Re Enzo, Via Santa Croce 26, ☎ 051 523322, fax 051 554035; comfortable and centrally located; moderate.
San Donato, Via Zamboni 16, ☎ 051 235395, fax 051 230547; recently renovated, in the Due Torri neighbourhood; moderate.
Touring, Via de' Mattuiani 1/2, ☎ 051 369893, fax 051 334763; calm, cosy and friendly, with great views from the rooftop terrace; moderate.
Tre Vecchi, Via dell'Indipendenza 47, ☎ 051 231991, fax 051 224143; a classic place to stay in Bologna, conveniently located between the station and Piazza Maggiore; moderate.
Youth hostels: *San Sisto* and *Due Torri*, Via Viadagola 14 and 5, ☎ 051 501810.
IMOLA *Molino Rosso*, Strada Statale Selice 49, ☎ 0542 6311, fax 0542 631163; in a recently renovated mill, with good restaurant; moderate.
LOIANO (36km south of Bologna off the A1) *Palazzo Loup*, Via Santa Margtherita 21, Località Scanello, ☎ 051 654 4040, fax 051 654 4040; small, quiet and restful, an 18C villa with gardens in a picturesque part of the Apennines; closed Dec–Feb; moderate.

 ### Eating out
BOLOGNA is full of excellent eating places.
Al Ghisello, Via Crocioni 7a, ☎ 051 614 6874; garden restaurant with outstanding Emilian fare; closed Mon and Aug; moderate.
Al Pappagallo, Piazza della Mercanzia 3c, ☎ 051 232807; good ambience and great food in the heart of the old city;

closed Sun; expensive.
Bitone, Via Emilia Levante 111, ☎ 051
546110; traditional Emilian recipes prepared with a personal twist; closed
Mon–Tues and Aug; moderate.
Da Sandro al Navile, Via del Sostegno
15, ☎ 051 634 3100; good food and
great wines from Emilia and other
regions; closed Sun, Dec–Jan and Aug;
moderate. ***Diana***, Via Indipendenza 24,
☎ 051 231302; delicious regional food
and wines—a favourite of the
Bolognese; closed Mon, Jan and Aug;
moderate.
Grassilli, Via del Luzzo 3, ☎ 051
222961; closed Wed, Sun evening (all
day Sun in Jul and Aug), Dec–Jan,
Jul–Aug; moderate.
Le Maschere, Via Zappoli 5b, ☎ 051
261035; famous for fish; closed Sun
and Aug; moderate.
Nuovo Notai, Via De Pignatari 1, ☎.
051 228694; traditional regional cuisine, in a historic building; closed Sun;
moderate.
Paradisono, Via Coriolano Vighi 33, ☎
051 566401; good trattoria specialising
in frogs and other Bolognese delicacies;
closed Tues (except in summer); inexpensive.
Rodrigo, Via della Zecca 2h, ☎ 051
220445; another famous fish restaurant, with excellent desserts; closed Sun;
expensive.
Torre de' Galluzzi, Corte de' Galluzzi
5a, tel. 051 267638; creative cuisine,
especially fish, in a medieval tower;
closed midday Sat Jun–Sep, Sun, Jan
and Aug; expensive.
**Cafés, confectioners, ice-cream
and pastry shops** include *Casa
Dolciaria Giuseppe Majani*, Via
Carbonesi 5, a historic confectioner.
Gelateria delle Moline, Via delle
Moline 13d, for Bologna's best ice-
cream. *Pasticceria Impero*, Via
Indipendenza 39, for coffee and pastries.
Other special food shops: *Antica*

Drogheria Calzolari, Via Petroni 9,
has a good selection of Bolognese food
and wines. ***Bottega del Vino Olindo
Faccioli***, Via Altabella 15b, ☎051
223171; wine bar offering good cold
dishes and a limited selection of hot
dishes; open evenings only, closed Sun;
inexpensive. ***Boutique del Formaggio***,
Viale Oriani 16 (near Santo Stefano), for
local and Italian cheeses. ***Cantina
Bentivoglio***, Via Mascarella 4b, ☎ 051
265416; another good wine bar; open
evenings only, closed Mon; inexpensive.
Osteria del Sole, vicolo Ranocchi 1, is a
wine bar that serves light snacks.
Picnic places in the Giardini
Margherita (**Map 16**).
CASTEL GUELFA DI BOLOGNA (13km
north of Imola) ***Locanda Solarola***, Via
Santa Croce 5,☎ 0542 670102; restaurant (with rooms) in an ancient farmhouse, offering the best in local cuisine
and well worth the drive; closed Jan and
Aug; expensive.
CASTEL SAN PIETRO TERME *Da
Willy*, Viale Terme 1010b, ☎ 051
944264; hotel restaurant popular with
locals; closed Mon, Jan and Aug; inexpensive.
IMOLA *Naldi*, Via Santerno 13, ☎
0542 29581; personal interpretations
of traditional Emilian recipes; closed
Sun, Jan and Aug; moderate.
Osteria del Vicolo Nuovo, Via
Cadronchi 6, ☎ 0542 32552; fine trattoria with a good wine list, in the town
centre; closed Sun–Mon, Jul–Aug; moderate. ***San Domenico***, Via Sacchi 1, ☎
0542 29000; restaurant widely
renowned for its creative interpretations
of traditional Emilian recipes; closed
Sun evening (all day Sun Jun–Aug) and
Mon, Jan and Jul–Aug; expensive.
LOIANO (36km south of Bologna off
the A1) ***Benvenuti***, Via Roma 13, ☎
051 654102; family-run restaurant
serving local dishes; closed Mon, Feb,
Jun and Oct; inexpensive.

Entertainment

Bologna probably has more theatres per square metre than any other Italian city. There are **opera**, **ballet** and **concert** programmes at the *Teatro Comunale*, late Oct–May, as well as numerous other **classical-music** series. Examples include *I Concerti di Musica Insieme*, Oct–Mar; *Balletti d'Autunno*, ballet, Oct–Mar; *Concerti d'Organo ai Servi*, organ concerts at Santa Maria dei Servi, Oct–May; *Il Sabato all'Accademia Filarmonica*, chamber music, Jan–Dec; *I Concerti del Circolo della Musica*, Oct–Mar; *I Concerti dell'Associazione Giovanile Musicale*, Oct–Mar; *Concerti d'Organo all'Antoniano*, Oct; *Immagini e Suoni nel Tempo*, concerts at the *Pinacoteca Nazionale*, Jan–May; *Conoscere la Musica*, spring concerts offered by the Conservatory, Feb–Apr; *Bologna Festival: I Grandi Interpreti*, Apr–Jun; *Organi Antichi*, organ concerts on antique instruments, Apr–Dec; *La Camera della Musica*, concerts in the *Cappella Farnese*, May; *Concerti di Villa Mazzacorati*, Oct–Apr and summer; *Concerti Capire la Musica*, autumn–winter; *Festival di Santo Stefano*, Jun; *Concerto del 2 Agosto*, memorial performance for the victims of the bomb of 2 Aug 1980.

Non-classical series include *Suoni nel Mondo*, ethnic music series, autumn–winter; *Rassegna Jazz alla Cantina Bentivoglio*, Oct–Jun; *Rassegna Jazz al Chet Baker*, Oct–Jun; *Concerti Jazz all'Osteria dell'Orsa*, autumn–spring; *Concerti Rock, Blues & Soul at Ruvido Club*, autumn–spring.

Plays and concerts are also held in *Palazzo dei Congressi* (Sala Europa) in the Quartiere Fieristica. For **theatre**: *Arena del Sole, Dehon, Duse, delle Celebrazioni, delle Moine, di Vita, San Leonardo-di Leo, San Martino* and *Testoni*. **Live music**, including Latin-American and jazz, likewise abounds at clubs and bars around the city.

Summer events include *Made in Bo'*, pop and jazz concerts and dancing, May–Jul; *Parco Cavaioni*, pop and jazz concerts and dancing, Jun–Aug; *Bologna Est*, festival with concerts, theatre, etc., Jul–Sep; and *Porretta Soul Festival*, at Porretta Terme, Jul. Open-air cinema at sites around the city in summer.

Shopping

The things to buy in Bologna are **eatables**: tortellini, raviole, mortadella, passatelli, etc. **Markets** are held on Fri and Sat in Piazza 8 Agosto (**Map 7**). Daily food markets in Via Ugo Bassi and Via Pescherie Vecchie. *Mostra Mercato dell'Antiquariato di Santo Stefano*, antiques market, second Sat and Sun of the month, except Jan, Jul and Aug. *Celò Celò Mamanca* collectables market, Thu except Jul–Aug, Via Valdonica and Piazza San Martino. *Decomela Art*, crafts fair, second weekend of the month (except Jul–Aug).

Special events

San Petronio, the patron saint, is celebrated on 4 Oct with a fair in Via Altabella; other religious festivals include *San Giuseppe*, Mar; *San Luca* and *Santa Rita*, May; *Sant'Antonio*, Jun; *Santa Lucia*, Nov–Dec.

Bologna hosts a number of trade fairs and exhibitions that are open to the public. Among the more interesting are *Arte Fiera*, annual art fair, Jan; *Children's Book Fair*, Apr; *Futurshow*, multimedia information technology, telematics, television and phototechnology salon, Apr; *Book Market*, Voltone del Podestà, Piazza Re Enzo, Oct–Nov and Mar–Apr; *Casa Dolce Casa*, linen and home furnishings show, spring; *Orchid Show*, spring; *Cactus Show*, Jun; *Bologna Biennale-Arteantiquaria*, biennial antiques fair, Nov; *Motorshow*, international automotive show, Dec.

Special sports events include the famous *Mille Miglia* antique car race, May; the *International Tennis Championship*, Jun; *Strabologna*, cycling race, May; and the *Gran Premio San Marino*, Formula 1 auto race, at Imola, May.

Sport

Professional **baseball**, **basketball**, **hockey**, **rugby** and **soccer** at Bologna. **Cycling** throughout the region (champion cyclist Marco Pantani is from Romagna). **Golf** courses at Monte San Pietro (*Golf Club Bologna*) and Monzuno (*Golf Club Molino Del Pero*). **Walking** and **climbing** in the Apennines.

History

Felsina, an important Etruscan city on the site of Bologna, was overrun by the Gauls in the 4C BC. They named their settlement Bononia, and the name was retained by the Romans when they conquered the plain of the Po in 225–191 BC. After the fall of the Western Empire, Bologna became subject to the Exarchs of Ravenna and later formed part of the Lombard and Frankish dominions. It was recognised as an independent commune by Emperor Henry V in 1116; its university first became prominent at about this time.

One of the foremost cities of the Lombard League (1167), Bologna reached the height of its power after the peace of Constance (1183) and sided with the Guelfs. Taddeo Pepoli founded a lordship here c 1337, which was held in turn by the Visconti, the Pepoli and the Bentivoglio, under the last of whom (Giovanni II Bentivoglio; 1463–1506) Bologna reached great fame and prosperity.

Pope Julius II reconquered the city in 1506, and for three centuries Bologna was incorporated into the Papal States, except for a brief interval (1796–1814) when it was part of Napoleon's Cisalpine Republic. In 1814 Bologna was occupied by a British force under General Nugent, in support of the Austrians against Napoleon. Unsuccessful insurrections broke out in 1831 and 1848 (the latter inspired by the eloquence of Ugo Bassi), and the town was held by an Austrian garrison from 1849 until the formation of the Kingdom of Italy in 1860. Bologna was for months the focal point of German resistance In the Second World War, but it escaped serious artistic damage.

Art and architecture

The predominant material in the architecture of Bologna has always been brick, for both structural and decorative purposes, and the late-Gothic buildings of the 14C show the height attained by local skill in brick designing. Sculptors who left important works in the city include Nicolò Pisano, Jacopo della Quercia and Giambologna. The wealthy court of the Bentivoglio attracted the painters Franceso Cossa, Ercole de'Roberti and Lorenzo Costa from Ferrara (c 1490). Francesco Francia was the founder of the Bolognese school of painting, which had an important revival at the end of the 16C with the Carracci (Lodovico and his cousins Annibale and Agostino). Their influence extended into the 18C, through Francesco Albani, Guido Reni, Domenichino and Guercino.

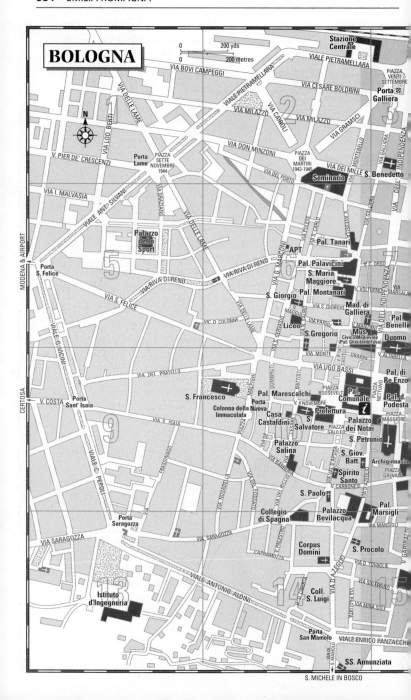

FERRARA

ZONA FIERISTICA & GALL. D'ARTE MODERNA

Stazione Centrale

PIAZZA VENTI SETTEMBRE

Porta Galliera

Bus Station

VIALE ANGELO MASINI

VIA STALINGRADO

Montagnola Giardino Pubblico

B. V. d. Soccorso

Porta Mascarella

VIALE C. B. PIGHAT.

VIA PEZZANA

V. DI LAVORO

S. Benedetto

PIAZZA OTTO AGOSTO

VIA IRNERIO

Istit. di Firsca

Istit. d'Anatomia

Porta S. Donato

VIA S. DONATO

S. Maria d. Purificazione

Pal. Bentivoglio

Pal. Biancomcini

Mus. Mineralogia

S. M. Maddalena

Pinacoteca Nazionale

Museo Geolog.

Stazione San Vitale

Teatro Contavalli

Casa Grassi

S. Martino

Teatro Comunale

Università

S. Sigismondo

Pal. Mazollini

Pal. Benelli

Pal. Malvezzi Campeggi

Pal. Salem

S. Giacomo Maggiore

SS. Vitale e Agricola

Porta S. Vitale

Duomo

Pal. Arcivescovile

Pal. Malvezzi De'Medici

S. Giobbe

Conservatorio

S. Vitale

Pal. di Re Enzo

Pal. d. Podesta

S. Bartolomeo

Pal. Sampieri

Casa Rossini

Pal. Fantuzzi

Due Torri

Casa Gionetti

S. M. d. Vita

Pal. Sanguinetti

Pal. Davia-Bargellini (Mus.)

Museo Civico Archeologico

Pal. di Mercanzia

Casa Reggiani

S. Caterina

Archiginnasio

S. Petronio

S. Stefano

S. M. dei Servi

Casa di Risparmio

Pal. Tacconi

Casa Saraceni

Pal. Loup

S. Giovanni in Monte

Palazzo Hercolani

Porta Maggiore

Pal. Marsigli

Casa Gradi

Palazzo Rossi

Palazzo Sanguinetti Vizani

Liceo

Teatro Duse

S. Domenico

Porta Castiglione

Casa Bolognese

Palazzo Agucchi

Casa di Carducci

Palazzo di Giustizia

SS. Trinità

VIA DANTE

SS. Giuseppe e Ignazio

S.M. del Baraccano

S. Giuliano

Porta S. Stefano

VIALE ENRICO PANZACCHI

Porta Castiglione

VIALE GIOVANNI GOZZADINI

Giardino Margherita

Ch. d. Misericordia

IMOLA & RAVENNA

Around Piazza Maggiore

In the centre of the city is the large, peaceful Piazza Maggiore (**Map 11**), known simply as *la piazza* to the Bolognese. It is adjoined by Piazza Nettuno, and both are surrounded by splendid public buildings. ***Palazzo del Podestà** was begun at the beginning of the 13C, but remodelled in 1484. At the centre of the building is the tall tower (Arengo) of 1212: two passageways run beneath it, and in the vault are statues of the patron saints of the city by Alfonso Lombardi (1525).

Fronting Via dell'Archiginnasio is the handsome long façade of **Palazzo dei Banchi** (1412, remodelled by Vignola 1565–68), once occupied by moneylenders. On street level are the Portico del Pavaglione and two tall arches that give access to side streets. You can see the dome of Santa Maria della Vita and the top of the Torre degli Asinelli above the roof of the palace.

On the other side of the great church is **Palazzo dei Notai**, the old College of Notaries, part of which was begun in 1381 and the rest completed by Bartolomeo Fieravanti (1422–40).

San Petronio

Although the immense church of *San Petronio was never the cathedral, it is the most important religious building in Bologna and one of the more remarkable brick buildings in existence. Begun in 1390 to designs by an otherwise unknown architect, Antonio di Vincenzo, it is dedicated to St Petronius, bishop of Bologna 431–450 and patron saint of the city. Medieval houses were demolished on this site so that the huge church could be erected here, at the political centre of the city, as a symbol of civic pride and independence. The church was designed to be twice this size; its construction went on until the mid-17C, when the nave-vault was completed.

San Petronio

Façade The immense, incomplete brick façade has a beautiful pink-and-white marble lower storey with three canopied doorways on which exquisite reliefs illustrate biblical history from the Creation to the time of the apostles. The central doorway is famous for its *sculptures, by Jacopo della Quercia. They are his masterpiece, begun in 1425 and left unfinished at his death in 1438. On the pilasters are ten bas-reliefs, mostly by assistants, illustrating the story of Genesis, and a frieze of half-figures of prophets. The architrave bears five scenes of the childhood of Christ. In the lunette are statues, also by Jacopo, of the *Madonna and Child with St Petronius* (St Ambrose was added in 1510). The archivolt above them is decorated with panels of prophets (1510–11); the central figure is by Amico Aspertini. The two lateral doorways (1524–30) have sculptures by Nicolò Tribolo, Alfonso Lombardo, Girolamo da Treviso, Amico Aspertini and others. The two sides of the building have a high marble basement beneath the large Gothic traceried windows.

Interior The great white and pink nave, 41m high, is lit by round windows and is separated from the aisles by ten massive compound piers. Because of its orientation (north to south), the church is unusually light. The splendid Gothic *vaulting of the nave dates from 1648; it is a masterpiece by Girolamo Rainaldi, who adapted the 16C designs of Terribilia and Carlo Cremona. The side chapels are closed by beautiful screens, many of them in marble dating from the late 15C, others in ironwork. The four 11C–12C crosses placed outside the chapels marked the limits of the late medieval city.

In the first chapel of the **south aisle** is a German *Madonna della Pace* of 1394, framed by a painting by Giacomo Francia. In the second chapel are a polyptych by Tommaso Garelli (1477) and early-15C frescoes. The third chapel has a frescoed polyptych of the school of the Vivarini; the fourth chapel, an early-16C crucifix and more 15C frescoes. The stained glass here is by Jacob of Ulm (1466). Fifth chapel: Amico Aspertini, *Pietà* (1519). Sixth chapel: Lorenzo Costa, *St Jerome*. Eighth chapel: carved and inlaid *stalls, by Raffaello da Brescia (1521). Ninth chapel: statue of *St Anthony of Padua* and monochrome frescoes by Girolamo da Treviso (1526). The design of the stained glass is attributed to Pellegrino Tibaldi. The screen of the tenth chapel is particularly beautiful; it dates from c 1460. The altarpiece is by Bartolomeo Passarotti. The eleventh chapel has a framed high relief of the *Assumption*, by Nicolò Tribolo (16C, with 18C additions) on the left wall. Beneath the organ, opposite, is a *Lamentation* group by Vincenzo Onofrio (1480).

The **choir** contains carved stalls by Agostino de'Marchi (1468–77). The organ on the right was built by Lorenzo di Giacomo da Prato in 1470–75. Before the high altar, Charles V was crowned Emperor in 1530 by Clement VII.

At the east end of the **north aisle** is a small museum (open 10.00–12.30 except Tues and Thur). It contains numerous drawings for the completion of the façade of the church, submitted right up to 1933 (including works by Baldassarre Peruzzi, Domenico Tibaldi and Palladio), and 16C–17C plans and models of the church (Girolamo Rainaldi, etc.). Also 17C–18C church vestments, reliquaries, church silver and illuminated choir books (some by Taddeo Crivelli).

In the eleventh chapel are two large painted panels by Amico Aspertini from the 15C organ. Ninth chapel: *St Michael* by Denys Calvaert (1582), and the Barbazzi monument with a bust by Vincenzo Onofrio (1479). Eighth chapel: *St Roch* by Parmigianino. In front of the monument of Bishop Cesare Nacci, by Vincenzo Onofrio (1479), begins the meridian line, nearly 67m long, traced in 1655 by the astronomer Gian Domenico Cassini. It has since been several times adjusted; a hole in the roof admits the sun's ray. The seventh chapel has a particularly fine screen attributed to Pagno di Lapo. The altarpiece is by Lorenzo Costa (1492). Here are Neo-classical funerary monuments of Felice Baciocchi and his wife Elisa Bonaparte by Cincinnato Baruzzi (1845; with two putti by Lorenzo Bartolini), and of their children. Sixth chapel: *Assumption* by Scarsellino (c 1600) and a statue of *Cardinal Giacomo Lercaro* by Giacomo

Manzù (1954). The huge wooden pulpit of unusual design is attributed to Agostino de'Marchi (c 1470). The fifth chapel was decorated in 1487–97. The *altarpiece is a late-15C Ferrarese work, and the paintings are by Francesco Francia and Lorenzo Costa. The stalls date from 1495, and in the pavement is enamelled tilework by Pietro Andrea da Faenza (1487). Between this chapel and the next is a fine late-14C statue of St Petronius in gilded wood.

The fourth chapel, the beautiful Cappella Bolognini, has another fine marble balustrade. The gilded polychrome wood Gothic *altarpiece was painted by Jacopo di Paolo in 1410. The remarkable *frescoes are by Giovanni da Modena. Outside is an 18C clock. The second chapel is a Baroque work by Alfonso Torreggiani (1743–50) with a fine grille and the tomb of Benedict XIV. Outside the chapel are frescoes by Lippo di Dalmasio and a *Madonna* attributed to Giovanni da Modena, who also executed the allegorical frescoes in the first chapel. Above the right door on the inside façade are *Adam and Eve*, attributed to Alfonso Lombardi.

Piazza Nettuno

In Piazza Nettuno (**Map 11**) is the *****Neptune Fountain**, designed by Tommaso Laureti and decorated with a splendid figure of Neptune and other bronze sculptures by Giambologna (1566). Fronting both Piazza Nettuno and Piazza Maggiore is the long façade of the huge **Palazzo Comunale** (**Map 10**), which incorporates Palazzo d'Accursio and is made up of several buildings of different dates, modified and restored over the centuries. The entrance gateway is by Galeazzo Alessi (c 1555), and the bronze statue above it of Pope Gregory XIII (Ugo Buoncompagni of Bologna, the reformer of the calendar), is by Alessandro Menganti (1580). To the left, under a canopy, is a *****Madonna* in terracotta by Nicolò dell'Arca (1478).

*****Palazzo d'Accursio**, to the left, with a tower (and clock of 1773), was acquired by the comune in 1287 from Francesco d'Accursio on his return from the court of King Edward I of England. The loggia was used as a public granary. Taddeo Pepoli began to unite various palaces on this site as a town hall in 1336, and in 1425–28 Fieravante Fieravanti rebuilt the palace to the right of the main entrance. The whole edifice was fortified in the 16C by the papal legates as their residence: the impressive battlemented walls (restored in 1887) extend along Via Ugo Bassi and Via IV Novembre.

From the courtyard the grand staircase, a ramp ascribed to Bramante leads up to the **first floor**, where the Chamber of Hercules contains a colossal terracotta statue by Alfonso Lombardi and a Madonna by Francesco Francia (1505). On the **second floor** the Sala Farnese has a good view of the piazza. It contains frescoes by Carlo Cignani and a copper statue of Pope Alexander VII (1660). The Cappella Farnese has 16C frescoes by Prospero Fontana. Here is the entrance to the **Collezioni Comunali d'Arte** and the **Museo Giorgio Morandi** (both open Tues–Sun 10.00–18.00; separate or cumulative ticket). The former is a well-displayed collection of paintings and furniture in 20 rooms of a wing of the Palazzo d'Accursio, used by the Cardinal legates of the city from 1506 up to the 19C. The long gallery was decorated in the 17C by the papal legate Pietro Vidoni. Other rooms have good 16C ceilings, late-18C decorations by Giuseppe Valliani and Vincenzo Martinelli (room **16**), and (room **17**) trompe-l'oeil frescoes by Dentone, Angelo Michele Colonna and Agostino Mitelli. The contents are well labelled and include works by Carlo Francesco Nuvolone, Artemisia Gentileschi, Ubaldo Gandolfi, Donato Creti (mostly painted in 1710–20), Jacopo di Paolo, Simone da Bologna, Vitale da Bologna, Francesco Francia (*Crucifixion*), Guido Cagnacci, Amico Aspertini, Lodovico Carracci, Giuseppe Maria Crespi, Francesco Hayez (*Ruth*), Jean Boulanger and Pelagio Pelagi.

The **Museo Morandi** contains the most representative collection in existence of works by Giorgio Morandi (1890–1964), a native of Bologna, donated by his family to the city. Well-displayed chronologically, it includes many of his paintings, watercolours, drawings and etchings. There are also works of art owned by the painter and a reconstruction of his studio.

Adjoining Palazzo del Podestà in Piazza Nettuno is the battlemented **Palazzo di Re Enzo**, built in 1246, which was the prison of Enzo (1225–72), King of Sardinia and illegitimate son of Emperor Frederick II, from his capture at Fossalta in 1249 until his death in 1272. The palace was radically restored in 1905–13.

The Museo Civico Archeologico

Via dell'Archiginnasio skirts the east flank of San Petronio. Beneath the marble-paved Portico del Pavaglione, with elegant uniform shopfronts, the windows enclosed in tall wooden frames, is the entrance to the *Museo Civico Archeologico, founded in 1881 and especially notable for its Etruscan material and Egyptian section (open Tues–Fri 09.00–14.00, Sat–Sun and holidays 09.00–13.00, 15.30–19.00).

In the **basement** the *Egyptian collection is one of the more important holdings of Egyptian antiquities in Europe. The first room has delicately carved limestone *reliefs from the tomb of Horemheb (1332–23 BC). The next section has a chronological display of funerary stelae, sarcophagi, objects in wood, bronzes, jewellery, etc., starting with the Old Kingdom (including a seated statuette of Neferhotep I). At the end of the hall are works from the Ptolomaic and Roman periods. The second wing has exhibits related to writing and the cult of the dead.

The **courtyard** contains a Roman lapidarium, and the **gipsoteca** has casts made at the end of the 19C of famous classical Greek masterpieces.

On the **first floor** the first door on the right leads into a room with a fine display of Villanovan finds (7C BC) from Verucchio, including beautiful amber, a reconstructed wooden throne, tables and foot-rests. Rooms **I** and **II** (still with their old-fashioned arrangement) contain prehistoric finds. The chronological display continues in the huge room **X**, with a vast collection of Villanovan and Etruscan *finds from the burial-grounds of Felsina, the Umbro-Etruscan predecessor of Bologna. The long gallery, decorated in the 19C with copies of Etruscan painted tombs, contains tomb-furniture illustrating the development of the Umbrian (9C–6C BC) and Etruscan (6C–mid-4C BC) civilisations. The Umbrian tombs contain urns with scratched, painted and (later) stamped geometric decoration, whereas the Etruscan tombs bear reliefs in sandstone and contain fine Attic vases (the so-called 'Etruscan' ware) and various objects of daily use in bronze, bone, etc. In Case 20 is a beautiful bronze *situla (6C BC), with exquisite reliefs of a ceremonial procession. Against the wall is a fine display of funerary stelae. At the end of the gallery are ivory and glass objects from the Tomba dello Sgabello (Case 33) and splendid finds from the Tomba Grande (5C BC) in Case 34. At the other end of the gallery is the entrance to room **XV** with a hoard of bronze fragments.

Off room **IX** (described below) is room **VI** with Greek works of art, including a *head of Minerva, said to be a copy of the Athene Lemnia of Phidias, and the 'Cup of Codrus', a fine red-figured Attic vase. Beyond room **VII** with Roman sculpture, room **VIII** contains Etruscan Bucchero ware, and engraved bronze mirrors (notably the '*patera cospiana*'). Room **IX** contains Roman glass, bronze statuettes, utensils and early-Christian ivory reliefs.

In the narrow road to the left of the museum, next to the indoor market, is the church of **Santa Maria della Vita**, rebuilt in 1687–90 with a cupola. It contains a dramatic *Lamentation over the Dead Christ*, in terracotta, a superb work by Nicolò dell'Arca, thought to date from 1463.

The Archiginnasio and San Domenico
Further along the Portico del Pavaglione is the **Archiginnasio**, built by Antonio Morandi in 1562–65 for the university, which had its seat here until 1800. The upper floor is shown by the doorman on request (open Mon–Sat 09.00–13.00). The wooden *anatomical theatre was built in 1637 by Antonio Levanti. By the 14C the university had acquired notoriety as the first school where the dissection of the human body was practised. The baldacchino over the Reader's chair is supported by two remarkable anatomical figures by Ercole Lelli (1734). In the Aula Magna, Rossini's *Stabat Mater* was given its first performance under the direction of Donizetti. From here you can see the long series of school rooms, now part of the Biblioteca Comunale, with c 700,000 volumes and 12,000 manuscripts.

A monument commemorating the physicist Luigi Galvani (1737–98) stands in front of the building. Across Via Farini, Via Garibaldi (left) continues to the cobbled Piazza San Domenico (**Map 15**). Here are tall columns bearing statues of St Dominic (1627) and the Madonna (1633), and the canopied tombs of Rolandino de'Passeggeri (1300) and Egidio Foscherari (1289).

Impressions of Bologna
Compare your impressions of Bologna to these, and see if they match:

Those who are not pleased with the entertainment they meet with at the inns in this city, it will be a difficult matter to please; they must be possessed of a degree of such nicety, both in their palates and temper, as will render them exceedingly troublesome to themselves and others, not only in their travels through Italy, but in the whole course of their journey through life.
John Moore, *A View of Society and Manners in Italy*, 1781

Among a revengeful people who seek satisfaction with the stilletto—these dark arcades afford the best opportunities at night to lie in wait and wreak their vengeance on an unsuspecting adversary.
Washington Irving, *Journal*, 24 April 1805

Wordsworth... has been all day very uncomfortable—annoyed by the length of the streets.
Henry Crabb Robinson, *Diary*, 7 June 1837

First thing at Bologna tried Bologna sausage on the principle that at Rome you go first to St Peter's.
Herman Melville, *Journal of a Visit to Europe and the Levant*, 30 March 1857.

The church of **San Domenico** (Map 15) was dedicated by Innocent IV in 1251 to St Dominic, founder of the order of Preaching Friars, who died here in 1221 two years after establishing the convent on this site. It is still one of the principal Dominican convents in Italy, with about 40 monks. The church was remodelled by Carlo Francesco Dotti (1728–31).

Inside, the Chapel of St Dominic was rebuilt in 1597–1605 (and restored in the 19C). Here you can see the saint's monumental **sarcophagus**, a master-piece of sculpture. It was carved with scenes from the saint's life in high relief in 1267 on a design by Nicola Pisano, mostly by his pupils, including Fra Guglielmo and Arnolfo di Cambio. The lid of the sarcophagus is decorated with statuettes and festoons by Niccolò dell'Arca, who took his name from this work. After Niccolò's death in 1492, Michelangelo—who was staying for a year in the city in 1495 (at the age of 20) with Gianfrancesco Aldovrandi—carved three statuettes: the right-hand angel bearing a candelabrum (the other is by Niccolò dell'Arca), St Petronius holding a model of Bologna, and (behind) St Proculus (with a cloak over his left shoulder). Girolamo Corbellini carved the last statue (St John the Baptist) in 1539. The sculpted scenes in relief below the sarcophagus and between the two kneeling angels are by Alfonso Lombardi (1532). The altar beneath dates from the 18C. Behind the tomb in a niche is a reliquary by Jacopo Roseto da Bologna (1383) holding the saint's skull. In the apse of the chapel is the **Glory of St Dominic**, by Guido Reni. Also here are two paintings by Alessandro Tiarini and Lionello Spada.

In the south transept is a painting by Guercino of *St Thomas Aquinas*. Here marquetry doors by Fra Damiano Zambelli (1538) lead into the **sacristy**. The lit-tle museum (open 10.00–12.00, 15.00–17.30 except Sun and holidays) con-tains damaged figures from a *Pietà* group by Baccio da Montelupo; a bust of **St Dominic** (1474), a very fine work in polychrome terracotta by Niccolò dell'Arca; paintings and frescoes by Lippo di Dalmasio, Lodovico Carracci and Bernardino Luini; intarsia panels by Fra Damiano; and books of anthems. On the floor above, another room contains 13C–15C reliquaries, including one made in France in the 13C, and a large chest of drawers with vestments (17C and later).

The choir has **stalls** in marquetry by Fra Damiano Zambelli (1541–51). The painting of the *Magi* is by Bartolomeo Cesi. A marquetry door opposite the sac-risty (usually unlocked) leads into the charming **Cloister of the Dead**, its fourth side closed by the exterior of the apse and cupola of the chapel of San Domenico. Here foreigners who died in Bologna were buried, including students and professors from the university. A simple tomb slab opposite the apse of the Chapel of St Dominic marks the burial place of the English.

Off the Chiostro Maggiore is St Dominic's cell (normally shown on request by a monk), with relics of the saint and a 13C painting of him.

The little chapel to the right of the choir (light on the right) contains a **Marriage of St Catherine** signed by Filippino Lippi (1501). In the north transept, an inscription of 1731 marks the tomb of King Enzo. The adjoining chapel holds a 14C wall monument (altered in the 16C) to Taddeo Pepoli and a painted crucifix signed by Giunta Pisano. In the Chapel of the Relics at the end of the transept is the tomb of Beato Giacomo da Ulma (Jacob of Ulm), the painter on glass, who died in Bologna in 1491.

In the north aisle, the chapel opposite that of St Dominic has an altarpiece incorporating small paintings of the *Mysteries of the Rosary* by Lodovico

Carracci, Bartolomeo Cesi, Dionigi Calvaert, Guido Reni and Francesco Albani. The painters Reni and Elisabetta Sirani are buried in this chapel (inscription on the left). In the porch leading to the side door is the funerary monument of Alessandro Tartagni by Francesco Ferrucci (1477). On the second altar, *St Raimondo* by Lodovico Carracci.

South of San Domenico, at the end of Via Garibaldi, the courthouse occupies Palazzo Ruini, with an imposing Palladian façade and courtyard (1584). North of San Domenico is Via Rolandino, with the 15C–16C Casa Gradi. The Casa Saraceni (Via Farini 15) is another fine late 15C building. Via Castiglione (**Map 11, 15**) is a handsome old street that leads away from the centre of the city to a city gate, past (no. 47) the 15C Casa Bolognesi.

The Due Torri area

Piazza di Porta Ravegnana is dominated by the famous *Due Torri* (**Map 11**), two leaning towers one of which is exceptionally tall. At one time some 180 towers existed in the city. The ***Torre degli Asinelli**, thought to have been built by the Asinelli family or by the comune (1109–19), is 97.5m high and leans 1.23m out of the perpendicular. The masonry at the base was added in 1488. A flight of 500 steps takes you up to the top (open daily 09.00–17.00 or 18.00).

The ***Torre Garisenda**, built by the Garisendi family at the same time as the other, was left unfinished owing to the subsidence of the soil and was shortened for safety in 1351–60. It is now only 48m high and leans 3.22m out of the perpendicular; but it was higher when Dante wrote the descriptive verses (*Inferno*, xxxi, 136) inscribed at the base of the tower.

No. 1 in the piazza is the Casa dei Drappieri (1486–96), with a balcony added in 1620. The narrow Via dell'Inferno, which leads out of the piazza, is on the site of the **ghetto** of Bologna (the synagogue was at no. 16). The new **Jewish Museum**, at Via Valdonica 1, is open Sun–Thur 10.00–18.00, Fri 10.00–16.00.

Five old roads lead from Piazza di Porta Ravegnana out of the city; each one ends in a gate on the line of the old city walls. The towers are now isolated by traffic; the wide Via Rizzoli, one of the less attractive streets in the centre of Bologna, is especially busy. The walkway beneath preserves Roman mosaics found during its construction. Adjoining Piazza di Porta Ravegnana is Piazza Mercanzia with the ***Palazzo della Mercanzia**, arguably the best-preserved example of ornamented Italian Gothic architecture in the city. It was built in 1382–84 from the plans of Antonio di Vincenzo and Lorenzo da Bagnomarino.

Via Santo Stefano (**Map 11, 16**) is lined by some fine 15C–16C *mansions, notably nos 9–11, Palazzo Salina-Bolognini, begun in 1525 in the style of Formigine, and nos 16–18, Palazzo Isolani by Pagno di Lapo Portigiani (1455). In Via de' Pepoli (right) is the 17C **Palazzo Pepoli-Campogrande** (with frescoes by Donato Creti and Giuseppe Maria Crespi), which houses some 18C paintings from the Pinacoteca; open Jul–Aug. Adjoining is Palazzo Pepoli (Via Castiglione 6–10), a huge Gothic building begun in 1344 by Taddeo Pepoli and restored in 1925.

Santo Stefano

The street opens out in front of an attractive piazza, in a peaceful corner of the town. At the east end stands the monastic complex of *Santo Stefano (**Map 11**), an ancient, picturesque group of buildings mentioned as early as 887 and dedicated as a whole to St Stephen the Martyr. Three churches face the piazza: Santi Vitale e Agricola, the oldest ecclesiastical building in the city, San Sepolcro, and the Crocifisso, with a 12C pulpit on its front.

The **Crocifisso**, restored in 1924, has a painted crucifix by Simone dei Crocifissi (c 1380) hanging in the raised choir. The crypt has some 11C details and a jumble of capitals. The 18C *Pietà* is the work of Angelo Piò, and the Aldovrandi tomb dates from 1438.

On the left is the entrance to the polygonal church of **San Sepolcro**, perhaps founded as a baptistery in the 5C but dating in its present form from the 11C. It has a brick cupola and interesting architectural details. The imagined imitation of the Holy Sepulchre at Jerusalem is partly hidden by the Romanesque pulpit and a stair and altar placed against it in the 19C. In the centre, behind a grille, is the tomb of St Petronius.

To the left again is the church of **Santi Vitale e Agricola**, a venerable building perhaps of the 5C, with massive columns and capitals, incorporating many fragments of Roman buildings. The three apses (rebuilt in the 8C and 11C) are lit by tiny alabaster windows. The altars in the side apses are 8C or 9C Frankish sarcophagi enclosing the relics of the 4C martyrs St Vitalis and St Agricola.

From San Sepolcro is the entrance to the **Cortile di Pilato** (12C); in the middle of this open court is 'Pilate's Bowl' (8C) bearing an obscure inscription relating to the Lombard kings Luitprand and Ilprand. Here you can see the beautifully patterned brickwork of the exterior of San Sepolcro. On a pillar in a little window is a delightful cockerel sculpted in the 14C.

Off the court is the church of the **Martyrium**, with a façade reconstructed in 1911. The chapel has good capitals and remains of 14C–15C frescoes. In the left chapel (light) is a charming group of wooden statues of the *Adoration of the Magi* painted by Simone dei Crocifissi (c 1370). The chapel of San Giuliano, also off the courtyard, has 14C frescoes. A door from the court leads into the *cloister*, which has two beautiful colonnades, the lower one dating from the 11C, and the upper from the 12C, with fine capitals. Here you can see the Romanesque campanile.

There is a small museum off the cloister (open daily 09.00–12.00, 15.30–18.15), in poor condition. It includes works by Jacopo di Paolo, Michele di Matteo, Simone dei Crocifissi and Lippo di Dalmasio. The Cappella della Benda holds several reliquaries, including that of St Petronius by Jacopo di Roseto, 1370.

San Giovanni in Monte

Across Via Santo Stefano and Via Farini, on a little hill, stands the church of *San Giovanni in Monte (**Map 11**). Of ancient foundation, in its present form it is a 13C Gothic building with extensive 15C additions. The façade has a great portal by Domenico Berardi (1474), and above it an eagle in painted terracotta by Niccolò dell'Arca. The campanile dates from the 13C–14C.

In the pleasant **interior** the columns are partly decorated with frescoes by Giacomo and Giulio Francia. The stained-glass tondo on the west wall is by the Cabrini on a design by Lorenzo Costa or Francesco del Cossa (1481). The Romanesque cross on an inverted Roman pillar capital bears a figure of Christ in fig wood attributed to Alfonso Lombardi. In the south aisle are altarpieces by Girolamo da Treviso, Bartolomeo Cesi, Pietro Faccini (**Martyrdom of St Lawrence*), Lippo di Dalmasio (fresco) and Lorenzo Costa (**Enthroned Madonna with Saints*, 1497). The sacristy conserves a precious collection of reliquaries, church silver, vestments, etc.

The inlaid stalls of the choir are by Paolo Sacca (1523). The **Madonna in Glory* on the east wall is another fine work by Lorenzo Costa, and the **crucifix is by Jacopino da Bologna. The north transept is a good architectural work of 1514 built for the blessed Elena Duglioli Dall'Oglio (1472–1520), who is buried here. She also commissioned the famous St Cecilia altarpiece for the chapel from Raphael: now in the pinacoteca, it is substituted here by a poor copy still enclosed in the original frame by Formigine. In the north aisle are works by Francesco Gessi, Luigi Crespi and (second chapel) Guercino.

Vicolo Monticelli descends to Via Castiglione, described above.

The Strada Maggiore

The Strada Maggiore (**Map 11, 12**) is an attractive old street running southeast on the line of the Via Emilia. Beside the Due Torri is the church of **San Bartolomeo**, where the rich decoration of the portico, by Formigine (1515), has been worn away (although it was restored in 1993). A 16C portal is in better condition. The ornate interior, with small domes over the side aisles, is largely the work of Giovanni Battista Natali (1653–84). In the fourth chapel of the south aisle is an **Annunciation* by Francesco Albani (1632). The tondo of the *Madonna* in the north transept is by Guido Reni.

A series of characteristic Bolognese mansions of all periods from the 13C–19C, some of them restored, can be seen further on in the Strada Maggiore. Among the better ones are the Casa della Fondazione Gioannetti (no. 13), with Gothic windows and polychrome decoration; **Casa Gelmi** (no. 26), built for the composer Gioacchino Rossini, from designs by Francesco Santini (1824–27); Casa Isolani (no. 19), a characteristic 13C house (restored), with a tiny upper storey on tall wooden brackets; Palazzo Sanguinetti (no. 34) with a rich 16C cornice; and Casa Reggiani (nos 38–40), a large 15C mansion with an arcaded court.

Beyond opens Piazza dei Servi (**Map 12**), with its porticoes. Here at no. 44 is Palazzo Davia-Bargellini, built in 1638, with two atlantes flanking the gateway. The fine staircase dates from 1730. The palace contains the **Museo Civico d'Arte Industriale e Galleria Davia-Bargellini** (open Tues–Sat 09.00–14.00; Sun and holidays 09.00–13.00), founded in 1924 by Malaguzzi Valeri and still preserving the character of its original arrangement. It includes domestic artefacts, wrought-iron work, ceramics, an 18C puppet theatre, a dolls' house, woodcarvings, Emilian furniture, and paintings by Vitale da Bologna, Bartolomeo Vivarini, Giuseppe Maria Crespi, Marcantinio Franceschini, Marco Meloni, Joseph Heintz the Younger, Bartolomeo Passarotti (portraits of the Bargellini family) and Prospero Fontana. There is also a good collection of terracottas by Giuseppe Maria Mazza and Angelo Piò.

The four porticoes of Piazza dei Servi, built in a consistent style at various periods from the 14C to 1855, are a continuation of the wide arcades in the Strada Maggiore alongside the church of **Santa Maria dei Servi** (**Map 12**). Begun in

1346 and enlarged after 1386, this is one of the more attractive Gothic buildings in Bologna.

The **interior** of the church is very dark. The fourth south chapel has a painting, by Denys Calvaert, of *Paradise* (1602). On the left pillar outside the sixth chapel is a fresco fragment attributed to Lippo di Dalmasio. The finely carved main altar is the work of Giovanni Angelo Montorsoli (1558–61). The choir, entered by a door off the ambulatory, contains good Gothic stalls (1450; completed in 1617). Outside the door into the sacristy are frescoes by Vitale da Bologna that survive from the 14C church. In the ambulatory are a polyptych by Lippo di Dalmasio (in very poor condition), and a delightful high relief in terracotta by Vincenzo Onofri. The chapel to the left of the east chapel preserves Cimabue's **Enthroned Madonna* (light) and a 15C fresco by Pietro di Giovanni Lianori. On the choir wall is the Grati monument by Vincenzo Onofri.

The sixth chapel of the north aisle has an *Annunciation* by Innocenzo da Imola (in a frame by Formigine); the fifth chapel, a Byzantine *Madonna and Child* (c 1261). Around the side door is an elaborate monument to Cardinal Gozzadini (d. 1536) by Giovanni Zacchi; in the second chapel, *Noli me Tangere* by Francesco Albani.

In Via Guerrazzi, to the south, are (no. 13) the Accademia Filarmonica, founded in 1666, to which Mozart was elected in 1770 at the age of 14, and (no. 20) the Flemish College (1650).

At Viale Carducci 5, on the right beyond Porta Maggiore, is the **Casa di Carducci** and **Museo del Risorgimento** (open Tues–Sun 09.00–13.00), where the poet Giosuè Carducci lived from 1890 to 1907. Here you can view a collection of manuscripts and a library of over 40,000 volumes. Outside is a monument by Leonardo Bistolfi (1928).

Piazza Aldrovandi, with chestnut trees and a street market, leads north to Via San Vitale. Here on the left, beyond an old city gate (11C–12C), is the church of **Santi Vitale ed Agricola** (Map 12), rebuilt in 1824, except for its 12C crypt. It is dedicated to two saints martyred under Diocletian in the arena, thought to have been in this area. Inside are works by Alessandro Tiarini and frescoes attributed to Giacomo Francia and Bagnacavallo.

Opposite is the long, oddly proportioned façade of **Palazzo Fantuzzi** (begun in 1517), decorated with two elephants in relief and with a Baroque staircase.

It is a short way back from here, by Via San Vitale, to the Due Torri.

San Giacomo Maggiore and its neighbourhood

Via Zamboni (Map 11, 7 and 8) leads away from the Due Torri and the centre of the city, to Piazza Rossini. Here the **Conservatorio Giovanni Battista Martini**, where Rossini studied in 1806–10, has one of the more important music libraries in Europe as well as a small portrait gallery. Opposite is Palazzo Malvezzi de'Medici, by Bartolomeo Triachini (1560).

On Via Zamboni, also facing the piazza, is **Palazzo Magnani** by Domenico Tibaldi (1577–87). The Salone (open to visitors when not in use) has a beautiful frescoed frieze of the *Founding of Rome* by the Carracci (1588–91). You can also view paintings by Tintoretto, Lodovico Carracci, Simone Cantarini, Domenico Induno, Giuseppe Maria Crespi and Guercino. Next door is Palazzo Malvezzi-Campeggi (no. 22), by Formigine, with a good courtyard.

The Romanesque church of *San Giacomo Maggiore (Map 7), was begun in 1267 (restored in 1915). The top of the façade has majolica decoration.

Inside, the aisleless nave is surmounted by a bold vault of unusually wide span. The chapels are crowned by a terracotta frieze of statues and urns (by Pietro Becchetti, 1765). On the south side are altarpieces by Bartolomeo Passarotti (1565), Innocenzo da Imola (in a frame by Formigine) and Lodovico Carracci. The eleventh chapel was designed by Pellegrino Tibaldi, who also painted the frescoes.

The ambulatory hosts a large painted crucifix by Jacopo di Paolo (c 1420), on the left wall. In the second chapel is Lorenzo Veneziano's polyptych of 1368. The damaged frescoes of the life of St Mary of Egypt are by Cristoforo da Bologna. In the third chapel are a polyptych by Jacopo di Paolo and a crucifix signed by Simone dei Crocifissi (1370). The fourth chapel holds late-13C frescoes (very damaged) from the façade. Opposite, on the choir wall, is the funerary monument of a philosopher and a doctor, both called Nicolò Fava, by a follower of Jacopo della Quercia.

The Cappella Bentivoglio (light switch on the floor), at the end of the north aisle, was founded in 1445 by Annibale Bentivoglio and enlarged for Giovanni II, probably by Pagno di Lapo Portigiani. Its *altarpiece is by Francesco Francia (c 1488). The *frescoes from the Apocalypse, of the *Triumph of Death* and of the *Enthroned Madonna* with charming portraits of Giovanni II Bentivoglio and his family, are all by Lorenzo Costa. The relief of Annibale I on horseback dates from 1458, the worn floor-tiles from 1489.

Opposite the chapel is the *tomb of Anton Galeazzo Bentivoglio, father of Annibale, one of the last works of Jacopo della Quercia (1435; with the help of assistants). The *Madonna in Glory* in the last chapel is by Bartolomeo Cesi.

The **Oratory of Santa Cecilia** (entered from no. 15 under the side portico of the church) has interesting *frescoes by Francesco Francia, Lorenzo Costa and their pupils, including Amico Aspertini. They were painted in 1504–06 by order of Giovanni II Bentivoglio. The altarpiece is also by Francia.

Along the side of the church, a delightful vaulted portico of 1477–81, with good capitals and decorated with terracotta (perhaps by Sperandio), connects Piazza Rossini with Piazza Verdi. Here is the best view of the fine brick campanile (1472). The **Teatro Comunale**, by Antonio Bibiena (1756; façade 1933), occupies the site of the great palace of the Bentivoglio, which was destroyed in a riot in 1507 and left in ruins until 1763 (the Bolognese called it *Il Guasto*—'The Ruin').

The university

Beyond, Via Zamboni is now lined with buildings used by the various faculties of the university (the *Studio*), the oldest in Italy, founded in the second half of the 11C and already famous just a century later. Its headquarters have been installed since 1803 in **Palazzo Poggi** (no. 33), built by Pellegrino Tibaldi (1549). The courtyard is ascribed to Bartolomeo Triachini. The palace contains frescoes of the story of Ulysses by Pellegrino Tibaldi.

The university **library** (Via Zamboni 35) contains over 800,000 volumes and 9000 manuscripts and autographs and has a fine 18C reading-room. Here Cardinal Mezzofanti (1774–1849), who spoke 50 languages and was called by Byron 'the universal interpreter', was librarian, and his own library is added to the collection.

You can visit the Museo Storico dello Studio, and numerous other scientific collections belonging to the university, by appointment. The Torre dell'Osservatorio dates from 1725.

The University of Bologna

Irnerius taught here between 1070 and 1100. He revived the study of the Roman system of jurisprudence, which his disciples spread over Europe—in 1144 Vacarius, founder of the law school at Oxford, was sent to England. In return, many Englishmen and Scotsmen served as rectors at Bologna. Here Petrarch was taught, and Copernicus started on the study of astronomy; and in 1789 the university became renowned for the discovery of galvanism. The number of its female professors is remarkable, among them being the learned Novella d'Andrea (14C), Laura Bassi (1711–88), mathematician, scientist and mother of 12, and Clotilde Tambroni, professor of Greek 1794–1817.

Today the university is renowned particularly for its School of Medicine and for its Division of Art, Music and Drama (DAMS). Umberto Eco, author of *The Name of the Rose*, teaches semiotics here.

The Pinacoteca Nazionale

The Accademia di Belle Arti occupies an old Jesuit college with a handsome courtyard in Via delle Belle Arti. In this building is the *Pinacoteca Nazionale, one of the more important collections of paintings in northern Italy (Map 8; open Tues–Sat 09.00–14.00, Sun and holidays 09.00–13.00). The gallery, especially important for its pictures of the Bolognese school, also has paintings by artists who worked in Bologna (including Giotto, Raphael and Perugino). Acquisitions have augmented the 17C and 18C works. The paintings are arranged by period and school. The rooms are unnumbered but have been numbered in the description below according to the ground plan on p 598.

At the top of the entrance stairs three galleries (4) around the cloister display works by the 14C Bolognese school, including Vitale da Bologna (*St George and the Dragon*), Jacopino da Bologna, Giovanni da Modena and Simone dei Crocifissi. In room 5 are works by Giotto and Lorenzo Monaco. In rooms 7–10 the 15C Bolognese school is represented by Michele di Matteo and Vitale da Bologna (detached *frescoes and sinopie).

The most important works of the 15C–16C are displayed in the **Long Gallery** (11). In the first section (A) the Venetian school is represented by Antonio and Bartolomeo Vivarini, Cima da Conegliano (*Madonna*) and Marco Zoppo. Beyond is the Ferrarese school (B), with Francesco del Cossa (*Enthroned Madonna*). Section C: Ercole de' Roberti (*St Michael Archangel*), Lorenzo Costa and Marco Palmezzano. Bolognese school (D and E): Francesco Francia (*Felicini Altarpiece*). Section F: Amico Aspertini. At the end (G), Raphael, *Ecstasy of St Cecilia*, one of his more famous works. Also here are works by Perugino, Giulio Romano, Franciabigio and Giuliano Bugiardini. Section K: Parmigianino (*Madonna and Saints*) and works by the 16C Emilian mannerists, including Bartolomeo Passarotti, Camillo Procaccini and Pellegrino Tibaldi. Section M: 15C–16C foreign schools, including El Greco. The fragment from a *Crucifixion* is by Titian.

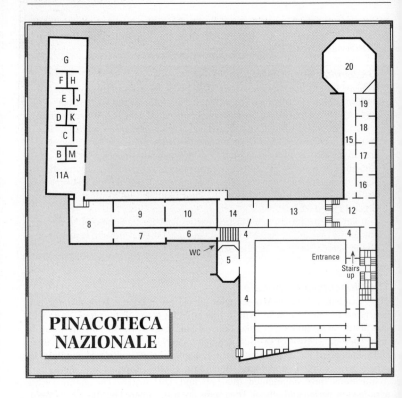

PINACOTECA
NAZIONALE

Return to the entrance, from which room **12** can be reached. It contains fine works by Guido Reni, including the large **Pietà dei Mendicanti*, with a model of Bologna. Room **13** has large *works by Annibale, Lodovico and Agostino Carracci, including the *Madonna Bargellini* by Lodovico and the *Last Communion of St Jerome* by Agostino. Room **14** contains works by Giorgio Vasari and Federico Barocci.

The long corridor (room **15**) off room 12 displays Bolognese 17C–18C paintings, including works by Francesco Albani. The small rooms off the gallery (16–19) contain works by Guercino, Domenichino, Francesco Albani, Giuseppe Maria Crespi, the Gandolfi and Donato Creti. The hall (20) at the end is hung with seven huge altarpieces by Domenichino, Guercino, Francesco Albani, Lodovico Carracci and Carlo Cignani.

Near the other end of Via delle Belle Arti is the majestic **Palazzo Bentivoglio** (no. 8; **Map 7**), built to a design perhaps by Bartolomeo Triachini in 1550–60. Further on, Via Mentana (left) leads to the basilica of **San Martino** (**Map 7**), founded in 1217. It was remodelled in the mid-15C, and the façade was rebuilt in 1879.

Inside, on the south, are altarpieces by Girolamo da Carpi and Amico Aspertini, and a fragment by Vitale da Bologna. The pretty organ in the sanctuary, by Giovanni Cipri, dates from 1556. On the north side, beside the sacristy door, are fresco fragments by Simone dei Crocifissi. The altarpieces are by Lorenzo Costa, Lodovico Carracci and Bartolomeo Cesi. The first chapel, built in 1506, contains paintings by Francesco Francia and Amico Aspertini. The statue of the *Madonna* is attributed to Jacopo della Quercia. Here also is a fresco fragment of the *Nativity*, recently uncovered and attributed to Paolo Uccello (very difficult to see).

The interesting Via Marsala, across Via Oberdan, has good medieval houses, one with high wooden brackets. At no. 12 is the late-13C Casa Grassi. The cathedral is a short way to the south.

West of the Cathedral

From Piazza Nettuno and Via Rizzoli (**Map 11**), Via dell'Indipenza, the busy, long main street, opened in 1888, leads north towards the railway station. A short way up on the right, is the **Cathedral** (**Map 7**). Probably founded before the 10C, it was rebuilt several times after 1605 and is now essentially a 17C Baroque building with an elaborate west front by Alfonso Torreggiani (18C). The nave is by Floriano Ambrosini, and the choir is the work of Domenico Tibaldi (1575). The crypt, campanile and two delightful red marble lions survive from the Romanesque building.

Inside, the second chapel of the south aisle preserves the skull of St Anne, presented in 1435 by Henry VI of England to Nicolò Albergati. Above the inner arch of the choir is an *Annunciation*, frescoed by Lodovico Carracci. A 12C *Crucifixion* group carved in cedar wood surmounts the high altar.

The area behind the cathedral is an interesting survival of medieval Bologna, with many old houses and remains of the towers erected by patrician families.

The Museo Medievale

On the opposite side of Via dell'Indipendenza, Via Manzoni leads to Via Galliera past the Madonna di Galliera, a church remodelled in 1479, with a Renaissance façade. Opposite, beneath a raised portico, is the entrance to Palazzo Ghisilardi-Fava, begun in 1483. Here is the *Museo Civico Medievale e del Rinascimento (**Map 6**; open Mon–Fri 09.00–14.00, Sat–Sun and holidays 09.00–13.00, 15.30–19.00), a beautifully arranged museum of medieval and Renaissance sculpture and applied arts.

Ground floor Rooms **1** and **2** illustrate the origins of the collections in the 17C and 18C, prior to the founding of the present museum in 1881. On the other side of the courtyard (which has 16C Jewish tombstones) is room **4** with 14C tombs by the Dalle Masegne. The second courtyard (on Via Porta di Castello) has a medieval lapidary collection. Rooms **5** and **6** display medieval metalwork and ivories, including a bronze 13C Mosen *ewer in the shape of a horse and rider. In room 5 you can see remains of the Roman imperial palace in the first city walls, destroyed in 1116. Room **7** is dominated by the over-life-size bronze and beaten-copper statue of Pope Boniface VIII by Manno Bandini (1301), formerly on the façade of Palazzo Pubblico. The 14C *cope is one of the finest works ever produced in *opus anglicanum* (English medieval embroidery). It includes scenes showing the martyrdom of St Thomas Becket.

Lower ground floor Stairs lead down to the lower ground floor. Room **9** has a statuette of St Peter Martyr by Giovanni di Balduccio. Room **10** has remains of a Roman building on this site, and charming 14C tombs of university lecturers. In room **11** is the red-marble tomb slab of Bartolomeo da Vernazza (d. 1348). Room **12**: **Triptych of the Madonna and Child with Saints*, carved in bas-relief by Jacopo della Quercia and assistants, and a terracotta *Madonna* in high relief, also by Jacopo. The interesting recumbent image of a saint in stuccoed and painted wood is by Antonio Federighi. Room **13** displays several 15C floor tombs and the tomb of Pietro Canonici (d. 1502), attributed to Vincenzo Onofrio.

First floor Room **15** has a major collection of bronzes, which include the *model for the *Neptune Fountain* by Giambologna, the first version of the famous *Mercury by the same artist, **St Michael and the Devil*, by Alessandro Algardi, and a bronze bust of Gregory XV by Gian Lorenzo Bernini. Rooms 17–22 contain the collection of applied arts. Among the more notable items are a ceremonial sword and sheath given to Lodovico Bentivoglio by Pope Nicholas V (**room 17**); a collection of European armour (room **18**); an ivory parade saddle (German, 15C) in room **19**; and Turkish armour and *bronzes from the 13C–15C (room **20**). In rooms **21** and **22** are northern European ivories, and Venetian and German glass, including a rare blue glass *cup with a gilt enamelled frieze, perhaps from the Barovier workshop in Murano (mid-15C), and two vessels probably made for the wedding of Giovanni Bentivoglio and Ginevra Sforza in 1464. Another room (**16**) has a fine display of illuminated choir books (13C–16C).

The collection of musical instruments, and the museum's celebrated holdings in majolica, are to be displayed in rooms frescoed by the Carracci.

Via Manzoni enters ***Via Galliera** (Map 6, 3), the main north–south artery of the city before Via dell'Indipendenza was built. It has been called the 'Grand Canal' of Bologna, from the splendour of its palazzi. A short way to the right is Palazzo Montanari (1725), next to the church of **Santa Maria Maggiore**, with 16C statues of *Mary Magdalen* and *St Roch* attributed to Giovanni Zacchi. In the other direction Via Porta di Castello ascends through an archway across Via Monte Grappa into the busy Via Ugo Bassi. Straight across, a road skirts the interesting exterior of the huge Palazzo Comunale into Piazza Roosevelt.

In Via Val d'Aposa is the charming façade of **Santo Spirito** (Map 10), a gem of terracotta ornament, in very good condition. Beyond is the church of San Paolo, by Giovanni Magenta (1611). The ***Collegio di Spagna** (Map 10, 14; open only by special permission) was founded by Cardinal Albornoz in 1365 for Spanish students. It is the last survivor of the many colleges, resembling those at Oxford and Cambridge, which existed in Bologna in the Middle Ages. It still has a high scholastic reputation. Ignatius Loyola and Cervantes are among its famous students. The main building is by Matteo Gattapone (1365); the gateway (1525) is probably the work of Bernardino da Milano. The handsome courtyard has a double gallery; the chapel has an altarpiece by Marco Zoppo.

Via Urbana follows the delightful garden wall of the college (you can see part of the external painted decoration on the building from here), back to Via Tagliapietre. Here on the right is the church of **Corpus Domini** (Map 14) built in 1478–80, with a terracotta portal by Sperandio. It contains frescoes by Marcantonio Franceschini in the cupola. In a 17C chapel (opened by a closed order of nuns) are preserved the relics of St Catherine de' Vigri (d. 1463), an erudite ascetic of Bologna, greatly venerated.

Nearby, at Via d'Azeglio 54, is **San Procolo** (**Map 14**), a church of ancient foundation, with a Romanesque façade. In the choir is an interesting Roman sarcophagus, probably decorated in the late 15C. **Palazzo Bevilacqua** (nos 31–33; **Map 10**) is a good example of the imported Tuscan style of 1474–82, with a splendid courtyard. The Council of Trent held two sessions in this building in 1547, having moved to Bologna to escape an epidemic. Beyond Via Farini, the attractive and peaceful Via d'Azeglio, one of the few old main streets without arcading, continues back to Piazza Maggiore.

To the north, at Piazza Roosevelt 26 is the enlarged Palazzo della Prefettura, of 1561–1603, perhaps by Terribilia. Via IV Novembre continues left past Palazzo Marescalchi (no. 5), in an early 17C style, and (no. 7) the birthplace of Guglielmo Marconi. Opposite is the huge Classical exterior of the flank of **San Salvatore**, with its façade on Via Battisti, by Giovanni Magenta and Tomaso Martelli (1605–23). The church contains the tomb of Guercino and works by Lippo di Dalmasio, Girolamo da Treviso, Girolamo da Carpi, Vitale da Bologna, Innocenza da Imola, Carlo Bononi and Garofalo.

San Francesco

Via Portanuova continues west from here to emerge beneath the Porta Nuova, one of the old city gates, into the long Piazza Malpighi beside the Colonna dell'Immacolata, with a copper statue designed by Guido Reni. Here is *San Francesco (**Map 10**), in many ways the most attractive church in Bologna. The churchyard holds the tombs of the Glossators, Accursio (d. 1260), Odofredo (d. 1265) and Rolandino de'Romanzi (d. 1284), restored in 1904. The church is in a more or less French Gothic style, begun in 1236, completed early in 1263, but considerably altered since. The façade (c 1250) has two carved 8C plutei and 13C–14C majolica plaques in the pitch of the roof. The smaller of the two towers was completed in 1261; the larger and finer, the work of Antonio di Vincenzo (1397–c 1402), is surrounded by decorative terracotta.

Inside are the terracotta tomb of Pope Alexander V, completed by Sperandio in 1482, in the north aisle; and the Fieschi tomb (1492), in the south aisle. The choir has a marble *reredos by Jacobello and Pier Paolo dalle Masegne (1388–92). On the sanctuary walls are frescoes by Francesco da Rimini, and a crucifix attributed to Pietro Lianori hangs in the east chapel of the ambulatory.

At Via dei Gombruti 23 (off Via Portanuova) the 'Old Pretender' stayed during several visits to Bologna. The most pleasant way back to Piazza Maggiore is to return along Via Portanuova and Via IV Novembre.

Via dell'Indipendenza ends at the **Montagnola** (**Map 3**), a public garden laid out around the mound formed over the ruins of the citadel of Galliera. Beyond it is Porta Galliera (1661). The **railway station** (**Map 2**) is just to the west. A bomb placed by right-wing terrorists in the station waiting-room in August 1980 killed 85 people and wounded 200 others; they are commemorated by a monument in the form of an irregular, slash-like window in the waiting-room wall, facing the tracks. On the other side of the railway is the **Sacro Cuore**, a large church in the Byzantine style, begun in 1877 and completed in 1912; the dome was rebuilt in 1934.

Around Bologna

In the southern part of the town are the pleasant Giardini Margherita (**Map 16**), laid out in 1875. The church of Santa Maria della Misericordia (**Map 15**), enlarged in the 15C, has stained-glass windows by Francesco Francia. The little church of the Madonna del Baraccano (**Map 16**) has a good fresco by Francesco Cossa. Further south, reached by Via Murri, at Via Toscana 19, is the Villa Aldovandi, with an 18C theatre (open on the first and third Thur of each month at 15.00).

On a hill to the southwest (**bus 30**) stands the former Olivetan convent of **San Michele in Bosco** (beyond Map 14), with a splendid view of Bologna. Here, on 1 May 1860, Camillo Cavour and Vittorio Emanuele II met to approve the sailing of the 'Thousand' to Sicily. The church, rebuilt since 1437 and completed in the early 16C, has a façade ascribed to Baldassarre Peruzzi (1523). It contains the tomb of the mercenary captain Armaciotto de'Ramazzotti, by Alfonso Lombardi (1526). The frescoes on the triumphal arch are by Domenico Maria Canuti. In the cloister are the remains of an important fresco cycle by Lodovico Carracci, Guido Reni and others. The primitive church of San Vittore, on the next hill to the south (at Via San Mamolo 40), dates from the 11C. It was enlarged in the 12C, altered in 1864, and later partly restored.

Just outside the Porta San Mamolo (**bus 29** from Via Ugo Bassi) stands the Observantine church of the **Annunziata** (**Map 14**). A Renaissance portico precedes the austere basilica of c 1475. Above are the Osservanza convent (1811–16) and the public park of Villa Ghigi.

The sanctuary of the **Madonna di San Luca** is a famous viewpoint. It is reached by **bus 20** from Via Indipendenza to the public park of **Villa Spada** (which contains a museum dedicated to fabrics, open Tues–Sun 09.00–13.00) in Via Saragozza (**Map 13**) at the foot of the hill of San Luca. From here a minibus (roughly every 30mins) ascends the hill. The church is connected with Porta Saragozza (**Map 13**), just over 3km away, by a *portico of 666 arches (1674–1793). Where the portico begins the ascent of the hill is the Arco del Meloncello, by Carlo Francesco Dotti (1718). The sanctuary, built by Dotti in 1725–49, contains a *Noli me Tangere* by Guercino, and paintings by Calvaert.

To the west, in the comune of Zola Predosa, is **Palazzo Albergati** with an unusual plain rectangular exterior built in 1659–94 on a plan by Giovanni Giacomo Monti. The huge Salone has stuccoes by Gian Filippo Bezzi, and other rooms have elaborate 17C–18C frescoes.

Outside Porta Sant'Isaia (**Map 9**) are the huge sports stadium, built in 1926, and the **Certosa** (**bus 14**), founded in 1334, suppressed in 1797, and consecrated in 1801 as the public cemetery of Bologna. It was much admired by Byron. The 14C–16C church contains marquetry stalls (1539) and frescoes by Bartolomeo Cesi. The tomb of Carducci lies near a statue of Murat, by Vincenzo Vela (1865). The Etruscan necropolis of *Felsina* was discovered in the precincts of the Certosa in 1869.

In the northeast part of the town (**buses 38** or **91** from Via Marconi via the station) is the Quartiere Fieristica, where important trade fairs are held. It has permanent exhibition halls, a conference centre and a theatre. Here, too, is the **Galleria d'Arte Moderna** (open Tues–Sun 10.00–18.00 or 19.00), with 20C works by artists from the region, most of which have been donated by the artists themselves.

Off the Via Emilia, 5km southeast of Bologna, is a British military cemetery.

Southeast of Bologna, on the Via Emilia, the town of **Imola** stands on the site of the Roman *Forum Cornelii*, founded by L. Cornelius Sulla in 82 BC. It still preserves the main outlines of its Roman plan.The cathedral was entirely rebuilt in the 18C. The early-14C castle was rebuilt by Gian Galeazzo Sforza, whose daughter Caterina married Girolamo Riario, lord of Imola, and held the fortress after his death until her defeat by Cesare Borgia (1500). It contains a collection of arms and armour. In the small pinacoteca is a painting by Innocenzo Francucci (da Imola; 1494–1550).

On the road from Imola to Florence, which ascends the valley of the Santerno, is **Castel del Rio**. It has a huge 13C castle of the Alidosi and a 16C palace (now the town hall) of the same family. Near Moraduccio is a British military cemetery. There are quarries of *pietra serena* (a dark grey sandstone) in the hills, which have interesting rock formations. The road continues into Tuscany (see *Blue Guide Tuscany*).

The Pistoia road, which leads south from Bologna, passes **Pontecchio Marconi**. This is the resting place of Guglielmo Marconi (1874–1937), whose first experiments in the transmission of signals by Hertzian waves were made at his father's Villa Griffone above the town. Marconi's mausoleum was designed by the prominent early Modernist architect Marcello Piacentini. In the park is a relic of the boat *Elettra* from which, while at anchor in the port of Genoa in 1930, Marconi lit up the lights of Sydney.

At **Marzabotto**, in the park of Villa Aria, are remains of an Etruscan city, thought to be *Misa* (6C–4C BC). Excavations have revealed traces of houses, temples and two necropoli. The site is open daily 08.00–19.00; the **Museo Nazionale Etrusco**, housing the finds, daily 09.00–12.00 and 15.00–18.30.

The road continues south to **Porretta Terme**, a little spa on the Reno, with warm springs of sulphurous and alkaline waters, beyond which it enters Tuscany (see *Blue Guide Tuscany*).

Ferrara and its province

Ferrara is famous as the residence of the Este dukes, whose court was one of the more illustrious of the Italian Renaissance. Its 15C walls are among the more extensive and interesting in Europe, and the huge Este castle survives right in the centre of the town. There are also numerous gardens and good museums, and important exhibitions and concerts are often held here. The town lies in a fertile plain near the right bank of the Po: extensive land-reclamation operations in the delta area brought back to Ferrara much of its old prosperity, and it is now an important market for fruit.

Practical information

Getting there
By air

Ferrara lies 45km from Bologna's Guilelmo Marconi Airport, with daily flights to and from domestic and international destinations.

By road

Ferrara has its own exit roughly halfway along the Padua–Bologna Autostrada (A13). It can also be reached from Bologna by 64, from Padua and Ravenna by 16, and from Mantua by 482. **Country buses** to Bologna, Modena and points throughout the province; **bus stations** at Rampari di San Paolo and Piazzale Stazione.

By rail

Ferrara is situated on the main rail line from Padua (50mins north) to Bologna (25mins south). From most other places to the south, east and west the quickest way to get there is via Bologna. Commuter trains connect to Rimini via Ravenna, and to Mantua via Suzzara.

Getting around
Car parks

In streets and squares throughout the city.

Bicycles

Can be hired on Corso Giovecca (next to the information office).

Buses

Buses 1 and 9 from the station to the castle. Services for the province (including Comacchio) depart from the bus station on Corso Isonzo (**Map 6**).

Information offices

FERRARA Corso Giovecca 21, ☎ 0532 209370. Offices are open in summer at **COMACCHIO**, **POMPOSA** and at the **LIDI** resorts.

Where to stay

FERRARA *Annunziata*, Piazza Repubblica 5, ☎ 0532 201111, fax 0532 203233; a friendly, family-run place, quiet and comfortable; moderate.

Astra, Viale Cavour 55, ☎ 0532 206088, fax 0532 764377; comfortable and well-managed, with antiques here and there; moderate.

Duchessa Isabella, Via Palestro 70, ☎ 0532 202121, fax 0532 202638; a beautiful, luxurious old townhouse with coffered ceilings, Ferrara-school frescoes and a good restaurant; closed Aug; expensive.

Locanda della Duchessina, Vicolo del Voltino 11, ☎ 0532 206981; a miniature version of the Duchessa Isabella (5 rooms), under the same management; closed Aug; moderate.

Locanda Borgonuovo, Via Cairoli 29, ☎ 0532 211100; even smaller than the Locanda della Duchessa (4 rooms), but just as nice; inexpensive.

Ripagrande, Via Ripagrande 21, ☎ 0532 765250, fax 0532 764377; in a Renaissance townhouse, with garden restaurant seating in summer; moderate.

Youth hostel near Palazzo dei Diamanti.

Eating out

FERRARA *La Providenza*, Corso Ercole I d'Este 92, ☎ 0532 205187; a restaurant known for its hearty local fare; closed Mon and Aug; moderate.

Il Bagattino, Via Correggiari 6, ☎ 0532 206387; trattoria, simple but good; closed Mon; inexpensive.

L'Oca Giuliva, Via Boccacanale di Santo Stefano 38, ☎ 0532 207628; wine bar offering good hot and cold meals; closed Mon, midday Tues and Jan; moderate.

Quel Fantastico Giovedì, Via Castelnuovo 9, ☎ 0532 760570; restaurant serving Emilian dishes with an innovative twist; closed Wed, Jan and Jul–Aug; moderate.

Among Ferrara's many good **cafés** are *Roverella* and *Europa*, in Corso Giovecca. *Al Brindisi*, Via Adelardi 11, a wine bar, serves good cold meals. *Perdonati*, Via San Romano 108, makes traditional Ferrarese breads.

Picnic places in Parco Massari, Parco Pareschi, and on the walls (especially pretty near the Baluardo San Tommaso).

SANT'AGOSTINO (22km southwest) *La Rosa*, Via del Nosco 2, ☎ 0532 84098; sophisticated country trattoria, offering delicious seasonal dishes using the freshest ingredients; closed Sun evening (and midday Sat Jun–Aug), Jan and Aug; moderate.

Entertainment

FERRARA Opera and concert season (Nov–May) and theatre performances at the *Teatro Comunale*. There is a summer festival of music, and concerts are sometimes held in palace courtyards. Ferrara is the seat of the European Youth Orchestra.

Shopping

Street markets in Ferrara Mon and Fri; antiques and crafts markets, first weekend of the month (except Aug), in Piazza Municipale and Piazza Savonarola.

Special events

The *Palio of Ferrara* (San Giorgio) is held at the end of May with races (horses, mules, etc.) in Piazza Ariostea; *Buskers Festival*, street musicians' festival, last week in Aug.

Sport

Cycling and **horse-riding** in the Parco Regionale del Delta del Po. **Golf** at Ferrara (*Cus Ferrara Golf*), Argenta (*Argenta Golf Club*) and Cento (*Golf Club Cento*).

FERRARA
• • • • • • • • •

Ferrara (population 137,000) is one of the more pleasing towns in northern Italy, well-administered and with a peaceful atmosphere. Cycling is the main means of getting about. The city is divided into two distinct parts: the southern district retains many attractive cobbled streets and medieval houses, whereas the area to the north, defined by Jacob Burckhardt as the first modern city of Europe, was laid out with spacious streets and fine palaces in the 15C by Ercole I d'Este.

History

Originating probably as a refuge of the Veneti in the marshes of the Po, Ferrara first became important under the Exarchate of Ravenna (6C). The Guelf family of Este, after a decisive defeat of the Ghibellines by Azzo Novello at Cassano in 1259, established the earliest and one of the greater northern Italian principalities here. Ferrara remained under the sway of the Este dukes until 1598, and their court attracted a great many poets, scholars and artists, while trade and commerce flourished. Nicolò II (1361–88) gave hospitality to Petrarch; Alberto (1388–93) founded the university; Nicolò III (1393–1441) was the patron of Pisanello, and in his city (1438) the eastern emperor John VI Palaeologus met Pope Eugenius IV for the ecumenical council, later transferred to Florence. Lionello (1441–50) inaugurated the age of artistic preeminence that Borso (1450–71) continued; Ercole I (1471–1505) laid out the northern district of the city; and Alfonso I (1505–34), husband of Lucrezia Borgia, was the patron of Ariosto and Titian. Ercole II (1534–59) exiled his wife Renée, the daughter of Louis XII of France and the protectress of John Calvin, who lived for a while in Ferrara under the assumed name of Charles Heppeville; Alfonso II (1559–97) was the patron of Tasso and began the reclamation of the marshes.

In 1598 the city was annexed to the States of the Church on the pretext that Cesare d'Este, heir apparent to the duchy in a collateral line, was illegitimate. The city soon lost importance; it suffered widespread bomb damage in the Second World War.

Art and architecture

Ferrara had a productive school of painting, including Cosmè Tura, 'the Mantegna of Ferrara', Francesco del Cossa, Ercole de'Roberti, Lorenzo Costa, Dosso Dossi and his brother Battista Luteri, and Il Garofalo, a pupil of Raphael.

Ferrara was the birthplace of a great sculptor, Alfonso Lombardi (1497–1537), and of a great architect, Biagio Rossetti (c 1447–1516). The composer Girolamo Frescobaldi (1583–1643) was also born here. At the end of the 16C the 'concerto delle donne' at the Este court had an important influence on the development of the madrigal. Robert Browning wrote several poems about Ferrara, and *My Last Duchess* (written in 1842) probably refers to Alfonso II and his wife. The writer Giorgio Bassani was born in Ferrara in 1916, and his novel *Il Giardino dei Finzi Contini* is set here.

The city centre

The centre of the city surrounds the *****Castello Estense** (Map 7; open Tues–Sun 09.30–17.30), the former palace of the dukes, a massive quadrilateral surrounded by a moat (still filled with water) and approached by drawbridges. The castle was begun in 1385 for Duke Nicolò II by Bartolino da Novara, who incorporated the 13C 'Torre dei Leoni' into the northern corner of the fortress and added three more identical towers. It was altered by Girolamo da Carpi in the 16C and readapted in the 20C to house the administrative offices of the province.

Castello Estense

After an earthquake in 1570 the piano nobile was refurbished to house the state apartments, as well as an antiquarium and a library. The overall plan was commissioned by Alfonso II d'Este (fifth Duke of Este) from Pirro Ligorio, the Neapolitan antiquary and architect who had been working at the Este court since 1568. Ligorio also designed the overall iconographic scheme underlying the painted decoration of the various rooms. The actual execution of the frescoes was entrusted to a group of artists active in Ferrara, including the local Camillo Filippi and his son Sebastiano (Il Bastianino), the Modenese Ludovico Settevecchi and Leonardo da Brescia. By that time the Este court had started to decline and had lost the role of cultural centre it held throughout the Renaissance, with great painters of the 15C such as Francesco del Cossa, Cosmè Tura and Ercole de'Roberti, followed in the 16C by Garofalo and Dosso Dossi.

Several rooms, restored in 1998, can be visited (open Tues–Sun 09.30–17.00). You enter from the lovely courtyard. The first two rooms on the ground floor display architectural remains from the castle, including reliefs with the Este coat of arms and carved keystones. The itinerary leads down a ramp into the kitchen, or **Sala del Caminetto**. Here are three badly ruined frescoes (1577) by Pirro Ligorio (the only ones to have survived the hundred that once decorated the courtyard), and a large-scale model of Ferrara after the plan published by Bolzoni. At the end of a corridor, wooden steps lead down to the grim **dungeons** beneath the Torre dei Leoni, where Parisina, wife of Nicolò III, and her lover Ugo, his illegitimate son, were imprisoned and murdered; the cells were last used for political prisoners in 1943.

An artillery ramp, by which the cannons were taken up to the bastions, leads up round the Torre dei Leoni past another prison,and a modern iron staircase continues up to the **first floor**. Here a loggia opens onto the **Giardino degli Aranci**, a charming little walled hanging garden designed by Girolamo da Carpi for the Este duchesses (with delightful views of the town). The **Camerino del Baccanali** is beautifully frescoed by Camillo Filippi and his sons Cesare and Sebastiano (Il Bastianino). The **Chapel of Renée of France** was one of the few Calvinist chapels in Italy to survive the Counter-Reformation. The **Sala dell'Aurora**, **Saletta dei Giochi** and **Salone dei Giochi** have delightful ceiling *frescoes by the Filippi (in the last two, around the walls, are copies made in 1911 of the frescoes in Palazzo Schifanoia). The tiny ***Stanzina delle Duchesse** was entirely decorated with grotesques by the Filippi c 1555–65.

The chapel of **San Giuliano** (1405) stands in the piazzetta on the west side of the castle. Off Corso Martiri della Libertà is a monument to the great reformer, Savonarola, born in Ferrara in 1452, by Stefano Galletti (1875). The **Palazzo Comunale** (**Map 7**), built for Azzo Novello (1243), was considerably altered in the late 15C by Pietro Benvenuti and Biagio Rossetti. The bronze statues of Nicolò III and Borso, on the Classical arch (on a design attributed to Leon Battista Alberti) and column in front, are 20C reproductions of the 15C originals destroyed in 1796. The arcaded courtyard has a fine staircase by Pietro Benvenuti (1481).

The Cathedral

The *Cathedral (**Map 11**), begun in 1135 for Guglielmo II degli Adelardi by the architect and sculptor Niccolò, was almost complete by the end of the 13C. The church was dedicated to the Virgin Mary and to St George, both of whom feature

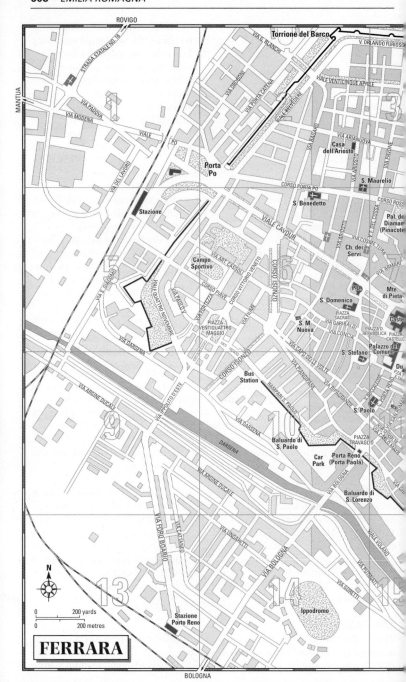

FERRARA

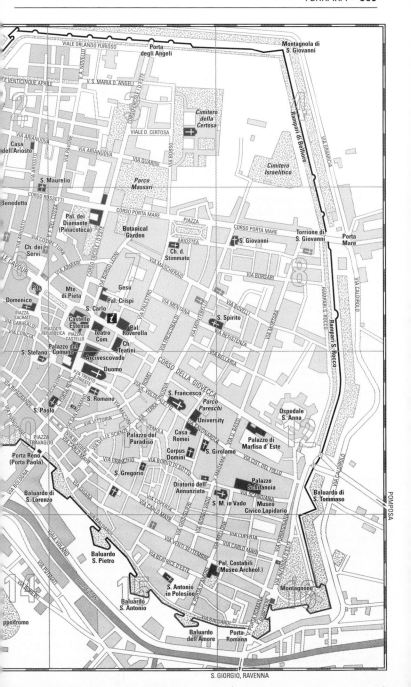

prominently on the **façade**. Niccolò's reliefs on the central portal include the architrave with scenes of the life of Christ (*Visitation, Nativity, Adoration of the Magi, Circumcision, Flight into Egypt* and *Baptism of Christ*), and a lunette with *St George Killing the Dragon*. The portal is crowned by an elaborate 13C *tribune housing a statue of the *Madonna and Child* by Cristoforo da Firenze (1427). Above is an architrave with the *Resurrection from the Graves*, and representations of the blessed and the damned, surmounted by a tympanum with the *Last Judgement*. The lunettes at the sides of the tribune show further scenes of the blessed and damned. The whole was carved by an unknown 13C sculptor. To the right of the side door is a statue of Alberto d'Este (1393). The south side is partly obscured by a charming little portico of shops added in 1473. The massive, unfinished campanile, southeast of the church, was built from 1412 to 1596 to a plan attributed to Leon Battista Alberti.

The **interior**, remodelled in 1712–18, is preceded by a narthex with a 5C sarcophagus and the original pilasters from the main portal. On the west wall are two detached frescoes by Garofalo, representing *St Peter* and *St Paul*. The north side has altarpieces by Garofalo (1524) and Francesco Francia. In the transepts are terracotta busts of the *Apostles* by Alfonso Lombardi. The south transept also has a *Martyrdom of St Laurence* by Guercino (1629) and the *altar of the Calvary, composed in 1673 from large 15C bronze groups of statuary by Niccolò and Giovanni Baroncelli and Domenico di Paris. Below is the effigy tomb of Bishop Bovelli (d. 1954). A *Last Judgement* by Bastianino (1580–83) adorns the apse.

A one-time ghost town

Fallen into decadence and plagued by malaria, Ferrara had been largely abandoned by the time most Grand Tourists of the 18C and 19C saw it. Here are a few of their remarks:

My pen was just upon the point of praising its cleanliness... till I reflected there was nobody to dirty it.
Hester Lynch Piozzi, *Observations... in the Course of a Journey*, 1789

You are in a dream, in the heart of a romance; you enjoy the most perfect solitude, that of a city which was once filled with "the busy hum of men", and of which the tremulous fragments at every step strike the sense, and call up reflection. In short, nothing is to be seen of Ferrara, but the remains, graceful and romantic, of what it was.
William Hazlitt, *Notes of a Journey through France and Italy*, 1826

More solitary, more depopulated, more deserted, old Ferrara than any city of the solemn brotherhood! The grass so grows up in the silent streets, that any one might make hay there, literally, while the sun shines. But the sun shines with diminished cheerfulness in grim Ferrara; and the people are so few who pass and repass through the places, that the flesh of the inhabitants might be grass indeed, and growing in the squares.
Charles Dickens, *Pictures from Italy*, 1846

The **Museo della Cattedrale** in the church of San Romano, opposite the south side of the cathedral in Piazza Trento e Trieste, is open Tues–Sat 10.00–12.00, 15.00–17.00, Sun and holidays 10.00–12.00, 16.00–18.00. It contains good

Flemish tapestries and illuminated choir books; *St George* and an **Annunciation* by Cosmè Tura (1469), from the doors of the old cathedral organ; the **Madonna of the Pomegranate* and a statuette of St Maurelius, both by Jacopo della Quercia (1408); and charming 12C reliefs of the **Months* (September, with the grape harvest, is particularly notable) from the old south doorway.

The **Seminario**, at Via Cairoli 32, occupies the 16C Palazzo Trotti, which contains two rooms frescoed by Garofalo (1519–20), with remarkable perspectives.

In the piazza south of the cathedral are the Torre dell'Orologio and a department store in an ugly building of 1957 on the site of the 14C Palazzo della Ragione. The pretty, arcaded Via San Romano leads south through an interesting medieval part of the town. The street ends at Porta Reno (or Porta Paolo), built in 1612 on a design by Giovanni Battista Aleotti. Nearby is the imposing church of San Paolo, begun in 1575 by the architect Alberto Schiatti. It contains 16C–17C paintings and frescoes by Girolamo da Carpi (*St Jerome*), Bastianino, Scarsellino (fresco in the apse with the *Abduction of Elias*) and Domenico Mona (*Adoration of the Magi, Conversion and Martyrdom of St Paul*, all in the presbytery). Along the aisles are some beautiful 18C terracotta sculptures by Filippo Bezzi and Francesco Casella.

Before the gate the pretty Via delle Volte (**Map 11**), which runs beneath numerous arches, leads left. It crosses Via Scienze, in which (at no. 17) is **Palazzo Paradiso**. The building dates from 1391 and has a façade of 1610 by Giovanni Battista Aleotti. In the library (Biblioteca Comunale Ariostea, open Mon–Fri 09.00–19.00, Sat 09.00–13.00) are the tomb of Ariosto, manuscript pages of Ariosto's epic poem *Orlando Furioso*, and autographs of Ariosto and Tasso. Nearby in Via Mazzini is the **synagogue** in the area which was the **ghetto** of Ferrara from 1627 to 1848, although a large Jewish community from Spain had lived freely in the town during the period of the Este dukes. The **Museo Ebraico di Ferrara**, at Via Mazzini 95, is open for guided tours Sun–Thur 10.00–11.00–12.00.

You can see well-preserved old houses of the 15C city and little churches in the narrow lanes lying between Via Scienze and Via Borgo Vado (**Map 11**). At Via Gioco del Pallone 31 is the house that belonged to Ariosto's family.

The attractive Via Voltapaletto (**Map 11**), east of the cathedral, leads past the handsome **Palazzo Costabili** (no. 11; 17C), decorated with busts and trophies, to the spacious church of **San Francesco**. The church was partly rebuilt in 1494 by Biagio Rossetti. The frescoes above the arches (Franciscan saints) and on the vault are good Ferrarese works of the 16C. In the north aisle are a fine fresco of the *Seizure of Christ in the Garden* (1524) by Garofalo and an altarpiece by Scarsellino.

The Casa Romei

Via Savonarola continues to the **Casa Romei (**Map 11**; no. 30; open Tues–Sat 08.30–19.00, Sun–Mon 08.30–14.00). The house is one of the best examples of aristocratic homes in 15C Ferrara. It was begun around 1440 for the wealthy Giovanni Romei, who served the Este court as a diplomat and (in 1474) married Polissena d'Este. In keeping with Giovanni's will the house was donated after his death to the Clarissan nuns of the adjacent convent of Corpus Domini and was used to house pilgrims and other visitors to the city (one of the guests was Lucrezia Borgia). It remained in the nuns' hands until the confiscation of monastic properties under Napoleon.

Off the central courtyard are two rooms with frescoes representing respectively the *Prophets,* with philosophical truths and biblical prophecies written on scrolls, and the *Sibyls* (probably executed after the wedding with Polissena d'Este). The frescoes in the courtyard date from the 16C. On the upper floor are frescoes by the Filippi (second half of the 16C) and a noteworthy collection of detached frescoes, mainly of the 14C, from Ferrarese churches that were either ruined or suppressed.

Across Via Savonarola is the seat of the university, founded in 1391. The church of **San Girolamo** (1712) faces the house (no. 19) where Savonarola passed the first 20 years of his life. The church of **Corpus Domini** has a 15C façade in Via Campofranco (if closed, enquire at the convent, Via Pergolato 4). After a fire that greatly damaged the interior, the church was refurbished in 1770 by Antonio Foschini. Most of the lavish painted decoration dates from that period. The capitular room at the back contains several floor tombs of members of the Este family, notably Alfonso I and II d'Este, and of Lucrezia Borgia (d. 1519) and two of her sons. Via Savonarola ends at the severe Palazzo Saracco.

Via Ugo Bassi, to the left, leads to Corso della Giovecca, where no. 174 is the **Palazzina di Marfisa d'Este** (Map 12; open daily 09.30–13.00, 15.00–18.00). Built in 1559 at the commission of Francesco d'Este for his daughter Marfisa, it was restored in 1938. The ceilings are decorated with grotesques and mythological scenes, by Camillo Filippi and his sons Sebastiano and Cesare, which were extensively restored in the late 19C. It also houses a good collection of period furniture, a supposed portrait of James I of England, and a damaged bust in profile of Ercole I d'Este, by Sperandio. The Loggia degli Aranci in the garden has a vault painted with trellised vines and birds.

Via Madama, to the right, continues as Via Borgo Vado, where the church of **Santa Maria in Vado**, another work of Rossetti (1495–1518), has a handsome interior covered with 17C and 18C paintings. Nearby, at Via Borgo di Sotto 47, is the **Oratorio dell'Annunziata** (Map 11; ring for admission at the convent at no. 49). The elegant façade is by the Ferrarese Gian Battista Aleotti (1612). The interior (open Mon–Sat 09.00–12.00 and 15.00–18.00; entered from the convent in Via Borgo di Sotto) is a rectangular room decorated in 1548 with frescoes attributed to Camillo Filippi, Pellegrino Tibaldi and Nicolò Rosselli, and trompel'oeil perspectives by Francesco Scala. The paintings were commissioned by the Confraternità della Buona Morte (a community service organisation) and represent the *Legend of the True Cross* according to the apocryphal text of Iacopo da Varagine. They are very damaged and in need of restoration. On the altar wall is a 15C *Resurrection* with members of the Confraternità (who assisted the condemned), and on the opposite wall an *Assumption* signed by Lamberto Nortense.

Palazzo Schifanoia

In Via Scandiana is Palazzo Schifanoia (entrance at no. 27; **Map 12**; open daily 09.00–19.00; closed the first Mon of the month), begun in 1385 and enlarged in 1391, 1458, and in 1469 by Pietro Benvenuti and Biagio Rossetti. Stairs lead up to the ***Salone dei Mesi**, decorated for Duke Borso d'Este with delightful frescoes of the months, one of the more renowned fresco cycles of the Renaissance of profane subjects (now in rather poor condition). They were painted by Francesco

Cossa with the help of Ercole de' Roberti and other (unidentified) masters of the Ferrarese school.

The frescoes follow a complicated decorative scheme referring to the months of the year in three bands: above are 12 scenes illustrating the triumph of a divinity; the middle band has the sign of the zodiac for that month, flanked by two symbolic figures, and the lower part of the walls are decorated with scenes from the court of Duke Borso.

The present entrance (formerly on the long north wall) is on the west wall. The scenes illustrating January and February are very ruined. The **east wall**, opposite the present entrance, is the best preserved and is known to have been decorated by Francesco Cossa. March: *Triumph of Minerva*, showing her on a chariot drawn by two unicorns; the sign of Aries; hawking scenes. April: *Triumph of Venus* (her chariot drawn by swans); Taurus; Duke Borso returning from the hunt and the Palio of St George. May: *Triumph of Apollo*; Gemini; fragments of farming scenes.

North wall: June: *Triumph of Mercury*; Cancer; scenes of the duke in a landscape. July: *Triumph of Zeus*; Leo; the duke receiving visitors, and scenes of women working hemp. August: *Triumph of Ceres*; Virgo. The scenes for September are usually attributed to Ercole de'Roberti: Triumph of Vulcan, with Vulcan's forge, and a love scene in bed thought to represent Mars and the vestal virgin Silvia, from whom Romulus and Remus were born; Libra; Borso receiving Venetian ambassadors. The south wall with the last three months is almost totally obliterated. There is a display of illuminated manuscripts here.

The *Sala degli Stucchi* (1468–70) has a delightful ceiling attributed to Domenico di Paris. The adjoining room has another good ceiling and a display of 14C–15C ceramics.

The main staircase leads back downstairs. Halfway down is the entrance to rooms that contain material from the municipal collections of **arts and antiquities**, including (in the first room) Egyptian works, two Greek red-figure vases and Roman glass. The next three rooms on a mezzanine floor (with remains of painted decoration on the walls) display 15C–16C ceramics. On the floor below are exhibited ivories and scenes of the Passion in alabaster, made in Nottingham in the early 15C; 15C intarsia stalls; plaques and medals by Pisanello, Matteo de' Pasti and Sperandio; sculptures including a bust by Guido Mazzoni and two Madonnas attributed to Domenico di Paris; 16C bronzes (Giovanni Francesco Susini, Giambologna and Duquesnoy), 18C marble busts, and a portrait of Cicognara by Canova (1822).

Across the street is the **Museo Civico Lapidario** (open as Palazzo Schifanoia), arranged in the 15C former church of Santa Libera. The collection of Roman works was formed in 1735 by Marchese Bevilacqua. Among the funerary stelae and sarcophagi are those of Annia Faustina and of the Aurelii (both dating from the 3C AD).

From the entrance to the lapidarium, Via Camposabbionario leads to the ruins of the once-imposing church of **Sant'Andrea**, one of the principal churches of Ferrara and former home to many of the frescoes and paintings now exhibited in the pinacoteca (including the beautiful *Costabili Polyptych* by Garofalo and Dosso Dossi). Until the 19C the church also held the remains of the great Ferrarese architect Biagio Rossetti, who was buried here in 1516. After a series of fires and earthquakes the ruined church was deconsecrated in 1867 and turned into a military warehouse. The north wall was destroyed in the 1960s to make way for an ugly concrete secondary school.

Via Camposabbionario ends in Via XX Settembre. Via XX Settembre 152 is the house that Biagio Rossetti (1445/47–1516) designed as his own home. It is now home to **Musarc** (open daily 10.00–13.00 and 15.00–18.00), a museum of architecture that has a permanent collection of Frank Lloyd Wright's plans and drawings for the Solomon R. Guggenheim Museum in New York and mounts three temporary exhibitions per year.

At Via XX Settembre 124 is *****Palazzo Costabili**, also called the Palazzo di Lodovico il Moro (**Map 15**). It was commissioned in 1495 from Biagio Rossetti by Antonio Costabili, who was the ambassador of the Este at the Sforza court of Lodovico il Moro in Milan (Lodovico married Beatrice d'Este in 1490). The building, one of Rossetti's masterpieces, was left unfinished in 1504. Off the beautiful square courtyard are two rooms decorated by Garofalo and his assistants around 1517. The first has lunettes with *Prophets* and *Sibyls*, and monochrome paintings on the ceiling; the second is painted with the *Story of St Joseph*. Off the portico on the south side of the courtyard is the so-called Aula Costabiliana or **Sala del Tesoro** with a stunning illusionistic ceiling depicting a polygonal dome and balcony with figures (members of the Costabili family) looking out at the viewer. The inspiration is clearly derived from Mantegna's Camera degli Sposi in the Palazzo Ducale at Mantua (see p 290). The three rooms are currently closed to the public.

A beautiful staircase leads up from the courtyard to the *****Museo Archeologico Nazionale** (open Tues–Sat 09.00–14.00, Sun and holidays 09.00–13.00). The museum was established in 1935 to hold finds from the necropolis of Spina in the Trebba Valley near Comacchio (excavated 1922–35). The collection was enlarged in the 1950s following the discovery of further tombs in the adjacent Pega Valley. By 1964 up to 4000 tombs had been excavated and their contents displayed in the museum. The artefacts buried in the tombs date between the 6C and the 3C BC and are mainly linked to the idea of banquets and symposia intended to accompany the dead, in a fitting manner, to the afterlife. Spina was an extremely rich port that traded extensively with Greece and Etruria. The relation with Greece is witnessed by a conspicuous number of Hellenic pottery of great quality (mainly Attic red-figure vases of the 5C BC) forming one of the richer collections of the kind in Italy.

Only six rooms are presently open to the public. Highlights include, in room **2**, a great kylix by the Pentesilea Painter and a krater by the Boreas Painter, both dated around 460 BC. In room **4** are some fine bronze objects, and room **5** has a beautiful krater by the Niobid Painter and an interesting anphora decorated by the Berlin painter in an old-fashioned black-figure style (it shows a racing chariot). Room **6** contains mainly local artefacts that mingle influences of Attic vases from Greece with Etruscan art. Atypical are the objects from a tomb associated with a Celtic youth (4C–3C BC) and a curious Punic mask in terracotta, used in funerary processions.

Gardens crown the ramparts of **Montagnone** (**Map 16**), and a park extends north above the walls built by Alfonso I (1512–18). Paths continue from here for c 5km around the walls as far as Porta Po, interrupted only at Porta Mare. The walls are described in greater detail below.

Via Porta Romana leads south through the walls and across the Po di Volano canal to the church of **San Giorgio** (beyond Map 16), which was the cathedral of Ferrara in the 7C–12C, then rebuilt in the 15C and partly renovated in the 18C. The campanile is by Rossetti (1485). Inside are the magnificent *tomb of Lorenzo Roverella, physician to Julius II and afterwards Bishop of Ferrara, by Ambrogio da Milano and Antonio Rossellino (1475); and the pavement tomb of Cosmè Tura. From Porta Romana a path takes you along a good stretch of walls built by Alfonso II.

Near Palazzo Costabili, off Via Beatrice d'Este, is the convent of **Sant'Antonio in Polesine** (ring for admission). The monastery was originally established in the late Middle Ages by the Eremitani di Sant'Agostino on what was then an island in the River Po. It then passed to a community of Benedictine nuns founded in 1254 by Beatrice II d'Este, who promoted the reconstruction of the complex. Beatrice died in 1264 and was beatified in 1270; her relics and marble tombstone (from which miraculous water issues) are kept on the side of the cloister flanking the church.

The **church** is divided into two parts, of which the oldest, to the east, houses the nuns' choir (with beautiful wooden stalls decorated with tarsia work of the late 15C) and three chapels with frescoes dating from the 14C to the 16C. The frescoes in the north chapel, executed in the early 14C, show a strong influence of Giotto and represent the lives of Christ and the Virgin. The iconography of some scenes is unusual: the *Visitation* includes Zacharias, who normally is not shown; the Nativity follows a Byzantine prototype with a double representation of Christ, one spiritual and prefiguring his death (hence the tomb), the other temporal and in need of human care (he is being washed by the midwives). The *Flight into Egypt* is absolutely unique in its representation of Jesus on Joseph's shoulder, instead of the Virgin's lap. On the left wall, the *Dormition of the Virgin* again follows a Byzantine scheme with Christ in a mandorla holding the personification of the Virgin's soul.

The cycle continues in the south chapel, with the scenes of the *Garden of Gethsemane*, *Judas's Betrayal* and the *Mocking of Christ* on the left wall, all belonging to the same school of painters that decorated the left chapel. The representation of Christ ascending the ladder to the Cross, painted in the lunette on the right wall, is highly unusual. Somewhat later in date (mid-14C) and belonging to a different school of painters (of Bolognese influence) are the scenes of the *Dance of Salome*, *Christ in Limbo*, *Crucifixion*, *Deposition* and *Entombment*, as well as the *St John the Baptist* and *St John the Evangelist* on either side of the window.

The frescoes in the central chapel date mainly from the 15C, whereas the vault is decorated with grotesques of the late 16C. The lunettes on the side walls depict the shell of Santiago de Campostela, as pilgrims travelling to the saint's shrine in Spain along the Via Romea departed from this church. On the walls are representations of the *Virgin Enthroned among Saints*, *Martyrs* and *Doctors of the Church*. Particularly interesting are a scene of the *Stoning of St Stephen* on the right wall, and the *Coronation of the Virgin*. The wooden crucifix at the top has been ascribed to the school of Cosmè Tura.

Behind the central chapel is a room decorated with 17C paintings inserted in the ceiling, a 16C panel with the *Virgin and the Mysteries of the Rosary* over the altar, and a fresco of the *Flagellation* attributed to Ercole de'Roberti on the entrance wall. At the other side of the choir is the newer part of the church, with an illusionistic ceiling painted in the 17C by Francesco Ferrari.

Palazzo dei Diamanti and north

The area of the city north of the castle and the broad, busy Corso della Giovecca (**Map 7, 11**, and **12**) was planned by Ercole I in the early 15C with wide thoroughfares and fine palaces and gardens.

Corso Giovecca 37 is a fragment of the old Arcispedale Sant'Anna, where Tasso was confined as a lunatic in 1579–86; behind is a 15C cloister of the former Basilian convent. The fine church of San Carlo is by Giovanni Battista Aleotti (1623). In Via Borgo Leoni is the church of the **Gesù**, which contains a *Pietà* in terracotta by Guido Mazzoni (1485). At Corso Giovecca 47 Palazzo Roverella has a beautiful terracotta façade of 1508, attributed to Biagio Rossetti. Nearby, at Via De Pisis 24, is the **Museo Civico di Storia Naturale** (open Tues–Sat 09.00–19.00, Sun and holidays 09.00–13.00, 15.00–19.00). On the other side of Corso Giovecca is the church of the **Teatini** (1653), which contains a *Presentation in the Temple* by Guercino. The Teatro Comunale, without a monumental façade, is attributed to Antonio Foschini (c 1780).

Palazzo dei Diamanti

The handsome, cobbled **Corso Ercole I D'Este** (**Map 7, 3**) leads north past several palaces and garden walls to Palazzo dei Diamanti (**Map 7**), begun by Rossetti for Sigismondo d'Este c 1492 and remodelled around 1565. It takes its name from the diamond emblem of the Este, repeated 12,600 times on its façade. The palace contains the **Pinacoteca Nazionale** (open Tues–Sat 09.00–14.00, Sun and holidays 09.00–13.00), especially notable for its paintings of the Ferrarese school. Important exhibitions are often held here.

The rooms are unnumbered, but the works are all labelled. The Vendeghini-Baldi collection (displayed in a room to the left) includes works by Garofalo, Michele Coltellini, Bartolomeo Vivarini, Andrea Mantegna, Ercole de'Roberti, Jacopo and Giovanni Bellini, and Gentile da Fabriano. Another series of rooms displays works by the 'Maestro di Figline', Simone dei Crocifissi, Ercole de'Roberti, Giuseppe Mazzuoli, the school of Piero della Francesca, and Cosmè Tura.

Early- and mid-16C painters represented include Giovan Francesco Maineri, Michele Coltellini, Domenico Panetti, Bastianino, and Lodovico and Agostino Carracci. The 17C and 18C works include paintings by Scarsellino, Guercino and Pietro della Vecchia.

The works from the Collezione Sacrati Strozzi, which were assigned to the city in 1992, include Madonnas by Biagio d'Antonio and Francesco Bianchi Ferrari, two 15C *muses, Christ in the Garden* attributed to Battista Dossi, and two interesting 16C views of Ferrara.

The **Salone d'Onore**, with a fine wooden ceiling of 1567–91, holds 13C–14C frescoes from the church of San Bartolo and the ruined Sant'Andrea, as well as frescoes by Serafino Serafini (*Apotheosis of St Augustine*) and Garofalo (the *Old and New Testament*, formerly in Palazzo Costabili). Also here are two works of 1565 by Camillo Bastiani and Bastianino.

The rooms beyond, part of the apartment of Cesare and Virginia d'Este, preserve their 16C decoration. Here are displayed a painting by Vittore Carpaccio and works by 16C painters from Ferrara (Ortolano, Mazzolino, Bastianino, Scarsellino and Carlo Bononi), with Garofalo and Dosso Dossi especially well represented (notice especially Garofalo's *Massacre of the Innocents* and the huge *Costabili Polyptych* from the church of Sant'Andrea, begun by Garofalo and finished by Dosso Dossi). The gallery also owns a good collection of etchings and engravings. Palazzo Prosperi Sacrati, on the opposite side of the Corso, with an elaborate 16C portal, is to be used as an extension to the gallery.

The northern districts
Beside Palazzo dei Diamanti, at no. 19, is the entrance to the handsomely arranged **Museo del Risorgimento e della Resistenza** (open Mon–Sat 09.00–14.00, 15.00–19.00; Sun and holidays 09.00–12.00, 15.30–18.30). At no. 17 is the **Museo Michelangelo Antonioni** (open daily 09.30–13.00, 15.00–18.00), with a collection documenting the work of the film director, who was born in Ferrara.

At the end of Corso Ercole I d'Este is the former **Porta degli Angeli (Map 3)** in the *walls of Ercole I. This was the gate by which the Este left Ferrara in 1598, and it was closed the following year. The walls were begun in 1451 at the southern limit of the city, and in 1492 Biagio Rossetti was commissioned to build the walls here around Ercole I's extension to the city. Alfonso I and Alfonso II strengthened the fortifications, and more work was carried out on them by the popes in the 17C and 18C. Their total length is c 9.2km, and paths and avenues surmount them for some 8.5km.

Eight semicircular towers survive to the left of Porta degli Angeli; at the northwest angle is the Torrione del Barco. The most interesting and best-preserved stretch of the walls (followed by a picturesque path open to cyclists) is from the Porta degli Angeli to the Porta Mare (**Map 8**). The view north extends across the former 'Barco', the ducal hunting reserve, as far as the Po, an area of some 1200h destined to become a park. Inside the walls you can see the orchards that surround the Certosa (see below) and the Jewish cemetery; in the distance are the towers of the castle.

Corso Porta Mare leads east from Palazzo dei Diamanti. At no. 2 is the **Orto Botanico** (open Mon–Sat 09.00–13.00, Tues and Thur 09.00–17.00). Beyond are the Parco Massari and Palazzo Bevilacqua Massari. The latter houses the **Museo d'Arte Moderna e Contemporanea** as well as the **Museo Boldini**, devoted to works by the Ferrarese painter Giovanni Boldini (1842–1931). Both museums are entered from Via Porta Mare 9 and are open 09.00–13.00 and 15.00–18.00.

The palazzo was built in the 16C and enlarged in the late 18C to house, on the *piano nobile*, an enfilade of 14 rooms that follows the model of French royal palaces. Today these richly decorated rooms display Boldini's paintings, from the beginning of his career in Italy to his French period, testifying to his interest in the work of the Impressionists. After his definitive move to Paris in 1870, Boldini soon became established as a painter of Parisian high society—an accomplishment best exemplified by the portraits of the *Comtesse de Rasty* (1878), the *Little Subercaseuse* (1891), *Princess Eulalia of Spain* (1898), and the magnificent *Lady in White* (1890) and *Lady in Pink* (1916). The rest of the first floor houses paintings of the 19C Italian school, as well as works of the Ferrarese symbolists Gaetano Previati (1852–1920) and Giuseppe Mentessi (1857–1931).

Twentieth century Italian art (paintings by Achille Funi, Robert Melli, Mario Pozzati, Filippo De Pisis) is shown on the **ground floor** galleries. Four rooms in the west wing accommodate the Malabotta collection of paintings and drawings by another celebrated Ferrarese artist, Filippo De Pisis (1896–1956). The latter collection was donated to the museum in 1996. The museum's collection of paintings by Giorgio De Chirico and the Metaphysical School of painters is currently not on display.

Metaphysical painting

This term is generally applied to the work of Giorgio De Chirico and Carlo Carrà from 1915 to 1918 and to that of Giorgio Morandi, who came together with Carrà toward the end of the war. The poet Alberto Savinio, brother of De Chirico, said that it involved 'the total representation of spiritual necessities within plastic limits—power to express the spectral side of things—irony'. De Chrico himself wrote in 1938: 'To be truly immortal a work of art must stand completely outside human limitations; logic and common sense are detrimental to it. Thus it approximates dream and infantile mentality.... One of the stronger sensations left to us by prehistory is that of presage. It will always be with us. It is as if it were an eternal proof of the non-sense of the universe.'

Although De Chirico had read Schopenhauer and Nietzsche, the actual metaphysics of the movement are obscure; in practice it involved using objects (often mannequins and statues) as signs, placing them in unusual combinations and strange architectural perspectives that create an atmosphere of mystery. De Chirico's earlier paintings (before 1915)—particularly those done in Paris, where he knew Picasso, Paul Guillaume and Apollinaire—already possessed these qualities, especially the powerful but mysterious sense of presage. They were intensified in the work he did when he was confined to hospital as a conscript at Ferrara in 1915.

Further on, on the right, is Piazza Ariostea (**Map 7**), with two Renaissance palaces and a statue of Ariosto (19C) on a column which in turn has carried statues of Duke Ercole I, Pope Alexander VII, Liberty and Napoleon.

Via Borso leads north to the **Certosa** (**Map 3**; 1452–61), with interesting cloisters, now occupied by a cemetery. The adjoining church of **San Cristoforo**, begun in 1498, probably by Rossetti, has good terracotta decoration. Off Via Borso, Via Guarini and Via Aria Nuova lead due west to the **Casa dell'Ariosto** (**Map 2**; Via Ariosto 67), the house built by the poet, who died here in 1533.

Around Ferrara

Ferrara has a small province, most of which is to the east of the town in the southern part of the Po Delta, where the Po di Volano reaches the sea in a nature reserve. The northern Po Delta, which lies in the Veneto, is described on p 494.

The Po River wetlands

The once marshy country between Ferrara and the sea, where the Po enters the Adriatic, has been the subject of land-reclamation schemes ever since the time of Alfonso II d'Este. It is a place of wild natural beauty: the dunes in the Po di Goro delta, in particular, are of great interest to naturalists. The Gran Bosco della Mesola on the Volano, one of the last wooded areas in the Po Delta, has been has been included in the recently-established **Parco Regionale del Delta del Po**, a nature reserve that you can explore by boat, on Camargue horses or by bike along the marshland banks (open Sun and holidays, 08.00–dusk). Yellow iris, waterlily and ditchreed offer a natural setting for numerous bird species, and the meanders of the delta host a large colony of European Pond Turtles. There is also sport fishing for eels, carp and perch. On the Po di Goro is the splendid **Castello di Mesola**, a hunting lodge of Alfonso II, built in 1583 by Antonio Pasi (on a design by Giovan Battista Aleotti), now used for exhibitions (open Mar–Nov, Tues–Sat 09.00–12.30 and 15.00 or 16.00–17.00 or 18.00).

The abbey of Pomposa

The isolated Benedictine abbey of *Pomposa, at Codigoro, was founded in the 7C–8C on what was then an island, but was gradually deserted in the 17C because of malaria. It is still one of the more evocative sites on the delta, marked by its fine *campanile, 48m high. The abbey is open daily, 09.00–12.00 and 14.00–19.00.

The church dates from the 8C–9C, and was enlarged in the 11C. It is preceded by an atrium with beautiful Byzantine sculptural decoration. The fine basilican **interior**, with good capitals and a mosaic floor from the 12C, is covered with charming 14C frescoes representing scenes from the Old and New Testament and the Apocalypse. Some of these, including the *Christ in Glory* in the apse, have been attributed to Vitale da Bologna.

The monastic buildings include the chapterhouse and refectory, both with important frescoes of the Bolognese school. There is a small **museum** above the refectory. Guido d'Arezzo (c 995–1050), inventor of the modern musical scale, was a monk here. The **Palazzo della Ragione** (abbot's justice court) is a beautiful 11C building, altered in 1396.

Comacchio, Spina and the coast

To the south are fields where rice is cultivated, and the marshes of the Valle Bertuzzi (visited by migratory birds). **Comacchio** is an interesting little town that grew to importance because of its salt-works. It is now important for fishing and curing eels—the huge shoals of eels that make for the sea in Oct–Dec are caught in special traps. The town was continuously attacked by the Venetians and destroyed by them in 1509. The pretty canal-lined streets are crossed by numerous bridges, notably the 17C Trepponti, which traverses no less than four canals. The Loggia dei Mercanti, duomo and Loggiata dei Cappuccini all date from the 17C.

In the drained lagoon northwest of Comacchio the burial-ground of the Greco-Etruscan city of **Spina** yielded a vast quantity of vases and other pottery (kept in the archaeological museum in Ferrara). Founded c 530 BC, it was a port carrying on a lively trade with Greece, but it barely outlasted the 4C BC. Part of the city itself, laid out on a regular grid plan with numerous canals, was located by aerial survey in 1956, and excavations continue.

The dwindling **Lago di Comacchio** is now more than two-thirds drained, to the detriment of the egrets, herons, stilts, terns and avocets that were once found here in profusion. It has recently been incorporated in the Parco Regionale del Delta del Po. At **Porto Garibaldi** (formerly Magnavacca) the Austrian navy captured the last 200 'Garibaldini', leaving Garibaldi alone with Anita and his comrade Leggero. Anita died at Mandriole, on the southern shore of the lake (monument), now in the province of Ravenna near the vast pine woods of San Vitale, which hide the view of the sea.

On the sandy coast are a line of popular resorts, including Lido delle Nazioni and Lido degli Estensi, known as the Lidi Ferraresi, with numerous hotels and camping sites, crowded with tourists in summer.

At **Argenta**, on the western side of the Valli di Comacchio, is a Marsh Museum (open Tues–Sun 09.30–13.00, 15.30–18.00) that documents land reclamation here over the centuries as well as the interesting flora and fauna of these wetlands.

On the western border of the province is the little town of **Cento**, the birthplace of Isaac Israeli, great-grandfather of Benjamin Disraeli, and of Guercino, whose painting is well represented in the Pinacoteca Civica. The church of the Rosario contains a chapel built for Guercino and a fine *Crucifixion* by him. Above the town rises the 14C rocca.

At **Pieve di Cento** a small Pinacoteca Civica in the main square preserves paintings by the Bolognese and Ferrarese schools (15C–19C), a wooden 14C *Madonna* and 18C reliquaries.

Modena and Reggio Emilia

Modena and Reggio Emilia are the first of the famous Emilian microcities you encounter travelling northwest from Bologna along the Via Emilia (the others are Parma, Fidenza and Piacenza). These places combine small-town scale with big-city amenities (symphony orchestras, opera, etc), and turn up each year in the list of Italy's most pleasant urban environments. Long studied by town planners, they are often overlooked by visitors.

Practical information

Getting there
By air

Bologna's Guilelmo Marconi Airport is 36km from Modena and 61km from Reggio Emilia. It handles daily flights to and from domestic and international destinations.

By road

Modena and Reggio Emilia are most quickly reached from the northwest or southeast by the A1 (Autostrada del Sole), the main artery connecting Milan and northern Italy to Rome and the south. Modena is located at the junction of this important road and the A22 (Autostrada del Brennero), which connects central Italy with Austria and Germany via the Brenner Pass.

Modena and Reggio Emilia also lie along the ancient Roman Via Emilia, now route 9, connecting Milan, Piacenza and Parma (to the northwest) with Bologna, Rimini and Ancona (southeast). Minor roads reach Modena from Verona via Mirandola (12) and from Carpi (413). Scenic mountain roads wind their way over the Apennines to Modena from Pistoia and Lucca (12) and to Reggio Emilia from La Spezia (63). The Pistoia/Lucca–Modena road passes through the principal ski resort in Tuscany, Abetone.

By rail

Italy's main north–south line closely follows the Via Emilia from Milan to Bologna. Some *Eurostar* and most *Intercity* trains stop at Reggio Emilia (1hr 20mins from Milan, 40mins from Bologna) and/or Modena (1hr 30mins from Milan, 30mins from Bologna). You can reach both cities without changing trains from Rome/Florence and from Bari/Ancona. Commuter trains (*Regionali* and *Interegionali*) connect Modena with Mantua and Verona, and Reggio Emilia with Guastalla and Sassuolo.

Getting around
Trains

Modena has two **railway stations**: Piazza Dante for all main line services of the *FS*; Piazza Manzoni for local trains to Fiorano and Sassuolo, run by the *Ferrovie Provinciali*.

Car parking

In Modena there is free parking outside the historic centre at Parco Novi Sad, Viale Vittorio Veneto, Viale Berengario, Viale Fontanelli and Viale

Sigonio. Pay parking in Piazza Roma. In Reggio Emilia, free parking on Via Cecati; pay parking along Via Nacchi and in the former Caserma Zucchi near the bus station.

Buses

MODENA Trolleybus 7 from the station to the museums and Via Emilia (for the duomo). *ATCM* also run services to localities in the province (including Maranello) from the bus station in Via Molza.

REGGIO EMILIA Minibus A from the station to Piazza del Monte. **Bus station** for the province (service operated by *Azienda Consorziale Trasporti*, ☎ 0522 431667) in the former Caserma Zucchi, Viale Allegri 9.

Information offices
MODENA Piazza Grande 21, ☎ 059 206660.
REGGIO EMILIA Piazza Prampolini 5, ☎ 0522 451152; www.hnet.it/news

Where to stay
MODENA *Canalgrande*, Corso Canal Grande 6, ☎ 059 217160, fax 059 221674; elegant and refined, in an 18C palace with luxuriant garden and excellent restaurant; moderate. *Centrale*, Via Rismondo 55, ☎ 059 218808, fax 059 238201; a recently renovated, simple place in the historic city centre; inexpensive. *Libertà*, Via Blasia 10, ☎ 059 222365, fax 059 222502; also central, in an ancient townhouse; inexpensive.
REGGIO EMILIA *Delle Notaria*, Via Palazzolo 5, ☎ 0522 453500, fax 0522 453737; a classic provincial hotel with a good restaurant; closed Aug; moderate. *Posta*, Piazza Del Monte 2, ☎ 0522 432944, fax 0522 452602; pleasant and comfortable, in the heart of town; moderate.
Youth hostel: *Tricolore*, Via dell'Abadessa 8, ☎ 0522 454795.

ALBINEA *Viganò*, Via Garibaldi 17, ☎ 0522 347292, fax 0522 347293; a simple, comfortable, family-run place with a pleasant garden 15km south of Reggio; inexpensive.

CARPI *Teresa Baldini*, Via Livorno 30, ☎ 059 662691; traditional osteria serving wholesome local dishes; closed evenings, Thu and Aug; inexpensive.

Pasticceria Portico San Nicolò, Via Berengario 42, for traditional cakes and pastries.

QUATTRO CASTELLA *Casa Matilde*, Località Puianello, ☎ 0522 889006, fax 0522 889006; an aristocratic villa in a shady park in the hills 14km south-west of Reggio; moderate.

 Eating out

MODENA *Compagnia di Via del Taglio*, Via Taglio 12, and *Stallo del Pomodoro*, Largo Hannover 63, are wine bars offering light meals. *Bianca*, Via Spaccini 24, ☎ 059 311524; good, upmarket trattoria; closed midday Sat, Sun, Dec and Aug; moderate. *Borso d'Este*, Piazza Roma 5, ☎ 059 214114; creative interpretations of regional dishes; closed midday Sat, Sun and Aug; moderate. *Fini*, Rua Frati Minori 54, ☎ 059 223314; the best place in town for traditional Modenese cuisine and fine wines; closed Mon–Tues, Dec and Jul–Aug; expensive. *Oreste*, Piazza Roma 31, ☎ 059 243324; more delicious Modenese specialities; closed Sun evening, Wed and Jul; moderate. *Vinicio*, Via Emilia Est 1526, Località Fossalta, ☎ 059 280313; personal interpretations of traditional recipes, with garden seating in summer; closed Sun–Mon, Dec–Jan and Aug; moderate.

Picnic places in the public gardens behind Palazzo Ducale.

REGGIO EMILIA *Caffè Arti e Mestieri*, Via Emilia San Pietro 16, ☎ 0522 451300; restaurant offering creative variations on traditional recipes; closed

Sun–Mon, Dec and Aug; moderate.

Cinque Pini-Da Pelati, Via Martiri di Cervarolo 46, ☎ 0522 553663; the best in town, serving regional cuisine with a personal twist; closed Tues evening, Wed and Aug; moderate.

Picnic places in the public gardens by the theatre.

NONANTOLA *Osteria di Rubbiara*, Via Risaia 2, Località Rubbiara, ☎ 059 549019; traditional osteria offering good Modenese cuisine, especially fresh pasta; closed Tues, Thur, Sun evening, Aug and Dec; moderate.

RUBIERA (12km west of Modena, 12km southeast of Reggio) *Da Arnaldo-Clinica Gastronomica*, Piazza XXIV Maggio 3, ☎ 0522 626124; hotel restaurant serving excellent local fare; closed Sun, midday Mon, Christmas, Easter and Aug; moderate.

SOLIERA (12km north of Modena) *Lancellotti*, Via Grandi 120, ☎ 059 567406; restaurant (with rooms) offering delicious seasonal delicacies; closed Sun–Mon, Dec–Jan and Aug; moderate.

 Entertainment

MODENA has two interesting theatres: *Storchi* (for prose) and *Comunale* (for music).

REGGIO EMILIA The *Teatro Municipale* has a renowned winter opera season; the *Ariosto*, music and drama.

 Shopping

REGGIO EMILIA Market on Tues and Fri in Piazza Prampolini and Piazza San Prospero.

 Special events

MODENA *San Geminiano* (patron saint), 31 Jan with a fair. *Carnival* celebrations on the Thur preceding Shrove Tuesday. *Pavarotti & Friends*, benefit concert, Jun; *International Military Band Festival*, Jul.

REGGIO EMILIA *Jazz Festival*, Apr. *Re Appennino*, Celtic folk festival, Jun–Jul.

San Prospero (patron saint), 24 Nov.

Sports

Professional **soccer** in Reggio Emilia (*Reggiana*), at Giglio Stadium. **Cycling** throughout the region. **Golf** courses at Colombaro di Formigine (*Golf & Country Club Modena*) and at San Bartolomeo (*Golf Club Matilde di Canossa*).

MODENA

Modena is an extremely prosperous provincial capital (population 176,000) that has figured prominently in Italian history. It has a very beautiful cathedral built by Lanfranco, with remarkable early-12C sculptures by Wiligelmus and later works by Campionese sculptors. A number of churches in the town have expressive works dating from the early 16C by the local sculptor Antonio Begarelli. The Galleria Estense has a very fine collection of paintings formed by the Este family in the early 16C, and the Musei Civici, recently well restored, have interesting local collections. The name of Modena is also associated with the Maserati motor works here and especially with the Ferrari works, founded by Enzo Ferrari (1898–1989) outside the town at Maranello.

History

The Roman colony of *Mutina*, established in the 2C BC on a site already inhabited by Gauls and Etruscans, diminished in importance under the Roman Empire. The present city dates its prosperity from the time of Countess Matilda of Tuscany (d. 1115), who supported the Guelfs and the pope's authority. After her death Modena became a free city and, in rivalry with Bologna, inclined more to the Ghibelline faction. In 1288 the Este family gained control of the city, and the duchy of Modena was created for Borso d'Este in 1452. It lasted until 1796 and was reconstituted in 1814–59 through an alliance of the Este with the house of Austria. Mary of Modena (1658–1718), queen of James II of England, was the daughter of Alfonso IV d'Este.

Exploring the town

The **Via Emilia** is the main thoroughfare of the city, and at its centre, behind the Torre Ghirlandina and the duomo, is the cobbled **Piazza Grande**.

The Duomo

The splendid Romanesque *Duomo was begun in 1099 on the site of two earlier churches built over the tomb of St Geminianus (d. 397), patron saint of the town. The architect Lanfranco worked together with Wiligelmus, who here produced some remarkable Romanesque sculptures. The work was continued by Campionese artists in the 12C–14C. The sculptures were beautifully restored and cleaned in 1972–91.

On the *façade, the west portal is a superb work by Wiligelmus (the two lions are restored Roman works). On the left of the door is the foundation stone of the church, to which was added a dedication to Wiligelmus. Across the front of the façade are four bas-reliefs with stories from Genesis, also by Wiligelmus (1100;

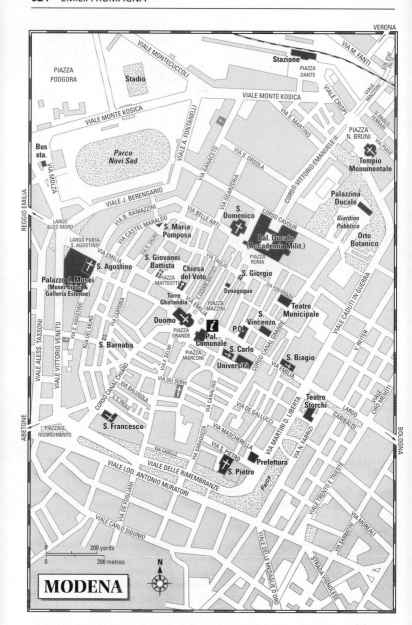

MODENA

they were formerly all aligned, but two were moved up when the side doors were added). Above the loggia, with finely carved capitals by the school of Wiligelmus and Campionese artists, is a large rose window by Anselmo da Campione (1200).

On the south side, which flanks the Piazza Grande, are more beautifully carved capitals by Wiligelmus and his school. The first door is the **Porta dei Principi**, also by Wiligelmus, with six very fine bas-reliefs of the life of San Geminianus. The lion on the right is a copy made in 1948 after damage to the porch. Above to the right is a very damaged bas-relief of Jacob and the Angel. The **Porta Regia** is by the Campionese school (1209–31). In the last arch on the south side are four reliefs describing the life of St Geminianus by Agostino di Duccio

The Porta Regia of the Duomo

(1442). The exterior of the apse is also very fine, and there is another inscription here of the early 13C, recording the foundation of the church by Lanfranco.

On the north side, the **Porta della Pescheria** has delightful carvings by the school of Wiligelmus on the archivolt, showing an assault on a castle.

Interior The beautiful *interior is of pale-red brick with a red-marble floor. The Romanesque arcades have alternate slender columns and composite piers that support an early-15C vault. The capitals are by Wiligelmus and his school. The two stoups are carved out of Roman capitals. In the south aisle, the Cappella Bellincini has frescoes by Cristoforo da Lendinara and his school dating from c 1475, with the *Last Judgement* and a frescoed triptych inside a terracotta arch. The small terracotta *Adoration of the Shepherds* is a beautiful work by Begarelli (1527). In the north aisle, the wooden statue of St Geminianus probably dates from the 14C. The elaborately carved terracotta ancona is attributed to Michele da Firenze, and the detached fresco of the *Madonna della Piazza* to Cristoforo da Modena (late 14C). The pulpit is by Enrico da Campione (1322). The second altarpiece is by Dosso Dossi. On the stairs is a wall monument to Claudio Rangoni (d. 1537) on a design by Giulio Romano.

The *rood-screen, supported by lions and crouching figures, forms the approach to the raised choir. The coloured sculptures are splendid works by Anselmo da Campione (1200–25). They represent the *Evangelists* (on the pulpit), and scenes of the Passion. Above hangs a wooden crucifix in high relief (1200).

In the choir, a screen of slender, red-marble coupled columns in two tiers by Campionese artists surrounds the beautiful altar table. In the apse is a restored statue in bronze and copper of *St Geminianus* by Geminiano Paruolo (1376). The stalls are by Cristoforo and Lorenzo da Lendinara. In the left apse is a polyptych by Serafino Serafini. The four inlaid portraits of the *Evangelists* are by Cristoforo da Lendinara, and there is more inlaid work by Lendinara in the sacristy.

In the **crypt** (with remarkable capitals, some attributed to Wiligelmus) are the tomb of St Geminianus and an expressive group of five terracotta statues known as the *Madonna della Pappa*, by Guido Mazzoni (1480). The tiny organ here by Domenico Traeri dates from 1719.

Around Piazza Grande

The north side of the duomo is connected by two Gothic arches to the *Torre Ghirlandina**, the beautiful detached campanile of the cathedral, 86m high and slightly inclined. It was begun at the same time as the cathedral, the octagonal storey being added in 1319; the spire was rebuilt in the 16C. The interior can be visited on Sun and holidays (open 31 Jan and Apr–Oct 10.00–13.00, 15.00–19.00; closed Aug). Nearby is the **Museo Lapidario**, at present closed. It contains sculpture from the cathedral, including eight 12C metopes from the south side.

In Piazza Grande is the **Palazzo Comunale**, with an arcaded ground floor and a clock tower. The building was first erected in the 12C, but dates in its present form from a reconstruction of 1624. The Sala del Fuoco has fine frescoes (1546) by Niccolò dell'Abate.

From Piazza della Torre beside the Torre Ghirlandina, the Via Emilia runs west through the centre of the town past the domed **Chiesa del Voto**, built in 1634 (with 17C works by Francesco Stringa and Lodovico Lana) and the church of San Giovanni Battista. On the other side of the Via Emilia is the church of **Sant'Agostino**, with a sumptuous interior designed by Giovanni Giacomo Monti in 1664. The *Deposition* here, with stucco figures bearing traces of colour, is the masterpiece of Antonio Begarelli (1524–26). The detached 14C fresco of the *Madonna and Child* is by Tommaso da Modena.

Galleria Estense

Next door is the huge Palazzo dei Musei, built in 1771 as a poorhouse. Since 1884 it has been the seat of the city's interesting museums. In the atrium and courtyard is a lapidary collection founded in 1828. On the top floor is the *Galleria Estense (open Tues, Fri and Sat 09.00–19.00, Wed–Thur 09.00–14.00, Sun and holidays 09.00–13.00), a fine collection of pictures put together by the Este family in the early 16C, notable especially for its works by the 15C–17C Emilian schools; it was first opened to the public in 1854. The most important part of the collection was sold to Dresden in the 18C. The rooms are not numbered, but the collection is displayed in roughly chronological order (although the paintings are often moved around). The room numbers given below correspond to the plan of the gallery on display.

In the atrium are cases containing a sampling of the Este collections, notably Egyptian and Italic antiquities and bronzes by L'Antico (including the Gonzaga vase).

The **long gallery** is divided into nine small rooms. Room **I** contains 14C–15C works including paintings by Tommaso da Modena and Barnaba da Modena. Room **II**: works by Cristoforo da Lendinara, Agnolo and Bartolomeo Erri and Bartolomeo Bonascia. Room **III** is devoted to Francesco Bianchi Ferrari and Marco Melonio. Room **IV** holds an interesting arrangement of terracotta statues by 16C Emilian artists. Room **V**: works by Francesco Botticini (*Adoration of the Child*), Giuliano Bugiardini and Andrea del Sarto (*Madonna and Child with St Elisabeth* *and St John*). Room **VI** contains Flemish works by Albrecht Bouts and Madonnas by Joos van Cleve and Mabuse. Room **VII**: *Deposition* by Cima da Conegliano and works by Vincenzo Catena and Giovanni Cariani. Room **VIII**: Filippo Mazzola and Francesco Maineri. Room **IX**: detached frescoes by Lelio Orsi, the *Madonna Campori* by Correggio, and works by Lelio Orsi. The room at the end (**X**) contains a beautiful 16C portable writing desk, and sculptures of lesser interest.

Room **XI** displays works by the Ferrara school, including Girolamo da Carpi and Dosso Dossi. Also here is the Estense harp, beautifully decorated at the end of the 16C. Room **XII** is the *Wunderkamera*, with an assembly of exotic and extravagant items from the Este collections. Room **XIII** has 16C Emilian paintings, including works by Garofalo. Room **XIV** has 16C–18C portraits, notably the portrait of *Francesco I* by Velazquez. Room **XV** preserves a collection of medals including some by Caradosso, Pisanello, Moderno, Bonacolsi and Giovan Cristoforo Romano. The marble head of a veiled lady is by Francesco Duquesnoy. Room **XVI** contains a carving by Grinling Gibbons.

The last four large rooms hold 16C–17C works. Room **1**: works by the Venetian school, including Tintoretto (notably the *octagons with scenes from Ovid's *Metamorphoses* for the villa of Vittore Pisani), Il Padovanino, Veronese (*Saints*), Palma il Giovane, Pietro Liberti and Jacopo Bassano. Rooms **2** and **3**: Emilian school: Guercino (*Martyrdom of St Peter*), Guido Reni, Lodovico Carracci, Prospero Fontana (*Holy Family*), Carlo Bononi, Scarsellino, Pier Francesco Cittadini (still lifes) and Carlo Cignani (*Flora*). A marble *bust of Francesco I d'Este, founder of the collection, by Gian Lorenzo Bernini (1652), stands near the entrance to this room. Room **4**: 17C works by Camillo and Giulio Cesare Procaccini, Pomarancio, Il Cerano, Rosa da Tivoli, Salvator Rosa, Niccolò Tournier, Domenico Fetti, Daniele Crespi and Charles le Brun; and 12 panels from the ceiling of Palazzo dei Diamanti in Ferrara by the Carracci and others.

On the floor below is the entrance to the **Museo d'Arte Medievale e Moderna** and the **Museo Archeologico Etnologico** (open Tues–Fri 09.00–12.00, Sat 09.00–13.00; Tues and Sat also16.00–19.00; Sun and holidays 10.00–13.00, 16.00–19.00). Both form part of the municipal museum founded in 1871 and recently sensitively restored, retaining its 19C appearance with old-fashioned showcases.

The medieval and 'modern' holdings include the terracotta *Madonna di Piazza* commissioned from Begarelli in 1523 for the façade of the Palazzo Comunale; reliquary crosses; musical instruments including a harpsichord by Pietro Termanini (1741) and flutes made by Thomas Stanesby (1692–1754) in London; scientific instruments including the microscope of Giovanni Battista Amici; ceramics; and arms. Room **8** preserves its furnishings of 1886, when it was opened to display the *Gandini collection of ancient fabrics, textiles and embroidered silks (with about 2000 fragments dating from the 11C to the 19C).

The large hall (**10**) displays the archaeological holdings, arranged chronologically from the palaeolithic era onwards. There is an important section devoted to Mutina, Roman Modena. The ethnological material is arranged in rooms **11**, **12** and **13**, with exhibits from New Guinea, pre-Columbian Peru, Asia, South America and Africa. The last room (**14**) displays the Matteo Campori (1857–1933) collection of paintings with 17C and 18C works, and a collection of cameos.

Also on the first floor is the city archive and the **Biblioteca Estense** (open daily except Sun and holidays, 09.00–13.00), with illuminated manuscripts, notably the *Bible of Borso d'Este*, illuminated by Taddeo Crivelli and Franco Russi; a 14C edition of Dante; and the missal of Renée of France, by Jean Bourdichon (16C).

Elsewhere in town

Via Sauro leads north from the Via Emilia to **Santa Maria Pomposa**, where Lodovico Antonio Muratori (1672–1750), provost of the church from 1716 and an eminent historian (nicknamed the 'Father of Italian History'), is buried. He lived and died in the adjacent house (now a museum, open daily 17.30–19.30), which preserves his autograph works and other mementoes

Via Cesare Battisti leads north from Piazza Grande to the church of **San Domenico**, rebuilt in 1708–31. In the baptistery is a colossal terracotta *statuary group by Begarelli, thought to represent *Christ in the House of Martha*. The huge *Palazzo Ducale**, now the Italian Military Academy, was begun in 1634 for Francesco I on the site of the old Este castle. The interesting interior (guided visits Sun, except holidays, 10.00 and 11.00 by reservation; ☎ 059 206660) has a fine courtyard and a monumental 17C staircase. In the state apartments, with numerous portraits and frescoes by Francesco Stringa, the Salone d'Onore has a ceiling fresco by Marcoantonio Franceschini, and the Salottino d'Oro elaborate decorations dating from 1751. There is also a museum illustrating the history of the academy, founded in 1669.

Behind the palace (entered from Corso Cavour) are pleasant public gardens laid out in 1602. The **Palazzina dei Giardini**, a garden pavilion begun in 1634 by Gaspare Vigarani (and altered in the 18C), is used for exhibitions by the Galleria Civica. It adjoins the botanical gardens (opened on request at the Istituto Botanico of the university) founded by Francesco III in 1758. Beyond the other end of the gardens is the huge Tempio Monumentale, a war memorial built in an eclectic style by Achille Casanova and Domenico Barbanti in 1929.

From Piazza Roma, in front of Palazzo Ducale, a narrow street leads south past the Baroque church of **San Giorgio**, by Gaspare Vigarani, to Piazza Mazzini and the **synagogue**, built in 1869–73 (open by appointment, ☎ 059 223978), which adjoins the Via Emilia.

In the southern part of the town, reached from the duomo by the arcaded Corso Canal Chiaro, is the church of **San Francesco** (1244; altered in the 19C), which contains a terracotta *Descent from the Cross* (1530–31), by Begarelli. To the east is the Baroque church of **San Bartolomeo**, with paintings by Giuseppe Maria Crespi and others. Further east the 15C church of **San Pietro**, with an ornamented brick front, contains sculptures by Antonio Begarelli, an organ with 16C paintings, and a good painting by Francesco Bianchi Ferrari. Beyond the church is a pleasant park with a war memorial of 1926 and the **Teatro Storchi** (1886), Modena's important prose theatre. Further west, near the Via Emilia, is the **university**, founded c 1178, in a building of 1773. North of Via Emilia rises the 17C church of **San Vincenzo**, with Estense tombs and paintings by Matteo Rosselli and Guercino.

The province of Modena

Carpi

The most interesting place in the province of Modena is the town of Carpi, with an attractive centre and some fine palaces, now surrounded by extensive industrial suburbs. From 1327 to 1525 it was a lordship of the Pio family, famous as patrons of the arts, who after 1450 were called Pio di Savoia. The huge *piazza, laid out in the 15C–16C, with a lovely portico, is particularly handsome.

Here the Pio Castle houses the **Museo Civico** (open Mar–Jun and Sep–Nov, Thur, Sat–Sun and holidays 10.00–12.30, 15.00–18.30; Jul–Aug, 10.00–13.00, 16.00–19.00), founded in 1914, which contains works by Bernardino Loschi, Vincenzo Catena, Mattia Preti, Scarsellino and Mastelletta, as well as some fine works in *scagliola*, a material made from selenite, which is used to imitate marble and pietre dure (the town was famous in the 17C–18C for its production of *scagliola* works). There is also a museum that commemorates the victims deported to Nazi concentration camps in Germany in the Second World War (open Jan–Jun and Sep–Dec, Thur, Sat–Sun and holidays 10.00–12.30, 15.00–18.30; Jul–Aug 10.00–13.00, 16.00–19.00). The largest Nazi internment camp set up in Italy in 1944 was at Fossoli, 5km outside Carpi; it was described at the beginning of *Se Questo E' un'Uomo* by the writer Primo Levi, who was deported from here to Auschwitz.

Beneath the portico in the piazza is a 19C pharmacy. The **Duomo**, begun by Baldassarre Peruzzi in 1514, contains terracottas and sculptures by Antonio Begarelli and paintings by Luca Ferrari, Giacomo Cavedoniand Sante Peranda. The Teatro Comunale (with a fine interior) dates from 1857–61. The Portico del Grano dates from the end of the 15C.

Behind the castle is the pieve of **Santa Maria in Castello** (known as La Sagra), with its tall campanile. The 12C church was greatly reduced in size in 1514. It contains the sarcophagus of Manfredo Pio (1351), a marble ambone attributed to Niccolò (12C) and two frescoed *chapels of the early 15C.

On Corso Manfredo Fanti is the late 17C church of **Sant'Ignazio**, which contains a fine high altar in *scagliola* (1696) and a large 17C painting by Bonaventura Lamberti. To the south is the church of **San Nicolò**, built on a central plan in 1494 (the nave was added in 1516 by Baldassarre Peruzzi). It also contains fine *scagliola* *altars. Further south are the Rococo church of the **Crocifisso** (with a *Madonna* by Begarelli) and **San Francesco**, with the tomb of Marco Pio attributed to the school of Jacopo della Quercia, and a fresco of the *Enthroned Madonna* attributed to Giovanni da Modena. Via Giulio Rovighi is on the site of the **ghetto**, where the Jewish community was forced to live between 1719 and 1796. The synagogue at no. 57 was in use until 1922.

North and east of Modena

Nonantola, with two 14C towers, is famous for its abbey, founded in 752 and rebuilt in brick in the 13C (open Mon–Sat 07.00–20.00, Sun 07.00–12.30, 15.00–20.00). The portal has reliefs by the school of Wiligelmus (1121). The church contains the tombs of Popes St Sylvester and Adrian III. In the refectory are fresco fragments dating from the early 12C.

Mirandola was a principality of the Pico family, the most famous member of which was Giovanni Pico (1463–94), noted for his wide learning, a typical figure of the Italian Renaissance. There are family tombs in the church of San Francesco and scanty remains of the Pico ducal palace in the main piazza. The Baroque church of the Gesù is also of interest.

At **San Felice sul Panaro** is a castle of the Este built in the 14C–15C, now the seat of an archaeological museum.

Finale Emilia is a pretty little town with a 14C castle, numerous fine palaces and interesting 16C–17C paintings in the Collegiata. In the Palazzo Comunale are 18C paintings by Fra' Stefano da Carpi.

South of Modena

South of Modena on the Panaro is **Vignola**, a fruit-growing centre, famous for its cherries. It was the birthplace of the architect Jacopo Barozzi, called Il Vignola (1507–73). The fine castle (open Tues–Sat 9.00–12.00, 14.30–18.00, summer 15.30–19.00; Sun and holidays 10.00–12.00 and 14.30–18.00, summer15.30–19.00) was built by Uguccione Contrari between 1401 and 1435. The chapel has very interesting late-Gothic frescoes by an unknown artist.

At **Maranello**, next to the Ferrari works, a museum (open Tues–Sun 09.30–12.30, 15.00–18.00), preserves mementoes of Enzo Ferrari, vintage cars, etc.

At **Sassuolo** is the important Palazzo Ducale, rebuilt for the Este in 1634, with an interesting park. A veritable gem of Baroque art and architecture, it contains decorations by Jean Boulanger (and by Angelo Michele Colonna and Agostino Mitelli in the Salone). It is open for special exhibitions.

On the road to Abetone across the Apennines are Pavullo nel Frignano, the 19C residence of the Dukes of Modena (now home to a small gallery of contemporary art, with works by local artists), and the resorts of Fiumalbo, Sestola and Pievepelago below **Monte Cimone** (2165m; skiing). Another beautiful road to Tuscany traverses the Passo delle Radici. At **San Pellegrino in Alpe**, next to the sanctuary where Saints Pellegrino and Bianco are buried, the old pilgrim hospice houses a Museo della Cività Montanara, with local ethnographic exhibits and archives.

REGGIO EMILIA

Reggio Emilia (or Reggio nell'Emilia) is the large, flourishing centre (population 131,000) of an important agricultural area. The inhabitants have a particularly good quality of life. Excellent Parmesan cheese (*parmigiano reggiano* or *grana*) is produced here. It was the Roman *Regium Lepidi* and is still divided in two by the Via Emilia: the southern part of the town retains a medieval pattern, whereas broad streets and open squares predominate to the north. The most settled period of Reggio's turbulent history was under the Este domination (1409–1796).

Exploring the town

In the centre of the Via Emilia is the little Piazza del Monte. Here is the altered 14C **Palazzo del Capitano del Popolo**, part of which is the Palazzo dell'Albergo Posta, transformed in the 16C into a hospice and restored in an eclectic style in 1910. It adjoins the central Piazza Prampolini. The Romanesque **Cathedral** has an unfinished façade added in 1555 by Prospero Sogari, who also carved the statues of *Adam and Eve* above the central door. The unusual tower bears a group of the *Madonna and Donors*, in copper, by Bartolomeo Spani (1522), who also carved the tomb of Valerio Malaguzzi, uncle of Ariosto, in the interior. The tomb of Bishop Rangone and the marble ciborium are by Sogari. In the **Palazzo Comunale** (begun in 1414), the green, white and red tricolour was proclaimed the national flag of Italy in 1797. The Sala del Tricolore has a small museum, shown on request. A passageway leads into the piazza in front of the church of **San Prospero**, guarded by six red marble lions. Rebuilt in 1514–27, it has a choir frescoed by Camillo Procaccini and fine inlaid stalls.

On the other side of the Via Emilia is the huge Piazza Martiri del 7 Luglio, with the **Musei Civici** (open Tues–Sun 09.00–12.00, Sun and holidays also 15.00–18.00). Here you can inspect various collections, still with their charming, old-fashioned displays. The Collezione Spallanzani, founded in 1772 and bought by the city in 1799, is a delightful natural history collection (including fossils). Upstairs are the Galleria Fontanesi, founded in 1893, with pictures by Emilian painters from the 15C to the 19C, and the Museo Chierici, with archaeological material (including Etruscan finds), arranged for study purposes. The numismatic collection has examples from the Reggio mint. The prehistoric finds from the locality include a 5C treasure dug up in 1957 (with a fine gold fibula). The Museo del Risorgimento e della Resistenza was closed at the time of writing.

Across the garden, with a harrowing bronze monument (1958) to Resistance martyrs, is the elegant **Teatro Municipale** (1852–57), with a high theatrical reputation. Behind the theatre are extensive **public gardens** in which a Roman family tomb of c 50 AD has been placed. In Piazza della Vittoria, beside the **Teatro Ariosto**, designed in 1741 by Antonio Cugini (and rebuilt after a fire in 1851), is the Gothic-revival spire of the **Galleria Parmeggiani**, with a fine 16C Hispano-Moresque doorway brought from Valencia. The eclectic collections include medieval metalwork and 14C–16C paintings of the Flemish and Spanish schools, including the *Redeemer* by El Greco.

Off the south side of the Via Emilia (reached from the broad Corso Garibaldi) is the splendid Baroque church of the *Madonna della Ghiara** (1597–1619), with a well-preserved interior (restored in 1996), its vaults and domes beautifully decorated with *frescoes and stuccoes by early-17C Emilian artists including Alessandro Tiarini, Lionello Spada and Camillo Gavasseti. An altarpiece by Guercino has been removed for restoration. A museum (open Sun 15.30–18.30) displays the cathedral treasury.

Around Reggio Emilia

There are at least half a dozen places in Reggio's small province you might want to visit.

Correggio was the birthplace of the painter Antonio Allegri (1489–1534), nicknamed 'Correggio', whose house is in Borgovecchio. The **Palazzo dei Principi**, begun in 1507, contains a small museum with 16C Flemish tapestries and a tempera *Head of Christ* by Mantegna. The 18C Teatro Asioli has been restored. San Quirino (1516–87) has an interesting interior.

Novellara has a castle (now town hall) of the Gonzaga, dating in part from the 14C. It contains a small museum with detached frescoes of the 13C–16C and a remarkable series of ceramic jars made for a pharmacy in the 15C–16C.

Gualtieri has the vast *Piazza Bentivoglio** as its main square (with a garden in the centre). It was begun in 1580 by Giovanni Battista Aleotti. Palazzo Bentivoglio, also by Aleotti, has 17C frescoes in the Salone dei Giganti.

Guastalla was once the capital of a duchy of the Gonzagas. In the square is a statue of the mercenary captain Ferrante Gonzaga (d. 1457), by Leone Leoni. The Basilica della Pieve is an interesting Romanesque church.

Brescello is a town of Roman origins. In the central piazza is a copy of a statue of Hercules by Jacopo Sansovino (the original is kept in the Museo Comunale). Sir Anthony Panizzi (1797–1879), librarian of the British Museum, was born in the town. The church of Santa Maria Maggiore (1830–37) was used as the setting of the film of *Don Camillo* (based on the book written in 1950 by Giovanni Guareschi), and there is a little museum with mementoes of the film.

The ruined **Castle of Canossa** (open Tues–Sun, summer 09.00–12.00, 15.00–18.30; winter 09.00–15.00) was the home of Countess Matilda of Tuscany, who was responsible for the submission of Emperor Henry IV to Pope Gregory VII in 1077. Only the foundations of the castle of that time remain; the ruins above ground date from the 13C and later.

Parma and Piacenza

Perhaps because of their nearness to the foggy Po, Parma and Piacenza are more sullen than their neighbours to the south. Their slightly melancholy air—which is shared by minor centres such as Fidenza and Firenzuola—is not unpleasant. Indeed, many residents—and visitors—see it as a virtue. Parma is famous for its architecture and its paintings by Correggio; Piacenza for its churches; and the whole area for its scrumptious cuisine.

Practical information

Getting there
By air

Parma's Giuseppe Verdi Airport has regular flights to Rome and Milan Malpensa, and seasonal flights to Olbia in Sardinia. Otherwise the airport nearest to Parma is Bologna Guilelmo Marconi (94km southeast), with daily flights to and from domestic and International destinations. If you're coming or going from Piacenza, you are better off using Milano Linate, Bergamo Orio al Serio or Brescia Montichiari, all of which also offer flights to destina-

tions in Italy and throughout Europe.

From Parma Giuseppe Verdi Airport to central Parma, **bus 11**. There are is no direct train or bus between Parma and Piacenza and the other airports.
By road

Parma and Piacenza are most quickly reached from the northwest or south-east by the A1 (Autostrada del Sole), the main artery connecting Milan and northern Italy to Rome and the south. Parma lies at the junction of this important road and the A15 from La Spezia and the Tyrrhennian coast; and at

Piacenza the A1 is joined by the A21 from Turin and Brescia. At Modena is the junction of the A1 and the A22 (Autostrada del Brennero), which connects central Italy with Austria and Germany via the Brenner Pass.

Parma and Piacenza also lie along the ancient Roman Via Emilia, now route 9, connecting Milan (to the northwest) with Modena, Bologna and Ancona (southeast). Minor roads reach Parma from La Spezia (62) and from Mantua (420); and Piacenza from Voghera (10). A scenic mountain road (45) winds through the Apennines to Piacenza from Genoa via Bobbio.

By rail

Italy's main north–south line closely follows the Via Emilia from Milan to Bologna. Some *Eurostar* and most *Intercity* trains stop at Parma (50mins from Milan, 1hr 20mins from Bologna) and/or Piacenza (40mins from Milan, 1hr 10mins from Bologna). You can reach both cities without changing trains from Rome/Florence and from Bari/Ancona. Commuter trains (*Regionali* and *Interegionali*) connect Modena with Mantua and Verona, and Reggio Emilia with Guastalla and Sassuolo.

Getting around

PARMA **Car parking** in Viale Mentana (free); underground car parks (fee): 'Toschi' on the river by Palazzo della Pilotta, and 'Goito', Strada Farina; other paid car parks on Viale Mentana and Via Tanzi. **Buses** from the bus station in Piazzale della Chiesa to the main places in the province, operated by *TEP* (☎ 0521 2141) and *APAM* (☎ 0376 2301). PIACENZA **Car parking** at the duomo and in streets and squares throughout the city centre. **Country buses** (operated by *ACAP*, ☎ 0523 337245) from Piazza Cittadella to places in the province and cities in Emilia.

Information offices

PARMA Via Melloni 1b, ☎ 0521 218889.
Informagiovani, Via Melloni 1b, ☎ 0521 218749.
PIACENZA Piazzetta dei Mercanti 10, off Piazza Cavalli, ☎ 0523 329324; *Informagiovani*, Via Taverna 37, ☎ 0523 334013.

Where to stay

PARMA *Grand Hotel Baglioni*, Viale Piacenza 12c, ☎ 0521 292929, fax 0521 292828; modern and fairly refined, with Art-Nouveau antiques; closed Aug; moderate.
Park Hotel Stendhal, Piazzetta Bodoni 3, ☎ 0521 208057, fax 0521 285655; modern and comfortable, with a good restaurant; moderate.
Park Hotel Toscanini, Viale Toscanini 4, ☎ 0521 289141, fax 0521 283143; overlooking the River Parma, also with a good restaurant; moderate.
Torino, Borgo Mazza 7, ☎ 0521 281047, fax 0521 230725; somewhat simpler than the others, but friendly and centrally located; closed Jan and Aug; moderate.
Villa Ducale, Via del Popolo 35, ☎ 0521 272727, fax 0521 780756; a renovated villa with park, 2km north on the road to Mantua; moderate.
Youth hostel: *Cittadella*, Parco Cittadella 5, ☎ 0521 961434.
PIACENZA *Grande Alberto Roma*, Via Cittadella 14, ☎ 0523 323201, fax 0523 330548; the classic place to stay, provincial elegance and a good restaurant with views; moderate.
Youth hostels: *Castell'Arquato*, ☎ 0523 805245; *Coli*, ☎ 0523 931117; *Il Riccio*, ☎ 0523 999637.

Eating out

PARMA *Al Tramezzino*, Via Del Bono 5b, Località San Lazzaro, ☎ 0521 484196; represents the culinary traditiion of Parma at its

best; closed Mon and Jul; moderate.
Angiol d'Or, Vicolo Scutellan 1, ☎.
0521 282632; another excellent taste
of tradition; closed Sun, Dec and Jan;
moderate.
Patrizzi, Strada della Repubblica 71, ☎
0521 285952; probably the best *cucina
parmense* in the city centre; closed 25
Dec, Mon and Sun evenings Jun–Aug;
moderate.
Cocchi, Via Gramsci 16a, ☎ 0521
981990; restaurant of the Hotel
Daniel—another good, conservative
place with an interesting wine list; closed
Sat, 24–26 Dec and Aug; moderate.
Il Cortile, Borgo Paglia 3, ☎ 0521
285779; a pleasant trattoria serving
delicious regional dishes; closed Sun,
midday Mon and Aug; inexpensive.
La Greppia, Strada Garibaldi 39a, ☎
0521 233686; the most creative of the
restaurants specialising in traditional
local cuisine; closed Mon–Tues and Jul;
moderate.
You can fine good **coffee and pastries** in Parma at *Le Bistrò* and
Orientale, both in Piazza Garibaldi.
There are also three excellent **wine
bars**—*Antica Osteria Fontana*, Via
Farini 24a, *Bottriglia Azzura*, Borgo
Felino 63 and *Grapaldo*, Borgo del
Correggio, 60a—all serving light meals.
Picnics in the Parco Ducale.
PIACENZA *Agnello*, Via Calzolai 2, ☎
0523 20874; trattoria offering good,
simple dishes at fair prices; closed Mon
and Aug; inexpensive.
Antica Osteria del Teatro, Via Verdi
16, ☎ 0523 323777; closed Sun
evening (also midday Sun in Jul), Mon,
Jan and Aug; expensive.
FORNOVO DEL TARO *Baraccone*, Via
XX Settembre 6, ☎ 0525 3427; good
tradtional osteria; closed midday Sun,
Mon and Aug; moderate.
Trattoria di Cafragna-Camorali,
Località Cafragna, ☎ 0525 2363; great
country trattoria, serving delicious renditions of local dishes; closed Sun

evening (also midday Sun in Jul),
Dec–Jan and Aug; moderate.
COLECCHIO *Villa Maria Luigi*, Via
Galaverna 28, ☎ 0521 805489; traditional regional food in a villa with garden seating in summer; closed Wed
evening, Thur and Jan; moderate.
BOBBIO *San Nicola*, Contrada
dell'Ospedale, ☎ 0523 932355; restaurant offering excellent regional food and
wines, in a former convent; closed Mon
evening and Tues; moderate.
FIDENZA *Astoria*, Via Gandolfi 7, ☎
0524 524588; good Emilian home
cooking; closed Mon; inexpensive.
I Gemelli, Via Gialdi 14, ☎ 0524
528506; an interesting seafood restaurant; closed Mon and Jun–Jul; moderate.
NOCETO *Aquila Romana*, Via Gramsci
6, ☎ 0521 625398; great food and outstanding value, in a historic building;
closed Mon–Tues and midday Jul–Aug;
inexpensive.
ROCCABIANCA *Hostaria da Ivan*, Via
Villa 73, Località Fontanelle, ☎ 0521
870113; simple osteria popular with
locals; closed Mon–Tues, Jan and Aug;
moderate.
SORAGNA *Antica Osteria Ardegna*,
Via Maestra 6, Località Diolo, ☎ 0524
599337; good local osteria; closed
Tues–Wed, Jan and Jul; moderate.

Entertainment

PARMA The *Teatro Regio* is
famous for **classical music**
(opera season Nov–Mar); the *Teatro
Cinghio* also has a concert series.
Drama at *Teatro Stabile-Teatro Due*,
Teatro delle Briciole-Teatro al Parco,
Teatro Lenz, *Teatro Pezzani*, *Teatro
Edison* and *Teatro Europa*. Bars with
live music at Parma, Fidenza and
Salsomaggiore Terme; **discos** (quite
popular with the *parmensi*) at Parma,
Albareto, Bardi, Berceto, Borgo Val di
Taro, Busseto, Collecchio, Felino,
Fidenza, Lesignano de Bagni, Medesano,
Montechiarugolo, Pellegrino Parmense,

Polesine Parmense, Salsomaggiore Terme, Solignano, Soragna and Tizzano. PIACENZA **Music and drama** at the *Teatro Municipale* and *Teatro San Matteo*. **Jazz and rock** at *Avila, Balzea, Sonnambula, Comogdia, Bartolomeo, Temple*.

Shopping

Italians from all over Emilia Romagna flood this area on weekends for the little markets of antiques and collectibles held in the various towns and villages. Parma is particularly well-known for its gastronomic specialities—notably Parmigiano Reggiano cheese; Parma ham (*prosciutto di Parma*) and various salames (*salame di Felino, culatello di Zibello, spalla cotta di San Secondo*); Fragno black truffles; Borgotaro mushrooms; *Lambrusco, Malvasia, Fortana, Profumo* and *Violetta di Parma* wines. Here is the schedule of markets at the time of writing. Naturally, it is subject to change.

PARMA Market in Piazzale della Pilotta, Wed and Sat. Antiques market on Via D'Azeglio, Thur.

PIACENZA Markets in Piazza Cavalli, Piazza Duomo and Chiostri del Duomo, Wed and Sat.

BARDI Antiques market, third Sat of the month, Apr–Sep.

COLORNO Antiques market, fourth Sun of the month, Jan–Dec.

FIDENZA Antiques market, first Sat of the month, Mar–Dec.

SALSOMAGGIORE Antiques market, third Sat of the month, Apr–Oct.

SAN SEDONCO Antiques market, second Sun of the month, Sep–Jul.

TRAVERSETOLO Antiques market, first Sun of the month, Jul–May.

FONTANELLATO Antiques market, third Sun of the month, Feb–Dec.

Special events

PARMA *Suoni nel Tempo*, classical music concert series at the *Galleria Nazionale*, *Teatro Farnese* and *Teatro Reggio*, Jan–May.

PIACENZA *Fiera di Sant'Antonio* and *Fiera di San Giuseppe*, with markets of local food and crafts. Other seasonal markets at Grazzano Visconti, Cortemaggiore, Castell'Arquato and Caorso.

BUSSETO Guided visit to places of Verdian significance, with music, monthly.

CASTEL ARQUATO Medieval market and banquet, May.

COLLECCHIO *Gran Premio Città di Collecchio*, amateur bicycle race, and *Palio Città di Collecchio*, amateur foot race, Mar. Summer film series, Jul–Aug.

FELINO Cinema and theatre festival, Mar.

FIDENZA Classical music and opera season, spring. *La Gostra di Maggio*, theatre festival, May.

FONTANELLATO Classical music and opera season, winter–spring.

GRAZZANO VISCONTI *Il Corteo*, historic pageant, May. *Alla Corte del Re*, music and dance in historic costume, first Sun of every month, Apr–Sep. *Notte di Faba*, medieval market and banquet, Jul.

SALSOMAGGIORE *Gino Gandolfi International Piano Competition*, March. *Premio Nazionale Bancarella*, national culture and entertainment awards, and International Chess Tournament, May. *Giuseppe Verdi International Choral Festival and Competition*, Jul.

Sports

Professional **soccer** at Tardini Stadium in Parma and Garilli Stadium in Piacenza. **Cycling** throughout the area, especially in the Apennine foothills. **Golf** courses at Sala Baganza (*La Rocca Golf Club*), Salsomaggiore (*Golf & Country Club Salsomaggiore*), Agazzano (*Golf Club La Bastardina*), Castell'Arquato (*Golf Club Castell'Arquato*) and Croara Nuova di

Gazzola (*Croara Country Club*). **Downhill skiing** at Lago Santo, Cervellino and Prato Spilla (above Parma), and at Passo Penice (Bobbio). **Walking** in the countryside around Parma; information from *CAI* (*Club Alpino Italiano*, ☎ 0521 984901) and *Corpo Forestale dello Stato* (☎ 0521 889146).

PARMA
• • • • • • •

Parma (population 169,000) is the second city of Emilia. It has some very fine works of art and important buildings, all grouped close together in the centre of the city. There is a beautiful baptistery, and delightful frescoed domes by Correggio (who arrived in the city around 1520) grace the Camera di San Paolo, the cathedral and the church of San Giovanni Evangelista. The huge Palazzo della Pilotta has at last been restored so that the splendid Farnese theatre can now be visited as well as the Galleria Nazionale, with a large collection of paintings of the highest interest—including masterpieces by Correggio and fine examples of the later Emilian schools. Parma is a gastronomic centre, famous for Parmesan cheese and Parma ham, and Italians from as far afield as Florence or Milan have been known to drive here for a Sunday lunch.

History

There was a Roman station here, on the Via Emilia. In the 12C–14C the town had a republican constitution, but from c 1335 onwards it was ruled by a succession of ducal families: the Visconti, Terzi, Este and Sforza. In 1531 it became a papal dominion and in 1545 Paul III passed it over, along with Piacenza, to his illegitimate son Pier Luigi Farnese, who was given the title of duke. The house of Farnese, and their heirs, the Spanish house of Bourbon-Parma, held the duchy until 1801. The Congress of Vienna assigned Parma to the ex-empress Marie-Louise in 1815, but in 1859 the widow of her son Charles III was obliged to hand it over to the King of Italy. It was heavily bombed in the Second World War, and unattractive new buildings were constructed in the historic city centre afterwards.

Baptistery

Exploring the town

The peaceful, cobbled **Piazza Duomo** is dominated by the pink-and-white ***baptistery**, a splendid octagonal building in red Verona marble. Its extremely interesting design shows the influence of French Gothic architecture and of ancient Roman buildings. Begun in 1196 by Benedetto Antelami, it was completed after 1216 by Campionese masters and consecrated in 1270.

The **exterior** has three doorways bearing splendid ***carvings** by Antelami. The lunette over the north door shows the *Madonna*,

Adoration of the Magi and *Dream of Joseph*. In the architrave beneath are the *Baptism of Christ*, *Banquet of Herod* and *Beheading of the Baptist*. The genealogical trees of Jacob and the Virgin adorn the door jambs. The west door depicts the *Last Judgement* in the lunette and architrave, and the south door illustrates the *Legend of Baalam and Josaphat*. Between the doors are blind arches with Classical columns, and a frieze of 79 small panels carved with stylised reliefs, fantastic animals, etc., which almost girdles the edifice. Four delicate galleries, with small columns, encircle the building's upper storeys.

The **interior**, on a different design from the exterior, is covered by a beautiful dome. It has more splendid *carvings by Antelami, including the fine capitals surmounting the tall columns on either side of the niches. Above is another series of columns in front of two galleries. There are coloured reliefs of the *Flight into Egypt*, *David* and the *Presentation in the Temple* over the doors and altar; between them are angels and the *Annunciation* figures, in the apses of the niches. Fourteen figures of the Months, Winter and Spring (some with reliefs of the signs of the zodiac below) have been set in the lower gallery. The red-porphyry altar is carved with the figures of John the Baptist, a priest and a Levite. In the centre is a font, and against the wall a stoup supported by a lion, also carved by Antelami. Six statues, formerly in niches on the exterior, are displayed around the walls.

The cupola has lovely *tempera paintings* of 1260–70, in a Byzantine style, with the *Story of Abraham*, *Life of St John the Baptist*, *Christ and the Prophets*, and the *Apostles* and the *Symbols of the Evangelists*. The painted decoration of the lunettes below dates from the same period. The lower part of the walls has 14C votive frescoes, including two attributed to Buffalmacco.

The Duomo

This splendid 11C church was modified by Antelami in the 12C. The projecting pink-and-white porch, supported by two huge lions, has reliefs of the *Months* added around the arch in 1281. The doors themselves date from 1494. The *campanile was built in 1284–94.

Inside, the Romanesque structure is still clearly visible, although it was entirely covered in later centuries by frescoes in the vault, nave, aisles and west end. Notice also the finely carved 12C capital—also Romanesque. High up on the inner façade is a fresco of the *Ascension* painted by Lattanzio Gambara (1573) with the help of Bernardino Gatti. More frescoes by Gambara, showing the *Life of Christ*, can be seen above the matroneum in the nave. The vault is frescoed by Girolamo Bedoli Mazzola (1557). The statue of the *Archangel Raphael* (formerly on the campanile) dates from c 1294.

In the cupola (light in the south transept) is the celebrated *Assumption* by Correggio (1526–30), one of the more remarkable dome frescoes in existence. The spandrels hold the four patron saints of Parma. The colossal figures of the apostles appear above, in a crowd behind a balustrade between the round windows. Christ descends from a golden Heaven to greet His mother, surrounded by angels and clouds. It is said that when Titian saw the dome he commented that if it were to be turned upside down and filled with gold, Correggio would still not receive the recompense he deserved for such a masterpiece.

The south aisle has ceiling frescoes by Alessandro Mazzola. In the last chapel is a *Crucifixion with Saints* by Bernardino Gatti. The south transept preserves a

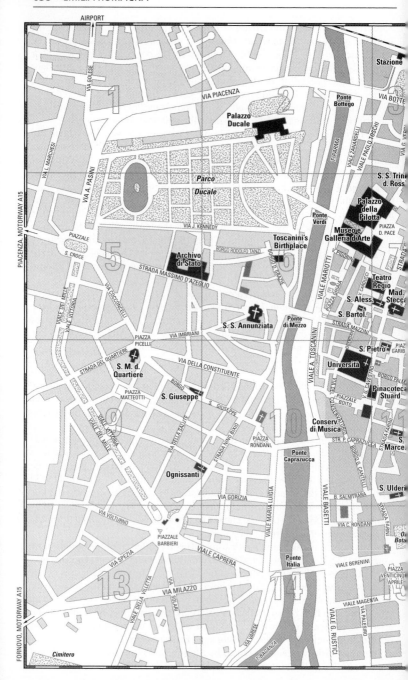

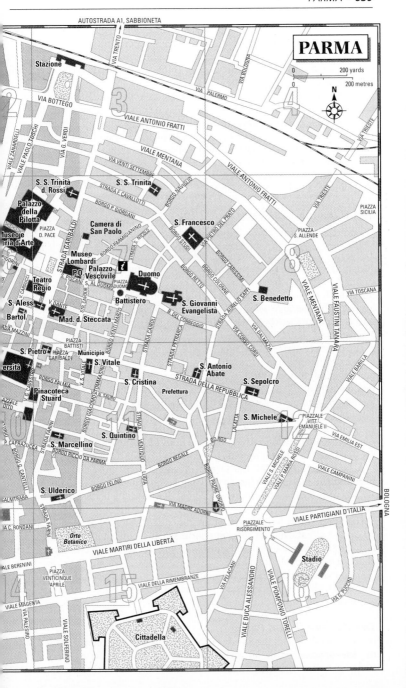

PARMA

AUTOSTRADA A1, SABBIONETA

VIA TRENTO

VIA BOLOGNA

Stazione

VIA PALERMO

0 ____ 200 yards
0 ____ 200 metres

N

VIA BOTTEGO

VIA G. VERDI

VIALE ANTONIO FRATTI

VIA TRIESTE

VIALE MENTANA

VIA VENTI SETTEMBRE

VIALE ANTONIO FRATTI

S. S. Trinita
d. Rossi

STRADA F. CAVALLOTTI

S. S. Trinita

BORGO NAVIGLIO

PIAZZA
SICILIA

BORGO P. GIORDANI

Palazzo
della
Pilotta

PIAZZA
D. PACE

Camera di
San Paolo

BORGO PARMIGIANINO

S. Francesco

BORGO STUDJ

VIA PIETRO DEL PRATO

BORGO CARISSIMI

PIAZZA
S. ALLENDE

Museo e
eria d'Arte

STRADA GARIBALDI

Museo
Lombardi

S. NICOLÒ

Palazzo
Vescovile

BORGO RETTO

BORGO COLONNE

VIA TRIESTE

Teatro
Regio

P.O.

S. PISCANI

S. AL DUOMO

Duomo

PIAZZA
DUOMO

S. Aless

V. DANTE

Battistero

S. Giovanni
Evangelista

B. DEL CORREGGIO

S. Benedetto

VIALE MENTANA

VIA FAUSTINI TANARA

VIA TOSCANA

. Bartol.

Mad. d. Steccata

STRADA PETRARCA

STRADA AURELIO SAFFI

VIA CORSO CORSI

VIA DALMAZIA

ADA MAZZINI

STRADA CAIROLI

BORGO FIENI MARZI

PIAZZA
BATTISTI

S. Pietro

PIAZZA
GARIBALDI

Municipio

V. S. VITALE

S. Vitale

VIA GIACOMO TOMMASINI

V. N. SAURO

S. Antonio
Abate

S. Sepolcro

VIALE BARILLA

ersità

Pinacoteca
Stuard

BORGO PALMIA

S. Cristina

STRADA DELLA REPUBBLICA

Prefettura

LA CATA

S. Michele

PIAZZALE
VITT.
EMANUELE II

AZZALE
DITO

BORGO G. CANTELLI

S. Marcellino

BORGO RICCIO DA PARMA

S. Quintino

STRADA VENTIDIO

LUGIA

BORGO REGALE

BORGO PADRE ONORIO

VIA EMILIA EST

VIALE S. MICHELE

VIALE P. MARIA ROSSI

VIA PICCININI

VIALE CAMPANINI

P. CAPRAZUCCA

STRADA FARINI

S. Ulderico

BORGO FELINO

VIA MADRE ADORNI

PIAZZALE
RISORGIMENTO

VIALE PARTIGIANI D'ITALIA

BOLOGNA

ALNITRARA

IA C. RONDANI

Orto
Botanico

VIALE MARTIRI DELLA LIBERTÀ

Stadio

LE BERENINI

PIAZZA
VENTICINQUE
APRILE

VIALE DELLA RIMEMBRANZE

VIA PELACANI

VIALE DUCA DI ALESSANDRO

VIALE POMPONIO TORELLI

VIALE MAGENTA

VIALE SOLFERINO

VIA PALESTRO

Cittadella

relief (from the pulpit) of the *Deposition* by Antelami, his earliest known work, signed and dated 1178 and surrounded by niello decoration.

A sarcophagus carved by Campionese sculptors serves as high altar. The choir (difficult to see) and apse have frescoes by Girolamo Mazzola Bedoli. The beautiful stalls are signed by Cristoforo da Lendinara, and the bishop's throne is by Benedetto Antelami. The **crypt** has good capitals and two fragments of Roman pavement. The last chapel in the north aisle was entirely frescoed in the 15C.

Opposite the duomo is **palazzo vescovile**, first built in the 11C, with a well-restored façade that shows successive additions of 1175 and 1234. The courtyard dates from the 16C. Just out of the piazza you can see a red palace on the site (plaque) of the birthplace of the chronicler Frate Salimbene (1221–c 1290). The 16C seminary, with a double blind arcade, and the early 20C doorway of a pharmacy, can be seen on the south side of the duomo.

San Giovanni Evangelista

Behind the duomo, facing its pretty apse, is the church of San Giovanni Evangelista, built over an earlier church in 1498–1510, with a façade of 1604–07. Its dome holds another splendid fresco by Correggio (1521), the *Vision of St John at Patmos* (light in the north transept), showing Christ surrounded by the apostles appearing to St John at his death. In the spandrels are the *Church Fathers*, and over the sacristy door in the north transept is a lunette fresco of the *Young St John Writing*, also by Correggio. The walls of the nave have a beautiful frieze by Francesco Maria Rondani (on cartoons by Correggio) of *Prophets and Sibyls*. The vault is frescoed by Michelangelo Anselmi.

The entrance arches of the first, second and fourth north chapels have lovely frescoes by Parmigianino: the first chapel has a font made out of a Roman urn, and delightful frescoed putti; the fourth chapel has an altarpiece by Girolamo Bedoli Mazzola. The frieze in the transepts dates from the late 15C or early 16C. Statues by Antonio Begarelli adorn the south transept. The *Crowning of the Virgin* in the main apse is a copy made in 1587 by Cesare Aretusi of a larger work, formerly here, by Correggio. On the high altar is a *Transfiguration* by Girolamo Bedoli Mazzola. The stalls date from 1513–38. In the sixth chapel in the north aisle is *Christ Carrying the Cross* by Michele Anselmi.

A door at the side of the façade of the church gives entrance to the **Benedictine monastery** (used by 20 monks; open daily 06.30–12.00, 15.30–18.30) with three lovely cloisters, a chapterhouse and a library (open on Sun and holidays only).

The **Spezeria di San Giovanni** (entrance at Borgo Pipa 1; open Tues–Sun 09.00–13.45), the monks' ancient pharmacy, was founded in 1298 and in use up to 1881. It preserves its 16C furnishings. You can also see 17C vases, mortars, pharmaceutical publications, etc.

From Piazza Duomo, Strada al Duomo leads to Strada Cavour, the main shopping street. This leads left to Piazza Garibaldi with the 17C Municipio and Palazzo del Governatore, and a number of cafés.

The Camera di San Paolo

In the other direction, the Strada Cavour ends at a war memorial tower. Just to the left, approached by an avenue of japonica trees, is the entrance to the *Camera di San Paolo (open daily 09.00–13.45), part of the private apartment of Abbess Giovanna Piacenza in the former Benedictine convent of San Paolo. Beyond several rooms with paintings by Alessandro Araldi, is the little room with celebrated *frescoes by Correggio, commissioned by the abbess in 1518 or 1519 (the artist's first commission in Parma). The Gothic umbrella vault is decorated with a dome of thick foliage supported by wickerwork (canes cover the ribs of the vault). The abbess' coat of arms appears in the centre, surrounded by drapes off which hang festoons of fruit. Through 16 oculi in the arbour you can see groups of putti at play, against the open sky. The monochrome lunettes below have painted trompe-l'oeil statues and reliefs of mythological subjects, and below is a frieze of rams' heads with veils stretched between in which are hung plates and pewterware (which may signify that the room was used as a refectory). Over the fireplace is Diana returning from the hunt, also by Correggio.

The significance of these remarkable Humanistic frescoes, in which the artist uses a careful play of light, is uncertain: the abbess was a particularly cultivated lady who lived in the convent for 17 years and was unsuccessful in her attempt to prevent it from becoming a closed community in 1524. The frescoes remained unknown to the outside world until the 18C, which probably accounts for their excellent state of preservation.

The room next door has another vault adorned with grotesques by Alessandro Araldi, painted four years earlier.

Strada Pisacane continues Strada al Duomo to Strada Garibaldi, which runs through one side of the huge, untidy Piazza della Pilotta. At Strada Garibaldi 15 is the **Museo Glauco Lombardi** (closed at the time of writing) with a collection relating to Empress Marie Louise. Just to the left is the **Teatro Regio** (open to visitors by appointment), which opened in 1829 with Bellini's *Zaira*. It is one of the more famous opera houses in Italy. The conductor Arturo Toscanini (1867–1957), who was born in Parma, played in the orchestra.

The Madonna della Steccata

Also in Via Garibaldi is the church of the *Madonna della Steccata, built in 1521–39 on a Greek-cross plan by Bernardino and Giovanni Francesco Zaccagni. The very fine exterior includes an elegant dome surrounded by a balustrade, and 18C statues on the roof.

The **interior** has superb frescoes by the Parma school, all carried out between 1530 and 1570. On the barrel vault between the dome and apse are six tempera *figures of the Virgins, Parmigianino's last work. The fresco of the *Assunta* in the dome is by Bernardino Gatti (inspired by Correggio). The side apses and arches are frescoed by Girolamo Bedoli Mazzola. The *Crowning of the Virgin* in the apse is by Michelangelo Anselmi (on a design by Giulio Romano). The organ doors are early works by Parmigianino (the organ itself was built in 1574 by Benedetto Antegnati and restored in 1780 by Negri Poncini). The tomb of Field-Marshal Count Neipperg (1775–1829), second husband of Marie Louise, is by Lorenzo Bartolini (1840). The Sagrestia Nobile (1670) has cupboards by Giovanni Battista Mascherone.

On the other side of Strada Garibaldi, on the bank of the river, is **Palazzo della Pilotta**, a gloomy, rambling palace built for the Farnese family c 1583–1622, but left unfinished; it was badly bombed, and half of it was demolished in the

Second World War. It contains the **Museo Archeologico Nazionale** (open Tues–Sun 09.00–19.00), Teatro Farnese and Galleria Nazionale (open Tues–Sun 09.00–13.45; admission with separate tickets). The entrance is under the portico towards the river.

The well-arranged Museo Archeologico Nazionale, founded in 1760, is interesting chiefly for its finds from Veleia. The visit begins on the **first floor**. Here you can see Roman statues from the Farnese and Gonzaga collections; a small Egyptian collection; a Roman copy of the Eros of Praxiteles and a head of Zeus; and finds from Veleia, including a fine group of Roman statues, the *tabula alimentaria* (the largest Roman bronze inscription known) and the bronze head of a boy (1C BC). The following rooms hold Greek, Italiot and Etruscan ceramics, and a relief of the head of an African river god in onyx (2C).

On the **lower floor** are palaeolithic finds from the region around Parma; material from the pile-dwellings of Parma and the lake-villages of its territory; and Roman inscriptions, bronzes, amphorae and mosaic pavements.

Teatro Farnese and Galleria Nazionale

Stairs ascend to the wooden door at the entrance to the Teatro Farnese and Galleria Nazionale. The huge ***Teatro Farnese** was built in 1617–18 in wood and stucco by Giovanni Battista Aleotti for Rannuccio I, Duke of Parma. It has a U-shaped cavea that could seat 3000 spectators. Above are two tiers of loggias, with arches modelled on Palladio's theatre at Vicenza, although the stage in this theatre had movable scenery. Used only nine times after its inauguration in 1628 (when it was flooded for a mock sea-battle), it fell into ruins in the 18C and was almost entirely destroyed by a bomb in the last war. It has been beautifully reconstructed. Most of the painted decoration (including the ceiling fresco) has been lost, although two painted triumphal arches survive at the sides, with stucco equestrian statues of Alessandro and Ottavio Farnese.

From the stage of the theatre you enter the ***Galleria Nazionale**, founded by Philip of Bourbon-Parma in 1752. A walkway leads into the Romanesque section, with 10C–11C wooden doors from San Bertoldo, and three *capitals carved by Benedetto Antelami. Beyond are exhibited early Tuscan works (Agnolo Gaddi, Nicolò di Pietro Gerini, Spinello Aretino, Fra Angelico); inlaid stalls by Bernardino di Lendinara; and local 15C works (*St Peter Martyr and Stories from his Life*, by the circle of Agnolo and Bartolomeo degli Erri). Beyond paintings by Francesco Francia and Cima da Conegliano (***Madonna and Child with Saints**) is an exquisite ***Head of a Girl** ('La Scapiliata') by Leonardo da Vinci (c 1508), owned by the Gonzaga in 1531. The two marble bas-reliefs are by Giovanni Antonio Amadeo.

Beyond a corridor with tiles made in Faenza in 1482 is a room with 16C Emilian works by Cristoforo Caselli, Filippo Mazzola, Garofalo and Dosso Dossi . Stairs lead up to another room with 16C Emilian works (Michelangelo Anselmi), and works by Giulio Romano, Holbein (portrait of *Erasmu*s), Sebastiano del Piombo and Bronzino. On the balcony above are interesting works by Girolamo Bedoli Mazzola and El Greco, and large works by the Carracci. The room below displays works by Guercino and Gian Lorenzo Bernini (two marble busts of Rannuccio II). At the end: portraits by Frans Pourbus the Younger; a portrait of *Isabella Clara Eugenia* and *Madonna and Child*, both by van Dyck; Flemish landscapes; and works by Canaletto and Bernardo Bellotto.

A walkway, with early maps and prints of Parma and 19C views of the city, leads back to the Teatro Farnese. Beneath the cavea is the entrance to the last section of the gallery, displayed in the small rooms of the Rocchetta, with the masterpieces of Correggio and Parmigianino. The works by Correggio include several frescoes and the *Madonna della Scodella* (his finest work, c 1525–30), *Madonna and Child, with St Jerome, an Angel, and Mary Magdalene* (1527–28), *Deposition* (1524), and the *Martyrdom of Four Saints*. Parmigianino is represented by a superb portrait known as the *Turkish Slave*, his self-portrait, and a fine collection of drawings.

In an oval room nearby are two colossal basalt statues dating from the 2C AD from the Orti Farnesiani on the Palatine in Rome, and a large Neo-classical hall exhibits 18C and 19C works including portraits by Zoffany and Jean Marc Nattier, and a seated statue of Maria Luigia by Canova. The last room has smaller 18C works (Zoffany, Maria Callani and Vigée-Lebrun).

The *Palatine Library* houses about 600,000 volumes, with editions and matrices of Giovanni Battista Bodoni, the printer, who set up his office in the palace in 1768–1813, and a section with musical manuscripts.

Across the river
On the other side of the Parma River, across Ponte Verdi, is the entrance to the **Parco Ducale**. Created in 1560 as the private park of Palazzo Ducale, these pleasant public gardens (worth a visit for their fine chestnut, beech and plane trees) are usually crowded with people. There is a second entrance on Viale Pasini. **Palazzo Ducale** (open by appointment, ☎ 0521 230023) was built as a summer residence for Ottavio Farnese by Giovanni Boscoli in 1564; it has a wing furnished in the French Neo-classical style.

A pretty road leads south from Ponte Verdi towards Borgo Rodolfo Tanzi. The house at no. 3 in this street is the simple **birthplace of Toscanini**, now a small museum with mementoes of the conductor (open Tues–Sat 10.00–13.00, 15.00–18.00; Sun and holidays 10.00–13.00). The nearby church of the Annunziata is an impressive Baroque building (1566); the graceful Ospedale della Misericordia, begun c 1214 and enlarged in the 16C, houses the state archives, with the archives of the duchy.

The southern quarters
In the southern part of the town, on the east bank of the river, the University of Parma occupies a 16C building ascribed to Galeazzo Alessi and Vignola. Nearby, at Via Cavestro 14, is the **Pinacoteca Stuard** (open Wed–Mon 09.30–18.00, Sun 09.00–13.20) with 14C–19C paintings (including works by Paolo di Giovanni Fei, Bernardo Daddi, Paolo Uccello, Lanfranco and Guercino). The church of Sant'Antonio Abate, in Strada della Repubblica to the east, was begun by Francesco Bibiena in 1712 and finished in 1766.

The **Museo Cinese ed Etnografico** (open Wed, Sun and holidays 15.00–18.00), in Via San Martino on the southern outskirts of the town, has a small collection of Asian art. In the Villetta Cemetery, further south, the embalmed body of Paganini rests beneath a classical canopy.

Around Parma

The province of Parma is at least as rich as the city itself in terms of things to see. To explore it in depth you should allow at least a couple of days.

Fidenza

The most important town in the province of Parma is Fidenza. Known as Borgo San Donnino from the 9C to 1927, it occupies the site of the Roman *Fidentia Iulia*, where St Domninus was martyred by the Emperor Maximian in 291. It was on the Via Francigena, the pilgrim route from Britain and France to Rome, and there are several carvings of pilgrims on the façade of its cathedral.

The ***Cathedral**, built during the 13C, has a façade with particularly interesting Romanesque *sculptures by Antelami and his school. On the left tower are two reliefs, one showing *Herod Enthroned*, and the other the *Three Kings* on horseback. In the tympanum of the left door are *Pope Hadrian II* and *St Domninus*, with *Charlemagne* on the left and a *Miracle of St Domninus* on the right. The arch is carved with figures of animals. The column on the right has a capital ingeniously carved with a scene of *Daniel in the Lions' Den*. On either side of the central door are fine *statues of *David* and *Ezekiel*, both by Antelami. The doorway has beautifully carved capitals and a relief of the *Martyrdom of St Domninus* in the architrave, with *Prophets, Apostles and Christ* in the lunette. On the right of the door is a relief showing an angel leading a group of poor pilgrims towards Rome. The right door is crowned by the figure of a *Pilgrim*, and beneath in the tympanum is *St Domninus*. The lunette is carved with figures of animals. On the right tower is another frieze showing a group of pilgrims. The exterior of the apse is also interesting.

In the beautiful **interior**, on the first right pillar (above the capital) is the figure of *Christ* with a relief of a *Battle of Angels* below, both by Antelami. The fourth south chapel (1513) has good terracotta decorations and frescoes. The stoup by the school of Antelami includes the figure of Pope Alexander II. In the last chapel on this side is a wooden statue of the Madonna and Child of 1626, and remains of very early frescoes. In the raised **choir**, high up between the apse vaults, are good sculptures, including a figure of *Christ as Judge* by Antelami and a fresco of the *Last Judgement* dating from the 13C. The **crypt** has interesting capitals, including one of *Daniel in the Lions' Den*. Here is displayed a seated statue of the *Madonna and Child* by Antelami (damaged in 1914) and the *Arca of St Domninus* with carved scenes of his life (1488). Nearer the altar is a 3C Roman sarcophagus.

Just off the piazza is the medieval Porta San Donnino. The restored town hall and the theatre, dating from 1812, face the main Piazza Garibaldi. At the end of Via Berenini, Palazzo delle Orsoline hosts the **Museo del Risorgimento** (entered from the street on the left, at no. 2; open Tues–Sat except holidays, 10.00–12.00; Thur and Sat also 15.30–18.00), with an interesting collection relating to the period from 1802–1946, excellently displayed. The huge Jesuit college and church dates from the end of the 17C.

Salsomaggiore

Salt was extracted from the waters of Salsomaggiore Terme from the Roman era until the mid-19C. After 1839 Salsomaggiore became one of the more famous spas of Italy; its saline waters are used even today to treat rheumatic, arthritic and post-inflammatory disorders. The Grand Hotel des Thermes (now a congress centre) was opened in 1901 and bought in 1910 by Cesare Ritz. It contains Art Nouveau works by Galileo Chini, who also decorated the spa building opened in 1923. There are still several Art Nouveau and Art Deco buildings in the town.

Mamiano

Mamiano lies near the Parma River south of Parma. The village itself is not very interesting, but the nearby Villa Mamiano, surrounded by a beautiful park, is well worth the drive down. It was the residence of the connoisseur, musicologist and art historian Luigi Magnani (d. 1984). His collections are now held by the **Fondazione Magnani**, and the remarkable private museum here is open Mar–Nov Tues–Sun 10.00–18.00. The *paintings include works by Dürer (*Madonna and Child*); Carpaccio (*Pietà*); Filippo Lippi (*Madonna and Child*); Gentile da Fabriano (*St Francis Receiving the Stigmata)*; van Dyck (equestrian portrait of *Giovanni Paolo Balbi*); Titian (*Madonna and Child with St Catherine, St Dominic and a Donor*, c 1512/14); and Goya (allegorical family portrait of the *Infante Luis de Bourbon*, a conversation piece of 1789). There is also a splendid Modern collection, with works by Monet, Renoir, Cézanne and Giorgio Morandi.

The Certosa

On the eastern outskirts of Parma is the Certosa di Parma (open Mon–Fri 08.00–12.00 and 14.00–17.00; Sat–Sun and holidays 08.00–12.00 only), from which the famous novel by the French novelist Stendhal, *La Chartreuse de Parme*, takes its name. First built in 1282, the Carthusian monastery has been enlarged and remodelled several times over the centuries. The present church contains frescoes by Sebastiano Galeotti, Francesco Natali and others.

Castles of the Parmigiano

Parma Province is rich in feudal strongholds. **Fontanellato** has a moated 13C *castle of the Sanvitale family (guided tours Oct–Mar, Tues–Sun 09.30–11.30, 15.00–17.00; Apr–Sep daily 09.30–11.30, 15.00–18.00). It contains a little room with delightful *frescoes by Parmigianino (1524), as well as 16C–18C furnishings, ceramics, etc. The Rocca Meli Lupi at **Soragna** has 16C works of art (guided tours daily 09.00–11.00, 14.00 or 15.00–16.30 or 18.00). The **synagogue**, with a Jewish museum, is open on Sun and holidays (10.00–12.30, 15.00–18.00).

Nearer the Po are the fortresses of the Rossi family at **Roccabianca** and **San Secondo Parmense** (open Apr–Sep for guided visits, Mon–Sat at 10.00, 11.00, 15.00, 16.00, 17.00, 18.00), with frescoes by the Campi. **Montechiarugolo** has a good castle of 1406 (guided visit Sat–Sun and holidays 15.00–18.00), and **Montecchio Emilia** preserves parts of the old ramparts. **Torrechiara** has the finest *castle (open Oct–Mar, Tues–Sun 08.30–13.15; Apr–Sep, Tues–Fri 09.00–13.45, Sat–Sun and holidays 09.00–18.15) in the province, built for Pier Maria Rossi (1448–60), with its 'golden room' frescoed by Benedetto Bembo (c 1463). Other rooms are decorated by Cesare Baglione and his followers.

home ground

...cole Verdi is the simple birthplace of the composer Giuseppe Verdi (...-1901), author of _Aida_, _Nabucco_ and many other famous operas. His hou... is open Mar–Oct, Tues–Sun 09.30–12.00, 15.00–19.00; Nov–Feb, Sat 14.30–17.30, Sun. 09.30–12.30, 14.30–17.30. **Busseto**, a charming small town, was the lordship of the Pallavicini in the 10C–16C. It has many buildings decorated with terracotta in the Cremonese style. The battlemented castle contains the town hall and the little Teatro Verdi (1868), and the Villa Pallavicino (attributed to Vignola) houses the civic museum (open Mar–Oct, Tues–Sun 09.30–12.30, 14.30–17.30) with mementoes of Verdi. At **Sant'Agata di Villanova sull'Arda** is the Villa Verdi, built by Verdi in 1849 as a summer residence. The house here is open Apr–Oct, Tues–Sun 09.00–12.00, 14.30 or 15.00–19.00; it contains relics and a bust by Vincenzo Gemito.

Other sights

Colorno has a grand ducal palace of the Farnese (open by appointment, ☎ 0521 312546), with a park and orangery. The church of San Liborio (begun in 1777) and several 18C oratories are also of interest.

In the broad valley of the Taro south of Parma, near Sala Baganza, are the **Boschi di Carrega**, a beautiful wooded area (now protected). The village of **Fornovo di Taro** was the scene of a battle, in 1495, in which the retreating Charles VIII of France defeated the Milanese and Venetians. The Romanesque church has fine 13C sculptures on its façade: Fornovo was on the Via Francigena, the medieval pilgrimage route to Rome, which ran south via **Berceto** (where there is a 13C church) and across the Apennines by the Passo della Cisa (1039m) to descend into the Magra Valley (see _Blue Guide Tuscany_).

PIACENZA
● ● ● ● ● ● ● ● ● ●

Piacenza (population 102,000), situated at the strategic point where the Via Emilia touches the Po, possesses a beautiful cathedral and several fine churches, as well as some interesting museums. Its name (the French for which is Plaisance) is derived from the Latin _Placentia_.

History

An important centre of trade since Roman times, Piacenza has an uncanny way of popping up almost at random in European history. The peace negotiations ratified at Constance (1183) between Frederick Barbarossa and the Lombard League were conducted in the church of Sant'Antonino here. In 1545 Pope Paul III created the dukedom of Parma and Piacenza for his illegitimate son Pier Luigi Farnese; the pope's grandson, Alessandro Farnese (1545–92), was governor of the Low Countries from 1578 until his death. Piacenza was the first city to join Piedmont by plebiscite in 1848.

Exploring the town

The centre of the old city is **Piazza Cavalli**, named after its pair of bronze equestrian statues of *_Duke Alessandro_ (1625) and his son and successor, *_Ranuccio_

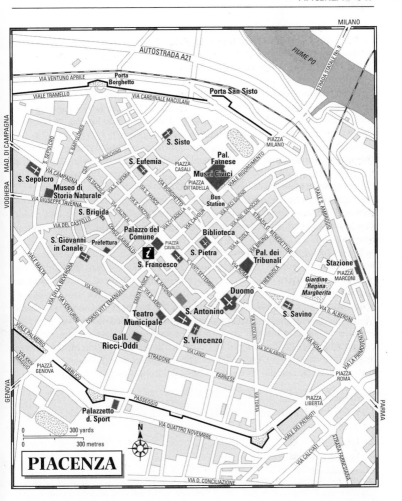

PIACENZA

Farnese (1620). The city commissioned these fine works from Francesco Mochi, who also designed the pediments. ***Palazzo del Comune** is a fine Gothic building begun in 1280, built of brick, marble and terracotta.

Via XX Settembre leads out of the square, past **San Francesco**, a church begun in 1278 with a transitional façade. The fine Gothic interior has a pretty apse with an ambulatory.

The ***Cathedral**, an imposing Lombard Romanesque church (1122–1240), stands at the end of the street. The beautiful polychrome ***façade**, in sandstone and red Verona marble, has recently been restored. The left porch and door are attributed to the school of Wiligelmus. The central door was heavily restored at the end of the 19C by Camillo Guidotti; the original elements include the archivolt with signs of the zodiac, the two telamones (supporting male figures), and capitals above. The lions were replaced in the 16C. The right door is by Niccolò. It has finely carved panels of the *Life of Christ*, including three unusual scenes of the *Temptations in the Desert*.

From the piazza on the south side you can see the exterior of the drum and the 14C campanile, crowned by a gilded angel, a weather vane placed here in the early 14C by Pietro Vago. Beyond the Chiostri del Duomo you can glimpse the exterior (from the Strada della Prevostura) of the early 12C apse, a carved window with four figures, and pretty loggias above.

Inside, massive cylindrical pillars divide the nave and aisled transepts. Set into the pillars are little square reliefs by local sculptors (c 1170) showing the work of the guilds that paid for the erection of each column. Above the arches are 12C figures of *Saints* and the *Madonna* (left) and *Prophets* (right). At the west end are two capitals attributed to Nicolò, one with the story of *Saul and David*, and one showing the *Stoning of St Stephen*. On the west wall are paintings by Camillo Procaccini and Lodovico Carracci. Three votive frescoes of the *Madonna*, dating from the 14C–15C, adorn a nave pillar.

The architecture of the transepts is particularly fine, and there are interesting remains of frescoes here (early 12C and c 1390). The frescoes in the vault of the central octagon were begun by Morazzone, but he completed just two sections before his death. The *frescoes in the rest of the vault (and the lunettes below) were completed by Guercino. A lunette over the entrance to the sacristy has a Giottesque Madonna. The two ambones are 19C reconstructions.

In the raised **choir** the high altar has a sculpted gilded reredos (late 15C), behind which are good stalls of 1471. The two large 18C Neo-classical paintings are by the local painter Gaspare Landi. The apse fresco and those in the sanctuary vaults are by Camillo Procaccini and Lodovico Carracci.

Unloved?

Piacenza was never particularly popular with Anglo-Saxons of old, as these comments make clear:

The Cathedral is among the rudest... in Italy.
Lady Morgan, *Italy*, 1820

A brown, decayed, old town, Piacenza is. A deserted, solitary, grass-grown place, with ruined ramparts; half-filled-up trenches, which afford a frowzy pasturage to the lean kine which wander about them: and streets of stern houses, moodily frowning at the other houses over the way. The sleepiest and shabbiest of soldiery go wandering about, with the double curse of laziness and poverty, uncouthly wrinkling their misfitting regimentals; the dirtiest of children play with their impromptu toys (pigs and mud) in the feeblest of gutters; and the gauntest of dogs trot in and out of the dullest of archways, in perpetual search of something to eat which they never seem to find.
Charles Dickens, *Pictures from Italy*, 1846

Via Chiapponi leads to the church of **Sant'Antonino**, rebuilt in the 11C with an octagonal lantern tower, which dates in part from the 10C, supported inside on a group of massive pillars. The huge north porch was added in 1350. The large paintings in the sanctuary are by Roberto De Longe (1693). A small museum contains parchments, illuminated codexes, and 15C–16C paintings.

Nearby is the **Teatro Municipale** (1803–10) with a little museum (ring for admission at Via Verdi 41). At Via San Siro 13 is the ***Galleria Ricci-Oddi**, with a representative collection of Italian 19C–20C painting (open Tues–Sun 10.00–12.00, 14.00 or 15.00–16.00, 17.00 or 18.00). The collection was begun in 1902 by Giuseppe Ricci Oddi (1868–1937) and donated by him to the city in 1924. The charming building, with excellent natural lighting, was built by Giulio Ulisse Arata for the collection, which is arranged in 25 rooms by schools and regions. Artists represented include Vito d'Ancona, Telemaco Signorini, Giovanni Boldini, Giovanni Fattori, Giuseppe Abbati, Vincenzo Cabianca, Antonio Fontanesi, Francesco Hayez, Girolamo Induno, Vincenzo Gemito, Federico Zandomeneghi, Antonio Mancini, Filippo Palizzi, Edoardo Dalbono, Domenico Morelli, Ettore Tito, Felice Casorati, Bruno Cassinari and Mario Cavaglieri.

Via Sant'Antonino is prolonged by the busy Corso Garibaldi. In this street are (right) the 12C front of Sant'Ilario, with a relief of Christ and the Apostles on the architrave, and (at the end of the street) Santa Brigida, also 12C. A little to the left is San Giovanni in Canale, a 13C and 16C church, well restored. Nearby in Via Taverna, at the Collegio Morigi, is a **Museo di Storia Naturale** (open Mon–Sat except holidays, 08.30–12.30, Thur also 15.00–17.30), with small natural history collections from the province of Piacenza and the Po River basin.

Via Campagna leads northwest from beyond Santa Brigida to (15mins walk) the church of the **Madonna di Campagna**, a graceful Renaissance building by Alessio Tramello (1522–28). On a Greek-cross plan, it has four little domed corner chapels. The central *dome, beautifully lit by small windows in a loggia, has frescoes by Pordenone (1528–31). The decoration of the drum and the pendentives was completed by Bernardino Gatti (1543). There are more works by Pordenone in other parts of the church, including a corner chapel with *scenes from the life of St Catherine, and another with scenes of the Nativity. Other paintings are by Camillo and Giulio Cesare Procaccini, Guercino and Camillo Boccaccino.

Via Sant'Eufemia leads northeast past the church of Sant'Eufemia, with an early 12C front (restored); straight ahead is **San Sisto**, another pretty church by Tramello (1499–1511), preceded by a courtyard. It was for this church that Raphael painted his famous '*Sistine Madonna*', sold by the convent to the elector of Saxony in 1754, and now at Dresden. On the north choir pier is the monument of Duchess Margaret of Parma (1522–86), governor of the Netherlands from 1559 to 1567; the fine stalls date from 1514.

Via Borghetto leads back towards the centre. On the left, in Piazza Cittadella, the huge **Palazzo Farnese** houses the **Musei Civici** (open Tues–Sun 09.00–12.30; Thur, Sat, Sun and holidays also 15.30–17.30, 18.00 and 18.30, respectively). The palace was begun for Duchess Margaret in 1558 by Francesco Paciotto and continued after 1564 by Vignola, but left only half-finished. It has a grand if plain exterior, divided in three floors by protruding cornices and numerous well-proportioned windows. Adjoining to the left is the smaller 14C Rocca Viscontea. In the courtyard you can see the 15C loggia of the castle and a huge double loggia with niches of the Palazzo Farnese.

Room **2** displays 16C paintings by Carlo Draghi and prints illustrating the history of the palace. Rooms **3** and **4** display 16C–18C ceramics and Venetian glass (16C–19C). Rooms **5–8** (the duke's apartment) are decorated with paintings by Sebastiano Ricci illustrating the life of the Farnese Pope Paul III, and by Giovanni Evangelista Draghi recounting the life of Alessandro Farnese, the Duke of Parma who waited in the Netherlands for the Armada. There are other Farnese portraits in room **7**. The large room **9** contains 14C frescoes. Rooms **10–14** display 12C–18C sculpture. Room **15** has a very fine display of arms and armour, mostly dating from the 16C and 17C.

The Risorgimento museum, on a **mezzanine** floor, documents the history of the city during the wars of independence against Austria.

In the **basement**, in remarkable vaulted rooms once used as kitchens and storerooms, is a fine collection of 50 *carriages dating from the 18C and 19C. Here begins the remarkable spiral staircase designed by Vignola that ascends to the top of the palace. Climb to the **second floor** for a glimpse of the deconsecrated *ducal chapel, built on an octagonal design in 1598.

Underground rooms in a wing of the palace are to exhibit the archaeological section, which includes the celebrated *Fegato di Piacenza*, an Etruscan divination bronze representing a sheep's liver, marked with the names of Etruscan deities.

The **pinacoteca**, approached through a beautiful iron *gate with the Farnese arms at the foot of the stairs, is housed in the duchess's apartments on the **second floor**. In room **16** are 16C paintings by Malosso, Girolamo Bedoli Mazzola, Camillo Boccaccino and Jan Sons. Room **17** has 17C works by Roberto De Longe, Paulus Moreelse and Justus Sustermans. A *tondo by Botticelli is displayed in room **18**. Room **20** has large canvases by Monti (Brescianino delle Battaglie) and Spolverini; Spolverini's illustrations of the life of Alessandro Farnese are in rooms **21–23**. Room **25** has Neo-classical works by Gaspare Landi.

Southeast of the Palazzo Farnese, on Via Roma, the Palazzo dei Tribunali is a 15C building with a sculptured doorway and a pretty courtyard. The Biblioteca Comunale Passerini-Landi has over 170,000 volumes and 3000 manuscripts (including some interesting psalters and codices). Further down Via Roma, **San Savino** is a 12C church with two mosaics of the 13C or earlier. Nearby is a pleasant public park in front of the railway station.

Beyond the southern outskirts of the city, at San Lazzaro Alberoni, is the **Collegio Alberoni**, with an important collection of works of art (open by appointment, ☎ 0523 613198), including *Christ at the Column* by Antonello da Messina; 18 Flemish tapestries; Flemish paintings (Mabuse, Provost, and still lifes); church silver and vestments; engravings by Piranesi; and scientific instruments. These belonged to Giulio Alberoni (1664–1752), a gardener's son who rose to be a cardinal and the able minister of Philip V of Spain.

Around Piacenza

On the northern border of Piacenza Province, on the Po, is **Monticelli d'Ongina**, with a 15C castle (opened on request) frescoed by Bonifacio Bembo, and an ethnographical museum illustrating life on the Po (open Sun and holidays 15.00–18.30).

Cortemaggiore, a 15C 'new town' built by the Pallavicini family, has two fine churches; the former Franciscan church has frescoes by Pordenone.

At Alseno the abbey of **Chiaravalle della Colomba** (open daily 09.00–

12.00, 14.00–18.00) has a Romanesque church and a 13C Gothic *cloister with coupled columns.

In the pretty Arda valley is **Castell' Arquato**, a picturesque hill-town with double gates. In the attractive Piazza stand the Palazzo Pretorio of 1293 and the Romanesque Collegiata with a 14C cloister, off which is a museum (open 10.00–12.00, 15.00–18.00) with church silver, sculpture and paintings. The 14C Rocca Viscontea can also be visited. The 16C Torrione Farnese is in the lower town, near the 13C fountain. A geological museum with marine fossils from the area, etc., is housed in the former hospital (16C). Another museum is dedicated to Luigi Illica, in the librettist's house.

Near Lugagnano Valdarda, in pretty countryside, is **Veleia** (open daily 09.00–dusk; Mon and Wed 09.00–15.00), the picturesque ruins of a small Roman town which flourished in the 1C BC, first excavated in the 18C. There is a small archaeological museum here.

Grazzano Visconti is an entire village rebuilt in medieval style at the beginning of this century.

Near Gazzola, above the Trebbia River, is the medieval **Castello di Rivalta** (privately owned; open at weekends or by appointment, ☎ 0523 978104), enlarged in the 15C and 18C, which retains its original furnishings and paintings by Pordenone.

Bobbio, in the southwest corner of the province, is noted for its learned monastery founded in 612 by the Irish Saint Columbanus, who died here in 615. The basilica, a 15C–17C building, has a crypt with some traces of the primitive church and the tomb of St Columbanus (1480). The museum is open daily except Mon and Thur 16.30–18.00), and contains a remarkable ivory Roman bucket with a representation of Orpheus (or David) in high relief (4C). The heavily-restored cathedral is 12C, and beyond, the 'humpback bridge', possibly Roman, probably 7C in part, crosses the River Trebbia.

Ravenna and its province

Ravenna (population 135,000) is unique in western Europe for the profusion of its Byzantine remains. Now 10km from the sea, it was once a flourishing Adriatic port and the capital of the Byzantine exarchs, whose semi-Oriental power is reflected by the magnificently coloured mosaics and imperial tombs. Numerous basilican churches with cylindrical bell-towers of the 9C–10C grace the quiet old centre (most of the residents use bicycles to get about). The Museo Nazionale has a particularly interesting collection. The modern town is without distinction and is surrounded by extensive industrial suburbs.

Practical information

Getting there
By air

Bologna's Guilelmo Marconi Airport, 86km west of Ravenna, handles daily flights to and from domestic and international destinations. Charter flights operate in summer from the small airport at Rimini.

By road

Ravenna is most quickly reached from Bologna by the A14 and A14 dir, a link road that also serves Lugo and Bagnacavallo. The fastest route from Rimini is 16, the Adriatic coast road. From Padua take the A13 to Ferrara Nord, then 16 south; from Venice, 309 via Chioggia.

By rail

Ravenna is not on a major rail line, but you can get there by commuter train (*Diretti* or *Regionali*) from Ferrara (50km in 1hr), Bologna (84km in 1hr 10mins) or Faenza (25km in 30mins).

Getting around
Car parking

In Ravenna (with hourly tariff and limited space) in and around the city centre.

Bicycles

Can be rented in Ravenna from the *Coop San Vitale*, Piazza Farini (at the station).

Buses

Buses 4 and **44** run on weekdays from the station to the basilica of Sant'Apollinare in Classe. Country buses (operated by *ATM*, ☎ 0544 689911) run from Piazzale Farini (opposite the train station) to places of interest in the province, including Bagnacavallo, Lugo and Brisighella, and to the resorts on the coast. Faenza is best reached from Ravenna by train.

Information offices

RAVENNA Via Salara 8–12, ☎ 0544 35404.
Informagiovani, Via Guido da Polenta 4, ☎ 0544 36494.
BRISIGHELLA Via De Gasperi 6, ☎ 0546 81166 and at the coastal resorts.

Where to stay

RAVENNA *Bisanzio*, Via Salara 30, ☎ 0544 39164, fax 0544 30001; central and fairly elegant, with a nice garden; moderate.
Centrale Byron, Via IV Novembre 14, ☎ 0544 212225, fax 0544 32539; warm and modern, in a well-renovated old townhouse; inexpensive.
Youth hostel: *Dante*, Via Nicolodi 12 , ☎ 0544 421164.
BRISIGHELLA *La Meridiana*, Viale delle Terme 19, ☎/fax 0546 81590; calm and quiet, with a shady garden on the River Lamone; closed Nov–Mar; inexpensive.
Terme, Viale delle Terme 37, ☎/fax 0546 81144; modern and comfortable, also with a garden; closed Oct–May, moderate.
Torre Pratesi, Località Cavina, ☎ 0546 84545, fax 0546 84558; the nicest place in the area, with just four rooms in a medieval watchtower; moderate.
LUGO *Ala d'Oro*, Corso Matteotti 56, ☎ 0545 22388, fax 0545 30509; in an aristocratic townhouse, with a good restaurant; moderate.
San Francisco, Via Amendola 14, ☎ 0545 22324, fax 0545 32421; quiet and comfortable; closed Dec–Jan and Aug; moderate.

Eating out

RAVENNA *Tre Spade*, Via Faentina 136, ☎ 0544 500522; elegant restaurant in a villa with park and outside seating in summer; closed Sun evening, Mon and Aug; moderate.

Picnic places in the public gardens of Rocca Brancaleone, or on the lawns around the Mausoleo di Teodorico.
BRISIGHELLA Gigiole, Piazza Carducci 5, ☎ 0546 81209; hotel restaurant offering traditional cuisine with an innovative twist; closed Mon and Feb–Mar; moderate.
La Grotta, Via Metelli 1, ☎ 0546 81829; very good regional cuisine at excellent prices; closed Tues, Jan and Jul; inexpensive.

Entertainment
RAVENNA **Classical music and theatre** at *Teatro Alighieri* and *Teatro Rasi*. **Live music** at bars and cafés around the town.

Children
RAVENNA *Mirabilandia* amusement park, on 16 at Savio (☎ 0544 561111).

Special events
RAVENNA *Mister Jazz*, jazz festival, Apr. *Ravenna Festival*, classical music festival in Jun–Jul. *Mosaico di Notte*, international organ music festival in Aug, with concerts every Mon in the basilica of San Vitale. *Feast of Sant'Apollinare*, 23 Jul. *Medieval market* second Sun in Sep. *Trofeo Callenge Roberto Trombini*, match race, Marina di Ravenna, Jul.

Sports
Professional **basketball** and **volleyball** at Palazzetto delle Arti e dello Sport in Ravenna. **Golf** course at Cervia (*Adriatic Golf Club Cervia*). **Swimming** and **water sports** at the seaside resorts.

History

The importance of Ravenna began with the construction, by Augustus, of the imperial port of *Classis*, to which the town was united by the Via Caesarea. Its greatest period, however, began in 401, when Honorius moved the imperial court and civil administration here from Milan, and Ravenna became the capital of the Western Empire. Honorius's sister, Galla Placidia, was the first to adorn the city with splendid monuments. Its importance continued under the successor of Honorius, Valentinian III.

The town also flourished under the German king Odoacer (473–93), who took up residence here. He was killed by the Ostrogoth Theodoric (493–526), who captured the city in 493 and proved to be a strong, effective ruler, respecting the traditions of Rome. The Byzantine general Belisarius conquered Ravenna in 540. A period of prosperity followed, under the Eastern Empire, when Justinian and his empress Theodora constructed some magnificent buildings here in the capital of the new exarchate.

Although the province passed into the hands of the Church in 757, Ravenna was still able to proclaim its independence as early as any town in Italy (1177). In the 13C–14C the city was governed by the Da Polenta family (of which Francesca da Rimini was a member), distinguished for their hospitality to Dante. Ravenna prospered as part of the Venetian Republic from 1441 to 1509, but the renewal of papal domination and the sack of the city in 1512, after the battle between Louis XII of France and the Holy League outside its walls, marked the beginning of its final decline. In 1849 Garibaldi found a brief refuge in the pine forest near the town, though his wife Anita died from the hardships of her flight from the Austrians. The city was finally united with the Kingdom of Italy in 1860; it was occupied by the Germans

September 1943 to December 1944. A busy industrial district has been built beyond the railway since the Second World War, and the port is again flourishing. The Candiano canal links the inner harbour of Ravenna with the sea at Marina di Ravenna.

Art and architecture

Ravenna is unequalled in western Europe as a centre for the study of Byzantine architecture, sculpture and mosaic. The plan of the churches had a widespread influence on later buildings in Italy, and the storeyed capitals at San Vitale are equal to the finest work in Constantinople itself. The mosaics show a progressive movement from the naturalism of the earlier work, inspired by Classical ideals (Tomb of Galla Placidia, the Baptisteries, Sant'Apollinare in Classe), to the hieratic decorative quality of the purely Byzantine style (San Vitale, and the processional mosaics in Sant'Apollinare Nuovo).

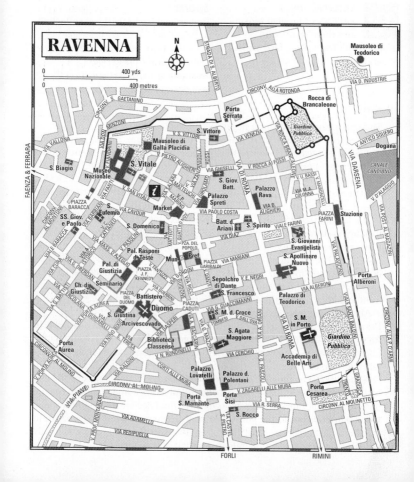

Exploring the city

In the central **Piazza del Popolo** are two Venetian columns with badly worn bases decorated by Pietro Lombardo (1483) and now bearing statues of St Apollinaris and St Vitalis (1644). A portico of eight 6C columns (four bearing the monogram of Theodoric) extends to the left of the crenellated Municipio. Byron lived with the Count and Countess Guiccioli, and wrote the end of *Don Juan*, *Marino Faliero*, and other poems, in Palazzo Guiccioli, at Via Cavour 54.

San Vitale

A garden in the northwest corner of the city centre surrounds Ravenna's most famous monumental complex, San Vitale and its former convent. San Vitale, the Mausoleum of Galla Placidia and the Museo Nazionale are now all approached through one entrance in Via San Vitale, at the end of Via Fanti. This itinerary may change as restoration of the convent buildings proceeds. There is plenty to see, so you would do well to visit the monuments first and the museum last.

- Open Tues–Sun 09.00–19.00; the best light in which to see the mosaics is usually between 12.00 and 13.00).

*San Vitale, the most precious example of Byzantine art extant in western Europe, is preceded by a small narthex. Founded by Julianus Argentarius for Bishop Ecclesius (521–34), the church was consecrated in 547 by Archbishop Maximian. The narthex, which stands obliquely to the church, was formerly preceded by an atrium. The octagonal building is surrounded by a double gallery and surmounted by an octagonal cupola.

Interior The impressive interior is famous for its decoration in marble and *mosaics (always partly under restoration). The remarkable plan, two concentric octagons with seven exedrae or niches and an apsidal choir, may have been suggested by Saints Sergius and Bacchus at Constantinople. The eight pillars that support the dome are encased in marble (largely renewed) and are separated by the exedrae with their triple arches. Higher up is the matroneum, or women's gallery, and above all is the dome, built—for lightness—from two rows of terracotta tubes laid horizontally and fitting into one another. The vault paintings are 18C; the intended mosaic decoration was probably never executed.

The chief glories of the church are in the *choir and *apse. On the triumphal arch are mosaics of **Christ and the Apostles with St Gervasius and St Protasius**, the sons of the patron saint. On either side are two constructions of antique fragments patched together in the 16C–18C, including four columns from the ancient ciborium (the first on the left is of rare green *breccia* from Egypt), and a fragment with putti of a Roman frieze known as

A capital in San Vitale

the 'Throne of Neptune'. Within the arch, on either side, are two *columns with lace-work capitals beneath impost blocks bearing the monogram of Julianus. In the lunettes are mosaics: on the right, *Offerings of Abel and of Melchizedech*; in the spandrels, *Isaiah and the Life of Moses*; on the left, *Hospitality and Sacrifice of Abraham*; at the sides, *Jeremiah and Moses on the Mount*. The upper gallery has magnificent capitals and mosaics of the *Evangelists*, and the vault mosaics of *Angels and the Paschal Lamb* amid foliage are also very fine. The stucco decoration beneath the arches is beautiful. In the centre is the reconstructed altar, with a translucent alabaster top (usually covered).

The apse has the lower part of its walls covered with marble inlay, a modern reconstruction from traces of the original plan. In the centre of the *mosaic, in the semi-dome, Christ (beardless) appears between two angels who present St Vitalis and Bishop Ecclesius (with a model of the church). On the side walls are two fine processional friezes: on the left, *Justinian with His Train* of officials, soldiers and clergy, among whom are Archbishop Maximian and Julianus Argentarius or Belisarius; on the right, *Theodora with Her Court*. In front of the apsidal arch are *Jerusalem*, *Bethlehem* and two *Angels*.

To the right of the apse, beyond an apsidal chamber, is the Sancta Sanctorum (kept locked). Further on is the former entrance to the campanile (originally one of the staircase towers giving access to the matroneum); beneath an adjoining arch are some fine stuccoes. The second staircase tower, still preserving some original work, is on the other side of the narthex; its stairs (now closed) ascend to the matroneum. Some early-Christian sarcophagi are kept in the church.

The tomb of Galla Placidia

From the north side of San Vitale a pathway leads across a lawn to the charming *tomb of Galla Placidia (open as San Vitale), a small cruciform building erected by Honorius's sister towards the middle of the 5C. The plain exterior is decorated with blind arcades and pilasters. The interior, lit by alabaster windows, is famous for its magnificent, predominantly blue *mosaics, especially interesting for the classic character of the figures and for their excellent state of preservation (although they are restored periodically).

Over the entrance is the *Good Shepherd*; in the opposite lunette, *St Laurence* with his gridiron; in the side lunettes, *Stags Quenching Their Thirst* at the Holy Fount. The vaults and arches of the longer arm of the cross are decorated to represent rich hangings and festoons of fruit. In the shorter arm are four *Apostles*; the other eight are on the drum of the cupola. The pendentives hold the symbols of the *Evangelists*. Above all is the *Cross* in a star-strewn sky. The three empty sarcophagi are no longer considered to have held the remains of Placidia, Constantius and Valentinian III; only one of them is of 5C workmanship.

The Museo Nazionale

The *Museo Nazionale (open Tues–Sat 08.30–19.00, Sun and holidays 08.30–22.00), which occupies the former Benedictine Monastery of San Vitale (founded in the 10C) contains an excellent, varied collection of treasures. The monastic collections were taken over by the municipality in 1804, and in 1887 the museum was nationalised. Recent archaeological finds from the territory are kept here.

A modern staircase leads up to a **mezzanine** floor, where a splendid collection of *coins is beautifully displayed in chronological order from the Roman period onwards. The stairs continue up to a group of rooms that were closed at the time of writing: a hall with a marble statue of Venice by Enrico Pazzi (1884), the first director of the museum, and recent donations; a large room displaying funerary stelae (1C BC–1C AD), many of them belonging to sailors, and finds (6C–5C BC) from the necropolis of San Martino in Gattara including a large Greek krater; and a corridor beyond, containing four mosaics decorated with birds.

The itinerary continues on the **first floor** through a large hall (once part of the monastery dormitory) displaying a collection of 16C–17C armour. Small rooms off the hall contain ceramics (Ravenna, Deruta, Faenza, Urbino, Castelli, etc.) and some detached frescoes (including one from San Vitale dating from the 13C). Beyond the hall is a corridor with an interesting collection of *icons of the Cretan-Venetian school, dating from the 14C to the 17C and arranged iconographically by type. Beyond this is a room with a large sinopia found beneath the apse mosaic in Sant'Apollinare in Classe. The next room contains marble reliefs from the so-called Palazzo di Teodorico.

You now come to the rooms that circle around the second cloister. Turning left, you enter a long hall displaying 6C transennae, including a relief of *Hercules and the Stag*, and the cross from the top of San Vitale. Next are Bronze Age ceramics and Roman finds from 20C excavations in Ravenna and Sant'Apollinare in Classe, including portrait heads and glass. Another room displays four Roman herms found offshore and an early-Christian sarcophagus of a child.

Continuing around the cloister, you reach a room containing a fine display of small 16C bronzes and plaquettes, and—at the end—a late-18C pharmacy (the ceramics date from the 17C–18C). Examples of 16C–18C furniture are also displayed. Further on is a hall with a beautiful collection of *ivories, including a relief of *Apollo and Daphne* (530 AD), a 6C diptych from Murano, and evangelistary covers. The last section holds a fine display of *medieval fabrics, among which are some precious examples from the tomb of St Julian at Rimini, and the so-called *Veil of Classis* with embroideries of Veronese bishops of the 8C–9C.

The three **cloisters** contain interesting sculptural fragments. The third cloister (18C) has a statue of Alexander VII (1699), and the second cloister (designed by Andrea da Valle in 1562), a seated statue of Clement XII (1738). The refectory contains detached *frescoes from Santa Chiara by Pietro da Rimini (mid-14C). In the first cloister, which dates from the early 16C, are Roman epigraphs and funerary stelae. From the little Renaissance portico near the east end of San Vitale you can see the terracotta frieze on the wall below the campanile.

The church of **Santa Maria Maggiore** (525–32, rebuilt 1671), adjoining the complex of San Vitale, preserves Byzantine capitals above Greek marble columns, and a tiny cylindrical campanile (9C–10C).

The Cathedral and the Battistero Neoniano

The Cathedral, founded early in the 5C by Bishop Ursus and often known as the *Basilica Ursiana*, was almost totally destroyed in 1733. The columns of the central arch of the portico and those on either side of the central door are from the original church. The round campanile, many times restored, dates from the 10C. In the nave is the 6C *ambo of St Agnellus, pieced together in 1913. The south transept chapel holds two huge 6C *sarcophagi. In the ambulatory is a good relief of St Mark in his study (1492, ascribed to Pietro Lombardo). The north transept chapel has an altarpiece and frescoes by Guido Reni and his school.

Adjoining the cathedral is the octagonal ***Battistero Neoniano** (or *Battistero degli Ortodossi*, open 09.30–18.30), converted from a Roman bath-house, perhaps by Bishop Neon (mid-5C). The plain exterior is decorated with vertical bands and small arches. The remarkable interior is entirely decorated with mosaics and sculptural details that blend with the architectural forms. The original floor is now more than 3m below the present surface.

Eight corner columns support arches decorated with mosaics of *Prophets*. In the niches and on the wall-spaces that are arranged alternately beneath the arches are mosaic inscriptions and marble inlaid designs from the original Roman baths. Each arch of the upper arcade encloses three smaller arches; the stucco decoration is very fine. In the dome, built from hollow tubes like that of San Vitale, are mosaics of the *Baptism of Jesus* (the old man with the reed represents the Jordan), the *Apostles*, the *Books of the Gospel* and four thrones, remarkable for their contrasting colours. The font is of the 12C–13C. In the niches are a Byzantine altar and a pagan marble vase.

The Museo Arcivescovile and Biblioteca Classense

Nearby, on the first floor of the arcivescovado, is the **Museo Arcivescovile** (open Apr–Sep 09.30–18.30; Oct, Nov, Mar 09.30–17.30; Dec, Jan, Feb 09.30–16.30), which contains some exquisite works and incorporates a little chapel with beautiful early 6C mosaics. In the first room are a lapidary collection, with fragments and mosaics from the original cathedral and from San Vitale; the silver *Cross of St Agnellus*, probably dating from 556–69 and restored in the 11C and 16C; a headless 6C porphyry statue, thought to be Justinian; and the marble pulpit from Santi Giovanni e Paolo (596). The so-called *Chasuble of St John Angeloptes* may be a 12C work.

On the left is a *chapel built by Bishop Peter II (494–519) and preceded by an atrium with a barrel vault covered with a delightful *mosaic of birds. The chapel also contains beautiful *mosaics in the vault.

In the end room is the famous ivory *Throne of Maximian*, an Alexandrine work of the 6C, exquisitely carved with the *Story of Joseph*, the *Life of Christ* and figures of *St John the Baptist* and the *Evangelists*.

The *Biblioteca Classense** (entered from Via Baccarini; open Sun–Fri 08.30–19.00), in a 16C–17C building, contains the former monastic library of the monastery of Sant'Apollinare in Classe, founded in 1515 and augmented by Pietro Canneti (1659–1730). The *Aula Magna, designed by Giuseppe Antonio Soratini, with stuccoes and a frescoed ceiling and carved bookcases, can be visited on request (daily except Sat afternoon and Sun and holidays, 08.00–19.00). The important library, owned by the municipality since 1803, has some 600,000 volumes, with 749 valuable codexes, including a 10C text of Aristophanes, illuminated manuscripts, choir books, works relating to Dante and a collection of Byron's letters.

Other sights around town

Across Piazza Caduti from the cathedral, the church of **San Francesco**, built by Bishop Neon in the 5C and remodelled in the 10C, was almost entirely rebuilt in 1793. The 10C campanile was restored in 1921. The lovely basilican interior has 22 columns of Greek marble. In the north aisle are three sarcophagi (including one with Christ and the apostles dating from the 5C), and the tombstone of Ostasio da Polenta (1396) in red marble (with his death mask). Beyond the tomb of Luffo Numai, by Tommaso Fiamberti (1509), the 4C *tomb of St Liberius serves as high altar. Steps beneath it lead down to an opening overlooking the 9C–10C crypt, partly flooded. Here you can see the foundations of an earlier church with its restored mosaic pavement. The first chapel on the south side has carved pilasters by Tullio Lombardo (1525).

On the left of San Francesco is the so-called Cappella di Braccioforte (1480, restored in 1920), containing several early-Christian sarcophagi. To the left again, by a little memorial bell-tower (1921) is the tomb of Dante (open daily 09.00–19.00). Dante, who is revered in Italy as Shakespeare is in the English-speaking world, was exiled from his native Florence and harried by his political enemies in 1317. He found refuge with the Da Polenta family of Ravenna, and he spent his last years with them, finishing the *Divina Commedia* under their patronage. He died on the night of 13–14 September 1321. The mausoleum was commissioned from Camillo Morigia by Cardinal Luigi Gonzaga in 1780 to enshrine an older tomb, with a relief by Pietro Lombardo (1483), and an epitaph by Bernardo Canaccio (1357). This in turn covers the antique sarcophagus in which the poet's remains were originally interred in the old portico of San Francesco. The bronze doors by Lodovico Pogliaghi and the coloured marble in the interior were added in 1921.

The **Museo Dantesco** (entered through a restored 15C cloister at Via Dante 4; open Tues–Sun, Apr–Sep 09.00–12.00, 15.30–18.00; Oct–Mar 09.00–12.00), first opened in 1921, has mementoes of the poet and material relating to various memorials to him. The room decorated by artists influenced by the Arts and Crafts movement in England was intended as a homage to Dante.

Of romance and ruin

You may recognise the city portrayed in these passages:

Ravenna itself preserves perhaps more of the old Italian manners than any City in Italy—it is out of the way of travellers and armies—and thus they have retained more of their originality. They make love a good deal, and assassinate a little.
Lord Byron, letter to Lady Byron, 20 July 1819

Ravenna, where Robert positively wanted to go to live once, has itself put an end to all those yearnings. The churches are wonderful: holding an atmosphere of purple glory, and if one could just live in them, or in Dante's tomb—well, otherwise, keep me from Ravenna. The very antiquity of the houses is white-washed, and the marshes on all sides send up stenches new and old, till the hot air is sick with them.
Elizabeth Barrett Browning, letter, 1848

Ravenna was my personal circus. It was what I came for.... The Ravenna churches with their mosaics... are a revelation of what can be done by an old civilisation when the gold-bug breaks down, and empires expire.
Henry Adams, letter to Elizabeth Cameron, 15 July 1896

We ended in Ravenna and felt the splendour of Rome dying among barbarians in a way that I never felt again until I reached the ruins of the Levant.
Freya Stark, *Traveller's Prelude*, 1950

Byron's first home in Ravenna (1819), Palazzo Rasponi, stood at the corner of Piazza San Francesco and Via Ricci; it has since been built over. Further south is the 5C basilican church of **Sant'Agata Maggiore**, which has a squat round campanile completed in 1560, and sarcophagi on the lawn outside. The basilican interior (if closed, ring at Via Mazzini 46), similar to San Francesco, contains Roman and Byzantine capitals, a very unusual fluted 7C pulpit, an early-Christian sarcophagus used as a high altar, and two Renaissance baldacchini over the altars at the east end.

Via Cerchio, to the south, ends opposite **Santa Maria in Porto**, a church begun in 1553 with a sumptuous façade by Morigia (1780). It contains fine stalls by Mariano (1576–93) and other French craftsmen, and (over the altar in the north transept) a marble Byzantine relief called *La Madonna Greca* (probably 11C). In the public gardens behind is the early-16C Loggetta Lombardesca.

The former monastery of the Canonici Lateranensi, adjoining the church, houses the Accademia di Belle Arti. The fine, large **Pinacoteca Comunale** here (open Mon–Sat 09.00–13.00, Tues and Thur also 16.00–19.00; Sun and holidays 16.00–19.00 only) is spaciously arranged around a pretty cloister in the well-lit rooms of the convent. It includes works by Taddeo di Bartolo, Paolo di Giovanni Fei, Lorenzo Monaco, Marco Palmezzano, Bernardino Zaganelli, Ludovico Brea, Antonio Vivarini, Gentile Bellini, Luca Longhi, Nicolò Rondinelli, Francesco di Santacroce, Palma Giovane and Paris Bordone. The effigy of Guidarello Guidarelli, killed at Imola in 1501, is the work of Tullio Lombardo (1525). The 19C–20C section includes works by Armando Spadini, Felice Carena, Giuseppe Abbati and Arturo Moradei.

The complex also houses a small **Museo Ornitologico e di Scienze Naturali** (open as above), with collections regarding the birds of Romagna, and butterflies, invertibrates, mammals, reptiles and crustaceans from Italy and abroad.

In Via di Roma, to the north, is the building known as the 'Palazzo di Teodorico', really the ruined church of **San Salvatore** (entered from Via Alberoni, open daily 08.30–19.00). Fine mosaics and part of a marble intarsia floor found in 1914 in a palace nearby are exhibited on the walls and on an upper floor, approached by a spiral stair.

Sant'Apollinare Nuovo

*Sant'Apollinare Nuovo (open 09.30–18.30) is one of the more beautiful basilicas in Ravenna. It was built by Theodoric in the early 6C; the mosaics are partly of this time, partly of the mid-6C. Dedicated originally to Jesus and later to St Martin, the church passed from the Arians to the Orthodox Christians under Archbishop Agnellus. Its present dedication dates only from the 9C. The façade with its portico was rebuilt in the 16C; adjacent is a fine 10C campanile.

The floor and the 24 Greek marble columns of the **interior** were raised in the 16C. They are surmounted by a panelled ceiling of 1611; the arcades bulge noticeably to the north. Two magnificent bands of *mosaics adorn the nave walls: that on the north side represents the port of *Classis*, with a procession of 22 virgin martyrs preceded by the Magi who offer gifts to the Infant Jesus seated on His mother's lap between four angels. On the south side are Ravenna, showing the façade of Theodoric's palace, and a procession of 26 martyrs approaching Christ enthroned. Above, on either side, are 16 fathers of the Church, or prophets; higher still, 13 scenes from the life of Christ.

The stucco decoration of the arches is very fine. The ambo in the nave dates from the 6C. In the apse, reconstructed in 1950 (and being restored), are the recomposed altar, transennae, four porphyry columns, and a marble Roman chair.

At the corner of Viale Farini, leading to the station, is Piazza Anita Garibaldi, adorned by a monument to the martyrs of the *Risorgimento* (with amusing lions). Here, the 14C marble doorway of the church of **San Giovanni Evangelista** has been reconstructed on a new wall that encloses a little garden in the church precincts. The church was built by Galla Placidia in fulfilment of a vow made in 424 during a storm at sea. It was well-restored after most of the façade and the first four bays were destroyed and the notable galleried apse, as well as the aisles, seriously damaged in the Second World War. The 10C–14C campanile survives (leaning to the west); two of the bells date from 1208.

In the basilican **interior** some columns, with their capitals and impost blocks, are original. Mosaics from the 13C floor, their naïve designs illustrating episodes from the Fourth Crusade, are displayed round the walls. Fresco fragments of the 14C Riminese school can be seen in a chapel off the north aisle. The chapel at the end of the south aisle has a little 8C carved altar.

The Battistero degli Ariani

Now return to Via Roma and turn north (right). The first lane on the left (Via degli Ariani) leads to the church of **Santo Spirito** (open Mon–Sat 09.30–12.30, 15.00–17.00 or 18.00; Sun 12.00–17.00), converted, like Sant'Apollinare, to the orthodox cult by Agnellus in the mid-6C. Fourteen columns and an ambo from the original church were retained after a rebuilding in 1543. Beside it is the tiny *Battistero degli Ariani* (now Santa Maria in Cosmedin; open daily 08.30–19.00), built by Theodoric in the early 6C. It contains splendidly preserved *mosaics of the *Baptism of Christ* and of the *Apostles* in the dome.

At Via Costa 8 is the Casa Stanghellini, a charming 15C Venetian house, and at the end of the street is the leaning 12C Torre Comunale. From here Via Rossi (right) leads to the church of San Giovanni Battista, with a cylindrical campanile; the interior, a 17C reconstruction, retains its ancient marble columns.

The Mausoleum of Theodoric

At the north end of Via di Roma is Porta Serrata, a gate of 1582. The Circonvallazione alla Rotonda leads east through unattractive suburbs past the rugged bastions of the Venetian **Rocca di Brancaleone**, which now enclose delightful public gardens. Beyond the railway (a rather unpleasant walk of c 20mins along a busy road), in a clump of trees to the left, is the *Mausoleum of Theodoric (open 08.30–19.00; **bus 2** from the station, every 30mins).

This remarkable two-storeyed tomb is unique in the history of architecture; its solid structure shows the influence of Syrian buildings as well as Roman models. Begun by the great Ostrogoth himself in c 520, it was built of hewn Istrian stone without mortar and crowned by an unusual monolithic roof. It was never finished, and for a time, until 1719, it was used as a monastic church (Santa Maria al Faro).

The ten-sided lower storey has a deep recess on every side. The upper floor, which is decorated with unfinished arcading, was approached by two 18C staircases, which collapsed in 1921. The monolithic cupola of Istrian limestone from Pola has a diameter of 11m and weighs about 300 tons. The crack, which is clearly visible, was probably the result of a harsh knock received during its installation. It is not known how the monolith was transported here. Inside is a porphyry bath which was used as the royal sarcophagus.

Sant'Apollinare in Classe

About 5km south of Ravenna and reached either by rail (Classe station, on the Rimini line), or—better—by road (buses 4 and 45 from Ravenna station) across the Ponte Nuovo (1736) and the site of *Classis*, is the basilica of *Sant'Apollinare Classe (open daily 09.00–19.00), built for Bishop Ursicinus by Julianus Argentarius in 535–38 and consecrated by Archbishop Maximian in 549. The narthex, which preceded the church, has been reconstructed. The magnificent late-10C *campanile is the tallest and most beautiful of all the towers of Ravenna.

The wide, bare **interior** has 24 lovely Greek marble-veined columns with square Byzantine bases and beautiful capitals. In the centre of the nave is the altar of Archbishop Maximian, restored in 1753. At the west end of the church are eight columns from the two original ciboria, and a fragment of the original mosaic floor. The aisles hold a series of magnificent sarcophagi, complete with lids, dating from the 5C to the 8C. At the end of the north aisle are a 9C ciborium and an interesting altar with a 5C relief of *Christ and the Apostles*.

The *mosaics of the apse are extremely interesting, though much altered. On the outside arch are five rows of symbolic mosaics, with figures of saints, palm trees, sheep, and *Christ* in a roundel with the symbols of the Evangelists. In the apse itself is a *Cross* on a blue ground with the symbol of the Transfiguration; below is a field of flowers and trees with birds and sheep and *St Apollonius* in prayer in the centre. Below this, to the right and left, are two large scenes, with the *Sacrifices of Abel, Melchizedech and Abraham*, and *Constantine IV* granting privileges for the church of Ravenna to Archbishop Reparatus in the 7C. Between the windows are the figures of the four bishops *Ursicinus, Ursus, Severus and Ecclesius* (6C). The arches of the windows are also decorated with columns in mosaic.

The **Pineta di Classe** (east of the basilica beyond the railway), whose sylvan grandeur was celebrated in poetry by Dante and Byron, is now sadly diminished. Although it has been designated a nature reserve, it is threatened by the industrial development on the outskirts of Ravenna.

Around Ravenna

Bagnacavallo is a small town with a charming theatre (1855) in its central piazza. In Via Garibaldi, next to a 13C tower, is the convent of San Giovanni where Allegra, daughter of Byron and Claire Claremont, died in 1821 at the age of five (plaque). Another former convent (the orchard of which is now a pretty public garden) houses a **pinacoteca** (open summer, Tues–Sat 16.00–19.00, Sun and holidays 10.00–12.00, 16.00–19.00; winter Tues–Sat 15.00–18.00, Sun ands holidays 10.00–12.00, 15.00–18.00) with paintings by Bartolomeo Ramenghi (1484–1542), called 'Il Bagnacavallo' after his native town, a local ethnographical museum, a library and a natural history museum. The Collegiata and Carmine also have paintings by Bagnacavallo. San Francesco, next to its huge convent, has a small Flemish painting and the tombstone of Tiberio Brandolini. Piazza Nuova is a charming little 18C oval cobbled marketplace surrounded by porticoes.

The church of **San Pietro in Silvis**, just outside the town (ring at the house next door if closed), has a lovely basilican interior of the Ravenna type, probably dating from the early 7C, with a raised presbytery above the crypt. It has *frescoes in the apse by Pietro da Rimini (c 1323; being restored).

At **Villanova**, on the river Lamone, is an interesting local museum illustrating life on the wetlands in the district, with handicrafts made from the reeds which grow in the marshes.

Lugo

The pleasant little town of Lugo has interesting 18C architecture. The *Teatro Rossini** was begun in 1757–59 by Francesco Petrocchi, and Antonio Bibiena designed the boxes, stage and three backcloths in 1761. It is built entirely of wood (with excellent acoustics), and the stage is the same size as the auditorium, which seats 500. Important opera productions were given here in the 18C, and concerts are now held in spring. The huge Neo-classical **Pavaglione** was built at the end of the 18C on the site of a marketplace in use since 1437; the arcading on one side dates from the early 16C. Beneath the porticoes are attractive shops with uniform fronts, and a market is held here on Wednesdays. Opera performances took place here in 1598 and again in the 17C.

The colossal incongruous monument (intended for another site) dedicated to Francesco Baracca, a First World War hero, was inaugurated here in 1936 by Mussolini. The Estense **Rocca** (the seat of the comune; open daily except Sun and holidays) dates in its present form from the 15C–16C. In the well restored courtyard is a 15C well-head. Upstairs, the Salotto Rossini has a portrait by Haudebourt Lescot (1828) of the composer, who lived in the town in 1802–04 as a child. The hanging garden is now a public park.

The church of the **Carmine** preserves an organ by Gaetano Callido (1797) used by Rossini. At Via Baracca 65 is the **Museo Francesco Baracca** (open daily 10.00–12.00, 16.00–18.00) with mementoes of the pioneer aviator (1888–1918), born in Lugo, including his plane used in the First World War. There was an important Jewish community in the town from the 15C onwards, and their cemetery survives.

Brisighella

Brisighella is a charming little town in the foothills of the Apennines, beneath three conical hills—one crowned by a clock-tower of 1290 (rebuilt in 1850), another by a 14C Manfredi **castle** with two drum towers (restored by the Venetians in the 16C; inside is a local ethnographical museum, open 15 Apr–15 Oct, Tues–Sun 10.00–12.00, 15.30–19.00 or 19.30; 16 Oct–14 Apr, Sat 14.30–16.30, Sun and holidays 10.00–12.00 and 14.30–16.30), and the third by a 17C sanctuary; all are reached by pretty paths. A delightful medieval pageant is held by candlelight in Jun and Jul in the town. Excellent olive oil is produced in the vicinity.

Above the main street runs the **Strada degli Asini**, a picturesque covered lane with a wooden vault and arches. The **Museo Ugonia** (open Tues–Sun 15.00–18.30, weekends also 10.00–12.00) contains a very interesting collection, beautifully displayed, of lithographs and watercolours by Giuseppe Ugonia (1880–1944). The town hall is in an imposing Neo-classical building of 1828. The church of the **Osservanza** contains fine stuccowork of 1634 and a painting by Marco Palmezzano.

Just outside the town is the 16C **Villa Spada** (with an 18C façade), surrounded by a large garden and containing a remarkable private art collection (not open to the public). A little beyond stands the *****Pieve del Thò** (ring for admission at the house on the right). This ancient church, first mentioned in 909, is thought to be on the site of a Roman building. The interior has primitive columns and capitals, on one of which is an inscription mentioning four late Roman emperors. It is thought that 'Thò' may come from 'ottavo', referring to the eighth mile on a Roman road from the Adriatic. You can see Roman remains beneath the church.

The stretch of Adriatic coast that lies within the province of Ravenna has numerous resorts with hotels of all categories. They include **Marina di Ravenna**, which developed round Porto Corsini (1736), and **Cervia**, to the south near pine woods, a small walled town built in 1698 on a regular plan, later surrounded by a large seaside resort and spa (with an 18-hole golf course).

In the **Pineta di San Vitale**, one of the few wooded areas left along the coast of Italy, is a reconstruction of the hut where Garibaldi lay in hiding in 1849; the original was burned in 1911. The Colonna dei Francesi (1557) on the Forlì road, marks the spot where Gaston de Foix fell mortally wounded in 1512 in the battle between the French and Julius II.

There are British and Canadian military cemeteries northwest of Ravenna and at Alfonsine: this area saw a lot of fighting during the Second World War during the Eighth British Army's advance on the Po.

The towns of Romagna

The towns of Romagna—the largest of which are Faenza, Forlì, Cesena and Rimini—are very different in atmosphere from their more industrialised neighbours to the north. Here the primary activity is still farming—except at Rimini, which in the mid-to-late-20C became famous throughout Europe as a meeting-place for young (and not so young) singles. But even here, the atmosphere is mellow and relaxed out of season. The countryside is green and gently rolling, and noteworthy monuments of art and architecture abound.

Practical information

Getting there
By air

For regular flights the airport nearest the towns of Romagna is Bologna Guilelmo Marconi, with daily flights to and from domestic and international destinations. Rimini's Miramare Airport (c 6km south of the city) has summer charter flights from all over Europe.

By road

The towns of Romagna are most quickly reached from Bologna and Ancona by the A14. Scenic mountain roads wind across the Apennines from Florence to Faenza (302) and to Forlì (67). The latter crosses the beautiful *Muraglione Pass (907m).

By rail

Italy's main Adriatic rail line closely follows the Via Emilia from Bologna to Rimini. Most *Eurostar* and *Intercity* trains stop at Faenza (30mins from Bologna), Forlì (40mins), Cesena (50mins) and Rimini 1hr 10mins). The area is accessible from the south by fast trains from Bari and Ancona. Commuter trains (*Regionali* and *Interegionali*) connect Imola and Faenza with Lugo and Ravenna, Faenza with Florence, and Rimini with Ravenna and Ferrara.

Getting around

RIMINI Car parking across Ponte d'Augusto e Tiberio, or in Largo Gramsci. **Trolley-buses** depart from Piazza Tre Martiri to the station and the shore, from where there are frequent services via Bellariva and Miramare to Riccione. **Country buses** run to destinations throughout the region.

Information offices

CESENA Piazza del Popolo 11, ☎ 0547 356327.

FAENZA Piazza del Popolo, ☎ 0546 25231.
FORLÌ Piazza Morgagni 9, ☎ 0543 714335.
RIMINI Piazza Malatesta 28, ☎ 0541 716371. Branch offices are open in summer at Santarcangelo di Romagna (Via Cesare Battisti 5) and at Verucchio (Piazza Malatesta 15).

Where to stay

FAENZA *Vittoria*, Corso Garibaldi 23, ☎ 0546 21508, fax 0546 29136; comfortable rooms and a good restaurant, in a 16C palace; moderate.
RIMINI At Rimini there are about 1400 hotels within the city limits, nearly all of them near the sea (and many with their own beaches). Although most are adequate, none are distinctive except:
Grand, Parco Fellini 2, ☎ 0541 56000, fax 0541 56866; a huge Belle Epôque affair, first opened on the seafront in 1908 and truly grand in elegance and service; expensive.
Duomo, Via Giordano Bruno 28, ☎ 0541 24215, fax 0541 27842; in a recently renovated building near the centre of the old town; moderate.
RICCIONE *Grand Hotel des Bains*, Viale Gramsci 56, ☎ 0541 601650, fax 0541 606350; a fine old property that lives up to its name, with three restaurants, two pools and every room a different colour; expensive.

Eating out

CASTGROCARO TERME (FORLÌ) *La Frasca*, Viale Matteotti 34, ☎ 0543 767471; restaurant (with rooms) offering excellent interpretations of regional recipes, with garden seating in summer; moderate.
CESENA *Casali*, Via Benedetto Croce 81, ☎ 0547 27485; restaurant of the Hotel Casali, offering good traditional

Emilian fare; closed Fri (Jun–Sept), Mon (Oct–May) and Jul–Aug; moderate.
Circolino, Corte Dandini 10, ☎ 0547 21875; traditional recipes with a creative twist; closed Tues and Jan; inexpensive.
Gianni, Via Dell'Amore 9, ☎ 0547 21328; regional cuisine and seafood; closed Thur; moderate.
CESENATICO *La Buca*, Corso Garibaldi 41, ☎ 0547 82474; more good regional cuisine and seafood; closed Mon and Jan; moderate.
Vittorio, Via Andrea Doria 3, Onda Marina harbour, ☎ 0547 81173; one of the better fish restaurants on the Costa Romagnola; closed Tues and Dec–Jan; expensive.
RIMINI *Lo Squero*, Lungomare Tintori 7, ☎ 0541 27676; genuine Emilian dishes, especially fish; closed Tues (in low season), Nov and Dec; moderate.
Cafés and cake shops include *Bar Dovisi*, Piazza Tre Martiri; *Pasticceria Vecchi*, Piazza Cavour.

Entertainment

RIMINI and the seaside resorts of the *Costa Romagnola* are famous for their **discotheques** and **live-music bars**. The best-known of all is probably the historic *Bandiera Gialla*. The *Rimini Chamber Orchestra* has a regular concert season (Jan–May) at the *Teatro Novelli* and occasional concerts at Bellaria Igea Marina, Cattolica, Misano Adriatico, Riccione, Rimini, San Giovanni in Marignano and Santarcangelo. The *Teatro Ermete Novelli*, Via Cappellini 3, offers drama as well as music.
ELSEWHERE Music and drama at Riccione, *Teatro Turismo*; Cattolica, *Teatro della Regina*; San Giovanni in Marignano, *Teatro Massari*.

Children

The *Costa Romagnola* is one of the few areas of northern Italy specifically equipped for kids. The area offers four water parks—*Aquafàn* (☎ 0541 603050) and *Beach Village* (☎ 0541 643723) in Riccione; *Acquabell* (☎ 0541 349710) at Bellaria; and *Acquamania* (☎ 0541 987642) at Morciano—and two amuseument parks—*Fiabilandia* in Rimini (☎ 0541 372064) and *Italia in Miniatura* at Viserba (☎ 0571 732004). There are also three dolphin show parks—*Show Park* in Rimini (☎ 0541 50298), *Delphinarium Riccione* (☎ 0541 601712) and *Delfinario Cattolica* (☎ 0541 951009).

Shopping

Market days: Cattolica, Piazza De Curtis, Sat. Rimini, around the Castle, Wed and Sat. Riccione, Piazza Unitè, Fri. Santarcangelo, Mon and Fri.

Antiques fairs at San Giovanni in Marignano, fourth Sun of the month, except Jul and Aug, and Santarcangelo, first Sun of the month, except Aug. Local crafts include ceramics, wrought iron, marble, wickerwork, hand-printed cloth and hand-made laces.

Special events

FAENZA The *Palio del Niballo*, a Renaissance tournament, takes place in Jun. At certain periods of the year (usually between Jun and Oct) a portable kiln (with a wood fire) is set up outside the duomo, and pottery is fired on the spot to be sold for charity.
RICCIONE *Premio Riccione per il Teatro and Riccione TTV*, theatre, television, video, May. *Ilaria Alpi Television Journalist Award*, May–Jun. *Riccione Moda Italia*, national competition for young fashion designers, Jul.
International Stamp Exhibition/Europa International Philatelic Exhibition/National Numismatic Meeting, Aug–Sep.

RIMINI *Sagra Musicale Malatestiana*, classical-music festival, dates announced annually

ELSEWHERE *Adriaticocinema*, film festival at Bellaria Igea Marina, Cattolica and Rimini, May–Jun. *Santarcangelo dei Teatri*, theatre festival, Santarchangelo, Jul. Food, music and pageantry on saints' days throughout the region.

Sports

Archery at Misano Adriatico. **Golf** at Veruccio (*Rimini Golf Club*) and at Riolo (*Golf Club La Torre*). **Horse-riding** at Rimini (*Club Ippico Riminese La Fenice*), Riccione (*La Perla Verde*), Verucchio (*Nanni Renato*). **Rowing** at *Canoa Club Rimini*, ☎ 0541 786451. Trap and skeet **shooting** at Rimini, Misano Adriatico and Torriana. **Swimming** and **water sports** at resorts up and down the coast. **Walking** and **mountain-biking**, throughout the region; maps and itineraries published by the Province of Rimini and distributed by the visitors' information office.

FAENZA

Faenza is a pleasant old town on the Lamone river, in the province of Ravenna, which has long been famous for its manufacture of the glazed and coloured pottery known as majolica or 'faience'. There are still some 60 working potteries in the town. The street names are indicated by faience plaques, and several houses have ceramic decoration. The town, still with its Roman plan, is divided into two by the Via Emilia (Corso Mazzini and Corso Saffi).

History

The powerful Manfredi family played a leading part in Faentine affairs from the early 13C until 1501, though they did not prevent the city from being severely damaged in 1241 by Holy Roman Emperor Frederick of Hohenstaufen, and again sacked in 1376 by the mercenary soldier Sir John Hawkwood, then in the papal service. In 1501 Cesare Borgia took the town and killed the last of the Manfredi, and from 1509 Faenza was included in the States of the Church.

The great period of Faentine majolica was 1450–1520, when the most famous of the 40 potteries in the town was that of the brothers Pirotti (the Ca' Pirota). The earliest authenticated specimen of faience, in the Cluny Museum in Paris, is a votive plaque dated 1475, though the technique (see below) is documented as early as 1142. Baldassare Manara (first half of the 16C) and Virgilio Calamelli (Virgiliotto da Faenza; later 16C) both produced distinguished work. The art had a second revival in the early 18C.

Exploring the town

The broad Viale Baccarini, which connects the station with the town, leads straight to the ***Museo Internazionale delle Ceramiche** (open Apr–Oct, Tues–Sat 09.00–19.00; Sun and holidays 09.30–13.00, 15.00–19.00; Nov–Mar 09.00–13.30, Sun and holidays also 15.00–18.00). The museum holds the best and most extensive collection of Italian majolica in Italy. Begun in 1908, the collection covers all periods and is beautifully displayed and well labelled (an excellent catalogue is also available).

Part of the lower floor is being rearranged. The museum includes superb examples of 15C–16C Faentine ware and ceramics from all the major Italian manufacturies. It also has pre-Columbian, Minoan, Greek and Etruscan ceramics, and an Oriental and Middle Eastern collection. The 20C works include pieces by Picasso and Matisse. The study collections are complemented by an excellent library and photographic collection.

A long hall on the **first floor** presents the evolution of Faentine ceramics from the early Middle Ages to the Renaissance. The section beyond samples Italian Renaissance ceramics produced in various regions. The finest examples are in room **2**. They include ceramics from Tuscany (notice the rare Medici porcelain dish shown in a separate vitrine), Umbrian ware from Gubbio and Deruta, and ceramics from Urbino, notably a dish with the *Adoration of the Magi* from the workshop of Guido Durantino, a cup with the Penitent St Jerome, and a cup with Venus, lovers and musicians. The next gallery illustrates standard formulas and the inevitable decline of majolica after the foundation of European porcelain manufactures (such as Sevres and Meissen) in the early 18C. A ramp leads down to the Modern and contemporary galleries, designed by the architects Piersanti and Rava.

A connoisseur's guide to faience

Use this quick history of faience to find your way among the museum's large and fascinating collections.

The so-called **archaic ware** produced from the mid-13C to the first half of the 15C has a white tin-glazed body decorated with two colours only (brown and green), which after 1350 were gradually replaced by blue. In the late 14C and early 15C the so-called **Zaffera ware** made its appearance, decorated with cobalt blue and manganese brown thickly applied on a white ground to produce a relief effect. In the 15C, the import of tin glazed wares from the island of Maiorca (hence the Italian name for faience, majolica) introduced the **lustre technique** as well as islamic decorative motifs. Their combination with the existing Italian tradition gave rise to an Italo-Moresque style which is particularly evident in the blue Zaffera ware that includes yellow and purple details to imitate the lustre effects of Hispanic wares.

Further influences in the 15C came from **Chinese porcelain** imported from Venice. The immediate consequence was the development of more delicate shapes (imitating Ming porcelain) and an enriched decorative repertoire, which found expression in a blue monochromy on white ground.

The typically Faentine motif of the **curled leaf** (or 'Gothic foliage') was developed in the late 15C and early 16C. The first **historiated wares** made their appearance around the same time, thanks to the crosslinks between potters and painters and to the circulation of illustrated books (after the invention of printing), which made famous paintings and woodcuts available to the *maiolicari* and introduced new themes such as mythology. The discovery of the **grotesques** of the Domus Aurea in Rome, and the decoration of the Vatican Logge by Raphael, provided further inspiration for subsequent ceramic production.

Monochrome ware was also highly valued from the 16C onwards. Examples include the beautiful **Faenza white**, with its characteristic shapes obtained from plaster moulds, and the blue-ground maiolica called **smalto berret-tino**, decorated with delicate grotesques.

The large, impressive **Piazza della Libertà**, with arcades and a fountain of 1619–21 (by Domenico Paganelli), is the centre of the town life. Here is the **cathedral**, begun by Giuliano da Maiano in 1474, a Renaissance building with an unfinished front. It contains good sculpture including a Bosi monument by the local sculptor Pietro Barilotti (1539), the reliquary urn of St Terenzio with beautiful *carvings in very low relief, and the *tomb of St Savinus (first bishop of Faenza, early 4C), with exquisite reliefs by Benedetto da Maiano (1474–76). An altarpiece by Innocenzo da Imola, in the fourth south chapel, represents the *Holy Family with the Infant St John and Sts Peter and Paul*.

On the other side of the Via Emilia is the picturesque arcaded **Piazza del Popolo** with a clock tower by Domenico Paganelli (reconstructed in 1944), **Palazzo del Podestà** (partly of the 12C) and the **municipio**, once the palace of the Manfredi. The **Voltone della Molinella** is a shopping arcade with a beautiful frescoed vault and grotteschi by Marco Marchetti (1566). The Bottega dei Ceramisti Faentini here exhibits and sells ceramics made in the town. In a pleasant cobbled courtyard is the Neo-classical *****Teatro Comunale Masini**. Designed by the local architect Giuseppe Pistocchi (1780–87), it has a charming interior with statues and reliefs by Antonio Trentanove.

Via Severoli leads right to the town pinacoteca (closed since 1982), with an interesting collection of works of art, including sculptures by Fra Damiano, Alfonso Lombardi and Donatello or his school (wooden statue of *St Jerome*), and paintings by Marco Palmezzano. The church of **Santa Maria dell'Angelo** (1621, by Girolamo Rainaldi) has a Spada tomb by Francesco Borromini and busts by Alessandro Algardi.

Further southwest, reached by Via Cavour, is *****Palazzo Milzetti** (open Mon–Sat 08.30–13.30; Thur also 14.00–17.00), a fine building by Giuseppe Pistocchi (1794–1802), with a Neo-classical interior on two floors and its decoration and furnishings intact. Many of the rooms have delightful tempera paintings by Felice Giani. On the *piano nobile* is an impressive octagonal room designed by Giuseppe Antonio Antolini, with stuccoes by Antonio Trentanove. The apartments on the lower floor are decorated with charming ceiling frescoes whose tiny, refined grotesques imitate Pompeiian styles. The oval bathroom, with grotesques on a black background, is particularly beautiful.

Nearby rises the 10C campanile of Santa Maria Vecchia. In Corso Mazzini, where there are several 18C and early 19C buildings, there are plans for **Palazzo Mazzolani** to one day house a local archaeological museum. In Borgo Durbecco, beyond the Lamone bridge, is the small Romanesque church of the **Commenda**, with a remarkable fresco by Girolamo Pennacchi the Younger (1533). The next street to the right, beyond the Barriera, leads to a British military cemetery.

Forlì

An undistinguished provincial capital (population 109,000) and agricultural centre, Forlì takes its name from the Roman *Forum Livii*, a station on the Via Emilia, which bisects the town. Its urban architecture suffered under the influence of Mussolini, born nearby.

In the central piazza is the church of **San Mercuriale** (12C–13C but altered later), dedicated to the first bishop of Forlì. It has a fine contemporary *campanile, 76m high, a high relief of the school of Antelami above the west door, and a graceful cloister. In the red-brick interior are paintings by Marco Palmezzano and the *tomb, by Francesco Ferrucci, of Barbara Manfredi (d. 1466), wife of Pino II Ordelaffi. Beneath the apse are remains of the 11C church and the crypt of 1176.

The **Palazzo del Municipio**, dating from 1459, was altered in 1826. Corso Garibaldi, with some 15C–16C mansions, leads to the **cathedral**, mainly an elaborate reconstruction of 1841, but preserving a huge tempera painting of the *Assumption*, the masterpiece of Carlo Cignani (1681–1706). The campanile, in Piazza Ordelaffi, was formerly the watchtower of the Orgogliosi, a rival family to the Ordelaffi, who ruled the town from 1315 to 1500.

At the south end of the town is the Rocca di Ravaldino (1472–82; now a prison), where Caterina Sforza was besieged by Cesare Borgia in 1499–1500. It was the birthplace of her famous son Giovanni delle Bande Nere (1498–1526).

A former hospital (1772) in Corso della Repubblica houses the **Pinacoteca Comunale Saffi** (open Tues–Fri 09.00–14.00; Sat 09.00–13.30; Sun and holidays 09.00–13.00), first opened to the public in 1846 and in this location since 1922. It is one of few museums in Italy to have preserved its old-fashioned arrangement. The gallery possesses only one work (the *pestapepe*, a druggist's street sign) attributed to the famous local painter Melozzo da Forlì (Melozzo degli Ambrogi; 1438–95), but it contains a fine collection of paintings by his most important follower, Marco Palmezzano (including an *Annunciation*), as well as paintings by Fra Angelico (two tiny panels of the *Nativity* and *Christ in the Garden*), Cavalier di Arpino, Livio Agresti, Lodovico Carracci, Carlo Cignani, Francesco Albani, Andrea Sacchi, Guido Cagnacci, Lorenzo Costa, Lorenzo di Credi, Bartolomeo Ramenghi and Silvestro Lega. It has sculptures by Bernardo and Antonio Rossellino, and Pier Paolo and Jacobello delle Masegne. On the upper floor is an ethnographical collection, and below is an archaeological collection.

There is a museum of musical instruments in Palazzo Gaddi. In the church of **Santa Maria dei Servi** the tomb of Luffo Numai (1502) has good reliefs by Tommaso Fiamberti.

In the Rabbi valley outside the town is a British military cemetery.

The town of **Predappio** was the birthplace of Benito Mussolini (1883–1945). The village, originally a hamlet called Dovia in the commune of Predappio Alta, received communal rank in 1925, and many new public buildings were erected. In the cemetery are Mussolini's remains, finally interred there in 1957, and those of his wife 'Donna Rachele' (Rachele Guidi), buried there in 1979. Predappio was taken from the Germans by Poles of the Eighth Army in October 1944. There is an Indian and British military cemetery nearby.

Cesena

Cesena now lacks distinction, although it enjoyed a period of brilliance under the Malatesta family (1379–1465). The most interesting building is the *Biblioteca Malatestiana* (open Mon–Sat 09.00–12.30, 15.00–18.00 or 16.00–19.00; Sun and holidays 10.00–12.30). Two Roman silver plates (early 5C AD) with banquet scenes in gold and *niello*, are displayed in the vestibule. A handsome doorway, with a relief of the Malatesta heraldic elephant, leads into the perfectly preserved *old library, a beautiful aisled basilica built in 1447–52 by Matteo Nuti for Domenico Malatesta Novello. Some precious old books, in their original presses, are still kept chained to the reading desks. The opaque windows look onto the cloister. Another room contains a display of some of the the 340 valuable manuscripts, including some with 15C illuminations, and 48 incunabula, which belong to the library.

Near the 15C **Palazzo del Ridotto** (rebuilt in 1782) is the church of the **Suffragio**, with a late-Baroque interior and a high altarpiece by Corrado Giaquinto (1752). The **cathedral**, begun in 1385, contains 15C sculpture. The theatre was opened in 1846.

The central Piazza del Popolo has a pretty fountain of 1583, opposite which steps lead up to the public gardens surrounding the 15C **Rocca Malatestiana** (open Tues–Sun 09.30–12.30, 15.00–19.00), which was a prison until 1969 and has been heavily restored. It contains 17C tournament armour and a Garibaldi collection. From the battlements are views of the coast, including the tower of Cesenatico, and inland to the Apennines. One of the towers houses a local ethnographical museum.

From Piazza del Popolo, Viale Mazzoni leads round the foot of the castle hill to San Domenico with 17C paintings. In Via Aldini is the Pinacoteca Comunale with works by Sassoferrato, Antonio Aleotti and Giovanni Battista Piazzetta.

Outside the town is the **Madonna del Monte**, a Benedictine abbey rebuilt in the 15C–16C with a collection of ex-votos and a *Presentation in the Temple* by Francesco Francia. A British military cemetery northeast of Cesena recalls the heavy fighting in this area by the Eighth Army in October 1944.

Cesenatico was the port of Cesena (designed in 1502 by Leonardo da Vinci for Cesare Borgia) from which Garibaldi and his wife Anita set sail on their flight towards Venice in August 1849. It is now the biggest of the numerous popular seaside resorts here, which stretch for some 30km south to Rimini and Pesaro. Near Gatteo a Mare is the mouth of the **Rubicone** river, the fateful Rubicon which Caesar crossed in defiance of Pompey in 49 BC. A Roman bridge (c 186 BC) survives over the river inland at **Savignano sul Rubicone**.

RIMINI

Rimini (population 128,000), capital of a province created in 1995, was first visited for its bathing beaches in 1843, and it was the largest seaside resort on the Adriatic by the 1950s. Its beaches, especially popular with German, French, British and Eastern European holidaymakers, extend along the shore in either direction; some 16 million tourists visit this coast every year (there are 2800 hotels in the province). The old city, over a kilometre from the sea front, is separated from it by the railway. Although Rimini is a somewhat characterless town, it contains the famous Tempio Malatestiano, one of the more important Renaissance buildings in Italy. It also has a good local museum, and it preserves a splendid Roman arch and bridge.

History

Rimini occupies the site of the Umbrian city of *Ariminum*, which became a Roman colony c 268 BC and was favoured by Julius Caesar and Augustus. In the 8C it became a papal possession, and it was contended between the papal and imperial parties in the 12C–13C. Neri da Rimini produced some beautiful illuminated manuscripts here from 1300 to 1323.

Malatesta di Verucchio (1212–1312), Dante's 'old mastiff', was the founder of a powerful dynasty of Guelf overlords, the most famous of whom was Sigismondo (1417–68), a man of violent character but an enthusiastic protector of art and learning. Malatesta's son, Giovanni the Lame, was the husband of the beautiful Francesca da Rimini (d. 1258), whose love for her brother-in-law Paolo inspired one of the tenderest passages in Dante's *Inferno* ('we read no more that day'). Pandolfo (d. 1534) surrendered the town to Venice, but after the battle of Ravenna (1512) it fell again into papal hands. In the Second World War Rimini, bombarded from sea or air nearly 400 times, was the scene of heavy fighting between the Germans and the Eighth Army and was captured by Canadians in September 1944. The film director Federico Fellini was a native of Rimini, and some of his films were inspired by the town.

Exploring the town

In the centre of the old town is the arcaded Piazza Tre Martiri, with the little **Oratory of St Anthony** on the spot where the saint's mule miraculously knelt in adoration of the Sacrament.

Tempio Malatestiano: tomb of Isotta degli Atti, wife of Sigismondo Malatesta

Via IV Novembre leads east to the ***Tempio Malatestiano** (open daily 07.00–12.00, 15.30–19.00), one of the outstanding monuments of the Italian Renaissance, built in Istrian stone. The original building (on the site of a 9C church) was a late 13C Franciscan church, used by the Malatesta family in the 14C for their family tombs. In 1447–48 Sigismondo Malatesta transformed this into a personal monument, as his own burial place. He commissioned Leon Battista Alberti to redesign it (with the help of Matteo de' Pasti in the interior) and had Agostino di Duccio decorate it with exquisite sculptural reliefs. The decline of Sigismondo's fortunes caused the suspension of the work in 1460, and the Franciscans completed the building.

The ***façade**, on a high basement, is inspired by the form of the Roman triumphal arch (and by the nearby Arch of Augustus, a Roman gate). One of the masterpieces of Alberti, it had a lasting effect on 16C and 17C church architecture in Italy. The upper part is incomplete. The two sides have wide arches surmounting the stylobate, beneath which (on the south side) are seven plain Classical sar-

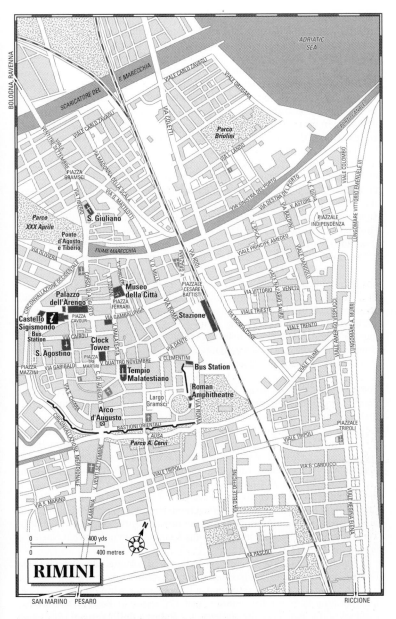

RIMINI

cophagi containing the ashes of eminent members of Sigismondo's court. Latin and Greek inscriptions record Sigismondo and his victories.

The *interior has been beautifully restored. The spacious nave is flanked by a series of deep side chapels connected by remarkably fine *sculptural decoration** by Agostino di Duccio, and closed by fine balustrades in red-and-white veined marble. The walls are covered with beautiful sculptural details (including the vaults and window frames). On the right of the entrance is the tomb of Sigismondo, whose armorial bearings (the elephant and rose) and initials (SI) recur throughout the church.

In the first chapel on the south side is a seated statue of *St Sigismund* supported by elephants' heads, and very low reliefs of angels, all elegant works of Agostino di Duccio. In the niches, statues of the Virtues and armour-bearers. The little **sacristy** (formerly the Chapel of the Relics), preserves its original doors surrounded by marble reliefs including two putti on dolphins. Inside is a damaged *fresco (above the door) by Piero della Francesca (1451), representing Sigismondo kneeling before his patron, St Sigismund of Burgundy, and relics found in Sigismondo's tomb. The third chapel has a frieze of putti at play on the entrance arch and (over the altar) *St Michael*, by Agostino. Here is the tomb of Isotta degli Atti, Sigismondo's mistress and later his third wife. The *crucifix was painted for the church by Giotto before 1312. The fourth chapel has more superb decoration representing the planetary symbols and signs of the zodiac, also by Agostino.

The fourth chapel on the north side is the masterpiece of Agostino, with reliefs representing the *Arts and Sciences*. The third chapel has particularly charming putti. In the first chapel (of the Ancestors) are figures of prophets and sibyls, a tiny *Pietà* (15C, French), above the altar, and the *Tomb of the Ancestors*, with splendid reliefs by Agostino.

The end chapels and presbytery do not belong to the original Malatesta building: the original design may have incorporated a dome at the east end. It was completed by the Franciscans (and rebuilt in the 18C and again after the Second World War). The temple has served as the cathedral of Rimini since 1809.

Behind the temple and across Largo Gramsci, in a residential area with a children's playground, you can see the fenced-off ruins of the **Roman amphitheatre**; only two brick arches remain above the foundations.

From Piazza Tre Martiri, Corso d'Augusto leads south to the ugly Piazza Giulio Cesare. The *Arco d'Augusto**, a single Roman archway (c 27 BC; restored) with composite capitals, marked the junction of the Via Emilia with the Via Flaminia here. It was later inserted into the medieval walls. At the opposite end of the corso is the *Ponte d'Augusto e Tiberio**, a five-arched bridge across the Marecchia begun by Augustus in the last year of his life and finished by Tiberius (21 AD). It is remarkably well-preserved (and used by cars and pedestrians). Its handsome dedicatory inscriptions are still in place in the centre of the bridge. The north arch was rebuilt after the Goths destroyed it in order to cut Narses off from Rome in 552.

In Corso d'Augusto the Cinema Folgor, built in the 1920s and often visited by Fellini as a child, is planned to become a study centre dedicated to the director. The corso runs through the south end of Piazza Cavour, with a fountain of 1543 incorporating Roman reliefs and a seated 17C statue of Paul V. Here are two restored Gothic buildings: the battlemented **Palazzo dell'Arengo** (1204), now used for exhibitions, and the 14C **Palazzo del Podestà**, now the town hall. At the end is the Neo-classical façade of the theatre, built in 1857 by Poletti, which hides the foyer (used for exhibitions): the theatre itself was bombed in the Second

World War and is still in ruins behind.

The **Castello Sigismondo**, which dates from 1446, is the seat of the **Museo delle Culture Extraeuropee**, founded by Delfino Dinz Rialto (1920–79) in 1972 (open Tues–Fri 08.30–12.30; Sat–Sun and holidays also 17.00–19.00). It contains a remarkable ethnological collection. The first section is dedicated to Oceania, on the lower floor is material from pre-Columbian America, and on the upper floor material from Africa.

In Via Sigismondo the Romanesque church of **Sant'Agostino** has a fine campanile, damaged 14C frescoes by local artists (including Giovanni da Rimini) and a huge painted 14C crucifix.

Via Gambalunga leads from Piazza Cavour past the town library to Piazza Ferrari, where excavations of a Roman house are in progress. Beyond the church of the Suffragio, at Via Tonini 1, in the ex-Jesuit college built by Alfonso Torreggiani in 1746–55, is the *****Museo della Città** (open Tues–Sat 08.00–12.30, 17.00–19.00; Sun and holidays 08.00–12.30, 16.00–17.00). Founded in 1871, it is particularly interesting for its works of art produced by Riminese artists.

The **ground floor** has Roman mosaics (including one, dating from the early 2C, showing boats in the port of Rimini), a Roman lapidarium and a large 14C fresco by the Riminese school.

On the **first floor** are paintings by the 14C Riminese school, including a fine crucifix by Giovanni da Rimini; *Last Supper* by Bartolomeo Coda; the two masterpieces of the collection—Giovanni Bellini's *****Dead Christ with Four Angels**, commissioned by Sigismondo Pandolfo Malatesta c 1460, and Domenico Ghirlandaio's *****Pala of St Vincent Ferrer**, commissioned by Pandolfo IV, with portraits of the Malatesta family—15C and 16C paintings, nine 17C Flemish tapestries, a bronze bust of Michelangelo attributed to Giambologna, and 14C–16C majolica.

Exhibits on the **second floor** include 17C Riminese paintings, three works by Guercino, a painting by Guido Reni, 18C and 19C works including portraits, and a painting of the Roman bridge of Rimini by Richard Wilson. The prehistoric and archaeological collection includes Etruscan tomb-furniture of the Villanovan period, with a remarkable axe-mould, and coins from the mint of *Ariminum*.

Other museums at Rimini include the **Museo dell'Aviazione**, Via Sant'Aquilina 58 (open daily 09.00–19.00), with historic European and American aircraft, anti-aircraft guns and radar, flight suits, medals and decorations; and the **Museo Nazionale del Motociclo**, Via Caslecchio 11 (open Tues–Sun 10.00–12.30, 15.00–19.00), where some 200 displays tell the sory of motorcycling by themes and periods. Many buffs come all the way to Rimini to consult the library (10,000 volumes) and archives before restoring their antique bikes.

The church of **San Giuliano**, in the suburb beyond the bridge, contains a fine *Martyrdom of St Julian* painted by Paolo Veronese. The pleasant public **Parco XXV Aprile** occupies the former bed of the river Marecchia (now channelled to the north).

Viale Principe Amadeo was laid out in the 19C to connect the old town with the sea. It is lined with pretty Art Nouveau villas with their gardens. By the railway line is the only skyscraper in the city. The sandy beaches along the coast northwest and southeast of Rimini, ruined by uncontrolled new building begun in the 1950s, attract millions of holidaymakers every year from all over Europe. There is a continuous line of resorts, including **Riccione**, with numerous hotels.

Around Rimini

In the pleasant, wide Marecchia valley, with hilly outcrops, is **Villa Verucchio**, with a Franciscan convent that may date from 1213. The church contains a 14C Riminese fresco.

Verucchio is an attractive hill-town from which the Malatesta clan set out to conquer Rimini. Its site, on a low hill where the river Marecchia emerges into the plain, has been of strategic importance since earliest times, and an Etruscan centre flourished here in the 7C BC. An ancient pieve lies at the foot of the hill. From the pretty Parco dei Nove Martiri an old walled mule path (to be reopened to the public) leads up to the Rocca. A lane descends to the former convent of Sant'Agostino, beautifully restored as the seat of the **Museo Civico Archeologico** (open Sun and holidays 10.00–12.30, 14.30–18.00; otherwise on request at the information office). Here, finds from an important Etruscan and Villanovan necropolis (9C–7C BC) excavated at the foot of the hill since 1894, are displayed. Particularly beautiful *amber and gold jewellery was found, as well as textiles and wooden objects (other material is displayed in the Archaeological Museum in Bologna).

The **rocca** (open as the Museum) has a splendid view of the Adriatic coast (Rimini and Cesenatico marked by their two skyscrapers) and inland to the Marche. The **Collegiata** has a 14C Riminese painted cross, and an early-15C cross attributed to Nicolò di Pietro in the north transept.

Montebello is a delightful little hamlet with just one street. Steps lead up to the entrance to the **Castello dei Guidi di Romagna**, still privately owned by the Guidi (open daily 14.30–18.30 or 19.30; in winter at weekends only). The old church is now used as a wine bar. There are fine views over the beautiful river valley and the former estate (now a nature reserve), which includes the castle of Saiano (reached by a path) with a church perched on an outcrop of rock. San Marino is also prominent. The courtyard is part-12C (with a tower built onto the rock), and part-Renaissance.

The **interior**, interesting for its architecture, has particularly good furniture in the Renaissance wing. A pretty angle room in the medieval part of the castle has an interesting collection of cassoni (marriage chests), including three dating from the 13C and 14C, an old oven, and a painted Islamic panel thought to date from the 11C. The family still owns a private archive dating from 980. There is a small garden inhabited by peacocks inside the walls. The castle was used for a time as German headquarters in the Second World War, and during a battle here 386 Gurkhas (part of the British Eighth Army) lost their lives; their military cemetery is on the San Marino road south of Rimini.

Sant'Arcangelo di Romagna is a pleasant small town. The **Sferisterio**, below the walls in the lower town, was built for ball games (and is now used for the game of *tamburello*). In Via Cesare Battisti are the fish market of 1829 and the Collegiata, with a Venetian polyptych. Also in this street is an old family-run shop where fabrics are still printed by hand (the wheel dates from the 17C); all the old books of samples have been preserved.

Uphill, Piazza delle Monache has a local museum of paintings and archaeology in a well-restored 17C palace. Also in the piazza is the entrance to a grotto (opened on request at the information office; ☎ 0541 624537), used as a wine cellar since the 16C. A passageway leads to a remarkable underground circular room with an ambulatory and niches carved in the tufa rock, possibly a pagan temple. There are many other similar grottoes beneath the town.

Further uphill is the picturesque old borgo, with three long straight streets of low houses leading from the Gothic-revival clock-tower to the 14C–15C rocca (still privately owned by the Colonna), recently restored and opened to the public (by appointment: ☎ 0541 620832). The **Museo Etnografico Usi e Costumi della Gente di Romagna**, in Via Montevecchi (open Tues–Sat, 09.00–12.00; Tues, Thur and Sat also 15.00–18.00; Sun and holidays 15.00–18.00), has collections documenting popular traditions (symbolism, social life, work, ritual aspects, arts) of southern Romagna.

San Marino

The tiny Republic of San Marino (6 sq km; population 23,000) lies a few kilometres south of Rimini, on the border with the Marche. The republic is famous for having preserved its independence for more than 16 centuries, since its alleged foundation c 300 by Marinus, a pious stonemason from Dalmatia who fled to the mountains to escape Diocletian's second persecution. Most of its territory consists of the peaks and slopes of the limestone **Monte Titano** (739m).

The capital, **San Marino**, is totally given over to the tourist trade. The three medieval citadels (Rocca, Cesta and Montale) are connected by a splendid *walkway that follows the crest of the hill and has fine views of the Adriatic coast. The church of **San Francesco** has a *St Francis* by Guercino and a *Madonna and Child* attributed to Raphael. The **Palazzo del Governo** dates from 1894. The legislative power is vested in a Council General of 60, from whom 10 (the Congress of State) are chosen as an executive, and 12 as a council that functions as a Court of Appeal; the chiefs of state are two 'regent captains' who hold office for six months (investiture April and October). San Marino has its own mint, postage stamps, police force and an army of about 1000 men.

Glossary of special terms

Ambo (pl. *ambones*), pulpit in a Christian basilica; two pulpits on opposite sides of a church from which the gospel and epistle were read

Amphora, antique vase, usually of large dimensions, for oil and other liquids

Ancona, retable or large altarpiece (painted or sculpted) in an architectural frame

Arca, wooden chest with a lid, for sacred or secular use. Also, monumental sarcophagus in stone, used by Christians and pagans

Architrave, lowest part of an entablature, horizontal frame above a door

Archivolt, moulded architrave carried round an arch

Atrium, forecourt, usually of a Byzantine church or a Classical Roman house

Attic, topmost storey of a Classical building, hiding the spring of the roof

Badia, *Abbazia*, abbey

Baldacchino, canopy supported by columns, usually over an altar

Basilica, originally a Roman building used for public administration; in Christian architecture, an aisled church with a clerestory and apse, and no transepts

Borgo, a suburb; street leading away from the centre of a town

Bottega, the studio of an artist: the pupils who worked under his direction

Bozzetto, sketch, often used to describe a small model for a piece of sculpture

Broletto, name often given to the town halls of northern Italy

Bucchero, Etruscan black terracotta ware

Bucrania, form of Classical decoration—heads of oxen garlanded with flowers

Campanile, bell-tower, often detached from the building to which it belongs

Canopic vase, Egyptian or Etruscan vase enclosing the entrails of the dead

Cantoria, singing-gallery in a church

Cartoon, from *cartone*, meaning large sheet of paper. A full-size preparatory drawing for a painting or fresco

Caryatid, female figure used as a supporting column

Cassone, a decorated chest, usually a dower chest

Cavea, the part of a theatre or amphitheatre occupied by the rows of seats

Cella, sanctuary of a temple, usually in the centre of the building

Cenacolo, scene of the Last Supper (often in the refectory of a convent)

Chalice, wine cup used in the celebration of Mass

Chiaroscuro, distribution of light and shade, apart from colour, in a painting

Ciborium, casket or tabernacle containing the Host

Cipollino, onion-marble; a greyish marble with streaks of white or green

Cippus, sepulchral monument in the form of an altar

Crenellations, battlements

Cupola, dome

Diptych, painting or ivory panel in two sections

Dossal, an altarpiece

Duomo, from the Latin *Domus dei*, 'house of God': cathedral

Ex-voto, tablet or small painting expressing gratitude to a pagan god or saint

Fresco (in Italian, *affresco*), painting executed on wet plaster. On the wall beneath is sketched the *sinopia*, and the *cartone* (see above) is transferred onto the fresh plaster (*intonaco*) before the fresco is begun, either by pricking the outline with small holes over which a powder is dusted, or by means of a stylus which leaves an incised line on the wet plaster. In recent years many frescoes have been detached from the walls on which they were executed

Gonfalon, banner of a medieval guild or commune

Graffiti, design on a wall made with an iron tool on a prepared surface, the design showing in white. Also used loosely to describe scratched designs or words on walls

Greek cross, cross with the arms of equal length

Grisaille, painting in various tones of grey

Grotesque, painted or stucco decoration in the style of the ancient Romans (found during the Renaissance in Nero's Golden House in Rome, then underground, hence the name, from 'grotto'). The delicate ornamental decoration usually includes patterns of flowers, sphinxes, birds, human figures, etc., against a light ground

Iconostasis, high balustrade with figures of saints, guarding the sanctuary of a Byzantine church

Impost block, a block with splayed sides placed above a capital

Intarsia (or *tarsia*), inlay of wood, marble or metal

Intrados, underside or soffit of an arch

Krater, Antique mixing bowl, conical in shape with rounded base

Latin cross, cross with a long vertical arm

Lavabo, hand basin usually outside a refectory or sacristy

Loggia, covered gallery or balcony, usually preceding a larger building

Lunette, semicircular space in a vault or ceiling, or above a door or window, often decorated with a painting or relief

Matroneum, gallery reserved for women in early Christian churches

Medallion, large medal; loosely, a circular ornament

Monochrome, painting or drawing in one colour only

Monolith, single stone (usually a column)

Narthex, vestibule of a Christian basilica

Niello, black substance used in an engraved design

Oculus, round window

Opera (del Duomo), the office in charge of the fabric of a building (i.e. the cathedral)

Pala, large altarpiece

Palaeochristian, from the earliest Christian times up to the 6C

Palazzo, any dignified and important building

Paliotto, the hanging that covers the front of an altar

Pendentive, concave spandrel beneath a dome

Pietà, group of the Virgin mourning the dead Christ

Pietre dure, hard or semi-precious stones, often used in the form of mosaics to decorate cabinets, table tops, etc.

Pieve, parish church

Plaquette, small metal tablet with relief decoration

Pluteus (pl. *plutei*), marble panel, usually decorated; series are used to form a parapet to precede the altar of a church

Polyptych, painting or panel in more than three sections

Predella, small painting or panel, usually in sections, attached below a large altarpiece, illustrating the story of a Saint, the life of the Virgin, etc.

Presepio, literally, crib or manger. A group of statuary of which the central subject is the Infant Jesus in the manger

Pronaos, porch in front of the cella of a temple

Putto (pl. *putti*), figure of a boy sculpted or painted, usually nude

Quadratura, painted architectural perspectives.

Reredos, decorated screen rising behind an altar

Rhyton, drinking horn usually ending in an animal's head

Rood-screen, a screen below the Rood or Crucifix dividing the nave from the chancel of a church

Scagiola, a material made from selenite, used to imitate marble and *pietre dure*

Schiacciato, term used to describe very low relief in sculpture, where there is an emphasis on the delicate line rather than the depth of the panel

Scuola (pl. *scuole*), Venetian lay confraternity, dedicated to charitable works

Sinopia, large sketch for a fresco made on the rough wall in a red earth pigment called sinopia (because it originally came from Sinope on the Black Sea). By detaching a fresco it is now possible to see the sinopia beneath and detach it

Situla, water bucket

Soffit, underside or intrados of an arch

Spandrel, surface between two arches in an arcade or the triangular space on either side of an arch

Stele, upright stone bearing a monumental inscription

Stemma, coat of arms or heraldic device

Stoup, vessel for holy water, usually near the west door of a church

Tessera, a small cube of marble, glass, etc., used in mosaic work

Thermae, Roman baths

Tondo, round painting or bas-relief

Transenna, open grille or screen, usually of marble, in early-Christian churches

Triptych, painting or panel in three sections

Trompe l'oeil, literally, a deception of the eye. Used to describe illusionist decoration, painted architectural perspectives, etc.

Villa, country house with its garden

The terms **quattrocento, cinquecento** (abbreviated in Italy '400, '500), etc., refer not to the 14C and 15C, but to the 'fourteen-hundreds' and 'fifteen-hundreds', i.e. the 15C and 16C, etc.

Index to artists

A

Abbati, Giuseppe (c 1830–68) 649, 660

Acquisti, Luigi (1745–1823) 225

Afro (Babaldella; born 1912) 519

Agostino di Duccio (1418–81) 158, 625, 672

Agresti, Livio (c 1580) 670

Albani, Francesco (1578–1660) 84, 264, 594, 595, 598, 670

Albertinelli, Mariotto (1474–1515) 149

Alberti, Giuseppe (1640–1716) 387

Alberti, Leon Battista (1404–72) 280, 284, 293, 607, 672

Albertini, Amadeo (born 1916) 91

Alberto da Milano (15C) 370

Albertolli, Giocondo (1742–1839) 147, 217, 226

Albini, Franco (1905–77) 544, 550

Aleotti, Giovanni Battista (1546–1636) 611, 612, 616, 632, 642

Aleotti dell' Argeuta, Antonio (active 1498) 671

Alessi, Galeazzo (c 1512–72) 137, 144, 145, 148, 163, 170, 186, 259, 541, 544, 547, 551, 553, 554, 555, 588, 643

Alfieri, Benedetto (1700–67) 80, 86, 88, 93, 113, 121

Algardi, Alessandro (1595–1654) 600, 669

Aliprandi, Michelangelo (active 1560–82) 373

Allori, Alessandro (1535–1607) 248

Altichiero, di Zevio (1320 or 1330–95) 368, 372, 374, 471, 480, 481

Amadeo, Giovanni Antonio (1447–1522) 139, 146, 167, 180, 183, 184, 185, 196, 210, 247, 276, 642

Amadeo, Giuseppe (18C) 137, 145, 275

Amalteo, Pomponio (1505–88) 439, 533, 534

Amati, Carlo (1776–1852) 144

Ambrogio da Milano (active 1450) 615

Ambrosini, Floriano (16C–17C) 599

Amigoni, Gasparo (active 1527–28) 294

Amigoni, Jacopo (1675–1752) 523

Ammannati, Bartolomeo (1511–92) 478

Amuzio da Lurago (16C) 217

Andrea da Milano see Solario

Andrea da Valle (16C) 475, 486, 487

Andrea del Castagno see Castagno

Andrea del Sarto (1486–1530) 118, 626

Andreasi, Ippolito (c 1548–1608) 289

Angelico, Fra (Giovanni da Fiesole; c 1395–1455) 84, 251, 642, 670

Angolo del Moro, Battista (active 1562) 369, 393

Anguissola, Sofonisba (c 1530–1629) 264

Annigoni, Pietro (1910–88) 393

Ansaldo, Giovanni Andrea (1584–1638) 550, 551

Anselmi, Giorgio (1723–97) 289, 293, 395

Anselmi, Michelangelo (1492–1554) 640, 641, 642

Anselmo, Giovanni (active 1470) 92

Anselmo da Campione (active 1160–80) 625

Antegnati, Benedetto (12C) 126, 173, 641

Antelami, Benedetto (c 1178–1230) 636, 637, 642, 644

Antico (Pier Jacopo Alari; 1460–1528) 478

Antonelli, Alessandro (1798–1888) 90, 120

Antonello da Messina (c 1430–79) 86, 159, 183, 219, 438, 549, 650

Antonio da Firenze (15C) 532

Antonio da Negroponte, Fra (15C) 457

Antonio da Osteno (15C) 529

Antonio da Treviso (15C) 406

Antonio da Viterbo (Pastura; c 1450–1516) 118

Antonio della Corna (early 16C) 276

Antonio di Vincenzo (c 1350–1401) 586, 601

Appiani, Andrea (1754–1817) 154, 166, 171, 175, 225, 253, 264

Araldi, Alessandro (1460–?1530) 641

Arcimboldo, Giuseppe (1527–93) 277

Aretusi, Cesare (1549–1612) 640

Arnolfo di Cambio (c 1245–1302) 591

Arp, Hans (1887–1966) 449

Arpino, Cavalier di (Giuseppe Cesari; 1568–1640) 264, 670

Arrighi, Alessandro (mid-17C) 275

Arrighi, Antonio (mid 18C) 277

Arrigone, Attilio (active 1695–1725) 174

C

H

I

J

K

M

General index

T

W

Z

Index to maps

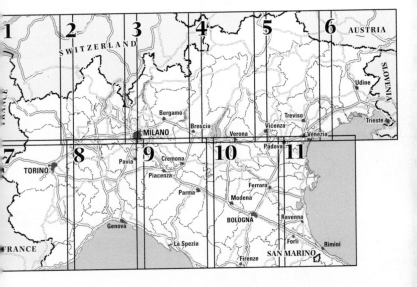

Key to maps

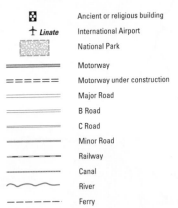

⊠	Ancient or religious building
✦ *Linate*	International Airport
▒	National Park
══════	Motorway
= = = = =	Motorway under construction
────────	Major Road
────────	B Road
────────	C Road
────────	Minor Road
─ ─ ─ ─	Railway
────────	Canal
～～～	River
─ ─ ─ ─ ─	Ferry

Scale to maps

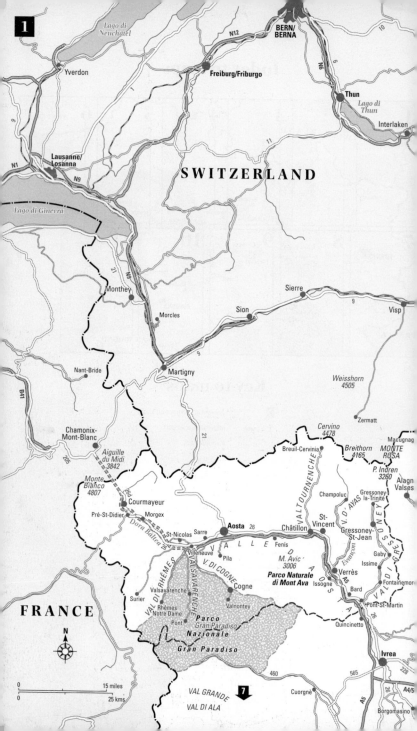

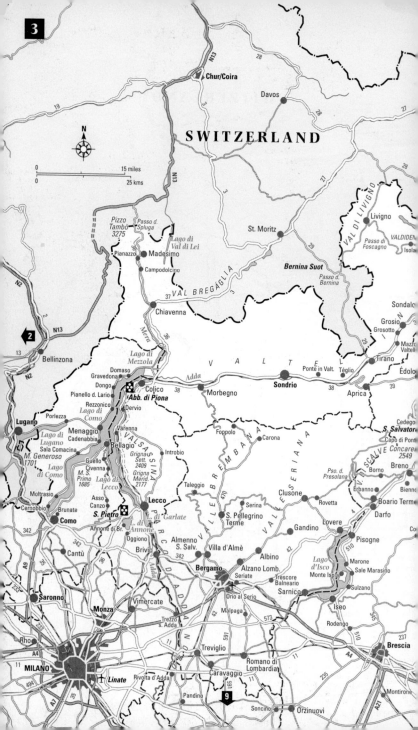

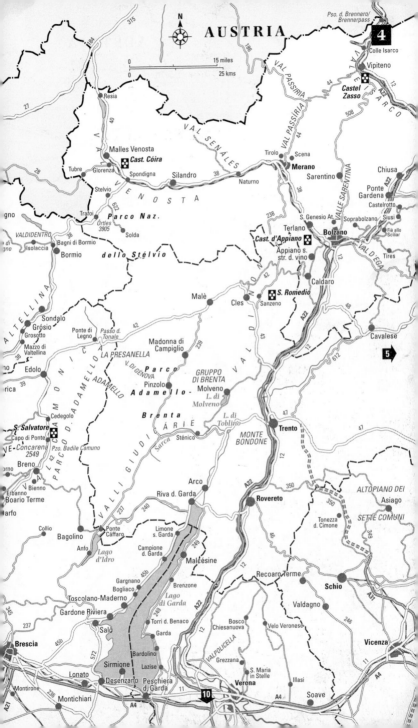

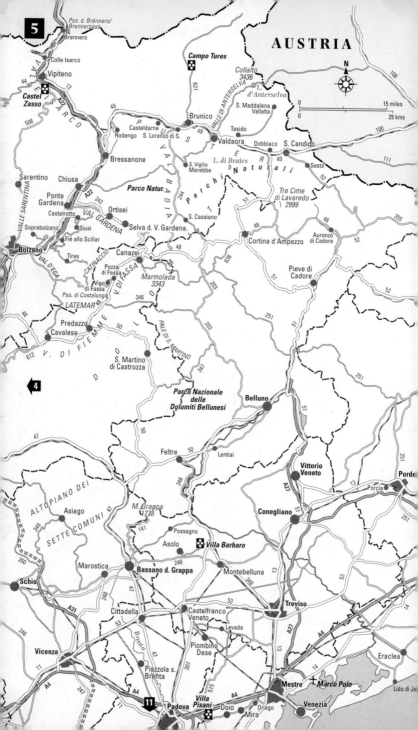

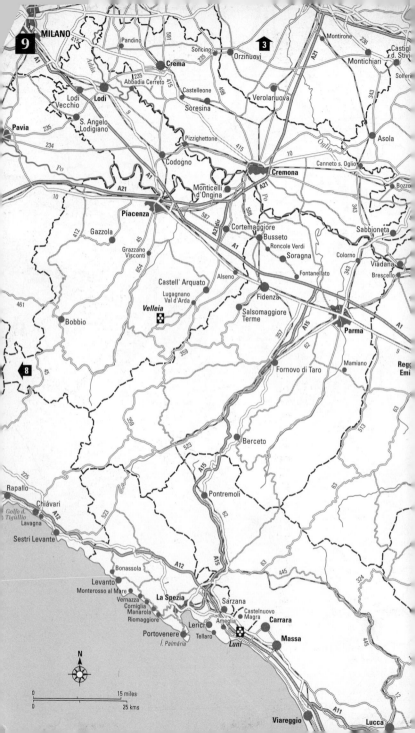